Commercial and Consumer Sales Transactions

Cases, Text and Materials

Fourth Edition

by Jacob S. Ziegel
Professor of Law Emeritus
Faculty of Law
University of Toronto

and

Anthony J. Duggan
Professor of Law
Faculty of Law
University of Toronto

2002
EMOND MONTGOMERY PUBLICATIONS LIMITED
TORONTO, CANADA

Emond Montgomery Publications Limited
60 Shaftesbury Avenue
Toronto ON M4T 1A3
http://www.emp.ca/lawschool

Printed in Canada.
Reprinted September 2011.

We acknowledge the financial support of the Government of Canada through the Canada Book Fund for our publishing activities.

Edited, designed, and typeset by WordsWorth Communications of Toronto, Canada.

Library and Archives Canada Cataloguing in Publication Data

Ziegel, Jacob S.
    Commercial and consumer sales transactions: cases, text and materials

4th ed.
Previously published as volume 1 of Commercial and consumer transactions.
ISBN 978-1-55239-054-2

    1. Commercial law—Canada—Cases.   I. Duggan, Anthony J.   II. Title.
III. Title: Commercial and consumer transactions.

KE919.Z53 2001   346.71'07   C2001-903721-X

To Alison, Rose and James Duggan

and to

Paul and Michal Staszewski

Preface to the Fourth Edition

Six years have elapsed since the publication of the third edition of this casebook and users of this new edition will want to know the important changes we have introduced in it. We are pleased to provide them with at least an outline of this information. Easily the most significant change is the fact that Professor Ziegel was able to persuade Professor Duggan to join him as co-editor of the new edition. Professor Duggan is a very distinguished Australian commercial and consumer law teacher and scholar, with a solid background of practical experience, and taught at the University of Melbourne and Monash University law schools for 25 years before joining the University of Toronto law school in 1999. One of the great advantages of having an antipodean collaborator is that it has enabled us to add relevant Australian cases and other materials in areas where there were no adequate Canadian counterparts.

We have divided the work of updating the casebook more or less evenly between us. In the interests of keeping individual chapters to a tolerable size, we have also subdivided several of the chapters in the third edition. Old chapter 6 has now been converted to three chapters: chapter 6 is now restricted to the seller's implied obligations with respect to title; chapter 7 addresses the implied obligation of quality of the goods; and chapter 8 deals with fitness of the goods for use, sales by sample, and (to avoid having to create yet another new chapter) private sales, as well as the impact of public law legislation in the food and drugs areas. Former chapter 10 has been subdivided into chapters 13 and 14, the first dealing with the transfer of title between seller and buyer, and the second with transfer of title by a non-owner. Similarly, old chapter 12 has been transformed into chapter 16 (buyer's right of rejection of non-conforming goods) and chapter 17 (buyer's claim for damages). Finally, chapter 18, formerly chapter 13, has been expanded with the addition of a new section on choice of law and jurisdictional clauses and the role of class actions in the resolution of sales disputes. We have also expanded the treatment of policy questions, particularly in relation to the doctrine of unconscionability (chapter 2), implied terms (chapter 8), and transfer of title by a non-owner (chapter 14).

It has long seemed to both of us that a treatment of sales law that focuses exclusively on the parties' substantive rights and obligations is seriously deficient. Just as important is an understanding of how the rights are enforced in practice (or, more often, not enforced), particularly in the consumer area. Our one regret is that space constraints prevented us from developing these adjectival aspects much more fully. However, there is nothing that precludes individual law teachers from adding further materials of their own.

It goes without saying that, in addition to the changes noted above, we have tried hard to update all the chapters, though we do not claim to have been totally successful. Some of the new additions are the following. In chapters 1 through 3 we have added extensive amounts of material on the impact of electronic commerce and the many new issues it raises inside as well as outside the contractual areas. In chapter 2, dealing with the definition of sale and the various types of near-sales, we have included the important English Court of Appeal decision in *Atari Corporation (U.K.) Ltd. v. Electronics Boutiquestores (U.K.) Ltd.*, [1998] QB 539 (CA), clarifying the parties' rights and obligations in consignment sales. Similarly, in chapter 17, in dealing with the buyer's claim to damages, we have added substantial extracts from the Court of Appeal's judgments in *Bence Graphics Ltd. v. Fasson U.K. Ltd.*, [1997] 1 All ER 979 (CA), adding yet another complicating twist to the uneasy relationship between the available market price measure of damages for the delivery of defective goods intended for resale and the buyer's actual damages.

We have incurred many debts in the preparation of this edition and are grateful for the opportunity to make the appropriate acknowledgments. Jason Kee, J.D. II, University of Toronto, worked very diligently for Professor Ziegel during the summer of 2001 and displayed great virtuosity in locating new sales materials on the internet and in converting the new edition into electronic format suitable for transmission to the publishers. Earlier in the year, Alba Sandre performed similar services with equal levels of skill for Professor Duggan. None of this would have been possible without the financial assistance generously made available by Dean Ron Daniels to pay for the students' help.

In Paul Emond, president of Emond Montgomery Publications, our publishers, and his associates, we were fortunate to find professional colleagues who were as efficient as they were courteous and, no less important, patient in indulging our requests for more time! WordsWorth Communications handled the editing of the new manuscript on behalf of Emond Montgomery. The pivotal persons here were Cindy Fujimoto and Paula Pike. We have nothing but praise for their meticulous attention to detail and their capacity for spotting errors that we should have avoided in the first place.

November 2001   J.S.Z.
                                                                          A.J.D.

Acknowledgments

A book of this nature borrows heavily from other published material. We have attempted to request permission from, and to acknowledge in the text, all sources of such material. We wish to make specific references here to the authors, publishers, journals, and institutions that have generously given permission to reproduce in this text works already in print. If we have inadvertently overlooked an acknowledgment or failed to secure a permission, we offer our sincere apologies and undertake to rectify the omission in the next edition.

CAMVAP. *Canadian Motor Vehicle Arbitration Plan.*

Canadian Bar Review. J.S. Ziegel, "The Future of Canadian Consumerism" (1973), 51 *Can. Bar Rev.* 191.

Carswell Co. Ltd. G.H.L. Fridman, *Sale of Goods in Canada*, 4th ed. (1995).

Clarendon Press. M.G. Bridge, *The Sale of Goods* (1997).

Ford Motor Co. of Canada. Warranty Guide 2001.

Longman Professional. A. Duggan, M. Bryan, and F. Hanks, *Contractual Non-Disclosure: An Applied Study in Modern Contract Theory* (1994).

Maclean Hunter Publications. J. Rogers and W. Lowther, "The Squeeze on Lemons," *Macleans*, July 11, 1983.

Mercer University. K.A. Strasser, "Magnuson-Moss Warranty Act: An Overview and Comparison with UCC Coverage, Disclaimer, and Remedies in Consumer Warranties" (1976), 27 *Mercer L Rev.* 1111.

Ontario Law Reform Commission. *OLRC Report on Consumer Warranties and Guarantees* (1972).

B. Sookman. "Electronic Commerce, Internet and the Law: A Survey of the Legal Issues" (1999), 48 *Univ. New Brunswick LJ* 119.

Sweet & Maxwell. A.H. Boulton, *The Making of Business Contracts*, 2nd ed. (1972).

Sweet & Maxwell. H. Street, *Principles of the Law of Damages* (1962).

Uniform Law Conference of Canada. T. Buckwold, *The Law of Commercial Leasing in Canada*, paras. 8-15 (1999).

University of Toronto Press. C. Rogerson and M. Trebilcock, "Products Liability and the Allergic Consumer: A Study in the Problems of Framing an Efficient Liability Regime" (1986), 36 *Univ. Tor. LJ* 52.

Short Table of Contents

Table of Contents

Table of Cases

(Page numbers in bold face type indicate that the text of the case or a significant extract therefrom is reproduced in this volume.)

Table of Abbreviations

A. REFERENCE TEXTS AND FREQUENTLY CITED TREATISES, REPORTS AND OTHER MATERIALS

ATIYAH — P.S. Atiyah, The Sale of Goods, 10th ed. (2001)

BENJAMIN — Benjamin's Sale of Goods, 5th ed. (1997)

FRIDMAN — G.H.L. Fridman, Sale of Goods in Canada, 4th ed. (1995)

GOODE — R.M. Goode, Commercial Law, 2nd ed. (1995)

INTERNATIONAL SALES CONVENTION — United Nations, Convention on Contracts for the International Sale of Goods, Vienna, 10 April 1980, UN Doc. A/Conf. 97/18

OLRC CONTRACT LAW AMENDMENT REPORT — Ontario Law Reform Commission, Report on Amendment of the Law of Contract (1986)

OLRC SALES REPORT — Ontario Law Reform Commission, Report on Sale of Goods (3 vols.) (1979)

OLRC WARRANTIES REPORT — Ontario Law Reform Commission, Report on Warranties and Guarantees (1972)

WHITE AND SUMMERS — J.J. White and R.S. Summers, Handbook of the Law under the Uniform Commercial Code, 5th ed. (1999)

WILLISTON — Williston on Sales (Revised ed., 4 volumes) (1990)

B. FREQUENTLY CITED STATUTES

BANK ACT

Bank Act, SC 1991, c. 46, as am.

BIA

Bankruptcy and Insolvency Act, RSC 1985, c. B-3, as am. SC 1992, c. 27, SC 1997, c. 12

BILL 100

Consumer Products Warranties Act, Bill 110, 1976 (Ont.) (not enacted)

BPA

Business Practices Act, RSO 1990, c. B.18

CA

Competition Act, RSC 1985, c. C-34, as am.

CPA

Consumer Protection Act, RSO 1990, c. C.31, as am.

OPPSA

Ontario, Personal Property Security Act, RSO 1990, c. P.10, as am.

SGA (BC)

Sale of Goods Act, RSBC 1979, c. 370, as am.

SGA (Ont.)

Sale of Goods Act, RSO 1990, c. S.1, as am.

SGA (UK, 1893)

Sale of Goods Act 1893, 56 & 57 Vict., c. 71

SGA (UK, 1979)

Sale of Goods Act 1979, c. 54, as am.[1]

SPPSA

Saskatchewan Personal Property Security Act, SS 1979-80, c. P-6.1, replaced by Personal Property Security Act 1993, SS 1993, c. P-6.2

UCC

Uniform Commercial Code (US)[2]

---

1 This is a consolidating Act and incorporates the amendments made to the 1893 Act.

2 References are to the 1991 Official Text unless otherwise indicated.

Concordance of the UK Sale of Goods Act 1893[1] and the Ontario Sale of Goods Act[2]

UK Section		Ontario Section
1	Definition of sale	2
2	Capacity	3
3	Formation of contract	4
4	Stat. of Frauds Provision—repealed in 1954	5 (repealed in 1994)
5-21		6-22
22	Sales in market overt	23 (excludes English rule)
23	Voidable title	24
24	Revesting of property in stolen goods—repealed in 1968	Omitted
25	Seller or buyer in possession	25
26	Effect of writs of execution	Omitted
27-39		26-38
40	Attachment by seller in Scotland	Omitted
41-58		39-56
59	Scottish law	Omitted
60	Repeals	Omitted
61(1)	Bankruptcy rules	Omitted
62	Definitions	1

---

1 Subsequent changes in the UK Act, particularly those introduced by the Misrepresentation Act 1967, the Supply of Goods (Implied Terms) Act 1973, the Unfair Contract Terms Act 1977, and the Sale of Goods Act 1979 (a consolidating Act), are not included.

2 RSO 1990, c. S.1, as am.

CHAPTER ONE

Evolution of Modern Sales and Consumer Law

SALES LAW[1]

The Anglo-Canadian Position

The principles of sales law as we know them today evolved very slowly and are mainly a product of late 18th century and particularly 19th century developments. The introduction of the action in assumpsit, while laying the theoretical foundations for the modern law, seemingly made little initial impact. Here, as elsewhere, economic and social conditions were the ultimate determinants of the pace of legal development, and the pressure for a detailed body of rules governing the law of sales did not really manifest itself until the arrival of the industrial revolution.

Events moved quickly during the 19th century and, by 1888, it was felt that the rules were sufficiently settled to warrant their being reduced to statutory form. This was the year when MacKenzie D. Chalmers, the author of the highly successful Bills of Exchange Act, 1882, was encouraged to draft a similar bill embracing the sales area. As Chalmers himself recorded, Lord Herschell's advice to him was to endeavour "to reproduce as exactly as possible" the existing law, leaving any amendments that might seem desirable to be introduced in committee on the authority of the legislature. Chalmers' labours eventually led to the enactment by the British Parliament of the Sale of Goods Act 1893.

Post-1893 Developments

The Imperial Act was quickly copied by most Commonwealth jurisdictions that followed the common law tradition. All of the common law provinces in Canada have adopted it, albeit with a number of minor changes. Manitoba was the first enacting province; for some unknown reason Ontario delayed its enactment until 1920.

In the intervening years, the UK Parliament has, on the whole, made only a modest number of changes to the 1893 Act that are of interest to Canadian lawyers. However, as in Canada's case, the sales rules codified in the 1893 Act have been affected by important

---

1 The account that follows is a condensed and updated version of the account appearing in the OLRC *Sale of Goods Report* (1979), at 7-22.

developments in the public and related private law areas. The most important changes are those effected by the following statutes:

1) The Law Reform (Enforcement of Contracts) Act, 1954. This Act repealed s. 4, the Statute of Frauds provision, in the parent Act of 1893.

2) The Misrepresentation Act, 1967. This Act amended the law of misrepresentation in important respects and also amended ss. 11(1)(c) and 35 of the Sale of Goods Act.

3) The Supply of Goods (Implied Terms) Act 1973. This Act amended ss. 12-14 of the Sale of Goods Act and, until superseded by the Unfair Contract Terms Act 1977, restricted or excluded the use of exception clauses in consumer sales and other sales transactions, including hire-purchase and conditional sales agreements.

4) The Unfair Contract Terms Act 1977. This Act, which came into force on February 1, 1978, introduced a comprehensive regime, not restricted to sales transactions, for the restriction or avoidance of exception clauses in consumer and non-consumer agreements.

5) The Supply of Goods and Services Act 1982. This Act applies to the transfer or supply of chattels not covered by the SGA or the English hire-purchase legislation, and introduces a statutory scheme for the implication of terms in contracts for the supply of services.

6) The Consumer Protection Act 1987. Part I of the Act implements an EEC Directive of July 25, 1985 imposing strict liability on a producer of goods for personal injury to a consumer or damage caused to the consumer's property because of a defective product.

7) The Sale of Goods (Amendment) Act 1994 (referred to hereafter as the "1994 Amendment Act"). The 1994 Amendment Act repealed the market overt rule.

8) The Sale and Supply of Goods Act 1994 (referred to hereafter as the "SSGA 1994"). SSGA 1994 implements the recommendations of the English and Scottish Law Commissions in their report on the Sale and Supply of Goods (Cmnd. 137, May 1987). It amends three of the earlier Acts and makes important amendments to the parent SGA.

9) The *Sale of Goods (Amendment) Act 1995* (referred to hereafter as the "1995 Amendment Act"). The 1995 Amendment Act deals with the sale of an undivided share in goods; the sale of unascertained goods forming part of a larger bulk; and ascertainment by exhaustion.

Because of the above and other statutory changes, the British Parliament adopted a consolidating statute in 1979, the Sale of Goods Act 1979. More recently, the UK government has indicated its willingness to consider adoption of a completely revised Sale of Goods Act, but nothing has materialized so far.

The UK statutory changes have had only a limited impact in Canada. Only British Columbia has copied the 1954 amendment,[2] and only one province, Saskatchewan, has adopted any of the 1973 amendments, and then only to a very limited extent. Disclaimer provisions, comparable to those in the 1973 Act, were anticipated in the Consumer Protection Acts of Ontario, Manitoba, and British Columbia. The Misrepresentation Act 1967 has attracted no followers and the prospect of the Unfair Contract Terms Act 1977 being copied verbatim seems equally doubtful in view of the trade practices legislation that

---

2 Ontario also repealed its Statute of Frauds provision (s. 5) in 1994, but this change was triggered by other factors and was not based on the British Legislation. See *infra* chapter 3. [ed.]

already covers a substantial part of the same ground in British Columbia, Alberta, Ontario, and other provinces.

This is not to suggest that the legislative scene in Canada has remained static; it has not. A large number of federal and provincial Acts have a direct and very important bearing on the parties' rights and obligations in the sale sector, and their number has rapidly increased in the post-war period. Many of them will be referred to hereafter.

American Sales Law

The Pre-Code Position

Nineteenth century American sales law largely followed English principles, but the laws of the individual states differed from each other and from the English rules on many points of detail and sometimes on points of substance. An important objective, therefore, of the Uniform Sales Act drafted by Professor Samuel Williston of the Harvard Law School, and adopted by the National Conference of Commissioners on Uniform State Laws (NCCUSL) in 1906, was to reconcile the conflicting state rules and to introduce a uniform body of law. Williston admired Chalmers' Act and followed it closely. Nevertheless a substantial number of differences survived between the Uniform Sales Act and the British Act. The more important differences included the wide definition of warranty in the American Act; the unitary classification of contractual terms; a significantly different regime of buyer's remedies; and the treatment of documents of title.

The Origins of the Uniform Commercial Code

At the time it was superseded by the Uniform Commercial Code, the Uniform Sales Act had been adopted by only thirty-six states. Williston's work has been called a "scholarly reconstruction of nineteenth century law." In any event, merchants on the Eastern seaboard felt that it no longer catered adequately to their needs and there was equal concern about the continuing lack of uniformity among the states. In 1936 the Merchants' Association of New York established a committee to prepare a federal Sales Act. In its subsequent Report the committee recommended extensive changes in the Uniform Act. A bill was drafted and introduced in the Congress in 1940.

The sponsors of the bill were persuaded to stay their hand pending the preparation of the revised Sales Act by the NCCUSL. Since the National Conference had also been responsible over the years for the preparation of other uniform acts in the commercial law area, it was decided to revise these as well. Thus was born the concept of a Uniform Commercial Code. In 1942 the American Law Institute agreed to co-sponsor the project.

The first "Official Draft" of the Code was published in 1952 and was approved with minor changes by the sponsoring organizations. Pennsylvania was the first state to enact the Code. One or other version of the Code was subsequently adopted by all the common law states and by the District of Columbia. Louisiana, a civil law jurisdiction, has adopted most of the Code, but not Article 2, the Sales Article. The Code has been officially revised or amended on many occasions, the most recent text for the whole Code being the 2001 Official Text. New Articles have also been added to reflect changing commercial practices and technological developments. However, not all the revisionary efforts have been successful. As noted below, the Code's sponsors have been unable to agree on the text for a revised Article 2 on Sales and were also unable to agree on the scope of a new Article 2B on Computer Information Transactions. In an effort to avoid unauthorized changes and to maintain a watchful eye over developments, the sponsoring organizations established a Permanent Editorial Board (PEB) of the Uniform Commercial Code in 1961. The Board issues frequent reports commenting on difficult points of interpretation, recommending desirable changes, and disapproving of unauthorized changes adopted by individual states. So far as the latter point is concerned, the Board has not been entirely successful in its mission since, over the years, a large number of unauthorized amendments have been made by individual states.

The Structure of the Uniform Commercial Code

The current Official Text is divided into 13 major parts, or Articles as they are called. Each Article deals with a separate area of substantive law, with the exceptions of Article 1, which deals with General Provisions, and Articles 10 and 11, which are concerned respectively with Effective Date and Transitional Provisions. The intervening Articles are devoted to the following topics:

Article 2:   Sales
Article 2A: Leases
Article 3:   Negotiable Instruments (revised in 1990)
Article 4:   Bank Deposits and Collections (amended in 1990)
Article 4A: Funds Transfers
Article 5:   Letters of Credit (revised in 1995)
Article 6:   Bulk Transfers: Repealer of Article 6 and [Revised] Article 6
Article 7:   Warehouse Receipts, Bills of Lading and other Documents of Title
Article 8:   Investment Securities (revised in 1994)
Article 9:   Secured Transactions; Sales of Accounts and Chattel Paper (revised in 1999)
Article 10: Effective Date and Repealer
Article 11: Effective Date and Transition Provisions

It will be seen, therefore, that despite its ambitious title the Code is not exhaustive: it does not include such important branches of commercial law as insurance law or agency, and it omits an equally extensive list of subjects falling within the jurisdiction of the US federal government. Nevertheless, the Code is a magnificent achievement. Equally impressive, from a Canadian point of view, is its enactment by all the common law states of the Union.

Article 2

As Professor Honnold observed in 1968, while it was the pressure for a revised uniform sales act that launched the Code project, in the end it was Article 9 on Secured Transactions, and its innovative solutions to the chaotic state laws governing chattel security, that ultimately commended the adoption of the Code to many of the state legislatures.

However, Article 2 is more than an amended version of the Uniform Sales Act. In style and organization it differs fundamentally from its predecessor, but the overall result is not a revolutionary blueprint for a new sales law. Rather, it meets two of the Code's own explicit objectives, "to simplify, clarify and modernize the law governing commercial transactions" and "to permit the continued expansion of commercial practices through custom, usage and agreement of the parties." The more important changes to the Uniform Sales Act effected by Article 2 are the following:[3]

1) Article 2 is more extensive in its coverage. It contains a substantial number of sections affecting the formation and construction of the contract of sale which have no counterpart in the Uniform Sales Act and which were designed to clarify or relieve the rigidities of the prior law.

2) The parties' freedom to shape the terms of their contract as they see fit remains a cardinal tenet, but is qualified by important behavioural baselines in Articles 1 and 2 which cannot be excluded and which are designed to prevent overreaching and to ensure fairness and standards of decency in commercial dealings.

3) The Code's basic framework of the seller's warranty obligations remains the same, but their scope is no longer restricted by traditional doctrines of privity. As a result of the alternative versions of s. 2-318, a seller's express or implied warranties extend to any person who may reasonably be expected to use, consume or be affected by the goods and who is injured by breach of the warranty.

4) The concept of title and its location, which played such a critical role in the Uniform Sales Act (as it still does in the UK and Ontario Acts) in furnishing the answer to widely disparate problems, has been dethroned. It has been replaced by an issue-oriented approach, which answers sale questions without regard to the locus of title.

5) The exceptions to the *nemo dat* rule have been enlarged; old and troublesome distinctions between void and voidable transactions have been eliminated; and the protection of third parties dealing in good faith with a merchant to whom the goods have been entrusted has been placed on a more rational footing.

6) The importance of a merchant's status has also been enhanced in other directions by imposing on the merchant, in the merchant's capacity as buyer or seller, a higher regime of obligations than is applied to non-merchants.

7) Article 2 places greater emphasis on the enforcement of bargains and discourages the rejection of goods based on trivial breaches or contrived excuses. Particularly noteworthy are the provisions on uncertainty (ss. 2-204, 2-306), the right to cure an imperfect tender (s. 2-508), and the substitutional methods of performance permitted in s. 2-614 in the case of unforeseen difficulties.

8) At the remedial level, important changes have been introduced with respect to the scope and enforcement of the rights of both parties. Save in exceptional circumstances, the seller can no longer sue for the price before the buyer has accepted the goods. On the other hand, the seller's right of stoppage *in transitu* is extended and he may, at his option, where the buyer is in breach, resell the goods and recover any actual deficiency without

---

3 As previously noted, Article 2 is in the course of being revised. The following summary is based on the existing text of the Article.

being bound by the traditional market price test. The unpaid seller is also given a limited right to recover his goods from an insolvent buyer. The buyer, for his part, enjoys more extended powers to seek an order for specific performance, and his right to "cover" in the event of the seller's failure to perform is the counterpart of the seller's right of resale. The conscious attempt to parallel the parties' rights is also seen in the retention of the Uniform Sales Act provision giving the buyer a lien on rejected goods in the buyer's possession and in his severely circumscribed right to recover goods identified to the contract where the seller has become insolvent after receiving all or part of the purchase price. Finally, attention should be drawn to the important right conferred on both parties to seek adequate assurance of performance (s. 2-609) where reasonable grounds for insecurity arise with respect to the other party's performance.

In the early 1990s, the Code's sponsors established a Committee to revise Article 2. The Committee laboured long and hard, but ultimately its efforts were not crowned with success. This was because of basic differences among the Committee members on such key issues as the characterization of "smart goods" (i.e., goods incorporating software essential for the functioning of the goods), the treatment of electronic contracts, revision of the "battle of the forms" provisions (2-207), and the need for additional consumer protection in other sections. The divisions came to a head in 1999 when, after a vigorous debate, the American Law Institute (ALI) members approved revised Article 2 as presented by the Committee. However, the executive of NCCUSL decided to table the report at its own annual meeting later that summer on the ground of strong industry opposition which, in the executive's opinion, made it unlikely that Revised Article 2 would be adopted in many states even if approved by NCCUSL. In light of these developments, the ALI and NCCUSL struck a new Committee to prepare a new revised Article 2 that hopefully would be able to resolve the earlier difficulties. The Committee reported in 2000 that its efforts had not been successful. The Code's sponsors thereupon decided to limit their efforts to an *amended* Article. These amendments were approved at the annual ALI meeting in May 2001 and will be presented for approval at NCCUSL's annual meeting in August 2001. See National Conference of Commissioners on Uniform State Laws, *Proposed Amendments to Uniform Commercial Code, Article 2—Sales*, ALI Tentative Draft for discussion at meeting on August 10-17, 2001.

Reform of Provincial Sales Law

The influence of Article 2 has also been felt in Canada. In 1979 the Ontario Law Reform Commission published a three-volume *Report on the Sale of Goods* (referred to hereafter as the "Sales Report") recommending the enactment of a revised Sale of Goods Act based on an amended version of Article 2. The Commission felt Article 2 was an appropriate precedent for Ontario because the United States was Canada's single largest trading partner and also because of its intrinsic merits as a functionally oriented modern sales law. One basic change recommended in an Ontario version of Article 2 was the adoption of a substantial breach test as the touchstone of a party's right to cancel the contract for breach by the other party or, where the buyer was the aggrieved party, to reject non-conforming goods in place of the Code's perfect tender rule. (See UCC 2-601, 2-703, 2-711 and OLRC Sales Report, c. 6(B), 16.1, and 17.1.)

On the initiative of the OLRC, its report was referred to the Uniform Law Conference of Canada (ULCC) with a view to seeing whether the OLRC recommendations could form the basis of a Uniform Sale of Goods Act. The ULCC established a special committee to investigate the question. The committee reported favourably in 1981 and submitted a draft Uniform Sale of Goods Act based on the Ontario draft Act but with a number of significant changes. See ULCC, Proc. 63rd Ann. Meeting, App. S, at 185 *et seq*. The Conference accepted the report and agreed to adopt the committee's draft Act as a new Uniform Sale of Goods Act after its style had been reviewed and put into an approved form by the Conference's Legislative Drafting Section. The Section's redrafted version appears in ULCC, 64th Ann. Proc., 1982, at 36 and App. HH. (Further drafting changes were made thereafter.)

Neither the OLRC draft Act nor the Uniform Act version has so far been adopted in any province. Nevertheless, the OLRC Report retains much pedagogical and intellectual value and it is frequently referred to in later chapters of this casebook. The Sales Report also led to a further report by the OLRC on *Amendment of the Law of Contract*, published in 1987, and some of its recommendations will also be referred to from time to time.

A series of papers and comments on the Sales Report will be found in *Papers and Comments Delivered at the Ninth Annual Workshop on Commercial and Consumer Law*, Toronto, November 2-3, 1979 (Butterworths, 1981). The Uniform Sale of Goods Act is discussed in Institute of Law Research and Reform, Alberta, Report No. 38, *The Uniform Sale of Goods Act* (Edmonton, October 1982).

In 1999 the ULCC embarked on a *Commercial Law Strategy* with a view to securing greater uniformity among the provincial commercial legislation. As part of the project, Professors Ziegel and Duggan were asked to prepare a report on whether they believed a new effort should be made to promote adoption of a Revised Sale of Goods Act. In their report to the August 2000 meeting of the ULCC the authors gave an affirmative reply because, in their view, "sales transactions continue to play a central role in the Canadian economy and therefore of Canadian law, and that a commercial law strategy that does not envisage a place for sales law would be seriously deficient." The authors also reported that they did not support the piecemeal approach to sales law reform adopted in the United Kingdom and, to a lesser extent, in Australia. See Jacob S. Ziegel and Anthony J. Duggan, *The Role of a Revised Sale of Goods Act in the Commercial Law Strategy of the Uniform Law Conference of Canada*, Uniform Law Conference of Canada, Proceedings of Annual Meetings, August 2000, Appendix F. However, as of this writing, the ULCC has decided that there is not sufficient support in the Canadian commercial community for a renewed attempt to secure adoption of a revised Sales Act.

International Developments

The need for uniform laws, or at least greater harmonization between national regimes, in the law and practices governing international trading transactions has long been obvious. Since the end of the Second World War, increasing efforts have been mobilized at both the governmental and non-governmental levels to advance this objective. As one of the world's major exporters and importers, Canada has an important stake in these developments. The legislative and other efforts to achieve international uniformity may also provide useful sources for national reforms and for uniformity within federal states, like Canada, where more than one legal system of private law obtains. Two legislative initiatives are of particular significance in the sales area.

The Hague Conventions of 1964

Formal efforts to draft a uniform law on international sales began in 1930 when the International Institute for the Unification of Private Law (UNIDROIT) appointed a committee for this purpose. Work on the project was suspended in 1939 but was resumed in 1951 under the auspices of the Dutch government. This resulted in the adoption in 1964 of two conventions, one on a Uniform Law on the International Sale of Goods (ULIS) and the other on a Uniform Law on the Formation of Contracts for the International Sale of Goods (ULFC). The conventions were not very successful. Before they were superseded in April 1980 by the Vienna Convention on Contracts for the International Sale of Goods (CISG), discussed below, they had only been ratified or acceded by nine, mainly smaller, countries. Canada and the United States were not among them.

The Vienna Sales Convention

The United Nations Commission on International Trade Law (UNCITRAL) was established by the General Assembly in 1966 with the object of promoting the progressive harmonization and unification of the law of international trade. The Commission consists of 29 elected members of the United Nations who are drawn from the various geographical regions and principal economic and legal systems of the world.

One of the first projects undertaken by the Commission was the preparation of a revised text of the two Hague conventions with a view to producing a new sales convention that would prove more acceptable to countries with different legal, social, and economic systems. The drafting work was completed in 1978 and, as previously noted, the Convention itself was approved at a UN sponsored diplomatic conference concluded on April 11, 1980. The Convention received the necessary ten ratifications or accessions in 1986 and came into force on January 1, 1988. The Convention is now in effect in 56 countries. These include the United States, Canada, Australia, China, most of the Western European countries, and the Russian Federation. The United Kingdom and Japan are two major trading nations which have not so far ratified the Convention. In Canada, the federal government ratified the Convention on April 23, 1991, with the concurrence of most of the common law provinces, pursuant to art. 93 of the Convention. It went into effect in those provinces on June 1, 1992, and for Saskatchewan and Quebec in June 1993. See Ziegel, "Canada Prepares to Adopt the International Sales Convention" (1991), 18 *CBLJ* 1.

The Convention has a very wide reach and it applies to contracts of sale between parties whose places of business are in different states: (1) when the states are contracting states; or (2) when the rules of private international law lead to the application of the law of a contracting state (art. 1(1)). The Convention does not apply if the contracting parties have excluded it pursuant to art. 6 of the Convention or if a Contracting State has excluded the conflict of laws basis for applying the Convention by making a declaration to this effect at the time of ratification (arts. 1(1)(b) and 95).

CISG has generated a large volume of case law, most of it over the past 13 years. (According to Professor Will's research,[4] there were 676 decisions during the period of 1988-98, of which 568 were court decisions and the remainder arbitral awards.) However, the common law jurisdictions—the United States, Canada and Australia—have produced only a trickle of cases: 18 from the United States, two from Australia, and two from Canada. The first Canadian decision on CISG was only rendered in 1998. See Ziegel, "Canada's First Decision on the International Sales Convention" (1999), 32 *CBLJ* 313. The paucity of CISG litigation in those countries is probably due to pervasive ignorance of the Convention, the widespread use of choice of law clauses in contracts adopting a law other than the CISG and practitioners' feelings that it is not worth making the intellectual efforts to become familiar with CISG because it is unlikely to affect the outcome of the case or because clients will not be willing to pay for the additional efforts involved. See Ziegel, "The Future of the International Sales Convention from a Common Law Perspective" (2000), 6 *NZ Bus. L Quar.* 336.

BIBLIOGRAPHICAL NOTE

The two leading commentaries on the Convention are by John Honnold, *Uniform Law for International Sales under the 1980 United Nations Convention*, 3rd ed. (Kluwer, 1999); and Peter Schlechtriem (ed.), *Commentary on the UN Convention on the International Sale of Goods (CISG)*, 2nd ed. (Clarendon Press, Oxford, 1998). A valuable set of comparative studies appears in Nina M. Glaston and Hans Smit (eds.), *International Sales: the United Nations Convention on Contracts for the International Sale of Goods*, (Matthew Bender, 1984). For discussions from a Canadian perspective see, *inter alia*, Jacob S. Ziegel and Claude Samson, *Report to the Uniform Law Conference of Canada: Convention on Contracts for the International Sale of Goods* (July 1981, mimeo, in English and French); and Louis Perret and Nicole Lacasse (eds.), *Actes du colloque sur la vente internationale*, (Wilson and Lafleur, 1989). There are a growing number of websites for the collection of CISG judgments and literature, of which the best known are those operated by the Pace University Law School, the Faculty of Law of Freiburg University, and UNCITRAL.

Note on Codification and Sources of Sales Law

There have been intermittent debates among common law academic lawyers about the virtues and vices of codification and some of the issues were resurrected (albeit in low key and without much fervour) during the Code's gestative period. See R.B. Schlesinger, "The Uniform Commercial Code in the Light of Comparative Law" (1959), 1 *Inter-Am. Law Rev.* 11. Its opponents argue that codification is incompatible with the "free" spirit of the common law and that it freezes its growth and responsiveness to changing conditions—qualities that are particularly important in the commercial law area. On the other hand, the supporters of codification urge that certainty and predictability are as important

---

4   M.R. Will (ed.), *Twenty Years of International Sales Law Under the CISG: International Bibliography and Case Law Digest (1980-2000)*, (Kluwer Law International, 2000).

as flexibility and that a busy practitioner should not be required to plough his way through many pages of frequently conflicting decisions to ascertain the law on a given point. Moreover, it is argued, in a federal system and at the international plane, meaningful uniformity can only be obtained by means of uniform legislation.

Whatever the merits of the criticism, they do not appear to have inhibited the movement towards codification of substantial areas of common law. But codification in this context does not have the same meaning as it has to the civilian. The Bills of Exchange Act (BEA), the Sale of Goods Act (SGA) and, now, the Uniform Commercial Code (UCC), preserve the common law rules except insofar as they are inconsistent with the express provisions of the statute, including, in particular, the general rules of contract. See, for example, SGA s. 57(1). Moreover, the SGA rules are generally so open-textured and broadly worded that there is ample scope for adaptation to changing circumstances in the hands of a creative judge.

Karl Llewellyn, the Chief Reporter of the Code, was particularly anxious to maintain this characteristic of commercial law and he inserted several key provisions which were designed to achieve this objective, *viz.*, UCC 1-102 (purposes and policies of the Code and rules of construction); 1-203, 2-103 (obligations of good faith); and 1-205 and 2-208 (course of dealing, course of performance, and usage of trade as normative and evidentiary sources to give meaning and to supplement or qualify terms of an agreement). Good faith and flexibility are important values in governing the consensual relationships of contracting parties, but of necessity they must yield to the higher value of certainty when conflicts with the claims of third parties are involved. Hence, Article 9 of the Code, which is concerned with secured transactions (that is, the law of chattel security), is more tightly drafted than Article 2 and unlike Article 2 has required some substantial amendments since it was first introduced.

Lord Herschell's judgment in *Bank of England v. Vagliano Bros.*, [1891] AC 107, at 144-45, touches on a minor issue of exegesis, *viz.*, the admissibility of prior case law to interpret the provisions of a codifying Act (in this case the BEA). Lord Herschell was of the view that the prior law is irrelevant. Rather, "the proper course is in the first instance to examine the language of the statute and to ask what is its natural meaning, uninfluenced by any considerations derived from the previous state of the law, and not to start with inquiring how the law previously stood, and then, assuming that it was probably intended to leave it unaltered, to see if the words of the enactment will bear an interpretation in conformity with this view." Do you share Lord Herschell's concern or is this a tempest in a teacup? As many of the cases in this volume illustrate, Lord Herschell's stricture is more honoured in the breach than by its observance. Recent examples may be seen in *Ashington Piggeries Ltd. v. Christopher Hill Ltd.* (*infra* chapter 6) and *Hardwick Game Farm v. SAPPA* (*infra* chapter 8), and in *Cehave NV v. Bremer Handelsgesellschaft mbH* (*infra* chapter 4). Do the courts use pre- or extra-code law to interpret the Act, to fill gaps, or to allow them to reflect changes in commercial practices or judicial ideology?

The SGA provisions are only presumptive and they may be "negatived or varied by express agreement or by the course of dealing between the parties, or by usage, if the usage is such as to bind both parties to the contract": SGA s. 53. The Act therefore makes it clear that course of dealing and usage of the trade are important sources in determining and explaining the parties' agreement. *Cf.* the Code's definition of "agreement" in UCC 1-201(3). "Course of dealing" and "usage" are not defined in the SGA but are carefully and comprehensively defined in UCC 1-205. A controversial feature of English law is the non-admissibility of course of performance of an agreement to assist in determining the meaning of the agreement. *L. Schuler AG v. Wickman Machine Tool Sales Ltd.*, [1974] AC 235 (HL). There is, however, contrary Canadian authority. The Code, in UCC 2-208, expressly recognizes the relevance of such evidence and this more liberal approach won the support of the OLRC. See OLRC Sales Report (1979), at 117-19.

THE DEVELOPMENT OF CANADIAN CONSUMER LAW

Jacob S. Ziegel
"The Future of Canadian Consumerism"
(1973), 51 *Can. Bar Rev.* 191, at 191-98 (Footnotes omitted)

I. Introduction

Fifty years ago the word consumerism had not been coined and the suggestion that consumer law should be taught as a separate intellectual discipline would have been regarded as fanciful. Today the one has become a household word and the other an accomplished fact.

Much has happened in the intervening period to justify this transformation. Concern about abuses in the marketplace is as old as the recorded history of civilized man, but the tempo of change in the character of the marketplace and the types of goods and services offered in it has been greater in this century than during any comparable period in Canadian history. From a predominantly agrarian society we have moved into a predominantly urbanized society. The simple wants of yesteryear have been replaced by the modern supermarket with its more than 7,500 items. The products of the agrarian society were for the most part uncomplicated, produced or manufactured locally, and buyer and seller dealt with each other on a basis of relative equality.

All this too has changed. Modern technology has placed at the disposal of the Canadian consumer a bewildering variety of highly complex products, consumable and non-consumable, many of which were unknown before the war. The notion of the consumer bargaining from a position of equal strength has become a fiction in any but the most attenuated sense. The contract of adhesion has replaced the handshake and a multi-billion-dollar credit industry is threatening to make the cash transaction a museum curiosity. The merchant himself has largely become a conduit pipe for goods manufactured and prepackaged often thousands of miles from the place of sale. The "medium is the message" accurately describes the modern salesman as a sophisticated advertising industry first creates the mass consumption markets and then sustains them by claims and images often far removed from reality.

The consumer's legitimate ignorance and his almost total dependence on the fairness and competence of those who supply his daily needs have made him a ready target for exploitation. The rapidly escalating number and variety of the complaints and enquiries received by Box 99, the federal consumer listening post, the provincial consumer protection bureaux, and the popular newspaper "action" columns attest to the consumer's concerns and vulnerability. It is not simply a matter of protecting him against outright frauds, although fraudulent transactions of all types still abound. The much greater challenge is to redress the serious imbalance in all aspects of the modern marketplace—a marketplace that encompasses the public sector no less than the private sector and the supply of services no less than the supply of goods—and this requires a magnitude of government involvement far transcending the modest levels experienced in earlier periods of Canadian history.

Despite these easily documentable facts, there are still many who question the vitality and the authenticity of the consumer movement. To some it is an ephemeral phenomenon ... . Others see the consumer movement as a left wing political plot in which consumer grievances are used as a Trojan horse to undermine the free market system. This view too will not bear the test of serious analysis. The leading consumer advocates on both sides of the border are drawn from all parts of the political spectrum or have no known political affiliations of any kind. Consumer concerns are as acute, perhaps more so, in communist countries as in countries enjoying a mixed type of economy. Consumerism is no more a political ideology than is labour law or poverty law although solutions to particular problems may be influenced by one's conceptions of the role of the modern marketplace.

A more challenging criticism comes from those who deny that there is a functional or intellectual unity to the proliferating variety of causes that are espoused by consumerists. In their view they are often only old problems represented under new labels such as the problems of landlord and tenant relations, warranty problems in the sale of goods and services, and the issue of safety, first, in the realm of food and drugs and, now, with respect to motor vehicles and hazardous household products. There is some substance to this argument but not enough to tilt the balance. Some overlapping occurs between many disciplines and it is no more harmful here than it is there.

Functionally, the thread that binds all consumer problems together is the perception that they affect the individual as a purchaser of goods and services for his personal use or consumption. Analytically, I believe it will be found that every consumer problem exhibits one or more of the following characteristics. First, a disparity of bargaining power between the supplier of goods or services and the consumer to whom they are being offered; secondly, a growing and frequently total disparity of knowledge concerning the characteristics and technical components of the goods or services; and, thirdly, a no less striking disparity of resources between the two sides, whether that disparity reflects itself in a consumer's difficulty to obtain redress unaided for a legitimate grievance or in a supplier's ability to absorb the cost of a defective product as part of his general overhead as compared to the consumer to whom its malfunctioning may represent the loss of a considerable capital investment.

Two other attacks on consumerism may be briefly noted. One is the self-serving argument that "we are all consumers." If this means no more than that consumerists have no monopoly of interest or concern, it is a legitimate point. But usually the protestation is offered by the suppliers of goods or services or their spokesmen, the inference being that their dual role as suppliers and consumers ensures automatic fair play when they appear as suppliers. This is palpably fallacious. The dominant interest of a supplier is to promote his business interests as he sees them; if he has any consumer concerns (which are in any event unlikely to coincide with his professional interests) they will quickly be suppressed in favour of those considerations that provide his profit or his livelihood.

But the self-operating character of the identity principle is far from self-evident. The evidence indeed points very much in the opposite direction. Almost every important piece of post-war consumer legislation has been opposed by some segment of the business community. However much that opposition may have been disguised in rhetoric about Big Brotherism and unjustifiable interference with the mechanism of the marketplace, the truth is that on those occasions the affected industries did not see regulation as being in their own best interests, whatever may have been the position from the consumer's point of view. There is nothing reprehensible about this pursuit of group interests. We take it for granted in all other spheres in our pluralistic society. What is surprising is that it should be thought that consumer-supplier relations are somehow exempt from this basic axiom of political and economic life.

Note on Post-War Canadian Consumer Protection Legislation[5]

Canadian consumerism is not a new phenomenon and consumer protection legislation can be traced to the early days of legislative activity of Upper and Lower Canada. The federal Food and Drugs Act is almost as old as Confederation and the Interest Act has an even longer history. Federal and provincial moneylending and pawnbroking legislation traces its roots to the beginning of the century.

What is true however is that, as in the United States and other Western industrialized nations, the post-war period spawned an enormous increase of interest in consumer problems and in the volume of remedial legislation at both the provincial and federal levels. The reasons for this phenomenon have been canvassed in the preceding article by Professor Ziegel. For a valuable collection of articles on the various aspects of Canadian consumerism, see Neilson (ed.), *Consumers and the Law in Canada* (1970); Law Society of Upper Canada, *Papers and Proceedings at Consumer Protection Conference*, Toronto, February 1973; C.S. Ackworthy, "Recent Developments in Consumer Law in Canada" (1980), 29 *ICLQ* 346; H. Buckwold, "Consumer Protection in the Community: The Canadian Experience" (1977-78), 2 *CBLJ* 182; E.P. Belobaba, "The Development of Consumer Protection Regulation: 1945-1984," in *Royal Commission on the Economic Union and Development Prospects for Canada*, Study Papers, vol. 50, at 1 (1985), and Symposium (1992), 21 *CBLJ* 70. A more recent compilation of notes and Commonwealth and US materials appears in Iain Ramsay, *Consumer Protection: Text and Materials* (Law in Context, 1989).

---

5 The citations for the statutes referred to in this note are found in the table immediately following the note. [ed.]

Provincial Legislation

So far as Ontario is concerned, the most important phase of post-war activity dates from 1965 when the Select Committee of the Ontario Legislature on Consumer Credit presented its *Final Report on Consumer Credit*. The Committee's recommendations led to the enactment of the Consumer Protection Act, RSO 1990, c. C.31, as am. (1966) and the Consumer Protection Bureau Act, RSO 1990, c. C.32, as am. (1966). Originally the CPA only dealt with three major issues: the licensing of itinerant sellers and the right of cancellation of door-to-door sales (see now Pt. II, Pt. II.1 and s. 21); writing requirements for "executory contracts" (Pt. II); and "truth in lending" disclosure requirements (Pt. III). Since then the scope of the Act has been substantially enlarged and it now includes the following provisions: s. 36(2) (avoidance of cut-off clauses in credit agreements);[6] s. 34(2) (avoidance of disclaimer clauses in consumer sales); s. 36(3) (regulation of unsolicited goods and credit cards); and s. 37 (prohibition of referral sales). Nevertheless, the CPA still falls short of a comprehensive consumer protection code even with respect to sales and credit transactions and, in general, its draftsmanship and enforcement leave much to be desired.

Apart from the CPA and CPBA, the province has adopted other important consumer protection legislation. In particular the student will need to familiarize himself with the following measures: Motor Vehicle Dealers Act, RSO 1990, c. M.42, as am. (primarily a licensing statute), the Motor Vehicle Repair Act, RSO 1990, c. M.43, as am., the Prepaid Services Act, RSO 1990, c. P.22, as am., the Unconscionable Transactions Relief Act, RSO 1990, c. U.2 (an old Act which empowers the courts to grant relief from usurious loan transactions), the Wages Act, RSO 1990 c. W.1 (this contains important provisions concerning wage assignments and the garnishment of earnings), and the Consumer Reporting Act, RSO 1990, c. C.33, as am. The Business Practices Act, RSO 1990, c. B.18, as am., first adopted in 1974 and conceptually a very important enactment, widens the scope of consumer rights by proscribing unfair as well as deceptive consumer "representations" and provides new methods of policing them. Several of the other provinces have comparable legislation.

With the introduction of the Personal Property Security Act, 1967, proclaimed in force as of April 1, 1976, Ontario became the first Canadian jurisdiction to adopt a modern law of secured transactions. The 1967 Act was repealed in 1989 and replaced by the Personal Property Security Act, 1989. PPS legislation is now also in force in all the other common law provinces and in the Yukon, the Northwest Territories, and Nunavut. Quebec has also adopted a much modified Article 9-type approach to the treatment of *sûretés mobilières* in the new Quebec civil code which went into effect in 1994. (For further details, see volume III of the previous edition of this casebook.) With few exceptions, the PPSA is not consumer oriented but it has an important bearing on consumer as well as commercial transactions in which a security interest in personal property is involved.

---

6 Ontario also repealed its Statute of Frauds provision (s. 5) in 1994, but this change was triggered by other factors and was not based on the British Legislation. See *infra* chapter 3. [ed.] This section has been amended by SO 1999, c. 12, Sched. F, and will be replaced by more comprehensive credit agreement provisions on proclamation.

In 1972, the Ontario Law Reform Commission published an important report on *Consumer Warranties and Guarantees in the Sale of Goods*, which recommended extensive and basic changes in this branch of the law. Bill 110, The Consumer Product Warranties Act, 1976, gave effect to some of the recommendations but the bill was allowed to die on the order paper. Paradoxically, many of the Commission's recommendations were implemented in the Saskatchewan Consumer Products Warranties Act, 1977, now replaced by the Consumer Protection Act, SS 1996, c. C-30.1, as am. The construction and sale of new homes raise problems similar to the sale of movable durable products. However, their treatment has fared better in Ontario as a result of the adoption of the Ontario New Home Warranties Plan Act, 1976.

The result of the foregoing enumeration leads to the inevitable conclusion that the modern Ontario commercial and consumer lawyer has to grapple with a formidable array of statutory provisions. The table following this note supplies a brief roadmap through the statutory jungle of federal and provincial legislation.

Federal Legislation

Federal intervention in the marketplace goes back to the earliest days of Confederation and, like the provincial legislation, increased rapidly in the post-World War II era.

The Small Loans Act, now repealed, was first adopted in 1939. It was designed, like its American counterpart, to encourage legitimate lenders to make loans to lower income borrowers and to combat usurious interest rates in small loans. The Act (which never applied to banks) imposed licensing requirements and set maximum interest rates for loans up to $1,500. In cases not governed by the Act, the Interest Act (a much older statute) allowed the parties to set their own rates subject to compliance with interest disclosure requirements relating to mortgages and other types of loan. Section 427 of the Bank Act, SC 1991, c. 46., and the regulations thereunder (historically a product of the 1967 decennial revision of the Bank Act) serve a similar purpose with respect to consumer loans made by the banks. These were designed to complement the parallel provincial truth-in-lending requirements adopted in the late 60s.

The federal credit and interest legislation is badly dated. In 1976 the federal government introduced a comprehensive Borrowers and Depositors Protection Act (Bill C-16) with a view to consolidating and updating its provisions. The bill was strongly opposed by many segments of the business community and also attracted substantial opposition from the provinces on constitutional grounds. As a result, after extensive committee hearings, the bill was abandoned by the Liberal government. It has been partly replaced by a series of fragmented amendments and revisions of the existing Acts. For further details, see J.S. Ziegel (ed.), *Seventh Annual Workshop on Commercial and Consumer Law* (1979), Part V. Bill C-44, which received the royal assent on December 17, 1980, repealed, *inter alia*, the licensing and graduated ceiling provisions in the Small Loans Act, and added a new s. 347 to the Criminal Code introducing a "criminal rate" of interest (that is, an effective annual rate of interest exceeding 60% of the credit advanced) for all types of credit, consumer and otherwise. The current Bank Act strengthens the earlier disclosure requirements and supplements them with rights of prepayment.

Part X of the Bankruptcy and Insolvency Act (BIA), first adopted in 1966 and which only applies in those Provinces which have requested its application, is designed to relieve the plight of overcommitted consumer debtors, and provides that the debtor may apply to the court to consolidate the debtor's debts into an orderly payment schedule. Part III, Division 2 of the BIA, which was added as part of an important package of amendments in 1992, allows an insolvent consumer debtor whose debts do not exceed $75,000 to make a proposal to the debtor's creditors for an extension of time for payment of the debts or a reduction of the debts, or both. Part V of the Bills of Exchange Act, added in 1970, allows consumers to assert against holders of negotiable instruments made or drawn by the consumer any defence the consumer would have been entitled to assert against the seller of the goods to which the instrument relates.

The Consumer Packaging and Labelling Act, enacted in 1971, prohibits deceptive packaging and labelling practices and imposes important disclosure requirements. The Food and Drugs Act and the Hazardous Products Act severally regulate or prohibit the manufacture and/or sale of an enormously wide range of consumer products. Also, with respect to safety, the Motor Vehicle Safety Act requires vehicles sold in Canada to have prescribed safety equipment, or to be safe in design to specifications. The Competition Act, previously known as the Combines Investigation Act, was amended in 1975 and now applies, *inter alia*, to a substantially enlarged range of false or deceptive representations and some types of unfair practices such as pyramidic sales, referral sales, and prize schemes. The then federal government also announced its intention to proceed with a "Stage Two" program which would include a comprehensive federal Trade Practices Act to supersede the existing consumer protection provisions in the Combines Act. The bill never materialized. However, in November 1977, the Liberal government introduced Bill C-13, an Act to amend the Combines Act, which, apart from its regulatory provisions on mergers, also introduced a federal consumer class action procedure for violations of the Act's Part V provisions. Both features of the bill were strongly opposed by the business community and the bill was allowed to lapse. Subsequent efforts then focussed on amending the merger and monopoly provisions in the Act and these finally succeeded in 1986.

The Competition Act was substantially amended in 1998 on both the commercial and the consumer sides. See SC 1999, c. 2. On the consumer side, misleading advertising offences are de-criminalized unless the Crown can show *mens rea* on the advertiser's part. Instead, the amending Act introduces administrative machinery to handle the new civil offences with appropriate remedial powers. There is also a right of appeal to the Competition Tribunal. Paradoxically, the new telemarketing provisions remain offences of strict liability—why, is not clear other than that the regulatory authorities in Canada and the United States regard misleading telemarketing as a particularly vicious form of preying on gullible consumers in their homes. See further, J.S. Ziegel, *Submissions to Standing Committee on Banking, Trade and Commerce on Bill C-20, Competition Act Amendment Bill*, November 25, 1998.

If it is accurate to describe the 1960s and much of the 1970s as the golden age of postwar consumerism, it seems equally safe to predict that historians will record the 80s as largely a period of consolidation and retrenchment and, in several provinces, even a period of dismemberment of programs already in place. See W.A.W. Neilson, "The Future of

Canadian Consumerism: A Retrospective and Prospective View," in Ziegel (ed.), *Papers and Comments delivered at the 10th Annual Workshop in Commercial and Consumer Law* (Butterworths, 1982), at 179, and Ziegel, "Is Canadian Consumer Law Dead?" (1995), 24 *CBLJ* 417, and compare Professor Belobaba's study noted earlier. There are a variety of reasons for this decline: the high rate of inflation which obtained at the beginning of the 1980s; two sharp recessions in a single decade and, in Canada's case, persistently high rates of unemployment; Canada's debt crisis and a general disenchantment with government intervention in the economy; and, not least, a weak and largely ineffectual consumer movement. However, even in its heyday there was often more form than substance to governmental commitment to consumer protection. Some of the provincial legislation was, and remains, badly drafted. Even more significant, it is unevenly enforced and frequently not at all, and, in some cases, is unenforceable. In almost all provinces, and increasingly at the federal level, the consumer protection agencies are chronically underfunded. The most telling example of the cumulative effect of these *malaises* is the merger, in the summer of 1993, of the federal Department of Consumer and Corporate Affairs with the Department of Industry, without any public discussion of the issue, and the marginalization of consumer programs in the merged Department.

The law and economics movement, which has had a powerful impact on other branches of law, has had a mixed effect on consumer law. It has contributed positively to the study of consumer issues by taking a hard-nosed look at the costs and benefits of interventionist legislation. Consumers have also benefitted through the movement's attack on vested interests and from its support for a more free and competitive marketplace. On the other hand the law and economics movement (or at least one branch of it) has had a negative influence in often seriously underestimating the imperfections of the modern marketplace and frequently in dismissing consumer legislation as costly and unnecessary without offering satisfactory alternatives.

Selected Table of Ontario and Federal Sales, Chattel Security and Consumer Protection Legislation

Federal Legislation

Bank Act, SC 1991, c. 46, as am.
Bankruptcy and Insolvency Act, RSC 1985, c. B-3, as am.
Bills of Exchange Act, RSC 1985, c. B-4
Competition Act, RSC 1985, c. 19 (2d Supp.), as am.
Consumer Packaging and Labelling Act, RSC 1985, c. C-38, as am.
Criminal Code, RSC 1985, c. C-46, s. 347 (criminal interest rate)
Food and Drugs Act, RSC 1985, c. F-27, as am.
Hazardous Products Act, RSC 1985, c. H-3, as am.
Interest Act, RSC 1985, c. I-15, as am.
Motor Vehicle Safety Act, RSC 1985, c. M-10, as am.
Personal Information Protection and Electronic Documents Act, SC 2000, c. 5

Ontario Legislation

Sales Legislation

Bulk Sales Act, RSO 1990, c. B.14, as am.
Electronic Commerce Act, SO 2000, c. 17
Factors Act, RSO 1990, c. F.1
Mercantile Law Amendment Act, RSO 1990, c. M.10
Sale of Goods Act, RSO 1990, c. S.1, as am.
Warehouse Receipts Act, RSO 1990, c. W.3

Consumer Legislation

Business Practices Act, RSO 1990, c. B.18, as am.
Class Proceedings Act, 1992, SO 1992, c. 6
Consumer Protection Act, RSO 1990, c. C.31, as am.
Consumer Protection Bureau Act, RSO 1990, c. C.32, as am.
Consumer Reporting Act, RSO 1990, c. C.33, as am.
Loan Brokers Act, SO 1994, c. 22, as am.
Ministry of Consumer and Business Services Act, RSO 1990, c. M.21, as am.[7]
Motor Vehicle Dealers Act, RSO 1990, c. M.42, as am.
Motor Vehicle Repair Act, RSO 1990, c. M.43, as am.
Ontario New Home Warranties Plan Act, RSO 1990, c. O.31, as am.
Prepaid Services Act, 1990, c. P.22, as am.
Real Estate and Business Brokers Act, RSO 1990, c. R.4, as am.
Travel Industry Act, RSO 1990, c. T.19, as am.
Unconscionable Transactions Relief Act, RSO 1990, c. U.2
Wages Act, RSO 1990, c. W.1, as am.

Bill 110, The Ontario Consumer Products Warranties Act, 1976 (not enacted)

Chattel Security Legislation

Personal Property Security Act, RSO 1990, c. P.10, as am.
Repair and Storage Liens Act, RSO 1990, c. R.25, as am.

---

7 Previously known as the Ministry of Consumer and Commercial Relations Act. The change was
   adopted in June 2001.

THE IMPACT OF ELECTRONIC COMMERCE ON COMMERCIAL AND CONSUMER TRANSACTIONS

Barry B. Sookman
"Electronic Commerce, Internet and the Law: A Survey of the Legal Issues"
(1999), 48 *Univ. New Brunswick LJ* 119 (Footnotes omitted)

Electronic commerce encompasses a wide spectrum of activities, some well established, most new. It is about doing business electronically; however, there is no single accepted definition of the term "electronic commerce." One reason for this is that new uses of the medium are emerging constantly. Electronic commerce can be defined to include any kind of transaction that is made using digital technology, including transactions over open networks such as the Internet, closed networks such as electronic data interchange (EDI) and debit and credit cards. Defined broadly it would include commercial transactions effected through any electronic means including facsimile, telex, and telephone.

The term "electronic commerce" can also be given a more limited interpretation to those trade and commercial transactions involving computer to computer communications whether utilizing an open or closed network. This "narrow" definition would include an enormous, growing and diverse range of activities including electronic trading of goods and services, on-line delivery of digital content, electronic banking, electronic payment and fund transfers, electronic bills of lading, commercial auctions, collaborative design, engineering services, public procurement, and direct consumer marketing and after sales services. So understood, electronic commerce would therefore include indirect electronic commerce (electronic ordering of tangible goods) as well as direct electronic commerce (on-line delivery of intangibles). It would also involve the transfer of products (such as consumer goods and services, information services, financial and legal services) and the dissemination of traditional activities such as health care and education, as well as activities such as shopping in virtual malls.

Electronic commerce is at the leading edge of the technological forces shaping the world economy. These forces are related and mutually reinforcing: improvements in information and communication technologies, globalization of markets and investment, and the shift to a knowledge-based economy. It has the potential to transform the way we work, the way we shop and the way we interact with government. The significant potential of electronic commerce to transform our economic and social life was recently summed up by the Minister of Revenue's Advisory Committee on Electronic Commerce which stated that electronic commerce "represents the most radical force of change that nations have encountered since the Industrial Revolution."

Since electronic commerce has the potential to transform the conduct of commercial transactions, the business of government and the delivery of goods and services and information, it is forcing us to think about how existing laws and regulations will apply to electronic commerce activities. In fact, over the last few years there has developed an enormous global recognition that existing legal frameworks need to adapt to cope with the challenges associated with electronic commerce. Much work in the area is being done by governments, businesses and other non-governmental organizations.

The following is a summary of some of the legal and regulatory issues pertaining to electronic commerce. Because of the large number of issues and their complexity, only a synopsis of the main issues is provided. As many of the novel legal issues have arisen as a result of the increasing use of the Internet for electronic commerce, the issues discussed below will focus predominantly on the legal issues arising from electronic commerce activities in the Internet and other open network environments.

The Jurisdiction Challenge

The Internet, being a new and rapidly developing means of mass communication and information exchange, raises difficult questions of private international law. A web site established in Canada, the United States or elsewhere can generally be accessed by any Internet user anywhere in the world. Advertising on a web site is capable of reaching not just the residents of the province, state or country from which the web site is operated, but residents living anywhere else in the world. Goods can be bought and sold over the Internet. Intangible products such as computer programs and sound recordings can also be bought and sold over the Internet and electronic copies can be transmitted or delivered to customers across the globe. Contracts of all types can be negotiated and concluded in cyberspace. Services can be performed or delivered over the Internet. A defamatory statement concerning a person can be posted on a UseNet site and be distributed to all other UseNet sites around the world, making the statement available to be read by anyone anywhere with access to the Internet. A copy of an infringing work uploaded to an Internet site will automatically be re-transmitted by Internet service providers to countless other sites around the world.

It is clear that activities carried on over the Internet can have consequences in many jurisdictions. Internet communications are almost universally unrestricted to a single territory. In fact, the Internet has no territorial boundaries. For practical purposes, when business is transacted over a computer network via a web site accessed by a computer in one state, it takes place as much in that state as it does anywhere. The Internet breaks down barriers between physical jurisdictions. When a buyer and seller consummate a commercial transaction over the Internet, there is no need for the traditional physical acts that often determine which jurisdiction's laws will apply and whether the buyer or seller will be subject to personal jurisdiction in the courts where the other is located … .

Regulatory Challenges Related to Electronic Commerce

Companies physically carrying on business in Canada must comply with a range of statutes, regulations, and common law and equitable rules pertaining to the business activities carried on. Canada, like many other countries of the world, has a myriad of federal, provincial and municipal statutory instruments which impact upon how business may be conducted and which affect the relationships between the businesses and persons with whom the businesses interact. In the Internet environment where the location of business activities are potentially everywhere there is Internet access, determining which jurisdictions' laws apply can be an exceptionally difficult task.

However, entities carrying on business over the Internet must consider the question or assume the consequences of failing to do so.

Set out below are some of the important types of laws and regulations which can impact businesses engaging in Internet based electronic commerce. The statutory frameworks described below relate principally to the laws of the Province of Ontario and the laws of Canada applicable therein. Companies carrying on business over the Internet must obviously consider what equivalent and/or additional provisions may be applicable in other jurisdictions. The laws and regulations described below are meant to be illustrative only of the types of legislative provisions which companies carrying on business over the Internet can expect to encounter.

· · ·

Licensing and Registration Requirements

Many statutes in the Province of Ontario require the licensing or registration of sellers of products and providers of services. Many of these statutes are intended to protect consumers. A person intending to establish a business or sell products in Ontario has to determine whether any specific legislation governs that business. The list set out below generally describes some of the types of businesses and persons that must be licensed or registered. The list, while not complete, is intended to indicate the types of businesses for which registration or licenses are required and to indicate the types of legislative regulation which may be mandated in other jurisdictions. For example:

Extra-Provincial Corporations: No extra-provincial corporation may carry on any of its business in Ontario without a licence under this Act to do so, and no person acting as representative for or agent for any such extra-provincial corporation shall carry on any of its business in Ontario unless the corporation has a licence.

Collection Agencies: No person may carry on the business of a collection agency or act as a collector unless the person is registered under the Limited Partnerships Act, RSO 1990, c. L-16. A collection agency includes people who hold themselves out to the public as providing a service or arranging payment of money owing to another person or who sells or offers to sell forms or letters represented to be a collection system or scheme.

Consumer Reporting Agencies: In order to conduct or act as a consumer reporting agency or as a personal information investigator, a person must be registered under the Consumer Reporting Act, RSO 1990, c. C-33.

Insurance Agents: To act as an insurance broker a person must be registered. Also, no person may hold himself, herself or itself out as an insurance broker or as the holder of a certificate unless the person is the holder of a certificate under the Registered Insurance Brokers Act, RSO 1990, c. R-19.

Travel Agencies: No person shall act or hold himself, herself or itself out as being available to act as a travel agent unless the person is registered as a travel agent by the registrar. Also, no travel agent may conduct business at a place at which the public is invited to deal unless it is named as an office in the registration.

· · ·

Consumer Protection and [Unfair Trade] Practices Legislation

Various statutes apply generally to persons carrying on business in Canada, or particular Provinces of Canada, that are designed to protect consumers or to promote specific social policies including those related to human rights and discriminatory business practices. It is possible that such legislation would apply to persons that are held to carry on business on-line or that offer goods or services over the Internet. For example:

Misleading Advertising: Under the Competition Act, RSC 1985, c. 34, s. 52(1), it is a criminal offence to make a representation to the public which is false or misleading in a material respect where the representation is made for the purpose of promoting, directly or indirectly, the supply or use of a product for the purpose of promoting, directly or indirectly, any business interest by any means whatsoever.[8] Further, under the Ontario Business Practices Act, RSO 1990, c. B-18 certain "unfair practices" are prohibited. Unfair practices include false, misleading or deceptive consumer representations including representations that the goods or services have sponsorship, approval, performance characteristics, accessories, uses, ingredients, benefits or quantities they do not have; a representation that goods are of a particular standard or quality, if they are not; a representation that a specific price advantage exists, if it does not; a representation that the proposed transaction involves or does not involve rights, remedies or obligations if the representation is false or misleading; a representation using exaggeration, innuendo or ambiguity as to material fact or failing to state a material fact if such use or failure deceives or tends to deceive; or a representation that misrepresents the purpose or intent of any solicitation of or any communication with the consumer.

Writing and Signature Requirements: Many jurisdictions have enacted or inherited legislation based upon the English Statute of Frauds. This legislation mandated formal writing requirements for certain classes of contracts such as contracts of guarantee, contracts for the sale of land, and contracts not to be performed within a year. Writing requirements have historically also been part of sale of goods legislation in the common law provinces. While several provinces have repealed certain of the statutory provisions requiring signatures and writings, writing requirements still exist. For example, under the Ontario Consumer Protection Act, RSO 1990, c. 31, 19(1)

---

8   Section 52(1) of the Competition Act was materially amended in the 1999 amendments to the Act, SC 1999, c. 2. Criminal misleading advertising offences are now mainly restricted to cases where there is a *mens rea*. In other cases the advertiser will be subject to administrative proceedings and civil penalties. See further, *infra*, chapter 4 in the section Public Law Aspects of False Advertising. [eds.]

[hereinafter OCPA], every executory contract for the sale of goods or services where the purchase price, excluding the cost of borrowing, exceeds fifty dollars (other than an executory contract under an agreement for variable credit) must be in writing and must contain certain prescribed information. Further, an executory contract is not binding on the buyer unless the contract is signed by the parties, and a duplicate original copy thereof is in the possession of each of the parties.

Privacy and Data Protection: The common law provinces do not recognize a general right of privacy such as a tort for the invasion of privacy. However, Four Canadian Provinces (Newfoundland, Saskatchewan, Manitoba and British Columbia) have enacted privacy statutes to create a statutory tort for a person who wilfully and without claim of right violates the privacy of another person. Under such legislation it is a tort to use a person's likeness, name or voice for advertising, sales promotion, or other commercial use without the person's consent. Under the Quebec Civil Code, Articles 35 and 36, an express right of privacy is also provided. This right of privacy includes the right in respect of the use of personal documents and appropriation of image. The Province of Quebec has also enacted data protection rules which extend to businesses in that Province. In October of 1998, the Federal Government also introduced into the House of Commons the Personal Information and Protection and Electronic Documents Act, Bill C-6.

. . .

Personal Jurisdiction Under Canadian Law—General Principles

The rules of civil procedure of most Provinces in Canada set out the circumstances in which a party to a proceeding may serve the originating process outside of the Province. For example, under the Rules of Civil Procedure applicable in the Province of Ontario, Rule 17.02, a party to a proceeding may, without court order, be served outside Ontario with an originating process where the proceeding against the party consists of a claim or claims, *inter alia*, in respect of real or personal property in Ontario; in respect of a tort committed in Ontario; in respect of damage sustained in Ontario arising from a tort or breach of contract, wherever committed; or against a person ordinarily resident or carrying on business in Ontario. The Ontario rules also provide that a court may grant leave in other circumstances to serve an originating process outside of Ontario.

To prevent overreaching, courts in Canada have developed rules governing and restricting the exercise of jurisdiction over extraterritorial and transnational transactions. For constitutional reasons, a court in Canada may exercise jurisdiction only if it has a "real and substantial connection" with the subject matter of the litigation. This requirement is intended to satisfy the principle of "order and fairness," a guiding element in Canadian law in the determination of an appropriate forum. The exact limits of what constitutes a reasonable assumption of jurisdiction are not rigid and they have not been fully refined in Canada. However, the test is intended to prevent a Canadian court from unduly entering into matters in which the jurisdiction in which the court is located has little interest.

A court in Canada may also refuse to exercise jurisdiction over extraterritorial or transnational transactions through the doctrine of *forum non-conveniens*. Under this doctrine, a court may refuse jurisdiction where there clearly is a more appropriate jurisdiction in which the case should be tried than the domestic jurisdiction chosen by the plaintiff. The choice of the appropriate forum is designed to ensure that the action is tried in the jurisdiction that has the closest connection with the action and the parties. All factors pertinent to making this determination must be considered.

Residents of Canada who use the Internet need to be concerned not only with the circumstances under which a court in another Province may assume jurisdiction with respect to Internet activities, but also whether courts in jurisdictions outside of Canada could assume jurisdiction. Because communications over the Internet have world-wide implications, it can be a daunting challenge to know with certainty when foreign courts will assume personal jurisdiction over Canadians with respect to Internet activities. ...

Carrying On Business and Personal Jurisdiction

Jurisdiction over a person is often asserted on the basis that the person carries on business or transacts business in the state. The wording of particular long-arm statutes creating personal jurisdiction on this basis often differs from jurisdiction to jurisdiction. For example, in the Province of Ontario, Rule 17.02 of the Rules of Civil Procedure expressly provides that a party to a proceeding may, without court order, be served outside Ontario with an originating process where the proceeding against the party consists of a claim or claims "against a person ordinarily resident or carrying on business in Ontario." In some states of the United States, the "transaction of any business" within the state allows the exercise of jurisdiction over non- residents, to the extent permissible under the Due Process clause.

It is not clear in what circumstances activities carried on over the Internet by a non-resident will be sufficient to fall within the "carrying on business" or "transacting of any business" requirements of long-arm statutes and satisfy the minimal contacts requirements with respect to the exercise of jurisdiction. In some Provinces of Canada, the phrase "carrying on business" ordinarily suggests that the business must have some fixed place in the jurisdiction and that the business must have been carried on for a substantial period of time. It also suggests some direct or indirect presence in the state asserting jurisdiction, accompanied by a degree of business activity which is sustained for a period of time. An isolated act does not constitute carrying on business within the jurisdiction. However, a marketing strategy which includes periodic visits to a Canadian Province and advertising in the Province may constitute carrying on business in the Province.

Is the "carrying on business" or "transaction of any business" requirement met by a person who conducts business outside of a State or Province over the Internet? The answer to this question is not yet completely settled, although a substantial amount of case law on this question exists in the United States. The trend in the cases on this issue is that the exercise of personal jurisdiction over a foreign defendant is directly proportionate to the nature and quality of the commercial activity that the entity conducts over the Internet. At one end of the spectrum are situations where a defendant clearly does business over the Internet. If the defendant enters into contracts with residents of a foreign jurisdiction that involve the knowing and repeated transmission of information over the Internet, personal jurisdiction is likely to be proper. At the opposite end of the spectrum are situations where a defendant has simply posted information on an Internet web site which is accessible to users in foreign jurisdictions. A passive web site that does little more than make information available to those who are interested in it, is unlikely to create grounds for the exercise of personal jurisdiction. The middle ground is occupied by interactive web sites where a user can exchange information with the host computer. In these cases, the exercise of personal jurisdiction is apt to be determined by examining the level of interactivity and commercial nature of the exchange of information that occurs on the web site. In this regard, the quality of the electronic contacts may be measured with reference to the intended object of the activity.

. . .

Contract Issues

Electronic commerce is dependent on the law of contract. Uncertainty as to the application of contract principles could impact on the willingness of persons to contract electronically.

Contractual issues pertaining to electronic commerce existed when most commerce was conducted over closed systems, such as electronic commerce using EDI. With the emergence of the Internet, more businesses and smaller businesses can access the advantages offered by EDI without expensive proprietary systems. However, The use of open networks and the expansion of commerce with persons unknown to one another, has raised a number of contract issues. These are summarized below.

Who Are the Contracting Parties?

The new virtual environment makes it difficult to determine who the contracting parties are and where they are located. It is essential that persons engaging in electronic commerce have the ability to validate the identity of the parties with whom they are conducting business. Some readers may be familiar with the cartoon depicting a dog seated at a computer surfing the Internet, the joke being that on the Internet no one knows that the dog is a dog. The problem with identifying the parties to electronic commerce transactions has important ramifications. Digital technology makes it inexpensive and simple to copy another person's trading name or image. The design and development of a glamorous web page is also far cheaper than the creation of an imposing shop front.

Some methods for identifying contractual parties electronically have been developed. The most widely used of these technologies is the digital signature. Digital signatures are an authentication technology which can be used to establish the identity of a person or a business, and to prove that a document is genuine and unaltered.

Secure technologies, most notably cryptography, also require a certification mechanism to independently verify information about transactions and transacting parties. There are still many unanswered questions concerning the use of cryptography and the status of certification authorities. These include:

1. How central is the role of certification?
2. Should certification be limited to certifying public (cryptographic) keys?
3. Is it important to clarify the liability of those entities that certify information and their responsibilities? If so, how can this be achieved?
4. What role, if any, should governments and international organizations play in ensuring international interoperability of certification mechanisms and mutual recognition of certification authorities?

Writing and Signature Requirements

Most commercial contracts need not take any particular form to be enforceable. However, some contracts must be "in writing" or be accompanied by a "signature" to be valid. For example, sale of goods legislation in some provinces require there to be a "writing" for sale of goods worth fifty ($50) dollars or more. The Statute of Frauds which has been adopted in most provinces requires, among other things, any contract that is not fully performed within one year to be evidenced by a written memorandum, signed by the party against whom the contract is to be enforced. Some consumer protection legislation, such as the OCPA requires "executory contracts" to contain specific types of information and be "signed" by each of the parties.

The need for some contracts to be "in writing" or to be "signed" by the parties raises questions as to whether these requirements are met when parties contract electronically. These issues are more complicated in transnational transactions where the formal requirements may be different in the *lex loci contractus*, and under the proper law of the contract. The weight of authority is that compliance with the *lex loci contractus* is sufficient for formal validity of a contract and, it appears as well, the contract will be considered to be formally valid if it complies with the proper law of the contract. However, the Statute of Frauds has been held to be procedural and therefore may apply to all contracts before a forum court regardless of the proper law of the contract.

To overcome the potential obstacles of the writing and signature requirements, the federal government introduced legislation in the fall of 1998 to allow departments to adopt a set of general provisions authorizing the use of electronic communications. Provinces and territories are being encouraged to undertake statutory reforms along similar lines using the Uniform Electronic Commerce Act approved in principle by the Electronic Commerce Project of the Uniform Law Conference of Canada (ULCC). The Uniform Electronic Commerce Act is modeled after the United Nations Commission on International Trade Law (UNCITRAL) Model Law on Electronic Commerce adopted in 1996.

Where and When a Contract is Formed

Where and when a contract is formed is determined objectively in light of the facts and circumstances of each case, including the place of contracting, the place of performance, the places of residence or business of the parties respectively, and the nature and subject matter of the contract. If both parties are in the same country at the time of the making of the contract, or if it is contained in a single document signed by both parties at the same place, there is no difficulty in determining where the contract is made. Where, however, contracts are concluded over great distances or by the use of novel communication technologies, a sophisticated analysis may be required to determine when and where a contract is formed.

The general rule is that a contract is formed when acceptance of an offer is communicated by the offeree to the offeror. If it is necessary to determine where a contract is formed, this is usually the place where acceptance is communicated to the offeror. This follows from the rule generally accepted under Canadian and English law that to make a binding contract, not only must an offer be accepted, but also the acceptance must be notified to the offeror. Consistent with this rule, the Canadian and English courts have held that even where there is not mutual presence at the same place and at the same time, if communication is instantaneous or near instantaneous, for example by telephone, radio communication or telex the contract is made when acceptance of the offer is communicated by the offeree to the offeror.

There are many different ways in which electronic messages are sent and received. Messages may be sent directly by a sender to a recipient. The messages may need to travel great distances and may traverse many parts of the Internet to ultimately reach the destination of the recipient. A message may also reach its destination, but not actually reach the person for whom it is intended immediately. There are questions as to whether the "instantaneous communication" rule will apply to these situations and if it does, the circumstances in which it will apply.

Need for Written Documents for Evidence

The law of evidence and many legal rules assume the existence of paper and signed or original records. Most electronic records are, in practice, being admitted in court. Nevertheless, it still is desirable to clarify the status of electronic records.

The Uniform Law Conference of Canada adopted the Uniform Electronic Evidence Act in August of 1998. This proposal for legislation focuses on questions of authentication, the best evidence rule and the relevance of recognized standards of record-keeping to the admissibility of the records. In October 1998, the Government of Canada introduced amendments to the Canada Evidence Act to make it consistent with the Uniform Law Conference of Canada Uniform Electronic Evidence Act.

Payment Systems and Electronic Money

Electronic commerce cannot develop without sound, user-friendly, efficient and secure electronic payment systems. The Internet facilitates transactions between parties who may be located on opposite sides of the globe, who are transacting business at any time of day or night, and for small or large amounts of money. Creating a user-friendly, efficient and secure electronic payment system in this context poses some challenging problems.

One of the most popular ways for paying for a consumer transaction completed on the Internet today is by credit card. There are security risks involved when credit card data is not transmitted through a secure server or is not encrypted before transmission. Credit cards are also not accepted for all forms of transactions. Alternate payment mechanisms have also been the focus of considerable attention. These include digital cash, digital cheques and smart cards or stored value cards. Credit card issuers are also collaborating on a Secure Electronic Transactions (SET) protocol for international electronic commerce.

Government concerns over electronic payment systems have focused on the impact these systems have on monetary policy and policies on financial markets, technology development and consumer protection. The first concern is that electronic payment systems may create new types of "currency" that may affect monetary policy. Some experts in governments have also expressed concern that electronic money may facilitate "money laundering" operations. One of the significant technology development issues is whether governments should take initiatives regarding methods of cryptography, protocols, or other systems standards, and, if so, to what extent they should be involved. There is concern that as almost all of the technologies and systems are still experimental and undergoing improvements, government policy on standard setting or technology could have a significant impact on the industry. Consumer protection issues include the qualification of electronic money issuers, operating conditions for payment systems and evaluation of systems from the perspective of consumer protection. Specific issues singled out for further study by the OECD are:

1. Liability of issuers in the case of loss or theft of electronic money;
2. Reimbursement of issuers if electronic money is damaged or value data is lost;
3. Consumer liability for unwittingly receiving forged electronic money;
4. Rules involving errors in downloading electronic money (by merchants);
5. Treatment of chargeback when transactions are canceled;
6. Rules for converting electronic money into currency; and
7. Government regulation of issuers and deposits.

Consumer Protection

From the consumer's perspective, electronic commerce offers significant benefits including convenience, increased access to information, lower prices and choice of products. However, electronic commerce also has properties that facilitate fraud and make prosecution difficult. Its international nature also raises the prospect that consumer protection legislation in the jurisdiction in which the consumer resides may not apply in the merchant's country. Studies have shown that building trust and confidence in electronic commerce is an essential prerequisite for businesses to win consumers over to electronic commerce. As such, finding appropriate frameworks to increase such trust and confidence will have favourable ramifications for business-to-consumer electronic commerce.

The issues most often identified as being in need of attention are fairness and truthfulness in advertising, labeling and other disclosure requirements such as warranties, guarantees, product standards and specifications, refund mechanisms in case of canceled orders, defective products, returned purchases and lost deliveries, and a means of qualifying merchants pertaining to the foregoing. The Canadian Working Group on Consumers and Electronic Commerce, composed of consumer and business associations and governments, is finalizing Canadian guidelines on consumer protection in electronic commerce. These guidelines are intended to define consumer protection requirements and provide the basis for development of voluntary and legislative measures related to consumer information, contract formation, privacy, security and redress. Canada is also taking part in the OECD project to develop international guidelines for consumer protection in electronic commerce.

A study entitled Consumer Protection Rights in Canada in the Context of Electronic Commerce was recently completed on behalf of Industry Canada. This study pointed out that most consumer statutes and programs at both the federal and provincial levels were developed in the 1960's and 1970's, based on prevailing government, market, legal and institutional conditions and attitudes and that the advanced technologies of the "new digital" economy often involve hidden features that are challenging traditional legal rules and principles. The report contains 16 specific recommendations to improving the current legislative framework to meet the basic needs of the on-line consumer across Canada.

Privacy

In repeated surveys, Canadians have expressed concerns about privacy in general and about the loss of control over personal information in particular. Using the Internet exposes consumers and businesses to privacy considerations that are not experienced in private, closed network environments. The protection of privacy in electronic commerce transactions has been identified by the Government of Canada, and others, as an essential ingredient to providing trust in the digital economy.

Currently, the federal government and most provinces have legislation governing the collection, use and disclosure of personal information held by governments. The federal Privacy Act adopted in 1982 applies to all federal government departments, most federal agencies and some federal crown corporations. To date, only Quebec has adopted comprehensive privacy legislation for the private sector.

Other countries have passed comprehensive privacy legislation. For example, such legislation exists in Germany, France and Sweden. In 1980, the Council of Europe adopted a Convention binding a number of countries to create legislation establishing fair information practices. In 1980, the OECD adopted a set of privacy principles. Canada signed these guidelines in 1994. The European Union has also passed a data protection directive protecting personal information and harmonizing privacy laws among its members. This directive requires all member companies to adopt privacy legislation or revise existing laws to comply with the directive. The directive also contains certain provisions requiring member states to block transfers of information to non-member states that do not provide an adequate level of protection.

In October of 1998 the federal government introduced the Personal Information Protection and Electronic Documents Act, Bill C-54. Part 1 of this bill addresses rights of privacy with respect to personal information that is collected, used or disclosed by an organization in the private sector. The legislation will initially apply to the federally-regulated private sector including telecommunications, broadcasting, banking and interprovincial transportation and to certain federal crown corporations. It will also cover federal entities not covered under the existing Privacy Act. Three years after coming into effect, the Act will apply to all personal information collected, used, or disclosed during the course of commercial activities. The legislation will not apply provincially where a province adopts legislation that is substantially similar to the privacy provision portions of the legislation. The privacy provisions of Bill C-54 are modeled on the Canadian Standards Association's (CSA) Model Code for the Protection of Personal Information, which is recognized as a national standard. ...

NOTE

The Uniform Electronic Commerce Act has now been adopted in most of the common law provinces. For the Ontario Act, see the list of legislation preceding Mr. Sookman's article. The federal government has also enacted the Personal Information Protection and Electronic Documents Act: see *supra*. Some of these provisions will be dealt with more fully in chapter 3, *infra*, which deals with formational problems in contracts of sale. The Consumer Measures Committee of the Internal Common Market also approved in 2001 the Internet Sales Contract Harmonization Template. For further details see, *infra*, chapter 3, note following the extract from the provisions of the Ontario Electronic Commerce Act.

CHAPTER TWO

Concept of Sale

INTRODUCTION

Section 2 of the SGA defines the meaning of sale. Every word of the definition is important and should be carefully studied in the light of the cases reproduced in this chapter. The obvious reason is that if a transaction does not satisfy the statutory definition then *prima facie* it is not governed by the Act (or any other Act which employs the same definition).

This does not mean that the sales rule should not be applied by analogy. It is always a relevant question whether there is any functional difference between a sale and the particular transaction in question and whether the rationale of the sales rule applies equally to both types of transaction.

The distinctions canvassed in the ensuing case material are between a sale and (1) a hire-purchase agreement or equipment lease; (2) a contract for labour and materials; and (3) selling agencies and consignment agreements. Omitted are cases dealing with the definition of goods, as to which see OLRC Sales Report, c. 4. Note that, in general, the SGA draws no distinction between commercial and consumer transactions, the character of the parties, or the purpose for which the goods are intended. An important exception occurs in the case of the implied conditions of fitness and merchantability (s. 15(1) and (2)). The condition of merchantability only applies to "a seller who deals in goods of that description," that of fitness to "goods of a description that it is in the course of the seller's business to supply." These phrases are not defined. Consider the broad definition of "merchant" in UCC 2-104(1) and see if it assists the exegesis of the SGA. Note too that Article 2 uses the merchant/non-merchant distinction much more extensively than does the SGA.

The scope of the SGA should be compared with the scope of the CPA, including the amplifying regulations under the latter Act. What are the important differences and what are their rationales? Can you suggest better definitions than those which appear in the CPA? Which of the following transactions are governed by the CPA or any part of it:

1) The repair of an automobile;
2) The rental of a colour TV set;
3) Subscription to a book club;
4) The rental of a cottage for the summer;

5) The purchase of a car by a lawyer who intends to use it partly in his business and partly for pleasure;

6) The purchase of wall-to-wall carpeting which is to be paid for within 90 days. The contract discloses no separate credit charge;

7) The purchase of a beverage vending machine which the purchaser intends to use to supplement his regular income?

The definitions in the CPA do not apply uniformly throughout the Act. For instance, s. 18 limits the application of Part II to executory contracts of sale. Part III applies to all consumer transactions involving the extension of credit.

Credit is defined differently in s. 36(1) and in s. 1.[1] Why? Section 37(1) defines buyer and seller more broadly than does s. 1. Considering the many types of consumer transactions, should the definitions in s. 37(1) be adopted generally for the CPA? For the SGA?

FURTHER QUESTIONS

1) Is the credit transaction of one who borrows money in order to purchase goods for use in her business protected by the CPA?

2) Does a professional carry on business?

3) A doctor buys a car and uses it for house calls and for pleasure driving. Does the CPA apply?

4) Do the definitions in s. 2(1) of the Regulations apply to transactions regulated in s. 36 of the Act? Is the recipient of unsolicited goods or credit cards a "buyer," a "borrower," or both?

5) Is the making of an appointment with a dentist an executory contract protected by Part II? What rights does the individual have if, when she leaves the dentist's chair, she is presented with an unexpectedly high bill?

Definition of "Goods" and Status of Software

There has been much discussion in the literature and some US and British litigation on how contracts for the supply of software should be characterized: whether they should be treated as sale contracts governed by sales law or whether the answer turns on whether the software was imbedded in "hard" goods or whether its supply constituted the primary purpose of the contract. Still further difficulties arise because the software may only be a licence to use from the author to the end user. Additional complications arise because a licence of the latter sort frequently contains conditions which may not be drawn to the user's attention until the user actually receives and opens the product (often referred to as the "shrinkwrap" problem). The following cases only address the characterization issue; the shrinkwrap problem is dealt with in chapter 3.

---

1   The definitions of credit in ss. 1 and 36(1) were substantially amended in S.O 1999, c. 12, Sched. F and come into effect on proclamation.

St Albans City and District Council v. International Computers Ltd.
[1996] 4 All ER 481 (CA)

SIR IAIN GLIDEWELL: ... before I turn to the subject of damages there is one aspect of the case on liability on which I wish to express my own opinion. This is the second issue to which I have already referred, namely, was the contract between the parties subject to any implied term as to quality or fitness for purpose, and if so, what was the nature of that term? Consideration of this question during argument led to discussion of a more general question, namely, "Is software goods?" To seek to answer this question, it is necessary first to be clear about the meaning of some of the words used in argument.

In his judgment, Scott Baker J adopted a description of a computer system which contains the following passage which I have found helpful:

> By itself hardware can do nothing. The really important part of the system is the software. Programs are the instructions or commands that tell the hardware what to do. The program itself is an algorithm or formula. It is of necessity contained in a physical medium.

A program in machine readable form must be contained on a machine readable medium, such as paper cards, magnetic tapes, discs, drums or magnetic bubbles.

In relation to COMCIS the property in the program, i.e. the intangible "instructions or commands," remained with I.C.L. Under the contract, St Albans were licensed to use the program. This is a common feature of contracts of this kind. However, in order that the program should be encoded into the computer itself, it was necessarily first recorded on a disc, from which it could be transferred to the computer. During the course of the hearing, the word "software" was used to include both the (tangible) disc onto which the COMCIS program had been encoded and the (intangible) program itself. In order to answer the question, however, it is necessary to distinguish between the program and the disc carrying the program.

In both the Sale of Goods Act 1979 section 61 and the Supply of Goods and Services Act 1982 section 18 the definition of "goods" "includes all personal chattels other than things in action and money ..." Clearly a disc is within this definition. Equally clearly, a program, of itself, is not.

If a disc carrying a program is transferred, by way of sale or hire, and the program is in some way defective, so that it will not instruct or enable the computer to achieve the intended purpose, is this a defect in the disc? Put more precisely, would the seller or hirer of the disc be in breach of the terms as to quality and fitness for purpose implied by section 14 of the Sale of Goods Act and section 9 of the Act of 1982? Mr Dehn, for I.C.L., argues that they would not. He submits that the defective program in my example would be distinct from the tangible disc, and thus that the "goods"—the disc—would not be defective.

There is no English authority on this question, and indeed we have been referred to none from any Common Law jurisdiction. The only reference I have found is an article published in 1994 by Dr Jane Stapleton. This is to a decision in *Advent Systems Ltd v. Unisys Corporation* 925 F.2d 670 that software is a "good"; Dr Stapleton notes the decision as being reached "on the basis of policy arguments." We were referred, as was Scott Baker J, to a decision of Rogers J in the Supreme Court of New South Wales, *Toby Construction Ltd v. Computa Bar (Sales) Pty Ltd* (1983) 2 NSWJR 48. The decision in that case was that the sale of a whole computer system, including both hardware and software, was a sale of "goods" within the New South Wales legislation, which defines goods in similar terms to those in the English statute. That decision was in my respectful view clearly correct, but it does not answer the present question. Indeed, Rogers J specifically did not answer it. In expressing an opinion I am therefore venturing where others have, no doubt wisely, not trodden.

Suppose I buy an instruction manual on the maintenance and repair of a particular make of car. The instructions are wrong in an important respect. Anybody who follows them is likely to cause serious damage to the engine of his car. In my view the instructions are an integral part of the manual. The manual including the instructions, whether in a book or a video cassette, would in my opinion be "goods" within the meaning of the Sale of Goods Act, and the defective instructions would result in a breach of the implied terms in section 14.

If this is correct, I can see no logical reason why it should not also be correct in relation to a computer disc onto which a program designed and intended to instruct or enable a computer to achieve particular functions has been encoded. If the disc is sold or hired by the computer manufacturer, but the program is defective, in my opinion there would prima facie be a breach of the terms as to quality and fitness for purpose implied by the Sale of Goods Act or the Act of 1982.

However, in the present case, it is clear that the defective program 2020 was not sold, and it seems probable that it was not hired. The evidence is that in relation to many of the program releases an employee of I.C.L. went to St Albans' premises where the computer was installed taking with him a disc on which the new program was encoded, and himself performed the exercise of transferring the program into the computer.

As I have already said, the program itself is not "goods" within the statutory definition. Thus a transfer of the program in the way I have described does not, in my view, constitute a transfer of goods. It follows that in such circumstances there is no statutory implication of terms as to quality or fitness for purpose.

Would the contract then contain no such implied term? The answer must be sought in the Common Law. The terms implied by the Sale of Goods Act and the Act of 1982 were originally evolved by the courts of common law and have since by analogy been implied by the courts into other types of contract. Should such a term be implied in a contract of the kind I am now considering for the transfer of a computer program into the computer without any transfer of a disc or any other tangible thing on which the program is encoded?

The basis upon which a court is justified in implying a term into a contract in which it has not been expressed is strict. Lord Pearson summarised it in his speech in *Trollope & Colls Ltd v. N.W. Metropolitan Regional Hospital Board* (1973) 1 WLR 601 at 609 when he said:

> An unexpressed term can be implied if and only if the court finds that the parties must have intended that term to form part of their contract; it is not enough for the court to find that such a term would have been adopted by the parties as reasonable men if it had been suggested to them; it must have been a term that went without saying, a term which, though tacit, formed part of the contract which the parties made for themselves.

In my judgment a contract for the transfer into a computer of a program intended by both parties to instruct or enable the computer to achieve specified functions is one to which Lord Pearson's words apply. In the absence of any express term as to quality or fitness for purpose, or of any term to the contrary, such a contract is subject to an implied term that the program will be reasonably fit for, i.e. reasonably capable of achieving the intended purpose.

In the present case if, contrary to my view, the matter were not covered by express terms of the contract, I would hold that the contract was subject to an implied term that COMCIS was reasonably fit for, that is, reasonably capable of achieving the purpose specified in the "Statement of User Requirements" in Chapter 5 of St Albans' Invitation to Tender, and that as a result of the defect in release 2020 I.C.L. were in breach of that implied term. ...

Beta Computers (Europe) Limited v. Adobe Systems (Europe) Limited
[1996] FSR 367 (Outer House, Scotland)

[The plaintiffs ("pursuers" in Scottish legalese) sued the defendants ("defenders") for the supply of computer software manufactured by a third party, which was treated by the parties as the owner of the copyright in the software. The defendants had placed an order with the plaintiffs for a standard upgrade package. The defendants placed the order by telephone and it was agreed that the package was not customized to the defendant's order. The plaintiffs procured and delivered the software. The software was packaged so as to indicate that it was subject to strict end user licence.

The shrinkwrapped package bore the words "Opening the ... software indicates your acceptance of these terms and conditions." The defendants never opened the package and they argued that the terms of delivery entitled them to reject the software and excused them from any obligation to pay for it. The plaintiffs argued that the defendants had placed an unconditional contract with the plaintiffs for the supply of the software and that the defendant's obligation to pay was not qualified by any rights they might have vis-à-vis the licensor of the software.

Lord Penrose found that every contract for the supply of software had to be determined on its own facts and held that this contract was a composite contract of which the defendant's acceptance of the licensing conditions was an integral part. Accordingly, not having opened the shrinkwrap package, the defendants were not obliged to pay the plaintiffs. The following extract from the judgment explains why Lord Penrose did not accept the suggestion that contracts for the supply of software involved a contract for the sale of goods:]

LORD PENROSE: ... In my view, any proper analysis of the transaction must begin by identifying what it was that the defenders sought to have supplied by the pursuers. In the end of the day it was a matter of substantial agreement between counsel that central to the defenders' requirements, on any view, was access to the intellectual property of Informix in a medium which they could use and from which they could copy program material electronically into their hardware system and so as to be able to employ it for their business purposes. The order was not an order for the supply of disks as such. On the other hand it was not an order for the supply of information as such. The subject of the contract was a complex product comprising the medium and the manifestation within it or on it of the intellectual property of the author, Informix, in the form of the program material contained. There are, perhaps, no true analogies of this type of product, and certainly none was brought to my notice. In an article in *Reed: Computer Law*, (2nd Ed.), at page 44, Mr Graham Smith says:

> What, then, is software? It is suggested that the answer is that at least where it is sup-
> plied on a physical medium it should be regarded as physical property, like a book or a
> record, even though the nature of the contract under which it is supplied will vary,
> depending on the circumstances.

The reference to the nature of the contract of supply may be clarified by the discussion of licensing. In relation to that, the author says:

> As Steyn J stated in *Eurodynamics Systems Plc v. General Automation Ltd* (6 Septem-
> ber 1988 unreported): "although the ideas and concepts involved in software remained
> [the defendant's] property, the reality of the transaction is that there has been a transfer
> of a product." It is submitted with respect that this is correct, and that where software is
> licensed there are effectively two contracts between the licenser and licensee: a con-
> tract for the supply of the physical manifestation of the software, and secondly the
> grant of a licence to use the software.

The contract relating to the medium would, on this approach, be a contract of sale or hire depending on whether property passed. Counsel were not able to provide a copy of Steyn J's opinion.

This reasoning appears to me to be unattractive, at least in the context with which this case is concerned. It appears to emphasise the role of the physical medium, and to relate the transaction in the medium to sale or hire of goods. It would have the somewhat odd result that the dominant characteristic of the complex product, in terms of value or of the significant interests of parties, would be subordinated to the medium by which it was transmitted to the user in analysing the true nature and effect of the contract. If one obtained computer programs by telephone, they might be introduced into one's own hardware and used as effectively as if the medium were a disk or CD or magnetic tape. One could not describe the supply of information over the telephone system for a price as a sale of goods. Once copied into the hardware, the differences relating to the medium would be irrelevant. On the other hand one could not properly ignore the physical medium where the software was provided on a disk. The physical entity might be defective or subject to damage as any other physical object. The floppy disk is constructed from components, any one of which might be so disconform to specification at the point of supply as to render the disk unusable whatever information it may have contained at some time in its existence. Similarly the information might have been corrupted at or prior to the point of supply. A contract for the sale of software, ignoring the ownership of the intellectual property at this stage, must, if it is to have business efficacy in any sense, procure the communication of the information required in a condition which will enable full and proper use to be made of it, and in a medium of such nature, quality and condition as will enable the purchaser to access the information and copy it. The analogy with a printed book is, in my opinion, false. Even if one considered the wider field of printed material, there would be no true analogy. A book typically is intended to be read, not copied, as a way of enjoying or using the object. The understanding of the reader may vary, of course, and the extent to which any reader may be able to make practical use of technical information contained in a book will vary according to his understanding and perhaps the means available to apply the information gleaned from the book in a practical way. But there are no limitations on accessing the information which affect readers generally and which are inherent in the medium ... .

NOTE

The characterization of sale contracts for goods that included software ("smart goods") was vigorously debated by the Committee drafting revised Article 2 of the UCC. The majority opinion was that "smart goods" should be treated as contracts for the sale of goods and that no distinction should be drawn between the goods' components and the software imbedded in the product. The majority of the Committee was strongly opposed to the solution propounded in the Uniform Computer Information Transactions Act (UCITA), which was intended to become new Article 2B of the UCC, but was ultimately rejected by the American Law Institute (ALI) as being too controversial.

The new Article 2 Drafting Committee that was struck after the withdrawal of the draft Revised Article 2 in 1998 changed tack and proposed adopting the UCITA approach in new s. 2-103.

This read in part as follows:

(b) If a transaction includes computer information and goods, this article applies to the goods but not to the computer information or informational rights in it. However, if a copy of a computer program is contained in and sold, or pursuant to Section 2.313A or 2.313B, leased as part of goods, this article applies to the copy and the computer program unless:

(1) the goods are a computer or computer peripheral; or

(2) giving the buyer or lessee of the goods access to or use of the program is ordinarily a substantial purpose of transactions in goods of the type sold or leased.

(c) In a transaction that includes computer information and goods, then with regard to the goods, including any copy of a computer program constituting goods under Section 2-102(a)(23), the parties may not by agreement alter a result that would otherwise be required by this article.

The draft comment to s. 2-103 explained:

> This section states, with a limited exception, that the rules in Article 2 do not explicitly apply
> to the computer information aspect of a transaction involving both the sale of goods and the
> transfer of an interest in computer information. In that case, if the State has not enacted a
> statute (such as the Uniform Computer Information Transactions Act) specifically dealing
> with computer information transactions, a court must select an appropriate rule to govern
> that aspect of the transaction.

The limited exception was that Article 2 would apply to the computer information aspect
of a transaction if a computer program is contained in the goods and supplied with them,
subject to the qualification that s. 2-103(b) mentions. So, for example, the computer program that controls a car's antilock braking system is governed by Article 2, as is the copy
in which the program is contained. However, an upstream contract to develop or supply
the program to the car manufacturer would be beyond the scope of Article 2. So would be
a separately licensed program for a digital camera that enables the camera to link to a
computer: Proposed Draft Comment.

However, this approach provoked a new round of controversy and the Proposed Amendments to Article 2 approved by the ALI in May 2001 (see, *supra*, chapter 1) are completely silent on the problem. In your view, what approach should be adopted in Canada?

Note on Barter or Exchange Transactions

OLRC Sales Report, at 65:

> Section 2 of The Sales of Goods Act stipulates that the price must be payable in money. An
> exchange or barter of goods will not satisfy the statutory test. This bland statement, how-
> ever, requires some important qualifications. It is clear, for example, that a price which is to
> be satisfied by the sale from the buyer to the seller of goods of equivalent or greater value,
> will meet the prescribed test. It is equally well settled that the price may be paid partly in
> cash and partly by means of a trade-in or other exchange, at any rate where the value of the
> trade-in is monetized. What remains excluded, therefore, is a pure barter agreement that is
> not tainted by any mention of a monetary figure.
>
> It is difficult to justify the insistence on a monetary consideration. UCC 2-304 does not
> do so. It provides as follows:
>
> > (1) The price can be made payable in money or otherwise. If it is payable in whole or
> > in part in goods each party is a seller of the goods which he is to transfer.
> >
> > (2) Even though all or part of the price is payable in an interest in reality the transfer
> > of the goods and the seller's obligations with reference to them are subject to this Article,
> > but not the transfer of the interest in reality or the transferor's obligations in connection
> > therewith.
>
> It may be argued that, where a simple exchange or other non-monetary form of considera-
> tion is involved, it will be difficult to assess damages if either party breaches his contract.
> But this will be true however the contract is characterized. The real question, in our opinion,
> is whether sales rules should be applied by analogy to a contract involving non-monetary

consideration, or whether it would be simpler to absorb such transactions into sales law by expanding the definition of price. While acknowledging that the problem is not of the first magnitude, we prefer the latter solution. We therefore recommend the adoption of the Code section, and our Draft Bill contains a provision to this effect.

What lends force to the OLRC recommendation is the fact that the rules governing the barter agreements are uncertain and surprisingly undeveloped. It was settled in the last century that they are not subject to s. 17 or the Statute of Frauds (until 1994 reproduced in Ontario's SGA s. 5); there is also "reasonable agreement among the authorities that it is not open to a disappointed party, who has parted with his goods without receiving the expected return, to sue for the value of the goods delivered as a price; his remedy is to claim unliquidated damages for non-delivery of the goods promised in exchange or possibly to sue the other party in fact on the basis that the property in such goods has passed to him": *Benjamin's Sale of Goods*, 5th ed., at paras. 1-025, and *cf. Messenger v. Greene*, [1937] 2 DLR 26 (NS CA) (How would these questions be decided under the Code?) Beyond these points, and perhaps a few others, there is much uncertainty as to the applicable law.

The uncertainty would not matter if one could safely assume that barter agreements are an historical curiosity and out of place in a modern industrialized society. The assumption cannot be made. In fact there is evidence of a remarkable resurgence of popularity in barter transactions of one description or another, both nationally and internationally.

At the national level, part of the popularity is explained by the emergence of an "underground" economy where tax avoidance may be an added incentive for barter transactions (for example, a farmer exchanging produce for an electrician's services), but it is clear that organized barter schemes, part of the "visible" economy, are also growing in importance. In 1998 they were said to have accounted for an estimated $7.5 billion worth of business worldwide. Due to the rapid development of e-commerce technology in recent years, and the ease with which it can facilitate barter transactions, the figure has undoubtedly risen substantially since then, and enterprises have sprung up which specialize in bringing bartering parties together.

At the international level, "countertrade" transactions became a well-established post-war trading phenomenon between socialist and capitalist countries and between developed and developing countries. The essential feature of a countertrade arrangement is that an exporter of goods obliges itself to import goods of equivalent value from the buyer country, in this way enabling the buyer country to conserve its limited reserves of foreign currency.

The countertrade may take the form of a straight barter (for example, the exporter's machinery for the buyer's vodka) or it may be in the form of a counterpurchase agreement. In the latter case, the exporter agrees to purchase from the buyer country commodities in amounts of the same monetary value or, increasingly often, somewhat less in value than the price of the exporter's goods. For further details, see Castel, deMestral and Graham, *International Business Transactions and Economic Relations* (1986), at 566-73.

LEASE OR SALE: THE FORM AND SUBSTANCE PROBLEM

Helby v. Matthews
[1895-99] All ER Rep. 821, [1895] AC 471 (HL)

LORD HERSCHELL LC: The appellant was the owner of a piano, of which he had given possession to one Charles Brewster, under an agreement in writing of Dec. 23, 1892, to the terms of which I shall have occasion to refer immediately. On July 21, 1893, Brewster, improperly and without the consent of the appellant, pledged the piano with the respondents, who are pawnbrokers, as security for an advance. The appellant, upon discovering this, demanded the piano from the respondents, and, on their refusing to deliver it, brought an action of trover. The defence set up by the respondents was that they had received the piano from Brewster in good faith and without notice of any claim on the part of the appellant, and that Brewster having "bought or agreed to buy" it from him, they were protected by s. 9 of the Factors Act, 1889.[2]

The county court judge held that the defence was not proved, and his judgment was upheld by the Divisional Court of the Queen's Bench. The Court of Appeal, however, came to the conclusion that the defence had been established, and reversed the judgment of the Divisional Court.

The only question is whether the respondents have made out that Brewster had bought or agreed to buy the piano. This depends upon the true effect of the agreement under which he obtained it. By that agreement Brewster, called therein the hirer, agreed to pay the "owner" on Dec. 23, 1892, a rent or hire instalment of 10s. 6d., and 10s. 6d. on the 23rd of each succeeding month, and to keep the instrument in the hirer's own custody at the address named in the agreement, and not to remove the same without the owner's previous consent in writing. He further agreed that if the hiring should be terminated by him under a subsequent clause of the agreement, and the instrument returned to the owner, the hirer should remain liable to the owner for arrears of hire up to the date of the return, and should not be entitled to any allowance, credit, return, or set-off for payments previously made. The owner, on the other hand, agreed that the hirer might terminate the hiring by delivering up the instrument to the owner, and, further, that if the hirer should punctually pay the full sum of eighteen guineas, by 10s. d. at the date of signing and by thirty-five monthly instalments of 10s. 6d. in advance as aforesaid, the instrument should become the sole and absolute property of the hirer. It was also agreed that unless and until the full sum of eighteen guineas was paid the instrument should be and continue the sole property of the owner.

It is said that the substance of the transaction evidenced by the agreement must be looked at, and not its mere words. I quite agree. But the substance must, of course, be ascertained by a consideration of the rights and obligations of the parties, to be derived from a consideration of the whole of the agreement. If Brewster agreed to

---

2   Section 9 of the British Factors Act, 1889, does not appear in the Ontario Factors Act, RSO 1990, c. F.1, but is reproduced almost verbatim in s. 25(2) of the Ont. SGA. [ed.]

buy the piano the parties cannot, by calling it a hiring, or by any mere juggling with words, escape from the consequences of the contract into which they entered. What then, was the real nature of the transaction? The answer to this question is not, I think, involved in any difficulty. Brewster was to obtain possession of the piano and to be entitled to its use so long as he paid the plaintiff the stipulated sum of 10s. 6d. a month, and he was bound to make these monthly payments so long as he retained possession of the piano. If he continued to make them at the appointed times for the period of three years the piano was to become his property, but he might at any time return it, and upon doing so, would no longer be liable to make any further payment beyond the monthly sum then due.

I cannot, with all respect, concur in the view of the Court of Appeal that, upon the true construction of the agreement, Brewster had "agreed to buy" the piano. An agreement to buy imports a legal obligation to buy. If there was no such legal obligation there cannot, in my opinion, properly be said to have been an agreement to buy. Where is any such legal obligation to be found? Brewster might buy or not just as he pleased. He did not agree to make thirty-six or any number of monthly payments. All that he undertook was to make the monthly payment of 10s. 6d. so long as he kept the piano. He had an option, no doubt, to buy it by continuing the stipulated payments for a sufficient length of time. If he had exercised that option he would have become the purchaser. I cannot see, under these circumstances, how he can be said either to have bought or agreed to buy the piano. The terms of the contract did not, upon its execution, bind him to buy, but left him free to do so or not as he pleased, and nothing happened after the contract was made to impose that obligation. The Master of the Rolls said:

> It is a contract by the seller to sell, and a contract by the purchaser, if he does not change his mind, to buy; and, if this agreement goes on to its end, it ends in a purchase. Therefore, it seems to me that the true and proper construction of this instrument, after all, is this—it is an agreement by the one to sell, and an agreement by the other to buy, but with an option on the part of the buyer if he changes his mind to put an end to the contract.

I cannot think that an agreement to buy, "if he does not change his mind," is any agreement to buy at all in the eye of the law. If it rests with me to do or not to do a certain thing at a future time, according to the then state of my mind, I cannot be said to have contracted to do it.

It appears to me that the contract in question was in reality a contract of hiring, and not in name or pretence only. But for the provision that if the hirer punctually paid the 10s. 6d. a month for thirty-six months, the piano should be his property, it could not be doubted that it was a mere agreement for its hire, and I cannot see how the fact that this provision was added made it any the less a contract of hiring until that condition had been fulfilled. I think it very likely that both parties thought it would probably end in a purchase, but this is far from showing that it was an agreement to buy. The monthly payments were no doubt somewhat higher than they would have been if the agreement had contained no such provision. One can well conceive cases, however, in which a person who had not made up his mind to continue the payment for three years, would nevertheless enter into such an agreement. It might be worth his while to make somewhat larger monthly payments for the use of the piano in order that he might enjoy that option if he chose to exercise it. In such a case how could it be said that he had agreed to buy when he had not only come under no obligation to buy, but had not even made up his mind to do so? The agreement is, in its terms, just as applicable to such a case as to one where the hirer had resolved to continue the payments for the three years, and it must be construed upon a considera- tion of the obligations which its terms create, and not upon a mere speculation as to what was contemplated, or what would probably be done under it.

It was said in the Court of Appeal that there was an agreement by the appellant to sell, and that an agreement to sell connotes an agreement to buy. This is undoubtedly true if the words "agreement to sell" be used in their strict legal sense; but when a person has, for valuable consideration, bound himself to sell to another on certain terms, if the other chooses to avail himself of the binding offer, he may, in popular language, be said to have agreed to sell, though an agreement to sell in this sense which is in truth merely an offer which cannot be withdrawn, certainly does not con- note an agreement to buy, and it is only in this sense that there can be said to have been an agreement to sell in the present case.

It was argued for the respondents that the case came within the mischief intended to be provided against by s. 9 of the Factors Act, 1889,[3] and that the enactment ought, therefore, to be so construed as to cover it. I can see no reason for thus straining the language of the enactment. A person who is in the possession of a piano under such an agreement as that which existed in the present case is no more its apparent owner than if he had merely hired it, and in the latter case any one taking it as security would have no claim to hold it as against the owner. Reliance was placed on the decision in *Lee v. Butler*, [1893] 2 QB 318, and it was said that the present case was not, in principle, distinguishable from it. There seems to me to be the broadest dis- tinction between the two cases. There was there an agreement to buy. The purchase money was to be paid in two instalments; but as soon as the agreement was entered into, there was an absolute obligation to pay both of them, which might have been enforced by action. The person who obtained the goods could not insist upon return- ing them and so absolve himself from any obligation to make further payment. Unless there was a breach of contract by the party who engaged to make the pay- ments the transaction necessarily resulted in a sale. That there was in that case an agreement to buy appears to me, as it did to the Court of Appeal, to be beyond ques- tion. It was further urged for the respondents that when Brewster pledged the piano with them it became impossible for him to return it to the appellant, and he became, therefore from that time bound to make the stipulated payment and to become the purchaser. I cannot accede to this argument. In my opinion, it is impossible to hold that Brewster, having only a right under the contract to buy, provided he complied with the prescribed conditions, could convert himself into a purchaser as against the

---

3 Section 9 of the British Factors Act, 1889, does not appear in the Ontario Factors Act, RSO 1990, c.
   F.1, but is reproduced almost verbatim in s. 25(2) of the Ont. SGA. [ed.]

owner by violating the conditions of the contract. I think the judgment appealed from must be reversed.

Appeal allowed.

[The other law lords delivered concurring judgments.]

Tamara M. Buckwold
The Law of Commercial Leasing in Canada
(1999), unpublished study prepared for the Uniform Law Conference of Canada, paras. [8]-[15] (Footnotes omitted)

Because modern lease transactions adopt a variety of legal and functional forms, it is virtually impossible to delineate discrete categories or kinds of lease. Furthermore, the descriptive terminology applied to these forms varies, and no apt labels exist for some leasing structures. One can only describe in general terms the nature and objective of the several leasing devices currently in use.

A lease transaction entails a contractual relationship between the lessor and the lessee, as well as a bailment. It thus invokes the traditional law of bailment along with the general principles of contract law. In its simplest form, there are only two parties to the transaction, the lessor, who owns the goods subject to the lease, and the lessee, who is entitled to their possession and use over a stipulated term in return for monetary payment, ordinarily by way of installments. The lessee may or may not be entitled to acquire title to the goods through the exercise of an option to purchase, usually at the end of the term. The lessor is generally a dealer who inventories goods for lease. Such transactions may range from the hourly rental of ski gear at a resort to the long term lease of business equipment.

The functional objectives of a transaction of this kind may vary. In its "pure" form, such a lease is designed simply to enable the lessee to use the lessor's property on a pay-as-you-go basis. Such a lease is sometimes described as an operating lease or in some contexts as a "true" lease, by way of distinction from a "security" lease, which lies at the other end of the spectrum.

A security lease is designed as a device for the acquisition of the leased goods under a deferred payment schedule, comparable in many respects to a conditional sale contract. As such, it is primarily a financing mechanism, though it may give rise to issues ordinarily arising in the context of a contract of sale or a true lease. In these transactions, the lessor retains title to the leased goods as security for payment of the sums stipulated in the contract through periodic installments of "rent," usually along with a terminal purchase option sum.

A simple lease may also function as a financing device if it is part of a "sale-leaseback" transaction. In that scenario, the original owner of the goods sells them to a financial institution, which then leases them back to the owner-cum-lessee. The lessor in such a relationship cannot be expected to assume any obligations relating to the quality or performance of the goods, which will have been acquired from another source whether contemporaneously with or some time prior to the financing transaction.

In the case of long term leases, a second contractual relationship is very often introduced into the picture through the assignment of the lessor's interest to a third party financer, who may or may not be related to the lessor. Functionally, this arrangement enables the lessee to finance the acquisition of goods through indirect resort to the assignee's capital, simultaneously facilitating the business operations of the lessor, who would otherwise not be in a position to inventory or acquire goods for lease to its customers. The assignee in this scenario is a provider of credit, not goods. It is therefore concerned to avoid any responsibility for the quality, performance or maintenance of the goods subject to the lease, while enjoying the benefit of the lessee's payment obligations thereunder.

The most complex variant of current leasing structures is what UCC Article 2A designates the "finance lease," terminology which is adopted in this context hereafter. In this situation, goods are sold by a supplier to a lessor, who then leases them to the lessee. The lessor is a financial institution whose role is to finance the acquisition of the goods in question by the lessee. It is ordinarily not related to the supplier, and is not involved in the selection or evaluation of the goods acquired for purposes of the lease. The lessee will have chosen the goods subject to the lease and dealt directly with the supplier in determining their performance attributes and suitability. However, there is no contractual relationship between the supplier and the lessee. The payment structure in the lease is designed to enable the lessor to recover its capital cost and a return on its investment. The lease is functionally a device for repayment over its term of the funds advanced for acquisition of the leased goods by the lessor. Legally, the transaction entails two related contracts: the contract of sale between the supplier and lessor, and the contract of lease between lessor and lessee. The adoption of the finance lease as a device for the acquisition of goods by the lessee reflects the taxation and financing strategies of the lessee and lessor, rather than a decision to "lease" goods in the traditional sense.

While the various kinds of lease transaction described above are legally and conceptually distinct in certain aspects, they share one functional objective. In today's commercial leasing market, a lease (other than one of short duration) is designed to finance the acquisition of goods, regardless of whether it is a "true" lease or a security lease. The assimilation of purchase and financing functions with a legal form historically intended simply to regulate the use of one person's goods by another has broadened and complicated the range of legal issues arising from these transactions, particularly insofar as those functions entail the introduction of a third party financer. Those issues may invoke aspects of the common law of bailment, contract and assignment, choses in action legislation, the statutory and common law of sales, the provincial and territorial Personal Property Security Acts and a variety of consumer protection statutes.

NOTES

1) The English conception of the hire-purchase agreement as a genuine lease with an option to purchase has created numerous difficulties, both on the contractual side and with

respect to the status of the agreement as a form of chattel security. (The chattel security aspects are discussed further in volume III of the previous edition of this casebook, chapter 2.) For a discussion of the English problems, see R.M. Goode and J.S. Ziegel, *Hire-Purchase and Conditional Sale: A Comparative Study* (1965), chapter 14. A leading textbook on the English law is R.M. Goode, *Hire-Purchase Law and Practice*, 2nd ed. (1970). Nevertheless, the English hire-purchase agreement has shown remarkable powers of survival and until quite recently it constituted the principal method for financing the acquisition of durable goods for business as well as consumer purposes.

2) This was never true in Canada. Nevertheless, until the introduction of the personal property security legislation, Canadian courts generally followed the English characterization and treated such agreements as true chattel leases unless they came within the *Lee v. Butler* type of exception discussed in *Helby v. Matthews*. See, for example, *Keneric Tractor Sales Ltd. v. Langille*, in volume III of the previous edition of this casebook, chapter 10, and earlier cases there referred to. English precedents were applied even though many of the provincial conditional sales acts (including Ontario's former Conditional Sales Act) defined a conditional sale as including a bailment with an option to purchase. The Crowther Committee in England recommended in 1971 the abolition of the hire-purchase agreement as a separate security device and its assimilation with other chattel security devices in a new Lending and Security Act. This step was not taken in England, but it was in Australia, at least in relation to consumer transactions. The Australian consumer credit laws deem a consumer hire-purchase agreement to be a sale of goods by instalments. Property in the goods is treated as having passed to the consumer on the date of delivery or the contract date, whichever is later, and the consumer is deemed to have given the supplier a mortgage over the goods to secure payment of the amount owing under the putative contract of sale: see Australian Consumer Credit Code, s. 10.

3) From an early date the Americans followed not the legal obligation test adopted in *Helby v. Matthews, supra*, but the intention, or substantial purpose, test. Under the substantial purpose test, the question is not whether the customer is obliged to pay the full purchase price and whether the customer becomes the owner of the goods at the end of the payments. Rather, the question is, what is the substantial effect of the total agreement? The test is a relative one, and it is not as easy to apply as the legal obligation test:

> "The difference between a true lease and a security transaction lies in whether the lessee acquires an equity of ownership through his rent payments. If the lessee can never become the owner it can be argued persuasively that the transaction is certainly a true lease. But who is the owner under a finance lease? While the lessee does not acquire title, the lessor has no equity because presumably the goods will be worn out or obsolete before they revert to him. His reversion rights, in short, are meaningless. At the same time the lessee has all the benefits of ownership": W.D. Hawkland, "The Impact of the Uniform Commercial Code on Equipment Leasing" [1972] *U. of Ill. Forum* 446 at 450.

See further, J.R. Peden, "The Treatment of Equipment Leases as Security Agreements under the Uniform Commercial Code" (1971), 13 *William and Mary L Rev.* 110, and volume III of the previous edition of this casebook, chapter 2.

UCC 1-201(37) contains a codified version of the substantial purpose test. It provides in relevant part as follows:

Whether a transaction creates a lease or security interest is determined by the facts of each case; however, a transaction creates a security interest if the consideration the lessee is to pay the lessor for the right to possession and use of the goods is an obligation for the term of the lease not subject to termination by the lessee, and

(a) the original term of the lease is equal to or greater than the remaining economic life of the goods,

(b) the lessee is bound to renew the lease for the remaining economic life of the goods or is bound to become the owner of the goods,

(c) the lessee has an option to renew the lease for the remaining economic life of the goods for no additional consideration or nominal additional consideration upon compliance with the lease agreement, or

(d) the lessee has an option to become the owner of the goods for no additional consideration or nominal additional consideration upon compliance with the lease agreement.

A transaction does not create a security interest merely because it provides that

(a) the present value of the consideration the lessee is obligated to pay the lessor for the right to possession and use of the goods is substantially equal to or is greater than the fair market value of the goods at the time the lease is entered into,

(b) the lessee assumes risk of loss of the goods, or agrees to pay taxes, insurance, filing, recording or registration fees, or service or maintenance costs with respect to the goods,

(c) the lessee has an option to renew the lease or to become the owner of the goods,

(d) the lessee has an option to renew the lease for a fixed rent that is equal to or greater than the reasonably predictable fair market rent for the use of the goods for the term of the renewal at the time the option is to be performed, or

(e) the lessee has an option to become the owner of the goods for a fixed price that is equal to or greater than the reasonably predictable fair market value of the goods at the time the option is to be performed.

For the purposes of this subsection (37):

(x) Additional consideration is not nominal if (i) when the option to renew the lease is granted to the lessee the rent is stated to be the fair market rent for the use of the goods for the term of the renewal determined at the time the option is to be performed, or (ii) when the option to become the owner of the goods is granted to the lessee the price is stated to be the fair market value of the goods determined at the time the option is to be performed. Additional consideration is nominal if it is less than the lessee's reasonably predictable cost of performing under the lease agreement if the option is not exercised;

(y) "Reasonably predictable" and "remaining economic life of the goods" are to be determined with reference to the facts and circumstances at the time the transaction is entered into; and

(z) "Present value" means the amount as of a date certain of one or more sums payable in the future, discounted to the date certain. The discount is determined by the interest rate specified by the parties if the rate is not manifestly unreasonable at the time the transaction is entered into; otherwise, the discount is determined by a commercially reasonable rate that takes into account the facts and circumstances of each case at the time the transaction was entered into.

4) OPPSA, s. 2 also adopts a substantial purpose test for distinguishing between true leases and security transactions. Unlike UCC 1-201(37), however, it does not spell out the criteria to be applied in administering the test. These have been left for the courts to develop. See the cases discussed in volume III of the previous edition of this casebook, chapter 2. The PPSAs in the other provinces have taken a different tack. With the exception of the enforcement provisions, they are expressed to apply to any lease of goods for a term of more than one year, *whether or not* the lease is intended as security. The purpose is to create a bright-line test for determining the application of the statute and to avoid the kind of litigation that has occurred in Ontario over the characterization of lease agreements. A similar provision has twice been recommended for Ontario, but the recommendations have not been adopted: Canadian Bar Association—Ontario, *Submission to the Minister of Consumer and Commercial Relations Concerning the Personal Property Security Act* (October 1998), para. 3. The Catzman Committee, which drafted the Revised OPPSA made a similar recommendation in its 1984 report. See further, volume III of the previous edition of this casebook, chapter 2.

5) Equipment leases of all types have grown greatly in value and popularity over the past 40 years—primarily for tax reasons but increasingly also for other reasons. According to the Buckwold study, *supra*, at para. [1]:

> Leasing as a device for the acquisition of goods has become an extremely important component of the Canadian and global economies. The Canadian Finance and Leasing Association, relying on World Bank and United Nations sources, recently advanced these statistics:
>
>> In 1978, annual plant and equipment leasing volumes worldwide (excluding vehicles and real estate) were about US $40 billion. By 1986, plant and equipment leasing had grown to almost US $175 billion and by 1996, worldwide annual plant and equipment leasing volumes had grown two and a half times to about US $430 billion. Canada ranks ninth in the world in annual plant and equipment leasing.
>
> The same organization estimates the leasing industry to have a total of over $60 billion in financing in place with businesses and consumers in Canada. In 1997, 25% of business investment in leasing and equipment was financed through leases, and 46% of new light passenger vehicles were leased, as compared with 34% acquired through loans and 20% purchased with cash.

Characterization of these agreements is of pervasive importance and affects, among other things, the following questions: (1) the capital cost write-off of the lessor, and the tax deductibility of the lease payments as current operating expenditures to the lessee; (2) the applicability of the SGA and the scope and liability of the lessor for breach of the implied warranties of quality; (3) the applicability of the OPPSA and comparable legislation in other provinces; (4) the rights and remedies of the lessor in the case of the lessee's default; and (5) the applicability of interest rate and consumer credit legislation.

The uncertainty governing these same questions in the United States prompted the sponsors of the Uniform Commercial Code—the National Conference of Commissioners on Uniform State Laws (NCCUSL) and the ALI—to promulgate a new Article 2A on leases in 1987. Article 2A has since been adopted by 48 states. In addition to Article 2A, state legislatures have enacted their own laws to govern consumer leasing transactions.

NCCUSL is in the process of drafting a model uniform statute to regulate consumer leases, the Uniform Consumer Leasing Act (UCLA). The main issues the UCLA will address are: (1) pre-contractual disclosure; (2) default and early termination payments; (3) risk of loss to consumers in connection with gap liability insurance; (4) excess wear and tear provisions; and (5) assignability.

There seems to be general agreement that a UCC Article 2A type statute is not warranted in Canada: Jacob S. Ziegel, "Should Canada Adopt an Article 2A Type Law on Personal Property Leasing?" (1990), 16 *CBLJ* 369; Ronald C.C. Cuming, "An Article 2A for Canada? A Comment on Professor Ziegel's Paper" (1990), 16 *CBLJ* 439; Buckwold, above. However, the Buckwold study concluded that there is a case for statutory reform limited to consumer lease transactions, because the law in this area is "substantially deficient, difficult to ascertain and lacking in uniformity": at para. [222]. The study also recommends legislation to address the tripartite aspect of finance lease transactions. The legislation would: (1) extend suppliers' and manufacturers' warranties to the lessee; (2) define the lessor's obligations to the lessee in connection with the goods, particularly in relation to matters of title and quiet possession; and (3) restrict the lessee's claims against the lessor in matters relating to the quality and performance of the goods: at para. [225].

6) The leasing of equipment also plays an important role in international trade and financing, and it is common to find high priced items (including such mobile goods as rolling stock, aircraft and ships) being acquired from a common supplier through a lease concluded with a financing lessor, which may or may not be related to the supplier. Many current systems of law lack modern rules to govern such transactions, and this led UNIDROIT to undertake the preparation of a convention on International Financing Leasing, which was adopted at a diplomatic conference held in Ottawa on May 28, 1988. See R.C.C. Cuming, "Legal Regulation of International Financial Leasing: The 1988 Ottawa Convention" (1989), 7 *Ariz. J Int'l & Comp. L* 39. The Convention received the necessary ratifications in 1994 and came into effect on May 1, 1995. The three ratifying countries are France, Italy, and Nigeria. Canada is considering joining the Convention but no decision has been made yet.

7) In the field of contracts of sale and lease-back, the English courts, arrestingly, have shown a much greater willingness to apply a substance test to determine the true nature of the transaction than in the case of hire-purchase agreements. (One of the reasons for the disparate treatment may be that many of the earlier cases involved attempts to bypass the English moneylenders' legislation). See A.L. Diamond, "Hire-Purchase Agreements as Bills of Sale" (1960), 23 *MLR* 399, 516. Section 57(3) of the Ontario SGA also makes it clear that the Act does not apply to any transaction in the form of a contract of sale that is intended to operate by way of mortgage, pledge, charge, or other security.

In Canada, so far as the sale and lease-back of chattels is concerned, such agreements will be caught by the provincial PPSAs if the agreement is in substance a security agreement. A leading decision to this effect is *Re Speedtrack Limited* (1980), 11 BLR 220 (Ont., Henry J), referred to in volume III of the previous edition of this casebook, chapter 2, in the context of the distinction between security and non-security chattel leases.

CONTRACTS FOR WORK AND MATERIALS

Borek v. Hooper
(1994), 18 OR (3d) 470 (Div. Ct.)

SOUTHEY J: This is an appeal from a judgment of His Honour Judge Lamb, pronounced in Small Claims Court on June 21, 1993, in which he awarded the plaintiff damages of $2,000, plus court costs and added disbursements of $976.93, for breach of an implied condition of merchantable quality under s. 15, para. 2 of the *Sale of Goods Act*, RSO 1990, c. S.1, in respect of a painting commissioned by the plaintiff from the defendant, a professional artist.

The case is one of first impression. Although counsel referred to several decided cases involving the contractual rights and obligations of artists, none dealt with problems of defective work or materials. The learned trial judge gave careful written reasons for his decision, and it is with regret that I find myself unable to agree with him. He was at a considerable disadvantage, because neither party was represented by counsel before him. I, on the other hand, had the benefit of able submissions from counsel on both sides.

The painting is large. Its dimensions are five feet × eight feet, with the horizontal being the longer edge. It was created expressly to fit a specific space in the plaintiff's home, and to fulfil her wish for a predominantly white painting to hang on a white wall. The painting is abstract. Its composition might be described, albeit crudely, as a relatively narrow, irregular shaped slash or splash of colour across a broad white background.

The artist created the painting in about three weeks. When he delivered it to the plaintiff and hung it, she was thrilled with it and paid him $4,000, which was the price that had previously been agreed upon. About three years later, in 1987, she noticed that the white areas in the painting were yellowing. In addition, by 1991, when the action was commenced, the surface of the painting had cracked and some flaking had occurred in the lower right portion. The plaintiff took the position that the painting she was left with was not the painting she had contracted for.

The learned trial judge found that the painting was of merchantable quality when delivered, but that it maintained its original characteristics for barely five years instead of an expected 10-year economic life, which he found would not have been unreasonable. This was the basis of his judgment for the plaintiff for 50 per cent of the purchase price.

It was held by the Court of Appeal in England in *Robinson v. Graves*, [1935] 1 KB 579, [1935] All ER Rep. 935, that the oral commissioning of the plaintiff, an artist, to paint a portrait was not a contract for the sale of goods, but was a contract for work and labour. The defendant customer in that case repudiated the contract after the plaintiff had commenced to paint the portrait. The portrait was never completed, but the plaintiff was found to be entitled to recover damages for breach of contract, despite the absence of any memorandum in writing of the contract, as would have been required under the *Sale of Goods Act*. Greer LJ said at p. 584:

I can imagine that nothing would be more surprising to a client going to a portrait painter to have his portrait painted and to the artist who was accepting the commission than to be told that they were making a bargain about the sale of goods. It is, of course, possible that a picture may be ordered in such circumstances as will make it an order for goods to be supplied in the future, but it does not follow that that is the inference to be drawn in every case as between the client and the artist. Looking at the propositions involved from the point of view of interpreting the words in the English language it seems to me that the painting of a portrait in these circumstances would not, in the ordinary use of the English language, be deemed to be the purchase and sale of that which is produced by the artist. It would, on the contrary, be held to be an undertaking by the artist to exercise such skill as he was possessed of in order to produce for reward a thing which would ultimately have to be accepted by the client. If that is so, the contract in this case was not a contract for the sale of goods within the meaning of s. 4 of the Sale of Goods Act, 1893.

At p. 585, he quoted with approval from the decision of Pollock CB in *Clay v. Yates* (1856), 1 H & N 73 at p. 78, 25 LJ Ex. 237: "My impression is, that in the case of a work of art, whether in gold, silver, marble or plaster, where the application of skill and labour is of the highest description, and the material is of no importance as compared with the labour, the price may be recovered as work, labour and materials." Greer LJ continued at pp. 587-88:

But if the substance of the contract, on the other hand, is that skill and labour have to be exercised for the production of the article and that it is only ancillary to that that there will pass from the artist to his client or customer some materials in addition to the skill involved in the production of the portrait, that does not make any difference to the result, because the substance of the contract is the skill and experience of the artist in producing the picture.

For these reasons I am of opinion that in this case the substance of the matter was an agreement for the exercise of skill and it was only incidental that some materials would have to pass from the artist to the gentleman who commissioned the portrait. For these reasons I think that this was not a contract for the sale of goods within the meaning of s. 4 of the Sale of Goods Act, 1893, but it was a contract for work and labour and materials.

Slesser LJ and Roche LJ gave reasons to the same effect. During the course of his reasons, Roche LJ said, at p. 593:

... I have no doubt that the proper conclusion to be drawn is that this was a contract not for the sale of goods but for the employment of an artist to do work which the defendant desired that he should do.

I am satisfied for the reasons given in *Robinson v. Graves* that the contract in the case at bar was not a contract to which the *Sales of Goods Act* applied, but was a contract for work and labour and materials.

The distinction between the two types of contract may be of no significance in the case at bar, because "a person contracting to do work and supply materials warrants that the materials which he uses will be of good quality and reasonably fit for the purpose for which he is using them, unless the circumstances of the contract are such as to exclude any such warranty" (*per* du Parcq J in *G.H. Myers & Co. v. Brent Cross Service Co.*, [1934] 1 KB 46, applied in the House of Lords in *Young & Marten Ltd. v. McManus Childs Ltd.*, [1969] 1 AC 454 at pp. 468 and 471, [1968] 2 All ER 1169).

There was ample evidence to support the finding of a breach of the implied condition of merchantability, if the *Sale of Goods Act* had been applicable. That same evidence would support a finding of a breach of the warranty I have found to have existed that the materials used by the defendant would be of good quality and reasonably fit for a purpose for which he used them. The uncontradicted evidence of the plaintiff was that the defendant, when he saw the yellowing after three years, acknowledged its existence and told the plaintiff that the painting should not do that. The evidence of expert witnesses called by the plaintiff was that the yellowing resulted from the defendant's choice of materials and that the cracks were caused by the materials and techniques of the artist.

In my opinion, the learned trial judge was right in holding the defendant liable to the plaintiff for damages, but I find for the reasons given above that the contractual provision breached was different from the one found by the learned trial judge.

· · ·

Judgment for plaintiff; case remitted to trial judge for assessment of damages.

Keillian West Ltd. v. Sportspage Enterprises Ltd.
(1982), 23 Alta. LR (2d) 199

VEIT J: This matter came before me for an order pursuant to R. 221(1) of the Rules of Court to determine and interpret the meaning of the following clause contained in sales agreement No. 2359, dated 21st July 1981:

> I agree to the terms and conditions of this agreement and further agree that Schedule "A" on the reverse side hereof constitutes and forms part of this agreement. I further acknowledge and agree, that in consideration of the services performed by Keillian West Ltd. related to this agreement, such services which were performed for the above-named company who [*sic*] is primarily liable, that I, in addition, am personally liable to Keillian West Ltd. for services rendered, notwithstanding where the billing is directed.

SIGNATURE: *R. Vogel*

· · ·

It is to be noted that the statement of defence of Richard Vogel is to the following effect:

1. He denies that he is indebted to the plaintiff;
2. He denies that goods were sold and delivered to him by the plaintiff;

3. He pleads the provisions of the Guarantees Acknowledgment Act, RSA 1980, c. G-12.

As to the interpretation of the clause, I have reached the following conclusions:

1. The clause constitutes a guarantee and not an indemnity: *Crown Lumber Co. v. Engel* (1961), 36 WWR 128, 28 DLR (2d) 762 (CA); Anson's Law of Contract, 23rd ed. (1969), at 69.

2. The guarantee was given on the sale of an interest in goods or chattels and not on the making of a contract for the provision of services.

(a) Goods v. services

Despite the word "services" which is used twice in the clause, and despite the contra preferentum doctrine, the essence of the contract was one for the provision of goods and not one for the provision of services. Although unable to find any specific authority on the interpretation of the words "goods and chattels" under the provisions of the Alberta Guarantees Acknowledgment Act, and that Act being the only one of its type in existence in Canada, I have reviewed some of the jurisprudence arising out of the interpretation of the Sale of Goods Act, SA 1980, c. S-2.

As to the definition of a "good" under that Act, I note that while there appears to have been some vacillation by senior courts in Canada between two lines of English cases, the better view is that the court must try to determine whether it was the work or the materials which constituted the essence of the contract.

In this case, the contract was for 20,000 44-page programmes, with a four-colour cover and eight inside colour pages for a total cost of $15,892.20. The sales agreement was between the plaintiff and Sportspage Enterprises Ltd. c/o Sportspage Celebrity Softball Classic. The ledger information concerning this client is entered under the name Sportspage Dining Lounge.

I have reviewed two cases involving printing. *Clay v. Yates* (1856), 1 H & N 73, 156 ER 1, 123, which is in fact a leading case on the meaning of goods, was a case in which the plaintiff printer verbally agreed to print for the defendant 500 copies of a treatise at a certain price per sheet, including paper. On reviewing the proof-sheet of the dedication of the treatise, the plaintiff concluded that it was libellous and refused to complete the printing. The court held that the contract was not a contract for the sale of goods and therefore the Statute of Frauds did not apply to it. The plaintiff, not being prevented by the Statute of Frauds from maintaining his action, was also held to have been correct in his identification of the material as libellous. The court there-fore held that the plaintiff was justified in refusing to complete the printing and was entitled to recover for printing.

Pollock CB made the following comment [see, *supra*, *Borek v. Hooper* (ed.)].

. . .

A Canadian printing case is the case of *Can. Bank Note Engraving & Printing Co. v. Toronto Ry.* (1895), 22 OAR 462. In that case the plaintiffs who carried on business as engravers and lithographers sued to recover the sum of $1,779, the price of certain bonds and coupons printed by them for the defendants, in a special form and with special wording, on paper purchased by the plaintiffs. At trial, Armour C.J. held that the Statute of Frauds applied, that the plaintiffs had not complied with it and therefore their claim could not be maintained. The Court of Appeal affirmed the trial judge's decision. However, of the four-judge court, Osler JA appears to have great reservations about the decision, Hagarty CJO appears to have decided the appeal on the basis of the terms, or lack thereof, of the contract itself and Burton and Maclennan JJA appear to express the view that a contract is for work if the product is worthless as a chattel and that a contract is for goods if the product can become the subject of a sale.

There was no evidence before me that the work put into the programme, as opposed to the programme itself, was material to the success of the softball tournament. There is no reason to suppose that the substance of the contract was the skill and labour involved in the production of the programmes rather than the programmes themselves. A work of art, for example, is likely to depend more on skill and labour than on the actual materials involved, and that is recognized usually in the price of a work of art which is typically higher than the cost of paper and pastel crayons used in the execution of the work: *Robinson v. Graves*, [1935] 1 KB 579, [1935] All ER Rep. 935 (CA). Nevertheless, some courts have even held such contracts to be contracts for the sale of goods: *Isaacs v. Hardy* (1884), 1 Cab. & El. 287. The Court of Appeal in the *Graves* case did not overrule the *Isaacs* case. If even such a contract can be classified as one for the sale of goods, a fortiori, so should this.

More recently, the Supreme Court of Canada has had to consider the distinction between a contract for services and one for goods. In *Preload Co. of Can. Ltd. v. Regina; Hayes v. Regina; Regina v. Hayes* (1958), 23 WWR 433, 13 DLR (2d) 305, affirmed [1959] SCR 801, 20 DLR (2d) 586, Culliton JA noted that the characterization of the contract depended on whether the purchaser was to pay substantially for the materials or substantially for the skill. He emphasized that the test was the same, notwithstanding that a high degree of skill goes into the making of the chattel.

The Supreme Court had earlier approved the judgment of the Court of Appeal of Ontario in which Roach JA had indicated that the contract before that court was not a contract for a chattel which could be delivered in its completed state: *Fairbanks Soap Co. v. Sheppard*, [1951] OR 860, [1952] 1 DLR 417, affirmed on this point [1953] 1 SCR 314, [1953] 2 DLR 193.

The contract before me was certainly one for the delivery of completed chattels in which the chattels themselves were more important than the skill applied to their production.

(b) Policy considerations

There is no particular explanation in the Act itself of the basis for distinguishing goods from services in the matter of guarantees. Report No. 5 of the Institute of Law Research and Reform on the Guarantees Acknowledgment Act, October 1970, does not point to any basis for distinction, at 13, 14. The guarantee signed by Mr. Vogel in this case was a sufficient memorandum in writing pursuant to the provisions of the Statute of Frauds and served the purpose of underlining his responsibility in law for the payment of the contract.

As a result of the conclusions earlier reached, I am of the view that the Guarantees Acknowledgment Act does not apply to Mr. Vogel. His guarantee was in writing and satisfies the Statute of Frauds. The guarantee is therefore binding on him.

. . .

Judgment for plaintiff.

Gee v. White Spot Ltd.
(1987), 32 DLR (4th) 238 (BCSC)

LEGG J: In the first action the plaintiff Mr. Gee claims damages for botulism poisoning which he alleges he suffered after consuming a meal on July 29, 1985, at the defendant's restaurant. In the second action the plaintiffs Mr. & Mrs. Pan claim damages for botulism poisoning which they allege they suffered after consuming a sandwich on September 4, 1985, at the same restaurant. All plaintiffs now bring applications that the following points of law arising from the pleadings be set down for hearing pursuant to the Rules of Court (BC), Rule 34, by consent of the parties. The wording of the questions is substantially the same in each application and I therefore need quote only from that filed by Mr. Gee, which is as follows:

> 1. Is the purchase of a meal from a restaurant to which the public has access a "contract of sale," and are the foods consumed pursuant to the said purchase "goods," within the meaning of the *Sale of Goods Act*, RSBC 1979, c. 370 (and amendments thereto);

. . .

Plaintiff's counsel submitted that the answer to the first question should be in the affirmative and that the purchase of a meal in a restaurant was a contract of sale of goods under the *Sale of Goods Act*, RSBC 1979, c. 370 ("the Act"), rather than a contract for services. Counsel submitted that there was an implied warranty or condition as to the quality or fitness of such a meal supplied by the defendant pursuant to s. 18 of the Act.

Although counsel were unable to find any authority binding on this court in support of that submission, cases decided in other provinces and the United Kingdom and the United States support an affirmative answer.

A copy of ss. 1 and 18 of the Act are annexed to these reasons. Section 1 defines "goods" as including all chattels personal and "sale" includes a sale and delivery. Although that wording is not conclusive on the entire question before me, I think that it is readily apparent that the sale of items of food is a contract of sale of goods under the Act. This was established as long ago as 1902 with the decision of *Wallis v. Russell*, [1902] 2 IR 585, in which the Court of Appeal held that s. 14(1) of the *Sale of Goods Act*, 1893 (UK), c. 71, applied to the sale of some "nice fresh crabs" which the plaintiff's granddaughter had purchased for her grandmother's tea from the defendant fish monger in Cork. Section 14 of the United Kingdom legislation was in substantially the same terms as s. 18 of the British Columbia Act. The defendant was held to be in breach of warranty under the section when the crabs proved to be poisonous. The Ontario Court of Appeal in *Shandloff v. City Dairy et al.*, [1936] 4 DLR 712, [1936] OR 379, held that the sale of a bottle of chocolate milk was covered by s. 15 of the *Sale of Goods Act*, RSO 1927, c. 163. That section was similar to s. 18 of the British Columbia Act.

In *Coote v. Hudson's Bay Co. et al.* (1977), 6 AR 59, a District Court judge in Alberta, Judge McFadyen, held that Hudson's Bay Company was liable in supplying a meat sandwich containing a sharp piece of wood to the plaintiff in the store cafeteria. Although the District Court judge did not refer to the Alberta *Sale of Goods Act*, RSA 80, c. S-2, he imposed liability in terms of the implied warranty found in s. 17 of that Act. He held that when the plaintiff purchased the food he impliedly made it known to the defendant that he would consume the food and relied upon the defendant's skill and judgment in the preparation of it. The judge held that the contract included an implied warranty that the food would be reasonably fit for human consumption.

In the United Kingdom Mr. Justice Tucker held in *Lockett v. A. & M. Charles, Ltd.*, [1938] 4 All ER 170, that the defendant restaurant operator was liable for breach of warranty to the female plaintiff who consumed a mouthful of whitebait supplied by the defendant and thereafter suffered food poisoning. At 172 Mr. Justice Tucker stated:

> Counsel for the plaintiffs is, in my opinion, right when he submits that, when persons go into a restaurant and order food, they are making a contract of sale in exactly the same way as they are making contract of sale when they go into a shop and order any other goods. I think that the inference is that the person who orders the food in a hotel or restaurant *prima facie* makes himself or herself liable to pay for it, and when two people—whether or not they happen to be husband and wife—go into a hotel and each orders and is supplied with food, then, as between those persons and the proprietor of the hotel, each of them is making himself liable for the food which he orders, whatever may be the arrangement between the two persons who are eating in the hotel. On the facts in this case, it is, in my opinion, right to hold that there was a contract implied by the conduct of the parties between the plaintiff, Mrs. Lockett, and the defendants when she ordered and was supplied with the whitebait at the Hotel de Paris.

At 173, Tucker J considered that the proper inference of law was that the person who ordered and consumed the food in a restaurant was liable to pay for it as between himself and the proprietor of the restaurant and then stated:

> If that is so, it follows beyond all doubt that there is an implied warranty that the food supplied is reasonably fit for human consumption. I hold that the whitebait delivered in this case were not reasonably fit for human consumption, and that there was a breach of warranty.

There are two general lines of authority in the United States to which counsel referred on the issue of a restauranteur's liability under an implied warranty. The numerical majority of judicial authority favours the view referred to as the "Massachusetts-New York rule" that a person serving food for immediate consumption on the premises impliedly warrants that the food served is wholesome and fit for human consumption and is liable for breach of an implied warranty. The numerical minority designated as the "minority Connecticut-New Jersey rule" drew an analogy between an Old English inn and a modern-day restaurant and reasoned that the serving of food in a restaurant constituted a service and was not a sale of goods, and in the absence of a sale refused to find any implied warranty and held that a restauranteur could be liable only for negligence. This divergence in the authorities is discussed in *Sofman v. Denham Food Service, Inc.* (1962), 37 NJ 304, 181 A.2d 168, in which the plaintiff succeeded against the defendant cafeteria operator in a claim for damages for injuries caused by the deleterious substance in the food which the plaintiff ate in the cafeteria.

At 170 the court stated:

> We see no resemblance between the operation of a cafeteria and the operation of the ancient inn. If it be assumed the inn did not 'sell' food but merely satisfied whatever might be the needs of its wayfarer guest, surely the same cannot be said of a cafeteria, at which the customer buys and pays for the food he wants and may carry it to wherever he wishes, on or off the premises. We can see no justification for applying the inn-keeper rule to a factual pattern in which the consideration underlying the innkeeper rule cannot be found.

Also persuasive was the reasoning of Justice Schettino who, at 170-71, stated:

> When a person orders food in a restaurant today, he selects a listed portion for which the restaurateur has set a fixed price. Reality would be ignored if it is said that a sale is not effected, at least as to that food which the patron consumes. Thus, while a distinction can be made between a cafeteria and a traditional restaurant, for present purposes the difference is so negligible that we should face the problem four square.

Later the justice stated that after balancing the views of the Connecticut-New Jersey rule against the Massachusetts-New York rule, he felt that the latter was more effective in securing the public health and safety and was more realistic.

I find that reasoning persuasive and adopt it here.

Another case cited by counsel in which a restaurant patron recovered for injuries caused by a chicken bone in a chicken sandwich purchased from the defendant restaurant is *Betehia v. Cape Cod Corp.*, 103 NWR 2d 64. At 66, Justice Hallows noted the difference between the minority Connecticut-New Jersey rule and the Massachusetts-New York rule and stated that to compare the modern restaurant with the old typical English inn was not appropriate. He stated at 66:

> These are old-fashioned concepts which do not fit modern-day practices. Food or meals may be sold in a restaurant or hotel not combined with any services such as lodging. The food furnished in a restaurant is paramount and the preparation and serving of it are incidental to the sale. Title under the sale theory passes when the food is put on the table, not piecemeal as it is consumed.

. . .

[2, 3] We adopt the better-reasoned majority rule and hold when a patron orders, and pays for, a meal or food at a public restaurant, there is a sale of such food within the

meaning of sec. 121.15, Stats., and there exists an implied warranty that the food so sold is reasonably fit for human consumption. We deem that a patron of a restaurant ordering a meal or food thereby makes known to the seller the particular purpose for which the food is required and by that act relies on the seller's skill and judgment in preparing such food.

In order to come within the *Sale of Goods Act*, a contract need not be one exclusively for the sale of goods. I rely, as did counsel, upon a passage in *Harbour Machine Ltd. v. Guardian Ins. Co. of Canada* (1985), 60 BCLR 360, at 364, 10 CCLI 72, in which Mr. Justice Esson of the Court of Appeal *in obiter dicta* referred to the decision in *Preload Co. of Canada Ltd. v. City of Regina; Hayes v. City of Regina; City of Regina v. Hayes et al.* (1958), 13 DLR (2d) 305, 24 WWR 433, at 422. In *Preload Co.*, Culliton JA, at 313-314 stated that whether a contract was one for sale of goods or was one for the sale of work and wages depended upon the essential character of the agreement and held that the contract in that case was a contract for the sale of goods because it was primarily for the purpose of producing a finished product.

I agree with counsel's submission that an item on a menu offered for a fixed price is an offering of a finished product and is primarily an offering of the sale of a good or goods and not primarily an offering of a sale of services.

Although the sale of a meal or food in a restaurant will normally carry with it the privilege of using the restaurant nevertheless the contract entered into between the customer of the restaurant and the operator of the restaurant is primarily for the purpose of consuming food or a meal and is, therefore, in my respectful opinion, a contract for a sale of goods. The service component offered with the meal or food is no different from a host of other transactions where the primary purpose is for the sale of goods.

For the foregoing reasons I answer the first question in the affirmative.

As to the second question, if the plaintiff is able to prove that:

(a) He purchased and consumed a meal sold by the defendant at its restaurant;

(b) He suffered injuries arising from botulism poisoning and the source of such botulism poisoning was the meal which he consumed; and

(c) It was in the course of the defendant's business to supply to members of the public foods of the type included in the meal;

then I consider the defendant would be liable under s. 18(a) of the *Sale of Goods Act* or, alternatively, under s. 18(b) of the *Sale of Goods Act*.

. . .

Answer accordingly.

Notes on Contracts for Work and Materials

1) *OLRC Report*. The OLRC Sales Report distinguishes between two types of contract for work and materials (at 45-46):

In the first case, the labour and skill are incorporated in the production of the finished chattel. In the second, however, labour or services are provided *in addition* to materials, although they constitute part of the same contract; the concept of incorporation is absent. In both types of case the question is one of characterization of the contract.

The first type of case is illustrated by a contract for a custom made man's suit, the tailor providing both skill and materials which "become" the final product. In this situation, the OLRC approves of the "property" test applied by Blackburn J in *Lee v. Griffith* (1861), 1 B. & S. 272, 30 LJQB 252, and reflected in the definition of contract of sale in SGA s. 2. The Commission disapproved of the "relative value" or "essential character" test adopted by the English Court of Appeal in *Robinson v. Graves, supra,* as, in their opinion (at 46), it

> draws an arbitrary and untenable distinction between a contract for the purchase of finished goods and a contract for an article that is to be made to the buyer's order. The essential character test, insofar as it differs from the relative value test, is equally open to criticism because it overlooks the fact that "what passes to the client is not the materials but the finished [product], of which both the work and materials are components."

The OLRC dismissed the concern that products such as portraits are different in nature from manufactured goods on the ground that the Sale of Goods Act is concerned with the transfer of title to all types of goods and not just commercial products.

The second type of "work and materials" contract is illustrated by a contract to perform work on a building under which both materials and labour are to be supplied. In *Young & Marten Ltd. v. McManus Childs Ltd.,* [1968] 3 WLR 630, [1969] 1 AC 454 (HL), a sub-contractor agreed to supply and install a particular brand of roof tile. The tiles used by the sub-contractor (which he had purchased from a supplier) had a latent defect which caused the tiles to break in cold temperatures. The builder brought an action against the sub-contractor for breach of an implied warranty of fitness with respect to the suitability of the tiles. The House of Lords, as a matter of principle (there being a dearth of authority on the question), agreed that the sub-contractor was deemed to have given a warranty of quality. However, this warranty, by analogy to the implied conditions of merchantability and fitness in the SGA, was limited to the materials themselves. The law lords reasoned that since there was no privity between the primary contractor and the manufacturer of the tiles the plaintiff would be remediless unless he could sue the sub-contractor who had installed the tiles. The sub-contractor in turn would have his remedy over against the manufacturer. In this way the claim of liability would run without interruption from the ultimate buyer of the home to the manufacturer of the defective goods. With regard to the labour component of the contract, the sub-contractor was only held to the standard of "proper skill and care," rather than the strict liability imposed for defects in materials. See also, *Dodd and Dodd v. Wilson and McWilliams,* [1946] 2 All ER 691 (KB), for a similar conclusion with respect to the liability of veterinarians for the injection of a contaminated serum and *G.H. Myers & Co. v. Brent Cross Service Co.,* [1934] 1 KB 46, with respect to the liability of an auto repair shop in supplying a defective part in the repair of a car.

The OLRC recommended that the implied warranties under the SGA be applied to goods supplied under contracts for work and materials, while the labour component in such contracts be left to judicial development. See the Draft Bill, s. 5.15(2) and Sales

Report, at 48. See also S.M. Waddams, "Strict Liability, Warranties, and the Sale of Goods" (1969), 19 *Univ. Tor. LJ* 157 for an excellent discussion of the anomalous consequences which follow when different warranty and tortious liability standards are applied to essentially similar transactions.

2) *American Approach*. The American courts have generally approached the issue of characterization from a functional point of view. See, for example, *Temple v. Keeler* (1924), 144 NE 635 (NYCA), in which it was held that when a customer "enters a restaurant, receives, eats, and pays for food, delivered to him on his order," the transaction is a sale of goods. The court reasoned that, even if services are performed, there is still a qualified sale of what is actually eaten. On the other hand, in another leading and very influential *Perlmutter v. Beth David Hospital* (1954), 123 NE 2d 792 (NYCA), the same court held that a blood transfusion for which a charge was itemized on the patient's bill was not a sales transaction, since the main object sought and contracted for was the care and treatment of the patient. The supplying of blood was held to be entirely subordinate to this. Both cases involved claims for damages for breach of the implied warranty of fitness. *Perlmutter* is generally regarded as a policy oriented decision designed to protect the solvency of public welfare institutions.

In *Newmark v. Gimbel's Inc.* (1969), 258 A.2d 697 (NJSC), the court held that the application by a beauty parlour of a permanent wave solution, which allegedly injured the plaintiff, was a hybrid transaction involving incidents of a sale and a service. Therefore, it was reasoned, an implied warranty of fitness of the products used existed with as much force as in the case of a simple sale. The court remarked that the overall price charged took into account the value of the product, and that the no-separate-charge argument of the defendant would, if adopted, place form over substance. As this illustrates, since the adoption of Article 2 the American courts have shown a ready disposition to assimilate near-sales to sales transactions for the purpose of applying the warranty provisions in the Code. For another familiar example, see *Hertz v. Transportation Credit Clearing* (1969), 289 NYS 2d 392, and *cf.* E.A. Farnsworth, "Implied Warranties of Quality in Non-Sales Cases" (1957), 57 *Col. L Rev.* 653.

What functional criteria have influenced the courts in these cases? Consider the trend towards strict liability for defective products and the evident reluctance to impose strict liability on a charitable institution such as a hospital. Are the functional criteria applied by the courts always clearly articulated? Should they be?

3) *Recent Canadian Medical Cases*. The issue of characterization—sale of a product versus a contract for the supply of services and medication—has recently come to the forefront in Canada as a result of the HIV crisis and the attempt by HIV victims to hold doctors and/or hospitals responsible for HIV-infected blood given the patient in a blood transfusion (*Pittman Estate v. Bain* (1994), 112 DLR (4th) 257 (Ont.)) or HIV-infected insemination serum administered to a woman seeking pregnancy (*Ter Neuzen v. Korn*, [1995] 3 SCR 674). Still another example is a claim against a medical practitioner for installing a defective breast implant (*Hollis v. Birch*, [1990] BCJ no. 1059; and see also *Dow Corning Corp. v. Hollis* (1993), 103 DLR (4th) 520 and [1995] 4 SCR 634).

In *Ter Neuzen* the doctor supplied the serum free of charge but subject to a small administration fee. The plaintiff, who contracted HIV, sued him (i) in tort for negligence, (ii) for breach of the implied condition of merchantability under the British Columbia

Sale of Goods Act, and (iii) for breach of the implied warranty of fitness at common law. The jury found the doctor had not been negligent in failing to appreciate or eliminate the HIV danger, and also apparently found that there was no contract of sale by description so that the condition of merchantability could not attach under the SGA. The jury was not asked to make a finding on the third ground of alleged liability.

On appeal, the BC Court of Appeal dealt with this issue as follows (*Ter Neuzen v. Korn* (1993), 103 DLR (4th) 473, at 517 (BCCA)):

> In our judgment, the wisdom of the common law has always recognized that warranties of quality for goods furnished under a contract may be excluded in appropriate circumstances. While this particular question has not been considered in this country, the above authorities from the United States provide useful precedents which, although not binding, are highly persuasive. They furnish strong support for the view we have reached that this claim for damages arising from a contract for AI, including the furnishing of semen in the course of medical services, should be confined to negligence. It would be inappropriate, in our view, for a warranty of quality to be implied in the circumstances of this case.

A similar approach to the scope of warranty liability was apparently adopted by Bouck J in *Hollis v. Birch, supra*. It is not clear, however, whether he would have drawn a distinction between the administration of a natural substance (like human semen) free of charge, and the provision of a commercially produced product (such as a breast implant) for which a charge is made.

All these issues were carefully explored in Lang J's comprehensive judgment in *Pittman Estate v. Bain, supra*. This involved an action by the plaintiff estate arising out of the administration of HIV-infected blood to the deceased. The plaintiffs sued the hospital, the Canadian Red Cross Society (CRCS), and the deceased's attending physician in negligence and, with respect to the first two defendants, for breach of the implied warranty of fitness. The warranty claim against the hospital was based on the argument that there was a contract between the deceased and the hospital for the purchase and sale of blood, and that the hospital had breached its statutory (and strict) obligation under the Ontario SGA to supply blood fit for the purpose, that is, free of HIV contamination. The plaintiffs also contended that even if the contract with the hospital was only a contract for the supply of services and materials, the hospital was still subject to the same strict warranty obligation to supply HIV-free blood.

Lang J held: (1) that there was no contract of sale between the deceased and the hospital since, although there was a contract between them, no money consideration passed from the deceased to the plaintiff so as to satisfy the definition of contract of sale in s. 2(1) of the Ontario SGA. She dismissed counsel's argument that the definition of "sell" in the Food and Drugs Act, RSC 1985, c. F-27, dispensed with the need for a money consideration on the ground that the expanded definition of sale under that Act existed for public safety purposes and had no bearing on the interpretation and scope of the SGA; and (2) that while ordinarily, in a contract for the supply of services and materials, there is a strict warranty of fitness with respect to the materials, there were strong policy reasons for not implying such a warranty in the case of blood, a natural product, which was supplied free of charge by the donor to the CRCS and free of charge by the CRCS to the hospital.

4) The Retail Sales Tax Act, RSO 1990, c. R.31, s. 1, as amended, sets out a very broad definition of "sale" encompassing, *inter alia*:

[any contract] whereby at a price or other consideration a person delivers to another person tangible personal property [para. a];

the provision of any charge or billing, including periodic payments upon rendering or providing or upon any undertaking to render or provide to another person a taxable service, or for or on account of a price of admission, including any admission sold on a subscription or season ticket basis [para. a.1];

the transfer or delivery in any manner of a computer program including the assumption of, or adherence to, a licence to use the program [para. a.3];

the furnishing, preparation or service for a consideration of food, meals, or drinks [para. d];

a transfer for a consideration of the title to or possession of tangible personal property that has been produced, fabricated, printed or imprinted to the order of the purchaser [para. f].

Should the SGA adopt a similar broad definition? Consider the different purposes of the two Acts. What concerns are addressed by the SGA that lie beyond the scope of the Retail Sales Tax Act, and vice versa?

CONSIGNMENT AGREEMENTS, CONTRACTS OF "SALE OR RETURN" AND SALES "ON APPROVAL"

Weiner v. Harris
[1910] 1 KB 285; [1909] All ER Rep. 405 (CA)

[The plaintiff was a manufacturing jeweller carrying on business in Hatton Garden, London. The defendant was a money-lender and pawnbroker and carried on business in Cardiff. The plaintiff brought the action to recover certain articles of jewellery pledged with the defendant by one Fisher as security for a loan.

Fisher travelled about the country selling jewellery. The articles in question had been entrusted to him by the plaintiff pursuant to the terms of a letter dated July 31, 1905, the relevant parts of which read as follows:

I acknowledge that I have from you on sale or return the goods entered up to this date in the book labelled "Goods sent to Mr. Fisher," which is in your possession, and which I have examined, and I admit that I have to account to you for such goods. The goods referred to in the book mentioned, and all further goods you may hereafter send to me, I admit are your property, and to remain so until sold or paid for, they being only left with me for the purposes of sale or return, and not to be kept as my own stock. The goods I receive from you are to be entered at cost price, and my remuneration for selling them is agreed at one-half of the profit—i.e., I retain one-half of the difference between the price at which I sell each article and the cost price of it, and immediately I receive the price of any article sold I am to remit to you the cost price and one-half of the profit as above. It is clearly understood you have no interest in my business, and I have none in yours, and that no partnership of any kind is existing or to exist between us, and that any goods I may at any time have from you are to be returned on demand.

At the trial of the action Pickford J held, on the construction of this letter, that there was no partnership between Fisher and the plaintiff, that title in the jewellery had never passed to Fisher and that he merely held it on a contract of sale or return, that he was not a mercantile agent entrusted with the plaintiff's goods, and that accordingly the defendant was not entitled to rely on the provisions of the Factors Act, 1889, Pickford J therefore gave judgment for the plaintiff. The defendant appealed.]

COZENS-HARDY MR: This appeal raises a question which is undoubtedly one of some difficulty, because the document upon which everything depends has been construed by two learned judges, for whom I have the most profound respect, in a manner which I am unable to adopt. [The Master of the Rolls stated the facts, and continued:] The only point which arises for consideration before us is what is the meaning and legal effect of a letter of July 31, 1905, upon the faith of which the business relations between the parties were carried on? That involves, before I read the letter, this important consideration: Was the transaction the ordinary well-known transaction of goods taken on sale or return, or was it a transaction under which Fisher was constituted agent for sale, with authority to sell, and bound to account to his principal for the proceeds of such sale? If it was the former, it is quite plain that the property never has passed from the plaintiff Weiner, and that Weiner is entitled to recover it; the Factors Act is altogether out of the question and does not require any consideration from us. If it was the latter, the Sale of Goods Act is equally out of the question, and we have only to consider what is the true meaning and effect of one or two sections of the Factors Act as between the plaintiff and the defendant. In my opinion this is not a transaction in which goods are sent on sale or return. It is quite plain that by the mere use of a well-known legal phrase you cannot constitute a transaction that which you attempt to describe by that phrase. Perhaps the commonest instance of all, which has come before the Courts in many phases, is this: Two parties enter into a transaction and say "It is hereby declared there is no partnership between us." The Court pays no regard to that. The Court looks at the transaction and says "Is this, in point of law, really a partnership? It is not in the least conclusive that the parties have used a term or language intended to indicate that the transaction is not that which in law it is." So here the mere fact that goods are said to be taken on sale or return is not in any way conclusive of the real nature of the contract. You must look at the thing as a whole and see whether that is the real meaning and effect of it. [The Master of the Rolls read the letter of July 31, 1905, and continued:] In my opinion it is impossible to say, on the fair construction of that letter, that the parties ever contemplated or intended that Fisher should be the purchaser of the goods, because on the very terms of it the price could not be ascertained until after he resold them, and he was not to put them in his stock. In the ordinary transaction of purchase and sale, directly one party to the contract says "I will not return, I will elect to take the goods," he becomes the buyer. This is plainly, as it seems to me, a transaction in which Fisher had no right to buy. Fisher only had a duty towards Weiner to sell, and he was to be remunerated for his services in selling the goods by half the excess of the cost price; no more. It is all the more extraordinary because he was not even accountable to Weiner for the so-called purchase price, that is to say, the cost price plus half the sale price, until he actually received the money from the buyer. I ought not to say "the ultimate buyer," because I do not consider that Fisher was a buyer at all. Take another instance: you never hear in an ordinary transaction of sale and return that the goods are only left with the man for the purposes of sale or return and not to be kept in his own stock. Then there was the phrase, although I do not attach too much importance to it, of accounting for the goods used in a simple transaction of sale and return. I have come unhesitatingly to the conclusion that this was a transaction in which Fisher was not and could not become the buyer of the goods, but a transaction in which Fisher was employed solely as agent, and as agent was to be remunerated by a certain percentage; and the very fact that he was to be remunerated for his services is alone, I think, almost sufficient to shew that he could not be a buyer, because it is quite plain that no person who is an agent, or is to be remunerated as agent, can be allowed to buy that which he is instructed and authorized to sell.

Appeal allowed.

[Fletcher Moulton and Farwell LJJ delivered concurring reasons.]

Atari Corporation (U.K.) Ltd. v. Electronics Boutiquestores (U.K.) Ltd.
[1998] QB 539 (CA)

WALLER LJ: This is an appeal from a decision of Hooper J., who upheld the decision of Master Foster granting summary judgment to the plaintiffs for the sum of £369,611.16.

The sum claimed by the plaintiff is the price of certain electronic computer games and hardware delivered to the defendants pursuant to orders made in August/October and November 1995. Details are conveniently set out in a schedule to the statement of claim. The first and largest order provided expressly for: "Payment 30 November 1995. Full S.O.R. until 31 January 1996." S.O.R. stood, of course, for sale or return.

The arrangement for sale or return was negotiated between the parties and the terms confirmed by two faxes. There is some dispute about what precisely was agreed, and indeed there may be a dispute as to the admissibility of any agreement said to have been reached outside the strict confines of the orders placed having regard to the defendants' terms of purchase. Suffice it to say that the plaintiffs will contend at any trial that sale or return applied only to the original stocking order in which it was specifically referred to and possibly one other order in which express reference is made to sale or return. They will say it did not apply to any other orders at all; and, indeed, if a later order repeated an item the subject of the original stocking order they will wish to contend that those items delivered under the original stocking order lost the sale or return element. The defendants contend that sale or return was to apply to any "first" order for items, and that, as regards orders repeating items the subject of the previous order, the agreement was that sale or return would not apply to the items the subject of the repeat orders, but would continue to apply to the items the subject of the "stocking" order. In the result, the defendants accept that, in relation to the contracts identified in the schedule to the statement of claim, there are three to which the sale or return term does not apply, and it is to those that the plaintiffs respondent's notice is applicable.

The original stocking order is the largest order, and accordingly it has been sensibly recognised that, for summary judgment purposes, the disputes as to whether sale or return applies to certain of the smaller orders, and as to whether some items, by virtue of repeat orders, lost their sale or return element, raise triable issues. On the application for summary judgment the point argued by the plaintiffs has simply been that the defendants have in any event failed to give notice of rejection of any goods which they held on sale or return.

As appears from the express terms of the first order which I have set out, it was the intention of the parties that payment would be made by 30 November 1995, albeit the defendants were to have the "right of sale or return" up until 31 January 1996. Furthermore, the defendants in fact confirmed their intention to pay, by fax dated 28 November 1995, but in the result the defendants have only paid very limited sums. It is the defendants' case that once 1 December went by, and it was appreciated that the goods were not selling well, some arrangement was reached under which the defendants only paid for those goods which they in fact sold. This is disputed by the plaintiffs and is a matter again which could only be resolved at a trial. The defendants further say that they in fact paid for the goods that were sold, and identified in schedules supplied monthly to the plaintiffs those items that had been sold and those that had not. The defendants then wrote the letter dated 19 January 1996 on which this appeal turns, which I should set out so far as material:

> "A review of all formats within the Electronic Boutique chain has recently taken place and the outcome was that Atari Jaguar is to be no longer stocked within the chain. Our decision was made on performance, participation, gross profit earned from footage allocated to product, and general market analysis on the Jaguar format. All stores have been requested to return all Jaguar stock to our central warehouse and when this is all received we will submit to you a complete list of what you will need to raise R.A."— agreed to mean return authorisation—"numbers against. This decision falls in line with our current trading agreement."

The response from the plaintiffs was by fax dated 22 January 1996, and so far as relevant read:

> On receipt of your fax we reviewed our files and have asked our solicitor to advise us, in particular about the sale or return arrangement. Our initial conclusion is that we believe that you have lost the right to return goods to us as you were in breach of contract by not settling the invoices relating to the initial order on the due date.

That was followed by a further fax of 25 January 1996 from the plaintiffs saying:

> For your information we have had confirmation from our legal people that your non-payment does constitute a breach of the original agreement, but we are willing to take back the unsold inventories subject to the agreement of a restocking charge.

. . .

Both parties commenced their arguments as to whether the defendants had successfully exercised their right under the term allowing for sale or return by reference to section 18 of the Sale of Goods Act 1979 [Ont. s. 19], which, so far as material, provides:

> Unless a different intention appears, the following are rules for ascertaining the intention of the parties as to the time at which property in the goods is to pass to the buyer ... Rule 4.— When goods are delivered to the buyer on approval or on sale or return or other similar terms the property in the goods passes to the buyer:— (a) when he signifies his approval or acceptance to the seller or does any other act adopting the transaction; (b) if he does not signify his approval or acceptance to the seller but retains the goods without giving notice of rejection, then, if a time has been fixed for the return of the goods, on the expiration of that time ...

We were also referred to *Benjamin's Sale of Goods*, 5th ed. (1997), pp. 216-217, para. 5-051, which deals with sale or return, and what Benjamin suggests constitutes a notice of rejection under section 18, rule 4. Authorities on the subject are sparse but the key sentence is:

> It is probable that any intimation to the seller which clearly demonstrates that the buyer does not wish to exercise his option to purchase will suffice, but it is open to the parties to agree that the buyer shall be entitled to reject only by returning the goods. (My emphasis.)

What that sentence demonstrates is that the starting point must be to construe the terms of the particular contract providing for sale or return, and decide what in the particular agreement the parties mean by sale or return or, as in this case, "Full sale or return until 31 January 1996." For example "full sale or return until 31 January 1996" could be construed as requiring the actual physical return of the goods to the seller prior to 31 January 1996; alternatively, it could be construed as requiring the buyers to have the goods which they intended to return available for collection prior to 31 January 1996 (and thus a requirement for notice to the plaintiffs to enable that to be achieved); alternatively, it could be construed as the buyers having the right until 31 January 1996 to notify the sellers that they were exercising the right to return the goods, the obligation thereafter being to have the same available after 31 January 1996; and there may be other possible constructions. If on a proper construction of the terms it is a case where a notice must be given, what the notice must contain and when it must be given will also need resolution. For example, (1) is it permissible to give a notice that goods will be available for collection at some future date, or must the notice allow the plaintiff to take immediate delivery in order to be effective? (2) Can the notice describe the goods generically for them to be specifically ascertained only at the time of collection?

The plaintiffs do not suggest that to exercise the right to return the goods the defendants had to physically return the goods to the plaintiffs' premises prior to 31 January 1996. It follows therefore that it is common ground that this is a notice case, i.e. what is required is some form of notice that the defendants are exercising their right to return goods the subject of the sale or return term. What, however, the plaintiffs stress is that the right to be exercised by the defendants is the right to return the goods, and thus they submit that, if the right to return the goods is to be exercised by a notice, that notice must conform to certain criteria. Mr. Leggatt on their behalf submitted that the letter of 19 January 1996 could not on any view be such a notice because it merely indicated that at some future date a list would be prepared. It was submitted in effect that what the letter was saying was that that list would constitute the rejection. In the alternative, and with greater emphasis, he submitted, first, that the notice must specify with precision the goods that are being returned and, second, that the buyers must have the goods physically available so that the sellers can come and collect the same immediately. He did accept that it might be possible to have a valid notice allowing for collection at some future date, but suggested that the defendants' case had always been that their notice was of immediate effect. Mr. Leggatt submitted there were three reasons why the notice should identify the goods with precision. First, he submitted that the whole purpose of having a notice was so that a seller would know precisely what was being rejected and what was not, and that it was of no comfort to the seller to be told that the answer could be objectively ascertained. Secondly, he submitted that certainty in commercial transactions was critical. Thirdly, he submitted that a seller might want to sell to others and accordingly must know precisely to what he now had the right to immediate possession.

· · ·

I admit to not having found this an easy case and it follows that if the question that had to be decided was simply whether leave to defend should be given, in my view leave to defend would be given. But it has certainly been the plaintiffs' submission that this is one of those cases where at the summary judgment stage the court is in as good a position as the trial judge to decide the point on construction of the contract and/or of the notice, and that thus the point should be decided under R.S.C., Ord. 14. In this court both sides were content to accept that if that was so then equally the point was capable of being decided under Order 14A in the defendants' favour were that to be the court's view. In other words, to save the costs of a full trial, if a clear view were formed on the point however difficult, the parties would like that view expressed.

My starting point is, as I have already indicated, to define what was intended by the term "full sale or return until 31 January 1996." It is possible, though it is unnecessary to decide the point, that the plaintiffs are right to this extent, that they were entitled to be put in a position to be able to collect any goods that the defendants were seeking to return by 31 January 1996. Even if that were right, it would merely show that to be effective as a notice of rejection that notice would have to be issued so as to enable the goods to be available for collection before that date, but the question would still remain whether the notice must give an immediate right of possession to the seller or a right to possession at some reasonable period from the notice.

It must on any view be right, whichever form of notice is appropriate, that, at least at the time of collection, the goods to be returned must be physically available for collection. There is, however, no requirement that a notice should be in writing, and I do not see why it is in any sense necessary to set out in detail the precise goods in the notice by which the defendants exercised their right as long as the notice, whether oral or in writing, referred clearly to the goods generically. Furthermore, certainly if a notice was sent or given which did suggest that goods were available for immediate collection, then a failure to hand over immediately would constitute a conversion of the goods by the buyer; it would not, however, invalidate the notice. Furthermore, if it were permissible to serve a notice prior to the date by which goods have to be returned, giving reasonable notice of some future date for collection, I can see no reason why there should be a requirement to have the goods physically available at the time of the notice as opposed to the time of collection, and once again a failure to have the goods available at the expiry of the reasonable notice would constitute a conversion but would not invalidate the notice. In my view in the context of this contract where goods were spread out in various different outlets, it was open to give a notice exercising the right to reject with the sellers' entitlement to collect the goods arising only at a reasonable time after the notice. Whether the sellers were entitled to insist that that reasonable time could not extend beyond 31 January 1996 does not arise for decision. ...

PHILLIPS LJ: [concurring]:

. . .

Benjamin's Sale of Goods, p. 49, para. 1-056, describes the effect of delivery on "sale or return" as follows:

> A person to whom goods are delivered on "sale or return" has a true option to buy, in the sense that he is free to buy or not as he chooses. In such a transaction the goods are bailed to a prospective buyer on the understanding that he may buy them at a stated price: he may elect either to buy or to return the goods, and by the terms of the agreement, or in accordance with the presumed intention of the parties set out in section 18, rule 4, of the Sale of Goods Act 1979, will be deemed to have bought them in certain events if he does not give notice of rejection. Since the property remains in the bailor until there is an election to buy, and the bailee is not until such time under any obligation to buy, there is no contract of sale within the meaning of the Act.

Where goods are supplied pursuant to a "sale or return" agreement, a contract is none the less concluded. Such a contract was described by Lord Esher MR in *Kirkham v. Attenborough*, [1897] 1 QB 201, 203:

> This contract is so common in business that it is well known to the courts, and has been interpreted, and all courts will now adopt the interpretation which has been put upon it. In the absence of other terms the contract does not pass the property in the goods

directly it is made. The person who has received them may return them, but the person who has entrusted them to another cannot demand their return, and his only remedy is to sue for their price or value.

. . .

An ordinary agreement for the supply of goods on sale or return thus has the following features: the seller cannot withdraw his offer to sell the goods; the buyer can accept by signifying acceptance to the seller, or by an act adopting the transaction, or by keeping the goods beyond the agreed period or, absent agreement, a reasonable period; the buyer can give a notice of rejection.

In my judgment the notice of rejection referred to by the Act of 1979 is no more than the notice that an offeree can always give that a contractual offer is rejected.

Until the property passes, the prospective buyer holds the goods as bailee. The Act makes no provision as to what he has to do with the goods if he gives notice of rejection. It seems to me that his duty at this point must depend upon the express or implied terms of the contract. He may simply have to hold the goods at the seller's disposal or he may have to return them to the seller. To be effective, a notice of rejection must be given before the property in the goods has passed. If a buyer so acts as to render it impossible for him to perform whatever the contract requires after rejection, e.g. if he ships the goods overseas to a potential sub-purchaser, such conduct is likely to constitute an act adopting the transaction, so that he cannot thereafter give a valid notice of rejection.

It is open to the parties to agree that the prospective buyer is not entitled to give a notice of rejection but will be deemed to have accepted the goods unless he returns them physically to the buyer within the "sale or return" period. Such a case was *Ornstein v. Alexandra Furnishing Co.*, (1895) 12 TLR 128. The plaintiffs accept that no such term falls to be implied in the present case ... .

Appeal allowed.

[Auld LJ also delivered a concurring judgment.]

Note on Consignment Agreements, Contracts of "Sale or Return" and Sales "On Approval"

The congeries of agreement denominated under the above titles have a common feature but also differ from each other in important respects. The common feature is that goods are delivered by their owner to a consignee for his prospective use or for sale or resale but that title is not to pass until some future event prescribed in the agreement between the parties has taken place. The differences reside in the character of the relationship established between the parties, the purpose of the agreement, and the rights of third parties dealing with the consignee. These questions cannot be answered by looking at the label which the parties themselves have attached to the agreement. Rather, as *Weiner v. Harris, supra*, makes clear, the answer depends on the substance of the agreement and the fair construction of its provisions.

More particularly:

1) the agreement is an *agency contract for sale* if the consignee of the goods undertakes to sell them as a disclosed or undisclosed agent for the owner;

2) the agreement is a *contract of "sale or return"* if the consignee will become the buyer of the goods on a prescribed event (usually the resale of the goods by him);

3) the agreement is a *security agreement* if, on an analysis of its terms, the consignee has essentially agreed to buy the goods and pay their price, and title in the meantime merely remains in the consignor by way of security (*cf. Re Stephanian's Persian Carpets Limited* (1980), 34 CBR (NS) 35 (Ont. SC in Bankruptcy) and see further, volume III of the previous edition of this casebook, chapter 2); and

4) the agreement is a *sale "on approval"* if the goods are delivered for the consignee's use or consumption but he wishes to examine them or to try them out before deciding whether to retain them. If he decides to retain them, or is deemed by his conduct to have so decided, the agreement ripens into a normal contract of sale.

In North American parlance the first three types of agreement are frequently referred to as "consignment agreements." It will be obvious, however, from the above analysis that the term is not a term of art and that it provides little guidance as to the true relationship between the parties. *Cf.* OLRC Sales Report, at 48-49. Nor do the existing statutory provisions. The Ontario Factors Act (RSO 1990, c. F.1), which is based on the British Factors Act of 1889, determines when a "mercantile agent" can make an effective disposition of the goods in favour of a third person. SGA s. 18, r. 4 provides a presumptive rule as to when the property in the goods passes to the buyer under a contract of sale or return or sale on approval, and s. 25(2) of the Act determines his powers of disposition before the property has passed. These provisions are quite different in concept and application from the provisions in the Factors Act. Again, OPPSA, RSO 1990, c. P.10, as am., s. 2(a)(ii) provides that the Act applies to a consignment "that secures payment or performance of an obligation" but provides no guidance as to how that question is to be answered in concrete cases. Once again, important rights and duties turn on the answer.

The OLRC Sales Report, at 49, felt that the rights of third parties dealing with the consignee should not depend on difficult questions of construction of the consignment agreement if the external appearances are the same. Chapter 12 of the Report offered some solutions. The Saskatchewan Law Reform Commission reached similar conclusions with respect to the artificiality of the distinction between true consignment agreements and consignment agreements intended as security. Accordingly SPPSA s. 3(2) provides that the Act applies to a commercial consignment "that does not secure payment or performance of an obligation."

"Commercial consignment" is defined in s. 1(h) as follows:

(h) "commercial consignment" means a consignment, pursuant to which goods are delivered for sale, lease, or other disposition to a consignee who, in the ordinary course of a consignee's business, deals in goods of that description, by a consignor who:

(i) in the ordinary course of the consignor's business deals in goods of that description; and

(ii) reserves an interest in the goods after they have been delivered;

but does not include an agreement pursuant to which goods are delivered:

(iii) to an auctioneer for sale; or

(iv) to a consignee for sale, lease or other disposition if the consignee is generally known to the creditors of the consignee to be selling or leasing the goods of others;

Similar provisions appear in the PPS Acts of the other common law provinces (but not in the Ontario PPSA). The effect of these provisions is that the consignor must comply with the perfection rules in the Act and is subject to its priority rules. Part V of the Act (remedies on default) will not apply, however. In Ontario, the Catzman Committee favoured the inclusion of commercial consignment agreements in the revised OPPSA even if the agreement was not substantively a security agreement, but the recommendation was not adopted by the government. See Report of the Advisory Committee (1984), p. 3 and draft Act, s. 2(1)(b). The question was revisited by the PPSL CBAO Committee in its 1998 submission to the Ontario government. The Committee did not recommend the inclusion of non-security consignments in the amended act because the Committee was concerned that some types of consignors, e.g., artists leaving work for sale with the art dealers, would not appreciate the need to perfect the consignment by filing a financial statement. See Canadian Bar Association (Ontario), Submission to the Minister of Consumer and Commercial Relations Concerning the Personal Property Security Act (1998).

For further discussion of the above issues see J.B. Colburn, "Consignment Sales and the Personal Property Security Act" (1981), 6 *CBLJ* 40; J.C. Macfarlane, "Sale of Goods on Consignment" (1973), 22 *Proc. Can. Bar Assoc.* 175; B. Geva, (1979), 25 *McGill LJ* 32, esp. at 53; and volume III of the previous edition of this casebook, chapter 2.

CHAPTER THREE

Formation of the Contract

INTRODUCTION

With modest exceptions, the Sale of Goods Act (SGA) does not attempt to codify the rules governing the formational elements of contracts of sale. The exceptions cover the contractual capacity of infants and others (s. 3), the form of the contract (s. 4), writing requirements (s. 5), contracts concluded under a mistaken assumption that the goods exist (s. 7), and determination of the price (ss. 9-10). In other cases, the general principles of contract continue to apply. See s. 57. True to its reform spirit the Uniform Commercial Code (UCC) contains a substantially larger number of formational rules. See in particular UCC 2-201 through 2-210; and 2-302 through 2-305; and 2-613.

For many years the Statute of Frauds requirement (Ont. s. 5) loomed large in the sales syllabuses of law schools and in the standard texts. In the post-war period the opinion of the legal profession has swung heavily against the utility of the requirement and, in England, s. 4 of the Sale of Goods Act (which corresponds to Ontario's s. 5) was repealed by the Law Reform (Enforcement of Contracts) Act 1954. While, until fairly recently, only British Columbia had followed the British precedent, there has been a marked decline in the number of reported Canadian cases in which the defence has been raised. Can you suggest why? In Ontario the OLRC recommended the repeal of s. 5. See Sales Report, at 110, but this recommendation, like the rest of the Report, lay fallow until it was suddenly resurrected in 1994. Section 54 of the Statute Law Amendment Act (Government Management and Services) Act 1994, SO 1994, c. 27, adopted that year repealed s. 5 of the SGA. The repeal was primarily motivated by the need to accommodate the growing practice of contracts for standard items being concluded electronically by data interchange (EDI), the position at that time being unsettled whether the courts will accept an electronic message as sufficient to satisfy the writing requirements of s. 5. See, *supra*, chapter 1, The Impact of Electronic Commerce on Commercial and Consumer Transactions and *infra*, this chapter, on the details of the new electronic commerce legislation.

The Americans still have a surprisingly strong attachment to the Statute of Frauds, and its sales component survived, albeit in a much modified form, the drafting of the Code. See UCC 2-201. During the revision of Article 2, there was a proposal to repeal the Statute of Frauds provision in its entirety, but the proposal was strongly resisted by industry representatives, and it was eventually dropped.

THE CONTRACTUAL PROBLEMS IN CONSUMER TRANSACTIONS

While the movement in commercial transactions has been *away* from formal requirements, the trend in consumer transactions has been strongly *toward* them. This is shown by a flock of post-war statutes, of which the Ontario Consumer Protection Act and its equivalent in the other provinces are the best known. Can you explain this paradox? Whatever the reason for the revival of interest in formal requirements in this area, do you think they accomplish their purpose? See the table following this note for a comparison of the formal requirements of the UCC, SGA, and CPA (Consumer Protection Act).

Interest in the contract-making process in consumer transactions is by no means confined to the evidentiary aspects and increasingly it embraces all aspects of the phenomenon. It is not difficult to see why. Nineteenth century contract law, strongly influenced by utilitarian concepts of the economy, idealized the process of private decision-making and felt that the parties to a contract were the best judges of what was in their interests. Twentieth century developments made the assumption increasingly suspect as highly urbanized life styles, complex products and mass-produced goods replaced the personal relationships and simpler products of an earlier and still predominantly agrarian age. The problem was compounded because, paradoxically, greater affluence gave the average consumer greater discretionary income and therefore made him more vulnerable to abuses in the modern marketplace.

As illustrated by the materials in this chapter, the courts and the legislatures have been challenged to fashion appropriate responses to two distinct types of problems. The first arises when a seller of goods or services takes advantage of the gullibility, weakness or ignorance of a consumer to strike a manifestly unfair bargain, or uses high-pressure sales techniques or other unethical selling practices to overcome the consumer's resistance. *W.W. Distributors & Co. Ltd. v. Thorsteinson; Gaertner v. Fiesta Dance Studios Ltd.*; and *Trans Canada Credit Corp. Ltd. v. Zaluski*, reproduced in this chapter, illustrate these forms of procedural unconscionability.

The second type of problem raises issues of substantive unconscionability. No unfair pressure has been brought to bear on the consumer to induce him to sign the contract. Nevertheless, the contract may still be objectionable because of its one-sided character and the overwhelmingly greater bargaining strength of the other party. Contracts of adhesion are the classical illustration of this type of problem.

As will be seen, the judicial reaction to both types of problem has been diverse and unpredictable as the courts have been torn between traditional respect for *pacta sunt servanda* principles and a desire to protect abused consumers. The legislative response has been much clearer. In Ontario's case, for example, the Ontario CPA addresses itself specifically to problems engendered by door-to-door sales, unsolicited goods and credit cards, "cut-off" clauses in consumer credit agreements, and disclaimers of warranty obligations in contracts of sale. Similar provisions will be found in many of the other provincial consumer protection acts.

A much more innovative approach was introduced in 1974 with the adoption of the British Columbia Trade Practices Act and the Ontario Business Practices Act.[1] While the

---

1   Several of the other provinces, e.g., Saskatchewan and Quebec, have followed suit.

two Acts differ widely on points of detail, they agree in seeking to substitute a generic approach to unfair or deceptive trade practices for the specifically oriented CPA provisions. In this respect they mirror comparable developments in the general contracts area as represented by such well known landmarks as UCC 2-302 and the British Unfair Contract Terms Act 1977. Needless to say, the theoretical soundness of these approaches has been much debated in Canada, the United States, and elsewhere. For a sampling of Canadian views see the "Symposium on Unconscionability in Contract Law" in (1979-80), 4 *CBLJ* 383; Michael J. Trebilcock, "An Economic Approach of Unconscionability," Study 11, in *Studies in Contract Law* (B. Reiter and J. Swan (eds.), 1980), at 379; and "Symposium: Certainty and Flexibility as Competing Contract Values and the OLRC Report" (1988), 14 *CBLJ* 1.

WRITING REQUIREMENTS

Post-1994 Comparison of Statutory Provisions

Contents of Provision	*UCC 2-201*	*SGA, s. 5 (Repealed)*	*CPA, s. 18*
1. Minimum monetary amount	$500[2]	$40	$50
2. Extent of writing required	Some writing sufficient to indicate that a contract for sale has been made between the parties	Note or Memorandum	"Executory contract" must be "in writing" and contain prescribed particulars
3. Notice of confirmation sufficient between merchants	Yes	No	Not applicable
4. Exception for specially manufactured goods	Yes	No	No
5. Alternatives to writing requirement	Yes	Yes	No
6. Disclosure of cost credit	No	No	Yes
7. Itemization of price	No	No	Yes

---

2   This has been increased to $5,000 in the Proposed Amendments to Article 2.

WRITING REQUIREMENTS IN THE DIGITAL AGE AND
THE SHRINKWRAP PROBLEM

Ontario Electronic Commerce Act

SO 2000, c. 17, ss. 4-7

4. Information or a document to which this Act applies is not invalid or unenforceable by reason only of being in electronic form.

5. A legal requirement that information or a document be in writing is satisfied by information or a document that is in electronic form if it is accessible so as to be usable for subsequent reference.

6.(1) A legal requirement that a person provide information or a document in writing to another person is satisfied by the provision of the information or document in an electronic form that is,

(a) accessible by the other person so as to be usable for subsequent reference; and

(b) capable of being retained by the other person.

(2) Subsection (1) is subject to section 16.

7.(1) A legal requirement that a person provide information or a document in a specified non-electronic form to another person is satisfied by the provision of the information or document in an electronic form that is,

(a) organized in the same or substantially the same way as the specified non-electronic form;

(b) Accessible by the other person so as to be usable for subsequent reference; and

(c) capable of being retained by the other person.

(2) Subsection (1) is subject to section 16.

Note on the Internet Sales Contract Harmonization Template[3]

In November 1999, federal, provincial, and territorial Ministers responsible for consumer affairs agreed on principles to make Internet sales and consumer legislation consistent throughout Canada. See Working Group on Electronic Commerce and Consumers, *Principles of Consumer Protection for Electronic Commerce*. To this end, the Consumer Measures Committee, a federal-provincial-territorial body of officials established under chapter 8 of the Agreement on Internal Trade, prepared a template to guide individual jurisdictions in drafting their own electronic sales legislation. It is entitled the Internet Sales Contract Harmonization Template, and was approved by the Ministers in May 2001. This model legislation differs from the Uniform Electronic Commerce Act adopted by the Uniform Law Conference of Canada (since passed in most provinces) in that it provides explicit protection for the electronic consumer, such as required information disclosure and cancellation rights under certain circumstances. Almost identical protections have already

---

3 This note was prepared by Jason Kee under the supervision of the editors of this volume.

been enacted in Manitoba under the Electronic Commerce and Information, Consumer Protection Amendment and Manitoba Evidence Amendment Act, SM 2000, c. E55, and similar action is anticipated in the other provincial jurisdictions in the foreseeable future.

Key aspects of the Template include a requirement for suppliers to provide prescribed information, including *inter alia* the supplier's name; contact information; a fair and accurate description of the goods or services being sold (including relevant technical specifications); an itemized list of the price of goods or services being sold, in addition to any delivery, postage and handling and insurance costs that are not included in the price of the goods or services; and all terms and conditions of sale (s. 3). Suppliers are also required to provide a copy of the contract (which must include all the prescribed information, the consumers name, and the date the contract was entered into) to the consumer in writing or electronic form within 15 days (s. 4). Failure to either disclose the required information or the written contract gives the consumer a right to cancel the contract, as does failure to provide the consumer an express opportunity to accept or decline the contract (s. 6). The Template also triggers a right to cancel where the goods or services purchased are not delivered within 30 days of the agreed delivery date, and contemplates a right to obtain a credit for credit card charges incurred (ss. 9-11).

Proposed Amendments to Uniform Commercial Code Article 2 as Approved by ALI, May 2001, ss. 2-204, 2-211, 2-212, and 2-213

Section 2-204: Formation in General.

(1) A contract for sale of goods may be made in any manner sufficient to show agreement, including offer and acceptance, conduct by both parties which recognizes the existence of such a contract, the interaction of electronic agents, or the interaction of an electronic agent and an individual.

(2) An agreement sufficient to constitute a contract for sale may be found even though the moment of its making is undetermined.

(3) Even though one or more terms are left open a contract for sale does not fail for indefiniteness if the parties have intended to make a contract and there is a reasonably certain basis for giving an appropriate remedy.

(4) Except as otherwise provided in Sections 2-211 through 2-213, the following rules apply:

(a) A contract may be formed by the interaction of electronic agents of the parties, even if no individual was aware of or reviewed the electronic agents' actions or the resulting terms and agreements.

(b) A contract may be formed by the interaction of an electronic agent and an individual acting on the individual's own behalf or for another person. A contract is formed if the individual takes actions that the individual is free to refuse to take or makes a statement that the individual has reason to know will:

(i) cause the electronic agent to complete the transaction or performance; or

(ii) indicate acceptance of an offer, regardless of other expressions or actions by the individual to which the electronic agent cannot react.

Section 2-211. Legal recognition of electronic contracts, records and signatures.

(1) A record or signature may not be denied legal effect or enforceability solely because it is in electronic form.

(2) A contract may not be denied legal effect or enforceability solely because an electronic record was used in its formation.

(3) This article does not require a record or signature to be created, generated, sent, communicated, received, stored, or otherwise processed by electronic means or in electronic form.

(4) A contract formed by the interaction of an individual and an electronic agent under Section 2-204(4)(b) does not include terms provided by the individual if the individual had reason to know that the agent could not react to the terms as provided.

Section 2-212. Attribution. An electronic record or electronic signature is attributed to a person if the record was created by or the signature was the act of the person or the person's electronic agent or the person is otherwise bound by the act under the law.

Section 2-213. Electronic communication.

(1) If the receipt of an electronic communication has a legal effect, it has that effect even though no individual is aware of its receipt.

(2) Receipt of an electronic acknowledgment of an electronic communication establishes that the communication was received but, in itself, does not establish that the content sent corresponds to the content received.

ProCD, Incorporated v. Matthew Zeidenberg and Silken Mountain Web Services, Inc.

(1996), 86 F.3d 1447 (CCA 7)

EASTERBROOK Circuit Judge: Must buyers of computer software obey the terms of shrinkwrap licenses? The district court held not, for two reasons: first, they are not contracts because the licenses are inside the box rather than printed on the outside; second, federal law forbids enforcement even if the licenses are contracts. 908 F.Supp. 640 (W.D.Wis. 1996). The parties and numerous *amici curiae* have briefed many other issues, but these are the only two that matter—and we disagree with the district judge's conclusion on each. Shrinkwrap licenses are enforceable unless their terms are objectionable on grounds applicable to contracts in general (for example, if they violate a rule of positive law, or if they are unconscionable). Because no one argues that the terms of the license at issue here are troublesome, we remand with instructions to enter judgment for the plaintiff.

I

ProCD, the plaintiff, has compiled information from more than 3,000 telephone directories into a computer database. We may assume that this database cannot be copyrighted, although it is more complex, contains more information (nine-digit zip codes and census industrial codes), is organized differently, and therefore is more original than the single alphabetical directory at issue in *Feist Publications, Inc. v. Rural Telephone Service Co.,* 499 US 340, 111 S.Ct. 1282, 113 L.Ed.2d 358 (1991). See Paul J. Heald, "The Vices of Originality" (1991), *Sup. Ct. Rev.* 143, 160-68. ProCD sells a version of the database, called SelectPhone (trademark), on CD-ROM discs. (CD-ROM means "compact disc—read only memory." The "shrinkwrap license" gets its name from the fact that retail software packages are covered in plastic or cellophane "shrinkwrap," and some vendors, though not ProCD, have written licenses that become effective as soon as the customer tears the wrapping from the package. Vendors prefer "end user license," but we use the more common term.) A proprietary method of compressing the data serves as effective encryption too. Customers decrypt and use the data with the aid of an application program that ProCD has written. This program, which is copyrighted, searches the database in response to users' criteria (such as "find all people named Tatum in Tennessee, plus all firms with 'Door Systems' in the corporate name"). The resulting lists (or, as ProCD prefers, "listings") can be read and manipulated by other software, such as word processing programs.

The database in SelectPhone (trademark) cost more than $10 million to compile and is expensive to keep current. It is much more valuable to some users than to others. The combination of names, addresses, and SIC codes enables manufacturers to compile lists of potential customers. Manufacturers and retailers pay high prices to specialized information intermediaries for such mailing lists; ProCD offers a potentially cheaper alternative. People with nothing to sell could use the database as a substitute for calling long distance information, or as a way to look up old friends who have moved to unknown towns, or just as an electronic substitute for the local phone book. ProCD decided to engage in price discrimination, selling its database to the general public for personal use at a low price (approximately $150 for the set of five discs) while selling information to the trade for a higher price. It has adopted some intermediate strategies too: access to the SelectPhone (trademark) database is available via the America Online service for the price America Online charges to its clients (approximately $3 per hour), but this service has been tailored to be useful only to the general public.

If ProCD had to recover all of its costs and make a profit by charging a single price—that is, if it could not charge more to commercial users than to the general public—it would have to raise the price substantially over $150. The ensuing reduction in sales would harm consumers who value the information at, say, $200. They get consumer surplus of $50 under the current arrangement but would cease to buy if the price rose substantially. If because of high elasticity of demand in the consumer segment of the market the only way to make a profit turned out to be a price attractive to commercial users alone, then all consumers would lose out—and so would the commercial clients, who would have to pay more for the listings because ProCD could not obtain any contribution toward costs from the consumer market.

To make price discrimination work, however, the seller must be able to control arbitrage. An air carrier sells tickets for less to vacationers than to business travelers, using advance purchase and Saturday-night-stay requirements to distinguish the categories. A producer of movies segments the market by time, releasing first to theaters, then to pay-per-view services, next to the videotape and laserdisc market, and finally to cable and commercial TV. Vendors of computer software have a harder task. Anyone can walk into a retail store and buy a box. Customers do not wear tags saying "commercial user" or "consumer user." Anyway, even a commercial-user-detector at the door would not work, because a consumer could buy the software and resell to a commercial user. That arbitrage would break down the price discrimination and drive up the minimum price at which ProCD would sell to anyone.

Instead of tinkering with the product and letting users sort themselves—for example, furnishing current data at a high price that would be attractive only to commercial customers, and two-year-old data at a low price—ProCD turned to the institution of contract. Every box containing its consumer product declares that the software comes with restrictions stated in an enclosed license. This license, which is encoded on the CD-ROM disks as well as printed in the manual, and which appears on a user's screen every time the software runs, limits use of the application program and listings to non-commercial purposes.

Matthew Zeidenberg bought a consumer package of SelectPhone (trademark) in 1994 from a retail outlet in Madison, Wisconsin, but decided to ignore the license. He formed Silken Mountain Web Services, Inc., to resell the information in the SelectPhone (trademark) database. The corporation makes the database available on the Internet to anyone willing to pay its price— which, needless to say, is less than ProCD charges its commercial customers. Zeidenberg has purchased two additional SelectPhone (trademark) packages, each with an updated version of the database, and made the latest information available over the World Wide Web, for a price, through his corporation. ProCD filed this suit seeking an injunction against further dissemination that exceeds the rights specified in the licenses (identical in each of the three packages Zeidenberg purchased). The district court held the licenses ineffectual because their terms do not appear on the outside of the packages. The court added that the second and third licenses stand no different from the first, even though they are identical, because they *might* have been different, and a purchaser does not agree to—and cannot be bound by—terms that were secret at the time of purchase. 908 F.Supp. at 654.

II

Following the district court, we treat the licenses as ordinary contracts accompanying the sale of products, and therefore as governed by the common law of contracts and the Uniform Commercial Code. Whether there are legal differences between "contracts" and "licenses" (which may matter under the copyright doctrine of first sale) is a subject for another day. ... Zeidenberg does argue, and the district court held, that placing the package of software on the shelf is an "offer," which the customer "accepts" by paying the asking price and leaving the store with the goods. *Peeters v. State,* 154 Wis. 111, 142 NW 181 (1913). In Wisconsin, as elsewhere, a contract includes only the terms on which the parties have agreed. One cannot agree to hidden terms, the judge concluded. So far, so good—but one of the terms to which Zeidenberg agreed by purchasing the software is that the transaction was subject to a license. Zeidenberg's position therefore must be that the printed terms on the outside of a box are the parties' contract—except for printed terms that refer to or incorporate other terms. But why would Wisconsin fetter the parties' choice in this way? Vendors can put the entire terms of a contract on the outside of a box only by using microscopic type, removing other information that buyers might find more useful (such as what the software does, and on which computers it works), or both. The "Read Me" file included with most software, describing system requirements and potential incompatibilities, may be equivalent to ten pages of type; warranties and license restrictions take still more space. Notice on the outside, terms on the inside, and a right to return the software for a refund if the terms are unacceptable (a right that the license expressly extends), may be a means of doing business valuable to buyers and sellers alike. See E. Allan Farnsworth, 1 *Farnsworth on Contracts* §4.26 (1990); *Restatement (2d) of Contracts* §211 comment a (1981) ("Standardization of agreements serves many of the same functions as standardization of goods and services; both are essential to a system of mass production and distribution. Scarce and costly time and skill can be devoted to a class of transactions rather than the details of individual transactions."). Doubtless a state could forbid the use of standard contracts in the software business, but we do not think that Wisconsin has done so.

Transactions in which the exchange of money precedes the communication of detailed terms are common. Consider the purchase of insurance. The buyer goes to an agent, who explains the essentials (amount of coverage, number of years) and remits the premium to the home office, which sends back a policy. On the district judge's understanding, the terms of the policy are irrelevant because the insured paid before receiving them. Yet the device of payment, often with a "binder" (so that the insurance takes effect immediately even though the home office reserves the right to withdraw coverage later), in advance of the policy, serves buyers' interests by accelerating effectiveness and reducing transactions costs. Or consider the purchase of an airline ticket. The traveler calls the carrier or an agent, is quoted a price, reserves a seat, pays, and gets a ticket, in that order. The ticket contains elaborate terms, which the traveler can reject by canceling the reservation. To use the ticket is to accept the terms, even terms that in retrospect are disadvantageous. See *Carnival Cruise Lines, Inc. v. Shute*, 499 US 585, 111 S.Ct. 1522, 113 L.Ed.2d 622 (1991); see also *Vimar Seguros y Reaseguros, S.A. v. M/V Sky Reefer*, 515 US 528, 115 S.Ct. 2322, 132 L.Ed.2d 462 (1995) (bills of lading). Just so with a ticket to a concert. The back of the ticket states that the patron promises not to record the concert; to attend is to agree. A theater that detects a violation will confiscate the tape and escort the violator to the exit. One *could* arrange things so that every concertgoer signs this promise before forking over the money, but that cumbersome way of doing things not only would lengthen queues and raise prices but also would scotch the sale of tickets by phone or electronic data service.

Consumer goods work the same way. Someone who wants to buy a radio set visits a store, pays, and walks out with a box. Inside the box is a leaflet containing some terms, the most important of which usually is the warranty, read for the first time in the comfort of home. By Zeidenberg's lights, the warranty in the box is irrelevant; every consumer gets the standard warranty implied by the UCC in the event the contract is silent; yet so far as we are aware no state disregards warranties furnished with consumer products. Drugs come with a list of ingredients on the outside and an elaborate package insert on the inside. The package insert describes drug interactions, contraindications, and other vital information—but, if Zeidenberg is right, the purchaser need not read the package insert, because it is not part of the contract.

Next consider the software industry itself. Only a minority of sales take place over the counter, where there are boxes to peruse. A customer may place an order by phone in response to a line item in a catalog or a review in a magazine. Much software is ordered over the Internet by purchasers who have never seen a box. Increasingly software arrives by wire. There is no box; there is only a stream of electrons, a collection of information that includes data, an application program, instructions, many limitations ("MegaPixel 3.14159 cannot be used with BytePusher 2.718"), and the terms of sale. The user purchases a serial number, which activates the software's features. On Zeidenberg's arguments, these unboxed sales are unfettered by terms— so the seller has made a broad warranty and must pay consequential damages for any shortfalls in performance, two "promises" that if taken seriously would drive prices through the ceiling or return transactions to the horse-and-buggy age.

· · ·

What then does the current version of the UCC have to say? We think that the place to start is §2-204(1): "A contract for sale of goods may be made in any manner sufficient to show agreement, including conduct by both parties which recognizes the existence of such a contract." A vendor, as master of the offer, may invite acceptance by conduct, and may propose limitations on the kind of conduct that constitutes acceptance. A buyer may accept by performing the acts the vendor proposes to treat as acceptance. And that is what happened. ProCD proposed a contract that a buyer would accept by *using* the software after having an opportunity to read the license at leisure. This Zeidenberg did. He had no choice, because the software splashed the license on the screen and would not let him proceed without indicating acceptance. So although the district judge was right to say that a contract can be, and often is, formed simply by paying the price and walking out of the store, the UCC permits contracts to be formed in other ways. ProCD proposed such a different way, and without protest Zeidenberg agreed. Ours is not a case in which a consumer opens a package to find an insert saying "you owe us an extra $10,000" and the seller files suit to collect. Any buyer finding such a demand can prevent formation of the contract by returning the package, as can any consumer who concludes that the terms of the license make the software worth less than the purchase price. Nothing in the UCC requires a seller to maximize the buyer's net gains.

Section 2-606, which defines "acceptance of goods," reinforces this understanding. A buyer accepts goods under §2-606(1)(b) when, after an opportunity to inspect, he fails to make an effective rejection under §2-602(1). ProCD extended an opportunity to reject if a buyer should find the license terms unsatisfactory; Zeidenberg inspected the package, tried out the software, learned of the license, and did not reject the goods. We refer to §2-606 only to show that the opportunity to return goods can be important; acceptance of an offer differs from acceptance of goods after delivery, see *Gillen v. Atalanta Systems, Inc.*, 997 F.2d 280, 284 n. 1 (7th Cir. 1993); but the UCC consistently permits the parties to structure their relations so that the buyer has a chance to make a final decision after a detailed review.

Some portions of the UCC impose additional requirements on the way parties agree on terms. A disclaimer of the implied warranty of merchantability must be "conspicuous." UCC §2-316(2), incorporating UCC §1-201(10). Promises to make firm offers, or to negate oral modifications, must be "separately signed." UCC §§2-205, 2-209(2). These special provisos reinforce the impression that, so far as the UCC is concerned, other terms may be as inconspicuous as the forum-selection clause on the back of the cruise ship ticket in *Carnival Lines*. Zeidenberg has not located any Wisconsin case—for that matter, any case in any state—holding that under the UCC the ordinary terms found in shrinkwrap licenses require any special prominence, or otherwise are to be undercut rather than enforced. In the end, the terms of the license are conceptually identical to the contents of the package. Just as no court would dream of saying that SelectPhone (trademark) must contain 3,100 phone books rather than 3,000, or must have data no more than 30 days old, or must sell for $100 rather than $150—although any of these changes would be welcomed by the customer, if all other things were held constant—so, we believe, Wisconsin would not let the buyer pick and choose among terms. Terms of use are no less a part of "the product" than are the size of the database and the speed with which the software compiles listings. Competition among vendors, not judicial revision of a package's contents, is how consumers are protected in a market economy. ... ProCD has rivals, which may elect to compete by offering superior software, monthly updates, improved terms of use, lower price, or a better compromise among these elements. As we stressed above, adjusting terms in buyers' favor might help Matthew Zeidenberg today (he already has the software) but would lead to a response, such as a higher price, that might make consumers as a whole worse off ... .

Appeal allowed.

NOTES

The 7th Circuit followed *ProCD* in another leading and equally controversial judgment, *Hill v. Gateway 2000, Inc.* (1997), 31 UCCC Rep. Serv. 2d 303. *Hill* was a class action and the plaintiff, who had bought one of the defendant's computers by phone, sued the defendant alleging breach of the civil Racketeer Influenced and Corrupt Organization Act (RICO) and other violations. The defendant relied on an arbitration clause appearing in the box in which the computer was shipped to the plaintiff after the defendant's receipt of the plaintiff's order. The trial judge refused to enforce the arbitration clause; the CCA 7 (again speaking through Easterbrook J) reversed and held that the warranty and other terms in the box constituted part of the contract between the parties. The only reported shrinkwrap case in Canada to date is Veit J's decision in *North American Systemshops Ltd. v. King*, [1989] AJ 512. The plaintiffs sued the defendant for breach of copyright in its software which the defendant had purchased in shrinkwrap form from an authorized dealer of the plaintiff. The package contained restrictions on buyers' right to make further copies of the software (other than for back up purposes) but these restrictions or a notice drawing buyers' attention to them were not visible on the outside of the package. Veit J approached the plaintiff's claim primarily through the prism of copyright and/or patent law and held that unless the copyright licensor makes it clear at the time of sale that there were restrictions, the buyer of the product was free to use it as it wished. However, and importantly, Veit J also found that the defendants had not in fact breached the licensing terms. Her judgment contains little discussion of the relevant contract principles (other than a long quotation from Sookman, *Computer Law*, at 2-48 *et seq*.) and of course no reference to the later contrary CCA 7 decisions.

As indicated below in the extracts from the Uniform Computer Information Transactions Act (UCITA), the *ProCD* highly functional approach is adopted by UCITA. However, the ALI refused to enforce UCITA for this and other reasons. The drafters of Revised Article 2 and, more recently, Amendments to Article 2, wrestled with the shrinkwrap problem but there was no consensus and so the existing Article 2 contract formation provisions were left as is. Conceptually, are you satisfied with Easterbrook J's approach or is the real issue the relief we should give the buyer in those rare cases where the buyer reads the licensing and other terms of the purchase after receipt of the software and is dissatisfied? Is it correct to say that the buyer can always reject the contract if she is dissatisfied with the fine print even if the seller's terms do not confer this right? Should we distinguish between different types of contracts? Should we rely on the courts' general policing powers against unconscionable terms, as indeed we do in those cases where the formal contracting rules have been satisfied?

Uniform Computer Information Transactions Act
(National Conference of Commissioners on Uniform State Laws, 2001)

Section 102. Definitions.

(55) "Record" means information that is inscribed on a tangible medium or that is stored in an electronic or other medium and is retrievable in perceivable form.

Section 202. Formation in General.

(a) A contract may be formed in any manner sufficient to show agreement, including offer and acceptance or conduct of both parties or operations of electronic agents which recognize the existence of a contract.

. . .

(e) If a term is to be adopted by later agreement and the parties intend not to be bound unless the term is so adopted, a contract is not formed if the parties do not agree to the term. In that case, each party shall deliver to the other party, or with the consent of the other party destroy, all copies of information, access materials, and other materials received or made, and each party is entitled to a return with respect to any contract fee paid for which performance has not been received, has not been accepted, or has been redelivered without any benefit being retained. The parties remain bound by any restriction in a contractual use term with respect to information or copies received or made from copies received pursuant to the agreement, but the contractual use term does not apply to information or copies properly received or obtained from another source.

Section 208. Adopting Terms of Records. Except as otherwise provided in Section 209, the following rules apply:

(1) A party adopts the terms of a record, including a standard form, as the terms of the contract if the party agrees to the record, such as by manifesting assent.

(2) The terms of a record may be adopted pursuant to paragraph (1) after beginning performance or use if the parties had reason to know that their agreement would be represented in whole or part by a later record to be agreed on and there would not be an opportunity to review the record or a copy of it before performance or use begins. If the parties fail to agree to the later terms and did not intend to form a contract unless they so agreed, Section 202(e) applies.

(3) If a party adopts the terms of a record, the terms become part of the contract without regard to the party's knowledge or understanding of individual terms in the record, except for a term that is unenforceable because it fails to satisfy another requirement of this [Act].

Section 209. Mass-market License.

(a) A party adopts the terms of a mass-market license for purposes of Section 208 only if the party agrees to the license, such as by manifesting assent, before or during the party's initial performance or use of or access to the information. A term is not part of the license if:

(1) the term is unconscionable or is unenforceable under Section 105(a) or (b); or

(2) subject to Section 301, the term conflicts with a term to which the parties to the license have expressly agreed.

(b) If a mass-market license or a copy of the license is not available in a manner permitting an opportunity to review by the licensee before the licensee becomes obligated to pay and the licensee does not agree, such as by manifesting assent, to the license after having an opportunity to review, the licensee is entitled to a return under Section 112 and, in addition, to:

(1) reimbursement of any reasonable expenses incurred in complying with the licensor's instructions for returning or destroying the computer information or, in the absence of instructions, expenses incurred for return postage or similar reasonable expense in returning the computer information; and

(2) compensation for any reasonable and foreseeable costs of restoring the licensee's information processing system to reverse changes in the system caused by the installation, if:

(A) the installation occurs because information must be installed to enable review of the license; and

(B) the installation alters the system or information in it but does not restore the system or information after removal of the installed information because the licensee rejected the license.

(c) In a mass-market transaction, if the licensor does not have an opportunity to review a record containing proposed terms from the licensee before the licensor delivers or becomes obligated to deliver the information, and if the licensor does not agree, such as by manifesting assent, to those terms after having that opportunity, the licensor is entitled to a return.

CONSEQUENCES OF NON-COMPLIANCE WITH CONSUMER WRITING REQUIREMENTS

J. Schofield Manuel Ltd. v. Rose

(1975), 9 OR (2d) 404 (Co. Ct.)

CORNISH Co. Ct. J: The defendants, on the advice of friends, decided to retain the services of the plaintiff company, a firm of interior decorators, in furnishing their new home at 47 Rondeau Drive. After some discussion and visits by Mr. Manuel, president of the plaintiff company, and Mrs. Christie Hansen, one of the firm's employees, Mr. Manuel supplied the Roses with three estimates of costs in duplicate.

The plaintiffs' total bills amounted to $11,758.05, particulars of which will be found in exs. 4, 5 and 6—dated June 7, 1972, June 9, 1972, and July 31, 1972, which estimates are signed by the defendant, Douglas Rose, but not by anyone on behalf of the plaintiff company. The balance of the charges appear to be in statements found in ex. 7 and dated August 29, 1972. Payments amounted to a total of $7,902.48. The plaintiff asks for judgment for the balance owing of $3,855.57 and interest at the rate of two per cent (2%) per month on this amount and the costs of this action.

The defence of the defendants to the plaintiff's claim for this balance rests on s. 31 of the Consumer Protection Act, RSO 1970, c. 82 [now RSO 1990, c. C.31, s. 19] so I will now quote it in full except for s. 31(3) which deals with trade in situations and is irrelevant to this case:

· · ·

Douglas Rose signed each of these [estimates] and returned one copy to the plaintiff and kept one copy for the use of his wife and himself.

It is to be noted that none of these documents were signed in the usual way by the plaintiff, nor do they contain a warranty or a statement that no warranty is being given, as required by s. 31(1)(f). It is open to argument prior to the work commencing that these documents are merely approved estimates and not contracts. I am of the opinion that, once the work commenced with the consent of the defendants, there can be no doubt that a contract has arisen between the parties unless such is prevented by s. 31 of the Consumer Protection Act.

In any event, the goods were delivered and the services completed by the end of August, 1972, and various payments on account were made. While the Roses expressed dissatisfaction with some of the plaintiff's work, I am of the opinion that it was only to be expected in a $10,000 contract that everything would not be completely pleasing to the customer. I find that their objections were minor and that the plaintiff did attempt to remedy these complaints. I am confirmed in this view by the fact that two months after these contracts were completed the defendants asked the plaintiff to give them an estimate on the furnishing of the den in this house.

The plaintiff made various attempts through his firm and through their lawyers (see exs. 1 and 2) to collect the balance owing, to which there was no reply, and then issued the writ in this action.

The statement of defence alleges that the defendants are not obliged to pay the balance owing on two grounds:

> I. The contract is an executory contract as defined in s. 1(h) of the Consumer Protection Act and since the plaintiff must comply with all the terms of s. 31 of the Act and it has not done so. The defendant does not ask for a refund of the moneys paid but merely declines to pay the balance, and thus apparently recognizes the contract as being valid and subsisting up to the amount paid but invalid as to the balance claimed as owing.
>
> II. The price charged by the plaintiff for goods delivered and services rendered were grossly excessive.

Let us now consider defence I: There is no doubt in my mind that the contract, if it is an executory contract as defined in s. 1(h), does not comply with s. 31(1)(f) above mentioned. This makes it unnecessary for me to spend much time on the question of whether it also offends s. 31(2) in that it did not bear the signature of the plaintiff, other than to say that Mr. Kohm presented an ingenious argument which impressed me that it should be considered as having been signed by the plaintiff because it was on the letterhead of the plaintiff and signed by the defendants and adopted by the plaintiff by carrying out its terms. In support of this proposition, he cited *Cohen v. Roche*, [1927] 1 KB 169, and other English cases quoted in the 8th edition of Cheshire and Fifoot, *The Law of Contracts* (1972), at 176.

Now let us consider whether this contract should be treated as an executory contract as defined in s. 1.

It is quite obvious that a contract which, at the time of signing, is an executory contract, can with the passage of time become a partly executed contract or a discharged contract or an executed contract.

In order to give this section of the Act any intelligent meaning, one must conclude that while the contract is in its executory stage the seller must comply with s. 31 and that, if he does not do so, the purchaser can consider the contract as void but that, once the contract becomes partly executed, the requirements of s. 31 are waived. If one does not adopt this interpretation, the only way one can avoid the statute producing a ridiculous result in such situations as we have here is by turning to the doctrine of *quantum meruit*.

If the framers of the statute wanted sellers to resort to *quantum meruit* to get redress in certain seller-buyer situations under the Act, they should have said so and they did not do so.

I find support for my view that this is not an "executory contract" governed by s. 31(1) by a perusal of s. 35 of the Act. This section provides that, where two-thirds of the purchase price has been paid on an executory contract, any provisions of that contract whereby the seller may retake possession of the goods upon default in payment is not enforceable except by leave of a Judge. This indicates to me that a contract must exist at the time two-thirds of the purchase price has been paid. If there was no contract at that time, title in the goods could not have passed to the purchaser and he could have no right to possession of the goods.

I have therefore come to the conclusion that the three contracts here in question are not governed by the requirements of s. 31 and are in fact binding contracts on the parties hereto.

. . .

There was a reference in argument to the proposition that the plaintiff, by reason of the failure to fully comply with s. 31, was—by s. 48 [now s. 39]—made guilty of an offence punishable on summary conviction and hence the contract was illegal. However, s-s. (4) of s. 48 provides that: "... an error or omission in any form prescribed ... by this Act or the regulations shall not be deemed to be in contravention of this Act ...," where it is proved that "the error or omission is a *bona fide* accidental or clerical error or omission. ..." I am satisfied that the plaintiff qualifies for this exception to the rule.

Judgment for plaintiff.

NOTES AND QUESTIONS

1) Do you agree with the court's reasoning? With the result? Could the result have been reached without doing violence to the meaning of "executory contract"? *Cf.* Judge Cornish's approach with Judge Borins' judgment in *Dominion Home Improvements Ltd. v. Knuude*, reproduced later in this chapter, and with the Divisional Court's decision (Steele J) in *Helman v. Gertner* (1990), 39 OAC 42. In the latter case, Steele J refused to enforce a contract for the services of a musical band between the plaintiffs and the defendant, one of the grounds being that the contract was not in writing as required by CPA, s. 19. *Schofield Manuel* was not referred to. However, the two cases are distinguishable on the ground that the defendant had repudiated the contract before the plaintiffs had an opportunity to display their musical talents.

On the other side of the coin, *Schofield Manuel* is supported by another Divisional Court decision (this one involving a three-member Court), *C. Battison & Sons Inc. v. Mauti* (1986), 34 DLR (4th) 700. The issue here was whether the plaintiff, a building renovator, could recover the agreed price for work done at the defendant's premises despite the plaintiff's being in breach of s. 10 of sch. 32 of Bylaw 107-78 enacted under the Municipality of Metropolitan Toronto Act. This provided that "before commencing any work a building renovator shall enter into a written contract with the person for whom the work is to be performed to be signed by the renovator and such person and to be in the form attached hereto ... ." The bylaw provided for a maximum penalty of $1,000. The plaintiff did the work without a written contract. The plaintiff asserted a construction lien and obtained a report from the master in its favour. This was set aside by a High Court judge on the ground that the contract was illegal and therefore unenforceable. On appeal, the Divisional Court disagreed on the ground that, in its view, the intention of the bylaw was not to affect contractual obligations, and because its purposes were adequately served by the penalty. (Do you agree with this construction of the bylaw? How often is the City of Toronto likely to lay such complaints and will a small penalty (probably well below $1,000) be a sufficient incentive to ensure that renovation contracts are reduced to writing?)

Leaving aside such constructional and restitutionary issues, would it be better to give courts an express dispensing power to waive technical breaches of the Consumer Protection Act? If so, what type of test would you recommend? Should CPA s. 39, discussed *supra*, be applied to civil as well as criminal sanctions?

2) *Disclosure Requirements.* While the purpose of the original Statute of Frauds writing requirement was primarily evidentiary (to avoid misunderstanding about the terms of the agreement and to prevent false allegations that an agreement had been concluded), modern writing requirements in consumer legislation are also intended to serve important cautionary and informational functions. The requirements in CPA s. 19, discussed in *J. Schofield Manuel Ltd. v. Rose, supra*, are one such example. The "truth in lending" disclosure requirements in the CPA, discussed *infra*, are another. Important disclosure requirements, not necessarily of a contractual character, will be found in the regulations adopted under such federal Acts as the Food and Drugs Act, RSC 1985 c. F.27 as am., the Consumer Packaging and Labelling Act, RSC 1985, c. C-38, as am., the Textile Labelling Act, RSC 1985, c. T-10 as am., and in such provincial legislation as the Ontario New Home Warranties Plan Act, RSO 1990, c. O.31, and the "additional written warranties" provisions in Saskatchewan's Consumer Products Warranties Act, s. 17. Such legislation is designed, *inter alia*, to assist the consumer to make more informed shopping decisions, to compare products and prices, and to appreciate better what the consumer is buying and the financial commitments she is being asked to make.

While the notion of legislating disclosure of information from sellers and other suppliers to consumers has gained widespread acceptance, the difficulties involved in this area should not be underestimated. For a comprehensive analysis of the problem as viewed from an American perspective, see W.C. Whitford, "The Functions of Disclosure Regulations in Consumer Transactions," [1973] *Wisc. L Rev.* 400. Whitford notes, for example, that almost all of the legislation in the area is aimed at the written contract, but that most consumers view the signing of the contract as little more than a formality, much like a handshake, and usually feel already morally bound to sign the contract once a verbal agreement has been reached. Whitford also observes that few consumers read the contract prior to signing and that, of those who do, many find the document incomprehensible even when the wording is specified by legislation. Do you think that "plain language" requirements adopted in New York state and other American states provide an appropriate answer?

There are many other problems. For example, how does one aid lower-income consumers through disclosure requirements when almost all of the literature suggests that middle-class consumers are the main beneficiaries of such legislation? Given the limited physical mobility of the poor, is greater disclosure going to benefit this group if it merely reveals that better prices are available in middle-class areas which are some distance from the poorer neighbourhoods?

A significant body of consumer literature exists with respect to the importance of information in transactional analyses. See, *inter alia*, Mackaay, "The Costliness of Information and its Effect on the Analysis of Law," in Ziegel (ed.), *Proceedings of the Seventh Annual*

Workshop on Commercial and Consumer Law (1979), at 121, and Stigler, "The Economics of Information" (1961), 69 *J Pol. Econ.* 213.

Note on Consumer Credit and "Truth in Lending" Disclosure Requirements

Consumer credit, a phenomenon now well over a century old, grew rapidly after World War II, from $870 million in outstanding balances in 1948 to more than $120 billion at the present time. See the table in chapter 1, volume III of the previous edition of this casebook. The types of credit grantors have also expanded rapidly. Before the war, most consumer credit was in the form of instalment credit extended by vendors of big ticket items ("vendor's credit"), particularly in connection with the sale of motor vehicles. Frequently, by pre-arrangement, the vendor assigned the instalment contract to a sales finance company, a financing technique that still exists and that in the past has given rise to many legal problems. See volume II of the previous edition of this casebook, chapter 3.

Until the late 1960s, Canadian banks played only a minor role in consumer credit financing. This was partly because the banks did not perceive it as a profitable source of business, and partly because the interest ceiling on loans under the Bank Act made it unattractive for them to make consumer loans. The ceiling was lifted in the decennial revision of the Bank Act in 1967 and thereafter the banks entered the consumer credit market in a major way. Today, the banks account for more than 60% of the outstanding balances of consumer credit. Revolving lines of consumer credit in the form of charge accounts with the credit grantor (for example, a department store or oil company) and multipurpose credit cards (such as Visa, Mastercharge, or American Express) have also expanded rapidly over the past 25 years. These too have generated their own problems.

The cost of consumer credit varies widely among the different types of credit and between credit grantors offering the same type of credit. For a long time, however, it was difficult for consumers to compare the different rates easily since the forms of disclosure of the cost varied widely. Sales finance companies usually expressed it in dollars and cents but not as a percentage of the balance of the purchase price. Others used a percentage "add on" rate, which was misleading since the rate was calculated on the amount of the initial sale price or loan and did not allow for the declining balance of the principal amount during the term of the contract. Yet another difficulty was that there was no standard formula for calculating the equivalent annual percentage rate.

The "truth in lending" movement, spearheaded by Senator Paul Douglas in the United States and vigorously supported by consumer activists in Canada, was designed to change all this by requiring all credit grantors to convert the cost of credit into a nominal annual interest rate and to require all components of the cost of credit (e.g., investigation fees, credit insurance, registration fees) to be included in the cost base. For the details of the debate, see J.S. Ziegel and R.E. Olley (eds.), *Consumer Credit in Canada* (U. of Sask., 1966).

The movement gained its first major victories in Canada where the federal and provincial governments agreed jointly in 1967 on uniform disclosure requirements expressed in terms of an annual nominal interest rate. The federal rules appear in regulations adopted under the Bank Act; the provincial rules appear in regulations adopted under provincial Consumer Protection Acts and, in several provinces, under separate Costs of Credit Disclosure Acts.

The consumer credit market has changed dramatically since the original truth in lending laws were enacted. In the 1960s, there were relatively few products. Closed-end contracts (loans and credit sales) were the norm and credit cards and other forms of open-end contract were in their infancy. Today's pattern is the reverse. Open-end credit contracts are widely used and closed-end transactions are in decline except for high cost items such as motor vehicles and, of course, real estate. There is also a much wider variety of products available to consumers, encompassing fixed and variable loan contracts, mortgage offset arrangements, combined credit and debit facilities, contracts offering flexible payment arrangements and the like. These developments raise questions about the premises underlying the truth in lending laws. For one thing, the more complex the market, the harder it is to ensure that consumers are provided with standardised credit cost information on a meaningful basis. There is a tension between pricing freedom and truth in lending objectives. Product differentiation increases the difficulty of comparison, but statutorily imposed product standardisation is likely to result in inefficient pricing practices (cross-subsidisation and the like). Another concern is that non-uniform truth in lending disclosure requirements enacted at the provincial level increase compliance costs for credit providers who operate nationally. For a fuller account of the policy arguments and proposals for reform, see Symposium, "Revision of the Federal Interest Act and Harmonization of Federal-Provincial Consumer Credit Disclosure Legislation" (1998) 29 *CBLJ* 161; Alberta Law Reform Institute, *Cost of Credit Disclosure* (Final Report, No. 82, February, 2000). The Ontario truth in lending laws are to be found in the *Consumer Protection* Act RSO 1990, c. C.31, as am. Part III was enacted in 1999, replacing 1960s-style truth in lending provisions: see SO 1999, c. 12.

There are very few reported cases in Canada of attempts by consumers or regulatory authorities to enforce the truth in lending legislation. A notable exception is *Motor Vehicle Manufacturers' Assn v. Ontario* (1988), 49 DLR (4th) 592 (Ont.), reproduced in volume I of the previous edition of this casebook at page 52. The recent amendments to the Ontario disclosure provisions (regressive in the view of one of the editors of this casebook) no longer make the decision a relevant one.

CONSUMER PROTECTION AND THE CONTRACT MAKING PROCESS: SPECIFIC RESPONSES

W.W. Distributors & Co. Ltd. v. Thorsteinson

(1960), 26 DLR (2d) 365, 33 WWR 669 (Man. CA)

FREEDMAN JA (for the court): Although this appeal raised two or three points of law—the exploration of which doubtless have been of some interest—I feel that this case can and should be disposed of on the basis of its particular facts.

Those facts show that the plaintiff (the appellant) brought to Court a contract that was tainted with misrepresentation; that the sale thereunder was effected by a combined process of pressure and deception; and that the signatures of the defendants thereto were procured by deliberate non-disclosure of certain very pertinent facts.

The plaintiff is a corporation engaged in the sale of cooking utensils. The defendants are mother and daughter—the latter having been an infant in July 22, 1959, when the contract was entered into, but being now of full age. On the date mentioned she was employed as a clerk and receptionist in a Winnipeg department store. She was engaged to be married to a young man whose wife she has since become.

While at work on July 22nd the infant defendant received a telephone call from a man who was a stranger to her. He told her that he had an engagement gift which he wished to present to her. She replied that she was busy at the time but suggested that he get in touch with her at her home in the evening. The caller was a salesman employed by the plaintiff company. The evidence does not show how he came to know of the infant defendant, but it was indicated to us by counsel in argument that the newspaper announcement of the young lady's engagement was the source of his information. Here we have a clue to the pattern of operation of the plaintiff company. This was the method of securing for its salesmen an "approach" to a member of the public who might be induced to become a purchaser.

One may perhaps disapprove of such a method, but it would be wrong to say that a contract arising therefrom would necessarily be invalid. In a free enterprise economy a reasonable latitude should be allowed for the play of individual initiative and originality. Hence I do not stress too strongly the somewhat covert method by which the plaintiff succeeded in getting into communication with the defendants. It is rather to what followed thereafter that we must look if we are to determine whether the plaintiff secured a contract which should be given the support and sanction of the Court.

The plaintiff's salesman and manager arrived at the home of the defendant on July 22, 1959, about 7 p.m. When they left two hours later they had succeeded in procuring the signatures of the infant and her mother to a contract for the purchase of three items of kitchen utensils, namely, a set of Queen Anne cookware, a set of Spring Tulip flatware, and an electric skillet. At the trial of this action a thoroughly qualified expert put the aggregate value of these three items at a maximum of $145.95. On July 23, 1959—that is to say, the day following the transaction in question—the plaintiff sued the defendants for payment under the contract. The amount claimed was $342.99. Such a claim in the circumstances becomes at once suspect. Close examination of the transaction shows that the contract cannot be maintained.

An exorbitant price is not in itself a ground for setting aside a contract of sale. But where the defence of misrepresentation has been raised, and where the evidence (at 52) indicates a specific warranty by the salesman that the defendants "were getting good value in exchange for their money," the Court must examine the circumstances of the transaction to determine whether what occurred was mere puffery by a salesman or whether it constituted a deliberate act of deception which could vitiate the contract. If, as was assuredly the case here, the representation was part of an entire pattern of improper conduct—consisting of material misstatements on the one hand and of wilful non-disclosure on the other—the Court is more easily led to a conclusion against the validity of the contract.

The actual sale price of the three items in the contract came to $239.50. How then did the plaintiff come to sue the next day for $342.99? The answer is to be found in a number of special provisions in the contract, some of them unusual in their nature and oppressive and onerous in their effect. There was, first of all, a service charge of $22.35 which, if it stood alone, could not be regarded as particularly objectionable as the contract called for a cash payment of $50 and then monthly payments of $20 extending over a period of 10 or 11 months. But then there was a recording fee of $2, which was simply for recording the contract in the office of the plaintiff. Another provision called for 10% interest after maturity. Finally it was provided that if the contract were placed in the hands of a solicitor the defendants should pay an additional 20% as solicitor's fees. The evidence of the infant and her mother makes it plain that these special provisions were not brought to their notice in any way. It is clear, too, from the judgment of Philp, Sr. Co. Ct. J, that he accepted the testimony of the defendants. It is true, of course, that as a general rule a person who signs a contract will be bound by its terms. But the rule is not inflexible. It may be departed from in appropriate cases, of which in my view this is one. Here it is clear that the representatives of the plaintiff not only did not provide an opportunity to the defendants to read and understand the contract, but by their tactics of pressure and speed deliberately sought to deny and succeeded in denying such opportunity to them. In such circumstances the Court may grant protection on grounds of equity, the more so where one of the victims is an infant.

What occurred at the home on the evening in question emerges from the evidence. The salesman, assisted by the manager, proceeded to give the infant plaintiff a demonstration of the cookware. Attempts on her part to ask pertinent questions were blocked by speedy interruptions on the part either of the salesman or of the manager. The infant plaintiff stated that she entered into the contract only as a result of the high-pressure tactics of the two men. The evidence reveals the picture of such tactics. As for the mother, the evidence indicates how her signature was procured. She had given a cheque for $50 for the cash payment merely by way of loan to her daughter. This was openly stated at the time, and indeed at the trial was admitted by the salesman and the manager. She was not a purchaser or intending to become a purchaser, yet they asked her to sign the contract. When she demurred the salesman said, "It is not important. It doesn't really mean anything except we would like to have your name on it with your daughter's." Clearly the salesman knew better. He was fully aware that if the mother signed the contract it would mean something. His statement was a deliberate act of deception designed to procure the mother's signature to the document.

Within minutes after the two men left, the infant and her mother sought to repudiate the contract but were unable to locate any representative of the plaintiff. The next morning payment on the cheque was stopped. When the salesman, after failing in his attempt to certify the cheque, called at the defendants' home he was at once informed of the repudiation of the contract. The defendants asked him to take the goods back. This he refused to do, saying that he had no such authority. The goods, still unused, are now exhibits in Court, available for return to the plaintiff.

Misrepresentation was raised as a defence, and the evidence amply confirms it. I think it would be unjust and inequitable to hold these ladies to a contract procured in the manner in which this one was. The learned trial Judge dismissed the plaintiff's action. I would dismiss the appeal, with costs.

Appeal dismissed.

Notes on Cooling Off Legislation and Unsolicited Goods

Cooling Off Legislation

1) *Thorsteinson* was decided before Manitoba adopted its cooling off legislation in the Manitoba Consumer Protection Act. All the provinces and many of the American jurisdictions now have such provisions. For the Ontario provisions, see CPA Pt. I and s. 21. For a general discussion of the Canadian legislation, see R.C.C. Cuming (1967), 32 *Sask. L Rev.* 113, and *cf.* Byron Sher (1968), 15 *UCLA L Rev.* 717. See also *Stubbe v. P.F. Collier & Son Ltd.* (1977), 74 DLR (3d) 605 (BCSC) and *Stubbe v. P.F. Collier & Son Ltd. (No. 2)* (1978), 85 DLR (3d) 77 (BCSC), decided under the BC Trade Practices Act, for a detailed description of practices held to be unfair in the door-to-door sale of the defendant's encyclopedias.

2) In the context of the Ontario provisions, consider the following questions:

a) What types of sale are caught by them? Are the definitional provisions in Pt. I and s. 21 consistent with one another? What is the meaning of "solicits, negotiates or arranges for the signing by a buyer ... at a place other than the seller's permanent place of business" in s. 21? Does "signing by a buyer" qualify "solicits, negotiates" as well as "arranges"? In what circumstances would a newspaper advertisement be deemed a solicitation?

b) Would it be practicable to extend the concept of a cooling off period to sales concluded at trade premises? If not, what alternative means can you suggest to protect a consumer against ill-considered and impetuous decisions?

c) The Ontario CPA used to require the licensing of itinerant salespersons. The requirement was repealed in 1999 because, according to the Minister's statement in the Ontario legislative assembly, it was found impractical to operate such a licensing scheme at the provincial level. He thought it could be done more efficiently at the municipal level. Do you agree? Do door-to-door sales still play an important role in the Canadian economy, or have they been replaced by e-commerce?

d) Consider the following situations and determine to what extent the statutory provisions apply to them:

    i) purchase through a mail-order catalogue;

    ii) purchase through an application form in a newspaper advertisement;

    iii) solicitation by telephone;

    iv) solicitation begun at consumer's home but contract completed at merchant's premises;

    v) contract signed at consumer's home after he has visited the merchant's premises;

    vi) contract signed at home by consumer who took contract away for further study.

3) Consider also these problems related to the buyer's right to rescind:

a) Where the vendor has not complied with s. 19, is the right to rescind still limited to 10 days?

b) How does the buyer learn of his right to rescind? *Cf. Zaluski's* case, *infra*, this chapter.

c) How can the buyer notify the seller of his decision to rescind? What if the seller's address is not shown on the contract?

d) The right to rescind only applies if the contract is for more than $50. Is this figure too high? Too low?

e) With respect to the provision "after the duplicate original copy of the contract first comes into the possession of the buyer" (s. 21(1)), how does this affect mail order sales, book club subscriptions, and similar transactions?

Unsolicited Goods and Services and Negative Option Schemes

A fertile source of consumer complaints over the years has been the practice of some suppliers of delivering goods such as books or periodicals that have not been requested and that are accompanied or followed by a demand for payment. Understandably, consumers were unsure of their rights and responsibilities in such circumstances. Section 36 of the Ontario CPA was enacted to give consumers some (additional) protection against claims involving unsolicited goods. Many of the other provinces have similar legislation.

What does s. 36 add to the common law position? Note the exclusions in s. 36(1)(b). How is the consumer to know of his or her rights under the section (or, for that matter, at common law)? If the "contract in writing" (s. 36(1)(b)) is for a consideration of more than $50, then presumably s. 19 will also apply. If it is for a lesser amount, what action by the consumer will be sufficient to show his acceptance of the goods?

A *negative option scheme* exists where a contract for the supply of goods or services (for example, a contract for the supply of books under a Book of the Month club or a contract for the supply of cable TV services) authorizes the seller to supply new goods or services, even if not previously requested, unless the consumer advises the supplier that she does not want the additional goods or services. The controversial nature of such provisions was highlighted at the beginning of 1995 with the attempt by Rogers Cable and other cable companies to bill subscribers for additional channels even though subscribers had not requested them. As a result of the public outcry the cable companies were forced to revise their strategies.

However, in many if not most of the provinces, negative option clauses are still perfectly legal although they may be vulnerable to attack under the trade practices legislation discussed later in this chapter. Nova Scotia is one of the provinces where such clauses (referred to as a "negative-option strategy") are now banned (but only in respect of services) and the seller is precluded from suing for the price of such additional services. See Consumer Protection Act, RSNS 1989, c. 92, as amended in 1994, c. 16, s. 2, adding s. 24A to the Act. Section 24A(1) defines a "negative-option strategy" as one where the seller delivers a service to a buyer after having, on or after April 26, 1994, first notified the buyer to the effect that (a) the seller proposes to deliver the service, and (b) the service will be delivered and the buyer will be billed for the service unless the buyer on or before the time specified in the notice or during a particular time period, instructs the seller not to deliver the services, and the buyer neither instructs the seller not to supply the services nor authorizes or requests the seller to deliver the services.

Gaertner v. Fiesta Dance Studios Ltd.

(1972), 32 DLR (3d) 639 (BCSC)

McKAY J (orally): The plaintiff is 31 years of age, unmarried and a registered nurse. She is claiming the return of $6,506 paid by her to the defendant, Fiesta Dance Studios Limited which carries on business under several names including Fred Astaire Dance Studios. This is one of several such claims now pending in this Court against the same defendant. This case has shown the incredible gullibility of some people and the readiness of others to take advantage of that gullibility. On October 24, 1969, the plaintiff entered into a contract with Fiesta for 32 hours of dancing lessons for a fee of $126 with $21 down and $21 a month. On October 31, 1969, one week later, the plaintiff entered into a second contract. This contract superseded the original one. It provided for 37 hours of private lessons and 37 hours of group lessons. The fee was $962 with the deposit from the first contract in the amount of $21 to be applied on the fee. On November 19, 1969, three weeks later, the plaintiff entered into yet another contract with Fiesta. This one provided for a further 65 hours of private lessons and 135 hours of group lessons for a fee of $2,340. This contract was not in substitution for the contract of October 31, 1969, but was in addition to that contract. Three weeks later on December 10, 1969, there was yet another contract. This one provided for a further 75 hours of private lessons and 150 hours of group lessons for a fee of $2,573. Again, this was in addition to the earlier contracts. On February 6, 1970, seven weeks later, the plaintiff entered into a contract to take a further 20 hours of private lessons for a fee of $685. On May 27, 1970, the plaintiff entered into a contract to take a further 25 hours of private lessons and 25 hours of group lessons for a fee of $650. Again, these latter two contracts were in addition to the earlier ones.

The plaintiff took lessons two or three times a week until February 13, 1971. At that time she had unused and due to her 118 hours of private lessons and 281 hours of group lessons. Thankfully, during the signing of the later contracts one of the clauses was deleted. It was a clause to the effect that all of the lessons had to be used up within a year. This poor lady would have been dancing night and day if that clause had not been deleted. Remarkable as it may seem, she was also taking dancing lessons on the side from a teacher who had departed from Fiesta and was conducting dancing lessons on his own. The reason given by the plaintiff for ceasing to take lessons was that she was not satisfied with the calibre of instruction she was receiving. In April, 1971, however, she wrote to the defendant enclosing a doctor's certificate to the effect that she had a bad knee and requested a refund for lessons not taken. There was no mention made as to the alleged inadequacies of her dancing instructors.

The evidence disclosed that there are various standards of dancing taught in chain studios of the defendant type. A student may progress, providing his or her ability, enthusiasm and finances permit (and it seems that the latter two are the most important) from the bronze standard to the silver standard to the gold standard and thence on to several other higher and exotic categories. The contract of October 31, 1969, was to cover the bronze standard but once embarked upon this she was encouraged by her instructors and the management to incorporate some of the silver standard steps with her bronze programme under a scheme called the silver amalgamation. This was the contract of November 19, 1969. The contract of December 10, 1969, relates to membership in the Gold Key Club to which I will later refer. The contract of February 2, 1970, was to prepare the plaintiff for a dance competition in Seattle referred to as the "Seattle Dance Olympics" which competition the plaintiff later attended. The final contract of May 27, 1970, purportedly covered supplemental lessons on styling.

Evidence was given by former instructors, both male and female, as to the various techniques used to induce some of the students to sign up for more and more lessons. This evidence satisfied me that the officers and employees of the defendant company are a thoroughly unscrupulous lot preying on lonely and foolish people. However, the evidence with respect to the techniques used on this plaintiff is not such as to permit me or the authorities to order rescission of the contracts except only the contract relating to the Gold Key Club.

Leaving that contract aside for the moment, the plaintiff's complaints are, first, the inadequacy of some of the instructors and, secondly, that the instructors talked in glowing terms of her dancing ability and by this means induced her to sign up for more and more lessons. In the case of *Miller et al. v. Lavoie et al.* (1966), 60 DLR (2d) 495, 63 WWR 359, the present Chief Justice of this Court was dealing with a case in which the provisions of the Contracts Relief Act had been invoked. That is not the case here, but his words are in my view appropriate and I quote [at 501]:

> This Court exists for many purposes and one of these purposes is the protection of unsophisticated and defenceless persons against the exactions of conscienceless persons who seek to take advantage of them. This legislation provides one method of exercising that benevolent authority. But the Courts are not empowered to relieve a man of the burden of a contract he has made under no pressure and with his eyes open, merely because his contract is an act of folly.

The situation with respect to the Gold Key Club is, however, in a different category. It was a demeaning, cruel and fraudulent device used to induce certain students, including the plaintiff, to sign up for lessons. Her instructor, Barnard, now the dance supervisor of the defendant organization, told her that because of her great ability and certain other qualities he was prepared to propose her as a member of the Gold Key Club. She was told that this was a great honour; that it was a special project of Fred Astaire's, that certain benefits would flow from membership including outings with male members of the staff; that she would, in effect, be an honorary member of the staff with certain special duties relating to new students and so on and so on. She was told she would have to dance before a three-member board of dance instructors and that the whole proceeding would have to be filmed with a movie camera and that the film would have to be sent to New York to obtain final approval of membership. She agreed to this great "honour." Arrangements were made. She appeared before a panel and danced with her partner. The movie camera was operated by the then manager of the organization. At the conclusion of this performance the staff members who had been present rushed up and congratulated her; champagne was opened; a cake was produced; still photographs were taken and then she was led off to the office of the manager at which time she was told that she had to sign up for some more lessons—$2,573 worth of lessons. This, said the manager, was to bring her up to the standards required of a Gold Key Member. The plaintiff objected but finally signed. The "queen for a day" routine made it difficult for her to back out. Unknown to the plaintiff, the whole performance was carried out without film in the camera. The procedure was a standing joke among the staff members. As I said before, it was a demeaning, cruel and fraudulent hoax perpetrated on this plaintiff and the contract cannot stand.

Counsel for the plaintiff took the position that the defendant was in breach of its contract in that it failed to supply the plaintiff with competent and qualified instructors. A clause in the contract reads as follows:

> Student hereby acknowledges that studio herein obligates itself to furnish student at all times herein set forth with a competent and qualified instructor but that studio is under no obligation whatsoever and is not agreed to provide a specific or designated instructor selected by student.

This strange wording indicates either sloppiness or deviousness in draftsmanship. Assuming, but without deciding, that the clause creates an obligation to supply competent and qualified instructors, I am of the view that the staff was reasonably competent to teach at the level required and was qualified within the staff qualification structure of the defendant company.

This submission is, in my view, without merit. There will be judgment for the plaintiff in the amount of $2,573 and costs.

Judgment for plaintiff.

Note on Long-Term Contracts and Rights of Cancellation

Gaertner's case is illustrative of a much larger number of service contracts in which consumers are persuaded, not always by reputable methods, to enter into long-term contracts involving substantial sums of money. If fraud can be shown, the consumer of course has well-established common law and equitable remedies, but what if this element is missing?

The New York City Department of Consumer Affairs has produced an interesting solution. Consumer Protection Law Reg. 16 provides that consumers who cancel future service contracts may not be charged more than 5% of the total cash price of the contract up to a maximum of $50 plus a pro-rated fee for lessons or services already used. The regulation covers such service contracts as dancing lessons, reducing salons, vocational training, correspondence courses, and other contracts which have been the subject of frequent complaints. Is the regulation too Draconian? Will it discourage reputable businessmen from engaging in capital intensive forms of consumer enterprises? What criteria would you adopt to determine the type of contracts that should be subject to a right of cancellation?

The BC Consumer Protection Act, RSBC 1996, c. 69, as am., ss. 11(8), (9) and 18(2), (3), contains a modified version of the NY provisions. The Quebec Consumer Protection Act, RSQ, c. P-40.1, ss. 189-196, generally follows the NY model.

In 1988, Ontario adopted the Prepaid Services Act, RSO 1990, c. P.22, as am. Services are defined in s. 1 as meaning facilities provided for, or instruction on, (a) health, fitness, modelling, talent development, diet or matters of a similar nature, or (b) martial arts, sports, dance or similar activities. The Act only applies (s. 2) to services or proposed services for which payment is required in advance. It does not apply to services provided (a) on a non-profit or co-operative basis; (b) by a private club primarily owned by its members (s. 2(2)).

The Act provides *inter alia* that every contract for services must be in writing (s. 3) and contain prescribed particulars (s. 4), and limits contracts for services to a maximum of one year after the day that all services are made available to the customer (s. 5). No further contract may be made between the parties during the subsistence of a contract (s. 6) unless the subsequent contract is for services that are distinctly different from services to be provided under the existing contract. In any event, a customer may rescind a contract by delivering written notice of rescission within 5 days after the contract is signed or the services are available, whichever is later (s. 9). Finally, a contract that provides for its automatic renewal must state that it is not renewable if the customer notifies the operator in writing, before the time for renewal, that the customer does not want to renew (s. 4(2)). In addition, at least 30 days before the renewal, the operator must send the customer a notice reminding the customer of the provision in s. 4(2) (s. 11).

Does the Ontario Act effectively deal with the type of abuses that occurred in *Gaertner v. Fiesta Dance Studios*? Is it as favourable to the consumer as New York City Reg. 16?

Trans Canada Credit Corp. Ltd. v. Zaluski

(1969), 5 DLR (3d) 702, [1969] 2 OR 496 (Co. Ct.)

LEACH Co. Ct. J: The plaintiff claims, as a holder in due course, against the defendants, as makers of a promissory note. The defendants allege that the execution of the note was obtained by the fraudulent misrepresentation of the agent of the third party and claim over against the third party for the amount of the plaintiff's claim.

The first concern of the Court was to determine if this action was a proper one for a claim for relief over against a third party under Rule 167 [rep. and sub. O. Reg. 180/64, s. 3] of the Rules of Practice. The Court is satisfied that the third party claim is proper as the same issue was raised in *Imperial Bank of Canada v. Wenige* (1924), 26 OWN 327. In that case the late Rose J, held it was proper for the defendant as maker of the note to claim over against the third party whose fraud it was alleged brought about its execution.

The plaintiff company is what is commonly known as a "finance company," and carries on business in St. Catharines and other parts of Ontario. The defendant, Peter Zaluski, is a garage mechanic, who was unemployed at the time of execution of the note. The defendants impressed the Court as being decent, simple people. The third party carries on the business of selling vacuum cleaners from door to door in the Niagara Peninsula and other parts of Canada.

On February 8, 1968, one Green, a salesman for the third party, attended at the defendant's home and Mrs. Zaluski answered the door. Green said he had something he would like to show her. Mrs. Zaluski told him if he was selling vacuum cleaners she was not interested as she had just purchased one, and furthermore her husband was out of work. Green denied he was selling vacuum cleaners, but wanted to show her a book of pictures which demonstrated the inventions of his company to ease the labour of the housewife. The ruse worked and he gained entrance to the house. Once inside he showed the booklet to Mr. and Mrs. Zaluski and their son Alan. It was apparently impressive. It showed pictures of motors, rockets and other advanced machinery. He then advised the Zaluski family he had a surprise for them, which was outside in the car. He was told not to bring it in if it was a vacuum cleaner. He then reappeared with a large box and asked them to guess what was inside it. Mr. and Mrs. Zaluski offered no guesses but Alan said he thought it was a vacuum cleaner. Green did not reply. He then opened the box and pulled out a vacuum cleaner. Mr. and Mrs. Zaluski reiterated the fact they did not want a vacuum cleaner as they had bought one a month previously. Green insisted on demonstrating it. Mr. Zaluski left for the basement in frustration, with Alan. Upon completion of the demonstration Green advised Mrs. Zaluski that he was not selling vacuum cleaners but was going to give her an opportunity to earn some money. Mrs. Zaluski, no doubt, was anxious to do so, as her husband was out of work. She allowed Green to continue with his proposal. He advised her that if she would write letters to her friends, his company would contact them and she would receive $25 for each sale of a vacuum cleaner. Green suggested thirty names and advised her if only nine persons bought, the vacuum cleaner would be hers to keep, free of charge. He further advised her he would pay the $19.90 deposit on the cleaner he would leave with her. Green then produced a conditional sales agreement (ex. 1) and a promissory note (ex. 2) which Mrs. Zaluski signed without reading. Mr. Zaluski was then called from the basement and requested to sign. Green advised him this was a chance to make some money. Upon this representation and some urging by his wife he signed the agreement and the note. He too did not read the documents. Green then prepared to leave and the defendants asked him to take the vacuum cleaner but he refused alleging he could not sell it as it was now used. The cleaner was then placed in the carton, where it remained unused to this date.

Green, before leaving, left with Mrs. Zaluski the form letter she was to write out to be sent to her friends. This letter (ex. 4) read as follows:

Dear Mary:

I know that you will be surprised to hear from me. John and I have recently been given the opportunity to see a most interesting exhibition plus a pleasant surprise and a chance to earn some extra money. I have arranged for you to have the same chance.

Mary you are under no obligation and, we feel, knowing you as we do, that you will be as impressed as we were. I have asked these people to come to see you both, and at the same time explain the contest to you.

I hope Bill will be able to arrange to see this exhibition as I am sure he would enjoy it.

Sincerely,
Joyce Smith

Mrs. Zaluski wrote out in her own handwriting 30 copies of this letter and forwarded them to the third party together with addressed envelopes. The third party then stamped the envelopes and mailed them out.

The third party on February 8, 1968, assigned the conditional sales contract and promissory note to the plaintiff who gave valuable consideration for the same.

On March 25, 1968, the defendants received a cheque for $25 from the third party representing their commission on the sale of a vacuum cleaner to one of the persons solicited by the defendant's letters. The defendants have not cashed the cheque. Shortly thereafter the defendants were contacted by the plaintiff for the payment of the first instalment on the note. This was the first notice the defendants received from the plaintiff since the transaction was carried out on February 8. The defendants have refused to pay the plaintiff and as a result this action was brought.

I shall deal firstly with the plaintiff's claim. I am satisfied on the evidence that the plaintiff is a holder in due course for valuable consideration without notice of the alleged fraudulent misrepresentation. The evidence further indicates there is no relationship between the plaintiff and the third party so as to effect the plaintiff with the inequities, as was held in *Federal Discount Corp. Ltd. v. St. Pierre*, [1962] OR 310, 32 DLR (2d) 86.

There will therefore be judgment for the plaintiff against the defendants for $252.72 and costs and counsel fee of $25.

Turning now to the defendant's claim over against the third party. Before dealing with the alleged fraudulent aspects of this transaction, I wish to give my reason for a ruling on evidence made during the course of the trial. Counsel for the third party submitted the Court should not admit any extrinsic evidence concerning the sale as this would offend against the parol evidence rule. This was so, he submitted the conditional sales agreement provided in fine print on the reverse side in para. 13:

> There are no representations, collateral agreements, conditions or warranties, express or implied by statute or otherwise on the part of Vendor or Trans Canada Credit with respect to the property or this contract or affecting the rights of the parties other than as specifically contained herein.

It is well-established law and the general rule that where the parties have embodied the terms of their contract in a written document then extrinsic evidence is not admissible to add to, vary, subtract from or contradict the terms of the written instrument: *Phipson on Evidence*, 9th ed., at 599.

There are, however, a number of situations in which the written instrument is not conclusive evidence of the contract alleged to be embodied in it. These situations may be recorded either as exceptions to the general rule or simply as cases falling outside the general rule: *Cross on Evidence* (1958), at 476.

Extrinsic evidence will always be admitted to defeat a deed or written contract on the grounds of fraud or misrepresentation: *Chitty on Contracts*, at 635, para. 633.

For the reasons given, *infra*, I am satisfied that the third party was guilty of fraudulent misrepresentation, and that the Court was correct in admitting extrinsic evidence to establish this fact.

The Court is satisfied on the evidence that the agent of the third party throughout misrepresented the transaction to the defendants. It was a clever, subtle and misleading scheme to sell a vacuum cleaner to persons who did not want one and could not afford it. From the time that Green appeared at the door until he left he stated he was not selling a vacuum cleaner but was giving the defendants an opportunity to earn money and receive a free vacuum cleaner as a bonus. The sample letter (ex. 4) verifies the subtlety of the scheme. In paragraph one it provides:

> John and I have recently been given the opportunity to see a most interesting exhibition plus a pleasant surprise and a chance to earn some extra money.

The agent Green paid the deposit which further indicates misrepresentation that the defendants would not be called on to pay.

The defendants were unwise in signing the promissory note and conditional sales agreement without reading them, but the Court is satisfied that any reasonable person subjected to such a deceptive, cunning sales scheme may have done the same.

Fraud is proved when it is shown that a false representation has been made, (1) knowingly, or (2) without belief in its truth or (3) recklessly, careless whether it be true or false. *Derry v. Peek* (1889), 14 App. Cas. 337. The Court is satisfied the agent Green fulfilled all these requirements amply. The third party as principal is responsible for the fraud committed by its agent within the scope of the agency. *Wilson v. Hotchkiss* (1901), 2 OLR 261.

The defendants will therefore have judgment against the third party for the amount of the judgment of the plaintiff against them, together with costs and a counsel fee of $25. Upon payment of the same, the defendants shall return the vacuum cleaner to the third party.

Judgment for plaintiff in action and
defendants in third party proceedings.

[The legal issues in this case arising out of the assignment of the conditional sales contract and the negotiation of the promissory note to Trans Canada Credit Corp. are discussed in volume II of the previous edition of this casebook, chapter 3.]

Note on Referral and Pyramidic Sales and Multi-Level Marketing Plans

1) *Referral Sales*. The referral sales plan described in *Zaluski*, *supra*, is fairly typical of the genre. For other descriptions of such plans and American legislative reactions, see W.G. Magnuson and J. Carper, *The Dark Side of the Marketplace* (1968), at 13-16 and 73-75.

Ontario's reaction to referral sales has had a checkered history. *The Report of the Minister's Committee on Franchising* (July 1971) recommended a regime of strict controls but not prohibition of the practice. The government apparently thought this too cumbersome and preferred to follow the abolition path now adopted by most of the other provinces. See CPA s. 37(2). Section 56 of the old Competition Act prohibited referral sales schemes except in respect of a scheme that is licensed or otherwise permitted by or pursuant to provincial legislation. However, the provision was repealed in the 1999 amendments for reasons which remain unclear.

2) *Pyramidic Sales.* Pyramidic selling schemes are a sophisticated version of referral selling and have spawned an even greater number of abuses. As a result, a substantial number of jurisdictions have adopted remedial legislation which subjects such schemes to strict licensing or prospectus clearance requirements coupled with rights of cancellation, or outlaws them altogether. In several provinces and American states the promoters have been successfully prosecuted for running an illegal lottery. For further details see Ontario, *Report of the Minister's Committee on Franchising* (July 1971).

The Committee's recommendations were implemented in the Pyramidic Sales Act, 1972 (SO 1972, c. 57). The Act was introduced because the Criminal Code had proved inadequate in controlling the proliferation of pyramidic schemes. The Pyramidic Sales Act attempted to regulate pyramidic selling by establishing, *inter alia*, a filing requirement and an escrow fund. The Act attracted few filings. The decline in the popularity of pyramidic schemes—attributed to government regulation—and the desire to eliminate schemes which benefitted from "the public's inability to understand the transaction" prompted the introduction and passage of the Pyramidic Sales Repeal Act, 1978 (SO 1978, c. 105). The Act's complicated repeal provisions froze the escrow fund and placed it under the registrar's direction, and provided for the appointment of an administrator to give notice to investors and advise them, and to set up dispute resolution procedures. The Act presumably made the federal prohibitory legislation (Competition Act amendments, 1975, adding ss. 36.3-36.4 (now s. 55.1)) operative in Ontario with respect to future pyramidic schemes. Section 55.1(2) of the Competition Act now outlaws pyramidic selling schemes altogether and the former provision (s. 55(4)) permitting pyramid selling where permitted under provincial law was repealed in 1992 (SC 1992, c. 14, s. 1).

However, s. 55 of the Act still permits *multi-level marketing plans* provided the operator of such a plan makes fair, reasonable and timely disclosure to a prospective participant in a plan of (a) compensation actually received by typical participants in the plan, or (b) compensation likely to be received by typical participants in the plan (s. 55(2.1)). "Multi-level marketing plan" is defined in s. 55(1) as "a plan for the supply of a product whereby a participant in the plan receives compensation for the supply of the product to another participant in the plan who, in turn, receives compensation for the supply of the same or another product to other participants in the plan."

What is there about multi-level marketing plans that makes them less objectionable than pyramidic selling plans? In either case, would it not be better to leave their regulation or prohibition to provincial securities law?

CONTRACT POLICING:
A GENERALIZED DOCTRINE OF UNCONSCIONABILITY

Judicial Developments

The topic of unconscionable contracts is concerned with the granting of relief on grounds that, for one reason or another, a contract was unfair. Relevant common law doctrines include the rules governing duress, the doctrines of unconscientious dealing and undue influence, the rules relating to penalties and forfeiture and the doctrine of fundamental breach and other judicial techniques for limiting exclusion clauses. Courts have from time to time attempted to restate the law in terms of a unified doctrine of unconscionability. A prominent example of this synthesizing trend is Lord Denning MR's statement in *Lloyds Bank Ltd. v. Bundy*, [1975] QB 326, at 336-37 and 339:

> There are cases in our books in which the courts will set aside a contract, or transfer of property, when the parties have not met on equal terms—when the one is so strong in bargaining power and the other so weak—that, as a matter of common fairness, it is not right that the strong should be allowed to push the weak to the wall. Hitherto those exceptional cases have been treated each as a separate category in itself. But I think the time has come when we should seek to find a principle to unite them ...
>
> ... [T]hrough all these instances there runs a single thread. They rest on "inequality of bargaining power." By virtue of it, the English law gives relief to one who, without independent advice, enters into a contract upon terms which are very unfair or transfers property for a consideration which is grossly inadequate, when his bargaining power is grievously impaired by reason of his own needs or desires, or by his own ignorance or infirmity, coupled with undue influences or pressures brought to bear on him by or for the benefit of the other.

This statement was later rejected by the House of Lords in *National Westminster Bank plc v. Morgan*, [1985] AC 686. Lord Scarman said:

> And even in the field of contract I question whether there is any need in the modern law to erect a general principle of relief against inequality of bargaining power. Parliament has undertaken the task (and it is essentially a legislative task) of enacting such restrictions on freedom of contract as are in its judgment necessary to relieve against the mischief: for example, the hire-purchase and consumer protection legislation, of which the Supply of Goods (Implied Terms) Act 1973, the Consumer Credit Act 1974, the Consumer Safety Act 1978, the Supply of Goods and Services Act 1982 and the Insurance Companies Act 1982 are examples. I doubt whether the courts should assume the burden of formulating further restrictions.

Lord Denning's generalized unconscionability doctrine has also not found favour in Australia. In *Commercial Bank of Australia Ltd. v. Amadio* (1983), 151 CLR 477, Mason J made it clear that the equitable doctrine of unconscientious dealing is limited to cases where the weaker party is at a special disadvantage. He said (at 462):

> I qualify the word "disadvantage" by the adjective "special" in order to disavow any suggestion that the principle applies *whenever there is some difference in the bargaining power of the parties* and in order to emphasize that the disabling condition or circumstance is one which seriously affects the ability of the innocent party to make a judgment as to his own best interests (emphasis added).

The problem with broad references to "inequality of bargaining power" is that they are indeterminate. Bargaining power is hardly ever equal. There will nearly always be some imbalance between contracting parties in terms of wealth, experience, information, and the like. If absolute equality was always insisted upon, there would be no more contracts. However, if the call is for less than absolute equality, it then becomes necessary to ask questions like, "how much?" and "of what kind?" Lord Denning's statement provides no guidance on this score.

By contrast, in Canada, Lord Denning's approach has been generally well received. It has been adopted in such cases as *McKenzie v. Bank of Montreal* (1975), 55 DLR (3d) 641 (OHC), aff'd. 70 DLR (3d) 113 (CA); *Royal Bank v. Hinds* (1978), 20 OR (2d) 613 (HCJ); *Buchanan v. Canadian Imperial Bank of Commerce* (1979), 100 DLR (3d) 624 (BCSC); *Harry v. Kreutziger* (1978), 9 BCLR 166, 95 DLR (3d) 231 (CA); and *Bertolo v. Bank of Montreal* (1987), 57 OR 577 (OCA). On the other hand, *Bundy* was distinguished on the facts in *Royal Bank v. Girgulus*, [1977] 6 WWR 439 (Sask. QB), rev'd. on other grounds, [1979] 3 WWR 451 (CA); *Thermo-flow Corp Ltd. v. Kuryluk* (1978), 84 DLR (3d) 529 (NSSC); *Ronald Elwin Lister Ltd. v. Dunlop Canada Ltd.* (1978), 19 OR (2d) 380 (HCJ); and by the majority in *Wallace v. Toronto-Dominion Bank* (1983), 41 OR (2d) 161 (OCA).

Canadian receptivity to the doctrine of unconscionability has been greatly strengthened by the Supreme Court of Canada's approval of the doctrine in *Hunter Engineering Co. v. Syncrude Canada Ltd.* (1989), 57 DLR (4th) 321, *infra*, chapter 18. See the judgments of Dickson CJ at 341-43 and Wilson J at 377-81. The case involved the validity of a disclaimer clause in a contract of sale where the seller was alleged to have delivered a seriously defective product. The Supreme Court upheld the disclaimer clause because there was no inequality of bargaining power between the parties, but made it clear that in appropriate circumstances an unconscionable clause would not be enforceable.

Section 2-302 of the United States Uniform Commercial Code is a statutory version of the unconscionability doctrine. It provides in part as follows:

> If the court as a matter of law finds the contract or any clause of the contract to have been unconscionable at the time it was made the court may refuse to enforce the contract, or it may enforce the remainder of the contract without the unconscionable clause, or it may so limit the application of any unconscionable clause as to avoid any unconscionable result.

The Official Comment to UCC 2-302 reads in relevant part as follows:

> This section is intended to make it possible for the courts to police explicitly against the contracts or clauses which they find to be unconscionable. In the past such policing has been accomplished by adverse construction of language, by manipulation of the rules of offer and acceptance or by determinations that the clause is contrary to public policy or to the dominant purpose of the contract. This section is intended to allow the court to pass directly on the unconscionability of the contract or particular clause therein and to make a conclusion of law as to its unconscionability. The basic test is whether, in the light of the general commercial background and the commercial needs of the particular trade or case, the clauses involved are so one-sided as to be unconscionable under the circumstances existing at the time of the making of the contract.

Modified versions of UCC 2-302 have been enacted in a number of other countries, including the United Kingdom (Unfair Contract Terms Act 1977), Australia (Trade Practices Act 1974 (Cth), Part IVA; Contracts Review Act 1980 (NSW)), and Canada (in provincial consumer sales practices legislation, discussed below).

Anthony J. Duggan
"Unconscionability"

in Peter Newman (ed.), *New Palgrave Dictionary of Economics and the Law*
(London: Macmillan, 1997) at 637-38 (Footnotes omitted)

Procedural and Substantive Unconscionability

There are two types of unconscionability, procedural and substantive. A court may find that a contract between A and B is unconscionable because of sharp dealing on B's part which affected the quality of A's consent to the transaction. This is procedural unconscionability. Alternatively, a court may conclude that a contract is unconscionable because, in its view, B is unduly favoured or A unduly disadvantaged. This is substantive unconscionability. Procedural unconscionability is unfairness in the bargaining process and substantive unconscionability is perceived unfairness in the bargaining outcome.

The following cases are examples of interventions based on procedural unconscionability grounds:

(1) A, a builder, is owed £500 by B. A, to B's knowledge, is in serious financial difficulties. B tells A that unless A is prepared to settle for £200, A will get nothing. A reluctantly agrees to accept the lesser sum. In subsequent proceedings, the court refuses to enforce the settlement agreement and orders B to pay the larger sum.

(2) A buys land from B for £45,000. The market value of the land at the time is £30,000. A has limited intelligence, is poorly educated and lacks business experience. B is aware of A's difficulties. A later refuses to go through with the transaction. The court denies B relief and sets the contract aside.

The following cases are examples of interventions based on substantive unconscionability grounds:

(3) A borrows money from B and mortgages the family home to B as security for repayment. A defaults and B takes steps to enforce the mortgage. Faced with eviction, A brings proceedings to have the contract set aside, pleading poverty. The court intervenes to protect A.

(4) A agrees to sell the family business to B for £50,000. The business had previously been valued at £60,000. A has Alzheimer's disease, but the condition is in its early stages and there is nothing in A's behaviour during negotiations which might alert B to the problem. A later regrets the decision to sell and brings proceedings to have the contract set aside. The court rules in A's favour.

Intervention on grounds of procedural unconscionability is easier to justify in economic terms than intervention on grounds of substantive unconscionability (Epstein, 1975), as the following analysis demonstrates.

Case (1) is similar to *D & C Builders Ltd. v. Rees.* There, a majority of the court held that the settlement agreement had been procured by intimidation. The plaintiffs had consented unwillingly to accept the lesser sum under the threat that they would receive nothing. The case is an example of ... a "structurally impaired market." A consented to the settlement agreement, but only because she had no effective choice. Given the circumstances, B enjoyed a situational monopoly over A which he exploited to his own advantage. The settlement agreement represented a misallocation of resources because it did not reflect A's preference given a workably competitive range of alternative choices. In this sense, there was an inequality of bargaining power between A and B, and the availability of the remedy acts as a deterrent against the exploitation of such positions of advantage in future cases.

Case (2) is a straightforward application of the equitable doctrine of unconscientious dealing. There are numerous decisions, many involving gifts, where the transaction has been set aside in similar circumstances (for example, *Wilton v. Farnworth*). The case is an example of … an "informationally impaired market." The arguments supporting judicial intervention in this kind of case are the same as for deliberate misrepresentation. B's conduct in exploiting A's disability is calculated to lead A into error just as surely as if B had lied to A. A mistake on A's part is likely to result in a misallocation of resources. Precautions to avoid A's mistake could in theory be taken by either party, but the efficient solution is for the lowest cost avoider to take the precautions. Where A's mistake is deliberately induced by B, B will always be the lowest cost avoider. All B has to do is refrain from the exploitative conduct, and that is a socially costless option. By contrast, precautions taken by or on A's behalf against exploitation will always entail some cost. It follows that, in the interests of preventing mistakes, the costs of exploitation should always be returned to the exploiter.

In contrast to Cases (1) and (2), there is no suggestion in Case (3) of any undue pressure or exploitative conduct on B's part. The court's concern is to relieve A's misfortune, not to punish B. Relief of poverty is sometimes cited as a sufficient ground for setting aside contracts under the doctrine of unconscientious dealing (for example, *Blomley v. Ryan,* 405). A similar motivation appears to underlie interest rate restrictions that are commonly found in money lending and consumer credit laws. However, such measures are likely over the longer term to end up doing more harm than good. The court's intervention in Case (3) effectively gives A the benefit of hindsight. It allows A to escape from a transaction which from an *ex post* perspective, was clearly not in her interests. The consequence is to make A herself better off, but the trade-off is increased transactions costs for future cases. A major function of contract is to reduce the cost of uncertainty in relationships. This function depends on the courts upholding the security of transactions. If a shift in A's preferences between the bargaining and performance stages of a contract was sufficient to have the contract set aside, B would have no guarantee of A's performance at the outset. In other words, B would be faced with the very uncertainty that it was the object of the transaction to avoid. B's likely response would be either to raise the price of dealing with A—and others like A—in future or, alternatively, to refuse to deal with A—and others like A—at all.

Case (4) is based loosely on *Hart v. O'Connor.* There, the New Zealand courts set aside the contract for unconscientious dealing, holding that the state of the purchaser's knowledge was irrelevant. However, the Privy Council on appeal rejected this view. In Case (4), given B's unawareness of A's disability, there is no element of exploitation in B's behaviour. Case (1) can be contrasted in this respect. If B has no knowledge of A's disability, then B is no longer self-evidently the party best placed to take precautions against A's mistake. There are certain threshold precautions a disadvantaged party can usually take to avoid misfortune in dealings. The most obvious course is to seek advice before entering into substantial transactions, or to entrust all business matters to a third party such as a lawyer or an accountant. Of course, A may be so seriously disadvantaged as to not appreciate the need for taking precautions at all. However, if that is the case A's incapacity is almost certain to be obvious to B. If the courts intervened regardless of whether B knew of A's disability, parties in A's position would in future be less inclined to take threshold precautions in their own interests. Correspondingly, parties in B's position would be faced with the prospect of investing resources to discover whether the other party might be the subject of a disadvantage likely to result in the transaction being set aside. The alternatives would be to incur this expenditure, or to take the risk of judicial intervention. Either way, transactions would become more costly.

Dominion Home Improvements Ltd. v. Irmgard Knuude

Unreported, Ont. DC, April 16, 1986

BORINS Dist. Ct. J (orally): ... In this case, the plaintiff is suing upon a contract to recover $3,400 representing the balance owing by the defendant for certain materials supplied and installed in the defendant's home by the plaintiff company. In addition to defending the plaintiff's claim, the defendant has counterclaimed for a declaration that the contract is not binding upon her for the return of a deposit of $300 paid to the plaintiff or, in the alternative, damages in the amount of $3,000. The essence of the defence is that the transaction between the parties should be set aside as unconscionable as it was induced by an inequality in the bargaining position of the parties and by dishonesty.

The plaintiff carries on the business of home improvements. In May of 1983 it had in its employ a Mr. Burke who sought contracts on behalf of the plaintiff by means of door-to-door solicitation. On May 11, 1983, he presented himself at the defendant's home in Toronto. The defendant had lived in the home since 1955. At that time she was an 80 year old widow who lived alone and who, because of her advanced age, experienced impairment in her sight and hearing. Central to the resolution of the case are the circumstances in which the contract was obtained and ultimately performed.

. . .

On May 11, 1983, after 2 p.m. Mrs. Knuude went to her front door to get the mail when she found a man there looking at her windows. He told her that the house needed new windows. Mrs. Knuude told him that the house had been rebuilt a few years earlier and that the only problem she had was on the interior east wall of the house on the first floor where an area of dampness caused the paint to blister and peel, and she showed it to the man. The man left and returned in a short time with Mr. Burke who examined the wall and said that the dampness was caused by faulty eavestroughs. Mr. Burke told her that replacement of the eavestroughs, soffit, and fascia would cure the problem of the dampness on the wall and quoted her a price of $3,900. Mrs.

Knuude said she did not want to have the work done and that, in any event, the price was too high. She showed Mr. Burke an estimate for $2,200 which she had received previously from another company to do similar work. She explained to the Court that she did not act on the previous estimate as she had received advice that the repairs were unnecessary. In the course of conversation, Mr. Burke asked Mrs. Knuude if she had any family, and she told him that she had a daughter in Quebec and a son in Mississauga.

Mrs. Knuude believed that Mr. Burke realized that she was uninterested in having the work done, but he kept insisting. After a while he jumped up and said, "You treat me like dirt." Mrs. Knuude wished him to leave her house, but he sat down and did not leave. She then asked Mr. Burke and the other man to leave. Mr. Burke instructed his assistant to leave. Then Mr. Burke sat down at the dining room table and said to Mrs. Knuude, "Why don't you scream?" She testified that when he said that she felt "the only thing was to keep calm." In the meantime he was preparing a contract. Mrs. Knuude said he came down in his price by $175. Eventually Mrs. Knuude signed the printed form contract. She also entered the figure "80" and her initials beside the word "age" because he told her to do so. Mrs. Knuude did not read the contract because she did not have her glasses, and it was not read to her. She believed that the contract was to cure the dampness on the east wall. Mrs. Knuude's explanation for signing the contract was "I knew I wouldn't get him out unless I signed the paper." Mr. Burke had also written out a cheque for $300 payable to the plaintiff as a deposit and got Mrs. Knuude to write her account number on it and sign it. It was about 5:45 p.m. when Mr. Burke eventually left the defendant's house.

Later that evening, using her glasses and a magnifying glass, she read the contract. She discovered that it said nothing about repairing the damp wall. That, of course, is true. The handwriting on the document is difficult to read. It appears to provide for the installation of aluminum soffit, fascia, and eavestroughs, and the re-calking of all of the windows. It provides for a total price of $3,700 with a down payment of $300 and a balance of $3,400 payable on completion of the work. It, indeed, makes no reference to the repair of the wall, nor does it set out in detail the various materials to be installed, the labour involved, and their respective costs.

Realizing that the contract did not provide for the repair of the wall, the first thing on the morning of the next day, May 12, Mrs. Knuude went to her bank where she stopped payment on the deposit cheque of $300. Somebody at the bank told her to telephone the plaintiff and cancel the contract. However, when she returned home, she found two employees of the plaintiff in her backyard. One was Henry Pyykko, an installer employed by the plaintiff. She told Mr. Pyykko she did not want to have the work done as the price was "outrageous." Mr. Pyykko, who testified on behalf of the plaintiff, said, "Okay" and he left. Within a short time, Mr. Burke and his assistant came running up the stairs of the defendant's home. Mr. Pyykko and his assistant also appeared. Mrs. Knuude said Mr. Burke was nearly crying. He sat down and put his head in his hands and said: "The men are here. They want to do the work." Mr. Burke told her he had spent half the night cutting the material for the job. This was clearly untrue as Mr. Pyykko explained that the material was all cut at the job site by his assistant when the work was to be done. Mrs. Knuude explained that Mr. Burke appeared so "heart broken" that she said that the plaintiff could do the work, and she re-instated the deposit cheque for $300.

Before she had told Mr. Burke to proceed with the work, Mr. Pyykko had climbed up on the roof and started to hammer on it. He did this for about a half hour. Mrs. Knuude was afraid this might cause the rain to leak in. Then Mr. Pyykko told her that he had to leave to go to another job and would not be available the next day, which was Friday, May 13. He said he would return on Monday, May 16, which he did. In the meantime, the president of the plaintiff company Mr. Julius Silver telephoned the defendant to inquire about her ability to pay for the work. She told him she could pay for it and expressed concern to him about what Mr. Pyykko had done to the roof and the possibility that it might cause the rain to leak in.

On May 16 and 17 Mr. Pyykko and his assistant installed the aluminum soffit, fascia, eavestroughing, and, as well, aluminum flashing. Also he re-calked all the windows and doors and re-painted the damp wall. After three weeks had passed, Mrs. Knuude telephoned Mr. Silver to say that the condition of the wall was worse than before it had been re-painted. He came to her home and on his arrival said: "You have a nice house. I'll put a lien on it." Mr. Silver told her he would fix the wall, but she first had to pay him $3,400. It was at that time that Mrs. Knuude first contacted a member of her family. She telephoned her daughter in Quebec. She explained that she had not contacted her family earlier by saying: "I had signed and I thought I had to go through with it."

In cross-examination, Mrs. Knuude said that she did not need the aluminum work done on her house and that, in any event, the price was too high. That was why she stopped payment on her cheque. She told plaintiff's counsel "I only wanted the wall painted." Mrs. Knuude said that she authorized the plaintiff to do the work because Mr. Burke on his return "made me believe everything was okay."

Peter Flicke testified on behalf of the defendant. He has 24 years experience as a general contractor, and for the last 18 years has been the owner of a company engaged in general home renovation. In my view, he is well qualified to comment upon the work performed by the plaintiff and the condition of the defendant's house which he examined. His opinion, which I accept, is that the installation of new eavestroughs could not have cured the problem of the damp wall. In other words, the work which the plaintiff did was not necessary to repair the wall. Mr. Flicke, of course, was unable to comment upon whether the soffit, fascia, and eavestrough on the defendant's house were in need of repair on the 11th of May, 1983. However, in Mr. Flicke's opinion the price charged by the plaintiff was excessive. He presented an estimate dated November 12, 1985, in the amount of $1,320 for the installation of a complete new aluminum overhang. He agreed that his estimate did not include certain additional work performed by the plaintiff and was prepared to increase his estimate to about $1,450 to take into account the additional work.

On the facts of this case I have no difficulty in concluding that the plaintiff cannot rely on the contract signed by the defendant on May 11, 1983. In doing so, I rely on the principle of unconscionability. This principle was discussed in detail by the British Columbia Court of Appeal in *Morrison v. Coast Financing Ltd.* (1965), 55 DLR (2d) 710 where Davey, JA stated at 713:

. . .

The *Morrison* case was followed by the British Columbia Court of Appeal in *Harry v. Kreutziger* (1979), 95 DLR (3d) 231 where, after a discussion of the authorities, McIntyre, JA, held at 237:

> From these authorities this rule emerges. Where a claim is made that a bargain is unconscionable, it must be shown for success that there was inequality in the position of the parties due to the ignorance, need or distress of the weaker, which would leave him in the power of the stronger, coupled with proof of substantial unfairness in the bargain. When this has been shown a presumption of fraud is raised and the stronger must show, in order to preserve his bargain, that it was fair and reasonable.

The *Harry* case was followed by the Ontario High Court in *Taylor v. Armstrong* (1979), 24 OR (2d) 614.

This entire transaction is coloured by unfairness and dishonesty and is evidenced by an obvious inequality in the position of the parties. In my view, throughout the entire transaction the plaintiff's employee Mr. Burke acted in a most reprehensible way. He dishonestly led the defendant to believe that the installation of a complete new aluminum overhang would cure the problem of the damp wall. He charged her an excessive price for the work and materials supplied by the plaintiff. After ascertaining that the elderly frail defendant lived alone, he would not leave her house until she signed the contract. He did not read the contract to her. The only way the defendant could get him to leave was to sign the contract. After she had cancelled the contract, Mr. Burke returned to her house and induced her to re-instate it by engaging her sympathy and falsely telling her that he had spent half the night cutting the materials for the job. Not only do these facts create a presumption of fraud, they constitute actual fraud … . In my view, the plaintiff has not succeeded in its burden of satisfying me that its bargain with the plaintiff was fair, just and reasonable. I have absolutely no doubt that in procuring the contract Mr. Burke deliberately sought to take advantage of the advanced age of Mrs. Knuude, her obvious frailty and the fact that she was living alone. He engaged in the lowest of business practices, and I am distressed that in light of this, the plaintiff even sought to attempt to enforce its contract. However, the plaintiff was within its rights in seeking to do so.

There is another ground upon which I would also decline to enforce the plaintiff's contract. It does not comply with the provisions of the *Consumer Protection Act*, RSO 1980, c. 87, s. 19(1)(b)(c), and by s. 19(2) [now RSO 1990, c. C.31] is not binding upon the defendant.

Counsel for the plaintiff has submitted that should I reach the conclusion that the contract is unenforceable, I should nevertheless award judgment for the plaintiff upon the basis of a *quantum meruit*. The plaintiff has not requested this relief in its statement of claim. Even if it had, I would not be prepared to make any award to the plaintiff. The payment of money on a *quantum meruit* is an equitable remedy and it is well established that an equitable remedy will not be granted to a plaintiff who seeks to recover it in circumstances which have arisen out of the plaintiff's own fraudulent conduct. It is true, of course, that there is no suggestion that the work performed by the plaintiff and the materials installed were in any way defective and that the defendant has received a substantial benefit. However, this is a risk that a person

takes when it conducts its business in the way in which the plaintiff conducted its
business. It follows that the plaintiff's action will be dismissed.

. . .

Action dismissed; counterclaim allowed.

NOTES AND QUESTIONS

1) Is the *Knuude* case an example of procedural or substantive unconscionability?
Can you think of any other grounds on which the case might have been decided? Was
resort to the unconscionability doctrine necessary? Can the decision be justified in economic terms?

2) An interesting approach to the generalized doctrine of unconscionability was taken
by Lambert JA in *Harry v. Kreutziger, supra.* He held that the principle of unconscionability adopted in the earlier cases was "only of the most generalized guidance," and that
the decisions in *Bundy* and *Morrison v. Coast Finance Ltd.* (1965), 55 DLR (2d) 710
(BCCA) were really aspects of a single question:

> whether the transaction, seen as a whole, is sufficiently divergent from community stand-
> ards of commercial morality that it should be rescinded (at 177).

This question, he added, must be answered by examining fact patterns in decided
cases. Cases closest in time and jurisdiction will be the most relevant in this regard. It
was also appropriate to seek guidance as to community standards of commercial morality
from contemporary provincial legislation. Lambert JA said he had taken into consideration the provisions of the BC Consumer Protection Act and Trade Practices Act. As a
result, he found the bargain before the court to be a "marked departure" from such standards and he agreed that it should be rescinded.

What objections, if any, might there be to deciding cases explicitly by reference to
"community standards of commercial morality"? Does unconscionability reduced to this
mean anything more than "the length of the Chancellor's foot"? (See *Hunter Engineering
Co. Inc. v. Synucrude Canada Ltd.* (1989), 57 DLR (4th) 321 at per Wilson J, (chapter 18,
infra). This question has been the subject of some debate in subsequent BC cases: see, for
example, *Smyth v. Szep,* [1992] 2 WWR 673 (BCCA); and *Gindis v. Brisbourne,* [2000]
BCJ No.162 (BCCA).

3) Does a doctrine of unconscionability have any place in commercial (i.e., non-
consumer) transactions? The Supreme Court of Canada in *Hunter Engineering* divided
on this question but at least a majority of the Court supported a general unconscionability
doctrine in dealing with disclaimer clauses. See, *infra*, chapter 18. There are also cases at
the provincial level which have answered the question in the affirmative: for example,
Atlas Supply Co. of Canada Ltd. v. Yarmouth Equipment Ltd. (1991), 103 NSR (3d) 1, 37
CPR (3d) 38 (NS CA), a case involving a franchise agreement. *Atlas* is extensively criticized in Vern W. Da Re, "Atlas Unchartered *(sic)*: When Unconscionability 'Says It All'"
(1996), 27 *CBLJ* 426.

UCC 2-302 extends to commercial transactions. The OLRC in its Sales Report thought
that this was the correct approach and recommended that no distinction should be drawn

between commercial and consumer transactions by the UCC 2-302-based provision in the revised Ontario Sale of Goods Act: see Sales Report, at 156. The Commission reaffirmed its position in its *Amendments to the Law of Contract* report in recommending the enactment of a general statutory doctrine of unconscionability (chapter 6, esp. at 135). Do you agree? Can the OLRC's position be reconciled with the need for certainty in the law governing commercial transactions?

Section 51AC of the Australian Trade Practices Act 1974 is an example of a statutory provision enacted specifically with commercial transactions in mind. The aim is to protect small business purchasers and suppliers in their dealings with large corporations. The section prohibits unconscionable conduct in trade or commerce in connection with the supply to a small business purchaser ("business consumer") or the acquisition from a small business supplier of goods or services. It does not apply if the small business consumer or the small business supplier is a public listed company, and it is limited to transactions where the price is $1 million or less. Remedies for contravention include damages, injunctions, and rescission orders. Examples of contracts to which the provision is directed include commercial leases, long-term contracts in the rural sector, and franchise agreements. Would Canadian small business benefit from a similar provision?

Tilden Rent-A-Car Co. v. Clendenning

(1978), 83 DLR (3d) 400, 18 OR (2d) 601 (CA)

DUBIN JA: Upon his arrival at Vancouver airport, Mr. Clendenning, a resident of Woodstock, Ontario, attended upon the office of Tilden Rent-A-Car Company for the purpose of renting a car while he was in Vancouver. He was an experienced traveller and had used Tilden Rent-A-Car Company on many prior occasions. He provided the clerk employed at the airport office of Tilden Rent-A-Car Company with the minimum information which was asked of him, and produced his American Express credit card. He was asked by the clerk whether he desired additional coverage, and, as was his practice, he said "yes." A contract was submitted to him for his signature, which he signed in the presence of the clerk, and he returned the contract to her. She placed his copy of it in an envelope and gave him the keys to the car. He then placed the contract in the glove compartment of the vehicle. He did not read the terms of the contract before signing it, as was readily apparent to the clerk, and in fact he did not read the contract until this litigation was commenced, nor had he read a copy of a similar contract on any prior occasion.

The issue on the appeal is whether the defendant is liable for the damage caused to the automobile while being driven by him by reason of the exclusionary provisions which appear in the contract.

On the front of the contract are two relevant clauses set forth in box form. They are as follows:

15 Collision Damage Waiver By Customers Initials "J.C."

In consideration of the payment of 2.00 per day customers liability for damage to rented vehicle including windshield is limited to NIL. But notwithstanding payment of said fee, customer shall be fully liable for all collision damage if vehicle is used, operated or driven in violation of any of the provisions of this rental agreement or off highways serviced by federal, provincial, or municipal governments, and for all damages to vehicle by striking overhead objects.

16 I, the undersigned have read and received a copy of above and reverse side of this contract

Signature of customer or employee of customer "John T. Clendenning"

(Emphasis added.)

On the back of the contract in particularly small type and so faint in the customer's copy as to be hardly legible, there are a series of conditions, the relevant ones being as follows:

6. The customer agrees not to use the vehicle in violation of any law, ordinance, rule or regulation of any public authority.

7. The customer agrees that the vehicle will not be operated:

(a) By any person who has drunk or consumed any intoxicating liquor, whatever be the quantity, or who is under the influence of drugs or narcotics;

The rented vehicle was damaged while being driven by Mr. Clendenning in Vancouver. His evidence at trial, which was accepted by the trial Judge, was to the effect that in endeavouring to avoid a collision with another vehicle and acting out of a sudden emergency, he drove the car into a pole. He stated that although he had pleaded guilty to a charge of driving while impaired in Vancouver, he did so on the advice of counsel, and at the time of the impact he was capable of the proper control of the motor vehicle. This evidence was also accepted by the trial Judge.

Mr. Clendenning testified that on earlier occasions when he had inquired as to what added coverage he would receive for the payment of $2 per day, he had been advised that "such payment provided full non-deductible coverage." It is to be observed that the portion of the contract reproduced above does provide that "In consideration of the payment of $2.00 per day customers liability for damage to rented vehicle including windshield is limited to NIL."

A witness called on behalf of the plaintiff gave evidence as to the instructions given to its employees as to what was to be said by them to their customers about the conditions in the contract. He stated that unless inquiries were made, nothing was to be said by its clerks to the customer with respect to the exclusionary conditions. He went on to state that if inquiries were made, the clerks were instructed to advise the customer that by the payment of the $2 additional fee the customer had complete coverage "unless he were intoxicated, or unless he committed an offence under the *Criminal Code* such as intoxication."

Mr. Clendenning acknowledged that he had assumed, either by what had been sold to him in the past or otherwise, that he would not be responsible for any damage to the vehicle on payment of the extra premium unless such damage was caused by reason of his being so intoxicated as to be incapable of the proper control of the vehicle, a provision with which he was familiar as being a statutory provision in his own insurance contract.

The provisions fastening liability for damage to the vehicle on the hirer, as contained in the clauses hereinbefore referred to, are completely inconsistent with the express terms which purport to provide complete coverage for damage to the vehicle in exchange for the additional premium. It is to be noted, for example, that if the driver of the vehicle exceeded the speed-limit even by one mile per hour, or parked the vehicle in a no-parking area, or even had one glass of wine or one bottle of beer, the contract purports to make the hirer completely responsible for all damage to the vehicle. Indeed, if the vehicle at the time of any damage to it was being driven off a federal, provincial or municipal highway, such as a shopping plaza for instance, the hirer purportedly would be responsible for all damage to the vehicle.

Mr. Clendenning stated that if he had known of the full terms of a written instrument, he would not have entered into such a contract. Having regard to the findings made by the trial Judge, it is apparent that Mr. Clendenning had not in fact acquiesced to such terms.

It was urged that the rights of the parties were governed by what has come to be known as "the rule in *L'Estrange v. F. Graucob, Ltd.*," [1934] 2 KB 394. ...

. . .

Consensus ad idem is as much a part of the law of written contracts as it is of oral contracts. The signature to a contract is only one way of manifesting assent to contractual terms. However, in the case of *L'Estrange v. F. Graucob, Ltd.*, there was in fact no *consensus ad idem*. Miss L'Estrange was a proprietor of a cafe. Two salesmen of the defendant company persuaded her to order a cigarette machine to be sold to her by their employer. They produced an order form which Miss L'Estrange signed without reading all of its terms. Amongst the many clauses in the document signed by her, there was included a paragraph, with respect to which she was completely unaware, which stated "any excess or implied condition, statement, or warranty, statutory or otherwise not stated herein is hereby excluded." In her action against the company she alleged that the article sold to her was unfit for the purposes for which it was sold and contrary to the *Sale of Goods Act*. The company successfully defended on the basis of that exemption clause.

Although the subject of critical analysis by learned authors (see, for example, J.R. Spencer, "Signature, Consent, and the Rule in *L'Estrange v. Graucob*," [1973] CLJ 104), the case has survived, and it is now said that it applies to all contracts irrespective of the circumstances under which they are entered into, if they are signed by the party who seeks to escape their provisions.

Thus, it was submitted that the ticket cases, which in the circumstances of this case would afford a ready defence for the hirer of the automobile, are not applicable.

As is pointed out in Waddams, *The Law of Contracts*, at 191:

> From the 19th century until recent times an extraordinary status has been accorded to the signed document that will be seen in retrospect, it is suggested, to have been excessive.

The justification for the rule in *L'Estrange v. F. Graucob, Ltd.*, appears to have been founded upon the objective theory of contracts, by which means parties are bound to a contract in writing by measuring their conduct by outward appearance rather than what the parties inwardly meant to decide. This, in turn, stems from the classic statement of Blackburn J, in *Smith v. Hughes* (1871), LR 6 QB 597, at 607:

> I apprehend that if one of the parties intends to make a contract on one set of terms, and the other intends to make a contract on another set of terms, as it is sometimes expressed, if the parties are not *ad idem*, there is no contract, unless the circumstances are such as to preclude one of the parties from denying that he is agreed to the terms of the other. The rule of law is that stated in *Freeman v. Cooke* (1848), 2 Ex. 654, 154 ER 652. *If, whatever a man's real intention may be, he so conducts himself that a reasonable man would believe that he was assenting to the terms proposed by the other party, and that other party upon that belief enters into the contract with him, the man thus conducting himself would be equally bound as if he had intended to agree to the other party's terms.*

(Emphasis added.)

Even accepting the objective theory to determine whether Mr. Clendenning had entered into a contract which included all the terms of the written instrument, it is to be observed that an essential part of that test is whether the other party entered into the contract in the belief that Mr. Clendenning was assenting to all such terms. In the instant case, it was apparent to the employee of Tilden-Rent-A-Car that Mr. Clendenning had not in fact read the document in its entirety before he signed it. It follows under such circumstances that Tilden-Rent-A-Car cannot rely on provisions of the contract which it had no reason to believe were being assented to by the other contracting party. ...

In ordinary commercial practice where there is frequently a sense of formality in the transaction, and where there is a full opportunity for the parties to consider the terms of the proposed contract submitted for signature, it might well be safe to assume that the party who attaches his signature to the contract intends by so doing to acknowledge his acquiescence to its terms, and that the other party entered into the contract upon that belief. This can hardly be said, however, where the contract is entered into in circumstances such as were present in this case.

A transaction, such as this one, is invariably carried out in a hurried, informal manner. The speed with which the transaction is completed is said to be one of the attractive features of the services provided.

The clauses relied on in this case, as I have already stated, are inconsistent with the over-all purpose for which the contract is entered into by the hirer. Under such circumstances, something more should be done by the party submitting the contract for signature than merely handing it over to be signed.

[Dubin JA quoted from Lord Devlin's judgment in *McCutcheon v. David MacBrayne Ltd.*, [1964] 1 WLR 125, at 132-34, reaffirming the general rule that "a signature to a contract is conclusive" and continued:]

An analysis of the Canadian cases, however, indicates that the approach in this country has not been so rigid. In the case of *Colonial Investment Co. of Winnipeg, Man. v. Borland*, [1911] 1 WWR 171, at 189, 19 WLR 588, 5 Alta. LR at 72 [affirmed 6

DLR 21, 2 WWR 960, 22 WLR 145, 5 Alta. LR 71], Beck J, set forth the following propositions:

> *Consensus ad idem* is essential to the creation of a contract, whether oral, in writing or under seal, subject to this, that as between the immediate parties (and merely voluntary assigns) apparent—as distinguished from real—consent will on the ground of estoppel effect a binding obligation unless the party denying the obligation proves:
>
> (1) That the other party knew at the time of the making of the alleged contract that the mind of the denying party did not accompany the expression of his consent; or
>
> (2) Such facts and circumstances as show that it was not reasonable and natural for the other party to suppose that the denying party was giving his real consent and he did not in fact give it;

In commenting on the *Colonial Investment Co. of Winnipeg v. Borland* case, Spencer, in the article above cited, observes at 121:

> It is instructive to compare a Canadian approach to the problem of confusing documents which are signed but not fully understood.

And at 122 the author concludes his article with the following analysis:

> Policy considerations, but of different kinds, no doubt lay behind both the Canadian and the English approaches to this problem. The Canadian court was impressed by the abuses which would result—and, in England, *have* resulted—from enabling companies to hold ignorant signatories to the letter of sweeping exemption clauses contained in contracts in standard form. The English courts, however, were much more impressed with the danger of furnishing an easy line of defence by which liars could evade contractual liabilities freely assumed. It would be very dangerous to allow a man over the age of legal infancy to escape from the legal effect of a document he has, after reading it, signed, in the absence of any express misrepresentation by the other party of that legal effect. Forty years later, most lawyers would admit that the English courts made a bad choice between two evils.

· · ·

In modern commercial practice, many standard form printed documents are signed without being read or understood. In many cases the parties seeking to rely on the terms of the contract know or ought to know that the signature of a party to the contract does not represent the true intention of the signer, and that the party signing is unaware of the stringent and onerous provisions which the standard form contains. Under such circumstances, I am of the opinion that the party seeking to rely on such terms should not be able to do so in the absence of first having taken reasonable measures to draw such terms to the attention of the other party, and, in the absence of such reasonable measures, it is not necessary for the party denying knowledge of such terms to prove either fraud, misrepresentation or *non est factum*.

In the case at bar, Tilden Rent-A-Car took no steps to alert Mr. Clendenning to the onerous provisions in the standard form of contract presented by it. The clerk could not help but have known that Mr. Clendenning had not in fact read the contract before signing it. Indeed the form of the contract itself with the important provisions on the reverse side and in very small type would discourage even the most cautious customer from endeavouring to read and understand it. Mr. Clendenning was in fact unaware of the exempting provisions. Under such circumstances, it was not open to Tilden Rent-A-Car to rely on those clauses, and it was not incumbent on Mr. Clendenning to establish fraud, misrepresentation or *non est factum*. Having paid the premium, he was not liable for any damage to the vehicle while being driven by him.

As Lord Denning stated in *Neuchatel Asphalte Co. Ltd. v. Barnett*, [1957] 1 WLR 356, at 360: "We do not allow printed forms to be made a trap for the unwary."

In this case the trial Judge held that "the rule in *L'Estrange v. Graucob*" governed. He dismissed the action, however, on the ground that Tilden Rent-A-Car had by their prior oral representations misrepresented the terms of the contract. He imputed into the contract the assumption of Mr. Clendenning that by the payment of the premium he was "provided full non-deductible coverage unless at the time of the damage he was operating the automobile while under the influence of intoxicating liquor to such an extent as to be for the time incapable of the proper control of the automobile." Having found that Mr. Clendenning had not breached such a provision, the action was dismissed.

For the reasons already expressed, I do not think that in the circumstances of this case "the rule in *L'Estrange v. Graucob*" governed, and it was not incumbent upon Mr. Clendenning to prove misrepresentation.

In any event, if "the rule in *L'Estrange v. Graucob*" were applicable, it was in error, in my respectful opinion, to impute into the contract a provision which Tilden Rent-A-Car had not in fact represented as being a term of the contract.

As was stated in *Canadian Indemnity Co. v. Okanagan Mainline Real Estate Board et al.*, [1971] SCR 493, at 500, 16 DLR (3d) 715, at 720, [1971] 1 WWR 289:

> A party who misrepresents, albeit innocently, the contents or effect of a clause inserted by him into a contract cannot rely on the clause in the face of his misrepresentation.

Under such circumstances, absent the exclusionary provisions of the contract, the defendant was entitled to the benefit of the contract in the manner provided without the exclusionary provisions, and the action, therefore, had to fail.

Appeal dismissed.

[Zuber JA concurred with Dubin JA; Lacourcière JA delivered a strong dissenting judgment.]

NOTES AND QUESTIONS

1) In your view, does *Clendenning* really come to grips with the problem of standard form agreements containing unfair provisions? Suppose that in *Clendenning*'s case the onerous clauses had been printed in bold type. Would this have helped Clendenning? Could he have rented a car elsewhere and, assuming he had the time to shop around, would he have found the other rental agreements significantly different?

One approach to the standard form conundrum in the consumer context, pioneered in the United States, is to require contracts to be written in simple and plain terms so that the average layperson can understand them. New York, Maine, and Connecticut and a number of other states have adopted such legislation. The New York statute provides that all written consumer contracts (including residential leases) must be written "in a clear and coherent manner using words with common and every day meaning" and "appropriately divided and captioned by its various sections". (Agreements involving amounts greater than $50,000 are excluded). Would a more clearly written agreement have met the objections to the insurance terms in the Tilden Rent-A-Car agreement?

2) Contrast the *Clendenning* case with *Fraser Jewellers (1982) Ltd. v. Dominion Electric Protection Co.* (1997), 34 OR (3d) 1 (CA). *Fraser Jewellers* involved a clause in a contract for the provision of a burglar alarm system which limited the supplier's liability to the customer if the system failed. Robins JA delivered the judgment of the court. The trial judge had ruled that the limitation clause was unconscionable. The part of Robins JA's judgment dealing with this question is as follows.

> As a general proposition, in the absence of fraud or misrepresentation, a person is bound by an agreement to which he has put his signature whether he has read its contents or has chosen to leave them unread: Cheshire, Fifoot & Furmston's *Law of Contract*, 13th ed. (1996) at p. 168. Failure to read a contract before signing it is not a legally acceptable basis for refusing to abide by it. A businessman executing an agreement on behalf of a company must be presumed to be aware of its terms and to have intended that the company would be bound by them. The fact that Mr. Gordon chose not to read the contract can place him in no better position than a person who has. Nor is the fact that the clause is in a standard pre-printed form and was not a subject of negotiations sufficient in itself to vitiate the clause: *L'Estrange v. F. Graucob Ltd.*, [1934] 2 KB 394 at p. 403, [1934] All ER Rep. 16 (DC); *Craven v. Strand Holidays (Canada) Ltd.* (1982), 40 OR (2d) 186 at p. 194, 142 DLR (3d) 31 (CA).
>
> This is not a case in which the clause limiting liability was so obscured as to make it probable that it would escape attention. This contract was printed and contained on essentially one sheet of paper. The limitation provision was highlighted in bold block letters. The language is clear and unambiguous. There was no need to resort to a magnifying glass to see it or a dictionary to understand it. Nothing was done to mislead a reader. Had Mr. Gordon perused the contract, he would have been aware of the limitation. The fact that he did not is irrelevant to the question of the fairness or conscionability of the contract.
>
> The trial judge held that it was the defendant's responsibility to bring the clause to the "specific attention" of the plaintiff and to explain its effect. Not to have done so, he found, constituted an "unacceptable commercial practice." As I view the matter, there was no special relationship existing between these parties that imposed any such obligation on the defendant. This is an ordinary commercial contract between business people. If anything, given that the plaintiff contacted the defendant to upgrade an existing system whose installation was governed by a contract containing a similar limitation provision, it could reasonably be assumed that the plaintiff was aware of the limitation imposed on ADT's potential liability. Be that as it may, in this commercial setting, in the absence of fraud or other improper conduct inducing the plaintiff to enter the contract, the onus must rest upon the plaintiff to review the document and satisfy itself of its advantages and disadvantages before signing it. There

is no justification for shifting the plaintiff's responsibility to act with elementary prudence onto the defendant.

It is not suggested that the plaintiff was rushed or pressured in any way into signing the contract. Nor is it suggested that the defendant engaged in any dubious conduct to achieve this end. The plaintiff had all the time needed to read the contract and consider its terms and, admittedly, could have questioned ADT's representative on any provision about which it may have had doubt. It accordingly must be treated in the same manner as a subscriber who signed the contract with full knowledge of the exclusion provision: see *Karroll v. Silver Star Mountain Resorts Ltd.* (1988), 33 BCLR (2d) 160, 40 BLR 212 (SC).

The trial judge was of the opinion that there was an inequality of bargaining position between the plaintiff, a small retailer, and the defendant, a large security protection firm, and treated this as militating in favour of striking the clause. While I agree that such inequality is a relevant criterion, the fact that the parties may have different bargaining power does not in itself render an agreement unconscionable or unenforceable. Mere inequality of bargaining power does not entitle a party to repudiate an agreement. The question is not whether there was an inequality of bargaining power. Rather, the question is whether there was an abuse of the bargaining power.

On the facts of this case, there is no evidence of any such abuse. Nothing in this record indicates that the defendant obtained the contract by any unfair use of its stronger position or sought to take undue advantage of the plaintiff or, indeed, that the plaintiff was victimized as a consequence of its weaker position. The fact that the plaintiff is a small business is not sufficient to justify the court's interference with the parties' contractual arrangements. Nor, as I indicated earlier, is the fact that the agreement is in the form of a standard printed contract.

The remaining question is whether the terms of the exclusion provision are, as the trial judge viewed them, so "unusual in character" or so unfair or unconscionable that their enforcement would constitute an "unacceptable commercial practice." In deciding this question, the provision, as I have already stated, must be considered in the light of the entire agreement.

Paragraph E makes it clear that ADT is not an insurer; that insurance, if any, should be obtained by the customer; that the amounts payable by the customer are based on the value of the services; and that the scope of liability is unrelated to the value of the customer's property.

Having regard to the potential value of property kept on a customer's premises, and the many ways in which a loss may be incurred, the rationale underlying this type of limitation clause is apparent and makes sound commercial sense. ADT is not an insurer and its monitoring fee bears no relationship to the area of risk and the extent of exposure ordinarily taken into account in the determination of insurance policy premiums. Limiting liability in this situation is manifestly reasonable. The clause, in effect, allocates risk in a certain fashion and alerts the customer to the need to make its own insurance arrangements. ADT has no control over the value of its customer's inventory and can hardly be expected, in exchange for a relatively modest annual fee, to insure a jeweller against negligent acts on the part of its employees up to the value of the entire jewellery stock whatever that value, from time to time, may be.

In *Fraser Jewellers* the contract was not a consumer one. Is this a sufficient ground for distinguishing it from *Clendenning*? Are there any other grounds on which the two cases can be distinguished?

3) Think about *Clendenning* and the questions raised in these notes in the light of the following extract.

Michael J. Trebilcock
The Limits of Freedom of Contract

(Harvard University Press, 1993), 119-20 (Footnotes omitted)

Standard Form Contracts

Standard form contracts have suffered a bad press from both judicial and academic members of the legal fraternity over many years. At least in a consumer setting, the hostility to standard form contracts is based on two principal propositions. First, it is said that the use of standard form contracts is a manifestation of monopoly. Second, it is pointed out that the use of standard form contracts is typically characterized by imperfect information on the part of some of the parties to them. In both cases, the legal implications are much the same: courts should be extremely cautious about enforcing such contracts. These two arguments require evaluation.

The monopoly argument essentially rests on the "take it or leave it" character of most standard form contractual offerings. However, as I have argued elsewhere, the principal justification for standard form contracts is the dramatic reduction in transaction costs that they permit in many contexts. That they may be offered on a take it or leave it basis is as consistent with the benign transaction cost conservation rationale for them as it is with a monopoly or collusion rationale. Simply observing the fact of standard form contracts yields no meaningful implications as to the under-lying structure of the market. Indeed, we observe them being used in many settings where manifestly the market is highly competitive, for example, in dry cleaning stores, hotel registration forms, insurance contracts, and so on. Indeed, even in the absence of standard form contracts, we see many goods being offered on a take it or leave it basis in some of the most competitive retail markets in the economy. For example, corner variety stores (mom and pop stores) typically offer their goods on a take it or leave it basis, presumably to avoid the transaction costs entailed in haggling over price or product offerings.

The imperfect information argument against standard form contracts is clearly more substantial. Almost necessarily implicit in the transaction cost justification for standard form contracts is the assumption that parties will often not read them or, if they do, will not wish to spend significant amounts of time attempting to renegoti-ate the terms. Thus, to hold parties bound to standard form contracts which they had entered into but which they had not read or understood does not rest comfortably with a theory of contractual obligation premised on individual autonomy and consent. Clearly, in many, perhaps most cases, meaningful consent is absent. Thus, to justify contractual enforcement of these kinds of standard form contracts requires us, once again, to move outside the purely internal, non-instrumental basis for contractual obliga-tion as deriving from the will of the parties and appeal instead to external benchmarks of fairness. In this respect, I have argued first that problems of unfairness resulting from imperfect information are not so severe as they might seem at first sight. To the extent that there is a margin of informed, sophisticated, and aggressive consumers in any given market, who understand the terms of the standard form contracts on offer and who either negotiate over those terms or switch their business readily to competing suppliers offering more favourable terms, they may in effect discipline the entire market, so that inframarginal (less well informed, sophisticated, or mobile) consumers can effectively free-ride on the discipline brought to the market by the marginal consumers, although there is the potential for a collective action problem if every consumer attempts to free-ride on the efforts of others in effective monitoring of contract terms. In addition, where suppliers are able either to term or to performance discriminate between marginal and inframarginal consumers, this generalized discipline will be undermined, and there is a clear risk that the inframarginal consumers will be exploited because of their imperfect knowledge of the contract terms. Here, I have proposed that courts, in evaluating the fairness of standard form contracts in particular cases, should investigate whether a particular consumer seeking relief from the contract or some particular provision in it has received a deal that is significantly inferior, in relation to either the explicit terms of the contract or the performance provided under it, to that realized by marginal consumers in the same market, with the economic as opposed to personal characteristics of consumers in these two classes held constant. In other words, where a supplier has deliberately exploited a consumer's ignorance of terms generally available, in the market for like goods or services, to consumers in an economically similar situation in order to exact terms substantially inferior to these generally prevailing terms, the supplier's actions should be viewed as unconscionable, perhaps again invoking the equal concern and respect basis for protection of individual autonomy. In markets which are so badly disrupted by imperfect information that there is no identifiable margin of informed consumers from which appropriate benchmarks can be derived, then judicial sniping in case-by-case litigation seems less appropriate than legislative or regulatory intervention of the kind that has occurred in many jurisdictions, for example, with respect to various classes of door-to-door sales.

NOTES

For a more detailed account of the economic approach to standard form contracts, see Don Dewees and Michael J. Trebilcock, "Judicial Control of Standard Form Contracts" in Paul Burrows and Cento Veljanovski (eds.), *An Economic Approach to Law* (1981), chapter 4; Michael J. Trebilcock, "An Economic Approach to the Doctrine of Unconscionability" in Barry Reiter and John Swan (eds.), *Studies in Contract Law* (1980), 379; Michael J. Trebilcock, "The Doctrine of Inequality of Bargaining Power: Post-Benthamite Economics in the House of Lords" (1976), 26 *UTLJ* 359.

Professor Trebilcock argues the case on economic grounds for legislative intervention to control standard form contracts in cases of severe market failure. The following extract, arguing from an opposing theoretical perspective, suggests that standard form contracts should be *routinely* controlled by legislation.

Reuben Hasson
"The Unconscionability Business—A Comment on
Tilden Rent-A-Car v. Clendenning"

(1978-79), 3 *CBLJ* 193-98

The sad fact is that, just as consideration performs an indifferent job in deciding which promises should be enforced, so does unconscionability serve as a poor device for regulating unfair provisions in standard form contracts.

It is the purpose of this brief comment to suggest that we should regulate standard form contracts which are commonly used by consumers by adopting mandatory statutory terms and conditions. These conditions would serve to protect the legitimate interests of the seller (or provider of services) as well as providing minimum protection for the buyer.

. . .

One senses that the result in the present case would have been different if the trial judge had found that the defendant was unable to control the vehicle because of intoxication. The question that then arises is why the court did not state this. The answer, of course, is that the common law tradition works by indirection and by "case-to-case sniping." The majority, rightly, felt it did not have the mandate to formulate a legislative rule. The question of what protection (if any) we want to give the people who damage cars as a result of drunken or reckless driving is a political one and it is one that should therefore be made by politicians. That point has been grasped in the area of tax discounting, an area in which there was at least one unconscionability precedent. I am not suggesting statutory standard form contracts for every single contractual transaction; there is no need, for example, to have a statutory contract dealing with alcoholics selling their property at gross undervalue, although that has been the subject of at least one reported case. I am also not opposed to using unconscionability as a means of striking out unfair provisions in standard form contracts, provided this device is recognized as being the poor second best that it is.

A Statutory Car Rental Contract

I shall resist the temptation of drafting a statutory car rental contract. I will do this because, like the judiciary, I know very little about the car rental business. Instead, I will set out the procedure that I think should be followed in drawing one up and an outline of what should be included in the contract. To deal with the procedure first: the Minister of Consumer and Corporate Affairs should consult with the car rental companies, insurance companies, Superintendent of Insurance and consumer organizations with a view to devising a statutory standard form contract. The contract should state *all* the disqualifying conditions with as much precision as possible; thus, if drunkenness is to be an excluded risk, drunkenness should be defined as precisely as possible. A disqualification which depended on the proportion of alcohol in a driver's blood would be better than one that depended on the trial judge's finding of whether the hirer was sufficiently impaired or not. Similarly, if a disqualification is to be made for driving at "an illegal, reckless or otherwise abusive speed," that speed should be quantified. If there is to be a deductible provision, the size of the deductible should be regulated.

Two arguments can be made against a statutory contract. In the first place, it might be argued that the resulting statutory contract will be an unhappy compromise between the interests of the car rental companies and consumers. This is likely to be true, but it is also true of every piece of legislation on the statute books. A statutory rental contract makes private legislation that previously was invisible and uncertain, visible and less uncertain.

The second fear that might be expressed is that a statutory standard form contract would merely restate the present horrific contract already used by car rental companies. This is a possibility but an exceedingly remote one. For one thing, it is difficult to believe that the executives of car rental companies will fight desperately to retain some of the clauses that presently appear in car rental contracts. Second, it would be a foolhardy Minister of Consumer and Corporate Affairs who would merely rubber-stamp the present car rental contracts. Experience with administrative control over insurance contracts shows that while it is difficult to counter "the significant role of industry representatives in drafting standard policies," some obnoxious clauses are removed. Further, those who are afraid of codifying contract terms, fail to take into account that we already have unfair contract terms. It is true that some of these unfair clauses can be successfully challenged but the consumer does not know which clauses will be held to be unfair and few will have the resources and tenacity of a Mr. Clendenning to pursue a challenge to the fairness of a particular clause up to the highest court in the land.

. . .

NOTE

Professor Hasson's views about the unsuitability of the judicial machinery for handling any but the simplest and most obvious cases of contract unconscionability are restated in "Unconscionability in Contract Law" and in "New Sales Act—Confessions of a Doubting Thomas" (1979-80), 4 *CBLJ* 383. For a spirited reply, see Barry Reiter, "Unconscionability: Is There a Choice?" (1979-80), 4 *CBLJ* 403.

Legislative Developments: Consumer Sales Practices Legislation

Until 1974, Canadian legislation adopted a piecemeal approach to unconscionable contracts and dealt with abuses largely on an individual footing. Ontario's Business Practices Act, RSO 1990, c. B.18 and the BC Trade Practices Act, RSBC 1996, c. 457, both first adopted in 1974, mark a decisive shift in legislative philosophy and legal techniques. Apart from British Columbia and Ontario, six other provinces have adopted some type of unfair trade practices legislation: Alberta, Unfair Trade Practices Act, RSA 1980, cu-3; Manitoba, Business Practices Act, SM 1990-1991, c. 6 and Trade Practices Inquiry Act,

RSM 1987, c. T110; Newfoundland, Trade Practices Act, RSN 1990, c. T-7; Prince Edward Island, Business Practices Act, RSPEI 1988, c. B-7; Quebec, Consumer Protection Act, RSQ 1981, c. P-40; and Saskatchewan, Consumer Protection Act, SS 1996, c. C-30.1.

Consider the following questions in relation to the Ontario and BC Acts.

1) Do they vest too much power in consumer protection agencies and/or the courts?

2) Is unconscionability or unfairness a defensible concept or does it merely sanction a new form of arbitrariness?

3) How helpful is the shopping list in s. 2(2) of the Ontario Act? What is the difference between an "excessively one-sided" transaction (clause (v)) and "inequitable" terms and conditions (clause (vi))? Could the shopping list be invoked to attack the following types of clause:

    a) A car rental agreement which holds the hirer responsible for any form of damage to the vehicle, whether caused through his negligence or not?

    b) "Cut-off" clauses and disclaimer clauses in consumer sales contracts discounted with a finance company?

    c) Acceleration clauses in consumer credit agreements?

    d) A holiday "package" tour which entitles the organizer to switch airlines or hotel accommodation without giving the consumer the option to cancel his reservation?

    e) A subscription to a book club which obliges the member to accept and pay for the monthly selection unless he has previously notified the club that he does not want the item?

4) To what extent does Ont. s. 2(2) distinguish between procedural and substantive unfairness?

The following extract addresses some of these issues in the context of corresponding Australian legislation, the Contracts Review Act 1980 (New South Wales).

Anthony J. Duggan
"Saying Nothing with Words"

in Jacob S. Ziegel (ed.), *New Developments in International Commercial and Consumer Law: Proceedings of the 8th Biennial Conference of the International Academy of Commercial and Consumer Law* (Oxford: Hart Publishing, 1998), 472-75 (Footnotes omitted)

The *Contracts Review Act* is contentious. Its architect, Professor John Peden, claimed that it was drafted with a view to making the law "sharp in focus, conceptually sound and explicit in its policy underpinnings," preserving judicial rigour in the application of the legislation and avoiding "ad hocery" in decision-making.

These claims are open to challenge. I have previously argued that the legislation is:

1) not "sharp in focus," because it does not distinguish between procedural unconscionability (where the contract is unjust because of deficiencies in the bargaining process) and substantive unconscionability (where the contract is unjust because the outcome is otherwise one-sided or unfair). The list of factors which the courts are directed to consider when deciding whether to grant relief is a jumble of proc-

ess-oriented and outcome-oriented considerations and no attempt is made to give them any relative weighting;

2) not "conceptually sound," because in so far as proof might be required of procedural unconscionability, no guidance is given as to how far this proof might legitimately be derived by inference from one-sided outcomes (the more readily such inferences are drawn, the less the distinction between procedural and substantive unconscionability will matter); and

3) not "explicit in its policy underpinnings," because it is quite unclear whether the legislation is motivated primarily (or at all) by economic efficiency considerations, loss distribution considerations or paternalistic concerns (depending on how it is interpreted, it could be made to relate to any of these goals).

In short, the legislation is indeterminate. This must be counted as a fundamental defect, given that the objective was to make the law more, rather than less, certain. The indeterminacy is a function of the legislature's failure to address key policy choices.

Three examples will serve to demonstrate the problem. Assume that A mortgages the family home to B as security for repayment of a loan made by B to C. C defaults in repayment, and B takes steps to enforce the security against A. Faced with eviction, A brings proceedings under the *Contracts Review Act* 1980 (NSW) to have the contract set aside. Neither B nor C was guilty of any wrongdoing towards A in the period leading up to the signing of the mortgage agreement. A might nevertheless argue that the contract is unjust within the meaning of the statute because it was not in her best interests, and that had she received independent advice at the time she would never have agreed to go ahead with the transaction. If the court is moved by compassion for A's plight, it may well he prepared to accept this argument. It might reason that the consequences to B if the mortgage is set aside will be less severe than the consequences to A if it is not, and that B is in a better position to spread the loss. This is essentially a loss distribution case in favour of intervention. Alternatively, the court might conclude that in the absence of any proof of wrongdoing on B's part, the contract is not unjust. To set aside a contract simply on the basis of the complaining party's assertion that she did not understand it would substantially undermine the security of transactions, and in this sense would be contrary to the public interest. Third party mortgages and guarantees would become less valuable to lenders as forms of security, and some classes of borrower might find it harder to obtain credit. This is essentially an economic efficiency case against intervention. Which of these competing views is correct—should the court be guided by loss distribution or economic efficiency considerations? For present purposes, the answer does not matter. What does matter is that the statute itself provides no guidance one way or the other. The statute is indeterminate.

Assume now that A agrees to buy property from B for $45,000. The market value of the property is $30,000. A has Alzheimer's disease, but the condition is in its early stages and there is nothing in A's behaviour during negotiations which might lead B to suppose that there is anything amiss. A later brings proceedings against B under the *Contracts Review Act* 1980 (NSW) to have the contract set aside. The issue in this case is whether proof that B knew of A's disability is required to support a finding that the contract was unjust. The question turns on whether the underlying concern of the statute is with relief of A's misfortune (a loss distribution concern) or prevention of B's wrongdoing (an economic efficiency concern). Which approach should the courts take? Again, the statute provides no guidance one way or the other. Not surprisingly, the courts have divided on the question.

Finally, assume that A holds a garage sale. Among the items for sale she includes a painting which she prices at $20. B, an art dealer, attends the sale and immediately recognises A's painting as a long lost masterpiece. B buys the painting from A for $20, without disclosing what he knows. The true value of the painting is $250,000. Could A have the contract set aside under the *Contracts Review Act* 1980 (NSW)? One approach might be to say that the contract is unjust within the meaning of the statute because, given B's superior information, there was a material inequality of bargaining power between the parties at the time of transacting or, alternatively perhaps, because B used unfair tactics in failing to disclose the information. This approach is consistent with a view that information should be shared between contracting parties (a distributive concern). An alternative approach might be to say that there is nothing wrong with a party trading on the basis of superior information. On the contrary, if B were required to disclose, he would end up having to share the gains from his discovery with A. A disclosure requirement, routinely imposed, would act as a disincentive to search and discovery. This approach is consistent with economic efficiency considerations. How should the court choose—in favour of a sharing rule, or in favour of exclusivity? Once again, the statute is no help. It is indeterminate.

Rushak v. Henneken

[1991] 6 WWR 596 (BCCA)

TAYLOR JA: With the advice and assistance of a gentleman friend who was knowledgeable about motor cars, the plaintiff in 1982 purchased a much-used but attractive 14-year-old Mercedes Benz sports car for $17,300 through the defendants, the agents of the vendor; this car was found by the trial judge to have been "of such peerless beauty that … she appears to have cast an hypnotic spell on all who had dealings with her."

Before purchasing the vehicle the plaintiff and her friend had a discussion about it with the defendant Hans Henneken, principal of the corporate defendant. Mr. Henneken knew something of the history of the vehicle, particularly that it had been imported from Germany and that rust was a problem in West German alpine areas. The trial judge found [[1986] BCWLD 2782] (at pp. 7-8):

> He [Mr. Henneken] conceded that a car as old as this one was bound to have rust and that cars developed rust within two months out of the factory. He said that rust occurs inside the metal of a car and works out to the surface and that post-factory undercoating would cover up any rust there was. The metal underneath a Mercedes Benz was smooth and for an undercoating to adhere the metal would have to have been ground and that the metal of this car had been ground.

In his evidence Mr. Henneken said he becomes suspicious when he sees post-factory undercoating because such undercoating does not stop or prevent rust. Mr. Henneken's evidence, in the words of the trial judge, was that "if anything, it traps the moisture, causing the rusting process to accelerate rather than to be retarded." He conceded that the only way to find out satisfactorily whether there was any rust lying at the back of post-factory undercoating would be to remove the undercoating.

When the plaintiff first looked at this vehicle it was in the possession of Mr. Henneken's salesman McAllister. Mr. McAllister pointed out to her several spots of rust visible under the fenders and recommended she take the car to a Mercedes Benz dealer for proper rust inspection.

The plaintiff then returned to speak with Mr. Henneken. He told her he knew the car by reason of doing repair work for the owner, who was selling it because of financial difficulties, and that the owner had been satisfied with its performance. Mr. Henneken added that the car was "a good vehicle," "one of the best of its kind in Vancouver," and "a very nice car."

The plaintiff was then given the car for the purpose of having it inspected by Mr. Kumar, an independent garage man. The opinion of Mr. Kumar, for which she paid a fee of $50, was generally favourable. Mr. Kumar reported "surface rust, minor underbody rust," and he, too, recommended that the plaintiff have it inspected by a Mercedes Benz dealer. Instead, the plaintiff and her friend, Mr. Hall, returned to Mr. Henneken, where they had the car put on a hoist so that Mr. Hall could look at its underside. A young employee of Mr. Henneken pointed out how clean the undercoating was. Mr. Henneken, who also looked at the undercoating, gave an opinion that the car was a good one.

On the basis of the foregoing investigation the plaintiff purchased the vehicle but found that she could not drive it because she could not get accustomed to its standard transmission. It was put into storage, and when she decided a year or so later to sell it, she found it was in a sad mechanical state, and rusted so badly that it would cost upwards of $10,000 just to repair the rust.

In a long and careful judgment, the learned trial judge made the following findings (at pp. 53-54):

1. The plaintiff delegated completely to Hall all decision-making powers in the matter of the examination of the car, its testing and reaching the conclusion to buy it.

2. Hall was far from being a neophyte in the buying of a car and his experience had taught him what questions to ask and where to look.

3. No pressure was put upon the plaintiff and Hall to buy; they were given every opportunity to have the car exhaustively examined and tested by experts of their choice.

4. Hall personally thoroughly examined the car not once but several times commencing with the first road test he made with the plaintiff as passenger and ending with the inspection of the undercarriage which he carried out in Henneken's garage having taken it there from Kumar's garage.

5. Both McAllister and Kumar urged Hall to have the car examined by the Mercedes Benz dealership but he chose not to have this done.

6. Both Henneken and Kumar carried out the tests which their training and years of experience had taught them to make and because of those tests believed and were justi-

fied in believing that the car was, as it appeared to be, in good condition for a car of its age and kind.

7. Both Henneken and Kumar specifically directed the attention of Hall to the matter of rust and Kumar in addition told him that he could not say what lay behind the undercoating but that he should have it looked at by a bodyman.

8. Hall, immediately after his discussions with Kumar, took the car to Henneken's garage and had it put on the hoist there so that he might carefully examine, as he did, the undercoating and undercarriage and satisfy himself, as he did, in the matter of rust.

9. Henneken did use commendatory language about the car in his statements to the plaintiff and Hall, for example, that in his opinion the car was one of the best of its kind in Vancouver; that it was a good vehicle and very nice; and that they could see for themselves that the car was in good shape.

10. That there was nothing in the appearance of the undercarriage of the car and in particular the undercoating to suggest to any of those who examined them, namely, Henneken, McAllister, Kumar and Hall, that behind the undercoating there was serious and widespread rust corrosion to the undercarriage metal.

The learned trial judge also found the following (at p. 58):

> The plaintiff has failed to satisfy me that in making statements to her about the car Henneken fell below the standard of care and skill possessed by a used car dealer in Vancouver in October 1982. The point is not whether he arrived at a correct conclusion about the soundness of the car but whether in reaching that conclusion he did or did not exercise, according to the standard of his peers, a reasonable and proper care, skill and judgment. c.f. Tindall CJ in *Chapman v. Walton* (1833), 10 Bing 57, 131 ER 826. On the evidence before me I cannot and do not find that he fell below that standard.

On the basis of these findings, the learned trial judge exonerated Mr. Henneken of all common law and *Sale of Goods Act*, RSBC 1979, c. 370, wrongs, but found he had committed a "deceptive act" under the *Trade Practice Act*, RSBC 1979, c. 406, and therefore awarded the plaintiff damages in the sum of $6,000.

The provisions of the *Trade Practice Act* relied upon by the plaintiff read as follows:

> 3(1) For the purposes of this Act, a deceptive act or practice includes
>
> (a) an oral written, visual descriptive or other representation, including a failure to disclose;
>
> (b) any conduct having the capability, tendency or effect of deceiving or misleading a person.
>
> (2) A deceptive act or practice by a supplier in relation to a consumer transaction may occur before, during or after the consumer transaction.
>
> (3) Without limiting subsection (1), one or more of the following, however expressed, constitutes a deceptive act or practice: ...
>
> (r) the use, in an oral or written representation, of exaggeration, innuendo or ambiguity as to a material fact, if the representation is deceptive or misleading.

The trial judge explained his view of the law in the following passage from his judgment (at p. 61):

The provisions of the Act were considered by Ruttan J in *Findlay v. Couldwell*, [1976] 5 WWR 340, 29 CPR (2d) 279, 69 DLR (3d) 320 (BC).

At p. 345 [WWR] he said:

> I should note here that a deceptive act does not necessarily involve deliberate intention to deceive. Deception need only have the capability of deceiving or misleading and it may be inadvertent yet still sufficient to avoid the transaction under the statute, which is directed to the welfare of the consumer, not the punishment of the vendor."

> At p. 346 he said that a representation constituted a deceptive act or practice under the statute if it led astray the representee or caused the representee to go in the wrong direction, that is, to bring about an error of judgment by the consumer.

> The philosophy and thrust of consumer legislation is very different from that of the common law in sale of goods. The former proceeds on the footing that a supplier who makes his livelihood out of supplying personal property to consumers, owes a positive duty of candour to the consumer and that duty embraces telling the consumer any material fact known to the supplier about the ware, the disposition of which to the consumer he is promoting. What is a material fact will depend upon the circumstances.

On the hearing of this appeal counsel for the plaintiff agreed that the learned trial judge, in the passage just quoted, was not establishing any new general positive duty of candour. He also confined his case to "misleading" representations falling within the definition of "deceptive act or practice" rather than to "deceptive" representations in the sense in which the word "deceptive" would normally be understood.

Counsel stressed, however, that there is clearly a duty to disclose any material fact the absence of which might mislead a purchaser. Counsel's position was simply that Mr. Henneken, knowing the probable history of the car in Germany, the usual progress of rust, and the properties and significance of post-factory undercoating, was under a duty to inform the plaintiff of all these matters, or at least a summary of them.

. . .

But it seems to me that the question raised is not so much whether Mr. Henneken was under a general duty to disclose what he knew about post-factory undercoating but whether his use of laudatory language to describe the car in circumstances where he knew there might be extensive rust under the undercoating was "conduct having the capability, tendency, or effect of misleading a person" within the meaning of s. 3(1)(b) of the Act.

Mr. Henneken's opinion was found by the trial judge to have been honestly held. Insofar as the important matter of rust was concerned, however, it was an opinion based solely on what little he saw on examining the undercarriage, and that examination had suggested to Mr. Henneken that his opinion could well be completely wrong, as it proved to be.

Mr. Henneken knew there might well be extensive rust deliberately covered over by brushed-on post-factory undercoating. That was something which made him suspicious because he was of the view that post-factory undercoating can only accelerate rusting, and that the only way to find out how much rust was there would be to take the undercoating off—if the owner would permit it. That knowledge, in my view, made the expression of his opinion without qualification something which Mr. Henneken must be taken to have known was capable of misleading a potential buyer.

It is, indeed, surprising that the *Trade Practice Act* has been little invoked in the courts, because I agree with the trial judge that it imposes a high standard of candour, especially on suppliers who choose to commend their wares.

Unfortunately, counsel did not direct us to cases decided under similar legislation in other provinces and elsewhere. Such legislation exists in the United Kingdom, Australia, at least four other Canadian provinces and several states of the United States. Section 4(1)(d) of the Alberta statute, *Unfair Trade Practices Act*, RSA 1980, c. U-3, includes in the definition of unfair practice "any ... conduct that ... might reasonably have the effect of ... misleading a consumer or potential consumer." Section 2(b)(vii) of the Ontario statute, the *Business Practices Act*, RSO 1980, c. 55, forbids the making by a supplier of any "unconscionable consumer representation," including "a misleading statement of opinion on which the consumer is likely to rely to his detriment." The Australian *Trade Practices Act*, 1974, forbids "conduct that is misleading or deceptive." A study of the cases under these statutes might possibly be helpful in interpreting our own, but that was not undertaken in the present case. I do not think it appropriate that the court embark on such a survey without having had the assistance of counsel.

There is, however, a decision in this province, cited but not explored on the appeal, which seems to me of potential assistance. In *British Columbia (Director of Trade Practices) v. Household Finance Corp.*, [1976] 3 WWR 731, 29 CPR (2d) 232 (BCSC) [affirmed [1977] 3 WWR 390, 33 CPR (2d) 284 (BCCA)] Mr. Justice Hutcheon said (at p. 736):

> Having in mind the examples of deceptive acts given in s. 2(3), I conclude that an act having the tendency of deceiving or misleading a person is one that tends to lead that person astray into making an error of judgment.

I think those words helpful in defining the scope of the section as it applies to this case.

Two other cases of assistance in determining the standard of candour imposed by the statute on suppliers are: *British Columbia (Director of Trade Practices) v. Lansdowne Pontiac Buick GMC Ltd.* (January 31, 1986), Vancouver Doc. C844175 (SC), [1986] BCWLD 1924; and *Stubbe v. P.F. Collier & Son Ltd.*, [1977] 3 WWR 493, 30 CPR (2d) 216, 74 DLR (3d) 605 (BCSC).

In the *Lansdowne Pontiac* case, the Director of Trade Practices alleged that the defendant had engaged in a deceptive act in the course of selling a motor vehicle to a customer at what was stated to be 14.2 per cent financing and thereafter advising them that the price would be increased by an additional $600 "to allow the company to provide the low rate of financing." It turned out that the cost to the dealer of participating in the financing programme was $500 per vehicle, and the sales managers had been instructed to obtain a price from the consumer that would cover this cost.

Mr. Justice Wallace found the defendant's practice in this regard to be deceptive. He said (at pp. 5-6):

> The fact that the Hunters concluded the transaction at the amended purchase price, after being told of the extra charge, does not, in my view, negate the deceptive nature of the transaction, which I find to be that of holding out to a prospective purchaser that he will receive the benefit of a low interest rate and then passing on to the purchaser the fee charged to the company for its participation in the programme, thereby in effect increasing the interest rate above that which had been represented. ...
>
> I do not think the defendant, in fact, realized it was misleading its customers when it followed the practice of seeking reimbursement from the customer for the participation fee it was required to pay GMAC under the financing programme. But whatever the intention of the defendant. I find that the financial arrangement described did constitute a deceptive practice and that the defendant acted in contravention of the *Trade Practice Act* in such circumstances.

In the *Stubbe* case, the defendant engaged in selling encyclopedias from door to door. The presentations given by the company's sales representatives were taken from "sales scripts" which were found to contain the following defects:

> 1. failing to disclose at the outset of the presentation that the purpose was to sell the encyclopedia;
>
> 2. falsely representing that the purpose of the call was to conduct a survey;
>
> 3. misrepresenting the amount of time required to complete the visit;
>
> 4. falsely representing that there were qualifications for purchasing the books other than credit worthiness;
>
> 5. placing a greater emphasis on the daily cost of the encyclopedia series than on the total cost; and
>
> 6. representing that the encyclopedia was completely new when it in fact was a revised edition.

With the exception of the third allegation, Mr. Justice Aikens found that these constituted deceptive practices under the Act. Referring to the fact that a card which was provided to the consumer at the outset disclosed the true purpose of the visit, the judge commented (at p. 510) [WWR]:

> Thus, on the one hand, by offering the card the representative gives the householder a chance to find out exactly what his intention is but, on the other hand, by the spoken words he leaves the impression that his visit is concerned with some sort of educational programme thus diluting the impact of the card if it has been read or, if not, directly deceiving the householder.
>
> In my view, the provisions of the Act must be construed so as to protect not only alert potential customers, but also those who are not alert, are unsuspicious and are credulous.

In dealing with the question whether the sales representatives committed a deceptive practice by focusing the potential purchaser's attention on the daily, as opposed to the total, cost of the encyclopedia, the judge observed (at p. 522) that it is sometimes "a difficult task to draw the line between legitimate salesmanship and salesmanship which is contrary to the Act."

While it used to be said that what is described in general terms as "puffery" on the part of a salesman does not give rise to legal consequences, I am not satisfied that the same can necessarily be said today in light of the provisions of the *Trade Practice Act*. "Puffery" cannot, in my view, excuse the giving of an unqualified opinion as to quality when the supplier has factual knowledge indicating that the opinion may in an important respect very well be wrong. Exaggeration or embellishment of qualities which a seller knows to exist may, perhaps, be excused as puffery, and particularly where the potential buyer is in as good a position as the supplier to form an opinion on the matter. That expression cannot, however, so far as the Act is concerned, be used to excuse a laudatory description given with specific factual knowledge not shared by the potential buyer which suggests the goods may, in fact, be in an important respect defective, and not therefore of the quality described at all.

I am of the view that the section must be taken to require that suppliers involved in the defined transactions refrain from any sort of potentially misleading statement, and that this must include an honestly held opinion given in circumstances in which the supplier knows that giving the opinion without appropriate qualification may mislead. It was not, in my view, open to the defendant to describe the car as "a good vehicle," "one of the best of its kind" and "very nice," without appropriate qualification, when he had reason to suspect that there might be extensive rust, and that the rust had been coated over with brushed-on undercoating so as to render it incapable of discovery by ordinary examination.

. . .

Appeal dismissed.

NOTES AND QUESTIONS

1) Would *Rushak v. Henneken* have been decided differently at common law in an action for innocent and/or negligent misrepresentation, in equity or in tort? Would the remedies have been the same? Does s. 3(1) of the BC Trade Practices Act require the consumer to have relied on the deceptive representation? Was the plaintiff prejudiced by Mr. Henneken's statement about the general condition of the vehicle? If Mr. Henneken had said nothing but had known or suspected that the car was badly rusted, would this have been a deceptive act or practice? What are the economic and social rationales for imposing liability in such circumstances? What impact will liability have on the availability and price of used cars? For discussion of these issues see Anthony T. Kronman, "Mistake, Disclosure, Information and the Law of Contracts" (1978), 7 *J Legal Studies* 1; R. Cooter and T. Ulen, *Law and Economics* (Scott Foresman & Co., 1988), at 257-67; Michael J. Trebilcock, *The Limits of Freedom of Contract* (Harvard University Press, 1993), chapter 5; Anthony Duggan, Michael Bryan and Frances Hanks, *Contractual Non-Disclosure: An Applied Study in Modern Contract Theory* (Melbourne: Longman Professional, 1994).

2) In *Memorial Gardens Ontario Ltd. v. Ont.* (1992), 2 OR (3d) 417 (CA), the appellant was charged under s. 17(2) of the Ontario BPA with engaging in an unfair practice "knowing it to be an unfair practice." The charge arose out of an agreement between the appellant and two executors of an estate for the sale and installation of a bronze memorial marker for the total price of $1,325. The executors did not proceed with the agreement and, instead, purchased a similar marker from a competitor at a saving of about $300. How should the case have been decided? How much of a *mens rea* is implied in the requirement in s. 17(2) that the defendant must "know" it is engaging in an unfair practice? What is a "grossly excessive price" for the purposes of s. 2(b) and s. 17(2) of the Act, and to what extent are the consumer's circumstances relevant in determining this question?

3) Both the BC Act (s. 22(1)(a)) and the Ontario Act (s. 4(2)) empower the court to impose punitive damages in a civil suit under the Act. When should the power be used? (*Cf. Novak v. Zephyr Ford Truck Centre Ltd.*, BCCA, Nov. 24, 1988, where the court affirmed the trial judge's award of punitive damages of $5,000. The seller had represented that a truck had never been involved in an accident requiring repairs costing more than $2,000 when the seller knew the truck had rolled over on the highway and had required repairs costing some $34,000.) Have the provisions become obsolete in light of the Supreme Court of Canada's acceptance of the availability of punitive damages in contract as well as tort cases?

CHAPTER FOUR

Scope of the Contract

The present chapter deals with a variety of issues, some old and some new, but all equally important. The first question is: how does the law distinguish between "mere" representations and those representations which are deemed to have become a term of the contract when the agreement has not been reduced to writing? Under existing law the distinction is fundamental because of the different remedies provided by the law in each of the two situations. A non-contractual misrepresentation only gives rise to equitable and sometimes tortious remedies whereas breach of a contractual representation provides the aggrieved party with a much more powerful range of remedies. So it is very much in the representor's interest to argue for a contractual characterization of the representation.

Assuming the first hurdle has been successfully overcome, there often arises a second: how is the contractual term itself to be characterized, for this too carries profoundly important remedial implications. As will be seen, such a seemingly simple question arouses strong emotions and equally varied responses depending on whether one prefers certainty over flexibility and predictability over good faith conduct in the individual situation.

The third question is very much a product of 20th century merchandising and distributive techniques, for it is concerned with the legal effect of a representation or promise made to the ultimate buyer by a manufacturer or other person in the distributive chain who is not in direct privity with the buyer. Analytically and functionally, the question is part of the broader issue of the manufacturer's responsibility for defective goods resulting only in economic loss. Anglo-Canadian law has been slow however to recognize the unity and it seems appropriate to approach the issues in two stages. The first, the manufacturer's responsibility for *express representations and promises*, is dealt with here; the second stage, the manufacturer's liability for breach of *implied warranties*, is dealt with in chapter 9.

PRIVATE LAW ASPECTS

Representations and Warranties

A.H. Boulton
The Making of Business Contracts

2nd ed. (1972), at 15-18

(i) *Definition of the contract*

As a general principle it will be universally agreed that the more precisely one can define the provisions of a contract the better, and it is desirable to be able to limit with certainty the documents which are to be examined in order to establish those provisions. This is not to say, however, that in any given contractual situation the parties will agree where the limit is to be drawn.

The Act [SGA (UK) 1893] does not give a great deal of assistance, and one is led back to the general law of contract, and to the necessity of defining a point at which it is possible to construe the documentation as constituting an offer and an acceptance of that offer. If, as often happens, the actual contract of sale comes at the end of a long period of negotiation in which a number of representations have been made regarding the goods, sometimes in an express and specific form, and sometimes by means of general statements in advertising media, it tends to be to the advantage of the buyer to regard all these representations as being germane to the contract, whereas it is to the advantage of the seller to set a clear limit to the number of documents that are to be relied upon. It is clearly established that unless the immediate terms of the contract expressly provide to the contrary a representation regarding the goods made by the seller before the sale, and designed to influence the buyer towards entering into the contract, is a condition of the contract. This doctrine has been recently extended by the courts, so that a buyer may be able to sue a manufacturer on a representation made by him regarding the goods sold by a distributor notwithstanding that the contract of sale was not made with the manufacturer but with the distributor.

The law has for a long time recognised that a distinction exists between a mere commendation of goods for the purpose of advertisement and a representation made in order to induce a buyer. Under the contemptuous expression "a mere puff" much of the output of the contemporary art of advertising may be dismissed. No action would lie at the instance of an aggrieved buyer who complained that a detergent advertised as washing "whiter than white" did no more than wash white, if only because it would be difficult to give any meaning to the phrase. But it is far from easy to determine exactly at what point a statement ceases to be a mere advertising commendation and becomes a representation to be imported into the contract.

The matter becomes more complicated when the goods of sale are technical products. The typical selling transaction today, outside the range of the retail market, takes place between the sales representative of manufacturing industry and the commercial buyer. In the case of technical products the commercial buyer may have to refer to specialists on his own side whose expertise is involved, and on the seller's side the transaction may move from the sales representative to the technologist. Not infrequently the final state is the evolution of a specification by negotiation between the parties. Over the course of the negotiations the seller may be represented at different times by different persons whose authority to make representations on his behalf may not be very clearly defined—and in this respect it is the representative's apparent authority that matters more than his real authority—so that it is possible for a number of assertions to be made as to the quality of the goods and in the case of machinery as to its anticipated performance. There may also be a wealth of published material in the shape of catalogues, specifications, and the like, all of which may be regarded as having influenced the buyer.

In view of this it is in the interest of the seller to make sure that, at the point of time at which the contract is entered into, all irrelevant and casual statements regarding the goods are clearly excluded from the scope of the contract proper. Thus in the typical BEAMA "A" conditions:

> All specifications, drawings and particulars of weights and dimensions submitted with our tender are approximate only, and the descriptions and illustrations contained in our catalogues, price lists and other advertisement matter are intended merely to present a general idea of the goods described therein, and none of these shall form part of the contract. After acceptance of our tender a set of certified outline drawings will be supplied free of charge on request.

This clause is skilfully drawn. It will be noted that it excludes from the scope of the contract particulars "submitted with" the tender, and contained in the more general sales literature, but does not exclude particulars that may be *contained in* tender, to do which would be unreasonable. In the interpretation of a contract governed by a clause of this kind it may therefore be important to determine whether a specification or drawing is "submitted with" the tender or is an integral part of the tender, a distinction which can be easily overlooked. There are practical reasons why, especially to a manufacturer of technical products which are in the course of constant development and refinement, such a safeguard is necessary. It is not practicable, every time some technical change of a minor type is made, for a complete scrutiny of all extant sales literature to be made and alterations effected in order to bring the literature into line with practice. However, the question must sometimes arise how far the protection which such a clause purports to give is reasonable. The wise buyer of a technical product will seek some assurance and guarantee of its specification and performance in a form that will bring it within the substantive contract, and will take steps to ensure that everything he has been told about the goods he is buying will not be arbitrarily excluded from the contract by such a clause.

It is not usual to find any clause matching this in conditions which buyers seek to impose. Naturally the interests of the buyer are best served by leaving the matter open so that any of the seller's negotiating representations can be relied upon. Buyers' conditions naturally tend to throw the emphasis upon the order as the ruling document without, however, expressly excluding other documents. Thus the Purchasing Officers Association conditions provide:

... the goods shall
> (i) conform, as to quantity, quality and description with the particulars stated in the order,
> (ii) be of sound materials and workmanship,
> (iii) be equal in all respects to the samples, patterns or specifications provided or given by either party.

The conditions put forward by a United Kingdom nationalised industry are of interest in this connection.

> The Articles shall be of the qualities and sorts described and equal in all respects to the Specifications, Patterns, Drawings and Samples which form part of the Contract Documents *or are otherwise relevant for the purposes of the Contract.* ...

The words italicised can open the door to a great deal of argument, and would seem to be wide enough to include practically any express statement regarding the goods.

Leaf v. International Galleries

[1950] 2 KB 86, [1950] 1 All ER 693 (CA)

[In March 1944 the plaintiff bought from the defendants an oil painting of Salisbury Cathedral for £85. During the negotiations for the purchase, the sellers represented that it was a painting by Constable. The trial judge found that that representation had been incorporated as one of the terms of the contract. Nearly five years later the buyer tried to sell the picture and then discovered that it was not a Constable. He asked the defendants to take back the picture and to return the purchase price. The defendants refused and adhered to their view that the painting was by Constable. As a result the plaintiff brought this action for rescission of the agreement. He did not seek damages.

The county court judge found that the defendants had made an innocent misrepresentation and that the picture was not by Constable. Nevertheless, he denied relief on the ground that the equitable remedy was not available in the case of an executed contract. The plaintiff appealed.]

DENNING LJ: The question is whether the plaintiff is entitled to rescind the contract on the ground that the picture in question was not painted by Constable. I emphasize that it is a claim to rescind only: there is no claim in this action for damages for breach of condition or breach of warranty. The claim is simply one for rescission. At a very late stage before the county court judge counsel did ask for leave to amend by claiming damages for breach of warranty, but it was not allowed. No claim for damages is before us at all. The only question is whether the plaintiff is entitled to rescind.

The way in which the case is put by Mr. Weitzman, on behalf of the plaintiff, is this: he says that this was an innocent misrepresentation and that in equity he is, or should be, entitled to claim rescission even of an executed contract of sale on that account. He points out that the judge has found that it is quite possible to restore the parties to their original position. It can be done by simply handing back the picture to the defendants.

In my opinion, this case is to be decided according to the well known principles applicable to the sale of goods. This was a contract for the sale of goods. There was a mistake about the quality of the subject-matter, because both parties believed the picture to be a Constable; and that mistake was in one sense essential or fundamental. But such a mistake does not avoid the contract: there was no mistake at all about the subject-matter of the sale. It was a specific picture, "Salisbury Cathedral." The parties were agreed in the same terms on the same subject-matter, and that is sufficient to make a contract: see *Solle v. Butcher*, [1950] 1 KB 671.

There was a term in the contract as to the quality of the subject-matter: namely, as to the person by whom the picture was painted—that it was by Constable. That term of the contract was, according to our terminology, either a condition or a warranty. If it was a condition, the buyer could reject the picture for breach of the condition at any time before he accepted it, or is deemed to have accepted it; whereas, if it was only a warranty, he could not reject it at all but was confined to a claim for damages.

I think it right to assume in the buyer's favour that this term was a condition, and that, if he had come in proper time he could have rejected the picture; but the right to reject for breach of condition has always been limited by the rule that, once the buyer has accepted, or is deemed to have accepted, the goods in performance of the contract, then he cannot thereafter reject, but is relegated to his claim for damages: see s. 11 sub-s. 1(c), of the Sale of Goods Act, 1893, and *Wallis, Son & Wells v. Pratt & Haynes*, [1910] 2 KB 1003.

The circumstances in which a buyer is deemed to have accepted goods in performance of the contract are set out in s. 35 of the Act, which says that the buyer is deemed to have accepted the goods, amongst other things, "when, after the lapse of a reasonable time, he retains the goods without intimating to the seller that he has rejected them." In this case the buyer took the picture into his house and, apparently, hung it there, and five years passed before he intimated any rejection at all. That, I need hardly say, is much more than a reasonable time. It is far too late for him at the end of five years to reject this picture for breach of any condition. His remedy after that length of time is for damages only, a claim which he has not brought before the court.

Is it to be said that the buyer is in any better position by relying on the representation, not as a condition, but as an innocent misrepresentation? I agree that on a contract for the sale of goods an innocent material misrepresentation may, in the proper case, be a ground for rescission even after the contract has been executed. The observations of Joyce J in *Seddon v. North Eastern Salt Co. Ld.*, [1905] 1 Ch. 326, are, in my opinion, not good law. Many judges have treated it as plain that an executed contract of sale may be rescinded for innocent misrepresentation: see, for instance, *per* Warrington LJ and Scrutton LJ in *T. & J. Harrison v. Knowles and Foster*, [1918] 1 KB 608, at 609, 610; per Lord Atkin in *Bell v. Lever Bros. Ld.*, [1932] AC 161, at 224; and *per* Scrutton LJ and Maugham LJ in *L'Estrange v. F. Graucob Ld.*, [1934] 2 KB 394, at 400, 405.

Apart from that, there is now the decision of the majority of this court in *Solle v. Butcher*, [1950] 1 KB 671, which overrules the first ground of decision in *Angel v. Jay*, [1911] 1 KB 666. But it is unnecessary to explore these matters now.

Although rescission may in some cases be a proper remedy, it is to be remembered that an innocent misrepresentation is much less potent than a breach of condition; and a claim to rescission for innocent misrepresentation must at any rate be barred when a right to reject for breach of condition is barred. A condition is a term of the contract of a most material character, and if a claim to reject on that account is barred, it seems to me *a fortiori* that a claim to rescission on the ground of innocent misrepresentation is also barred.

So, assuming that a contract for the sale of goods may be rescinded in a proper case for innocent misrepresentation, the claim is barred in this case for the self-same reason as a right to reject is barred. The buyer has accepted the picture. He had ample opportunity for examination in the first few days after he had bought it. Then was the time to see if the condition or representation was fulfilled. Yet he has kept it all this time. Five years have elapsed without any notice of rejection. In my judgment he cannot now claim to rescind. His only claim, if any, as the county court judge said, was one for damages, which he has not made in this action. In my judgment, therefore, the appeal should be dismissed.

Appeal dismissed.

[Jenkins LJ and Evershed MR delivered concurring judgments.]

NOTES

1) The judgments in *Leaf* seem to favour a merger of the remedies of rescission where the representation gives rise both to an equitable action for misrepresentation and an action for breach of condition. Is there any justification for retaining the equitable remedy at all where the representation amounts to a term of the contract? *Riddiford v. Warren* (1901), 20 NZLR 572 (CA), foll'd in *Watt v. Westhoven*, [1933] VLR 458, held that the equitable remedies have not survived the SGA because s. 57(1), in preserving the general principles of law, only refers to "the rules of the common law." This rather subtle distinction has not been adopted in any reported Anglo-Canadian case and it did not appeal to the OLRC (Sales Report, at 142), which recommended against formal abolition of the equitable remedy. The same position, albeit in a broader setting, has been adopted in s. 1 of the British Misrepresentation Act 1967.

2) In *Leaf*'s case the plaintiff does not appear to have pleaded common mistake. What would have been the effect of his doing so?

3) *Ennis v. Klassen* (1990), 70 DLR (4th) 321 (Man. CA). In this case a divided Manitoba Court of Appeal debated at length the availability of rescission for innocent misrepresentation in an executed contract for the sale of a motor vehicle and the merits of making the remedy available where the representation also constitutes a term of the contract. The defendant originally bought a BMW car second hand from a third party believing it to be a 733 model. Shortly after taking delivery of the vehicle he discovered that it had been imported illegally into Canada and that it was a 728 model. There was no market for the model in Canada, spare parts would have to be imported from Germany, and the vehicle had negligible commercial value. The defendant, after learning these facts, adver-

tised the car for sale and described it in the classified advertisement and in the bill of sale as a "BMW 733." The plaintiff agreed to purchase the vehicle for $9,000 after he had examined and test driven it. The plaintiff knew (and was also told by the defendant) that the vehicle did not have an injection fuel system but still believed he was buying a "733" model. The defendant apparently did not disclose his own experience with the vehicle.

Shortly after having paid for and taken delivery of the vehicle, the plaintiff discovered it was only a "728" model. He drove it no more and demanded cancellation of the contract. Several months later he commenced an action for rescission, also alleging fraud on the defendant's part. He did not plead breach of the implied condition of description (see Ont. SGA, s. 14; *infra*, chapter 6). The trial judge found no fraudulent representations and dismissed the action.

On appeal, the majority (Huband JA, Monnin CJM) allowed rescission on the basis of innocent misrepresentation and held that rescission was available even in the case of an executed contract where the representation was fundamental in character. Taddle JA, dissenting, was of the view that the plaintiff had waited too long to claim rescission but that he should be allowed to amend his pleadings to claim damages for breach of the condition of description. The following passage (at 334-36) contains his reasoning on these points:

> To me, the essential fact is that the plaintiff bought the car on the basis of its description in the bill of sale as a "BMW 733." But the plaintiff's action was not based, as it surely might have been, on a breach of the implied condition that the car would correspond to its description. Instead, the plaintiff alleged fraud.
>
> It is unfortunate that the plaintiff chose to rely on a misrepresentation to found a cause of action when there was a much more straightforward basis of advancing the claim. The plaintiff could obtain the same remedies for breach of the condition as he could for fraudulent misrepresentation. And he would not have the burden of proving fraud.
>
> By the time the action came on for trial, the plaintiff must have realized that the evidence of fraud was weak. Although no amendment was made to the pleadings, it is clear from the judgment of Lockwood J that the plaintiff was then relying, in the alternative, on innocent misrepresentation as a basis for rescission.
>
> The law of innocent misrepresentation, in the case of a contract which has been performed, is in a state of doubt. Professor Waddams in his text, *The Law of Contracts*, 2nd ed., at p. 315, says this area of the law is "extraordinarily complex" and Professor Fridman in an article, "Error In Substantialibus. A Canadian Comedy of Errors," 56 Can. Bar Rev. 603 (1978), suggests that this area of law is erroneously dealt with in a number of decisions.
>
> This court might consider the point in some depth. But to what end? We might conclude that Lord Denning's dictum in *Leaf v. International Galleries*, [1950] 1 All ER 693 (CA), to the effect that innocent misrepresentation can give rise to rescission even where the purchase price of goods sold has been paid and delivery of them taken, should be followed. But we are still left with Lord Denning's own acknowledgment that rescission for innocent misrepresentation cannot be obtained where it is not available for breach of a condition.
>
> · · ·
>
> The real issues in this action are two. Should the plaintiff at this stage of the proceedings be allowed to rescind for breach of condition? If not, should he be allowed to amend his claim to include a claim for damages?

The great disadvantage of relying on an innocent misrepresentation, as distinct from a breach of condition, is that there is in law no alternative remedy to rescission. And if that right is lost, as it was in *Leaf v. International Galleries, supra*, and in *Long v. Lloyd*, [1958] 2 All ER 402, [1958] 1 WLR 753 (CA), the plaintiff gets nothing. On the other hand, a breach of a condition, even where the right to rescission has been lost, gives rise to a claim for damages.

I suspect that many of the decisions to which Professor Fridman refers in his article, were reached due to a reluctance on the part of judges to deny a wronged plaintiff a remedy. This is an understandable way of dealing with the problem, but is no substitute for law reform as exemplified by the *Misrepresentation Act, 1967* (UK), c. 7, which sanctioned damages as a remedy for innocent misrepresentation.

Section 13(3) of the *Sale of Goods Act*, RSM 1987, c. S10, provides as follows: [see Ont. SGA, s. 12(3)].

Section 37 of the same statute provides as follows: [see Ont. SGA, s. 34].

It is question of fact in every case as to whether breach of a condition entitles the buyer to rescind or, by reason of his acceptance of the goods, entitles him to damages only. In the present case, the learned trial judge did consider the availability of rescission, even though it was for misrepresentation rather than breach of contract, but said no. I do not believe this to be a case in which this court is justified in reaching a conclusion different from that of the learned trial judge.

This is a case in which the nature of the goods sold makes rescission an undesirable remedy. We are not talking about a painting, as was the case in *Leaf v. International Galleries, supra*, or some other item which retains its value and can be returned in exchange for the price without unfairness to the seller. What we have here is a motor car, an item which depreciates rapidly and which, left out in the open in Winnipeg, might well be the subject of physical deterioration.

Even if we accept that the plaintiff did the best he could to abort the sale once he discovered that the car had been misdescribed, there was a three-month delay before any formal step was taken to claim rescission and then the claim was made only on the ground of fraud, a ground rejected by the learned trial judge.

What we are being asked to do is order rescission well over two years after the car was delivered to the plaintiff and when timely repudiation, rejected by the trial judge, was at best poorly communicated to the defendant. To say that the equitable remedy of rescission is an appropriate one in such circumstances would be to cause much uncertainty as to ownership in cases, such as this, where there is a dispute as to the availability of the remedy. The better course, in my view, is to compensate the plaintiff in damages. Other buyers in similar circumstances would then know that they must mitigate their loss and not leave the property to depreciate and deteriorate to the eventual loser's cost.

Esso Petroleum Co. Ltd. v. Mardon

[1976] 2 WLR 583, [1976] 2 All ER 5 (CA)

[Mr. Mardon entered into a contract with Esso for the lease of an Esso service station in Southport. Before the contract was signed Mardon was told by Esso's officials that the estimated throughput of the service station was 200,000 gallons a year. The estimate was far out and the actual throughput turned out to be only 60,000 to 70,000 gallons a year. As a result the lease was a financial disaster for Mardon and he lost all the money he had invested in it. The parties' relationship deteriorated and eventually Esso sued for possession of the service station; Mardon counterclaimed seeking damages for breach of warranty and for negligent misrepresentation based on the false estimate of probable throughput of the service station.

The following extract from Lord Denning's judgment deals with the legal aspects of Mr. Mardon's counterclaim.]

LORD DENNING MR: Such being the facts, I turn to consider the law. It is founded on the representation that the estimated throughput of the service station was 200,000 gallons. No claim can be brought under the Misrepresentation Act 1967, because that Act did not come into force until April 22, 1967: whereas this representation was made in April 1963. So the claim is put in two ways. First, that the representation was a collateral warranty. Second, that it was a negligent misrepresentation. I will take them in order.

Collateral warranty

Ever since *Heilbut, Symons & Co. v. Buckleton*, [1913] AC 30, we have had to contend with the law as laid down by the House of Lords that an innocent misrepresentation gives no right to damages. In order to escape from that rule, the pleader used to allege—I often did it myself—that the misrepresentation was fraudulent, or alternatively a collateral warranty. At the trial we nearly always succeeded on collateral warranty. We had to reckon, of course, with the dictum of Lord Moulton, at 47, that "such collateral contracts must from their very nature be rare." But more often than not the court elevated the innocent misrepresentation into a collateral warranty: and thereby did justice—in advance of the Misrepresentation Act 1967 I remember scores of cases of that kind, especially on the sale of a business. A representation as to the profits that had been made in the past was invariably held to be a warranty. Besides that experience, there have been many cases since I have sat in this court where we have readily held a representation—which induces a person to enter into a contract— to be a warranty sounding in damages. I summarised them in *Dick Bentley Productions Ltd. v. Harold Smith (Motors) Ltd.*, [1965] 1 WLR 623, at 627, when I said:

> Looking at the cases once more, as we have done so often, it seems to me that if a representation is made in the course of dealings for a contract for the very purpose of inducing the other party to act upon it, and actually inducing him to act upon it, by entering into the contract, that is prima facie ground for inferring that it was intended as a warranty. It is not necessary to speak of it as being collateral. Suffice it that it was intended to be acted upon and was in fact acted on.

Mr. Ross-Munro retaliated, however, by citing *Bisset v. Wilkinson*, [1927] AC 177, where the Privy Council said that a statement by a New Zealand farmer that an area of land "would carry 2,000 sheep" was only an expression of opinion. He submitted that the forecast here of 200,000 gallons was an expression of opinion and not a statement of fact: and that it could not be interpreted as a warranty or promise.

Now I would quite agree with Mr. Ross-Munro that it was not a warranty—in this sense—that it did not *guarantee* that the throughput *would be* 200,000 gallons. But, nevertheless, it was a forecast made by a party—Esso—who had special knowledge and skill. It was the yardstick (the e.a.c.) by which they measured the worth of a filling station. They knew the facts. They knew the traffic in the town. They knew the throughput of comparable stations. They had much experience and expertise at their disposal. They were in a much better position than Mr. Mardon to make a forecast. It seems to me that if such a person makes a forecast, intending that the other should act upon it—and he does act upon it, it can well be interpreted as a warranty that the forecast is sound and reliable in the sense that they made it with reasonable care and skill. It is just as if Esso said to Mr. Mardon: "Our forecast of throughput is 200,000 gallons. You can rely upon it as being a sound forecast of what the service station should do. The rent is calculated on that footing." If the forecast turned out to be an unsound forecast such as no person of skill or experience should have made, there is a breach of warranty. Just as there is a breach of warranty when a forecast is made—"expected to load" by a certain date—if the maker has no reasonable grounds for it: see *Samuel Sanday and Co. v. Keighley, Maxted and Co.* (1922), 27 Com. Cas. 296; or bunkers "expected 600/700 tons": see *Efploia Shipping Corporation Ltd. v. Canadian Transport Co. Ltd. (The Pantanassa)*, [1958] 2 Lloyd's Rep. 449, at 455-57 by Diplock J. It is very different from the New Zealand case where the land had never been used as a sheep farm and both parties were equally able to form an opinion as to its carrying capacity: see particularly *Bisset v. Wilkinson*, [1927] AC 177, at 183-84.

In the present case it seems to me that there was a warranty that the forecast was sound, that is, Esso made it with reasonable care and skill. That warranty was broken. Most negligently Esso made a "fatal error" in the forecast they stated to Mr. Mardon, and on which he took the tenancy. For this they are liable in damages. The judge, however, declined to find a warranty. So I must go further.

Negligent misrepresentation

Assuming that there was no warranty, the question arises whether Esso are liable for negligent misstatement under the doctrine of *Hedley Byrne & Co. Ltd. v. Heller & Partners Ltd.*, [1964] AC 465. It has been suggested that *Hedley Byrne* cannot be used so as to impose liability for negligent pre-contractual statements: and that, in a pre-contract situation, the remedy (at any rate before the Act of 1967) was only in warranty or nothing. Thus in *Hedley Byrne* itself Lord Reid said, at 483: "Where there is a contract there is no difficulty as regards the contracting parties: the question is whether there is a warranty." And in *Oleificio Zucchi S.P.A. v. Northern Sales Ltd.*, [1965] 2 Lloyd's Rep. 496, at 519, McNair J said:

> ... as at present advised, I consider the submission advanced by the buyers, that the ruling in [*Hedley Byrne*, [1964] AC 465] applies as between contracting parties, is without foundation.

As against these, I took a different view in *McInerny v. Lloyds Bank Ltd.*, [1974] 1 Lloyd's Rep. 246, at 253 when I said:

> ... if one person, by a negligent misstatement, induces another to enter into a contract—with himself or with a third person—he may be liable in damages.

In arguing this point, Mr. Ross-Munro took his stand in this way. He submitted that when the negotiations between two parties resulted in a contract between them, their rights and duties were governed by the law of contract and not by the law of tort. There was, therefore, no place in their relationship for *Hedley Byrne*, [1964] AC 465, which was solely on liability in tort. He relied particularly on *Clark v. Kirby-Smith*, [1964] Ch. 506 where Plowman J held that the liability of a solicitor for negligence was a liability in contract and not in tort, following the observations of Sir Wilfrid Greene MR in *Groom v. Crocker*, [1939] 1 KB 194, at 206. Mr. Ross-Munro might also have cited *Bagot v. Stevens Scanlan & Co. Ltd.*, [1966] 1 QB 197, about an architect; and other cases too. But I venture to suggest that those cases are in conflict with other decisions of high authority which were not cited in them. These decisions show that, in the case of a professional man, the duty to use reasonable care arises not only in contract, but is also imposed by the law apart from contract, and is therefore actionable in tort. It is comparable to the duty of reasonable care which is owed by a master to his servant, or vice versa. It can be put either in contract or in tort: see *Lister v. Romford Ice and Cold Storage Co. Ltd.*, [1957] AC 555, at 587 by Lord Radcliffe and *Matthews v. Kuwait Bechtel Corporation*, [1959] 2 QB 57. The position was stated by Tindal CJ, delivering the judgment of the Court of Exchequer Chamber in *Boorman v. Brown* (1842), 3 QB 511, at 525-26:

> That there is a large class of cases in which the foundation of the action springs out of privity of contract between the parties, but in which, nevertheless, the remedy for the breach, or non-performance, is indifferently either assumpsit or case upon tort, is not disputed. Such are actions against attorneys, surgeons, and other professional men, for want of competent skill or proper care in the service they undertake to render: ... The principle in all these cases would seem to be that the contract creates a duty, and the neglect to perform that duty, or the nonfeasance, is a ground of action upon a tort.

That decision was affirmed in the House of Lords in (1844), 11 Cl. & Fin. 1, when Lord Campbell, giving the one speech, said, at 44:

> ... wherever there is a contract, and something to be done in the course of the employment which is the subject of that contract, if there is a breach of a duty in the course of that employment, the plaintiff may either recover in tort or in contract.

To this there is to be added the high authority of Viscount Haldane LC, in *Nocton v. Lord Ashburton*, [1914] AC 932, at 956:

> ... the solicitor contracts with his client to be skilful and careful. For failure to perform his obligation he may be made liable at law in contract or even in tort, for negligence in breach of a duty imposed on him.

That seems to me right. A professional man may give advice under a contract for reward, or without a contract, in pursuance of a voluntary assumption of responsibility, gratuitously without reward. In either case he is under one and the same duty to use reasonable care: see *Cassidy v. Ministry of Health*, [1951] 2 KB 343, at 359-60. In the one case it is by reason of a term implied by law. In the other, it is by reason of a duty imposed by law. For a breach of that duty he is liable in damages: and those damages should be, and are, the same, whether he is sued in contract or in tort.

It follows that I cannot accept Mr. Ross-Munro's proposition. It seems to me that *Hedley Byrne & Co. Ltd. v. Heller & Partners Ltd.*, [1964] AC 465, properly understood, covers this particular proposition: if a man, who has or professes to have special knowledge or skill, makes a representation by virtue thereof to another—be it advice, information or opinion—with the intention of inducing him to enter into a contract with him, he is under a duty to use reasonable care to see that the representation is correct, and that the advice, information or opinion is reliable. If he negligently gives unsound advice or misleading information or expresses an erroneous opinion, and thereby induces the other side to enter into a contract with him, he is liable in damages. This proposition is in line with what I said in *Candler v. Crane, Christmas & Co.*, [1951] 2 KB 164, at 179-80, which was approved by the majority of the Privy Council in *Mutual Life and Citizens' Assurance Co. Ltd. v. Evatt*, [1971] AC 793. And the judges of the Commonwealth have shown themselves quite ready to apply *Hedley Byrne*, [1964] AC 465, between contracting parties: see in *Sealand of the Pacific Ltd. v. Ocean Cement Ltd.* (1973), 33 DLR (3d) 625; and New Zealand *Capital Motors Ltd. v. Beecham*, [1975] 1 NZLR 576.

Applying this principle, it is plain that Esso professed to have—and did in fact have—special knowledge or skill in estimating the throughput of a filling station. They made the representation—they forecast a throughput of 200,000 gallons—intending to induce Mr. Mardon to enter into a tenancy on the faith of it. They made it negligently. It was a "fatal error." And thereby induced Mr. Mardon to enter into a contract of tenancy that was disastrous to him. For this misrepresentation they are liable in damages.

Defendant's appeal allowed;
plaintiff's cross-appeal dismissed.

[Ormrod and Shaw LJJ delivered concurring judgments.]

NOTES

1) *The test for collateral warranty*

(a) This is the first of the two major issues dealt with in *Esso v. Mardon*. The other one is the relationship between the *Hedley Byrne* doctrine and contractual warranties. It is discussed in note 2, *infra*. In *Heilbut, Symons & Co. v. Buckleton*, [1913] AC 30, which Lord Denning mentions in *Esso v. Mardon*, the House of Lords said that a statement cannot be classified as a warranty unless the representor made it with promissory intent ("*animus contrahendi*"). Otherwise the statement is a mere representation and this means the representee cannot sue *in contract* for damages. When is a statement made with promissory intent? The case law on this question is inconclusive. In *Esso v. Mardon*, Lord Denning quoted from his own judgment in *Dick Bentley Productions Ltd. v. Harold Smith (Motors) Ltd.*, [1965] 1 WLR 623, saying that if a representation has the purpose and effect of inducing the other party to enter into a contract, that is *prima facie* ground for inferring that a promise was intended. The textbooks by and large support this view. See, for example: S.M. Waddams, *The Law of Contracts*, 4th ed. (1999), at 294-97; Gunter Treitel, *The Law of Contract*, 10th ed. (1999), at 325-30. The courts infer that a representation had the purpose and effect of inducing a contract if, for example: (i) the representation diverted the representee from making independent inquiries to reveal the truth; (ii) but for the representation, the representee would not have entered into the contract at all; or (iii) the representor is in a better position than the representee to know the truth of the statement (for example, where the representor is a dealer and the representee is a private buyer): Treitel, at 327-29. A statement of opinion that is so vague that it cannot be verified is a "mere puff" and is not actionable, but a statement of opinion may imply that the representor has reasonable grounds for making it and the implied statement may be a term of the contract: Treitel, at 329.

To qualify as an actionable misrepresentation, a statement must be a material statement of fact which induced the representee to make the contract. The test of materiality is whether the statement would induce a reasonable person to enter into the contract. There are two relevant considerations: (i) what the statement is about (would a reasonable person have thought the statement was important?) and (ii) the circumstances in which the statement was made (would a reasonable person have taken the representor seriously?) A representation is material in these two senses if a reasonable person would not have entered into the contract but for the representation at least without making her own inquiries first: Treitel, at 310-16.

It will be apparent that the question of whether a statement amounts to an actionable misrepresentation turns on more or less the same variables as the question of whether a statement is a term of the contract. This suggests that the representation-contractual warranty distinction is a purely formal one—a distinction without a difference. Why do the courts maintain it? A possible reason is that the distinction provides a way out in cases where the court thinks that contract damages are inappropriate. The consequence of saying that the statement was a mere representation and not a warranty will be to deny the representee compensation for expectation losses. The representee may still have an action for damages, but the action will be in tort, not contract, and in tort compensation is typically limited to the plaintiff's reliance loss. This rationalization assumes a rigid distinction between the contract and tort measure of damages which the case law does not necessarily support: see further, (e), below.

(b) Formally, Anglo-Canadian law still says that the test of a warranty turns on proof of promissory intention, but if the representation was made with the purpose and effect of inducing the contract, the court will typically infer the representor's intent: see (a), above. Compare the reliance test, first formally adopted in American law in s. 12 of the American Uniform Sales Act (1906) on the initiative of its drafter, Professor Williston. The reliance test makes no reference to promissory intent, but turns simply on whether the representee reasonably relied on the representor's statement when entering into the contract. Williston's historical research convinced him that the claim for breach of warranty was originally an action on the case for deceit (that is, a tortious claim) and that only in the second half of the 18th century did such claims sound in contract. Williston thought that *Heilbut, Symons & Co. v. Buckleton*, [1913] AC 30 (HL) was wrongly decided. See his "Representation and Warranty in Sales—*Heilbut v. Buckleton*" (1913), 27 *Harv. L Rev.* 1, as well as his earlier "What Constitutes an Express Warranty in the Law of Sales?" (1908), 21 *Harv. L Rev.* 555. The Ontario Law Reform Commission endorsed the reliance test in its Report on Warranties and Guarantees (at 28-29) and its Report on Sale of Goods (at 135 *et seq.*) The Saskatchewan Consumer Protection Act, SS 1996, c. C-30.1, s. 45(1) provides as follows:

> Any promise, representation, affirmation of fact or expression of opinion or any action that reasonably can be interpreted by a consumer as a promise or affirmation relating to the sale or to the quality, quantity, condition, performance or efficacy of a consumer product or relating to its use or maintenance, made verbally or in writing directly to a consumer or through advertising by a retailer seller or manufacturer, or his agent or employee who has actual, ostensible or usual authority to act on his behalf, shall be deemed to be an express warranty if it would usually induce a reasonable consumer to buy the product, whether or not the consumer actually relies on the warranty.

This is a broad statutory version of the reliance test. It is broad in the sense that it applies whether or not the consumer representee actually relied on the warranty. Compare Consumer Product Warranty and Liability Act, SNB 1980, s. C-18.1, s. 4.

The US Uniform Sales Act 1906 has been replaced by UCC 2-313, which governs express warranties. It provides in part that "any affirmation of fact or promise made by the seller to the buyer which relates to the goods and becomes part of the basis of the bargain creates an express warranty that the goods shall conform to the affirmation or promise." The provision substitutes "basis of the bargain" for reliance as the test of an express warranty. The basis of the bargain test raises questions that are just as difficult as the English requirement for proof of promissory intent. Proposed amendments to Article 2 are currently under consideration, but the most recent draft under consideration (and approved by the ALI in May, 2001: see, *supra*, chapter 1) makes no changes to the law in this respect.

(c) Should representations by private sellers be treated on the same footing as dealer representations? The English case law on this question is unsettled. In *Oscar Chess Ltd. v. Williams*, [1957] 1 WLR 370, the defendant (a private individual) sold his car to the plaintiff (a dealer) for 280 pounds. The defendant mistakenly described the car as a 1948 Morris 10, whereas in fact it was a 1939 model worth 175 pounds. The court held the statement was not a term of the contract, mainly because the buyer was in at least as good a position as the seller to know whether the statement was true. *Dick Bentley Productions Ltd. v. Harold Smith (Motors) Ltd.* represents the reverse case. There the seller was a dealer and the buyer was a private individual. The court held that the seller's incorrect statement about the car's age was a warranty. The two cases together suggest that it *does* matter to know whether the representor was a dealer. However, in *Beale v. Taylor*, [1967] 1 WLR 1193, reproduced in Chapter 6, *infra*, a car was sold by a private seller to a private buyer. The seller misstated the car's age, and the court treated the representation as a term of the contract. The seller (who represented himself) apparently did not argue that the statement was a "mere representation." The case seems to be inconsistent with *Oscar Chess Ltd. v. Williams*, but it may be distinguishable on the ground that in *Oscar Chess* the seller was a dealer. As between a private seller and a private buyer, where neither party is an expert, it is not as obviously true to say that the buyer is in at least as good a position as the seller to discover the truth. In fact, the seller may have the advantage because being in possession of the goods gives her an ongoing opportunity for inspection and discovery, whereas a buyer will typically have only a one-off opportunity of examination at the point of purchase.

(d) In the *Dick Bentley* case, Lord Denning said that if a statement has the purpose and effect of inducing a contract, that is *prima facie* ground for inferring that a promise was intended: see (a), above. However, he went on to say that the inference could be rebutted by proof that the representor was not negligent. This additional statement has not been well received. As Treitel points out (at 328), it is hard to reconcile with cases where representors have escaped liability for breach of contract without having disproved fault. The landmark case of *Redgrave v. Hurd* (1881), 20 Ch. D 1 is a prime example. In *Esso v. Mardon*, the representor's negligence was relevant to the warranty question, but that was because of what the warranty said. The court found a warranty on Esso's part that it had used reasonable care and skill in making the forecast. This meant that Esso's negligence went to the question of breach. It is quite a different thing to say that the representor's negligence also has a bearing on the question of whether a statement amounts to a warranty in the first place.

The justification for holding a representor liable for negligent misstatements is clear enough. Proof of negligence implies that there were cost-effective precautions the representor could have taken to discover the truth. A ruling in favour of the representee gives the representor in future cases an incentive to take precautions. What is the justification for imposing strict liability on the representor? The answer is that a strict liability rule gives representors an incentive to be careful in a secondary sense: it encourages them to be circumspect in cases where they cannot be sure of their information by adding a qualification or disclaimer. A disclaimer is a signal to the representee that there is no cost-effective way of discovering the truth or, alternatively, that it is cheaper for the representee to investigate. The effect of the disclaimer is to transfer to the representee the risk of loss if the statement turns out to be untrue. If there is no cost-effective way of discovering the truth, the representee will then have to decide whether to terminate the negotiations or to carry on, perhaps seeking an adjustment of the contract price to compensate for the risk of an unfavourable outcome. Alternatively, if it is cheaper for the representee to investigate, the representee will have to decide whether the cost of investigation is worthwhile given the value of the contract opportunity. Either way, the effect of the disclaimer is to minimize the risk of mistakes: see Bishop, "Negligent Misrepresentation Through Economists' Eyes" (1980), 96 *LQR* 360.

(e) Breach of contract typically entitles the plaintiff to recover expectation or loss of bargain damages and it is this consideration that lies at the heart of the representation-warranty characterization debate: see (a), above. However, there is no reason in principle why the plaintiff should *necessarily* be entitled to expectation damages. The outcome should turn on the nature of the promise. The cases tend to bear this out. *Esso v. Mardon* itself is a case in point. Esso was held liable in tort for negligence and also for breach of warranty, but the damages on both counts were the same. Given the nature of Esso's promise, the claimant was not entitled to expectation damages on the breach of warranty ground. What Esso warranted was not the truth of its forecast, but simply that it had used reasonable care and skill in making it. In *Marks v. GIO Holdings Australia* (1998), 196 CLR 494 (High Court of Australia), Gaudron J stressed that the expectation and reliance measures of damages signify different kinds of loss. The successful plaintiff in a breach of contract case typically recovers expectation damages because the plaintiff's loss is the non-performance of the contract. In tort, no question of expectation loss can arise. The plaintiff's complaint is not about the defendant's failure to keep a promise. It is about the defendant's failure to leave the plaintiff alone. The general principle underlying both damages measures is the same, namely that compensation is for loss actually suffered. The implication is that for some breaches of warranty the reliance measure of damages, rather than the loss of bargain measure, may be the appropriate one. See also *British Columbia Hydro and Power Authority v. BG Checo International Ltd.* (1993), 99 DLR (4th) 577, at 591-94 *per* La Forest and McLachlin JJ (on damages in contract and tort in cases of concurrent liability).

2) *The* Hedley Byrne *doctrine and warranty law*

(a) *Esso v. Mardon* establishes that an action may lie in tort for negligent misstatement based on *Hedley Byrne & Co. Ltd. v. Heller & Partners Ltd.,* [1964] AC 465, in respect of wrong information or advice given by one contracting party to another in the course of precontractual negotiations. Canadian law is the same: see especially *BG Checo*, above and *Queen v. Cognos Inc.* (1993), 99 DLR (4th) 626. These and other cases are discussed in Lewis N. Klar, *Tort Law*, 2nd ed. (Carswell, 1996), at 192-96. However, there must be a duty of care arising out of a special relationship between the parties. The mere fact that the statement was made in the course of precontractual negotiations is not enough to satisfy this requirement. According to Klar (*op. cit.*, at 182-88), in determining whether or not a special relationship exists, the courts have focussed on factors such as the following: (i) the skill of the advisor; (ii) the skill of the advisee; (iii) the nature of the occasion; (iv) whether the advice was solicited; and (v) the nature of the advice (was it a statement of fact or an expression of opinion, was it firm or speculative, was it qualified in any relevant way?).

(b) In the circumstances these guidelines refer to, it will often be found that the statement in issue is promissory. If so, the representee will have an action for breach of warranty against the representor and will not need to sue in tort. The significance of the tort action's availability depends on how liberally warranty law is applied. The more strictly the courts insist on proof of contractual intention to support a warranty, the more the alternative cause of action in tort will matter. Conversely, the closer the courts move to a simple reliance test, the less work there will be for the alternative cause of action in tort to do.

(c) But for the Supreme Court of Canada's decision in *J. Nunes Diamonds Ltd. v. Dominion Electric Protection Co.*, [1972] SCR 769, one would anticipate little difficulty about Canadian courts following *Mardon's* case on the availability of the tortious claim in addition to any claim for breach of contract regardless of when the negligent representation was made.

The reasoning, if not the actual decision, in *Nunes'* case has been widely criticized by commentators and subsequent Canadian courts have shown a ready willingness to distinguish it and to follow *Mardon*. *Mardon* was followed, *inter alia*, by the Ontario Court of Appeal in *Sodd Corp. v. Tessis* (1977), 79 DLR (3d) 632, where Lacourcière JA, speaking for the court, held the defendant, a chartered accountant and licensed trustee in bankruptcy, liable for a negligent misrepresentation respecting the value of a bankrupt's inventory offered for sale. *Nunes* was distinguished as not involving an independent tort, whereas the case at bar, like *Mardon*, was concerned with a pre-contractual representation which induced the formation of the contract. See also *Ronald Elwyn Lister Ltd. v. Dunlop Canada Ltd.* (1978), 85 DLR (3d) 321 (Ont. HC), where Rutherford J found that *Nunes* presented no bar to recovery in tort for pre-contractual negligent misrepresentations, and *Sealand of the Pacific Ltd. v. Robert C. McHaffie Ltd.* (1974), 51 DLR (3d) 702 (BCCA) where a similar distinction was drawn. Can or should a distinction be drawn between pre-contractual and intra-contractual representations in terms of the *Hedley Byrne* doctrine? What little credibility *Nunes Diamonds* retains as a substantive doctrine appears to have been undermined by the Supreme Court's decision in *Central Trust Co. v. Rafuse,* [1986] 2 SCR 147, reaffirmed in *Winnipeg Condominium Corp. No. 36 v. Bird Construction Co.* (1995), 121 DLR (4th) 193, holding that the existence of a contractual relationship (in this case between a solicitor and his client) does not preclude the existence of an action in tort. Of course, a contract can always exclude any other remedy but this is a question of documentary construction, not of substantive law.

For further discussion of the above issues see B. Reiter, "Contracts, Torts, Relations and Reliance," Study 8 in B. Reiter and J. Swan (eds.), *Studies in Contract Law* (1980), at 235; S. Schwartz, "Annual Survey of Canadian Law: Part 3: Contracts" (1976), 8 *Ott. L Rev.* 588, at 618-26; and J. Blom, "The Evolving Relationship between Contract and Tort" (1985), 10 *CBLJ* 257.

3) *The parol evidence rule*

(a) A well-drafted sales agreement will invariably contain a "merger" clause precluding the admissibility of extrinsic evidence to prove representations or terms not contained in the contract document: see *supra*. Even if there is no merger clause, the parol evidence rule may apply. The parol evidence rule says that extrinsic evidence is not admissible to modify the terms of a written contract. The justification for merger clauses and the parol evidence rule is easy enough to see. They give the seller a way of preventing unauthorised representations by employees and perhaps also unverifiable claims by the buyer. Both equally destroy the predictability and efficiency of the seller's standard form contract. On the other hand, an indiscriminate application of the parol evidence rule—with or without the support of a merger clause—may cause serious injustice by defeating the parties' real intentions.

(b) In *Mendelssohn v. Normand Ltd.*, [1970] 1 QB 177, the English Court of Appeal laid down the following rule (at 183-84):

> There are many cases in the books when a man has made, by word of mouth, a promise or a representation of fact, on which the other party acts by entering into the contract. In all such cases the man is not allowed to repudiate his representation by reference to a printed

condition, ... nor is he allowed to go back on his promise by reliance on a written clause ... The reason is because the oral promise or representation has a decisive influence on the transaction—it is the very thing which induces the other to contract—and it would be most unjust to allow the maker to go back on it. The printed condition is rejected because it is repugnant to the express oral promise or representation.

However, the Supreme Court of Canada has repeatedly held that evidence of a collateral warranty is inadmissible unless it is consistent with the main contract: *Hawrish v. Bank of Montreal*, [1969] SCR 515; *Bauer v. Bank of Montreal* (1980), 110 DLR (3d) 424; *Carman Construction Ltd. v. CPR*, [1982] 1 SCR 958. These cases seem to suggest that a written document is binding according to its terms regardless of what the parties say and do in the lead-up to signature. They are open to criticism on the ground that a party who induces signature to a document by saying something inconsistent with its contents cannot be said to have a reasonable expectation of the other party's assent; the representor cannot reasonably suppose that the signer intended the document to prevail over what the representor said: Waddams, at 247. The passage from *Mendelssohn v. Normand* quoted above was approved by the British Columbia Court of Appeal in *Zippy Print Enterprises Ltd. v. Pawliuk*, [1995] 3 WWR 324. See also *Gallen v. Allstate Grain Co. Ltd.* (1984), 9 DLR (4th) 496 (BCCA) and *Corey Developments Inc. v. Eastbridge Developments (Waterloo) Ltd.* (1997), 34 OR (3d) 73 (Gen. Div.) aff'd. (1999), 44 OR (3d) 95 (CA). However, the law remains unsettled pending the Supreme Court's reconsideration of the issue.

(c) Section 4(7) of the Ontario Business Practices Act in effect abolishes the parol evidence rule for consumer transactions. See also Trade Practices Act, RSBC 1996, c. 457, s. 29; Consumer Protection Act, SS 1996, c. C-30.1, s. 46; and Consumer Product Warranty and Liability Act, SNB 1978, c. C-18.1, s. 5. The English Law Commission, in a 1976 Working Paper, took the much bolder step of recommending abolition of the rule for *all* purposes: see English Law Commission, Working Paper No. 70, *Law of Contracts, The Parol Evidence Rule*.[1] The recommendation was endorsed by the OLRC with respect to contracts for the sale of goods (see OLRC Sales Report at 110-16) and, *semble,* for all contractual purposes by the Law Reform Commission of British Columbia in its Report No. 44 on *The Parol Evidence Rule* (1979). The OLRC reaffirmed its earlier position in its *Amendment of the Law of Contract* report, chapter 8, especially at 163. None of these recommendations has so far been implemented.

Abrogation of the rule does not mean, of course, that the extrinsic evidence must be believed; it simply means the court is free to review all the relevant evidence with a view to determining the true agreement between the parties. Nevertheless, businesses may wonder how, without the benefit of the parol evidence rule, they are able to protect themselves against unauthorized representations or invest any confidence in the conclusiveness and finality of their standard form agreements. What answer would you give?

---

1 The Law Commission changed its position in its final report. It did so on the ground that, properly understood, the rule requires no legislative amendment and that the rule only amounts to the proposition that if parties intend a document to be the exclusive record of their agreement, that intention will prevail. See further, Waddams, "Two Contrasting Approaches to the Parol Evidence Rule" (1986-87), 12 *CBLJ* 207.

Do you see any intermediate solution between abrogation of the parol evidence rule and maintenance of the status quo?

4) *Statutory developments*

(a) *United Kingdom.* The Misrepresentation Act 1967 (UK) among other things: (i) introduced a statutory damages remedy for non-fraudulent misrepresentation; (ii) removed various common law barriers to rescission for non-fraudulent misrepresentation; (iii) gave the courts a discretion to disallow rescission and award damages instead; and (iv) limited the representor's right to rely on exclusion clauses. Section 2(1) is the damages provision. It provides:

> Where a person has entered into a contract after a misrepresentation has been made to him by another party thereto and as a result thereof he has suffered loss, then, if the person making the misrepresentation would be liable to damages in respect thereof had the misrepresentation been made fraudulently, that person shall be so liable notwithstanding that the misrepresentation was not made fraudulently, unless he proves that he had reasonable ground to believe and did believe up to the time the contract was made that the facts represented were true.

The provision gives the representee a right of action for damages without the need to prove fraud on the representor's part or that the representation amounted to a promise. Nor does the representee have to prove negligence, but the representor can escape liability by proving that "he had reasonable ground to believe" that the facts represented were true. The reference to fraud imports the tort, or reliance, measure of damages.

(b) *United States.* UCC 2-313 governs express warranties. Section 2-313 currently provides as follows:

> Express warranties are created by the seller as follows:
>
> (a) Any affirmation of fact or promise made by the seller to the buyer which relates to the goods and becomes part of the basis of the bargain creates an express warranty that the goods shall conform to any affirmation or promise.
>
> (b) Any description of the goods which is made part of the basis of the bargain creates an express warranty that the goods shall conform to the description.
>
> (c) Any sample or model which is made part of the basis of the bargain creates an express warranty that the whole of the goods shall conform to the sample or model.

The provision creates a statutory right of action for damages, but only in relation to representations that become "part of the basis of the bargain."

Section 2-313 imposes obligations on the seller to the immediate buyer only. Proposed amendments to Article 2 are currently under consideration. The latest draft (May, 2001) adds two new provisions, ss. 2-313A and 2-313B, which impose warranty-type obligations on the seller to remote purchasers in certain cases: see further, *infra.*

(c) *Business practices laws.* The Business Practices Act, RSO 1990, c. B.18, s. 4, creates a statutory right of action for damages in relation to false and misleading consumer representations. It also confers a right of rescission and allows for an award of compensation in lieu of rescission. Other provinces have similar legislation. The federal Competition Act, RSC 1985, c. C-34, s. 36(1), is a similar provision, but it is limited in effect to (i) representations in advertising that (ii) (since 1999 amendments) are know-ingly or recklessly false or misleading (i.e., fraudulent). The Australian Trade Practices Act, 1974 (Cth), (TPA), also creates a statutory right of action for damages in relation to false or misleading representations. However, in contrast to the Canadian Competition Act, the TPA imposes strict liability on the representor and it is not limited to advertising representations. Moreover, in contrast to the Ontario and other provincial laws, the TPA misleading conduct provision is not limited to consumer transactions. It is a measure of general application. There are not many reported cases on the Canadian provisions. By contrast, the TPA misleading conduct provision is probably the most heavily litigated statu-tory provision in Australia and it is certainly one of the most significant reforms to have been made to Australian commercial law. The case law decided under it has radically transformed the law of misrepresentation. The most noteworthy features are as follows: (i) the test of a misleading statement is an objective one and it is determined by the likely effect of the statement on a typical member of the audience to which the statement is directed; (ii) damages are available without proof of fault on the representor's part and whether or not the statement was promissory; (iii) the measure of damages is the amount of the claimant's loss as a result of the misrepresentation and this is to be determined on first principles rather than by drawing analogies with tort and contract cases; (iv) dam-ages can be awarded against the representor or other persons involved in the contraven-tion, such as the representor's directors, employees, or agents; (v) discretionary relief, including rescission, contract variation and restitution orders, can be given as an alterna-tive to a damages award; and (vi) liability cannot be excluded except to the extent that a disclaimer has the effect of (A) negating the misleading tendency of the representor's other statements, or (B) breaking the chain of causation between the representor's con-duct and the representee's loss. The main limitations on the TPA provision are that it applies only if: (i) the representor's conduct was "in trade or commerce"; and (ii) as a general rule, the representor is a corporation. The first limitation means in effect that the representation must relate to a business transaction of some kind (though not necessarily a retail sale). The TPA provision does not apply to private dealings. The second limitation derives from the fact that the Commonwealth parliament does not have plenary power under the Australian Constitution to legislate with respect to trade and commerce. The TPA is an exercise mainly of the power to legislate with respect to corporations. How-ever, the States have enacted mirror-image fair trading laws to fill the gap. The State fair trading laws cover all persons, not just corporations.

CHARACTERIZATION OF CONTRACTUAL TERMS

Cehave N.V. v. Bremer Handelsgesellschaft m.b.H.

[1976] 1 QB 44 (CA)

LORD DENNING MR: In 1970, the sellers, a German company, agreed to sell to the buyers, a Dutch company, 12,000 metric tons of US citrus pulp pellets. Those pellets are a by-product of oranges. The juice is extracted and tinned. The orange rinds are dried and made into pellets. The pellets are used as an ingredient in making cattle food.

In September 1970, there were two contracts of sale, each for 6,000 metric tons, delivery in bulk [to] be made by six instalments of 1,000 tons each over the first six months of 1971. Under the first contract of September 24, the price was $73.50 per metric ton. Under the second contract of September 28, the price was $73.75. In each case c.i.f. Rotterdam. Each contract incorporated the terms issued by the Cattle Food Trade Association, form 100, for shipment of feeding stuffs in bulk "Talequale c.i.f. terms." That form contained two sentences material to this dispute in clause no. 7: "Shipment to be made in good condition ... each shipment shall be considered a separate contract."

The first three or four shipments were quite satisfactory. This case is concerned with a shipment made early in May 1971. It was by the German vessel the *Hansa Nord*. She took on about 3,400 metric tons of citrus pulp pellets at Port Manatee in Florida. Four bills of lading were issued. They were appropriated by the sellers as follows: two were for 1,000 tons each on the second contract. One for 1,000 tons and one for 419,856 tons on the first contract. But there was no physical appropriation of the cargo as between the two contracts.

On May 14 the buyers paid the price and got the shipping documents. The *Hansa Nord* arrived in Rotterdam on Friday, May 21, and started unloading on Saturday, May 22. It was finished by May 25. The cargo was discharged into lighters. The out-turn weights were:

Ex-hold no. 1 ... 1,260 metric tons
Ex-hold no. 2 ... 2,053 metric tons.

It is to be noticed that by this time the market price had fallen greatly. The contract price for these 3,400 tons was (when converted into sterling) about £100,000. But the market price on May 24 in Rotterdam was, for sound goods, only £86,000. This may give an explanation of subsequent happenings.

The cargo ex. no. 2 hold (2,053 tons) was in good condition. But some of the cargo ex. no. 1 hold (1,260 tons) was found to be damaged. On May 24 the buyers rejected the whole cargo (both no. 2 and no. 1 holds) on the ground that it was not shipped in good condition and they claimed repayment of the purchase price of £100,000. On the next day the sellers refused, saying that the goods were shipped in good condition: and that the damage must have occurred at sea and that the buyers ought to lodge their claim with the insurers.

So there it was. The goods were in the lighters with both sellers and buyers disclaiming ownership. Now comes an astonishing sequence of events. There was a Mr. Baas in Rotterdam who was an importer of feeding products (including citrus pulp pellets). On May 29, 1971, if not before, he inspected the cargo in the lighters. On June 1, 1971, the lighter owners applied ex parte to the Rotterdam County Court, the Commercial Court I expect, asking it to authorize a sale of the goods. They applied by their lawyer, a Mr. Driessen. The sellers were not told of this application. But the buyers were. They were represented by the same lawyer as the lighter owners, Mr. Driessen. On the same day this court granted the application and authorised the sale. It appointed agents to make the sale. The agents approached Mr. Baas. They did not approach any other possible bidders. They sold the whole cargo to Mr. Baas (out of both no. 2 and no. 1 holds) for a sum equivalent to £33,720. The expenses of sale were deducted, leaving the net proceeds at £29,903. These were paid into a Dutch bank "to the order of whom it may concern." On the self-same day, Mr. Baas sold the whole cargo to the buyers (i.e., the original buyers under the two contracts) at the same price and upon the same terms as he had himself bought them from the agents of the court. The board of appeal found:

> as a fair inference from the evidence … that the buyers and Mr. Baas intended that he (Baas) should acquire the cargo for their (the buyers') benefit, or on their behalf.

> . . .

Having bought the whole cargo from Mr. Baas, the buyers transported it in the same way as they would have done if it had never suffered any damage. They took the lighters by canal to their plant at Veghel, a journey of some 60 miles. The buyers then used the entire cargo to manufacture cattle food at their processing plant at Veghel. They used it in the self-same way as they would sound goods except that they used "smaller percentages in their compound feeds than would be normal with sound goods." This difference in manufacture did not cause them any loss. At any rate, there is no finding that it did. And it was surely for them to prove it.

The upshot of it all was, therefore, that the buyers took the whole cargo and used all of it for their business just as if they had never rejected it save for the smaller percentages. So the ubiquitous Mr. Baas had helped them greatly. They paid only £33,720 for it instead of the contract price of £100,000. The board of appeal of the trade association felt it necessary to make this comment:

> We wish to record that we are not satisfied that we have been presented with a full account of how the goods were disposed of in Rotterdam after rejection by the buyers. The witnesses produced by the buyers gave contradictory evidence on this question, as well as on other less vital issues.

That is a devastating comment. The buyers must have known the truth. But they did not tell it to the board of appeal. At any rate, not the whole truth.

Nevertheless, despite that devastating comment, the board of appeal made their award in favour of the buyers. They ordered the sellers to repay to the buyers the £100,000 with interest, and directed the proceeds of sale (£29,903) to be repaid to the sellers. So the buyers have got the entire cargo and used it for their cattle food, but instead of paying £100,000 for it, they have only paid them £30,000. The judge has upheld this award [1974] 2 Lloyd's Rep. 216, at 227. The sellers appeal to this court. They recognise that they may have to pay something by way of damages for the damaged goods, but they deny that the buyers had any right to reject the whole cargo.

The board of appeal found a breach of the express clause "Shipped in good condition." They said:

> … on the balance of probability, not all the goods in hold no. 1 were shipped in good condition as required by the contract, nor on balance of probability were they reasonably fit to be carried on the contemplated voyage.

The board of appeal also found a breach of the implied condition as to merchantability contained in section 14(2) of the Sale of Goods Act 1893. They said:

> The goods in hold 1 were "merchantable" on arrival in Rotterdam in a commercial sense, though at a lower price than would be paid for sound goods: we find and hold, however, that they were not "of merchantable quality" within the meaning of the phrase when used in the Sale of Goods Act 1893.

The board of appeal did not find a breach of the implied condition of fitness contained in section 14(1) of the Act. They found all the elements about reliance and so forth, but they did not find that the goods were unfit. They could hardly have found them unfit, seeing that they were in fact used for that purpose.

"Shipped in good condition"

The judge held that, in contracts for the sale of goods, a stipulation must either be a "condition" or a "warranty" and that there could be no tertium quid. Accepting that distinction, he held that this stipulation "shipped in good condition" was a "condition" and not a "warranty" [1974] 2 Lloyd's Rep. 216, at 225; so that, for any breach of it by the seller, the buyer was entitled to treat the contract as repudiated.

Those decisions by the judge are so important that they deserve careful consideration.

The general law apart from the sale of goods

For the last 300 or 400 years the courts have had to grapple with this problem: in what circumstances can a party, who is in breach himself of a stipulation of the contract, call upon the other side to perform his part or sue him for non-performance? At one time the solution was thought to depend on the nature of the stipulation itself, and not on the extent of the breach or its consequences. Under the old forms of pleading, a plaintiff had to aver and prove that he had performed all conditions precedent or that he was ready and willing to perform them. The question, therefore, was whether the stipulation (which he had broken) was a condition precedent or not; or, in the terminology of the 18th century, whether it was an *independent* covenant (the breach of which did not debar him from suing the other side), or a *dependent* covenant (the breach of which did debar the plaintiff because the performance by the other was *dependent* on the plaintiff performing his). This distinction was well stated by Serjeant Williams in his notes to *Pordage v. Cole* (1969), 1 Wms. Saund. 319, at 320(b):

> ... where there are several covenants, promises or agreements, which are *independent* of each other, one party may bring an action against the other for a breach of his covenants, etc. without averring a performance of the covenants, etc. on his, the plaintiff's part; and it is no excuse for the defendant to allege in his plea a breach of the covenants, etc. on the part of the plaintiff; ... But where the covenants, etc. are *dependent*, it is necessary for the plaintiff to aver and prove a performance of the covenants, etc. on his part, to entitle himself to an action for the breach of the covenants on the part of the defendant; ...

Although that division was treated as exhaustive, nevertheless, when the courts came to apply it, they had regard to the extent of the breach. This was done by Lord

Mansfield in 1777 in the great case of *Boone v. Eyre (Note)* (1777), 1 Hy. Bl. 273, of
which there was no satisfactory record until Lord Kenyon in 1796 produced a manuscript note of it: see *Campbell v. Jones* (1796), 6 Term Rep. 570, at 573 and *Glazebrook
v. Woodrow* (1799), 8 Term Rep. 366, at 373. It is summarised in the notes to *Cutter
v. Powell* (1795), 6 Term Rep. 320 (*Smith's Leading Cases*, 13th ed. (1929), vol. 2,
at 16-17). The plaintiff conveyed to the defendant a plantation in the West Indies,
together with the stock of negroes on it, in consideration of £500 down and an annuity of £100 a year, and covenanted that he had a good title to the plantation and was
lawfully possessed of the negroes. Some time later the defendant discovered that the
plaintiff had no title to the negroes and stopped paying the annuity. The court held
that the defendant was liable to pay the annuity. He could not escape simply because
the plaintiff had not "a title to a few negroes." His remedy was to bring a cross-action
for damages. It would be different "if the plaintiff had no title at all to the plantation
itself" (see 8 Term Rep. 366, at 374): for then the plaintiff could not have recovered
the annuity. In the language of those times, if the breach went to the whole consideration, the covenant was considered to be a condition precedent and the defendant could
plead the breach in bar of the action: but if the breach went

> only to a part, where a breach may be paid for in damages, there the defendant has a
> remedy on his covenant, and shall not plead it as a condition precedent (1 Hy. Bl. 273n.).

In short, if the breach went to the root of the matter, the stipulation was to be
considered a condition precedent: but if the breach did not go to the root, the stipulation was considered to be an independent covenant which could be compensated for
in damages: see *Davidson v. Gwynne* (1820), 12 East 381, at 389, *per* Lord Ellenborough
CJ; *Ellen v. Topp* (1851), 6 Exch. 424, at 441; and *Graves v. Legg* (1854), 9 Exch.
709, at 716.

Apart from those cases of "breach going to the root," the courts at the same time
were developing the doctrine of "anticipatory breach." When one party, before the
day when he is obliged to perform his part, declares in advance that he will not perform it when the day comes, or by his conduct evinces an intention not to perform it,
the other may elect to treat his declaration or conduct as a breach going to the root of
the matter and to treat himself as discharged from further performance: see *Hochster
v. De la Tour* (1853), 2 E & B 678. By his prior declaration or conduct, the guilty
party is said to repudiate the contract. The word "repudiation" should be confined to
those cases of an *anticipatory* breach, but it is also used in connection with cases of
an *actual* breach going to the root of the contract: see *Heyman v. Darwins Ltd.*, [1942]
AC 356, at 378-79 by Lord Wright. All of them were gathered together by Lord
Blackburn in his famous speech in *Mersey Steel and Iron Co. Ltd. v. Naylor, Benzon
& Co.* (1884), 9 App. Cas. 434, at 443-44:

> The rule of law, as I always understood it, is that where there is a contract in which
> there are two parties, each side having to do something (it is so laid down in the notes to
> *Pordage v. Cole*, 1 Wms. Saund. 319, at 320) if you see that the failure to perform one
> part of it goes to the root of the contract, goes to the foundation of the whole, it is a
> good defence to say, "I am not going on to perform my part of it when that which is the

root of the whole and the substantial consideration for my performance is defeated by your misconduct." … I repeatedly asked Mr. Cohen whether or not he could find any authority which justified him in saying that every breach of a contract … must be considered to go to the root of the contract, and he produced no such authority. There are many cases in which the breach may do so; it depends upon the construction of the contract.

Those last words are clearly a reference to a "condition" strictly so called, in which any breach entitled the other to be discharged from further performance. But the earlier words are quite general. They refer to all terms other than conditions strictly so called.

The Sale of Goods Act

Such was the state of the law when the Sale of Goods Act 1893 was passed on February 20, 1894. I have studied the then current edition of *Benjamin, Sale of Personal Property*, 4th ed. (1888), and the little books which Judge Chalmers wrote before (1890) and after the Act (*Chalmers' Sale of Goods Act*, 1893, 1st ed. (1894)), and the proceedings in Parliament. These show that until the year 1893 there was much confusion in the use of the words "condition" and "warranty." But that confusion was removed by the Act itself and by the judgment of Bowen LJ in *Bentsen v. Taylor, Sons & Co.*, [1893] 2 QB 274, at 280. Thenceforward those words were used by lawyers as terms of art. The difference between them was that if the promisor broke a *condition* in any respect, however slight, it gave the other party a right to be quit of his obligations and to sue for damages: unless he by his conduct waived the condition, in which case he was bound to perform his future obligations but could sue for the damage he had suffered. If the promisor broke a *warranty* in any respect however serious, the other party was not quit of his future obligations. He had to perform them. His only remedy was to sue for damages: see *The Mihalis Angelos*, [1971] 1 QB 164, at 193 and *Wickman Machine Tool Sales Ltd. v. L. Schuler A.G.*, [1972] 1 WLR 840, at 851.

Now that division was not exhaustive. It left out of account the vast majority of stipulations which were neither "conditions" nor "warranties" strictly so called: but were intermediate stipulations, the effect of which depended on the breach. The cases about these stipulations were legion. They stretched continuously from *Boone v. Eyre (Note)*, 1 Hy. Bl. 273, in 1777 to *Mersey Steel and Iron Co. Ltd. v. Naylor, Benzon & Co.* (1884), 9 App. Cas. 434. I cannot believe that Parliament in 1893 intended to give the go-by to all these cases: or to say that they did not apply to the sale of goods. Those cases expressed the rules of the common law. They were preserved by section 61(2) of the Act of 1893, which said:

> The rules of the common law, including the law merchant, save in so far as they are inconsistent with the express provisions of this Act … shall continue to apply to contracts for the sale of goods.

There was nothing in the Act inconsistent with those cases. So they continued to apply.

In 1962 in the *Hong Kong Fir Shipping Co. Ltd. v. Kawasaki Kisen Kaisha Ltd.*, [1962] 2 QB 26, the Court of Appeal drew attention to this vast body of case law.

They showed that, besides conditions and warranties, strictly so called, there are many stipulations of which the effect depends on this: if the breach goes to the root of the contract, the other party is entitled to treat himself as discharged: but if it does not go to the root, he is not. In my opinion, the principle embodied in these cases applies to contracts for the sale of goods just as to all other contracts.

The task of the court can be stated simply in the way in which Upjohn LJ stated it at 64. First, see whether the stipulation, on its true construction, is a condition strictly so called, that is, a stipulation such that, for any breach of it, the other party is entitled to treat himself as discharged. Second, if it is not such a condition, then look to the extent of the actual breach which has taken place. If it is such as to go to the root of the contract, the other party is entitled to treat himself as discharged: but, otherwise, not. To this may be added an anticipatory breach. If the one party, before the day on which he is due to perform his part, shows by his words or conduct that he will not perform it in a vital respect when the day comes, the other party is entitled to treat himself as discharged.

"Shipped in good condition"

This brings me back to the particular stipulation in this case: "Shipped in good condition." Was this a condition strictly so called, so that *any* breach of it entitled the buyer to reject the goods? Or was it an intermediate stipulation, so that the buyer cannot reject unless the breach is so serious as to go to the root of the contract?

If there was any previous authority holding it to be a *condition* strictly so called, we should abide by it, just as we did with the clause "expected ready to load": see *Finnish Government (Ministry of Food) v. H. Ford & Co. Ltd.* (1921), 6 Ll. L Rep. 188; *The Mihalis Angelos*, [1971] 1 QB 164. But, there is no such authority with the clause "shipped in good condition." I regard this clause as comparable to a clause as to quality, such as "fair average quality." If a small portion of the goods sold was a little below that standard, it would be met by commercial men by an allowance off the price. The buyer would have no right to reject the whole lot unless the divergence was serious and substantial: see *Biggin & Co. v. Permanite Ltd.*, [1951] 1 KB 422, at 439, *per* Devlin J and *Christopher Hill Ltd. v. Ashington Piggeries Ltd.*, [1972] AC 441, at 511, *per* Lord Diplock. That is shown in this very case by clause 5 in form no. 100 which contains percentages of contamination, below which there is a price allowance, and above which there is a right in the buyer to reject. Likewise with the clause "shipped in good condition." If a small portion of the whole cargo was not in good condition and arrived a little unsound, it should be met by a price allowance. The buyers should not have a right to reject the whole cargo unless it was serious and substantial. This is borne out by the difficulty which often arises (as in this case) on a c.i.f. contract as to whether the damage was done before shipment or took place after shipment: for in the latter case the buyer would have no claim against the seller but would be left to his claim against the insurers. So, as matter of good sense, the buyers should be bound to accept the goods and not reject them unless there is a serious and substantial breach, fairly attributable to the seller.

In my opinion, therefore, the term "shipped in good condition" was not a condition strictly so called: nor was it a warranty strictly so called. It was one of those intermediate stipulations which gives no right to reject unless the breach goes to the root of the contract.

On the facts stated by the board of appeal, I do not think the buyer was entitled to reject these instalments of the contract. The board only said that "not all the goods in hold no. 1 were shipped in good condition." That does not say how many were bad. In any case, their condition cannot have been very bad, seeing that all of them were in fact used for the intended purpose. The breach did not go to the root of the contract. The buyer is entitled to damages, but not to rejection.

Appeal allowed.

[Roskill and Ormrod LJJ delivered concurring judgments.]

Bunge Corporation v. Tradax Export S.A.

[1981] 1 WLR 711, [1981] 2 Lloyd's Rep. 1 (HL)

[In January 1974 the buyers agreed to buy from the sellers 15,000 tons of US soya bean meal, shipment to be made at the rate of 5,000 tons in each of May, June and July 1975 f.o.b. one US Gulf port at seller's option. Each of the parties issued its own contract note which, while differing slightly (and, as was found, inconsequentially) in language, agreed in requiring the buyers to give the sellers 15 days' loading notice. The contract also included the terms and conditions of GAFTA 119, cl. 7 of which provided:

7. Period of delivery: During _____ at Buyers' call. Buyers shall give at least _____ consecutive days notice of probable readiness of vessel(s) and of the approximate quantity required to be loaded ...

The parties agreed that, in the light of the contract notes, cl. 7 should be read as if it required the buyer to give at least 15 days' notice of probable readiness of vessel.

The parties subsequently agreed to extend the time for delivery of the May shipment until June. The sellers received notice of readiness to load at 08:46 hours on June 17, 1975, i.e., less than 15 days before the extended shipment date. They rejected the notice because of its lateness and subsequently claimed damages from the buyers for breach of contract. The dispute was referred to arbitration. The umpire found in the sellers' favour. The Board of Appeal of GAFTA affirmed his decision subject to stating a special case for the court's opinion.

On the hearing of the special case Parker J reversed the Board of Appeal's decision on the ground that cl. 7 of GAFTA 119 was an innominate term; that after receiving the notice the sellers were still left with 4/5 of the stipulated period of notice and that the shortfall did not come near to depriving them of substantially the whole benefit which it was intended they should obtain from the contract.

The Court of Appeal unanimously reversed. The House of Lords, equally unanimously, affirmed.]

LORD WILBERFORCE: The appeal depends upon the construction to be placed upon clause 7 of GAFTA form 119 as completed by the special contract. It is not expressed as a "condition" and the question is whether, in its context and in the circumstances it should be read as such.

Apart from arguments on construction which have been fully dealt with by my noble and learned friend, the main contention of Mr. Buckley for the appellant was based on the decision of the Court of Appeal in *Hongkong Fir Shipping Co. Ltd. v. Kawasaki Kisen Kaisha Ltd.*, [1962] 2 QB 26, as it might be applied to clause 7. Diplock LJ in his seminal judgment illuminated the existence in contracts of terms which were neither, necessarily, conditions nor warranties, but, in terminology which has since been applied to them, intermediate or innominate terms capable of operating, according to the gravity of the breach, as either conditions or warranties. Relying on this, Mr. Buckley's submission was that the buyer's obligation under the clause, to "give at least [15] consecutive days' notice of probable readiness of vessel(s) and of the approximate quantity required to be loaded," is of this character. A breach of it, both generally and in relation to this particular case, might be, to use Mr. Buckley's expression, "inconsequential," i.e. not such as to make performance of the seller's obligation impossible. If this were so it would be wrong to treat it as a breach of condition: *Hongkong Fir* would require it to be treated as a warranty.

This argument, in my opinion, is based upon a dangerous misunderstanding, or misapplication, of what was decided and said in *Hongkong Fir*. That case was concerned with an obligation of seaworthiness, breaches of which had occurred during the course of the voyage. The decision of the Court of Appeal was that this obligation was not a condition, a breach of which entitled the character to repudiate. It was pointed out that, as could be seen in advance the breaches, which might occur of it, were various. They might be extremely trivial, the omission of a nail; they might be extremely grave, a serious defect in the hull or in the machinery; they might be of serious but not fatal gravity, incompetence or incapacity of the crew. The decision, and the judgments of the Court of Appeal, drew from these facts the inescapable conclusion that it was impossible to ascribe to the obligation, in advance, the character of a condition.

Diplock LJ then generalised this particular consequence into the analysis which has since become classical. The fundamental fallacy of the appellants' argument lies in attempting to apply this analysis to a time clause such as the present in a mercantile contract, which is totally different in character. As to such a clause there is only one kind of breach possible, namely, to be late, and the questions which have to be asked are, first, what importance have the parties expressly ascribed to this consequence, and secondly, in the absence of expressed agreement, what consequence ought to be attached to it having regard to the contract as a whole.

The test suggested by the appellants was a different one. One must consider, they said, the breach actually committed and then decide whether that default would deprive the party not in default of substantially the whole benefit of the contract.

They invoked even certain passages in the judgment of Diplock LJ in the *Hongkong Fir* case, [1962] 2 QB 26 to support it. One may observe in the first place that the introduction of a test of this kind would be commercially most undesirable. It would expose the parties, after a breach of one, two, three, seven and other numbers of days to an argument whether this delay would have left time for the seller to provide the goods. It would make it, at the time, at least difficult, and sometimes impossible, for the supplier to know whether he could do so. It would fatally remove from a vital provision in the contract that certainty which is the most indispensable quality of mercantile contracts, and lead to a large increase in arbitrations. It would confine the seller—perhaps after arbitration and reference through the courts—to a remedy in damages which might be extremely difficult to quantify. These are all serious objections in practice. But I am clear that the submission is unacceptable in law. The judgment of Diplock LJ does not give any support and ought not to give any encouragement to any such proposition; for beyond doubt it recognises that it is open to the parties to agree that, as regards a particular obligation, any breach shall entitle the party not in default to treat the contract as repudiated. Indeed, if he were not doing so he would, in a passage which does not profess to be more than clarificatory, be discrediting a long and uniform series of cases—at least from *Bowes v. Shand* (1877), 2 App. Cas. 455 onwards which have been referred to by my noble and learned friend, Lord Roskill. It remains true, as Lord Roskill has pointed out in *Cehave N.V. v. Bremer Handelsgesellschaft m.b.H. (The Hansa Nord)*, [1976] QB 44, that the courts should not be too ready to interpret contractual clauses as conditions. And I have myself commended, and continue to commend, the greater flexibility in the law of contracts to which *Hongkong Fir* points the way (*Reardon Smith Line Ltd. v. Yngvar Hansen-Tangen (trading as H.E. Hansen-Taggen)*, [1976] 1 WLR 989, at 998). But I do not doubt that, in suitable cases, the courts should not be reluctant, if the intentions of the parties as shown by the contract so indicate, to hold that an obligation has the force of a condition, and that indeed they should usually do so in the case of time clauses in mercantile contracts. To such cases the "gravity of the breach" approach of the *Hongkong Fir Case*, [1962] 2 QB 26 would be unsuitable. I need only add on this point that the word "expressly" used by Diplock LJ at 70 of his judgment in *Hongkong Fir* should not be read as requiring the actual use of the word "condition": any term or terms of the contract, which, fairly read, have the effect indicated, are sufficient. Lord Diplock himself has given recognition to this in this House: *Photo Production Ltd. v. Securicor Transport Ltd.*, [1980] AC 827, at 849. I therefore reject that part of the appellants' argument which was based upon it, and I must disagree with the judgment of the learned trial judge in so far as he accepted it. I respectfully endorse, on the other hand, the full and learned treatment of this issue in the judgment of Megaw LJ in the Court of Appeal.

. . .

LORD ROSKILL: ... In short, while recognising the modern approach and not being overready to construe terms as conditions unless the contract clearly requires the court so to do, none the less the basic principles of construction for determining whether or not a particular term is a condition remain as before, always bearing in mind on the one hand the need for certainty and on the other the desirability of not, when legitimate, allowing rescission where the breach complained of is highly technical and where damages would clearly be an adequate remedy. It is therefore in my opinion wrong to use the language employed by Diplock LJ in the *Hongkong Fir* case, [1962] 2 QB 26 as directed to the determination of the question which terms of a particular contract are conditions and which are only innominate terms.

. . .

NOTES

1) As will be seen in subsequent chapters, the seller's implied obligations in SGA ss. 13-16 of title, description, merchantability, fitness for purpose, and conformity to sample are all treated as conditions. Is this wise in the light of what occurred in *Cehave, supra,* and having regard to the many other reported illustrations of the operation of the implied terms? The OLRC Sales Report (at 145-47) felt that a system of *a priori* characterization was too rigid and could lead to inefficient results. The Report therefore favoured eliminating the distinction in the SGA between warranties and conditions, and substituting a common nomenclature of warranties to describe express or implied terms relating to goods. The Report further recommends the adoption of a unitary concept of substantial breach to determine the remedies available for breach of contract by the seller or buyer and, in particular, to determine when an aggrieved party may cancel the contract because of breach by the other. In the light of Lord Wilberforce's reasoning in *Bunge* do these recommendations err too much on the side of flexibility?

2) As the Sales Report notes, the Vienna Sales Convention also avoids *a priori* characterization of terms. Instead, the parties' remedies under the Convention depend on whether or not the breach is of a fundamental character. See arts. 49 and 64. According to art. 25, a breach is fundamental,

> if it results in such detriment to the other party as substantially to deprive him of what he is entitled to expect under the contract, unless the party in breach did not foresee and a reasonable person of the same kind in the same circumstances would not have foreseen such a result.

How would a court applying this test determine the dispute in *Bunge Corp. v. Tradax*?

3) Amendments in 1994 to the English Sale of Goods Act 1979 added a new s. 15A, which reads in part as follows:

> (1) Where in the case of a contract of sale—
>> (a) the buyer would, apart from this subsection, have the right to reject goods by reason of a breach on the part of the seller of a term implied by section 13, 14 or 15 above, but
>> (b) the breach is so slight that it would be unreasonable for him to reject them,
>
> then, if the buyer does not deal as a consumer, the breach is not to be treated as a breach of condition but may be treated as a breach of warranty.
>
> (2) This section applies unless a contrary intention appears in, or is to be implied from, the contract.
>> (3) It is for the seller to show that breach fell within subsection (1)(b) above.

The provision is based on recommendations made by the English and Scottish Law Commissions in their report on the *Sale and Supply of Goods* (Cmn 137, May 1987). How is this reform different from what the OLRC had in mind? What is the justification for limiting the reform to non-consumer transactions?

In Australia, the New South Wales Sale of Goods Act 1923 was amended in 1988 to include the following provision:

> Nothing in this Act shall be construed as excluding a right to treat a contract of sale as repudiated for a sufficiently serious breach of a stipulation that is neither a condition nor a warranty but is an intermediate stipulation.

How does this provision compare with s. 15A of the English Act?

4) Outside sales law, American law generally adopts an innominate term test in determining the consequences of a breach of contract. In the area of sales law, however, American law has long adopted "the perfect tender" rule (that is, a rule of strict compliance with all terms of the sales contract), and this rule appears in UCC 2-601. However, this Draconian rule is tempered in important respects by offsetting provisions in other parts of Article 2. See *infra*, chapter 16, Note on "Recasting the Buyer's Rights of Rejection."

MANUFACTURERS' REPRESENTATIONS

Seller's Adoption of Manufacturer's Representations

Cochran v. McDonald

(1945), 161 P.2d 305 (Wash. Sup. Ct.)

GRADY J: This action was originally brought by O.K. Cochran against Winterine Manufacturing Company, a corporation, to recover damages for breach of warranty. In an amended complaint H.D. McDonald, doing business as McDonald & Company, was joined as a defendant. The plaintiff was unable to secure legal service of process upon Winterine Manufacturing Company, and the case proceeded to trial against McDonald & Company as the sole defendant. At the close of the evidence submitted by the plaintiff its sufficiency was challenged by the defendant, which challenge was sustained by the court and a judgment was entered dismissing the action. The motion of the plaintiff for a new trial was denied and this appeal followed.

The factual situation as disclosed by the record is as follows: Winterine Manufacturing Company manufactured a product known as Antarctic Antifreeze to be used in motor vehicles to prevent freezing in cold weather. The company assigned to respondent the western part of Washington for the distribution of its product and he purchased from it a large quantity of the antifreeze. The antifreeze was put up in sealed gallon jugs and to each jug the manufacturer affixed a label upon which was printed the following:

> Antarctic Antifreeze. The Manufacturer's Guarantee on Antarctic Antifreeze is Insured by an Old Line Casualty Company. Manufactured by Winterine Manufacturing Company, Denver, Colorado.

Guarantee. The Manufacturer of this Antifreeze Guarantees: 1. If used according to directions, in a normal cooling system, Antarctic Antifreeze will protect the cooling system from freezing for a full winter season. 2. It will not cause rust or deteriorate the hose, radiator or engine of your car. 3. It will not cause damage to the finish of your car. 4. It will not evaporate. 5. It will not leak out of a cooling system tight enough to hold water.

Directions for Use. Do not mix with any other antifreeze. Drain cooling system, make certain it is clean and leakproof. Put in proper amount of Antarctic to afford the required freezing protection. (See your dealer's "Protective Chart.") Add water. Fill to within about 2 inches of top of radiator.

The respondent sold a quantity of the antifreeze to Huletz Auto Electric Co. and resold it to a Texaco service station. The appellant purchased a gallon jug of the antifreeze from the service station. Before making the purchase appellant read what was on the label. He testified that this induced him to buy the antifreeze and that he relied upon the representations printed thereon. Appellant put the antifreeze in the radiator of his automobile. Damage was done to the radiator and motor of appellant's automobile. An analysis of the antifreeze showed that it contained highly corrosive elements and was unfit for the purpose designed. The inherently dangerous character of the article was not known to respondent and there was nothing about it as handled by him indicating anything out of the ordinary. It was only upon use of the antifreeze that its character became known.

The appellant presents three grounds of liability of respondent to him:

(1) Upon the express warranty printed upon the label affixed to the article by the manufacturer.

(2) Upon an implied warranty of fitness for the purpose intended when the article resold is noxious and dangerous to property.

(3) Upon an implied warranty of fitness for the purpose intended under the Uniform Sales Act.

We shall discuss the foregoing in the order set forth.

(1) The question presented is whether a wholesaler, who purchases goods from the manufacturer of them who has affixed a written warranty of quality or fitness for the purpose intended by reselling the goods to a vendee, is liable upon the warranty to an ultimate purchaser who relies upon the warranty in making his purchase, puts the goods to use and suffers damage to his property by reason of a breach of the warranty.

In our discussion of this branch of the case we shall refer only to express warranties as the subject of implied warranty is treated later in this opinion.

We have not found in our research many cases dealing with the precise question we are now considering, but the courts passing upon the question, and the text writers, seem to agree that the applicable principle of law is that a dealer is not liable upon an express warranty of a manufacturer which is put out with or attached to the goods manufactured unless he, in some way, adopts the warranty and makes it his own when selling the goods to others, and that by merely selling the goods he does not adopt the warranty of the manufacturer as his own. *Pemberton v. Dean*, 88 Minn. 60, 92 NW 478, 60 LRA 311, 97 Am. St. Rep. 503; *Cool v. Fighter*, 239 Mich. 42,

214 NE 162; *Wallace et al. v. McCampbell*, 178 Tenn. 224, 156 SW 2d 442, 55 CJ Sales, 684, 687.

In 55 CJ, *supra*, the author states:

> A purchaser of personal property with warranty, who in reselling it to another adopts, by his conduct at the resale, the warranty of his seller, thereby assumes a warranty of the same character as that which was expressly accorded to him. The fact of resale does not itself constitute an adoption of prior warranties so as to render the seller liable for failure of the goods to comply with such warranties, and this is true even though the words of warranty are physically affixed to the goods.

. . .

Judgment affirmed.

NOTES

1) See also *Courtesy Ford Sales, Inc. v. Farrior* (1974), 298 So. 2d 26 (Ala. CA) and *Bill McDavid Oldsmobile, Inc. v. Mulcahy* (1976), 533 SW 2d 160 (Tex. CA), in both of which the courts held that an automobile dealer was not a party to the manufacturer's warranty delivered by him to the buyer at the time of sale. In *Farrior* the court said (at 31):

> The question then arises as to whether the dealer can be held liable for the guarantees of the manufacturer. We have been cited to no cases, nor have we found any, so holding. It has been decided, however, that unless a dealer specifically adopts the warranty of the manufacturer then he is not bound thereby. *Cool v. Fighter*, 239 Mich. 42, 214 NW 162; *Pemberton v. Dean*, 88 Minn. 60, 92 NW 478; *Wallace v. McCampbell*, 178 Tenn. 224, 156 SW 2d 442; *Cochran v. McDonald*, 23 Wash. 2d 348, 161 P. 2d 305. There is no evidence that Courtesy Ford adopted the warranty sued on. Appellate argues that Courtesy Ford is bound by the warranty issued by Ford Motor Company and cites *General Motors v. Earnest*, 279 Ala. 299, 184 So. 2d 811 as authority. In the *Earnest* case, the dealer admitted that he was liable under the manufacturer's warranty, but in the instant case, the dealer has steadfastly maintained that it was not liable under the manufacturer's warranty. Therefore, we do not perceive how *Earnest* could be apt authority for the contention that Courtesy Ford is bound by Ford Motor's warranty.

Can one fairly draw a distinction between adoption of a manufacturer's labelling on a package (for example, identifying the goods, their weight, or the purpose for which they are to be used) and adoption of a manufacturer's performance warranty? If there is no distinction, and there is no presumption of adoption in either case, how does one determine what the merchant has agreed to sell and what his responsibilities are under the implied conditions of description and merchantability in SGA ss. 14 and 15? Despite its obvious importance, there does not appear to be a reported English or Canadian case in which the merchant seller's deemed adoption of the manufacturer's description of the goods or a warranty relating to the goods has squarely arisen for decision.

2) UCC 2-314(2)(f) provides that, to be of merchantable quality, goods must conform to promises or statements of fact appearing on the label or container. Compare this approach with Ontario's Bill 110, s. 7(2), which would hold a retailer jointly liable with the manu-

facturer for express warranties made in writing or published or broadcast by the manufacturer. Contrast Competition Act s. 52(2), which deems a representation of the types described (including a representation expressed on an article offered or displayed for sale, its wrapper or container) to be made to the public by, and only by, the person to be so expressed, made or contained.

3) In its Sales Report, the OLRC recommended (at 204) that:

> the general proposition should be that a description of the goods given by a third person is binding on the seller only if by his words or conduct he has adopted the description as his own.

See also Draft Bill, s. 5.11(2).

This general recommendation was qualified in two respects. First, in its Report on Consumer Warranties and Guarantees the OLRC had recommended that, in a consumer sale, promises or affirmations on or accompanying goods should be deemed to be an express warranty by the seller, whether or not the seller had actually caused the promise or statement to be made. Second, with respect to all sales by merchants, the Sales Report recommended a slightly enlarged version of UCC 2-314(2)(f) as one of the requirements of the warranty of merchantability. The Commission reasoned that this imposed no greater hardship on the merchant than holding him responsible for the merchantability and fitness of goods produced by someone else and that the merchant, if sued, would be entitled to claim indemnity from the party actually responsible for the labelling. See OLRC Warranties Report, at 34-35, and OLRC Sales Report, at 204-6. Compare Consumer Protection Act, SS 1996, c. C-30.1, s. 47:

> (1) A retail seller shall be deemed to be a party to express warranties contained on labels or packages accompanying or attached to a consumer product sold by him to a consumer unless he has made it clear to the consumer prior to the sale that he does not adopt the express warranties.
>
> (2) Subject to subsection (3), no retail seller shall be deemed to be a party to any express warranties contained in any advertisement originating from or carried out by a manufacturer unless he expressly or impliedly adopts such warranties.
>
> (3) Notwithstanding that retail seller does not adopt the express warranties mentioned in subsections (1) and (2), any descriptive statements that appear on the label or container or otherwise accompany the consumer product shall, for the purposes of paragraph 3 of section 11, be deemed to be part of the description of the product.

See also Consumer Product Warranty and Liability Act, SNB 1978, c. C-18.1.

Green v. Jo-Ann Accessory Shop Ltd.

(1983), 21 Man. R 261

FERG CCJ: Plaintiff sues for $238.30, under Part II of the County Courts Act, the sum claimed being $168.00 for "failure to receive refund from defendant of garment which is unsatisfactory" and $70.30 claimed as out-of-pocket expenses.

. . .

The "garment" in question is a Kappi, 100% polyester, black and white dress. The plaintiff's complaint is as described in a letter by the plaintiff to the manufacturer, Dolman Dress Company, Montreal as follows:

> This dress has been worn three times and it requires a pressing after each wearing. The dress creases so badly that after a brief period it looks like circular accordion pleats in front and of course, is very creased if I have been sitting. The label states the dress is 100% polyester.

In addition, the plaintiff sent the dress to the Manitoba Department of Health for testing. Eleanor Menzies a clothing and textile specialist reported by mail (Exhibit #5) in part as follows:

> The dress was tested at the University of Manitoba Textile Lab and was found to be 100% polyester. The labelling is correct.
> ... Polyester has always been, and still is, noted for its crease resistance and easy care. There is no new polyester fibre on the market, but the way in which it is used in some yarns does not meet our expectations of being crease-resistant.

The plaintiff as well complained to the Consumer and Corporate Affairs Canada, Winnipeg office who in part replied,

> I am at a loss as to why this garment made out of 100% polyester would crease to that extent as one of the good characteristics of polyester is crease resistance ...

Dolman Dress in a letter to the plaintiff states in part, (Exhibit #9),

> The word polyester on the label denotes only the type of yarn in the cloth, which could make the fabric washable or dry cleanable. However, very few woven garments are completely crease resistant. Garments made in a knitted polyester fabric are the most crease resistant. This is not the case in the dress you purchased and therefore it has to be touched up with the iron.

Here, it must be noted as it is very significant that the label on the dress contains an emblem in red, an iron with an "X" over it signifying "Do Not Iron or Press" as set out in the National Standard of Canada publication Can. 2-86.1-M 79 (Exhibit #20).

The plaintiff's contention, quite understandable, is that she, as a consumer upon seeing that symbol is entitled to expect that the dress would not crease or certainly not to the extent her undisputed evidence indicated it did crease after wear, as no "ironing or pressing" is indicated or necessary.

It is significant too that Consumer and Corporate Affairs Canada in a letter to the plaintiff (Exhibit #16) states in part:

> I have to agree there is no such thing as 100% crease resistant polyester, that is why we advise consumers when buying such garments to do a hard wrinkle test in order to determine whether the garment will crease or not. The only course of action that could be taken is if there are some type of care instructions on the label such as "do not iron." If there is please advise me and I will advise our office in Montreal to pursue this course.

This "course" was pursued, and the court was told by Mr. Russell Dolinski of the Brandon office of Consumer and Corporate Affairs Canada, that the Manufacturer Dolman Dress, have now changed the label by deleting the iron symbol entirely— thus obviously admitting, in the court's opinion, that the "Do not iron or press" symbol on the label was in fact misleading and as it in fact did mislead the plaintiff, she stating that the symbol "do not iron" led her to believe the dress would not crease to the extent it did or at all.

The defendant refused to make a refund or any adjustment and relied on the correspondence indicating the dress was indeed 100% polyester, and the label was not misleading. The court rejects that defence as the fact is, as indicated, the label was misleading to the extent noted and since rectified by the manufacturer.

· · ·

There is no doubt in this court's opinion, that the "Do Not Iron or Press" symbol on the dress label, was misleading and the dress purchased was not what the symbol would lead an ordinary consumer to believe, that is, that the dress would be practically crease resistant which in fact it was not. Here, there has been a breach of an implied condition and under s. 13(3) of the *Sale of Goods Act*, RSM 1987, c. S.10, that breach is to be treated as a breach of warranty, the plaintiff having paid for and accepted the dress.

The plaintiff is entitled to damages which in this case would be the cost of a replacement dress to the same value, namely, $168.00. The judgment will be against the corporate defendant only, the other defendant not having had any personal connection at all with the sale and purchase.

Judgment for plaintiff in part.

QUESTIONS

Was this case correctly decided? Is it consistent with the reasoning in *Cochran v. McDonald*? Should Ms Green have been required instead to sue the manufacturer of the dress or of the fabric and, if so, on what basis?

The Privity Issue: Manufacturers' Liability for Express Representations

Murray v. Sperry Rand Corp.

(1979), 5 BLR 284, 96 DLR (3d) 113 (Ont. HC)

REID J: This action concerns the purchase by the plaintiff of a forage harvester.

At the relevant times:

(a) Plaintiff was a farmer.

(b) Sperry Rand Corporation was the American manufacturer of the forage harvester.

(c) Sperry Rand Canada Limited was the Canadian distributor of the machine.

(d) Farm Supplies and Services was a business carried on by the late Charles Church in Barrie, Ontario. It was the New Holland dealer. For convenience I refer to this company, and the late Charles Church, as "Church."

(e) The forage harvester was the New Holland S.P. 818. "S.P." stood for "self-propelled."

A forage harvester simultaneously cuts and chops hay and grass crops. Plaintiff had been thinking for some time about purchasing a new forage harvester. He owned one and had used it for some time. It was not a self-propelled type. That is, it had to be pulled by a tractor. He was particularly interested in a self-propelled type because he had a back problem. He hoped to avoid having to twist in his seat on the tractor, a necessary part of pulling a harvester.

He had seen the S.P. 818 in action at a ploughing match and, on a later occasion, displayed at a stand operated by Church at the 1967 Barrie Fall Fair. He discussed the machine with Church's salesman Hogarth, who was at the stand. Hogarth gave him a sales brochure describing the machine. Plaintiff took the brochure home and read it for several nights. It described the machine's features and performance. He was particularly interested in the "fineness of the cut," that is to say, the size to which the machine would chop the crops it harvested. The quality of silage rose as the fineness increased. He was also interested in the productive capacity of the machine for he was planning to expand his operations. On these points the brochure said:

> You'll fine-chop forage to $3/16$ of an inch ... season after season!
>
> You'll harvest over 45 tons per hour with ease, ...
>
> Under test conditions, the big New Holland harvesters have harvested well over 60 tons per hour.
>
> And Micro-Shear cutting action gives you a choice of crop fineness—from $3/16$ of an inch to $2\frac{1}{4}$.

In consequence of his interest, Church and Hogarth visited plaintiff's farm. So did William Hutchinson, a representative of Sperry Rand Canada. In the course of the conversations that occurred on these visits, plaintiff explained his type of farming and the operation for which he intended the machine. He received assurances that the harvester would perform as described in the brochure, that it was ideally suited to plaintiff's type of farming, and that it would do a better job than his existing machine.

In the result, plaintiff placed an order for the harvester. It was dated September 26, 1967, addressed to Farm Supplies and Services and signed by plaintiff as purchaser. It was accepted by Hogarth on behalf of Church as vendor. The order was written out on the date it bears by Hutchinson at plaintiff's farm. This was on the occasion of a meeting between plaintiff and Hutchinson at plaintiff's farm when the S.P. 818 was discussed at length.

The price was $12,600.

The harvester was delivered to plaintiff. He began to use it. This litigation arose out of his repeated but unsuccessful attempts to operate the harvester at anything like the promise of the brochure.

During the long course of these attempts plaintiff complained to Chuch and both Sperry Rand Companies. These complaints were responded to with interest and reasonable alacrity. The machine suffered from the problem, described by the experts who testified, of "wrappage." That is to say, the crop being cut fouled the cutting apparatus. This caused frequent stops to free it. The result was repeated delays. Defendants sent machines and technicians to the farm. They inspected and adjusted, replaced and modified parts over several years.

There is absolutely no question, however, that despite all their efforts Church and the Sperry Rand Companies were unable to achieve the level of performance set forth in the brochure, or get reasonably near it. After their best efforts the manufacturer's representatives were able to achieve a rate of only 16 tons per hour while operating it themselves at plaintiff's farm. This corresponds with plaintiff's calculations in July 1970. This was a far cry from the 46-60 tons per hour advertised in the sales brochure.

The abject failure of the machine seriously delayed plaintiff's harvest. This had a number of unfortunate consequences. Part of the crop was lost entirely. Much of what was harvested was over-ripe. This reduced the value of the silage made from it. Plaintiff's plans to raise and board cattle were frustrated. Ultimately he sold the harvester and gave up farming.

. . .

On the evidence I make the following findings:

(1) Plaintiff was induced to purchase the harvester through oral representations made by the personnel of Church and Sperry Rand Canada and through the sales brochure prepared and published by Sperry Rand Corporation.

(2) The performance of the machine fell seriously short of that represented in the sales brochure.

In relation to liability, the real questions in this litigation are not questions of fact. There is no doubt about the failure of the machine. It was confirmed very clearly by the evidence of both defendants. Defendants' attempts, particularly those of Sperry Rand Corporation, to blame the failure of the machine upon plaintiff were unsuccessful. There is no question in my mind that the machine failed because of an inherent defect or because the machine was not suitable for plaintiff's farming conditions, or both. Defendant manufacturer denied that the machine suffered from an inherent defect. Yet it was not able to explain why in the hands of its own people the machine would not perform properly.

(3) I find also that the consequence of the machine's failure was damage suffered by plaintiff.

[Reid J found that (1) Church was liable as a signatory to the contract and as a party to the representations; (2) the representations made to the plaintiff were collateral warranties because they were made with the intention of inducing contractual relations; (3) the plaintiff was entitled to the benefit of the implied conditions of fitness for purpose and merchantable quality in SGA s. 15; and (4) the contract's disclaimer clause was ineffective in its attempt to exclude the implied conditions or the collateral warranties. Reid J continued:]

The Liability of the Manufacturer

Sperry Rand Corporation was not a party to the written contract between plaintiff and Church. It had manufactured the harvester. It had also published the sales brochure.

I refer to it as a sales brochure notwithstanding evidence from an official of Sperry Rand Corporation that it was not intended to persuade people to buy the machines it describes. That view is, in my opinion, contradicted by the brochure itself. Its tone is strongly promotional. It goes far beyond any simple intention to furnish specifications. It was, in my opinion, a sales tool. It was intended to be one and was used in this case as one.

The representations contained in it, so far as they related to this litigation have already been set out. In the circumstances of this case those representations amounted to collateral warranties given by the manufacturer.

It is, in my opinion, the law that a person may be liable for breach of a warranty notwithstanding that he has no contractual relationship with the person to whom the warranty is given: *Shanklin Pier Ltd. v. Detel Products Ltd.*, [1951] 2 KB 854, [1951] 2 All ER 471, [1951] 2 Lloyd's Rep. 187; *Traders Finance Corpn. v. Haley; Haley v. Ford Motor Co.* (1966), 57 DLR (2d) 15, at 18, affirmed 62 DLR (2d) 329 (SCC); *Andrews v. Hopkinson*, [1957] 1 QB 229, [1956] 3 All ER 422. See also K.W. Wedderburn, *Collateral Contracts* (1959), *Cambridge LJ* 48, at 68 and Cheshire and Fifoot, *The Law of Contract* (7th ed.), at 54-56.

It has been stressed that the intention behind the affirmations govern. I can see no difference whether the affirmations are made orally or in writing.

I have given my opinion that the brochure was put out to entice sales. I can see no other purpose for it. It contained a number of warranties that were proven to be inaccurate. The breach of these creates liability upon the dealer. I can see no legal basis for differentiating between dealer and manufacturer in relation to collateral warranties. The manufacturer initiated the affirmations; it was the manufacturer who apparently prepared and certainly published the brochure. The dealer would perforce have to rely on the manufacturer.

The dealer induced a sale through the use of the brochure and thus acquired liability. Should the manufacturer who published the brochure in an obvious attempt to induce sales be shielded from liability because it had no direct contact with plaintiff?

In *Shanklin Pier Ltd.*, *supra*, McNair J was dealing with a case in which a paint manufacturer made representations concerning the qualities of its paint to pier owners. Owners caused the paint to be specified in a contract for painting the pier. The painting contractors therefore purchased the paint and applied it to the pier. The paint failed. The owners sued the manufacturers: a mirror image of this case.

McNair J held that the representations were warranties given by manufacturers to owners. The defence submitted that "in law a warranty could give rise to no enforceable cause of action except between the same parties as the parties to the main contract in relation to which the warranty was given."

McNair J said [at 856]:

> In principle this submission seems to me to be unsound. If, as is elementary, the consideration for the warranty in the usual case is the entering into of the main contract in

relation to which the warranty is given, I see no reason why there may be an enforceable warranty between A and B supported by the consideration that B should cause C to enter into a contract with A or that B should do some other act for the benefit of A.

In other words, manufacturers would have been liable if they had supplied the paint directly to the owners and were equally liable in supplying the paint indirectly.

I see no significant difference between the oral warranties given by the paint manufacturer in that case and the written warranties given by the harvester manufacturer in this. The intention was the same in both cases, viz., to induce the recipient of such representations to purchase the product described. I see no real difference either in the way in which the representations were placed before the prospective purchasers. Dissemination of a sale brochure through dealers is a well-known and normal method of distribution for manufacturers whose products are not sold directly to the public. Through the brochure, the manufacturer presents his case to the potential customer just as directly as he would if they were sitting down together to discuss the matter.

Plaintiff's purchase from the dealer in this case seems clearly to be "some other act for the benefit of the manufacturer" contemplated by McNair J.

Traders Finance Corpn. v. Haley, supra, involved somewhat different circumstances. There, a sale of trucks had been arranged between a prospective purchaser and the manufacturer, Ford. It was held that statements made by a Ford officer to purchaser amounted to warranties. Hall J said in the appeal to the Supreme Court of Canada (*Ford Motor Co. v. Haley*, 62 DLR (2d) 329):

> To conform with the appellant's agency arrangements, the deal was put through in the name of Universal Garage as vendor although Universal Garage had no actual part or interest in the transaction.

The sale was financed by Traders Finance.

The case differs from this one in that Ford was held to be the seller within The Sale of Goods Act. Nevertheless, it was recognized that the warranties had been given by a person who was a third party to the agreement. The words of Johnson JA in the Court of Appeal are therefore apposite. He said, at 18 of the report (57 DLR (2d)):

> The learned trial Judge has found, and the evidence amply bears him out, that a warranty was given by the respondent (Ford). Such warranty, although given by a person not a party to the agreement, is nonetheless binding upon him.

In *Shanklin Pier Ltd.*, McNair J referred to the case of *Brown v. Sheen & Richmond Car Sales Ltd.*, [1950] 1 All ER 1102. There judgment was given against a motor car dealer on an express oral warranty given in relation to the purchaser of a car, notwithstanding that the transaction had been "carried through with the assistance of a finance company" and there was not "in any legal sense any agreement to sell between the [purchaser] plaintiff and the defendants [dealer]" [at 857].

In *Andrews v. Hopkinson, supra*, another decision of McNair J the basic situation in *Brown v. Sheen, supra*, was repeated. It led to the same result.

I cannot see any significant difference in the situation of the paint manufacturer in *Shanklin*, the car manufacturer in *Haley* (apart from the question who was "seller") and the harvester manufacturer in this case.

The Liability of the Distributor

It could hardly be argued that Sperry Rand Canada Ltd. was not the agent of Sperry Rand Corporation. Its liability could rest on that ground. It seems to me, however, to be a fair inference from the evidence that this defendant is directly liable as a warrantor in the same way in which I have held the manufacturer liable.

Again, the evidence is not overwhelming. Plaintiff's recollection was less than precise on the point. Yet the evidence given on behalf of this defendant tended to support the impression that warranties of the same type that were given by Church and the manufacturer were also given by this defendant.

Mr. William Hutchinson said that he had visited the farm before the sale. He called on plaintiff on September 26, 1967 in response to a retail inquiry. He met plaintiff. The meeting lasted from two to three hours. Plaintiff described his interest and the crops he proposed to cut. He was interested in the length of cut. They discussed a self-propelled forage harvester. They went through the New Holland product book. He was there with another person, other than plaintiff.

This resulted in his writing up the order and plaintiff's signing it.

I think it is a fair inference from this and plaintiff's evidence that the product book was the sales brochure and that Hutchinson gave plaintiff the same type of assurances given by Church.

While I recognize difficulties with this evidence, I am satisfied that this has been established on the balance of probabilities.

The defendant is therefore liable to plaintiff directly for breach of warranty.

Judgment for the plaintiff.

NOTES

1) When *Sperry Rand* was first reported in the media it was described as a revolutionary decision. Do you agree? To what extent does it expand the doctrine in *Shanklin Pier*? Although the precedent is frequently overlooked, one of the earliest examples of the courts constructing a collateral contract between manufacturer and a consumer is *Carlill v. Carbolic Smoke Ball Co.*, [1893] 1 QB 256 (CA). *Sperry Rand* has been well received by subsequent Canadian courts. One such judgment (although basing itself on *Carlill* rather than *Sperry Rand*) is that of La Forest JA in *Hallmark Pool Corp. v. Storey* (1983), 144 DLR (3d) 56 (NBCA), in which warranty liability was imposed on a swimming pool manufacturer for advertising, *inter alia*, that its pool would give the consumer "… a glamorous in-ground pool that's weatherproof, from 50-below in Canada to searing heat in the Southwest."

2) In the light of *Esso Petroleum v. Mardon, supra*, could the plaintiff in *Sperry Rand* also have brought a successful action under the *Hedley Byrne* doctrine? Would it have been to his advantage to have done so in view of the fact that he was also claiming damages for lost profits?

3) The doctrine of collateral contract as a method for avoiding privity problems with respect to manufacturers' representations does not surmount all the difficulties. For example, can the doctrine be invoked by a buyer who did not himself see the representation but relied on the information of a friend who had seen or heard about it? Should it also be

necessary for the buyer to prove he relied on the representation, or should it be sufficient to show that the representation was generally calculated to induce reliance by members of the public and would normally do so in whole or in part? (*Cf. Naken v. General Motors of Canada Ltd.* (1979), 21 OR (2d) 780 (CA) and *Lambert v. Lewis, infra*, note 5.) Many representations by manufacturers are contained inside the product's packaging (for example, the warranty card for an electric toaster) and would normally not be seen by a purchaser until the sale has been completed. Could reliance sufficient to satisfy the doctrine be shown under such circumstances? *Cf.* the shrinkwrap cases referred to *supra*, chapter 3, and the CCA decisions in *ProCD, Inc. v. Zeidenberg* and *Hill v. Gateway 2000, Inc.*

4) Compare the following statutory responses to the privity problem.

a) Consumer Protection Act, SS 1996, c. C-30.1, s. 55:

In any action brought pursuant to this Part against a manufacturer, retail seller or warrantor for breach of a statutory, express or additional written warranty, lack of privity of contract between the person bringing the action and the retail seller, manufacturer or warrantor is not a defence, and the retail seller, manufacturer or warrantor is presumed conclusively to have received consideration.

b) Australian Trade Practices Act 1974 (Cth), s. 74G(1):

Where:

(a) a corporation, in trade or commerce, supplies goods (otherwise than by sale by auction) manufactured by the corporation to a consumer; or

(b) a corporation, in trade or commerce, supplies goods manufactured by the corporation to another person who acquires the goods for re-supply and a person (whether or not the person who acquired the goods from the corporation) supplies the goods (otherwise than by way of sale by auction) to a consumer;

and:

(c) the corporation fails to comply with an express warranty given or made by the corporation in relation to the goods; and

(d) the consumer or a person who acquires the goods from, or derives title to the goods through or under, the consumer suffers loss or damage by reason of the failure;

the corporation is liable to compensate the consumer or that other person for the loss or damage and the consumer or that other person may recover the amount of the compensation by action against the corporation in a court of competent jurisdiction.

c) Proposed Amendments to Uniform Commercial Code Article 2—Sales (Tentative Draft May 2001)

S. 2.313A. Obligation to Remote Purchaser Created by Record Packaged with or Accompanying Goods

(1) This section applies only to new goods and goods sold or leased as new goods in a transaction of purchase in the normal chain of distribution. In this section:

(a) "Immediate buyer" means a buyer that enters into a contract with the seller.

(b) "Remote purchaser" means a person that buys or leases goods from an immediate buyer or other person in the normal chain of distribution.

(2) If a seller in a record packaged with or accompanying the goods makes an affirmation of fact or promise that relates to the goods, provides a description that relates to the goods, or makes a remedial promise and the seller reasonably expects the record to be, and the record is, furnished to the remote purchaser, the seller has an obligation to the remote purchaser that:

    (a) the goods will conform to the affirmation of fact, promise or description unless a reasonable person in the position of the remote purchaser would not believe that the affirmation of fact, promise or description created an obligation; and

    (b) the seller will perform the remedial promise ... ."

S. 2.313B. Obligation to Remote Purchaser Created by Communication to Public

(1) This section applies only to new goods and goods sold or leased as new goods in a transaction of purchase that occurs in the normal chain of distribution. In this section:

    (a) "Immediate buyer" means a buyer that enters into a contract with the seller.

    (b) "Remote purchaser" means a person that buys or leases goods from an immediate buyer or other person in the normal chain of distribution.

(2) If a seller in advertising or a similar communication to the public makes an affirmation of fact or promise that relates to the goods, provides a description that relates to the goods, or makes a remedial promise and the remote purchaser enters into a transaction of purchase with knowledge of and with the expectation that the goods will conform to the affirmation of fact, promise or description, or that the seller will perform the remedial promise, the seller has an obligation to the remote purchaser that:

    (a) the goods will conform to the affirmation of fact, promise or description unless a reasonable person in the position of the remote purchaser would not believe that the affirmation of fact, promise or description created an obligation; and

    (b) the seller will perform the remedial promise ...

Section 2-313A is meant to deal with so-called "pass-through warranties." The typical case is where a manufacturer sells packaged goods to a retailer and includes in the package a record that sets out the obligations the manufacturer is willing to assume in favour of the end consumer. Section 2-313B will typically apply where a manufacturer makes statements in its advertising which, if made to an immediate buyer, would amount to an express warranty or remedial promise under s. 2-313; the goods are sold to a person other than the recipient of the advertising, and are then sold or resold to the recipient. By imposing liability on the seller, the section adopts the approach of cases such as *Randy Knitwear Inc. v. American Cyanamid Co.*, reproduced *infra*, this chapter.

How do these provisions address the issues raised in note 3, above? See further, OLRC Sales Report, at 138-39.

5) *Lambert v. Lewis*. The decisions and approaches in *Esso Petroleum v. Mardon, supra*, and *Murray v. Sperry Rand, supra*, should be compared with the decision of the English Court of Appeal in *Lambert v. Lewis*, [1980] 2 WLR 299, [1980] 1 All ER 978 (CA), rev'd. on other grounds, [1981] 1 All ER 1185, *infra*, chapter 17. The owner of a Land Rover purchased a towing hitch from a firm of retailers who operated a garage. The towing hitch was manufactured by a reputable company which had widely advertised the towing hitch, by means of brochures and otherwise, as being foolproof and requiring no maintenance. The retailers had bought the towing hitch from one of the wholesalers with

whom they dealt. However, they were unable to identify the particular wholesaler from whom they bought this towing hitch.

The owner used the article to attach a trailer to his Land Rover. The towing hitch suffered from a serious design defect. As a result, while an employee was driving the Land Rover, the trailer became detached and careened across the road into the path of an oncoming car killing the driver of the car and his son and injuring his wife and daughter.

The wife and daughter brought an action for damages against the driver of the Land Rover, its owner, the retailers, and the manufacturers of the towing hitch based on the alleged negligence of each of them. The owner brought third-party proceedings against the retailers claiming an indemnity in contract for any damages for which he might be held liable to the plaintiffs on the ground that the retailers had breached the implied conditions of fitness and merchantability under s. 14 of the British Sale of Goods Act 1893. The retailers in turn claimed an indemnity or contribution in tort or contract from the manufacturers. The trial judge found the driver, the owner, and the manufacturers liable in negligence and assessed the driver's and owner's liability at 25 per cent and that of the manufacturers at 75 per cent. He dismissed the plaintiff's claim against the retailers and the third-party proceedings against the retailers by the owner. He did not therefore have to adjudicate the retailers' claim over against the manufacturers but stated that had it been necessary for him to decide the question he would have dismissed the claim over.

On appeal the Court of Appeal reversed the trial judge's dismissal of the owner's claim against the retailers and allowed the owner's claim in full.[2] It therefore became necessary for the Court of Appeal to consider the merits of the retailer's claim for an indemnity or contribution from the manufacturers. The retailers based their claim on three grounds: (a) breach of collateral warranty; (b) negligent misrepresentation; and (c) negligent manufacture of the towing hitch. The Court of Appeal unanimously rejected all three grounds. The present note is only concerned with the first two grounds. (The third ground is considered in chapter 9, *infra*.)

a) *Collateral warranty*. Speaking for the court, Stephenson LJ said (at 326-27):

> We accept Mr. Turner's submission that not much is needed to conclude that when a warranty of suitability for a particular purpose is expressed or implied in a contract of sale that warranty has been relied on by the purchaser: *Hardwick Game Farm v. Suffolk Agriculture Poultry Producers Association*, [1969] 2 AC 31, *per* Lord Reid at 84 and *per* Lord Pearce at 115; *Christopher Hill Ltd. v. Ashington Piggeries Ltd.*, [1972] AC 441, at 495, *per* Lord Wilberforce. But the difficulty is to show that what the manufacturers stated in the literature advertising and accompanying their products as to their safety and suitability was intended to be a contractual warranty or binding promise. It is one thing to express or imply it in a contract of sale, another to treat it as expressed or implied as a contract, or a term of a contract, collateral to a contract of sale. There may be cases where the purchase from an intermediate seller may be regarded as fortuitous and the original supplier or seller can properly be held liable for breaches of warranty given by the intermediate seller as well as for those given by him: *Wells (Merstham) Ltd. v. Buckland Sand and Silica Ltd.*, [1965] 2 QB 170. But that is not, in our judgment, this case.

---

2 This aspect of the Court of Appeal's judgment is considered below in chapter 17.

He distinguished *Carlill v. Carbolic Smoke Ball Co., supra,* on the ground that the manufacturer's promise there was made directly to the plaintiff, and was meant to be binding, and that the case was no authority for holding that the manufacturers were saying to the retailers: "if you acquire our product we promise it is safe and merchantable and if it is not we will pay you such damages as the law requires." Stephenson LJ accepted the interpretation of *Shanklin Pier Ltd. v. Detel Products Ltd.* adopted by the trial judge in the present case, *viz.* that "consideration for the representation was the procurement by the plaintiffs of a contract of sale by their contractors with the defendants." The trial judge had also found that the retailers had not purchased the towing hitch in reliance on the alleged warranty, although apparently there was ample evidence that the retailers' employees had seen and accepted at face value the manufacturers' sales literature. Stephenson LJ did not find it necessary to rest his rejection of the collateral warranty claim on this ground.

b) *Negligent misrepresentation—the Hedley Byrne doctrine.* The trial judge dismissed the claim based on the *Hedley Byrne* doctrine on the ground apparently that there was no enquiry from the retailers to the manufacturers that prompted the manufacturers to make the claims about their product—they did it voluntarily. Counsel argued that a request for the information was not an essential ingredient in an action for negligent misrepresentation if the statement was made seriously, intended to be acted upon, and in fact acted upon. Stephenson LJ replied as follows (at 328-29):

> This may sometimes be so. A doctor who goes to the help of an unconscious patient will be liable to him if he injures him by negligent treatment. But we cannot regard the manufacturer and supplier of an article as putting himself into a special relationship with every distributor who obtains his product and reads what he says or prints about it and so owing him a duty to take reasonable care to give him true information or good advice. Bearing in mind what for instance Lord Reid said in the *Hedley Byrne* case, [1964] AC 465, at 482 and what Lord Pearce said at 539, we consider that cases of liability for statements volunteered negligently must be rare and that statements made in such circumstances as these are not actionable at the suit of those who have not asked for them. To make such statements with the serious intention that others will or may rely on them—and here parol evidence of intent may be admissible—is not, in our opinion, enough to establish a special relationship with those others or a duty to them.

Stephenson LJ neither referred to nor discussed the Court of Appeal's judgment in *Esso Petroleum v. Mardon, supra,* although one would have thought it relevant both on the definition of collateral warranty and on the scope of the *Hedley Byrne* doctrine. Do you see any incompatibility between the ethos of the two judgments? Why should the Court of Appeal in *Lambert v. Lewis* have been so anxious to protect the manufacturers from the retailers' claim? The student will find it instructive to compare the Court of Appeal's conservative position with the judgment of the New York Court of Appeals in *Randy Knitwear Inc. v. American Cyanamid Co.* which follows.

Randy Knitwear Inc. v. American Cyanamid Co.

(1962), 181 NE 2d 399 (NYCA)

FULD Judge: "The assault upon the citadel of privity," Chief Judge Cardozo wrote in 1931, "is proceeding in these days apace." (*Ultramares Corp. v. Touche*, 255 NY 170, 180, 174 NE 441, 445, 74 ALR 1139.) In these days, too, for the present appeal, here by leave of the Appellate Division on a certified question, calls upon us to decide whether, under the facts disclosed, privity of contract is essential to maintenance of an action against a manufacturer for breach of express warranty.

American Cyanamid Company is the manufacturer of chemical resins, marketed under the registered trade-mark "Cyana," which are used by textile manufactures and finishers to process fabrics in order to prevent them from shrinking. Apex Knitted Fabrics and Fairtex Mills are manufacturers of fabrics who were licensed or otherwise authorized by Cyanamid to treat their goods with "Cyana" and to sell such goods under the "Cyana" label and, with the guaranty that they were "Cyana" finished. Randy Knitwear, a manufacturer of children's knitted sportswear and play clothes, purchased large quantities of these "Cyana" treated fabrics from Apex and Fairtex. After most of such fabrics had been made up into garments and sold by Randy to customers, it was claimed that ordinary washing caused them to shrink and to lose their shape. This action for breach of express warranty followed, each of the 3 parties being made the subject of a separate count. After serving its answer, Cyanamid, urging lack of privity of contract, moved for summary judgment dismissing the cause of action asserted against it, and it is solely with this cause of action that we are concerned.

Insofar as relevant, the complaint alleges that Cyanamid "represented" and "warranted" that the "Cyana" finished fabrics sold by Fairtex and Apex to the plaintiff would not shrink or lose their shape when washed and that the plaintiff purchased the fabrics and agreed to pay the additional charge for the cost involved in rendering them shrink-proof "in reliance upon" Cyanamid's representations. However, the complaint continues, the fabrics were not as represented since, when manufactured into garments and subjected to ordinary washing, they shrank and failed to hold their shape. The damages suffered are alleged to be over $208,000.

According to the complaint and the affidavits submitted in opposition to Cyanamid's motion, the representations relied upon by the plaintiff took the form of written statements expressed not only in numerous advertisements appearing in trade journals and in direct mail pieces to clothing manufacturers, but also in labels or garment tags furnished by Cyanamid. These labels bore the legend

A
CYANA
FINISH
This Fabric Treated for
SHRINKAGE
CONTROL
Will Not Shrink or
Stretch Out of Fit
CYANAMID

and were issued to fabric manufacturers using the "Cyana Finish" only after Cyanamid had tested samples of the fabrics and approved them. Cyanamid delivered a large number of these labels to Fairtex and Apex and they, with Cyanamid's knowledge and approval, passed them on to garment manufacturers, including the plaintiff, so that they might attach them to the clothing which they manufactured from the fabrics purchased.

As noted, Cyanamid moved for summary judgment dismissing the complaint against it on the ground that there was no privity of contract to support the plaintiff's action. The court at Special Term denied the motion and the Appellate Division unanimously affirmed the resulting order.

Thirty-nine years ago, in *Chysky v. Drake Bros. Co.*, 235 NY 468, 139 NE 576, 27 ALR 1533, this court decided that an action for breach of implied warranty could not succeed, absent privity between plaintiff and defendant and, some time later, in *Turner v. Edison Storage Battery Co.*, 248 NY 73, 161 NE 423, we reached a similar conclusion with respect to express warranties, writing, "There can be no warranty where there is no privity of contract" (at 74, 161 NE at 424). This traditional privity limitation on a seller's liability for damage resulting from breach of warranty has not, however, been adhered to with perfect logical consistency (see e.g., *Ryan v. Progressive Grocery Stores*, 255 NY 388, 175 NE 105, 74 ALR 339; *Bowman v. Great A. & P. Tea Co.*, 308 NY 780, 125 NE 2d 165; *Mouren v. Great A. & P. Tea Co.*, 1 NY 2d 884, 154 NY 2d 642, 136 NE 2d 115) and, just a year ago, in *Greenberg v. Lorenz*, 9 NY 2d 195, 213 NYS 2d 39, 173 NE 2d 773, we noted the definite shift away from the technical privity requirement and recognized that it should be dispensed with in a proper case in the interest of justice and reason. More specifically, we held in *Greenberg* that, in cases involving foodstuffs and other household goods, the implied warranties of fitness and merchantability run from the retailer to the members of the purchaser's household, regardless of privity of contract. We are now confronted with the further but related question whether the traditional privity limitation shall also be dispensed with in an action for breach of express warranty by a remote purchaser against a manufacturer who induced the purchase by representing the quality of the goods in public advertising and on labels which accompanied the goods.

It was in this precise type of case, where express representations were made by a manufacturer to induce reliance by remote purchasers, that "the citadel of privity" was successfully breached in the State of Washington in 1932. (See *Baxter v. Ford Motor Co.*, 168 Wash. 456, 12 P.2d 409, 15 P.2d 1118, 88 ALR 521; same case after new trial, 179 Wash. 123, 35 P.2d 1090.) It was the holding in the *Baxter* case that the manufacturer was liable for breach of express warranty to one who purchased an automobile from a retailer since such purchaser had a right to rely on representations made by the manufacturer in its sales literature, even though there was no privity of contract between them. And in the 30 years which have passed since that decision, not only have the courts throughout the country shown a marked, and almost uniform, tendency to discard the privity limitation and hold the manufacturer strictly accountable for the truthfulness of representations made to the public and relied upon by the plaintiff in making his purchase, but the vast majority of the authoritative commentators have applauded the trend and approved the result.

The rationale underlying the decisions rejecting the privity requirement is easily understood in the light of present-day commercial practices. It may once have been true that the warranty which really induced the sale was normally an actual term of the contract of sale. Today, however, the significant warranty, the one which effectively induces the purchase, is frequently that given by the manufacturer through mass advertising and labeling to ultimate business users or to consumers with whom he has no direct contractual relationship.

The world of merchandising is, in brief, no longer a world of direct contract; it is, rather, a world of advertising and, when representations expressed and disseminated in the mass communications media and on labels (attached to the goods themselves) prove false and the user or consumer is damaged by reason of his reliance on those representations, it is difficult to justify the manufacturer's denial of liability on the sole ground of the absence of technical privity. Manufacturers make extensive use of newspapers, periodicals, and other media to call attention, in glowing terms, to the qualities and virtues of their products, and this advertising is directed at the ultimate consumer or at some manufacturer or supplier who is not in privity with them. Equally sanguine representations on packages and labels frequently accompany the article throughout its journey to the ultimate consumer and, as intended, are relied upon by remote purchasers. Under these circumstances, it is highly unrealistic to limit a purchaser's protection to warranties made directly to him by his immediate seller. The protection he really needs is against the manufacturer whose published representations caused him to make the purchase.

The policy of protecting the public from injury, physical or pecuniary, resulting from misrepresentations outweighs allegiance to an old and out-moded technical rule of law which, if observed, might be productive of great injustice. The manufacturer places his product upon the market and, by advertising and labeling it, represents its quality to the public in such a way as to induce reliance upon his representations. He unquestionably intends and expects that the product will be purchased and used in reliance upon his express assurance of its quality and, in fact, it is so purchased and used. Having invited and solicited the use, the manufacturer should not be permitted to avoid responsibility, when the expected use leads to injury and loss, by claiming that he made no contract directly with the user.

It is true that in many cases the manufacturer will ultimately be held accountable for the falsity of his representations, but only after an unduly wasteful process of litigation. Thus, if the consumer or ultimate business user sues and recovers, for breach of warranty, from his immediate seller and if the latter in turn, sues and recovers against his supplier in recoupment of his damages and costs, eventually, after several separate actions by those in the chain of distribution, the manufacturer may finally be obliged "to shoulder the responsibility which should have been his in the first instance." (*Hamon v. Digliani*, 148 Conn. 710, 717, 174 A.2d 294, 297; see *Kasler & Cohen v. Slavouski*, [1928] 1 KB 78, where there were a series of 5 recoveries, the manufacturer ultimately paying the consumer's damages, plus a much larger sum covering the costs of the entire litigation.) As is manifest, and as Dean Prosser observes, this circuity of action is "an expensive, time-consuming and wasteful process, and it may be interrupted by insolvency, lack of jurisdiction, disclaimers, or the statute of limitations." (Prosser, "The Assault upon the Citadel" [Strict Liability to the Consumer], 69 *Yale LJ* 1099, at 1124.)

Indeed, and it points up the injustice of the rule, insistence upon the privity requirement may well leave the aggrieved party, whether he be ultimate business user or consumer, without a remedy in a number of situations. For instance, he would be remediless either where his immediate seller's representations as to quality were less extravagant or enthusiastic than those of the manufacturer or where—as is asserted by Fairtex in this very case (7 NY 2d 791, 194 NYS 2d 530, 163 NE 2d 349; see, also, *supra*, 11 NY 2d at 9, n. 1, 226 NYS 2d 365, 181 NE 2d 400)—there has been an effective disclaimer of any and all warranties by the plaintiff's immediate seller. Turning to the case before us, even if the representations respecting "Cyana" treated fabric were false, the plaintiff would be foreclosed of all remedy against Fairtex, if it were to succeed on its defense of disclaimer, and against Cyanamid because of a lack of privity. (*Cf. Baxter v. Ford Motor Co.*, 168 Wash. 456, 12 P.2d 409, 15 P.2d 1118, 88 ALR 521; same case, 179 Wash. 123, 35 P.2d 1090, *supra*.)

Although we believe that it has already been made clear, it is to be particularly remarked that in the present case the plaintiff's reliance is not on newspaper advertisements alone. It places heavy emphasis on the fact that the defendant not only made representations (as to the nonshrinkable character of "Cyana Finish" fabrics) in newspapers and periodicals, but also repeated them on its own labels and tags which accompanied the fabrics purchased by the plaintiff from Fairtex and Apex. There is little in reason or logic to support Cyanamid's submission that it should not be held liable to the plaintiff even though the representations prove false in fact and it is ultimately found that the plaintiff relied to its harm upon such representations in making its purchase.

We perceive no warrant for holding—as the appellant urges—that strict liability should not here be imposed because the defect involved, fabric shrinkage, is not likely to cause personal harm or injury. Although there is language in some of the opinions which appears to support Cyanamid's contention (see *Worley v. Procter & Gamble Mfg. Co.*, 241 Mo. App. 1114, 1121, 253 SW 2d 532; *Dimoff v. Ernie Majer, Inc.*, 55 Wash. 2d 385, 347 P.2d 1056; see, also, *Laclede Steel Co. v. Silas Mason Co., D.C.*, 67 F Supp. 751), most of the courts which have dispensed with the requirement of privity in this sort of case have not limited their decisions in this manner. (See, e.g., *Burr v. Sherwin Williams Co.*, 42 Cal. 2d 682, 696-97, 268 P.2d 1041 [insecticide; damage to crops]; *State Farm Mut. Auto Ins. Co. v. Anderson-Weber, Inc.*, 110 NW 2d 449 [Iowa] [automobile; property damage]; *Graham v. John R. Watts & Son*, 238 Ky. 96, 36 SW 2d 859 [mislabeled seed; wrong crop]; *Silberman v. Samuel Mallinger Co.*, 375 Pa. 422, 428-29, 100 A.2d 715 [glass jars; commercial loss]; *United States Pipe & Foundry Co. v. City of Waco*, 130 Tex. 126, 108 SW 2d 432, cert. den. 302 US 749, 58 S. Ct. 266, 82 L.Ed. 579 [cast iron pipes; property damage].) And this makes sense. Since the basis of liability turns not upon the character of the product but upon the representation, there is no justification for a distinction on the basis of the type of injury suffered or the type of article or goods involved.

We are also agreed that the present case may not be distinguished, and liability denied, on the ground that the article sold by the appellant, *resin*, is different from that purchased by the plaintiff, *fabric*. To be sure, as Cyanamid urges, the failure to render the fabric shrink-proof may rest with Fairtex and Apex, but the short and simple answer is that Cyanamid actually and expressly represented that fabrics accompanied by the labels which it supplied were "Cyana Finish" and would not shrink or lose their shape. Since it made such representations, Cyanamid may not disclaim responsibility for them. If the ultimate fault for the plaintiff's loss is actually that of Fairtex and Apex, Cyanamid's appropriate recourse is against them.

Nor may it be urged that section 93 of the Personal Property Law renders privity of contract necessary. The Legislature has there defined a warranty as "affirmation" (or "promise") made by a seller, but the section nowhere states that liability for breach of express warranty extends only to the warranting seller's immediate buyer and cannot extend to a later buyer who made the purchase from an intermediate seller but in foreseeable and natural reliance on the original seller's affirmations. Indeed, we made the matter clear in *Greenberg v. Lorenz* when, after observing that the rule requiring a direct contractual relationship between the plaintiff and the defendant is of "judicial making," we went on to say, "our statutes say nothing at all about privity" (9 NY 2d 195, 200, 213 NYS 2d 39, 42, 173 NE 2d 773, 775).

In concluding that the old court-made rule should be modified to dispense with the requirement of privity, we are doing nothing more or less than carrying out an historic and necessary function of the court to bring the law into harmony "with modern-day needs and with concepts of justice and fair dealing." (*Bing v. Thunig*, 2 NY 2d 656, 667, 163 NYS 2d 3, 11, 143 NE 2d 3, 9; see *Greenberg v. Lorenz*, 9 NY 2d 195, 200, 213 NYS 2d 39, 42, 173 NE 2d 773, 775, *supra*; *Woods v. Lancet*, 303 NY 349, 355, 102 NE 2d 691, 694, 27 AL 2d 1250.)

The order appealed from should be affirmed, with costs, and the question certified answered in the negative.

NOTES AND QUESTIONS

1) What is the practical difference between the Anglo-Canadian approach and the American approach to a manufacturer's liability for false representations concerning its goods made to the public? Does the non-contractual approach adopted in *Randy Knitwear* mean that neither party would be able to rely on the provisions of the sales article of the Code, or does the case create a hybrid cause of action, combining elements of both tort and contract? Chief Justice Traynor's judgment in *Seely v. White Motor Co.* (1965), 403 P.2d 145 (Cal. SC), quoted in *Morrow v. New Moon Homes Inc.* (*infra*, chapter 9), clearly assumes the Code provisions would apply to false representations resulting only in economic loss. This willingness to blur traditional contract-tort boundaries, although not unknown in Anglo-Canadian law, is a much more distinctive feature of the realist approach in modern American law and won the support of the OLRC Sales Report. The recommended definition of express warranty in s. 5.10 of the draft bill applies to representations or promises made by the "seller, manufacturer or distributor of the goods" and regardless of whether "there is privity of contract between the person making the representation or promise and the buyer" or where "it was made with a contractual intention."

2) Suppose Mrs. M purchased a garment to which there was attached the "Cyana" label. Would she have a remedy against Cyanamid on the ground that the garment was not shrink-proof? Against Randy Knitwear? Would it make any difference if she did not notice the label until she unwrapped the package at home?

Suppose she had given the garment to her daughter as a birthday present, what would be her daughter's position? How do the amended Article provisions quoted earlier in this chapter address these questions? See further, OLRC Warranties Report, c. 5 and Ontario Sales Report, c. 10. See also chapter 9, *infra*.

Liability of Testing or Sponsoring Organizations

PROBLEM

H purchased a new pair of shoes. Because of the design and construction of the soles they were allegedly slippery and unsafe on vinyl-covered floors. Unaware of this defect, H wore the shoes and, on the same day she purchased them, slipped and injured herself on the vinyl floor of her kitchen. The shoes had been advertised in Good Housekeeping magazine and, with the consent of the magazine's publisher, bore the "Good Housekeeping's Consumers' Guaranty Seal" both in advertisements and in labels affixed to the container of the shoes. With respect to the seal, the magazine stated: "We satisfy ourselves that products advertised in Good Housekeeping are good ones and that the advertising claims for them in our magazine are truthful." The seal itself contained the promise, "If the product or performance is defective, Good Housekeeping guarantees replacement or refund to consumer."

H brings an action for damages against the publishers of Good Housekeeping magazine. Should she recover and, if so, on what theory of liability (express warranty, *Donoghue v. Stevenson*, *Hedley Byrne*)? Is a claim for damages excluded by the terms of the seal? See *Hanberry v. Hearst Corp.* (1969), 276 Cal. App. 2d 680, 81 Cal. Rptr 519 and *Hempstead v. General Fire Extinguisher Corp.* (1967), 269 F. Supp. 109 (US Dist. Ct. Del.), and contrast *Benco Plastics, Inc. v. Westinghouse Electric Corp.* (1974), 387 F. Supp. 772, esp. at 786 (US Dist. Ct. Tenn.). See also M.P. Diepenbrock, "Annotation—Liability of Product Indorser or Certifier for Product Caused Injury" (1971), 39 ALR 3d 181 and Comments in (1970), 74 *Dick. L Rev.* 792; (1970), 4 *Ga. L Rev.* 260; and (1970), 5 *U San Francisco L Rev.* 137.

PUBLIC LAW ASPECTS OF FALSE ADVERTISING

A General Overview

The Victorians had a lax attitude toward false and wildly exaggerated advertising claims, as may be seen by studying turn of the century newspapers and catalogues. Outside the public health area, they made few attempts to restrain them through public law sanctions. This indulgence may be ascribed to a variety of factors: the relative novelty of the "penny" press and the undeveloped state of mass communication techniques, the limited purchasing power of most consumers, a still heavily agrarian society, and no doubt a stronger belief than we would entertain today in the capacity of the average reader or listener to separate the chaff from the wheat. See further E.S. Turner, *The Shocking History of Advertising* (1965).

Changes in public attitudes only came slowly, with the Americans apparently taking the first initiatives. The Federal Trade Commission Act (38 Stat. 717) adopted by the Congress on September 26, 1914, declared unlawful "unfair methods of competition" and conferred broad powers on the newly created Federal Trade Commission to enjoin such practices by means of "cease and desist" orders. Section 5 of the Act was broad enough to include false or deceptive advertising claims but only, as the US Supreme Court subsequently held in *FTC v. Raladam Co.* (1931), 283 US 643, if the advertisements injured or tended to injure competition. The thrust of the original Act, in other words, was to encourage honest competition and not consumer protection *per se*. The Act was amended in 1938 (52 Stat. 111) and the Commission's powers were extended to the policing of "unfair or deceptive acts or practices" in interstate commerce, without regard to their effect on competition. The Act has been amended again since then (and most recently in 1980: see the Federal Trade Commission Improvements Act of 1980, PL 96-252, 94 Stat. 374), but s. 5 remains an anchor section in the overall scheme of the Act. For the current provisions see 15 USC ss. 45 *et seq.*

The FTC Act has been copied at the state level in the form of "little FTC" acts. The National Conference of Commissioners on Uniform State Legislation has also adopted a Uniform Consumer Sales Practices Act. Nevertheless, the FTC has retained its preeminent position in the United States as the senior and generally most active watchdog of unfair market practices. Even then its level of performance attracted much criticism in the '60s. See, for example, the lively account by Edward Cox, Robert Felmeth and John Schultz, *The Consumer and the Federal Trade Commission*, also reprinted in 115 Cong. Rec. (daily ed.), Jan. 22, 1969, and compare the *Report of the ABA Commission to Study the Federal Trade Commission* (Sept. 15, 1969).

General public law legislation dealing with false representations did not materialize in the United Kingdom until the adoption of the Trade Descriptions Act 1968. The Act is exclusively criminal in character and, unlike the FTC Act, spells out the proscribed types of representation with considerable specificity. Another distinctive feature of the Act is that its enforcement is entrusted primarily to local inspectors of weights and measures. The provisions of the 1968 Act were supplemented by the Fair Trading Act 1973 (UK Statutes 1973, c. 41). This established the Office of Fair Trading headed by a Director General of Fair Trading. Under Part II of the Act the director may refer to the Consumer Protection Advisory Committee the question whether a misleading or confusing consumer trade practice adversely affects the economic interests of UK consumers (s. 14(1)), and he can make proposals for the creation of new criminal offences by statutory orders (ss. 13-26). Part III of the Act provides novel powers to cope with rogue traders who have persistently broken the law to the detriment of consumers. In such cases the director must use his "best endeavours" to obtain a satisfactory written assurance from the trader that he will refrain from continuing to break the law and, if the trader refuses to give the assurance, the director may seek a court injunction. These provisions appear to have been influenced by American precedents and, as has been seen previously (*supra*, chapter 3), have their counterparts in the provincial trade practices Acts. See further, Gordon Borrie,

"The Office of Fair Trading," in Ziegel (ed.), *Proc. 7th Ann. Workshop on Commercial and Consumer Law* (1979), at 49.

In Australia, misleading advertising is regulated at the federal level by the Trade Practices Act 1974 (Cth), Part V, Div. 1 and at the State level by fair trading legislation. TPA, Part V, Div.1 and the State fair trading statutes are substantially uniform. The legislation comprises a general prohibition on misleading conduct and a series of specific prohibitions on false and misleading representations relating to product quality, price, country of product origin, and so on. Contravention of the specific prohibitions is a criminal offence, subject to penalties of up to $200,000 in the case of a corporation. The prohibitions impose strict liability, but there is a due diligence defence. If an advertisement is misleading, the supplier, the advertising agency and the publisher are all liable to prosecution, but there is a special defence for publishers which is meant to take account of their limited capacity for monitoring the accuracy of advertising copy submitted to them. In an appropriate case, company directors, employees, agents or other individuals who were involved in the contravention may also be prosecuted. The Australian Competition and Consumer Commission is the main enforcement agency. There have been numerous successful prosecutions. Contravention of the general prohibition is not a criminal offence, but the enforcement agency can bring proceedings for an injunction or a corrective advertising order and the like. These orders can also be sought where a specific prohibition is breached. Contravention of the general and specific prohibitions also attracts civil liability. Any person who suffers loss or damage as a result of the contravention can sue for damages or apply for a discretionary order such as rescission, contract variation or restitution: *supra*.

The Canadian public law response to false representations has its own distinctive history and characteristics. A section dealing with false advertising claims was added to the Criminal Code as early as 1914 (4-5 Geo. V, SC 1914, c. 24, adding s. 406A, subsequently renumbered with amendments as section 306). However, between this date and the transfer of the section to the Combines Investigation Act in 1969 there was only one reported prosecution under it. Obviously the provinces did not attach much importance to this species of white collar crime.

A new, much more activist, era was ushered in with the addition of s. 33C to the Combines Investigation Act (now the Competition Act) dealing with misrepresentations as to the ordinary price of goods (SC 1960, c. 45, s. 13). This was followed, in 1969, by the transfer to the Act of s. 306 of the Criminal Code in the form of a new s. 33D (SC 1968-69, c. 38, s. 116; ss. 33C and 33D were renumbered respectively ss. 36 and 37 in the 1970 RSC revision. See now RSC 1985, c. C-34, ss. 52-53). In the same year the Economic Council of Canada published its *Interim Report on Competition Policy* (Ottawa, July 1969) and this event, coupled with the need to remove some obvious technical differences between ss. 33C and 33D, led to the introduction of a series of abortive government bills to amend the Combines Investigation Act (Bill C-256, 1971 Bill C-227, 1973, Bill C-7, 1973), culminating in Bill C-2, which was adopted in 1975 and came into effect on January 1, 1976 (SC 1974-75-76, c. 76). As previously indicated, in 1986 the title of the Act was changed to the Competition Act.

The provinces introduced trade practices legislation from 1974 onwards which included provisions governing false representations in advertising and elsewhere. Before this, there had been various provisions scattered throughout provincial statutes, such as CPA (Ont.),

s. 38. However, as with former s. 306 of the Criminal Code, these provisions were largely conspicuous by their non-enforcement. The track record under the trade practices legislation has been better (though it varies widely among the provinces) but still leaves a great deal to be desired.

Federal prosecutions under the Competition Act acquired a significantly higher profile, both because of their longer history and because of their predominantly curial, non-administrative character. However, amendments to the Act in 1999 mark a significant change in philosophy. The purpose of the 1999 amendments is to reduce reliance on the criminal law to control misleading advertising and to increase the use of administrative sanctions. Section 52 of the Act used to be a strict liability provision, subject to a due diligence defence. The 1999 amendments added a *mens rea* component so that now the section only applies where the representation was made "knowingly or recklessly." The penalty has been increased to $200,000 to reflect the seriousness of the offence to which the section is now limited. Non-fraudulent misrepresentation in advertising and the like is no longer a criminal offence. Instead it is governed by a newly created Part VII.1, Deceptive Market Practices. Part VII.1 provides for the imposition of civil penalties in relation to "reviewable conduct," including misleading advertising. It gives the Competition Tribunal power, on application by the Commissioner, to impose cease and desist orders, to require the publication of corrective statements and to impose administrative monetary penalties. Under the old law, a person who suffered loss or damage as a consequence of misleading advertising could sue to recover compensation. As a consequence of the 1999 amendments, private remedies under the statute are now only available in two cases: (1) where the defendant contravenes s. 52 (i.e., the representation is fraudulent); and (2) in the case of a non-fraudulent representation, where the defendant fails to comply with a tribunal order under Part VII.1: Competition Act, s. 36 (as amended).

The above description of legislative developments in Canada and other countries discloses a wide diversity of regulatory philosophies and means used to restrain false advertisements. Here is a short list of some of the numerous issues that call for consideration:

1) *How important is the phenomenon of false advertisements?* Are advertising agencies right in claiming that the worst offenders are small enterprises and that the national advertisers exercise stringent internal controls?

2) *In Canada, who should have principal responsibility for policing advertisements*: the federal government or the provinces? Assuming they both have constitutional policing powers, how should they allocate responsibility between themselves? And regardless of where the jurisdiction lies, should the actual enforcement of the laws be entrusted to local Crown prosecutors or consumer protection officials, or should it be centralized (as it largely is at the present time)? Do we have something to learn in this respect from the British experience?

3) *The types of advertisements proscribed*: should they be limited to false or misleading advertisements or should they include, *pace* s. 5 of the FTC Act, "unfair" claims? *Cf.* BPA ss. 2(2) and 3. Should the offending types of representation be spelled out in detail, as is done in the British Act, or is it better to use general prohibitory language? Should there be regulation-making power, as in CPLA s. 18(1)(g) and BPA s. 16(1)(c), allowing government officials to define what is deemed to be false or deceptive, or is such power incompatible with the rule of law?

4) *How should the legislation be enforced?* By use of criminal sanctions, by administrative cease and desist provisions, or both? What role is there for private law enforcement of misleading advertising laws, through the bringing of damages claims and the like?

5) *Should the offences be absolute or strict in character (that is, without requirement of proof of mens rea)?* If not, what defences should be permitted? Compare *R v. City of Sault Ste. Marie*, [1978] 2 SCR 1299, with CA s. 60(2). For the Charter impact on this issue, see *Reference re s. 94(2) of the Motor Vehicle Act*, [1985] 2 SCR 486; *R v. Westfair Foods Ltd.* (1986), 11 CPR (3d) 345 (Man. QB); and *R v. Wholesale Travel Group Inc.*, [1991] 3 SCR 154, 84 DLR (4th) 161, aff"g. (1990), 63 DLR (4th) 325 (Ont. CA). Have the 1999 amendments to the Competition Act gone too far in confining misleading advertising offences to cases of dishonesty? Are the new administrative remedies a sufficient counterweight? Contrast the Australian laws, which provide for criminal sanctions alongside administrative orders as well as allowing for private remedies.

For useful Canadian materials on many of these questions, see Canadian Consumer Council, S*ymposium on Misleading Advertising* (December 1970); R.I. Cohen and J.S. Ziegel, *A Proposal for Consumer and Misleading Trade Practices Legislation for Canada* (1976); Trebilcock *et al.*, *A Study on Consumer Misleading and Unfair Trade Practices* (DCCA, 1976); M.S. Moyer and J.C. Banks, "Industry Self-Regulation: Some Lessons from the Canadian Advertising Industry," in D. Thompson (ed.), *Problems in Canadian Marketing* (1977), chapter 8; and Scott Requadt, "Regulatory Offences since *Wholesale Travel*: The Need to Re-evaluate Sections 1, 7 and 11(d) of the Charter" (1993), 22 *CBLJ* 407.

Constitutional Position

As in other areas of commercial and consumer law, the rational and efficient resolution of the above issues is bedevilled by an increasingly complex and conflicting overlay of jurisprudence affecting the distribution of constitutional powers between the federal and provincial governments. In *Proprietary Articles Trade Assn. v. AG Can.*, [1931] AC 310, the Privy Council upheld the anti-conspiracy provisions of the then Combines Act as a legitimate exercise of the criminal law power. While the criminal law characterization may also safely be assumed to apply to the misleading advertising provisions, until recently it was not clear whether the federal government could prosecute them without provincial concurrence.

The difficulty arises because the administration of justice in each province is a provincial responsibility and because s. 91(27) of the Constitution Act, 1867, restricts the federal power to the enactment of criminal laws, "including the Procedure in Criminal Matters." In *R v. Hauser*, [1979] 1 SCR 984, which involved a prosecution under the federal Narcotics Control Act, the intervening provinces argued vigorously that only the provinces have the power to enforce the criminal law because of the provisions of s. 92(14). The majority of the Supreme Court of Canada side-stepped the issue by validating the Act as an exercise of the federal government's peace, order and good government power. Mr. Justice Dickson delivered a scholarly and powerful dissent. The question was raised again, *inter alia*, before Linden J in *R v. Hoffman-Laroche Limited* (1980), 14 CR (3d) 289 (Ont. HC), aff'd. 125 DLR (4th) 607 (Ont. CA), which involved a prosecution under s. 34 of the (then) CIA. He read s. 91(27) broadly to include the determination of prosecutorial powers. On the other hand, Wetmore CCJ in *R v. Kripps Pharmacy Ltd.* (1980), 114 DLR (3d) 457 (BC Co. Ct.); mandamus refused, [1981] 1 WWR 753 (BCSC), aff'd. 129 DLR (3d) 566, (BCCA), rev'd. sub nom. *R v. Wetmore* (1983), 2 DLR (4th) 577 (SCC), preferred Dickson J's dissenting judgment to Linden J's view. The issue was finally resolved by the Supreme Court of Canada in *AG Can. v. Can. National Transport Ltd.* (1983), 3 DLR (4th) 16, where a majority of the Court held that the federal government's criminal law power included the power to prosecute federal offences. (Dickson J reiterated his earlier position but agreed with the majority in the result on the ground that the Competition Act was a valid exercise of the federal government's trade and commerce power.) The Supreme Court reaffirmed its majority ruling in *R v. Wetmore, supra*, with Dickson J again dissenting.

There are other constitutional problems. Prior to the Supreme Court's decision in *General Motors v. City National Leasing*, [1989] 1 SCR 641, the lower courts were sharply divided with respect to the validity of CA s. 31.1 empowering the recovery of civil damages by an injured person as a result of conduct contrary to Part V of the Competition Act. For a sampling of the lower court decisions, see *Rocois Construction Inc. v. Quebec Ready Mix Inc.* (1979), 105 DLR (3d) 15; *Henuset Bros. Ltd. v. Syncrude Canada Ltd.* (1980), 114 DLR (3d) 300, (Alta. QB); *Seiko Time Canada Ltd. v. Consumers Distributing Co. Ltd.* (1980), 112 DLR (3d) 500 (Ont. HCJ), rev'd. 10 DLR (4th) 161 (Ont. CA); and *cf. R v. Zelensky*, [1978] 2 SCR 940; *MacDonald v. Vapor Canada*, [1977] 2 SCR 940; and Calvin S. Goldman, "The Constitutionality of the Combines Investigation Act Civil Damages Remedy" (1985-86), 11 *CBLJ* 385. The Supreme Court upheld s. 31.1 as a valid exercise of the federal government's general power to regulate trade and commerce under s. 91(2) of the Constitution Act. See Peter W. Hogg, *Constitutional Law of Canada* (Carswell looseleaf), Vol. I, at 18-15–18-16 and 20-15–20-16. *General Motors* is difficult to reconcile with earlier decisions of the Supreme Court in the agricultural products and food and drugs acts areas (*viz.*, *Dominion Stores v. The Queen* (1979), 106 DLR (3d) 581, and *Labatt Breweries of Canada Ltd. v. AG Can*, [1980] 1 SCR 914, giving a narrow reading to the trade and commerce power, and their authority may now be undermined. The significance of *General Motors* is that it no longer restricts the federal government to use of the criminal law power to regulate misleading advertising and unfair practices, and enables it to deploy a wider range of techniques (for example, administrative and recovery of damages by injured parties) to discipline anti-competitive conduct.

For further discussion of the above issues, see P.W. Hogg and W. Grover, "The Constitutionality of the Competition Bill" (1975-76), 1 *CBLJ* 197; James C. MacPherson, "Economic Regulation and the British North America Act: Labatt Breweries and other Constitutional Imbroglios" (1981), 5 *CBLJ* 172; and *infra*, chapter 8 in the section on Public Control of Food, Drugs, and Hazardous Products.

The adoption of the Canadian Charter of Rights and Freedoms has added another complicating element to the constitutional picture. See the Charter decisions referred to above in Question 5 and *Irwin Toy Ltd. v. AG Que.* (1989), 58 DLR (4th) 577 (SCC) upholding Quebec's restrictions on children's advertising on TV as a valid restriction on free speech. See further, "Symposium on Commercial Free Speech and the Canadian Charter" (1990), 17 *CBLJ* 2. In *RJR–MacDonald v. Canada*, [1995] 3 SCR 199, the court held that the anti-advertising provisions in the federal Tobacco Products Control Act were unconstitutional. The Act infringed s. 2(b) of the Charter and a majority of the court concluded that the Act could not be justified under s. 1. There was enough evidence to establish a causal connection between the advertising ban and the objective of reducing consumption. However, the majority was not prepared to accept that a total ban on all forms of advertising, including purely informational advertising, was the least drastic means of achieving the objective. The court would have upheld a ban more carefully targeted at the recruitment of new smokers: see Hogg, *Constitutional Law of Canada, looseleaf ed.,* Vol. II, at 40.19-40.20.

CHAPTER FIVE

Seller's Implied Obligations: Title, Quiet Possession and Freedom from Encumbrances

OLRC Report on Consumer Warranties and Guarantees

(1972), at 31-32

In practice the buyer with defective goods on his hands is more likely to complain of breach of one of the implied quality obligations in the Sale of Goods Act than of a breach by the seller of an express warranty. How is he likely to fare? The answer is, on the whole, very well, assuming the absence of an effective disclaimer clause or other debilitating circumstance.

The Research Team for this project reported finding that among laymen, including many government officials, there is still a surprising lack of knowledge about the seller's implied obligations at law, and an extremely strong belief that the only obligations binding on a seller are those expressly assumed by him. The source of this misunderstanding appears to be the idea of "let the buyer beware"—expressed in the legal maxim "*caveat emptor*"—and the assumption that this maxim is the foundation of the common law of sales.

Historically this is an inaccurate description of the law.[1] The maxim apparently is not of Roman origin. It was well established in the classical period of Roman law that a buyer who had been sold goods with a latent defect was entitled to bring an action *in quanti minoris* for a reduction of the purchase price, or a redhibitory action for rescission of the sale. The maxim equally did not reflect the state of early English law, and a learned writer has shown that medieval society imposed sanctions of one kind or another on a seller who was guilty of sharp practices or unfair dealing. The maxim is first cited by Fitzherbert in the 16th century (without authority to support it) but did not make its appearance in the scant and not always relevant case law until the 17th century.

Its life as an accurate reflection of the law was relatively short-lived. Erosions of the rule that a seller did not vouch his title began as early as the middle of the 18th

---

1 See generally, Hamilton, "The Ancient Maxim *Caveat Emptor*" (1933), 40 *Yale LJ* 1133.

century and the implied condition of merchantability in the case of manufacturers and non-specific goods was established by 1815. The implied condition of fitness followed in 1829, and in 1877 it was authoritatively settled that a seller was strictly liable for latent defects even though they could not have been avoided by the exercise of reasonable care and skill on his part. By the time Chalmers began to draft his Sale of Goods Act, the contours of the modern sales rules had been substantially settled. The only areas in which the maxim still has any vitality (ignoring again for this purpose the impact of disclaimer clauses) is with respect to private sales and sales of specific goods where the buyer has inspected the goods and is deemed to have bought them subject to such defects as his examination ought to have revealed.

Niblett Ltd. v. Confectioners' Materials Co. Ltd.

[1921] 3 KB 387, [1921] All ER Rep. 459 (CA)

BANKES LJ: In this case the buyers seek to recover damages from the sellers on the ground that the goods delivered were not in accordance with the contract of sale. The case as presented to us rests on one or another of three enactments. It is said that the buyers had a right of action under s. 12 or under s. 14 of the Sale of Goods Act, 1893, or under s. 17 of the Merchandise Marks Act, 1887. Upon this last alternative I need say nothing. No reference was made to it at the trial. If it had been insisted on it would have required evidence which the respondents had no opportunity of giving in the Court below, and the appellants ought not to be allowed to make that point now. I therefore confine myself to the claims under s. 12 and s. 14 of the Sale of Goods Act, 1893, though it does not appear that s. 14 was much relied on by counsel or considered by the judge at the trial.

In August, 1919, the parties entered into a contract for the sale of 3000 cases of condensed milk. The contract was originally made at an interview, but it was subsequently confirmed by writing in the form of a sold note dated August 18 sent by the respondents to the appellants with a request that they would sign a counterpart, that is to say, a bought note, in the same terms, which the appellants did. The contract appears to be wholly embodied in the writing. Notwithstanding this both parties seem to have treated the contract as partly oral and partly in writing, and to have adduced parol evidence as to its terms, and counsel for the respondents have contended that it was agreed that one or more of three brands of condensed milk, including the "Nissly" brand, might be delivered by fulfilment of the contract, and Bailhache J appears to have dealt with the case on that footing. Two thousand cases were delivered, and give rise to no question. One thousand arrived bearing labels with the word "Nissly" upon them. It came to the knowledge of the Nestlé and Anglo-Swiss Co. that parcels of condensed milk were being imported with this label upon them, and they took up the position that these 1000 cases infringed their registered trade mark. They objected to these goods being dealt with in any way. The justice of their objection was admitted by the respondents, who gave an undertaking not to sell, offer for sale, or dispose of any condensed milk under the title of "Nissly." The appellants did their best to sell, exchange, or export the goods, but found that the only possible way of dealing with them was to strip them of their labels and sell them without marks or labels.

Bailhache J came to the clear conclusion that if s. 12 of the Sale of Goods Act, 1893, is to be construed literally the respondents had no right to sell the goods as they were, and that the appellants were not enjoying and never had enjoyed quiet possession of the goods; that they could never get them from the Commissioners of Customs, and that if they had got them they were never in a position to deal with them, because of the Nestlé Co.'s threat. But he felt himself bound by the judgment of Lord Russell CJ in *Monforts v. Marsden* (1895), 12 RPC 266, to give to s. 12 a meaning and effect which he would not have attributed to it but for that case. With the greatest respect to Lord Russell CJ I think the doubts cast by Bailhache J upon that decision are justified. The case was heard and decided by Lord Russell CJ on circuit. He took the view that s. 12 was to be read with qualifications like those which limit the implied covenant for quiet enjoyment in a conveyance of real property by a grantor who conveys as beneficial owner under s. 7 of the Conveyancing Act, 1881, and he imposed upon the implied obligations in s. 12 of the Sale of Goods Act, 1893, a restriction limiting their operation to acts and omissions of the vendor and those acting by his authority. I cannot agree with the view thus expressed by Lord Russell. I think s. 12 has a much wider effect, and that the language does not warrant the limitation imposed by Lord Russell. I express no opinion as to what "circumstances" of a contract are "such as to show a different intention," to use the earlier words of s. 12. Mr. Spence contended that these circumstances are not confined to matters relating to the making of the contract, but would include the fact that at the time of making a written contract for the sale of goods it was understood that the goods would be of one or another brand. He argued that this was a circumstance which would show an intention to exclude the warranties otherwise implied. But assuming that goods of one or more of three brands might be delivered under the contract, that circumstance does not show any intention that if two of those brands are free from objection, and the third is an infringement of trade mark rights, the vendor may tender goods of the third brand in fulfilment of his contract. The goods tendered must still be goods which the vendor has a right to sell. Therefore in my opinion the appellants have established a right of action under s. 12, sub-s. 1, of the Act.

Appeal allowed.

Rowland v. Divall

[1923] 2 KB 500, [1923] All ER Rep. 270 (CA)

BANKES LJ: Whatever doubt there may have been in former times as to the legal rights of a purchaser in the position of the present plaintiff was settled by the Sale of Goods Act, 1893, by s. 12 of which it was provided that: "In a contract of sale, unless the circumstances of the contract are such as to show a different intention, there is (1.) An implied condition on the part of the seller that ... he has a right to sell the goods." The facts are shortly these. The plaintiff bought a motor car at Brighton from the defendant in May, 1922. He took possession of it at once, drove it to his place of business at Blandford, where he exhibited it for sale in his shop, and ultimately sold it to a purchaser. It was not discovered that the car was a stolen car until September, when possession was taken of it by the police. The plaintiff and his purchaser between them had possession of it for about four months. The plaintiff now brings his action to recover back the price that he paid to the defendant upon the ground of total failure of consideration. As I have said, it cannot now be disputed that there was an implied condition on the part of the defendant that he had a right to sell the car, and unless something happened to change that condition into a warranty the plaintiff is entitled to rescind the contract and recover back the money. The Sale of Goods Act itself indicates in s. 53 [Ont. s. 51] the circumstances in which a condition may be changed into a warranty: "Where the buyer elects, or is compelled, to treat any breach of a condition on the part of the seller as a breach of warranty" the buyer is not entitled to reject the goods, but his remedy is in damages. Mr. Doughty contends that this is a case in which the buyer is compelled to treat the condition as a warranty within the meaning of that section, because, having had the use of the car for four months, he cannot put the seller in statu quo and therefore cannot now rescind, and he has referred to several authorities in support of that contention. But when those authorities are looked at I think it will be found that in all of them the buyer got some part of what he contracted for. In *Taylor v. Hare* (1805), 1 B & P (NR) 260, at 262, the question was as to the right of the plaintiff to recover back money which he had paid for the use of a patent which turned out to be void. But there the Court treated the parties, who had made a common mistake about the validity of the patent, as being in the nature of joint adventurers in the benefit of the patent; and Chambre J expressly pointed out that "The plaintiff has had the enjoyment of what he stipulated for." The language there used by Heath J, though it may have been correct as applied to the facts of that case, is much too wide to be applied to such a case as the present. In *Hunt v. Silk* (1804), 5 East 449, at 452 Lord Ellenborough went upon the ground that the plaintiff had received part of what he bargained for. He said: "Where a contract is to be rescinded at all, it must be rescinded *into*, and the parties put in statu quo. But here was an intermediate occupation, a part execution of the agreement, which was incapable of being rescinded." And *Lawes v. Purser* (1856), 6 E & B 930 proceeded on the same ground, that the defendant had derived benefit from the execution of the contract. But in the present case it cannot possibly be said that the plaintiff received any portion of what he had agreed to buy. It is true that a motor car was delivered to him, but the person who sold it to him had no right to sell it, and therefore he did not get what he paid for—namely, a car to which he would have title; and under those circumstances the use of the car by the purchaser seems to me quite immaterial for the purpose of considering whether the condition had been converted into a warranty. In my opinion the plaintiff was entitled to recover the whole of the purchase money, and was not limited to his remedy in damages as the judge below held.

SCRUTTON LJ: [B]efore the passing of the Sale of Goods Act there was a good deal of confusion in the authorities as to the exact nature of the vendor's contract with respect to his title to sell. It was originally said that a vendor did not warranty his title. But gradually a number of exceptions crept in, till at last the exceptions became the rule, the rule being that the vendor warranted that he had title to what he purported to sell, except in certain special cases, such as that of a sale by a sheriff, who does not so warrant. Then came the Sale of Goods Act, which re-enacted that rule, but did so with this alteration: it re-enacted it as a condition, not as a warranty. Sect. 12 [Ont. s. 13] says in express terms that there shall be "An implied condition on the part of the seller that … he has a right to sell the goods." It being now a condition, wherever that condition is broken the contract can be rescinded, and with the rescission the buyer can demand a return of the purchase money, unless he has, with knowledge of the facts, held on to the bargain so as to waive the condition. But Mr. Doughty argues that there can never be a rescission where a restitutio in integrum is impossible, and that here the plaintiff cannot rescind because he cannot return the car. To that the buyer's answer is that the reason of his inability to return it—namely, the fact that the defendant had no title to it—is the very thing of which he is complaining, and that it does not lie in the defendant's mouth to set up as a defence to the action his own breach of the implied condition that he had a right to sell. In my opinion that answer is well founded, and it would, I think, be absurd to apply the rule as to restitutio in integrum to such a state of facts. No doubt the general rule is that a buyer cannot rescind a contract of sale and get back the purchase money unless he can restore the subject matter. There are a large number of cases on the subject, some of which are not very easy to reconcile with others. Some of them make it highly probable that a certain degree of deterioration of the goods is not sufficient to take away the right to recover the purchase money. However I do not think it necessary to refer to them. It certainly seems to me that, in a case of rescission for the breach of the condition that the seller had a right to sell the goods, it cannot be that the buyer is deprived of his right to get back the purchase money because he cannot restore the goods which, from the nature of the transaction, are not the goods of the seller at all, and which the seller therefore has no right to under any circumstances. For these reasons I think that the plaintiff is entitled to recover the whole of the purchase money as for a total failure of consideration, and that the appeal must be allowed.

ATKIN LJ: I agree. It seems to me that in this case there has been a total failure of consideration, that is to say that the buyer has not got any part of that for which he paid the purchase money. He paid the money in order that he might get the property, and he has not got it. It is true that the seller delivered to him the de facto possession, but the seller had not got the right to possession and consequently could not give it to the buyer. Therefore the buyer, during the time that he had the car in his actual possession had no right to it, and was at all times liable to the true owner for its conversion. Now there is no doubt that what the buyer had a right to get was the property in the car, for the Sale of Goods Act expressly provides that in every contract of sale there is an implied condition that the seller has a right to sell; and the only difficulty that I have felt in this case arises out of the wording in s. 11, sub-s. 1(c) [Ont. s. 12(3)], which says that: "Where a contract of sale is not severable, and the buyer has accepted the goods … the breach of any condition to be fulfilled by the seller can only be treated as a breach of warranty, and not as a ground for rejecting the goods and treating the contract as repudiated, unless there be a term of the contract, express or implied, to that effect." It is said that this case falls within that provision, for the contract of sale was not severable and the buyer had accepted the car. But I think that the answer is that there can be no sale at all of goods which the seller has no right to sell. The whole object of a sale is to transfer property from one person to another. And I think that in every contract of sale of goods there is an implied term to the effect that a breach of the condition that the seller has a right to sell the goods may be treated as a ground for rejecting the goods and repudiating the contract notwithstanding the acceptance, within the meaning of the concluding words of sub-s. (c); or in other words that the sub-section has no application to a breach of that particular condition. It seems to me that in this case there must be a right to reject, and also a right to sue for the price paid as money had and received on failure of the consideration, and further that there is no obligation on the part of the buyer to return the car, for ex hypothesi the seller had no right to receive it. Under those circumstances can it make any difference that the buyer has used the car before he found out that there was a breach of the condition? To my mind it makes no difference at all. The buyer accepted the car on the representation of the seller that he had a right to sell it, and inasmuch as the seller had no such right he is not entitled to say that the buyer has enjoyed a benefit under the contract. In fact the buyer has not received any part of that which he contracted to receive—namely, the property and right to possession—and, that being so, there has been a total failure of consideration. The plaintiff is entitled to recover the 334*l*. which he paid.

Appeal allowed.

Butterworth v. Kingsway Motors Ltd.

[1954] 1 WLR 1286, [1954] 2 All ER 694 (QB)

PEARSON J: The subject-matter of this litigation is a Jowett Javelin motor-car which was first registered in November, 1949. We have no evidence as to what happened to it between November, 1949, and about the end of 1950, but Miss Rudolph, the fifth party, became interested in it late in the year 1950. On January 3, 1951, she took it from Messrs. Bowmaker Ld. on a hire-purchase agreement containing no unfamiliar provisions.

. . .

Miss Rudolph paid some of the monthly payments due under the hire-purchase agreement, but she had not paid all of them nor, of course, had she exercised the option to purchase by August 1, 1951, when she purported to sell this Jowett Javelin car to a motor dealer named Leonard Kennedy, the fourth party. The price was £1,000 and that was paid by him by means of a cash payment of £350 and the delivery of an AC shooting brake, which was valued for the purpose of that transaction at £650.

That sale was wrongful because the car still belonged to Bowmaker Ld., and Miss Rudolph had no right to sell it. There was, therefore, a clear breach of the implied condition under section 12(1) of the Sale of Goods Act, 1893. It may well be that Miss Rudolph did not then realize that she was acting in an unlawful manner, but it is quite clear that she was.

On or about August 11, the fourth party, Mr. Kennedy, purported to sell this car for a little more than he had given for it—namely, £1,015—to Hayton, the third party. Hayton was a produce merchant and, so far as Kennedy knew, Hayton required the car for his own use and not for re-sale. This second transaction was again a completely wrongful sale as the car still belonged to Bowmaker Ld., so that, again, there was a breach of the same implied condition, but I find that he acted in good faith in believing he had a right to sell the car.

On the same day, August 11, Hayton, the third party, purported to sell the car for £1,030, to the defendants, Kingsway Motors, who are motor dealers, and Hayton knew that they were buying the car for re-sale. Here again, the sale was wrongful as the car still belonged to Bowmaker Ld., so that there was a breach of the same implied condition. Hayton also acted in good faith in believing that he had a right to sell the car.

After certain negotiations from about August 15 onwards, the defendants, on or about August 30, 1951, purported to sell the car to the plaintiff for £1,275, which was paid by means of certain cash payments amounting to £550 and the delivery of a Standard car which for this purpose was considered to be worth £725. Here, again, there was a wrongful sale as the car still belonged to Bowmaker Ld. and the defendants had no right to sell it, so there was a breach of the same implied condition. Here, also, the defendants acted in good faith, believing that they had a right to sell.

It appears from the registration book that the plaintiff was registered as owner on January 15, 1952. From the time of its acquisition on about August 30, 1951, until some time in July, 1952, he made full use of the car, fully believing that it was his car and that he had every right to use it. Miss Rudolph continued to make some monthly payments to Bowmaker Ld., under the hire-purchase agreement. In the end, however, she learned that she ought not to have sold the car as she had done and she informed Bowmaker Ld. of the actual position. Her conduct in those two respects, of course, affords strong evidence that she was acting in good faith and not with any intention of deceit, but it was a wrongful sale.

On July 15, 1952, Bowmaker Ld. wrote to the plaintiff in these terms:

Re: Jowett Javelin—Regd. No. HGA 4. We have reason to believe that the vehicle described above is at present in your possession and we wish to advise you that it is our property the subject of a hiring agreement into which we entered with a Miss G. Rudolph. Assuming our information to be correct, we have to ask you to be good enough to arrange at once for the vehicle to be returned into the possession of our Liverpool office, and we shall be obliged if you will confirm that you have given effect to our requirements. It occurs to us that you might perhaps like the opportunity to acquire title in the vehicle and quite without prejudice, we would be prepared to allow you to do so in consideration of an immediate payment of £175 14s. 2d.

If the plaintiff had been willing to enter into some agreement on the lines suggested by Bowmaker Ld., a great deal of trouble would have been saved because no doubt it would have been possible to arrange what ultimately happened in fact, that Miss Rudolph herself would repay the outstanding balance to Bowmaker Ld. The plaintiff would then have had what he had originally bargained for at the price he originally agreed to pay, and did pay, and it would have saved a great deal of expense to everybody. On the other hand, he would have lost the chance he had in 1952 of reclaiming the full 1951 price in return for giving up this motor-car in July, 1952, by which time it had substantially depreciated in its realizable value by reason of a general fall in the market price of second-hand cars, but I do not think those considerations ultimately affect the legal issue here. I only mention them to show that I have not left out of consideration possible arguments on the grounds of hardship. In my view, the plaintiff's position is somewhat lacking in merits.

On July 17, 1952, acting very promptly in the matter, the plaintiff's solicitors wrote to the defendants:

> We have been consulted by Mr. H. Butterworth of 44, Dee Lane, West Kirby, who informed us that he purchased a Jowett Javelin car for £1,275 on August 30 last. We are instructed that this motor-car was not yours to sell, and in the circumstances our client will expect the return of the money paid.

That shows that the plaintiff is claiming the repayment of the money and not wishing to retain the car. That second point becomes even more clear in later letters. On July 18 there is a reply from the defendants' solicitors to the plaintiff's solicitors:

> ... The allegations that the Jowett Javelin car was not the property of our clients to sell has come as a complete surprise. Our clients purchased the car from a motor dealer. ...

On July 23 Bowmaker Ld. wrote to the plaintiff's solicitors:

> *Re: Miss G. Rudolph Agreement No.___:* ... Since we wrote to Mr. Butterworth, we have received from our hirer a post-dated cheque which, if met, will be sufficient to discharge our interests and to enable us to release the vehicle to Mr. Butterworth. The cheque in question is dated [July 25], so we propose to write you again during the course of a day or two.

· · ·

On those facts, the first question is the relation between the plaintiff and the defendants, and a very important question is whether the plaintiff, by his letter of July 17, 1952, duly and effectually rescinded the contract of sale between him and the defendants. I hold, first, that that letter of July 17, as a matter of construction, constituted a rescission of that contract of sale. When I say "a rescission of the contract of sale," I am using the wording which was used in the Court of Appeal in *Rowland v. Divall*, [1923] 2 KB 500, and without prejudice to the question whether it could also be put in rather a different way: that there was a fundamental breach by the defendants and the plaintiff elected to treat that breach as a repudiation of that contract of sale. I do not think that it makes any difference which way one looks at it in the end.

Secondly, I hold that, on the authority of *Rowland v. Divall*, the plaintiff was on that date entitled to rescind that contract of sale. The possible contention for the defendants that such rescission was precluded by the plaintiff's use of the car for a substantial period and the deterioration in its condition and/or depreciation in its market value during that period is answered by the reasoning of Bankes LJ (at 503) in that case. Another possible contention that such rescission was precluded by the plaintiff's acceptance of the motor-car when it was delivered or after delivery is answered by the reasoning of Atkin LJ (at 506).

The contention mainly relied upon by Mr. Atkinson for the defendants as against the plaintiff was that there was not a total failure of the consideration. That question he said was to be determined as at the date of the issue of the writ, and that, as at that date, the plaintiff was still in undisturbed possession of the car; there was no outstanding adverse claim against him because Miss Rudolph had paid the outstanding instalments and the hire-purchase money, and Bowmaker Ld. were willing to accept such payment in full discharge of their interest in the car and to release the vehicle to the plaintiff. The answer to that contention is that on July 17 the plaintiff was entitled to, and did, rescind the contract of sale and thereby he established, and in a sense crystallized, his right to receive repayment of the purchase price as money paid in consideration for the sale of the motor-car. He could not consistently with that claim for repayment of the purchase also claim to retain possession of the car, but at all times it was sufficiently clear that he was not adopting any attitude of seeking to retain possession of the car. He was holding the car at the disposal of the defendants. I further hold that after he had written that letter the plaintiff was entitled to, and did, maintain his position of having no claim to possession of the car, but having a right to repayment of the purchase price. Having regard to that, whatever the general merits of his position may be, I hold that the plaintiff is in law entitled to recover, and there will be judgment for £1,275 against the defendants.

The next question is as to the present ownership of the car. The various purported sales all took place at times when Bowmaker Ld. were still the owners of the car, so that all the purported sellers in this rather long chain had no title to it at the times when the sales, or purported sales, were made; but on or about July 25, 1952, Miss Rudolph acquired a good title from Bowmaker Ld. or, at any rate, made a payment to Bowmaker Ld. which extinguished their title and induced them to relinquish any claim they had to the car. I think the right view is that Miss Rudolph did acquire the title as between her and Bowmaker Ld., but I further hold on authority that the title so acquired went to feed the previously defective titles of the subsequent buyers and enured to their benefit. It is a rather curious position but I so hold mainly on the authority of the Court of Appeal decision in *Whitehorn Brothers v. Davison*, [1911] 1 KB 463.

. . .

The next set of questions is concerned with the rights of the defendants against Hayton, and Hayton against Kennedy, and Kennedy against Miss Rudolph. The defendants are entitled to claim damages against Hayton for breach of the condition as to good title to the car, but that breach of the condition is now reduced to a breach of warranty and damages can be claimed on that basis. In consequence of that breach, the defendants lost the purchase price of £1,275 but, on the other hand, they eventually acquired ownership of the car. For the value of that car which they so acquired, they must give credit in reduction of the prima facie sum of £1,275.

The next question is: At what date is the value of the car to be assessed? One possible argument for the third party would be that it was a duty of the defendants to mitigate the damage by taking all reasonable steps to dispose of the car and it would have been reasonable for the defendants at once, in July or August or thereabouts in 1952, to take the car and dispose of it at the price it would then fetch in order to avoid further depreciation. It may be that there was a duty to mitigate the damage in that way, but the argument to the contrary is formidable: namely, that the defendants at that time were faced with a difficult legal position, and they were entitled to maintain their attitude against the plaintiff that the car belonged to him and it did not belong to them and they were not liable. I think there is a possibility of a good deal of argument as to what the "reasonable" steps to mitigate the damage would be, but I think this problem can be solved much more simply.

What the defendants gained was the ownership and right to possession of that car and, when one comes to assess the value of what they gained, one should take it at the date when it was gained. That is the position here. Then one has to arrive as best one can at the proper value of that car in or about July, 1952. [His Lordship referred to the evidence and continued:] The present value of this car is something like £450 and, making the best assessment I can, I assess its value in July, 1952, at £800. Therefore, the net claim of the defendants against the third party, all questions of the parties' costs being left over, is £475; that is to say, the difference between the full claim of £1,275 and the £800 deducted for the value of the car, leaving a difference of £475, and the decision is that the defendants are entitled to recover that sum from the third party.

The next step in the chain is the claim of Hayton, the third party, against Kennedy, the fourth party. This is possibly complicated by the fact that so far as the fourth party knew at the time of the contract of sale, Hayton was buying for his own use and not for re-sale; but Hayton paid £1,015 for the ownership of the car and he received initially no ownership at all so there was at that time a clear breach of contract. Prima facie his claim would be for the whole sum of £1,015 because he paid £1,015 and received nothing in exchange. In fact, subsequent events have reduced his claim. He has not suffered as much damage as that, but I think the fair view is that the subsequent events have to be taken as a whole and the effect is that his net claim against the fourth party is for £475, always leaving aside any question as to the parties' costs in this matter.

Similarly, I think the same result can be arrived at between Kennedy and Miss Rudolph. The previously mentioned complication does not exist here because Miss Rudolph knew that Kennedy was a motor dealer and was buying for re-sale. I do not think that that ultimately alters the result. Mr. Kennedy's claim against Miss Rudolph is £475, leaving aside the question of costs.

Judgment for the plaintiff.

Patten v. Thomas Motors Pty. Ltd.

(1965), 65 NSWR 458 (Australia)

[The following statement of facts is taken from the judgment of Collins J.

The case concerns the adventures of a Fiat motor car concerning which, one Ingeborg Persch, on 19th August, 1960, entered into a hire-purchase agreement with Commercial & General Acceptance Ltd. The hire-purchase agreement contained, *inter alia*, the following usual terms whereby the hirer agreed:

> 3(g) Not to conceal the goods or to part with personal possession or control of the same without due consent.
>
> 4(a) Not unlawfully to sell dispose of or encumber the goods or any right title or interest therein or attempt purport or agree to do so.
>
> 10. I may elect to become the owner of the goods by paying the total rent and fulfilling my other obligations hereunder or by compliance with section 11 of the Act. Until then I shall have no property in the goods and shall be only a bailee.

In April, 1961, while the agreement was still effective, Miss Persch purported to sell the car to the fifth party, Clinton Motors Pty. Ltd. Thereafter the vehicle changed hands rather rapidly until on 22nd April, 1961, the defendant, Thomas Motors Pty. Ltd., purported to purchase the vehicle. Then on 26th May, 1961, the plaintiff purported to purchase the vehicle from the defendant. All these transactions, including the intermediate transactions, were found by the learned trial judge to have been entered by the successive purchasers in good faith.

The plaintiff used the car for over two years until a demand was made upon him to surrender it by a finance company, Deposit & Investment Co. Ltd. The plaintiff refused to accede to this demand, whereupon on 15th July, 1963, Deposit & Investment Co. Ltd. seized the car and the plaintiff was thereafter deprived of its possession.

Deposit & Investment Co. Ltd. came into the picture in this way: On 1st August, 1961, over two months after the appellant had purported to buy the car from the respondents, Miss Persch inquired of Commercial & General Acceptance Ltd. the "pay-out figure" on the vehicle. Having ascertained this amount, she then fraudulently obtained from Deposit & Investment Co. Ltd. a loan, giving as security a bill of sale over, *inter alia*, the car in question. The amount so raised was used to discharge the amount outstanding under the hire-purchase agreement to Commercial & General Acceptance Ltd. and that company accepted the payment in discharge of its interest in the car.]

COLLINS J: This is an appeal by a plaintiff in a District Court action against the decision of his Honour Judge Bruxner, sitting without a jury, to return verdict and judgment in favour of the defendant.

The action was a claim for damages for breach of warranty of title of a motor vehicle purported to be purchased by the appellant Denis Frank Patten from Thomas Motors Pty. Ltd., the respondent to this appeal. The defendant had joined a third party in the action and successively the other parties were joined, including a fifth party, Clinton Motors Pty. Ltd. ...

[His Honour here stated the facts as set out above, and continued:]

The question which has provoked the debate in the present appeal is whether that payment "fed" the contract that Miss Persch had entered into with Clinton Motors and all the subsequent contracts so as to bestow upon the appellant plaintiff the legal estate in the car. The theory is that on discharging her obligation under the hire-purchase agreement, the property in the vehicle passed from Commercial & General Acceptance Ltd. to Miss Persch for a *scintilla temporis* and then instantaneously, as it were, passed along the line of succession until it vested in the appellant. If that be so, then on 9th August, 1961, the appellant acquired the legal title in the motor car and any cause of action that he may have had for damages for breach of warranty of title under s. 17(1) of the *Sale of Goods Act*, 1923-1953, from the date that he acquired the vehicle, namely 20th May, 1961, up to that date was thereupon extinguished. So that thereafter, on 24th September, 1963, when he took the proceedings by way of ordinary summons and particulars of claim in the District Court against the respondent, he had no cause of action.

The phrase "feeding the contract" is an unusual one, but it is derived from law of real property, where the phrase "feeding the estoppel" has been sanctioned by long usage. The rule applies if a vendor, not having the legal estate but being estopped from denying that he has it, conveys property; then his subsequent acquisition of the legal estate "feeds the estoppel" and the legal estate vests in the purported purchaser (*Doe d. Christmas v. Oliver* (1829), 109 ER 418; *General Finance, Mortgage & Discount Co. v. Liberator Permanent Benefit Building Society* (1878), 10 Ch. D. 15; *Church of England Building Society v. Piskor*, [1954] Ch. 553).

. . .

In *Whitehorn Bros. v. Davison*, [1911] 1 KB 463, a dealer in jewellery obtained possession of a valuable necklace from the plaintiffs, who were manufacturing jewellers, by false pretences, that is to say, fraudulently. He then pledged the necklace with the defendant, who was a pawnbroker. Subsequently the dealer bought the necklace from the plaintiffs, who accepted bills for the price.

In an action by the manufacturing jewellers against the pawnbroker for detinue of the necklace the jury found that the dealer obtained possession of the necklace by fraud and that the pawnbroker had acted in good faith, and on those findings Bray J gave judgment for the plaintiff. The Court of Appeal set aside this judgment and entered judgment for the defendant on the ground that the title acquired by the dealer having been perfected, it went to feed the title of the defendant with the result that, as he had not acted in bad faith and had no notice of the fraud of the dealer, he had a good title to the necklace.

. . .

In the present appeal Mr. Byron, on behalf of the appellant, advanced the contention that the doctrine "feeding the contract" or "feeding the estoppel" could only apply in a case where title acquired by the innocent purchaser was merely voidable and had no application where no title (or a so-called void title) passed. If goods are obtained by fraud then a voidable title passes, but if the goods are obtained by larceny by a trick, or indeed any form of larceny, no title passes. The bailee, Miss Persch, had no better title when she purported to sell the car to Clinton Motors than a thief would have had. As no title passed as a result of the transaction between her and Clinton Motors, the doctrine of feeding the title could not apply. He submitted then that Lord Pearson erred when, in *Butterworth's* case, he considered that the rule of feeding the contract applied.

I am of opinion that Mr. Byron's argument fails.

Although *Whitehorn Bros. v. Davison* did deal with a voidable contract, Vaughan Williams LJ in his judgment, said: "It is by reason of this event that I have come to the conclusion that the question of larceny by a trick becomes of no importance in this case. The title of Bruford (the jewellery dealer) to the necklace was, at any rate for the time being, perfected by that transaction, and would go to feed the title of the defendant, his pledgee, the result being that, if the defendant's title is not vitiated by bad faith on his part or notice, he has a good title." Buckley LJ said in terms at 481: "If ... (the dealer) had stolen it he had that which is sometimes incorrectly called a void title, but which is really no title at all ... (the dealer) could not then give the defendant a title. Upon this hypothesis the defendant on August 5th got no title but afterwards when ... (the dealer) became the owner of the necklace and had property in it, his title would go to feed the defendant's title; and as from that time it appears to me to be immaterial whether ... (the dealer) originally stole the necklace or not. From that time the defendant had a title." Each of these statements is strong authority against Mr. Byron's contention.

I now turn to Mr. Byron's contention that Lord Pearson erred in holding in *Butterworth's* case that the rule of feeding the contract applied in the circumstances of that case. He further suggested that there was an inconsistency between that view and his Lordship's ultimate verdicts in favour of the defendant and certain other added parties, so that his statement that the rule applied may be disregarded as being either irrelevant or merely obiter. In that case a car, having been sold wrongfully by a hirer under a hire-purchase agreement in the usual terms, passed through a number of hands by way of further purported sales until it was ultimately sold by the defendant to the plaintiff. After he had used the vehicle for an appreciable time, the plaintiff learned of the true facts and rescinded the contract with his vendor and demanded the return of his purchase price. Lord Pearson held this to be a valid rescission. After this rescission the original bailee of the car paid out her indebtedness under the hire-purchase agreement and the true owners accepted this payment in discharge of their interest in the vehicle.

This, in my opinion, is the critical matter of distinction between the facts of *Butterworth's* case and the facts of the present case. In *Butterworth's* case the plaintiff's rescission of his contract with the defendant took place before the wrongdoer had perfected her title by paying out the owner. In distinction, the wrongdoer in the present case paid out the true owner before the plaintiff became aware of the true facts and, on becoming aware of them he did not, nor did he attempt to, rescind his contract with the defendant.

In *Butterworth's* case the plaintiff never at any time had title to the vehicle. Having rescinded and demanded the return of his purchase price, he then sued for the return of the price in a common money count of money had and received as on a total failure of consideration (*Rowland v. Divall*). This act of rescission had the consequence that the spurious contract between the plaintiff and his vendor, the defendant, could not be legitimated by the subsequent acquisition of title by the bailee; it had then ceased to exist by reason of the rescission and there was nothing to be fed. All the other parties with the exception of the original wrongdoer obtained verdicts for damages for breach of warranty of authority from their respective vendors. It is these verdicts that Mr. Byron alleges are inconsistent with Lord Pearson's acceptance of the rule of feeding the title. Although Lord Pearson did not elaborate on his reasons, it is my view that it may well be that the purported rescission had a second consequence, namely, that immediately on rescission the vendor, having thereupon become liable to the plaintiff, immediately suffered damage from the breach of condition of title in the transaction in which he had been the purchaser and so did each other purchaser in his turn, in a kind of chain reaction in reverse. A simpler explanation may be that an examination of Lord Pearson's reasons strongly suggests that every moving party other than the plaintiff elected to reduce the breach of the condition to a breach of warranty and sued only for damages. Certainly in assessing the damages to be awarded to the defendant in his turn from his purported vendor, Lord Pearson treated as a matter of mitigation the fact that he had obtained a good title to the car on the basis of the rule of feeding the contract.

In the present case there was no act of rescission to break the chain. In my opinion the weight of authority compels the view that Miss Persch perfected her title when she paid out Commercial & General Acceptance Ltd. and that company accepted the payment in discharge of their interest in the vehicle. The title immediately passed down the line of successive purchasers until it vested in the appellant. The consequence was that when the appellant took proceedings in the District Court he no longer had any cause of action against the defendant.

Appeal dismissed.

NOTES

1) Plaintiff purchased electrical lamps from the defendant for resale. Upon taking delivery of the initial shipment it was discovered that the lamps had not been approved by the Canadian Standards Association as required by British Columbia law. Plaintiff sued for breach of s. 16 of the British Columbia SGA (Ont. SGA, s. 13), arguing that since the lamps could not lawfully be sold where the purchaser wanted to resell them, there was no right in the defendant to sell the goods. What result? See *J. Barry Winsor & Associates Ltd. v. Belgo Canadian Manufacturing Co. Ltd.* (1975), 61 DLR (3d) 352 (BCSC); aff'd. 76 DLR (3d) 685 (CA).

2) Section 13(a) deems the seller to warrant that he has "a right to sell," not simply that he has a right to convey title to the goods. Is there a difference? Examine again the definition of contract of sale in SGA s. 2(1). Cases such as *Niblett, supra,* and *J. Barry*

Winsor & Associates, supra, suggest that there is a difference and that s. 13(a) means that the seller may lawfully "deal" with the goods. What are the implications of this gloss? If A, a distributor of B's goods, agrees not to sell them to discount stores, will A commit a breach of s. 13(a) if he ignores the prohibition?

Note too that the seller must have the "right" to sell; a "power" to convey good title (by virtue of such exceptions to the *nemo dat* rule as appear in SGA ss. 25(1) and (2), the Factors Act, s. 2, and OPPSA, s. 28(1)) is not sufficient. Does this distinction make sense? What difference does it make to the buyer whether his seller has a right or merely a power to pass good title to the goods?

3) SGA s. 13(a) deems the seller to warrant his title at the time he purports to transfer it to the buyer. Literally interpreted, this means that in a conditional sale agreement in which the seller retains title until completion of the buyer's payments the seller would not be deemed to warrant his title until the buyer has finished his payments—a manifestly unsatisfactory result. A similar result would follow in hire-purchase agreements and other types of lease with an option to purchase. Happily, the courts have navigated their course around this obstacle. See *Karflex Ltd. v. Poole*, [1933] 2 KB 251, extended in *Warman v. Southern Counties Car Finance Corp. Ltd.*, [1949] 2 KB 576 and *cf. Sloan v. Empire Motors Ltd.* and *Vancouver Finance Co.* (1956), 3 DLR (2d) 53 (BCCA) and OLRC Sales Report, at 195-96 and 223-26. Note however the impact of the PPSA on the characterization of conditional sale agreements and at least some types of hire-purchase and equipment leases and the effect this may have on the implied condition of title under s. 13(a). See *infra*, this chapter, Note on the Implied Warranty of Freedom from Encumbrances.

4) What do you make of the doctrine of "feeding the estoppel" as applied in *Butterworth v. Kingsway Motors, supra*, and *Patten v. Thomas Motors, supra*? Whose estoppel is being fed? Could the results in these cases not be rationalized on a more apt basis, for example, that a buyer cannot rescind the purchase if the seller has in fact cured the defect in title? (On the right to cure a tender of non-conforming goods, now explicitly recognized in UCC 2-508, see, *infra*, chapter 16.) If the seller has a right to cure a defect in title before the buyer becomes aware of the defect and rescinds the transaction, why should the seller not have a like right to cure even after the buyer has learned of the defect, assuming the seller's offer to cure is made promptly and in good faith?

5) As *Rowland v. Divall, supra*, and *Butterworth v. Kingsway Motors, supra*, show, where the seller has breached his condition of title the buyer is entitled to recover the price without any allowance being made for the use of the goods. Various commentators have argued that the result is unjust. See for example, Atiyah, *The Sale of Goods*, 10th ed., at 109 *et seq.* The OLRC Sales Report (at 506-9) reviewed several earlier suggested solutions and then reached the following conclusion:

> In our opinion, restitutionary claims for defects in title should be put on the same footing as claims arising out of other defects that entitle the buyer to claim the return of the price. We have previously recommended that where the buyer has received the goods any claim by a buyer to recover so much of the price as has been paid should be subject to such a reduction on account of any benefits derived by him from the use or possession of the goods as is just in the circumstances. In our view this recommendation should also apply to a buyer's claim to recover the purchase price where there is a defect in the seller's title and we so recommend.

In addition, following our earlier recommendations the seller will have an opportunity to cure the defect in title if he satisfies the requirements generally applicable to a seller's right to cure a non-conforming tender or delivery.

Microbeads AG v. Vinhurst Road Markings Ltd.

[1975] 1 All ER 529, [1975] 1 WLR 218 (CA)

LORD DENNING MR: This case raises a new and interesting point on the sale of goods. The defendants, an English company ("Vinhurst"), bought some special machinery from the plaintiffs, a Swiss company. They used the machines for making white lines on roads. Two or three years later another English company, who owned a patent, came along and said that these machines infringed their patent. They sought an injunction to prevent the use of the machines. Have the English company, who bought the machines, a cause of action against the Swiss company who sold them?

The dates are important. I will start with the owners of the patent. They are an English company, Prismo Universal Ltd. ("Prismo"), who carry on business near Crawley in Sussex. They hold a patent for an apparatus for applying markings on roads. It is done by the machine which carries a spray gun and a quantity of thermo-plastic material. This gun sprays the material on to the roads so as to make a white and yellow line.

For some time the invention was kept secret. The application for a patent was filed on 28 December 1966. The complete specification was filed on 28 December 1967. The Patent Office made their various examinations. Eventually, on the 11th November 1970, the complete specification was published. It was on that date that it became open to the world to learn about it. It was only after that date that the patentee had any right or privileges in respect of it: see ss. 13(4) and 22 of the Patents Act 1949. On 12th January 1972 letters patent were granted to Prismo in respect of the invention. It was only then the patentee was entitled to institute proceedings for infringement: see s. 13(4) of the 1949 Act.

Now, before that invention was made public, Vinhurst bought some road marking machines and accessories from the Swiss company. These machines were sold and delivered to Vinhurst between January and April 1970, that is some months before the Prismo specification was published in November 1970. The price of the machines and accessories was nearly £15,000 of which Vinhurst paid £5,000, leaving the £10,000 balance to be paid. The buyers, Vinhurst, did not know anything about the patent. They had no idea that the machines might be infringing machines. They took them in good faith and used them. But they found the machines very unsatisfactory. They were dissatisfied. They did not pay the balance of the price.

On 30th November 1970 the sellers, the Swiss company, sued Vinhurst for the balance of £10,000 owing for the machines. At first Vinhurst put in a defence saying that the machines were not reasonably fit for the purpose of marking roads.

But then in 1972 Prismo came down on Vinhurst and said these machines (supplied by the Swiss company) infringed their patent. Thereupon Vinhurst amended their defence so as to set up the infringement as a defence and counterclaim. The point was set down as a preliminary issue. The judge found that the sellers, the Swiss company, were not guilty of a breach of contract in this respect. The buyers appeal to this court.

The preliminary issue was directed on these assumptions: (1) that the letters patent were valid; (2) that the machines sold by the Swiss company to Vinhurst were such as to fall within the scope of the claims in the specification; (3) that the property in each of the machines was to pass prior to November 1970. On those assumptions the point of law was whether there was any breach of contract on the part of the Swiss company under s. 12(1) or s. 12(2) of the Sale of Goods Act 1893 having regard to the dates of filing and publication of the specification and of the grant of the patent.

Before the judge most of the discussion was on s. 12(1). It says that there is an "implied condition on the part of the seller that … he has a right to sell the goods …." That means that he has, *at the time of the sale*, a right to sell the goods. The words "a right to sell the goods" means not only a right to pass the property in the machines to the buyer, but also a right to confer on the buyer the undisturbed possession of the goods: see *Niblett Ltd. v. Confectioners' Materials Co. Ltd.*, [1921] 3 KB 387, at 402, by Atkin LJ. Now, at the time of the sale in January 1970 the Swiss company were able to confer those rights. They had made the machines out of their own materials and they could undoubtedly pass the property in them to the buyers. Moreover there was no one at that time entitled to disturb their possession. There was then no subsisting patent. The specification had not been published. No one could sue for infringement. The buyer could, *at that time*, use the machines undisturbed. So I agree with the judge that there was no breach of s. 12(1).

Now I turn to s. 12(2). It says that there is an "implied warranty that the buyer shall have and enjoy quiet possession of the goods." Taking those words in their ordinary meaning, they seem to cover this case. The words "shall have and enjoy" apply not only to the time of the sale but to the future; "shall enjoy" means in the future. If a patentee comes two or three years later and gets an injunction to restrain the use of the goods, there would seem to be a breach of the warranty. But it is said that there are limitations on the ordinary meaning such limitations being derived from the civil law (as suggested by Benjamin on Sale) or from conveyancing cases.

One such limitation is said to follow from the words of Lord Ellenborough CJ in *Howell v. Richards* (1809), 11 East 633, at 642, when he said:

> The covenant for title is an assurance to the purchaser, that the grantor has the very estate in quantity and quality which he purports to convey, viz, in this case an indefeasible estate in fee simple. The covenant for quiet enjoyment is an assurance against the consequences of a defective title, and of any disturbances thereupon.

Counsel for the Swiss company said that Lord Ellenborough CJ there meant a defective title existing at the time of the sale. The covenant, he said, did not apply to a defective title which only appeared some time after the sale. The defect here appeared after the sale; it [appeared] in November 1970 when the complete specification was published.

The other limitation, derived from the conveyancing cases, was that the covenant for quiet enjoyment protected the purchaser or tenant only from the acts or operations of the vendor or lessor and those claiming under him, but not against the acts or operations of those claiming by title paramount: see *Jones v. Lavington*, [1903] 1 KB 253. Counsel for the Swiss company submitted that that conveyancing rule applied to s. 12(2) also. Here the claim by the patentee was by title paramount.

There is one case which supports this contention. It is a decision of Lord Russell of Killowen CJ in 1895 when he was on the Northern Circuit. It is *Monforts v. Marsden* (1895), 12 RPC 266. But that case was disapproved by this court in *Niblett Ltd. v. Confectioners' Materials Co. Ltd.* and must be taken to be overruled. Afterwards in *Mason v. Burningham*, [1949] 2 KB 545, at 563, Lord Green MR made it clear that the conveyancing cases should not be applied to s. 12 of the Sale of Goods Act 1893. He said:

> It is to be observed that in the language used in the Sale of Goods Act, 1893, s. 12(2), there is no exception for any disturbance by title paramount. The words are as I have quoted them, "that the buyer shall have and enjoy quiet possession of the goods." I invited counsel for the defendant to refer us to any authority that would justify the insertion into that statutory phrase of an exception in the case of disturbance by title paramount, but he was unable to do so, and, in the absence of any authority, I can only express my opinion that the statute means what it says and is not to have any such gloss put on it.

I would follow the guidance of Lord Greene MR. Even if the disturbance is by title paramount—such as by the patentee coming in and claiming an injunction to restrain the use of the machine—there is a breach of the implied warranty under s. 12(2).

But the main point of counsel for the Swiss company before us—a point which the judge accepted—was that the defects of title must be present *at the time of the sale*. That is why so much turned on the date of publication, 11th November 1970. After that date the Swiss company, could by taking reasonable steps, have known that their machines were infringing machines and that they could not have a right to use them. So, if they had sold after 11th November 1970, they would be in breach of s. 12(2) and of s. 12(1) also. But counsel for the Swiss company says that before that date the Swiss company may have been perfectly innocent. Nothing had been published about this patent. The machines were sold in January and April 1970. There was no defect in title existing at the time of the sale. Accordingly counsel submitted there was no breach of s. 12(2).

I cannot accept this submission. It means putting a gloss on section 12(2), by introducing a qualification which is not there. It seems to me that when a buyer has bought goods quite innocently and later on he is disturbed in his possession because the goods are found to be infringing a patent, then he can recover damages for breach of warranty against the seller. It may be the seller is innocent himself, but when one or other must suffer, the loss should fall on the seller: because, after all, he sold the goods and if it turns out that they infringe a patent, he should bear the loss. In the present case the Prismo company can sue for infringement now and stop the buyer using the machines. That is a clear disturbance of possession. The buyer is not able to enjoy the quiet possession which the seller impliedly warranted that he shall have. There is a breach of section 12(2).

Appeal allowed.

NOTES

1) Is the construction placed in *Microbeads* on the seller's implied warranty of quiet possession too harsh? Would the court have reached the same conclusion if the sale had not been in the ordinary course of the seller's business? *Cf.* OLRC Sales Report, at 196-97.

2) It will be noted that *Microbeads* really involved the seller's liability for innocent patent infringement. Unlike the SGA, the UCC contains a separate provision under this head and only holds a *merchant seller* liable for such infringements [UCC 2-312(3)]. Why should a private seller be held strictly responsible for the defects in his title and not be held responsible for defects arising out of patent or trade mark infringements? Happily, patent and trademark owners do not generally appear to be concerned with private infringements—at least judging by the absence of reported Canadian cases. A partial explanation may be s. 56 of the (Canadian) Patent Act, RSC 1985, c. P-4, as am., 1993, c. 44, s. 194, which provides in part:

> 56(1) Every person who, before the earlier of the date of filing of an application for a patent and the priority date of the application, if any, has purchased, constructed or acquired the invention for which a patent is afterwards obtained under this Act, has the right to use and sell to others the specific article, machine, manufacture or composition of matter patented and so purchased, constructed or acquired without being liable to the patentee or the legal representatives of the patentee for so doing.

3) In *Ahlstrom Canada Ltd. v. Browning Harvey Ltd.* (1987), 31 DLR (4th) 316 (Nfld. CA), B, a bottler of soft drinks, placed an order with A, a manufacturer of bottles, for a quantity of 1.5-litre glass bottles. The bottles were delivered in June 1979 and paid for. In August of the same year the use of 1.5-litre bottles for soft drinks was prohibited under the Hazardous Products Act, RSC 1985, c. H-3. (On the provisions of the Act, see, *infra*, chapter 8.) B shipped the bottles back to A, which accepted them without prejudice to its position that it had no such obligation.

B brought an action for recovery of the price and succeeded at trial on the ground that this result was "fair, reasonable and equitable." The decision was reversed on appeal since, in the view of the Court of Appeal, A had not breached any of its warranty obligations under the SGA. Gushue JA said (at 320):

> When the contract was completed, Browning Harvey had obtained exactly what it had bargained for and, at that time, in accordance with the provisions of s. 22 (and other sections) of the *Sale of Goods Act*, the risk passed from Ahlstrom to Browning Harvey. Thus, any loss sustained by reason of the ban, imposed some months later, against the use of these bottles, had to be born by the purchaser, Browning Harvey Limited.

He did not refer to *Microbeads* nor did he examine the effect of an order under the HPA. Had A committed a breach of the implied condition of title? Of the implied warranty to give quiet possession?

Note on the Implied Warranty of Freedom from Encumbrances (Section 13(c))

There appears to be very little significant jurisprudence on s. 13(c), presumably because buyers prefer to rest their case on ss. 13(a) or (b). Like the implied warranty of quiet possession, s. 13(c) seems to have borrowed from land law, where it occupies a well-established niche. Section 13(c) may grow in importance in view of the conceptual changes brought about by the various Personal Property Security Acts. In particular, since a conditional sale agreement is now treated as a full-fledged security agreement, there seems little justification for saying that a buyer under such an agreement who resells the goods without disclosing the security interest is guilty of a breach of the implied condition of title. The correct answer should be that he has breached the warranty under s. 13(c).

However, Canadian courts have become so accustomed to treating an undisclosed conditional sale as a breach of title that it may be difficult for them to change their attitude. Would this be calamitous? Is there a good reason for treating the right to sell as a condition and treating freedom from encumbrances as a mere warranty?

CHAPTER SIX

Seller's Implied Obligations with Respect to Description

SGA s. 14 imposes on the seller the fundamental obligation to supply goods that conform to the contract description. The meaning of "description" is not self-evident and the materials in the present section illustrate the various contexts in which the courts and other agencies have had to grapple with the question. What gives particular thrust to s. 14 is the fact that it applies to *all* sellers and that the obligation is characterized as a condition with the important remedial consequences that this entails.

The term "description" is also used in several other places in the Act, *viz.* ss. 15(1), 15(2), r. 5(i), and 29(3). Initially there was a tendency to interpret the term uniformly, without regard to its particular context, but this liberal approach appears to have been arrested by the judgment of the law lords in the *Ashington Piggeries* case (*infra*, this chapter) that "description" in s. 15 does not have the same meaning as in s. 14. On this terminological point see further, OLRC Sales Report, at 205-6, 208.

Determining the meaning of "description" in its various settings in the SGA has been complicated by the blurring of lines between a sale "by description" and a sale of specific goods. A sale of specific goods carried great significance before the adoption of the SGA, and much of this significance has been retained in the Act: see, for example, SGA ss. 7-8, 12(3), 19, r. 1, and s. 50. In the 19th century too the implied conditions of quality (and quality in an extended sense included the implied condition of description: see the judgment of Mellor J in *Jones v. Just* (1868), LR 3 QB 197, at 202-3) did not apply to a sale of specific goods when the goods were available for inspection. Traces of this rule may be found in the requirement of SGA 15(2), dealing with the condition of merchantability, that the goods must be bought "by description." See further *Benjamin's Sale of Goods*, 3rd ed., §756; S.J. Stoljar (1952), 15 *Mod. L Rev.* 425; (1953), 16 *Mod. L Rev.* 174. As will be seen, however, from the cases in this section, so far as the obligation to deliver goods of the right description and merchantable quality are concerned, any lingering distinction between a sale of specific and non-specific goods has been substantially abandoned in the post-1893 jurisprudence.

Andrews Brothers (Bournemouth) Ltd. v. Singer & Co. Ltd.

[1934] 1 KB 17, [1933] All ER Rep. 479 (CA)

SCRUTTON LJ: This is an appeal from a judgment of Goddard J in an action by the plaintiffs, a company carrying on business at Bournemouth, who in the agreement between them and the defendants out of which the dispute has arisen are called agents for manufacturers, which is quite a misleading term inasmuch as they are really purchasers of motor cars which they intend to sell. They brought their action against Singer & Co. alleging that the latter delivered a car which did not comply with the terms of the contract.

The facts which are fully set out in the careful judgment of Goddard J may be shortly summarised: the description of the kind of car the plaintiffs wanted could have been satisfied by delivery to them of a new car; but the particular car which Singer & Co. tendered to them was in this position. Another agent, who thought he had in view a purchaser for the car, had it sent to Darlington and thence it was driven some distance further to show to the prospective customer, but as that person did not like it the agent returned it to Singer & Co., the result being that it had run a very considerable mileage with the consequence no doubt that certain changes had taken place in it. When the car was tendered to the plaintiffs' representative he noticed or suspected that it had run a considerable distance, but he took it, doing nothing, however, so far as I can see, to abandon any claim for damages on the ground that it was not a new car.

At the trial two points arose: First, the plaintiff said that the car was not a new car as that term was understood in the trade. The defendants on the other hand said it was. Goddard J came to the conclusion that it was not a new car, and in this Court his decision on that point has not been questioned and I therefore proceed on the assumption that the defendants, who were bound to supply a new car, tendered a car which was not a new one. The defendants contended secondly that they are exempted from liability by reason of clause 5 of the agreement entered into. That clause reads as follows: "All cars sold by the company are subject to the terms of the warranty set out in Schedule No. 3 of this agreement and all conditions, warranties and liabilities implied by statute, common law or otherwise are excluded." The defendants say that their obligation to supply a car complying with the description in the contract is a condition implied by statute, and as the plaintiffs accepted the car under the agreement containing clause 5 they cannot bring an action in respect of the supplying of a car which was not a new one. Clause 5 is, I take it, a sequel to *Wallis, Sons & Wells v. Pratt & Haynes*, [1910] 2 KB 1003. In that case the subject matter of the sale was "common English sainfoin," and the contract contained this clause: "Sellers give no warranty express or implied as to growth, description or any other matters." What in fact was sold under the contract was not "common English sainfoin" but something quite different, namely, "giant sainfoin." On discovering this the purchasers sued for damages, to which claim the sellers replied that they gave no warranty express or implied as to description. The Court of Appeal (Moulton LJ dissenting) took the view that the clause excluded any liability even though the seed supplied was not of the description contracted to be supplied. The House of Lords adopted Moulton LJ's judgment and said that the goods tendered should comply with the description in the contract, which description was not a warranty but a condition, and as the clause relied on did not include "condition" it did not operate to protect the sellers. Those advising the present defendants in preparing this agreement appear to have thought that by the inclusion of the word "conditions" in the relevant clause liability would be excluded, although what was supplied did not comply with the description. The question therefore is whether the defendants have succeeded in excluding liability in this case—whether they can tender under the contract goods not complying with the description in the contract and say that the plaintiffs having accepted the car cannot now sue for breach of contract.

In my opinion this was a contract for the sale of a new Singer car. The contract continually uses the phrase "new Singer cars." At the end of the agreement I find this: "In the event of the dealer having purchased from the Company during the period of this agreement 250 new cars of current season's models"; and in the very beginning of the agreement I find this: "The company hereby appoint the dealer their sole dealer for the sale of new Singer cars." The same phrase also occurs in other parts of the agreement, and the subject-matter is therefore expressly stated to be "new Singer cars." The judge has found, and his view is not now contested, that the car tendered in this case was not a new Singer car. Does then clause 5 prevent the vendors being liable in damages for having tendered and supplied a car which is not within the express terms of the contract? Clause 5 says this: "All conditions, warranties and liabilities implied by statute, common law or otherwise are excluded." There are well-known obligations in various classes of contracts which are not expressly mentioned but are implied. During the argument Greer LJ mentioned an apt illustration, namely, where an agent contracts on behalf of A he warrants that he has authority to make the contract on behalf of A although no such warranty is expressed in the contract. Mr. Pritt relied on s. 13 of the Sale of Goods Act, 1893, which provides that "where there is a contract for the sale of goods by description, there is an implied condition that the goods shall correspond with the description ...," and from that he says it follows that this particular condition comes within the words employed by the section. That, I think, is putting a very strained meaning on the word "implied" in the section. Where goods are expressly described in the contract and do not comply with that description, it is quite innaccurate to say that there is an implied term; the term is expressed in the contract. Suppose the contract is for the supply of a car of 1932 manufacture, and a car is supplied which is of 1930 manufacture, there has not been a breach of an implied term; there has been a breach of an express term of the contract. It leads to a very startling result if it can be said that clause 5 allows a vendor to supply to a purchaser an article which does not comply with the express description of the article in the contract, and then, though the purchaser did not know of the matter which prevented the article supplied from complying with the express terms of the contract, to say, "We are under no liability to you because this is a condition implied by statute and we have excluded such liability."

In my view there has been in this case a breach of an express term of the contract. If a vendor desires to protect himself from liability in such a case he must do so by

much clearer language than this, which, in my opinion, does not exempt the defendants from liability where they have failed to comply with the express term of the
contract. For these reasons I think Goddard J came to a correct conclusion, and this
appeal therefore fails.

Appeal dismissed.

[Greer LJ and Eve J delivered concurring judgments.]

NOTES

1) Scrutton LJ is no doubt correct in his assertion that analytically words of description are an express part of the contract in which they appear. It is equally clear however
that Chalmers, following 19th century usage, treated the descriptive language as giving
rise to an *implied* obligation on the seller to deliver goods conforming to the description.
See, for example, *Chalmer's Sale of Goods Act*, 18th ed. (1981), at 119, note (r), and
cases cited in note (h). That being the case, should Scrutton LJ not have respected the
SGA's characterization of the obligation?

2) UCC 2-313(1)(b) provides that "any description of the goods which is made part of
the basis of the bargain creates an express warranty that the goods shall conform to the
description." The OLRC Sales Report, at 202-3, and draft bill s. 5.11(1)(a), favoured a
similar treatment of the obligation in the revised Sale of Goods Act. The English and
Scottish Law Commissions, in their *First Report on Exemption Clauses in Contracts*
(1969), para. 22, admitted the anomalous characterization in the UK Act but felt it was
harmless and that it served the useful purpose of making it clear that the term amounts to
a condition and is not a mere warranty. Do you agree?

Varley v. Whipp

[1900] 1 QB 513, 69 LJQB 333 (Div. Ct.)

[In June 1899 the plaintiff and the defendant met in Huddersfield, at which time the
plaintiff offered to sell to the defendant for £21 a second-hand self-binding reaping
machine, which the plaintiff said was then at Upton, and he also said it had been new
the previous year, and had only been used to cut fifty or sixty acres. The defendant
had not then seen the machine but he agreed to buy it. The machine was not then the
plaintiff's property, but he bought it immediately afterwards for £18. On June 28 the
plaintiff put the machine on the railway to send to Beverley.

On July 2, the defendant wrote the plaintiff as follows: "I have had a look at the
'self-binder' you sent me but it is not what I expected; it is a very old one and has
been mended and you told me that it had only cut about 50 acres, and was practically
new. I think you must never have seen it. It will be no use to me as I don't care about
old things, and especially machinery, but I shall be at Huddersfield this week ... where
I shall be pleased to see you." After some further correspondence the defendant re-

turned the machine on August 14, and the plaintiff brought this action to recover the price. The county court judge held that the contract was a sale by description, and that the defendant could only treat the misdescription as a breach of warranty but not as a ground for rejecting the machine. He therefore gave judgment for the plaintiff for the amount claimed. The defendant appealed.]

CHANNELL J: I am of opinion that this appeal ought to be allowed. The case turns on a fine point, namely, whether the words used by the seller with regard to the machine were part of the description, or merely amounted to a collateral warranty. If the property in the machine passed prior to July 2, nothing that the buyer could do afterwards would divest it. The question is, did the property pass? The machine which was to be sold had never been seen by the buyer, and it was not the property of the seller at the time. It was described as being at Upton, as being a self-binder, as being nearly new, and as having been used to cut only about fifty or sixty acres. All these statements were made with regard to the machine, and we have to consider how much of these statements was identification of the machine, and how much was mere collateral warranty. If a man says that he will sell the black horse in the last stall in his stable, and the stall is empty, or there is no horse in it, but only a cow, no property could pass. Again, if he says he will sell a four-year old horse in the last stall, and there is a horse in the stall, but it is not a four-year old, the property would not pass. But if he says he will sell a four-year old horse, and there is a four-year old horse in the stall, and he says that the horse is sound, this last statement would only be a collateral warranty. The term "sale of goods by description" must apply to all cases where the purchaser has not seen the goods, but is relying on the description alone. It applies in a case like the present, where the buyer has never seen the article sold, but has bought by the description. In that case, by the Sale of Goods Act, 1893, s. 13, there is an implied condition that the goods shall correspond with the description, which is a different thing from a warranty. The most usual application of that section no doubt is to the case of unascertained goods, but I think it must also be applied to cases such as this where there is no identification otherwise than by description. Then the sale being a sale by description, when did the property pass, if it did not pass when the bargain was made? The section of the Sale of Goods Act dealing with the passing of the property is s. 17, by which "(1.) where there is a contract for the sale of specific or ascertained goods, the property in them is transferred to the buyer at such time as the parties to the contract intend it to be transferred. (2.) For the purpose of ascertaining the intention of the parties regard shall be had to the terms of the contract, the conduct of the parties, and the circumstances of the case." It is impossible to imagine a clause more vague than this, but I think it correctly represents the state of the authorities when the Act was passed. Sect. 18 does not apply; the only clause in that section which could possibly apply would be rule 1, but I do not think that this was "an unconditional contract of the sale of specific goods." Then when did the property pass? Not when the machine was put on the railway for the vendor could not make the property pass by putting on the railway that which did not fulfill the implied condition. The earliest date therefore at which the property could be said to pass would be when the machine was accepted by the purchaser. But it never was accepted. I am doubtful whether the letter of July 2 could be treated as amounting to a rejection, but the purchaser certainly did not accept the machine by that letter, and therefore the property never had passed. The result is that the defendant is entitled to judgment, and the appeal must be allowed.

BUCKNILL J: I am of the same opinion. The county court judge has found that there was a sale by description, and I think that finding is right. The machine was sold as a self-binder, which was then at Upton, was nearly new, and had only been used to cut fifty or sixty acres. Was that a collateral warranty, or was it the description of the article intended to be sold? I am of opinion that it was the description, and that there was a contract for sale by description, within the meaning of s. 13 of the Sale of Goods Act. The machine was put on the railway, and got to the defendant's place of business. He could then accept or reject it. He wrote the letter of July 2, by which, though possibly he did not reject the machine, certainly he did not accept it. I am of opinion that the appeal must be allowed, and judgment given for the defendant.

Appeal allowed.

NOTES

1) *Varley v. Whipp* cannot be properly understood without recalling the anomalous rule in what was then s. 11(1)(c) of the UK Act [Ont., s. 12(3)] that where the contract is for the sale of specific goods, the property in which has passed to the buyer, the breach of any condition to be fulfilled by the seller can only be treated as a warranty and not as a ground for rejecting the goods. See *infra*, chapter 16. Thus the Divisional Court had to consider two separate issues: (1) had the seller committed a breach of the implied condition of description; and (2) if he had, did this prevent the presumptive transfer of title as envisaged in s. 18, rule 1 [Ont. s. 19, r. 1] of the Act? The writers have generally concentrated on the latter question and less on the court's analysis of the meaning of description in s. 13 of the UK Act. See, *inter alia*, P.S. Atiyah, *The Sale of Goods*, 7th ed. (1985), at 224-25, and G.H.L. Fridman, *The Sale of Goods in Canada*, 4th ed. (1995), at 82. On SGA s. 12(3), see also *Home Gas Ltd. v. Streeter*, *infra*, chapter 16, and *Wojakowski v. Pembina Dodge Chrysler Ltd.*, [1976] 5 WWR 97 (Man.), discussed in Notes following *Home Gas*.

2) *Williston on Sales*, rev. ed., at 224-25, is critical of the broad meaning given to "description" in *Varley v. Whipp* and other post-1893 English cases. He argues that the term should be confined to cases where the identification of the goods which are the subject-matter of the bargain depends upon the description. He points out that the English courts have been forced to give an extended meaning to the term in order to provide the disappointed buyer with an effective right of rejection, and that the difficulty does not arise under the American Uniform Sales Act (now replaced, of course, by Article 2 of the UCC) since that Act generally allows rescission for breach of warranty whether or not the implied term of description, strictly construed, has been breached. Williston's strictures derive some support from several of the law lords' judgments in the *Ashington Piggeries* case and from Lord Wilberforce's judgment in the *Reardon Smith Line* case (both *infra*,

this chapter) but for a different reason, *viz.* that a right of rejection should not be recognized for inconsequential breaches that can be adequately compensated for in damages. For a searching examination of the meaning of description, see also R.M. Goode, *Commercial Law,* 2nd ed. (1995), at 293 *et seq.*

3) Section 11(1)(c) of the UK Act 1893 [now SGA 1979, s. 11(4)] was amended by the Misrepresentation Act 1967, s. 4(1), which omitted the words "or where the Canadian contract is for specific goods, the property in which has passed to the buyer." None of the provincial SGAs appears so far to have copied the amendment.

Beale v. Taylor

[1967] 3 All ER 253, [1967] 1 WLR 1193 (CA)

SELLERS LJ: I have come to the conclusion that this appeal should be allowed. It is an unfortunate case which I would have hoped might have been disposed of satisfactorily within the confines of the county court, either by the learned judge in the first instance or on an application to him to hear the matter again if, as it is suggested here, there was some misunderstanding as to the contentions on behalf of the plaintiff. However, it has now come on appeal and this court has to decide it. It is an unusual case, and for both parties—who, as the judge said, are both innocent in the matter—an unfortunate one.

The defendant seller, Mr. Taylor, had a car which he believed to be a Herald convertible, 1961, 1200 twin-carburetter car. He apparently had driven it for some time and done a considerable mileage with it and wished to dispose of it. I think that it had been in an accident, and certainly it was not in very good condition. The seller inserted an advertisement in about April, 1966, in a well-known paper for the sale of secondhand cars. That was in these terms: "Herald convertible, white, 1961, twin carbs., £190. Telephone Welwyn Garden," and it gives a telephone number, "after 6:00 p.m." The plaintiff buyer, who was born in 1946 and has been driving cars for some little time, or his mother, or both, saw the advertisement, got in touch with the seller, and went along to his home to see the car. They saw it and had a run in it. The buyer did not drive because there was no insurance for him. I do not know whether his mother went in the car too. After that run and some discussion the buyer made an offer, or his mother made an offer to buy the car for £160, which the seller accepted. There was a little delay while the balance of the purchase price was paid, and then the buyer drove it away. From the outset apparently the buyer found that the steering was pulling to the left-hand side, so much so that he said that, in his journey from Welwyn Garden City to St. Albans, his arms ached; and he eventually after a short time put it in a garage to be checked over. Then it was found by the garage people that, instead of being a car of that description—that being a 1961 1200 Triumph Herald convertible—it was in fact a car which was made up of two cars. The back portion apparently was of that description but the front portion, which had been welded on about half-way, somewhere under the driver's seat, and which contained the engine, was an older, earlier model, the 948 c.c. model, and these two parts had been made into this one structure. Having regard to the nature of the welding of the two chassis together, as described by the expert who was called, it is not surprising that the car was not running properly. It had also apparently had an accident, as I have said, and it was condemned as being unsafe to take on the road.

The question then arose what was to happen with regard to the purchase price which the buyer had paid to the seller. Instead of the matter being settled amicably, which might have been the wisest thing to do in order to save the money which has been involved in costs, the matter went to court. The buyer relied on the fact that there had been a description of this vehicle as a Triumph Herald 1200 motor car with the registration number 400 RDH and that the vehicle which was delivered did not correspond with that description. The seller, who conducted his own defence and apparently put in his written defence as well, denied that it was a sale by description and said that, on the contrary, it was

> the sale of a particular car as seen, tried and approved, the [buyer] having an abundant opportunity to inspect and test the car.

He denied that the buyer had in the circumstances suffered any loss or damage. Of course a person may purchase a commodity relying entirely on his own judgment in the matter, and there may be no representation at all. Perhaps one hundred years ago more credence might have been given to the seller's defence than is given now, but, since the Sale of Goods Act, 1893, the rule caveat emptor has been very much modified. Section 13 of the Sale of Goods Act, 1893, provides that

> Where there is a contract for the sale of goods by description, there is an implied condition that the goods shall correspond with that description;

and certainly there is good authority for saying that, if the buyer has not seen the goods, then in the ordinary way the contract would be one where the buyer relied on the description alone. Sale of goods by description may, however, apply where the buyer has seen the goods if the deviation of the goods from the description is not apparent; but even then (and I am quoting now from a well-known text book, *Chalmers' Sale of Goods* (15th ed.)), when the parties are really agreed on the thing sold a misdescription of it in the contract may be immaterial.

The question in this case is whether this was a sale by description or whether, as the seller contends, this was a sale of a particular thing seen by the buyer and bought by him purely on his own assessment of the value of the thing to him. We were referred to a passage in the speech of Lord Wright in *Grant v. Australian Knitting Mills, Ltd.*, [1936] AC 85, at 100, which I think is apt as far as this case is concerned. Lord Wright said:

> It may also be pointed out that there is a sale by description even though the buyer is buying something displayed before him on the counter; a thing is sold by description, though it is specific, so long as it is sold not merely as the specific thing but as a thing corresponding to a description, e.g., woollen under-garments, a hot water bottle, a secondhand reaping machine, to select a few obvious illustrations

and, I might add, a secondhand motor car. I think that, on the facts of this case, the buyer, when he came along to see this car, was coming along to see a car as advertised, that is, a car described as a "Herald convertible, white, 1961." When he came along he saw what ostensibly was a Herald convertible, white, 1961, because the evidence shows that the "1200" which was exhibited on the rear of this motor car is the first model of the "1200" which came out in 1961; it was on that basis that he was making the offer and in the belief that the seller was advancing his car as that which his advertisement indicated. Apart from that, the selling of a car of that make, I would on the face of it rather agree with the submission of the seller that he was making no warranties at all and making no contractual terms; but fundamentally he was selling a car of that description. The facts as revealed very shortly afterwards show that that description was false. It was unfortunately not false to the knowledge of the owner who was selling nor of the buyer, because no one could see from looking at the car in the ordinary sort of examination which would be made that it was anything other than that which it purported to be. It was only afterwards that, on examination, it was found to be in two parts. I think that that is a sufficient ground on which to decide this case in favour of the buyer.

Appeal allowed.

NOTES

1) Suppose in *Beale v. Taylor* the defendant had advertised the vehicle for sale as a "used car" and that when the plaintiff phoned and enquired what type of vehicle it was the defendant had replied "Herald convertible 1961," would this have made a difference to the outcome? Would it make a difference if the plaintiff had only asked the question after he had inspected and testdriven the vehicle?

2) In view of the modern judicial tendency to apply SGA s. 14 to the sale of specific as well as future or unascertained goods, can you think of a situation in which a sale of specific goods will not be treated as a sale by description?

3) In *Speedway Safety Products Pty. Ltd. v. Hazell & Moore Industries Pty. Ltd.*, [1982] 1 NSWLR 255 (Australia), the respondent company, a distributor of Suzuki motorcycles, was in receivership. It had a spare parts division at Wentworth St. The appellant was an importer of motorcycle parts and accessories and carried accessories for Suzuki motorcycles.

The appellant's managing director was interested in buying some of the respondent's assets including its stock of spare parts. He visited the Wentworth St. premises on four or five occasions and looked at the stock. On the third occasion he carried out a test check to determine the average age of the stock and the range of models of motorcycles to which the items related. On April 1, 1977 the parties reached an agreement which was recorded in a letter of the same date from the receiver to the appellant. According to the letter, the appellant had agreed to the purchase "of the plant and equipment and ... purchase of the stock situated at the premises 74-78 Wentworth Avenue ... ." The agreement also provided for the appellant taking over the lease of the premises on Wentworth St.

The appellant paid part of the purchase price and went into occupation of the premises. It then complained that there were errors in the previous stocktake by the receiver and that some of the items among the goods bought by it were obsolete or damaged or affected by rust and unsaleable. The appellant therefore refused to pay the balance of the price.

The New South Wales Court of Appeal held that there had been no sale by description and that the appellant was not entitled to invoke the implied condition of merchantability in s. 19(2) of the NSW Sale of Goods Act [Ont., s. 15(2)]. Samuels JA said:

> I do not regard this formula [*viz.* "the stock situated at"] as establishing a sale by description within the meaning ascribed to that phrase in the authorities to which I have referred. It is true, of course, that the use of the word "stock" identifies the goods, and may thus be regarded as supplying the minimum referential description mentioned by Dixon J. But it cannot be extended to answer the further requirement that a description properly so-called indicates a classification or asserts some attribute or quality to which the goods must correspond.

Do you agree with this conclusion? Could it be argued that referring to the "stock situated at ..." is merely a compendious way of identifying all the items making up the stock? Can the decision be justified on other grounds, for example, that the appellant had inspected the stock prior to purchase and must be deemed to have been aware of its condition or, alternatively, that the other requirements of s. 15(2) were not satisfied?

Harlingdon and Leinster Enterprises Ltd. v. Christopher Hull Fine Art Ltd.

[1990] 3 WLR 13 (CA)

NOURSE LJ: It is a matter of common knowledge that the market value of a picture rests largely on its authorship. Frequently the seller makes an attribution to an artist, although the degree of confidence with which he does so may vary considerably. In some cases the attribution may be of sufficient gravity to become a condition of the contract. In others it may be no more than a warranty, either collateral or as a term of the contract. Or it may have no contractual effect at all. Which of these is in point may depend on the circumstances of the sale; there being, for example, a difference between a sale by one dealer to another and one by a dealer to a private buyer. Remarkably, there is little authority as to the legal consequences of these everyday transactions. Here, in a sale by one London dealer to another of a picture which was later discovered to be a forgery, the judge in the court below, finding that the buyer did not rely on the seller's attribution, gave judgment for the seller. The buyer nevertheless contends that there was a contract for the sale of goods by description and a breach of the condition implied by section 13(1) of the Sale of Goods Act 1979. He also claims that there was a breach of the condition as to merchantable quality implied by section 14(2) of the Act.

. . .

The defendant company carries on business from a gallery in Motcomb Street, London, SW1, being owned and controlled by Mr. Christopher Hull. In the autumn of 1984 he was asked to dispose of two oil paintings which were described in a copy of an auction catalogue of 1980 as being the work of Gabriele Müntel (1877-1962), an artist of the German expressionist school. The true position was that the painting with which this action is concerned was not a work of hers but a forgery. Mr. Hull, who specialises in the works of contemporary British artists of the younger generation, had no training, experience or knowledge which would have enabled him to conclude from an examination of the paintings whether they were by Münter or not. He took them to Christies, who expressed interest. Before that he had been told by Mr. Evelyn Joll, a director of Thomas Agnew & Sons Ltd., that the plaintiff company, which carries on business as Leinster Fine Art from a gallery in Hereford Street, London, W2, had a good reputation as dealers in German art. In fact they had a special interest in buying and selling German expressionist paintings. The plaintiff company is owned and run by Mr. and Mrs. Holger Braasch and in the autumn of 1984 one of their employees in the business was Mr. Klaus Runkel.

Mr. Hull, acting on Mr. Joll's recommendation, telephoned the plaintiffs and spoke to Mr. Braasch. Mr. Hull said that he had come across, and was in the position to sell, two paintings by Gabriele Münter. Having seen the auction catalogue and consulted Christies, Mr. Hull had reasonable grounds for believing, and did believe, that they had been executed by that artist. Mr. Braasch expressed interest in the paintings. On some date at the end of November 1984 Mr. Runkel visited Motcomb Street in order to view them. There he met Mr. Hull, who did not need to repeat, and did not repeat, what he had already said to Mr. Braasch about having two paintings by Münter. It was obviously and clearly understood between Mr. Runkel and Mr. Hull that the former had come to decide whether the plaintiffs might purchase a painting or paintings which the latter had said were by Münter. Mr. Hull said that he did not know much about the paintings, that he had never heard of Gabriele Münter and that he thought little of her paintings. He made it absolutely plain that he was not an expert in them. By some form of words which neither party could precisely remember at the trial, Mr. Hull to a certain extent made it clear that he was relying on Mr. Runkel.

Mr. Runkel examined the paintings. Neither he nor Mr. Braasch had special expertise or training in the assessment of German expressionist painting, and Mr. Runkel's examination neither would nor ought to have revealed that the painting in question was not by Münter. Mr. Runkel saw a copy of the auction catalogue, in which the relevant entry (translated from the German) was:

Village Street in Upper Bavaria

22 000.—

Oil on cardboard. 39 × 48 cm.—Framed. Monogrammed, bottom left: MÜ. Gummed label on back with stamp of the estate of Gabriele Münter.

Alongside a massive wall surrounding a yard the street leads steeply into the background. Three separate women on the path. Warm sunlight from the right.

Reproduction Table 25

Mr. Runkel asked no questions about the provenance of the paintings. He did not ask for any opportunity to make further inquiries. He expressed no reservations about the degree of his own knowledge or experience. Neither he nor Mr. Hull expressed any doubt as to whether either or both of the paintings were executed by Münter. There was bargaining as to price, but Mr. Hull kept to his asking price of £6,000 for the painting in dispute. By the end of the meeting Mr. Hull and Mr. Runkel had agreed that that painting should be sold by the defendants and purchased by the plaintiffs at a price of £6,000 if and when the plaintiffs found a customer of their own who agreed to purchase it from them, failing which the painting would be returned to the defendants. That is the agreement with which this case is concerned.

On 1 December 1984 both pictures were delivered to the plaintiffs' gallery in Hereford Street. On 3 December the plaintiffs notified Mr. Hull that they had found a customer of their own who had agreed to purchase the painting from them and they requested Mr. Hull to make out an invoice to them. The invoice was in these terms:

Leinster Fine Art
9 Hereford Road
London W.2.

FFAI 84209
3 December 1984

GABRIELE MUNTER, 1877-1962
Dorfstrasse in Oberbayern
oil on board,
39 × 48cm
MS No 961

£ 6,000

The judge found that no addition was made to the terms of the sale when the invoice was made out. It merely gave effect to the earlier agreement between Mr. Hull and Mr. Runkel.

The judge found that both at the time when the agreement was made and subsequently when the invoice was made out both Mr. Hull and Mr. Runkel believed that the painting was by Münter and that, if either had not believed that, the deal would not have been made. He made the following further findings.

... that the plaintiffs did not rely on the description of the painting as one by Gabriele Münter. They relied only on their own assessment. ...

Before Judge Oddie and initially in this court the plaintiffs' case was put in four different ways. First, it was said that there was a contract for the sale of goods by description within section 13(1) of the Act of 1979; secondly, that the painting was not of merchantable quality within section 14(2) and (6); thirdly, that there was a breach of the implied condition that the painting would be reasonably fit for a particular purpose made known to the defendants within section 14(3); and, fourthly, that the defendants made an actionable misrepresentation inducing the plaintiffs to enter into the contract and entitling them to recover damages under the Misrepresentation Act 1967. Judge Oddie held in favour of the defendants on all four points. In this court the third and fourth points were abandoned by Mr. Crystal, for the plaintiffs. We have therefore to consider only the questions of sale by description and merchantable quality.

Section 13(1) of the Sale of Goods Act 1979 [Ont. s. 14] is in these terms: ...

The sales to which the subsection is expressed to apply are sales "by description." Authority apart, those words would suggest that the description must be influential in the sale, not necessarily alone, but so as to become an essential term, i.e. a condition, of the contract. Without such influence a description cannot be said to be one *by* which the contract for the sale of the goods is made.

I think that the authorities to which we were referred are consistent with this view of section 13(1). In *Varley v. Whipp* [1900] 1 QB 513 [see *supra* this chapter (ed.)] ... Channell J said, at p. 516:

> The term "sale of goods by description" must apply to all cases where the purchaser has not seen the goods, but is relying on the description alone. It applies in a case like the present, where the buyer has never seen the article sold, but has bought by the description, which is a different thing from a warranty. The most usual application of that section no doubt is to the case of unascertained goods, but I think it must also be applied to cases such as this where there is no identification otherwise than by description.

Bucknill J agreed. In that case section 13 was held to apply to a contract for the sale of specific goods, that is to say goods identified and agreed on when the contract was made, which had not been seen by the buyer. Channell J said that the buyer had been "relying" on the description alone, and that he had bought "by" the description. The buyer's reliance on the description showed that it was an essential term of the contract.

Other authorities show that section 13(1) may apply to a contract for the sale of specific goods which have been seen by the buyer, provided that their deviation from the description is not apparent on a reasonable examination: see *Chalmers' Sale of Goods*, 18th ed. (1981), p. 120 and the cases cited in footnote (a), to none of which we were referred in argument. We were, however, referred to another authority in the same category: see *Couchman v. Hill* [1947] 1 KB 554, where the plaintiff purchased from the defendant at auction a heifer which was described in the sale catalogue as "unserved." Later, having been found to be in calf, she died as a result of carrying it at too young an age. After the plaintiff had overcome an objection which is immaterial for present purposes, it was held by this court that the description of the heifer as unserved constituted a condition of the contract. Scott LJ, with whose judgment Tucker and Bucknill LJJ agreed, said, at p. 559: "as a matter of law, I think every item in a description which constitutes a substantial ingredient in the 'identity' of the thing sold is a condition. ..." We may be sure that the heifer had been seen by the buyer, but that the fact of her being in calf was not apparent on a reasonable examination. The buyer must have relied on the description. Although he did not rely on the description alone, it was held to be a substantial ingredient in the identity of the heifer or, if you prefer, an essential term of the contract.

· · ·

In *Gill & Duffus S.A. v. Berger & Co. Inc. (No. 2)* [1984] AC 382, the facts of which need not be stated, Lord Diplock, with whose speech the other members of the House of Lords agreed, said this of section 13, at p. 394:

while "description" itself is an ordinary English word, the Act contains no definition of what it means when it speaks in that section of a contract for the sale of goods being a sale "*by* description." One must look to the contract as a whole to identify the kind of goods that the seller was agreeing to sell and the buyer to buy ... where, as in the instant case, the sale (to use the words of section 13) is "*by* sample as well as *by* description," characteristics of the goods which would be apparent on reasonable examination of the sample are unlikely to have been intended by the parties to form part of the "description" *by* which the goods were sold, even though such characteristics are mentioned in references in the contract to the goods that are its subject matter.

Those observations, in emphasising the significance to be attached to the word "by," show that one must look to the contract as a whole in order to identify what stated characteristics of the goods are intended to form part of the description *by* which they are sold.

We were also referred to the decision of Sellers J in *Joseph Travers & Sons Ltd. v. Longel Ltd.* (1947), 64 TLR 150, where it was held that, since the buyers had placed no reliance on a descriptive name for rubber boots, the sale was not one by description. The decision is chiefly of value for Sellers J's approval, at p. 153, of the following passage in *Benjamin on Sale*, 7th ed. (1931), p. 641:

Sales by description may, it seems, be divided into sales: 1. Of unascertained or future goods, as being of a certain kind or class, or to which otherwise a "description" in the contract is applied. 2. Of specific goods, bought by the buyer in reliance, at least in part, upon the description given, or to be tacitly inferred from the circumstances, and which identifies the goods. So far as any descriptive statement is a mere warranty or only a representation, it is no part of the description. It is clear that there can be no contract for the sale of unascertained or future goods except by some description. It follows that the only sales not by description are sales of specific goods *as such*. Specific goods may be sold as such when they are sold without any description, express or implied; or where any statement made about them is not essential to their identity; or where, though the goods are described, the description is not relied upon, as where the buyer buys the goods such as they are.

It is suggested that the significance which some of these authorities attribute to the buyer's reliance on the description is misconceived. I think that that criticism is theoretically correct. In theory it is no doubt possible for a description of goods which is not relied on by the buyer to become an essential term of a contract for their sale. But in practice it is very difficult, and perhaps impossible, to think of facts where that would be so. The description must have a sufficient influence in the sale to become an essential term of the contract and the correlative of influence is reliance. Indeed, reliance by the buyer is the natural index of a sale by description. It is true that the question must, as always, be judged objectively and it may be said that previous judicial references have been to subjective or actual reliance. But each of those decisions, including that of Judge Oddie in the present case, can be justified on an objective basis. For all practical purposes, I would say that there cannot be a contract for the sale of goods by description where it is not within the reasonable contemplation of the parties that the buyer is relying on the description. For those purposes, I think that the law is correctly summarised in these words of *Benjamin on Sale*, which should be understood to lay down an objective test: "Specific goods may be sold as such ... where, though the goods are described, the description is not relied upon, as where the buyer buys the goods such as they are."

In giving his decision on this question, Judge Oddie said:

> There can clearly be a sale by description where the buyer has inspected the goods if the description relates to something not apparent on inspection. Every item in a description which constitutes a substantial ingredient in the identity of the thing sold is a condition.

Later, having said that he had not been referred to any similar case where a sale in reliance on a statement that a painting was by a particular artist had been held to be a sale by description, the judge continued:

> In my judgment such a statement could amount to a description and a sale in reliance on it to a sale by description within the meaning of the Act. However, on the facts of this case, I am satisfied that the description by Hull before the agreement was not relied on by Runkel in making his offer to purchase which was accepted by Hull. I conclude that he bought the painting as it was. In these circumstances there was not in my judgment a sale by description.

I agree. On a view of their words and deeds as a whole, the parties could not reasonably have contemplated that the plaintiffs were relying on the defendants' statement that the painting was by Gabriele Münter. On the facts which he found the judge could not, by a correct application of the law, have come to any other decision.

[Nourse LJ then proceeded to discuss the plaintiff's claim of breach of the implied condition of merchantable quality [UK SGA, ss. 14(2) and (6)] and rejected it for the same reasons as the trial judge had. He found that the painting still had aesthetic value (thus satisfying the "use" test of merchantibility) and that it could also be resold in its existing condition (thus satisfying the test of "exchange value"). He rejected the argument that the price paid for the paintings should be taken into consideration in determining the exchange value (price is one of the criteria of merchantable quality mentioned in s. 14(6) of the UK Act) on the grounds that the plaintiff had taken a calculated risk in paying such a high price and that the plaintiff's mistaken belief about the authenticity of the paintings could not be used in determining their exchange value. Without this mistaken belief, the paintings would have been worth £50 to £100 and the plaintiff would have been able to resell them for this amount. Nourse LJ concluded his judgment with the following reflections of one obviously interested in fine art (at 23-24):]

Although that is enough to dispose of this appeal in favour of the defendants, I desire to add some general observations about sales of pictures by one dealer to another where the seller makes an attribution to a recognised artist. The huge additional value of an authentic attribution has, from the earliest periods of European art, seduced a corresponding volume of skill and energy into the production of fakes, even in the lifetime of the artist. An early example was Dürer (1471-1528), who had to enlist the support of the Emperor Maximilian I in order to prevent the imitation of his woodcuts and engravings. With the great expansion in royal and noble collections which took place in the 18th century, faking became an art of its own. It has even been known for a faker, Hans van Meegeren who between 1935 and 1945 produced forgeries of the works of Vermeer, to become almost as famous as the artist himself. Modern advances in technology, while in some respects increasing the possibilities of detection, have in others assisted the faker to apply his skill with ever increasing ingenuity. Even if fakes are put on one side, many old master paintings cannot be safely attributed to a particular member of a group of artists, some of whom may still remain obscure.

All this is a matter of common knowledge amongst dealers in the art market and, I would expect, amongst all but the most inexperienced or naive of collectors. It means that almost any attribution to a recognised artist, especially of a picture whose provenance is unknown, may be arguable. In sales by auction, where the seller does not know who the buyer will be, the completeness with which the artist's name is stated in the catalogue, e.g. "Peter Paul Rubens," "P.P. Rubens" or "Rubens," signifies in a descending scale the degree of confidence with which the attribution is made. Nowadays an auctioneer's conditions of sale usually, perhaps invariably, so declare and, further, that any description is an opinion only. But in sales by private treaty by one dealer to another there is no such practice. That would suggest that there the seller's attribution is not a matter of importance. Indeed, Mr. Evelyn Joll, who gave evidence at the trial as to the professional practices of art dealers, went further. The effect of his evidence was that neither of the conditions implied by sections 13(1) and 14(2) could apply to a sale by one dealer to another. He said that an art dealer's success depended on, and was judged by, his ability to exercise his own judgment. It was not customary for a dealer to rely in any way on the judgment or representations of the dealer from whom a picture was being purchased.

Understandably enough, the judge was not satisfied on Mr. Joll's evidence that there was any usage or custom in the London art market which would exclude the application of the material provisions of the Act of 1979. But he did, I think, accept it as showing that many dealers habitually deal with each other on the principle caveat emptor. For my part, being confident that that principle would receive general acceptance amongst dealers, I would say that the astuteness of lawyers ought to be directed towards facilitating, rather than impeding, the efficient working of the market. The court ought to be exceedingly wary in giving a seller's attribution any contractual effect. To put it in lawyers' language, the potential arguability of almost any attribution, being part of the common experience of the contracting parties, is part of the factual background against which the effect, if any, of an attribution must be judged.

[Slade LJ wrote a concurring judgment. Stuart-Smith LJ dissented. He rejected the argument that reliance is an essential component of a sale by description; on the contrary, if it was "a term of the contract that the painting is by Münter, the purchaser does not have to prove that he entered into the contract in reliance on this statement." This distinguished a contractual term or condition from a mere non-contractual representation inducing a purchaser to enter into a contract where reliance is a prerequisite to the granting of relief. He continued (at 26):]

STUART-SMITH LJ: In my judgment, the matter can be tested in this way. If following the telephone conversation Mr. Runkel had arrived at the gallery, seen the painting, bargained about the price and agreed to buy it, it seems to me beyond argument that it would have been a sale by description. And indeed Mr. Rueff was at one time disposed to concede as much. Had the invoice been a contractual document, as it frequently is, again, it seems to me clear that the sale would have been a sale by description. In fact the invoice was written out subsequently to the oral contract; but the judge held, rightly as it seems to me, that it gave effect to what had been agreed. It was cogent evidence of the oral contract.

   How does it come about that what would otherwise be a sale by description in some way ceased to be one? It can only be as a result of the conversation between Mr. Hull and Mr. Runkel before the bargain was actually struck. If Mr. Hull had told Mr. Runkel that he did not know one way or the other whether the painting was by Münter in spite of the fact that he had so described it or that he could only say that the painting was attributed to Münter, and that Mr. Runkel must make up his mind for himself on this point, I can well see that the effect of what had previously been said about the identity of the painter might have been cancelled or withdrawn and was no longer effective at the time of the contract. But Hull did not say that, as the judge found. And I cannot see that this is the effect of what was said. Merely to say that he knew nothing of the painter and did not like her paintings does not in any way to my mind necessarily mean that he was cancelling or withdrawing what he had previously said, based as it was on the auction catalogue. Nor does the fact that it was recognised that the plaintiffs were more expert in German expressionist art than Mr. Hull advance the matter. It would in my judgment be a serious defect in the law if the effect of a condition implied by statute could be excluded by the vendor's saying that he was not an expert in what was being sold or that the purchaser was more expert than the vendor. That is not the law; it has long been held that conditions implied by statute can only be excluded by clear words. There is nothing of that kind in this case.

OLRC Sales Report

(1979), at 203-4

(b) Sales in Self-Service Stores

The second question that arises in connection with the implied condition of description concerns sales in self-service stores. As noted, there may still be some doubt as to whether such a sale is a sale "by description." The English and Scottish Law Commissions recommended resolving this problem by adding a new subsection to section 13 of the UK Sale of Goods Act, the provision equivalent to section 14 of the Ontario Act. This has now been done. The new clause provides as follows:

13.(2) [now s. 13(3)] A sale of goods shall not be prevented from being a sale by description by reason only that, being exposed for sale or hire, they are selected by the buyer.

A similar, but enlarged, recommendation appears in the New South Wales Working Paper. The problem to which the UK amendment is addressed arises because of earlier doubts as to whether the seller in a self-service store warrants the merchantable quality of his goods. These doubts were raised in part because section 15.2 of the existing [Ontario] Act only applies where goods are bought "by description." Later in this chapter, we recommend deletion of this phrase in section 15.2, with the result that this particular problem will cease to exist. It is also probable that a court today would have little hesitation in holding that a sale, at least of labelled goods, in a self-service store is a sale by description; as an earlier American court remarked about such a sale (*Corvan N. Harris v. Ezy-Way Foodliner Co.* (1961), 170 A.2d 160 (Me. Sup. Ct.)), "the printed word [is] the silent salesman." Nevertheless, to resolve any lingering doubts, we recommend the adoption of a provision comparable to section 13(2) of the UK Act in the revised Ontario Act.

Arcos, Limited v. E.A. Ronaasen and Son

[1933] AC 470, [1933] All ER Rep. 646 (HL)

LORD ATKIN: My Lords, the question between the parties arises on an award stated in the form of a special case by an umpire appointed under a submission contained in two contracts for the sale of timber. The contracts were in the White Sea 1928 C.I.F. form and were between the appellants, Arcos, Ld., sellers, and the respondents, E.A. Ronaasen & Son, buyers.

It is unnecessary to set them out at length. The substance was that the sellers agreed to sell to the buyers "the wood goods hereinafter specified" subject to a variation of 20 per cent in sellers' option on any item, to be shipped from Archangel "during the summer 1930." The first contract specified "Redwood and whitewood staves bundled:

90 standards ½ inch by 28 inches by 2 inches to 5 inches.
10 standards ½ inch by 17 inches by 2½ inches to 5 inches.

Messrs. Arcos, Ld., promise to do their best to induce the shippers not to cut any 2 inches in the ½ inch by 17 inches headings, but should a few 2 inches width fall [*sic*] buyers agree to take same at a reduction in price of 40s. per standard." There were further conditions on the back of the contract which it is unnecessary at present to consider.

The second contract was in identical terms save as to quantities of standards and provided for 135/180 and 27 standards of 28 inches length, and 15/20 and 3 standards of 17 inches length.

The staves were required by the buyers for making cement barrels, and this was made known to the sellers in circumstances that implied a condition that they should be fit for that purpose. The goods in question were shipped under the contracts in

October. When the shipping documents were tendered the buyers refused them on the ground that there had not been a summer shipment. There was an arbitration to determine this dispute, and the umpire held that the shipment was a summer shipment.

The buyers thereupon examined the goods which had been landed and claimed to reject them on the ground that they were not of contract description. This dispute went to arbitration and the umpire made his award in the form of a special case in which, after stating the facts, he awarded subject to the opinion of the Court that the buyers were not entitled to reject. On the hearing of the special case Wright J, and on appeal the Court of Appeal, differed from the umpire and held that the buyers were entitled to reject. The simple question is whether the goods when shipped complied with the implied condition (see the Sale of Goods Act, 1893, s. 13) that they should correspond with the description.

When the umpire inspected them on July 9, 1931, some nine months after landing and exposure to rain, he found the actual measurements to be as follows:

28-inch staves.
  None less than ½ inch.
  4.3 per cent. were ½ inch.
  85.3 per cent. between ½ and 9/16 inch.
  9.4 per cent. between 9/16 inch and 5/8 inch.
  1 per cent. between 5/8 and 3/4 inch.
  None over 3/4 inch.
17-inch staves.
  None less than ½ inch.
  6.4 per cent. were ½ inch.
  75.3 per cent. between ½ inch and 9/16 inch.
  18.3 per cent. between 9/16 inch and 5/8 inch.
  None over 5/8 inch.

He found that they were all fit for use in the manufacture of cement barrels. He was unable with accuracy to say what was their thickness when shipped, but, he stated, "their thickness was closer to ½ inch than it is now and I am satisfied that the staves when shipped were commercially within and merchantable under the contract specification."

The decisions of the learned judge and of the Court of Appeal appear to me to have been unquestionably right. On the facts as stated by the umpire as of the time of inspection only about 5 per cent of the goods corresponded with the description: and the umpire finds it impossible to say what proportion conformed at the time of shipment.

It was contended that in all commercial contracts the question was whether there was a "substantial" compliance with the contract: there always must be some margin: and it is for the tribunal of fact to determine whether the margin is exceeded or not. I cannot agree. If the written contract specifies conditions of weight, measurement and the like, those conditions must be complied with. A ton does not mean about a ton, or a yard about a yard. Still less when you descend to minute measurements does ½ inch mean about ½ inch. If the seller wants a margin he must and in my experience does stipulate for it. Of course by recognized trade usage particular figures may be given a different meaning, as in a baker's dozen; or there may be even incorporated a definite margin more or less; but there is no evidence or finding of such a usage in the present case.

No doubt there may be microscopic deviations which business men and therefore lawyers will ignore. And in this respect it is necessary to remember that description and quantity are not necessarily the same: and that the legal rights in respect of them are regulated by different sections of the code, description by s. 13, quantity by s. 30. It will be found that most of the cases that admit any deviation from the contract are cases where there has been an excess or deficiency in quantity which the Court has considered negligible. But apart from this consideration the right view is that the conditions of the contract must be strictly performed. If a condition is not performed the buyer has a right to reject. I do not myself think that there is any difference between business men and lawyers on this matter. No doubt, in business, men often find it necessary or inexpedient to insist on their strict legal rights. In a normal market if they get something substantially like the specified goods they may take them with or without grumbling and a claim for an allowance. But in a falling market I find that buyers are often as eager to insist on their legal rights as courts of law are ready to maintain them. No doubt at all times sellers are prepared to take a liberal view as to the rigidity of their own obligations, and possibly buyers who in turn are sellers may also dislike too much precision. But buyers are not, as far as my experience goes, inclined to think that the rights defined in the code are in excess of business needs.

It may be desirable to add that the result in this case is in no way affected by the umpire's finding that the goods were fit for the particular purpose for which they were required. The implied condition under s. 14, sub-s. 1, unless of course the contract provides otherwise, is additional to the condition under s. 13. A man may require goods for a particular purpose and make it known to the seller so as to secure the implied condition of fitness for that purpose: but there is no reason why he should not abandon that purpose if he pleases, and apply the goods to any purpose for which the description makes them suitable. If they do not correspond with the description there seems no business or legal reason why he should not reject them if he finds it covenient so to do.

Agreeing as I do with the reasoning of the judgments below, I find it unnecessary to say more than that I agree that the appeal should be dismissed with costs.

Appeal dismissed.

[Concurring judgments were delivered by Lord Buckmaster and Lord Warrington.]

NOTES

1) Do you agree with Lord Atkin's reasoning or, in your opinion, is the "perfect tender" rule, *viz.* the rule that the goods tendered must conform in every respect with the contract description, too harsh? Should the law draw a distinction between major and minor breaches of the descriptive terms and limit the buyer to a claim for damages in a breach of the latter type? Does the Sale of Goods Act, ss. 29, 33, draw any distinction

with respect to the severity of breach and the buyer's right of rejection? Would the case be decided differently today in the light of *Cehave, supra*, chapter 4, and *Reardon Smith Line Ltd. v. Hansen-Tangen, infra*? Is this the type of situation in which s. 15A of the UK SGA, adopted in 1994, denying a non-consumer buyer the right to exercise a right of rejection if "(b) the breach is so slight that it would be unreasonable for him to reject them." Sharp market price fluctuations are a frequent cause of commodity buyers' seeking to reject goods on minor grounds. See Eno, "Price Movement and Unstated Objections to the Defective Performance of Sales Contracts" (1935), 44 *Yale LJ* 782.

2) A very modest exception to the perfect tender rule is found in the judicially evolved gloss that "a deficiency or excess in quantity which is microscopic and which is not capable of influencing the mind of the buyer will not entitle him to reject the goods, for *de minimis non curat lex*" (*Benjamin's Sale of Goods*, 3rd ed. (1987), §609). Benjamin continues:

> Some slight elasticity in carrying out a commercial contract for the supply of goods in bulk is unavoidable, and the courts will not allow the buyer to take advantage of a merely trivial difference in quantity if the delivery is substantially of the quantity named. Thus, in *Shipton Anderson and Co. v. Weil Brothers & Co.* (1912), 1 KB 524, an excess of 55 lb. of wheat over and above an agreed limit of 4,950 tons was held to fall within the rule. It seems, however, that the seller cannot invoke the rule except as a defence to an allegation that he has not substantially performed his obligation under the contract of sale and the burden of proving that the deficiency or excess falls within the rule rests upon him. The *de minimis* rule does not apply to documentary credits.

Ashington Piggeries Ltd. v. Christopher Hill Ltd.;
Christopher Hill Ltd. v. Norsildmel

(Conjoined Appeals)
[1972] AC 441 (HL), [1971] 1 All ER 847

[The following statement of facts is taken from the judgment of LORD HODSON:]

In July 1961 the first case was noticed of a new and hitherto unknown disease afflicting mink which are bred in a large number of farms in this country. A male kit was found with a grossly enlarged abdomen and died within a few days. Similar cases were reported from that time onwards in various parts of the country. The common factor was that all the afflicted mink had been fed a fortified cereal mink food marketed under the brand name "King Size" and made up according to a formula. This formula emanated from a Mr. Udall who, since the early nineteen-fifties, had been concerned with the breeding of mink in the Wimborne area and was recognised as an expert on mink farming. The company, Ashington Piggeries Ltd., the defendants in the action, was controlled by Mr. Udall. In 1960 he approached a Mr. Granger, who was the personal assistant to the managing director of the plaintiff company (Christopher Hill Ltd.) with a view to the latter company compounding for him a mink food to be called "King Size" in accordance with a formula prepared by himself. This last-named company is an old-established and well-known animal feeding stuff compounder carrying on business at Poole. At this time the company was compounding 167 varieties of feeding stuffs principally for poultry, pheasants, calves and pigs but, until the events giving rise to this case, had had no experience or knowledge of mink.

To put the matter shortly, the ingredients were to be supplied by the plaintiffs and were to be of the best quality available. These were commodities which the plaintiffs were in the habit of handling in the course of their business and the manufacture of compounds for animal feeding to customers' formula was something which the trial judge found the plaintiffs habitually undertook. The contract of sale was entered into in May 1960 and deliveries of "King Size" commenced immediately either to the defendants or to their customers. Between May 1960 and the end of March 1961 "King Size" had been supplied to about 100 farms, but no real trouble arose until the end of July 1961. Mr. Udall's herd of mink was affected and began to suffer increasing losses. "King Size" came under suspicion as being the cause of the outbreak of the severe liver disease from which the animals were suffering.

These proceedings were started by the plaintiffs claiming the price of goods sold and delivered, namely, the "King Size." To this the defendants answered that the goods were worthless and relied in the first instance on a change made in the formula of the goods without their consent, making their attack on the use of an anti-oxidant called Santoquin No. 6 as being the cause of the liver disease in the mink. After several days this attack was abandoned and in its place the attack was directed against Norwegian herring meal claimed to have been included in "King Size" and to have been the cause of the toxin which killed the mink. It was said that the meal was manufactured from herring preserved with sodium nitrite in circumstances which rendered the meal toxic to animals and in particular mink. The substance said to be toxic was dimethyinitrasomine (DMNA) which was not a constituent of the formula. There was at the trial a conflict as to causation which no longer subsists. The findings of fact made at the trial and no longer disputed are that the cause of the liver disease in the mink was "King Size" and that the toxic element was DMNA which was in the herring meal because of the use of sodium nitrite for preservation purposes.

[The following extract from L. Wilberforce's judgment deals with the appellants' argument that the respondents had committed a breach of the condition of description. (Other extracts from the decision dealing with the implied condition of fitness are reproduced *infra*, chapter 8.)]

LORD WILBERFORCE:

1. *Section 13 of the Act*: The question is whether the compound mink food sold by the respondents (under the name "King Size") corresponded with the description. The appellants' case was that the food was to be made up according to a formula which identified generically the ingredients and specifically the chemical additives, quantifying precisely the proportions of each ingredient. One of these ingredients was herring meal. The food delivered in certain relevant months, it was claimed, did not correspond with the description because it contained a significant quantity of DMNA.

The proposition is that "King Size" made partly of herring meal which contains DMNA does not correspond with the description "King Size." This can be reduced to the proposition that the herring meal ingredient did not correspond with the description because it contained DMNA. The analogy was invoked, inevitably, by the appellants of copra cake with castor seed; the respondents invoked that of oxidised iron. The learned judge accepted the former, the Court of Appeal the latter.

Whether in a given case a substance in or upon which there has been produced by chemical interaction some additional substance can properly be described or, if one prefers the word, identified, as the original substance qualified by the addition of a past participle such as contaminated or oxidised, or as the original substance plus, or intermixed with, an additional substance, may, if pressed to analysis, be a question of an Aristotelian character. Where does a substance with a quality pass into an aggregate of substances? I do not think that it can be solved by asking whether the chemical interaction came about by some natural or normal process, e.g., preservation by the addition of salt (sodium chloride), or by some alien intrusion by the production of DMNA from sodium nitrite through a heating effect. I cannot see any distinction in principle in this difference. Further I do not believe that the Sale of Goods Act was designed to provoke metaphysical discussions as to the nature of what is delivered, in comparison with what is sold. The test of description, at least where commodities are concerned, is intended to be a broader, more common sense, test of a mercantile character. The question whether that is what the buyer bargained for has to be answered according to such tests as men in the market would apply, leaving more delicate questions of condition, or quality, to be determined under other clauses of the contract or sections of the Act. Perhaps this is to admit an element of impression into the decision, but I think it is more than impression which leads me to prefer the answer, if not all of the reasoning, of the Court of Appeal that the defect in the meal was a matter of quality or condition rather than of description. I think that the buyers and sellers and arbitrators in the market, asked what this was, could only have said that the relevant ingredient was herring meal and, therefore, that there was no failure to correspond with description. In my opinion, the appellants do not succeed under section 13.

[The other law lords, Lord Dilhorne dissenting, agreed with Lord Wilberforce's interpretation of the meaning of description in UK SGA, s. 13 (Ont. s. 14).]

Reardon Smith Line Ltd. v. Yngvar Hansen-Tangen (The "Diana Prosperity")

[1976] 2 Lloyd's Rep. 621, [1976] 3 All ER 570 (HL)

[This case involved a charter-party and a sub-charter-party, both relating to a new oil tanker to be built in Japan. By the time the tanker was ready for delivery the market had collapsed because of the 1974 oil crisis. It was therefore in the interests of the charterers to try to escape from their obligations by rejecting the ship. They sought to do so on the ground that the tanker tendered did not correspond with the contractual description.

For the purposes of the appeals it was assumed that the vessel complied in all respects with the detailed particulars contained in a form incorporated in the agreements. However, the appellants seized upon a provision in the sub-charter (referred to in the judgment of Lord Wilberforce as the "box") which made reference to "... (the) good Japanese flag (subject to Clause 41) ... Newbuilding motor tank vessel called Hull No. 354 at Osaka Zosen," as well as apparently a clause in an addendum to the intermediate charter which read, in part, "the vessel to perform this Charter is to be built by Osaka Shipbuilding Co. Ltd. ... ." In fact, because the vessel was too large to be built at the Osaka yards, Osaka entered into a joint venture for production of the ship at another yard 300 miles away.

The following extract from Lord Wilberforce's judgment reflects his view of the changing character of "description" in the law of sales and the characterization of sales terms generally:]

LORD WILBERFORCE: The appellants sought, necessarily, to give to the "box" and the corresponding provision in the intermediate charter contractual effect. They argued that these words formed part of the "description" of the future goods contracted to be provided, that, by analogy with contracts for the sale of goods, any departure from the description entitled the other party to reject, that there were departures in that the vessel was not built by Osaka Shipbuilding Co. Ltd., and was not hull no. 354. I shall attempt to deal with each of these contentions.

In the first place, I am not prepared to accept that authorities as to "description" in Sale of Goods cases are to be extended, or applied, to such a contract as we have here. Some of these cases either in themselves, e.g., *Moore v. Landauer*, [1921] 2 KB 519, or as they have been interpreted, e.g., *Behn v. Burness* (1863), 3 B & S 751, I find to be excessively technical and due for fresh examination in this House. Even if a strict and technical view must be taken as regards the description of unascertained future goods (e.g., commodities) as to which each detail of the description must be assumed to be vital, it may be, and in my opinion is, right to treat other contracts of sale of goods in a similar manner to other contracts generally so as to ask whether a particular item in a description constitutes a substantial ingredient of the "identity" of the thing sold, and only if it does to treat it as a condition, see *Couchman v. Hill*, [1947] 1 KB 554, at 559, *per* Lord Justice Scott. I would respectfully endorse what was recently said by Lord Justice Roskill in *Cehave N.V. v. Bremer Handelsgesellschaft m.b.H. (The Hansa Nord)*, [1975] 2 Lloyd's Rep. 445, at 458; [1976] 1 QB 44, at 71:

> In principle it is not easy to see why the law relating to contracts for the sale of goods should be different from the law relating to the performance of other contractual obligations, whether charter-parties or other types of contract. Sale of goods law is but one branch of the general law of contract. It is desirable that the same legal principles should apply to the law of contract as a whole and that different legal principles should not apply to different branches of that law.

and similarly by Mr. Justice Devlin in *Cargo Ships "El-Yam" Ltd. v. Invoer-En Transport Onderneming "Invotra,"* [1958] 1 Lloyd's Rep. 39, at 52. The general law of contract has developed, along much more rational lines, for example, *Hong Kong Fir*

Shipping Co. Ltd. v. Kawasaki Kisen Kaisha Ltd., [1961] 2 Lloyd's Rep. 478; [1962] 2 QB 28, in attending to the nature and gravity of a breach or departure rather than in accepting rigid categories which do or do not automatically give a right to rescind, and if the choice were between extending cases under the Sale of Goods Act, 1893, into other fields, or allowing more modern doctrine to infect those cases, my preference would be clear. The importance of this line of argument, is that Mr. Justice Mocatta and Lord Denning, MR, used it in the present case so as to reject the appellants' argument on "description" and I agree with them. But in case it does not appeal to this House, I am also satisfied that the appellants fail to bring the present case within the strictest rules as to "description."

CHAPTER SEVEN

Seller's Implied Obligations with Respect to Quality

SGA s. 15.2 implies in the buyer's favour a condition of the merchantable quality of the goods. Both the expression "merchantable quality" and the implied condition of merchantable quality are frequently ascribed to an early 19th century decision, *Gardiner v. Gray* (1815), 171 ER 46, which involved a contract for the sale of 12 bags of waste silk. The sale note said nothing about the quality of the silk. On their arrival the buyer found the silk much inferior in quality to the sample that had previously been supplied to his agent, and of a quality not saleable under the denomination of "waste silk." The buyer pleaded the seller's promise to be that the silk should be waste silk of a good and merchantable quality. In allowing the buyer's claim Lord Ellenborough said, "the intention of both parties must be taken to be, that it shall be saleable in the market under the denomination mentioned in the contract between them. The purchaser cannot be supposed to buy goods to lay them on a dunghill." As will be noted, Lord Ellenborough's test of merchantable quality is a relative one—what is acceptable in the marketplace. Not surprisingly this allows much room for differences of opinion and much of the jurisprudence has been concerned to give some content to the term in the widely varying circumstances in which the problem arises for decision.

Two preliminary points deserve to be made about the structure of SGA s. 15. First, the preamble to the section suggests that *caveat emptor* is the dominant rule and the implied conditions of merchantability and fitness the exceptions to it. The OLRC Sales Report (at 207) thought this anomalous since the great majority of sellers are professionals to whom one or the other of the two implied terms, and frequently both, will apply unless they have been successfully excluded. The Commission therefore recommended the deletion of the preamble, a change that appears in UCC 2-314 and 2-315.

The second point arises out of the fact that s. 15 places the implied condition of fitness before the implied condition of merchantability. This seems anomalous since merchantable quality is broader in scope than fitness for purpose, although frequently the two overlap. The explanation is historical and is given in *Benjamin's Sale of Goods* at para. 352. Since circumstances have changed in the interval, the English and Scottish Law Commissions recommended the reversal of the two subsections and this recommendation was implemented in the Supply of Goods (Implied Terms) Act, 1973. See now UK SGA 1979, s. 14. In the Code the implied warranty of merchantability also appears before the implied warranty of fitness. See UCC 2-314 and 2-315. In view of these considerations, the materials on merchantability in the present chapter precede those on fitness.

Sale "by Description," Character of Seller, and Sale by an Agent

1) *Sale "by description."* See Lord Wright's judgment in *Grant v. Australian Knitting Mills Ltd.*, [1936] AC 85, at 100, cited in *Beale v. Taylor*, *supra*, chapter 6.

2) *Character of seller*. See the extract from Lord Wilberforce's judgment in *Ashington Piggeries Ltd. v. Christopher Hill Ltd.*, *infra*, chapter 8, and note the following observations in the OLRC Sales Report, at 209, on the amendment to the implied conditions of merchantability and fitness now appearing in ss. 14(2) and 14(3) of the UK Sale of Goods Act 1979:

> Section 15.2 of the Ontario Act not only requires a sale "by description," but also requires that the goods be purchased from a seller "who deals in goods of that description." In the amended UK Act, it need only be shown that the seller sold the goods "in the course of *a* business" [emphasis in original]. In our view, undesirable results could flow from imposing a condition of merchantability on a business seller, regardless of whether he deals, or has ever purported to deal, in goods of the kind offered for sale. As commentators have noted a literal reading of the UK language would lead, as the Law Commissioners apparently intended it to lead, to liability attaching to a seller who was disposing of a piece of capital equipment that had become surplus to his requirements; for example, disposition of a truck by a fuel supplier.
>
> If the only result of the British approach were to entitle the buyer to a reduction in the price if the truck turned out to be in poorer condition than the buyer had a right to assume, we could accept it with equanimity. Indeed, a persuasive argument could be made for permitting such an action *in quanti minoris* against any seller.[1] It seems reasonable to assume, however, that, under the UK approach, the seller's liability would encompass the full measure of damages recoverable under the rule in *Hadley v. Baxendale*, including any consequential damages suffered by the buyer. We do not think this desirable. Accordingly, we recommend that the warranty of merchantability should be restricted in the revised Act to a seller who deals in goods of the kind supplied under the contract of sale. We note that this is the same test as is used in UCC 2-314(1), although the Code employs slightly different language.

---

1 The *actio redhibitoria* and action *in quanti minoris* were permitted in classical Roman law for rescission of the sale or a reduction in the price if the goods suffered from a latent vice unknown to the buyer and which he could not have discovered by reasonable examination before the purchase. The seller's knowledge of the defects was equally immaterial. Apparently the remedies were not restricted to suits against commercial sellers. See Buckland, *A Text-Book of Roman Law from Augustus to Justinian*, 3rd ed. (1966), at 491 *et seq.* These grounds of relief, seemingly rooted in concepts of unjust enrichment and fair dealing, survive in modern civil law systems. See, for example, Québec C. Civ., arts. 1726 *et seq.* (entitled "Warranty of Quality"); and compare, Treitel, "Remedies for Breach of Contract," in *International Encyclopedia of Comparative Law*, vol. VII, at 16-57 to 16-60.

3) *Retailers and manufacturers.* Section 15 does not distinguish between the liability of retailers, manufacturers and other types of merchant. In fact, s. 15.1 makes it clear that there is no distinction ("whether the seller is the manufacturer or not") for the purpose of determining the seller's liability for breach of the implied condition of fitness. From time to time it has been suggested that this is a harsh rule and that it is not fair to hold a retailer liable for defects in goods manufactured by someone else, especially since liability under s. 15 is strict and does not depend on any showing of negligence. *Cf.* Waite, "Retail Responsibility and Judicial Law Making" (1936), 34 *Mich. L Rev.* 494. In its *Report on Consumer Warranties and Guarantees in the Sale of Goods* (1972), at 73, the OLRC gave the following reasons for not excusing a retailer from liability under s. 15:

> We have considered this line of reasoning but have rejected it on a number of grounds. First, the large Canadian department stores are economically as powerful as many manufacturers of domestic goods. Second, many manufacturers, especially manufacturers of soft goods and of accessories, are quite small in size. In the third place, relief from liability would discourage retailers from exercising such residual choice of manufacturers as remains to them. In some consumer goods areas—for example furniture—the choice is still quite substantial. To limit the retailer's liability to cases where negligence is proven would place an unfair burden on the consumer. Finally, the consumer will still find it easier in many instances to seek redress from the dealer from whom he bought the goods than to pursue the manufacturer. A dealer who cares for his reputation ought not to mind this; but whether he does so or not, the knowledge that he may be held responsible together with the manufacturer will encourage him to spur the manufacturer to greater responsiveness to the consumer's complaint.

4) *Liability of private sellers (OLRC Sales Report, at 207)*:

Section 15 only applies to merchant sellers, and the last question is whether either of the implied warranties should be extended to private sellers. The traditional justifications for the restriction to merchant sellers are threefold: namely, that a merchant seller holds himself out as possessing special skill and knowledge with respect to the goods; that he sells for profit; and, that he is in a better position to absorb, or to pass on, any loss resulting from undiscoverable defects than the average buyer. None of these considerations applies to a non-merchant seller. We accept the continuing validity of this reasoning, and do not recommend that the implied terms of merchantability and fitness be extended to private sales. This recommendation does not, however, resolve the question whether a private seller should at least be under an obligation to disclose defects in the goods that are actually known to him, and that are not obvious from a visual inspection of the goods. The question does not lend itself readily to statutory resolution and is, in our view, best left for judicial development by means of the doctrines of good faith and fair dealing, mistake, and constructive fraud.

The Meaning of Merchantable Quality

Hardwick Game Farm v. Suffolk Agricultural and
Poultry Producers Association[2]

[1969] 2 AC 31, [1968] 2 All ER 444 (HL)

LORD REID: My Lords, in the summer of 1960 very large numbers of young turkeys died in what appeared to be an epidemic of an unknown disease. But the outbreaks were curiously patchy and the trouble was soon traced to feeding stuffs. Such birds are generally fed on mixtures of various ingredients. It was common to include up to about ten per cent of groundnut extractions, and it was found that in the mixture fed to these birds there had been a proportion of groundnut extractions imported from Brazil. Then it was found that much of this Brazilian food was contaminated by a poison, aflatoxin, to amounts up to five parts per million. Then it appeared that, owing to climatic conditions in Brazil, spores of a fungus, aspergillus flavus, had caused a mould to grow on the groundnuts and secrete this poison. Groundnut extractions had for many years been imported from India. It has now been found that the Indian product sometimes contains some of this poison, though generally in smaller amounts, but in 1960 there was no reason to suspect that any groundnut extractions might contain this poison.

The plaintiffs, Hardwick Game Farm, had about 2,000 breeding pheasants. The eggs were collected and hatched and the young pheasants reared in much the same way as chickens and turkeys. A large number of them died in 1960 from this poison and it is not disputed that it was contained in compound feeding stuffs supplied by a local compounder referred to in this case as SAPPA. They sued SAPPA and SAPPA agreed to pay £3,000 damages. That settlement is admitted to have been reasonable and proper. But SAPPA brought in their suppliers, Grimsdale and Lillico and they in turn brought in their suppliers, Kendall and Holland Colombo. It has been held that Grimsdale and Lillico are liable to SAPPA and that Kendall and Holland Colombo are liable to Grimsdale and Lillico. In the first appeal Kendall and Holland Colombo maintain that they are not liable. Lillico do not appeal. But Grimsdale in effect maintains in the second appeal that, if they cannot recover from Kendall and Holland Colombo, then SAPPA cannot recover from them. I need make no further mention of Lillico and Holland Colombo and it will be clearer simply to have in mind the chain, Kendall to Grimsdale to SAPPA to the game farm.

Kendall and Grimsdale are both members of the London Cattle Food Traders' Association. Brazilian groundnuts had not been imported until 1959 but early in 1960 there were large shipments. Kendall had acquired a large quantity and while the goods were afloat Kendall sold a considerable quantity in the London Market to Grimsdale.

---

2 The case is also reported and cited under the name of *Henry Kendall & Sons v. William Lillico & Sons Ltd.*, two of the parties involved in this multipartite litigation. We have adopted the above style of cause for reasons of consistency with the judgments in the *Ashington Piggeries* case, *supra*, chapter 6. [ed.]

Then Grimsdale sold a part of this to SAPPA at the market at Bury St. Edmunds; SAPPA took delivery shortly after the arrival of the goods in London.

The case raises a number of points and I shall first consider the position under the Sale of Goods Act, 1893, section 14. The relevant subsections are [see Ont. SGA, s. 15]. ...

Conflicting arguments have been submitted about the meaning of almost every part of these subsections. If one puts aside for the moment the encrustations of authority their meaning appears to me to be reasonably clear. But, if a whole chapter of the law is compressed into one section of a code, one cannot expect its words to apply to unusual cases without expansion or adaptation. That is the task of the court: but it is not in my view legitimate to substitute for the words of the code some general words used by an eminent judge in a particular case and treat them as a test of universal application. Where that has been done in other chapters of the law it has led to trouble, and there has been a tendency to do that here.

I take first subsection (2) because it is of more general application. It applies to all sales by description where the seller deals in such goods. There may be a question whether the sale of a particular article is not really a sale by description but that does not arise here: these are clearly sales by description. Then it is a condition (unless excluded by the contract) that the goods must be of merchantable quality. Merchantable can only mean commercially saleable. If the description is a familiar one it may be that in practice only one quality of goods answers that description—then that quality and only that quality is merchantable quality. Or it may be that various qualities of goods are commonly sold under that description—then it is not disputed that the lowest quality commonly so sold is what is meant by merchantable quality: it is commercially saleable under that description. I need not consider here what expansion or adaptation of the statutory words is required where there is a sale of a particular article or a sale under a novel description. Here the description groundnut extractions had been in common use.

The novel feature of this case is that whereas in 1960 there appears to have been thought to be only one quality of this product, subject to minor variations, it has now been discovered that particular parcels though apparently of the usual quality may really be of a very different quality because they are contaminated by minute quantities of a powerful poison. So the question at once arises—do you judge merchantable quality in light of what was known at the time of the sale or in light of later knowledge?

It is quite clear that some later knowledge must be brought in for otherwise it would never be possible to hold that goods were unmerchantable by reason of a latent defect. By definition a latent defect is something that could not have been discovered at the time by any examination which in light of then existing knowledge it was reasonable to make. But there is a question as to how much later knowledge ought to be brought in. In the present case it had become well known before the date of the trial that the defect was that these Brazilian groundnut extractions were contaminated by poison: but it had also become well known that, while this poison made the goods unsuitable for inclusion in food for poultry, it was generally regarded as proper to include such extractions in cattle food, provided that the proportion included did not exceed 5 per cent of the whole. The question is whether this latter fact should be taken into account in deciding whether these goods were of merchantable quality in 1960.

I think it would be very artificial to bring in some part of the later knowledge and exclude other parts. In this case it is quite true that there was a period, after the nature and effect of this contamination had been discovered but before it had become accepted that small quantities of contaminated goods could safely be included in cattle foods, during which contaminated groundnut extractions were virtually unsaleable. But suppose that in this case it had been discovered at an early stage that these goods could be used for cattle food, so that there never was a period during which they were unsaleable. In that case I would not think it possible to take into account the nature of the defect but to exclude from consideration the effect which knowledge of the defect had on the market.

There is clear evidence that before the date of the trial Indian groundnut extractions so contaminated were sold under the ordinary description and were not rejected by the buyers when the contamination was discovered; a director of British Oil and Cake Mills who are by far the largest compounders in this country said that they bought these goods untested and then tested them. If they were found to be very highly contaminated they were destroyed: but otherwise they were included in feeding stuffs for cattle. This company apparently did not claim any relief on the ground that such goods were of defective quality or were of no use if highly contaminated. And it appears that other buyers who found poison in the goods which they bought did not try to reject the goods but merely asked for rebates on the price: they never got any rebates and the evidence is that they did not press their claims. So I think that it sufficiently appears that groundnut extractions contaminated to an extent not said to be different from the contamination of the Brazilian product were regarded as of merchantable quality under the ordinary description at the date of the trial.

I do not think I am precluded from taking this view of the meaning of subsection (2) by any of the authorities.

A statement with regard to the meaning of section 14(2) which has been commonly accepted is that of Lord Wright in *Cammell Laird & Co. v. The Manganese Bronze and Brass Co.*, [1934] AC 402. In that case the respondents contracted to supply two specially designed ship's propellers. They first supplied propellers which were unsatisfactory and it was only at a third attempt that they supplied propellers which were satisfactory. Cammell Laird sued for damages caused by the delay. They succeeded on the terms of the contract and under section 14(1). But Lord Wright went on to consider the application of section 14(2). Apart from a short general statement at the end of the speech of Lord Tomlin, at 413, none of the other noble and learned lords said anything about section 14(2) or Lord Wright's gloss on it. Lord Wright said, at 430:

> In earlier times, the rule of caveat emptor applied, save only where an action could be sustained in deceit on the ground that the seller knew of the defect, or for breach of express warranty (warrantizando vendidit). But with the growing complexity of trade, dealings increased in what are now called "unascertained or future goods," and more generally "goods sold by description." As early as 1815 in *Gardiner v. Gray* (1815), 4

Camp. 144, Lord Ellenborough stated the rule. Goods had been sold as waste silk; a breach was held to have been committed on the ground that the goods were unfit for the purpose of waste silk and of such a quality that they could not be sold under that denomination. What subsection (2) now means by "merchantable quality" is that the goods in the form in which they were tendered were of no use for any purpose for which such goods would normally be used and hence were not saleable under that description.

I feel sure that Lord Wright did not really mean this to be a test of universal application in the form in which he stated it. If he did I disagree for reasons which I shall state. In the *Cammell Laird* case, if the propellers were of no use for the ship for which they had been designed it was true to say that they were of no use for any other ship and therefore unsaleable as propellers. But there are many cases in which different qualities of a particular kind of goods are commonly sold under different descriptions. Suppose goods are sold under the description commonly used to denote a high quality and the goods delivered are not of that high quality but are of a lower quality which is commonly sold under a different description, then it could not possibly be said that the goods in the form in which they were tendered were of no use for any purpose for which those goods would normally be used. They would be readily saleable under the appropriate description for the lower quality. But surely Lord Wright did not mean to say that therefore they were merchantable under the description which was appropriate for the higher quality. They plainly were not. Lord Wright said, [1934] AC 402, at 430, "no use for any purpose for which *such goods* would normally be used." Grammatically "such goods" refers back to "the goods in the form in which they were tendered." But what he must have meant by "such goods" were goods which complied with the description in the contract under which they were sold. Otherwise the last part of the sentence "and hence were not saleable under that description" involves a non sequitur. If I now set out what I am sure he meant to say I think it would be accurate for a great many cases though it would be dangerous to say that it must be universally accurate. The amended version would be:

> "What subsection (2) now means by 'merchantable quality' is that the goods in the form in which they were tendered were of no use for any purpose for which goods which complied with the description under which these goods were sold would normally be used, and hence were not saleable under that description." This is an objective test: "were of no use for any purpose ..." must mean "would not have been used by a reasonable man for any purpose. ..."

That would produce a sensible result. If the description in the contract was so limited that goods sold under it would normally be used for only one purpose, then the goods would be unmerchantable under that description if they were of no use for that purpose. But if the description was so general that goods sold under it are normally used for several purposes, then goods are merchantable under that description if they are fit for any one of these purposes: if the buyer wanted the goods for one of those several purposes for which the goods delivered did not happen to be suitable, though they were suitable for other purposes for which goods bought under that description are normally bought, then he cannot complain. He ought either to have taken the necessary steps to bring subsection (1) into operation or to have insisted that a more specific description must be inserted in the contract.

That would be in line with the judgment of Mellor J in *Jones v. Just* (1868), LR 3 QB 197, which has always been regarded as high authority. He said, at 205:

> It appears to us that, in every contract to supply goods of a specified description which the buyer has no opportunity to inspect, the goods must not only in fact answer the specific description, but must also be saleable or merchantable under that description.

The buyer bought manilla hemp: on arrival the goods were found to be damaged to such an extent as not to be saleable under that description and the buyer resold under the description "Manilla hemp with all faults" and received about 75 per cent of what merchantable manilla hemp would have fetched. So it certainly could not be said that the goods were of no use. But the buyer recovered, as damages for breach of the implied warranty, the difference between what the hemp would have been worth if merchantable as manilla hemp and what he was able to get for it when sold "with all faults."

It would also be in line with what Lord Wright said in *Canada Atlantic Grain Export Co. v. Eilers* (1929), 35 Ll. L Rep. 206, at 213:

> ... if goods are sold under a description which they fulfil, and if goods under that description are reasonably capable in ordinary use of several purposes, they are of merchantable quality within section 14(2) of the Act if they are reasonably capable of being used for any one or more of such purposes, even if unfit for use for that one of those purposes which the particular buyer intended.

There is another statement by Lord Wright regarding section 14(2) in *Grant v. Australian Knitting Mills Ltd.*, [1936] AC 85, at 99:

> The second exception (i.e., section 14(2)) in a case like this in truth overlaps in its application the first exception (i.e., section 14(1)); whatever else merchantable may mean, it does mean that the article sold, if only meant for one particular use in ordinary course, is fit for that use; merchantable does not mean that the thing is saleable in the market simply because it looks right.

That too appears to me to be in line with my amended version of what he said in the *Cammell Laird case*, [1934] AC 402, at 413.

Another explanation of the phrase "merchantable quality" which has frequently been quoted is that of Farwell LJ in *Bristol Tramways, etc., Carriage Co. Ltd. v. Fiat Motors Ltd.*, [1910] 2 KB 831, at 841, CA:

> The phrase in section 14(2) is, in my opinion, used as meaning that the article is of such quality and in such condition that a reasonable man acting reasonably would after a full examination accept it under the circumstances of the case in performance of his offer to buy that article whether he buys for his own use or to sell again.

I do not find this entirely satisfactory. I think what is meant is that a reasonable man in the shoes of the actual buyer would accept the goods as fulfilling the contract which was in fact made. But if the description was so wide that goods required for different purposes were commonly bought under it and if these goods were suitable for some of those purposes but not for the purpose for which the buyer bought them, it would have to be a very reasonable buyer indeed who admitted that the goods were merchantable, and that it was his own fault for not realising that goods might be merchantable under that description although unsuitable for his particular purpose.

There was also another explanation brought to our attention. In *Australian Knitting Mills Ltd. v. Grant* (1933), 50 CLR 387, at 413, Dixon J said:

> The condition that goods are of merchantable quality requires that they should be in such an actual state that a buyer fully acquainted with the facts and, therefore, knowing what hidden defects exist and not being limited to their apparent condition would buy them without abatement of the price obtainable for such goods if in reasonable sound order and condition and without special terms.

I would only qualify this by substituting "some buyers" for "a buyer." "A buyer" might mean any buyer: but for the purposes for which some buyers wanted the goods the defects might make the goods useless, whereas for the purposes for which other buyers wanted them the existence of the defects would make little or no difference. That is in fact the position in the present case. I think that it must be inferred from the evidence that buyers who include groundnut extractions in their cattle foods are prepared to pay a full price for goods which may be contaminated. But buyers who only compound poultry foods would obviously not be prepared to buy contaminated goods at any price. Nevertheless contaminated groundnut extractions·are merchantable under the general description of groundnut extractions because, rather surprisingly, some buyers appear to be ready to buy them under that description and to pay the ordinary market price for them.

LORD PEARCE (dissenting): In my opinion, the definition of Farwell LJ, [1910] 2 KB 831, at 840, as amplified by Dixon J, 50 CLR 387, at 418, is to be preferred to that of Lord Wright, [1934] AC 402, at 430, which has, I think, the following weakness. The suggestion, without more, that goods are merchantable unless they are no use for any purpose for which they would normally be used and hence would be unsaleable under that description may be misleading, if it contains no reference to price. One could not say that a new carpet which happens to have a hole in it or a car with its wings buckled are of no use for their normal purposes and hence would be unsaleable under that description. They would no doubt, if their price was reduced, find a ready market. In return for a substantial abatement of price a purchaser is ready to put up with serious defects, or use part of the price reduction in having the defects remedied. In several classes of goods there is a regular retail market for "seconds," that is, goods which are not good enough in the manufacturer's or retailer's view to fulfil an order and are therefore sold off at a cheaper price. It would be wrong to say that "seconds" are necessarily merchantable.

Sir Owen Dixon was clearly right in saying (above) that in order to judge merchantability one must assume a knowledge of hidden defects, although these do not manifest themselves or are not discovered until some date later than the date of delivery which is the time as at which one must estimate merchantability (see also Atkin

LJ in *Niblett Ltd. v. Confectioners Materials Co. Ltd.*, [1921] 3 KB 387, at 404: "No one who knew the facts would buy them in that state or condition; in other words they were unsaleable and unmerchantable.") But what additional after-acquired knowledge must one assume? Logic might seem to indicate that the court should bring to the task all the after-acquired knowledge which it possesses at the date of trial. But I do not think that this is always so. For one is trying to find what market the goods would have had if their subsequently ascertained condition had been known. As it is a hypothetical exercise, one must create a hypothetical market. Nevertheless the hypothetical market should be one that could have existed, not one which could *not* have existed at the date of delivery. Suppose goods contained a hidden deadly poison to which there was discovered by scientists two years after delivery a simple, easy, inexpensive antidote which could render the goods harmless. They would be unmarketable at the date of delivery if the existence of the poison was brought to light, since no purchase could then have known the antidote to the poison. Hypothesis is no reason for complete departure from possibility. One must keep the hypothesis in touch with the facts as far as possible. But I do not think that the point is important on the present facts.

Appeals dismissed.

NOTES

1) Lord Morris concurred with Lord Reid on the issue of merchantability, preferring the view of Lord Wright in *Cammell Laird* to that of Farwell LJ in *Bristol Tramways*. Lord Guest felt that the test under s. 14(2) must be "whether the article is saleable in the ordinary market for such goods under that description" (at 108). He held that Lord Wright's test was but one factor in the determination of merchantability, and could not be determinative since it omits all reference to price. Lord Guest preferred the test formulated by Dixon J in *Grant v. Australian Knitting Mills*. Lord Wilberforce expressed no opinion on the application of s. 14(2) to the facts, but agreed with Lord Pearce on the interpretation of the subsection.

The law lords' position on the applicability of the implied condition of fitness to the facts at bar is dealt with later in this chapter.

For a classic article on the meaning of merchantability, see W.L. Prosser, "The Implied Warranty of Merchantable Quality" (1943), 21 *Can. Bar Rev.* 446.

2) *Aswan Engineering Establishment Co. v. Lupdine Ltd.* Section 14(6) of the UK Sale of Goods Act contains the following definition of merchantable quality. It was first introduced in the Supply of Goods (Implied Terms) Act 1973 on the recommendation of the English and Scottish Law Commissions:

> Goods of any kind are of merchantable quality within the meaning of subsection (2) above if they are as fit for the purpose or purposes for which goods of that kind are commonly bought as it is reasonable to expect having regard to any description applied to them, the price (if relevant) and all the other relevant circumstances.

The meaning of the words "if they are as fit for the *purpose or purposes* for which goods of that kind are commonly bought" was a key issue in *Aswan Engineering Establishment v. Lupdine Ltd.*, [1987] 1 All ER 135 (CA).

Lupdine were manufacturers of a waterproofing compound known as "Lupguard." Awsan was a construction company carrying on business in Kuwait. In June 1980 it bought about 35,100 kg of Lupguard for shipment to Kuwait. The Lupguard was packed in plastic pails manufactured and supplied by Thurgar Bolle (TB). Each pail held about 25 kg of Lupguard. The pails were stacked five or six high in 20-foot containers, 702 pails per container. The containers were shipped to Kuwait between July and September 1980. When the containers arrived they were left standing on the quayside in full sunshine. As a result the temperature inside the containers reached 70° C or 158° F. "It was as if the plastic pails had been put in an oven." The plastic pails collapsed and there was a total loss of the Lupguard.

Aswan brought action against Lupdine. Lupdine brought in TB as third parties. Aswan then amended its claim and joined TB as second defendants. The agreed expert evidence offered at the trial showed that the pails could withstand temperatures up to 52° C without special precautions and could have withstood much higher temperatures if the rows of pails had been separated horizontally with wooden battens.

Neill J held that Aswan was entitled to succeed in contract against Lupdine but he dismissed Lupdine's claim against TB. He held that the pails were of merchantable quality within the meaning of s. 14(6) of the 1979 Act, and that there was no express or implied term that the pails were to be fit for the journey to Kuwait. He dismissed Aswan's claim in negligence against TB on the ground that TB owed no duty of care to Aswan.

Aswan and Lupdine appealed the dismissal of the claims against TB. They argued *inter alia* that the test of merchantable quality adopted in *Hardwick Game Farm* was no longer good law and that as a result of the statutory definition goods had to be reasonably fit for "all the purposes for which goods of any kind are normally bought." The Court of Appeal rejected the argument and Lloyd JA reasoned as follows (at 145-46):

> The argument of counsel for the appellants is undoubtedly attractive at first sight. If Parliament had intended to enact Lord Reid's formulation, it might have been expected that the definition would have referred to *one* of the purposes for which goods are commonly bought. But there is an equally strong, and perhaps even stronger, argument the other way. If Parliament had intended to enact what counsel for the appellants submits is the meaning of s. 14(6), then the definition would surely have referred specifically to all purposes, not just the purpose or purposes. The reason why Parliament did not adopt either of those courses is, I think, to be found in the speech of Lord Reid in *Henry Kendall & Sons Ltd. v. William Lillico & Sons Ltd.* In the passage which I have already quoted, Lord Reid points out that goods of any one kind may be sold under more than one description, corresponding to different qualities.
>
> To take the facts of the present case, heavy duty pails are no doubt of higher quality than ordinary pails, and for that reason no doubt command a higher price. Pails which are suitable for the lower quality purpose may not be suitable for the higher quality purpose. It would obviously be wrong that pails sold under a description appropriate to the higher quality should be held to be merchantable because they are fit for a purpose for which pails

are sold under the description appropriate to the lower quality. Since the definition presup-poses that goods of any one kind may be sold under more than one description, it follows that the definition had, of necessity, to refer to more than one purpose. In my opinion, this is the true and sufficient explanation for the reference to "purposes" in the plural. The refer-ence to *the* purpose in the singular was required in order to cover one-purpose goods, such as the pants in *Grant v. Australian Knitting Mills Ltd.* It would be wrong to infer from the use of the phrase "purpose or purposes" that Parliament intended any such far-reaching change in the law as that for which counsel for the appellants contends. On the contrary, I agree with counsel for Thurgar Bolle that the definition is as accurate a reproduction of Lord Reid's speech in *Henry Kendall & Sons v. William Lillico & Sons Ltd.* as it is possible to compress into a single sentence.

Lloyd JA pointed out that counsel had been invited by the court to refer to the Law Commission's Report that preceded the adoption of the definition of merchantable qual-ity in 1973, but that they had both declined to do so! (In fact, the 1967 Report casts no light on the Commission's reasons for adopting the "purpose or purposes" language in the definition of merchantable quality.)

3) In its Sales Report the Ontario Law Reform Commission rejected the narrow con-struction of merchantable quality adopted in *Hardwick Game Farm, supra.* The commis-sion reasoned that the law lords' test led to arbitrary results and was inconsistent with the broad meaning of the implied condition of fitness also adopted in *Hardwick Game Farm.* See Report, at 212. The Commission therefore recommended adoption of the following definition of merchantable quality (Draft Bill, s. 5.13(1)(a)):

(1) In this section merchantable quality means,

(a) that the goods, whether new or used, are as fit for the one or more purposes for which goods of that kind are commonly bought and are of such quality and in such condition as it is reasonable to expect having regard to any description applied to them, the price, and all other relevant circumstances.

As will be noted, the definition was much influenced by the Law Commission's defini-tion, although there are also some important differences between the two definitions which will be discussed later.

4) The 1994 amendment to the UK SGA amended s. 14 (the merchantability section) by deleting the term "merchantability" and instead deeming an implied "term" (*sic*) in a contract by a seller selling goods in the course of a business "that the goods supplied are of *satisfactory quality*" (s. 14(2)) (italics added). Subsections (2A) and (2B) provide:

(2A) For the purposes of this Act, goods are of satisfactory quality if they meet the standard that a reasonable person would regard as satisfactory, taking account of any descrip-tion of the goods, the price (if relevant) and all the other relevant circumstances.

(2B) For the purposes of this Act, the quality of goods includes their state and condition and the following (among others) are in appropriate cases aspects of the quality of goods—

(a) fitness for all the purposes for which goods of the kind in question are commonly supplied,

(b) appearance and finish,

(c) freedom from minor defects,

(d) safety, and

(e) durability.

Do you prefer this formulation to the OLRC's formulation, or does your preference turn on the language of the implied condition of fitness and the extent to which it meets any gaps in the scope of the implied term of satisfactory quality? How does one determine the meaning of "reasonable person" for the purpose of the new English test?

B.S. Brown & Son Ltd. v. Craiks Ltd.

[1970] 1 WLR 752, [1970] 1 All ER 823 (HL)

LORD REID: My Lords, this case arises out of two orders given by the appellants, who are textile merchants, to the respondents, who are cloth manufacturers. Those orders were for the manufacture of considerable quantities of rayon cloth to a detailed specification. There was a misunderstanding as to the purpose for which the buyers wanted the cloth. They wanted it to fulfil contracts for cloth for making dresses. The sellers thought it was for industrial use. The Lord Ordinary found that they were "astounded" when they first heard, some months after deliveries had commenced, that it was to be used for dresses, and they would not have accepted the order if they had known that. When the contract was determined both parties were left with considerable quantities on their hands.

The buyers sue for damages. Admittedly this was a sale by description within the meaning of the Sale of Goods Act, 1893, and the cloth delivered complied with the description. But the buyers alleged breach of the conditions implied by section 14(1) and (2) of the Sale of Goods Act, 1893. The Lord Ordinary held there was no breach and assoilzied the defenders. The buyers accepted this decision as regards section 14(1) but reclaimed as regards section 14(2). They accept all the Lord Ordinary's findings of fact. The First Division adhered to the Lord Ordinary's interlocutor. The only question now before your Lordship is whether the goods were of merchantable quality within the meaning of section 14(2) which is as follows:

> Where goods are bought by description from a seller who deals in goods of that description (whether he be the manufacturer or not), there is an implied condition that the goods shall be of merchantable quality; provided that if the buyer has examined the goods, there shall be no implied condition as regards defects which such examination ought to have revealed.

It is common ground that the cloth, though complying with the contract description, was not suitable for making dresses—apparently because of irregular weaving. But it was suitable for a number of industrial uses, such as making bags. Was it therefore of merchantable quality?

The Lord Ordinary found (1969 SLR 107, at 108) that the contract price was a low price for cloth of that description for making dresses but

> higher than would have been normal for it as an industrial fabric, but not unreasonably high for the sellers constructing it for such a purpose.

There is no doubt that cloth of this or very similar description was in common use for making dresses. There was no evidence that cloth of this precise description had been used for industrial purposes, but there is a finding that the respondents "had made rayon material of a very similar construction for industrial use before." The Lord Ordinary appears to have accepted the evidence of an expert who said that he had never seen this particular construction of cloth before because the material was viscose, not cotton.

It is evident that at the proof the appellants put most weight on their case under section 14(1), so it is not surprising that the findings of fact with regard to their case under section 14(2) are not as detailed as one might have desired. Certainly this kind of cloth of the quality delivered was suitable for industrial use, but we do not know why it was not more frequently used for industrial purposes. There is no suggestion in the findings that the manufacturers, as dealers in goods of that description, ought to have known, or even suspected, that these goods were not intended for industrial use.

All the well-known authorities were cited on the proper interpretation of "merchantable quality." Some importance was attached to what I said in *Hardwick Game Farm v. Suffolk Agricultural Poultry Producers Association*, [1969] 2 AC 31, at 75:

> If the description is a familiar one it may be that in practice only one quality of goods answers that description—then that quality and only that quality is merchantable quality. Or it may be that various qualities of goods are commonly sold under that description—then it is not disputed that the lowest quality commonly so sold is what is meant by merchantable quality: it is commercially saleable under that description.

I see no reason to alter what I said, but judicial observations can never be regarded as complete definitions: they must be read in light of the facts and issues raised in the particular case. I do not think it is possible to frame, except in the vaguest terms, a definition of "merchantable quality" which can apply to every kind of case. In the *Hardwick* case no question as to price arose because the evidence showed that, even when all the facts were known, the market price was the same for tainted and untainted goods. But suppose that the market price for the better quality is substantially higher than that for the lower quality. Then it could not be right that, if the contract price is appropriate for the better quality, the seller should be entitled to tender the lower quality and say that, because the lower quality is commercially saleable under the contract description, he had fulfilled his contract by delivering goods of the lower quality. But I think that the evidence in this case with regard to prices is much too indefinite to support a case on that basis.

The appellants mainly relied on the contention that, whereas cloth of this description had been commonly used for making dresses, there was no evidence that such cloth had ever been put to an industrial use. There is, I think, some ambiguity in saying that goods are of the same description where the contract description is a precise and detailed description, and that may be novel: or one may mean of the same general description, and that may be common. In most of the authorities the latter meaning seems to have been adopted. Here, as I read the findings of fact, it is not clear whether cloth had commonly been made to this precise specification: but it is clear that cloth of this general description had commonly been used for making dresses and had sometimes been put to an industrial purpose.

Of the various general statements of the law I think that the most applicable to the present case is that of Lord Wright in *Cammell Laird & Co. Ltd. v. Manganese Bronze & Brass Co. Ltd.*, [1934] AC 402, at 430. In the *Hardwick* case, [1969] 2 AC 31, at 77, I suggested that a slight alteration was necessary and that this statement should read:

> What subsection (2) now means by "merchantable quality" is that the goods in the form in which they were tendered were of no use for any purpose for which goods which complied with the description under which these goods were sold would normally be used, and hence were not saleable under that description.

The question, then, is whether this cloth "would normally be used" for industrial purposes. It was suitable for such use. Moreover, the manufacturers assumed it was for such use and their good faith is not disputed: there is no finding that other skilled and knowledgeable manufacturers would have thought differently. So I cannot find any ground for holding that the cloth delivered would not normally be used for any industrial purpose. And if one is entitled to look at the facts and the statutory condition apart from authority, I would not hold that it had been proved that the cloth delivered was not of merchantable quality. I would, therefore, dismiss this appeal.

LORD GUEST: ... Passing now to the question of price, this does not seem to have bulked very largely in the arguments before the courts below. In my view, this case must be approached on the basis that the goods were not one-purpose-only goods but goods which were reasonably capable of being used for more than one purpose, as the Lord Ordinary has found. In the case of such dual purpose goods it is not, in my opinion, legitimate for the purpose of deciding whether the goods are of merchantable quality to compare the contract price too closely with the price at which the goods were sold for the secondary purpose. There will always be a discrepancy in cases of breach of contract; otherwise there could be no claim of damages. The assumption is that the goods are merchantable for a secondary purpose and unless the price is what has been described as a "throw away price" the discrepancy sheds little or no light on the question of merchantable quality. "Commercially saleable" suggests that the price must be unreasonably low. The Lord Ordinary has disposed of the question of price upon the footing that it only arises where there is a case of latent defect, which was the case in *Hardwick Game Farm v. Suffolk Agricultural Poultry Producers Association*, [1969] 2 AC 31. I am not satisfied that this is a sound distinction. I cannot, for my part, see that the question of latent defect makes any difference. I would hold to the view I expressed in *Hardwick*, [1969] 2 AC 31, at 108 that price cannot be omitted entirely but, on mature reconsideration, I think that the test of Dixon J in *Australian Knitting Mills Ltd. v. Grant* (1933), 50 CLR 387, at 418 which I approved was expressed too broadly. The expression he used: "without abatement of the price obtainable," cannot be construed strictly. It cannot be a necessary requirement of merchantability that there should be no abatement of price. If the difference in price is substantial so as to indicate that the goods would only be sold at a "throw away price," then that may indicate that the goods were not of merchantable quality. In the present case the difference in price of 6.25d. on 30.25d. is not, in my view, so material as to justify any such inference. The Lord Ordinary finds, 1969 SLT 107, at 108:

> The price of 36.25d. per yard was higher than would have been normal for it as an industrial fabric, but not unreasonably high for the defenders constructing it for such a purpose. On the other hand, this price of 36.25d. per yard was low for a dress fabric, and the defenders' price for constructing it as a dress fabric would have been higher.

Appeal dismissed.

[Lords Wilberforce and Hodson concurred with Lord Guest. Viscount Dilhorne concurred for separate reasons.]

International Business Machines Co. Ltd. v. Shcherban

[1925] 1 DLR 864, [1925] 1 WWR 405 (Sask. CA)

HAULTAIN CJS (dissenting): The defendants refused to accept a counting device or computing scale, valued at $294, because a piece of glass which covered the dial, and which could be replaced for 25 or 30¢, was broken.

The only ground upon which the defendants can be justified in refusing to accept the scale is, that it is not of merchantable quality as required by s. 16(2) of the Sale of Goods Act, RSS 1920, c. 197.

With deference and a great deal of diffidence, I cannot agree with the other members of the Court that such a trivial defect justified the rejection of the scale. …

The article in question in this case was bought for the defendants' own use. I should gather from its description that it is rather a complicated bit of machinery. So far as we know it was in perfect working order, and the absence of a piece of glass worth 30¢ in no way affected the efficiency of the machine. Under all the circumstances, the case seems to come within the maxim "*de minimis non curat lex*," and I cannot agree that the defendants in rejecting the machine were "reasonable men acting reasonably."

The facts in *Jackson v. Rotax Motor Cycle & Co.*, [1910] 2 KB 937, distinguish it from the present case. In that case 364 out of 609 motor horns delivered under contract were defective, and it would have cost at least £35 to put them in proper condition. The Court of Appeal held that the horns were not merchantable. Cozens-Hardy MR, at 945, said:

> It is true that a large proportion of the goods were merchantable, but that does not justify an action by the vendor for the price of the goods unless he can prove that he was ready and willing to deliver and had delivered or had tendered all the goods in a merchantable condition and of the quality required, subject, of course, to the qualification, if it be necessary to mention it, that the law does not regard as an exception that to which the rule of de minimis can apply; but, subject only to that qualification, it is for the vendor in a case like this to prove that he has delivered or has tendered delivery of goods which were in accordance with the contract.

Farwell LJ, in the same case, at 945 says:

> Of the tubes in question more than half were defective and of the horns also a very considerable number were defective, so that a very large number of the aggregate were in fact unmerchantable. It may well be that in the case of a single horn out of hundreds or a tube or two out of hundreds the rule de minimis would apply, and it would be open to the jury, or to the official referee, to find that, notwithstanding the fact that one or two items were unmerchantable, the consignment as a whole, treating the contract as for a consignment, was merchantable.

While the decision in that case was in favour of the purchaser, the passages I have quoted from the judgments seem to support the conclusion I have arrived at on the question of merchantable quality.

As the other members of the Court are for allowing the appeal, it will be unnecessary for me to say any more with regard to the judgment appealed from, except that, in my opinion the trial Judge proceeded on a wrong principle in awarding damages. If the defendants were not justified in rejecting the scale, the plaintiff was only entitled to damages as provided for in s. 48 of the Sale of Goods Act.

LAMONT JA: Whatever the terms of the agreement between the parties as to payment may have been, one thing is clear, and that is, that the scale was to be delivered at Hafford. The first scale was so delivered. Then the plaintiffs agree to ship a new scale and take back the first one shipped. This was done. Whether we look upon this as merely a substitution of one scale for another under an original verbal contract, or as delivery of a machine under a new contract, as contended by counsel for the defendants, is, in my opinion, immaterial; for the second scale when it arrived at Hafford was not in a deliverable condition, and this was recognized by the plaintiffs when, in their letter of December 8 they asked the defendants to have the repairs made and they would pay for them. The scale delivered, therefore, was not of merchantable quality, as required by s. 16(2) of the Sale of Goods Act … .

The "quality" of goods includes their state or condition (s. 2(10)).

In *Bristol Tramways, etc. Co. v. Fiat Motors Ltd.*, [1910] 2 KB 831, Farwell LJ, at 841, said: … .

Applying the test there laid down, we have to ask ourselves here if a reasonable man, buying the scale in question to resell it to a customer, would accept it with the glass of the dial broken. In my opinion, he would not. The glass must have been intended to fill some useful purpose, or it would not have been put over the dial. The object of having it there was presumably to protect the dial, and to keep the dust out of the delicate machinery. Without that protection, it is improbable that the machine would work efficiently for the same length of time as with it. The defendants were, therefore, in my opinion, within their strict legal rights in refusing to accept the scale until it was put into a merchantable shape.

For the plaintiffs it was contended that, as the cost of a new glass was trifling—some 30¢—the Court could apply the maxim *de minimis non curat lex*. This maxim is frequently applied where trifling irregularities or infractions of the strict letter of the law are brought to the notice of the Court. (*Broom's Legal Maxims*, 9th ed., at 102) I am of opinion, however, that the present is not a case for the application of the maxim. ...

[After quoting from the judgments in *Jackson v. Rotax Motors*, Lamont JA continued:]

A fortiori, where the consignment contains but a single article which is unmerchantable, the maxim has no application. To be immediately saleable or merchantable, the sale required the glass over the dial. It was the plaintiff's duty to put it on. A vendor who contracts to sell a new scale complete, cannot compel the acceptance of one with a broken part when the defect is objected to by the purchaser. He must, before he is entitled to damages for non-acceptance, put the scale in deliverable shape, that is, he must tender in fulfilment of his contract a machine which is of "merchantable quality." This the plaintiffs did not do. That they were most anxious to meet the demands of the defendants in every way they could, and were exceedingly generous in varying the terms of payment to suit their convenience, does not, in my opinion, affect the question; for the defendants clearly set up that the scale tendered was a damaged machine.

Appeal allowed, judgment for defendants.

NOTES

1) Could the court in *Shcherban* have distinguished *Jackson v. Rotax Motors* and, if so, how? Even accepting the desirability of a strict performance test in relation to express and implied conditions (recall our earlier discussion of the Sale of Goods' *a priori* classification of sale terms), why should this preclude the seller from making a bona fide offer to cure the defect where cure can be affected without prejudice to the buyer's interests? As will be explained again, *infra* chapter 16, UCC 2-509(2) recognizes such a right and the right has been expanded in the amended version of Article 2 approved by the ALI in May 2001. A right to cure is now also recognized in Canadian real estate law where a buyer refuses to close on the contract date because of a lien or other cloud on the seller's title. See *Garrett v. Ayr Ventures Inc.* (1995), 21 OR (3d) 407, and earlier authorities there cited. *Shcherban's* case was referred to and followed in *Winsley Brothers v. Woodfield Importing Company*, [1929] NZLR 480, which involved the sale of a "thicknessing machine." The machine had been delivered with a broken shield which could be replaced for £1. The New Zealand Supreme Court, reversing the lower court, held that because of this defect the machine was not merchantable and the buyer was entitled to reject it. The trial judge had held the defect was *de minimis* and had allowed the seller recovery of the price of the machines less a £1 deduction on account of the defect. See also Trueman JA's judgment in *Scott v. Rogers Fruit Co.*, [1928] 1 DLR 201, at 206-8 (Man. CA).

2) *IBM v. Shcherban* was also referred to in *Friskin v. Holiday Chevrolet-Oldsmobile Ltd.* (1976), 72 DLR (3d) 289 (Man. CA). The case involved the right of the buyer of a used car to reject it for non-merchantability. The dealer argued that s. 58(1) of the Manitoba Consumer Protection Act, RSM 1970, c. C200 (which implies a condition of merchantable quality in retail sales of goods governed by the Act) should be construed in such a way as

to give a vendor a reasonable opportunity to make the goods merchantable or reasonably fit for the purpose intended. The argument was unequivocally rejected. Speaking for the court, O'Sullivan JA said in part (at 291):

> ... once it is established that there has been a breach, the plaintiff has the right to reject the goods. The defendant cannot say he has not had an opportunity to remedy the defects. The warranty is not a warranty to render merchantable or to render fit. It is a warranty (or condition) that the goods are, at the time of sale and delivery, merchantable or reasonably fit.

(The second sentence is a reference to the fact that the dealer did in fact have an opportunity to cure the defects.)[3] Once again therefore these cases raise the basic issue whether the seller of non-conforming goods should have a right of cure.

3) *Shcherban* and *Jackson v. Rotax Motors, supra,* show that in order to be merchantable the goods must be saleable in their then condition as well as being fit for their general use or, to put it slightly differently, merchantability implies *use value* and *exchange value.* See further Prosser, "The Implied Warranty of Merchantable Quality" (1943), 21 *Can. Bar Rev.* 446, at 450 *et seq.* Unfit goods obviously are not saleable at the same price as fit goods but it does not follow that the goods are merchantable because they are fit to be used. A serious cosmetic or other nonfunctional defect (such as a tear in a coat or a significant blemish in the body of a new automobile) may make the goods equally unappealing.

The distinction is important because of the definition of "merchantable quality" in (old) s. 14(6) of the UK Sale of Goods Act 1979. To repeat, the definition read:

> Goods of any kind are of merchantable quality within the meaning of subsection (2) above if they are as fit for the purpose or purposes for which goods of that kind are commonly bought as it is reasonable to expect having regard to any description applied to them, the price (if relevant) and all the other relevant circumstances [1979, c. 54, s. 14(6)].

Some UK observers felt that the definition was too narrow and that the reference to the goods being "as fit" for the purpose or purposes for which goods of that kind are commonly bought excluded cosmetic and other defects which, although reducing their resale value or acceptability, do not affect the functional or use value of the goods. (The 1994 amendment to the UK SGA seems to have addressed the problem by substituting a test of "satisfactory quality." See *supra* this chapter.)

The Ontario Law Reform Commission sought to avoid this "unjustifiably narrow" construction of the meaning of fitness and to resolve the doubt created by these words. It

---

3 For strikingly similar sentiments see the recent judgment of the English Court of Appeal in *Rogers v. Parish (Scarborough) Ltd.,* [1987] 2 All ER 232, in the course of which Mustill LJ said (at 236): "In the passage already quoted [the trial judge] gave much weight to the fact that the defects were capable of repair and that the defendants had in some measure been able to repair them. Yet the fact that a defect is repairable does not prevent it from making the res venditur unmerchantable if it is of a sufficient degree (see *Lee v. York Coach and Marine,* [1977] RTR 35). The fact, if it was a fact, that the defect had been repaired at the instance of the purchaser, which in the present case does not appear to be so, might well have had an important bearing on whether the purchaser had by his conduct lost his right to reject, but it cannot in my view be material to the question of merchantability, which falls to be judged at the moment of delivery."

did so by recommending that the definition of merchantable quality be amended to read that merchantable quality means "that the goods, whether new or used, are as fit for the one or more purposes for which goods of that kind are commonly bought *and are of such quality and in such condition* as it is reasonable to expect ... ." (italics added). See Draft Bill, s. 5.13(1)(a). The italicized words were added to make it clear that merchantable quality is not limited to the use value of the goods. See OLRC Sales Report, at 212, and generally, at 210-15. Note also that the definition applies to used as well as new goods. This aspect of the concept of merchantability is dealt with below.

Merchantability and Motor Vehicles

As will be obvious from earlier materials in chapters 6 and 7, motor vehicles have contributed more than their share of litigation to this branch of sales law and indeed to all aspects of sales law. The present subsection looks at the dealer's warranty obligations in the sale of used vehicles and at more refined statutory solutions than those offered in the SGA that have been adopted in several jurisdictions in the post-war period.

Bartlett v. Sidney Marcus Ltd.

[1965] 1 WLR 1013, [1965] 2 All ER 753 (CA)

LORD DENNING MR: This case raises the question on the sale of a secondhand car: What is the effect of the statutory conditions implied therein?

The defendants are very reputable dealers in secondhand cars. The plaintiff was minded in January, 1964, to buy a secondhand Jaguar motor car. He bought it from the defendants for the sum of £950. They took his Ford Zodiac in exchange for £400, so he paid on balance £550. This is what happened: Walker, the salesman for the dealers, took the car down from Sloane Street to Romford to show to the plaintiff. On his way through the City he noticed that there was something wrong with the clutch and with the oil pressure gauge. He thought himself that *either* the clutch needed bleeding, that is, to get the air out, *or* there was a leak between the principal and the slave cylinders. Neither of those would be a very serious matter. When Walker took the car out to the plaintiff, he told him about those defects. He mentioned the clutch and the oil pressure. He suggested two alternative reasons: either it needed bleeding or there was a leak between the cylinders. Then they discussed the price. He asked £600. The plaintiff said only £500. Then there was a question about repairs to the clutch. Then Walker said: "I will take it back and have it attended to and you pay £575, or you can have it done yourself and have it at £550." That is what they agreed, that the plaintiff should take the car and repair the clutch himself. So he had it for £550.

A written contract was drawn up in which it was said, after noting the price: "Oil pressure and filter circuit to be checked. Clutch to be bled, At client's expense." There were printed terms and conditions, none of which apply here. The plaintiff took the car and drove it for at least a fortnight. He thought it was in good condition and it seemed to be running smoothly. He noticed the oil consumption was considerable and something was wrong with the clutch, but he was not unduly alarmed about it because he had been told of it. He drove it for another fortnight and then he took it in to the garage to be repaired. At the garage it was found that there were a number of things wrong with it and a lot of things worn. Most serious of all was this: the clutch thrust was found to be worn away. This was a far more serious defect to the clutch than either Walker or the plaintiff had imagined. The work was done. The engine had to be taken down, and whilst it was taken down, they repaired other things. Because the clutch thrust was so worn out the cost of putting it right came to some £45. The plaintiff claimed that sum as damages from the defendants. He alleged that there was an express term that the car was in perfect condition except that the clutch needed bleeding. The judge held there was no such express term and there is no appeal from that finding. The plaintiff alleged also that the defendants were in breach of the conditions in section 14 of the Sale of Goods Act.

I think there was an implied condition under section 14(1). The plaintiff did make known to the dealer the purpose for which he wanted the goods, so as to show that he relied on his skill and judgment. There was therefore an implied condition that the goods were reasonably fit for the purpose, that is, as a motor car to drive along the road. I think also there was an implied condition under section 14(2). These goods were bought by description from a seller who dealt in goods of that description. There was therefore an implied condition that they should be of merchantable quality. The judge has found that both these conditions were broken and has awarded damages of £45. The defendants now appeal.

Sir John Hobson, for the plaintiff, said that in this case the two implied conditions came very much to the same thing. But he seemed to rely most on the implied condition as to merchantability under section 14(2). I have always understood that the condition under section 14(2) is less stringent than the condition under section 14(1). But nevertheless I agree with Sir John that they do in this case overlap. I will approach this case, as he did, on section 14(2). I take the tests as to merchantability stated by Lord Wright in *Cammell Laird & Co. v. Manganese Bronze and Brass Co. Ltd.*, [1934] AC 402, at 430 and *Grant v. Australian Knitting Mills Ltd.*, [1936] AC 85, at 99. In the *Cammell Laird* case, Lord Wright said the goods were unmerchantable if they were "of no use" for any purpose for which such goods would normally be used. In the *Grant* case (at 100 AC) he said that merchantable meant that the article, if only meant for one particular use in the ordinary course, is "fit for that use." It seems to me that those two tests do not cover the whole ground. There is a considerable territory where on the one hand you cannot say that the article is "of no use" at all, and on the other hand cannot say that it is entirely "fit for use." The article may be of some use though not entirely efficient use for the purpose. It may not be in perfect condition but yet it is in a usable condition. It is then, I think, merchantable. The propeller in the *Cammell Laird* case was in a usable condition: whereas the underpants in the *Grant* case were not. I prefer this test to the more complicated test stated by Farwell LJ in *Bristol Tramways & Co. Ltd. v. Fiat Motors Ltd.*, [1910] 2 KB 831, at 841. It means that on a sale of a secondhand car, it is merchantable if it is in usable condition, even though not perfect. This is very similar to the position under section 14(1). A secondhand car is "reasonably fit for the purpose" if it is in a roadworthy condition, fit to be driven along the road in safety, even though not as perfect as a new car.

Applying those tests here, the car was far from perfect. It required a good deal of work to be done on it, but so do many secondhand cars. A buyer should realise that when he buys a secondhand car defects may appear sooner or later; and, in the absence of an express warranty, he has no redress. Even when he buys from a dealer the most he can require is that it should be reasonably fit for the purpose of being driven along the road. This car came up to that requirement. The plaintiff drove the car away himself. It seemed to be running smoothly. He drove it for four weeks before he put it into the garage to have the clutch repaired. Then more work was necessary than he anticipated. But that does not mean that, at the time of the sale, it was not fit for use as a car. I do not think that, on the judge's findings, there was any evidence of a breach of the implied conditions.

On the whole I would find that this car was reasonably fit for use as a car on the road and in those circumstances there was no breach of either section 14(1) or (2) and I would allow the appeal accordingly.

Appeal allowed.

[Danckwerts and Salmon LJJ delivered concurring judgments.]

Crowther v. Shannon Motor Co.

[1975] 1 WLR 30, [1975] 1 All ER 139 (CA)

LORD DENNING MR: Mr. Crowther is a young man interested in art. In 1972 he bought a secondhand motor car from reputable dealers in Southampton. It was a 1964 Jaguar. He bought it on July 17, 1972, for the sum of £390. The dealers commended it. They said that "it would be difficult to find a 1964 Jaguar of this quality inside and out." They added that for a Jaguar "it is hardly run in." Mr. Crowther looked carefully at it. He took it for a trial run. The next day it was tested by the Ministry of Transport officials. The report of the test was satisfactory. So Mr. Crowther bought the Jaguar. He did not take the words of puff seriously. But he relied on the sellers' skill and judgment. There was clearly an implied condition under section 14(1) of the Sale of Goods Act 1893 that the car was reasonably fit for the purpose for which he required it and which he made known to the seller.

That was July 17, 1972. The mileage as stated on the mileometer at that time was 82,165 miles. Mr. Crowther took the car. He drove it on some long journeys. He went up to the North of England and back. He went round Hampshire. He went over 2,000 miles in it. He found that it used a great deal of oil. But he managed to drive it for three weeks. Then on August 8, 1972, when he was driving up the M3 motorway, it came to a full stop. The engine seized up. The car was towed into a garage. The engine was found to be in an extremely bad condition. So much so that it had to be scrapped and replaced by a reconditioned engine. The car was out of use for a couple of months or so.

Mr. Crowther brought an action in the county court for damages from the dealers. He called as a witness a previous owner of the car, a Mr. Hall. He gave evidence that he had bought it from these selfsame dealers about eight months before. He had paid them about £400 for it. He had used it for those eight months and then sold it back in July 1972 to these very dealers. When he resold it to them he knew the engine was in a very bad state, but he did not disclose it to them. He left them to find out for themselves. He was himself an engineer. He gave a trenchant description of the engine:

> At the time of resale I though the engine was clapped out. I do not think this engine was fit to be used on the road, not really, it needed a rebore.

The judge accepted the evidence of Mr. Hall. He held that there was a breach of section 14(1) of the Act. He awarded Mr. Crowther damages in the sum of £460.37 with costs. Now there is an appeal to this court by the dealers. They say there was no justification for the finding that this car was not reasonably fit for the purpose. The mileage when they sold it was 82,165 miles. The mileage when it clapped out was 84,519 miles. So that in three weeks it had gone 2,354 miles.

Mr. Rudd, who put the case very cogently before us, submitted that a car which had covered 2,354 miles must have been reasonably fit for the purpose of driving along the road. He drew attention to the case some years ago in this court of *Bartlett v. Sydney Marcus Ltd.*, [1965] 1 WLR 1013. We emphasised then that a buyer, when he buys a secondhand car, should realise that defects may appear sooner or later. In that particular case a defect did appear in the clutch. It was more expensive to repair than had been anticipated. It was held by this court that the fact that the defect was more expensive than had been anticipated did not mean that there had been any breach of the implied condition. But that case seems to me to be entirely distinguishable from the present case. In that case it was a minor repair costing £45 after 300 miles. Here we have a very different case. On the dealers' own evidence, a buyer could reasonably expect to get 100,000 miles life out of a Jaguar engine. Here the Jaguar had only done 80,000 miles. Yet it was in such a bad condition that it was "clapped out" and after some 2,300 miles it failed altogether. That is very different from a minor repair. The dealers themselves said that if they had known that the engine would blow up after 2,000 miles, they would not have sold it. The reason obviously was because it would not have been reasonably fit for the purpose.

Some criticism was made of a phrase used by the judge. He said "What does 'fit for the purpose' mean?" He answered: "To go as a car for reasonable time." I am not quite sure that that is entirely accurate. The relevant time is the time of sale. But there is no doubt what the judge meant. If the car does not go for a reasonable time but the engine breaks up within a short time, that is evidence which goes to show it was not reasonably fit for the purpose at the time it was sold. On the evidence in this case, the engine was liable to go at any time. It was "nearing the point of failure," said the expert, Mr. Wise. The time interval was merely "staving off the inevitable." That shows that at the time of the sale it was not reasonably fit for the purpose of being driven on the road. I think the judge on the evidence was quite entitled to find there was a breach of section 14(1) of the Sale of Goods Act 1893 and I would therefore dismiss the appeal.

Appeal dismissed.

[Orr and Browne LJJ delivered short concurring judgments.]

QUESTIONS

1) Do you find Lord Denning's explanation of the distinction between *Crowther* and *Bartlett v. Sidney Marcus Ltd.* persuasive? What is the economic effect of holding a used-car dealer responsible for defects of which he could not reasonably have been aware at the time of sale? Does CPA s. 34 allow him to exclude or limit his warranty liabilities under SGA s. 15?

2) The Commonwealth jurisprudence on a dealer's warranty liability on the sale of used (and new) cars is reviewed in Whincup, "Reasonable Fitness of a Car" (1975), 38 *Mod. L Rev.* 660. He concludes (at 670) that the applicable standard is that the car must "at the time of sale and for a reasonable time thereafter be free of any material defect making it incapable of safe and lawful use." "Reasonable time," in his view, will be determined by the price, age and condition of the car but the buyer may expect to incur incidental but possibly expensive repairs. Does the decision in *Crowther* meet Mr. Whincup's criteria?

3) A car dealer knew that a 1968 Firebird in his inventory had been used extensively for drag racing. He sold the car to G in 1972 for $2,895, the price of such a car in good condition, without disclosing the car's unusual history. G bought it as an ordinary used car for normal driving purposes. But the car was not suitable for highway driving and its engine exploded two days after the sale was completed. G sues for the return of his money. What result? See *Green v. Holiday Chevrolet-Oldsmobile Ltd.* (1975), 55 DLR (3d) 637 (Man. CA).

Note on Used-Vehicle Warranty and Disclosure Legislation

Used vehicles have been a more fertile source of complaints and litigation than any other group of used goods, and for this reason there has been a growing tendency for the provinces to legislate separately in this area. The legislation takes two forms. The first is a licensing requirement for motor vehicle dealers and their salesmen. We have encountered this type of control mechanism before and will encounter it again. The advantages of this type of approach—an *ex ante* screening mechanism coupled with powerful *post factum* sanctions for violations—are offset by the reluctance of licensing agencies to deprive a licensee of his livelihood even when persistent misconduct is involved. In Ontario, appeals from a refusal by the Registrar of Motor Vehicle Dealers and Salesmen to grant or renew a licence, or a proposal by him to suspend or cancel a licence, are heard by the Commercial Registration Appeals Tribunal (CRAT).

The second type of legislation is represented by ss. 88 to 100 of the Ontario Highway Traffic Act, RSO 1990, c. H.8, as am., partly reproduced below, which has its counterpart in some of the other provinces. The legislation has had an interesting evolution. Originally a dealer was merely enjoined not to sell a vehicle that was unroadworthy. This standard was found to be too vague and was therefore supplemented by specific regulations. This too was found insufficient since the dealer was not required to certify anything in writing. This led to the introduction of a Certificate of Mechanical Fitness. However, difficulties continued to subsist. Some of them are related in the OLRC Warranties Report, c. 9, at 141 *et seq.* Particularly important were the following difficulties:

1) There was a ready traffic in false and even forged certificates. Motor vehicle mechanics were not subject to the jurisdiction of the Registrar of Motor Vehicle Dealers, and the Apprenticeship and Tradesmen's Qualifications Act did not, it was claimed, permit the cancellation of a mechanic's licence on grounds of moral turpitude.

2) The title of the certificate was misleading since most of the checks performed for the purposes of the certificate were (and are) directed to the roadworthiness of the vehicle and not to its mechanical condition.

3) Dealers frequently took the position that they were not civilly responsible for the consequences of a false certificate. Section 74(3) [now 90(3)] did not address this question and the jurisprudence, though favourable to the buyer, did not firmly settle the point. Section 73 was repealed in 1982 and it is no longer obligatory for the seller of a used vehicle to provide the buyer with a Safety Standards Certificate. (The section was apparently repealed because licence plates now remain with their owner and no longer travel with the vehicle). However, apparently dealers continue to offer the certificate as a selling aid and even if the seller can no longer be held contractually liable for an inaccurate certificate unless the dealer adopts it as his own, the inspection station issuing the certificate should remain liable for breach of warranty if the certificate was issued to induce the recipient to buy the vehicle or otherwise act to her detriment in reliance on the certificate. Apart from the certificate itself, the inspection station doing the inspection will be liable for breach of contract if its services were retained by the purchaser. Finally, the issuer of the certificate may also be liable to the recipient in negligence under the *Hedley Byrne* doctrine.

The first two difficulties related above were largely taken care of in the 1973 amendments to the Highway Traffic Act (SO 1973, c. 167) and, as indicated, the name of the certificate was changed to "Safety Standards Certificate." In one respect the buyer is now worse off than before in so far as the dealer is no longer statutorily obliged to furnish the buyer with a Safety Standards Certificate.

The typical used-car agreement used to exclude the statutory implied warranties and substitute a 30-day or (less frequently) 60-day 50–50 warranty. See the warranty given in *Presley v. MacDonald, infra*. For the current form of agreement adopted by the Ontario Automobile Dealers Association for new and used vehicles see the Appendix of this casebook. It is not clear to what extent the new agreement is intended to supersede the old 50–50, 30-day warranty.

A different approach to protecting the buyer civilly from undisclosed mechanical defects has been adopted in New Zealand and many of the Australian states. Under the terms of this type of legislation, the dealer is deemed to warrant the vehicle's mechanical fitness for a stipulated time and number of miles depending on the price unless he has disclosed the defects and given a reasonably accurate estimate of the cost of repair. If the vehicle does suffer from undisclosed defects, the dealer is responsible for the cost of repair. He is likewise responsible for any substantial inaccuracy in his estimate of the cost of repairing disclosed defects. Do you support this type of approach to the problem of used cars? According to earlier reports, the Australian schemes appeared to be working well, although some observers claim that they are economically inefficient and help to inflate the price of used cars. Why should this be so and, assuming the legislation does lead to increased prices, is this fatal to its soundness?

Apparently, Quebec is so far the only Canadian jurisdiction to have followed the Australasian precedents. See the Quebec Consumer Protection Act 1978, Division IV, also reproduced below.

Highway Traffic Act

RSO 1990, c. H.8

88. In this section and in sections 88 to 100,

"Director" means the Director of Vehicle Inspection Standards appointed under section 89; ("directeur")

"licensee" means a person who is the holder of a motor vehicle inspection station licence issued under section 91; ("titulaire de permis")

"motor vehicle inspection mechanic" means a person who certifies by means of a safety standards certificate that a motor vehicle complies with the equipment and performance standards prescribed by the regulations; ("mécanicien préposé à l'inspection des véhicules automobiles")

"motor vehicle inspection station" means any premises maintained or operated for the inspection of motor vehicles and the issuance of safety standards certificates or vehicle inspection stickers in respect of the motor vehicles; ("centre d'inspection des véhicules automobiles")

"registrant" means a person who is registered as a motor vehicle inspection station mechanic under section 92; ("mécanicien inscrit")

"vehicle inspection record" means a form required to be completed in accordance with the regulations prior to the issue of a vehicle inspection sticker; ("fiche d'inspection de véhicule")

"vehicle inspection sticker" means the device issued as evidence that the inspection requirements and performance standards referred to in section 85 have been complied with. ("vignette d'inspection de véhicule")

. . .

90. (1) No person other than a licensee or a person authorized in writing by the licensee shall issue a safety standards certificate.

(2) No person other than a licensee, a motor vehicle inspection mechanic or a person authorized in writing by the licensee shall affix a vehicle inspection sticker to a vehicle.

(3) A safety standards certificate in respect of a motor vehicle shall not be issued or a vehicle inspection sticker affixed to a vehicle unless,

(a) the vehicle has been inspected by a motor vehicle inspection mechanic in the motor vehicle inspection station and the vehicle complies with the inspection requirements and performance standards prescribed by the regulations; and

(b) the safety standards certificate or a vehicle inspection record,

(i) is made by the motor vehicle inspection mechanic who inspected the vehicle, and

(ii) is countersigned by the licensee or a person authorized in writing by the licensee.

. . .

92. (1) No person shall sign a vehicle inspection record as mechanic or certify in a safety standards certificate that a vehicle complies with the standards of equipment and performance prescribed by the regulations unless the person is registered by the Director as a motor vehicle inspection mechanic in a motor vehicle inspection station and the Director may so register any person for whom application is made under subsection (2).

(2) Where a licensee or an applicant for a motor vehicle inspection station licence applies for the registration as a motor vehicle inspection mechanic in the motor vehicle inspection station of the licensee or in the proposed motor vehicle inspection station of the applicant for a licence, as the case may be, of any person who meets the requirements of this Act and the regulations, the person is entitled to be registered as a motor vehicle inspection mechanic in the motor vehicle inspection station.

Quebec Consumer Protection Act

SQ 1978, c. 9, P-40.1, as am.

[Division IV]

§2.—Contracts of sale and long-term contracts of lease of used automobiles and used motorcycles

155. The merchant must affix a label on every used automobile that he offers for sale or for long-term lease.

The label must be so affixed that it may be read entirely from outside the automobile.

156. The label must disclose:

(a) if the used automobile is offered for sale, its price, and, if it is offered for long-term lease, its retail value;

(b) the number of miles or kilometres registered on the odometer, and the number of miles or kilometres actually travelled by the automobile, if different from that indicated on the odometer;

(c) the model year ascribed by the manufacturer, the serial number, the make, the model and the cubic capacity of the engine;

(d) if such is the case, the fact that the automobile has been used as a taxi-cab, a drivers' school automobile, a police car, an ambulance, a leased automobile, an automobile for customers or as a demonstrator and the identity of every business or of every public agency that owned the automobile or rented it on a long-term basis;

(e) if such is the case, every repair done on the used automobile since it has been in the possession of the merchant;

(f) the class provided for in section 160;

(g) the characteristics of the warranty offered by the merchant;

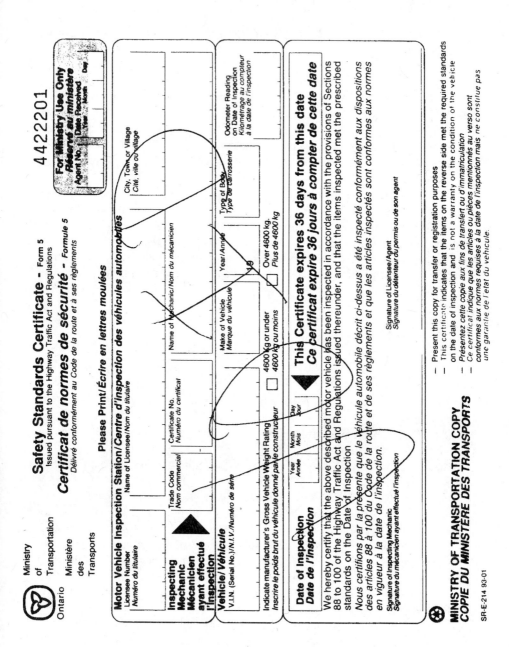

(h) that a certificate of mechanical inspection issued under the Highway Safety Code (c. C-24.2) will be given to the consumer upon the signing of the contract;

(i) that the merchant must, at the request of the consumer, provide him with the name and telephone number of the last owner other than the merchant.

For the application of paragraphs b and d of this section, the merchant may base himself on a written declaration of the last owner unless he has reasonable grounds to believe that it is false.

157. The label must be appended to the contract or, in the case of a long-term contract of lease which is not evidenced in writing, given to the consumer at the making of the contract.

All that is disclosed on the label forms an integral part of the contract, except the price at which the automobile is offered and the specifications of the warranty, which may be changed.

158. The contract of sale must be evidenced in writing and indicate:

(a) the number of the licence issued to the merchant under of [*sic*] the High-way Safety Code (c. C-24.2) (Note: misprint in Revised Statutes text omits section number);

(b) the place and date of the contract;

(c) the name and address of the consumer and of the merchant;

(d) the price of the automobile;

(e) the duties chargeable, under a federal or provincial act;

(f) the total amount the consumer must pay under the contract; and

(g) the specifications of the warranty.

159. The sale or long-term lease of a used automobile carries with it a warranty that the automobile will remain in good working order

(a) for a period of six months or 10 000 kilometres, whichever occurs first, in the case of a class A automobile;

(b) for a period of three months or 5 000 kilometres, whichever occurs first, in the case of a class B automobile;

(c) for a period of one month or 1 700 kilometres, whichever occurs first, in the case of a class C automobile.

160. For the application of section 159, used automobiles are divided into the following classes:

(a) class A automobiles, namely, where not more than two years have elapsed between the date the manufacturer put his automobiles of the same model and of the same model year on the market and the date of the sale or long-term lease contemplated in the said section, provided that the automobile has not covered more than 40 000 kilometres;

(b) class B automobiles, namely, where they are not contemplated in paragraph *a* and not more than three years have elapsed between the date the manufacturer put his automobiles of the same model and of the same model year on the market and the date of the sale or long-term lease contemplated in the said section, provided that the automobile has not covered more than 60 000 kilometres;

(c) class C automobiles, namely, where they are not contemplated in paragraph a or b and not more than five years have elapsed between the date the manufacturer put his automobiles of the same model and of the same model year on the market and the date of the sale or long-term lease contemplated in the said section, provided that the automobile has not covered more than 80 000 kilometres;

(d) class D automobiles, namely automobiles not contemplated in any of paragraphs a, b and c.

161. The warranty provided for by section 159 does not cover:

(a) normal maintenance service and the replacement of parts resulting from it;

(b) interior upholstery or exterior decorative items;

(c) damage resulting from abuse by the consumer after delivery of the automobile; and

(d) any accessory provided for by regulation.

162. Where the merchant offers a class A, B or C automobile for sale or long-term lease, he may indicate on the label all the defects which exist in the automobile, with an estimate of the cost of repair thereof. The merchant is bound by the estimate and he guarantees that the repair may be carried out for the price mentioned in the estimate.

In that case, the merchant is not subject to the obligation of warranty for the defects mentioned on the label.

163. The warranty takes effect upon the delivery of the used automobile.

. . .

166. Section 155 to 165 do not apply to a new automobile which has been the object of a contract of lease comprising an option to purchase of which the lessee decides to avail himself or comprising a right of acquisition in section 150.29 or 150.30 which the consumer decides to exercise.

Presley v. MacDonald

(1963), 38 DLR (2d) 237, [1963] 1 OR 619 (Co. Ct.)

KENNEDY Co. Ct. J: About July 3, 1961, the plaintiff Presley, who was then 20 years old, went to see the defendant MacDonald in Cornwall, where the latter carried on business under the name of Uptown Motor Sales, and looked at a 1956 Oldsmobile sedan and went for a ride in it. He asked the defendant MacDonald what kind of warranty he would get with the car, whereupon the defendant MacDonald said he would give him a "30-day 50–50 mechanical warranty." The plaintiff Presley thereupon purchased the car for $1,095 and a purchase order dated July 3, 1961, was executed by the plaintiff Presley and by Uptown Motor Sales.

The purchase order (ex. 1) has the following words in brackets written on the face of it:

(30-day 50–50)
(mechanical)
(warranty)

Also on the front of the purchase order appear the following words: "The front and back of this order comprise the entire agreement affecting this purchase and no other agreement or understanding of any nature concerning same has been made or entered into, or will be recognized."

Notwithstanding the wording of the purchase order a "certificate of mechanical fitness" dated July 3, 1961, (ex. 2) was executed by Uptown Motor Sales and delivered to the plaintiff Presley who signed this name thereon acknowledging the receipt thereof, which (after stating that certain parts of the car, which have nothing to do with the accident, had been checked), states as follows: "We hereby certify that the above described motor vehicle is in a safe condition to be operated on a highway." This certificate of mechanical fitness was not properly pleaded in the statement of claim but was produced by the plaintiff Presley while he was being cross-examined by counsel for the defendant MacDonald and was marked as ex. 2 without objection.

A day or two after the plaintiff Presley signed the purchase order and was given the certificate of mechanical fitness he took delivery of the car and drove it from Cornwall to Lindsay. Later on July 8, 1961, he drove the car from Lindsay to Oshawa and on the return journey while driving from Oshawa to Lindsay there was a "bang," the car started to "shake," the rear wheels seized, the car skidded sideways, went into a ditch and rolled over with the result that the car was wrecked and the plaintiff Presley and one of his passengers were injured.

The police officer who investigated the accident found on the road oil and pieces of metal and tire marks indicating that as the car travelled over a small knoll it started to travel sideways along the road and the shoulder thereof for some 160 ft. until it went into a ditch and turned over. On examining the car after the accident he found that the transmission of the car was broken and that the pieces of metal he had picked up on the road matched the metal of the transmission of the car.

The special and general damages claimed by the plaintiff have been agreed upon by the parties at the sum of $950 which I presume includes an allowance for the sale price of the wrecked car.

I think it is well-established law, that if a prospective purchaser chooses an article such as a second-hand car from a second-hand car dealer, and in the exercise of his own judgment buys the car without any warranty or misrepresentation by the seller, the purchaser in such case would have no cause of action against the seller for any defect in the car.

In this case, however, in my opinion, there were two warranties consisting, firstly of the certificate of mechanical fitness (ex. 2), and secondly of the "30-day 50–50 mechanical warranty" (ex. 1). I must therefore endeavour to reach a conclusion as to what were the terms of each warranty.

The Sale of Goods Act, RSO 1960, c. 358, s. 1(n) defines a warranty as follows: …

And s. 51(1), leaving out the words which are not applicable, provides the following remedy for a breach of warranty: …

I will deal first of all with the warranty contained in the certificate of mechanical fitness (ex. 2).

Section 49 of the Highway Traffic Act, RSO 1960, c. 172, provides as follows:

49(1) When a used motor vehicle is sold by a dealer in used motor vehicles, the dealer shall deliver to the purchaser at the time of the sale a certificate of mechanical fitness signed by the dealer stating that the motor vehicle is, or is not, in a safe condition to be operated on a highway, and such certificate shall be on a separate form from any bill of sale or other document.

(2) Every dealer who contravenes any of the provisions of subsection 1 or who makes a false statement in any such certificate is liable to a fine of not less than $50 and not more than $300.

Pursuant to such section the defendant MacDonald gave to the plaintiff Presley the certificate of mechanical fitness (ex. 2) executed by Uptown Motor Sales which (after stating that certain parts of the car, which had nothing to do with the accident, had been checked) states as follows: "We hereby certify that the above described motor vehicle is in a safe condition to be operated on a highway." Since the Highway Traffic Act by s. 49 creates a duty and provides a penalty for the breach thereof, it seems to me that I should record the reasons why, in my opinion, the rights of the plaintiff Presley are not affected by the general rule applicable to the interpretation of such statutory provision.

The cases indicate that the general rule of interpretation applicable to a statute which creates a duty and imposes a penalty for a breach thereof is that

(a) when a statute creates a duty and does not provide any remedy for the breach of the duty, an individual is entitled to bring an action for damages for any special damages he may have suffered by reason of the breach,

(b) but when a statute creates a duty and provides a special remedy for the breach of it, there is a presumption that the statute intended to exclude any other remedy. If the plaintiff Presley was suing the defendant Macdonald for damages for a breach of the duty imposed on the defendant MacDonald by s. 49 to "deliver to the purchaser at the time of the sale a certificate of mechanical fitness ..." the rule of interpretation mentioned in para. (b) above might be applicable. But in the instant case the defendant Macdonald did in fact deliver to the plaintiff Presley at the time of the sale a certificate of mechanical fitness as required by s. 49, and the plaintiff Presley is not suing the defendant MacDonald for damages for breach of any statutory duty but is suing the defendant MacDonald for damages for the breach of a warranty which the defendant MacDonald gave with the car when he sold it to the plaintiff Presley. In such circumstances, in my opinion, the rule of interpretation mentioned in para. (b) is not applicable and the plaintiff Presley has a right to maintain an action against the defendant Macdonald for damages for a breach of the warranty given to him by the defendant MacDonald.

· · ·

In my opinion, when the defendant Macdonald gave to the plaintiff Presley a certificate of mechanical fitness (ex. 2) which states "We hereby certify that the above described motor vehicle is in a safe condition to be operated on a highway," such certificate constitutes a warranty or an agreement within the meaning of s. 1(n) the plaintiff Presley was "in a safe condition to be operated on a highway," and that when the transmission broke causing the rear wheels to lock and the motor vehicle to go into the ditch and be wrecked, there was a breach of such warranty which entitled the plaintiff Presley to "maintain an action against the seller for damages for the breach of warranty, ... the measure of damages for breach of warranty [being] the estimated loss directly and naturally resulting in the ordinary course of events from the breach of warranty."

It seems to me that the general and special damages suffered by the plaintiff Presley which have been agreed at $950 represent "loss directly and naturally resulting in the ordinary course of events from the breach of the warranty" and that, if it were not for the "30-day 50–50 mechanical warranty" the plaintiff Presley would be entitled to judgment against the defendant MacDonald for $950 and costs. (It will be noted that the defendant MacDonald did not introduce any evidence as to what if any tests were made to see that the car was "in a safe condition to be operated on the highway.")

I will now deal with the purchase order (ex. 1) which in my opinion contains a further warranty. The plaintiff Presley at the trial testified to the effect that when he was negotiating for the purchase of the car with the defendant MacDonald he asked him what kind of warranty he would get with the car and the defendant MacDonald agreed to give him a "30-day 50–50 mechanical warranty," and these words were then written on the face of the purchase order. The plaintiff Presley impressed me as being a truthful witness, and I have no doubt that he understood the words to mean as he said several times with slight variations when he was being examined, "I figure if anything mechanical went wrong with the car any damage caused by it would be paid one-half by the garage." It seems to me that a reasonable interpretation of the words, "30-day 50–50 mechanical warranty" and of the evidence of the plaintiff Presley is that if within 30 days of the sale, any of the parts of the car became defective the defendant MacDonald would repair or replace them and would pay one-half of the cost thereof and that if the car was damaged by reason of a mechanical defect the defendant MacDonald would pay one-half of the cost of repairing the damage, and since in the instant case the car was by reason of a mechanical defect damaged beyond repair, it seems to me it follows as a logical sequence that the defendant Macdonald is liable to pay one-half the damages suffered by the plaintiff Presley. Since the defendant MacDonald did not testify or call any evidence, it seems to me that the uncontradicted evidence given by the plaintiff Presley in this connection which is against his own interest and the above reasonable interpretation of the words in question should be accepted.

Counsel for the defendant if I understand his argument correctly, has argued that the "30-day 50–50 mechanical warranty" only meant that if within 30 days of the sale any of the parts of the car became defective the defendant MacDonald would repair or replace them and would pay one-half the cost thereof. This argument, if carried to its conclusion, would mean in this case, that when the transmission broke and as a consequence the car went off the road and was wrecked, all that the defendant MacDonald would have to do would be to pay one-half of the cost of a new transmission. If the argument of counsel for the defendant MacDonald is to prevail, then in such circumstances it seems to me that the plaintiff Presley as previously stated would be entitled under the warranty contained in the certificate of mechanical fitness (ex. 2) to the full sum of $950. But, unfortunately for the plaintiff Presley, he has in my opinion, through an abundance of precaution by insisting on the "30 day 50–50 mechanical warranty" reduced the liability of the defendant MacDonald to 50% of the damage he has suffered. In such circumstances there will be judgment for the plaintiff Presley for $475 and costs.

Judgment for plaintiff.

QUESTIONS AND NOTES

1) Do you agree with the decision in *Presley*? Had there been a breach of the certificate of mechanical fitness? If there had, could its civil consequences be reduced by a disclaimer clause? What would have been the position if the plaintiff or a passenger in the vehicle had been injured as a result of the accident? Are the answers to the foregoing questions affected by a licensee's or mechanic's negligence in carrying out the certified inspection? See *Hawke v. Waterloo-Wellington Flying Club Ltd.* (1972), 22 DLR (3d) 266 (Ont. Co. Ct.); *L.G. Wilson Motors Ltd. v. Woods* (1970), 2 NBR (2d) 581 (SC); and *Henzel v. Brussels Motors Ltd.*, [1973] 1 OR 339, 31 DLR (3d) 131 (Co. Ct.), esp. at 136-40.

2) The leading case on the civil consequences of breach of a statutory duty where the statute itself only provides for a penalty is *R v. Saskatchewan Wheat Pool*, [1983] 1 SCR 205. Dickson J, giving the judgment of the Supreme Court, laid down the following principles: (1) civil consequences of breach of statute should be subsumed in the law of negligence; (2) the notion of a nominate tort of statutory breach giving a right of recovery merely on proof of breach and damages should be rejected, as should the view that an unexcused breach constitutes negligence *per se* giving rise to absolute liability; (3) proof of statutory breach, causative of damages, may be evidence of negligence; and (4) the statutory formulation of the duty may afford a specific, and useful, standard of reasonable conduct. Dickson J did not address himself to situations like those in *Presley v. MacDonald* where the defendant is sued for breach of a certificate.

3) *Motor Vehicle Repairs.* Over the years there have been many complaints about abuses in the car repair industry. The complaints include overcharging for repairs, work being done that had not been authorized, and offers of "free estimates" that turn out not to be free if the customer fails to authorize the repairs. Another well-documented abuse involving transmission estimates concerns repair shops that refuse to reassemble the transmission parts after the transmission has been dismantled if the customer fails to authorize the installation of a new transmission.

Legislation such as the Ontario Motor Vehicle Repair Act, RSO 1990, c. M.43, as amended, is designed to curb the abuses. The Act applies (s. 1) to any vehicle as defined in the Highway Traffic Act ("vehicle"), to a person who works on or repairs vehicles for compensation ("repairer"), and to an individual who contacts a repairer for an estimate, work or repairs to a vehicle ("customer"). The Act provides *inter alia* that where a customer asks for a written estimate no repairer shall charge for any work or repairs unless the repairer first provides the customer with a written estimate of cost that contains prescribed particulars (s. 2). No fee may be charged for an estimate unless a customer is told in advance that a fee will be charged and the amount of the fee (s. 3(1)). No fee may be charged for an estimate if the work is authorized and carried out (s. 3(2)).

No work or repairs may be charged for that is not authorized by the customer (s. 4(1)), and an authorization by telephone is not effective unless the person receiving the authorization records the name and telephone number of the person giving the authorization and the date and time of the authorization (s. 5). On completion of work or repairs the repairer must give the customer a detailed invoice with prescribed particulars (s. 8). All parts and labour in a repair job (other than in relation to a motorcycle) are deemed to be warranted for 90 days or 5000 km, whichever comes first (s. 9(1)). A charge made in contravention of the Act is non-collectable and non-recoverable, and may be recovered by the customer in a civil action if it has been paid (s. 11). A violator is also subject to criminal sanctions—a maximum fine of $2,000 or imprisonment for up to a year in the case of an individual, and a maximum fine of $25,000 in the case of a corporation (s. 12).

How much do the above provisions add to the common law? Could motor vehicle repair abuses also be dealt with under the Business Practices Act? How effective is the MVRA likely to be in practice? Who will monitor compliance with the Act? Will it prevent overcharging for repairs or the giving of inflated estimates?

Merchantability and the Durability of Goods

Mash & Murrell Ltd. v. Joseph I. Emanuel Ltd.

[1961] 1 WLR 862, [1961] 1 All ER 485 (QB)

[The plaintiffs carried on business in the United Kingdom as dealers in potatoes fit for human consumption. The defendants were also dealers in and importers of potatoes. On July 8, 1957, the defendant's agents agreed to sell the plaintiffs 2,000 half-bags of Cyprus potatoes, then afloat the S.S. *Ionian*, at 16s. per half-bag, c. & f. Liverpool, plus commission.

The potatoes had been loaded on the *Ionian* on June 29, 1957, at Limassol on the south coast of Cyprus for shipment to Liverpool and, after several intervening port calls, reached Liverpool on July 18. On their arrival there the potatoes were found to be rotten and were condemned by the port authorities as unfit for human consumption.

The plaintiffs brought this action for damages alleging breach of several implied warranties as described in Diplock J's judgment below. The defendants denied liability.]

DIPLOCK J: The plaintiffs claim that they are entitled to recover damages from the defendants arising out of the state of the goods on arrival at Liverpool. They rely on the rotten state of the potatoes on arrival and ask me to infer that the potatoes shipped cannot have been fit to travel at the time of shipment. By "fit to travel" I mean fit to be carried to Liverpool so as to arrive in a condition fit for the purpose for which they would normally be used.

There is no doubt at all that on arrival the potatoes were rotten and were wholly unfit for human consumption. As this is the purpose for which Cyprus spring crop potatoes would normally be used, I do not think it is seriously contended that they were then merchantable. I find that on arrival at Liverpool they were unmerchantable.

. . .

On those findings of fact a question of law, which has been hotly debated, arises. I have so far travelled through my legal life under the impression, shared by a number of other judges who have sat in this court, that when goods are sold under a contract such as a c.i.f. contract, or f.o.b. contract, which involves transit before use, there is an implied warranty not merely that they shall be merchantable at the time they are put on the vessel, but that they shall be in such a state that they can endure the normal journey and be in a merchantable condition upon arrival. But it has been strenuously argued by Mr. Roskill for the defendants that that impression under which I have been for so long is quite erroneous and, like a similar impression of Lord Atkin when he was Atkin J, is founded on a misreading of the famous old case about rabbits, *Beer v. Walker* (1877), 46 LJQB 677. It is, therefore, necessary to analyse the way in which the plaintiffs put their case.

They have put their case in three different ways. First, founding themselves on section 14(1) of the Sale of Goods Act, 1893, they say that here was a case where the buyer by implication made known to the seller the particular purpose for which the goods were required so as to show that they relied on his skill and judgment, and that, accordingly, they rely on the implied condition that the goods were fit for that purpose, namely, the purpose of being carried by the *Ionian* on her voyage to Liverpool, and for the purpose of being carried to Liverpool for sale for use for human consumption after arrival.

Alternatively, they put their case on section 14(2), namely, the warranty as to merchantable quality, and they say the merchantable quality as regards these potatoes is that at the time of shipment they should be merchantable as potatoes sold for carrying and delivery to Liverpool by the *Ionian*.

The third way they put it is that there is an implied warranty in a c.i.f. or c. & f. contract, as this was, that the goods should be fit to stand the voyage from Cyprus to Liverpool on which the *Ionian* was about to embark, a normal voyage from Cyprus to Liverpool, and should arrive sound and fit for sale for human consumption after arrival.

For those propositions, Mr. Roche relies primarily on *Beer v. Walker, Ollett v. Jordan*, [1918] 1 KB 41 (DC), and, for the last proposition, on a decision of McCardie J in *Evangelinos v. Leslie & Anderson* (1920), 41 Ll. LR 17. I shall have to examine those cases a little more carefully.

It does not seem to me that there is really any very great distinction between the three alternative ways in which the plaintiffs put their case. Had the case been tried before the Sale of Goods Act, 1893, it would have been unnecessary to put it in the first two ways, and it seems to me, in a case of this kind, that subsections (1) and (2) of section 14 of the Act are really two sides of the same coin. If a buyer makes known a particular purpose—those, of course, are the words of the subsection—to the seller so as to show that he relies on the seller's skill and judgment, then the suitability for that particular purpose is a warranty and implied condition of the contract. If he does not make known any particular purpose, then, the assumption being that he requires them for the ordinary purposes for which such goods are intended to be used, the implied condition is one that they are fit for those ordinary purposes, that is to say, that they are merchantable, and I venture to think there is no other distinction between subsection (1) and subsection (2).

If it were possible for the coin to have three sides, I should have said the implied term on which Mr. Roche relies as a third ground, applicable to c.i.f., c. & f. and f.o.b. contracts, was a third side of the same coin. I think it really comes to no more than this, that merchantability in the case of goods sold c.i.f. or c. & f. means that the goods must remain merchantable for a reasonable time, and that, in the case of such contracts, a reasonable time means time for arrival and disposal upon arrival.

However, I think it is necessary, in the way this case has been argued, that I should deal with the three alternatives. So far as section 14(1) is concerned, the evidence which I have already alluded to shows, first, that the defendants' agents knew the nature of the plaintiffs' business; they knew it as the result of having had dealings with them for many years; indeed, there was produced by Mr. Mash a letter from them of 1951 which refers particularly to their hotel and ships' stores trade in which they say they know him to be well established.

It is also plain from the evidence that Mash made it clear to the defendants' agents that he wanted the potatoes for use in his trade in this country. Mr. Roche, in those circumstances, relies on the well-known case of *Manchester Liners Ltd. v. Rea Ltd.*, [1922] 2 AC 74 (HL), which he says, I think rightly, establishes the proposition that if the particular purpose is made known by the buyer to the seller, then, unless there is something in effect to rebut the presumption, that in itself is sufficient to raise the presumption that he relies upon the skill and judgment of the seller; and Mr. Roche relies particularly on a passage in Lord Atkinson's speech. ...

If that is so—and Mr. Roskill, of course, contests it—I do not think he contests that the decision of the Divisional Court in *Beer v. Walker*, 46 LJQB 677 does get the plaintiffs home. I think it is right, however, that I should deal with the second way in which the plaintiffs put it, namely, "merchantability," because I think the result is the same. So far as merchantability is concerned, it is, I think, convenient for me to take, as the definition of "merchantable quality"—to follow the words of section 14—a statement again in Lord Wright's speech in the *Cammell Laird* case, where he says, [1934] AC 402, at 430:

> What subsection (2) now means by "merchantable quality" is that the goods in the form in which they were tendered were of no use for any purpose for which such goods would normally be used and hence were not saleable under that description.

I do not think it is seriously contended, as I have said, that these goods were fit for any purpose for which Cyprus spring potatoes in bags would be normally used, which is human consumption, at the time of their arrival.

The question, therefore, is whether merchantability in a contract of this kind does require that they should remain, from the time of delivery, which is, of course, in a c.i.f. contract, the time of shipment, in a merchantable condition until arrival at destination and for a reasonable time for disposal. The authority for the affirmative proposition relied on by Mr. Roche is *Beer v. Walker*, 46 LJQB 677.

. . .

That was a case of rabbits being sent from London to Brighton. The rabbits were of merchantable quality, that is to say, fit for human consumption, when they were sent from London, but when they were delivered to the defendants in Brighton they were putrid and valueless. The case came before the Divisional Court on appeal from the county court. I think it is necessary to read a little of the judgment from which the appeal came. The deputy county court judge said:

> When the rabbits were sent from London they were in good order and condition, but when they were delivered to the defendant they were putrid and valueless. The question in the case is, upon whom is the loss to fall? There is no doubt that in such a case there was an implied warranty that the rabbits would be merchantable, but I am of opinion that that condition was satisfied if they were delivered in good order and condition to the railway in London: see *Dawes v. Peck* (1799), 8 Term Rep. 330, and *Dutton v. Solomonson* (1803), 3 Bos. & P. 582. There is, therefore, no breach of warranty, and the plaintiff is entitled to be paid the contract price for the rabbits. There will, therefore, be judgment for the plaintiff with costs.

The report goes on:

> From this judgment the defendant appealed. The questions for the opinion of the court were: (1) Whether there was, under the said circumstances, such an implied warranty. (2) Whether such implied warranty (if any) was satisfied by the delivery of the said rabbits to the railway company in the order, condition and state so warranted.

the implied warranty referred to being an implied warranty that the rabbits would be merchantable. I think that statement of the questions for the opinion of the court is probably the statement by the editor of the report.

I think I must read the judgment in full. Grove J said (at 678):

> The case finds that what took place was in the ordinary course of business, so that there was nothing in the mode of sending the rabbits which was out of the usual course, and therefore the rabbits which were unfit for human food had become so in the ordinary course of transit. Then, that being so, the question is, was there an implied warranty that they should be fit for food? It cannot, I think, be contended that when a person undertakes to supply another with goods which are not specific goods, there is not an implied warranty that the goods shall be fit for the purpose for which they ordinarily would be intended to be used, and that with regard to animals used for human food that they are fit to be so used.

I emphasise those words, because they are an exact definition of what is meant by "merchantable quality," almost the *ipsissima verba* of Lord Wright in the *Cammell Laird* case. The judgment goes on:

> Then the second, and in fact the only question, which is really arguable in this case is, whether such a warranty was satisfied by the delivery to the railway company at their station in London, or whether the warranty was not such that if nothing happened out of the ordinary course, the rabbits should reach the person for whom they were destined in good order and fit for human food. Now I am of opinion that the implied warranty extended to the time at which, in the ordinary course of transit, the rabbits should reach the defendant, and not only to that time, but that it continued until the defendant should

have a reasonable opportunity of dealing with them in the ordinary course of business. Our judgment, therefore, will be for the appellant.

Remembering that *Beer v. Walker* was decided before the Sale of Goods Act, 1893 (so there was no particular magic in fitness for a purpose of merchantable quality), it seems to me to be clear that the court in that case was dealing with a warranty which today would be called a "warranty of merchantable quality," and I respectfully agree with Atkin J's analysis of what the decision in *Beer v. Walker* really meant.

Judgment for plaintiff.

NOTES

Diplock J's decision was reversed on appeal, [1962] 1 WLR 16, on questions of fact. The Court of Appeal did not adopt any position with respect to the issue of durability. For a later Canadian decision supporting the same view of the law as Diplock J's, see *Georgetown Seafoods Ltd. v. Usen Fisheries Ltd.* (1977), 78 DLR (3d) 542 (PEISC), and *cf.* the following statement by Laidlaw JA in *Tregunno v. Aldershot*, [1944] 1 DLR 102 (Ont. CA) at 107-8, in dealing with a shipment of peaches:

> The contract to be considered is between the grower as plaintiff and the wholesale dealer as defendant. Importing into that contract the implied condition that the goods shall be of merchantable quality and applying the proper principle of law, I think the condition is satisfied after the defendant had a reasonable opportunity of dealing with the goods in the ordinary course of business at the place where delivery of them in that condition was made to it by the plaintiff.

See also Fridman, *Sale of Goods in Canada*, 4th ed., at 210-13.

Nevertheless, Diplock's exposition of the law remains controversial—at least in the eyes of English authors who argue that it should be limited to perishable goods or to goods in transit, although in the latter case this view encounters the difficulties of SGA s. 32. See *Benjamin's Sale of Goods*, 5th ed., para. 11-052, and *cf.* R.M. Goode, *Commercial Law*, 2nd ed. (1995), at 324-25. Diplock himself remained quite unrepentant. Writing for a unanimous House of Lords in his new incarnation as a law lord, he said in *Lambert v. Lewis*, [1982] AC 225, at 276 (for the facts of the case, see, *supra*, chapter 4):

> The implied warranty of fitness for a particular purpose relates to the goods at the time of delivery under the contract of sale in the state in which they were delivered. I do not doubt that it is a continuing warranty that the goods will continue to be fit for that purpose for a reasonable time after delivery, so long as they remain in the same apparent state as that in which they were delivered, apart from normal wear and tear. What is a reasonable time will depend on the nature of the goods, but I would accept that in the case of the coupling the warranty was still continuing up to the date, some three to six months before the accident, when it first became known to the farmer that the handle of the locking mechanism was missing.

As will be noted, Lord Diplock does not indicate how he would determine the period of reasonable durability or how he would apply the test to a complex chattel made up of many components. Does the extract from the OLRC Warranties report, reproduced below, answer these questions? Is there a simple answer?

Apart from the Canadian cases, involving perishable goods, and cited above, more recent Canadian cases seemed to have felt no difficulties about expanding the requirement of reasonable durability to other types of goods. A strong example is *Fording Coal Ltd. v. Harnischfeger Corp. of Can. Ltd.* (1990), 1 BLR (2d) 313 (BCBD, Macdonald J), aff'd. (1991), 8 BAC 250. The plaintiff purchased an electric mining shovel from the defendant for a sum in excess of $5 million for use at the plaintiff's mine site. The shovel was operated virtually continuously for some 5 years and 25,000 hours when the failure of a small component part, a roller, led to the shut down of the whole machine. Macdonald J found that the defect existed at the time of the sale of the shovel and that the failure of the roller occurred well before the roller's anticipated life span. The purchase agreement contained a negotiated 1-year unlimited hours warranty in lieu of the defendant's standard warranty of 1 year or 3,000 hours. The defendant's standard form of warranty excluded all other warranties, express or implied, but the provision had not been included in the negotiated warranty.

Macdonald J found that the failure of the roller was a breach of the implied conditions of fitness and merchantability (at 318) and that the express warranty negotiated between the parties did not preclude the plaintiff from invoking the statutory warranties. With respect to the first point, he reasoned that "Fitness is not required merely on the date of sale, but for the reasonably anticipated life span of the goods, provided they are used throughout their life span for the purpose intended." (See *BC Rail Ltd. v. Canadian Pacific Consulting Services* (1988), 23 BCLR (2d) 357, at 384-85 (at 318-19).)

OLRC Warranties Report

at 37-38

(i) *Durability.* It is often said that it is no part of the condition of merchantability that the goods or, in the case of mechanical products, the particular components making up the article, shall last for any particular period of time. As a matter of common sense this proposition cannot be correct and it appears to conflict with both the concept of fitness, general or particular, and the relevance of price as an indication of the quality of goods which the buyer is entitled to expect. Nevertheless, there is a surprising dearth of authority on the question. The reported cases appear to be confined to perishable goods and to deal with the issue whether the seller impliedly warrants that the goods will reach their destination in a merchantable condition.

The Commission recommends that the position be clarified, and that the condition of merchantability be expanded to include a requirement that the goods shall be durable for a reasonable length of time, having regard to the price and the other surrounding circumstances. This recommendation is not particularly novel. The farm implements legislation of several of the Western provinces has long contained provisions governing this aspect of a seller's obligations.

It is a common practice for many manufacturers to undertake to replace some or all parts of a product sold by them which turns out to be defective within a prescribed period. The question that arises is whether, in the same vein, a seller should be entitled to limit his obligation to supply goods that remain fit for their purpose by reference to a time period, or whether the statutory test should always be paramount. As will be shown in a later chapter, manufacturers' and sellers' warranties vary widely with respect even to the same type of product and, in the case of new cars, fluctuate from year to year. Some warranties are of very limited value or even worthless.

In the opinion of the Commission, it is no more consistent with public policy to allow sellers to limit the duration of their warranties unilaterally than it is to allow them to exclude their implied obligations of quality altogether. It is therefore recommended, subject to what we say hereafter, that the statutory test of reasonable durability should remain the paramount test and that a buyer should not be precluded from challenging the adequacy of an express warranty of durability. In reaching this conclusion, the Commission has considered, but does not agree with the policy expressed in the Alberta and Prince Edward Island Farm Implements Acts. These Acts provide that a manufacturer's express warranty of durability shall supersede the statutory warranty of reasonable durability. The proposed legislation should not, of course, preclude or discourage the giving of express warranties of durability by manufacturers, since they may wish, for competitive reasons, to assume by contract a higher duty than required by the statute. Where an express warranty of durability is given by a manufacturer, it should be operative unless it is inconsistent with the minimum terms and conditions of the statutory warranty of reasonable durability.

NOTE

An implied warranty of durability was adopted in s. 4(a) of Ontario's Bill 110 and also appears in s. 48(g) of the Saskatchewan Consumer Protection Act, SS 1996, c. C-30.1, as amended. In the latter case the retail seller is deemed to have given the following warranty:

> (g) that the product and all its components are to be durable for a reasonable period, having regard to all the relevant circumstances of the sale, including:
>> (i) the description and nature of the product;
>> (ii) the purchase price;
>> (iii) the express warranties of the retail seller or manufacturer; and
>> (iv) the necessary maintenance the product normally requires and the manner in which it has been used; ...

Section 26(3)(j) of the Nova Scotia Consumer Protection Act, RSNS 1989, c. 92, provides that, notwithstanding any agreement to the contrary, there is implied in every consumer sale:

> (j) a condition that the goods shall be durable for a reasonable period of time having regard to the use to which they would normally be put and to all the surrounding circumstances of the sale.

These provisions have been applied in such cases as *MacIsaac v. Chebucto Ford Sales Ltd.* (1989), 89 NSR (2d) 322 and *Zarubin v. Yorkton Carpet Land Ltd.* (1990), Oct. 25, 1990, Sask. QB, No. 314 AD 1990.

The Canadian Manufacturers' Association, in a brief submitted to the Ontario government in 1973, strongly objected to the recommendations in the Warranties Report. The brief argued that a reasonable period of durability was too vague and would lead to much uncertainty and increased costs. It also pointed out that the price of a product was no reliable indicator of its quality since price is also determined by many other factors. The brief recommended instead the adoption of a "minimum statutory warranty period." The duration of this period "would be determined by regulation for each product grouping having similar characteristics and functions."

The OLRC Sales Report did not feel that the CMA's recommendations were practicable in the context of a general sales act, "which must of necessity encompass an infinite range of goods." The OLRC did however modify its earlier recommendation to the extent of recommending that reasonable durability be treated in the revised SGA as one of the requirements of the implied warranty of merchantability, and not as a wholly separate warranty. See OLRC Sales Report, at 215-16 and draft bill, s. 5.13(1)(b)(vi).

Compliance with Public Law of Buyer's Jurisdiction

Sumner, Permain & Co. v. Webb & Co.

[1922] 1 KB 55, [1921] All ER Rep. 680 (CA)

SCRUTTON LJ: The defendants sold f.o.b. in England to the plaintiffs a large quantity of "Webb's Indian Tonic" of which the defendants were the manufacturers, and which they knew was intended to be sent out to the Argentine where the plaintiffs carry on business. Unknown to the plaintiffs, the defendants' tonic contained a small proportion of salicylic acid, a fact which by reason of a certain law of the Argentine rendered it legally unsaleable in that country. The plaintiffs now contend that the impossibility of legally selling it in the market for which it was intended constitutes a breach of the implied condition that the goods should be of merchantable quality. In *Niblett v. Confectioners' Materials Co.*, [1921] 3 KB 381, at 398, which has been referred to, I agreed with my brothers' view under s. 12, sub-s. 1, that the sellers had broken the implied condition that they would have a right to sell the goods, but as Bankes LJ has pointed out, I did not discuss s. 14, sub-s. 2, further than to say this: "I have not been able to trace the origin or history of the condition that goods shall be of merchantable quality. If I had to express my present opinion it is that the condition does not touch the title to the goods or the right to sell them." I have looked a little further into the matter and can now finally express my opinion that "merchantable quality" does not cover legal title to goods or the legal right to sell. In my view "merchantable quality" means that the goods comply with the description in the contract, so that to a purchaser buying goods of that description the goods would be good tender. It does not mean that there shall in fact be persons ready to buy the goods. For instance take the case that I put during the argument; if you sell "vestings" of a particular fancy pattern for sale in China, you do not warrant that the Chinese buyer will like that pattern and will buy it when it goes out there; if the goods are vestings of the pattern contracted for, they are merchantable though nobody likes the pattern or is willing to buy. Similarly I do not think "merchantable quality" means that there can legally be buyers of that article. If the goods are of the contract description the possibility of legally making a sale of them does not in my view come within the expression "merchantable quality." I am still not quite clear when that expression first began to be used. I see that in *Randall v. Newson*, 2 QBD 102, Lord Esher (or Brett JA as he then was) appears to have thought that it was first used in *Gardiner v. Gray* (1815), 4 Camp. 144, at 145. There was in that case a count "that the silk should be waste silk of a good and merchantable quality," and it was in reference to that count that Lord Ellenborough used the language which has repeatedly been quoted in other cases. "The intention of both parties must be taken to be that it shall be saleable in the market under the denomination mentioned in the contract between them. The purchaser cannot be supposed to buy goods to lay them on a dunghill"; and that particularly picturesque passage has been cited by judge after judge in cases on this point ever since. Now, when Lord Ellenborough there uses the word "saleable" I do not think he means "legally saleable." As explained by Lord Esher himself in *Randall v. Newson*, the fundamental thing is that "the article offered or delivered shall answer the description of it contained in the contract." And in a passage a little later on he adds: "If that subject matter be merely the commercial article or commodity, the undertaking is, that the thing offered or delivered shall answer that description, that is to say, shall be that article or commodity, saleable or merchantable," or in other words shall be a good tender under a contract for a sale of goods of that description. I am quite unable to find that any case since has ever dealt with the possibility of legally selling the goods in the particular market and has treated that possibility as included in the definition of "merchantable." For these reasons I disagree with the view taken by Bailhache J.

Appeal allowed.

[Concurring judgments were delivered by Banks and Atkin LJJ]

NOTES

1) Do you agree with Scrutton LJ's reasoning? Is it consistent with the test of merchantability adopted in *Hardwick Game Farm, supra*? With the decision in *Niblett v. Confectioners' Materials Co., supra*, chapter 5? Would the court in *Sumner, Permain* have reached the same conclusion if the tonic water had failed to comply with the requirements of the British food and drug legislation, or is such compliance better left as an aspect of the implied condition of fitness? In discussing whether a revised Ontario Sale of Goods Act should address itself to the problem of the merchantability of goods not in compliance with the law of the buyer's jurisdiction, the remarks (at 218):

> It would not be right, as a general proposition, to oblige a seller to familiarize himself with the requirements of every jurisdiction to which his goods may be exported. If the foreign buyer seeks compliance with this own law, he should bring this home to the seller. In our view, the implied warranty of fitness is sufficiently flexible to cope with this problem.

Do you agree? For the modern scope of the implied condition of fitness see *infra*.

2) For a case distinguishing *Sumner, Permain*, see *Egekvist Bakeries v. Tizel & Blinick*, [1950] 1 DLR 585. The defendant, a firm of brokers in Toronto, sold the plaintiff bakery company in Minneapolis a consignment of blueberries then in cold storage in Chicago. The defendant had previously shipped the blueberries from Hamilton, Ontario to Chicago. A sample of the blueberries had been taken by US Customs at the border and, at the time the defendant sold the blueberries to the plaintiff, they were subject to an order by the US Food and Drug Administration requiring the blueberries to be kept intact until released by the appropriate authority. The defendant had ignored the order in reselling and shipping the blueberries to the plaintiff. At all material times the blueberries were in a mouldy condition and were subsequently ordered to be destroyed by a US District Court. The plaintiff, which had already paid for the blueberries, sued the defendant for damages for breach of contract.

LeBel J found in the plaintiff's favour. He held, following *Niblett Ltd. v. Confectioners' Materials Co.*, *supra*, chapter 5, that the defendant had breached SGA s. 13(a) since, as a result of the FDA order, it had no right to sell the blueberries to the plaintiff. He also said (at 591):

> A good deal may be said in support of the proposition that a person selling goods in a foreign market does not impliedly warrant that he has the right to sell them in that market, for example, that the goods conform with whatever enactments or regulations that may exist there, particularly where the goods are sold f.o.b. the seller's country, but that is a different thing from the case of a vendor selling f.o.b. the foreign market as here, with knowledge that he cannot lawfully sell in that market until he has discharged some legal condition, and that until he has done so he can be prevented by lawful authority from selling.

LeBel J expressed no view on the applicability of SGA ss. 15.1 or 15.2.

3) In *Sumner, Permain* the buyer also claimed relief under the implied condition of fitness. The court held that the condition had not been breached because the buyers were unable to show that they relied on the sellers' skill and judgment to supply tonic water that complied with the law of the Argentine. The lord justices were influenced in this conclusion by the fact that the plaintiffs had for years sold this tonic water in the Argentine without objection. For a similar conclusion on the facts see *Teheran-Europe Co. Ltd. v. S.T. Belton (Tractors) Ltd.*, [1968] 2 QB 545 (CA). Diplock LJ said (*ibid.*, at 560-61):

> Where a foreign merchant buys by description goods, not for his own use, but for resale in his own country of which he has no reason to suppose the English seller has any special knowledge, it flies in the face of common sense to suppose that he relies on anything but his own knowledge of the market in his own country and his own commercial judgment as to what is saleable there. To hold the contrary would mean that whenever anyone known by the seller to be a foreign merchant bought from a seller in England goods for sale in his own country there would arise automatically an undertaking on the part of the seller, unless he expressly disclaimed it, that the goods would be suitable for sale in the market of which the foreign buyer knew everything and he, the seller, knew nothing. With great respect, that would be nonsense.

4) An important constitutional question is whether the buyer's province can oblige a seller to comply with its sales legislation where the seller has his place of business in another jurisdiction and the "proper law of the contract" (in the conflict of law sense) is not the law of the buyer's province. In *R v. Thomas Equipment Ltd.* (1979), 96 DLR (3d) 1, the Supreme Court of Canada, distinguishing its earlier decision in *Interprovincial Co-operatives Ltd. v. The Queen*, [1976] 1 SCR 477, upheld Alberta's constitutional power to enforce its Farm Implement Act, RSA 1970, c. 136, against a New Brunswick manufacturer which had terminated the selling agency of an Alberta dealer. The decision has important implications for the general reach of provincial consumer and business protection laws. See, further, Robert K. Paterson, "Do Unto Others: The Extraterritorial Reach of Regulatory Legislation in Canada" (1980-81), 5 *CBLJ* 114.

Examination Under Section 15.2

Thornett & Fehr v. Beers & Son

[1919] 1 KB 486, 24 Com. Cas. 133

[The plaintiffs, merchants in vegetable glues, sued the defendants for £363.1s, being the balance of the price of certain barrels of vegetable glue sold by them to the defendants. The defendants pleaded that the sale was a sale by sample, that this term had been mistakenly omitted from the sold note, and that the glue was not equal to the sample. In the alternative, they claimed that the glue was not merchantable, and they also counterclaimed for the return of £3,000 which they had paid, and for damages, on the ground that the glue was valueless.

Bray J found on the facts that the sale was not a sale by sample, and the balance of his judgment (reproduced below) is concerned with the applicability of the proviso to s. 14(2) [Ont. s. 15(2)].

The evidence on this point was that the parties had agreed that they should meet at Nottingham where the glue, in barrels, was lying in a warehouse, so that the defendants could see it. On September 18, 1918, the defendants wrote to the plaintiffs: "We are arranging for our representative who is at present in Birmingham to visit Nottingham tomorrow morning in order to inspect the thirty-five tons of adhesive in question." Mr. Anholt, the plaintiffs' representative, went down to Nottingham, and attended at the warehouse on the following morning. He remained there till 12, but the defendants did not materialize. He had other business to do, so he left word where he could be found, and that he would return if called. He also told the foreman at the warehouse to give the defendants' representative every facility for inspection. The defendants' representatives, a Mr. Halfhide and a Mr. Beers, called between 12 and 1:30 but when Mr. Anholt returned at 1:30 they had left. Mr. Halfhide stated in evidence that they did not have any of the casks opened and only looked at the outside, but he admitted they had been offered every facility and had received Mr. Anholt's message that he would come. However they had no time as they had another appointment. Mr. Anholt stated that the foreman told him that the defendants had seen two or three casks which had been opened. The foreman was not called by either side. The next day the defendants told Mr. Tobias, another representative of the plaintiffs, that they had inspected the parcel and offered him £90 a ton for it. A deal was ultimately struck at £95 a ton.]

BRAY J: The next question is whether under s. 14, sub-s. 2, of the Sale of Goods Act, 1893, there was an implied condition that the goods should be merchantable. This raises a somewhat difficult question. The sub-section is as follows: "Where goods are bought by description from a seller who deals in goods of that description ... there is an implied condition that the goods shall be of merchantable quality; provided that if the buyer has examined the goods, there shall be no implied condition as regards defects which such examination ought to have revealed." First, were the goods bought by description? In *Varley v. Whipp*, [1900] 1 QB 513, the headnote, which I think accurately states the actual decision, reads thus: "The expression 'contract for the sale of goods by description,' in the Sale of Goods Act, 1893, s. 13, applies to all cases where the buyer has not seen the goods, but relies solely on the description given by the seller." I do not think it can be said here that the buyers relied solely on the description. They had seen the goods, and certainly relied partly on what they had seen. I infer this from what they stated on September 20 when Mr. Halfhide began by saying, "I have inspected the goods." I do not think, however, that it is necessary for the decision to lay down so broad a proposition that there could not be a sale by description where the buyer had seen the goods, and relied only partly on the description. I desire to leave that question open and not to decide that there was no implied condition that the goods were merchantable on the ground that it was not a sale by description.

Proceeding with the section, it is not disputed that the plaintiffs were sellers who dealt in vegetable glue. I now come to the proviso. Before the passing of the Act I think the law stood as laid down in *Jones v. Just* (1868), LR 3 QB 197, at 202, where it is said that "where goods are in esse, and may be inspected by the buyer, and there is no fraud on the part of the seller, the maxim caveat emptor applies." The sub-section, however does not use the words "where the goods may be inspected by the buyer," but "if the buyer has examined the goods." In other words, it is not sufficient that the buyer should have had the opportunity of inspecting the goods, he must have examined them. I think the change of language must have been intentional, and I must see whether the buyers examined the goods. I do not think the statute requires a full examination, because the words that follow show that the proviso deals with the case where the buyer has not made a full examination. Was there an examination? I find that on September 18 both parties intended a full examination. The facts that both parties were to be present, that the foreman was told by the plaintiffs to offer the defendants every facility, and the defendants' letter of September 18 go to show this. I think I must take it that the defendants did not in fact have any barrels opened, but I think that the reason was that they had no time; they were satisfied with their inspection of the barrels, and they were willing to take the risk, the price being so low, and Mr. Halfhide himself, as I have found, told the plaintiffs at the beginning of the interview when the bargain was made that he had inspected the parcel. It may be a question whether, after this statement, the defendants could be heard to say that they had not examined the glue, but however that may be, I think they examined the goods within the meaning of the sub-section. There can be no doubt that revealed the defects complained of. The defects complained of were apparent the moment the casks were opened. The examination agreed to on September 18, which they had full opportunity of making on September 19, would involve the opening of a sufficient number of casks to ascertain the condition of the glue. I hold that this case falls within the proviso, and consequently there was no implied condition. Having found that it was not a sale by sample, and that there was no implied condition that the glue was merchantable, the defence fails, and the plaintiffs are entitled to judgment.

Judgment for plaintiffs.

OLRC Sales Report

at 218-19

Section 15.2 of the Ontario Sale of Goods Act provides that, if the buyer has examined the goods, the condition of merchantable quality does not apply as regards defects that "*such* examination ought to have revealed." this test has been criticized as being too favourable to the buyer. First, it is said, it encourages the buyer not to examine the goods. Secondly, even if he does examine the goods, the buyer is only deemed to have notice of defects that "such" (that is, his actual) examination ought to have revealed. On a literal reading of this proviso, the buyer is under no obligation to conduct a reasonably careful examination. It will be observed, however, that the test is not wholly subjective, since the buyer will be deemed to be aware of defects which his examination "ought to have revealed." A further criticism is that section 15.2 is not consistent with the buyer's position in the case of a sale by sample, dealt with in section 16(2)(c) of the existing Act, since, in this instance, the seller's warranty only extends to freedom from defects that would not be apparent on "reasonable examination of the sample." The test here is wholly objective.

As to the latter criticism, it is our view that the inconsistency between sections 15.2 and 16(2)(c) is more apparent than real, since the purpose of a sample is to enable the buyer to determine for himself the quality of the goods offered. The first criticism was examined by the English and Scottish Law Commissions. The Commissions concluded that it would not be desirable to return to the pre-1893 position, which deemed the buyer to have notice of any defects discoverable on examination whether or not he had examined the goods. We agree with this conclusion. We are somewhat more troubled by the criticism that the buyer who conducts a perfunctory examination of the goods may be better off than the diligent buyer, especially since the code has avoided this anomaly. On balance, however, we have decided to recommend no change. The problem does not appear to be of great practical importance, and we believe there is sufficient elasticity in the language of the proviso, coupled with the general requirement of good faith, to enable a court to avoid its unfair operation against either party. Accordingly, our Draft Bill provides that the implied warranty of merchantability does not apply, if the buyer examined the goods before the contract was made, "with respect to any defect that such an examination ought to have revealed."

The Law Commissions did not, however, consider the present statutory provision to be entirely satisfactory. The Commissions recommended extending the proviso in one direction by excluding the condition of merchantability with respect to defects in the goods specifically drawn by the seller to the buyer's attention. We support this change and recommend that a similar provision be incorporated in the revised Act.

CHAPTER EIGHT

Seller's Implied Obligations: Fitness for Use, Sales by Sample, Private Sales, and Food and Drug Laws

As will have been noted from the cases on merchantability, there is a good deal of overlap between the implied conditions of merchantability and fitness; frequently the two conditions may be successfully invoked in the same case. This conclusion would not be obvious from a literal reading of SGA s. 15.1, and at first sight its requirements would appear to impose formidable burdens on a buyer seeking to hold the seller liable for breach of the implied condition of fitness. As will be seen however from the cases that follow, the courts have so successfully eroded the requirements that s. 15.1 can no longer be regarded as an accurate reflection of the modern position.

The Scope of Section 15.1

Hardwick Game Farm v. Suffolk Agricultural and Poultry Producers Association

[1971] 2 AC 31, [1968] 2 All ER 444 (HL)

[For the facts of this case, see *supra*, chapter 7. The following extract deals with the general scope of the implied condition of fitness and its application to the facts at bar.]

LORD PEARCE: The judge and the Court of Appeal held that the purpose of Grimsdale was "a particular purpose" within section 14(1). It was argued that such a purpose was too wide and had not enough particularity to constitute a particular purpose. I do not accept this contention. Almost every purpose is capable of some subdivision, some further and better particulars. But a particular purpose means a given purpose, known or communicated. It is not necessarily a narrow or closely particularised purpose (see *Benjamin on Sale* (1950), 8th ed., at 630: "A particular purpose is not some purpose necessarily distinct from a general purpose"). A purpose may be put in wide terms or it may be circumscribed or narrowed. An example of the former is to be found in *Bartlett v. Sydney Marcus Ltd.*, [1965] 1 WLR 1013, where the purpose was that of a car to drive on the road. See also *Baldry v. Marshall*, [1925] 1 KB

260 ["a comfortable car suitable for touring purposes"]. A somewhat narrower purpose was to be found in *Bristol Tramways, etc., Carriage Co. Ltd. v. Fiat Motors
Ltd.*, [1910] 2 KB 831 ["an omnibus for heavy traffic in a hilly district"]. The less
circumscribed the purpose, the less circumscribed will be, as a rule, the range of
goods which are reasonably fit for such purpose. The purpose of a car to drive on the
road will be satisfied by almost any car so long as it will function reasonably; but the
narrower purpose of an omnibus suitable to the crowded streets of a city can only be
achieved by a narrower range of vehicles. This, however, is a question of fact and
degree. Lord Herschell said in *Drummond v. Van Ingen*, 12 App. Cas. 284, at 293:

> Where the article may be used as one of the elements in a variety of other manufactur-
> ers, I think it may be too much to impute to the maker of this common article a knowl-
> edge of the details of every manufacture into which it may enter in combination with
> other materials.

In general it would be wrong to say, as was suggested in argument, that a wide purpose is unfair to the seller because it purports to require fitness for every conceivable
subdivision of purpose within the main purpose.

I would expect a tribunal of fact to decide that a car sold in this country was reasonably fit for touring even though it was not well adapted for conditions in a heat
wave; but not, if it could not cope adequately with rain. If, however, it developed
some lethal or dangerous trick in very hot weather, I would expect it to be found
unfit. In deciding the question of fact the rarity of the unsuitability would be weighed
against the gravity of its consequences. Again, if food was merely unpalatable or
useless on rare occasions, it might well be reasonably suitable for food. But I should
certainly not expect it to be held reasonably suitable if even on very rare occasions it
killed the consumer. The question for the tribunal of fact is simply "were these goods
reasonably fit for the specified purpose?"

"To resell in smaller quantities to be compounded into food for cattle and poultry"
was therefore a particular purpose within section 14(1). If a particular purpose is
made known, that is sufficient to raise the inference that the buyer relies on the seller's skill and judgment unless there is something to displace the inference. There is
no need for a buyer formally to "make known" that which is already known. See
Manchester Liners Ltd. v. Rea Ltd., [1922] 2 AC 74, at 92; *Cammell Laird & Co. v.
The Manganese Bronze & Grass Co.*, [1934] AC 402; *Mash and Murrell Ltd. v. Joseph
I. Emanuel Ltd.*, [1961] 1 WLR 862, at 867 (a sale from one merchant to another).
The reliance need not be exclusive. Partial reliance will suffice.

The judge considered that the inference that the buyer relied on the seller's skill
and judgment was displaced by the fact that Grimsdale and Kendall were members of
the same Association, the London Cattle Food Traders Association. I do not, with
respect, accept this view. The whole trend of authority has inclined towards an assumption of reliance wherever the seller knows the particular purpose. And where
there are several subsales and the purpose is obvious, the liability is frequently passed
up the line. To cut the chain of liability at one particular point is not fair unless there
is some cogent reason for doing so. In the present case I see no ground for holding
that Kendall were in any relevantly different position from Grimsdale. The fellow-

membership of the CTFA was irrelevant. One member may rely on another member just as much as he relies on an outside trader. The fellow-membership may even increase his reliance.

Reliance is not excluded by the fact that the seller may not himself have seen the goods he sells. In *Bigge v. Parkinson* (1862), 7 H & N 955, at 959, where it was implied that stores for troops in India must be fit for their purpose, Cockburn CJ said:

> Where a person undertakes to supply provisions, and they are supplied in cases hermetically sealed, but turn out to be putrid, it is no answer to say that he has been deceived by the person from whom he got them.

The seller, not the buyer, is aware of the provenance of the goods and has chosen to acquire them for disposal. It would, therefore, be not unreasonable that the buyer should rely on the seller's "knowledge and trade wisdom" to use a phrase quoted in *Australian Knitting Mills Ltd. v. Grant*, 50 CLR 387, at 446, by Evatt J from *Ward v. Great Atlantic & Pacific Tea Co.* (1918), 231 Mass. 90, at 93, 94. And Walton J in *Preist v. Last* (1903), 89 LT 33, at 435, refers to the buyer's reliance that the seller will not sell him "mere rubbish." This expression is echoed in the evidence in the present case where Mr. Brown of Lillico said that they relied on Kendall "not to sell what they knew was rubbish" (Appendix 2, at 208).

It is argued that the width of the purpose should prevent one from inferring that there was reliance. I do not think so. The compounders of food for cattle and poultry need healthy ingredients, as the seller knew. The parties were not considering what admixture of healthy groundnut meal would be good for particular animals or birds, but whether assuming a certain quantity of groundnut meal would be a fit ingredient, the goods delivered would be healthy or harmful groundnut meal. It was reasonable that the buyer should rely on the seller to deliver groundnut meal which would, as groundnut meal, be a healthy and not a harmful ingredient in a compound.

In my opinion, there was on the circumstances of this case sufficient to establish reliance by Grimsdale on Kendall and a resulting condition.

The condition did not mean that the food was fit, however strange or unsuitable the proportions of the compound might prove to be. It meant that the food was fit if compounded reasonably and competently according to current standards. Goods are not fit if they have hidden limitations requiring special precautions unknown to the buyer or seller. The groundnut meal delivered was plainly not fit for the purpose of reselling in small lots to compounders of food for cattle and poultry. It was highly toxic. It is beside the point that Kendalls were unaware of the proportions in which it was to be compounded. It was unfit for use in the normal range of proportions. The evidence shows that 10 per cent was included in the feeding stuff for pheasants. This was not abnormal. When the toxicity had been discovered and investigated the recommendation of a reputable working party was that not more than 5 per cent of meal with a high toxicity should be included even in cattle rations and none should be included in rations for birds. Moreover, while its toxicity was unknown, the meal was thereby far more harmful and dangerous. Even had the buyer known of its toxic qualities, it was not fit for compounding for poultry. For a compounder's business is to mix healthy foods in suitable compounds. It is quite unsuitable that he should get toxic meal which can be only used by inserting it in quantities so abnormally small that the dilution of other compounds removes its lethal effect. All the courts below have held rightly without any dissent that this meal was not reasonably fit for the purpose for which it was supplied by Kendall to Grimsdale.

Ashington Piggeries Ltd. v. Christopher Hill Ltd.; Christopher Hill Ltd. v. Norsildmel

(Conjoined Appeals)
[1972] AC 441, [1971] 1 All ER 874 (HL)

[For the facts of this case, see *supra*, chapter 6. The following extract from Lord Wilberforce's judgment deals with the applicability of SGA s. 14(1) [Ont. s. 15.1] to the facts at bar.]

LORD WILBERFORCE:

2. *Section 14(1) of the Act*: I do not think it is disputed, or in any case disputable, that a particular purpose was made known by the buyers [Ashington Piggeries] so as to show that they relied on the sellers' skill and judgment. The particular purpose for which "King Size" was required was as food for mink.

Equally I think it is clear (as both courts have found) that there was reliance on the respondents' skill and judgment. Although the Act makes no references to partial reliance, it was settled, well before the *Cammell Laird* case, [1934] AC 402, was decided in this House, that there may be cases where the buyer relies on his own skill or judgment for some purposes and on that of the seller for others. This House gave to that principle emphatic endorsement.

The present is certainly such a case. In the words of Milmo J, [1968] 1 Lloyd's Rep. 457, at 480:

> On the one hand Mr. Udall was relying on his own judgment as to what his formula should contain and the levels at which the various ingredients in it should be included. On the other, he was relying, and had no alternative but to rely, upon the [respondents] to obtain the ingredients, to see they were of good quality and not to use ingredients which, as a result of contamination, were toxic.

The word "toxic" will require some examination but, subject to this, I consider that this passage correctly states the position as regards reliance.

The field thus left to the sellers can be described in terms of their responsibility as merchants, to obtain and deliver ingredients, and relevantly herring meal, not unfit by reason of contamination, to be fed to animals, including mink. The field reserved to the buyers, on the other hand, was that of particular or specific suitability for mink. There was no doubt that herring meal, as such, was suitable for mink; on the other hand, the particular consignments supplied in 1961 were unsuitable because of the presence of DMNA. What, then, was the nature of this unsuitability?

If mink possessed an idiosyncrasy, which made the food as supplied unsuitable for them though it was perfectly suitable for other animals, this would be the buyers' responsibility, unless, as is not the case here, they made this idiosyncrasy known to the sellers so as to show reliance on them to provide for it. But any general unsuitability would be the sellers' responsibility. Although the evidence was not very complete, it is sufficiently shown, in my opinion, that mink are more sensitive to DMNA than most other animals to whom compound foods would be sold. Chicken and pigs are among the least sensitive, next cattle and then sheep, with mink at the top of the scale. So the question arises, what does the buyer, alleging unfitness, have to prove? If the fact were that the herring meal supplied, while damaging to mink, was perfectly harmless to all other animals to whom it might be fed, it would be unjust to hold the sellers liable. If, on the other hand, the herring meal was not only lethal to mink but also deleterious, though not lethal, to other animals, the sellers' responsibility could be fairly engaged. A man can hardly claim that the product he sells is suitable, especially if that is a foodstuff, merely because it fails to kill more than one species to which it is fed.

In this case, because of the difficulty of tracing the lethal element, the evidence as to its presence, its strength and its effect was not scientifically complete. It was not until 1964 the DMNA was identified. By that time all the infected herring meal had been disposed of, and all other animals to which it had been fed had died. The critical question in this part of the appeal is whether the buyers proved enough to show that their mink died because of some general, that is, non-specific, unsuitability of the herring meal through contamination. The burden was upon the buyers to show that this was so.

· · ·

In my opinion, the appellants made good their case: they proved the cause of their losses to lie in the inclusion of a generally (viz. non-specific as regards mink) toxic ingredient in the food. It was not for them to show that this same food killed, or poisoned, other species. So to require would place far too high a burden on a buyer. The buyer may have no means of ascertaining what the effect on other species may be. The whole of the contaminated consignment may have been fed to the buyer's animals: is the buyer to fail because he cannot show that this particular consignment killed, or at least injured, other animals? He must, I think, carry his proof to the point of showing that the guilty ingredient has some generally (as opposed to specifically) toxic quality. But once he has done this, has he not shown, at least with strong prima facie force, that a feeding stuff which contained it was unsuitable? Is he not entitled to throw on to the seller the burden of showing, if he can, that the damage to the buyer's animals was due to some factor within the field of responsibility reserved to the buyer? I would answer yes to these questions. In the end, it is for the judge to decide whether, on the evidence, the buyers have proved their case. Milmo J's conclusions are expressed in three passages, one in the main action, the others in the third party proceedings (the whole case was heard together):

Herring meal does not normally contain a poison. The herring meal which killed the English mink contained DMNA which is a poison, and it contained it at a level sufficiently high to be lethal to mink, which are animals to which herring meal can properly be fed. All animals are sensitive to DMNA poisoning, though mink are more sensitive than most. ([1968] 1 Lloyd's Rep. 457, at 481.)

I find that the meal which poisoned the English mink was not reasonably fit for use as an ingredient in animal foodstuffs because of the fact that it contained in substantial and significant quantities DMNA which is a toxic substance to which all animals are sensitive. (at 487.)

While I accept that there was no evidence that the meal *had a deleterious effect* upon any animal or other type of livestock other than mink, I do not consider that it was proved affirmatively that the meal which killed the mink *could have been fed with impunity* to all other types of livestock. (at 486 — emphasis supplied.)

This is precisely the position: coupled with the general finding as to toxicity (something to which all animals are sensitive, i.e., liable to suffer liver damage) it amounts to a rejection of the only line of defence open to the respondents—namely, that the relevant consignment was fit to be fed to all normal animals and only unfit to be fed to mink.

In my opinion, these findings were justified and correct.

So much for the facts, but there remains one legal argument on this part of the case. Section 14(1) contains the words "and the goods are of a description which it is in the course of the seller's business to supply." The respondents relied on these words and persuaded the Court of Appeal to decide that the requirement was not satisfied because, briefly, the respondents were not dealers in mink food. A similar argument was put forward on the words in section 14(2) "where goods are bought by description from a seller who deals in goods of that description." The Court of Appeal decided this point, too, in the respondents' favour. The respondents, they held, did not deal in mink food, or "King Size," before Mr. Udall placed with them the orders which produced the defective goods. I have some doubt whether this argument is even correct on the facts, because Mr. Udall had been ordering "King Size" for several months before he ordered the fatal consignment. But we must deal with the legal argument because it is clearly of general importance. It appears never previously to have been accepted and it substantially narrows the scope of both subsections. It rests, in the first place, upon a linguistic comparison of the meaning of the word "description" in the three places where it appears and on the argument that it must mean the same in each place.

I do not accept that, taken in its most linguistic strictness, either subsection bears the meaning contended for. I would hold that (as to subsection (1)) it is in the course of the seller's business to supply goods if he agrees, either generally, or in a particular case, to supply the goods when ordered, and (as to subsection (2)) that a seller deals in goods of that description if his business is such that he is willing to accept orders for them. I cannot comprehend the rationale of holding that the subsections do not apply if the seller is dealing in the particular goods for the first time or the sense of distinguishing between the first and the second order for the goods or for goods of the description. The Court of Appeal offered the analogy of a doctor sending a novel prescription to a pharmacist, which turns out to be deleterious. But as often happens to arguments of this kind, the analogy is faulty: if the prescription is wrong, of course the doctor is responsible. The fitness of the prescription is within his field of responsibility. The relevant question is whether the pharmacist is responsible for the purity of his ingredients and one does not see why not.

But, moreover, consideration of the preceding common law shows that what the Act had in mind was something quite simple and rational: to limit the implied conditions of fitness or quality to persons in the way of business, as distinct from private persons. Whether this should be the law was a problem which had emerged, and been resolved, well before 1893. The first indication of the point arose in *Jones v. Bright* (1829), 15 Bing. 533 (copper sheathing). Two of the judges regarded it as an essential allegation that the defendant should have been the manufacturer of the defective copper. Part J in fact, at 546, used the words "distinguishing, as I do, between the manufacturer of an article and the mere seller." In *Brown v. Edgington* (1841), 2 Man. & G 279, at 291 (the crane rope) we find a description of the defendant by Bosanquet J as "a dealer in articles of that description," clearly a reason for holding him liable though he was not the manufacturer. The distinction between the dealer and the private seller is clearly brought out in *Burnaby v. Bollet* (1847), 16 M & W 644, where a man bought a carcass in the market but later sold it to another farmer. His exemption from liability for defects in the carcass was explicitly based on his private character; he was "not clothed with any character of general dealer in provisions" (at 649), he was "not dealing in the way of a common trade" (at 655). And finally in the forerunner case of *Jones v. Just* (1868), LR 3 QB 197, we find Mellor J in his fourth and fifth categories, which anticipate respectively section 14(1) and 14(2) of the Sale of Goods Act 1893, referring to a manufacturer or dealer contracting to supply an article which he manufactures or produces, or in which he deals, and to a manufacturer undertaking to supply foods manufactured by himself or in which he deals, so clearly following and adopting the prior accepted division between sales by way of trade and private sales.

One asks, therefore, what difference the insertion in the Sale of Goods Act of the word "description" made to these well-accepted rules. It seems at least clear that the words now appearing in section 14(1) "and the goods are of a description which it is the seller's business to supply" cannot mean more than "the goods are of a kind. ..." "Description" here cannot be used in the sense in which the word is used when the Act speaks of "sales by description," for section 14(1) is not dealing with sales by description at all. If this is so, I find no obstacle against reading "goods of that description" in a similar way in section 14(2). In both cases the word means "goods of that kind" and nothing more. Moreover, even if this is wrong, and "description" is to be understood in a technical sense, I would have no difficulty in holding that a seller deals in goods "of that description" if he accepts orders to supply them in the way of business; and this whether or not he has previously accepted orders for goods of that description.

So, all other elements being present as I have tried to show, I would hold that section 14(1) applies to the present case. I would agree with the judge that section

14(2) equally applies and disagree with the reasons (based on the "description" argument) which led the Court of Appeal to a contrary opinion.

That the goods were unmerchantable was conceded in both courts—in my opinion, rightly so. Goods may quite well be unmerchantable even if "purpose built." Lord Wright made this quite clear in the *Cammell Laird* case, [1934] AC 402; so equally with "King Size" mink food.

I would therefore allow the appeal.

The appeal of Christopher Hill Ltd. (the respondents) against Norsildmel ("the third parties") raises different, and, in one respect at least, more difficult issues. The goods supplied were in this case Norwegian herring meal and they were supplied under the terms of a commodity market contract in writing. A number of points arise under it. On the following I express my concurrence with others of your Lordships, and do not think it necessary to add reasons of my own.

1. The respondents were not in breach of a term in the contract implied by virtue of section 13 of the Sale of Goods Act 1893. The goods supplied were, in my opinion, Norwegian herring meal. The words "fair average quality of the season" were not in this contract part of the description. I do not find it necessary to consider whether, if they were, there was a breach of any implied condition that the goods should correspond with this description. They were not relied upon as themselves importing a warranty; but, if the contention is open, I am in agreement with my noble and learned friend, Lord Diplock, for the reasons which he gives, that they do not cover the particular defect which existed.

2. The exemption clause contained in general condition 3 does not exclude a claim for breach of any warranty implied under section 14(1) of the Act.

This leaves the substantial question whether a term as to reasonable fitness ought to be implied under section 14(1) of the Act. There was also raised a question as to remoteness of damage but, in the view which I take, this depends on the same considerations as those necessary for determination of liability under section 14(1). I now consider this question.

In so doing I should make it clear that, although I refer to Norsildmel as the third parties, and actual contract for sale was made with a committee called Sildemelutvalget to whom Norsildmel succeeded in 1964, but no distinction has been made between these organisations. What is necessary to determine is whether any particular purpose for which the goods were required was made known by the buyers to the sellers so as to show that the buyers relied on the sellers' skill and judgment: what the particular purpose was: finally, whether the particular purpose included feeding to mink. The particular purpose relied upon by the respondents was that the meal was required for inclusion in animal feeding stuffs to be compounded by them. They do not contend that feeding to mink was explicitly stated as a purpose; but they say that feeding to mink was known to both parties as a normal user for herring meal, and that it was sold without any reservation or restriction as to the use to which it might be put. The sale was negotiated through an agent in England—C.T. Bowring & Co. on behalf of Sildmelutvalget, but no point has been taken as to any limitation upon their knowledge as compared with that of their principals.

The scope and application of section 14(1) of the Sale of Goods Act 1893 was fully considered by this House in *Hardwick Game Farm v. Suffolk Agricultural Poultry Producers Association Ltd.*, [1969] 2 AC 31. The opinion expressed in that case endorsed a tendency which other cases (such as *Manchester Liners Ltd. v. Rea Ltd.*, [1922] 2 AC 74) had shown, to expand the scope of section 14(1) so as to cover territory which might otherwise, on a first reading, have been thought to belong to section 14(2). I think that this tendency essentially reflects a reversion to the more general approach to questions of the seller's liability under implied warranty adopted by the common law, as contrasted with the compartmentalisation into separate, but inevitably overlapping, provisions adopted by the Sale of Goods Act. *Naturam expellas furca* is a maxim which tends to apply to codifications. At any rate it is clear that this House in the *Hardwick* case, [1969] 2 AC 31, accepted that the "making known" so as to show reliance which the section requires is easily deduced from the nature and circumstances of the sale, and that the word "particular" means little more than "stated" or "defined." As Lord Pearce said in *Hardwick*, at 115: "There is no need for a buyer formally to 'make known' that which is already known": and here there is no doubt that the third parties, through their selling agents C.T. Bowring & Co. Ltd., and also directly, knew what the herring meal was required for, namely, for inclusion in animal feeding stuffs to be compounded by the buyers, and no special purpose in relation to mink was relied on. The third parties were, moreover, a committee, or cooperative, of manufacturers of herring meal: in this case, whether one speaks of implication or presumption, the conclusion can hardly be otherwise than that of reliance by the buyers to produce a product reasonably fit for the purpose. I observe, indeed, that my noble and learned friend, Lord Guest, who felt difficulty in *Hardwick* as to the application of section 14(1) against persons who were dealers in the market, said that he could well understand, where the sale is by a manufacturer to a customer, that the inference (sc. of reliance) can easily be drawn (at 106). I agree with Milmo J that it ought to be drawn in this case.

Then was the purpose, to be used for inclusion in animal feeding stuffs to be compounded by the buyers, a particular purpose? In my opinion, certainly yes. It is true that the purpose was wide, wider even than the purpose accepted as particular in *Hardwick* (for compounding into food for cattle and poultry), and, if one leaves aside a possible alternative use as fertiliser, on which there was some indefinite evidence, the purpose so made known covers a large part of the area which would be within section 14(2). But I do not think, as the law has developed, that this can be regarded as an objection or that in accepting a purpose so defined, as a "particular purpose," the court is crossing any forbidden line. There remains a distinction between a statement (express or implied) of a particular purpose, though a wide one, with the implied condition (or warranty) which this attracts, and a purchase by description with no purpose stated and a different condition (or warranty) which that attracts. Moreover, width of the purpose is compensated, from the seller's point of view, by the dilution of his responsibility: and to hold him liable under an implied warranty of fitness for the purpose of which he has been made aware, wide though this may be, appears as fair as to leave him exposed to the vaguer and less defined standard of merchantability. After all, the seller's liability is, if I may borrow the expression of my noble and learned friend, Lord Morris of Borth-y-Gest, no more than to meet the requirement of a buyer who is saying to him "that is what I want it for, but I only want to buy if you sell me something that will do." I think that well expresses the situation here.

[Lord Wilberforce went on to find that feeding herring meal to mink was a normal user in 1961 and known as such to the third party, that the respondents were entitled to rely on the third party to supply herring meal suitable for their purposes, and that the consignment was in fact unsuitable so that a breach of the implied condition under s. 14(1) had been proved.]

Appeals allowed.

NOTES

1) Lord Hodson, Lord Guest, Viscount Dilhorne, and Lord Diplock concurred with Lord Wilberforce on the interpretation of s. 14(1) and its application to the contracts between the appellants and the respondents and between the respondents and the third party. With respect to the phrase in s. 14(1), "goods are of a description which it is ... the seller's business to supply," Lord Hodson and Viscount Dilhorne found that the respondents' business was to make compounds for animal feeding. In producing the mink food they were only using raw materials which it was in the course of their business to supply. Lords Guest and Diplock agreed with Lord Wilberforce that "description" was not here used in the same sense as in "sale by description," but rather in a wider sense to mean goods "of that kind." Lord Guest further agreed with Lord Wilberforce that it was in the course of a seller's business to supply goods if he agreed, either generally or in a specific case, to supply them in the way of business, regardless of whether he had entered into a similar agreement before.

2) Lord Diplock, in a long and thoughtful judgment, dissented from the majority both on the proper interpretation of s. 14(1) and its relationship to s. 14(2), and on whether there had been sufficient disclosure by the respondents to the third party of the intended purpose of the herring meal so as to trigger the operation of s. 14(1). The following extracts illustrate Lord Diplock's position:

a) *The interpretation of s. 14(1) and its relationship to s. 14(2)* (*ibid.*, at 506-7):

The key to both subsections is reliance—the reasonable reliance of the buyer upon the seller's ability to make or select goods which are reasonably fit for the buyer's purpose coupled with the seller's acceptance of responsibility to do so. The seller has a choice whether or not to accept that responsibility. To enable him to exercise it he must be supplied by the buyer with sufficient information to acquaint him with what he is being relied upon to do and to enable him to appreciate what exercise of skill or judgment is called for in order to make or select goods which will be fit for the purpose for which the buyer requires them.

This consideration, in my view, throws light upon two matters arising under section 14. The first is the meaning of "particular purpose" in subsection (1). The second is the application of the doctrine of "partial reliance" under both subsection (1) and subsection (2).

To attract the condition to be implied by subsection (1) the buyer must make known the purpose for which he requires the goods with sufficient particularity to enable a reasonable seller, engaged in the business of supplying goods of the kind ordered to identify the characteristics which the goods need to possess to fit them for that purpose. If all that the buyer does make known to the seller is a range of purposes which do not all call for goods possessing identical characteristics and he does not identify the particular purpose or purposes within that range for which he in fact requires the goods, he does not give the seller sufficient information to enable him to make or to select goods possessing a characteristic which is needed to make them fit for any one of those purposes in particular, if the same characteristic either is not needed to make fit, or makes them unfit, for other purposes within the range.

A "range of purposes" case thus poses a stark question of legal policy as to whether the seller's responsibility ought to be to supply goods which are fit for at least one of the purposes within the range or to supply goods which are fit for all of those purposes unless he expressly disclaims responsibility for their fitness for any one or more of them. The answer to this question of policy has, in my view, been pre-empted by subsection (2) of section 14 of the Sale of Goods Act 1893:

The commonest way in which a buyer makes known to the seller a range of purposes for which the goods are required is by the description by which he buys them and by nothing more. This is the case that is contemplated by subsection (2). This, as it has been authoritatively construed by the courts, provides that the only condition to be implied as to the responsibility of the seller is that the goods should be reasonably fit for one of the purposes within the range.

To supplement the description by which the goods are bought, or to replace it if they are not bought by description, the buyer may identify with greater precision the purpose for which the goods are required, by making it known to the seller in some other way. This is the case contemplated by subsection (1). He may do this expressly or by implication. At any rate, if he does so expressly he can make it known to the seller that he relies upon the seller to supply goods that are fit for more than one purpose or, indeed, for all possible purposes which lie within a range. But the mere fact that the seller knows that the buyer is engaged in a business in which goods of the description by which they are bought *may* be needed for any one of a number of purposes within the range of those for which goods of that description are normally used, adds nothing to what he might reasonably infer from the fact that the buyer ordered the goods by a description which covers goods fit for a range of purposes, without particularising which of those purposes he requires goods for. It might be otherwise if the seller knew that the buyer was engaged in a business in which goods of the description by which they were needed for one or more only of the purposes within the whole range.

It would, in my view, conflict with the principle of reliance which underlies section 14(1) and (2) and would be a misuse of a statutory code of this kind, to treat a range of purposes for any one of which the buyer *may* require the goods, on the one hand, as constituting "the particular purpose for which the goods are required" and so giving rise to an implied condition under subsection (1) that they shall be reasonably fit for all purposes within the range, if the seller's knowledge of the *range* is derived in whole or in part from some circumstance other than the description by which the goods are ordered; and, on the other hand, as giving rise to an implied condition under subsection (2) that the goods need only be fit for one of the purposes within the range, if the seller's knowledge of the *range* is derived solely from the description by which the goods are ordered. So to construe the code would for practical purposes deprive subsection (2) of any effect.

b) *Adequacy of disclosure of purpose to third party* (*ibid.*, at 512):

I turn next to section 14(1) upon which Hill also relies. The most that Hill made known to the Norwegians about the purposes for which the herring meal was required was what I have previously termed a "range of purposes." The extent of that range was limited to what their agent in London had learnt from Hill in the course of previous dealings as to the nature of Hill's business. The range so made known included use as an ingredient in feeding-stuffs for many kinds of domestic animals and poultry. What it did not include was use as an ingredient in feeding-stuffs for mink. This seems to me to be conclusive that even if the Norwegians knew that Norwegian herring meal was a commodity which might be used as an ingredient in the diet of mink, use for that purpose can neither be nor form any part of the particular purpose for which the goods were required which was *made known by the buyer to the seller*, so as to give rise to the implied condition under section 14(1) that they should be reasonably fit for feeding mink.

My Lords, it will already be apparent that, for the reasons which I have already advanced in discussing "range of purposes," the decision of this House in *Hardwick Game Farm v. Suffolk Agricultural Poultry Producers Association*, [1969] 2 AC 31, that the fourth parties were liable to the third parties for breach of the condition implied under section 14(1) in my view goes to the utmost limit of what can be held to be a "particular purpose" within the meaning of that section without amending the Act itself. However desirable it may be to make such an amendment, to do so lies beyond the competence of this House of Parliament acting alone—even in its judicial capacity. I myself would distinguish that part of the decision in the *Hardwick Game Farm* case whenever I can. I do not think that it is open to your Lordships to extend it.

3) In the light of the broad scope given by the majority of the law lords in the *Hardwick Game Farm* and *Ashington Piggeries* cases to the implied condition of fitness and the ready implication of reliance on the seller's skill and knowledge even in dealings between merchants, what significant differences remain between the condition of merchantability and the condition of fitness? Was Lord Diplock (in *Ashington Piggeries*) right in complaining that the scales had been tipped too generously in the buyer's favour? To what extent were the law lords in both cases influenced by the lethal nature of the defect in the goods? Would it be better to treat the cases as examples of the American inspired movement to hold manufacturers, producers and distributors strictly liable in tort for the supply of defective goods causing injury to person or other property? (On this aspect of the modern law of sales see further *infra*, chapter 9.)

4) Given the ready implication of reliance, the English and Scottish Law Commissions recommended modifying s. 14(1) of the UK Act to give effect to the judicial interpretation. The recommendation was adopted in the Supply of Goods (Implied Terms) Act 1973. Section 14(3) of the UK Sale of Goods Act 1979 now reads as follows:

(3) Where the seller sells goods in the course of a business and the buyer, expressly or by implication, makes known—

(a) to the seller, or

(b) where the purchase price or part of it is payable by instalments and the goods
were previously sold by a credit-broker to the seller, to that credit-broker,

any particular purpose for which the goods are being bought, there is an implied condition
that the goods supplied under the contract are reasonably fit for that purpose, whether or not
that is a purpose for which such goods are commonly supplied, except where the circumstances show that the buyer does not rely, or that it is unreasonable for him to rely, on the
skill or judgment of the seller or credit-broker.

Does s. 14(3) put to rest the proper meaning of "any particular purpose"? The OLRC
Sales Report (at 221) supported the British changes, with the exception of the reference
in the opening line of s. 14(3) to a sale by the seller "in the course of a business." On this
point the Commission explained its position as follows (*ibid*.):

The exception to which we refer relates to the opening line of section 14(3) of the UK Act,
which makes the implied warranty of fitness applicable to all sales by a seller "in the course
of a business." Here, consistently with the position adopted by us with respect to the condition of merchantable quality, we recommend that the new warranty of fitness continue to be
restricted to sales by a seller who deals in goods of the kind supplied under the contract of
sale. We realize that, where the seller does not deal in goods of the kind supplied under the
contract, there will be no warranty of fitness. This should not, however, preclude a buyer
from being able to show that, even though the seller was not a merchant with respect to the
goods sold to the buyer, there was communicated reliance on his skill and judgment, and
that the seller had expressly warranted the fitness of the goods for the indicated purpose. In
such circumstances, we think it better that the burden should rest on the buyer to make out
such a case; the seller should not have to show, as apparently he would have to show under
the UK amendment, that the buyer did not rely, or that it was unreasonable for him to rely,
on the seller's skill and judgment.

Allergies and Other Abnormal Product Use Cases

Ingham v. Emes

[1955] 2 All ER 740, [1955] 2 QB 366 (CA)

DENNING LJ: Mrs. Ingham, the second plaintiff, is the wife of the licensee of the
Sun Hotel, Dunsfold. In March, 1954, she had her hair dyed by the ladies' hairdresser
called Maison Emes in Godalming. The preparation which was used was called Inecto
Rapid. As a result of it she suffered acute dermatitis and she brings this action against
the hairdresser for damages.

The story starts, however seven years before, in 1947, when the second plaintiff
was attending another hairdresser. She then had her hair dyed with Inecto and after
about two days her eyes became puffy. She consulted a doctor and he suspected that
it might be the Inecto which caused the trouble. After that experience she did not
have Inecto for a long time because she knew it might have a bad effect on her. In
September, 1951, she started going to Maison Emes in Godalming where she was
attended by an assistant named Mrs. Hughes. Thenceforward for two and a half years

the second plaintiff regularly had her hair tinted by Mrs. Hughes with henna and they were on excellent terms with one another. During one of these visits the second plaintiff may well have told Mrs. Hughes about her previous Inecto experience, but rather in a gossipy manner, not in such a way as to make any impression on Mrs. Hughes' mind. In March, 1954, the second plaintiff had a coming engagement, when she was going with her husband to see the brewers and she wanted to look her best. She was getting tired of the henna shampoos, as they needed to be done so often and were expensive. Thereupon, the assistant, Mrs. Hughes, suggested that the second plaintiff should try Inecto, and went on to say that, if she tried Inecto, she must have a test first, because it was dangerous. There was a conflict between the two ladies whether the second plaintiff on that occasion reminded Mrs. Hughes of her previous experience with Inecto. The second plaintiff says that she reminded Mrs. Hughes of it. Mrs. Hughes says that she did not. The judge found that Mrs. Hughes was right about this, because he did not think that Mrs. Hughes would have been so rash as to go on with Inecto if she had known of previous trouble. On Mar. 9, 1954, the second plaintiff went to have the test to see if she was likely to be harmed by Inecto. Mrs. Hughes opened a package of Inecto and put the instructions on the table. The second plaintiff read them. The instructions said:

> The manufacturers … draw attention below to a simple and easy test, which in the opinion of eminent skin specialists will disclose any predisposition to skin trouble from the use of dye. The test must, as a matter of routine, be employed on each occasion prior to using the dye, regardless of the fact that it has been used with success on the same person on a previous occasion.

Then follows in large letters "It may be dangerous to use Inecto Rapid without this test." The test is then described of applying a little Inecto behind the ear, painting a film of collodion over it and leaving it for forty-eight hours. The instructions then say:

> If no irritation has been experienced and there is no redness or inflammation then the skin is free from predisposition and the colouring may be used.

On Mar. 9 Mrs. Hughes applied the test in exact accordance with the instructions. On Mar. 11 the second plaintiff returned. Mrs. Hughes examined the patch and said her skin was perfectly clear. She told the second plaintiff that she was not a reactor and that she was a safe person to have Inecto. The second plaintiff thereupon made an appointment to have her hair dyed with Inecto on Mar. 16. It was done on that day, and within a few days the plaintiff was suffering from acute dermatitis. There is no doubt that it was due to the Inecto.

It appears from the evidence that the test is not infallible. Dr. Hassan, the expert called by the defendant, described Inecto as "an extremely dangerous substance." In very rare cases, even when the test is negative, the subject herself may be sensitive to it. For instance, she may be negative when the test is done, but sensitive a few days later when the dye is applied. Or she may not react to the small test but may react to the full dose. The judge came to the conclusion that the second plaintiff was "of the rare type to whom the ordinary test will not apply but who is allergic to a large dose," and he found that there was "no fault of either party." He dismissed the claim, therefore, founded on negligence, but he found in favour of the second plaintiff on the ground of breach of warranty. He found that there was a warranty by the hairdresser that the Inecto was suitable for this particular person, the second plaintiff, and that the defendant was liable when it turned out not to be suitable. If the second plaintiff had not had any previous trouble with Inecto, then I think the judge would have been right. She was apparently a perfectly normal person, and Mrs. Hughes said, or as good as said, to her: "If you pass the test you may safely have Inecto." There would be, I think, in those circumstances, an implied term that Inecto was reasonably fit for the purpose of dyeing the hair of this particular person, the second plaintiff, if she passed the test. But the second plaintiff to her own knowledge was not in this regard a perfectly normal person. She had experienced Inecto before and she knew that it might have a bad effect on her. In the modern phrase she knew that she was allergic to it. She ought clearly to have made that known to Mrs. Hughes; and she knew that she ought to have done so. That is shown by the fact that she herself insisted at the trial that she had told Mrs. Hughes about it on the very day that Inecto was suggested; but, unfortunately for her, the judge did not accept her evidence on this point. If she had made it known, Mrs. Hughes would never have gone on with the Inecto. It is rather like the case which I put in the course of the argument: if a doctor suggests penicillin, and the patient knows by experience that he is allergic to penicillin, he ought to tell the doctor so. I appreciate that cases of medical treatment are very different from the present, but there is in each case a duty to use reasonable care to disclose known peculiarities. The second plaintiff ought to have brought home to Mrs. Hughes that she was allergic to Inecto.

The difficulty that I have felt is that this looks to me like a plea of contributory negligence, or a plea that the second plaintiff was the author of her own misfortune; and that has never been pleaded or found. But I think the same result is reached by saying that the implied term as to fitness is dependent on proper disclosure by the customer of any relevant peculiarities known to her, and in particular of the fact that she knew by experience that Inecto might have a bad effect on her. The way this result is reached in law is this: in a contract for work and materials (such as the present), there is an implied term that the materials are reasonably fit for the purpose for which they are required: see *G.H. Myers & Co. v. Brent Cross Service Co.*, [1934] 1 KB 46. This term is analogous to the corresponding term in the sale of goods: see *Stewart v. Reavell's Garage*, [1952] 1 All ER 1191. In order for the implied term to arise, however, the customer must make known to the contractor expressly or by implication the "particular purpose" for which the materials are required, so as to show that he relies on the contractor's skill or judgment. The particular purpose in this case was to dye the hair, not of a normal person, but of a person known to be allergic to Inecto. The second plaintiff did not make that particular purpose known to Mrs. Hughes. She cannot therefore recover in the implied terms.

I ought perhaps to say that I do not think this case is governed by the Harris tweed case, *Griffiths v. Peter Conway, Ltd.*, [1939] 1 All ER 685. In that case a lady suffered from dermatitis owing to wearing a Harris tweed coat, which was specially made for her, and she failed to recover. Harris tweed is not a dangerous thing and it is reasonably fit for any normal person, test or not test: whereas Inecto is a dangerous thing which is not reasonably fit for anyone unless she passes a test. The manufacturers in their instructions represent in effect that, if a person passes the test, Inecto is safe. The hairdresser passed on that representation to her customer on her own account. That brings an implied term into operation in favour of all persons who pass the test except those, such as the second plaintiff, who know that they are allergic and do not disclose it. I would therefore allow the appeal and give judgment for the defendant.

Appeal allowed.

[Birkett and Romer LJJ delivered concurring judgments.]

Carol Rogerson and Michael Trebilcock
"Products Liability and the Allergic Consumer: A Study in the Problems of Framing an Efficient Liability Regime"

(1986), 36 *Univ. Tor. LJ* 52 (Footnotes omitted)

A significant portion of the population is affected by allergies, and the numbers appear destined to grow both with improvements in the diagnostic skills of medical science and with the ever-expanding role of new chemical products in our daily lives. It has been estimated that approximately 35 million people in the United States suffer from allergies. While most of these are victims of asthma and hay fever, the remainder, an estimated 10 million, constitute a still substantial class of people who suffer allergic reactions from other sources. It is this area in particular that provides grist for legal analysis, raising problems of products liability in cases involving the purchase and use of a variety of natural and man-made products. Even a brief foray through the products liability case-law involving allergic consumers reveals a surprisingly wide array of common domestic products which have the propensity to spark allergic reactions: hair dyes, permanent wave solutions, lipsticks, nail polishes, sun-tan lotions, depilatories, toothpastes, deodorants, bathsalts, laundry soaps, fabric dyes, hatbands, Harris tweed cloth, and even eye-glass frames. Natural products are no less fraught with hazard to the allergic consumer than the complex substances compounded by manufacturers. The allergenic properties of such foods as strawberries, citrus fruits, eggs, milk products, and shellfish are so well known as to have passed into the realm of community folk-wisdom. Case-law involving the liability of drug manufacturers for unintended side-effects of otherwise beneficial drugs is also closely related to the problem of the allergic consumer that allergic reactions are one type of side-effect suffered by hypersensitive users. Current scientific thinking has it that nearly every product intended for personal bodily use possesses the potential to cause an allergic reaction in some percentage of the population.

Allergic reactions can run the gamut of severity from mild cases of rash and hives to extremely painful skin blistering, nervous conditions, kidney disorders, damage of the optic nerves, and, as in one American case, a rare and usually fatal disease of the arteries. Reactions from some drugs and certain foods, such as nuts and seafood, have proved fatal. As well as experiencing pain and suffering, the consumer who suffers an allergic reaction may face out-of-pocket costs for medical expenses and/or foregone income. It is the purpose of this paper to examine and evaluate the response of civil liability regimes to the problem of the allergic consumer.

As in any products liability case, civil liability regimes expose both the supplier and the manufacturer of the product to the possibility of being made a defendant in a suit brought by the allergic consumer-plaintiff. In its present state, Anglo-Canadian law would allow such an action to be framed either in the tort of negligence or in contract for breach of warranty under the Sale of Goods Act, the latter form of recovery conventionally being regarded as constituting a form of strict liability. The former would normally be used in an action against the manufacturer, the latter when recovery is sought against the retailer or the manufacturer in the event that the manufacturer is also the direct supplier. American law has gone one step further with the adoption in many jurisdictions of a form of strict tortious liability which applies to all suppliers of products, be they manufacturers, retailers, or distributors.

· · ·

In the negligence context, the courts have typically, as in other abnormal use cases, approached the allergy problem through the concept of reasonable foreseeability, imposing liability upon suppliers in cases where they knew or ought to have known of the harm and where a reasonable person possessing such knowledge would have taken precautions either in the form of a product modification or, more commonly, a warning. The reported cases appear generally to have eschewed any delicate balancing of injury costs and precaution costs, instead translating the collapsed concepts of reasonable foreseeability and standard of care into a narrow formulaic requirement that a certain percentage of persons must suffer an allergic reaction from the product before the manufacturer will be held liable. A singular lack of consensus exists as to the threshold percentage for the imposition of liability. This test of significant numbers has been most explicitly espoused by the American courts in the form of the "recognized" or "appreciable class" test, and consequently the American case-law reveals most clearly the inconsistent application and unpredictable results of the test.

In two remarkably similar cases involving dermatitis contracted from deodorants, recovery was allowed against one manufacturer, who had sold over 82 million jars of the product and received only 373 complaints, but denied against the other, who had received the statistically higher number of 4 complaints in a year in which 600,000 sales of the product had been recorded. A more startling discrepancy exists between a case such as *Braun v. Roux Distributing* in which recovery was allowed even though there had been no other reported cases of injury in 50 million packages of the defendant's hair dye sold and the danger had only been discussed in scientific literature, and one such as *Bennett v. Pilot Products,* where recovery was denied even though the manufacturer had actual knowledge that one out of every thousand persons was allergic to one of the chemical ingredients in its permanent wave solution. The U.S. case-law is further confused by the sub-theme of the duty to warn. The courts have been unable to come to grips with the problem raised by a situation where harm to an appreciable class is foreseeable but a warning would have proved futile because of the plaintiff's lack of knowledge of his or her susceptibility. Some cases have denied recovery where a warning would have been ineffective even if provided; others have disregarded this factor and imposed liability in the absence of a warning.

The Anglo-Canadian courts are in an even greater state of confusion, refusing to commit themselves to anything so concrete as a numbers test and approaching the problem indirectly through the vague concept of "dangerousness." The concept would appear to have implicit in it a combined recognition of probability of harm and seriousness of harm (that is, expected injury cost), but it does not distinguish between avoidably and unavoidably dangerous products and also tends to skew decision-making because of its emotive connotations. This is aptly illustrated in *Ingham v. Emes* by the English Court of Appeal's categorical rejection of the idea that Harris tweed, a venerable British institution, could be conceived of as a dangerous product and its all too eager assumption that hair-dye, even accompanied by a patch test that would identify the large majority of potentially allergic users of the risks, fell into such a category. The general absence in Anglo-Canadian case-law of a coherent theoretical framework to justify the imposition or denial of liability with respect to the supplier is reflected in an arbitrary reliance on labels such as "idiosyncratic," "peculiarly sensitive," or "abnormal," connoting some degree of rarity in the occurrence of the harm.

As the courts have themselves recognized, not without a certain degree of perplexity, the test of significant numbers obviously breaks down in the case of common allergies, such as food allergies, where the affected group is often relatively large but where the courts intuitively perceive the inappropriateness of imposing liability. The factors which lie behind the seemingly arbitrary distinction between natural and manufactured products have not been carefully analysed. Plagued by a desire to maintain a consistent position, some courts have gone so far as to argue backwards from the food cases for a complete abandonment of the significant numbers test and a blanket denial of liability in all allergy cases on the grounds that an allergic reaction is always caused by the buyer's peculiar idiosyncracy and not by want of appropriate precautions on the part of the supplier.

In summary, in the negligence case-law a narrow focus on a quantitative requirement has left the courts with little guidance as to the relevance of other factors, such as the social value of the product, the availability of substitutes, the seriousness of harm, the consumer's access to information on allergic reactions, and the cost and effectiveness of preventive measures.

The complexities of the existing allergy case-law are compounded when one moves from a negligence context to one of strict liability. In Anglo-Canadian law this means the context of the implied warranties under the Sale of Goods Act. Given the "lowest common denominator" approach which the courts have adopted in interpreting the warranty of merchantability (a product will be regarded as merchantable if it is fit for any *one* of the purposes to which the product as described in the contract is normally applied), the warranty of reasonable fitness for purpose as embodied in section 15(1) of the Ontario Sale of Goods Act generally offers allergic consumers their best hope of recovery. The strictness of liability for breach of the implied warranty of fitness has been taken to mean that liability will be imposed regardless of the fact that the seller has taken all reasonable care to avoid or detect the presence of a defect and even if the defect was undiscoverable. As Lord Reid stated in *Kendall v. Lillico*:

If the law were always logical one would suppose that a buyer, who has obtained a right to rely on the seller's skill and judgment, would only obtain thereby an assurance that proper skill and judgment had been exercised, and would only be entitled to a remedy if a defect in the goods was due to failure to exercise such skill and judgment. But the law has always gone farther than that. By getting the seller to undertake to use his skill and judgment the buyer gets under sec. 14(1) [s. 15(1) of the Ontario act] an assurance that the goods will be reasonably fit for his purpose and that covers not only defects which the seller ought to have detected but also defects which are latent in the sense that even the utmost skill and judgment on the part of the seller would not have detected them.

One would have expected, given the explicit distinction which is conventionally made between the negligence requirements of fault and the "no-fault" aspects of strict liability, that the allergic consumer would have generous prospects of recovery under implied warranty. However, such has not been the case. Liability under the implied warranties is not absolute, and unusual risks are not automatically covered.

Hovering in the background of the courts' interpretation of the warranties is the somewhat nebulous concept of a defect, implying the courts' involvement in the setting of objective quality standards. With regard specifically to the warranty of fitness, the concept of a defect is worked in through the interpretation of the terms "particular purpose" and "reasonably fit for such purpose." In what is a somewhat surprising development, the courts have tended to rely upon a Learned Hand-style negligence formula of probability of harm times seriousness of harm (a risk-utility analysis) in determining whether the degree of risk created warrants the imposition of liability upon the supplier. Lord Pearce's judgment in *Kendall v. Lillico* provides the clearest statement of the convergence of the theories of negligence and warranty:

I would expect a tribunal of fact to decide that a car sold in this country was reasonably fit for touring even though it was not well adapted for conditions in a heat wave, but not if it could not cope adequately with the rain. If, however, it developed some lethal or dangerous trick in very hot weather, I would expect it to be found unfit. In deciding the question of fact *the rarity of the unsuitability should be weighed against the gravity of the consequences.* Again, if food was merely unpalatable or useless on rare occasions, it might well be reasonably suitable for food. But I should certainly not expect it to be held reasonably suitable if even on very rare occasions it killed the consumer.

It would appear that the major distinction between the negligence and warranty regimes is that under implied warranty the seriousness of the risk is determined on the basis of the court's knowledge at the time of trial when the risk has in fact materialized (regardless of whether this knowledge was available to or could have been generated by the supplier prior to the transaction), whereas under negligence it is determined on the basis of what the supplier knew or ought to have known at the time of the transaction. Also, it would not appear as if the cost of prevention figures in the warranty formula for the imposition of liability, although, as has been shown, the courts have not clarified the role of this factor even in the negligence cases.

. . .

However, even if the considerations canvassed in this section seem, at a general level, persuasive in favouring strict product liability over negligence, several critical issues which bear on this judgment remain to be resolved within the framework of a strict liability regime. These issues are particularly problematic in the allergies cases.

· · ·

First, what is the meaning of a "defect"? Strict liability is not conventionally understood to imply absolute liability in the sense that a supplier of a product is liable for all losses causally related to a product, however arising. Strict liability in theory entails liability for product defects without proof of negligence. In the allergies context, the products in question are typically not defective in construction relative to other units of the same product, and are invariably entirely suitable in design or composition for most consumers who use them. On what basis, if any, should they be regarded as defective when used by an allergic consumer? In what way, if at all, is the allergic consumer conceptually different from the congenitally clumsy person who cuts himself on a kitchen knife or the congenitally inept person who falls off or over a ladder or chair? In neither case does it seem intuitively sensible to hold the supplier of the knife, ladder, or chair liable, despite the fact that suppliers thereof must be aware that such accidents are not especially uncommon. Doctrinally, this conclusion might be supported by finding that the product is not defective, or that there has been a voluntary assumption of risk or contributory negligence. However, whatever the doctrinal rationalization for the conclusion, the intuitive sense of it seems to revolve around the proposition that the avoidance precautions available to the person injured were less costly than any available to the supplier, or alternatively, if the consequences of congenital clumsiness or ineptitude cannot readily be avoided by the injured party, the costs of avoidance precautions to the supplier (and ultimately other consumers) are wholly disproportionate to the benefits derived generally by consumers. But determining whether a product is defective on this basis involves a form of cost-benefit analysis familiar in a negligence regime but ostensibly irrelevant to strict liability.

NOTES

1) The Rogerson and Trebilcock article goes on to propose a new liability regime for allergy cases, one that is based on efficiency considerations. The authors identify three kinds of cases. In Case (1), the consumer has full knowledge of her allergic propensities and the allergenic properties of the product. In Case (2), the consumer has knowledge of either her allergic propensities or the allergenic properties of the product, but not both. In Case (3), the consumer has no knowledge of either her allergic propensities or the allergenic properties of the product. They argue that in Case (1), the consumer should generally bear the loss. In Case (2), the consumer should bear the loss unless, in a particular case, the supplier is shown to be the better cost avoider. Precautions a supplier might take to avoid the loss include: (a) modifying the product; (b) communicating information to consumers about risks and precautions; and (c) withdrawing the product. Precautions open to the consumer include: (a) modifying her use of the product; (b) getting information for herself about her likely reaction to the product; and (c) substituting another product. In

Case (3), the supplier should be liable unless it takes precautions, such as attaching a warning to the product about its allergenic propensities. A step like this will take the fact situation out of Case (3) into Case (2).

For a different view, see James A. Henderson Jr., "Process Norms in Product Liability for Allergic Reactions" (1990), 51 *Univ. Pitts. LR* 761. Henderson argues for a no liability rule in allergy cases on process (ease of judicial administration) grounds.

2) The rule that the implied condition of fitness only applies to a normal user of the goods (unless, of course, she has disclosed her particular condition at the time of purchase) also applies to the *manner* in which the goods are used. Thus it has been held that a buyer of infected pork chops cannot complain if proper cooking would have eliminated the problem and she failed to follow the normal procedure. See *Yachetti v. John Duff & Sons Ltd.*, [1943] 1 DLR 194, foll'd. in *Heil v. Hedges*, [1951] 1 TLR 512. In cases of this nature, is it open to the court to apportion liability between the buyer and seller on a basis analogous to contributory negligence? See the note on *Lambert v. Lewis*, [1982] AC 225, *infra*, chapter 17.

3) The abnormal use rule is not limited to cases of allergic reactions, or to cases involving consumer product liability claims. In *James Slater and Hamish Slater (a firm) v. Finning Ltd.*, [1997] AC 473, the rule was applied in a quite different factual context to deny the buyer relief. The case concerned a contract for the supply of component parts for a boat engine. The parts failed, but the evidence showed that the problem was due to factors external to the parts themselves. *Slater v. Finning* was applied in *Innovative Automation Ltd. v. Candea Inc.* (1998), 38 OR (3d) 324 (Ont. Ct. (Gen. Div.)).

Patent or Trade Name Exception

Baldry v. Marshall

[1925] 1 KB 260, [1924] All ER Rep. 155 (CA)

BANKES LJ: This is an appeal from a judgment of Greer J, and upon the facts as found by the learned judge his conclusion was in my opinion quite right. It appears that the plaintiff wrote to the defendants, "Can you tell me if the Bugatti eight cylinder is likely to be on the market this year, if so will you send particulars?" indicating that according to his impression this was a new type of car that was going to be put on the market. In their reply the defendants said: "As no doubt you are already aware, we specialize in the sale of these cars, and are in a position to supply you with all information necessary," thereby intimating that the plaintiff might regard them as persons upon whose skill and judgment he could safely rely. Those letters were followed by an interview at which the plaintiff made plain to the defendants the purpose for which he required the car. Then came the contract, which was on a printed form. It was in the form of a request by the plaintiff to the defendants to supply him with "one eight cylinder Bugatti car fully equipped and finished to standard specification as per the car inspected." On the back of the contract there was printed "The company reserves the right to withdraw any model or alter specifications or prices without notice. Illustrations and specifications must be taken as a general guide and not as binding in detail," and under the heading "Guarantee" the words, "The same as received by us from the manufacturers." The guarantee which they had so received from the manufacturers was expressed to be "against any breakage of parts due to faulty material," and contained the following clause: "Cars are sold on condition that the foregoing guarantee is accepted instead of and expressly excludes any other guarantee or warranty, statutory or otherwise." It is said that by the use of that language the defendants meant to exclude conditions as well as warranties; but they have not done so, and if there is one thing more clearly established than another it is the distinction which the law recognizes between a condition and a warranty. In *Wallis v. Pratt*, [1911] AC 394, the sellers by a clause stating that "Sellers give no warranty express or implied" endeavoured to exclude the condition implied under s. 13 of the Sale of Goods Act, that the goods sold should correspond with the description, but the House of Lords held that they had not used apt words to effect that purpose. So here the defendants have not used the necessary language to exclude the implied condition which arises under s. 14 as to fitness for the particular purpose of which the plaintiff had given them notice. But then it is said that even if the implication of that condition is not excluded by the terms of the contract it is excluded by the proviso to sub-s. 1 on the ground that the car was sold under its trade name. It is however clear to my mind upon evidence that it was not in fact sold under a trade name within the meaning of the proviso. The mere fact that an article sold is described in the contract by its trade name does not necessarily make the sale a sale under a trade name. Whether it is so or not depends upon the circumstances. I may illustrate my meaning by reference to three different cases. First, where a buyer asks a seller for an article which will fulfil some particular purpose, and in answer to that request the seller sells him an article by a well-known trade name, there I think it is clear that the proviso does not apply. Secondly, where the buyer says to the seller, "I have been recommended such and such an article"—mentioning it by its trade name—"will it suit my particular purpose?" naming the purpose, and thereupon the seller sells it without more, there again I think the proviso has no application. But there is a third case where the buyer says to a seller, "I have been recommended so and so"—giving its trade name—"as suitable for the particular purpose for which I want it. Please sell it to me." In that case I think it is equally clear that the proviso would apply and that the implied condition of the thing's fitness for the purpose named would not arise. In my opinion the test of an article having been sold under its trade name within the meaning of the proviso is: did the buyer specify it under its trade name in such a way as to indicate that he is satisfied, rightly or wrongly, that it will answer his purpose, and that he is not relying on the skill or judgment of the seller, however great that skill or judgment may be? Here there is nothing to show that the plaintiff when describing the car in the contract as an "eight cylinder Bugatti car," after he had communicated to the defendants the purpose for which he wanted it, meant to intimate that he was not relying on their skill and judgment. The evidence seems to be all the other way. In my opinion the appeal must be dismissed.

Appeal dismissed.

[The concurring judgments of Atkin and Sargant LJJ are omitted.]

G.H.L. Fridman
Sale of Goods in Canada

4th ed. (1995), at 200-2

It is provided in section 15(1) of the Ontario Act that "in the case of a contract for the sale of a specified article under its patent or other trade name, there is no implied condition as to its fitness for any particular purpose." The meaning and application of this proviso have caused some difficulty. The proviso assumes the absence of any express assurance by the seller and deals only with cases of express or implied information by the buyer of the purpose for which he requires the article, so framed as to show that the buyer relies on the seller's skill or judgment. The idea behind the proviso is that by ordering an article under its patent or trade name the buyer is explicitly not relying on the seller's skill or judgment as to the fitness of the article for its intended purpose. Hence to make a sale, one under a trade or other patent name, the buyer must "specify it under its trade name in such a way as to indicate that he is satisfied, rightly or wrongly, that it will answer his purposes and that he is not relying on the skill or judgment of the seller." As *Baldry v. Marshall* shows, there may be a sale under a trade name but not within the proviso, by the reintroduction of the concept of reliance: a point that was reiterated by Masten JA, in *Advance-Rumely Thresher Co. v. Lister*, [1927] 4 DLR 51. In the case of *Bristol Tramways & Carriage Co. Ltd. v. Fiat Motors Ltd.*, [1910] 2 KB 831, a sale of a 24/40 h.p. Fiat omnibus and six 24/40 h.p. motor chassis was not a sale under a patent or trade name and the condition implied by the subsection applied. This was because "Fiat" had not become a trade or patent name, and the proviso was held to be confined to articles which in fact had a patent or trade name under which they could be ordered. Such a name is acquired by user, and whether or not it has been so acquired is a question of fact in each case. In *Baldry v. Marshall*, it was said that although a "Bugatti" car was ordered, the proviso might not apply to an article like a motor car which was sold under a very elaborate and specific description. A sale of "Coalite," however, was held to be a sale under a trade or patent name in *Wilson v. Rickett Cockerell & Co. Ltd.*, [1954] 1 QB 598, thereby excluding the operation of the implied condition as to fitness for purpose where explosive material was mixed with the "Coalite" and caused damage to the room of the purchaser. Similarly in *O'Fallon v. Inecto Rapid (Can.) Ltd.*, [1940] 2 WWR 714, a sale of a specific hair dye was held to be outside the protection of the implied condition as to fitness because the dye was bought under a trade name. Though the manufacturer and wholesale distributor could be liable (for negligently failing to warn of the possible damages to inexperienced users) the retailer, who was not negligent, could not. And in *Simon v. Imperial Oil Ltd.* a sale of a drum of "Esso stove oil" came within the basis of negligence. However, in *Fillmore's Valley Nurseries Ltd. v. North Amer. Cyanamid Ltd.* (1958), 14 DLR (2d) 297 the sale of chemical "amino triazole," a herbicide used to control weeds in the growing of pansy plants, was held not to be a sale of a specified article under its trade name. Nor was the sale of the insecticide and herbicide in *Willis v. F.M.C. Machinery & Chemicals Ltd.* (1976), 68 DLR (3d) 127. In these cases, therefore, the implied condition was not excluded.

The proviso may be excluded, as seen above, by the circumstances, from which it may be deduced that the sale was not in actuality one under a trade or patent name. The possibility of this occurring seems to make the utility of the proviso questionable. Moreover, where the operation of the proviso renders the condition implied as to fitness inapplicable, it may well be that the implied condition as to merchantability can still operate for the benefit of the buyer. This, as will be seen has been the effect of the judicial interpretation of the language of the two subsections now contained in s. 15(1)(2) of the Ontario Act. Consequently, and justifiably it may be admitted, as is shown by the redrafting of the law on this subject in the USA by the Uniform Commercial Code, it has been argued that the differentiation between the conditions implied in the two subsections is outmoded, and indeed has been outflanked by the decisions of the court.

NOTE

Saskatchewan never adopted the trade name proviso. The proviso was eliminated in the British Supply of Goods (Implied Terms) Act 1973, s. 3. See now UK Sale of Goods Act 1979, s. 14(3). The OLRC has also recommended the abolition of the proviso. See Sales Report, at 220-21, and draft bill, s. 5.14.

THE IMPLIED CONDITIONS IN A SALE BY SAMPLE

Steels & Busks Ltd. v. Bleecker Bik & Co. Ltd.

[1956] 1 Lloyd's Rep. 228 (QB)

[Steels & Busks Ltd. required rubber for use in the manufacture of suspenders on corsets. In May of 1949 a representative of the company first approached the sellers. The sellers were informed that Steels & Busks required crepe rubber for manufacturing suspenders and that a light colour for the rubber was important because of the delicate colour of the suspender ends. A discussion ensued, chiefly involving the relative merits and prices of "water white crepe" and "first grade pale crepe." On May 5, 1949, the representative of Steels & Busks placed an order referring to a particular sample ("Ref. 601"). Subsequently, all orders by the buyers with the sellers were made "as previously delivered" or in like terms.

In September of 1951 the buyers began to receive complaints from their customers. An expert hired by the buyers determined that a chemical, "PNP," in the rubber supplied by the sellers had caused discoloration and stains on the manufactured corsets. In March of 1953 the buyers brought an action against the sellers claiming, *inter alia*, that the rubber did not conform in quality with the sample or that supplied under previous contracts.]

SELLERS J: The question of law for the decision of the Court is whether on the facts as found the goods delivered were or were not in accordance with the contractual terms.

. . .

The buyers wanted the pale crepe rubber for the manufacture of the ends of suspenders for use on corsets. The earlier deliveries had proved suitable for this purpose after whatever processing took place. The final delivery, while apparently suitable in the course of processing and manufacture, proved as to part of the delivery unsuitable because the garments became stained in the boxes in which they were packed and in the shops, due to the presence of a chemical conveniently described as "PNP." These defects were traced to 21 bales which alone are the subject of complaint in these proceedings.

At the time of the sale neither of the parties was aware that "PNP" was used in the treatment of rubber or that it might be detrimental, as it proved to be in this case. Indeed, no thought was given to the matter at all. By reason of the presence of "PNP" in the 21 bales, the buyers' loss, as alleged, has been heavy.

. . .

If the buyers are to succeed in their claim, it must, I think, only be on the ground that the 21 bales did not comply with the sample, that is, the first delivery. In one respect the bales complained of did not so comply. They contained "PNP," whereas the sample did not, and it was submitted that Sect. 15(2)(a) of the Sale of Goods Act [Ont., s. 16(2)(a)] had not been complied with as the bulk did not correspond with the sample in quality. Sect. 15(2) of the Act [Ont., s. 16(2)] is as follows ...

Sect. 15(2) is not inconsistent with the view that where there is (as here) a defect not apparent on reasonable examination of the sample, the buyers' rights arise, if at all, under sub-s. (2)(c) and not under sub-s. (2)(a), but it is not, I think, conclusive as a matter of construction.

The law arising on Sect. 15 has recently been considered by Mr. Justice Devlin in *F.E. Hookway & Co., Ltd. v. Alfred Isaacs & Sons and Others*, [1954] 1 Lloyd's Rep. 491. It was submitted by Mr. Mocatta that this case was wrongly decided and I was asked to take a different view. In that long and somewhat complicated case it appears that the parties traded in a commodity called shellac, a substance used in the manufacture of gramophone records. In the case of the delivery contract, business was done upon the basis of a "standard sample" kept in the offices of the Association and which was selected from time to time with great care to represent a standard in each of the qualities of shellac in which the market deals. There was no official analysis of the sample, comparisons were always made visually by those skilled in the trade. Any member could obtain a part of the sample for his own use, so that it diminished in size and had to be renewed. Any member might have what he got analysed. Quality under the delivery was judged entirely visually except with regard to the presence of resin, which called for an analysis. I take a considerable extract from the judgment, commencing at 511:

> ... the clause "Quality equal to London standard" has the effect of making this contract analogous to the contract for sale by sample which is dealt with in the Sale of Goods Act, 1893, Sect. 15. Instead of a specific sample being given in each case to the seller, there is one standard sample with which the bulk must correspond in quality. But the word "quality," in my judgment, is in its place in this contract confined—as it would be

in the case of the ordinary sale by sample—to such qualities as are apparent on an ordinary examination of the sample as usually done in the trade.

James Drummond & Sons v. E.H. Van Ingen & Co. (1887), 12 App. Cas. 284, is the case upon which Sect. 15 is largely based. In that case, the cloth sold had a latent defect which was not apparent on a reasonable examination of the sample, which had the same latent defect. The House of Lords held that it was not sufficient that the goods should correspond with the sample; they must also be merchantable and fit for the purpose for which they were required. The seller was therefore responsible for the latent defect. In a famous passage, Lord Macnaghten, at 297, describes the function of the sample:

> After all [he says], the office of a sample is to present to the eye the real meaning and intention of the parties with regard to the subject-matter of the contract which, owing to the imperfection of language, it may be difficult or impossible to express in words. The sample speaks for itself. But is cannot be treated as saying more than such a sample would tell a merchant of the class to which the buyer belongs, using due care and diligence, and appealing to it in the ordinary way and with the knowledge possessed by merchants of that class at the time. No doubt the sample might be made to say a great deal more. Pulled to pieces and examined by unusual tests which curiosity or suspicion might suggest, it would doubtless reveal every secret of its construction. But that is not the way in which business is done in this country.

In that case [that is, the *Drummond* case], the contract expressly provided that quality and weight should be equal to certain numbered samples; and the Earl of Selborne, LC, at 288, said this about its construction:

> I think that the word "quality" as used in the contracts, ought to be restricted to those qualities which were patent or discoverable from such examination and inspection of the samples as, under the circumstances, the respondents might reasonably be expected to make.

In *James Drummond & Sons v. E.H. Van Ingen & Co.*, the House of Lords was able, by giving the sample clause a restricted meaning, to hold that its terms did not exclude an implied warranty covering latent defects. It is of the essence of this reasoning that a clause of this sort does not cover latent qualities or defects at all. In that case it was the seller's argument that was defeated by this construction. But, by the same token, it is not open to a buyer to submit a sample to an analysis unusual in the trade so as to reveal it in certain attributes or qualities hitherto unsuspected, and then to require, by virtue of the sample clause alone, that the bulk should contain the same qualities. If, for example, a buyer, to use the words of Lord Macnaghten, pulls a sample of cloth to pieces and discovers by means of analysis that the dye contains a certain proportion of a certain chemical, he cannot by virtue of the same clause require that the dye in the bulk shall contain the same proportion of the same chemical. He may, of course, complain that if it does not contain that proportion it would be unmerchantable or would fail to satisfy some other express or implied condition as to quality; but he cannot say that it breaks the condition that the bulk shall correspond with the sample in quality, for that condition is dealing only with apparent quality. There is abundant evidence in this case that in the shellac trade, as in most other trades, the method of examination usual in the trade is the visual method. As flow is not a quality detectable by the visual method, it follows that a defective flow cannot be a breach of the sample clause.

I am in complete agreement with that construction of Sect. 15(2)(a), and I am grateful for that passage, which I adopt and apply here. *James Drummond & Sons v. E.H. Van Ingen & Co., supra*, as Mr. Justice Devlin indicates, is the forerunner very largely of Sect. 15. Although it is before the Act and therefore perhaps not technically an authority, I should not feel emboldened to disregard it even if I wished to do so.

The extent to which a sample may be held to "speak" must depend on the contract and what is contemplated by the parties in regard to it. A sample may be analysed, X-rayed—tested to destruction. In the present case the parties were content, in accordance with the normal practice of the trade, to rely on a visual examination. Neither "PNP" nor, I think, any other chemical in general use for coagulation and preservation or either is detectable by visual examination, and therefore the presence or absence of the chemical cannot in itself be a breach of the sample clause. It is like the "flow" in the shellac case.

The buyers had in fact used the first delivery and found it satisfactory and that no doubt resulted in the repeat orders. The crude rubber had received treatment and processing by them and revealed no defect. Such circumstances would not enlarge the liability of the sellers, as the contract remained, as far as the compliance with a sample was concerned, a contract which called for compliance in those matters revealed by visual examination and those matters only.

In my judgment, the Appeal Committee (and also, indeed, the original arbitrators) were entitled to come to the decision that the goods delivered under the last contract were in accordance with the contractual terms, and I answer the question raised accordingly.

Award upheld.

NOTE

For a Canadian application of the rules in UK s. 15(2), see *Gordon Campbell Ltd. v. Metro Transit Operating Co.* (1983), 23 BLR 177 (BC).

PRIVATE SALES

Frey v. Sarvajc

[2000] SJ no. 382 (Sask. QB)

WILKINSON J: The plaintiffs seek damages for the cost of repairs ($6,695.25) and for the diminution in value ($4,400) in respect of a 1992 Dodge Dakota truck they purchased from the defendant by private sale on October 14, 1997. The plaintiffs claim the defendant failed to advise that the truck was previously a "total loss" vehicle that had been repaired using parts from three different vehicles and that the defendant represented the truck had never been in an accident. The defendant denied he was asked whether the truck was ever in an accident and relies on the express terms of the bill of sale which states the truck is sold "as is."

. . .

This was a transaction between private individuals. As a result, the plaintiffs gain no protection either from The Consumer Protection Act, SS 1996, c. C-30.1 or from the implied conditions as to quality and fitness under s. 16 of The Sale of Goods Act, RSS 1978, c. S-1. The defendant was not in the business of selling used vehicles.

The oft-quoted authority in transactions of this kind is *Bartlett v. Sidney Marcus Ltd.*, [1965] 2 All ER 753 at page 755 where Lord Denning MR stated:

> ... A buyer should realize that, when he buys a secondhand car, defects may appear sooner or later; and, in the absence of an express warranty, he has no redress. ...

Here, the truck was sold "as is" without express warranty of any kind. There have been cases holding that a sale "as is" does not relieve the vendor of liability where there has been fundamental breach of the contract, i.e. a breach that deprives the buyer of substantially the whole benefit they were to obtain under the agreement. See, for example, *Keefe v. Fort* (1978), 27 NSR (2d) 353, 89 DLR (3d) 275 (NS CA) where engine failure in a second-hand sports car shortly after purchase was held not to constitute fundamental breach, despite the fact that the repairs very nearly equalled the purchase price of the vehicle. See also *Schofield v. Gafco Enterprises Ltd.*, [1983] 4 WWR 135 (Alta CA). In contrast, in *Ronak v. Jones*, [1996] 3 WWR 283 (Alta. QB), the Court found fundamental breach where the vehicle sold was subsequently certified unfit for use on Alberta highways. The Court distinguished that from the so-called "lemon" cases and stated that neither party to the transaction had in their contemplation that the term of sale designating it "as is" would have application to a fundamental breach. In the case before me, the truck was not so completely unroadworthy that it can be said there was a fundamental breach going to the root of the contract or that deprived the buyers of substantially the whole benefit of what they bargained for.

If the buyers wish to obtain an express warranty that the vehicle has not been in an accident, it is incumbent upon them to include it in the bill of sale. In *Jim Gauthier Chevrolet Olds Cadillac Ltd. v. Saunders*, [1995] MJ no. 194 (QB), there was a representation in the bill of sale that "the vehicle has not been an insurance write-off." As it transpired, the vehicle was an amalgam of two other vehicles, one of which had been a write off. The seller was held liable for breach of the express warranty in the bill of sale.

Faced with the application of the principle "caveat emptor," the buyers argued latent structural defect, relying on principles drawn from cases on real property law. Those cases hold that if latent defects are actively concealed by the seller, or if a seller conducts himself in a manner calculated to mislead a purchaser or lull his suspicions with regard to a defect known to the seller, the rule of caveat emptor does not apply.

In *Rowsell v. Auto Source Inc.*, [2000] NJ no. 33 (Nfld. Prov. Ct.), there is a review of the application of these principles to a commercial transaction for the sale of a vehicle. The Court notes that the general rule is that the maxim caveat emptor prevails. What is expected of the buyer varies a great deal depending on the circumstances, with particular emphasis being placed on the relative bargaining positions of the parties to the transaction, their experience in matters of that nature, the type of goods they are dealing in and, especially, what opportunity was available to the buyer to inspect the goods before the deal was made.

In the *Rowsell*, supra, case, Handrigan PCJ refers to *Kinch v. Sharbell* (1999), 173 Nfld. & PEI R 336 (PEI SC) and the following statement of principle:

> Under common law, where there is no evidence of fraud, the purchaser of a product may not complain of defects in a product that the purchaser has had an opportunity to inspect before purchase. This is referred to as the maxim caveat emptor. It is expected that if the vendor has not been fraudulent in the sale of the product, it is the responsibility of the purchaser to have obtained a warranty on the item before agreeing to buy it. The definition attributed to caveat emptor in *Black's Law Dictionary* is "let the buyer beware."

He turns to the question of how fraud impacts on the rule of caveat emptor, quoting from the Ontario Court of Appeal decision in *McGrath v. MacLean* (1979), 95 DLR (3d) 144 (Ont. CA) at page 150 as follows:

> ... Fraud can be a rather elastic conception, and there are cases which show a tendency to find fraud when there has been concealment by the vendor of latent defects. ... On the other hand, a latent defect of quality ... which is either unknown to the vendor or such as not to make him chargeable with concealment or reckless disregard of its truth or falsity will not support any claim of redress by the purchaser.

The application of these principles to the sale of used cars is summarized in the comments of Gow J in *Rushak v. Henneken*, [1986] BCJ no. 3072 (SC) where he states:

> At a common law in the absence of a fiduciary or analogous relationship, there is not as between negotiating parties any duty of disclosure. Almost always the seller of a used car knows of its defects, or at least some of them, but he is not under any duty to disclose them to a potential buyer, unless there has been on his part active concealment, that is, he has done something to the car with intent to prevent the defect being discovered. *Leeson v. Darlow*, [1926] 4 DLR 415 at p. 432; *Allen v. McCutcheon* (1979), 10 BCLR 149. *Sorensen v. Kaye Holdings Ltd.* (1979), 14 BCLR 204 per Lambert, JA at p. 235. The common law rule is caveat emptor. The underlying philosophy of the law of contract is that "a party is expected to look out for himself, and make his own bargains. If he has done foolishly, this is his own fault and he is left to his own devices."

The distinction between patent and latent defects is described in *Halsbury's Laws of England* (3d ed.) Vol. 34, page 211, para. 353 as follows:

> Defects of quality may be either patent or latent. Patent defects are such as are discoverable by inspection and ordinary vigilance on the part of a purchaser; latent defects are

such as would not be revealed by any inquiry which a purchaser is in a position to make before entering into the contract for purchase. As regards patent defects, the vendor is not bound to call attention to them; the rule is caveat emptor; a purchaser should make inspection and inquiry as to that which he is proposing to buy.

Relying on these authorities, the Court in *Rowsell* held that the defects in that case were of the latent variety, consisting of damage to the frame cleverly hidden between the veneer of repairs and discoverable only by extensive testing and probing. The seller was found in any event to have no knowledge of the condition of the vehicle and therefore the principle of caveat emptor applied.

The facts of the case before me are different. The fact that the serial numbers for the engine and frame did not match were readily discoverable on inspection and were discovered by Auto Clearing on examining the engine. The facts are distinguishable from *Rowsell* where the veneer of the vehicle concealed the damage. Likewise, the facts are different from *Thomas v. Blackwell*, [1999] SJ no. 769 (QB) (a real property case relied on by the plaintiffs), where the structural defects in a wall were concealed by the interior wood panelling and decorative parging. Dismantling a wall is not a reasonable or ordinary inspection on the part of a buyer of a home. Stripping the veneer off a vehicle is not a reasonable or ordinary inspection on the part of a prospective purchaser. Here, mismatched serial numbers were determinable on visual inspection by a mechanic. An inspection by a mechanic is a matter of ordinary vigilance on the part of many purchasers. It is an inquiry the purchasers here were in a position to make and there is no indication the seller obstructed them from doing so. I conclude the defects, as such, were patent and discoverable by inspection and ordinary vigilance on the part of the purchasers. Accordingly the rule of *caveat emptor* applies.

NOTES AND QUESTIONS

1) According to Wilkinson J, the defects were patent in the sense that the mismatched serial numbers should have alerted the plaintiffs to the fact that the engine had been replaced. However, the court ended up finding in the plaintiffs' favour on a second ground, namely misrepresentation. The truck's odometer reading was 58,000 kilometres. Wilkinson J said that "to advertise the truck as a 1992 Dodge Dakota with 58,000 kilometres as though it were an entire homogenous unit, all of whose parts had been exposed to the same use (58,000 kilometres), was misleading." The plaintiffs were awarded damages for breach of warranty on this basis. For a remarkably similar Australian case, see *Treloar v. Ivory* (1991), ASC s. 56-076 (Sup. Ct of West. Aust.).

2) In the case of a private sale, the default rule for defective goods (quality and fitness) is *caveat emptor*. In the case of a dealer sale, the statutory implied terms of quality and fitness apply, and this means the default rule is reversed. Why shouldn't the default rule be the same for both cases?

3) What is the default rule for correspondence with description in the case of a private sale? (*Frey v. Sarvajc* is similar to *Beale v. Taylor*, chapter 6, *supra*, on this point). What is the default rule in the case of a dealer sale? What is the rationale?

4) Consider the following case:

S owns a boat. She places it with A, a boat dealer, to sell on her behalf. A sells the boat to B. B does not know that A is S's agent (ie., S is an undisclosed principal). The boat breaks down. Can B sue S for breach of the implied condition of quality or fitness?

The implied conditions of quality and fitness do not cover private sales. Assuming S herself is not a boat dealer, the sale to B is a private sale. It makes no difference that A is a dealer, because A is only an intermediary. S, not A, is the seller.

The UK SGA was amended in 1973 to address cases like this. The amendment reads as follows:

> The preceding provisions of this section [merchantable quality and fitness for purpose] apply to a sale by a person who in the course of a business is acting as agent for another as they apply to a sale by a principal in the course of a business, except where that other is not selling in the course of a business and either the buyer knows that fact or reasonable steps are taken to bring it to the notice of the buyer before the contract is made

(Sale of Goods Act 1979, s. 14(5)).

In the circumstances it refers to, the provision could be read as meaning that A, not S, is liable to B. However, in *Boyter v. Thomson*, [1995] 2 AC 628, the House of Lords rejected this construction. The court said that the provision "is applicable to any sale by an agent on behalf of a principal disclosed or undisclosed, where circumstances giving rise to the exception do not exist. When the subsection applies, the normal common law rules of principal and agent also apply." In other words, if S is a disclosed principal, B can sue S and if S is an undisclosed principal B can sue either A or S.

The OLRC Sales Report recommended against the adoption of a similar provision in Ontario. It said (at 210):

> It appears to us that the equities are fairly evenly divided as between the private seller and the buyer, and that an insufficient case has been made out for changing the existing law. Let us suppose, for example, that a dealer who holds goods on consignment from a non-merchant seller fails to disclose his agency capacity to the buyer. Although, under existing law, the buyer would appear to be unable to sue the undisclosed principal for breach of the warranties of merchantability or fitness, he would still have his remedy against the agent. It would seem less obvious that the principal would have a right of indemnity against the agent for failure to disclose his agency capacity, if the U.K. amendment were adopted, unless a provision to this effect were also added. Again, it would not occur to the average principal that he must instruct his agent to be sure to disclose not only his status as agent, but also the fact that he is acting for a private seller. Moreover, if he did give such instructions, it is not clear whether they would satisfy the requirements of section 14(5) of the U.K. Act that "reasonable steps" must be taken to bring the facts to the notice of the buyer before the contract is made. In the result, the U.K. amendment raises as many difficulties as it purports to resolve.

Do you agree?

5) Compare the following cases:

a) S offers a car for private sale. The bodywork is rusted. S paints over the rust-affected areas. B buys the car, but does not discover the defect until later.

b) S offers a car for private sale. The bodywork is rusted. A previous owner has painted over the rust-affected areas. S knows this, but does not tell B. B buys the car, but does not discover the defect until later.

c) S, a dealer, offers a car for sale. The bodywork is rusted. A previous owner has painted over the rust-affected areas. S is unaware of this. B buys the car, but does not discover the defect until later.

In which, if any, of these cases will B have a claim against S? Do the legal distinctions make any sense? Consider the following explanation.

It is customary to think of productive facts in terms of good news (the discovery that an asset has positive attributes that enhance its social value). However, bad news (the discovery that an asset has negative attributes, or defects, that lower its social value) may also be productive because the timely revelation of bad news may help to avert further loss. For example, if a house is infested with termites, the damage will get worse until someone discovers the problem and does something about it.

A disclosure rule is unlikely to discourage property owners (sellers) from searching out bad news concerning their assets. A home-owner might pay a pest exterminator to check periodically for termites, but typically home-owners conduct investigations of this sort in order to protect their own investments ... . Their purpose is not to gain an advantage over intending purchasers. Therefore, in most cases a home-owner will have an adequate incentive to check for termites, even if the law requires disclosure of the results. In any event, many termite infestations are discovered without deliberate search, but simply by living in the house—something the home-owner will generally do whether disclosure is required or not. Similarly, it is unlikely that a rule requiring disclosure of defects would discourage retailers from developing expertise regarding the quality and attributes of the products they stock. This kind of knowledge carries with it numerous advantages. For example, it enables a retailer to be more efficient in purchasing [stock], and it reduces the likelihood of the retailer failing to identify any special advantage the goods enjoy (and therefore underselling them). A disclosure rule is unlikely to offset these influences ... . Accordingly [in product defect cases] the need for preservation of incentives to search is not a reason for permitting non-disclosure. On the contrary, there are good reasons for requiring disclosure. Where the undisclosed defect is of a degenerative nature (such as termite infestation in a house, or rust in the body of a motor vehicle), repairs should be carried out as soon as possible. A non-disclosure rule confronts the seller with the incentive to do nothing, so as to transfer the repair costs to the buyer. In the meantime, however, the defect will get worse. By contrast, a rule requiring disclosure removes the disincentive to taking early remedial action ... .

In the case of a non-degenerative defect, these considerations do not arise so that the governing economic consideration lies with the prevention of mistakes. In this connection, the main consideration is the identity of the lowest-cost information gatherer. This is likely to vary depending on the circumstances—in particular, whether the defect is patent or latent ... . When the defect is a patent one and the seller knows that the buyer has not detected it, then a rule requiring disclosure is likely to be economically justified: it is cheaper for the seller to point out the buyer's oversight than it is for the buyer to rectify the situation. On the other hand, if the seller is not aware of the buyer's error, and has no reason to know of it, a disclosure rule would be uneconomical because it is likely to result in sellers telling buyers all sorts of things they already know. Communications of this kind needlessly increase transactions costs ... . Furthermore, a blanket disclosure requirement would significantly increase the risks of transacting. It would provide a buyer who had spotted a better deal with a basis for rescission, so facilitating opportunistic behaviour and, in effect, converting the contract into an option ... .

Where the defect is a latent one, and the seller is aware of it but the buyer is not, disclosure should be required. A rule favouring the seller in these circumstances might result in excessive transactions costs—where, for instance, a succession of prospective buyers hire mechanics to inspect a car before purchase ... . Where neither party is aware of the defect, it may still be efficient to allocate responsibility to the seller, on the basis that, of the two parties, the seller is likely to be better placed to discover the defect more cheaply ... . This is most likely to be true where:

- the property is in the seller's possession, because a seller in possession will usually have better opportunities than the buyer for discovering the defect; or
- the seller is a dealer, because the expertise acquired by dealers in relation to the goods they stock will often give them a comparative advantage over buyers in the detection of faults prior to purchase.

Where the seller is a dealer, sale of goods law conforms to the pattern just described. The sale of goods by a dealer is subject to statutory implied terms relating to quality and fitness for purpose. These function as a surrogate for disclosure requirements ... . However, such laws go further than the normal disclosure rule by imposing liability regardless of whether the dealer knows of the defect. The statutory implied terms do not expressly discriminate between patent and latent defects, but they do indirectly limit the seller's liability in the case of patent defects [consider, for example, the operation of the examination proviso in relation to the implied condition of merchantable quality, and the operation of the reliance requirement in relation to the implied condition of fitness for purpose]. Private sales (where the seller is not a dealer) are for the most part not subject to the statutory implied terms, and the general rule at common law is *caveat emptor*. A *caveat emptor* rule is difficult to justify economically in the case of:

- degenerative defects; and
- non-degenerative defects of which, to the seller's knowledge, the buyer is ignorant.

On the other hand, the *caveat emptor* rule will be displaced if the court can imply a misrepresentation arising out of the seller's conduct, and silence in either of these two circumstances is especially likely to attract the implied misrepresentation doctrine.

(Anthony Duggan, Michael Bryan, and Frances Hanks, *Contractual Non-Disclosure: An Applied Study in Modern Contract Theory* (Melbourne, Australia: Longman Professional, 1994), at 157-60.) For additional reading, see Anthony T. Kronman, "Mistake, Disclosure, Information and the Law of Contracts" (1978), 7 *J Legal Studies* 1; Robert Cooter and Thomas Ulen, *Law and Economics* (Glenview, Illinois: Scott Foresman & Co., 1988), at 259-65.

PUBLIC CONTROL OF FOOD, DRUGS AND HAZARDOUS PRODUCTS

Foods and Drugs

Note on the History of Food and Drug Legislation in Canada[1]

The need for strict food and drug laws and their enforcement has become painfully apparent in the post-war period in the light of the thalidomide tragedy and the discovery or apprehension of carcinogenic properties in food additives, artificial sweeteners, synthetic growth hormones and other products of the modern laboratory. The need for watchfulness has been accentuated by the rapid strides of food technology and the pharmacological sciences and by the proliferation of items on the typical supermarket and drugstore shelves.

It is therefore surprising to find that until a hundred years ago no such protective legislation existed in Canada at all. In England it took a number of scandals, such as the case of the adulteration of lozenges with arsenic instead of the usual plaster of Paris, resulting in more than fifteen deaths and affecting more than 400 people, to prod the British Parliament into action. The first British Act to deal with this danger to public health was adopted in 1860. What might be considered as the first real food and drug legislation in Canada was passed in 1874 (SC 1874, c. 8), more than twenty-five years before similar legislation was enacted by the US Congress. These first efforts were mainly directed at the sale of adulterated liquor; protection of the public was of secondary importance. The main objectives of the Canadian Act were the imposition of licensing fees on the compounders of spirits and the imposition of various duties on these same individuals. Significantly, the legislation was adopted as an amendment to the Internal Revenue Act.

In 1884 (SC 1884, c. 34) the legislation was removed from the Internal Revenue Act and put into a separate Act, best known as the Adulteration Act. That Act, for the first time, provided an extensive definition of the term "adulterated." What has turned out to be one of the most important provisions of what is now known as the Food and Drugs Act was introduced in 1890 (SC 1890, c. 26)—the provisions authorizing the government to prescribe standards for foodstuffs. The first such standards were promulgated in 1910 and today they govern, *inter alia*, such matters as food enrichment, food additives and vitamins, and cover many hundreds of items.

Amendments in 1920 (SC 1920, c. 27) provided for an even more detailed definition of the terms "adulterated food" and "adulterated drugs." Still more important was the provision dealing with "misbranding," that is, the mislabelling of products. This provision is still extremely important today. The Act was again amended in 1934 (SC 1934, c. 54) to prohibit the sale of products labelled or advertised as remedies for a wide variety of illnesses (set out in Schedule A). In 1939 (SC 1939, c. 3), this power of prohibition was extended to therapeutic devices and cosmetics.

In the post-war period there have been several major amendments. An amendment in 1961 (SC 1960-61, c. 37) permitted the authorities to deal with the possession of and

---

1 Professor Ziegel is particularly indebted to Eric Gertner and Terry Burgoyne, two former students of his, for researching and, to a substantial extent, preparing the original version of this note. Once again, for reasons of space, the materials in this section have been condensed (albeit in a modestly updated form) and readers are referred to the first edition, at 306-22, for the full text of the original materials. [eds.]

trafficking in certain drugs, known as "controlled drugs" (now set out in Schedule G), which may be considered to be dangerous. Similar legislation was enacted a few years later with respect to "restricted drugs" (set out in Schedule H). In 1969 (SC 1968-69, c. 41), Parliament also empowered the government to regulate or prohibit the importation of any drug manufactured outside Canada and the distribution, sale and possession for sale of any such drug.

Besides the substantive provisions outlined above, the present Act (RSC 1985, c. F-27) provides for administration and enforcement of the provisions of the Act by inspectors appointed by the government. An inspector is given substantial powers by s. 22 of the Act, including the right to "enter any place where on reasonable grounds he believes any article to which this Act or its regulations apply is manufactured, prepared, preserved, packaged or stored" (s. 23(1)). In addition, the Act makes it an offence to obstruct an inspector in the carrying out of his or her duties (s. 24(1)) or knowingly to make any false or misleading statement (s. 24(1)).

By far the most important section of the Act is s. 30, which sets out the regulatory powers of the government. This allows the government to give flesh to the skeletal bones of the Act, including the power to declare any food or drug adulterated (s. 30(1)(a)), the power to act with respect to labelling and packaging to prevent the consumer or purchaser from being deceived or misled as to its design, construction, performance, intended use, quantity, character, value, composition, merit or safety, or to prevent injury to the health of the consumer or purchaser" (s. 30(1)(b)) and the power to prescribe standards of composition, strength, potency, purity, quality or other property of any article, drug, cosmetic or device (s. 30(1)(c)). Anyone found to be in contravention of the Act or its regulations is guilty of an offence and liable to a fine or imprisonment or both (ss. 31 and 31.1).

An example of the exercise of the regulatory power for the protection and safety of the public are those regulations dealing with the introduction of new drugs. Before new drugs may be sold or even advertised for sale, the manufacturer must provide the Minister with a "new drug submission," which must include details of the tests to be applied to control the potency, purity, stability and safety of the new drug, detailed reports of the tests made to establish the safety of the new drug for the purpose and under the conditions of use recommended, and substantial evidence of its clinical effectiveness. If satisfied that the submission meets the requirements of Reg. C.08.002(2) the Minister will issue a notice of compliance. However, the notice may be suspended where the Minister believes it is necessary to do so in the interests of public health because, for instance, new evidence reveals that the drug is not safe for the use represented, or because upon the basis of new information there is a lack of substantial evidence that the drug will have the effect represented or because it has been found that the labelling of the drug is false, misleading or incomplete. The extensive regulations under the Act can be found at CRC 1978, c. 869-871.

Before the Second World War the constitutionality of the Food and Drugs Act was affirmed on two occasions as a proper exercise of the criminal law power, s. 91(27) of the BNA Act, of the federal government. See *Standard Sausage Co. v. Lee*, [1934] 1 DLR 706 (BCCA) and *R v. Goldsmid* (1932), 45 BCR 435. The constitutionality of the drug provisions were reaffirmed in *R v. Wetmore* (1983), 2 DLR (4th) 577 (SCC), but the so-called "recipe" provisions affecting the nomenclature of food products were ruled unconstitutional in the *Labatt Breweries* case, [1980] 1 SCR 915. See further, *R v. Hydro-Quebec*, [1997] 3 SCR 213 which discusses *Wetmore* and other cases. See also the notes in chapter 4 (under "Public Law Aspects of False Advertising") and Ziegel, "The Food and Drugs Act ...," *The Can. Consumer*, October 1980, at 15. As in the case of the false advertising provisions of the Competition Act, Charter challenges may also be expected to be launched against important sections of the Food and Drugs Act.

Hazardous Products

Surprising as it may seem, until the enactment of the Hazardous Products Act (HPA) in 1969 (SC 1968-69, c. 42; RSC 1985, c. H-3, as am.), there was no general federal legislation regulating the importation or sale of dangerous household products not intended for human consumption or application to the human body, or prohibiting the sale of such products altogether. The HPA was designed to fill this important gap. Similar legislation has been adopted in other Western countries, including the United Kingdom and the United States of America. In the United States, Congress adopted the Consumer Products Safety Act (CPSA) in 1972.

The heart of the HPA lies in ss. 4, 5, and 6. Section 4 provides that no person shall advertise, sell, or import into Canada a hazardous product included in Part I of the Schedule. A similar prohibition applies to hazardous products included in Part II of the Schedule "except as authorized by the regulations."

Pursuant to s. 5, the Governor General in Council may, *inter alia*, make regulations:

> (a) authorizing the advertising, sale or importation of any restricted product and prescribing the circumstances and conditions under which and the persons by whom the restricted product may be advertised, sold or imported;
>
> (b) prescribing the procedures to be followed by a board of review established pursuant to section 9 in conducting an inquiry; and
>
> (c) generally for carrying out the purposes and provisions of this Part.

Pursuant to s. 6(1),

> 6.(1) The Governor in Council may, by order, amend Part I or Part II of Schedule I by adding thereto
>
> (a) any product, material or substance that is or contains a poisonous, toxic, flammable, explosive, corrosive, infectious, oxidizing or reactive product, material or substance or other product, material or substance of a similar nature that the Governor in Council is satisfied is or is likely to be a danger to the health or safety of the public; or
>
> (b) any product designed for household, garden or personal use, for use in sports or recreational activities, as life-saving equipment or as a toy, plaything or equipment for use by children that the Governor of Canada is satisfied is or is likely to be a danger to the health or safety of the public by reason of its design, construction or contents.

Pursuant to s. 6(2),

> The Governor in Council may, by order, amend Part I or II of Schedule 1 by deleting therefrom any product, material or substance if the Governor in Council is satisfied that the inclusion of the product, material or substance in that Part is no longer necessary.

Section 21 provides for the appointment of inspectors and analysts; ss. 22 to 26 confer powers of search, seizure, and forfeiture of products that are in violation of the Act or its regulations. Under ss. 8 and 9, where a product or substance is added to Part I or Part II, any manufacturer or distributor of that product or substance, or any person having the product in his possession for sale, may request that the order be referred to a board of review (an ad hoc body established by the Minister of Health), which is then obliged to submit a report to the Minister together with its recommendations. The constitutionality of the HPA rests on the same basis as the Food and Drugs Act: *R v. Hydro-Quebec*, above.

The Canadian Act raises a substantial number of legal and practical problems which have assumed increasing importance in the light of well-publicized incidents such as lead soldering in electric kettles and large pop bottles that explode upon impact. Some of the more important questions are the following:

1) What is the criterion for determining whether a product is hazardous? Should cost-benefit analysis play a role in such a determination?

2) Should there be a more systematic effort to determine the safety of the major household items in current use?

3) Should manufacturers be under statutory obligation to notify the Department of any dangers associated with their product which come to their attention, or are there sufficient private law incentives on manufacturers to dispense with such a regulatory requirement?

4) When a product is put on the prohibited list, prohibiting the further sale of the product, what is the position of distributors, retailers, and consumers who have previously purchased the item and still have it in their possession? Should the manufacturer be obliged to accept the goods back and make an appropriate refund of all or part of the purchase price? Should there be any deduction for use? (*Cf.* the U.S. Consumer Product Safety Act, ss. 12 and 15, which makes provisions for such civil remedies.) Does existing sales law already take care of the problem and, if so, how?

5) Should a consumer be entitled to petition to have a product placed on the restricted list and to have the petition referred to the Board of Review?

General References (Canadian and US): *Canadian Product Safety Guide*, CCH Canadian Ltd., 2 vols.; Kimble, *Federal Consumer Product Safety Act* (West, 1975); J.C. Shaul and M.J. Trebilcock, "The Administration of the Federal Hazardous Products Act" (1982-83), 7 *CBLJ* 2.

CHAPTER NINE

Manufacturer's Liability for Defective Goods: The Privity Problem

INTRODUCTION

Since the Sale of Goods Act is based on contractual relationships, it is only concerned with the warranty claims of a buyer against the person from whom he bought the goods. The Act has nothing to say about the buyer's rights against prior parties in the distribution chain and in particular it is silent about the buyer's rights against the manufacturer of the goods where the manufacturer is not the immediate seller.

We have previously encountered the problem in chapter 5 in the context of a manufacturer's liability for express warranties. We saw there how the courts in England, Canada and the United States have surmounted the privity problem by relying on theories of collateral contracts (Anglo-Canadian courts) or on the hybrid origins of the action for breach of warranty (US courts). A much more difficult question, both conceptually and in terms of public policy, is whether the walls of privity should be breached to hold the manufacturer liable in damages to the ultimate buyer for breach of implied statutory warranties resulting only in economic loss.

As will be seen, with the notable exceptions of the Supreme Court of Canada's decision in the *Kravitz* case, a civil law decision, and the Supreme Court's decision in *Winnipeg Condominium Corp. No. 36 v. Bird Construction Co. Ltd.* (1995), 121 DLR (4th) 193, both discussed in this chapter, the wall is still firmly in place in Canada but somewhat less so in the United States. In both countries, some important inroads, at least for consumer goods and agricultural machinery, have been made by legislation. In reading the materials in the present chapter the student is urged to bear in mind the important distinctions between consumer and non-consumer goods, and between defective goods causing injury to persons or other property, and defective goods only resulting in economic loss to the buyer.

OLRC Report on Consumer Warranties

(1972), at 65-68

a. *Introduction*

It has often been remarked that in the modern marketing milieu it is the manufacturer who plays the dominant role. It is he who is responsible for putting the goods into the stream of commerce and, in most cases, of creating the consumer demand for them by continuous advertising. The retailer is little more than a way station. It is the manufacturer who endows the goods with their characteristics and it is he who determines the type of materials and components that shall be used and who establishes the quality control mechanism. It is also he who determines what express guarantees shall be given to the consumer and who is responsible for the availability of spare parts and the adequacy of servicing facilities. Almost all the consumer's knowledge about the goods is derived from the labels or markings attached to the goods or the sales literature that accompanies them—and these too originate from the manufacturer.

These are not the only factors that strongly militate in favour of holding the manufacturer responsible for breach of any express warranties and the warranties implied under The Sale of Goods Act. The present Anglo-Canadian law involves circuity of actions and an unnecessary multiplication of costs and proceedings. Typically the buyer sues the retailer who then joins the wholesale distributor or importer, and they in turn will bring in the manufacturer. If the retailer is insolvent or has otherwise closed his business for any reason, the consumer may even be able to initiate an action. If the consumer has moved a substantial distance from the original place of purchase or to another province, he will be faced with new procedural hurdles. If the cause of the breakdown of the goods is disputed, the buyer will not have the right to obtain discovery of documents from the manufacturer or to examine his officers, although the manufacturer rather than the retailer is likely to be in possession of all the pertinent facts.

The retailer's lot is also an unhappy one. Ontario law has no procedural rule comparable to the American device of "vouching over" and the retailer is forced to go to the expense and trouble of formally joining the person next in the distributive link as a third party. If the consumer for some reason has delayed his action against the retailer, the retailer may find that the prescriptive period has lapsed, and that it is too late for him to issue a third party notice.

Despite these weighty reasons, Anglo-Canadian law has made little progress in permitting the consumer to proceed directly against the manufacturer. The doctrine of privity still remains a most formidable barrier. For practical purposes there appear to be very few exceptions to the rule. The rule in *Donoghue v. Stevenson*, [1932] AC 562 does not apply to actions in negligence for pure economic losses. It is conceivable that the consumer may have an action against the manufacturer for negligent misstatements of fact under the *Hedley Byrne* doctrine, but such an action would place a very heavy onus on the plaintiff. A more promising avenue would be via the concept of "collateral warranties" or "collateral contract." It is now well established that a manufacturer may be liable for breach of an express warranty if the warranty is intended to induce the buyer to order the manufacturer's product from another person. The English courts have applied the doctrine in a wide variety of situations but we have not been able to find a reported case in which the Anglo-Canadian courts have applied it to a consumer transaction.[1]

In principle, however, there appears to be no reason why it should not apply and, in particular, why it should not apply to a manufacturer's express guarantee. But even allowing for this possibility, the consumer still faces several major difficulties. In the first place, the doctrine only applies to express representations. Second, the consumer must show that the representation was intended to have contractual force and, third, that he saw or knew of the representation *before* making his purchase and relied on it—that is, intended to accept the offer implicit in the representation. It is apparent that the doctrine of collateral warranty is not the full answer to the practical problems faced by the consumer.

In the light of the foregoing considerations the Commission recommends that the proposed Act contain a clearly stated statutory rule holding a manufacturer liable for breach of any express representations, and also deeming him to have given the same implied warranties as are attributed to the immediate seller under our sales law. For the purpose of this rule, the doctrine of privity of contract should be abolished in warranty claims by a buyer against the manufacturer of the goods.

b. *Canadian Precedents*

The change which we propose in Ontario law is not novel in Canada. At the turn of the century much new farming machinery was being introduced in the prairie provinces. The machinery did not always work satisfactorily and there was also widespread concern about the use of disclaimer clauses. To meet these difficulties, remedial legislation was adopted in Alberta as early as 1913[2] and was copied during the next six years by Saskatchewan and Manitoba. Similar legislation was adopted in Prince Edward Island at a much later date. Today, all of these acts imply various warranties in favour of the retail buyer of the equipment and all of them provide, in slightly varying language, that the manufacturer or provincial distributor as well as the dealer "are liable to the purchaser to observe, keep and perform the warranties" and that the purchaser "may maintain an action against any such manufacturer or general provincial distributor, as well as against the vendor, or against any one or more of them, for any breach of any of these warranties."[3] So far as we have been able to ascertain, these provisions, which clearly breach the walls of privity, have not created any particular difficulties.

---

1 Note that the OLRC Report was published in 1972; *Murray v. Sperry Rand, supra*, chapter 4, was decided in 1979, although it too was not a consumer case.

2 The Farm Implements Act, SA 1913, c. 15.

3 The Agricultural Implements Act, 1968, SS 1968, c. 1, as am., s. 24.

c. *American Developments*

American developments provide another and still more important source of precedents. In discussing the developments it is important to distinguish between two separate problems, first, the liability of the manufacturer for defective goods that cause personal injuries or physical damage to the property of the buyer or some other person and, second, the liability of the manufacturer for defective goods that only cause economic losses. We are primarily concerned with the second problem, though, for reasons stated later in this chapter, the two problems interact closely.

As early as 1933 the Supreme Court of Washington held the Ford Motor Company liable for breach of an express warranty that the windshield on its passenger cars was shatter-proof.[4] This precedent was followed in another landmark decision, *Randy Knitwear Inc. v. American Cyanamid Co.*,[5] in which the New York Court of Appeals held a manufacturer of chemical resins liable for a false representation that fabrics treated with the resin were shrink-proof. In both these and other cases technical requirements of privity were ignored and liability was based on some other ground. One of the grounds was the hybrid nature of the action for breach of warranty, which was said to sound both in contract and in tort. The courts did not rely on the English doctrine of collateral contracts.

An important turning point in the development of this branch of American law occurred in *Henningsen v. Bloomfield Motors* (1960), 161 A.2d 69. In this historic decision the New Jersey Supreme Court held the Chrysler Corporation strictly responsible for a defect in one of its cars which caused a serious accident resulting in injuries to the buyer's wife and the total loss of the vehicle. Liability was predicated upon a theory of implied warranties running with the vehicle from the manufacturer to the ultimate buyer or user, and again any requirement of privity of contract was expressly rejected. In *Greenman v. Yuba Power Products, Inc.* (1963), 377 P.2d 897, the California Supreme Court abandoned the rationale of implied warranties as fictitious and held that the manufacturer's liability was imposed as a rule of public policy and was tortious in character. Many other courts have since followed this characterization.

This issue which still remains unresolved is whether the theory of strict tortious liability also applies to defects causing only economic loss. In *Santor v. A. & M. Karagheusian Inc.* (1965), 207 A.2d 305, another New Jersey decision, the court held that it did, but in *Seely v. White Motor Co.* (1965), 403 P.2d 145, the California Supreme Court rejected the merger and held that sales law principles (including particularly Article 2 of the Uniform Commercial Code) continued to govern claims for economic losses. Subsequent courts have been divided in their approach, as have the authors of numerous law review articles. We shall return to this conflict.

---

4 *Baxter v. Ford Motor Co.* (1933), 12 P.2d 409, 15 P.2d 1188, 88 ALR 521.

5 (1962), 181 NE 2d 399 (NYCA). This was said to be based on the history of the action for breach of warranty. Later American decisions base their reasoning squarely on grounds of public policy.

There have also been some developments at the legislative level. Article 2-318 of the 1962 official text of the Uniform Commercial Code provided that:

> A seller's warranty whether express or implied to any natural person who is in the family or household of his buyer or who is a guest in his home if it is reasonable to expect that such person may use, consume or be affected by the goods and who is injured in person by breach of the warranty. A seller may not exclude or limit the operations of this section.

It was widely felt that this version was too restrictive and that it was out of step with the developing case law. The disapproval was reflected in unauthorized versions of the section adopted by a substantial number of Code states. With a view to discouraging the further proliferation of non-uniform versions the sponsors of the Code promulgated a revised Article 2-318 in 1966. This contains three alternatives, Alternatives A, B and C. Alternative A corresponds to the previous version of the section. Alternatives B and C read as follows.

Alternative B
A seller's warranty whether express or implied extends to any natural person who may reasonably be expected to use, consume or be affected by the goods and who is injured in person by breach of the warranty. A seller may not exclude or limit the operation of this section.

Alternative C
A seller's warranty whether express or implied extends to any person who may reasonably be expected to use, consume or be affected by the goods and who is injured by breach of the warranty. A seller may not exclude or limit the operation of this section with respect to injury to the person of an individual to whom the warranty extends.

These alternatives go considerably beyond Alternative A. Alternative B extends the seller's express or implied warranties to *any* natural person who may reasonably be expected to use, consume or be affected by the goods. Unlike his counterpart in Alternative A, the beneficiary is not restricted to a member of the buyer's family or household or to a guest—a restriction that in most cases would make Alternative A inapplicable against the manufacturer. On the other hand, Alternative B is still limited to claims arising out of personal injuries. A critical difference between Alternative B and C is that Alternative C applies, it seems, to any injury. However, it is not clear whether a claim solely for economic losses is deemed to be an "injury."

It seems clear that the seller contemplated in Alternatives B and C includes the manufacturer of the goods if the other conditions of the provisions are satisfied. A number of Congressional bills on product warranties that have been introduced in recent years would have imposed liability on a manufacturer towards a consumer buyer for breach of the implied warranties. So far none of them has been enacted. More progress has been made at the state level, and several state acts now impose such liability. One of them is the Song-Beverley Consumer Warranty Act, which was adopted in California in 1970.

NOTE

The OLRC Report on Consumer Warranties was written in 1972. There have been important developments since then in the theoretical literature on products liability law, particularly from the law and economics perspective. The issue that has most interested law and economics scholars is the choice between strict liability and negligence liability for product defects.

Under a negligence regime, the manufacturer is only liable if there were cost-justified precautions it could have taken to avoid the loss. A cost-justified precaution is a precaution the cost of which is less than the amount of the loss the defect causes, discounted by the probability of the loss occurring. This is a particular application of Judge Learned Hand's negligence formula: *United States v. Carroll Towing Co.*, 159 F.2d 169 at 173 (2d Cir. 1947). The theory is that by holding a manufacturer liable in negligence, the court creates an incentive for manufacturers in future to take cost-justified precautions against product defects. The result will not be to eliminate defects altogether, but to reduce them to the point where any further expenditure on product improvements would be uneconomical. Sometimes, the consumer may be able to take precautions more cheaply than the manufacturer. Assume M manufactures kitchen knives. There is a 0.1% chance of the knife causing injury to the user. The cost of an injury if it occurs is $2000. Therefore the expected loss is $2.00. M could reduce this cost to $1.50 by fitting a guard to each knife at a cost of 25 cents per unit. But consumers could achieve the same saving at a cost of only 10 cents per unit by taking basic precautions when using the knife. In this case, the precautions open to both the manufacturer and the consumer are both cost-effective relative to the expected loss, but the manufacturer's precaution costs are higher than the consumer's. The economical solution is for the consumer to take precautions. The function of the contributory negligence defence is to create an incentive for this to happen. It is true that, in many cases, investment in goodwill will act as a sufficient incentive for the manufacturer to take care, while concern for personal health, safety, and economic well-being will motivate the consumer to be careful. However, economists believe that deterrence considerations remain important at the margin.

Note that the economic justification for negligence liability assumes that consumers systematically underestimate the risk of product defects. If consumers were fully informed, there would be no need for a negligence rule because then the parties would bargain their own way to the most economic outcome. The consumer would pay the manufacturer a premium up to the amount of the expected loss saving in exchange for the precaution. This is the Coase theorem at work. The assumption of consumer-manufacturer information asymmetry is made in nearly all the law and economics literature on product liability, but it has not gone unchallenged. See, for example, Alan Schwartz, "Proposals for Product Liability Reform: A Theoretical Synthesis" (1988), 97 *Yale LJ* 353, at 374-84.

Under a strict liability regime, the manufacturer is liable for product-related losses whether there were cost-justified precautions open to it or not. The difference between negligence and strict liability is that under negligence the consumer bears the risk of "unavoidable" losses, whereas under strict liability the manufacturer bears the risk. Strict liability impounds the full cost of defects in the explicit price of the product, whereas under negligence the cost of "unavoidable" losses will not be accounted for. It is part of the implicit price that the consumer should factor in before deciding to buy. However, if it is right to assume that consumers systematically underestimate the risk of product defects, then it is likely that they will fail to make the correct price adjustment. This means that the product will seem cheaper to them than it actually is, and they will buy more of the product than is warranted by its true cost. The more of a product consumers purchase, the higher the incidence of defect-related losses will be. In other words, defect related-losses are a function not only of the level of care manufacturers and consumers take, but also of product activity level (how much of the product is bought and used). The standard economic justification for strict liability is that it makes prices reflect all defect-related losses and this will reduce the amount of the product purchased to an efficient level. It is widely agreed that strict manufacturer liability should be coupled with a contributory negligence defence to induce consumers to take whatever cost-justified precautions against loss that may be open to them: For an accessible account of the economic arguments, see A. Mitchell Polinsky, *An Introduction to Law and Economics*, 2nd ed. (1989), chapter 11.

Posner says that "the kind of product failures against which manufacturers expressly warrant their products are frequent and hence familiar to consumers and therefore enter into their buying decisions. But product failures that cause serious personal injuries are extremely rare, and the cost to the consumer of becoming informed about them is apt to exceed the expected benefit": *Economic Analysis of Law*, 5th ed. (1998), at 198. This implies that strict manufacturer liability is warranted for personal injury cases but not claims for economic loss alone. White and Summers share this view: *Uniform Commercial Code*, 5th ed. (2000), at 407 (see *infra* in the Notes following *Morrow v. New Moon Homes*). Do you agree? Are there other economic considerations that might be relevant? The OLRC relied in part on administrative cost considerations (avoidance of circuity of action and multiplicity of proceedings) in support of its recommendation for a strict liability rule extending to economic losses. Is this a sufficient justification?

JUDICIAL AND LEGISLATIVE DEVELOPMENTS

United Kingdom

M.G. Bridge
The Sale of Goods

(Oxford: Clarendon Press, 1997), at 370-76 (Footnotes omitted)

The Liability of Remote Sellers

Under this heading, we may group a number of parties in the distribution chain, such as producers, importers, and wholesalers, who are not privy to the final contract between the consumer buyer of new goods and his immediate seller. Landmark decisions on the implied terms of satisfactory quality and fitness for purpose have been actuated by the judicial policy of pushing responsibility for defective goods back up the distribution chain to the responsible source. This will be the producer or, if the producer is abroad and unamenable to suit, the importer. Nevertheless, the proper plaintiff in each case is the immediate buyer, though related actions by each buyer in the distribution chain, which ranges from the producer to the consumer buyer, may be conjoined or consolidated in one set of proceedings. Apart from actions on the implied terms in the Sale of Goods Act, a remote seller, such as the producer, may incur liability on an express warranty or guarantee forming part of a contract collateral to the contract of sale. In addition, there may be liability in the tort of negligence for personal injury and property damage, and liability under the Consumer Protection Act 1987. There are also proposals afoot to affirm, in so far as it needs to be affirmed, the liability of a producer on a guarantee and to make the producer liable directly to the consumer buyer in respect of the implied term of satisfactory quality in the Sale of Goods Act.

The Indemnity Chain

To understand the difficulties facing a buyer in mounting a claim for defective goods against a party other than the immediate seller, the starting point is the doctrine of privity of contract whereby only parties to the contract may derive rights and liabilities from it. In products liability jargon, "vertical privity" prevents a buyer from suing on a warranty in a contract further up the chain, between, for example, the wholesaler and retailer. "Horizontal privity" prevents persons altogether outside the distribution chain, such as a non-purchasing user of the goods or an outsider injured by goods under the control of the buyer or a user, from moving laterally into the buyer's shoes to launch against his seller a warranty action. Were outsiders able to overcome the horizontal privity obstacle, they would still have to deal with vertical privity in pursuing sellers further up the chain.

The privity doctrine is closely associated with the rule that consideration must move from the promisee, and emerged when distribution chains were rudimentary, and a contract formed directly between producer and consumer buyer not at all uncommon. The later development of lengthier distribution chains, before the tort of negligence had expanded to give consumer buyers and users some recourse against producers, served to insulate producers from consumer grievances and stimulated the growth of strict warranty liability against retail sellers, even when those sellers had resold packaged goods they could not have examined.

Strict though the liability of the immediate seller is, and sympathetic as courts are to the pushing of liability up the distribution chain, this process of indemnification, based upon a system of third-party notices, can break down for a number of reasons at some point in the chain. There might, for example, be an intervening bankruptcy, or an exemption clause in one of the contracts may bring liability to a halt, or the disclosure of one of the buyer's purposes may not be precise enough to allow indemnification, or one of the buyers may have difficulty identifying his seller, or a limitation period may toll so as to arrest the process of indemnification.

Negligence

Where a buyer suffers personal injury or property damage, a claim in negligence may be launched directly against the producer. In the case of design faults, it may be difficult to establish negligence in fact but aberrant products fresh from the assembly line so loudly bespeak negligence, once fault by the buyer and anyone else between him and the producer has been eliminated, that one may as well speak of an evidentiary presumption of negligence, of whatever strength, on the part of the producer. Some goods are not so much defective as suitable for use only if the producer issues an adequate warning or instructions about their proper use: a failure to issue such a warning will be treated as negligence. Similarly, an immediate seller may also incur liability in negligence for a failure to warn or instruct, the existence of a contract of sale being no bar to such a tort action.

With respect to economic loss caused by defective goods, exemplified by loss of profits attributable to inefficiency in the goods, the cost of repairing them, or an inherent loss of value, the courts have generally held fast against an extension of negligence liability. But some exceptions have emerged. Recovery is likely to be permitted where the buyer expends money on the goods in order to avert the risk of physical loss posed by a defect. In addition, where the buyer suffers physical loss, recovery will be allowed in respect of economic loss consequent upon that physical loss. The House of Lords decision in *Junior Books Ltd. v. Veitchi Co. Ltd*, marooned by recent decisions of the same court drawing back the tide of economic loss liability in negligence, allowed a privity-vaulting factory owner to recover directly from a flooring subcontractor the cost of prematurely having to replace a defective floor. No explanation was given for why the factory owner chose not to sue the main contractor. In *Lambert v. Lewis,* the House of Lords stated its willingness to allow the retail seller of a defective towing hitch to recover the damages liability it owed to the buyer, not from the wholesaler, who could not be identified, but directly from the producer. Since the retail seller was held not liable, however, the claim did not in the end have to be pressed. It is by no means certain that a court would now be so sympathetic to the buyer.

It would be wrong to see in the above developments an opening up of liability for economic loss that would make deep inroads into the privity of contract doctrine. The recent retrenchment of liability for economic loss has occurred hand in hand with the direction that plaintiffs should protect themselves from loss by contract and seek recourse against their contractual partners. This accords with buyers pursuing their sellers rather than producers. One obvious objection to extending the liability in negligence of the producer is that it outflanks a producer's attempt to limit or exclude contractual liability by a clause to that effect in the contract with the immediate buyer. After initially being attracted to the idea, the House of Lords now prefers to deny recovery altogether than to mould the content of any negligence duty, sounding in economic loss and owed, for example, by a producer to a consumer buyer, to fit the contractual duty of the producer at the top of the distribution chain. Since producers can be reached by way of the indemnity process, it seems a somewhat technical defence to allow them to invoke privity when they are not sheltering behind a wall of limited or excluded liability contained in the immediate purchase contract.

Express Warranty and Guarantee

If producers choose to promote their products and stimulate sales at the retail level so as to feed commercial activity further down the distribution chain, a strong case can be made for making them liable to the consumer buyer. Unlike their American counterparts, English courts have not been prepared to give such buyers extended implied warranty rights against producers. Nevertheless, there is the possibility of express warranty liability arising out of advertising and of rights promised in producers' guarantees addressed to the consumer buyer.

Although it has been established for over 100 years that a producer reaching out to a consumer can incur liability on a collateral contract, reported instances of such liability are rare and tend not to involve mass advertising. Where a statement is made by a third party to a consumer contract of sale, the tortious characteristics of warranty are heightened. Suppose that A, a producer, makes a statement to B, a consumer buyer, who then purchases goods from C, a retail seller. According to collateral contract analysis, A, to be liable, should bargain for B's entry into the contract with C, and B should do so in a way suggestive of accepting an offer of liability from A if the statement turns out to be incorrect. Courts are rarely so pedantic as to observe the niceties of these legal steps in actual decision-making. What appears to count is B's reliance upon the statement. Where a retailer sued a producer on a statement that its towing hitch needed no maintenance and was fool-proof, however, the Court of Appea showed a surprising reluctance to infer a contractual intention on the part of a producer in respect of the contents of its sales literature. The trial judge showed a corresponding readiness to believe that the retailer relied upon the producer's reputation rather than its statements, as though any neat separation could be made between the two.

Whether the looser approach to analysing the steps in a collateral contract is adopted, or a rigorous analysis preferred, many producers' guarantees fall outside a collateral contract since they come too late to affect the consumer buyer's decision to enter into the contract with the retail seller. A good example of this is the guarantee that is to be found inside the packaged goods once purchased.

The inference of warranty on the part of a third party such as a producer is commonly a device that serves to prevent the doctrine of privity of contract from diluting contractual responsibility. Statements from a producer may appease a buyer who then desists from securing a corresponding warranty from the retail seller or from displaying his reliance upon the skill and judgement of that seller. The collateral contract breaks down the insulation of the producer from that retail contract. Though Lord Moulton said over eighty years ago that the incidence of collateral contracts was rare, his words do not accurately record the modern tolerance of collateral warranties. With the disappearance of the parol evidence rule, it is somewhat incongruous to speak of two contracts between the same parties arising out of the same contractual adventure, as opposed to the one contract that is a blend of writing and informal collateral warranty. Nevertheless, Lord Moulton's words may still retain some vitality. In *Lambert v. Lewis,* the Court of Appeal indicated that the requirement of contractual intention was harder to satisfy where the alleged collateral warranty came from a third party to the supply contract.

Doubts as to the legal liability of a producer on a guarantee have been addressed by the Department of Trade and Industry in a consultative paper, which canvasses the possibility of making guarantees civilly enforceable by statutory means. The Department has also sought guidance on the appropriate measure of damages (tort or contract?) and has at this stage ruled out prescriptive measures to determine the scope and duration of any guarantee that a producer chooses to give. A further question being asked is whether the retailer should be jointly and severally liable with the producer on the latter's guarantees. This initiative seems to have been overtaken for practical purposes by a European Commission green paper which, in the context of exploring a unified European approach, is seeking reactions to a range of solutions to the problem of "commercial" guarantees. These would range from compulsory to voluntary schemes of regulation, and from the enforcement of guarantees only in the country where they are given to their portability throughout the countries of the European Union.

A final point arising from producers' guarantees concerns their use as a medium for conveying a clause exempting the producer from liability at common law for negligence. Apart from any difficulty the producer might have at common law in inferring consent to the exemption from a consumer's acceptance of the guarantee, the Unfair Contract Terms Act 1977 denies legal effect to such exemptions. First of all, liability for death or personal injury may not by "any contract term or ... notice" be excluded or restricted. Secondly, "the negligence of a person concerned in the manufacture or distribution of goods" may not be excluded or restricted by a contract term or notice contained in or referring to a guarantee, where goods ordinarily supplied for private use or consumption turn out to be defective when in consumer use. Goods are treated as being in consumer use whenever they are not used exclusively in the course of a business.

Canada

Chabot v. Ford Motor Co. of Canada Ltd.

(1983), 39 OR (2d) 162 (HCJ)

[The plaintiff bought a vehicle in Winnipeg from the defendant dealer, South Park Mercury. The vehicle was manufactured by the Ford Motor Co. and sold by Ford Motor Co. of Canada to the dealer. Shortly after its purchase the vehicle was destroyed by fire. The fire was caused by a defectively installed drain plug in the oil pan. The plaintiff sued all the defendants in damages for the loss of his vehicle: he sued the dealer in contract for breach of warranty and he sued the other defendants in tort for negligent manufacture of the vehicle and in contract for breach of Ford's manufacturer's warranty. The following extract from Eberle J's comprehensive judgment deals with the tortious claim, having regard to the fact that the plaintiff was not alleging that he had suffered personal injury as a result of the accident or that there had been damage to property other than to the vehicle itself (at 189-91):]

EBERLE J: ... This raises the question of what damages are recoverable in tort against the Ford companies. In tort claims, a plaintiff may be precluded from recovering certain kinds of damage from the manufacturer of a defective article. In *Rivtow Marine*

Ltd. v. Washington Iron Works et al., [1974] SCR 1189, 40 DLR (3d) 530, [1973] 6 WWR 692, Mr. Justice Ritchie, writing for the majority, said at 1207 SCR:

> ... the liability for the cost of repairing damage to the defective article itself and for the economic loss flowing directly from the negligence, is akin to liability under the terms of an express or implied warranty of fitness and as it is contractual in origin cannot be enforced against the manufacturer by a stranger to the contract.

The breadth of this language might at first seem to suggest that the plaintiff in the instant case cannot recover from the manufacturers of the truck damages for its destruction, caused by the defective parts. But I think this view would be incorrect, for it fails to pay due regard to the particular facts in *Rivtow*, and the special nature of the damages there in issue.

That case involved claims for damages against the manufacturer of two cranes for the cost of repairing manufacturing defects and economic loss suffered consequent upon the cranes being withdrawn from service to effect the repairs. No accident had occurred and accordingly the defects had not caused further damage, either to the cranes or other property or to persons.

In the instant case, the plaintiff is not claiming damages for the cost of repairing the defective parts of the truck, nor is he claiming economic loss resulting from effecting such repairs. He is claiming compensation for the damage done to his truck by the defect. This case, therefore, is not within the factual ambit of *Rivtow*. In addition, in *Trans World Airlines, Inc. v. Curtiss-Wright Corp., et al.*, 148 NYS 2d 284 (1955), a case referred to in *Rivtow*, Eder J drew a distinction between cases where the defective article causes an accident, and cases where the defective article does not do so, and accordingly must be regarded merely as a substandard article. I quote from 290:

> TWA was not without remedy. Until an accident attributable to a defective engine happened, its only remedy was to hold Lockheed, the seller, for breach of warranty. It is only when the danger inherent in a defectively made article causes an accident that a cause of action against the manufacturer also arises.
>
> If the ultimate user were allowed to sue the manufacturer in negligence merely because an article with latent defects turned out to be bad when used in "regular service" without any accident occurring, there would be nothing left of the citadel of privity and not much scope for the law of warranty. There seems to me to be good reason for maintaining that, short of an accident, the citadel should be preserved. Manufacturers would be subject to indiscriminate lawsuits by persons having no contractual relations with them, persons who could thereby escape the limitations, if any, agreed upon in their contract of purchase. Damages for inferior quality, per se, should better be left to suits between vendors and purchasers since they depend on the terms of the bargain between them.

These words seem peculiarly apt in the present case, in which an accident occurred, causing total loss of the vehicle. The plaintiff is not claiming damages for the poor quality or poor installation of the drain plug, but for the destruction of his vehicle.

I am of the view, therefore, that *Rivtow* does not apply to this case. Even if it does apply to reduce the plaintiff's claim by the cost of effecting the repairs to the defective parts, the cost of properly tightening the drain plug is for all practical purposes negligible. The plaintiff accordingly is entitled to recover his damages from the Ford companies unless precluded by the new vehicle warranty.

Since Ford US is not referred to in the manufacturer's new vehicle warranty, it cannot appeal to the exclusion clauses thereof to avoid its tortious liability. The question remains whether Ford Canada can shield itself from tortious liability by those clauses.

Much of what I say on this issue will recall my earlier comments regarding exclusion of contractual liability.

Do the exclusionary clauses in Ford Canada's warranty apply to and effect only that express warranty, or do they go beyond it, and exclude tortious liability? If it has the latter effect, it does so without any assent by the plaintiff. The purchase agreement told the plaintiff he was getting a warranty from Ford Canada, an additional benefit. Neither by the purchase agreement nor from any other source was the plaintiff told that his rights against Ford Canada in tort were to be taken away from him. That was something to which the plaintiff never agreed, and was never asked to agree. Ford Canada cannot shield itself from tortious liability unless it can show that the plaintiff understood, or must be taken to have understood, that he was renouncing his common law rights. It has not shown that. The exclusionary aspects of Ford Canada's warranty should be viewed as applying only to limit the liability it assumed by the express warranty.

One must be careful about imposing additional tort liabilities on a party whose position and obligations are already spelled out in contract. I am mindful of the principles enunciated in *J. Nunes Diamonds Ltd. v. Dominion Electric Protection Co.*, [1972] SCR 769, 26 DLR (3d) 699, to that effect. However, the situation is different where the tort arises quite independently of the performance of the contract.

That, I believe, is the case here. The tort of which the plaintiff complains did not arise in the performance of the manufacturer's warranty. It arose much before the effective date of the warranty; it arose during the process of manufacture of the vehicle. This is so even though the damages did not occur until after the warranty came into effect, for the damages did not flow from any promise in the warranty, but from an entirely separate and antecedent tort.

Winnipeg Condominium Corp. No. 6 v. Bird Construction Co. Ltd.

(1995), 121 DLR (4th) 193 (SCC)[6]

[A land developer contracted with the respondent (Bird Construction) to build an apartment building in accordance with plans and specifications prepared by the inter-

---

6 The statement of facts appearing below is largely based on the official summary appearing in the headnote preceding the Supreme Court judgment.

venor, an architectural firm. The respondent subcontracted the masonry portion of the work. The building was converted into a condominium in 1978, when the appellant (Winnipeg Condominium) became the registered subsequent owner of the land and building. In 1982, the appellant's directors became concerned about the masonry work on the exterior cladding of the building. They retained the architects (the intervener) and a firm of consulting engineers to inspect the building. The architects and engineers expressed the opinion that the building was structurally sound. In 1989, a storey-high section of the cladding fell from the ninth storey level of the building but without injuring anyone or causing damage to other property. The appellant had further inspections undertaken which revealed structural defects in the masonry work. Following these inspections, the entire cladding was replaced at the appellant's expense at cost of $1.5 million.

The appellant commenced an action in negligence against the respondent, the architects and the subcontractor. The statement of claim detailed alleged inadequacies in design and workmanship without assigning specific blame to one defendant or another. The respondent and the subcontractor filed notices of motion for summary judgment and notices of motion to strike the claim as disclosing no reasonable grounds of action with the Manitoba Court of Queen's Bench. Both motions were dismissed. The defendant appealed but the subcontractor did not. The appeal was dismissed with respect to the motion for summary judgment but allowed with respect to the motion to strike, and the statement of claim was struck out against the respondent.

The appellant appealed to the Supreme Court of Canada. The issue before the Supreme Court was whether a general contractor responsible for the construction of a building may be held tortiously liable in negligence to a subsequent purchaser of the building, who is not in contractual privity with the contractor, for the cost of repairing defects in the building arising out of negligence in its construction.

In a unanimous judgment, delivered by La Forest J, the Supreme Court reversed the judgment of the Manitoba Court of Appeal and upheld the appellant's right to sue the respondent in negligence. In La Forest's words (at para. 43):

> The law in Canada has now progressed to the point where it can be said that contractors (as well as subcontractors, architects and engineers) who take part in the design and construction of a building will owe a duty in tort to subsequent purchasers of the building if it can be shown that it was foreseeable that a failure to take reasonable care in constructing the building would create defects that pose a substantial danger to the health and safety of the occupants. Where negligence is established and such defects manifest themselves before any damage to persons or property occurs, they should, in my view, be liable for the reasonable cost of repairing the defects and putting the building back into a non-dangerous state.

The Court of Appeal had followed the reasoning in *D & F Estates Ltd. v. Church Commissioners for England,* [1988] 2 All ER 992, where, in a comparable situation, the House of Lords had rejected the right of an owner to sue a contractor in negligence for the cost of repairing a dangerously defective structure where the defect was discovered before it caused injury to persons or other property. La Forest J held that the Manitoba Court of Appeal was mistaken in doing so because the House of Lords' decision was based on two premises neither of which applied in Canada. The first premise was rejection of Lord Wilberforce's judgment in *Anns v. Merton London Borough Council,* [1977] 2 All ER 492 embracing a general principle of liability in negligence for foreseeable losses. The second premise was that a tortious action will not lie where the parties' relationship is in contract.

Justice La Forest noted that the principle enunciated in *Anns* was alive and well in Canada even though it had now been formally repudiated in England in *Murphy v. Brentwood District Council,* [1990] 2 All ER 908 (HL), and had been reaffirmed by the Supreme Court as recently as *Canadian National Rly Co. v. Norsk Pacific Steamship Co.,* [1992] 1 SCR 1021. So far as the second point was concerned, the Supreme Court had upheld the independent character of actions in tort and in contract in *Central Trust Co. Rafuse,* [1986] 2 SCR 147, therefore removing the second objection to the plaintiffs' action in the present case.

On the merits of allowing a plaintiff to recover the costs of preemptive repairs to avoid putative harm to persons and property, La Forest J gave the following policy reasons:]

La FOREST J: Apart from the logical force of holding contractors liable for the cost of repair of dangerous defects, there is also a strong underlying policy justification for imposing liability in these cases. Under the law as developed in *D & F Estates* and *Murphy*, the plaintiff who moves quickly and responsibly to fix a defect before it causes injury to persons or damage to property must do so at his or her own expense. By contrast, the plaintiff who, either intentionally or through neglect, allows a defect to develop into an accident may benefit at law from the costly and potentially tragic consequences. In my view, this legal doctrine is difficult to justify because it serves to encourage, rather than discourage, reckless and hazardous behaviour. Maintaining a bar against recoverability for the cost of repair of dangerous defects provides no incentive for plaintiffs to mitigate potential losses and tends to encourage economically inefficient behaviour. The Fourth District Court of Appeal for Florida in *Drexel Properties, Inc. v. Bay Colony Club Condominium, Inc.*, 406 So.2d 515 (1981), at p. 519, explained the problem in the following manner:

> Why should a buyer have to wait for a personal tragedy to occur in order to recover damages to remedy or repair defects? In the final analysis, the cost to the developer for a resulting tragedy could be far greater than the cost of remedying the condition.

Woodhouse J in *Bowen v. Paramount Builders Ltd.*, [1977] 1 NZLR 394, at p. 417, described the problem in similar terms:

> It would seem only common sense to take steps to avoid a serious loss by repairing a defect before it will cause physical damage; and rather extraordinary if the greater loss when the building falls down could be recovered from the careless builder but the cost of timely repairs could not.

Allowing recovery against contractors in tort for the cost of repair of dangerous defects thus serves an important preventative function by encouraging socially responsible behaviour.

[La Forest J rejected the respondent's argument that allowing recovery in tort would create great confusion in contractual relationships, impair a contractor's ability to limit his potential liability for defective work, and impose unlimited liability towards an indeterminate number of future owners and occupants of a building. He dealt with these objections in the following passages:]

The Concern with Overlap Between Tort and Contract Duties

Turning to the first concern, a duty on the part of contractors to take reasonable care in the construction of buildings can, in my view, be conceptualized in the absence of contract and will not result in indeterminate liability to the contractor. As I mentioned earlier, this Court has recognized that a tort duty can arise concurrently with a contractual duty, so long as that tort duty arises independently of the contractual duty; see *Rafuse, supra; Edgeworth, supra*. As I see it, the duty to construct a building according to reasonable standards and without dangerous defects arises independently of the contractual stipulations between the original owner and the contractor because it arises from a duty to create the building safely and not merely according to contractual standards of quality. It must be remembered that we are speaking here of a duty to construct the building according to reasonable standards of safety in such a manner that it does not contain *dangerous* defects. As this duty arises independently of any contract, there is no logical reason for allowing the contractor to rely upon a contract made with the original owner to shield him or her from liability to subsequent purchasers arising from a dangerously constructed building.

The tort duty to construct a building safely is thus a circumscribed duty that is not parasitic upon any contractual duties between the contractor and the original owner. Seen in this way, no serious risk of indeterminate liability arises with respect to this tort duty. In the first place, there is no risk of liability to an indeterminate class because the potential class of claimants is limited to the very persons for whom the building is constructed: the inhabitants of the building. The fact that the class of claimants may include successors in title who have no contractual relationship with the contractors does not, in my view, render the class of potential claimants indeterminate. As noted by the New Jersey Supreme Court in *Aronsohn v. Mandara*, 484 A.2d 675 (1984), at p. 680, "[t]he contractor should not be relieved of liability for unworkmanlike construction simply because of the fortuity that the property on which he did the construction has changed hands."

[T]here is no risk of liability in an indeterminate amount because the amount of liability will always be limited by the reasonable cost of repairing the dangerous defect in the building and restoring that building to a non-dangerous state. Counsel for Bird advanced the argument that the cost of repairs claimed for averting a danger caused by a defect in construction could, in some cases, be disproportionate to the actual damage to persons or property that might be caused if that defect were not repaired. For example, he expressed concern that a given plaintiff could claim thousands of dollars in damage for a defect which, if left unrepaired, would cause only a few dollars damage to that plaintiff's other property. However, in my view, any danger of indeterminacy in damages is averted by the requirement that the defect for which the costs of repair are claimed must constitute a real and substantial danger to the inhabitants of the building, and the fact that the inhabitants of the building can only claim the reasonable cost of repairing the defect and mitigating the danger. The burden of proof will always fall on the plaintiff to demonstrate that there is a serious risk to safety, that the risk was caused by the contractor's negligence, and that the repairs are required to alleviate the risk.

Finally, there is little risk of liability for an indeterminate time because the contractor will only be liable for the cost of repair of dangerous defects during the useful life of the building. Practically speaking, I believe that the period in which the contractor may be exposed to liability for negligence will be much shorter than the full useful life of the building. With the passage of time, it will become increasingly difficult for owners of a building to prove at trial that any deterioration in the building is attributable to the initial negligence of the contractor and not simply to the inevitable wear and tear suffered by every building; for a similar view, see Sachs LJ in *Dutton, supra*, at p. 405.

The Caveat Emptor Concern

Turning to the second concern, *caveat emptor* cannot, in my view, serve as a complete shield to tort liability for the contractors of a building. In *Fraser-Reid, supra,* this Court relied on the doctrine of *caveat emptor* in rejecting a claim by a buyer of a house for the recognition of an implied warranty of fitness for human habitation. However, the Court explicitly declined to address the question of whether *caveat emptor* serves to negate a duty in tort (pp. 726-27). Accordingly, the question remains at large in Canadian law and must be resolved on the level of principle.

In *Fraser-Reid*, Dickson J (as he then was) observed that the doctrine of *caveat emptor* stems from the *laissez-faire* attitudes of the eighteenth and nineteenth centuries and the notion that purchasers must fend for themselves in seeking protection by express warranty or by independent examination of the premises (at p. 723). The assumption underlying the doctrine is that the purchaser of a building is better placed than the seller or builder to inspect the building and to bear the risk that latent defects will emerge necessitating repair costs. However, in my view, this is an assumption which (if ever valid) is simply not responsive to the realities of the modern housing market. In *Lempke, supra*, at p. 295, the Supreme Court of New Hampshire made reference to a number of policy factors that strongly militate against the rigid application of the doctrine of *caveat emptor* with regard to tort claims for construction defects:

> First, "[c]ommon experience teaches that latent defects in a house will not manifest themselves for a considerable period of time … after the original purchaser has sold the property to a subsequent unsuspecting buyer. …"
>
> Second, our society is rapidly changing.

We are an increasingly mobile people; a builder-vendor should know that a house he builds might be resold within a relatively short period of time and should not expect that the warranty will be limited by the number of days that the original owner holds onto the property.

... Furthermore, "the character of society has changed such that the original buyer is not in a position to discover hidden defects. ..."

Third, like an initial buyer, the subsequent purchaser has little opportunity to inspect and little experience and knowledge about construction. "Consumer protection demands that those who buy homes are entitled to rely on the skill of a builder and that the house is constructed so as to be reasonably fit for its intended use. ..."

Fourth, the builder/contractor will not be unduly taken unaware by the extension of the warranty to a subsequent purchaser. "The builder already owes a duty to construct the home in a workmanlike manner. ..." ... And extension to a subsequent purchaser, within a reasonable time, will not change this basic obligation.

Fifth, arbitrarily interposing a first purchaser as a bar to recovery "might encourage sham first sales to insulate builders from liability."

Philip H. Osborne makes the further point in "A Review of Tort Decisions in Manitoba 1990-1993," [1993] *Man. LJ* 191, at p. 196, that contractors and builders, because of their knowledge, skill and expertise, are in the best position to ensure the reasonable structural integrity of buildings and their freedom from latent defect. In this respect, the imposition of liability on builders provides an important incentive for care in the construction of buildings and a deterrent against poor workmanship.

My conclusion that a subsequent purchaser is not the best placed to bear the risk of the emergence of latent defects is borne out by the facts of this case. It is significant that, when cracking first appeared in the mortar of the building in 1982, the Condominium Corporation actually hired Smith Carter, the original architect of the building, along with a firm of structural engineers, to assess the condition of the mortar work and exterior cladding. These experts failed to detect the latent defects that appear to have caused the cladding to fall in 1989. Thus, although it is clear that the Condominium Corporation acted with diligence in seeking to detect hidden defects in the building, they were nonetheless unable to detect the defects or to foresee the collapse of the cladding in 1989. This, in my view, illustrates the unreality of the assumption that the purchaser is better placed to detect and bear the risk of hidden defects. For this Court to apply the doctrine of *caveat emptor* to negate Bird's duty in tort would be to apply a rule that has become completely divorced, in this context at least, from its underlying rationale.

NOTES

The Impact of Bird Construction

1) *Recovery for negligent defects constituting a danger to persons or other property.* The preceding cases deal with the question of a manufacturer's liability for product defects where: (1) there is no privity of contract between the claimant and the manufacturer; and (2) the claim is for purely economic loss. In *Rivtow Marine Ltd. v. Washington Iron Works*

(1973), 40 DLR (3d) 530, [1974] SCR 1189, a case involving the manufacture and supply of a defective crane, the majority upheld part of the plaintiff's claim, but it disallowed the cost of repairs to the crane. The basis of the decision was that in the particular circumstances of the case, the defendant was under a duty to warn the plaintiff promptly of the defect so that it could be repaired as soon as possible. Laskin J, dissenting, would have held the defendant liable on the broader ground that it was negligent in having produced a defective crane in the first place. He thought that a plaintiff should be allowed to recover repair costs where the defective product is dangerous and the repairs are necessary to prevent physical injury or damage to other property. In *Bird Construction*, the Supreme Court effectively adopted Laskin J's position. La Forest J, speaking for the court, said that contractors and others who take part in the design and construction of a building "all owe a duty in tort to subsequent purchasers of the building if it can be shown that it was foreseeable that failure to take reasonable care in the construction of the building would create defects that pose a substantial danger to the health and safety of the occupants." It is true that *Bird Construction* was a building case, but the reasoning is clearly applicable also to defective products.

2) *English and American law compared.* The law in England is much less favourable to plaintiffs. There repair costs are not recoverable in tort even if the repairs are necessary to avoid the risk of injury or damage to other property: see *D & F Estates Ltd. v. Church Commissioners for England*, [1989] AC 177 and *Murphy v. Brentwood District Council*, [1991] AC 898, both discussed in the remarks preceding the *Bird Construction* extract, *supra*. Contrast *Anns v. Merton London Borough Council*, [1978] AC 728, which *Murphy v. Brentwood* expressly overrules and *Junior Books Ltd. v. Veitchi Co.*, [1982] 1 AC 520, which *Murphy v. Brentwood* overrules by implication. A substantial number of American cases have allowed recovery in tort for a dangerously defective chattel resulting only in damage to the chattel itself. These are not referred to in *Bird Construction*. See Annotations, 72 ALR (4th) 12, esp. at s. 6; Speiser, Krause and Gans, *The American Law of Torts* (1989 and 2000 Supplement), Vol. 6, s. 18.140; *Pennsylvania Glass Sand Corp. v. Caterpillar Tractor Co.*, 652 F.2d 1165 (CCA 3, applying Pa. Law); and *Northern Power & Engineering Corp. v. Caterpillar Tractor Co.*, 623 P.2d 324 (Alaska). The US Supreme Court disapproved these cases in *East River S.S. Corp. v. Transamerica Delaval Inc.*, 106 S.Ct. 2295 (1986), on the grounds that allowing tort recovery in such circumstances was too indeterminate and that so long as no person and no other property was harmed such claims should be governed by warranty law. *East River* was an admiralty decision and it is therefore not binding on State courts. For example, it was not followed by the Alaska Supreme Court in *Pratt & Whitney Canada Inc. v. Sheehan*, 852 P.2d 1173 (1993). There the court allowed recovery in tort for a defective propeller which forced the owner of the airplane to make an emergency landing resulting in extensive damage to the aircraft.

3) *The "complex structures" theory.* While it is clear that a manufacturer is liable under the rule in *Donoghue v. Stevenson* for damage to property other than the chattel containing the defect, it is unclear whether the manufacturer will also be held liable if the defect causes physical damage to *other* parts of the chattel containing the defective component.

In *Chabot's* case, *supra*, Eberle J answered yes to the question but his reasoning is skimpy. The only precedent he cites is *TWA v. Curtiss-Wright Corp.*, but it is not clear from the passage in Eder J's judgment quoted by Eberle J whether Eder J meant to draw a distinction between "internal" and "external" harm caused by the defective part. It is true that Laskin J's dissenting judgment in *Rivtow Marine* speaks of the threat of physical harm "to the defective product" (see *supra*), but we are not told whether he meant to override the traditional distinction between internal and extraneous harm. Laskin J's formulation of the rule was not essential to his position since in *Rivtow*'s case there was a threatened injury to persons (those using the crane or working on the barge) as well as potential harm to the barge if the crane collapsed.

In *Junior Books Ltd. v. Veitchi Co.*, [1982] 3 WLR 447, at 499, Lord Brandon clearly was of the view that a manufacturer would only be held liable for physical damage caused to extraneous property. In *D & F Estates*, *supra*, at 1006-7, on the other hand, Lord Bridge thought it was arguable that, in the case of complex structures, one element of the structure should be regarded, for *Donoghue v. Stevenson*-type purposes, as distinct from another element so as to allow recovery for damage to the other element. However, he resiled from this position in *Murphy*, *supra*, at 926-28, and rejected the complex structures theory. Nevertheless, he was prepared to retain a distinction between a part of a complex structure which only constitutes a "danger" because it does not perform its proper function in sustaining the other parts and some distinct item incorporated in the structure "which positively malfunctions so as to inflict positive damage on the structure in which it is incorporated." As examples of the latter type of situation he cites a defective central heater boiler which explodes and damages a house or a defective electrical installation which causes a fire and damages the house. The defective plug in *Chabot*'s case, *supra*, seems to fall into this second category. Unfortunately, Lord Bridge only speaks of allowing recovery against the manufacturer of the boiler or the installer of the defective wiring (whose liability easily falls under *Donoghue v. Stevenson*) and does not refer to the builder's liability.

In *Bird Construction*, *supra*, La Forest J said (at para. 15) that he agreed with Lord Bridge's criticism of the complex structures theory, but also added that since the theory merely served to circumvent and obscure the underlying questions he preferred to address the issue of liability for a dangerously defective chattel directly.

A substantial number of American courts do permit recovery where a "calamitous," "catastrophic," or "dangerous" accident causes a defective component to damage the rest of the chattel, for example, a propeller which falls off an aircraft forcing the aircraft to crash land. See the sources cited *supra*. It is not clear, however, to what extent these decisions also require proof of imminent danger to persons or other property or whether it will be presumed as a matter of law because of the nature of the accident. (Such proof, for example, was not required in *Sheehan*'s case although the pilot of the plane was obviously exposed to great danger.)

4) *Recovery for negligent defects not constituting a danger to person or other property.* It is a necessary inference from La Forest J's judgment that his judgment is not to be construed as imposing liability on builders (and therefore on manufacturers) for negligently performed work (or manufactured chattels) not constituting a hazard for the benefit of subsequent purchasers not in privity with the builder or manufacturer. However, part of his reasoning is just as apt to cover this type of claim as well given that his starting point was reaffirmation of the Supreme Court's approval of Lord Wilberforce's judgment in *Anns v. Merton London Borough Council*.

Lord Wilberforce's proposition was the basis of the majority decision in *Junior Books Ltd. v. Veitchi Co.*, [1982] 3 All ER 201 (HL), holding a subcontractor liable to the owner of factory premises for a faulty floor laying job. The decision was roundly criticized at the time, in Canada as well as in England. See, *inter alia*, Waddams, "Comment" (1983-84), 8 *CBLJ* 101 and Symposium, "Economic Loss: Where Are We Going after *Junior Books*?" (1987), 12 *CBLJ* 241, especially the papers by B. Feldthusen and J. Bloom.

The criticism focused on two key points: (a) Lord Roskill's "heresy" in suggesting that there is no difference in principle between a *Donoghue v. Stevenson* type of claim for physical harm and a claim in negligence for pure economic loss, and (b) the effect of the decision in imposing a warranty-type liability on a sub-contractor (and, by a parity of reasoning on a manufacturer) not in privity with the owner or the builder and without giving him the benefit of any disclaimer or limited liability clause in his contract with the head-contractor. (In fairness to Lord Roskill, it must be added that he was not called upon to deal with the relevance of exclusionary clauses since the House of Lords had no evidence before it of the terms of the agreement between the sub-contractor and the contractor.) Is Professor Blom correct, however, in suggesting in (1986-87), 12 *CBLJ* 275, at 289 that consumers do not need an economic remedy against the manufacturer and that they should be content with the warranty protection they are entitled to receive from the seller from whom they bought the goods? If he is correct, why do manufacturers regularly provide performance warranties and why do consumers show so much interest in them?

Since the House of Lords has now repudiated the *Anns* doctrine in its entirety, inferentially *Junior Books* has fallen by the wayside as well. The Canadian position is less clear but our own hunch is that when the issue arises before the Supreme Court it will be decided on the footing that the answer more appropriately lies in warranty law and that if current warranty law is inadequate (because of privity barriers and such like) it would be better to expand the warranty rules than to burden a manufacturer with unbounded economic negligence claims.

5) *Distinguishing dangerous defects from non-dangerous ones*. If the law is limited as suggested in note 4, above, then the courts will have to distinguish between dangerous and non-dangerous product and building defects. This may not be easy to do. Klar says that "although heavy cladding which falls is certainly dangerous, the matter may not be so clear in other cases: leaky roofs and cracked foundations, for example": *Tort Law*, 2nd ed. (1996), at 218. On leaky roofs and the like, see further *Symposium*, "The Leaky Condo Problem on the West Coast" (1999), 31 *CBLJ* 335. On cracked foundations and the like, see *Alie v. Bertrand & Frere Construction Co.*, [2000] OJ no. 1360 (the "Eastern Ontario cement case").

Retailer's Right to Indemnity

In *Lambert v. Lewis*, [1980] 2 WLR 299 (CA), the facts of which have been given previously (*supra*, chapter 4), the retailers argued that they were entitled to rely on the doctrine of *Donoghue v. Stevenson*, [1932] AC 562 (HL), to recover damages from the manufacturers of the towing hitch coextensive with their liability to the owner even though the defect had only caused the retailers economic loss. Counsel for the retailers distinguished *SCM (UK) Ltd. v. W.J. Whittal & Son Ltd.*, [1971] 1 QB 337 and *Spartan Steel & Alloys*

Ltd. v. Martin & Co. (Contractors) Ltd., [1973] 1 QB 27, on the ground that in the present case there was a limited number of contractors buying and selling, and stocking and distributing the manufacturers' article, and that the manufacturers could expect any and all of these couplings which they manufactured to go through the chain of such contractors to the ultimate consumer with some such result of their use as happened in this case of physical damage and consequent legal liability.

Speaking for the court, Stephenson LJ rejected the argument on the following grounds (*ibid.*, at 331):

> The answer seems to us to be found in principle and on authority, in particular the authority of those two recent decisions of this court, not in a detailed examination of the cases nor in a logical analysis of the distinction between physical damage to the owner's trailer and physical injury to the first plaintiff and her family, or between loss of profits and financial loss incurred by legal liability to pay damages, but in applying common sense to draw a line between circumstances where the financial loss can and cannot be held to be recoverable for a breach of duty owed the party who incurs the loss. Whether we follow the first thoughts of Lord Denning MR in *SCM (United Kingdom) Ltd. v. W.J. Whittall & Son Ltd.*, [1971] QB 337 with which Winn LJ agreed, and consider remoteness, or his second thoughts in *Spartan Steel & Alloys Ltd. v. Martin & Co. (Contractors) Ltd.*, [1973] QB 27 with which Lawton LJ agreed, and discard everything but policy in setting bounds to duty and damage, we reach the conclusion that the loss which the retailers incurred by their liability to indemnify the owner against his legal liability to compensate the plaintiffs cannot be recovered from the manufacturers.

Stephenson LJ also observed (at 331):

> There comes a point where the logical extension of the boundaries of duty and damage is halted by the barrier of commercial sense and practical convenience. In our judgment, the facts of this case do not enable the retailers to push that barrier back as far as to include themselves and their damage within the range of the manufacturers and the towing hitch which they put into the market, or to surmount the barrier where we think common sense would place it.

Are you persuaded by this reasoning? In the House of Lords ([1981] 1 All ER 1185, at 1192), Lord Diplock expressly left open the question for future consideration.

The Quebec Civil Law Position

In *General Motors Products of Canada Ltd. v. Kravitz*, [1979] 1 SCR 790, the Supreme Court of Canada considered a claim by a buyer that an automobile manufacturer is liable under the Quebec Civil Code for latent defects in a new vehicle purchased by the buyer from one of the manufacturer's authorized dealers, quite apart from the dealer's liability to the buyer and notwithstanding the absence of privity between the parties. Kravitz brought an action against GM and the dealer claiming: (1) that his tender of the automobile to GM be declared valid; (2) that the sale of the automobile to him by the dealer be cancelled; and (3) that GM and the dealer be compelled jointly and severally to pay back the purchase price of the automobile and to pay incidental damages. The Quebec Court of Appeal upheld the Superior Court judgment. This found that the presence of serious latent defects in the automobile justified cancellation of the sale and that GM and the dealer were liable for the defects. Only GM appealed.

A unanimous Supreme Court of Canada, speaking through Pratte J, upheld the Court of Appeal's decision. The Court found that the "no-warranty" provision in the contract of sale between the dealer and Kravitz was null and void on the principle adopted by the French courts and consistent with the Civil Code that a manufacturer or professional seller cannot "contract out of the [Code's (Article 1522)] legal warranty against latent defects or limit the liability resulting from such warranty." The GM standard new car warranty given to Kravitz when he bought the automobile was also no bar to Kravitz's claim because to accept its limitation would be in effect "to relieve GM from its liability under the legal warranty for latent defects ... ." On the important question of whether Kravitz could exercise a direct remedy against GM, the Court found that the legal warranty against latent defects given by GM in its sale to the dealer was effective not only between the parties to the immediate contract but also enured for the benefit of a subsequent purchaser:

> A claim in warranty against latent defects is not one that is personal to the purchaser in the sense that he is entitled to it *intuitu personae*; the purchaser is entitled to it as the owner of the thing. As we have seen, it is a claim that is tied to the thing to which it relates. It is therefore transferred to the successors by particular title at the same time as the thing itself, in that the initial seller is liable on it to any purchaser of the thing sold. This solution is in keeping with the relevant articles of the *Civil Code* and with the principles on which they are based. [at 496-97, DLR]

The court found that as Kravitz "became the creditor of GM's warranty against latent defects" he could bring an action for cancellation and damages against GM.

As will be seen from the above extract, the court's reasoning is strikingly reminiscent of the theory of liability adopted by the court in *Henningsen's* case, except that there the plaintiffs were suing to recover for personal injuries as well as other heads of damages. In *Kravitz's* case, on the other hand, the car had not been involved in an accident and the plaintiff was not basing his claim on any delictual liability of GM. *Kravitz* therefore stands for the important proposition that, under Quebec law, a manufacturer is liable to the ultimate buyer for breach of the implied (legal) warranty that his goods are free from inherent defects. This goes much further than any comparable jurisprudence on the common law side though it remains to be seen whether *Kravitz* will be extended to non-consumer cases and to cases where the manufacturer's product is processed, transformed, or otherwise changed before it reaches the ultimate buyer's hands. All the earlier Quebec cases referred to in Pratte J's judgment involved consumer products, usually motor vehicles.

See the special issue of the *McGill Law Journal* on the *Kravitz* decision: (1980), 25 *McGill LJ* 296 *et seq*. See also Schwartz, "The Manufacturer's Liability to the Purchaser of a 'Lemon': A Review of the Situation in Canada After *General Motors Products of Canada Ltd. v. Kravitz*" (1979), 3 *Ottawa L Rev*. 583, and Wm. E. Tetley, QC, in J. Ziegel (ed.), *Papers and Comments, Ninth Annual Workshop on Commercial and Consumer Law* (1981), at 244 *et seq*.

Legislative Developments

The extract from the OLRC Report on Consumer Warranties, *supra*, shows that as early as 1913 remedial legislation in Alberta breached the walls of privity in order to protect retail buyers of new farm machinery. The Ontario Law Reform Commission, building upon this precedent and grounding manufacturers' liability in sales law rather than in tort, recommended that the privity requirement be abolished in warranty claims by a consumer buyer against the manufacturer of the goods. They recommended that a manufacturer be held liable for breach of any express warranties and that the manufacturer be deemed to have given the consumer buyer (whether or not the goods were purchased directly from the manufacturer) implied warranties comparable to those that run from retailer to buyer.

The OLRC's recommendations were incorporated into Bill 110, the Consumer Products Warranties Act 1976, which received a first reading on June 16, 1976. The Bill did not proceed beyond its introduction and it has not been reintroduced since then. Apparently, industry opposition and the government's hope that agreement would be reached among the provinces on a substantially uniform bill account for the lack of progress. Bill 110 contains, among other things, four implied warranties deemed to be given by the manufacturer and retailer jointly to a consumer buyer: (1) that the product corresponds to its description where the sale is "by description made by a person other than the retail seller"; (2) that the product will perform for a reasonable length of time; (3) that the product is in such a condition that a consumer buyer fully aware of the product's defects would buy without price abatement; and (4) that "spare parts and reasonable repair facilities will be available for a reasonable period of time."

The Saskatchewan Consumer Products Warranties Act 1977 (RSS 1978, c. C-30, now re-enacted as Part III of the Consumer Protection Act, SS 1996, c. C-30.1) has adopted the OLRC's recommendation to abolish the doctrine of privity for consumer warranty claims (see s. 14(1) of the original Act, s. 55 of the 1996 Act, and L.J. Romero, "The Consumer Products Warranties Act" (1978-1979), 43 *Sask. L. Rev.* 181, at 187-89). The Saskatchewan Act also provides statutory warranties similar to those found in Bill 110. New Brunswick has enacted broadly comparable legislation in its Consumer Product Warranty and Liability Act, SNB 1978, c. C-18.1. See I.F. Ivanovich, "Consumer Products in New Brunswick: *Fidem Habeat Emptor*" (1983), 32 *UNBLJ* 123 (Part I), (1984), 33 *UNBLJ* 43 (Part II).

The OLRC's recommendations on manufacturers' liability have also had an influence outside Canada. In Australia, the federal Trade Practices Act 1974 was amended in 1977 to incorporate a new Part V, Div. 2A, headed "Actions against Manufacturers and Importers of Goods." The 1977 amendments make manufacturers statutorily liable to consumers for losses caused by product defects. Liability extends to persons who derive title to the goods through or under a consumer, but not to other third parties who may suffer loss, for example, users and bystanders. The provisions are limited to consumer goods (goods of a kind that are ordinarily acquired for personal, domestic, or household use or consumption). As in the case of Ontario's Bill 110 and the Saskatchewan and New Brunswick laws, the basic scheme is to make the manufacturer liable to the consumer on the same footing that the retailer is liable. So, for example, a manufacturer may be required to pay damages if the product is not of merchantable quality or fit for its purpose, or if it does not correspond with a description the manufacturer has applied to it. There are also requirements governing reasonable availability of spare parts and repair facilities and manufacturers' express warranties. New Zealand has also enacted comparable legislation: see Consumer Guarantees Act 1993.

In Australia, the waters were muddied in 1992 when the Trade Practices Act was amended again to incorporate a new Part VA which comprises an additional set of provisions governing manufacturers' liability. The new provisions were meant to give effect to recommendations made by the Australian Law Reform Commission and the Law Reform Commission of Victoria in their joint report, *Product Liability* (ALRC Report No. 51, VLRC Report No. 27, 1989). The text of Part VA is based on the European Community Product Liability Directive. It is similar to Consumer Protection Act 1987 (UK), Part I. Part V, Div. 2A of the Australian Trade Practices Act is still in force. The two sets of manufacturers' liability provisions overlap and are to some extent inconsistent. The main differences are as follows: (1) the 1977 provisions are an extension of contract law, whereas the 1992 provisions are an extension of tort law; (2) the 1977 provisions apply to goods that are defective in the sale of goods sense, namely goods that are not of merchantable quality, fit for their purpose, and so on, whereas the 1992 provisions define "defect," in a tort sense, by reference to a standard of safety that "persons generally are entitled to expect"; (3) the 1977 provisions cover all kinds of loss that are recoverable in contract, including economic loss, whereas the 1992 provisions, consistently with a tort-based approach, are limited to personal injury, loss relating to other goods, and loss relating to buildings; (4) the 1992 provisions are not limited to consumer goods, though they do not apply to losses that are recoverable under workers' compensation laws and so most industrial claims are excluded; (5) the 1992 provisions include a contributory negligence defence and a state of the art defence; and (6) the 1977 provisions benefit the immediate consumer and any person who derives title to the goods through or under a consumer, while the 1992 provisions extend to other third parties as well.

Three other developments also merit attention. The first involves the Quebec Consumer Protection Act 1978. Title I, Chapter III, Division I of the Act deals with warranties. Section 54 in effect deems the manufacturer to have given warranties similar to those imposed upon the retail seller. These provisions appear to have been influenced by the corresponding developments in the common law provinces described above. For an analysis see Applebaum, "The Law of Warranty in the Province of Quebec," *Meredith Memorial Lectures 1979*, at 71.

Second, in its *Report on Products Liability* (1979), the OLRC made the following recommendations (at 129):

> 1. Ontario should enact a principle of strict liability in accordance with recommendations 2 and 3 below.
>
> 2. A person who supplies a defective product that causes injury should be strictly liable in tort for damages.
>
> 3. A person who supplies a product and who makes a false statement concerning the product, reliance upon which causes injury, should be strictly liable in tort for damages, whether or not the reliance is that of the person injured.
>
> 4. Subject to recommendation 5, the principle of strict liability proposed in recommendations 2 and 3 should cover personal injury and damage to property, together with economic loss directly consequent thereon.

5. The principle of strict liability proposed in recommendations 2 and 3 should not extend to damage to property used in the course of carrying on a business.

6. The principle of strict liability proposed in recommendations 2 and 3 should not extend to pure economic loss.

Recommendation 6 is of particular interest in the present context. It seems to mean that *Rivtow Marine* and its progeny (including of course the Supreme Court's decision in *Bird Construction, supra*) would retain their relevance, assuming the Commission's recommendations are ever implemented. So far the Ontario government has shown little interest in doing so.

The third development concerns the OLRC's approach in its Sales Report to extending a manufacturer's warranty liability in the context of claims for pure economic losses. As will be seen from the extract below, the Commission chose not to take a firm position but preferred to put forward some tentative recommendations for discussion purposes.

OLRC Sales Report

at 247-48

The Commission supports in principle the desirability of extending the express and implied warranties of a seller in favour of a subsequent buyer. After careful deliberation, however, we have decided not to take a firm position on the issue at this time, but to postpone a final decision until interested parties have had an opportunity to express their views. We adopt this position primarily because of the novelty and importance of the issue in Ontario, and because of the absence of hard data on the probable impact of such an extension of warranty liability. The only precedent in Canada appears to be the farm implement and agricultural machinery legislation in the Prairie Provinces and Prince Edward Island. These are useful guides if one is considering an incremental approach, but they provide little assistance in seeking to assess the impact of a general change in warranty law.

There appears to be an equal paucity of precedents in other common law jurisdictions. American law is still in a state of flux. We noted in our *Warranties Report*, the decision of the New Jersey Supreme Court in *Santor v. A. & M. Karagheusian, Inc.* (1965), 207 A.2d 305 (NJSC). In that case, the Court extended the concept of tortious liability for personal injury and physical damage caused by a defective product to purely economic losses in the case of consumer goods. This extension was disapproved in the majority judgment of the Supreme Court of California in *Seeley v. White Motor Co.* (1965), 403 P.2d 145 (Cal. SC) and has been rejected by the majority of other courts. American courts have been equally divided with respect to whether the remote seller can be sued on a theory of implied warranty running with the goods. On the strength of the recent decision of the Supreme Court of Alaska in *Morrow v. New Moon Homes Inc.* (1976), 548 P.2d 279 (Ala. SC) there appears, however, to be a trend in favour of allowing consumer claims, subject to the usual defences available to a seller under the Uniform Commercial Code. The question of the manufacturer's liability to the ultimate buyer in non-consumer transactions remains at large.

Finally, reference should be made to the important recommendations in the New South Wales *Working Paper on the Sale of Goods*. This Working Paper, basing itself in part on our *Warranties Report*, recommended extending the warranty of merchantable quality in favour of a remote buyer, but without confining it to consumer goods. The remote buyer's claim would, however, generally be subject to any defence that would have been available to the remote seller in an action for breach of warranty by the immediate buyer. We consider other aspects of the New South Wales recommendations more fully below.

The Commission's exposure draft statutory provision will be found in s. 5.18. (In considering the Commission's cautiousness bear in mind that the Sales Report is concerned with all types of sale of goods and not only with consumer goods.)

United States

Morrow v. New Moon Homes, Inc.

(1976) 548 P.2d 279 (SC of Alaska) (Footnotes omitted)

RABINOWITZ Chief Justice: This appeal raises questions concerning personal jurisdiction over, and the liability of, a nonresident manufacturer of a defective mobile home that was purchased in Alaska from a resident seller.

In October of 1969, Joseph R. and Nikki Morrow bought a mobile home from Golden Heart Mobile Homes, a Fairbanks retailer of mobile homes. A plaque on the side of the mobile home disclosed that the home had been manufactured in Oregon by New Moon Homes, Inc. The Morrows made a down payment of $1,800, taking out a loan for the balance of the purchase price from the First National Bank of Fairbanks. The loan amount of $10,546.49, plus interest of 9 percent per year, was to be repaid by the Morrows in 72 monthly installments of $190.13 each.

At the time of the purchase, the Morrows inspected the mobile home and noticed that the carpeting had not been laid and that several windows were broken. Roy Miller, Golden Heart's salesman, assured them that these problems would be corrected and later made good his assurances. Miller also told the Morrows that the mobile home was a "good trailer," "... as warm as ... any other trailer." After the sale, Miller moved the Morrows' mobile home to Lakeview Terrace, set it up on the space the Morrows had rented, and made sure the utilities were connected. Then the troubles started.

On the first night that the mobile home's furnace was in use, the motor went out and had to be replaced. The electric furnace installed by the manufacturer had been removed by someone who had replaced the original with an oil furnace. The furnace vent did not fit, and consequently the "stove pipe" vibrated when the furnace was running. Subsequent events showed the furnace malfunction was not the primary problem with the mobile home.

About four days after the mobile home had been set up, the Morrows noticed that the doors did not close all the way and that the windows were cracked. The bathtub leaked water into the middle bedroom. In March of 1970 when the snow on the roof began to melt, the roof leaked. Water came through gaps between the ceiling and the wall panels, as well as along the bottom of the wallboard. A short circuit developed in the electrical system; the lights flickered at various times. When it rained, water came out of the light fixture in the hallway. Other problems with the mobile home included the following: the interior walls did not fit together at the corners; the paneling came off the walls; the windows and doors were out of square; the door frames on the bedroom doors fell off and the closet doors would not slide properly; the curtains had glue on them; and the finish came off the kitchen cabinet doors.

Despite all these problems, the Morrows continued to live in the mobile home and make the loan payments. Golden Heart Mobile Homes was notified many times of the difficulties the Morrows were having with their mobile home. Roy Miller, the Golden Heart salesman with whom the Morrows had dealt, did put some caulking around the bathtub, but otherwise he was of little assistance. Finally, sometime before April 1, 1970, Nikki Morrow informed Miller that if Golden Heart did not fix the mobile home the Morrows wanted to return it. Miller said the Morrows would "[h]ave to take it up with the bank." Subsequently, Golden Heart went out of business.

The First National Bank of Fairbanks was more sensitive to the Morrows' plight. Upon being informed by the Morrows that they intended to make no further payments on the mobile home, bank personnel went out and inspected the home several times. In addition, on May 17, 1970, the bank wrote to New Moon Homes, Inc. in Silverton, Oregon. Its letter informed New Moon of the problems the Morrows were having with their New Moon mobile home and asked whether New Moon expected to send a representative to Fairbanks since Golden Heart, the dealer, was no longer in business. Apparently, New Moon did not respond to the bank's letter.

A short time later the Morrows' counsel wrote a letter to New Moon Homes notifying New Moon that the Morrows intended to hold the company liable for damages for breach of implied warranties. About a month later the Morrows separated, with Nikki Morrow continuing to live in the mobile home. She continued to make payments to First National because she "couldn't afford Alaskan rents." Nikki Morrow eventually moved out of the mobile home but made no effort to sell or rent it because she considered it "not fit to live in." In October of 1971 the Morrows filed this action against both New Moon Homes and Golden Heart Mobile Homes, alleging that defendants had breached implied warranties of merchantability and fitness for particular purpose in manufacturing and selling an improperly constructed mobile home. ...

The heart of this appeal concerns the remedies which are available to a remote purchaser against the manufacturer of defective goods for direct economic loss. The superior court held that the Morrows had no legal claim against New Moon because they were not in privity of contract with New Moon. The first argument advanced here by the Morrows amounts to an end run around the requirement of privity. The Morrows contend that their complaint asserted a theory of strict liability in tort. They further argue that they should have prevailed irrespective of any lack of privity of contract between New Moon and themselves, because lack of privity of contract is not a defense to a strict tort liability claim. It is true that in *Bachner v. Pearson*, 479 P.2d 319 (Alaska 1970), we held:

that implied warranty and strict products liability are sufficiently similar to require that a complaint worded in terms of the former theory should be deemed to raise a claim under the latter theory.

Thus, although the Morrows' complaint sounded in breach of implied warranties, it also raised a strict liability claim if such a claim is legally cognizable against New Moon.

In *Clary v. Fifth Avenue Chrysler Center, Inc.*, 454 P.2d 244 (Alaska 1969), Alaska adopted the *Greenman v. Yuba Power Products, Inc.*, 377 P.2d 897 (Cal. 1962), rule of strict products liability, which provides that

[a] manufacturer is strictly liable in tort when an article he places on the market, knowing that it is to be used without inspection for defects, proves to have a defect that causes injury to a human being.

By its terms the *Greenman* formulation applies only when the defective product causes personal injury. Since the Morrows did not sustain any personal injuries which were caused by the defects in their mobile home, strict liability is seemingly unavailable to them in the instant case. However, the Morrows argue that strict liability should nonetheless apply in the situation where a consumer sues a manufacturer solely for economic loss attributable to the manufacturer's defective product. This precise contention presents a question of first impression in Alaska.

The issue whether strict liability in tort should extend to economic loss has prompted no small amount of discussion in legal journals. The two leading judicial opinions are probably *Santor v. A. and M. Karagheusian, Inc.* 44 NJ 52, 297 A.2d 305 (1965), and *Seely v. White Motor Co.*, 63 Cal. 2d 9, 45 Cal. Rptr. 17, 403 P.2d 145 (1965). In the former case, Santor purchased from a retailer certain carpeting manufactured and advertised by Karagheusian. Almost immediately after the carpet was laid, Santor noticed an unusual line in it. As the pile wore down, the line became worse and two additional lines appeared. Since the retailer had gone out of business, Santor sued the manufacturer for damages for breach of the implied warranty of merchantability. In a unanimous decision, the Supreme Court of New Jersey held that the plaintiff, as the ultimate purchaser of defective carpeting, could maintain an action against the manufacturer on either of two theories, breach of implied warranty of reasonable fitness or strict liability in tort. Privity of contract was not necessary in order to pursue either theory, although damages were limited to loss of value of the carpeting. Although the opinion emphasized the widespread advertising carried on by Karagheusian, the Santor court made clear that "strict liability in tort is not conditioned upon advertising to promote sales."

[W]hen the manufacturer presents his goods to the public for sale he accompanies them with a representation that they are suitable and safe for the intended use. ... [S]uch a representation must be regarded as implicit in their presence on the market. ... The obligation of the manufacturer thus becomes what in justice it ought to be—an enterprise liability and one which should not depend on the intricacies of the law of sales. The purpose of such liability is to insure that the cost of injuries or damage, either to the goods sold or to other property, resulting from defective products, is borne by the makers of the products who put them in the channels of trade, rather than by the injured or damaged persons who ordinarily are powerless to protect themselves.

Barely four months after *Santor* came down, its strict liability holding was rejected by the Supreme Court of California in *Seely v. White Motor Co., supra.* Seely purchased a truck manufactured by White Motor Co. for use in his heavy duty hauling business. Upon taking possession of the truck, Seely found that it bounced violently. This "galloping" continued for 11 months until the truck's brakes failed and the truck overturned, sustaining in excess of $5,000 in damages. Seely was not injured in the incident.

Seely sued White Motor Co. seeking damages for the cost of repairing the truck and for both the money paid on the purchase price and the profits lost in his business because he was unable to make normal use of the truck. The Supreme Court of California affirmed the trial court's award of damages in the amount of the payments made plus lost profits, on the grounds that White Motor Co. had breached an express warranty to Seely, the ultimate purchaser. The majority opinion, written by Chief Justice Traynor, condemned in broad dicta Santor's application of strict liability principles to a case involving only economic loss ... .

Seely appears to enjoy the support of the vast majority of the other courts which have considered the question whether strict liability in tort should extend to instances of economic loss. We also prefer the result in *Seely*, although our reasoning differs slightly in emphasis from that of the *Seely* court. Under the Uniform Commercial Code the manufacturer is given the right to avail himself of certain affirmative defenses which can minimize his liability for a purely economic loss. Specifically, the manufacturer has the opportunity, pursuant to AS 45.05.100, to disclaim liability and under AS 45.05.230 to limit the consumer's remedies, although the Code further provides that such disclaimers and limitations cannot be so oppressive as to be unconscionable and thus violate AS 45.05.072. In addition, the manufacturer is entitled to reasonably prompt notice from the consumer of the claimed breach of warranties, pursuant to AS 45.05.174(c)(1).

In our view, recognition of a doctrine of strict liability in tort for economic loss would seriously jeopardize the continued viability of these rights. The economically injured consumer would have a theory of redress not envisioned by our legislature when it enacted the UCC, since this strict liability remedy would be completely unrestrained by disclaimer, liability limitation and notice provisions. Further, manufacturers could no longer look to the Uniform Commercial Code provisions to provide a predictable definition of potential liability for direct economic loss. In short, adoption of the doctrine of strict liability for economic loss would be contrary to the legislature's intent when it authorized the aforementioned remedy limitations and risk allocation provisions of Article II of the Code. To extend strict tort liability to reach the Morrow's case would in effect be an assumption of legislative prerogative on our part and would vitiate clearly articulated statutory rights. This we decline to do. Thus, we hold that the theory of strict liability in tort which we recognized in *Clary* does not extend to the consumer who suffers only economic loss because of defective goods.

The principal theory of liability advocated by the Morrows at trial was that New Moon had breached statutory warranties which arose by operation of law with the manufacture and distribution of this mobile home. Specifically, the Morrows rely upon AS 45.05.096 and AS 45.05.098 of the Uniform Commercial Code as enacted in Alaska. The former section provides for an implied warranty of "merchantability" in the sale of goods governed by the Code; the latter establishes an implied warranty that the goods are fit for the particular purpose for which they were purchased. The superior court was of the view that these code warranties operated only for the benefit of those purchasing directly from a manufacturer or seller. Since the Morrows were not in privity of contract with New Moon, the superior court concluded that a warranty theory based on AS 45.05.096 and AS 45.05.098 could not serve as a basis for liability.

There is little question that the Code applies to the distribution of mobile homes. New Moon qualifies as a "merchant" within the meaning of the relevant section, AS 45.05.042, and mobile homes, being highly movable, are "goods" as defined in AS 45.05.044. Further, in *George v. Willman*, 379 P.2d 103 (Alaska 1963), we held that the implied warranty of merchantable quality established by the Code's predecessor, the Uniform Sales Act, was fully applicable to the sale of mobile homes. The result is no different under AS 45.05.096 and AS 45.05.098 of the Code.

It is equally clear that in this jurisdiction the Morrows, as immediate purchasers, can recover against their seller for breach of the Code's implied warranties. Indeed, this was the theory upon which the default judgment against Golden Heart Mobile Homes was predicated. The critical question in this case is whether the Morrows, as remote purchasers, can invoke the warranties attributable to the manufacturer which arose when New Moon passed title of the mobile home to the next party in the chain of distribution. In other words, do the implied warranties of merchantability and fitness run from a manufacturer only to those with whom the manufacturer is in privity of contract?

Although sometimes criticized, the distinction between horizontal and vertical privity is significant in this case. The issue of horizontal privity raises the question whether persons other than the buyer of defective goods can recover from the buyer's immediate seller on a warranty theory. The question of vertical privity is whether parties in the distributive chain prior to the immediate seller can be held liable to the ultimate purchaser for loss caused by the defective product. The Code addresses the matter of horizontal privity in AS 45.05.104, extending the claim for relief in warranty to any "... person who is in the family or household of his buyer or who is a guest in his home if it is reasonable to expect that the person may use, consume, or be affected by the goods. ..." With regard to vertical privity, the Code is totally silent and strictly neutral, as Official Comment 3 to AS 45,05.104 makes eminently clear. The Code leaves to the courts the question of the extent to which vertical privity of contract will or will not be required. ...

The dispute here is whether the requirement of vertical privity of contract should be abolished in Alaska. This battle has already been waged in many jurisdictions, and the results are well known; the citadel of privity has largely toppled. The course of this modern development is familiar history and we need not recount it at length here. Contrived "exceptions" which paid deference to the hoary doctrine of privity while obviating its unjust results have given way in more recent years to an open frontal assault. The initial attack came in *Spence v. Three Rivers Builders & Masonry Supply, Inc.*, 353 Mich. 120, 90 NW 2d 873 (1958), but the leading case probably remains *Henningsen v. Bloomfield Motors Inc.*, 32 NJ 358, 161 A.2d 69 (1960), in which the New Jersey Supreme Court held liable for personal injuries and property damages both the manufacturer of an automobile and the dealer who sold the vehicle. The rationale for the widespread abolition of the requirement of privity stems from the structure and operation of the free market economy in contemporary society; it was succinctly summed up not long ago by the Supreme Court of Pennsylvania (*Kassab v. Central Soya*, 246 A.2d 853 (1968)):

> Courts and scholars alike have recognized that the typical consumer does not deal at arms length with the party whose product he buys. Rather, he buys from a retail merchant who is usually little more than an economic conduit. It is not the merchant who has defectively manufactured the product. Nor is it usually the merchant who advertises the product on such a large scale as to attract consumers. We have in our society literally scores of large, financially responsible manufacturers who place their wares in the stream of commerce not only with the realization, but with the avowed purpose, that these goods will find their way into the hands of the consumer. Only the consumer will use these products; and only the consumer will be injured by them should they prove defective.

The policy considerations which dictate the abolition of privity are largely those which also warranted imposing strict tort liability on the manufacturer: the consumer's inability to protect himself adequately from defectively manufactured goods, the implied assurance of the maker when he puts his goods on the market that they are safe, and the superior risk bearing ability of the manufacturer. In addition, limiting a consumer under the Code to an implied warranty action against his immediate seller in those instances when the product defect is attributable to the manufacturer would effectively promote circularity of litigation and waste of judicial resources. Therefore, we decide that a manufacturer may be held liable for a breach of the implied warranties of AS 45.05.096 and AS 45.05.098 without regard to privity of contract between the manufacturer and the consumer.

The more difficult question before this court is whether we should extend this abolition of privity to embrace not only warranty actions for personal injuries and property damage but also those for economic loss. Contemporary courts have been more reticent to discard the privity requirement and to permit recovery in warranty by a remote consumer for purely economic losses. In considering this issue we note that economic loss may be categorized into direct economic loss and consequential economic loss, a distinction maintained in the Code's structure of damage remedies. One commentator has summarized the distinction:

> Direct economic loss may be said to encompass damage based on insufficient product value; thus, direct economic loss may be "out of pocket"—the difference in value between what is given and received—or "loss of bargain"—the difference between the value of what is received and its value as represented. Direct economic loss also may be measured by costs of replacement and repair. Consequential economic loss includes all indirect loss, such as loss of profits resulting from inability to make use of the defec-

tive product. [Note *Economic Loss in Products Liability Jurisprudence*, 66 *Colum. L Rev.* 917, 918 (1966).]

A claim of the Morrows in this case is one for direct economic loss.

A number of courts recently confronting this issue have declined to overturn the privity requirement in warranty actions for economic loss. One principal factor seems to be that these courts simply do not find the social and economic reasons which justify extending enterprise liability to the victims of personal injury or property damage equally compelling in the case of a disappointed buyer suffering "only" economic loss. There is an apparent fear that economic losses may be of a far greater magnitude in value than personal injuries, and being somehow less foreseeable these losses would be less insurable, undermining the risk spreading theory of enterprise liability.

Several of the courts which have recently considered this aspect of the privity issue have found those arguments unpersuasive. We are in agreement and hold that there is no satisfactory justification for a remedial scheme which extends the warranty action to a consumer suffering personal injury or property damage but denies similar relief to the consumer "fortunate" enough to suffer only direct economic loss. Justice Peter's separate opinion in *Seely v. White Motor Co.*, 63 Cal. 2d 9, 45 Cal. Rptr. 17, 24, 403 P.2d 145, 152 (1965), persuasively establishes that the cleavage between economic loss and other types of harm is a false one, that each species of harm can constitute the "overwhelming misfortune" in one's life which warrants judicial redress. The Supreme Court of New Jersey is also in complete agreement with this view: ...

The fear that if the implied warranty action is extended to direct economic loss, manufacturers will be subjected to liability for damages of unknown and unlimited scope would seem unfounded. The manufacturer may possibly delimit the scope of his potential liability by use of a disclaimer in compliance with AS 45.05.100 or by resort to the limitations authorized in AS 45.05.230. These statutory rights not only preclude extending the theory of strict liability in tort, *supra*, but also make highly appropriate this extension of the theory of implied warranties. Further, by expanding warranty rights to redress this form of harm, we preserve "... the well developed notion that the law of contract should control actions for purely economic losses and that the law of tort should control actions for personal injuries." We therefore hold that a manufacturer can be held liable for direct economic loss attributable to a breach of his implied warranties, without regard to privity of contract between the manufacturer and the ultimate purchaser.[7] It was therefore error for the trial court to dismiss the Morrows' action against New Moon for want of privity.

---

7 We recognize that the arguments against the abolition of privity are more compelling when the injury alleged is damages of a consequential nature many times the value of the manufacturer's product. See, for example, Note, "Economic Loss in Products Liability Jurisprudence" (1965), 66 *Colum. L. Rev.* 917, 965-66. We do not speak today to the issue of consequential economic loss, other than to note that AS 45.05.222 governs the recovery of such damages and requires, among other things, that said damages must have been foreseeable by the manufacturer. *Adams v. J.I. Case Co.*, 125 Ill. App. 2d 388, 261 NE 2d 1 (1970).

Our decision today preserves the statutory rights of the manufacturer to define his potential liability to the ultimate consumer, by means of express disclaimers and limitations, while protecting the legitimate expectation of the consumer that goods distributed on a wide scale by the use of conduit retailers are fit for their intended use. The manufacturer's rights are not, of course, unfettered. Disclaimers and limitations must comport with the relevant statutory prerequisites and cannot be so oppressive as to be unconscionable within the meaning of AS 45.05.072. On the other hand, under the Code the consumer has a number of responsibilities if he is to enjoy the right of action we recognize today, not the least of which is that he must give notice of the breach of warranty to the manufacturer pursuant to AS 45.05.174(c)(1). The warranty action brought under the Code must be brought within the statute of limitations period prescribed in AS 45.05.242. If the action is for breach of the implied warranty of fitness for particular purpose, created by AS 45.05.098, the consumer must establish that the warrantor had reason to know the particular purpose for which the goods were required and that the consumer relied on the seller's skill or judgment to select or furnish suitable goods. In the case of litigation against a remote manufacturer, it would appear that often it will be quite difficult to establish this element of actual or constructive knowledge essential to this particular warranty.

. . .

Appeal allowed.

NOTES

1) The privity of contract doctrine has two aspects, "vertical privity" and "horizontal privity." "The 'vertical' non-privity plaintiff is a buyer within the distributive chain who did not buy directly from the defendant. For example, a man who buys a lathe from a local hardware store and then later sues the manufacturer is a 'vertical' non-privity plaintiff. The 'horizontal' non-privity plaintiff is not a buyer within the distributive chain but one who consumes or uses or is affected by the goods. For example, a woman poisoned by a bottle of beer that her husband purchased from a local grocer is a horizontal non-privity plaintiff. So, too, is a son who is injured by the new lawnmower his father bought, and the employee hurt by equipment purchased by her employer, and so on": White and Summers, *Uniform Commercial Code*, 5th ed. (2000), at 399. *Morrow v. New Moon Homes* is a vertical privity case. So are the other cases dealt with so far in this chapter. Horizontal privity is dealt with in the next section, *infra*.

2) Uniform Commercial Code 2-318 governs third-party beneficiaries of express and implied warranties. It gives states a choice between three alternative forms of privity rule: Alternative A, Alternative B, and Alternative C. The extract from the OLRC Report on Consumer Warranties, *supra*, sets out the text of these three alternatives and also explains the history of UCC 2-318.

Alternative A reproduces the original version of UCC 2-318 as adopted in 1952 and continued by the 1962 Code. Twenty-nine states have adopted Alternative A or a similar provision. Alternative A makes limited inroads into the horizontal privity requirement, but it says nothing about vertical privity. Comment 3 to UCC 2-318 says that "beyond [the horizontal privity reform] the section in this form is neutral and is not intended to enlarge or restrict the developing case law on whether the seller's warranties, given to his buyer who resells, extend to other persons in the distributive chain." It follows that in states which have adopted Alternative A, the courts are free to go their own way on the vertical privity issue, and so the law varies from state to state. According to White and Summers (at 406):

> the law permits a non-privity buyer to recover for direct economic loss if the remote seller has breached an *express* warranty. Where the buyer cannot show reliance on express representations by the remote seller, however, the case law is in conflict. Many courts still hold that, absent that reliance, a non-privity buyer cannot recover for direct economic loss on either an express or implied warranty theory. But a growing number of courts now allow non-privity plaintiffs to recover for direct (and even consequential) economic loss.

Morrow v. New Moon Homes is an early example of a case in the second category (Alaska has adopted Alternative A).

Uniform Commercial Code 2-318, Alternative B attacks both horizontal and vertical privity limitations for plaintiffs who are natural persons and who have suffered personal injuries. Beyond that it is silent. Alternative C is broader still. Some courts have read it as eliminating both vertical and horizontal privity requirements altogether, but whether it allows a non-privity plaintiff to recover damages for economic loss as opposed to personal injury or property damage is an arguable point. Six states have adopted Alternative B, and at least eight have adopted Alternative C or a similar provision. Seven other states have enacted their own provisions. In some Alternative B and Alternative C states, the courts have made additional inroads into the privity doctrine: see, generally, White and Summers, at 401-8.

3) White and Summers distinguish between direct and consequential economic loss. "Direct economic loss" is damage that flows directly from insufficient product quality. It includes ordinary loss of bargain damages: the difference between the actual value of the goods accepted and the value they would have had if they had been as warranted. Courts frequently measure direct economic loss by the purchaser's cost of replacement or repair. "Consequential economic loss" covers all economic loss a purchaser suffers beyond direct economic loss, including loss of profits, loss of goodwill, and loss of business reputation (at 405). White and Summers are critical of the case law allowing recovery for direct and consequential economic loss. They say (at 406, 407):

> A number of problems remain for courts that allow recovery to non-privity plaintiffs for direct economic loss. In our view, the remote seller's standard of responsibility (and, therefore, the appropriate measure of recovery) cannot be set solely in light of the terms of the transaction between the ultimate buyer and the immediate seller. In some cases it would plainly be unfair to hold the remote seller to the terms between the plaintiff and his seller. To cite an obvious case, assume … a remote seller who sells second hand goods to a dealer who passes them off as new to the plaintiff. The remote seller should not be held to have warranted the goods as new. Similarly, a manufacturer should not be held answerable for the difference between the *retail* price and the value of the goods delivered

and

more than in personal injury and property damage cases, it is appropriate to recognize the traditional rights of parties to make their own contract. If remote sellers wish to sell at a lower price and exclude liability for consequential economic loss to sub-purchasers, why should we deny them that right? Why should we design a system that forces a seller to bear the unforeseeable consequential economic losses of remote purchasers? Indeed, by forcing the buyer to bear such losses we may save costly law suits and even some economic losses against which buyers, knowing they have the responsibility, may protect themselves. In short, we believe that a buyer should pick its seller with care and recover any economic loss from that seller and not from parties remote from the transaction. Put another way, we believe the user is often the "least cost risk avoider." By placing the loss on the users or by forcing them to bargain with their immediate sellers about the loss, we may minimize the total loss to society. If manufacturers are not the least cost risk avoider, but must nevertheless bear the loss, we may cause them to spend more of society's resources than optimal to avoid the loss and may unnecessarily increase the cost of the commodity sold.

Do you agree? Does the judgment in *Morrow v. New Moon Homes* satisfactorily address these concerns? Recall the statutory developments in Canada and elsewhere, discussed *supra*. How does the legislation deal with White and Summers' point that in some cases it would be unfair to hold the remote seller to the terms between the plaintiff and his seller? How does it address their concerns about consequential economic loss awards? Note in this last connection that the legislation is limited to consumer transactions. How might this be relevant?

THE PROBLEM OF HORIZONTAL PRIVITY AND THE POSITION OF SUBSEQUENT TRANSFEREES

OLRC Report on Consumer Warranties

(1972), at 74-76

It frequently happens that goods are bought by a consumer not for his own use or enjoyment but for the use of the members of his family or to be given as a gift to a friend. Or again, the consumer may be moving to another city or another province and may not wish to take all his household goods with him. Another common situation arises where appliances are installed in a new home and the builder sells the home to a consumer or the home is sold by one consumer to another. In all these cases, if the goods turn out to be defective the person who received or purchased the goods directly or indirectly from the original buyer would have no contractual rights of recovery against the retailer or manufacturer because of the absence of privity of contract between him and them. If he is prescient, he might have obtained an assignment to him of the original buyer's rights, but even this measure of foresight may not help him much, since it is doubtful whether such an assignment is valid at common law. To compound the third party's difficulties, he will usually have no right of recourse against his immediate seller (assuming he bought the goods and did not receive them as a gift) because neither the quality warranties appearing in The Sale of Goods Act nor the warranties recommended by us for inclusion in the proposed Consumer Products Warranties Act will apply to private sellers. In the case of passenger cars a second purchaser may be able to invoke the manufacturer's express warranty since such warranties usually apply, with or without qualifications, to the first and second owner. In the case of other durable goods, the warranty is usually silent on the question of its assignability or the warranty is expressly restricted to the first buyer.

We see no reason however why the right of a consumer with a derivative title to enforce the express or implied warranties which accompanied the first retail sale of the goods should depend on the largesse of the manufacturer or retailer, or on the consumer's somewhat tenuous ability to prove some kind of a collateral contract between him and the retailer or manufacturer. It seems to us that the reasoning which militates in favour of allowing the retail buyer to sue the manufacturer directly without a showing of privity applies at least as strongly in the present circumstances. Indeed, it can be argued that the consumer with a derivative title has a stronger case. The retailer buyer at least has a right of recourse against the dealer whereas the later consumer at present is left remediless. It may also be remarked that the current legal position provides an undeserved windfall for the retailer, since in many instances it may not be practicable for the original buyer to lay a complaint. Even if he could be persuaded to do so, his damages would not necessarily coincide with the damages suffered by his successor in title.

Accordingly, the Commission recommends that the rights of the successor in title be expressly recognized by statute. The change can probably be effected most easily by defining "consumer buyer" to include any person deriving his interest in the goods from or through the original purchaser, whether by purchase, gift, operation of law or otherwise. Such a definition will also make it clear that the rights of the successor in title are derivative and are no greater than those of the original buyer.

This recommendation is not a novel one. By invoking a doctrine of implied warranties running with the goods, the Supreme Court of New Jersey in the *Henningsen* case discussed above extended protection both to the buyer and his wife (albeit only for the purpose of a personal injury claim) and, as has been seen, section 2-318 of the Uniform Commercial Code and its revised versions contemplate warranties running directly to third parties, at least where injury to person or to property is involved. In the opinion of the Commission, for the purpose of applying express or implied warranties, it would be illogical to distinguish between physical injury or damage and pure economic losses, assuming both were reasonably foreseeable. It is not anticipated that the relaxation of the horizontal rules of privity will lead to a flood of unwarranted claims. The successor in title will still have to show that the malfunction in the article was due to a defect in the manufacturing process and not to some intervening cause and, in the absence of long term express warranties, most of the claims are likely to be brought within a short period following the original purchase.

NOTES

1) Section 41 of the Consumer Protection Act, SS 1996, c. C-30.1 provides as follows:

(1) Subject to subsection (2), persons who derive their property or interest in a product from or through the consumer, whether by purchase, gift, operation of law or otherwise, are, regardless of their place in the sequence of dealings respecting the product, deemed:

(a) to be given by the retail seller or manufacturer the same statutory warranties that the consumer was deemed to have been given pursuant to sections 48 and 50;

(b) to receive from the warrantor the same additional written warranties that the consumer received and, for the purposes of any provision of this Part, unless otherwise provided in this Part:

(i) have rights and remedies against the retail seller, manufacturer or warrantor equal to but not greater than the rights and remedies the consumer has pursuant to this Part; and

(ii) are subject to any defences or rights of set-off that could be raised against the consumer pursuant to this Part.

(2) No retail seller who acquires a product from or through a consumer for the purposes of resale or for use predominantly in a business has any rights pursuant to subsection (1) respecting that product.

This provision implements the OLRC's recommendations. Compare s. 55:

In any action brought pursuant to this Part against a manufacturer, retail seller or warrantor for breach of a statutory, express or additional written warranty, lack of privity of contract between the person bringing the action and the retail seller, manufacturer or warrantor is not a defence, and the retail seller, manufacturer or warrantor is conclusively presumed to have received consideration.

Would s. 41 have assisted the plaintiff in the *Lyons* case, extracted below? What about s. 55? What is the relationship between ss. 41 and 55?

2) Section 23 of the New Brunswick Consumer Product Warranty and Liability Act, SNB c. C-18.1 reads as follows:

Where the seller is in breach of warranty provided by this Act, any person who is not a party to the contract but who suffers a consumer loss because of the breach may recover damages against the seller for the loss if it was reasonably foreseeable at the time of the contract as liable to result from the breach … .

"Consumer loss" is defined broadly in s. 1(1) to include all non-business losses. How is this provision different from s. 41 of the Saskatchewan Act?

3) For the US position on horizontal privity, see the Notes following *Morrow v. New Moon Homes, supra.*

Lyons v. Consumer Glass Co. Ltd.

(1981), 28 BCLR 319

MacDONELL LJSC: All the parties to the proceedings have concurred in stating a question of law in the form of a special case for the opinion of the court under R. 33 of the Supreme Court Rules.

The opinion sought of the court is: "May John Earl Lyons bring an action against Senum for breach of contract or for breach of any warranty or condition implied by the provisions of the Sale of Goods Act, RSBC 1960, chapter 344 [now RSBC 1979, c. 370]?"

The plaintiff is a four-year-old infant bringing an action by his guardian ad litem, John Lyons, his father. It is agreed that the mother of the infant bought from Senum a glass "evenflo" baby bottle for the feeding of the infant. Upon returning home from the store the mother filled the bottle with milk and placed it on a table in the kitchen of her home. In the later afternoon the baby bottle fell to the floor and broke into a number of pieces of glass and one of the pieces struck the plaintiff in the eye.

The plaintiff brings action against the manufacturer and the retail store which sold the bottle to the mother of the plaintiff.

The plaintiff relies on the Sale of Goods Act [RSBC 1979], s. 18, to found its action against the storekeeper. Its action against the other defendants must, of necessity, be founded upon negligence. The purpose of the special case is to determine whether s. 18 of the Sale of Goods Act is available to the plaintiff where the contract for the purchase of the bottle was between the mother of the plaintiff and the storekeeper. Section 18 of the Sale of Goods Act reads as follows [Ont. SGA, s. 15(1)]

. . .

It is argued for the plaintiff that the child was entitled to the benefit of the Sale of Goods Act, notwithstanding there was no privity of contract between the infant and the merchant. The reasoning is that the mother was acting as the agent of the child in obtaining the bottle for the use of the child. This position is opposed on the basis that the facts do not warrant the finding of agency and, in any event, an implied agency cannot be found in the case of the baby bottle which is not for the child but for the benefit of the parent in helping feed the baby milk. It is further argued by the defence that the Sale of Goods Act is only available to a buyer, and for liability to be extended under the Sale of Goods Act the definition of buyer would have to be expanded to include those for whose benefit the purchase is made.

I have examined the authorities cited and conclude that there are no Canadian cases supporting the plaintiff's position. The case of *Varga v. John Labatt Ltd.*, [1956] OR 1007, 6 DLR (2d) 336, Ontario High Court, supports the defendants' position. In that action proceedings were taken with respect to injuries sustained by the plaintiff from a chlorine solution contained in a bottle of beer. The plaintiff was successful against the manufacturer. The claim against the hotel was dismissed as there was no privity of contract between the plaintiff and the hotel, the plaintiff having received the bottle as a treat from a friend in the hotel beverage room.

The closest counsel for the plaintiff was able to come was the English case of *Lockett v. A. & M. Charles Ltd.*, [1938] 4 All ER 170. This was an action by a husband and wife for food poisoning suffered by the wife following lunch at a hotel. It was agreed that both ordered their food; however, the husband paid for the meal. It was held that the wife was entitled to succeed as she was entitled to recover damages for breach of the implied warranty that the food supplied was fit for human consumption. The question of who paid for the meal was discounted by the learned trial judge as an important fact as he said [at 172]:

I think that the inference is that a person who orders the food in a hotel or restaurant *prima facie* makes himself or herself liable to pay for it, and when two people—whether or not they happen to be husband and wife—go into a hotel and each orders and is supplied with food, then, as between those persons and the proprietor of the hotel, each of them is making himself liable for the food which he orders, whatever may be the arrangement between the two persons who are eating at the hotel.

It can be seen in that case the court did not rely on agency but treated the husband and wife as both contracting parties with the restaurant.

A somewhat different approach was taken by the English Court of Appeal in *Jackson v. Horizon Holidays*, [1975] 1 WLR 1468, [1975] 3 All ER 92. The plaintiff booked a holiday for himself and his family and was successful in recovering damages in respect of the disappointment and distress suffered by his wife and children when the holiday turned out to be inferior to what the defendant had promised. The judgment of Lush LJ in *Lloyd's v. Harper* (1880), 16 Ch. D. 290 (CA), was relied upon and was quoted in part as follows [at 95]:

> I consider it to be an established rule of law that where a contract is made with A for the benefit of B, A can sue on the contract for the benefit of B, and recover all that B could have recovered if the contract had been made with B himself.

This approach has not been followed in Canada and, apparently, it has not yet been applied in England for personal injuries. Such an approach would not be possible in this case as action has not been taken by the mother claiming a contract made for the benefit of the child. Additionally, it is questionable in any event in this case that the parent can be said to be contracting for the benefit of the child.

The state of the law of Canada which, in my opinion, requires privity of contract to found a claim on the warranty contained in the Sale of Goods Act has been considered in several Canadian provinces. The Ontario Law Reform Commission, in its Report on Products Liability (1979), commented on the state of the law in Canada and recommended that Ontario bring in a principle of strict liability to overcome this problem and others. The province of Saskatchewan in the Consumer Products Warranties Act, 1977 (Sask.), c. 15 [now RSS 1978, c. C-30], gave the benefit of consumers' products warranties, inter alia, to persons who may:

> 5. ... reasonably be expected to use, consume or be affected by a consumer product and who suffers personal injury as a result of a breach, by a retail seller or manufacturer ...

It can be seen that not only do persons who use or consume or are affected by a consumer product have a right of action against the seller, that right of action is also extended to the manufacturer.

New Brunswick has passed somewhat similar legislation in the Consumer Product Warranty and Liability Act, 1978 SNB, c. C-18.1.

It is my opinion that the plaintiff is not able to rely on the Sale of Goods Act of British Columbia to support his claim for personal injuries against the seller of the baby bottle as there is no privity of contract between the plaintiff and the defendant Senum Brothers Enterprises Ltd.

Plaintiff not entitled to rely on the Sale of Goods Act.

CHAPTER TEN

Manufacturer's Express Performance Warranties

Manufacturers of high-value goods in North America have long offered end buyers express warranties concerning the soundness and performance characteristics of their products. Such warranties are regarded both as important sales tools and as expressions of the manufacturer's confidence in the quality of his product. However, in the past, the actual terms of manufacturers' warranties have often fallen short of their ostensible goals. The present chapter explores some of these problems and also shows how, in the motor vehicle field, manufacturers have responded to longstanding concerns by consumers over the difficulty of resolving warranty disputes by introducing what is now a Canada-wide arbitration plan.

Henningsen v. Bloomfield Motors Inc.

(1960), 161 A.2d 69 (NJSC)

[Mr. Henningsen purchased a Plymouth automobile from the defendant dealer for his wife as a Mother's Day gift. The purchase order was a printed form of one page, the reverse side of which contained the manufacturer's warranty. The warranty by its terms expressly limited the manufacturer's obligation to make good at its factory any part or parts that were returned within ninety days after delivery of the vehicle to the original purchaser or before the vehicle had been driven 4,000 miles, whichever event occurred first. The warranty further stated that it was given expressly in lieu of all other warranties expressed or implied, and all other obligations or liabilities on the part of the manufacturer.

Mrs. Henningsen was driving the car when she lost control and crashed into a highway sign and a brick wall. The vehicle was a total loss and the collision insurance carrier, after inspection, advanced the opinion that something definitely went "wrong from the steering wheel down to the front wheels" and that the untoward happening must have been due to mechanical defect or failure.

The trial court felt that the proof was not sufficient to make out a *prima facie* case as to the negligence of either the manufacturer or the dealer, but plaintiffs succeeded against both on the ground of breach of warranty.

The extract which follows contains the court's observations on Chrysler's express performance warranty.]

FRANCIS J (for the court): The terms of the warranty are a sad commentary upon the automobile manufacturers' marketing practices. Warranties developed in the law in the interest of and to protect the ordinary consumer who cannot be expected to have knowledge or capacity or even the opportunity to make adequate inspection of mechanical instrumentalities, like automobiles, and to decide for himself whether they are reasonably fit for the designed purpose. *Greenland Develop. Corp. v. Allied Heat. Prod. Co.*, 184 Va. 588, 35 SE 2d 801, 164 ALR 1312 (Sup. Ct. App. 1945); 1 Williston, *supra*, at 625, 626. But the ingenuity of the Automobile Manufacturers Association, by means of its standardized form, has metamorphosed the warranty into a device to limit the maker's liability. To call it an "equivocal" agreement, as the Minnesota Supreme Court did, is the least that can be said in criticism of it. *Federal Motor Truck Sales Corporation v. Shamus*, 190 Minn. 5, 250 NW 713, 714 (SC 1933).

The manufacturer agrees to replace defective parts for 90 days after the sale or until the car has been driven 4,000 miles, whichever is first to occur, *if the part is sent to the factory, transportation charges prepaid, and if examination discloses to its satisfaction that the part is defective*. It is difficult to imagine a greater burden on the consumer, or less satisfactory remedy.

Aside from imposing on the buyer the trouble of removing and shipping the part, the maker has sought to retain the uncontrolled discretion to decide the issue of defectiveness. Some courts have removed much of the force of that reservation by declaring that the purchaser is not bound by the manufacturer's decision. *Mills v. Maxwell Motor Sales Corporation*, 105 Neb. 465, 181 NW 152, 22 ALR 130 (SC 1920); *Cannon v. Pulliam Motor Company*, 230 SC 131, 94 SE 2d 397 (SC 1956). In the *Mills* case, the court said:

> It would nevertheless be repugnant to every conception of justice to hold that, if the parts thus returned for examination were, in point of fact, so defective as to constitute a breach of warranty, the appellee's right of action could be defeated by the appellant's arbitrary refusal to recognize that fact. Such an interpretation would substitute the appellant for the courts in passing upon the question of fact, and would be unreasonable. *Supra*, 181 NW, at 154.

Also suppose, as in this case, a defective part or parts caused an accident and that the car was so damaged as to render it impossible to discover the precise part or parts responsible, although the circumstances clearly pointed to such fact as the cause of the mishap. Can it be said that the impossibility of performance deprived the buyer of the benefit of the warranty?

Moreover, the guaranty is against defective workmanship. That condition may arise from good parts improperly assembled. There being no defective parts to return to the maker, is all remedy to be denied? One court met that type of problem by holding that where the purchaser does not know the precise cause of inoperability, calling a car a "vibrator" would be sufficient to state a claim for relief. It said that such a car is not an uncommon one in the industry. The general cause of the vibration is not known. Some part or parts have been either defectively manufactured or improperly assembled in the construction and manufacture of the automobile. In the operation of the car, these parts give rise to vibrations. The difficulty lies in locating the precise spot and cause. *Allen v. Brown*, 181 Kan. 301, 310 P.2d 23 (SC 1957). But the warranty does not specify what the purchaser must do to obtain relief in such case, if a remedy is intended to be provided. Must the purchaser return the car, transportation charges pre-paid, over a great distance to the factory? It may be said that in the usual case the dealer also gives the same warranty and that as a matter of expediency the purchaser should turn to him. By under the law the buyer is entitled to proceed against the manufacturer. Further, dealers' franchises are precarious (see, *Automobile Franchise Agreements*, Hewitt (1956)). For example, Bloomfield Motors' franchise may be cancelled by Chrysler on 90 days' notice. And obviously dealers' facilities and capacity, financial and otherwise are not as sufficient as those of the primarily responsible manufacturer in his distant factory.

The matters referred to represent only a small part of the illusory character of the security presented by the warranty. Thus far the analysis has dealt only with the remedy provided in the case of a defective part. What relief is provided when the breach of the warranty results in personal injury to the buyer? (Injury to third persons using the car in the purchaser's right will be treated hereafter.) As we have said above, the law is clear that such damages are recoverable under an ordinary warranty. The right exists whether the warranty sued on is express or implied. ... And, of course, it has long since been settled that where the buyer or a member of his family driving with his permission suffers injuries because of negligent manufacture or construction of the vehicle, the manufacturer's liability exists. Prosser, *supra*, §§83, 84. But in this instance, after reciting that defective parts will be replaced at the factory, the alleged agreement relied upon by Chrysler provides that the manufacturer's "obligation under this warranty" is limited to that undertaking; further, that such remedy is "in lieu of all other warranties, express or implied, and all other obligations or liabilities on its part." The contention has been raised that such language bars any claim for personal injuries which may emanate from a breach of the warranty. Although not urged in this case, it has been successfully maintained that the exclusion "of all other obligations and liabilities on its part" precludes a cause of action for injuries based on negligence. *Shafer v. Reo Motors*, 205 F.2d 685 (3 Cir. 1953). Another Federal Circuit Court of Appeals holds to the contrary. *Doughnut Mach. Corporation v. Bibbey*, 65 F.2d 634 (1 Cir. 1933). There can be little doubt that justice is served only by the latter ruling.

NOTES

1) If a manufacturer's express performance warranty purports to exclude "all other obligations and liabilities on its part," would such a disclaimer be binding under Anglo-Canadian law? Would the answer be different if the buyer signed and returned a "warranty card" to the manufacturer accepting the manufacturer's offer to be enrolled in his warranty program, or if the buyer received service under the manufacturer's warranty?

2) In a carefully documented and tightly reasoned study ("A Theory of the Consumer Product Warranty" (1981), 90 *Yale LJ* 1297), Professor Priest examines the two main current theories of the consumer product warranty and advances a new one of his own. The two main theories are the exploitation theory and the signalling theory. The exploitation theory "derives from the presupposition of overwhelming manufacturer market power" and, in Professor Priest's view, has greatly influenced the policy of enterprise liability and modern judicial treatment of consumer product warranties. However, he feels that "the connection remains vague between the extent of market power and the specific definition of warranty coverage."

The signalling theory focuses on the difficulty consumers face at the time of purchase in estimating the risk of product defects. It regards express warranties as messages "signalling the mechanical attributes of goods" and proceeds from the assumption of consumer misperception of product risks. Professor Priest argues however that consumer perceptions are very difficult to identify or to measure. As a consequence, "hypotheses concerning the relationship between perceptions and specific warranty provisions are highly speculative and essentially nonfalsifiable."

Professor Priest's own theory is that a warranty is a contract "that optimizes the productive services of goods by allocating responsibility between a manufacturer and a consumer for investments to prolong the useful life of a product and to insure against product losses." The novelty of the theory is its "emphasis on the variety of allocative investments that consumers may make to extend productive capacity and its consideration of the difficulties of drafting warranty contracts to encourage such investments." (at 1298)

Professor Whitford and Professor Priest subsequently engaged in a debate on the merits of Professor Priest's analyses and of his new theory. See Whitford, (1982), 91 *Yale LJ* 1371 and Priest, *ibid.*, at 1386.

3) Since *Henningsen*'s case, *supra*, automobile manufacturers' warranties have changed significantly and generally for the better. See, for example, the *Ford Motor Company of Canada Warranty Guide: 2001 Model Ford and Mercury Cars and Light Trucks* reproduced below. What changes do you observe? What problems, if any?

NOTES

1) In *Chabot*'s case, *supra*, chapter 9, Eberle J considered Ford's contractual liability to the plaintiff under the terms of Ford's then new vehicle warranty:

> By it, Ford Canada promised that, within certain limiting circumstances which are not relevant in this case, the defendant South Park would repair, replace or adjust free of charge any parts (except tires) found to be defective in materials or workmanship. It matters not whether South Park also promised it would do such work; Ford Canada independently warranted that South Park would do so.

His conclusion was that (at 191-92):

> On the facts as found, the part consisting of the oil pan, gasket and drain plug assembly was defective. It would be possible to regard the entire engine of the truck as being defective, but I think it is more reasonable to draw the line at the smallest collection of components which together exhibit the material defect.

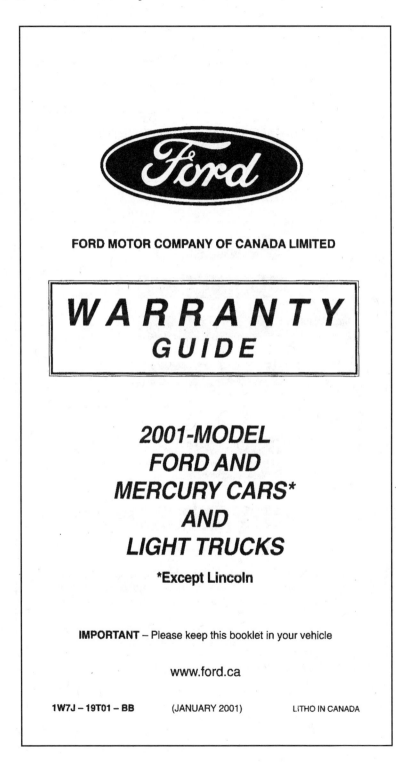

FORD MOTOR COMPANY OF CANADA LIMITED

WARRANTY
GUIDE

2001-MODEL
FORD AND
*MERCURY CARS**
AND
LIGHT TRUCKS

**Except Lincoln*

IMPORTANT – Please keep this booklet in your vehicle

www.ford.ca

1W7J – 19T01 – BB   (JANUARY 2001)   LITHO IN CANADA

HOW LONG THE COVERAGES LAST

This chart shows you how long the warranty coverages last.

WARRANTY TIME AND KILOMETRE COVERAGE AT A GLANCE

COVERAGE	Months					
	12 24 36		60 72		96	
Basic	60,000 km.					
Corrosion			unlimited distance			
Direct Injection Diesel Engine	160,000 km.		$100 deductible after 36/60			
Safety Restraint System	80,000 km.					
Emissions:						
Defect	60,000 km.					
Performance	60,000 km.					
Certain Emission Parts	130,000 km.					

This chart shows only general information. Refer to the detailed information on the following pages for what is covered and what is not covered under each of these coverages.

**FORD MOTOR COMPANY OF CANADA, LIMITED
THE CANADIAN ROAD,
OAKVILLE, ONTARIO L6J 5E4**

THE NEW VEHICLE WARRANTY
FOR YOUR
2001 MODEL VEHICLE

NEW VEHICLE LIMITED WARRANTY

Ford Motor Company of Canada, Limited warrants **that its authorized dealers** will repair, replace or adjust those parts on 2001 Ford of Canada cars and light trucks, that are found to be defective in materials or workmanship made or supplied by Ford for the periods described below. **The defects must occur under normal use of the vehicle during the warranty coverage period.**

Ford recommends that you take your vehicle to your selling dealer who wants to ensure your continued satisfaction with the vehicle you purchased. You must, however, take your Ford of Canada car or light truck to a Ford dealer authorized to service your vehicle. Certain warranty repairs require special training and/or equipment, so not all dealers are authorized to perform all warranty repairs. That means that, depending on the warranty repair needed, the vehicle may need to be taken to another dealer. In certain instances Ford may authorize repairs at other than Ford dealer facilities. A reasonable time must be allowed to perform a repair after taking the vehicle to the dealership. Repairs will be made using Ford or Motorcraft Parts or remanufactured or other parts that are authorized by Ford.

– 1 –

Who Pays for Warranty Repairs

There is no charge for warranty repairs performed under the Basic (except for the Direct Injected Diesel engine deductible after 36 months/60,000 kilometres), Corrosion, Emission, or Safety Restraint Coverages during the time and distance travelled limits of the New Vehicle Limited Warranty.

Federal or provincial governments may require an environmental or disposal tax (levy) on all or a portion of a warranty repair. Where federal or provincial law allows, this tax (levy) must be paid by you, the owner of the vehicle.

When Warranty Begins

The warranty begins on the original retail delivery date, or on the date of first use, whichever occurs first ("original warranty start date").

BASIC COVERAGE

Under this Basic Coverage, the complete vehicle (except those components coming under the other coverages listed below and those items listed under "Items Not Covered Under This New Vehicle Limited Warranty" on pages 10, 11 and 12) is covered for 36 months or 60,000 kilometres, whichever occurs first.

SAFETY RESTRAINT COVERAGE

Safety belts and air bag Supplemental Restraint Systems (SRS) are covered against defects in factory-supplied materials or workmanship. Safety restraint system coverage begins on the original warranty start date and lasts for 60 months or 80,000 kilometres, whichever occurs first.

-2-

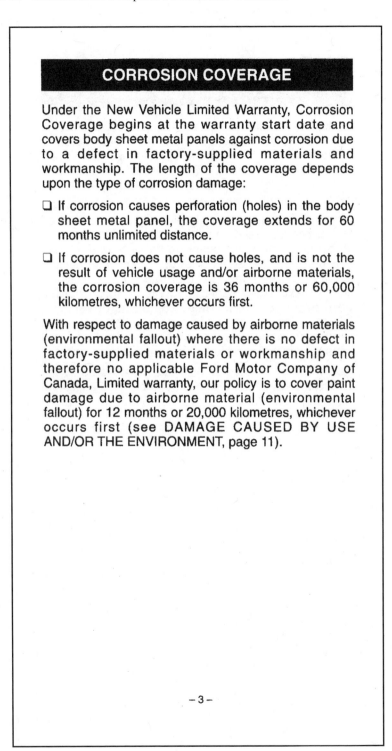

CORROSION COVERAGE

Under the New Vehicle Limited Warranty, Corrosion Coverage begins at the warranty start date and covers body sheet metal panels against corrosion due to a defect in factory-supplied materials and workmanship. The length of the coverage depends upon the type of corrosion damage:

❑ If corrosion causes perforation (holes) in the body sheet metal panel, the coverage extends for 60 months unlimited distance.

❑ If corrosion does not cause holes, and is not the result of vehicle usage and/or airborne materials, the corrosion coverage is 36 months or 60,000 kilometres, whichever occurs first.

With respect to damage caused by airborne materials (environmental fallout) where there is no defect in factory-supplied materials or workmanship and therefore no applicable Ford Motor Company of Canada, Limited warranty, our policy is to cover paint damage due to airborne material (environmental fallout) for 12 months or 20,000 kilometres, whichever occurs first (see DAMAGE CAUSED BY USE AND/OR THE ENVIRONMENT, page 11).

– 3 –

7.3L DIRECT INJECTION
DIESEL ENGINE COVERAGE

Certain direct injection diesel engine components are covered against defects in factory-supplied materials or workmanship for 60 months or 160,000 kilometres, whichever occurs first. A $100 deductible per repair visit applies after the Basic Coverage period (36 months or 60,000 kilometres, whichever occurs first).

Covered components: cylinder block, heads and all internal parts, intake and exhaust manifolds, flywheel, timing gear, harmonic balancer, valve covers, oil pan and pump, water pump, fuel pump and fuel system (excluding fuel lines and fuel tank), high pressure lines, gaskets and seals, glow plugs, turbocharger, powertrain control module, electronic driver unit, injectors, injection pressure sensor, high pressure oil regulator, exhaust back pressure regulator and sensor, camshaft position sensor, accelerator switch.

Note: Some components also may be covered by the Emissions Warranties with no deductible. See pages 5-8 for more information.

– 4 –

EMISSION CONTROL SYSTEMS COVERAGE

Emissions Defects Warranty Coverage

Under the emissions Defects Warranty, Ford provides coverage for 3 years or 60,000 kilometres (whichever occurs first) for passenger cars and light duty trucks. Certified heavy duty engines (vehicles with a GVWR over 3,856 kg. (8,500 pounds) are provided coverage of 5 years or 80,000 kilometres (whichever occurs first).

During this coverage period, Ford warrants that:

❑ your vehicle or engine is designed, built and equipped – at the time it was sold – to meet with the Emission Regulation under the Canadian Environmental Protection Act.

❑ your vehicle or engine is free from defects in factory-supplied material and workmanship that could prevent it from conforming with those applicable Emissions regulations.

❑ you will not be charged for repair, replacement or adjustment of defective emission-related parts listed under **What Is Covered?** on page 7.

Under the Emissions Defects Warranty for passenger cars and light duty trucks under 3,856 kg. (8,500 pounds) Ford also provides coverage, including labour and diagnosis, for 8 years or 130,000 kilometres, (whichever occurs first) for these emissions parts:

❑ Catalytic Converter

❑ Electronic Emissions Control Unit (PCM)

❑ Onboard Emissions Diagnostic Device

– 5 –

Emissions Performance Warranty Coverage

(Not applicable to vehicles rated at more than 3,856 kg. (8,500 pounds) GVWR).

If your vehicle is registered in a province where the province or local government has an approved Inspection and Maintenance (I/M) program, you are eligible for the Emissions Performance Warranty Coverage for 3 years or 60,000 kilometres (whichever occurs first) if you meet certain conditions.

Under the Emissions Performance Warranty Coverage, Ford will repair, replace or adjust – with no charge for labour, diagnosis, or parts – any emissions control device or system if you meet all these conditions:

❑ You have maintained and operated your vehicle according to the instruction on proper care as set forth in the **Owner's Guide**, the **Service Guide**, and this booklet.

❑ Your vehicle fails to conform during the warranty coverage period of 3 years or 60,000 kilometres (whichever occurs first) to the applicable I/M standards.

❑ You are subject to a penalty or sanction under local, provincial, or federal law because your vehicle has failed to conform to the emissions standards. (A penalty or sanction can include being denied the right to use your vehicle.)

❑ Your vehicle has not been tampered with, misused, or abused.

The Emissions Performance Warranty will not apply to your vehicle if:

❑ the vehicle is tested at high altitude, but is certified to meet standards only at sea level.

❑ the vehicle will pass the applicable provincial or local I/M test using approved procedures and standards set by these jurisdictions.

– 6 –

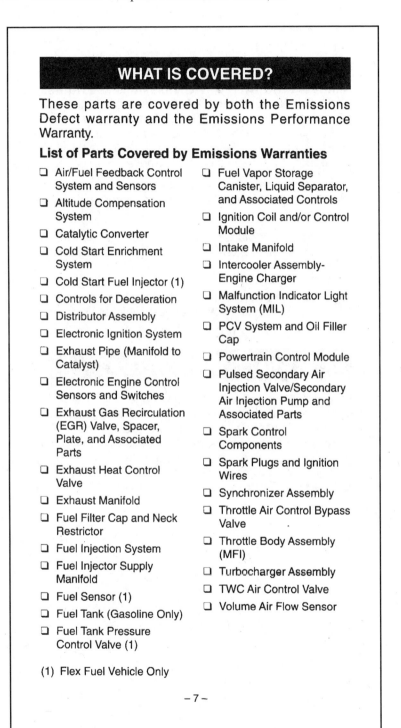

WHAT IS COVERED?

These parts are covered by both the Emissions Defect warranty and the Emissions Performance Warranty.

List of Parts Covered by Emissions Warranties

- ❏ Air/Fuel Feedback Control System and Sensors
- ❏ Altitude Compensation System
- ❏ Catalytic Converter
- ❏ Cold Start Enrichment System
- ❏ Cold Start Fuel Injector (1)
- ❏ Controls for Deceleration
- ❏ Distributor Assembly
- ❏ Electronic Ignition System
- ❏ Exhaust Pipe (Manifold to Catalyst)
- ❏ Electronic Engine Control Sensors and Switches
- ❏ Exhaust Gas Recirculation (EGR) Valve, Spacer, Plate, and Associated Parts
- ❏ Exhaust Heat Control Valve
- ❏ Exhaust Manifold
- ❏ Fuel Filter Cap and Neck Restrictor
- ❏ Fuel Injection System
- ❏ Fuel Injector Supply Manifold
- ❏ Fuel Sensor (1)
- ❏ Fuel Tank (Gasoline Only)
- ❏ Fuel Tank Pressure Control Valve (1)

- ❏ Fuel Vapor Storage Canister, Liquid Separator, and Associated Controls
- ❏ Ignition Coil and/or Control Module
- ❏ Intake Manifold
- ❏ Intercooler Assembly-Engine Charger
- ❏ Malfunction Indicator Light System (MIL)
- ❏ PCV System and Oil Filler Cap
- ❏ Powertrain Control Module
- ❏ Pulsed Secondary Air Injection Valve/Secondary Air Injection Pump and Associated Parts
- ❏ Spark Control Components
- ❏ Spark Plugs and Ignition Wires
- ❏ Synchronizer Assembly
- ❏ Throttle Air Control Bypass Valve
- ❏ Throttle Body Assembly (MFI)
- ❏ Turbocharger Assembly
- ❏ TWC Air Control Valve
- ❏ Volume Air Flow Sensor

(1) Flex Fuel Vehicle Only

– 7 –

Important Information about the List of Parts.

Also covered by the two emissions warranties (3 year/60,000 kilometre Defect and Performance) are all emission-related bulbs, hoses, clamps, brackets, tubes, gaskets, seals, belts, connectors, gasoline fuel lines, and wiring harnesses that are used with components on the List of Parts, above.

Parts that should be replaced on a certain recommended maintenance schedule remain under warranty until:

(A) the first replacement time that is specified in your **Owner's Guide** and the **Service Guide**;

or

(B) the time or distance travelled limits of the Defect and Performance Warranties (whichever occurs first).

WHAT IS NOT COVERED?

Ford will deny you warranty coverage if your vehicle or part has failed because you abused or neglected it, did not maintain it properly, added unapproved modifications, used improper fuel/fluids that it was not designed for, or experienced any item included in **Items Not Covered Under This New Vehicle Limited Warranty**, pages 10, 11 and 12.

– 8 –

FORD ROADSIDE ASSISTANCE

Your vehicle is eligible, within Canada or the United States, for the Ford Roadside Assistance Program. This Program is separate from the New Vehicle Limited Warranty, but the coverage is concurrent with the 36/60 "Basic Coverage" period.

Under this Program, Ford will cover towing (to the nearest Ford dealership), spare tire mounting, fuel delivery, dead battery service, lockout problems and customized trip routing.

For emergency roadside assistance, call
1-800-665-2006 24 hours a day.

Please refer to the Ford Roadside Assistance booklet for complete details regarding this Program. This booklet is included with the glove box package that comes with your vehicle.

The benefits of the Ford Roadside Assistance Program are transferred (within the 36/60 "Basic Coverage" period), at no charge, to subsequent owners of your vehicle when the vehicle ownership is transferred.

For uninterrupted Roadside Assistance coverage, you may purchase extended coverage prior to your Basic Warranty's Roadside Assistance expiring. For more information and enrollment, contact
1-877-294-2582

or visit our website at:
www.ford.ca

Towing necessitated by a warrantable failure beyond the "Basic Coverage" is covered under the applicable warranty.

– 9 –

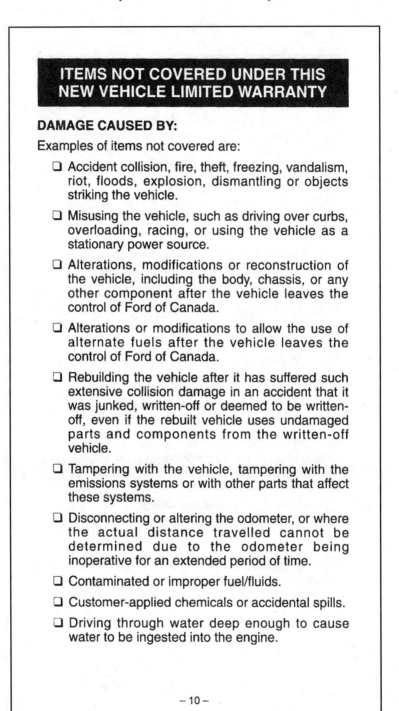

ITEMS NOT COVERED UNDER THIS NEW VEHICLE LIMITED WARRANTY

DAMAGE CAUSED BY:

Examples of items not covered are:

❏ Accident collision, fire, theft, freezing, vandalism, riot, floods, explosion, dismantling or objects striking the vehicle.

❏ Misusing the vehicle, such as driving over curbs, overloading, racing, or using the vehicle as a stationary power source.

❏ Alterations, modifications or reconstruction of the vehicle, including the body, chassis, or any other component after the vehicle leaves the control of Ford of Canada.

❏ Alterations or modifications to allow the use of alternate fuels after the vehicle leaves the control of Ford of Canada.

❏ Rebuilding the vehicle after it has suffered such extensive collision damage in an accident that it was junked, written-off or deemed to be written-off, even if the rebuilt vehicle uses undamaged parts and components from the written-off vehicle.

❏ Tampering with the vehicle, tampering with the emissions systems or with other parts that affect these systems.

❏ Disconnecting or altering the odometer, or where the actual distance travelled cannot be determined due to the odometer being inoperative for an extended period of time.

❏ Contaminated or improper fuel/fluids.

❏ Customer-applied chemicals or accidental spills.

❏ Driving through water deep enough to cause water to be ingested into the engine.

– 10 –

❏ Non-Ford parts installed after the vehicle leaves Ford of Canada's control. For example, but not limited to, cellular phone, alarm systems, and remote starting systems

NOTE: Warranty coverage will be invalidated on parts affected by such damage.

DAMAGE CAUSED BY USE AND/OR THE ENVIRONMENT

The New Vehicle Limited Warranty does not cover surface rust and deterioration of paint, trim, upholstery and other appearance items that results from use and/or exposure to the elements. Examples are:

❏ Stone Chips, Scratches. (some examples are on paint and glass)
❏ Road Salt, Tree Sap.
❏ Lightning, Hail.
❏ Earthquake.
❏ Cuts, Burns, Punctures or Tears
❏ Dings/Dents.
❏ Bird and Bee Droppings.
❏ Windstorm.
❏ Water or Flood.

DAMAGE CAUSED BY IMPROPER MAINTENANCE

The New Vehicle Limited Warranty does not cover damage caused by failure to maintain the vehicle, improperly maintaining the vehicle, or using the wrong part, fuel, oil, lubricants, or fluids (see important information on maintaining your vehicle on page 14). See the **Owner's Guide** for correct fluid specifications and levels, and consult the **Scheduled Maintenance Service Guide** for the proper ways to maintain your vehicle.

Failure to perform maintenance as specified in the Owner Guide and Service Guide will invalidate warranty coverage on parts affected by the lack of maintenance.

MAINTENANCE/WEAR

The New Vehicle Limited Warranty does not cover: (1) parts and labour needed to maintain the vehicle and (2) the replacement of parts due to normal wear and tear. You, as the owner, are responsible for these items. Here are examples.

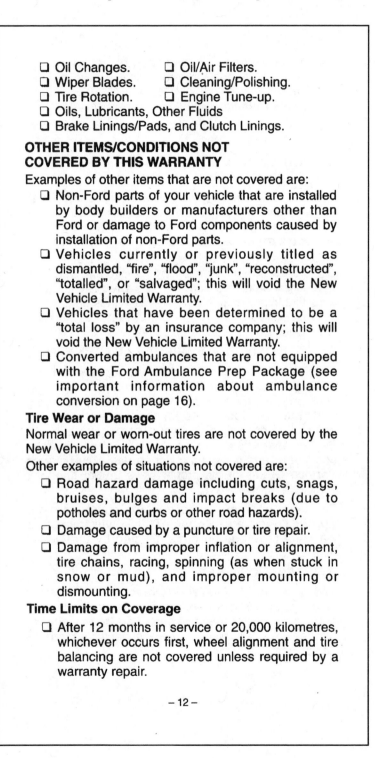

❏ Oil Changes.   ❏ Oil/Air Filters.
❏ Wiper Blades.   ❏ Cleaning/Polishing.
❏ Tire Rotation.   ❏ Engine Tune-up.
❏ Oils, Lubricants, Other Fluids
❏ Brake Linings/Pads, and Clutch Linings.

OTHER ITEMS/CONDITIONS NOT COVERED BY THIS WARRANTY

Examples of other items that are not covered are:

❏ Non-Ford parts of your vehicle that are installed by body builders or manufacturers other than Ford or damage to Ford components caused by installation of non-Ford parts.

❏ Vehicles currently or previously titled as dismantled, "fire", "flood", "junk", "reconstructed", "totalled", or "salvaged"; this will void the New Vehicle Limited Warranty.

❏ Vehicles that have been determined to be a "total loss" by an insurance company; this will void the New Vehicle Limited Warranty.

❏ Converted ambulances that are not equipped with the Ford Ambulance Prep Package (see important information about ambulance conversion on page 16).

Tire Wear or Damage

Normal wear or worn-out tires are not covered by the New Vehicle Limited Warranty.

Other examples of situations not covered are:

❏ Road hazard damage including cuts, snags, bruises, bulges and impact breaks (due to potholes and curbs or other road hazards).

❏ Damage caused by a puncture or tire repair.

❏ Damage from improper inflation or alignment, tire chains, racing, spinning (as when stuck in snow or mud), and improper mounting or dismounting.

Time Limits on Coverage

❏ After 12 months in service or 20,000 kilometres, whichever occurs first, wheel alignment and tire balancing are not covered unless required by a warranty repair.

– 12 –

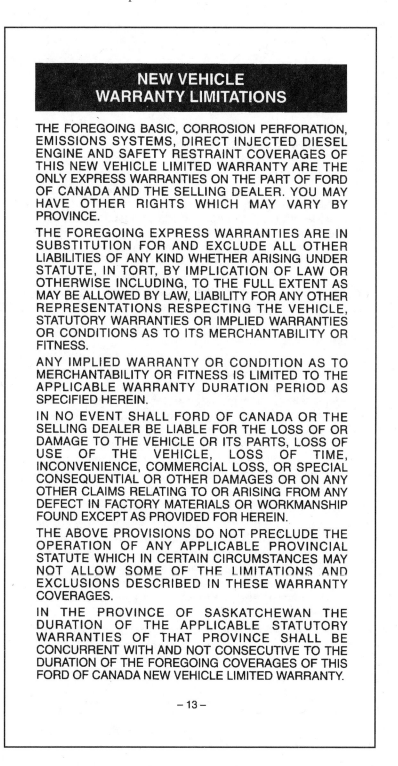

NEW VEHICLE WARRANTY LIMITATIONS

THE FOREGOING BASIC, CORROSION PERFORATION, EMISSIONS SYSTEMS, DIRECT INJECTED DIESEL ENGINE AND SAFETY RESTRAINT COVERAGES OF THIS NEW VEHICLE LIMITED WARRANTY ARE THE ONLY EXPRESS WARRANTIES ON THE PART OF FORD OF CANADA AND THE SELLING DEALER. YOU MAY HAVE OTHER RIGHTS WHICH MAY VARY BY PROVINCE.

THE FOREGOING EXPRESS WARRANTIES ARE IN SUBSTITUTION FOR AND EXCLUDE ALL OTHER LIABILITIES OF ANY KIND WHETHER ARISING UNDER STATUTE, IN TORT, BY IMPLICATION OF LAW OR OTHERWISE INCLUDING, TO THE FULL EXTENT AS MAY BE ALLOWED BY LAW, LIABILITY FOR ANY OTHER REPRESENTATIONS RESPECTING THE VEHICLE, STATUTORY WARRANTIES OR IMPLIED WARRANTIES OR CONDITIONS AS TO ITS MERCHANTABILITY OR FITNESS.

ANY IMPLIED WARRANTY OR CONDITION AS TO MERCHANTABILITY OR FITNESS IS LIMITED TO THE APPLICABLE WARRANTY DURATION PERIOD AS SPECIFIED HEREIN.

IN NO EVENT SHALL FORD OF CANADA OR THE SELLING DEALER BE LIABLE FOR THE LOSS OF OR DAMAGE TO THE VEHICLE OR ITS PARTS, LOSS OF USE OF THE VEHICLE, LOSS OF TIME, INCONVENIENCE, COMMERCIAL LOSS, OR SPECIAL CONSEQUENTIAL OR OTHER DAMAGES OR ON ANY OTHER CLAIMS RELATING TO OR ARISING FROM ANY DEFECT IN FACTORY MATERIALS OR WORKMANSHIP FOUND EXCEPT AS PROVIDED FOR HEREIN.

THE ABOVE PROVISIONS DO NOT PRECLUDE THE OPERATION OF ANY APPLICABLE PROVINCIAL STATUTE WHICH IN CERTAIN CIRCUMSTANCES MAY NOT ALLOW SOME OF THE LIMITATIONS AND EXCLUSIONS DESCRIBED IN THESE WARRANTY COVERAGES.

IN THE PROVINCE OF SASKATCHEWAN THE DURATION OF THE APPLICABLE STATUTORY WARRANTIES OF THAT PROVINCE SHALL BE CONCURRENT WITH AND NOT CONSECUTIVE TO THE DURATION OF THE FOREGOING COVERAGES OF THIS FORD OF CANADA NEW VEHICLE LIMITED WARRANTY.

– 13 –

THINGS YOU SHOULD KNOW ABOUT THIS NEW VEHICLE WARRANTY

PAINT, SHEET METAL AND OTHER APPEARANCE ITEMS

Defects or damage to paint, sheet metal or other appearance items may occur during assembly or when the vehicle is in transit to the dealer. Normally, these defects are noted and corrected at the factory or by your dealer during new vehicle inspection. Paint, sheet metal or appearance defects present at the time your vehicle is delivered to you are covered by this warranty. For your protection, we suggest that if you do find any such defects, you notify your dealer within one week of the vehicle's delivery to you, as normal deterioration due to use and exposure is not covered by this warranty.

GENERAL

Please note the distinction between "defects" and "damage" as used in the warranty. Defects are covered because we, the manufacturer, are responsible. This includes defects in Ford-supplied parts used in making warranty repairs as well as in the original parts of the vehicle. On the other hand, we have no control over damage caused by such things as collision, misuse and lack of maintenance. Therefore, damage for any reason is not covered under this warranty.

MAINTAINING YOUR VEHICLE PROPERLY

Your glove compartment contains an **Owner's Guide** and a **Scheduled Maintenance Service Guide** which indicate the scheduled maintenance required for your vehicle. Proper maintenance guards against major repair expense resulting from neglect or inadequate maintenance, and may help increase the value you receive when you sell or trade your vehicle.

It is your responsibility to make sure that all of the scheduled maintenance is performed and that the materials used meet Ford engineering specifications. Failure to perform scheduled maintenance as

– 14 –

specified in the **Scheduled Maintenance Service Guide** will invalidate warranty coverage on parts affected by the lack of maintenance. Make sure that receipts for completed maintenance work are retained with the vehicle and confirmation of maintenance work is always entered in your **Scheduled Maintenance Validation Record**.

Your Ford dealership has factory-trained technicians who can perform the required maintenance using genuine Ford parts. The dealership looks forward to meeting your every service need to maximize your satisfaction with your vehicle.

OBTAINING REPAIRS

To obtain warranty repairs, you must take your vehicle to a Ford dealership. While any Ford dealership handling your vehicle line will provide warranty service, we recommend you return to the dealership that sold you your vehicle.

Certain warranty repairs require special training and/or equipment, so not all dealers are authorized to perform all warranty repairs. That means that, depending on the warranty repair needed, the vehicle may need to be taken to another dealer. In certain instances Ford may authorize repairs at other than Ford dealer facilities.

WARRANTY APPLIES

The New Vehicle Limited Warranty described in this booklet applies to your vehicle if:

❑ it was originally sold or leased by a Ford of Canada dealer; <u>and</u>

❑ it was originally registered/licensed and operated in Canada or the United States.

WARRANTY DOES NOT APPLY

The New Vehicle Limited Warranty described in this booklet does not apply if the vehicle was purchased in Canada and:

❑ Is subsequently shipped out of Canada to a foreign country specifically for the purpose of resale in that country, or

❑ Is registered / licensed for use in countries other than Canada, or the United States.

TRAVELLING

If you travel with this vehicle outside of Canada or the United States, it may be necessary for you to pay the servicing Ford dealer in a foreign country for a repair that could be covered under this New Vehicle Limited Warranty. When this occurs, you should present the paid repair order/invoice to a Ford of Canada dealer for refund consideration.

IMPORTANT INFORMATION ON AMBULANCE CONVERSIONS

Ford vehicles are suitable for producing ambulances only if equipped with the **Ford Ambulance Prep Package.** In addition, Ford urges ambulance manufacturers to follow the recommendations of the **Ford Incomplete Vehicle Manual** and the **Ford Truck Body Builders Layout Book** (and pertinent supplements).

Using a Ford vehicle without the Ford Ambulance Prep Package to produce an ambulance voids the Ford New Vehicle Limited Warranty and may void the Emission Control Systems Coverage under this warranty. Vehicles used as ambulances without the Ford Ambulance Prep Package could experience elevated underbody temperature, fuel overpressurization and the risk of fuel expulsion and fires. Whether the vehicle is equipped with the **Ford Ambulance Prep Package** may be determined by inspecting the information plate on the driver's rear door pillar. Whether the ambulance manufacturer has followed Ford's recommendations can be determined by contacting your vehicle's ambulance manufacturer.

– 16 –

TIRES

Two separate warranties apply to the tires on your new vehicle. The New Vehicle Limited Warranty provides no cost coverage for tire repairs, replacements or adjustments due to defects in factory-supplied materials or workmanship during the Basic Coverage period. The tire manufacturer also provides you with a separate tire warranty that may extend beyond the Basic Coverage terms or period. You will find the manufacturer's tire warranty with the owner literature supplied with your new vehicle.

During the Basic Coverage period, your authorized Ford of Canada dealer wants to ensure your complete satisfaction at no out-of-pocket cost to you. In addition, you have the option of having a tire warranty repair performed by the manufacturer's authorized service centre. If you go to a tire service centre during the Ford Basic Coverage period for a covered repair (replacement or adjustment), you may be charged a prorated amount for wear or other charges. If so, you should present your paid invoice detailing the nature of the charges to any authorized Ford of Canada dealership for refund consideration.

CUSTOMER ASSISTANCE

The steps to take

Your satisfaction is important to Ford of Canada and to your dealer. Normally, matters concerning your vehicle will be resolved by your dealer's Sales or Service Department. Ford recommends that you take these steps:

1. First talk with your dealer's Service Manager or Sales Manager. Most problems will be resolved at this level. However, if the matter is not resolved to your satisfaction, you should consider steps 2 and 3.

– 17 –

2. Discuss the problem with the owner or General Manager of the dealership.

3. If you still cannot come to an agreement, contact the Ford of Canada Customer Assistance Centre at:

1-800-565-3673 (FORD)

FORD EXTENDED SERVICE PLAN

You can get more protection for your new car or light truck by purchasing a Ford Extended Service Plan (ESP). Ford ESP is the only service contract backed by Ford Motor Company of Canada, Limited. It provides:

❏ benefits during the warranty period depending on the plan you purchase (such as: reimbursement for rentals; coverage for certain maintenance and wear items); and

❏ protection against repair costs after your Basic Warranty expires.

You may purchase Ford ESP from any Ford of Canada dealer. There are several Ford ESP plans available in various time, distance and deductible combinations. Each plan is tailored to fit your own driving needs, including reimbursement for towing and rental.

When you purchase Ford ESP, you receive peace-of-mind protection throughout Canada and the United States, provided by a network of more than 5,000 Ford Motor Company dealers.

NOTE: Repairs performed outside Canada and the United States are not eligible for Ford ESP coverage.

This information is subject to change. Ask your dealer for complete details about Ford ESP coverage.

MEDIATION/ARBITRATION PROGRAM (CANADA ONLY)

In those cases where you continue to feel that the efforts by Ford and the dealer to resolve a factory-related vehicle service concern have been unsatisfactory, Ford of Canada participates in an impartial third party mediation/arbitration program administered by the Canadian Motor Vehicle Arbitration Plan (CAMVAP).

The CAMVAP program is a straight forward and relatively speedy alternative to resolve a disagreement when all other efforts to produce a settlement have failed. This procedure is without cost to you and is designed to eliminate the need for lengthy and expensive legal proceedings.

In the CAMVAP program, impartial third-party Arbitrators conduct hearings at mutually convenient times and places in an informal environment. These impartial Arbitrators review the positions of the parties, make decisions and, where appropriate, render awards to resolve disputes. CAMVAP decisions are fast, fair and final as the arbitrator's award is binding on both you and Ford of Canada.

The CAMVAP services are available in all Canadian territories and provinces (in Quebec commending on January 25, 2001). For more information, without charge or obligation, call your CAMVAP Provincial Administrator directly at 1-800-207-0685.

– 19 –

> South Park has not repaired or replaced this defective part; it has opposed the plaintiff's claim for relief. Accordingly, Ford Canada is liable, in warranty, for the cost of such service. I realize this is a measure of relief of little use to the plaintiff.

Is this a reasonable construction of the warranty or is it more likely that Ford expected the plaintiff to be indemnified under the terms of his motor vehicle owner's insurance policy against an accident leading to the total destruction of the vehicle?

2) *Henningsen*'s case, *supra*, expresses judicial dissatisfaction with the state of automobile warranties in the early 1960s. A number of later American and Canadian studies have documented the same dissatisfaction at the non-judicial level and with respect to a broader range of goods. See for example Federal Trade Commission, *Staff Report on Automobile Warranties* (1968); Federal Trade Commission, *Staff Report on Automobile Warranties* (1970); and OLRC Warranties Report, chapter 9, *supra*.

This dissatisfaction led to the adoption of remedial legislation in the United States and Canada. The best known, and most important, of the American initiatives is the Magnuson-Moss Warranty—Federal Trade Commission Improvement Act (1975), 15 USC §2301-2312, the contents of which are summarized below in the extract from Professor Strasser's article.

Canadian reactions to some extent antedate American post-war developments. The various Prairie farm implement Acts have to a varying degree regulated the form and content of express and implied warranties in the sale of such products since before the Second World War. For details, see OLRC Warranties Report, Table 10, at 98-99. The Prairie legislation was of course restricted in its scope but it served as a precedent for the OLRC recommendation that the proposed Consumer Products Warranties Act contain basic guidelines with respect to the form and content of written (performance) warranties for consumer products. See the Warranties Report, at 101-2. Once again Saskatchewan has been more persuaded by the Commission's reasoning than Ontario itself: see the Saskatchewan Consumer Products Warranties Act 1976, RSS 1978, c. C-30, as am. ss. 17-18, but apparently not yet in force, and L.J Romero, "The Consumer Products Warranties Act" (1978-79), 43 *Sask. L Rev.* 81.

3) If a consumer is entitled to the benefit of non-excludeable implied warranties (as is true in Ontario as a result of CPA s. 34(2)), why is it necessary to regulate express performance warranties as well? Should one or the other suffice?

K.A. Strasser
"Magnuson-Moss Warranty Act: An Overview and Comparison with UCC Coverage, Disclaimer, and Remedies in Consumer Warranties"

(1976), 27 *Mercer L Rev.* 1111, at 1113-14

The Act was passed in response to the specific consumer problems discussed above and to the generalized feeling of consumer helplessness in the face of warrantors' practice of using existing state law to effectively deny the consumer redress under consumer warranties. The Act was passed to make warranties more understandable to the consumer and to insure that obligations arising under either express or implied warranties are enforceable. As stated in the House Committee Report, the Act is designed to solve consumer warranties problems by:

1. [R]equiring that the terms and conditions of written warranties on consumer products be clearly and conspicuously stated in simple and readily understood language,

2. [P]rohibiting the proliferation of classes of warranties on consumer products and requiring that such warranties be either a full or limited warranty with the requirements of a full warranty clearly stated,

3. [S]afeguards against the disclaimer or modification of the implied warranties of merchantability and fitness on consumer products where a written warranty is given with respect thereto, and

4. [P]roviding consumers with access to reasonable and effective remedies where there is a breach of a warranty on consumer products.

The Senate consideration of the matter added consumer need for greater product reliability. This need would be met, it was thought, by making it economically rewarding for a manufacturer to build in better quality. Under the present system, to achieve a competitive price, a manufacturer must make products as cheaply as possible and then must disclaim all warranties possible. The Act rewards those manufacturers who make the more reliable products by giving them the competitive sale advantage of a "full" warranty. By making warranties more understandable, the Act will permit the consumer to make an informed choice between products on the basis of their warranties and will make consumer warranties a more important factor in the competition for sales. Thus, the legislation is an attempt to change the "rules of the warranty game":

Only when the rules of the warranty game are clarified so that the consumer can look to the warranty duration of the guaranteed product as an indicator of product reliability (because all costs of breakdown have been internalized) will consumers be able to differentiate on the basis of price between more reliable and less reliable products. This ability to differentiate should produce economic rewards from increased sales and reduce service costs to the producer of more reliable products. ...

Only a warrantor giving this type of "full" warranty is in a position to increase his profit, by making product reliability or service capability improvements. Furthermore, to the extent that consumer choice in the market place is guided by the desire for product reliability measured by the duration of the warranty, there will be an incentive for suppliers of consumer products to offer full warranties of relatively long duration. Therefore, there is a need to identify for the consumer which products are fully warranted and to create standards for "full" warranties.

The Act is also designed to help the consumer by strengthening the enforcement powers of the Federal Trade Commission which is the consumer's primary protector in the market place. This aspect of the Act is dealt with in Title Two and is beyond the scope of this discussion.

SELECTED BIBLIOGRAPHY ON THE MAGNUSON-MOSS WARRANTY ACT

D.G. Adams and M.F. Schwartz, "Consumer Protection—The Magnuson-Moss Act," [1976] *Ann. Survey Am. L* 257.

K.R. Guerin, "Clash of the Federal Titans: The Federal Arbitration Act v. The Magnuson-Moss Warranty Act—Will the Consumer Win or Lose?" (2001), 13 *Loy. Consumer L Rev.* 4.

M.E. Gunter, "Can Warrantors Make an End Run? The Magnuson-Moss Act and Mandatory Arbitration in Written Warranties" (2000), 34 *Ga. L Rev.* 1483.

M.T. Hymson, "The Magnuson-Moss Warranty—Federal Trade Commission Improvement Act: Should the Consumer Rejoice?" (1976-77), 15 *J Family L* 77.

W.R. Kutner, "Consumer Product Warranties Under the Magnuson-Moss Warranty Act and the Uniform Commercial Code" (1977), 62 *Corn. L Rev.* 738.

P.D. Rothschild, "The Magnuson-Moss Warranty Act: Does It Balance Warrantor and Consumer Interests?" (1976), 44 *Geo. Wash. L Rev.* 335.

Enforcing Warranty Claims

One of the enduring problems of consumer law is how to provide simple and inexpensive remedies for legitimate consumer grievances where the parties have not been able to settle their differences by negotiation. Consumers have a deep-seated and understandable aversion to litigation. Even the Small Claims Court, which historically was intended to provide a low cost and readily accessible forum for disputes involving small amounts, has failed to attract significant consumer support.

Various solutions have been propounded, of which industry sponsored resolution panels, mediational boards, "substitute actions" brought on behalf of the consumer by a public official (see the British Columbia Trade Practice Act, s. 24), and consumer class actions are some examples. See, further, OLRC Warranties Report, c. 8; OLRC Report on Class Actions (1982), and Ramsay, "Consumer Redress Mechanisms for Poor Quality and Defective Products" (1981), 31 *UTLJ* 117.

In the automobile warranty context, two approaches specifically geared to problems in this area have been introduced since the early 1980s. The first, of American origin, consists of the enactment of so-called "Lemon" laws—that is, laws designed to deal with the problem of defective cars that the dealer or manufacturer has been unable or unwilling to put right. The second approach involves the introduction of voluntary motor vehicle arbitration plans, such as the Ontario Motor Vehicle Arbitration Plan (OMVAP), which became operational in Ontario in November 1986. Such plans give the consumer the option of submitting his grievance to arbitration instead of having to litigate. The materials that follow deal with these solutions and some related issues.

June Rogers and William Lowther
"The Squeeze on Lemons"

Maclean's Magazine, July 11, 1983

Almost from the moment Josiane Rivet drove her new 1983 Renault Alliance off a Montreal lot last August, she had problems. First, oil began to leak from the brakes and the universal joint. Then the electrical system and the transmission faltered. Over a five-month period her $9,600 car was in the dealer's garage 30 days. In April she wrote Renault threatening to sue if the company did not replace her car. The manufacturer referred her to the dealer, who, in turn, conceded that her complaints were justified. Before the company would give her a new vehicle, though, she was asked to pay an additional $300. She refused. But finally, just last month, the company offered her a demonstrator with 1,100 km on the odometer and a six-month warranty, and she took it. Said Rivet: "I think that was all I could expect to get."

Compared to many of the roughly 700,000 owners of 1983 vehicles in Canada, Rivet was fortunate. Dissatisfied buyers who decide to sue car manufacturers can spend years in court, and even then they often end up empty-handed. But if Rivet and other disgruntled owners lived in any of 12 states across the border—from California to Maine—that have passed "lemon laws" over the past nine months, their cases could have been solved within 40 days. What is more, they would have had the choice of receiving either a new car or the cash equivalent.

In Canada consumers who buy faulty vehicles are not directly protected under law. There are no precise figures on the number of faulty vehicles sent onto the market. But "the need for recourse is growing," says Phillip Edmonston, president of the Automobile Protection Association (APA), a nonprofit consumer advocacy group based in Montreal. "We receive thousands of complaints on new cars every year—and some are real horror stories." In Quebec and Saskatchewan dissatisfied car buyers can resort to tough consumer protection acts. But neither jurisdiction specifically spells out redress in the case of a new vehicle that does not function properly. In Ontario, New Democrat MPP Edward Philip has tabled a private member's bill modelled on the "Lemon Aid Act" in Connecticut. Although it is unlikely to be adopted, the Conservative government is "looking into the lemon laws," says a spokesman for the ministry of consumer and commercial relations. As well, the 15,000-member APA has formed a task force to draft a comprehensive automobile protection act.

All the US lemon laws passed so far, and 14 more pending in other states, are based on the Connecticut definition of a lemon. It requires that a car be replaced or a refund granted if the vehicle cannot be fixed in four attempts, or needs 30 days or more of garage repairs for a single problem in the first year. Almost all the laws also stipulate that the consumer first resort to arbitration procedures that the carmakers have drawn up in recent years to handle customer disputes. They include meetings with the dealers and manufacturers. In some cases, the Better Business Bureau is called in to negotiate. But the arbitration is not binding, and if the consumer is not satisfied he can turn to the courts.

The state representative who drafted the Connecticut law, lawyer John Woodcock, is pleased with its performance since it went into effect nine months ago. "There is far more sensitivity on the part of car dealers and manufacturers to lemon car problems," he said. As a result, 20 to 30 new cars have already been replaced.

Evan Johnson, a staff attorney with the Center for Auto Safety in Washington, DC, an advocacy group that consumer activist Ralph Nader founded in 1970, says research suggests that as many as one in every 1,000 new cars may be a lemon. With eight million new cars sold in the United States last year, that would mean that about 8,000 of them could have been lemons. Said Johnson: "We think that lemon laws will encourage better quality manufacturing and better inspection by the dealer before delivery."

Still, the major car manufacturers insist that their arbitration programs are sufficient to resolve consumer complaints. Nick Hall, manager of media relations for GM Canada in Oshawa, Ont., says that in the past three years 376 complaints across the country have been resolved at the dealership level and another 83 have been settled with the help of the Better Business Bureau. While the BBB panels have made GM pay some "hefty repair bills," says Hall, they have not yet ordered that a new car be replaced. But Jeffrey Gray, legal counsel for the APA in Toronto, dismisses GM's program as "a bunch of baloney." He particularly objects to the fact that a consumer who takes part in GM's final step of mediation by the BBB must sign a commitment to abide by the decision.

But the mere existence of the lemon laws in the United States has already made manufacturers more cautious, says Paul Tuz, president of the Better Business Bureau of Metropolitan Toronto. Still, he thinks that the growing US consumer awareness is bound to rub off on Canadians. "My guess," says Tuz, "is that we will have lemon laws here within the next 10 years."

Note on Automobile Lemon Laws

As of 1994, all American states and the District of Columbia had adopted some type of automobile lemon law and there is a substantial volume of law review literature describing and critiquing the legislation. See, for example, "Comment" (1988-89), 57 *U. Cincinnatti L Rev.* 1015; Vicki D. Rau, "New Remedies for Defective Automobile Purchasers: A Proposal for a Model Lemon Law" (1988), 23 *Valparaiso U. L Rev.* 145; and James A. Lack, "U.S. Lemon Laws vs. The Canadian Motor Vehicle Arbitration Plan: Two Approaches to Resolving New Car Defect Issues" (1995), 19 *Suffolk Transnat'l L Rev.* 315. The lemon laws were designed to enable auto buyers to bypass the intricacies of the Article 2 sales rules and to remedy the shortcomings of the Magnuson-Moss Act, but they suffer from significant weaknesses of their own which impair their effectiveness. The weaknesses include lack of uniformity (which creates compliance problems for auto manufacturers and dealers), lack of definitive and workable standards (leaving the consumer guessing whether his claim will meet the statutory criteria), and non-applicability of many of the laws to breach of implied warranties under Article 2. For further details see Rau, *supra*.

The Canadian Motor Vehicle Arbitration Plans (CAMVAP)

After studying for several years the idea of introducing an American-style "lemon" law, the Ontario government decided in 1985 to proceed instead with an industry supported voluntary arbitration plan. The Ontario Motor Vehicle Arbitration Plan became operational in November 1986. OMVAP was incorporated as a non-profit corporation under Ontario law. Its board of directors was composed of representatives from the Ontario Branch of the Consumers' Association of Canada, the automobile industry, the Ministry of Consumer and Commercial Relations, the Better Business Bureau of Metro Toronto, and the Arbitrators' Institute of Canada. The corporation had a full-time executive director. As its name indicates, OMVAP's purpose was to provide aggrieved buyers of automobiles with a cost-less, accessible, and efficient arbitral mechanism for resolving warranty disputes with auto manufacturers.

In September 1989 OMVAP published a *Two Year Review of the Ontario Motor Vehicle Arbitration Plan* prepared by Professor Peter Mercer of the University of Western Ontario at the request of OMVAP's board of directors. Some of the statistical results collected by the Report were the following. In the two-year period 1987 and 1988 the Plan received a total of 6,049 inquiries. 742 consumer complaints were settled, representing a settlement ratio of 31.1%, and on average 107 cases were being processed or waiting to be arbitrated. Of the 742 settled complaints, 263 (35%) were settled in favour of the consumer, 242 (33%) were settled in favour of the company, and 237 complaints (32%) were mediated without arbitration. Overall, in 64.5% of the cases (500 out of 742) the consumer received either a cash or non-cash (that is, repair) award or settlement. The average cash award was $2,833. There were 40 buy-back awards in the two-year period involving an average dollar amount of $11,649. The Report's overall conclusion was that OMVAP had proved its value and should become a permanent feature of the settlement of motor vehicle warranty disputes in Ontario, but with some changes in the operational structure of the program and in the terms of the arbitration agreement.

OMVAP was replaced by CAMVAP early in 1994, presumably because it was felt that the benefits of the arbitral plan should be made available to auto buyers in all the provinces. The Plan was brought in incrementally and is now in force across Canada. The principles and operational structure of CAMVAP are basically the same as those of OMVAP, but the details differ. The following information is a summary of the CAMVAP Guide and Arbitration Agreement.[1]

Canadian Motor Vehicle Arbitration Plan

About the Program

- CAMVAP is designed to specifically deal with consumers' problems about *their* automobile. There is no cost to the consumer. The process does not require a lawyer and, in fact, almost all consumers are not represented by counsel. The manufacturers do not use counsel and might only do so if the matter is particularly contentious and the consumer is using counsel. Consumers can bring witnesses to support their case.
- CAMVAP's hearings are much less formal and generally do not have the adversarial tone of a court appearance. The arbitration is done in the consumer's home community—an important factor if you happen to live in a rural community such as Fort St. John, British Columbia or Dryden, Ontario.
- CAMVAP is entirely voluntary. Consumers who want to use the traditional court systems instead of CAMVAP are free to do so.

---

1 The following information was originally supplied to Professor Ziegel in 1995 by Stephen Moody, General Manager of CAMVAP in Toronto, and has been updated.

- The arbitrator's decision is final—on both the consumer *and* the manufacturer. Much like small claims court, appeal of the arbitrator's decision is limited to substantive errors in law made by the arbitrator or judge.
- CAMVAP covers vehicles from new through to four model years old (1997 model year). The entrance standards are set out on page 9 of the brochure.
- The results of individual arbitrations are confidential. Therefore, as there is not a public scorecard, the issue is more often problem resolution rather than one of strict liability. The arbitrator's award is based on a balance of probabilities after hearing the evidence presented at the Hearing. Often, the consumer, arbitrator and manufacturer's representative will test drive the vehicle to view the problem first-hand.
- CAMVAP is the same for all consumers in Canada.
- CAMVAP is an alternative to the court system. Consumers may choose to use CAMVAP or to proceed through the court system. Small claims courts in Canada have maximum limits that range from $3,000 to $6,000 and in one case $10,000. CAMVAP awards frequently exceed these limits.
- CAMVAP is currently the largest consumer products arbitration plan in Canada, and arbitrates between 350 and 400 cases across the country each year.

About the Awards

- Our awards from 1994 to 1999 show a breakdown of 71% in favour of the consumer and 29% where the arbitrator found no liability on behalf of the manufacturer. Based on awards for the 5 model years covered by CAMVAP, the results were 11% buybacks; 26% for repairs; 10% for monetary payment of repairs previously paid for by the consumer; 16% conciliated; 8% were buy-backs with reduction in price; and 29% no liability on the manufacturer.

About the Organizational Structure

- CAMVAP is a contractual agreement between the provincial and territorial governments, the industry associations for both the domestic and import manufacturers and the Consumers' Association of Canada. There is no government funding of the program.
- CAMVAP is a balanced partnership among Governments, manufacturers, dealers and consumer groups. The Program has 16 members. They are the Provincial and Territorial Governments (12), the Motor Vehicle Manufacturers' Association, the Association of International Automobile Manufacturers of Canada, the Consumers' Association of Canada (CAC) and the Canadian Automobile Dealers Association.
- CAMVAP's Board has 11 members, those being, one Government member representing the Western Provinces and Territories; one Government member representing Atlantic Canada; one Government member representing Ontario, one Government member representing Quebec; 2 industry members representing the MVMA member manufacturers; 2 industry members representing the AIAMC member manufacturers; 2 consumer members represented by the CAC; and one member representing CADA member dealers. It is important to note that each of the Govern-

ment Board members have [*sic*] responsibility for automobile related consumer issues in their respective Governments. The two CAC Board members were selected by their National Headquarters with one member being from Alberta and the other from Newfoundland. Both have been CAC provincial chapter Presidents. CAMVAP's Board has very effective and very strong consumer representation.

CAMVAP Agreement for Arbitration[2]

Purpose of the CAMVAP Program

The purpose of the Canadian Motor Vehicle Arbitration Plan (CAMVAP) is to establish a voluntary arbitration program for residents of Canada which will resolve disputes between automobile Manufacturers and their customers in a fair, inexpensive and fast manner. The Agreement for Arbitration and the Rules of Arbitration are meant to achieve this result, are to be interpreted accordingly and are not intended to reduce or diminish consumer rights granted to Canadian consumers by any Provincial or Territorial legislation.

Key Terms

In this Agreement, certain important words appear with the first letter of the word capitalized. These important words also have special meanings and the meanings are set out in the Key Terms section at the end of this Agreement.

1. *Eligibility*

A. *Residence and Ownership*

To have your dispute arbitrated under the Plan you must be a resident of Canada in a participating Province or Territory and be the Owner or Lessee of the Vehicle in respect of which your Claim is being made. In the case of an owned Vehicle, you must have been the registered owner at the time when the dispute with the Manufacturer first started and you must continue to be the Owner throughout the arbitration of your Claim. In the case of a leased Vehicle, you must be a single user Lessee under a lease agreement with a term of not less than 12 months. In addition, you must have the consent of the Lessor to the arbitration of your Claim and the Lessor's agreement to accept the decision of the Arbitrator.

B. *Disputes Which Can Be Arbitrated*

You can arbitrate disputes relating to the following:
(a) The interpretation, application or administration of the Manufacturer's new vehicle warranty; or

---

2 The following text reproduces the text of the original Agreement. The current CAMVAP Agreement is substantially longer, but the two Agreements cover the same ground. We have retained the original version in the interests of saving space.

(b) Allegations of defect in workmanship or materials affecting your Vehicle as delivered by the Manufacturer to an Authorized Dealer.

C. *Disputes Which Cannot Be Arbitrated*

You cannot arbitrate the following types of disputes:

(a) Involving personal injury or property damage resulting from the use, ownership or operation of your Vehicle;

(b) Involving claims for consequential or incidental damages, loss of profits, inconvenience, loss of use or availability of your Vehicle, or punitive damages, other than as specified in Section 2C(a)(2);

(c) Involving the same claims you are now making but which have previously been settled with the Manufacturer or an Authorized Dealer;

(d) Involving claims strictly relating to a dispute between you and an Authorized Dealer;

(e) Involving claims which have been or are presently being arbitrated or mediated outside the Plan, or being litigated before the courts, either by yourself or as part of a class action;

(f) Involving vehicles used primarily for business or commercial purposes;

(g) Involving motorhomes;

(h) Involving vehicles built to non-Canadian specifications and intended for sale outside Canada;

(i) Relating to service contracts, extended warranties, or third party warranties which are not part of the Manufacturer's new vehicle warranty;

(j) Relating to tire defects except where the defect is directly related to some other defect in workmanship or materials which affects your Vehicle;

(k) Relating to options or accessories which were not authorized by the Manufacturer and were not ordered and installed by an Authorized Dealer at the time that your Vehicle was sold to the original retail customer; and

(l) Relating to rustproofing applied other than by the Manufacturer.

D. *Eligible Models*

To arbitrate your Claim, your Vehicle must originally have been purchased from an Authorized Dealer and it must be of the current or previous four (4) model years. In addition, your Claim Form and Agreement for Arbitration must be received by the Provincial Administrator on or before the applicable filing date set out below:

Vehicle Model Year	Last Filing Date
1997	September 30, 2001
1998	September 30, 2002
1999	September 30, 2003
2000	September 30, 2004
2001	September 30, 2005
2002	September 30, 2006
2003	September 30, 2007
2004	September 30, 2008

Your Claim Form and Agreement for Arbitration must be sent to the Provincial Administrator office in the Province or Territory in which you reside. The filing date for your Claim is the date when your completed Claim Form and this Agreement, signed by you and, if applicable, the Lessor, is received at the Provincial Administrator office.

2. *Awards*

Under the Plan, the Arbitrator can make one or more of the following awards:

A. *Repairs*—That your Vehicle be repaired by an Authorized Dealer.

Where the Arbitrator makes this award, the Manufacturer will arrange to have such repairs carried out in a good and workmanlike manner within 30 working days of receipt of the Arbitrator's order. This 30 working day period can be extended by a reasonable period of time to allow for the delivery of authorized replacement parts to the Manufacturer or to the Authorized Dealer.

When the Arbitrator makes this award, the Arbitrator will remain responsible for the case for 90 days from the date the repairs are completed. If the repairs are not carried out in a good and workmanlike manner, you may, through your Provincial Administrator office, ask the Arbitrator to recall the Parties to a hearing in order to make an additional award.

B. *Buy-Back*—That the Manufacturer buy back your Vehicle.

Where the Arbitrator makes this award, the buy-back price will be subject to a reduction for use of your Vehicle calculated using the following formula.[3]

When the Arbitrator makes this award, you are responsible for recovering, where allowable, any Provincial or Territorial sales tax paid at the point of purchase of your Vehicle.

When the Arbitrator makes this award, the amount of the award shall not exceed the Purchase Price of your Vehicle. The Manufacturer will refund any Goods and Services Tax (GST) paid on the purchase of your Vehicle which will be adjusted to take into account any reduction for use of your Vehicle.

Where the Arbitrator makes an award requiring the Manufacturer to buy back your Vehicle, the following requirements apply:

(a)   You must represent and warrant that your Vehicle is free and clear of all third party security interests, mortgages and liens;

---

3   The reduction for use is calculated by dividing the Purchase Price of your Vehicle by 160,000 km and then multiplying that result by the number of kilometres shown on your Vehicle's odometer on the date of the hearing. The Arbitrator may choose not to make any reduction for use where your Vehicle has been in service for less than 365 days from its original in-service date on the date this Agreement, signed by you and, if applicable, the Lessor, is received by the Provincial Administrator.

(b) If your Vehicle is subject to a lien, the Manufacturer shall make payment jointly to you as Owner and to the lienholder. If your Vehicle is leased, the Manufacturer shall make payment jointly to you as Lessee, and to the Lessor and the lienholder;

(c) Either as Owner or Lessee, as the case may be, you must provide an indemnity agreement for any claims that may be made by lienholders against the Manufacturer with respect to your Vehicle;

(d) You must agree to deliver your Vehicle to the Manufacturer or an Authorized Dealer agreeable to you and the Manufacturer within 14 days of receipt of the Arbitrator's order. Your Vehicle must be delivered in substantially the same condition that it was in at the time of the hearing. The Manufacturer or the Authorized Dealer is entitled to inspect your Vehicle before taking delivery in order to check its condition. The Manufacturer or the Authorized Dealer can refuse to take delivery of your Vehicle if it has been damaged, or there are components missing, since the time of the hearing; and

(e) You must provide all documents necessary to transfer the ownership of your Vehicle.

When the Arbitrator makes this award, the Arbitrator will remain responsible for the case until the buy-back is completed. If the buy-back is not completed under this Section, the Manufacturer may ask the Arbitrator to recall the Parties to a hearing in order to adjust the award.

C. *Other Awards*

(a) *Monetary Awards*—An order awarding an amount of money for:

(1) a refund of the cost of repairing your Vehicle;

(2) a refund of reasonable and documented expenses incurred for car rentals, accommodation, towing, taxis and diagnostic testing not to exceed $350.00 in total;

(b) *Replacement*—If your Vehicle is of the current model year only, an order for replacement of your Vehicle with an equivalent model year vehicle equipped with the same options and accessories, where possible;

(c) *No Liability*—A finding that the Manufacturer is not responsible for your Claim; or

(d) *No Jurisdiction*—The Arbitrator shall determine whether or not he/she has jurisdiction to hear and determine your Claim which will include considerations of whether or not your Claim is eligible for arbitration under the Plan.

3. *Documents*

Your problems with your Vehicle must be set out completely in the Claim Form. The Arbitrator will only look at those problems. You must use your best efforts to give the Arbitrator all documents relevant to your Claim. To ensure that the arbitration goes smoothly, you and the Manufacturer must agree on the documents which are relevant and those which are not relevant to your Claim. If you and the Manufacturer cannot agree on the relevance of any documents, or if you refuse to hand over any documents which the Arbitrator reasonably believes are necessary for the determination of that issue, the Arbitrator may disallow all or part of your Claim.

4. *Decisions of the Arbitrator*

All decisions of the Arbitrator are final and binding on the Parties. Subject to the law of the Province or Territory in which you reside, the Arbitrator's award may be enforced in court in the same way as a Judgment or Order.

5. *Release of Claims*

Where the Arbitrator makes an award and the Manufacturer complies with the award, your Claim will come to an end and the Manufacturer will be released from any responsibility to you with respect to all issues related to your Claim.

6. *Suspension of Legal Rights*

You may not start any legal action or proceeding against the Manufacturer or any Authorized Dealer with respect to your Claim once you have filed your Claim with the Provincial Administrator. Any legal action or proceeding which has been started must be discontinued by you before you file your Claim with the Provincial Administrator. You may not apply for arbitration of any dispute which was previously litigated in the courts. You may not litigate any dispute in the courts which previously went to arbitration unless the next Section applies to you.

7. *Arbitrator's Failure To Give a Decision*

If the Arbitrator does not make a final decision with respect to your Claim within 21 days after the hearing of your Claim, you may start a legal action against the Manufacturer in respect of the matters relating to your Claim. Before doing this, however, you must give the Provincial Administrator notice in writing by registered mail. The notice must be sent to the same Provincial Administrator's office where you sent your Claim and must refer to the CAMVAP file number which was assigned to your Claim. The notice must say that the Arbitrator has not made a decision with respect to your Claim and you must give CAMVAP 30 days from receipt of your notice to resolve the matter with the Arbitrator. CAMVAP may either get the Arbitrator's final decision, which will be sent to you, or may appoint a replacement Arbitrator to rehear your Claim.

8. *Confidentiality*

All Parties involved in the arbitration of your Claim must agree to keep all proceedings involving the arbitration of your Claim confidential. This means that all information, documents and testimony presented during the arbitration proceedings and the award must be kept confidential and are not to be disclosed to any third party or used in connection with any matter not related to the arbitration of your Claim.

9. *Class Actions*

If your dispute with the Manufacturer is already included in a representative or class action in the courts, it cannot be arbitrated under the Plan. To have your Claim arbitrated, you must opt out of or stop your participation in the representative or class action.

10. *Governing Law*

This Agreement shall be governed by the laws of the Province or Territory in which you reside as disclosed on your Claim Form. If you move permanently to another Province or Territory before the hearing of your Claim begins, you must notify the Provincial Administrator and your Claim will be transferred to the Provincial Administrator in the Province or Territory of your new residence. Your Claim will then be governed by the laws of the Province or Territory of your new residence.

QUESTIONS

1) Is it correct to claim, as the Rogers-Lowther *Maclean's* article does, that Canadian consumers have no recourse for lemon cars under existing provincial law, other than in Saskatchewan and Quebec?

2) What advantages would a lemon-type law give Canadian consumers that they do not already enjoy under existing law?

3) When would you advise a Canadian consumer to arbitrate a grievance under CAMVAP and when would you recommend suit in the regular courts?

4) Is an arbitration award under CAMVAP limited to the terms of the manufacturer's warranty? Can the arbitrator take into consideration the warranty provisions in the SGA and the CPA? See Agreement for Arbitration cl. 1(C).

5) From the consumer's point of view, is it desirable to keep confidential the results of arbitration? Will it hinder consumers in determining whether or not to proceed under CAMVAP?

6) Should there be a right of appeal from the decision of an arbitrator in all cases or only on questions of law? (Under the Ontario Arbitration Act, SO 1991, c. 17, the arbitrator may be required to state a case for the opinion of the court on a point of law.)

CHAPTER ELEVEN

Seller's Delivery Obligations

MEANING OF DELIVERY

OLRC Sales Report

at 331-33

A number of preliminary observations are in order. First, by virtue of sections 26 and 27 of the Ontario Sale of Goods Act, the seller's basic obligation to deliver the goods .conditions his *prima facie* right to payment and acceptance by the buyer. However, delivery also has other important consequences, both under existing Anglo-Canadian law and even more so under Article 2 of the Uniform Commercial Code. Under the Sale of Goods Act, delivery affects the seller's lien rights and the rights of third parties who deal in good faith with a buyer who has been entrusted with goods or with the documents of title thereto. Further, in the case of a sale of future or unascertained goods, delivery usually coincides with the transfer of title, and therefore determines the time for the transfer of risk.

These important consequences have not been diminished by the Code. Indeed, Article 2 has increased their number. It may, therefore, fairly be said that, while the role of title has been demoted under the Code, that of delivery has been enhanced. This is not surprising, since most buyers are more conscious of the need to obtain possession of the goods, than they are to ascertain the status of an abstraction; the seller's right to sell is usually taken for granted. All this leads to the conclusion that there is no difference in doctrinal approach with respect to problems of delivery between the Sale of Goods Act and Article 2. The difference lies in matters of detail, and in the greater particularization of rules and situations adopted in Article 2. There is a further point. The Article 2 rules differ from the Ontario provisions in that they are closely integrated with the other Articles of the Code on Documents of Title (Article 7) and Secured Transactions (Article 9). The Ontario seller, on the other hand, is confronted with a large variety of statutes, federal as well as provincial, which are not necessarily consistent with one another or with the provisions of the Sale of Goods Act, and which need to be consulted for a full statement of his delivery obligations.

Delivery, as defined in the Sale of Goods Act, does not coincide with the layman's understanding of the term. It means the transfer of possession of goods from the seller to the buyer. The concept does not require the physical movement of goods. Regret-

tably, neither the Code nor the Act is consistent in the use of the term. Delivery is
sometimes used in its broad generic sense, and sometimes to describe the manner in
which a transfer of possession may be effected: for example, by shipment or dispatch. Further terminological confusion may be engendered by the failure to distinguish adequately between a *tender of delivery* and *delivery*. The two concepts are
distinct, and trigger different results and different obligations. Article 2 has made
some progress in sorting out the terminological muddle. The process is not, however,
complete, and a further effort seems worthwhile, particularly in the light of the precedents afforded by the Hague Uniform Law on the International Sale of Goods and
the draft UNCITRAL Convention. So far, the terminological confusion seems to have
caused the courts little difficulty. While we do not wish to exaggerate the importance
of the problem, we nevertheless recommend that the revised Act should strive for
greater clarity in the use of the term "delivery" and its various derivatives, and that it
should also distinguish more clearly between "tender of delivery" and "delivery."

TIME OF DELIVERY

Hartley v. Hymans

[1920] 3 KB 475, [1920] All ER Rep. 328

McCARDIE J: In the first place I think that time was here of the essence of the
contract. This, indeed, was not really disputed by the plaintiff. It is curious that s. 10
of the Sale of Goods Act, 1893, deals so ambiguously with this point. That section
provides: "(1.) Unless a different intention appears from the terms of the contract,
stipulations as to time of payment are not deemed to be of the essence of a contract
of sale. Whether any other stipulation as to time is of the essence of the contract or
not depends on the terms of the contract." This section gives a very slender notion of
the existing law, and it is well to remember s. 61 which provides (*inter alia*): "(2.) the
rules of the common law, including the law merchant, save in so far as they are inconsistent with the express provisions of this Act ... shall continue to apply to contracts
for the sale of goods." Now the common law and the law merchant did not make the
question whether time was of the essence depend on the terms of the contract, unless
indeed those terms were express on the point. It looked rather to the nature of the
contract and the character of the goods dealt with. In ordinary commercial contracts
for the sale of goods the rule clearly is that time is prima facie of the essence with
respect to delivery: see per Lord Cairns LC in *Bowes v. Shand* (1877), 2 AC 455, 463,
464 (the sale of rice); per Cotton LJ in *Reuter v. Sala* (1879), 4 CPD 239, 249 (sale of
pepper); and per Lord Esher MR in *Sharp v. Christmas* (1892), 8 TLR 687 (the sale
of potatoes). In *Paton & Sons v. Payne & Co.* (1897), 35 SLR 112, however, it was
held by the House of Lords that in a contract for the sale and delivery of a printing
machine time was not of the essence. This point is not fully dealt with in *Benjamin on
Sale*, 5th ed., at 588 *et seq.*, and no general rule appears to be stated in that treatise.
But in *Blackburn on Sale*, 3rd ed., at 244 *et seq.*, the matter is more clearly treated
and it is laid down that "In mercantile contracts, stipulations as to time (except as

regards time of payment) are usually of the essence of the contract." I may add that the relevant decisions on the point are excellently summarized in *Halsbury's Laws of England*, vol. xxv., at 152, in the section on *Sale of Goods* written by Sir Mackenzie Chalmers and Mr. W.C.A. Ker. With the above text-books may be contrasted the passage in *Addison on Contracts*, 11th ed., at 543.

Now, if time for delivery be of the essence of the contract, as in the present case, it follows that a vendor who has failed to deliver within the stipulated period cannot prima facie call upon the buyer to accept delivery after that period has expired. He has himself failed to fulfil the bargain and the buyer can plead the seller's default and assert that he was not ready and willing to carry out his contract. That this is so seems clear. It is, I take it, the essential juristic result, when time is of the essence of the contract. This is cogently shown by the judgment in *Plevins v. Downing*, 1 CPD 220 where the plaintiff vendors agreed to deliver iron in the month of July; as Brett J put it (at 226) when delivering the opinion of the Court: "The day after the end of July they could not have insisted on an acceptance of iron then offered to the defendant": see also per Martin B. in *Coddington v. Paleologo* (1867), LR 2 Ex. 193, at 196-97; and upon an analogous point see *Pearl Mill Co. v. Ivy Tannery Co.* [1919] 1 KB 78, at 83.

NOTES AND QUESTIONS

1) For a general discussion of the treatment of time as a contractual term, see S.J. Stoljar, "Untimely Performance in the Law of Contract" (1955), 71 *LQR* 527. See also *Bunge Corp. v. Tradax, supra*, chapter 4.

2) Why should the common law distinguish between the importance of time for purposes of delivery and the importance of time for the purposes of payment by the buyer?

3) SGA s. 27 provides that, unless otherwise agreed, delivery and payment are concurrent conditions. Does this import a qualification to SGA s. 11, and mean that in cash transactions the buyer is in breach of a condition unless he is able and willing to pay for the goods at the time of delivery? See OLRC Sales Report, at 147-48, 350, and 391, and *infra*, chapter 15.

Allen v. Danforth Motors Ltd.

(1957), 12 DLR (2d) 572 (Ont. CA)

SCHROEDER JA (for the court): The defendant appeals from the judgment of Smily J pronounced on June 10, 1957, whereby it was adjudged that the plaintiff do recover from the defendant the sum of $2,477 and costs.

The plaintiff, a married woman, entered into a contract with the defendant, a motor car dealer, to purchase a Regent Sedan motor car from the defendant, an enfranchised dealer in Dodge Motor products. The contract was in writing and was executed on April 9, 1957. The price of the car was stated to be $2,877 less a discount of $400, so that the net price was $2,477. Although the price was payable "cash on delivery of car," the plaintiff gave the defendant a cheque for the full purchase-price on the date of the contract.

After some discussion it was agreed that the defendant would provide a motor vehicle of a "heron grey colour with grey trim." No delivery date was specified in the written contract which contained the following terms: "The undersigned hereby purchases from you for delivery on or about ..."

This is followed by a description of the motor car and particulars of the price. The contract also contains the following terms:

I clearly understand that delivery of this car is contingent upon strikes, fires and other causes beyond your control, and hereby agree to extend delivery date (as may be reasonably required accordingly.)

and—

It is mutually agreed that there are no warranties or representations except as stated herein and made in writing.

The plaintiff was permitted to give evidence of a discussion which took place between her and the defendant's general manager as to the time of delivery. She stated: "It didn't seem there was any question of delivery on the colour. It would be a matter of three days or twenty-four hours. He would let me know if he could get it." Apparently, however, the manager found that he would have some difficulty in finding a car of the colour specified and informed the plaintiff of his difficulty two or three days later. The plaintiff stated that she informed the defendant's representative that she required the vehicle on Saturday, April 14th, as she had planned to take a trip to Buffalo with some friends during that weekend. She herself was not a licensed driver but only a learner and it had been arranged that a friend would drive the motor vehicle for her. When he was unsuccessful in obtaining a car of the desired colour from other dealers in Toronto, the defendant's manager offered her a blue car which she declined to accept. In order that she might have her contemplated trip to Buffalo, he offered to let her have the use of a new motor car of the same make and model as the one which she had ordered but she did not take advantage of this offer.

The plaintiff further testified that the defendant's manager telephoned her on Monday, April 16th, or Tuesday, April 17th, to state that he had been obliged to put in a special order with the manufacturer and that she then repudiated the contract and cancelled the order "because I couldn't wait as I wanted it to practise on for lessons." Her evidence as to the discussion relating to the time of delivery was substantially corroborated by Mr. George Cartwright who had been instrumental in bringing the parties together.

There was a conflict between the evidence of the plaintiff and the defendant's general manager as to the delivery date. Mr. Stratton, the manager, testified that no delivery date had been specified. He alleged that he had told the plaintiff that the normal delivery period was within two or three weeks but admitted that he had agreed "to get in touch with Mrs. Allen within two or three days and advise her what had taken place."

On the conflicting evidence the learned trial Judge made the following finding: "I think I must find on this evidence that the defendant agreed to deliver the car which the plaintiff agreed to purchase, within a few days, two or three or at least by the end of the week as the plaintiff has said." Mr. Stratton stated that as a result of the rush order which he had submitted to the manufacturer, a motor car answering the description of the motor car described in the written contract was available for delivery to the plaintiff on April 19th, ten days after the date of the contract; that he advised the plaintiff to this effect but she refused to accept delivery.

In this action the plaintiff sought to recover the sum of $2,477 paid by her as the purchase-price of the automobile.

The contract being one for the sale of goods of the value of more than $40, it is one required by the statute to be in writing; s. 5(1) Sale of Goods Act, RSO 1950, c. 345. [Now RSO 1990, c. S.1.]

It is provided by s. 26 of the Act that the seller is under a duty to deliver the goods and the buyer to accept and pay for them in accordance with the terms of the contract of sale. I refer also to s. 28(1) and (2) relating to the rules as to delivery under a contract for the sale of goods. Under the Act, as under the common law, where no time for delivery of the goods is fixed, they are to be delivered within a reasonable time.

If extrinsic evidence were admissible, the finding of the learned trial Judge as to the date fixed for delivery must be treated as having established the governing date, but in the present case not only have the parties reduced the transaction to writing, but the contract is one which is required by law to be in writing. Extrinsic evidence is, therefore, inadmissible to contradict, vary, add to or subtract from the terms of the document. Where a contract, not required by law to be in writing, purports to be contained in an instrument which the Court infers was not intended to express the whole agreement between the parties, proof may be given of any omitted or supplemental oral term expressly agreed upon before or at the time of executing a document but only if it is not inconsistent with the documentary terms. We are concerned here, however, with a formal contract in writing and one which is required by law to be in writing.

One of the incidents of a contract for the sale of goods where no date of delivery is specified is that the goods must be delivered within a reasonable time. The incidents which are impliedly contained in a written contract, whether by construction of its terms or by implication of law, are as much within the general rule as if expressed in written terms in the instrument, and it cannot be varied or contradicted by extrinsic evidence: *Heyworth v. Knight* (1864), 17 CBNS 298, 144 ER 120; *Burges v. Wickham* (1863), 3 B & S 669, 122 ER 251.

It has been held that a written contract for the sale of goods expressing no time for payment and delivery and therefore importing by construction of law a sale for ready money, does not admit of evidence of credit given except under a general usage of the trade: *Ford v. Yates* (1841), 2 Man. & G. 549, 133 ER 866. In that case the contract of sale was silent as to the time of payment but was construed by the Court to be a sale for cash on delivery, and evidence of a course of dealing by which the purchaser was allowed 6 months' credit was held inadmissible.

I refer also to *Greaves v. Ashlin* (1813), 3 Camp 426, 170 ER 1433. There the vendor had agreed in writing, sufficient under the Statute of Frauds, to sell certain goods, the contract being silent as to the time of delivery. Since this imported a reasonable time for the removal of goods by the buyer, oral evidence that he was to take them away immediately was held to be inadmissible.

It has been well settled that if the real contract of the parties is reduced into writing, whether it be a contract required by the Statute of Frauds to be in writing or not, verbal evidence is not allowed to be given of what passed between the parties either before the written instrument was made or during the time that it was in a state of preparation so as to add to or subtract from or in any manner vary or qualify the written contract: *Hickman v. Haynes* (1875), LR 10 CP 598; *Goss v. Lord Nugent* (1833), 5 B & Ad. 58, 110 ER 713; *Evans v. Roe* (1872), LR 7 CP 138. In *Inglis v. Buttery & Co.* (1878), 3 App. Cas. 552, it was held that even deleted words could not be looked at. The same point arose for determination in *King's Old Country Ltd. v. Liquid Carbonic Can. Corp.*, [1943] 1 DLR 538, 50 Man. R 359. There the contract in writing for the sale of goods called for delivery "as soon as possible" and it was held that those words could not be qualified or altered by a prior oral agreement by which the seller gave an unconditional promise to deliver before a fixed date; that there was no way by which the parol undertaking by the defendant to deliver the subject matter of the sale on or before May 15th could qualify the written agreement or resolve it into an operative prior and collateral agreement.

It is provided by s. 54 of the Sale of Goods Act that where in the Act any reference is made to "reasonable time," the question of what is a reasonable time is a question of fact. The uncontradicted evidence adduced by the defendant on this point is that if a car were specially ordered from the manufacturer, as was done in this case, it was impossible to secure delivery in less than 2 weeks. In the present case the car was available for delivery within 10 days of the date of the contract.

Even if the plaintiff were entitled to prove by extrinsic evidence that Saturday, April 14, was the date stipulated for delivery to be made, there is no term or provision of the contract nor is there anything in the surrounding circumstances from which it can be inferred that the time so stipulated was of the essence of the contract. Nor is there any finding upon that issue. Section 11 of the statute provides that unless a different intention appears from the terms of the contract, stipulations as to time of payment are not deemed to be of the essence of a contract of sale and whether any other stipulation as to time is of the essence or not depends on the terms of the contract. Assuming that April 14th had been established as the date of delivery, I am not convinced that it would be a stipulation constituting a condition, performance of which went to the whole consideration of the purchaser, for a breach of which she was entitled to reject the motor car in question and treat the contract as repudiated. It is unnecessary, however, to decide this point.

The crucial question to be determined in this case arises from the construction of the contract and, in my view, it is unquestionably a contract which required performance by the defendant within a reasonable time. The defendant offered to make delivery of the motor vehicle within a reasonable time and the plaintiff was not, in my opinion, entitled to refuse acceptance.

Appeal allowed.

QUESTIONS

1) In cases such as the above, should the plaintiff forfeit his whole payment? What was the defendant's measure of damages? See *Charter v. Sullivan* (*infra*, chapter 15) and *cf. Dies v. British and International Mining and Finance Corp. Ltd.*, [1939] 1 KB 724 and *Stockloser v. Johnson* (*infra*, chapter 15). Was Schroeder JA influenced in his judgment by the apparent unreasonableness of the plaintiff's conduct? Is it proper to invoke the parol evidence rule where the contract says nothing about the time of delivery? If the action were brought today, would the plaintiff be able to rely on s. 4(7) of the Ontario Business Practices Act?

2) S ordered a steel building from I at a price of $11,485, delivery to be made in the first week of June. S paid a deposit of $2,485. I failed to deliver on time and S agreed to wait until the end of June. By the end of July delivery had not been made, so S ordered another building from a different supplier without informing I. In late August, I notified S that it could then deliver. S refused delivery, informing I that it now had a substitute, and sued for the return of its deposit. What result? See *Sunstrum Ranching Co. Ltd. v. International Building Systems Ltd.*, [1975] 4 WWR 86 (Sask. Dist. Ct.).

Chas. Rickards Ltd. v. Oppenheim

[1950] 1 KB 616, [1950] 1 All ER 420 (CA)

[The defendant ordered from the plaintiff a Rolls-Royce chassis, which was delivered on July 30, 1947. At the request of the defendant, who wanted a body built on the chassis, the plaintiffs contacted various coachbuilders, one of which said it would be able to complete the work "within six or, at the most, seven months." On that footing the defendant gave the work order to the plaintiffs, who subcontracted with the coachbuilders. On August 20, 1947, the specifications for the body were finally agreed upon, placing the time for delivery, at the latest, at March 20, 1948.

The work was not completed by that date. Evidence indicated that the subcontractors were plagued by labour and materials problems. The defendant continued to press for delivery, choosing not to cancel the contract. He requested delivery in time for Ascot, 1948, but received no compliance. On June 29, 1948, the defendant wrote to the coachbuilders, referring to their latest promise of delivery of two weeks, as follows:

> I regret that I shall be unable, unless my plans change, to accept delivery of the Rolls you are making for me after July 25. For six months I have had a reservation to take a car abroad on August 3 for my holiday and it would appear to me to be impossible to alter this date. I shall, therefore, have to buy another car.

On July 8, 1948, the defendant was informed that the car would not be ready by July 25, whereupon he purchased another car and claimed from the plaintiffs £2,041, the amount he had paid for the chassis. The car was completed and tendered on October 18, 1948, but the defendant refused to accept delivery.

In this action the plaintiffs claimed £4,530 from the defendant, representing the balance of the price of the car under the agreement, or a similar amount for work and materials with respect to the body. The defendant counterclaimed for the chassis or, alternatively, its value. Finnemore J held that as the work on the car had not been completed by July 25 the defendant was entitled to cancel the contracts and gave judgment in his favour on both the claim and the counterclaim. The plaintiffs appealed.]

DENNING LJ: It is clear on the finding of the trial judge that there was an initial stipulation making time of the essence of the contract between the plaintiffs and the defendant: the body of the car was to be completed "within six, or, at the most seven months." Mr Sachs (for the plaintiffs) did not seek to disturb that finding; indeed, he could not successfully have done so. But what he did say was that that stipulated time was waived. His argument was that, the stipulated time having been waived, the time became at large, and that thereupon the only obligation of the plaintiffs was to deliver within a reasonable time. He said that "a reasonable time" meant, in accordance with well-known authorities, a reasonable time in the circumstances as they actually existed, that is, that the plaintiffs would not exceed a reasonable time if they were prevented from delivering by causes outside their control, such as strikes or the impossibility of getting parts, and events of that kind; and that on the evidence in this case it could not be said that a reasonable time was in that sense exceeded. He cited the well-known words of Lord Watson in *Hick v. Raymond and Reid*, [1893] AC 22, 32, 33, that where the law implies that a contract shall be performed within a reasonable time, it had "invariably been held to mean that the party upon whom it is incumbent duly fulfils his obligation, notwithstanding protracted delay, so long as such delay is attributable to causes beyond his control and he has neither acted negligently nor unreasonably." These words, he said, supported the view that in this case, on the evidence, a reasonable time had not been exceeded.

If this had been originally a contract without any stipulation as to time and, therefore, with only the implication of reasonable time, it may be that the plaintiffs could have said that they had fulfilled the contract; but in my opinion the case is very different when there was an initial contract, making time of the essence of the contract: "within six or at the most, seven months." I agree that that initial time was waived by reason of the requests that the defendant made after March, 1948, for delivery; and that, if delivery had been tendered in compliance with those requests, the defendant could not have refused to accept the coachbody. Suppose, for instance, that delivery had been tendered in April, May, or June, 1948: the defendant would have had no answer. It would be true that the plaintiffs could not aver and prove they were ready and willing to deliver in accordance with the original contract. They would have had, in effect, to rely on the waiver almost as a cause of action. At one time there would have been theoretical difficulties about their doing that. It would have been said that there was no consideration; or, if the contract was for the sale of goods, that there was nothing in writing to support the variation. There is the well-known case of *Plevins v. Downing* (1876), 1 CPD 220, coupled with what was said in *Bessler, Waechter, Glover & Co. v. South Derwent Coal Co. Ld.*, [1938] 1 KB 408, which gave rise to a good deal of difficulty on that score; but all those difficulties are swept away now. If the defendant, as he did, led the plaintiffs to believe that he would not insist on the stipulation as to time, and that, if they carried out the work, he would accept it, and they did it, he could not afterwards set up the stipulation as to the time against them.

Whether it be called waiver or forbearance on his part, or an agreed variation or substituted performance, does not matter. It is a kind of estoppel. By his conduct he evinced an intention to affect their legal relations. He made, in effect, a promise not to insist on his strict legal rights. That promise was intended to be acted on, and was in fact acted on. He cannot afterwards go back on it. I think not only that that follows from *Panoutsos v. Raymond Hadley Corporation of New York*, [1917] 2 KB 473, a decision of this court, but that it was also anticipated in *Bruner v. Moore*, [1904] 1 Ch. 305. It is a particular application of the principle which I endeavoured to state in *Central London Property Trust Ld. v. High Trees House Ld.*, [1947] KB 130.

So, if the matter had stopped there, the plaintiffs could have said, notwithstanding that more than seven months had elapsed, that the defendant was bound to accept; but the matter did not stop there, because delivery was not given in compliance with the requests of the defendant. Time and time again the defendant pressed for delivery, time and time again he was assured he would have early delivery; but he never got satisfaction; and eventually at the end of June he gave notice saying that, unless the car were delivered by July 25, 1948, he would not accept it.

The question thus arises whether he was entitled to give such a notice, making time of the essence, and that is the question that Mr. Sachs has argued before us. He agrees that, if this were a contract for the sale of goods, the defendant could give such a notice. He accepted the statement of McCardie J, in *Hartley v. Hymans*, [1920] 3 KB 474, at 494-95, as accurately stating the law in regard to the sale of goods, but he said that that did not apply to contracts for work and labour. He said that no notice making time of the essence could be given in regard to contracts for work and labour. The judge thought that it was a contract for the sale of goods. But in my view it is unnecessary to determine whether it was a contract for the sale of goods or a contract for work and labour, because, whatever it was, the defendant was entitled to give a notice bringing the matter to a head. It would be most unreasonable if the defendant, having been lenient and waived the initial expressed time, should, by so doing, have prevented himself from ever thereafter insisting on reasonably quick delivery. In my judgment he was entitled to give a reasonable notice making time of the essence of the matter. Adequate protection to the suppliers is given by the requirement that the notice should be reasonable.

So the next question is: was this a reasonable notice? Mr. Sachs argued that it was not. He said that a reasonable notice must give sufficient time for the work, then outstanding, to be completed. He says that, on the evidence in this case, four weeks was not a reasonable time because it would, and did in fact, require three and a half months to complete it. In my opinion, however, the words of Lord Parker in *Stickney v. Keeble*, [1915] AC 386, at 419 apply to such a case as the present just as much as they do to a contract for the sale of land. He said that

in considering whether the time so limited is a reasonable time the court will consider all the circumstances of the case. No doubt what remains to be done at the date of the notice is of importance, but it is by no means the only relevant fact. The fact that the purchaser has continually been pressing for completion, or has before given similar notices which he has waived, or that it is specially important to him to obtain early completion, are equally relevant facts to which I would add, in the present case, the fact that the original contract made time of the essence of the contract. In this particular case, not only did the defendant press continually for delivery, not only was he given promises of speedy delivery, but on the very day before he gave this notice he was told by the works manager in charge of the work that it would be ready within two weeks. Then he gave a four weeks' notice. The judge found that it was a reasonable notice, and, in my judgment, there is no ground on which this court could in any way differ from that finding. The reasonableness of the time fixed by the notice must, of course, be judged at the time at which it is given. It cannot be held to be a bad notice because, after it is given, the suppliers find themselves in unanticipated difficulties in making delivery.

Appeal dismissed.

[Singleton LJ delivered a reasoned concurring judgment; Bucknill LJ concurred without separate reasons.]

NOTES AND QUESTIONS

1) Compare *Oppenheim* with *McNeill v. Associated Car Markets Ltd.* (1962), 35 DLR (2d) 581 (BCCA). On the many meanings of waiver in the common law see *Banning v. Wright*, [1972] 1 WLR 972, esp. Lord Reid, at 981 and Lord Simon of Glaisdale, at 990. For the Code provisions on modification of contractual terms and waiver, see UCC 2-209.

2) Why did the plaintiff sue in this case? Was it because it had completed the work and a benefit had been conferred on the defendant (because the body had been built on the chassis) even though the plaintiff was in breach of the time of delivery? Was the plaintiff's only alternative to dismantle the body and simply return the chassis to the defendant, or would this have amounted to an act of conversion? Could theories of unjust enrichment be invoked here to prevent unjust results? How would you formulate them for this purpose?

A.H. Boulton
The Making of Business Contracts
2nd ed. (1972), at 27-31

There is little doubt that the most intractable problem in the attempt to create completely fair and workable conditions to operate between the buyer and seller of goods is this one of the sanction to be applied in the event of late delivery, and consequently the means available to the buyer to ensure that he obtains his goods at the time he needs them. It has been seen that the typical conditions extant fall into three groups. Sellers' conditions seek to avoid liability, buyers' to fix full responsibility, including consequential damages, and more moderate conditions provide for liquidated damages. In modern industry the problem of late dispatch is a serious one, and in the opinion of many observers failure to keep quoted dispatch times is the prime sin of modern industry. There are both reasons and excuses for lateness, however, and the problem is not as easy in practice as it appears to the lawyers in the uncomplicated atmosphere of a court. It may therefore be of value to stand back from this problem and, forgetting the wording of rival conditions, attempt to see it whole and objectively. Upon almost every other point in the cleavage of interest between buyer and seller a compromise can readily be found by negotiation. Upon this, however, the difference of approach between the two parties is so fundamental that the unsatisfactory compromise of "liquidated damages" is very frequently adopted simply because it is difficult to find a better.

It is unsatisfactory for a number of reasons. The very fact that the adverse consequences to the seller of defaulting in the matter of time can be measured with accuracy may constitute a temptation to allow in his costing for a measure of "penalty" to be applied, and then to hope for the best. If pressures develop which give rise to a general deterioration in the delivery position the manufacturer will naturally balance penalty against penalty and bias his production plans so as to operate to his least disadvantage in this respect, rather than consider the extent to which his customers will in fact be damaged by his default. The reduction in price which the application of "liquidated damages" affords to the buyer seldom matches the damage actually suffered. Sometimes the buyer who is kept waiting for his goods loses nothing thereby, but if he suffers at all his loss is likely to exceed anything he may receive as liquidated damages. Thus the device fails in its ostensible purpose, in that it is seldom a genuine pre-estimate of the damage that will be suffered by the buyer. It is normally qualified by a provision under which the seller is entitled to call for an extension of time if delay is due to circumstances over which he has no control, and it is so easy for the seller to make such a claim with his full knowledge of the circumstances and to find plausible excuses, and so difficult for the buyer to refute it, that in practice it is found that to invoke the liquidated damages clause is to invite vexatious argument and to generate ill-will.

In this book the attempt throughout is to concentrate upon typical situations, and the typical situation in which the maintenance of delivery promises is of vital importance is that in which the goods to be supplied are made specially for the customer, and are such that their manufacture is a relatively lengthy process. In other situations the problem is not acute. If the goods of like kind can be readily purchased elsewhere the buyer can help himself out of the difficulty by buying in the market, and the seller who is left with goods on his hands can similarly sell them on the market. The damage which either suffers if there is a breach of contract is easily measurable as the difference in price, and the situation is adequately dealt with in the Sale of Goods Act, which, as has already been observed, grew out of the decisions of the courts made over a period when the contract of sale was mostly a matter for merchants dealing with commodities. When, however, an order is placed for goods which are specially made, the buyer has placed himself in the hands of the seller in a quite different way. Probably only those concerned in manufacturing industry can have a proper sense of the problems that arise when default occurs, or properly assess the difficulties that may be the cause of default. It is by no means unusual for the construction of a complicated machine, or, indeed, for a relatively standard article, if it is large and made only to order, to occupy a year of factory time. It is easy for the law to apply principles, valid enough in their proper place, granting the aggrieved buyer the right to repudiate the contract breached by the defaulting seller and to buy the goods elsewhere, but in practice that is the last thing he is likely to do, because to do it is to sacrifice such progress as has been made in the factory, and to recommence, with a new manufacturer, the long waiting period required for design and the organisation of manufacture. If he does cancel the contract the true reason may be that he has changed his plans and is using the opportunity thus gratuitously offered to escape from his commitments. Looking at the same situation from the point of view of the seller, it is equally easy for the law to say that he has defaulted and has failed to deliver the goods at the proper time so that the buyer is released from the contract and that he, as the seller, has only himself to blame. But to be left with a nearly completed machine for which there is no immediate prospect of sale and which represents the investment of many thousands of pounds in production costs is a major catastrophe which he cannot contemplate with any equanimity. Thus, once an order for this type of article is placed, the two parties are deeply commited to each other by the practical realities of the situation.

From the point of view of the buyer, however, the availability of the goods at the time contracted for may be absolutely vital. He may himself have entered into commitments upon the strength of the seller's undertakings. When the goods are themselves to be used for production purposes as earning assets, delay may involve him in trading losses and in breach of his own undertakings. Of what value to him is a liquidated damages clause yielding a maximum of £1,000, if, as a result of the delay he loses profits worth ten times as much, involves himself in lawsuits from the breach of his own contracts, and suffers a loss of reputation which cannot be appraised? For him, the best position is to be able to recognise time as of the essence of the contract, and to rest upon the common law principle expressed in the Sale of Goods Act, "The measure of damages is the estimated loss directly and naturally resulting in the ordinary course of events from the seller's breach of contract." As has been seen, the damages recoverable at common law by the application of this principle can be very heavy and can include loss of profits.

But the seller also has his point of view. When he quotes a time for the supply of the goods he is looking into the future, which is always a risky business. It is not merely a matter of fire, flood, act of God, industrial dispute, embargo, riot, or any other hair-raising possibilities which legal draftsmen love to write into their escape clauses. His chief designer may fall sick, or find another job, or a flaw may be found in a major casting, so that it has to be replaced from the foundry, or he may be kept waiting for components he has ordered from other suppliers. He may find it difficult to work to required tolerances without seeking new standards of material. It may simply happen that a job takes longer than he had expected, or that a sub-assembly has to be redesigned because of teething troubles. Just how far can he expect to stretch an escape clause based upon the magical words "circumstances beyond his reasonable control"? The two things he dare not expose himself to are to have his custom built machine left on his hands and to be held liable to damages when he has genuinely done his best to fulfil his promises.

Now practical men can see these two points of view. Buyers are not, as human beings, unreasonable, nor are sellers. There is, none the less, real importance in the principle that promises are made to be kept, and that the seller who breaks his promises should be held responsible. The truth is that the practice which buyers wish to be armed against is the tendency of sellers to quote delivery times frivolously or recklessly or fraudulently. This last is a strong word to use, but one that is sometimes justified. It is very frequently the case that the time quoted for delivery is of more significance in the award of a competitive tender than is the price quoted. If the earning power of a production machine is £2,000 per month it is better to buy it for £10,000 and have it in six months than to pay £8,000 and to wait for a year. It is plainly fraudulent for a manufacturer in order to obtain business against honest competitors who have quoted realistically, to add ten per cent to his proper price and state a delivery date which he well knows is impossible of achievement, offering a liquidated damages clause which at the maximum will absorb the loading he has injected into his price. It is fraudulent, but that is not to say that it has never been done.

What are the possible sanctions for non-delivery at the promised time, and when, in fairness, ought they to be applied? It is suggested that the reasonable answers are as follows:

(a) The right of the buyer to cancel the contract and to buy elsewhere. This, as has been shown, is often impracticable, and operates unjustly against the seller who has made a reasonable effort to fulfil his obligations, but has met with unexpected difficulties, even though those difficulties do not come within the usually accepted meaning of *force majeure*. It is, however, a sanction which should be available as a last resort to relieve the buyer from a contract in the event of complete incompetence on the part of the seller.

(b) The right on the part of the buyer to claim damages at large, which can include loss of profits provided they are reasonably foreseeable. This operates excessively harshly against an honest seller who has met with unexpected difficulties, but is fully justifiable against a seller who has quoted recklessly or fraudulently in the matter of delivery time.

(c) Liquidated damages, usually subject to an escape clause dealing with the more obvious kinds of *force majeure*. This is unlikely to recompense the aggrieved buyer adequately, but provides an incentive to a seller to do his utmost to minimise delays which occur in respect of promises made in good faith, but arise in the course of manufacture when there has been some lack of alertness on the part of the manufacturer.

NOTE

In view of the difficulties to which Boulton alludes, what type of clause dealing with the time of delivery and the buyer's remedies for breach thereof would fairly balance both parties' interests? Examine also cl. 9 in the *Vehicle Purchase Agreement* reproduced in the appendix to this volume. Does it fairly balance the interests of the dealer and buyer? Is Boulton right in characterizing as fraudulent a seller's promise to deliver by a given date when he knows he cannot meet the deadline? What remedies does the law give the buyer in such circumstances? It is often said that the common law recognizes no doctrine of good faith in bargaining or in the performance of contracts. Does this example (among others) prove the need for such a doctrine, a doctrine that is familiar in many civilian systems?

See, generally, OLRC Sales Report, *supra*, chapter 9, and for a survey of recent common law developments in Canada, S. O'Byrne, "Good Faith in Contractual Performance: Recent Developments" (1995), 74 *Can. Bar Rev.* 70 and *Wallace v. United Grain Growers Ltd.* (1997), 152 DLR (4th) 1, at 33 and 44-45 (SCC).

USE AND INTERPRETATION OF MERCANTILE SHIPPING TERMS

OLRC Sales Report

at 346-50

4. The Use of Mercantile Terms

For over 150 years, the custom of merchants dealing in international trade has been to describe their mutual obligations of performance in a symbolic shorthand of initials and words. The commonest of these are "f.o.b." and "c.i.f.," which signify "free on board" and "cost, insurance and freight" respectively. In North America, these terms have not been restricted to use in export transactions, or to shipment by sea. Their earliest use in Canada was in connection with the internal or domestic Great Lakes grain trade, but they were soon extended to carriage by rail, and are now also used in truck shipments. The different types of shipping terms, and the frequency of their use among the respondents to the CMA Questionnaire, are shown in Table 2, set out below.

Table 2   SHIPPING TERMS

	Always or often %	Mid %	Rarely or never %
(a) Ex works (factory, warehouse, etc.)	42.1	22.3	35.5
(b) F.O.R.—F.O.T. (free on rail—truck) named departure point	8.0	14.4	77.6
(c) F.A.S. (free along ship) named port of shipment	2.6	9.0	88.5
(d) F.O.B. (free on board) named port of shipment	36.6	22.6	40.7
(e) C. & F. (cost and freight) named port of destination	4.1	10.8	85.1
(f) C.I.F. (cost, insurance, freight) named port of destination	6.9	15.7	77.5
(g) Freight or carriage paid to named point of destination (inland)	20.5	30.8	48.7
(h) Ex ship—named port of destination	1.2	3.7	95.7
(i) Ex quay—named port of destination	0.8	2.3	96.5
(j) Other	7.7	3.7	88.5

It will be noted that, while shipment "ex works" is the single most common term, "f.o.b. named port of shipment" comes a close second, and that, when combined, the various other forms of shipment terms substantially exceed in frequency sales made "ex works." However, frequency of use is not coterminous with agreement as to the meaning of the terms used, or variations thereof. To what extent, therefore, should the revised Ontario Act follow the lead of Article 2 in providing an authoritative catalogue of definitions? The preliminary, but far from exhaustive, inquiries made on our behalf indicate considerable sympathy for such an enterprise. The Canadian decisions interpreting the meaning of shipping terms are modest in number, and the courts have generally resorted to British precedents. We were advised that, even among shipping managers, the terms are not always fully understood, and that their statutory codification might help to dispel some of the uncertainty.

It goes without saying that no final decision should be taken without further and comprehensive consultation with the interested parties. Assuming the reaction remains positive, two further questions arise: (a) which model should be adopted; and, (b) what provision should be made with respect to the impact of containerization?

(a) *Which Model?*

There are only two approaches that seriously commend themselves as precedents: namely, the provisions in sections 2-319 to 2-323, of the Uniform Commercial Code, and the *Incoterms* adopted by the International chamber of Commerce. The two sets of terms have been compared for us, and the overall conclusion appears to be that the differences between them are modest. Nevertheless, there is little doubt in our minds that the Code terms make a more logical choice. We say this for two reasons. In the first place, the United States is our closest trading partner, and it is obviously desirable that Canadian and American businessmen should attach the same meaning to each other's trade terms. Secondly, the Article 2 definitions are better geared to North American practices and traditions since, unlike the *Incoterms*, they are not restricted to foreign trade contracts. Accordingly, we recommend that the revised Act incorporate a definition of common trade terms. The definitions contained in UCC 2-319 to 2-323 should be adopted in preference to the *Incoterms* promulgated by the International Chamber of Commerce.

(b) *Impact of Containerization*

Containerization is a mode of shipment in which large numbers of packages or units are stored in sealed metal crates. The primary advantages of containerization are simplicity of handling and increased security. The container revolution, which began in the middle 1960's, has had its most significant impact so far on the overseas shipping trade. To a lesser extent, it has influenced domestic shipping, with most container carriage going to those carriers, known as "combined transport operators," who containerize the shipper's goods in anticipation of their shipment by sea. In the future, intermodal domestic containerization may be expected to grow as regulatory difficulties are solved and shipper awareness of its advantages is increased.

The containerization process differs from traditional breakbulk carriage in many ways. First, it eliminates the individual handling of packages by carriers and forwarding agents, thus making traditional bills of lading inappropriate for such carriage. Secondly, it complicates the process of determining which carrier is liable for damage to the goods, because the container is sealed by the first carrier, usually the combined transport operator, bearing a greater burden of liability than in the past; it further points out the incongruous limitations on liability to which the various modes of carriage are now subject. Thirdly, it raises new problems of passage of title and risk of loss as between buyer and seller, especially where the contract is f.o.b. or c.i.f. and the seller is obliged to obtain a bill of lading. The reason, as some commentators have pointed out, is that a clean bill of lading for "shipped" not "received" goods may not be obtainable. Fourthly, questions of what constitutes a package for purposes of liability limitations have only begun to be litigated, and no uniform principles have yet emerged.

As now constituted, the usual requirements of a bill of lading (that is, that it be issued by a shipowner, not a forwarding agent, that the goods be "on board" or "shipped" and not "received," that it be "clean," and that it should confirm storage under deck) cannot ordinarily be satisfied by container carriage. This fact indicates that the traditional rules will have to be adapted in time to conform to this new, and vastly more efficient, means of transportation. It may be that the terms f.o.b. and c.i.f. will have to be redefined to encompass container transport. Or, it may be that commerce will develop a new term or terms to signify the rights and duties of the parties where goods are shipped in this manner.

Many problems have yet to be litigated, and commercial handling of these transactions is still evolving. We therefore conclude that any attempt to codify the law regarding the rights and obligations of sellers and buyers under a container transport of goods at this time would be premature, and might stunt the development of containerization.

Note on Containerization

As the OLRC Report indicates, the introduction of containerization has numerous legal implications, some of which still have to be worked out. For a sampling of some of the voluminous literature in this area, see D.M. Sassoon, "Trade Terms and the Container Revolution" (1969-70), 1 *J Mar. L & Comm.* 73; S. Simon, "Container Law: A Recent Reappraisal" (1976-77), 8 *J Mar. L & Comm.* 489; *Benjamin's Sale of Goods*, 5th ed., paras. 21-071 *et seq.*; and de Wit, *Multimodal Transport* (1995).

Beaver Specialty Ltd. v. Donald H. Bain Ltd.

(1973), 39 DLR (3d) 574, [1974] SCR 903

RITCHIE J (for the Court): This is an appeal by Beaver Specialty Limited (hereinafter referred to as "Beaver") from a judgment of the Court of Appeal for Ontario varying the judgment rendered by King J at trial and directing that the respondent, Donald H. Bain Limited (hereinafter referred to as "Bain") recover the sum of $31,616.48, together with interest from February 7, 1963, from Beaver in respect of the purchase price of 2,000 cases of Chinese walnuts which had become unmerchantable in the course of transit between Vancouver from whence they had been shipped by Bain and Toronto where Beaver had refused to accept delivery of the cargo.

There was also an appeal by Pacific Inland Express Limited (hereinafter referred to as "PIX"), the truckers responsible for the carriage of the cargo, against the finding of the Court of Appeal that Beaver was entitled to recover $19,269.75 from that company in respect of the loss of value of the walnuts through damage in transit and also for storage charges.

This litigation arises out of a contract for purchase and delivery of the 2,000 cases of walnuts entered into by Beaver in Toronto through the Toronto office of Bain which was engaged in the business of wholesale commission merchants and brokers having its head office in Winnipeg and branch offices at both Toronto and Vancouver.

The original order was for 4,000 cases of these walnuts and it was passed on in this form by Bain (Toronto) to its Vancouver office by telephone on January 16, 1963, and by confirmatory letter of the same day, whereupon Bain's Vancouver office appears to have at once prepared a contract note addressed to Beaver in the following terms:

Order 508

Vancouver, B.C. January 16, 1963
Canada

Messrs. Beaver Specialty Company, Ltd.
Toronto, Ontario.

We have this day booked for you as per your order to—

Donald H. Bain Limited,
159 Bay St., Toronto, Ont.

4,000 cases CHINESE 1961 crop Light Dry Cracked
walnut meats PIECES, packed in veneer
cases, parchment paper lined of 55
net shipping weight each   @per lb.
Can. $.59

"Seller to supply original Chinese Quality Certificates"
Prices as above f.o.b. Toronto, Ont.
Terms NET CASH

Shipment 2,000 cases to be invoiced and
transferred to buyer's account in warehouse January 31, 1963. Balance of
2,000 cases to be invoiced and transferred to buyer's account in warehouse
February 28, 1963.

This contract is made subject to terms
printed on the reverse side of this form.

Yours truly,
DONALD H. BAIN LTD.
Agents

The 2,000 cases first referred to in this note were not transferred to the buyer's (*i.e.*, Beaver's) account in the warehouse but by agreement between the parties were delivered to PIX for shipment to Beaver in Toronto. The agreement between the parties in this regard is evidenced by the further contract note of the same date which contains the following and was marked ex. 7 at the trial:

Prices	all charges paid Toronto in truckload quantities,
Terms	Net Cash,
Shipment	To be taken by Beaver Specialty Co., Toronto—
	2,000 cases by January 31/63—2,000 cases by February 28/63.

and is further corroborated by the terms of a letter dated January 18, 1968, from Bain Toronto to Bain Vancouver, which contains the following paragraph:

> Our buyer, Beaver Specialty Company, Toronto, has asked that 2,000 cases of their contract be shipped January 31st, 1963 to them, by Pacific Inland Express trucks. They do not want these goods before that time, but want them shipped on the date they are to come out. Please invoice them also, at the same time.

PIX undertook to transport these walnuts from Vancouver to Toronto under protective service at temperatures between 45° and 50°. These shipments arrived at the Federal Cold Storage in Toronto on February 5, 6, and 7, 1963, and there is no dispute, at least between Bain and Beaver that the walnuts arrived in Toronto in seriously damaged condition apparently occasioned by freezing.

The question at issue between Beaver and Bain is as to which company had title to the walnuts while they were in transit and the difference arising between the trial Judge and the Court of Appeal is that the trial Judge proceeded on the basis that the goods remained the property of Bain until delivery "f.o.b. Toronto" to Beaver, whereas the Court of Appeal interpreted the evidence as disclosing that the 2,000 cases were transferred to Beaver's account when they were delivered to PIX for transportation. The question is a very narrow one and turns on the interpretation of the contract note, and upon a consideration of the provisions of the Sale of Goods Act. There appears to be no doubt that the contract was for sale by description rather than by sample, and the respondent accordingly invokes the provisions of s. 19, Rule 5 of the Sale of Goods Act, RSO 1960, c. 356 [now RSO 1990, c. S.1]. This section reads: ...

The appellant on the other hand invokes the provisions of s. 33 of the same Act which read as follows:

The appellant contends, as the trial Judge found, that the intention of the parties is made manifest by the contract note to which I have referred and by the documents which accompanied its execution and that that intention was that the goods were to be shipped "f.o.b. Toronto, Ont." and that it was never intended that title should pass to Beaver until its acceptance of delivery in Toronto.

The respondent Bain contends, in conformity with the reasons for judgment of the Court of Appeal, that the words "f.o.b. Toronto, Ont." as they occur in the contract note have reference entirely to the price of the goods and this is because, as I have indicated, they are found in one line of the contract which reads: "Prices as above f.o.b. Toronto, Ont." The absence of any punctuation after the word "above" in this line cannot, in my opinion, be treated as meaning that the words and letters "f.o.b. Toronto, Ont." were referable only to the price. "Prices as above" is a clear reference to the fact that the prices had been designated in the earlier part of the contract note.

In the course of the reasons for judgment rendered orally by Mr. Justice Kelly on behalf of the Court of Appeal [11 DLR (3d) 432, [1970] 2 OR 555], he expressed the view that the contract [at 435-6]

> … contemplated that Bain should fulfil it by transferring, in the Vancouver warehouse, to Beaver's order, successively two lots of 2,000 cases each and that upon each such transfer Bain would be entitled to the payment for the purchase price of such 2,000 cases; that the revised instructions substituted for the first transfer in the warehouse, the physical delivery of the 2,000 cases to the carrier; that when such delivery was made, the contract in respect of that 2,000 cases was fully performed by Bain and Bain was entitled to payment, the cases thereafter being at the risk of Beaver.

With the greatest respect for this view, it appears to me to ignore the circumstances which surrounded the preparation of the contract note. When Beaver gave its original instructions to Bain (Toronto) Mr. Carter of that firm took a handwritten note regarding the order which was preserved and became ex. 5 at trial. This memorandum reads as follows:

16 Beaver Spec. Co. Toronto
4000 cs Chinese LDC walnuts
      Pe's 55 #—59¢
      Dev'd Toronto in
      truck loads.
2000 by Jan. 31/63 from Vancouver
2000 by Feb. 28/63 from Vancouver
Invoiced by DHB Ltd. Vancouver.

At the hearing before us the abbreviations in this note were explained by appellant's counsel and were not questioned on behalf of other counsel and are as follows:

In the first line "16" refers to January 16, 1963.
In the 2nd line LDC means "Light Dry Cracked"
In the 3rd line Pe's indicates the price 55 lbs. at 59¢ per lb.
In the 4th line "Dev'd" means "delivered"
In the last line "DHB Ltd." refers to "Donald H. Bain Limited."

. . .

It thus appears to me to have been established that when issuing the contract note to Beaver, Bain was carrying out the intention of the parties made manifest by the telephone call from Beaver to Bain (Toronto) and the pencil note made at the time. I am therefore of opinion that the entry "f.o.b. Toronto, Ont." occurring on the contract note is to be read in conjunction with the pencilled memorandum of the order given by Beaver and accepted by Bain which provided for "delivery Toronto in truck loads," which in my view means that Beaver was to take delivery in Toronto. This is confirmed by the letter of January 18th and by ex. 7, to both of which I have made reference.

In this regard, the case of *Winnipeg Fish Co. v. Whitman Fish Co.* (1909), 41 SCR 453, appears to me to be highly relevant. There a contract was made in Winnipeg between the agents of the shippers (Whitman Fish Co.) and the purchasers (Winnipeg Fish Co.) for the shipment of a car load of fish from Canso, NS, where the shippers' plant was located to Winnipeg. The sale was by sample and the written order as conveyed by the shippers' agent in Winnipeg to his company in Canso contained the words "On condition you ship them the same quality haddies as sample."

Under the terms of the contract the goods were to be shipped "f.o.b. Winnipeg" and in the course of the reasons for judgment rendered by Mr. Justice Davies and concurred in by Mr. Justice Duff, it was said at 460:

> I agree with the holding of the Court of Appeal that the contract in the case must in the circumstances under which it was made be held to have "required delivery of the fish in Winnipeg and that the property in the fish did not pass until such delivery." Such a determination does not necessarily follow from the use of the letters and words "f.o.b. Winnipeg" in the contract made. There is room for much contention as to their real effect and the language may be said to be ambiguous. But when we consider the circumstances surrounding the making of the contract, that the agent of the plaintiffs and of the defendants were both in Winnipeg, when they made it and that the fish were to be shipped from Canso, Nova Scotia, thousands of miles from Winnipeg and delivered "f.o.b. Winnipeg," that they were to be in accordance with a sample then and there produced and that the plaintiffs in suing upon the contract in expressly setting forth another claim that their goods were to be delivered in Winnipeg, I agree that the contention [*sic*] of the parties must fairly be determined to have been that the property in the fish should not pass until they were in Winnipeg ready for delivery to the defendants.

In the course of his reasons for judgment in the Court of Appeal in the present case, Mr. Justice Kelly found himself able to distinguish the *Winnipeg Fish Co.* case on the ground that in that case the plaintiffs included in their statement of claim a paragraph alleging that the fish were "to be delivered at Winnipeg."

I appreciate that this was an added factor favouring the purchasers' contention in that case, but in the present case the circumstances surrounding the making of the contract were that the agents of Beaver and Bain were both in Toronto when they made it; that the walnuts were to be shipped from Vancouver thousands of miles from Toronto and delivered "f.o.b. Toronto"; and I find that the pencilled note taken by Mr. Carter of Bain when the Beaver order was given and specifying that the goods were to be "delivered Toronto in truck loads" is sufficient to resolve any ambiguity to which the letters and words "f.o.b. Toronto" might give rise in favour of the primary meaning attributed to this phrase by leading authorities on the sale of goods.

In this regard I have reference to what is said in Mr. Williston's work on *The Law Governing Sales of Goods*, rev. ed. (1948), s. 280(b), where it is said:

> As it is a necessary implication in f.o.b. contracts that the buyer is put at all expense in regard to the goods after the time when they are delivered f.o.b., the presumption follows that the property passes to the buyer at that time and not before, ... *and the further presumption follows that the place where the goods are to be delivered f.o.b. is the place of delivery to the buyer.*

(The italics are my own.) Further authority to the same effect is to be found in Vold on *The Law of Sales*, 2nd ed., s. 33, where it is said:

> Under shipment "f.o.b. destination" the presumption is that the property interest was not meant to pass until the goods reached destination.

In the case of *Steel Co. of Canada Ltd. v. The Queen*, [1955] 2 DLR 593, [1955] SCR 161, [1955] CTC 21, certain manufactured goods had been shipped by the appellant in Montreal and delivered by it to Canada Steamship Lines Limited for shipment to various companies beyond the Head of the Lakes and the contract contained a printed heading: "f.o.b." under which was typed "Hd. of Lakes." The vendors, like Bain in this case, relied on the provisions of s. 20 of the Manitoba Sale of Goods Act and particularly Rule 5 thereof. (This section is the almost exact equivalent of s. 19, Rule 5 of the Ontario Sale of Goods Act hereinbefore referred to.) In the course of his reasons for judgment which he delivered on behalf of himself and Mr. Justice Fauteux, Kerwin CJC, had occasion to say, at 595-6:

> I agree with the contention on behalf of the appellant that, while it might have been argued that the goods were unconditionally appropriated to the contracts by the marks, or tags, and by the delivery of them to the carrier, if "F.O.B. Hd. of Lakes" had not appeared in the invoices, the presence of these words brings the case within the opening part of s. 20 of the Manitoba Sale of Goods Act "Unless a different intention appears." The authorities justify the statement in *Benjamin on Sale*, 8th ed., at 691: "The meaning of these words [f.o.b.] is that the seller is to put the goods on board at his own expense on account of the person for whom they are shipped; delivery is made, and the goods are at the risk, of the buyer, from the time when they are so put on board." This does not mean that in all F.O.B. cases the property in the goods contracted to be sold passes only when the goods are so put on board, but the circumstances in the present instance do not take it out of the general rule. The duty of the appellant to pay the freight to the Head of the Lakes is one that would usually accompany the obligation to put the goods Free on Board.

Having regard to all the above, it will be seen that I take the view that the circumstances surrounding and immediately preceding the issuance of the contract note are such as to support the contention of the appellant that this note evidenced the intention of the parties that the walnuts were to be delivered to Beaver in Toronto and this being the case the provisions of s. 33(1) of the Sale of Goods Act to which I have already referred, apply and Beaver which had had no reasonable previous opportunity of examining the goods must be deemed not to have accepted them and was therefore fully justified in its refusal of the cargo.

Appeal allowed.

QUESTIONS

What is the ratio of this decision—that in an f.o.b. destination contract, title, and therefore risk, does not pass to the buyer until the goods are delivered at destination? Suppose the parties *do* intend that title shall pass to the buyer before the goods are delivered to him (as will typically be true in a documentary sale where the buyer receives the bill of lading and pays for the goods before the goods have reached their destination), does this mean that risk passes to the buyer at the earlier date? On the relationship between risk and the transfer of title, see further, *infra*, chapter 12, and *cf.* UCC 2-319. On time of delivery and transfer of title, see also SGA s. 19, rule 5 and *Caradoc Nurseries v. Marsh, infra*, chapter 13.

DELIVERY AND DOCUMENTS OF TITLE

Nature of Document of Title

OLRC Sales Report

at 319-22

A document of title, as commonly understood in the sales context, is a writing, generally issued by a person in the business of warehousing or transporting goods, purporting to cover goods in his possession, and entitling the holder of the writing to deal with the goods. There are two kinds of documents of title: (1) a bill of lading, being an acknowledgment by a carrier that the goods have been received for carriage; and (2) a warehouse receipt, being an acknowledgment by a bailee that goods have been received for storage. Documents of title are comparable to bills of exchange, notes and cheques in that, in the ordinary course of commerce, the rights represented by the document can be transferred by transferring possession of the document itself, with any necessary endorsement. They are also similar in that a bill, note or cheque represents the right to receive payment, while a document of title represents the right to receive possession of goods. However, the comparison is not exact. The incidents attached to bills, notes and cheques are clearly established as a result of comprehensive federal legislation, while the incidents attached to documents of title are less clear. Moreover, both at common law and under the relevant statutes, there are important differences in these incidents.

We have not undertaken an exhaustive examination of the law relating to documents of title, but their role cannot be ignored. They are mentioned in several sections of the existing Sale of Goods Act and affect some basic issues of sales law.

These issues include the effect of documents of title on the following: (1) the passing of title and risk between seller and buyer; (2) the seller's delivery obligations; (3) the seller's remedies; and, (4) the operation of the *nemo dat* rule and the statutory protection given to innocent third parties. In examining these issues we have encountered two basic difficulties with the existing law. The first difficulty is the lack of codification of the law relating to documents of title in Ontario. The second difficulty concerns the nature of the legislative changes that have been made to the common law.

As to the first difficulty, there is, as stated, no modern comprehensive codification of the law relating to documents of title in Ontario. Nor are documents of title governed by a clear body of common law. We are told by Falconbridge that, by the late nineteenth century, bills of lading were instruments well known to commerce and that, by the custom of merchants, peculiar incidents were attached to them. Peculiar incidents were not, on the other hand, attached by custom to warehouse receipts. There are few modern Canadian cases dealing with the law relating to documents of title, and some of the older cases are inconsistent with the assumptions underlying modern usage of these documents.

This point can be illustrated by examining a distinction commonly made in modern commercial practice. Borrowing ideas and nomenclature from other branches of negotiable instrument law, and perhaps relying upon American precedents, it is common in practice to distinguish between negotiable and non-negotiable documents of title. This distinction may center, according to trade usage, on one or more of a number of things. First, it may go to the issue of whether the document is transferable at all. Secondly, the distinction may relate to the form of the transfer; that is, whether the bailee must acknowledge or attorn to the transferee before the transferee has any right under the document. Thirdly, the distinction between negotiable and non-negotiable documents of title may determine whether the document is intended to be assignable free from the equities existing between the original parties; that is, whether the bailee can raise any claim or defence that he had against the original holder against a subsequent holder of the document. Fourthly, the distinction may be relevant in determining whether a transferee of an apparently regular document, who takes in good faith for value and without notice of a defect in the title of his transferor, or the want of title of his transferor, takes free from that defect or want of title.

In contexts other than documents of title, it is primarily the fourth meaning that is the essence of negotiability. Yet at common law, according to Falconbridge,

> A bill of lading, and *a fortiori* any other document of title to goods, is not negotiable in the same sense as a bill of exchange may be negotiable, and therefore the mere honest *possession* of a bill of lading endorsed in blank, or in which the goods are made deliverable to the bearer, is not such a title to the goods as the like possession of a bill of exchange would be to the money promised to be paid by the acceptor. The endorsement of a bill of lading gives no better right to the goods than the endorser himself had. ...

By the Warehouse Receipts Act [RSO 1990, c. W.3.], negotiable warehouse receipts are given incidents of negotiability similar to those attached to bills and notes. However, there is no federal or provincial legislation that does the same for bills of lading.

Since the documents themselves seldom set out what is meant by "negotiable" or "non-negotiable," the parties are left, in the event of a dispute, to establish the meaning of these terms by trade usage. This they must do against a background of common law rules, which have developed little since the last century and which seem flatly to contradict the parties' assumptions.

The second basic difficulty with the existing law governing documents of title is the nature of the legislative changes that have been made to the common law. There are references to documents of title scattered throughout several Ontario statutes, including the Sale of Goods Act, the Factors Act, the Personal Property Security Act, the Mercantile Law Amendment Act and the Warehouse Receipts Act. In addition, there is federal legislation covering some aspects of bills of lading, such as the Bills of Lading Act and the regulations made pursuant to the Railway Act. The provincial legislation is marked by significant inconsistencies, much duplication and numerous gaps. The inconsistencies include such a basic matter as the lack of a uniform definition of documents of title. Further, these inconsistencies extend to the radically different treatment accorded to warehouse receipts and bills of lading: the former are covered by fairly comprehensive legislation, while the latter are governed by the common law. The duplication in provincial legislation centers on the overlapping protection given to innocent holders of documents of title. They are protected by provisions in four acts: namely, the Sale of Goods Act, the Factors Act, the Mercantile Law Amendment Act and the Warehouse Receipts Act. These acts do not, however, adopt any consistent theory as to the circumstances in which innocent holders should be protected from defects of title. The gaps in provincial legislation relate primarily to bills of lading, rather than to warehouse receipts. They include such basic matters as the formal requirements of a document of title, the obligations of a bailee who holds goods under a document of title, the extent of the bailee's lien, and the form and effect of negotiation or transfer of these instruments.

Documents of Title and the Seller's Delivery Obligations

OLRC Sales Report

at 326-27

The existing Sale of Goods Act says little about the effect of the issuance of a document of title on the seller's obligation to deliver the goods. Two provisions of the Act merit reference. Cases in which a document of title has been issued are specifically excluded from the operation of section 28(3), which controls the time of delivery where goods are held by a bailee that are not to be shipped. Section 31(1) of the Sale of Goods Act, which deals with the effect of delivery to a carrier where the seller is authorized or required to send the goods to the buyer, does not specifically exclude from its operation cases where documents of title have been issued. The courts have, however, arrived at this result by emphasizing that section 31 is only a *prima facie* rule. We turn now to consider the situations contemplated by these provisions.

(i) *Goods Held by a Bailee That Are Not To Be Shipped*

As noted, cases in which a document of title has been issued are expressly excluded from the operation of section 28(3) of the Sale of Goods Act. As a result, what constitutes an effective tender of delivery where goods are covered by a document of title is left to be resolved by the common law and other statutes. In Ontario, sections 21 and 22 of the Warehouse Receipts Act provide that a transferee of a warehouse receipt receives "the benefit of the obligation of the warehouseman to hold possession of the goods for him ... ." A similar, but more elaborate, rule is found in UCC 2-503(4). This provision contains additional qualifications that clarify the circumstances in which failure by the bailee to honour a document of title will defeat the seller's tender. We think that the provisions of UCC 2-503(4) as they relate to documents of title would be useful additions to our revised Act, and recommend their adoption in lieu of the provisions of section 28(3) of the existing Act. Our Draft Bill contains a provision giving effect to this recommendation.

(ii) *Goods Authorized or Required To Be Shipped*

The *prima facie* rule found in section 31(1) of the Ontario Sale of Goods Act, that delivery to the carrier is delivery to the buyer, may be displaced where the seller reserves a right of disposal in the goods. Section 20(2) provides that, where the goods are shipped and by the bill of lading the goods are deliverable to the order of the seller or his agent, the seller is prima facie deemed to reserve the right of disposal. In this way a bill of lading may determine whether there has been delivery of the goods and, arguably, locate the place of the buyer's right of inspection, since delivery and the right of inspection are usually treated as coterminous events. In contrast, the Code has specific provisions for inspection in section 2-513, which are functionally oriented and divorced from questions of delivery. In addition, as indicated, section 2-505 has recognized that the reservation of a right of disposal has the limited purpose of giving the seller a security interest, and has no bearing on other issues. Finally, sections 2-503(2) and (3) and 2-504 set out more fully the seller's general duty of tender and delivery in shipment and destination contracts, including those involving documents of title. These provisions are examined in greater detail in chapter 14. We also explain elsewhere, in a more general context, the advantages of the Code's separate provisions for inspection, and its limitation of the seller's right of disposal to a security interest. The rationale that supports these provisions is equally applicable where documents of title are involved. Accordingly, we recommend that the revised Act should incorporate provisions similar to UCC 2-503(2) and (3), and UCC 2-504 with respect to the role of documents of title affecting the seller's delivery obligations in shipment and destination contracts. As under the Uniform Commercial Code, the revised Act should incorporate separate rules, unconnected with questions of delivery, with respect to the effect of the reservation of a right of disposal and the place of inspection of goods after delivery.

CHAPTER TWELVE

Risk of Loss and Frustration of the Contract of Sale

RISK OF LOSS

OLRC Sales Report

at 265-66

Multiple hazards can accompany goods between the time of their identification to the contract and the time of their actual receipt by the buyer. This possibility has led to the adoption of rules governing the location of the risk of loss that go back at least to Roman times.

Risk rules and rules of frustration intersect; but they are not the same. Unless otherwise provided, a frustrating event discharges both parties from further obligations under the contract. This result does not, however, necessarily follow from loss of, or damage to, the goods. If risk of loss at the material time lies with the buyer, he remains liable for the price; obviously, the contract is not discharged so far as he is concerned. Conversely, if the risk is with the seller, the buyer will be excused from further obligations, but whether the seller will also be relieved will turn on other factors. In this Report, therefore, it will be convenient to postpone discussion of frustration problems to a later chapter.

Four basic tests have been adopted by different legal systems to determine the time when risk of loss passes from the seller to the buyer. According to these tests, risk passes as follows: (a) when the contract is concluded; (b) when title in the goods is transferred; (c) when the seller has delivered the goods, actually or constructively; and, (d) when the buyer has actually received the goods. Roman law was the source of the first test. It is a test that survives in a substantial number of civil law jurisdictions, including Switzerland, the Netherlands, Japan and members of the Latin American legal system. The title or property test has been adopted in France, among other jurisdictions. This test was also part of the common law, and was codified in the UK Sale of Goods Act, 1893. It is reproduced in section 21 of the Ontario Act. The "delivery" test is in force in the Scandinavian countries and, as will be seen, has been substantially adopted in the Uniform Commercial Code. The fourth test, the one that turns on transfer of possession, obtains under German and Austrian law, and under the laws of various Eastern European countries. An important aspect of it also appears in the Code.

If one groups together, as others have done, the first two and the last two tests, it will be seen that there are only two basic tests: namely, those that turn upon identification and appropriation of the goods to the contract, and those that apply a delivery or control test.

Illustrations of the Operation of the Current Rules

Jerome v. Clements Motor Sales Ltd.

(1958), 15 DLR (2d) 689, [1958] OR 738 (CA)

SCHROEDER JA: This action arose out of the following circumstances: The plaintiff had entered into negotiations with the appellant for the purchase of a used 1955 Nash sedan in the month of July, 1957. The bargain was reduced to a formal contract in writing bearing the date July 8, 1957. Under the terms of the agreement the total purchase-price of the 1955 Nash sedan was $2,395. The appellant agreed to accept in trade a used Ford car owned by the plaintiff's daughter for which it made an allowance of $1,000 and a 1951 Nash motor car owned by the plaintiff for which it agreed to allow the sum of $495, the balance of $900 to be paid in cash. On the same date, the plaintiff gave the appellant her cheque for $902 to cover the balance of the purchase-price and to provide for the transfer fee of the motor-vehicle permit for the 1955 Nash motor car. At the same time the plaintiff delivered to the appellant the motor-vehicle permits in respect of the two cars which were being accepted in trade, the transfer form on which were signed by the plaintiff's daughter and the plaintiff respectively. It was arranged between the parties that the plaintiff should retain possession and enjoy the use of the 1951 Nash car until she obtained delivery of the 1955 Nash automobile. The agreement also contained the following clause: "No warranties or representations whatever are made upon any secondhand car or used car ordered (unless specified hereon in writing), said car being purchased in its present condition and having been examined and accepted by me, and subject to any repairs above provided for." The agreement provided for the installation of a new tail pipe, checking of an oil leak on the rear wheel and the changing of the battery. This involved the removal of the comparatively new battery in the 1951 Nash motor car to the 1955 Nash motor car, an operation which was to be effected at the time that delivery of the motor car was taken by the plaintiff. The appellant agreed to effect the repairs which were specifically mentioned in the agreement and certain other minor repairs not set forth in the document without cost to the plaintiff.

It was stated in evidence that all the repairs to the 1955 Nash, with the exception of the installation of the battery, were effected on Thursday July 11th, on which date the motor car was removed from the repair shop and placed in the defendant's showroom. A fire of undetermined origin occurred on these premises at 3 o'clock in the morning on Friday July 12, 1957, in the course of which the repair shop and the showroom were laid waste and the motor car in question was seriously damaged and greatly deteriorated in value. As the appellant was unable to make delivery of the motor car, the plaintiff instituted action to recover the $900 paid by her in addition to the value of the two motor cars which the appellant had agreed to accept in trade on the terms hereinbefore stated.

[Schroeder JA referred to the plaintiff's alternative claim against the respondent insurance company, and continued]:

The question of substance in this action is whether at the time of the fire the motor vehicle in question was at the seller's risk or at the buyer's risk. Section 21 of the Sale of Goods Act, RSO 1950, c. 345 [Now RSO 1990, c. S.1, s. 21] provides as follows: ...

The rules governing the transfer of property from a seller to a buyer are set forth in ss. 18 and 19 of the Sale of Goods Act, and I shall refer to those portions thereof which are relevant: ...

The learned trial Judge came to the conclusion that there was nothing in the terms of the contract or the conduct of the parties or the circumstances of the case on which he could base a finding as to the time at which the parties to the contract intended the property in the motor vehicle to be transferred to the buyer and that it was therefore necessary to resort to the provisions of the Rules contained in s. 19 of the Act to ascertain their intention. He held that under the contract the appellant, as the seller, was bound to do something to the motor vehicle for the purpose of putting into a deliverable state and that although the repairs, except the installation of the battery, were said to have been completed on Thursday July 11th, the buyer did not have notice of that fact, and accordingly the property in the vehicle had not passed to the purchaser at the time of the fire.

The fact that the things which were required to be done to the vehicle to put it into a deliverable state were trivial in nature does not affect the question. In *Wilde v. Fedirko* (1920), 13 SLR 190, the plaintiff had undertaken to place certain fire bricks in the engine of a threshing machine to enable straw to be burned and it was held that the placing of the bricks in position was a condition precedent to the passing of the property. In *McDill v. Hilson* (1920), 53 DLR 228, 30 Man. R. 454, a decision of the Manitoba Court of Appeal, it was held that the undertaking to polish furniture and remedy the chipped condition thereof not having been carried out by the vendor, the goods were not in a deliverable state, and that this prevented the property therein from passing to the purchaser.

It is not seriously contended that *R. 2* of s. 19 is not applicable to this contract, having regard to those things which under the contract the vendor was bound to do for the purpose of putting the vehicle into a deliverable state but it is argued that it can be inferred from the terms of the contract, the conduct of the parties and the surrounding circumstances, that the parties intended that the property in the motor vehicle was to be transferred to the purchaser on July 8, 1957, the date of the contract, so that "a different intention appears." The burden of showing that "a different intention appears" within the meaning of *R. 2* of s. 19, lies upon the appellant who so alleges.

In his work on Sales, Lord Blackburn pointed out that where the vendor has undertaken to perform certain things to the subject-matter of the sale, it is important to ascertain whether the performance thereof is meant to precede the vesting of the property or not. This, he states, is a question of the construction of the agreement; that it may often happen that the parties have expressed their intention in a manner that leaves no room for doubt. When, however, they have not done so in express terms, their intention must be collected from the whole agreement. He then refers to Rules, such as are now found in s. 19 of the Sale of Goods Act, which were adopted in the English Courts since the beginning of the Nineteenth Century as rules of construction "which are perhaps some of them a little artificial." In the opinion of Lord Blackburn, the Rule as set forth in *R. 2* of s. 19, seems to be founded in reason. He states that in general it is for the benefit of the vendor that the property should pass. The risk of loss is thereby transferred to the purchaser, and as the vendor may still retain possession of the goods, so as to retain security for payment of the price, the transference of the property is to the vendor pure gain. It is therefore reasonable that where, by the agreement, the vendor is to do something before he can call on the purchaser to accept the goods as corresponding to the agreement, the intention of the parties should be taken to be that the vendor was to do this before he obtained the benefit of the transfer of the property. He adds: "The presumption does not arise if the things might be done after the vendor had put the goods in the state in which he had the right to call upon the purchaser to accept them, and would be unreasonable where the acts were to be done by the buyer who would thus be rewarded for his own default." This passage was quoted in the judgment of King J, in *McLellan v. Nor. British & Mercantile Ins. Co.* (1891), 30 NBR 363, at 376; aff'd (1892), 21 SCR 288.

There is no doubt but that the operation of *R. 2*, s. 19 is subordinated to the real intention of the parties as to when the property in the subject-matter of the sale should pass to the purchaser if that intention has been manifested in some other manner.

It is contended on behalf of the appellant that the work to be done to the 1955 Nash motor car was completed on Thursday July 11th, and that the plaintiff must be taken to have notice thereof because the appellant had agreed to make delivery to the plaintiff on Thursday July 11th. Under the Sale of Goods Act, one of the incidents of a contract for the sale of goods where no date of delivery is specified in the written contract (as in this case), is that the goods must be delivered within a reasonable time and what is a reasonable time is a question of fact: see s. 28(2) and s. 54. In *Allen v. Danforth Motors Ltd.* (1958), 12 DLR (2d) 572, this Court held that where a contract for the sale of an automobile, whether it be one required by law to be in writing or one which purported to express the whole agreement between the parties, contained no specification of the date of delivery, the implication arose under the statute that delivery would be made within a reasonable time; that the incidents which were impliedly contained in a written contract, whether by construction of its terms or by the implication of law, were as much within the general rule as if expressed in written terms in the instrument and could not be varied or contradicted by extrinsic evidence. It cannot be said, therefore, that this contract provided for delivery of the motor car to the purchaser on Thursday July 11th, if the appellant relies upon an oral agreement fixing that date as the date of delivery, since that would be a term clearly at variance with the terms and provisions of the written document. I am therefore unable to give effect to this argument advanced by the appellant. There is, however, this further fallacy in that argument, namely, that the time at which the buyer has notice of the performance of the things required to be done by the seller under the terms of the contract referred to in *R. 2* relates to a period of time at, or after, which the work is completed. That burden cannot be discharged in advance by inserting an express stipulation in the contract that the work is to be performed by a specified date. The crucial question is—did the buyer actually have notice or knowledge of the performance of these things at the time of the destruction of the motor vehicle by fire on Friday July 12, 1957? The final words "and the buyer has notice thereof" were not found in the common law rule but, as was pointed out by Chalmers in his work on the *Sale of Goods*, 11th ed., at 66, these words were added in Committee on a suggestion from Scotland that it was unfair that the risk should be transferred to the buyer without notice. The rule is expressed negatively and under it the property *does not pass* until the things required to be done by the vendor are done *and the buyer has notice thereof.*

Counsel for the appellant contends that the fact of payment of the purchase-price in advance, the transfer of the two motor-vehicle permits for the motor cars which were being traded in by the purchaser, and the payment by her of the transfer fee in respect of the 1955 Nash motor car indicated a contrary intention within the meaning of s. 19. *McDill v. Hilson* and *Wilde v. Fedirko*, *supra*, and the cases therein cited are authority for the proposition that payment of the purchase-price could not be indicative of such a contrary intention. No more can it be said, in my opinion, that the transfer of the two motor-vehicle licences previously mentioned justify drawing the inference of a contrary intention. The manager of the appellant company stated in evidence that a motor-vehicle permit for the 1955 Nash automobile, made out in the name of the plaintiff, was in his possession on July 9th and had been placed in the motor car to be delivered to the plaintiff when she was given possession of the vehicle. At the time of the fire this permit was still in the possession of the vendor and I would not regard the issuance of the new permit as having any significant bearing upon the question of the intention of the parties as to the passing of the property in the vehicle.

It was further contended that the condition of the contract providing for the reservation of the title and right of possession in the motor car to the vendor until the full purchase-price was paid in money, was a term of vital significance. The sum of $900, the monetary consideration required to be paid by the purchaser, having been paid on July 8th, the appellant maintained that the title and right to possession which theretofore had been vested in the vendor, *ipso facto* became vested in the purchaser. This, it was argued, was a clear manifestation of a different intention. The provision of the agreement upon which this contention is based reads as follows:

"The title to and right of possession in said motor car shall remain with you until conveyed or until the full purchase price is paid in money." In the view which I have formed this provision of the contract has no bearing on the issue whatsoever. It is important to ascertain the reason for the inclusion of this term in the contract. Under s. 38 of the Sale of Goods Act, it is provided that notwithstanding that the property in goods may have passed to a buyer, the unpaid seller has by implication of law a lien on the goods or right to retain them for the price while he is in possession of them.

Under the provision of s. 41, however, he loses his lien or right of retention thereon when he delivers the goods to a carrier or other bailee for the purpose of transmission to the buyer without reserving the right of disposal of the goods or when the buyer or his agent lawfully obtains possession of the goods. It is plainly evident that the real purpose of inserting this particular term or provision in the contract, was to protect the seller against loss of its lien if the subject-matter of the sale came into the possession of the purchaser before the payment of the full purchase-price. In any event, the word "property" as used in ss. 18 and 19 of the Act, is used in a distinct and specific sense and must be given the particular meaning assigned to it under the provisions of s. 1(i) where the word "property" is defined as meaning "general property in goods and not merely a special property." The essence of sale, as pointed out in *Burdick v. Sewell* (1884), 13 QBD 159 at 175; 10 App. Cas. 74 at 93, is the transfer of the ownership or general property in goods from seller to buyer for a price. The definite article "the" preceding the word "property" indicates the general property as distinguished from "a" property, that is merely a special property. The general property in certain goods may be in one person while a special property in them is in another person, as in the case of a pledge where the pledge has only a special property or interest, the general property remaining in the pledgor: *Halliday v. Holgate* (1868), LR 3 Ex. 299. So, therefore, the general property in goods may be transferred to one person, subject to a special property or interest in another: *Franklin v. Neate* (1844), 13 M. & W. 481, 153 ER 200. A person therefore to whom the general property in a material object is transferred becomes the owner thereof who owns a right to the aggregate of its uses. The person upon whom the ownership of a thing devolves has the general property therein whereas he who has merely a special interest in it is not an owner of the thing but merely an encumbrancer of it.

Where the general property in a material object is vested in A, although it may be subject to lien or some other kind of encumbrance held by B, A is nevertheless still entitled to the residue of its uses, and whatever right over the object is not vested in B is vested in A. That residuary use may be of lesser dimensions or less valuable than the rights of B, but the ownership is in A and not in B. When B's right is determined in some manner, A's right, relieved from the encumbrance weighing it down, will immediately assume its full stature and will once more have its full effect. That which is a right of ownership when there are no encumbrances, remains a right of ownership notwithstanding any number of them.

The appellant's argument is predicated on the premise that on July 8th the purchaser had paid the full purchase of the motor car, hence the title and right to possession thereof could not be said to remain with the vendor and since it had to vest somewhere it must be deemed to have vested in the purchaser. Even if this argument were otherwise sound, the words "full purchase price as paid in money" must, of necessity, where part of the consideration was paid by the trading in of two other motor cars, be given a broader interpretation and the word "money" should be construed as including "money's worth." In that aspect of the matter, since the plaintiff still had possession of the 1951 Nash car for which an allowance of $495 was to be made, the full purchase-price could not be said to have been paid to the appellant on

July 8th. It would therefore be open to the plaintiff to argue that if any significance were to be attached to this provision as bearing upon the question of the transfer of the general property in the 1955 Nash car the title thereto and the right of possession thereof were still vested in the vendor on the date of the fire. As stated, however, I am unable to hold that the reservation of this special property in the motor car to the vendor could prevent the passing of the general property therein to the purchaser within the meaning of ss. 18 and 19 of the statute, once the intention of the parties is established.

In my opinion, the learned trial Judge has rightly determined that at the time of the fire on the appellant's premises, the property in the 1955 Nash motor car had not passed from the seller to the purchaser and that it was therefore at the appellant's risk. Accordingly the appeal should be dismissed as against the plaintiff with costs. The plaintiff still has the 1951 Nash motor car in her possession and evidently intends to retain it. The judgment should, therefore, be varied by reducing the amount of the recovery to $1,900.

Appeal dismissed.

[McGillvray JA delivered a concurring judgment; Laidlaw JA dissented.]

QUESTIONS

1) Suppose the vehicle had been in a deliverable condition at the time of the contract of sale and the defendant had not agreed to make repairs. Suppose further the plaintiff said he needed several days to raise the purchase price and had requested a delay in delivery until then, would the result have been different? Should it have been?

2) Suppose the dealer had gone bankrupt before the vehicle had been delivered to the buyer. Would it then have been in the buyer's interest to argue that the title had passed to him and that he was entitled to claim release of the vehicle? *Cf. Carlos Federspiel & Co. S.A. v. Chas. Twigg & Co. Ltd., infra,* chapter 13. Does this demonstrate the undesirability of linking risk rules to title questions?

3) *A.J. Herscovici Furs Ltd. v. TNT Can. Inc.* (1989), 97 AR 243 (CA), aff'g. (1987), 85 AR 67 (QB). The appellant fur coat retailer purchased coats from the respondent manufacturer on earlier occasions and on all such occasions transportation costs were paid by the retailer. By a letter, the retailer directed the manufacturer to ship all goods via a specific land transport business, and also provided detailed declaration instructions that limited the declared value of the goods. Previously, the coats had been shipped by air express and the full value had been declared. Nineteen coats were shipped by the manufacturer by the new mode, but did not reach their destination. What is the result? Would the result have been different if the manufacturer had reserved title in the coats until payment and payment had never been made? Would it have made a difference if the retailer had never changed the mode of transport and the declaration of value?

Critique of the Current Rule; Other Approaches

OLRC Sales Report

at 266-69

The title test adopted by the common law is difficult to justify functionally. It may seem reasonable to argue that the party in whom ownership is vested at the material time should also assume the risks incident to ownership. However, as has also been observed of the Roman test, it shows little concern for practical considerations. The title test ignores insurance factors; it disregards the fact that the party in possession of the goods is best able to ensure their safekeeping and to determine the cause of an accident; and, it overlooks the fact that until the seller has delivered the goods, he has not completed his contractual obligations. A strict application of the title test leads to anomalous results that run counter to the expectations of practical persons. It would greatly surprise a consumer buyer, and no doubt his seller, to be told that, by selecting a particular item on the seller's floor for subsequent delivery to his home, he could be deemed to have assumed the risk forthwith. Conversely, a seller would find it difficult to understand why, following delivery, the risk of loss should remain with him simply because he retained title until payment of the price. These difficulties have not gone unobserved. In overseas shipment contracts, the business community long ago rejected the title test by the adoption of trade terms, such as "f.o.b." and "c.i.f." These terms transfer the risk of loss to the buyer when the goods are delivered to the carrier, regardless of the locus of title. The courts, too, carved out an important exception in the case of the sale of a part of a larger bulk of goods in storage that is accompanied by the transfer of a delivery warrant. Technically, there is no transfer of title in such a case, since no particular part of the bulk has been appropriated to the contract; nevertheless, in the interests of mercantile convenience, the courts found an implied intention that risk was to pass upon delivery of the warrant.

These exceptions demonstrate the fundamental weakness of the title test and the superiority of the delivery test. As has been observed, the "passing of risk upon actual delivery is the modern solution. It conforms with commercial views and practices; it has been adopted by the more recent national and international codifications." The Uniform Commercial Code, too, has adopted the "modern" solution.

This solution is contained in section 2-509, which reads as follows:

> **2-509**(1) Where the contract requires or authorizes the seller to ship the goods by carrier
>
>   (a) if it does not require him to deliver them at a particular destination, the risk of loss passes to the buyer when the goods are duly delivered to the carrier even though the shipment is under reservation (Section 2-505); but
>
>   (b) if it does require him to deliver them at a particular destination and the goods are there duly tendered while in the possession of the carrier, the risk of loss passes to the buyer when the goods are there duly so tendered as to enable the buyer to take delivery.

(2) Where the goods are held by a bailee to be delivered without being moved, the risk of loss passes to the buyer

    (a) on his receipt of a negotiable document of title covering the goods; or

    (b) on acknowledgment by the bailee of the buyer's right to possession of the goods; or

    (c) after his receipt of a non-negotiable document of title or other written direction to deliver, as provided in subsection (4)(b) of Section 2-503.

(3) In any case not within subsection (1) or (2), the risk of loss passes to the buyer on his receipt of the goods if the seller is a merchant; otherwise the risk passes to the buyer on tender of delivery.

(4) The provisions of this section are subject to contrary agreement of the parties and to the provisions of this Article on sale on approval (Section 2-327) and on effect of breach on risk of loss (Section 2-510).

The first three subsections of section 2-509 distinguish between three types of situations. The first involves contracts that require or authorize the seller to ship the goods by independent carrier ("shipment contracts"). Here, the risk passes to the buyer when the goods are delivered to the carrier, unless the seller is required to deliver them at a particular destination ("destination contracts"). In the latter event, risk passes when the goods are there duly tendered while in the hands of the carrier. The second type of situation concerns goods in the hands of a bailee that are to be delivered without being moved. Here, risk of loss passes upon the buyer's receipt of a document of title or acknowledgment by the bailee of the buyer's right to possession. Finally, in cases not falling within the preceding rules, risk of loss passes to the buyer upon his receipt of the goods, if the seller is a merchant, and, if he is not, upon tender of delivery. It should be noted that, by virtue of section 2-509(4), the provisions of subsections (1), (2) and (3) are subject, *inter alia*, to contrary agreement of the parties.

It will be observed that a common thread runs throughout these rules: that is, the transfer of possession of the goods from the seller to the buyer, or a tender thereof. The *situs* of title plays no role whatever. It has been said that section 2-509 has been very successful in its objectives and that, unlike pre-Code law, it has generated very little litigation. We support the general philosophy of section 2-509 and recommend the adoption of a comparable provision in the revised Act.

UN Convention on Contracts for the International Sale of Goods

[Reproduced below are the risk provisions in the Convention. How do they differ from the Code provisions?]

Article 66

Loss of or damage to the goods after the risk has passed to the buyer does not discharge him from his obligation to pay the price, unless the loss or damage is due to an act or omission of the seller.

Article 67

(1) If the contract of sale involves carriage of the goods and the seller is not bound to hand them over at a particular place, the risk passes to the buyer when the goods are handed over to the first carrier for transmission to the buyer in accordance with the contract of sale. If the seller is bound to hand the goods over to a carrier at a particular place, the risk does not pass to the buyer until the goods are handed over to the carrier at that place. The fact that the seller is authorized to retain documents controlling the disposition of the goods does not affect the passage of the risk.

(2) Nevertheless, the risk does not pass to the buyer until the goods are clearly identified to the contract, whether by markings on the goods, by shipping documents, by notice given to the buyer or otherwise.

Article 68

The risk in respect of goods sold in transit passes to the buyer from the time of the conclusion of the contract. However, if the circumstances so indicate, the risk is assumed by the buyer from the time the goods were handed over to the carrier who issued the documents embodying the contract of carriage. Nevertheless, if at the time of the conclusion of the contract of sale the seller knew or ought to have known that the goods had been lost or damaged and did not disclose this to the buyer, the loss or damage is at the risk of the seller.

Article 69

(1) In cases not within articles 67 and 68, the risk passes to the buyer when he takes over the goods or, if he does not do so in due time, from the time when the goods are placed at his disposal and he commits a breach of contract by failing to take delivery.

(2) However, if the buyer is bound to take over the goods at a place other than a place of business of the seller, the risk passes when delivery is due and the buyer is aware of the fact that the goods are placed at his disposal at that price.

(3) If the contract relates to goods not then identified, the goods are considered not to be placed at the disposal of the buyer until they are clearly identified to the contract.

Article 70

If the seller has committed a fundamental breach of contract, articles 67, 68 and 69 do not impair the remedies available to the buyer on account of the breach.

Risk of Loss and the Effect of the Party's Breach

A difficult question is whether and to what extent normal rules for transfer of risk of loss should be modified when one or the other party is in breach of his contractual obligations at the time of loss. The only express provision in the SGA which deals with this situation is s. 21(a), which provides that

> where delivery has been delayed through the fault of either the buyer or seller, the goods are at the risk of the party in fault as regards any loss that might not have occurred but for such fault. …

The comparable Code rules appear in UCC 2-510 and are much more detailed than s. 21(a):

> **2-510**(1) Where a tender or delivery of goods so fails to conform to the contract as to give a right of rejection the risk of their loss remains on the seller until cure or acceptance.
>
> (2) Where the buyer rightfully revokes acceptance he may to the extent of any deficiency in his effective insurance coverage treat the risk of loss as having rested on the seller from the beginning.
>
> (3) Where the buyer as to conforming goods already identified to the contract for sale repudiates or is otherwise in breach before risk of their loss has passed to him, the seller may to the extent of any deficiency in his effective insurance coverage treat the risk of loss as resting on the buyer for a commercially reasonable time.

J.J. White and R.S. Summers, *Uniform Commercial Code*, 5th ed. (2000), at para. 5.5, criticize 2-510 on the ground that "the draftsmen never clearly articulated why the party in breach should bear the risk of loss in certain circumstances when he would not bear that risk were he not in breach." They admit, however, that the section has given rise to little appellate litigation, an observation that in Canada applies to risk of loss cases generally. (Can you suggest why?)

At first blush, s. 21(a) appears to differ fundamentally from 2-510. Section 21(a) presents, however, a very incomplete statement of existing Anglo-Canadian law on the effect of breach and, taking this into consideration, the OLRC came to the conclusion that the Code provision was substantially consistent with existing law and supported its adoption with some modifications (Sales Report, at 273-75). Note, however, the influence of insurance coverage and the non-subrogation effect of UCC 2-510(2) and (3).

Allied Mills Ltd. v. Gwydir Valley Oil Seeds Pty Ltd.

[1978] 2 NSWLR 26 (CA)

MOFFITT P: I agree with the judgments of Hutley JA and of Mahoney JA.

HUTLEY JA: This is an appeal by the defendant from a verdict and judgment of Coates DCJ, given on 25th November, 1977.

The appellant was the seller and the respondent was the buyer, of 130 tonnes of linseed meal in store at the seller's place of business in Moree. His Honour found that the contract was for the unconditional sale of specific goods in a deliverable state, so that the property passed on the making of the contract, on or prior to 4th February, 1975.

The terms of the contract were embodied in two documents. There was a purchase order which was signed by the seller, followed by a written contract in the seller's form. The only difference is that the seller's form of contract contained the following clause: "Sellers shall not be liable in any respect for failure or delay in fulfilment and performance of this contract or any part thereof if hindered or prevented directly or indirectly by an Act of God, Riots, Rebellion, Strikes, Lockouts or by any cause beyond their control."

Delivery was to take place during February 1975, and the goods were to be picked up by the buyer's agent. In breach of contract, and for its own purposes, the seller declined to deliver 100 tonnes during February, and on 21st March, 1975, there was a fire in the shed in which it was stored.

The buyer had resold the linseed meal. It was forced to enter the market to obtain other meal to satisfy its contracts, and bought this meal at a higher price, $85 per tonne, that is $30 per tonne higher than the sale price. It sued to recover the sum of $3,000, being the extra expense to which it was put in buying linseed meal at a higher price. It recovered this sum.

· · ·

No challenge was made to his Honour's finding that, under this contract, the property in the goods passed to the buyer on 4th February, 1975. His Honour applied the first proviso in s. 25 of the *Sale of Goods Act*, 1923 [Ont. s. 21]. This section is in the following terms: "Unless otherwise agreed, the goods remain at the seller's risk until the property therein is transferred to the buyer, but when the property therein is transferred to the buyer, the goods are at the buyer's risk, whether delivery has been made or not:

"Provided that where delivery has been delayed through the fault of either buyer or seller, the goods are at the risk of the party in fault as regards any loss which might not have occurred but for such fault:

"Provided also that nothing in this section shall affect the duties or liabilities of either seller or buyer as a bailee of the goods of the other party."

He held that the goods were at the risk of the seller, because of its breach of contract and, further, that the loss which was suffered might not have occurred, but for such fault. On the facts found by him, his decision was correct. This proviso has received surprisingly little judicial consideration. The only case to which the Court was referred was *Demby Hamilton & Co. Ltd. v. Barden*. This was a case in which the buyer was in breach, in that he did not accept delivery of goods, which deteriorated during storage and, applying the proviso, the goods were at the buyer's risk, and he had to pay the purchase price.

The first submission for the seller is that the judgment under appeal was wrong, because the proviso quoted above only exonerated the buyer from the necessity of paying for the goods which were burnt, and did not give him a cause of action in damages. This conclusion does not follow from the above case; the most which can be said is that it provides no authority in a case such as the present.

Some support is provided for this contention by the second proviso which preserves the law of bailment, and it may be that it is in the relationship of bailor and bailee that the relevant rights of these parties is to be found. It is not, in my opinion, necessary to decide this question as even, on this basis, I consider the judgment under appeal plainly right.

The appellant submitted that the seller was the bailee, and the buyer the bailor. This is correct. The first proviso which reversed the risk by reason of the fault of the seller did not, however, alter their respective titles, as it is not necessary in law for the risk and the ownership to be coincidental. As Benjamin, *Sale of Goods*, 1974 ed., p. 197, par. 417 says: "If the property has passed to the buyer under the contract of sale, but the seller remains in possession of the goods, it appears that he does so as a bailee for reward until the time for delivery has arrived"; and the learned author further states at p. 198, par. 418: "... , if the risk has passed to the buyer, but delivery is delayed due to the seller's fault, the seller must assume the risk of any loss which might not have occurred but for such fault, and in addition must take reasonable care of the goods."

It would seem clear to me that, where a seller who is a bailee for reward does not deliver the goods in accordance with the contract, as here, he cannot take advantage of his own wrong and contend that he has a lower degree of responsibility than he had pursuant to the contract itself. The bailee here, having failed to deliver the goods, is liable to the buyer, unless it is able to establish that it had taken reasonable care of the goods which, in this case, means it had established that it had not stored them under conditions under which they might be damaged: see Paton, *Bailment in the Common Law*, p. 168.

There is no evidence which would justify a finding that it had discharged its burden. Even though his Honour found the evidence which was called by the plaintiff (the buyer) unhelpful, the burden lay upon the seller (the defendant) to establish affirmatively that the damage which was suffered was not its fault.

The conditions of sale above referred to did not help the defendant, because its failure to fulfil the performance of this contract was not due to a cause beyond its control. It was due to a cause within its control. If it had complied with the terms of the contract, the goods would not have been in the place where the fire occurred and, further, it failed to establish that it had no responsibility for the occurrence of the fire.

The seller sought to rely upon the doctrine of frustration. This contract was not frustrated in any legal sense, that is, brought to an end by the appearance of a situation to which the contract could not, on its true construction, apply: *Davis Contractors Ltd. v. Fareham Urban District Council* (2), per Lord Reid. The contract applies perfectly to the new situation. The seller just did not fulfil its contract, that is, by delivering the goods, and for this the law gives a remedy—damages. In order to comply with the contract, delivery had to take place during the month of February. The buyer did not release the seller from that obligation by rescinding the contract, so that the seller remained liable to deliver at any reasonable time. Being unable to deliver, and being unable to prove that it had discharged its responsibilities as a bailee for reward, it cannot escape liability by invoking the doctrine of frustration.

In my opinion, the appeal should be dismissed with costs.

MAHONEY JA: I am satisfied that, at the time when the goods were destroyed by fire, the property in the goods had passed to the buyer, their delivery had been delayed by the fault of the seller, and the goods were, therefore, at the risk of the seller "as regards any loss which might not have occurred but for such fault": s. 25 of the *Sale of Goods Act*, 1923, first proviso. The goods were, in my opinion, destroyed by such a "loss." The relationship between the loss, and the event which caused it, and the fault of the seller is described merely by the words "might not have occurred but for such fault." I do not think that it is necessary to attempt to delimit the ambit of that relationship in the abstract; it is sufficient for present purposes to conclude that the events which happened fall within it.

Putting the matter at the lowest against the seller, the goods were retained where they were by it; they remained there by reason of its refusal to offer delivery of them, and they would not have been destroyed by the fire, unless they were where they were. I think this is sufficient for the purpose of the section.

The seller advanced an alternative argument. It submitted that the destruction of the goods by fire absolved it from its obligation in respect of the delivery of them. Two possible bases of this argument were advanced: s. 12 of the Act, and the common law doctrine of frustration.

I do not think that s. 12 is applicable: the goods were specific goods but, as the learned judge held, the property in the goods and, therefore, the risk as to them passed to the buyer on the making of the agreement. It is not necessary to consider whether s. 12 can apply, if the risk thereafter passes back from the buyer to the seller, because that did not happen in the present case: s. 25 operates only to put the goods at the risk of the seller in relation to the limited categories of loss to which the proviso to that section refers.

The common law doctrine of frustration was also referred to, but the Court did not have the benefit of any detailed analysis of the cases. The arguments of counsel raised the question whether, apart from s. 12, a party who, in accordance with the Act, bears the risk in respect of goods can rely upon the common law doctrine of frustration as a defence to an action for the price of specific goods, or for the failure to give, or accept, delivery of them. I do not think it is necessary to express an opinion upon this question. The seller was sued for breach of its obligation under the agreement for sale to deliver the goods; it was in those terms that the buyer's claim was framed. In order to rely upon the doctrine of frustration, if it be available, the seller must show that the delivery was prevented by supervening events, and it must not appear that those events were the result of a default, of the relevant kind, on the seller's part: *Joseph Constantine Steamship Line Ltd. v. Imperial Smelting Corporation Ltd.*

The learned trial judge did not find it necessary to make findings of fact as to the cause of the fire. But the question was dealt with in evidence, and it is open to this Court to make the appropriate finding. In my opinion, the proper inference to be drawn is that the fire resulted from default on the part of the seller. I need not repeat the facts. Looking at the matter upon the basis of the probabilities, I think the fire arose from a cause for which the seller was, or ought to have been, aware and against which it took no proper precautions. Assuming that the doctrine of frustration be relevant, that which prevented the delivery of the goods was a default of the seller such as would prevent it relying upon that doctrine.

I agree with the orders which have been proposed.

Appeal dismissed.

FRUSTRATION OF CONTRACT OF SALE

Frustration Through Casualty to the Goods

OLRC Sales Report

at 365-68

1. *Introduction*

Like the law of mistake, the rules governing the frustration of agreement belong to one of the most difficult branches of contract law. The relatively small number of Canadian sales cases involving frustration issues and the infrequency with which the parties themselves may encounter the problem in periods of national and international stability mask the legal difficulties. In an environment of intense inflation and rapidly changing economic and political conditions, the parties are often faced with contingencies not foreseen at the time of contracting or which undermine their common assumptions. *Force majeure* clauses are a regular feature in well drafted contracts, and the parties may seek to protect themselves against future imponderables by the insertion of other appropriate clauses in their contracts. These drafting devices may diminish the need for clear rules; they do not replace them.

With the exception of section 8, the Sale of Goods Act does not purport to codify the law of frustration in its relation to contracts of sale. Cases falling outside the provisions of section 8 continue to be governed by common law principles. The common law position, though much litigated in this century in the United Kingdom, is far from clear, and both the theory of frustration and its scope as a defence remain unsettled. There is, therefore, much to be said for an attempt to clarify the present law. As will be seen, the Uniform Commercial Code contains a substantial number of provisions which, while disclaiming any pretence at a comprehensive statement, do clarify and improve the existing position in important respects in so far as contracts of sale are concerned. For a number of reasons, we support a similar approach in the revised Act to that adopted in the Code. The desirability of a general restatement of frustration principles should, we believe, be left for future consideration as part of our proposed Law of Contract Amendment Project.

2. *The Sale of Goods Act, Section 8*

Section 8 of the Sale of Goods Act deals with one aspect of the law of frustration in relation to a contract of sale; that is, the loss of specific goods. The section provides as follows:

> **8**. Where there is an agreement to sell specific goods and subsequently the goods without any fault of the seller or buyer perish before the risk passes to the buyer, the agreement is thereby avoided.

The effect of section 8 is to discharge the seller's obligation to deliver and the buyer's obligation to pay the price. The section should be read in conjunction with its companion provision, section 7, which applies similar principles to determine the effect on the contract of the parties' mistaken assumption with respect to the existence of the goods. As was noted in an earlier chapter, section 7 raises problems of construction. This is also the case with section 8. The section is, moreover, seriously incomplete. We turn now to consider the deficiencies of section 8.

First, section 8 deals only with the loss of "specific" goods. It is not clear whether the term "specific" is to be interpreted as referring solely to goods in existence at the time of making the contract. The Act defines "specific goods" in section 1(1)(m) as "goods identified and agreed upon at the time the contract of sale is made." In *Howell v. Coupland* (1876), 1 QBD 258 (CA), however, a seller was excused from a contract of sale of potatoes to be grown on his land when the crop failed. This case, decided before the enactment of the Sale of Goods Act, 1893, and other similar decisions, have raised the possibility of the application of section 8 to "quasi-specific goods." The law has not, however, developed.

Secondly, it will be noted that section 8 of the Sale of Goods Act only applies where the goods "perish." In chapter 5 of this Report, in the context of mistake, we considered the question when goods have "perished" within the meaning of section 7 of the Act. The term "perish" raises similar problems of interpretation in the context of section 8. For example, it is difficult to determine what degree of deterioration of the subject matter will bring the section into operation. There is some authority, disputed though it is, that the concept of perishment includes deterioration that alters, but does not destroy, the goods. Similarly, the concept of perishment causes difficulty in indivisible contracts where part of the subject matter of the contract is destroyed. There is authority that partial destruction will result in frustration of an indivisible contract, with the result that, even though the buyer is willing to take the remaining goods, he cannot force the seller to deliver.

Thirdly, it is not clear to what extent "fault" includes loss due to negligence. Section (1)(f) of the Sale of Goods Act defines "fault" to mean "a wrongful act or default." This definition is wide enough to embrace negligent conduct, and such a reading would be consistent with the rule applied in the case of self-induced frustration. Still, a small amendment to the definition would put the point beyond doubt.

Fourthly, difficulties are created by the restriction of section 8 to an "agreement to sell." By virtue of section 2(3) of the Sale of Goods Act, there is an agreement to sell where there has been no transfer of property in the goods to the buyer, but where such transfer is to take place at a future time or subject to some condition to be fulfilled thereafter. It seems clear, therefore, that section 8 has no application to contracts of sale where property or title has passed to the buyer. Yet, where title has passed, risk may nevertheless remain with the seller by agreement, or control of the goods may not have passed to the buyer. In the latter case, it is true that the line between frustration concepts and the seller's obligation to deliver the goods blurs. Nevertheless, it may well be argued that the doctrine of frustration should apply in the situation discussed above, notwithstanding that title may have passed to the buyer.

Fifthly, similar difficulties arise because section 8 is restricted to cases where goods perish "before the risk passes to the buyer." The section will not apply, therefore, where risk of loss has been assumed by the buyer, even though property in and possession of the goods remain with the seller. Indeed, there might be a difficulty in applying the concept of frustration to this situation: to discharge the seller from his obligation to deliver, on the ground of frustration, would also discharge the buyer from his obligation to pay the price, and this would conflict with the term of the contract placing the risk of loss on the buyer. Professor Glanville Williams would resolve this dilemma by applying frustration only to the obligation of the seller to deliver and not to the contract as a whole.

Sixthly, section 8 contains no reference to the relevance of foreseeability. A literal application of the section would lead to the conclusion, contrary at least to one line of frustration theory, that the seller is excused from non-performance, even though he could reasonably foresee a substantial risk of loss of or damage to the goods.

Apart from these constructional points, section 8 is open to the further objection of serious incompleteness. The section fails to deal with accepted forms of frustration, other than those where specific goods have perished. For example, it omits any reference to impossibility with reference to the designated means of delivery, illegality, or frustration of purpose. Such cases are left to the common law for resolution. Again, there would appear to be no justification for the distinction drawn by the section between specific and unascertained goods, if one accepts, as we do, that frustration doctrines can apply just as readily to agreed or assumed sources of supply as to goods identified at the time of the formation of the contract. The courts have applied common law frustration concepts where the contractual source of supply fails, but have not extended this analysis to the area of so-called "economic frustration"; that is, situations where alternative sources of supply, or performance generally, have become prohibitively expensive or otherwise burdensome.

Howell v. Coupland

[1874-80] All ER Rep. 878, 1 QBD 258 (CA)

LORD COLERIDGE CJ: I am of opinion that the judgment of the Court of Queen's Bench should be affirmed. The contract here is a contract between the plaintiff and the defendant, that the defendant shall sell and the plaintiff shall buy 200 tons of Regent potatoes, grown on land belonging to the defendant in Whaplode, at a certain rate per ton. From the facts found in the case, it appears that at the time of making the contract the defendant had sixty-eight acres ready for potatoes, twenty-five acres had been already sown, the other forty-three acres were afterwards sown, an amount which by ordinary calculation would be enough to raise the stipulated quantity of potatoes. Before the time for delivery it is found that the potato disease had appeared—a disease which it is expressly found no amount of skill, care, or diligence on the part of the defendant could prevent. The crop is attacked by this disease, and by it reduced so low as to make it impossible for the defendant to deliver the requisite quantity of potatoes; and it is also found that at the time the disease was discovered to have made its appearance, the defendant had no other land suitable for the purpose of sowing other potatoes so as to supply, if possible, the deficiency in the quantity contracted to be delivered. Under these circumstances the Court of Queen's Bench have held that the principle of *Taylor v. Caldwell* (1863), 32 LJQB 164 and *Appleby v. Myers* (1867), LR 2 CP 651 applies, and the defendant is excused from the performance of his contract.

It appears to me that the true ground of construction on which this contract should be interpreted, and I believe the ground on which the Court of Queen's Bench have decided, is that by the clear and simple construction of the contract both parties agreed there should be a condition that the potatoes should be or have been in existence at the time named for the performance of the contract. They had been in existence, and had been destroyed by causes over which the defendant had no control, and, therefore, it became impossible for him to perform his contract, and according to the law in such case, as applicable to the condition both parties agreed to be bound by, he is excused. It was not an absolute contract to deliver under all circumstance, but it was a contract to deliver a certain quantity of potatoes of a specific crop, and if at the time of delivery such quantity is not forthcoming through reasons over which the defendant has no control, such condition will exempt the defendant from performance of the contract.

Judgment of the Court of Queen's Bench affirmed.

[Concurring judgments were delivered by James and Mellish LJJ, Baggallay JA, and Cleasby B.]

OLRC Sales Report

at 370-73

It will be recalled that we have already discussed UCC 2-613 in chapter 5 of this Report, in the context of section 7 of the Sale of Goods Act. In chapter 5, we recommended that the revised Act should adopt, in place of section 7 of the existing Act, a provision comparable to UCC 2-613 with respect to the effect on the contract of the parties' mistaken assumption as to the existence of the goods. In the context of our discussion of frustration, it will be convenient to set out, once again, the provisions of UCC 2-613, which read as follows:

> **2-613.** Where the contract requires for its performance goods identified when the contract is made, and the goods suffer casualty without fault of either party before the risk of loss passes to the buyer, or in a proper case under a "no arrival, no sale" term (Section 2-324) then
>
> (a) if the loss is total the contract is avoided; and
>
> (b) if the loss is partial or the goods have so deteriorated as no longer to conform to the contract the buyer may nevertheless demand inspection and at his option either treat the contract as avoided or accept the goods with due allowance from the contract price for the deterioration or the deficiency in quantity but without further right against the seller.

This section felicitously fuses the old provisions in section 7 and 8 of the Uniform Sales Act. As has been previously noted, it improves on them, and *a fortiori* on the provisions of section 8 of the Ontario Act, insofar as it confers an option on the buyer to obtain the surviving or deteriorated goods with an abatement in the price. Further, in our view, the term "casualty" is more meaningful to express the applicability of the Code section to all forms of loss or damage affecting the goods, without regard to the extent or value of the loss or damage, and overcomes the difficulties inherent in the use of the word "perish" in our Sale of Goods Act. But the section also has its weaknesses and, in our view, could be improved or clarified in a number of respects. We therefore recommend adoption in the revised Act of a provision similar to UCC 2-613 with respect to casualty to identified goods, but subject to the following amendments.

First, the section should not be confined to "goods identified when the contract is made." This phraseology continues the present requirement of specific goods, with its attendant problems. There appears to be no sufficient reason why the rule should not also apply where goods are subsequently identified to the contract with the consent of both parties. Accordingly, we recommend that the provision in the revised Act comparable to UCC 2-613 should apply to "goods identified when the contract is made or goods that have been subsequently identified to the contract with the consent of the buyer and the seller."

Secondly, the application of the section should not be confined, as under section 8 of the Sale of Goods Act, to cases in which goods suffer casualty "before the risk" passes to the buyer. As Glanville Williams first suggested, this linking of discharge of the seller to the location of risk is misconceived. Earlier in this chapter, we discussed the difficulties that can arise where risk has passed to the buyer, but property in and possession of the goods remains with the seller. These difficulties may occur equally under UCC 2-613. The function of the rules governing passage of risk, which in Ontario are contained in section 21 of the Sale of Goods Act, is to determine which party to a contract bears the risk of loss of, or damage to, the goods. Section 21 does not, of itself, answer the question whether, where the goods have suffered casualty, the seller is discharged from his obligation to perform. That function is served by the doctrine of frustration. In our opinion, the question of who bears the risk of loss at the time of casualty. Furthermore, the seller's right to be discharged, in whole or in part, from the performance of his obligations should not affect the buyer's obligation to pay the price if he has assumed the risk of loss. Accordingly, we recommend that the application of the provision in the revised Act comparable to UCC 2-613 should not be restricted to cases where goods suffer casualty before risk of loss has passed to the buyer. This recommendation is subject to the qualification that the buyer should retain the right to compel partial performance, with due allowance, in the case of partial loss or destruction of the goods, where the risk of such casualty has not passed to him. Where the risk of casualty is with the buyer, he should also have the right to claim the remaining goods, but without an abatement in the price. It follows from what we have said that the section in the revised Act comparable to UCC 2-613 should expressly provide that, in the case of casualty to goods, the seller's obligation is discharged, but the buyer is discharged from the obligation to pay the price only if the risk of such loss has not passed to the buyer.

Thirdly, like its predecessors, section 2-613 appears to operate absolutely, without regard to the foreseeability of the casualty, or to any undertaking on the seller's part to assume liability for delivery in any event. To cover this contingency, it has been suggested to us that the operation of the section be excluded where the promisor has special knowledge leading him to "anticipate" the casualty which he does not communicate to the buyer, even though he has reason to believe that the buyer does not possess the knowledge. A further suggestion is that the section should not apply where the seller assumes responsibility for the continued and unblemished existence of the goods. We think that both these factors can be accommodated by making it clear that the section applies "unless the circumstances indicate that either party has assumed a greater obligation." We therefore recommend that these words be added to the provision in the revised Act corresponding to UCC 2-613. Any remaining *lacunae* will be picked up by the existing requirement in UCC 2-613 that both parties must be "without fault," and by the general requirement of good faith applicable throughout the revised Act.

Earlier in this chapter, we indicated that it is unclear whether "fault," as used in section 8 of the Sale of Goods Act, includes loss due to negligence. Comment 1 to UCC 2-613 states that "'fault' is intended to include negligence and not merely wilful wrong." We are of the view that "fault" as used in the revised Act should include loss due to negligence, and accordingly recommend that the revised Act adopt the Code definition of "fault."

While we do not favour retaining even an improved version of section 8 of the Ontario Act as an isolated provision governing one aspect of the rules of frustration, we support a provision comparable to UCC 2-613 in the context of a larger group of frustration provisions. We appreciate that it may be contended that UCC 2-613 deals with but one instance of the application of the broader rule codified in UCC 2-615, and that no good purpose would be served by including such a provision in the revised Act. We are not, however, persuaded by this line of reasoning, and favour a specific provision along the lines of UCC 2-613 on two grounds. First, it would set forth expressly the buyer's rights in the event of the seller's discharge, whereas such a provision is lacking at present in section 2-615. Secondly, it would make it clear that casualty to identified goods is unarguably a frustrating event.

Commercial Frustration

Ocean Tramp Tankers Corp. v. V/O Sovfracht (The "Eugenia")

[1964] 1 All ER 161, [1964] 2 QB 226 (CA)

[The present case was one of a series of cases arising out of the closure of the Suez Canal in 1956. The parties had entered on September 8, 1956, into a charterparty for the leasing of the Eugenia "for a trip out to India via Black Sea." The vessel entered the Suez Canal on October 31 but was unable to leave the canal because the canal was blocked. On January 4, 1957, the charterers claimed that the contract had been frustrated by the blocking of the canal. The owners denied that there had been a frustration and treated the conduct of the charterers as a repudiation.

Lord Denning's judgment is reproduced here for his interpretation of current frustration theory in English law.]

LORD DENNING MR: The second question is whether the charterparty was frustrated by what took place. The arbitrator has held that it was not. The judge has held that it was. Which is right? One thing that is obvious is that the charterers cannot rely on the fact that the Eugenia was trapped in the canal; for that was their own fault. They were in breach of the war clause in entering it. They cannot rely on a self-induced frustration; see *Maritime National Fish, Ltd. v. Ocean Trawlers, Ltd.*, [1935] AC 524. But they seek to rely on the fact that the canal itself was blocked. They assert that, even if the Eugenia had never gone into the canal but had stayed outside (in which case she would not have been in breach of the war clause), nevertheless she would still have had to go round by the Cape; and that, they say, brings about a frustration, for it makes the venture fundamentally different from what they contracted for. The judge has accepted this view. He has held that, on Nov. 16, 1956, the charterparty was frustrated. The reason for his taking Nov. 16, 1956, was this: Prior to Nov. 16, 1956, mercantile men (even if she had stayed outside) would not have formed any conclusion whether the obstructions in the canal were other than temporary. There was insufficient information available to form a judgment. On Nov. 16, 1956, mercantile men would conclude that the blockage of the southern end would last till March or April, 1975; so that, by that time, it would be clear that the only thing to do (if the ship had never entered the canal) would be to go round the Cape. The judge said:

> I hold that the adventure, involving a voyage round the Cape, is basically or fundamentally different from the adventure involving a voyage via the Suez Canal.

So he held that the contract was frustrated. He was comforted to find that, in *Société Franco Tunisienne D'Armement v. Sidermar SPA*, [1961] 2 QB 278 at 307, Pearson J came to a similar conclusion. I must confess that I find it difficult to apply the doctrine of frustration to a hypothetical situation, that is, to treat this vessel as if she had never entered the canal and then ask whether the charter was frustrated. The doctrine should be applied to the facts as they really are. But I will swallow this difficulty and ask myself what would be the position if the vessel had never entered the canal but stayed at Port Said. Would the contract be frustrated? This means that, once again, we have had to consider the authorities on this vexed topic of frustration. But I think that the position is now reasonably clear. It is simply this: If it should happen, in the course of carrying out a contract, that a fundamentally different situation arises for which the parties made no provision—so much so that it would not be just in the new situation to hold them bound to its terms—then the contract is at an end.

It was originally said that the doctrine of frustration was based on an implied term. In short, that the parties, if they had foreseen the new situation, would have said to one another: "If that happens, of course, it is all over between us." But the theory of an implied term has now been discarded by everyone, or nearly everyone, for the simple reason that it does not represent the truth. The parties would not have said: "It is all over between us." They would have differed about what was to happen. Each would have sought to insert reservations or qualifications of one kind or another. Take this very case. The parties realised that the canal might become impassable. They tried to agree on a clause to provide for the contingency. But they failed to agree. So there is no room for an implied term.

It has frequently been said that the doctrine of frustration only applies when the new situation is "unforeseen" or "unexpected" or "uncontemplated," as if that were an essential feature. But it is not so. It is not so much that it is "unexpected," but rather that the parties have made no provision for it in their contract. The point about it, however, is this: If the parties did not foresee anything of the kind happening, you can readily infer that they have made no provision for it. Whereas, if they did foresee it, you would expect them to make provision for it. But cases have occurred where the parties have foreseen the danger ahead, and yet made no provision for it in the contract. Such was the case in the Spanish Civil War when a ship was let on charter to the Republican Government. The purpose was to evacuate refugees. The parties foresaw that she might be seized by the Nationalists. But they made no provision for it in their contract. Yet, when she was seized, the contract was frustrated: see *W.J. Tatem, Ltd. v. Gamboa*, [1939] 1 KB 132. So, here, the parties foresaw that the canal might become impassable. It was the very thing that they feared. But they made no provision for it. So the doctrine may still apply, if it be a proper case for it.

We are thus left with the simple test that a situation must arise which renders performance of the contract "a thing radically different from that which was undertaken by the contract": see *Davis Contractors, Ltd. v. Fareham UDC*, [1956] AC 696 at 729, *per* Lord Radcliffe. To see if the doctrine applies, you have first to construe the contract to see whether the parties have themselves provided for the situation that has arisen. If they have provided for it, the contract must govern. There is no frustration. If they have not provided for it, then you have to compare the new situation with the old situation for which they did provide. Then you must see how different it is. The fact that it has become more onerous or more expensive for one party than he thought is not sufficient to bring about a frustration. It must be more than merely more onerous or more expensive. It must be positively unjust to hold the parties bound. It is often difficult to draw the line. But it must be done, and it is for the courts to do it as a matter of law: see *Tsakiroglou & Co., Ltd. v. Noblee & Thorl G.m.b.H.*, [1962] AC 93 at 116, 119, *per* Viscount Simonds and *per* Lord Reid.

Appeal allowed.

[Donovan and Danckwerts LJJ concurred.]

OLRC Sales Report

at 374-77

Section 2-615 of the Uniform Commercial Code provides as follows:

2-615. Except so far as a seller may have assumed a greater obligation and subject to the preceding section on substituted performance:

(a) Delay in delivery or non-delivery in whole or in part by a seller who complies with paragraphs (b) and (c) is not a breach of his duty under a contract for sale if performance as agreed has been made impracticable by the occurrence of a contingency the non-occurrence of which was a basic assumption on which the contract was made or by compliance in good faith with any applicable foreign or domestic governmental regulation or order whether or not it later proves to be invalid.

(b) Where the causes mentioned in paragraph (a) affect only a part of the seller's capacity to perform, he must allocate production and deliveries among his customers but may at his option include regular customers not then under contract as well as his own requirements for further manufacture. He may so allocate in any manner which is fair and reasonable.

(c) The seller must notify the buyer seasonably that there will be delay or non-delivery and, when allocation is required under paragraph (b), of the estimated quota thus made available for the buyer.

This section has three principal components. Paragraph (a) states the circumstances in which a "delay in delivery or non-delivery in whole or in part" will be excused on grounds of frustration. Paragraph (b) introduces the principle of apportionment where, following the frustrating event, the seller is not left with sufficient supplies to meet all legitimate demands. Paragraph (c) imposes a notice requirement on the seller and follows logically from the duty to allocate and the right of election conferred on the buyer under section 2-616. It will be convenient to postpone discussion of paragraph (c) until we consider the provisions of UCC 2-616.

Paragraph (a) of UCC 2-615 raises the question of the basic purposes and applications of the doctrine of frustration. Various theories of the true "basis" of the frustration doctrine have been judicially asserted. One theory was stated by Lord Blackburn in *Taylor v. Caldwell* (1863), 3 B & S 824, 122 ER 309 (QB), and holds that, from the nature of the contract, the courts find an implied term to the effect that, on the occurrence of certain events, performance will be excused. A second theory, which has its origins in the dissenting opinion of Viscount Haldane in *F.A. Tamplin Steamship Co. Ltd. v. Anglo-Mexican Petroleum Products Co. Ltd.*, [1916] 2 AC 397 (HL), would view the contract as vanishing with the disappearance of the foundations of the contract. A third theory sees frustration as a device by which courts may reach the result that justice demands. The first theory has come under attack lately in England and in Canada, and the third theory has gained in popularity. By contrast, UCC 2-615 follows the middle path; that is, the theory that the contract vanishes with the disappearance of its foundations.

Apart from the possible theoretical basis of the doctrine of frustration, there is the question of the situations to which the doctrine applies. Since *Taylor v. Caldwell*, no one has questioned the application of a doctrine of frustration, however it is rationalized, to situations where performance has become impossible. The case of *Krell v. Henry*, [1903] 2 KB 740 (CA) expanded the application of the doctrine to instances where literal performance remained possible, but the underlying purpose of the contract seemed defeated. This extension, by means of a frustration of purpose test, met with mixed criticism; and its status was uncertain in Ontario, at least until recently, and still remains so in England. A third possible situation to which the frustration doctrine might be applied is the case where performance is possible, but would impose severe hardship upon the promisor. This extension has received little judicial encouragement. It is to the second situation, that is, to frustration of the underlying purposes of the contract, that UCC 2-615 appears to address itself by applying a test of commercial impracticality, or commercial frustration. The question that needs consideration is whether this test should now be formally adopted in the revised Sale of Goods Act. Such a step would not be radical, and, we believe, can be justified on two grounds.

First, the existing law is not simply a test of literal impossibility. The frustration of purpose test has been present, though little used, in Anglo-Canadian law since at least *Krell v. Henry*, in which Vaughan Williams LJ stated a test of frustration, extending *Taylor v. Caldwell* in terms not dissimilar to those adopted by the draftsmen of UCC 2-615. While, as noted, the courts have been divided in their reaction to *Krell v. Henry*, the Ontario Court of Appeal, in *Capital Quality Homes Ltd. v. Colwyn Construction Ltd.* (1975), 61 DLR (3d) 385,[1] recently gave new life to the principle expressed in that decision. The Court of Appeal held that a contract for the sale of land was frustrated by the enactment of certain provisions of the Planning Act that prevented subdivision of the land. The Court stated as follows with respect to the "supervening event" that gives rise to frustration:

> The supervening event must be something beyond the control of the parties and must result in a significant change in the obligation assumed by them.

This language clearly supports a frustration of purpose test, and is consistent with the Code's test of commercial impracticability or frustration. The Court also emphasized that, in its view, the theory of the implied term "has been replaced by the more realistic view that the Court imposes upon the parties the just and reasonable solution that the new situation demands." Since the buyer's known purpose to subdivide the land could not be realized, the contract was frustrated.

The second reason for believing the change is not radical lies in the draftsmen's own interpretation of the scope of section 2-615(a), and in the cautious attitude toward this provision displayed by American courts. Official Comment 4 to section 2-615 makes it clear that "increased cost alone does not excuse performance unless the rise in cost is due to some unforeseen contingency which alters the essential nature of performance." Something more substantial is required. The American courts have moved hesitantly in granting a non-performing party the shelter of UCC 2-615(a). A good example is the recent case of *Eastern Airlines Inc. v. Gulf Oil Corp.* (1975), 19 UCC Rep. 721 (SD Fla.). This case involved a contract for the supply of oil by Gulf Oil to Eastern Airlines. The contract rate was frozen because it had been pegged to a certain index for Texas oil that was itself artificially frozen by the US Government. World prices, which Gulf had to pay, had, on the other hand, risen 400%. Gulf argued that it was a basic assumption of the contract that the index for Texas oil would continue to reflect world prices. On the basis of the available evidence and all the surrounding circumstances, the Court refused to make such a finding, and accordingly held that the contract had not been frustrated. The same reluctance has been shown by other

---

1 Subsequently distinguished, however, in *Victoria Wood Devpt. Corp. v. Ondrey* (1978), 22 OR (2d) 1, 92 DLR (3d) 229 (CA).

American courts confronted with a defence under UCC 2-615, and one must look hard to find a case where frustration was permitted on grounds other than impossibility.

There is little danger, therefore, that the adoption in Ontario of a provision similar to paragraph (a) of section 2-615 would result in ready acquiescence by the courts to attempts by dissatisfied buyers and sellers to seek relief from contracts that have lost their initial attraction. Further, we feel that the provision has positive merit, in that it leads to a more direct canvassing by the courts of the factors underlying the parties' common assumptions, and the important role played by economic considerations in shaping those assumptions.

We accept the test of commercial impracticability or frustration contained in UCC 2-615(a). Subject to the following consequential issues, we recommend that a provision comparable to UCC 2-615(a) be incorporated in the revised Ontario Act.

Michael J. Trebilcock
The Limits of Freedom of Contract

(Harvard University Press, 1993), at 130-36 (Footnotes omitted)

The Superior Risk-Bearer Approach

Frustration

A sophisticated recent attempt by Posner and Rosenfield to reconceptualize the traditional approach of contract law to gap-filling shows how intractable the difficulties associated with it inherently are. In the context of frustration, they propose that discharge should be allowed where the promisee is the superior risk-bearer; if the promisor is the superior risk-bearer, non-performance should be treated as a breach of contract. They acknowledge that if the parties have expressly assigned the risk to one of them, there is no occasion to inquire who is the superior risk-bearer. They claim that the inquiry is merely "an aid to interpretation." In suggesting this, Posner and Rosenfield are not at all clear about whether it is to be assumed that the parties must have intended to assign the risk to the superior risk-bearer (with appropriate compensation paid for bearing the risk), in which case the two basic questions in this context of whether there is a contractual gap and how to fill it are elided, or whether, irrespective of their intentions, instrumental efficiency considerations are being invoked to impose this rule on the parties in the interest of efficient resource (or risk) allocation in general (and despite the lack of compensation for bearing the risk). In other words, it is not clear whether their approach is based on actual consent to contractual obligations or whether Kaldor-Hicks notions of efficiency are being invoked to assign obligations to the parties. In operationalizing their superior risk-bearer approach, Posner and Rosenfield propose the following framework of analysis:

> It does not necessarily follow from the fact that the promisor could not at any reasonable cost have prevented the risk from materializing that he should be discharged from his contractual obligations. Prevention is only one way of dealing with risk; the other is

insurance. The promisor may be the superior insurer. If so, his inability to prevent the risk from materializing should not operate to discharge him from the contract, any more than an insurance company's inability to prevent a fire on the premises of the insured should excuse it from its liability to make good the damage caused by the fire.

The factors relevant to determining which party to the contract is the cheaper insurer are (1) risk-appraisal costs and (2) transaction costs. The former comprise the costs of determining (a) the probability that the risk will materialize and (b) the magnitude of the loss if it does materialize. The amount of risk is the product of the probability of loss and of the magnitude of the loss if it occurs. Both elements—probability and magnitude—must be known in order for the insurer to know how much to ask from the other party to the contract as compensation for bearing the risk in question.

The relevant transaction costs are the costs involved in eliminating or minimizing the risk through pooling it with other uncertain events, that is, diversifying away the risk. This can be done either through self-insurance or through the purchase of an insurance policy (market insurance).

. . .

Thus, issues of fault are usually irrelevant to the assignment of liability for losses from such contingencies. Indeed, it is well-established law that "self-induced" (avoidable) alleged frustrating events cannot attract relief under the frustration doctrine.

While Posner and Rosenfield believe that many U.S. frustration cases implicitly reflect the economic logic of the framework of analysis they propose, many of the cases that they discuss seem readily susceptible of analysis within their own framework so as to yield opposing results. For example, they discuss the case of *Transatlantic Financing Corp. v. United States*, where a shipowner argued (unsuccessfully) that its contract with the U.S. government to transport wheat from the United States to Iran should be discharged by virtue of the closing of the Suez Canal. They cite the following passage from the decision of Judge Wright as support for their framework:

> Transatlantic was no less able than the United States to purchase insurance to cover the contingency's occurrence. If anything, it is more reasonable to expect owner-operators of vessels to insure against the hazards of war. They are in the best position to calculate the cost of performance by alternative routes (and therefore to estimate the amount of insurance required), and are undoubtedly sensitive to international troubles which uniquely affect the demand for and cost of their services.

Posner and Rosenfield comment as follows:

> The shipowner is the superior risk bearer because he is better able to estimate the magnitude of the loss (a function of delay, and of the value and nature of the cargo, which are also known to the shipowner) and the probability of the unexpected event. Furthermore, shipowners who own several ships and are engaged in shipping along several different routes can spread the risks of delay on any particular route without purchasing market insurance or forcing their shareholders to diversify their common-stock portfolios. And the shipping company could, if it desired, purchase in a single transaction market insurance covering multiple voyages. Of course, the shipper in the particular case—the United States Government—was well diversified too, but the decision should

(and here did) turn on the characteristics of shippers as a class, if an unduly particularistic analysis is to be avoided.

This seems a largely spurious rationalization of the decision. On the particular facts, surely the U.S. government was much better placed than the carrier to appraise the risks of the outbreak of war in the Middle East; better placed than the carrier to evaluate the consequences of delayed arrival of the goods; and better placed than the carrier to self-insure or otherwise diversify away the risk of canal closure.

The objection that these considerations are unduly particularistic seems unconvincing. If the decision should turn on the characteristics of shippers and carriers as classes, what empirical intuitions or generalizations can confidently be offered, or at least are likely to be accessible to a court, as to which class can better determine the probability of given contingencies occurring, can better evaluate the consequences of interrupted or aborted performance should it occur, or as to which class of actors can more cheaply self-insure, market insure, or otherwise diversify away the risks in question? Moreover, why should a court confine its search for the superior risk-bearer to the immediately contracting parties? If one of the contracting parties would have insured the risk with a third party, had the risk been contemplated, why not make the third party liable anyway by judicially constructing a notional, Kaldor-Hicks efficient contract with that party (despite the violence that this would do to the autonomy basis for contractual obligation)?

Similar ambiguities attend another class of case which Posner and Rosenfield discuss—contracts for the supply of agricultural products:

> [This group of cases] illustrates how the courts can arrive at an economically efficient result yet disguise it as an apparently meaningless semantic distinction. The cases have similar facts. A supplier contracts to deliver a particular quantity and quality of an agricultural product; an unexpected event such as a flood or an exceptionally severe drought prevents delivery; the buyer seeks damages. The courts generally discharge the contract where the supplier is a grower, but enforce it where the supplier is a wholesaler or large dealer. The result is both consistent and efficient; it places the risk of extreme weather conditions on the superior risk bearer. The purchaser from the grower can reduce the risk of adverse weather by diversifying his purchases geographically; there is empirical evidence to suggest that in some climatic regions geographical separation of only a few miles can dramatically reduce the risk of a large loss. When the seller is a wholesaler or large dealer there is no reason to allow discharge since he can diversify his purchases and thereby eliminate the risk of adverse weather.

Again, this reasoning seems dubious at best. One could just as easily argue that growers are likely to be better able than perhaps distant wholesalers to estimate the probability of a contingency such as adverse climatic conditions or disease interfering with the production of a crop. Buyers, conversely, may be better able to evaluate the consequence of non-performance. As to who can better diversify away the risk, while it may be true that buyers can diversify their purchases geographically, growers can buy crop insurance, diversify their crop production geographically, or, at least in the case of disease, diversify their product mix, or plant or develop more robust strains of crops. The last possibility raises the risk-incentive trade-off. Providing implicit insurance against the risk of crop failure reduces long-run incentives to avoid the insured contingency, that is, it creates a problem of moral hazard. How should courts weigh this trade-off? Indeed, in Posner and Rosenfield's discussion of the frustration case-law, it is sometimes difficult to be sure whether their analysis turns on least-cost insurer or least-cost avoider considerations. Superior knowledge of the probability of a given contingency materializing, which is presumably relevant to both tests for assignments of liability, is particularly ambiguous in this respect.

Another case that well illustrates these ambiguities is the *Westinghouse* case. Here, Westinghouse entered into long-term contracts to supply uranium fuel at agreed prices to twenty-seven public utilities. Commitments under these contracts substantially exceeded uranium supplies in inventory or under contract to Westinghouse. Apparently, a combination of the OPEC-induced oil price shock and the formation of a cartel of major uranium producers drove the price of uranium up to several times Westinghouse's price commitments under its contracts with the utilities, generating a potential loss of about two billion dollars, and the company sought discharge of the contracts under s. 2-615 of the Uniform Commercial Code on grounds of "commercial impracticability." On the one hand, it could be argued that Westinghouse was better placed than the utilities to estimate the probability of disruption to the uranium supply market (having closer familiarity with it) and perhaps was also better placed than the utilities to evaluate the magnitude of the price increases that might be associated with such disruption. On the other hand, it might be argued that the utilities were better placed than Westinghouse to diversify away (spread) the risk through their substantial customer, shareholder (many probably institutional), and employee bases, to whom the costs of the price increases could variously have been shifted. However, these factors would need to be compared with Westinghouse's opportunities to have hedged more fully in the upstream uranium market. The litigation was subsequently settled, apparently for about half the claimed losses that full contract enforcement would have entailed. Obviously, the latter option would have been of little value to the utilities if it had forced Westinghouse into bankruptcy.

A similar case is that of *Florida Power and Light Co. v. Westinghouse Electric Corp.*, where, in a contract between Westinghouse and Florida Power for the sale of a nuclear reactor, Westinghouse agreed to remove and dispose of spent reactor fuel. Changes in government policy after the signing of the contract precluded disposal of the waste as originally contemplated, and Westinghouse, instead of making an anticipated profit of twenty million dollars on reprocessing the waste, now stood to lose eighty million dollars from performance of this obligation. The court relieved Westinghouse of its obligation on grounds of commercial impracticability. But, as Sykes points out, it is difficult to discern any basis for concluding that Florida Power could better bear the burden of waste disposal than Westinghouse.

Even in cases where the contract subject matter is physically destroyed, rendering performance impossible, the analysis is not necessarily any more straightforward. For example, in the classic case of *Taylor v. Caldwell*, where a music hall which had been rented to a concert group burned down before the scheduled concerts, leading the court to treat the rental contract as frustrated, it may well have been the case (or at least is likely to be in contemporary circumstances) that the hall owner would be insured against the loss of the hall, leaving only the losses sustained by the concert group to be borne by the contracting parties. It is far from clear who of the two parties would be better placed to bear these losses.

Posner and Rosenfield acknowledge that often (I would be inclined to argue, typically) the criteria they propose for identifying the most efficient insurer or risk-bearer will point in opposite directions—one party is better placed to estimate the probability of a given contingency materializing (typically the party whose performance is in issue); the other party, who is to receive the performance in issue, can better evaluate the magnitude of the loss if the contingency does materialize; and either party may be better placed to diversify away or absorb the risk through self-insurance, market insurance, or, more debatably, superior wealth. Uncertainties surrounding these issues are likely to render judicially determined insurance extremely expensive compared with most forms of explicit first-party insurance. Moreover, in contractual settings such as entailed in the frustration cases, at least in the absence of major information asymmetries between the parties, it is not clear that the courts are likely to improve on the risk allocations of the parties by engaging in highly particularistic *ex post* assignments of losses.

A clear, albeit austere, rule of literal contract enforcement in most cases provides the clearest signal to parties to future contractual relationships as to when they might find it mutually advantageous to contract away from the rule. It must be acknowledged, however, that even if one dispensed with or severely circumscribed the scope of the doctrine of frustration, courts would still remain free, and indeed would be unable to avoid, issues of contractual interpretation as to whether given risks fall within the scope of the promised performance. However, … a strong presumption to this effect would seem to minimize uncertainties for contracting parties and provide them with incentives to adapt their contractual relationship *ex ante* as they feel appropriate and not cast this burden *ex post* on the publicly subsidized court system. In long-term relationships, where negotiating complete contingent claims contracts may be infeasible, a variety of adaptive mechanisms available to the parties for *ex ante* or ongoing allocations of risks make it presumptively unlikely that *ex post* judicial assignments of losses on a case-by-case basis will achieve a superior risk allocation, at least on insurance grounds. Although the availability of this range of adaptive mechanisms in various transactional settings might suggest that a single categoric presumption (for example, the promisor is presumed in most cases to have assumed the risk) will be ill-adapted to all of the vast range of settings to which it might be applied, Scott persuasively argues that generalized default or interpretative rules and individualized contractual alternatives together reduce the costs and errors of contracting.

CHAPTER THIRTEEN

Property (Title) Aspects of the Contract of Sale: Transfer of Title Between Seller and Buyer

OLRC Sales Report

at 259-62

The focal role occupied by property concepts in traditional sales law is hardly surprising, since the overriding purpose of a contract of sale is to transfer the general property in goods from the seller to the buyer. Its importance, moreover, is greatly enhanced in existing Anglo-Canadian law in two respects. First, there are the rules in the Act dealing with the following matters: namely, the transfer of risk; the right to payment of the price; the right to reject specific goods; and the seller's rights of resale and the measurement of damages. These rules are presumptively linked to, or affected by, the locus of title. Second, there is the much broader range of non-sales rules whose operative effect turns on the same question. Examples are as follows: namely, the existence of an insurable interest; the right to replevy or to claim goods in bankruptcy; the right to sue third parties in conversion and for injury to the goods; exigibility of goods by execution; exposure to various forms of taxation; liability as "owner" under motor vehicle acts; and, criminal liability under a variety of penal or regulatory statutes. A sales act cannot be expected to regulate all the non-sales incidents of transfer of title, but it may well be asked, as it has been asked, what features the questions of risk, price, rejection, and rights of resale have in common that cause them to be governed by the same metaphysical abstraction.

The picture is further complicated. The rule adopted by the Ontario Sale of Goods Act to determine the time of transfer of title are so complex, and frequently turn on such highly subjective factors, that accurate prediction of the outcome of a litigated issue is well nigh impossible, and incongruous results may well occur. The existing Sale of Goods Act proceeds from two basic principles, and then elaborates a series of presumptive rules to assist the court in discharging its task. The overriding principles are contained in sections 17 and 18 of the existing Act, and may be stated in this way. First, title cannot pass before the goods have been ascertained. Second, where there is a contract for the sale of specific or ascertained goods, the parties' own intentions govern as to the time of transfer.

If a different intention has not been manifested (and many contracts are silent on the question) then the presumptive rules in section 19 of the Act, relating to the intention of the parties as to the time at which the property in the goods is to pass, come into play. These rules are notoriously difficult to apply and, not surprisingly, different courts have often reached different results on substantially similar facts. The difficulties are particularly acute in the case of a contract involving the sale of future or unascertained goods. In such a case, in one set of circumstances, the presumptive rule in section 19, Rule 5(i) of the Act requires the court to inquire not only whether goods of the correct "description" and in a "deliverable state" were "unconditionally" appropriated to the contract, but also whether the buyer gave his "assent" to the appropriation and whether the assent was "express" or "implied." The resulting confusion was aptly described by Lord Cresswell in a judgment written more than a century ago [*Gilmour v. Supple* (1858), 14 ER 803, at 809 (PC)] This description remains very relevant today. Lord Cresswell stated:

> It is impossible to examine the decisions on this subject without being struck by the ingenuity with which sellers have contended that the property in goods contracted for had, or had not, become vested in the buyers, according as it suited their interests; and buyers, or their representatives, have, with equal ingenuity, endeavoured to show that they had, or had not, acquired the property in that for which they contracted; and Judges have not unnaturally appeared anxious to find reasons for giving a judgment which seemed to them most consistent with natural justice. Under such circumstances, it cannot occasion much surprise if some of the numerous reported decisions have been made to depend upon very nice and subtle distinctions, and if some of them should not appear altogether reconcilable with each other.

If the courts manipulate the rules to achieve equitable results, would it not be simpler, it may well be asked, to achieve the same results by providing issue-oriented rules that are not geared to an elusive "title"?

A further group of difficulties arises from the failure of the Act to distinguish between a reservation of title by the seller before the goods have been delivered to the buyer, and those situations in which the seller reserves title after delivery to secure payment of the price. Only recently, with the adoption of the Personal Property Security Act, has this anomaly been removed. It may well be, however, that part of this anomaly continues to survive in cases where a bill of lading is issued in the seller's favour after shipment of the goods, and before the bill is endorsed to the buyer.

Section 19, Rules 1 and 2

Varley v. Whipp

See *supra*, chapter 6

Jerome v. Clements Motor Sales Ltd.

See *supra*, chapter 12

Section 19, Rule 5

Royal Bank of Canada v. Saskatchewan Telecommunications

[1985] 5 WWR 333 (Sask. CA)

WAKELING JA: The rights of the parties to this appeal turn on a decision as to when property passed in respect of certain buildings being constructed by Tritec Developments Ltd. (hereinafter called "Tritec") for Saskatchewan Telecommunications (hereinafter "Sask Tel"). The buildings were being constructed at the premises of Tritec according to plans and specifications provided by Sask Tel for eventual delivery to sites in Northern Saskatchewan. Prior to the completion of the buildings the Royal Bank of Canada, acting under a debenture securing the indebtedness of Tritec, placed the said company in receivership.

The buildings were released to the appellant upon payment of the sum of $20,000 and the parties have agreed that if title had passed to Sask Tel prior to the appointment of the receiver it would be entitled to payment of this sum, but otherwise it would be retained by the receiver. It is for this reason that the parties made application for a ruling as to when title to the buildings could be said to have passed from Tritec to Sask Tel.

Both counsel agree this transaction is either a sale of goods or a building contract for provision of materials and services and that in either case, if the intention of the parties as to when ownership passes can be determined from the contract, that intention will prevail. If such intention cannot be ascertained from the contract, then resort must be had to certain rules to ascertain intention. If it is a sale of goods, these rules are as set forth in the Sale of Goods Act, RSS 1978, c. S-1, s. 20, and if it is a building contract, a somewhat different set of rules apply as are extracted from decided cases.

Because it may be helpful in the determination of whether a discernible intention of the parties can be identified, it seems appropriate to first determine whether the contract is dealing with the sale of goods or is a building contract.

During argument, counsel for the appellant suggested the buildings were never to be affixed to the realty but merely transported to the site and slid onto treated timbers. The factual integrity of this statement was not easy to confirm from the plans and specifications, and it was agreed the appellant should present further information on the point and the respondent would have leave to reply. This information is now available and, once again, the information is not entirely conclusive but only helpful in the determination of whether the "work" eventually became a fixture.

It appears that the diesel buildings and radio buildings were to be placed on treated timbers embedded in the ground and affixed to such timbers by lag bolts. The outhouses were built on treated skids, which skids would be secured to the ground by 1000 mm anchor rods.

The parties agree that the proper test for determining whether or not such buildings are to be treated as fixtures was articulated in *Stack v. T. Eaton Co.* (1902), 4 OLR 335 at 338 (CA), by Meredith CJ:

· · ·

The reasonable assumption is that the buildings were merely bolted to the timbers so they could be readily moved elsewhere if the need arose. In these circumstances, the decision of this court in *Morrison v. Thomas*, 15 Sask. LR 110, [1922] 1 WWR 215, 65 DLR 364 (CA), supports the conclusion that the buildings in this case are chattels and not fixtures.

In the recent decision of *Taypotat v. Surgeson*, [1985] 3 WWR 18, 18 ETR 195, 37 Sask. R 205 (sub nom. *Re Kenron Homes Ltd.; Taypotat v. Surgeson*), this court had reason to review this question with respect to homes that were originally intended for construction in the usual fashion on concrete foundations located on residential lots, but for special reasons were constructed elsewhere to be moved onto the lots later. It was decided the homes were the subject of building contracts, and in reaching that conclusion emphasis was placed on the fact the buildings were originally intended to have been constructed on the foundations at the site and the change of the place of construction did not serve to change the general nature of the contract from a building contract to a sale of goods. The relevant portion of the judgment of Tallis JA is as follows [at 33]:

> The contract does not expressly deal with the ownership of the home as it passes through the various stages of construction. *However, when we consider the entire contract we are of the opinion that the parties intended, at the time of execution, that the owner was to acquire a legal proprietary interest in the home as it progressed through the various stages of construction. This is manifested, among other things, by the fact that the houses were to be affixed to the appellants' realty. Does the change in arrangements between the parties, as evidenced by App. A to each contract, alter the legal relationship between them? We think not.* The variation in terms which permitted the contractor to build the homes on its property in Yorkton and then haul them to the respective sites on the reserve with prepared basement walls and foundations in place does not change the nature of the contract between the parties. (The italics are mine.)

The determination that this contract deals with the sale of goods is consistent with the finding in the *Kenron Homes* judgment, in that the underlined portion shows the significance that was placed on the fact the buildings were destined to be affixed to a firm foundation on the eventual owner's property.

· · ·

The next consideration should be to find out whether there is a discernible intention of the parties from a review of the contract and the conduct of the parties. The result of this consideration dictates whether there is need to resort to the implied rules in s. 20 of the Sale of Goods Act to determine when title passes.

There is clearly no succinct provision in the contract indicating when ownership passes, and any conclusion as to what was intended by the parties will have to come from inferences arising from the interpretation of the contract or the conduct of the parties.

A careful review of the terms of the contract with particular reference to such indicators as insurance arrangements, assumption of risk, the specific nature of the buildings, inspection and warranty has not produced a clear or even identifiable signal of the intention of the parties. However, while considering the content of the contract, it is appropriate to point out that particular emphasis was placed during argument on the fact the contract called for monthly or progress payments in the following terms:

1A.26 1. Applications for payment on account may be made monthly as the work progresses.

2. Applications for payment shall be dated the last day of the agreed monthly payment period and the amount claimed shall be the value, proportionate to the amount of the Contract, of work performed and products delivered to the site of that date.

1A.27 1. SASK TEL shall, within thirty (30) days of receipt of an application for payment from the Contractor submitted in accordance with Article 1A.26 make payment to the Contractor on account in accordance with the provisions of the Agreement. If SASK TEL amends the application, it shall promptly notify the Contractor in writing giving reasons for the Amendment.

These provisions indicate Tritec may bill monthly for work done and materials actually incorporated in the building and for materials on site destined for incorporation into the building, and if Tritec did send an interim monthly bill, Sask Tel was required to make payment.

Based on a series of decisions that are generally known as the shipbuilding cases, having application to the sale of goods, counsel for the appellant suggests title to what had been constructed passed to Sask Tel on the payment of the first monthly account. Counsel for the respondent suggests that a monthly payment is not the same as a progress payment which is related to a payment due when a structure reaches a stage of construction, and the shipbuilding cases only have application to progress payments.

Since monthly accounts were not mandatory, it is a less compelling argument to suggest they were intended to signal the point at which property passes. After all, if no monthly account had been sent, then property would not pass until final acceptance and payment. It seems illogical to assume the whole basis of transfer of title and ownership should hang on such a tenuous and uncertain thread. Nonetheless, the shipbuilding cases have indicated some form of acceptance of the structure or unit is required to acknowledge the passage of ownership and it has been held that the submission and acceptance of a progress payment is an indication of such acceptance. That form of acceptance can be said to exist here as monthly accounts were sent and payments duly made, so a further consideration of these cases seems appropriate.

The shipbuilding cases can be taken to have indicated that where progress payments are involved, a presumption may arise that it is the intention of the parties that title is to pass on payment of the first progress payment. Indeed, this is what was stated by way of dicta by Lord Watson in *Seath v. Moore* (1888), 11 App. Cas. 350 at 380 (PC):

> ... where it appears to be the intention, or in other words the agreement, of the parties to a contract for building a ship, that at a particular stage of its construction, the vessel, so far as then finished, shall be appropriated to the contract of sale, the property of the vessel as soon as it has reached that stage of completion will pass to the purchaser, and subsequent additions made to the chattel thus vested in the purchaser will, accessione, become his property ... *such an intention or agreement ought (in the absence of any circumstances pointing to a different conclusion) to be inferred from a provision in the contract to the effect that an instalment of the price shall be paid at a particular stage,* coupled with the fact that the instalment has been duly paid, and that until the vessels reached that stage the execution of the work was regularly inspected by the purchaser, or some one on his behalf. (The italics are mine.)

In the above case the ship had already been registered in the name of the buyer before the builder went into bankruptcy, so there was other firm support for the intent of the parties without reliance on the suggested presumption.

It is also clear from the same quotation that Lord Watson had a firm understanding that payment by instalments was a useful method of determining when the unfinished vessel had been appropriated to the contract and not proof by itself of the intent of the parties. In any event, the more recent judgment of the House of Lords in *Sir James Laing & Sons Ltd. v. Barclay, Curle & Co.*, [1908] AC 35, also dealing with a shipbuilding contract, has made it clear that the making of progress payments is but one factor to be considered in the determination of the intent of the parties.

Lord Loreburn said at 43:

> It may be a very useful guide to look at other decisions, but, after all, the question is what the parties said and intended. The facts referred to by Mr. Clyde and Mr. Smith, namely, that the ship was to be paid for by instalments, and that there was a power of inspection on the part of the purchasers, may be marks pointing to the property passing, but it is not conclusive, and the question still remains as to what the contract really means.
>
> I think the contract was for a completed ship, and the risk lay upon the builders until delivery, and there was no intention to make delivery or to part with the property until the vessel was completed.

For the reasons mentioned, it would seem a very contrived and superficial treatment of the contract to suggest that the monthly statements in this case were very meaningful in determining the intent of the parties relative to ownership.

Having failed to find a satisfactory indication of the intent of the parties from either their conduct or the terms of the contract, and having also decided the contract is one relating to the sale of goods, resort must be had to s. 20 of the Sale of Goods Act. Clearly, RR. I, II, III and IV of that section do not have application, and R. V(1), which is set out below, is the only one which appears applicable.

· · ·

On the application of R. V(1), the title and ownership did not pass until the goods in a deliverable state were unconditionally appropriated to the contract. That had not happened when Tritec was placed in receivership, so Tritec still had title and ownership to the buildings in question at that time and the respondent is therefore entitled to retain the said payment of $20,000.

Appeal dismissed.

Carlos Federspiel & Co., S.A. v. Chas. Twigg & Co., Ltd.

[1957] 1 Lloyd's Rep. 240 (QBD)

MR. JUSTICE PEARSON: In this case the basic facts are agreed and all the evidence is contained in agreed documents. The only remaining issues are (1) whether the ownership of certain goods passed from the defendant company, as sellers, to the plaintiffs, as buyers, in which case both defendants would be liable to the plaintiffs for conversion of their goods; (2) if there is liability, whether the sum described as loss of profit can, under any guise, be included in the damages. The defendant company has taken no part in the trial, and the contest has been between the plaintiffs and the second defendant, who is receiver for a debenture-holding company. The figures of damage, in the event of liability being established, are agreed at, I think, £646 5s. without the sum for loss of profit, and that sum, if it is to be added, is agreed at a figure which I think is £89 7s. 8d.

As stated in par. 1 of the statement of claim, the plaintiffs are a company incorporated in San Jose, Costa Rica, who were at all material times carrying on business as merchants in Costa Rica. The defendant company at all material times in the early part of 1953 carried on business as manufacturers of children's bicycles and tricycles at Lye in the County of Worcester. Then, as stated in par. 4 of the statement of claim, and admitted in the defence, in about June, 1953, the plaintiffs agreed to buy and the defendant company agreed to sell and deliver at a price of 1820 US dols., certain goods which are set out in that paragraph of the statement of claim, namely, cycles, tricycles and certain accessories. As stated in par. 5 of the statement of claim and admitted in the defence, the agreement was contained in or evidenced by an order in writing from the plaintiffs to the defendant company dated June 16, 1953, and an acceptance in writing of the said order from the defendant company to the plaintiffs, dated June 25, 1953. Then it is also common ground that, as stated in par. 6 of the statement of claim, pursuant to the said agreement, the plaintiffs on or about July 1, 1953, paid the said price to the defendant company by cheque of that date, and the receipt of it was acknowledged by the defendant company on July 7, 1953. Then it appears from par. 2 of the defence which is similar to, but as to the date more accurate than, par. 3 of the statement of claim, that on July 28, 1953, the second defendant, Mr. H.J. Patience, was appointed receiver and manager of the defendant company by the debenture holders. Thereafter all goods belonging to the defendant company, which were charged to the debenture holders by virtue of their debentures, passed into his management and control. On Oct. 2, 1953, the second defendant, Mr. Patience, the receiver, refused to deliver to the plaintiff company any goods in fulfilment of the contract of sale which had been made in June, 1953. Then on Nov. 17, 1953, the company being insolvent, a compulsory winding-up order was made.

[Pearson J reviewed the pleadings and continued:]

That, therefore, is the main issue: whether or not the goods were appropriated to the contract by the sellers with the consent of the buyers so as to pass the ownership to the buyers; and the buyers are the plaintiff company. I should have said that the defence to which I have referred is the defence of the defendant Patience only. As I have said, the defendant company have taken no part in the trial, and they did not even deliver a defence at the earlier stage.

· · ·

Now I will come to the set of documents in this case which constitute the contract. First, there is the sellers' price list, which quotes the prices f.o.b. English port inclusive. That only states the price, so I think it is not of great significance. Then there is a letter of May 20, 1953, from the buyers to the sellers, saying:

> To-day we are able to inform you that we received your first shipment, according your invoice No. ... and found that the cycles and tricycles are made of a good quality and are satisfactory.
>
> For the above mentioned, we would like to place a new order and would appreciate very much if you would send us by airmail, your last catalogue and complete price list. We do not have it complete and would like to place a new order for rush shipment.

The only significance of this is, I think, that at this early stage, as one will find throughout the correspondence, the emphasis is on shipment as indicating the intention of the parties that shipment should be a decisive act of performance by the seller.

Then there is a letter of June 6 from the sellers to the buyers, and they say, among other things:

> ... as we should very much like to extend our business relationship with your goodselves, we have pleasure in offering you a commission of 5 per cent. (on the f.o.b. value exclusive of packing) on all orders which you place with us. This commission would be in addition to the 2½ per cent cash discount which we allow for payment in advance or by confirmed irrevocable letter of credit.

On June 16, there is the offer. It is addressed by the buyers to the sellers, and it says:

> Gentlemen,
>
> Regarding to your letter dated June 6th, we are agreed at the *present* with your indications in regard to the representation, but hope that in a very near future you are going to accede to our request naming us your exclusive agents for this territory.
>
> For the following order we beg you to send us two pro-forma invoices to be able to make advance payment reducing the 5 per cent and 2½ per cent discounts. Please pre-

pare shipment to be able to ship with direct ship to our Port Limon, as soon as you receive our advance payment remittance.

Then they set out the goods for which the order is given, being cycles, and so on. Then there is the provision:

All boxes have to be marked: C.F. & Co., San Jose—Costa Rica, Port Limon.

The answer, which is the acceptance, is on June 25. There is a letter and an enclosed confirmation of export order and an enclosed pro forma invoice. The material parts of the letter from the sellers to the buyers are at the beginning:

Dear Sirs,
   We thank you for your letter of the 16th June and are very pleased to have your second order for cycles and tricycles.
   This has been entered by us under reference P/1052 and we are enclosing herewith our official acknowledgment form. Attached also is our pro-forma invoice, in duplicate, on which we have given the approximate c.i.f. charges and deducted the 5 per cent commission and 2½ per cent cash discount. This will enable you to remit to us, as suggested, and we look forward to receiving your cheque in due course.
   Meanwhile, we have placed the order on our works and can assure you that we will have the goods ready for shipment at the earliest possible moment.

Confirmation of export order was enclosed, and it contains these provisions:

Shipping Marks: C.F. & Co., San Jose, Costa Rica, Port Limon.
Delivery: f.o.b. UK Port.
Packing: Extra.—No. 4—As per our pro-forma invoice dated 25.6.53.
Freight: Extra.
Insurance: Extra.
Payment: In advance.—As per your letter dated 16.6.53.

The goods are set out, and there is the provision:

All shipments will be invoiced at prices ruling at the date of despatch, irrespective of anything shown to the contrary on your order sheet.

Then there is the enclosed pro forma invoice, which sets out the goods, sets out the shipping mark and numbers as before: "C.F. & Co., San Jose, Costa Rica, Port Limon. 1/up." Then certain packing charges are set out, and then there are these words: "Approximate c.i.f. charges—£60." Then there is a deduction made for the two commissions, 5 per cent on the f.o.b. value, exclusive of packing, and 2½ per cent cash discount on the same sum for payment in advance.

Then on July 1, there is a letter from the buyers to the sellers, saying:

To-day we received your letter dated June 25th from which we separate your two pro forma invoices.
   To cover these pro forma invoices we are sending you herewith our cheque 2376 against our account at the National City Bank of New York in the amount of USA $1820.

We beg you to acknowledge receipt of this remittance any difference will be paid as soon as we receive your definitive invoices and two original shipping documents.

Please follow the shipping instructions given in our order of June 16 regarding marks, etc., etc.

To avoid difficulties with the custom house it is indispensable that you send us with the five invoices, 5 packing lists indicating what contains on each box, with the indication of the No. of each cycle (serial No.) that would help us very much.

Thanking you in advance for the soon shipment of that order, we remain,

Yours truly,

Carlos Federspiel & Co., SA

Then there is the receipt for the cheque, dated July 7, 1953.

Then on July 9 the sellers write to the buyers saying:

We thank you for your letter of the 1st July together with cheque for the amount of $1820 and have pleasure in enclosing our official receipt.

Your instructions regarding marks, etc., will be complied with and immediately we have some definite information as to the date of shipment we will write to you again.

When we forward the documents we will let [you] have a statement showing the actual position of the account, and you can then remit to us any balance which may be due.

You may be assured that the order is having our best attention, and we anticipate that the goods will be ready for despatch in the very near future.

That is the end of the contractual documents, and the question arises: what is the nature of this contract? I agree with Mr. Lyell that fundamentally it is to be regarded as an f.o.b. contract, but one has to add that it has some c.i.f. features attached to it. The delivery expressly is to be f.o.b., but freight and insurance are to be extras, and they are stated at an approximate figure of £60. It would seem that the intention is that the sellers are, in the first instance, to arrange the insurance and the contract of affreightment, and they are to pay the freight and insurance and charge them as extras to the buyers; and the intention seems to be that they should charge the cost price to the buyers, so that any rise or fall in rates of freight or insurance would be for the account of the buyers and of no interest to the sellers. That seems to be the nature of the contract.

· · ·

[Pearson J reviewed the authorities on the time of transfer of the property in a contract for the sale of future or unascertained goods, and continued:]

On those authorities, what are the principles emerging? I think one can distinguish these principles. First, Rule 5 of Sect. 18 of the Act [Ont., s. 19, r. 5] is one of the Rules for ascertaining the intention of the parties as to the time at which the property in the goods is to pass to the buyer unless a different intention appears. Therefore the element of common intention has always to be borne in mind. A mere setting apart or selection of the seller of the goods which he expects to use in performance of the contract is not enough. If that is all, he can change his mind and use those goods in performance of some other contract and use some other goods in performance of this contract. To constitute an appropriation of the goods to the contract, the parties must have had, or be reasonably supposed to have had, an intention to attach the contract irrevocably to those goods, so that those goods and no others are the subject of the sale and become the property of the buyer.

Secondly, it is by agreement of the parties that the appropriation, involving a change of ownership, is made, although in some cases the buyer's assent to an appropriation by the seller is conferred in advance by the contract itself or otherwise.

Thirdly, an appropriation by the seller, with the assent of the buyer, may be said always to involve an actual or constructive delivery. If the seller retains possession, he does so as bailee for the buyer. There is a passage in *Chalmers' Sale of Goods Act*, 12th ed., at 75, where it is said:

> In the second place, if the decisions be carefully examined, it will be found that in every case where the property has been held to pass, there has been an actual or constructive delivery of the goods to the buyer.

I think that is right, subject only to this possible qualification, that there may be after such constructive delivery an actual delivery still to be made by the seller under the contract. Of course, that is quite possible, because delivery is the transfer of possession, whereas appropriation transfers ownership. So there may be first an appropriation, constructive delivery, whereby the seller becomes bailee for the buyer, and then a subsequent actual delivery involving actual possession, and when I say that I have in mind in particular the two cases cited, namely, *Aldridge v. Johnson* (1857), 7 E & B 885 and *Langton v. Higgins* (1859), 4 H & N 402.

Fourthly, one has to remember Sect. 20 of the Sale of Goods Act [Ont., s. 21] whereby the ownership and the risk are normally associated. Therefore as it appears that there is reason for thinking, on the construction of the relevant documents, that the goods were, at all material times, still at the seller's risk, that is *prima facie* an indication that the property had not passed to the buyer.

Fifthly, usually but not necessarily, the appropriating act is the last act to be performed by the seller. For instance, if delivery is to be taken by the buyer at the seller's premises and the seller has completed his part of the contract and has appropriated the goods when he has made the goods ready and has identified them and placed them in position to be taken by the buyer and has so informed the buyer, and if the buyer agrees to come and take them, that is the assent to the appropriation. But if there is a further act, an important decisive act to be done by the seller, then there is *prima facie* evidence that probably the property does not pass until the final act is done.

Applying those principles to the present case I would say this. Firstly, the intention was that the ownership should pass on shipment (or possibly at some later date) because the emphasis is throughout on shipment as the decisive act to be done by the seller in performance of the contract. Secondly, it is impossible to find in this correspondence an agreement to a change of ownership before the time of shipment. The letters, especially those of Aug. 27 and Sept. 14, which are particularly relied on by the plaintiff, do not contain any provision or implication of any earlier change of ownership. Thirdly, there is no actual or constructive delivery; no suggestion of the seller becoming a bailee for the buyer. Fourthly, there is no suggestion of the goods being at the buyer's risk at any time before shipment; no suggestion that the buyer should insist on the seller arranging insurance for them. Fifthly, the last two acts to be performed by the seller, namely, sending the goods to Liverpool and having the goods shipped on board, were not performed.

Therefore, my decision that the *prima facie* inference which one would have drawn from the contract is that the property was not to pass at any time before shipment, is in my view not displaced by the subsequent correspondence between the parties. It follows, therefore, that there was no appropriation of these goods and therefore the action fails.

Judgment for defendants.

Caradoc Nurseries Ltd. v. Marsh

(1959), 19 DLR (2d) 491, [1959] OWN 123 (Ont. CA)

MORDEN JA: The defendant appeals from the judgment of His Honour Judge McCallum, sitting as Judge of the First Division Court of the County of Middlesex, awarding the plaintiff the sum of $123.75.

By the written agreement, dated October 22, 1957, the defendant agreed to purchase from the plaintiff specified quantities of various shrubs and trees. Sometime in the winter of 1958, the defendant called at the plaintiff's place of business at which time the contract was slightly varied by the substitution of two items for different types of trees. Except for a large silver maple which was on this occasion tagged by an employee of the plaintiff in the presence of the defendant, the contract was, in my view, one for the sale of unascertained goods. In April, 1958 the plaintiff sent the goods by its deliveryman to the defendant who refused to accept them. The plaintiff sued for the sale price. In his dispute and at the trial the defendant stated that the contract called for delivery in the fall of 1957 and as the goods were admittedly not tendered or delivered then, he was under no liability to the plaintiff. On the other hand, the plaintiff maintained that the parties had agreed upon a spring delivery. This was the sole issue raised at the trial and it was resolved by the learned trial Judge in the plaintiff's favour.

. . .

Mr. Rowan in an able and full argument submitted that s. 48(1) and (2) of the Sale of Goods Act, RSO 1950, c. 345 was applicable. On the other side, Mr. Shortt contended that the relevant provision was s. 47(1). I set them out: ...

The determination of this appeal turns upon whether or not in the circumstances disclosed by the evidence the property in the goods passed to the defendant. If it did, then the plaintiff is entitled to the sale price; if it did not so pass, then there will have to be a new trial to ascertain the damages in accordance with s. 48(2). There is noth-

ing in the written agreement expressing the intentions of the parties with respect to the passing of the property and it is therefore necessary to fall back upon s. 19 of the Act, particularly Rule 5(i) which is as follows: ...

In this case upon the facts there was no appropriation by the buyer; if there was any it was by the seller. The buyer did not expressly assent but his assent can be implied from the terms of the contract—the plaintiff was obligated to deliver the goods to the defendant and before he could do this he had to select the various shrubs and trees to complete the order. Implied assent to appropriation is discussed in *Benjamin on Sale of Personal Property*, 8th ed., pp. 327 *ff.* and I quote from 328 the following extract from Lord Blackburn's authoritative treatise: "It follows from this, that where from the terms of an executory agreement to sell unspecified goods the vendor is to dispatch the goods, or to do anything to them that cannot be done till the goods are appropriated, he has the right to choose what the goods shall be; and the property is transferred the moment the dispatch or other act has commenced, for then an appropriation is made finally and conclusively by the authority conferred in the agreement, and in Lord Coke's language, 'the certainty, and thereby the property, begins an election' (*Heyward's Case* (1595), 2 Co. Rep. 37A). But, however clearly the vendor may have expressed an intention to choose particular goods, and however expensive may have been his preparations for performing the agreement with those particular goods, yet until the act has actually commenced the appropriation is not final, for it is not made by the authority of the other party, nor binding upon him." See also *Aldridge v. Johnson* (1857), 6 El. & Bl. 885 at 901, 119 ER 1476.

The appropriation by the plaintiff was not final, was not unconditional when the particular shrubs and trees were selected, nor when they were uprooted, nor when they were loaded on the plaintiff's truck and being carried to the defendant's house. During those times the plaintiff could have changed its mind, recalled the truck and substituted other shrubs and trees. But when the truck arrived at the defendant's house and the goods were tendered then I say the appropriation became unconditional and the property in the goods was transferred to the plaintiff. At that point of time the seller's election had become irrevocable. It is not essential for a final appropriation by a seller that the delivery be completed by the buyer's acceptance; tender is sufficient: *Mason & Risch Ltd. v. Christner* (1918), 46 DLR 710 at 716, 44 OLR 146 at 153 and *Scythes & Co. v. Dods Knitting Co.* (1922), 52 OLR 475 at 477-78. There is no evidence, in fact no suggestion that the goods tendered were not those described in the contract.

The property in the goods having passed to the defendant, the plaintiff was entitled to the sale price which was what the learned trial Judge awarded him. Accordingly the appeal must be dismissed with costs including a counsel fee of $15.

Appeal dismissed.

[*Cf. Colley v. Overseas Exporters, infra*, chapter 15 of this volume.]

Sells v. Thomson

(1914), 17 DLR 737 (BCCA)

MacDONALD CJA: The defendants, a company of booksellers doing business in Vancouver, ordered from the plaintiffs, a publishing company doing business in London, England, but licensed in this province, twenty-five volumes of a book having the title of "British Columbia," etc. These volumes were to be taken out of stock, and would have to be appropriated to the contract in order to pass the property therein to the defendants. The contract falls within rule 5, sub-sec. (1) of the Sale of Goods Act, ch. 203, RSBC, 1911, ch. 26, which reads as follows:

> Where there is a contract for the sale of unascertained or future goods by description, and goods of that description and in a deliverable state are unconditionally appropriated to the contract, either by the seller with the assent of the buyer, or by the buyer with the assent of the seller, the property in the goods thereupon passes to the buyer. Such assent may be express or implied, and may be given either before or after the appropriation is made.

I take it that in this case there would be an implied assent to the appropriation of the goods by the seller. Until such an appropriation the contract would be an executory one of bargain and sale.

The defendants cabled to the plaintiffs cancelling the order for the balance of 13 volumes which had not then been sent out. Counsel for the plaintiffs admitted that no appropriation of these had been made prior to the receipt of the cablegram. The plaintiffs nevertheless thereafter appropriated 13 volumes to this contract, and the defendants having refused to accept the books action was brought for the price as upon a contract for goods sold and delivered. I have therefore to ask myself whether or not the implied assent of the defendants, to the future appropriation of goods, to the contract, was withdrawn or destroyed by the notification that they would not accept the goods; in other words, whether or not the plaintiffs, after receipt of that notification, could proceed to convert the executory agreement into an executed one by setting the goods apart as applicable to the contract and thus pass the property in them to the defendants against their will. I have not been able to find any direct authority upon this point. I am, however, of opinion that the implied assent to an appropriation of the goods was withdrawn by the notice, and that the plaintiffs could not thereafter without defendant's assent convert the executory contract into an executed one.

The case relied upon by Mr. Buchanan, counsel for the plaintiffs, *Tredegar v. Hawthorn* (1902), 18 Times LR 716, does not in my opinion assist him. That was an action for damages for breach of a contract and not for the price. The repudiation there was made before the time had arrived for the delivery of the coals. The sellers declined to accept the repudiation, but waited until the time for delivery and then brought their action for damages for non-acceptance of the coals. The point in issue was this; the defendants claimed that the measure of damages was the difference between the market price at the date of repudiation and the sale price; whereas the plaintiffs claimed, and the Court held, that it was the difference between the market price, at the date when performance was due and the sale price. In other words, that the sellers were not bound to re-sell immediately they got notice of the buyer's intention not to take the goods, but might, if they chose, wait until the time for performance had arrived and sue on the footing of the transaction at that date. In that case there was no attempt to appropriate the coals to the contract and convert what was an executory agreement into an executed one and sue for the price. The case is really of no assistance in the determination of the question now under consideration.

The action is grounded solely upon a contract for goods sold and delivered, and no alternative claim is made for damages for breach of the executory agreement of bargain and sale. As the action is, therefore, in my opinion not properly founded, I would allow the appeal and direct that the action be dismissed. ...

Appeal allowed.

[Concurring judgments were delivered by Irving JA and McPhillips JA.]

In re Wait

[1927] 1 Ch. 606 (CA)

ATKIN LJ: This case has resulted in a decision which if correct will have far-reaching effects upon commercial transactions. It has the support of the judgments of both learned judges below, and also of Sargant LJ, and therefore in expressing my opinion that it was wrongly decided I feel bound to examine in some detail the facts and contentions relied on by the parties.

Both the debtor and the claimant are grain merchants in Bristol. On November 20, 1925, by a written contract of form 22 of the London Corn Trade Association Messrs. W.H. Pim, Junior & Co., Ld., acting for Messrs. Balfour Williamson & Co., of London, agreed to sell to the debtor 1000 tons Western White wheat. Shipment was to be in good condition per motor vessel *Challenger*, expected to load between December 16-31, 1925, from Oregon and/or Washington as per bill or bills of lading to be dated accordingly when the goods were actually on board. ... [This] is an ordinary commercial contract for the sale c.i.f. of grain to be imported to England from the United States of America. It is a contract for the future shipment of grain not, at the time, ascertained. It is not the sale of a cargo. Apart from some appropriation of the goods to the buyer with his express or implied assent at or after shipment, which would, I think, be unusual, the buyer would acquire no property in any grain until he took up the documents in exchange for cash or acceptance.

On November 21, 1925, the debtor by a contract in writing agreed to sell to the claimants 500 tons Western White wheat per motor vessel *Challenger*, expected to load between December 16-31, 1925, bill of lading to be dated accordingly ...

It appears that by other contracts the debtors had agreed with other sellers for the purchase from them of further grain to be shipped per the *Challenger*. He had a contract for the delivery of a further 500 tons of Western White wheat and 1500 tons of

No. 2 Northern wheat. All this wheat was shipped on the *Challenger* on bills of lading bearing dates that conformed to the contracts of sale. The wheat was shipped in bulk. Of the Western White wheat 1190 tons were shipped in the after-hold, and 310 tons in No. 2 hold. On February 28 the *Challenger* arrived at Avonmouth bringing the wheat as described above. Meanwhile other events material to this decision had occurred. On December 22 the debtor gave the claimants particulars of the date of the bill of lading for motor vessel *Challenger* to satisfy the contract of November 21. On January 4 the bills of lading arrived in this country and were sighted by the consignees making the prompt date under the contract February 6. On the same date the debtor rendered to the claimants a provisional invoice for 5933*l*. 5*s*., the price of the 500 tons less freight; on February 3 the debtors passed to the claimants a debit note for Western White wheat for 5933*l*. 5*s*. stating the prompt date to be February 6, which was a Saturday, with a note appended: "Kindly let us have your cheque for the above amount on Friday morning, and oblige." And on the Friday, February 5, the claimant gave the debtor a cheque for 5933*l*. 5*s*., which was paid in to the general credit of the debtor's account with the Westminster Bank, Bristol. ...

On February 23 the debtor, who was in difficulties, called a meeting of his creditors, and on February 24 on his own petition a receiving order was made, and he was adjudicated bankrupt, Mr. Collins being appointed special manager of the estate. On March 5 he was appointed trustee in bankruptcy of the estate. On February 27 Mr. Collins took up from the bank the bills of lading, giving them a cheque for the full amount less the sum of 5933*l*. 5*s*., which the bank allowed to be treated as a credit against the advance. Having received the bills of lading he was able to deal with the wheat. Of the 1500 tons Western White wheat, 830 tons were delivered to Messrs. Spiller & Baker ex ship; some further wheat was delivered to the purchasers; and at the time the motion was launched the trustee had in warehouse 530 tons available for performance of the contract with the claimants, but which was in fact property of the debtor or possibly only of the trustee available for distribution amongst the creditors generally.

· · ·

I now proceed to discuss the suggestion that apart from the right to specific performance under s. 52 of the Code [Ont. s. 50], there was in this case an equitable assignment to the claimants of 500 tons of flour which entitled them to claim from the trustee delivery of 500 tons out of the 530 tons remaining in his possession, and, indeed, gave the claimants a charge or lien over the whole 1000 tons to which the debtor was entitled under his contract with Balfour Williamson & Co. In the view that I have taken of the facts of this case, I have already said that the goods were never so ascertained that specific performance could have been ordered of them. This consideration would appear to defeat the supposed equitable assignment, and I will not repeat the passages referred to by the Master of the Rolls which establish the test. I have already indicated my own view of the claimants' contract of November 21 and suggested that the debtor does not in fact agree to sell to the claimants any aliquot part of the 1000 tons, which in fact he had agreed to buy from Balfour Williamson & Co. But even if he had, I do not think that at any time here there was an equitable assignment which ever gave the claimants a beneficial interest in these goods. It has been difficult to elicit the moment of time at which the beneficial interest came into existence. At various times in the argument it has been the moment when the 1000 tons were shipped; when they were declared to the debtor by Balfour Williamson & Co.; when the bills of lading came into the possession of the bank; when the claimants paid the 5933*l*. 5*s*. to the debtor; when the goods were taken up by the trustee; and when the 530 tons came into the possession of the trustee. The difficulty illustrates the danger of seeking to conduct well established principles into territory where they are trespassers. Without deciding the point, I think that much may be said for the proposition that an agreement for the sale of goods does not import any agreement to transfer property other than in accordance with the terms of the Code, that is, the intention of the parties to be derived from the terms of the contract, the conduct of the parties and the circumstances of the case, and, unless a different intention appears, from the rules set out in s. 18. The Code was passed at a time when the principles of equity and equitable remedies were recognized and given effect to in all our Courts, and the particular equitable remedy of specific performance is specially referred to in s. 52. The total sum of legal relations (meaning by the word "legal" existing in equity as well as in common law) arising out of the contract for the sale of goods may well be regarded as defined by the Code. It would have been futile in a code intended for commercial men to have created an elaborate structure of rules dealing with rights at law, if at the same time it was intended to leave, subsisting with the legal rights, equitable rights inconsistent with, more extensive, and coming into existence earlier than the rights so carefully set out in the various sections of the Code.

The rules for transfer of property as between seller and buyer performance of the contract, rights of the unpaid seller against the goods, unpaid sellers' lien, remedies of the seller, remedies of the buyer, appear to be complete and exclusive statements of the legal relations both in law and equity. They have, of course, no relevance when one is considering rights, legal or equitable, which may come into existence dehors the contract for sale. A seller or a purchaser may, of course, create any equity he pleases by way of charge, equitable assignment or any other dealing with or disposition of goods, the subject-matter of sale; and he may, of course, create such an equity as one of the terms expressed in the contract of sale. But the mere sale or agreement to sell or the acts in pursuance of such a contract mentioned in the Code will only produce the legal effects which the Code states.

But without deciding this point, we have to apply the words of Lord Westbury in *Holroyd v. Marshall* (10 HLC 191, 209): "In equity it is not necessary for the alienation of property that there should be a formal deed of conveyance. A contract for valuable consideration, by which it is agreed to make a present transfer of property, passes at once the beneficial interest, provided the contract is one of which a Court of equity will decree specific performance. In the language of Lord Hardwicke, the vendor becomes a trustee for the vendee; subject, of course, to the contract being one to be specifically performed. And this is true, not only of contracts relating to real estate, but also of contracts relating to personal property, provided that the latter are such as a Court of equity would direct to be specifically performed." It must be remembered that while Lord Westbury's proposition that a contract for valuable consideration, by which it is agreed to make a present transfer of property, passes at once the beneficial interest, provided the contract is one of which a Court of equity will decree specific performance, may be beyond dispute, the converse that when there is a contract of which the Court of equity will decree specific performance the beneficial interest has passed is not logically true, and is not the law. Nor is it true that in equity when a man agrees in a contract for the sale of goods to sell part of a specified whole, he agrees to make a transfer of property either present or when the property is in fact acquired. Agreements by a farmer to sell a lamb out of his flock, a ton of potatoes out of his crop grown on his farm, a bushel of apples from his orchard, a gallon of milk from this morning's milking, an egg out of the eggs collected yesterday, seem to me not to amount to an equitable assignment of any of the matters sold, or to give an equitable charge or lien over the whole subject-matter to secure the delivery of the part. The doctrine asserted seems to produce the result that in every case of the sale of future goods, as soon as the goods have become identifiable, the beneficial interest in them passes to the buyer, notwithstanding the provision in the Code that, in the absence of express intention, the property only passes when goods of that description and in a deliverable state are appropriated to the contract, either by the seller with the assent of the buyer, or by the buyer with the assent of the seller, and apparently notwithstanding an express agreement that the property shall not pass except on payment. So to hold would be to defeat the intention of the parties, either express or to be implied from their contract being bound by the terms of the Code, and it appears to me not to accord with the principles of equity to impose upon the parties rights which are contrary to their manifest intention.

Does it make any difference that the creditors here paid their purchase money in advance of the due date, and in any case before they could get delivery under the contract? I think not. So far as specific performance is concerned, the right seems to exist, if at all, independently of whether one party or the other has performed his part of the contract and I have already dealt with the objections to the demand for specific performance under the provisions of s. 52 of the Code.

Lord Westbury in *Holroyd v. Marshall* (10 HLC 191, 211) uses wide words in the passage beginning: "But if a vendor or mortgagor agrees to sell or mortgage property, real or personal, of which he is not possessed at the time, and he receives the consideration for the contract, and afterwards becomes possessed of property answering the description in the contract, there is no doubt that a Court of equity would compel him to perform the contract, and that the contract would, in equity, transfer the beneficial interest to the mortgagee or purchaser immediately on the property being acquired. This, of course, assumes that the supposed contract is one of that class of which a Court of equity would decree the specific performance. If it be so, then immediately on the acquisition of the property described the vendor or mortgagor would hold it in trust for the purchaser or mortgagee, according to the terms of the contract. For if a contract be in other respects good and fit to be performed, and the consideration has been received, incapacity to perform it at the time of its execution will be no answer when the means of doing so are afterwards obtained. "I cannot help thinking that in his reference to property real or personal, the learned Lord was not directing his mind to contracts for the sale of goods which ordinarily would not be of that class of which a Court of equity would decree the specific performance." I cannot believe he intended that in the cases suggested above the farmer, the seller, would hold the lamb, or the potatoes, or the bushel of apples, or the egg in trust for the purchaser as soon as they were ascertained, much less, as these words are supposed to mean, as soon as they were acquired by the seller. Similarly, I fail to see how the payment of the price can convert that which was not an equitable assignment before the payment into an equitable assignment after the payment. Payment of the price has no doubt been material in considering a different question—namely, the right of the purchaser in a contract for the sale of real property, who pays the price or portion of the price before conveyance, to be given a lien on the land for his purchase price. The right is correlative to and appears to be derived from the right of the unpaid vendor of real property to claim a lien on the land after conveyance for the unpaid purchase price. But the latter lien in my judgment does not exist in the case of an ordinary sale of goods. The remedies are defined. The unpaid vendor has a lien which is a possessory lien; and has a right of stoppage in transitu; but in my experience no one has ever claimed or been given in the countless cases that have arisen of vendors of goods remaining unpaid after delivery, a right to a lien over the goods in the possession of the purchaser. Similarly, the purchaser who in pursuance of the contract of sale has paid the purchase price, or part of it, before delivery has never claimed or received a lien over the property which is in the hands of the vendor. I am satisfied that such liens would be quite inconsistent with the provisions of the Code, and do not exist.

It is, however, said, "does not common honesty demand that such a beneficial interest should be created?" The answer is, I think, that the test of honesty is inadequate, it is too narrow or too wide. The sphere of honesty is not confined to dealings with beneficial interests in property. Many would think that deliberately to break a contract for the sale of future goods, where no question of property at law or in equity could arise, would be dishonest; but the law gives only a remedy in damages. In the simple cases suggested, which I hesitate to repeat, the farmer might be acting dishonestly in parting with the whole of his flock, his apples, his potatoes or his eggs to a different purchaser; but I venture to think that if he does the purchaser even with notice acquires a complete title to the property bought.

This brings me to the last subject of this too lengthy judgment. If the contentions put before the Court for the claimants be correct and beneficial interests in property are created as suggested, the whole course of business transactions will be fundamentally affected. Many large business transactions such as this, indeed nearly all import transactions, are financed by banks or financial houses, as this was. It is quite common for the banker to be given information of sub-sales, indeed he often asks for it, or it is proffered voluntarily as some guarantee of the stability of the bank's customer. Such notice was given here. If notice of the sub-sale under a contract which becomes specific when delivery is made is notice of equitable interests in the subpurchasers, the bank would be affected even though by taking the bills of lading, or other documents, they acquired the legal title. They would have to satisfy themselves on being paid off that the equitable interests were not being defeated, and their own powers of disposition if their customer made default would be enormously restricted.

Presumably they would have to communicate with each sub-purchaser. The effect of the decision below when once appreciated would throw the business world into confusion, for credit would be seriously restricted.

The net result of this decision is that the buyer of goods in these circumstances is in no better position in bankruptcy than a seller. If a seller of goods delivers them to the buyer before payment, trusting to receive payment in due course, and the buyer becomes bankrupt, the seller is restricted to a proof, and can assert no beneficial interest in the goods. There seems no particular reason why a different principle should prevail where a buyer hands the price to the seller before delivery of the goods trusting to receive delivery in due course. In both cases credit is given to the debtor, and the buyer and the seller respectively take the well known risk of the insolvency of their customer.

I regret to differ from the opinion of the judges below and my brother Sargant. I do not think that there is any difference as to the existence of the principles of equity which are involved. They are well settled, and beyond doubt in their own sphere beneficial. The difference has been as to their application to such facts as appear in this case and I feel bound to repel the disastrous innovations which in my opinion the judgments under review would introduce into well settled commercial relations.

Appeal allowed.

[Lord Hanworth MR delivered a concurring judgment; Sargant LJ dissented.]

In re Goldcorp Exchange Ltd.

[1995] AC 74 (PC)

LORD MUSTILL: On 11 July 1988 the Bank of New Zealand Ltd. ("the bank") caused receivers to be appointed under the terms of a debenture issued by Goldcorp Exchange Ltd. ("the company"), dealer in gold and other precious metals. The company was then and still remains hopelessly insolvent. Amongst its assets is a stock of gold, silver and platinum bullion. Even if the company had not been brought down by dealings unconnected with bullion this stock would have been far short of what was needed to satisfy numerous contracts under which members of the public had purchased precious metals for future delivery. The discovery that not only was there a shortfall in available bullion but also that the stock of bullion had been dealt with internally in a manner quite different from what had been promised by the vendors in their promotional literature has aroused great indignation amongst the members of the public (more than 1,000) whose faith in the promises made by the vendors has proved to be misplaced. These feelings were exacerbated when it was realised that the debt secured by the debenture and the floating charge which it created were in excess of the entire assets of the company, including the stocks of bullion, so that if the secured interest of the bank is satisfied in preference to the claims of the purchasers, the latter will receive nothing at all. This has impelled the private investors (hereafter collectively referred to as "the customers") to assert in the liquidation of the company, not their unanswerable personal claims against the company for damages or for the repayment of sums paid in advance, but claims of a proprietary nature; in the first instance as regards the remaining stock of bullion, and at a later stage of the litigation asserted by reference to the moneys paid under the various purchase contracts, or to a proportion of the company's general assets seen as representing the moneys so paid.

In response, the receivers applied to the High Court under section 345 of the Companies Act 1955 for directions concerning the disposal of the remaining bullion. They have pursued proceedings of great complexity, very skilfully marshalled by Thorp J in such a manner as to enable decisions to be given in principle with regard to various categories of customer and thus to minimise the inevitable cost and delay involved in the investigation of so many and diverse claims. The outcome has been the settlement, or disposal by court decisions against which there is no appeal, of claims by several types of customer. There remain three categories, forming the subject matter of the present appeal. The first and largest category comprises the first respondents, those customers who have come to be known as "non-allocated claimants." These were customers who had purchased bullion for future delivery. At the time when the bank's floating charge crystallised upon the appointment of receivers, there had not been any appropriation of specific and segregated parcels of bullion to the individual purchase contracts. The second category of claimant has only one member, namely the second respondent Mr. S.P. Liggett, whose case resembles that of the non-allocated claimants but has certain additional features upon which he relies to contend that his claim will succeed even if the rights of the non-allocated claimants are subordinated to those of the bank. The third category of claimant consists of those who had made contracts for the purchase of bullion from Walker & Hall Commodities Ltd. before the business of that company was acquired by the company in 1986.

In the High Court all the claims were founded on the proposition that the customers had, or must be deemed to have, proprietary interests in bullion which could be traced into the stock remaining on liquidation. Thorp J rejected the claims of the non-allocated claimants and of the second respondent (save in one respect which is not directly before the Board), but allowed the claims of the Walker & Hall claimants. In the case of the latter the judge limited the amount of the remedy by reference to a question of tracing to which their Lordships must later refer. On appeal, the Court of Appeal [1993] 1 NZLR 257 agreed with Thorp J in holding that the first two categories of customer had no proprietary rights to the bullion. The scope of the debate was, however, enlarged to embrace a new claim to a proprietary remedy related directly or indirectly to the original payments of price by the customers under the purchase contracts. On this part of the appeal the court was divided in opinion. Cooke P and Gault J found in favour of the non-allocated claimants and second respondent, albeit for reasons which were not identical, and went on to hold that the entire amount of the purchase moneys could be traced into the general assets of the company. McKay J rejected this basis of claim. The position as regards the Walker & Hall claimants was the subject of procedural complications which their Lordships must later describe.

The receivers and the bank have appealed to the Board in relation to all three categories of customer.

Non-allocated claimants

I. The facts

Dealings in gold coins and ingots as consumer products are a comparative innovation in New Zealand. In the forefront of developing the market was a predecessor of Goldcorp Exchange Ltd. (Details of the alterations in the management and corporate structure of the concerns which acted as vendors in the transactions giving rise to the present litigation are complex, but they are not material to the issues now before the Board, and it is convenient to refer simply to "the company.")

Although the course of business between the company and the non-allocated claimants was not wholly consistent, and the documents varied somewhat from time to time, the general shape of the business was always as follows. Sales were promoted in various ways, particularly through glossy, illustrated brochures. So far as presently material the brochures offered two methods of purchasing bullion: "The first is what we call physical delivery and the second is non-allocated metal." After explaining how purchases of granules, ingots and coins could be made for physical delivery a typical brochure described the procedure for purchasing non-allocated metal, which (it was said) was "preferred by the majority of investors and … recognised as the most convenient and safe way of purchasing metal." According to this brochure:

> Basically, you agree to buy metal at the prevailing market rate and a paper transaction takes place. [The company] is responsible for storing and insuring your metal free of charge and you are given a "non-allocated invoice" which verifies your ownership of the metal. In the case of gold or silver, physical delivery can be taken upon seven days notice and payment of nominal delivery charges.

A later version of the brochure said:

> Basically, you agree to buy and sell as with physical bullion, but receive a certificate of ownership rather than the metal. The metal is stored in a vault on your behalf. …
> What protection have I that Goldcorp will deliver?
> The metal stocks of Goldcorp are audited monthly by Peat Marwick, to ensure there are sufficient stocks to meet all commitments.

If a member of the public decided to make a purchase on the non-allocated basis he or she received a certificate stating: "This is a certificate for non-allocated metal stored and insured by [the company]. Delivery may be taken within seven days upon payment of delivery charges."

Later, the certificate was altered so as to read:

> This is to certify that [name] is the registered holder of [quantity] fine gold. The above metal is stored and insured *free of charge* by Goldcorp Exchange Ltd. on a non-allocated basis. Delivery may be taken upon seven days' notice and payment of deliv-

ery charges. The owner shall be entitled to the collection of the bullion, or funds from the sale of bullion, only upon presentation of this certificate.

In addition to the documentation there were of course preliminary discussions between the customer and the company. Whilst these varied in detail from one occasion to another the following general description by McKay J [1993] 1 NZLR 257, 296-297, was accepted as correct for the purposes of argument:

> The wording makes it clear that the investor is not merely depositing money or acquiring a contractual right to be supplied at some later date after giving seven days' notice. The wording describes an actual purchase of gold or silver which will then be stored free of charge and insured by Exchange. Delivery is available on seven days' notice and on payment of a small fee for ingotting. This suggests that although there will be physical bullion held in storage for the investor and insured for him, it will be part of a larger bulk and will require ingotting before he can take delivery of his specific entitlement. In the meantime, he will have an interest, along with other investors, in the bulk which is being held and stored by Exchange for him and for other investors.

> That certainly was the perception of investors. As the judge said: "No one could read the claimants' affidavits, still less hear the evidence given by them on cross-examination, without being convinced of the depth and genuineness of their belief that by accepting the invitation to purchase on a non-allocated basis they were not simply buying 'gilt edged investments,' but gold itself. The speed and strength of their reaction to advice that Exchange had not stored bullion sufficient to cover their 'bullion certificates' made that plain." In an appendix to his submissions on behalf of the non-allocated claimants Mr. Finnigan collected numerous extracts from the affidavits filed on their behalf. These amply support the judge's finding. They depose to the various statements made to them on behalf of Exchange, all emphasising the absence of security problems, the fact that their bullion would be stored in safe keeping and would be safer than if they took delivery of it, the risks of storing bullion at one's own home, and the safety and security offered by storage with Exchange. Verbal assurances were also given that not only was the bullion insured, but the metal stocks were audited monthly by a large and respected firm of chartered accountants. Some deponents relied particularly on this factor as a guarantee that there would always be sufficient bullion to cover all the certificates issued by Exchange as was indicated in its brochures. Others refer to correspondence with Exchange which reinforced their belief that their metal was physically stored in vaults on their behalf. A number of investors received letters in connection with Exchange's audit asking them to confirm "the amount of non-allocated bullion we hold on your behalf as at 31 March. ..." Exchange's evidence as to what investors were told is more consistent with Exchange's brochures and with the evidence of investors. Mr. Campbell, who was bullion manager from January 1984 until the receivership, said at para. 7.2 that it was invariably explained to the non-allocated investors that the bullion purchased "was not set aside as that person's metal, but instead was stored as part of the company's overall stock of bullion," that "the bullion was stored and insured by the company," and as to safe keeping that "they would not have to worry about security problems of storing the bullion in their own homes." This suggests that the bullion

would be stored in bulk rather than on an allocated basis, but that it would be physically stored and held safely for the investor.

II. The issues

As already seen, by the time the judgment in the Court of Appeal [1993] 1 NZLR 257 had been delivered the proprietary claims of the customers had been widened to comprise not only bullion but also the general assets of the company, to an extent representing the sums originally paid by way of purchase price. The following issues now arise for consideration. (i) Did the property in any bullion pass to the customers immediately upon the making of the purchases—(a) simply by virtue of contract of purchase itself, or (b) by virtue of the written and oral statements made in the brochures and by the company's employees? (Although these were referred to in argument as representations their Lordships believe them to be more in the nature of contractual undertakings, and therefore call them "the collateral promises"). (ii) Did the property in any bullion subsequently acquired by the company pass to the customer upon acquisition? (iii) When the customers paid over the purchase moneys under the contract of sale, did they retain a beneficial interest in them by virtue of an express or constructive trust? (iv) Should the court now grant a restitutionary remedy of a proprietary character in respect of the purchase moneys?

If the answer to any of these questions is in the affirmative it will be necessary to consider the extent to which the customer's rights in the relevant subject matter can be applied to the bullion or other assets now in the possession of the company.

III. Title to bullion: the sale contracts

Their Lordships begin with the question whether the customer obtained any form of proprietary interest, legal or equitable, simply by virtue of the contract of sale, independently of the collateral promises. In the opinion of their Lordships the answer is so clearly that he did not that it would be possible simply to quote section 18 of the Sale of Goods Act 1908 (New Zealand) (corresponding to section 16 of the Sale of Goods Act 1893 (56 & 57 Vict. c. 71))[1] and one reported case, and turn to more difficult issues. It is, however, convenient to pause for a moment to consider why the answer must inevitably be negative, because the reasons for this answer are the same as those which stand in the way of the customers at every point of the case. It is common ground that the contracts in question were for the sale of unascertained goods. For present purposes, two species of unascertained goods may be distinguished. First, there are "generic goods." These are sold on terms which preserve the seller's freedom to decide for himself how and from what source he will obtain goods answering the contractual description. Secondly, there are "goods sold ex-bulk." By this expression their Lordships denote goods which are by express stipulation to be supplied from a fixed and a pre-determined source, from within which the seller may make his

---

1 And s. 17 of the Ont. SGA. [ed.]

own choice (unless the contract requires it to be made in some other way) but outside which he may not go. For example, "I sell you 60 of the 100 sheep now on my farm."

Approaching these situations a priori common sense dictates that the buyer cannot acquire title until it is known to what goods the title relates. Whether the property then passes will depend upon the intention of the parties and in particular on whether there has been a consensual appropriation of particular goods to the contract. On the latter question the law is not straightforward, and if it had been decisive of the present appeal it would have been necessary to examine cases such as *Carlos Federspiel & Co. S.A. v. Charles Twigg & Co. Ltd.* [1957] 1 Lloyd's Rep. 240 and other cases cited in argument. In fact, however, the case turns not on appropriation but on ascertainment, and on the latter the law has never been in doubt. It makes no difference what the parties intended if what they intend is impossible: as is the case with an immediate transfer of title to goods whose identity is not yet known. As Lord Blackburn wrote in his treatise on *The Effect of the Contract of Sale* (1854), pp. 122-123, a principal inspiration of the Sale of Goods Act 1893:

> The first of [the rules] that the parties must be agreed as to the specific goods on which the contract is to attach before there can be a bargain and sale, is one that is founded on the very nature of things. Till the parties are agreed on the specific individual goods, the contract can be no more than a contract to supply goods answering a particular description, and since the vendor would fulfil his part of the contract by furnishing any parcel of goods answering that description, and the purchaser could not object to them if they did answer the description, it is clear there can be no intention to transfer the property in any particular lot of goods more than another, till it is ascertained which are the very goods sold.
>
> This rule has existed at all times; it is to be found in the earliest English law books. ... It makes no difference, although the goods are so far ascertained that the parties have agreed that they should be taken from some specified larger stock. In such a case the reason still applies: the parties did not intend to transfer the property in one portion of the stock more than in another, and the law which only gives effect to their intention, does not transfer the property in any individual portion.

Their Lordships have laboured this point, about which there has been no dispute, simply to show that any attempt by the non-allocated claimants to assert that a legal title passed by virtue of the sale would have been defeated, not by some arid legal technicality but by what Lord Blackburn called "the very nature of things." The same conclusion applies, and for the same reason, to any argument that a title in equity was created by the sale, taken in isolation from the collateral promises. It is unnecessary to examine in detail the decision of the Court of Appeal in *In re Wait* [1927] 1 Ch. 606 for the facts were crucially different. There, the contract was for a sale ex-bulk. The 500 tons in question formed part of a larger quantity shipped on board a named vessel; the seller could supply from no other source; and once the entire quantity had been landed and warehoused the buyer could point to the bulk and say that his goods were definitely there, although he could not tell which part they were. It was this feature which prompted the dissenting opinion of Sargant L.J. that the sub-purchasers had a sufficient partial equitable interest in the whole to found a claim for measuring out and delivery of 500 tons. No such feature exists here. Nevertheless, the reasoning contained in the judgment of Atkin LJ, at pp. 625-641, which their Lordships venture to find irresistible, points unequivocally to the conclusion that under a simple contract for the sale of unascertained goods no equitable title can pass merely by virtue of the sale.

This is not, of course, the end of the matter. As Atkin LJ himself acknowledged, at p. 636:

> [The rules in the statute] have, of course, no relevance when one is considering rights, legal or equitable, which may come into existence dehors the contract for sale. A seller or a purchaser may, of course, create any equity he pleases by way of charge, equitable assignment or any other dealing with or disposition of goods, the subject matter of sale; and he may, of course, create such an equity as one of the terms expressed in the contract of sale.

Their Lordships therefore turn to consider whether there is anything in the collateral promises which enables the customers to overcome the practical objections to an immediate transfer of title. The most direct route would be to treat the collateral promises as containing a declaration of trust by the company in favour of the customer. The question then immediately arises—What was the subject matter of the trust? The only possible answer, so far as concerns an immediate transfer of title on sale, is that the trust related to the company's current stock of bullion answering the contractual description; for there was no other bullion to which the trust could relate. Their Lordships do not doubt that the vendor of goods sold ex-bulk can effectively declare himself trustee of the bulk in favour of the buyer, so as to confer pro tanto an equitable title. But the present transaction was not of this type. The company cannot have intended to create an interest in its general stock of gold which would have inhibited any dealings with it otherwise than for the purpose of delivery under the non-allocated sale contracts. Conversely the customer, who is presumed to have intended that somewhere in the bullion held by or on behalf of the company there would be stored a quantity representing "his" bullion, cannot have contemplated that his rights would be fixed by reference to a combination of the quantity of bullion of the relevant description which the company happened to have in stock at the relevant time and the number of purchasers who happened to have open contracts at that time for goods of that description. To understand the transaction in this way would be to make it a sale of bullion ex-bulk, which on the documents and findings of fact it plainly was not.

Nor is the argument improved by reshaping the trust, so as to contemplate that the property in the *res vendita* did pass to the customer, albeit in the absence of delivery, and then merged in a general equitable title to the pooled stock of bullion. Once again the argument contradicts the transaction. The customer purchased for the physical delivery on demand of the precise quantity of bullion fixed by his contract, not a shifting proportion of a shifting bulk, prior to delivery. It is of course true that a vendor may agree to retain physical possession of the goods on behalf of his purchaser after the sale has been completed, and that there may be a constructive delivery and redelivery of possession, so as to transform the vendor into a bailee or pledgee without the goods actually changing hands: see *per* Lord Atkinson in *Dublin City Distillery*

Ltd. v. Doherty [1914] AC 823, 844. Lord Atkinson was there contemplating a situation, such as existed in the *Dublin City* case itself, where the goods held in the warehouse were already identified (by numbers on the casks: see p. 825), so that the contract was one for the sale of specific goods under which the property would pass at once to the vendee. The case is, however, quite different where the sale is of generic goods. Even if the present contract had been a sale ex-bulk, in the sense that the contractual source was the bulk of bullion in the store, section 18 of the Act of 1908 would have prevented the property from passing on sale: see *Laurie and Morewood v. Dudin & Sons* [1926] 1 KB 223 and *Whitehouse v. Frost* (1810) 12 East 614. The present case is even more clear, since the customers contracted to purchase generic goods without any stipulation as to their source.

The next group of arguments for the non-allocated claimants all turn on an estoppel, said to derive from the collateral promises. Their Lordships derive no assistance from cases such as *Waltons Stores (Interstate) Pty Ltd. v. Maher* (1988) 164 CLR 387 and *Commonwealth of Australia v. Verwayen* (1990) 95 ALR 321 which show that on occasion a party may estop himself from relying on the protection of the statute. No such estoppel could assist the customers here, for the problem facing them at every turn is not section 18 of the Sale of Goods Act 1908, but the practical reality underlying it which Lord Blackburn called "the very nature of things": namely that it is impossible to have a title to goods, when nobody knows to which goods the title relates. The same objection rules out reliance on cases such as *In re Sharpe (A Bankrupt), Ex parte Trustee of the Bankrupt's Property v. The Bankrupt* [1980] 1 WLR 219 concerning what is called a proprietary estoppel.

A more plausible version of the argument posits that the company, having represented to its customers that they had title to bullion held in the vaults, cannot now be heard to say that they did not. At first sight this argument gains support from a small group of cases, of which *Knights v. Wiffen* (1870), LR 5 QB 660 is the most prominent. Wiffen had a large quantity of barley lying in sacks in his granary, close to a railway station. He agreed to sell 80 quarters of this barley to Maris, without appropriating any particular sacks. Maris sold 60 quarters to Knights, who paid for them and received in exchange a document signed by Maris addressed to the station master, directing him to deliver 60 quarters of barley. This was shown by the station master to Wiffen who told him that when he got the forwarding note the barley would be put on the line. Knights gave a forwarding note to the station master for 60 quarters of barley. Maris became bankrupt, and Wiffen, as unpaid vendor, refused to part with the barley. Knights sued Wiffen in trover to which Wiffen pleaded that the barley was not the property of the plaintiff. A very strong court of Queen's Bench found in favour of the plaintiff. Blackburn J explained the matter thus, at pp. 665–666:

> No doubt the law is that until an appropriation from a bulk is made, so that the vendor has said what portion belongs to him and what portion belongs to the buyer, the goods remain in solido, and no property passes. But can Wiffen here be permitted to say, "I never set aside any quarters?" ... The defendant knew that, when he assented to the delivery order, the plaintiff, as a reasonable man, would rest satisfied. ... The plaintiff may well say, "I abstained from active measures in consequence of your statement, and I am entitled to hold you precluded from denying that what you stated was true."

There may perhaps be a shadow over this decision, notwithstanding the high authority of the court: see the observations of Brett LJ in *Simm v. Anglo-American Telegraph Co.* (1879), 5 QBD 188, 212. Assuming that the decision was nevertheless correct the question is whether it applies to the present case. Their Lordships consider that, notwithstanding the apparent similarities, it does not. ...

All this aside, there is another reason why the argument founded on estoppel cannot prevail. The answer is given by Mellor J in *Knights v. Wiffen* itself, where, quoting from *Blackburn's Contract of Sale*, p. 162 he says, at pp. 666-667:

> This is a rule [i.e. the estoppel], which, within the limits applied by law, is of great equity; for when parties have agreed to act upon an assumed state of facts, their rights between themselves are justly made to depend on the conventional state of facts and not on the truth. The reason of the rule ceases at once when a stranger to the arrangement seeks to avail himself of the statements which were not made as a basis for him to act upon. They are for a stranger evidence against the party making the statement, but no more than evidence which may be rebutted; between the parties they form an estoppel in law.

· · ·

Similar statements can be found in several texts, such as for example *Palmer on Bailment*, 2nd ed. (1991), p. 1374.

To this the customers respond that they are not obliged to assert the same proprietary interest against the bank as they would do if their opponents were strangers to the entire relationship. By taking a floating rather than an immediate fixed charge the bank accepted the risk of adverse dealings by the company with its assets, and when the charge crystallised the bank "stood in the shoes" of the company, taking those assets with all the detrimental features which the company had attached to them. If the estoppel binds the company, then it must bind the bank as well.

Attractive as this argument has been made to seem, their Lordships cannot accept it. The chargee does not become on the crystallisation of the charge the universal successor of the chargor, in the same way as the trustee in bankruptcy or personal representative, who is as much subject to the personal claims of third parties against the insolvent as he is entitled to the benefit of personal claims of which the insolvent is the obligee. Rather, the chargee becomes entitled to a proprietary interest which he asserts adversely to the company, personified by the liquidator and all those general creditors who share in the assets of the company. The freedom of the chargor to deal with its assets pending the crystallisation of the charge does not entail that the chargee's right to the assets is circumscribed by an indebtedness of a purely personal nature. The most that the *Knights v. Wiffen*, LR 5 QB 660, line of authority can give to the purchaser is the pretence of a title where no title exists. Valuable as it may be where one party to the estoppel asserts as against the other a proprietary cause of action such as trover, this cannot avail the purchaser in a contest with a third party creditor possessing a real proprietary interest in a real subject matter, whereas the purchaser has no more than a pretence of a title to a subject matter which does not actually exist.

· · ·

Their Lordships must also reject a further variant of the argument, whereby a trust in respect of bullion came into existence as an aspect of a bailment, so that even if title *stricto sensu* did not pass nevertheless the fruits of the breach of trust may be traced into the existing stock of bullion. In other circumstances it might be necessary to look more closely at those elements of the argument which seek to attach the characteristics of a trust to a relationship of bailment, which does not ordinarily have this character, and also at the feasibility of tracing. There is no need for this, however, since there was never any bailment, and no identifiable property to which any trust could attach.

IV. Title to after-acquired bullion

Having for these reasons rejected the submission that the non-allocated claimants acquired an immediate title by reason of the contract of sale and the collateral promises their Lordships turn to the question whether the claimants later achieved a proprietary interest when the company purchased bullion and put it into its own stock. Broadly speaking, there are two forms which such an argument might take.

According to the first, the contracts of sale were agreements for the sale of goods afterwards to be acquired. It might be contended that quite independently of any representation made by the company to the non-allocated claimants, as soon as the company acquired bullion answering the contractual description the purchaser achieved an equitable title, even though the passing of legal title was postponed until the goods were ascertained and appropriated at the time of physical delivery to the purchaser. In the event this argument was not separately pursued, and their Lordships mention it only by way of introduction. They will do so briefly, since it was bound to fail. The line of old cases, founded on *Holroyd v. Marshall* (1862) 10 HL Cas. 191 and discussed in *Benjamin's Sale of Goods*, 3rd ed. (1987), pp. 80, 218-219, paras. 106 and 357, which might be said to support it, was concerned with situations where the goods upon acquisition could be unequivocally identified with the individual contract relied upon. As Lord Hanworth MR demonstrated in *In re Wait*, [1927] 1 Ch. 606, 622, the reasoning of these cases cannot be transferred to a situation like the present where there was no means of knowing to which, if any, of the non-allocated sales a particular purchase by the company was related. Since this objection on its own is fatal, there is no need to discuss the other obstacles which stand in its way.

The second category of argument asserts, in a variety of forms, that the collateral promises operated to impress on the bullion, as and when it was acquired by the company, a trust in favour of each purchaser. Before looking at the arguments in detail it is necessary to mention a problem which is very little discussed in the judgments and arguments. It will be seen that the analysis to date has involved two markedly different assumptions. The first relates to the expectation of the customer in the light of the collateral promises. The customer is assumed to have believed that it would make no difference whether he took immediate delivery of the bullion and put it in a bank, or left it with the company—except that in the latter case he would avoid the trouble, risk and expense of storage. In law this expectation could be fulfilled only by a system under which the company obtained bullion either by an outside purchase or transfer from its own stock, and immediately stored it separately in the name of the customer, leaving it untouched until the moment of delivery or repurchase. The second assumption relates to the obligations which the company actually undertook. It has not been suggested that this matched the customer's expectation, for there is nothing in the collateral promises, either written or oral, entitling the customer to separate and individual appropriation of goods. Instead, as shown by the passage already quoted from the judgment of McKay J [1993] 1 NZLR 257, 296-297, the arguments proceed on the basis that the company promised to maintain bullion, separate from its own trading stock, which would in some way stand as security, or reassurance, that the bullion would be available when the customer called for delivery. But what kind of security or reassurance? If the scheme had contemplated that, properly performed, it would have brought about a transfer of title to the individual customer before that customer's appropriated bullion was mixed in the undifferentiated bulk, analogies could have been drawn with decisions such as *Spence v. Union Marine Insurance Co. Ltd.* (1868), LR 3 CP 427, *South Australian Insurance Co. v. Randell* (1869), LR 3 PC 101, *Indian Oil Corporation Ltd. v. Greenstone Shipping S.A. (Panama)*, [1988] QB 345, and the United States silo cases of which *Savage v. Salem Mills Co.* (1906), 85 P 69 is an example. Since, however, even if the company had performed its obligations to the full there would have been no transfer of title to the purchaser before admixture, these cases are not in point. The only remaining alternative, consistently with the scheme being designed to give the customer any title at all before delivery, is that the company through the medium of the collateral promises had declared itself a trustee of the constantly changing undifferentiated bulk of bullion which should have been set aside to back the customers' contracts. Such a trust might well be feasible in theory, but their Lordships find it hard to reconcile with the practicalities of the scheme, for it would seem to involve that the separated bulk would become the source from which alone the sale contracts were to be supplied: whereas, as already observed, it is impossible to read the collateral promises as creating a sale ex-bulk.

This being so, whilst it is easy to see how the company's failure to perform the collateral obligations has fuelled the indignation created by its failure to deliver the bullion under the sales to non-allocated purchasers, their Lordships are far from convinced that this particular breach has in fact made any difference.

Let it be assumed, however, as did McKay J [1993] 1 NZLR 257, 284 in his dissenting judgment, that the creation of a separate and sufficient stock would have given the non-allocated purchasers some kind of proprietary interest, the fact remains that the separate and sufficient stock did not exist.

The customers' first response to this objection is that even if the concept of an immediate trust derived from a bailment arising at the time of the original transactions cannot be sustained, the collateral promises created a potential or incomplete or (as it was called in argument) "floating" bailment, which hovered above the continuing relationship between each purchaser and the company, until the company bought and took delivery of bullion corresponding to the claimant's contract, whereupon the company became bailee of the bullion on terms which involved a trust in favour of the purchaser. Their Lordships find it impossible to see how this ingenious notion, even if feasible in principle, could be put into practice here, given that the body of potential beneficiaries was constantly changing as some purchasers called for and took delivery whilst others came newly on the scene, at the same time as the pool of available bullion waxed and waned (sometimes to zero as regards some types of bullion) with fresh deliveries and acquisitions. Even if this is left aside, the concept simply does not fit the facts. True, there is no difficulty with a transaction whereby B promises A that if in the future goods belonging to A come within the physical control of B he will hold them as bailee for A on terms fixed in advance by the agreement. But this has nothing to do with a trust relationship, and it has nothing to do with the present case, since in the example given A has both title to the goods and actual or constructive possession of them before their receipt by B, whereas in the present case the non-allocated claimants had neither. The only escape would be to suggest that every time the company took delivery of bullion of a particular description all the purchasers from the company of the relevant kind of bullion acquired both a higher possessory right than the company (for such would be essential if the company was to be a bailee) and a title to the goods, via some species of estoppel derived from this notional transfer and retransfer of possession. Their Lordships find it impossible to construct such a contorted legal relationship from the contracts of sale and the collateral promises.

Next, the claimants put forward an argument in two stages. First, it is said that because the company held itself out as willing to vest bullion in the customer and to hold it in safe custody on behalf of him in circumstances where he was totally dependent on the company, and trusted the company to do what it had promised without in practice there being any means of verification, the company was a fiduciary. From this it is deduced that the company as fiduciary created an equity by inviting the customer to look on and treat stocks vested in it as his own, which could appropriately be recognised only by treating the customer as entitled to a proprietary interest in the stock.

· · ·

Here, the argument assumes that the person towards whom the company was fiduciary was the non-allocated claimant. But what kind of fiduciary duties did the company owe to the customer? None have been suggested beyond those which the company assumed under the contracts of sale read with the collateral promises; namely to deliver the goods and meanwhile to keep a separate stock of bullion (or, more accurately, separate stocks of each variety of bullion) to which the customers could look as a safeguard for performance when delivery was called for. No doubt the fact that one person is placed in a particular position vis-à-vis another through the medium of a contract does not necessarily mean that he does not also owe fiduciary duties to that other by virtue of being in that position. But the essence of a fiduciary relationship is that it creates obligations of a different character from those deriving from the contract itself. Their Lordships have not heard in argument any submission which went beyond suggesting that by virtue of being a fiduciary the company was obliged honestly and conscientiously to do what it had by contract promised to do. Many commercial relationships involve just such a reliance by one party on the other, and to introduce the whole new dimension into such relationships which would flow from giving them a fiduciary character would (as it seems to their Lordships) have adverse consequences far exceeding those foreseen by Atkin LJ in *In re Wait*, [1927] 1 Ch. 606. It is possible without misuse of language to say that the customers put faith in the company, and that their trust has not been repaid. But the vocabulary is misleading; high expectations do not necessarily lead to equitable remedies.

Let it be assumed, however, that the company could properly be described as a fiduciary and let it also be assumed that notwithstanding the doubts expressed above the non-allocated claimants would have achieved some kind of proprietary interest if the company had done what it said. This still leaves the problem, to which their Lordships can see no answer, that the company did not do what it said. There never was a separate and sufficient stock of bullion in which a proprietary interest could be created. What the non-allocated claimants are really trying to achieve is to attach the proprietary interest, which they maintain should have been created on the non-existent stock, to wholly different assets. It is understandable that the claimants, having been badly let down in a transaction concerning bullion should believe that they must have rights over whatever bullion the company still happens to possess. Whilst sympathising with this notion their Lordships must reject it, for the remaining stock, having never been separated, is just another asset of the company, like its vehicles and office furniture. If the argument applies to the bullion it must apply to the latter as well, an obviously unsustainable idea.

Finally, it is argued that the court should declare in favour of the claimants a remedial constructive trust, or to use another name a restitutionary proprietary interest, over the bullion in the company's vaults. Such a trust or interest would differ fundamentally from those so far discussed, in that it would not arise directly from the transaction between the individual claimants, the company and the bullion, but would be created by the court as a measure of justice after the event. Their Lordships must return to this topic later when considering the Walker & Hall claimants who, the trial judge has held, did acquire a proprietary interest in some bullion, but they are unable to understand how the doctrine in any of its suggested formulations could apply to the facts of the present case. By leaving its stock of bullion in a non-differentiated state the company did not unjustly enrich itself by mixing its own bullion with that of the purchasers: for all the gold belonged to the company. It did not act wrongfully in acquiring, maintaining and using its own stock of bullion, since there was no term of the sale contracts or of the collateral promises, and none could possibly be implied, requiring that all bullion purchased by the company should be set aside to fulfil the unallocated sales. The conduct of the company was wrongful in the sense of being a breach of contract, but it did not involve any injurious dealing with the subject matter of the alleged trust. Nor, if some wider equitable principle is involved, does the case become any stronger. As previously remarked the claimants' argument really comes to this, that because the company broke its contract in a way which had to do with bullion the court should call into existence a proprietary interest in whatever bullion happened to be in the possession and ownership of the company at the time when the competition between the non-allocated claimants and the other secured and unsecured creditors first arose. The company's stock of bullion had no connection with the claimants' purchases, and to enable the claimants to reach out and not only abstract it from the assets available to the body of creditors as a whole, but also to afford a priority over a secured creditor, would give them an adventitious benefit devoid of the foundation in logic and justice which underlies this important new branch of the law.

V. Conclusion on property in bullion

For these reasons their Lordships reject, in company with all the judges in New Zealand, the grounds upon which it is said that the customers acquired a proprietary interest in bullion. In the light of the importance understandably attached to this dispute in the courts of New Zealand, and the careful and well-researched arguments addressed on this appeal, the Board has thought it right to approach the question afresh in some little detail. The question is not, however, novel since it has been discussed in two English authorities very close to the point.

The first is the judgment of Oliver J in *In re London Wine Co. (Shippers) Ltd.*, [1986] PCC 121. The facts of that case were not precisely the same as the present, and the arguments on the present appeal have been more far-reaching than were there deployed. Nevertheless their Lordships are greatly fortified in their opinion by the close analysis of the authorities and the principles by Oliver J, and in other circumstances their Lordships would have been content to do little more than summarise it and express their entire agreement. So also with the judgment delivered by Scott LJ in *Mac-Jordan Construction Ltd. v. Brookmount Erostin Ltd.*, [1992] BCLC 350 which is mentioned by Gault J [1993] 1 NZLR 257, 284, but not discussed since it was not then reported in full. This was a stronger case than the present, because the separate fund which the contract required the insolvent company to maintain would have been impressed with a trust in favour of the other party, if in fact it had been maintained and also because the floating charge which, as the Court of Appeal held, took priority over the contractual claim, expressly referred to the contract under which the claim arose. Once again, their Lordships are fortified in their conclusion by the fact that the reasoning of Scott LJ conforms entirely with the opinion at which they have independently arrived.

VI. Proprietary interests derived from the purchase price

Their Lordships now turn to the proposition, which first emerged during argument in the Court of Appeal, and which was not raised in the *London Wine* case [1986] PCC 121, that a proprietary interest either sprang into existence on the sales to customers, or should now be imposed retrospectively through restitutionary remedies, in relation not to bullion but to the moneys originally paid by the customers under the contracts of sale. Here at least it is possible to pin down the subject matter to which the proprietary rights are said to relate. Nevertheless, their Lordships are constrained to reject all the various ways in which the submission has been presented, once again for a single comparatively simple reason.

The first argument posits that the purchase moneys were from the outset impressed with a trust in favour of the payers. That a sum of money paid by the purchaser under a contract for the sale of goods is capable in principle of being the subject of a trust in the hands of the vendor is clear. For this purpose it is necessary to show either a mutual intention that the moneys should not fall within the general fund of the company's assets but should be applied for a special designated purpose, or that having originally been paid over without restriction the recipient has later constituted himself a trustee of the money: see *Quistclose Investments Ltd. v. Rolls Razor Ltd.* [1970] AC 567, 581-582. This requirement was satisfied in *In re Kayford Ltd. (In Liquidation)*, [1975] 1 WLR 279 where a company in financial difficulties paid into a separate deposit account money received from customers for goods not yet delivered, with the intention of making withdrawals from the account only as and when delivery was effected, and of refunding the payment to customers if an insolvency made delivery impossible. The facts of the present case are, however, inconsistent with any such trust. ...

The same insuperable obstacle stands in the way of the alternative submission that the company was a fiduciary. If one asks the inevitable first question—What was the content of the fiduciary's duty?—the claimants are forced to assert that the duty was to expend the moneys in the purchase and maintenance of the reserved stock. Yet this is precisely the obligation which, as just stated, cannot be extracted from anything express or implied in the contract of sale and the collateral promises. In truth, the argument that the company was a fiduciary (as regards the money rather than the bullion) is no more than another label for the argument in favour of an express trust and must fail for the same reason.

Thus far, all the arguments discussed have assumed that each contract of sale and collateral promises together created a valid and effective transaction coupling the ordinary mutual obligations of an agreement for the sale of goods with special obligations stemming from a trust or fiduciary relationship. These arguments posit that the obligations remain in force, albeit unperformed, the claimants' object being to enforce them. The next group of arguments starts with the contrary proposition that the transactions were rendered ineffectual by the presence of one or more of three vitiating factors: namely, misrepresentation, mistake and total failure of consideration. To these their Lordships now turn.

It is important at the outset to distinguish between three different ways in which the existence of a misrepresentation, a mistake or a total failure of consideration might lead to the existence of a proprietary interest in the purchase money or its fruits superior to that of the bank.

1. The existence of one or more of these vitiating factors distinguished the relationship from that of an ordinary vendor and purchaser, so as to leave behind with the customer a beneficial interest in the purchase moneys which would otherwise have passed to the company when the money was paid. This interest remained with the customer throughout everything that followed, and can now be enforced against the general assets of the company, including the bullion, in priority to the interest of the bank.

2. Even if the full legal and beneficial interest in the purchase moneys passed when they were paid over, the vitiating factors affected the contract in such a way as to revest the moneys in the purchaser, and, what is more, to do so in a way which attached to the moneys an interest superior to that of the bank.

3. In contrast to the routes just mentioned, where the judgment of the court would do no more than recognise the existence of proprietary rights already in existence, the court should by its judgment create a new proprietary interest, superior to that of the bank, to reflect the justice of the case.

With these different mechanisms in view, their Lordships turn to the vitiating factors relied upon. As to the misrepresentations these were presumably that (in fact) the company intended to carry out the collateral promise to establish a separate stock and also that (in law) if this promise was performed the customer would obtain a title to bullion. Whether the proprietary interests said to derive from this misrepresentation were retained by the customers from the moment when they paid over the purchase moneys, or whether they arose at a later date, was not made clear in argument. If the former, their Lordships can only say that they are unable to grasp the reasoning for if correct the argument would entail that even in respect of those contracts which the company ultimately fulfilled by delivery the moneys were pro tempore subject to a trust which would have prevented the company from lawfully treating them as its own. This cannot be right. As an alternative it may be contended that a trust arose upon the collapse of the company and the consequent non-fulfilment of the contracts. This contention must also be rejected, ...

Furthermore, even if this fatal objection could be overcome, the argument would, in their Lordships' opinion, be bound to fail. Whilst it is convenient to speak of the customers "getting their money back" this expression is misleading. Upon payment by the customers the purchase moneys became, and rescission or no rescission remained, the unencumbered property of the company. What the customers would recover on rescission would not be "their" money, but an equivalent sum. Leaving aside for the moment the creation by the court of a new remedial proprietary right, to which totally different considerations would apply, the claimants would have to contend that in every case where a purchaser is misled into buying goods he is automatically entitled upon rescinding the contract to a proprietary right superior to those of all the vendor's other creditors, exercisable against the whole of the vendor's assets. It is not surprising that no authority could be cited for such an extreme proposition. The only possible exception is *In re Eastgate; Ex parte Ward*, [1905] 1 KB 465. Their Lordships doubt whether, correctly understood, the case so decides, but if it does they decline to follow it.

Similar objections apply to the second variant, which was only lightly touched upon in argument: namely, that the purchase moneys were paid under a mistake. Assuming the mistake to be that the collateral promises would be performed and would yield a proprietary right, what effect would they have on the contracts? Obviously not to make them void ab initio, for otherwise it would mean that the customers had no right to insist on delivery. Perhaps the mistake would have entitled the customers to have the agreements set aside at common law or under statute, and upon this happening they would no doubt have been entitled to a personal restitutionary remedy in respect of the price. This does not, however, advance their case. The moneys were paid by the customers to the company because they believed that they were bound to pay them; and in this belief they were entirely right. ...

Their Lordships are of the same opinion as regards the third variant, which is that a proprietary interest arose because the consideration for the purchase price has totally failed. It is, of course, obvious that in the end the consideration did fail, when delivery was demanded and not made. But until that time the claimants had the benefit of what they had bargained for, a contract for the sale of unascertained goods. Quite plainly a customer could not on the day after a sale have claimed to recover the price for a total failure of consideration, and this at once puts paid to any question of a residuary proprietary interest and distinguishes the case from those such as *Sinclair v. Brougham*, [1914] AC 398, where the transactions under which the moneys were paid were from the start ineffectual; and *Neste Oy v. Lloyds Bank Plc.*, [1983] 2 Lloyd's Rep. 658, where to the knowledge of the payee no performance at all could take place under the contract for which the payment formed the consideration.

There remains the question whether the court should create after the event a remedial restitutionary right superior to the security created by the charge. The nature and foundation of this remedy were not clearly explained in argument. This is understandable, given that the doctrine is still in an early stage and no single juristic account of it has yet been generally agreed. In the context of the present case there appear to be only two possibilities. The first is to strike directly at the heart of the problem and to conclude that there was such an imbalance between the positions of the parties that if orthodox methods fail a new equity should intervene to put the matter right, without recourse to further rationalisation. Their Lordships must firmly reject any such approach. The bank relied on the floating charge to protect its assets; the customers relied on the company to deliver the bullion and to put in place the separate stock. The fact that the claimants are private citizens whereas their opponent is a commercial bank could not justify the court in simply disapplying the bank's valid security. No case cited has gone anywhere near to this, and the Board would do no service to the nascent doctrine by stretching it past breaking point.

Accordingly, if the argument is to prevail some means must be found, not forcibly to subtract the moneys or their fruits from the assets to which the charge really attached, but retrospectively to create a situation in which the moneys never were part of those assets. In other words the claimants must be deemed to have a retained equitable title: see Goff and Jones, *The Law of Restitution*, 4th ed., p. 94. Whatever the mechanism for such deeming may be in other circumstances their Lordships can see no scope for it here. So far as concerns an equitable interest deemed to have come into existence from the moment when the transaction was entered into, it is hard to see how this could coexist with a contract which, so far as anyone knew, might be performed by actual delivery of the goods. And if there was no initial interest, at what time before the attachment of the security, and by virtue of what event, could the court deem a proprietary right to have arisen? None that their Lordships are able to see. Although remedial restitutionary rights may prove in the future to be a valuable instrument of justice they cannot in their Lordships' opinion be brought to bear on the present case.

. . .

VII. Non-allocated claimants: conclusions

Their Lordships fully acknowledge the indignation of the claimants, caught up in the insolvency of the group of which the company formed part, on finding that the assurances of a secure protection on the strength of which they abstained from calling for delivery were unfulfilled; and they understand why the court should strive to alleviate the ensuing hardship. Nevertheless there must be some basis of principle for depriving the bank of its security and in company with McKay J [1993] 1 NZLR 257, 284-306, they must find that none has been shown.

. . .

Appeal allowed.

NOTES

1) For a detailed discussion of *In re Goldcorp Exchange Ltd.*, see J. Beatson, "Proprietary Claims in the Law of Restitution" (1995), 25 *CBLJ* 66 and Donovan Waters, "Proprietary Relief—Two Privy Council Decisions—A Canadian Perspective" (1995), 25 *CBLJ* 90.

2) Section 17 of the SGA provides that in a contract for the sale of unascertained goods, no property in the goods is transferred to the buyer until the goods are ascertained. As *In re Wait* and *In re Goldcorp Exchange Ltd.* demonstrate, this means that a person who buys goods forming part of a larger bulk can have no interest in the goods unless and until they are separated out of the bulk. The English and Scottish Law Commissions in their *Report on Sale of Goods Forming Part of a Bulk* (Law Comm. No. 215, Scots Law Comm. No. 145, 1993) were critical of this rule on a number of grounds. Most importantly:

a) It produced anomalies such as the following:

- If the seller sold and delivered to other customers the entire bulk of the buyer's entitlement, then property in what was left would pass to the buyer under the doctrine of ascertainment by exhaustion, but if the residual bulk comprised goods even slightly in excess of the buyer's entitlement property would not pass.
- If the contract identified the buyer's entitlement in terms of quantity, weight or some other measure, property would not pass until the goods were separated out, but if the contract gave the buyer a fixed share of the bulk, the buyer became an owner in common of the bulk.

b) The rule meant that if the buyer prepaid the contract price and the seller became insolvent before the goods could be delivered, the buyer had no claim to the goods themselves against the seller's trustee in bankruptcy, but was limited to proving in the bankruptcy for the amount of the payment. The Law Commissions thought it was unjust that a prepaying buyer should stand to lose both the price and the goods on the seller's insolvency.

c) The rule was an impediment to freedom of contract. Parties may have wanted property to pass when the price was paid in exchange for documents, such as a bill of lading, but the rule prevented this outcome.

The Commissions recommended that where there is a contract for the sale of a speci-fied quantity of goods forming part of an identified bulk, a buyer who has paid for some or all of the contract goods should obtain an undivided share in the bulk and become a tenant in common of the whole. When the buyer's share of the bulk is separated out and ascertained, property in the goods would pass to the buyer in accordance with the normal rules on the passing of property.

The Sale of Goods Act 1979 (UK) was amended in 1995 to give effect to these recom-mendations. The amending Act inserted a new s. 20A, which reads as follows:

(1) This section applies to a contract for the sale of a specified quantity of unascertained goods if the following conditions are met—

(a) the goods or some of them form part of a bulk which is identified either in the contract or by subsequent agreement between the parties; and

(b) the buyer has paid the price for some or all of the goods which are the subject of the contract and form part of the bulk.

(2) Where this section applies, then (unless the parties agree otherwise), as soon as the conditions specified in paragraphs (a) and (b) of subsection (1) above are met or at such later time as the parties may agree—

(a) property in an undivided share in the bulk is transferred to the buyer, and

(b) the buyer becomes an owner in common of the bulk.

(3) Subject to subsection (4) below, for the purposes of this section, the undivided share of a buyer in bulk at any time shall be such share as the quantity of goods paid for and due to the buyer out of the bulk bears to the quantity of goods in the bulk at that time.

(4) Where the aggregate of undivided shares of buyers in a bulk determined under sub-section (3) above would at any time exceed the whole of the bulk at that time, the undivided share in the bulk of each buyer shall be reduced proportionately so that the aggregate of the undivided shares is equal to the whole bulk.

(5) Where the buyer has paid the price for only some of the goods due to him out of a bulk, any delivery to the buyer out of the bulk shall, for the purposes of this section, be ascribed in the first place to the goods in respect of which payment has been made.

(6) For the purposes of this section, payment of part of the price for any goods shall be treated as payment for a corresponding part of the goods.

New s. 20B says that co-owner A is deemed to have consented to any dealing with goods in the bulk by co-owner B insofar as the goods fall within B's undivided share. The purpose is to facilitate dealings in the individual shares.

The 1995 Amendment Act also added new provisions to s. 18, Rule 5. These read as follows:

(3) Where there is a contract for the sale of a specified quantity of unascertained goods in a deliverable state forming part of a bulk which is identified either in the contract or by subsequent agreement between the parties and the bulk is reduced to (or to less than) that quantity, then, if the buyer under that contract is the only buyer to whom goods are then due out of the bulk—

(a) the remaining goods are to be taken as appropriated to that contract at the time when the bulk is so reduced; and

(b) the property in those goods passes to that buyer.

(4) Paragraph (3) above applies also (with the necessary modifications) where a bulk is reduced to (or to less than) the aggregate of the quantities due to a single buyer under separate contracts relating to that bulk and he is the only buyer to whom goods are then due out of that bulk.

The purpose is to codify the doctrine of ascertainment by exhaustion: *Wait & James v. Midland Bank* (1926), 31 Co. Cas. 172.

None of these changes have yet been adopted in Canada. For discussion of s. 20A see M.G. Bridge, *The Sale of Goods* (1997), at 83-90.

3) The UK amendments provide a measure of protection to the prepaying buyer, but only in the case where goods are bought out of a contractually designated bulk. They do not apply where, for example, the buyer prepays for goods (a) to be manufactured by the seller or to the seller's order, or (b) to be obtained by the seller from an unspecified source. In cases like this, the buyer will be at risk if the seller becomes insolvent before the goods are appropriated to the contract (see, for example, *Carlos Federspiel & Co., S.A. v. Chas. Twigg & Co., Ltd., supra*). This kind of case has attracted a fair amount of attention in recent years, particularly in the context of consumer transactions. The following are some of the solutions that have been proposed.

a) To have the agreement provide that title will pass to the buyer as soon as the seller begins work on the chattel and the buyer has made the first payment. This approach is often adopted in contracts for the construction of vessels, aircraft, and other high-cost, purpose-built goods. It is not a practicable solution in the case of mass-produced items because of the problem of identification and the difficulties it would create for manufacturers.

b) To require the seller to hold the buyer's advances in trust until the goods are ready for delivery. In *Quistclose Investments Ltd. v. Rolls Razor Ltd.*, [1970] AC 567, the House of Lords affirmed the effectiveness of contractual stipulations requiring a recipient of funds to use them only for designated purposes and finding a resulting trust if the funds are not or cannot be used as intended. The *Quistclose* doctrine is now also an established part of Canadian law. The difficulty with a trust clause is that most sellers would find it an unacceptable restriction since the whole purpose of asking for advance payment is to finance the production of future goods (where the seller is a manufacturer) or to enable the seller to acquire the goods from a third party (where the seller is not the manufacturer).

c) To ask the court to declare a remedial constructive trust in favour of the prepaying buyer on the grounds (i) that, not having performed its part of the bargain, it would be unjust to allow the seller to retain the purchase price, and (ii) that the seller's assets should not be augmented for the benefit of the seller's secured and unsecured creditors.

The advantage of the remedial constructive trust is that it does not require the plaintiff to prove any subsisting *in rem* rights after the monies have been paid over to the seller, whether in the monies themselves or other assets of the defendant; unlike the traditional English constructive trust, it is a wholly restitutionary and discretionary remedy. Since the Supreme Court's decision in *Lac Minerals Ltd. v. International Corona Resources Ltd.*, [1989] 2 SCR 574, the remedial constructive trust has become an established doctrine of Canadian law and is increasingly invoked in practice. What remains unclear is whether, and to what extent, Canadian courts will allow the remedy where the defendant is insolvent and the remedy would prejudice the rights of the defendant's secured and unsecured creditors. The remedy was allowed in such circumstances in *Taypotat v. Surgeson*, [1985] 3 WWR 18 (Sask. CA); *Waselenko v. Touche Ross Ltd.*, [1988] 3 WWR 38 (Sask. CA); and *Barnabe v. Touhey* (1994), 18 OR (2d) 370.

English commentators have expressed much hostility toward the remedial constructive trust because of its unpredictability and adverse impact on third-party interests. The device was treated inconsistently in the Privy Council's judgment in *Re Goldcorp, supra*. In the context of the buyers' claim to recover the purchase price of the bullion, Lord Mustill said that "Their Lordships must firmly reject any such approach." (AC, at 104). On the other hand, when dealing with the Walker & Hall claims (in a section of the judgment not reproduced in the extract preceding these Notes), and in a more cautious vein, we are told that "the law relating to the creation and tracing of equitable property interests is still in a state of development." (AC, at 109.)

d) To adopt a provision similar to UCC 2-502 entitling the buyer to recover goods identified to the contract where the seller becomes insolvent within 10 days of receiving the first instalment of the price. The OLRC Sales Report, at 265, thought the section was of negligible value and also queried whether a province could constitutionally adopt such a provision.

e) To allow the buyer to acquire a buyer's purchase money security interest (BPMSI) in respect of his prepayments similar to the purchase-money security interest available to the unpaid seller under the PPS acts. See A. Dadson, "A Fresh Plea for the Financing Buyer" (1985-86), 11 *CBLJ* 171. Purchase-money security interests are discussed in volume III of this casebook. There would be considerable difficulties in adapting the provincial acts to provide a BPMSI; none of the acts has so far made the effort.

f) In the case of consumer buyers, to confer a statutory non-possessory lien in favour of the buyer along the lines proposed in the BC Law Reform Commission's *Report on the Buyer's Lien: A New Consumer Remedy* (LRC 93, 1987) and discussed in Wood (1988), 14 *CBLJ* 118. The recommendations were implemented in the Consumer Protection Statutes Amendment Act, 1993, SBC 1993, c. 39, which added a new Part 9 to the BC Sale of Goods Act. Part 9 is reproduced at the end of these notes. See also Arthur Close, "The British Columbia Buyer's Lien—A New Consumer Remedy" (1995), 25 *CBLJ* 127.

g) To establish a compensation fund for the reimbursement of buyers comparable to the compensation funds established in several provinces for the protection of travellers and buyers of motor vehicles. Is it practicable to establish such a scheme for every type of retail merchant or even a majority of merchants?

h) To require the seller under the contract to provide a "stand-by" letter of credit (SLOC) in the buyer's favour, which the buyer can invoke if he does not receive the goods for which he has paid. SLOCs are discussed in volume II of the previous edition of this casebook. They are becoming increasingly common, in domestic as well as international transactions; but only a buyer in a strong bargaining position can hope to secure one. Even then it will not be worth the trouble unless there is a substantial sum of money at risk.

BC Sale of Goods Act, Part 9

Buyer's Lien

Interpretation

73. In this Part

"buyer's lien" means a lien arising under section 74;

"payment" includes an obligation incurred by the buyer to a person, other than the seller, to whom the buyer remains liable notwithstanding a default by the seller;

"seller" includes

(a) a successor in interest or title of a seller, and

(b) a trustee;

"trustee" means a person who assumes control of a seller's property by operation of law, under legal process or under the terms of a security agreement and includes a sheriff, a trustee in bankruptcy, a liquidator and a receiver.

Buyer's lien

74.(1) Where in the usual course of a seller's business the seller makes an agreement to sell goods and

(a) the buyer pays all or part of the price,

(b) the goods are unascertained or future goods, and

(c) the buyer is acquiring the goods in good faith for use primarily for personal, family or household purposes,

then the buyer has the lien described in subsection (2).

(2) The lien under subsection (1) is for the amount the buyer has paid towards the purchase price of the goods and is against

(a) all goods

(i) that are in or come into the possession of the seller and are held by the seller for sale,

(ii) that correspond with the description of or with any sample of the goods under the agreement to sell, and

(iii) the property in which has not passed to a different buyer under a different contract of sale, and

(b) any account in a savings institution in which the seller usually deposits the proceeds of sales.

Termination of lien

75.(1) A buyer's lien is discharged when the seller

(a) fulfills the contract of sale by causing property in goods to pass to the buyer in accordance with the contract of sale, or

(b) refunds to the buyer the money that the buyer has paid towards the purchase price of the goods.

(2) Whether a buyer's lien is to be discharged under subsection (1)(a) or under subsection (1)(b) is at the option of the seller, but a discharge of the lien under subsection (1)(b) does not affect any right of action the buyer may have for a breach of the contract of sale.

(3) A buyer's lien ceases to bind goods that are appropriated to a sale made in good faith to a different buyer, whether or not that sale is in the usual course of the seller's business.

Priority

76.(1) For the purposes of subsection (2) "security interest" has the same meaning as in the *Personal Property Security Act.*

(2) A buyer's lien has priority over other security interests.

Trustee's duty

77.(1) A trustee who assumes control of a seller's property is, with respect to any valid and existing buyer's lien of which the trustee has knowledge, under a duty to ensure that property subject to the lien is dealt with for the benefit of the buyer in accordance with this Part.

(2) A trustee who deals with property that is subject to a buyer's lien is not liable to the buyer if the trustee acts in good faith and without knowledge of the lien.

Proceedings

78.(1) Subject to subsection (3), a person entitled to a buyer's lien on goods may commence a proceeding to enforce the lien in whatever court has monetary jurisdiction and the jurisdiction shall be determined by reference to the amount the buyer has actually paid.

(2) In a proceeding to enforce the lien the court may make one or more of the following orders:

(a) an order declaring that the buyer's lien exists;

(b) an order that goods be seized and sold and the proceeds applied to the discharge of one or more buyers' liens;

(c) an order that goods be seized and delivered to the holder of a buyer's lien to discharge the lien.

(3) No proceeding may be brought under this section to enforce a buyer's lien against goods that are in the possession, custody or control of a trustee.

Several liens

79.(1) Where there are 2 or more buyers' liens over the same property and

(a) the seller fails, or is unable, to discharge the liens, and

(b) on the enforcement of the liens, insufficient money is realized to satisfy the claims of those buyers,

(2) The equitable principles respecting the marshalling of claims apply to competing buyers' liens.

Application

80.(1) The provisions of this Part and the regulations made under it apply notwithstanding any waiver or agreement to the contrary.

(2) Nothing in this Part derogates from the rights of a buyer under a contract of sale, including the right of a buyer to

(a) reject goods where the buyer would otherwise be entitled to do so, or

(b) claim damages in respect of defective or deficient goods.

QUESTIONS

What difficulties (if any) do you see with these provisions? Do they apply to contracts for work and materials? To contracts for the supply of services? Should they? What is the impact of restricting Part 9 to contracts of sale involving unascertained or future goods, and to restricting the buyer's lien (s. 74(2)(ii)) to goods in the seller's possession that "correspond with the description" of the goods under the agreement to sell? In the light of the buyer's lien, what advice would you give to a lender who is being asked to give a line of credit to a retail merchant against the security of the merchant's inventory?

The Consequences of the Passing of Property

The most important practical consequences that flow from the passing of property to the buyer are as follows.

1) If property has passed, the buyer will generally have good title if the seller becomes insolvent while the goods are still in the seller's possession.

2) If the goods are delivered subject to a reservation of title (or property) by the seller, the seller may have a good title if the buyer becomes insolvent (subject to the requirements of the PPS acts).

3) The right to sue a third party for damage to or loss of the goods may depend on who has the property.

4) The risk passes *prima facie* when the property passes.

5) Generally speaking, the seller can only sue for the price if property has passed.

6) Where the contract involves a sale of specific goods the title in which has passed to the buyer, the buyer may lose the right of rejection (SGA, s. 12(3)). (This rule was deleted from the British Act in 1967.)

On the other hand, the passing of property does not affect the following questions:

1) The buyer's non-entitlement to possession until he has paid the price (SGA ss. 27, 39);

2) The power of a seller in possession to pass good title to a third party acting in good faith and without notice (SGA s. 25(1));

3) The seller's possessory lien for the unpaid price and the right to resell the goods in case of default (SGA s. 46(3)); and

4) The buyer's right to reject non-conforming goods (SGA ss. 33-34); and

5) the locus of the risk of loss where delivery has been delayed through the default of one of the parties (SGA s. 21(b)).

Karl Llewellyn, the Chief Reporter of the Uniform Commercial Code and principal architect of Article 2, was averse altogether to the "lump concept" approach to title in the Uniform Sales Act (and therefore also in the SGA) on the grounds that such unrelated issues as the transfer of risk or the seller's rights to claim the price should not depend on the same metaphysical abstraction. He preferred "narrow issue thinking" in which the several questions were decided on their individual merits without reference to title. See K.N. Llewellyn, "Through Title to Contract and a Bit Beyond" (1938), 15 *NYULQ Rev.* 159.

Despite Williston's objections (63 *Harv. L Rev.* 561, 566 *et seq.*) the Code's sponsors approved Llewellyn's functional approach, as may be seen from the following Article 2 provisions:

UCC 2-501—(insurable interest)

    2-502—(buyer's rights to goods on seller's insolvency)

2-509–510—(risk of loss)

    2-709—(seller's right to sue for price)

    2-716—(buyer's right to replevy identified goods and to sue for specific performance).

    2-722—(right to sue for third-party injury to goods)

The UN International Sales Convention has adopted a similar functional approach (see Articles 67-69) and intentionally abstained from adopting any rules on the transfer of title (see Article 4(b)). The OLRC Sales Report (at 280-82) supports the Code solution and recommends it for adoption in a revised Ontario Act.

If the Code approach is adopted, does it dispense with the need to have general title rules to govern situations not covered by specific rules, for example, to determine tax liabilities or tort liability in the case of a motor vehicle driven by a person with the "owner's" consent? *Cf.* UCC 2-401(1), which contains general rules for the passing of title "[i]nsofar as situations are not covered by the other provisions of this Article and matters concerning title become material ...".

CHAPTER FOURTEEN

Property (Title) Aspects of the Contract of Sale: Transfer of Title by Non-Owner

INTRODUCTION

A.J. Duggan
"Personal Property Security Interests and Third Party Disputes: Economic Considerations in Reforming the Law"

in Michael Gillooly (ed.), *Securities over Personalty*
(Sydney: Federation Press, 1994), at 234, *passim* (Footnotes omitted)

There are three main sets of circumstances, which may give rise to third party claims to personal property. The first case is where property owned by A is misappropriated by X and sold or otherwise disposed of to B. For example: (1) X steals the property from A; (2) X tricks A into giving up possession of the property (*Ingram v. Little*, [1961] 1 QB 31; *Lewis v. Averay*, [1972] 1 QB 198); (3) X is a bailee (having legitimately obtained possession from A), but the sale to B occurs without A's authority.[1] This kind of case involves competing claims to ownership. If A wins, the consequence is that B will be treated as never having obtained title, whereas if B wins A's title will be extinguished. The second case is where A holds a security interest and X (the debtor), without A's consent, sells the asset to B who buys it without knowing of the security arrangement. This kind of case involves a claim to ownership by B in

---

1 In (3), the bailment agreement between A and X might be, for example:

   (a) a warehousing contract;

   (b) a contract of carriage;

   (c) a repair or maintenance agreement;

   (d) a consignment for sale; or

   (e) a conditional sale or hire-purchase agreement.

Example (e) is different from the others, because in substance the contract between A and X is a security agreement. A is only nominally the owner of the collateral. Therefore, example (e) is really an illustration of the second kind of third party claim described in the text, rather than the first.

competition with A's security interest. If A wins, the consequence is not that B gets nothing (as in the first case), but that B takes the asset subject to A's security interest. Conversely, if B wins, the consequence (as in the first case) is that A's security interest is extinguished. The third case is where A holds a security interest and X (the debtor) without A's consent creates another security interest in the asset in favour of B who transacts without knowing of A's prior entitlement. This kind of case involves competing claims to priority. If A wins, the consequence is that (as in the second case), B takes the asset subject to A's security interest. If B wins, the consequence is not that A gets nothing (as in the second case), but that A's security interest is postponed to B's. Whoever wins gets first claim to the asset. The other party gets any surplus after the winner's debt has been satisfied.

In each of these cases, the dispute between A and B is not of their own making in any direct sense. The wrongdoer is X, but often X is likely to be judgment-proof. Accordingly, the law is faced with the dilemma of having to choose between two innocent parties. The intractability of the problem is reflected in the fact that the law has fluctuated down the centuries between two opposing principles:

> [T]he first is for the protection of property; no-one can give a better title than he himself possesses. The second is for the protection of commercial transactions; the person who takes in good faith and for value without notice should get a better title.

The first principle is embodied in the Latin maxim, nemo dat quod non habet. It favours A. The second principle is known to civilian law as possession vaut titre. It favours B. The conflict of principle means that there can never be an entirely satisfactory ex post solution to these kinds of problems. In certain circumstances, registration may be an appropriate form of ex ante solution. The purpose of registration is to give B a means of discovering the existence of A's interest before B transacts with X. If A's interest is registered, B should discover it by searching. Then, assuming B is honest, the transaction with X will not go ahead and the problem of conflict is avoided. This will not be the outcome if A fails to register or B fails to search, but then, in either case, there is a clear principled basis for arriving at an ex post solution.

· · ·

Misappropriation

(a) The Current Law

In a sale of stolen property, current law strongly favours the original owner (A) over the purchaser (B). The general rule is nemo dat quod non habet ... . Where A is fraudulently induced to sell goods to X and they are later resold to B, the general rule is, again, nemo dat quod non habet, but subject to an exception concerning voidable title. This is to the effect that if, at the time X sells the goods to B, the contract between A and X has not been avoided then B acquires a good title provided B buys the goods in good faith and without notice of X's defect of title. Where A entrusts the goods to X, and X wrongfully sells them to B, the exceptions to the nemo dat rule are rather more numerous, largely as a consequence of the *Factors Acts*. In particular, the nemo dat rule is likely to be displaced in favour of the bona fide purchaser rule if X is: (1) a mercantile agent; (2) a buyer who has been entrusted with possession of the goods by the seller (A) in advance of the transfer of property; or (3) a seller who has been left in possession of the goods by the buyer (A) following the transfer of property.

Two intriguing questions emerge from this pattern of regulation: (1) why should the law favour A in cases of theft; and (2) why should a different position be taken in cases of misappropriation other than theft? Alternative rules for the theft case are possible, as an examination of other legal systems reveals, and it is by no means self-evident that the approach which has been taken in modern Anglo-Australian law represents the optimal solution. One alternative approach would be to adopt a rule favouring B. This was, for example, the ancient Babylonian rule under the Code of Hammurabi in relation to stolen slaves. (A was entitled to recover the slave from B, but only upon reimbursing B the price B paid X and without deduction for the use B had had of the slave in the meantime.)

A second alternative approach would be to adopt a mixed rule, favouring either A or B depending on the circumstances. An example is provided by the concept of renunciation, developed in post-biblical Jewish law: the rule of law favours A for as long as A continues to search actively for the stolen property, but once the search stops A is taken to have legally renounced title and X is in a position to transfer ownership to B. A third alternative would be to adopt a sharing rule, as was done by the Mongolians in cases of cattle theft. (In that context, A was favoured in the sense of being entitled to the head—the better part of the animal—while B had to be content with the rump—the inferior part.)

Economic considerations throw some light on the issues raised above. From an economic perspective, there are three sets of considerations involved in the resolution of third party property disputes: (1) market considerations; (2) loss avoidance considerations; and (3) administrative cost considerations.

(b) The Economic Perspective

1. Market Considerations

A reason commonly given in support of the rule nemo dat quod non habet is that other alternatives would encourage theft and fraud. This is because, if B were to prevail in such cases, X would obtain a better price on resale. People will pay more for a clear title than a doubtful one. As Posner puts it, "we do not want an efficient market in stolen goods." Admittedly, the criminal law can be invoked to counter the incentives which the adoption of an alternative rule might create. For example, the penalties for theft and fraud could be increased, or additional resources could be allocated to the detection and prosecution of these crimes. In practice, however, there are limits to the possible improvements on either front. Therefore, the choice of rule to govern the dispute between A and B can be expected to have a marginal (but not insignificant) effect on X's behaviour.

A rule favouring A may reduce the incidence of theft. However, a countervailing consideration is that such a rule will also make it harder for owners to sell their goods in the secondhand market. The likely consequences are: (1) reduced demand for secondhand goods, in favour of new goods; and (2) an increased preference among buyers for dealing with sellers who have an established reputation for honesty. In both respects, the rule benefits retailers and respectable secondhand dealers at the expense of private sellers.

2. *Loss Avoidance Considerations*

Market considerations are not the only relevant factor. It also needs to be asked which of the parties, A or B, is best placed to avoid the loss (in other words, who can most readily take precautions to prevent the sale by X to B from occurring?). If it is cheaper for A to do so, the law should favour B by adopting the bona fide purchaser rule. This will induce A to take the necessary precautions. If the law were to favour A (by adopting the nemo dat rule), then the incentive would lie with B to take precautions and this would necessarily entail a waste of resources if the loss can be avoided more readily by A. Conversely, if it is cheaper for B to take precautions then the appropriate choice of legal rule, from a loss avoidance perspective, is nemo dat quod non habet.

The most obvious precaution against theft open to A is to increase expenditure on security (locks, alarms, guard dogs and the like). The possibilities open to B include investigating X's title and avoiding shady dealers. There are limits to how far B can be expected to go in requiring proof of title, particularly in a system where proof of title is not customarily required in connection with the purchase and sale of assets. Nevertheless, there are certain basic precautions which, at least in some circumstances, may be feasible (for example, asking X for the name and address of the previous owner). Again, B will not always be in a position to tell that X is a shady dealer, but B always has the option of refusing to deal with any person who does not have a known reputation for honesty. In any event, if B does choose to deal with X, factors such as price, location and X's appearance and demeanour may be enough to raise suspicion.

3. *Administrative Cost Considerations*

Administrative cost considerations relate to the cost to society of policing and enforcing a particular rule. Other things being equal, the simpler the rule, the less costly it will be to administer. On this basis, the nemo dat rule seems superior to the bona fide purchaser rule, because it gives rise to fewer issues. Under the bona fide purchaser rule, the court must be satisfied that B was honest, gave value and had no notice of A's title. By contrast, under the nemo dat rule, issues relating to blame-worthiness do not arise. On the other hand, there are still plenty of issues open for litigation under a nemo dat rule (for example: whether the asset was stolen or taken under circumstances in which B might have a claim to title; questions relating to damages: and whether A is, in fact, the rightful owner).

Administrative cost considerations may also help to explain why the law does not adopt a sharing rule (apportionment of the loss between A and B). A sharing rule would be expensive to administer because it will nearly always require an assessment of the value of the property to reach the correct compromise between A and B. The problems will be particularly acute where, as often happens, A places a high subjective valuation on the stolen item (whether for sentimental reasons or otherwise). A sharing rule made sense in the context of Mongolian cattle theft, because: (1) the property was about to be compromised (slaughtered) anyway; and (2) there was likely to have been substantial agreement among the herdsmen about the value of cattle heads and rumps. However, in modern times these conditions will not often obtain.

4. *Assessment*

On the basis of what has been said so far, it might be thought that the best approach would be not to have a general rule governing third party disputes over stolen goods at all, but instead to rely on case-by-case determinations with outcomes geared to the net efficiency effects of each particular set of circumstances. Under this kind of approach, the court would be required to investigate whether: (1) in the particular circumstances of the case, A or B is the lowest cost loss avoider; (2) loss avoidance considerations outweigh market considerations (is it more important to encourage the relevant party to be careful than it is to inhibit dealings in stolen goods or facilitate secondhand dealings, as the case may be?); and (3) administrative cost considerations outweigh loss avoidance or market considerations (are the savings from applying the nemo dat rule sufficient to offset any losses that may result on either or both of the other two fronts?). This simple description of what would be entailed is enough to demonstrate the impracticality of a case-by-case approach. It would be prohibitively expensive to administer (this is a second-order administrative cost issue), and the law would be uncertain so that its capacity for influencing commercial behaviour would be reduced (this is a second-order loss avoidance issue).

It follows that resort to general rules is the only viable alternative (second-order efficiency considerations clearly trump the first-order considerations). Formulation of a general rule inevitably means that: (1) assumptions must be made about what is more likely than not to be true across classes of cases; and (2) the possibility of exceptions is to be disregarded. A rule strongly favouring A in cases of theft can be explained by saying that, on balance, market considerations, loss avoidance considerations and administrative cost considerations all point in the same direction. In other words, it is a product of the assessments that, on balance: (1) the benefits of restricting the market for stolen goods outweigh the benefits of facilitating the secondhand goods market; (2) purchasers (B) can be more readily encouraged than owners (A) to take marginal additional precautions against theft; and (3) the nemo dat rule is cheaper to administer than the bona fide purchaser rule. In other times and places, different conditions may affect these assessments and result in a different rule. For example, the market overt rule can be explained on the basis that it reflects a different view about the importance of facilitating dealings in secondhand goods relative to the other competing considerations. More broadly, as Levmore argues, the variety of legal rules relating to dealings in stolen goods from time to time and place to place can be seen as a product of differences in local and temporal circumstances affecting the assessments which underlie the balancing of competing policy considerations.

Where the goods are misappropriated by means other than theft, the law's commitment to the nemo dat rule is somewhat weaker. The reasons for this are not hard to find. In the case where X tricks A into giving up possession of the property, A deals directly with X. A therefore has the opportunity to observe X's demeanour and physical appearance and to verify X's identity and reliability. By contrast, the precautions open to B are no different than in the case of theft. In these circumstances, the voidable title rule (which favours B) might be explained by saying that: (1) on balance, loss avoidance considerations point in this direction; and (2) generally speaking, encouraging A to be careful is more important than competing market considerations and administrative cost considerations. The rules relating to mercantile agents are subject to similar considerations. Furthermore, where X is a mercantile agent A will also have some opportunities for monitoring X's conduct (for example, by checking from time to time that the goods are still in X's keeping, or by signalling to third parties that X is not the owner). In these circumstances, it makes sense for the law to favour B. On the other hand, the law does not favour B in every case where X is an untrustworthy bailee. For example, where X is a carrier, repairer or warehouser, the nemo dat rule will ordinarily apply. In these cases, the nature of X's occupation should be sufficient to raise in B's mind the possibility that the goods might belong to someone else. It is therefore reasonable to expect that B should make inquiries, and the nemo dat rule encourages the taking of such precautions. By contrast, where X is a mercantile agent, B will not necessarily have any reason to suppose either that X does not own the goods or that X lacks A's authority to sell them on the terms proposed. In these circumstances, a rule favouring A would encourage secondhand buyers to take excessive precautions, and would therefore unduly limit the market for secondhand goods.

NOTES

1) For further reading, see Levmore, "Variety and Uniformity in the Treatment of the Good Faith Purchaser" (1987), 16 *J Legal Studies* 43; Weinberg, "Sales Law, Economics and the Negotiability of Goods" (1980), 9 *J Legal Studies* 509; and Baird and Jackson, "Information, Uncertainty and the Transfer of Property" (1984), 13 *J Legal Studies* 299.

2) The introductory part of the extract identifies three cases which may involve third party claims to personal property: (1) misappropriation; (2) fraudulent conversion of collateral by a debtor; and (3) the creation by a debtor of successive security interests in the same collateral. The second part of the extract discusses Case (1). The balance of the paper, which is omitted from the extract, discusses Cases (2) and (3).

In Canada, Cases (2) and (3) are governed mostly by the provincial personal property security statutes. The PPSAs, which are based on UCC, Article 9, adopt a registration scheme that covers: Case (2) where the collateral is a motor vehicle and, in provinces other than Ontario, other serial numbered goods as well; and Case (3). The PPSAs are dealt with in detail in volume III of the previous edition of this casebook.

3) As discussed in the extract, in Anglo-Canadian law the general rule governing Case (1) is *nemo dat quod non habet*. However, there are exceptions to the rule. In Ontario, the main ones are as follows:

    a) conduct precluding the true owner of the goods from denying either the seller's ownership of the goods or her authority to sell them (estoppel) (SGA, s. 22);

    b) sale by a mercantile agent (Factors Act RSO 1990, c. F-1);

c) sale by a seller in possession (SGA, s. 25(1));

d) sale by a buyer in possession (SGA, s. 25(2)); and

e) sale under a voidable title (SGA, s. 24). ·

Each of these five exceptions will now be studied in turn.

ESTOPPEL

Leonard v. Ielasi

(1988), 46 SASR 495 (Full Ct. SC S. Aust.)

MILLHOUSE J: This is an appeal from Senior Judge Brebner in an action in which he decided that the plaintiffs (the respondents before us), rather than the claimant (now the appellant) were entitled to a motor car.

The facts are these. The respondents or perhaps only the female respondent—she seems to have been the actor throughout, presumably with the assent of the male respondent—I shall refer only to her—in April 1984 bought a motor car for $3,000. Soon afterwards a man named Christianos asked her if he could borrow it. She allowed him to do so. Either before or soon after the loan was agreed the registration ran out. Without the respondent's knowledge or assent, Christianos registered it in his own name. Later she found out about this and wanted the registration transferred into her name again but Christianos assured her it was alright as it was. The respondent accepted his assurance and the car remained registered in Christianos' name. He then—again without her knowledge or assent—sold the car to a used car dealer. We were told from the Bar table that the dealer is now out of business and I gather is not worth powder or shot: that no doubt is why he has no part in these proceedings. The dealer registered the car in his own name and later sold it to the appellant. The appellant paid the dealer and had no idea that she was not getting a good title to the car: she acted in good faith. Soon afterwards the car was seized by the police to whom the respondent had complained when she found out what Christianos had done.

This is one of those unfortunate situations in which an innocent party, be it appellant or respondent, must be out of pocket.

Several authorities were cited to us by Mr Gabriel Wendler for the appellant and by Mr Russell Jamison for the respondents. I need go only to two, for in them, all the relevant cases are considered. Those two are, the decision of the House of Lords in *Moorgate Mercantile Co. Ltd. v. Twitchings*, [1977] AC 890 and the decision of the New South Wales Court of Appeal in *Thomas Australia Wholesale Vehicle Trading Co. Pty. Ltd. v. Marac Finance Australia Ltd.* (1985), 3 NSWLR 452.

In each, the Court had to consider the equivalent of s. 21(1) of our *Sale of Goods Act* 1895 (it is s. 26(1) in the NSW Act) [Ont. s. 22]:

> Subject to the provisions of this Act, where goods are sold by a person who is not the owner thereof, and who does not sell them under the authority or with the consent of the owner, the buyer acquires no better title to the goods than the seller had, unless the owner of the goods is by his conduct precluded from denying the seller's authority to sell.

The facts in *Moorgate Mercantile Co. Ltd. v. Twitchings* are set out in the judgment of Lord Wilberforce (at 901):

> The appellant finance company ("the plaintiffs"), as owners, let a motor car on hire-purchase to one McLorg. It was their intention, as it was their normal practice, to register the agreement with HPI.

> HP Information Ltd. (HPI) was a company with which the great majority of hire-purchase agreements were registered—registration was neither compulsory nor universal and some transactions escaped it: both appellants and respondents subscribed to HPI.

> By some failure, which has not been identified, but which on the probabilities occurred within the plaintiffs' organisation, the agreement was not registered. Consequently when the defendant, a motor dealer, who contemplated buying the car from McLorg, inquired from HPI whether there was any hire-purchase agreement registered or recorded against the car, McLorg having concealed it, he received a negative answer. He proceeded with the purchase and resold the car. The plaintiffs, learning of this, sued the defendant for damages for conversion and succeeded in the county court. The Court of Appeal, however, by a majority allowed the defendant's appeal; Geoffrey Lane LJ dissented, and the majority decided as they did on different grounds.

Lord Wilberforce, having considered one of the defences of the respondent and having, with the majority, rejected it, turned to the question of estoppel— "… that the plaintiffs are estopped from asserting their ownership of the car by their conduct, that is, by their negligent omission to register their agreement."

Having pointed out that what was relied on was "inaction or silence rather than positive conduct" Lord Wilberforce went on (at 902-903):

> English law has generally taken the robust line that a man who owns property is not under any general duty to safeguard it and that he may sue for its recovery any person into whose hand it has come.
>
> In order that silence or inaction may acquire a positive content it is usually said that there must be a duty to speak or to act in a particular way, owed to the person prejudiced, or to the public or to a class of the public of which he in the event turns out to be one.

He then propounded the test to be applied:

> My Lords, I think that the test of duty is one which can safely be applied so long as it is understood what we mean. I have no wish to denigrate a word which, to modern lawyers, has become so talismanic, so much a universal solvent of all problems, as the word "duty," but I think that there is a danger in some contexts, of which this may be one, of bringing in with it some of the accretions which it has gained—proximity, propinquity, foreseeability—which may be useful, or at least unavoidable in other contexts. What I think we are looking for here is an answer to the question whether, having regard to the situation in which the relevant transaction occurred, as known to both parties, a reasonable man, in the position of the "acquirer" of the property would expect

the "owner" acting honestly and responsibly, if he claimed any title in the property, to take steps to make that claim known to, and discoverable by the "acquirer" and whether, in the fact of an omission to do so, the "acquirer" could reasonably assume that no such title was claimed.

Applying that test, Lord Wilberforce thought that the appellant, belonging as it did to the HPI scheme, was under a duty towards dealers to take reasonable care to register a hire-purchase agreement: it had failed in that duty. Lord Wilberforce would have dismissed the appeal. He, with Lord Salmon, was in the minority. The majority expressed the opinion that the appellant was under no duty to register the hire-purchase agreement with HPI and that a dealer who bought a car after receiving a negative report from HPI was to be regarded as taking a reasonable business risk: the respondent could not therefore plead that the appellant was estopped.

The second case is *Thomas Australia Wholesale Vehicle Trading Co. Pty. Ltd. v. Marac Finance Australia Ltd.* This too concerns a hire-purchase agreement. The facts are set out by Glass JA (at 466):

> The plaintiff company sued the defendant company in the District Court claiming damages for breach of warranty as to the title of a certain Mercedes Benz sedan. The claim was heard by Nash DCJ who on 7 February 1984 directed the entry of judgment for *$50,374.94* including interest. The defendant appeals against the judgment on two grounds.
>
> The defendant is a car dealer which specialises in buying and selling prestige vehicles. On 8 January 1983 it acquired the Mercedes for $33,000 from one John Kenneth Kerr (Kerr), who had no title and no right to sell it. The car was then the property of Barclays Australia (Finance) Ltd. (Barclays) which had purchased it on 19 May 1982 for $50,000 and leased it to International Capital Corporation Ltd. (ICC), a shelf company controlled by Kerr. The plaintiff is a finance company. On 14 February 1983 it bought the car from the defendant for $45,000 and leased it to a third party. On an unspecified date in May 1983 Barclays repossessed the car as a result of the default of ICC under the lease to it. The plaintiffs loss at the time of repossession as a result of the breach of warranty was assessed by the judge at $46,374.94.

The car had been registered by Kerr in the name of Kerr Real Estate Pty. Ltd., through which company Kerr traded.

Glass JA having quoted Lord Wilberforce's test said (at 468):

> ... in the absence of a register and of any relevant transaction known both to Barclays as owner and the defendant as acquirer there are no circumstances which would raise a duty of care.

Apart from Kirby P, to whose judgment I shall come, the third member of the Court of Appeal was McHugh JA. He agreed with the view of Glass JA and cited (at 469), amongst others, the *Moorgate* case (supra):

> The section (s. 26(1) of the *Sale of Goods Act* 1923 (NSW)) creates a statutory estoppel. An owner may be precluded from denying the seller's authority by reason of his conduct which, expressly or impliedly, constitutes an unambiguous representation to the

buyer that the seller has his authority to make the sale: ... In some cases, the omission of the owner to take steps to prevent the sale may also estop him from asserting his title: Throughout the history of the law of sale of goods, conduct, which stops short of a representation, has only estopped the owner from claiming his goods when it constitutes a breach of a duty of care which he owed to the buyer.

Kirby P agreed with the other two members of the Court in the result of the appeal. He did so because he thought (at 465) that s. 26(1) "in the facts proved ... is not attracted to the relief of the purchaser." However, he expressed his strong view (which the other members of the Court were at pains to attempt to refute) that the courts have imparted to s. 26(1) "an alien gloss which defeats the intentions of the legislature" (the words are those of Glass JA (at 469) in referring to the judgment of Kirby P). Two quotations from the learned President's comprehensive and most able judgment (I speak with respect) make plain his view (at 458-459):

> The result of the line of authority which I have reviewed is that a gloss has been placed upon the language of the statute. There is nothing in the *Sale of Goods Act* 1923 (NSW), s. 26(1), which pre-conditions the disentitling conduct (by which the owner will be precluded from denying the seller's authority to sell) to the existence of a duty relationship between the owner and the innocent purchaser. That duty relationship has been read into the legislation by a long series of decisions which, in my view, reflect a fascination with the law of estoppel which preceded the enactment of the *Sale of Goods Act* 1893 (UK), s. 21 (now in this State, the *Sale of Goods Act* 1923, s. 26).
>
> In short, in an area of the law where it has long been recognised that inconsistent decisions have complicated and obscured the operation of the statute (*cf.* Walsh J in *Motor Credits (Hire Finance) Ltd. v. Pacific Motor Auctions Pty. Ltd.* (1962), 79 WN 684, at 689 (NSW)) and where, beyond duty relationships, practices and commercial realities are changing and developing all the time, it is illegitimate, as it seems to me, to bridle the statutory language by imposing the requirement of a precondition of a duty relationship which is not to be found in that language, is not necessary for its operation, can be explained by reference to pre-existing law and which frustrates the purpose of the statute and its beneficial operation in the just resolution of the claims of innocent purchasers who will otherwise suffer by virtue of careless conduct on the part of the owner.

The learned President then considered *Moorgate Mercantile Co. Ltd. v. Twirchings* and pointed out (at 459-460) that:

> although entitled to high respect, (it) does not bind us. It perpetuates an erroneous approach to the section and contains, in any case, powerful statements of dissent by Lords Wilberforce and Salmon.

I must admit both to being greatly attracted by the persuasiveness of Kirby P and to preferring his view, following as it does the opinions expressed by such as Lord Denning MR (in his judgment in the Court of Appeal) and Lord Wilberforce, to that of the views of the two other Justices of Appeal. If it were necessary to do so I should be prepared to follow Kirby P rather than the majority in *Thomas v. Marac* (supra).

However it is not, it seems to me, necessary to take that step.

The facts of this appeal may be distinguished from those both in *Moorgate v. Twirchings* and *Thomas v. Marac*.

In this appeal Christianos acted without the knowledge or assent of the respondent in registering the motor car in his own name. In neither of the other cases, so far as I can see, did the seller act wrongfully over registration or with the knowledge of the owner.

Even though in a dissenting opinion the test propounded by Lord Wilberforce seems to have been accepted by all the members of the New South Wales Court of Appeal, I respectfully agree with them in accepting it and set it out again:

> ... whether, having regard to the situation in which the relevant transaction occurred, as known to both parties, a reasonable man, in the position of the "acquirer" of the property would expect the "owner" acting honestly and responsibly, if he claimed any title in the property, to take steps to make that claim known to, and discoverable by the "acquirer" and whether, in the fact of an omission to do so, the "acquirer" could reasonably assume that no such title was claimed. ((1977) AC 890 at 903.)

Acting "honestly and responsibly": how can it possibly be said that the respondent acted "responsibly" in doing nothing after she found out that Christianos had already registered the car in his name? In my view she cannot be said to have acted "responsibly." She should have taken some action, when she found out about the registration, to get the car back. Instead she allowed herself to be conned by Christianos and did nothing. This gave Christianos the opportunity to sell the car. The owner, having done nothing in these circumstances, the "acquirer" (the appellant) "could reasonably assume that no ... title was claimed." The respondent is precluded by her conduct from denying Christianos' authority to sell: as a result the dealer gained a good title to the car and was able to pass a good title to the appellant.

The learned senior judge considered that neither registration in Christianos' name nor his possession was: "sufficient to constitute an unambiguous representation to a buyer that Christianos had authority to make the sale." He referred, amongst other cases, to *Moorgate v. Twitchings* and *Thomas v. Marac*. He concluded that the respondent owed no duty to the appellant: in that, for the reasons I have given, I think the learned senior judge was in error.

Appeal allowed.

[Johnston J agreed with Millhouse J. Jacobs J dissented.]

NOTES AND QUESTIONS

1) The orthodox position is that carelessness alone is not enough to found an estoppel by negligence against the true owner (A). The buyer (B) has to show that: (1) A owed B a duty to be careful; (2) A was negligent in breach of that duty; and (3) A's negligence was the proximate cause of B's entry into the transaction with the seller (X). Contrast Kirby P's view in the *Marac Finance* case. What is wrong with saying that carelessness alone

on A's part is enough to found an estoppel? In many, if not most, cases where A is dis-possessed of goods by X, A will have been careless at least to some degree. As Jacobs J puts it in *Leonard v. Ielasi*, charges of carelessness are easy to lay, particularly with the wisdom of hindsight. Estoppel is supposedly an exception to the general rule *nemo dat quod non habet*, but if A's carelessness alone is enough to found an estoppel, isn't there a danger of the exception overtaking the rule? In *Leonard v. Ielasi*, all three judges accepted the orthodox position concerning estoppel by negligence, though with varying degrees of reluctance. Do you agree with the majority's conclusion as a matter of law? Was there anything special about the facts of the case to justify characterizing the plaintiff's con-duct as more than just carelessness? As a matter of policy, do the economic considera-tions discussed in the Introduction to this chapter help at all in determining what the outcome of the case should have been? Can the distinction the courts purport to maintain between carelessness and negligence in the strict sense be justified in economic terms?

2) For a case similar to *Leonard v. Ielasi*, see *Shaw v. Commissioner of Police of the Metropolis*, [1987] 3 All ER 405 (CA), extracted later in this chapter under the Buyer in Possession heading. Are the two cases consistent? In *Shaw*, the court held that because the estoppel provision (s. 22 of the SGA in Ontario) is limited to cases "where goods are sold by a person who is not their owner," it does not apply if there is only an agreement to sell. Is this an unduly restrictive interpretation of the provision? Was there anything special about the facts of the case that might help to explain the result?

3) *Moorgate Mercantile Co. v. Twitchings*, which Millhouse J discusses in *Leonard v. Ielasi*, concerned a financier's failure to register a hire-purchase agreement under the British HPI scheme. The HPI scheme is not a statutory one—it is privately run—and registration is not compulsory. The House of Lords, by a majority, held that failure to register did not estop a financier from asserting its ownership of the motor vehicle against a third-party purchaser. Contrast the Canadian position. What are the conse-quences of failing to register a security interest to which the PPSA applies? See OPPSA s. 20(1)(c), discussed in volume III of the previous edition of this casebook, chapter 5. If the OPPSA (or comparable legislation) had applied to the facts in the *Marac Finance* case, also discussed in Millhouse J's judgment, how would it have affected the outcome?

4) *Motor Credits (Hire Finance) Ltd. v. Pacific Motor Auctions Pty., Ltd.* (1963), 109 CLR 87 concerned a dealer who held motor vehicles from a financier subject to a floor plan arrangement. The financier owned the vehicles, but it hired them to the dealer on terms authorizing the dealer to sell them by retail on its behalf. The dealer got into financial difficulties and the financier withdrew its authority to sell. The dealer, in disregard of the authority withdrawal, sold a number of the vehicles to a trade buyer outside normal business hours and on unusual terms. The question was whether the third-party buyer obtained a good title to the vehicles *vis-à-vis* the financier. The trial judge concluded that the finan-cier had given the dealer apparent authority to sell the vehicles (why not actual author-ity?) and this estopped it from denying the buyer's title. This decision was overturned on appeal by a majority of the High Court of Australia. The following is an extract from Owen J's judgment.

As stated above, the learned trial judge proceeded upon the basis that the effect of the "display plan" arrangement between the plaintiff and Motordom was to vest in the plaintiff as purchaser from Motordom the title to cars originally bought by Motordom on its own behalf and subsequently accepted by the plaintiff for inclusion in the "display plan" arrangement, such cars thereafter being held by Motordom as a bailee from the plaintiff for the purposes of resale on the terms of that arrangement. That being so, the question is whether the plaintiff, to adopt the words of s. 26(1) of the Sale of Goods Act, "is by its conduct precluded from denying" Motordom's authority to deal with the sixteen cars in question in the way in which it did. There can be no doubt that had Motordom sold the cars in the ordinary course of its business, the defendant would have got a good title to them notwithstanding the fact that the plaintiff had revoked Motordom's authority to sell. The case would then have fallen within the terms of s. 5 of the Factors Act. But the transaction between Motordom and the defendant was not one in the ordinary course of Motordom's business as a dealer in cars and that section cannot therefore operate. Nor can the defendant rely upon s. 28(1) of the Sale of Goods Act since Motordom was not in possession of the goods merely as the seller of them to the plaintiff, but as a bailee under the "display plan" arrangement: *Staffs Motor Guarantee Ltd. v. British Wagon Co. Ltd.*, ([1934] 2 KB 305); *Eastern Distributors Ltd. v. Goldring (Murphy, Third Party)*, ([1957] 2 QB 600). It was necessary, therefore, for the defendant to show that it had been induced by the plaintiff's conduct to believe that Motordom was entitled to deal with the cars in a manner which was outside the ordinary course of a dealer's business. Motordom professed to sell the cars as the owner of them but there is nothing in the evidence which would justify the conclusion that in the particular transaction with which this case is concerned the plaintiff was privy to that representation. In that respect the facts differ from those in the *Eastern Distributors' Case*. There Murphy, the owner of the vehicle, agreed that another person, Coker, should pretend to the plaintiff, a hire purchase company, that he, Coker, owned the vehicle in order to induce the plaintiff to buy it from Coker and the plaintiff, in reliance upon the representation that Coker was the owner, bought the vehicle. But that is not this case. By allowing the cars which it owned to be in the possession of Motordom the plaintiff unquestionably held that company out as having authority to sell them in the ordinary course of its business as a dealer and, for the purposes of such sales, to represent that it was the owner of cars sold. And any such sale would have been effective to pass title to an innocent purchaser notwithstanding the revocation of Motordom's authority since a purchaser of goods from one whose business it is to buy and sell goods of that description is entitled to assume that the seller has authority to sell, in the ordinary course of his business, goods of that description which are in his possession. But a purchaser is not entitled to assume that the seller has authority to deal with such goods otherwise than in the ordinary course of business unless there be some further act by the true owner leading the purchaser to believe that the seller is clothed with authority to enter into such a transaction.

In the present case I can see nothing to support such a conclusion and thus preclude the plaintiff from denying Motordom's authority to deal with the cars in the way in which it did. In other words, the plaintiff did no more than hold out Motordom as having authority to dispose of its cars in the ordinary course of its business as a dealer.

The case was further appealed to the Privy Council: *Pacific Motor Auctions Pty. Ltd. v. Motor Credits (Hire Finance) Ltd.*, [1965] A 867. The Privy Council decided the case in the buyer's favour, relying on Sale of Goods Act 1923 (NSW), s. 28 (s. 25(1) of the

Ontario SGA, the "seller in possession" provision): see *infra*. It declined to rule on the estoppel point.

5) What would the outcome be on a set of facts like the ones in *Pacific Motor Auctions* if the PPSA applied? See OPPSA, ss. 25 and 28, discussed in volume III of the previous edition of this casebook, chapter 9.

MERCANTILE AGENTS

St. John v. Horvat

(1994), 113 DLR (4th) 670 (BC CA)

CUMMING JA: This is an appeal from the order of Mr. Justice KC Mackenzie, pronounced October 23, 1992, vesting title to, and possession of, a 1982 travel van in Dalas May St. John, the respondent.

Facts

On August 10, 1990, the respondent delivered her van to E & E Travel Easy R.V. Sales Ltd. (E & E), to be sold on consignment. The respondent authorized E & E to obtain a firm offer of sale and instructed them to contact her when they obtained a firm offer so that she could then sign the necessary documents to transfer ownership in the van to the purchaser. She did not authorize E & E to sell the van.

On September 27, 1990, E & E sold the van to the appellant for $13,500 without notifying, or obtaining authorization from, the respondent. The appellant intended to resell the van and, after purchasing it, left it with E & E for that purpose.

At the time of the sale to the appellant, the van was still registered in the name of the respondent. On October 2, 1990, E & E registered with the Motor Vehicle Branch a forged transfer of ownership of the van from the respondent to itself.

In May, 1991, the appellant decided to retain the van for his own use and asked E & E to transfer the van into his name. On May 13, 1991, the appellant registered a transfer form that purported to transfer ownership of the van from E & E to himself.

On May 18, 1991, the respondent discovered that the appellant had purchased the van from E & E and was in possession of it.

. . .

The respondent brought an action against the appellant for the return of the travel van or, alternatively, damages for conversion. The respondent then brought an application pursuant to Rule 18A requesting that the van be transferred into her name.

The learned chambers judge allowed the respondent's application on the ground that the appellant could not rely on s. 58(1) of the Sale of Goods Act, RSBC 1979, c. 370.

The issues on this appeal can be summarized as follows:

(a) ... .

(b) Does s. 58 of the Sale of Goods Act give the appellant good title to the van?

(c) Does s. 26 of the Sale of Goods Act assist the respondent?

Discussion

. . .

(b) Does s. 58 of the Sale of Goods Act [for Ontario, see Factors Act, RSO 1990,
c. F.1, s. 2—eds.] *give the appellant good title to the van?*

Section 58(1) of the Sale of Goods Act reads:

> 58(1) Where a mercantile agent is, with the consent of the owner, in possession of
> goods or of the documents of title to goods, any sale, pledge or other disposition of the
> goods made by him when acting in the ordinary course of business of a mercantile
> agent is, subject to this Act, as valid as if he were expressly authorized by the owner of
> the goods to make the same, if the person taking under the disposition acts in good
> faith, and has not at the time of the disposition notice that the person making the dispo-
> sition has not authority to make the same.

In order to avail himself of the protection of s. 58(1), the appellant must show that
the following elements exist: (1) a mercantile agent, (2) who was in possession of
goods, (3) with the consent of the owner; and (4) made a sale in the ordinary course
of business of a mercantile agent, (5) where the buyer has acted in good faith and without notice that the mercantile agent did not have authority to enter the transaction.

"Mercantile" is defined in the Shorter Oxford English Dictionary as, "Of or belonging to merchants or their trade; commercial."

"Mercantile agent" is defined in s. 1 of the Sale of Goods Act:

> "mercantile agent" means a mercantile agent having, in the customary course of his
> business as an agent, authority either to sell goods, or to consign goods for the purpose
> of sale, or to buy goods or to raise money on the security of goods;

E & E was in the business of selling recreational vehicles to the public. The important question is whether E & E customarily had authority to sell the vehicles delivered into its possession. There does not appear to be any evidence that E & E did not
customarily have such authority. In my view, the chambers judge did not err in concluding that E & E was a mercantile agent.

Counsel for the respondent submitted that valid transfer papers, executed by the
respondent and left in E & E's possession, are necessary before E & E can be said to
have been in possession of the van within the meaning of s. 58. In support of this
proposition, she cited the judgment of Willmer LJ in *Stadium Finance Ltd. v. Robbins*,
[1962] 2 QB 664 (CA) at pp. 673-4. However, Willmer LJ was in the minority on that
issue. Ormerod and Danckwerts LJJ were of the opinion that the automobile was in
the possession of the mercantile agent for the purpose of sale, despite the fact that the
mercantile agent did not have possession of the ignition key or the registration book.

A motor vehicle falls within the definition of "goods" in s. 1 of the Act; therefore,
the questions of when a sale of a motor vehicle has occurred, or when property in
a motor vehicle has passed, are to be determined under the Act. It follows that the
question as to whether the van was in the "possession" of E & E should also be
determined under the Sale of Goods Act.

It is not necessary for a mercantile agent to obtain transfer papers or a bill of sale in order to be in possession of other chattels for purposes of the Sale of Goods Act; I fail to see why an automobile should be any different. I conclude that a mercantile agent does not have to be in possession of transfer papers in order to be in "possession" of a motor vehicle for the purpose of s. 58 of the Sale of Goods Act.

It is clear that the respondent consented to E & E's possession of the van.

The question of whether E & E disposed of the van "in the ordinary course of business of a mercantile agent" requires an analysis of the purpose of s. 58.

Sections 58 through 67 of the Sale of Goods Act were taken from the Factors Act, 1889 (UK), c. 45. The Factors Act was designed to deal with the situation where the owner of goods had delivered them to a mercantile agent for sale but the mercantile agent did not sell according to the instructions of the owner, or failed to pay the proceeds of sale to the owner. The Act reflects the policy that, despite the fact that the seller does not have a right to sell, people who buy goods in good faith should be protected, and that in such a situation the principal, the person who chose the agent, should bear the loss if the agent acts outside the scope of his or her actual authority.

Tied to this development was the emergence in agency law of the doctrine of ostensible or apparent authority, by which a principal is liable for the acts of an agent within the agent's apparent authority: see Fridman, *Sale of Goods in Canada*, 3rd ed. (Toronto: Carswell, 1986), at p. 131. The important question thus relates to the perception of the person dealing with the agent as to the extent of the agent's authority; did the agent appear to have authority to act on behalf of his or her principal?

The policy issue underlying the doctrine of apparent authority, i.e., whether the principal who chose the agent, or the innocent third party, ought to bear the loss, calls for an objective test to determine whether the disposal of the goods was done "in the ordinary course of business of a mercantile agent." Would a reasonable person have believed that the mercantile agent was disposing of goods in the ordinary course of business? This test protects buyers where the mercantile agent appeared to have authority to sell the goods but in so doing was acting outside his or her actual authority. Likewise, it protects the initial owner of the goods where the circumstances surrounding the sale should have put a reasonable buyer on notice that the sale was not a transaction in the ordinary course of business.

There is no evidence that any of the circumstances surrounding the sale of the van by E & E to the appellant would have put a reasonable person on notice that E & E did not have authority to sell the van in the ordinary course of its business.

Counsel for the respondent argued that when E & E, without authority, sold the van to the appellant, forged the transfer papers to transfer the van from the respondent to itself, and then transferred title in the van to the appellant, it took itself out of the category of a mercantile agent disposing of goods in the ordinary course of business. In *Chester Industrial Tool Supply Ltd. v. Cantec Wire and Cable Ltd.* (October 14, 1988), Vancouver Registry C854119 (BCSC) [summarized 12 ACWS (3d) 92], an obiter comment was made to the effect that a mercantile agent, by conduct about which the purchaser was unaware, could take a transaction outside of s. 58. But that case is readily distinguishable for there, unlike the present case, there was no willing transfer of possession by the owner to the agent, and the agent was not in possession.

Section 58 was designed to deal with situations where a mercantile agent in possession with the consent of the owner acts improperly. The question, therefore, is not whether the mercantile agent did something to take itself out of the category of mercantile agent disposing of goods in the ordinary course of business, but whether a reasonable person purchasing from the mercantile agent would have believed that the sale to him was a sale in the ordinary course of business. For example, in *Stadium Finance Ltd.*, supra, the sale of a used car without the ignition key and the documentation necessary to register the vehicle was held not to be a sale in the ordinary course of business of a mercantile agent, presumably because a reasonable buyer would have expected to receive them if it were a sale in the ordinary course.

The mere fact that the mercantile agent has acted outside his or her actual authority does not take a sale out of the ordinary course of business; s. 58 is designed to cure such a defect: see Atiyah, *The Sale of Goods*, 8th ed. (London: Pitman Publishers, 1990), at pp. 364-5. If the words "in the ordinary course of business of a mercantile agent" were defined in such a way that lack of authority to sell or fraud on the part of the mercantile agent would take the transaction out of s. 58, the entire purpose of that provision—to promote efficiency in commercial transactions and protect buyers who, without any indication that the mercantile agent does not have authority to sell, purchase goods from one who does not have such authority—would be defeated. What takes a sale out of the ordinary course of business is conduct of the seller or other circumstances that would put a reasonable buyer on notice that this was not a sale in the ordinary course of business.

I am of the opinion that "ordinary course of business of a mercantile agent" in s. 58 of the Sale of Goods Act means "ordinary course of business of a mercantile agent as perceived by a reasonable buyer."

As previously stated, transfer papers are not required under the Sale of Goods Act for a "sale" of a motor vehicle, which can be sold like any other chattel; nor are they necessarily required for a sale in the ordinary course of business. (The issue of what documents are required in order to register and insure a motor vehicle is separate from the question of whether a sale or a sale in the ordinary course of business has occurred.)

The presence or absence of transfer papers will be relevant to the question of whether a reasonable buyer would have been put on notice that the sale is not in the ordinary course of business. Absence of transfer papers might, in certain circumstances, be evidence that the sale is not one in the ordinary course, but they are not necessary for a sale; therefore, they are not an essential requirement of an ordinary course sale of a motor vehicle. Each situation will have to be considered in light of its particular facts.

In the present case, after purchasing the van, the appellant intended to resell it and left it with E & E for that purpose. Given those circumstances, it is reasonable and understandable that he did not at that time require transfer documents in order to register it in his own name. Later, when he changed his mind and decided to keep the van for himself, the transfer from E & E to him was recorded on the motor vehicle transfer form printed by the Motor Vehicle Branch. E & E was named on the form as the seller and there was nothing in the circumstances that should have put the appellant on notice that this was not a sale in the ordinary course of business. There would be no reason for him to ask to see the previous transfer form from the respondent to E & E, but even if he had, there was nothing on that transfer form to cause him to suspect that it was a forgery. In short, the evidence does not indicate that a reasonable buyer would have suspected that this was other than a sale in the ordinary course of business.

I find that the appellant has established that he acted in good faith and without notice that E & E did not have authority to sell the van.

All of the essential elements of s. 58 are present; consequently, the appellant is entitled to possession and ownership of the van unless, as counsel argued, s. 26 is of assistance to the respondent.

(c) Does s. 26 of the Sale of Goods Act assist the respondent?

Section 26 of the Sale of Goods Act [see Ont. s. 22] preserves the nemo dat rule, subject to other provisions of the Act. It reads: ... .

The object of the nemo dat rule is the protection of the owner's right to his goods. However, this objective must be balanced against the competing objectives of promoting commerce and protecting consumers and other innocent purchasers, which are embodied in ss. 28, 30 and 58 of the Act. Section 28 (sale under voidable title), s. 30 (seller or buyer in possession after sale) and s. 58 (disposition by mercantile agent), are exceptions to s. 26 and represent encroachments on the traditional nemo dat rule.

Section 26 protects owners whose goods are sold by someone who does not have the authority to sell. Section 58 promotes commerce and protects consumers by allowing bona fide purchasers to keep the goods they have purchased from mercantile agents who do not have authority to sell. Under s. 58, the mercantile agent must be in possession of the goods with the consent of the owner, the goods must be sold in the ordinary course of business of a mercantile agent, and the buyer must act in good faith, without notice of the mercantile agent's lack of authority. When it applies, s. 58 creates an exception to the nemo dat rule preserved in s. 26. In the present case all of the requirements of s. 58 have been satisfied; therefore, s. 26 does not assist the respondent.

Disposition

This case raises a difficult question: Which of two innocent parties should bear the loss occasioned by E & E's conduct? The law of British Columbia is that where there are two innocent parties, and all of the requirements of s. 58 are satisfied, the party who chose to leave his or her goods in the possession of the mercantile agent should bear the loss. The respondent freely chose to deliver her van into the possession of E & E so that E & E could solicit offers from prospective purchasers. She chose the agent; thus, it is appropriate that she bear the loss occasioned by E & E's conduct, and that the appellant be allowed to keep the van.

Appeal allowed.

NOTE

See also *Patry v. General Motors Acceptance Corporation of Canada*, [2000] OJ No. 1618 (OCA) on the meaning of "good faith" in relation to the purchase of goods from a mercantile agent.

SELLER IN POSSESSION

Pacific Motor Auctions Pty., Ltd. v. Motor Credits (Hire Finance) Ltd.

[1965] 2 All ER 105, [1965] AC 867 (PC)

[The facts of this case are summarized in Note 4 under the Estoppel heading, *supra*.]

LORD PEARCE [His Lordship set out the facts and history of the case in the lower courts. He continued as follows.]:

The appellant contended before their lordships both that the respondent was estopped or precluded from denying Motordom's authority as the learned trial judge had found, and also that the appellant obtained a good title under s. 28(1) of the Sale of Goods Act, 1923-1953, of New South Wales. Owing to the view taken by their lordships on the effect of s. 28(1), it became unnecessary to consider the difficult question of estoppel. The point under s. 28(1) turns on the construction of the words "Where a person having sold goods continues or is in possession of the goods." Are those words to be construed in their full sense, so that wherever a person is found to be in possession of goods which he had previously sold he can, whatever be the capacity in which he has possession, pass a good title? Or is some, and if so what, limitation to be placed on them by considering the quality and title of the seller's possession at the time when he sells them again to an innocent purchaser? Section 28(1) does not limit its effect to a sale "made in the ordinary course of business," as does s. 5(1) of the Factors (Mercantile Agents) Act, 1923, and the corresponding English provision. Counsel for the respondent, however, urged their lordships to limit the application of s. 28(1) in a like manner, since Motordom was in fact a mercantile agent and, therefore, it was not right to attribute to it a wider authority than was provided by the section particularly directed to its activity. Their lordships are unable to accept this view. Section 28(1) is not limited to any particular class of seller; it applies to a purchase from any kind of seller made in good faith and without notice of the previous sale.

The English statutory provision which was the origin of s. 28(1) was introduced in 1877 with the object of mitigating the asperity of the common law towards an innocent party purchasing goods from a person who has all the trappings of ownership but in truth has no proper title to the goods. Nemo dat quod non habet. The purchaser had no defence at common law against the true owner, subject to certain exceptions which are set out by Willes J, in *Fluentes v. Montis* (1868), LR 3 CP 268 at 276-77. In *Johnson v. Credit Lyonnais Co.* (1877), 2 CPD 224 an innocent purchaser attempted to establish that the true owner had "so conducted himself as to have lost the right to follow his own goods into the hands of the purchaser or pledgee." The true owner had in that case left in the hands of the seller the documents of title to the goods which he had bought, and had failed to have any entry made in the books of the dock company which had custody of the goods, thus facilitating the fraudulent second sale. Denman J held that there was no estoppel. As a direct consequence statutory protection was given to purchasers by s. 3 of the Factors Act Amendment Act, 1877. When *Johnson's* case was dismissed on appeal, Cockburn CJ said (1877), 3 CPD 32 at 36:

> And I am strongly fortified in this view by the fact that, as soon as the decisions here appealed from had been made public, the legislature by statute (40 & 41 Vict. c. 39) at once proceeded to settle the question in that view in the future by applying the protection given by the Factors Acts to persons acquiring title from agents, to innocent parties purchasing or making advances in such cases as the present. Whether, prior to and independently of such legislation, the law as it stood would have afforded protection is a different matter.

There is thus no doubt about the general intention of the original provision and the general mischief at which it was aimed. It is intended as a protection to innocent purchasers in cases where estoppel gave insufficient protection.

Section 3 of the Factors Act Amendment Act, 1877, dealt only with sellers who continued in possession of documents of title, but later s. 8 of the Factors Act, 1889, which took its place, dealt with the seller's continued possession both of goods and of documents of title. The wording of this latter section was included in identical terms in the Sale of Goods Act, 1893 (s. 25(1)). In the Sale of Goods Act, 1923-1953, New South Wales adopted the same form of words as that contained in two English sections. The first reported question that arose about the construction of those same words is to be found in *Mitchell v. Jones* (1905), 24 NZLR 932, a case under the New Zealand Sale of Goods Act, 1895. There the owner of a horse sold it to a buyer and some days later obtained it back from him on lease. Then, having possession of the horse in the capacity of lessee, he sold it a second time to an innocent purchaser. The full court held that the innocent purchaser was not protected. Stout CJ said (at 935):

> The point turns on how the words "or is in possession of the goods" ... are to be construed ... The meaning is—first, that if a person sells goods and continues in possession, even though he has made a valid contract of sale, provided that he has not delivered them, he may to a bona fide buyer make a good title; and, secondly, the putting-in of the words "or is in possession of the goods" was meant to apply to a case of this character: If a vendor had not the goods when he sold them, but they came into his possession afterwards, then he would have possession of the goods, and if he sold them to a bona fide purchaser he could have made a good title to them. He would be in the same position as if he had continued in possession of the goods when he made his first sale. In such a case as that he could make a good title to a bona fide purchaser. That is not this case. In this case the person who sold the goods gave up possession of them, and gave delivery of them to the buyer. The relationship, therefore, of buyer and seller between them was at the end. It is true that the seller got possession of the goods again, but not as a seller. He got the goods the second time as the bailee of the buyer, and as

the bailee he had no warrant, in my opinion, to sell the goods again, nor could he make a good title to them to even a bona fide purchaser.

And Williams J said (at 936) that the section "does not ... apply where a sale has been absolutely final by delivery, and possession has been obtained by the vendee." It has not been doubted in argument nor do their lordships doubt that that case was rightly decided.

In 1934, however, MacKinnon J, founding on that case, put a further gloss on the statutory provision in *Staffs Motor Guarantee, Ltd. v. British Wagon Co., Ltd.*, [1934] 2 KB 305. In April, one Heap agreed with a finance company to sell his lorry to it and then to hire it from the company on hire-purchase terms. He filled up a proposal form which was accepted, and a hire-purchase agreement, dated May 2, was signed. During the term of the hiring he sold it to an innocent purchaser. It seems that there was an interval between the agreement to sell and the hire-purchase agreement, but it does not appear from the report that there was any physical delivery or interruption of Heap's physical possession. MacKinnon J held that:

> Heap's possession of the lorry [at the time of the second sale] ... was not the possession of a seller who had not yet delivered the article sold to the buyer, but was the possession of a bailee under the hire-purchase agreement. ...

Although the sale had not been completed by physical delivery nor had there been interruption of the seller's physical possession, he held that the case was covered by the principle in *Mitchell v. Jones*. In *Union Transport Finance, Ltd. v. Ballardie*, [1937] 1 KB 510, du Parcq J, while not doubting the correctness of the decision of MacKinnon J came to a contrary conclusion in slightly different circumstances. One Clark sold his car to a finance house with a view to its being let on hire-purchase to his employee. The employee signed the agreement, but the whole transaction was colourable and Clark at all times was intended to keep possession of the car. The learned judge held that, at different stages, the finance house and the employee had a right to the possession of the car but that neither had exercised the right at the date of delivery of the car to the innocent purchaser. Clark had never attorned to the employee so as to make his possession a bailment under the hire-purchase. The section, therefore, applied. This conclusion is, in their lordships' opinion, correct. In *Olds Discount Co., Ltd. v. Krett and Krett*, [1940] 2 KB 117, Stable J accepted the decision of MacKinnon J There, a finance house agreed with Goldstein that it would buy his goods whenever he could negotiate a contract with somebody who would hire the goods on hire-purchase from the finance house. He did so. The finance house bought the goods from Goldstein and the hirer took possession of them. He defaulted, however, and Goldstein, as agent for the finance house, took possession and then dishonestly sold them to an innocent purchaser. Stable J rightly held that it was a mere accident that the agent to whom the finance house subsequently gave their mandate to hold the goods was the person who had sold them to a finance house. That decision, in their lordships' opinion, is clearly maintainable on the principle of *Mitchell v. Jones*. Finally, a judgment of the Court of Appeal delivered by Devlin J, in *Eastern Distributors, Ltd. v. Goldring*, [1957] 2 QB 600 on one point in a complicated case accepted and followed the decision in *Staffs Motor Guarantee, Ltd. v. British Wagon Co., Ltd.* without discussing it or questioning its validity. There is thus no case which holds that the section does not apply where, after the sale, the seller simply attorns to the buyer and holds the goods as his bailee.

It is plainly right to read the section as inapplicable to cases where there has been a break in the continuity of the physical possession. On this point, their lordships accept the observation of the learned judges in *Mitchell v. Jones* as to the words "or is" which are the sold grounds for any doubt on this point. What is the justification, however, for saying that a person does not continue in possession where his physical possession does continue, although the title under or by virtue of which he is in possession has changed? The fact that a person having sold goods is described as *continuing* in possession would seem to indicate that the section is not contemplating as relevant a change in the legal title under which he possesses. For the legal title by which he is in possession *cannot* continue. Before the sale he is in possession as an owner, whereas after the sale he is in possession as a bailee holding goods for the new owner. The possession continues unchanged, but the title under which he possesses has changed. One may, perhaps, say in loose terms that a person having sold goods continues in possession as long as he is holding because of, and only because of, the sale; but what justification is there for imposing such an elaborate and artificial construction on the natural meaning of the words? The object of the section is to protect an innocent purchaser who is deceived by the vendor's physical possession of goods or documents and who is inevitably unaware of legal rights which fetter the apparent power to dispose. Where a vendor retains uninterrupted physical possession of the goods, why should an unknown arrangement, which substitutes a bailment for ownership, disentitle the innocent purchaser to protection from a danger which is just as great as that from which the section is admittedly intended to protect him? Since the original provision under the Factors Act Amendment Act, 1877 (s. 3), dealt only with the continuing in possession of documents of title to goods, it seems clear that it was intending merely to deal with the physical possession of the documents and that it did not intend that a consideration of the legal quality of the possession of the documents should have any relevance. When the Factors Act, 1889 (s. 8), added continuance in possession of the goods themselves to continuance in possession of the documents, it can hardly be suggested that the word "possession" was intended to have any more esoteric meaning in relation to goods than it had in relation to documents of title. Moreover, such a construction would be in direct conflict with the definition (s. 1(2) of the Factors Act, 1889) whereby

> A person shall be deemed to be in possession of goods or of the documents of title to goods, where the goods or documents are in his actual custody or are held by any other person subject to his control or for him or on his behalf.

When s. 8 of the Factors Act, 1889, came to be enacted again as s. 25(1) the Sale of Goods Act, 1893, the identical words cannot have been intended to bear a different meaning from that which by definition they bore under the Act of 1889.

Further, s. 25(1) of the Sale of Goods Act, 1893, was accompanied by subs. (2) which was in identical terms with s. 9 of the Factors Act, 1889 (originally s. 4 of the

Factors Act Amendment Act, 1877), and dealt with a person who, having bought or agreed to buy goods, obtained possession of the goods. Possession under sub-s. (1) must surely mean the same as possession under sub-s. (2), which has been held to mean actual custody. In sub-s. (2) there is a reference to "mercantile agent" which, by sub-s. (3), "has the same meaning as in the Factors Acts." In *Hugill v. Masker* (1889), 22 QBD 364 at 370, Lord Esher MR, said of sub-s. (2):

> It is to be observed that the section is not dealing with the rights of the parties to that contract as against each other, but with the rights of third persons who enter into another transaction on the faith of the possession which the vendee under that contract has obtained of the documents of title.

Again in *Cahn and Mayer v. Pockett's Bristol Channel Steam Packet Co., Ltd.*, [1899] 1 QB 643 at 658, Collins LJ, with reference to sub-s. (2), said:

> "Possession" by the Factors Act, 1889, s. 1(2), means actual custody. The Factors Act, 1889, which is thus referred to, and as to part of it in terms again enacted, in the Sale of Goods Act, is the last of a series of statutes whereby the legislature has gradually enlarged the powers of persons in the actual possession of goods or documents of title, but without property therein, to pass the property in goods to bona fide purchasers. Possession of, not property in, the thing disposed of is the cardinal fact. From the point of view of the bona fide purchaser the ostensible authority based on the fact of possession is the same whether there is property in the thing, or authority to deal with it in the person in possession at the time of the disposition or not.

The climate of legislative opinion was, at the time of the passing of the Factors Act, 1877 and 1889, favourable to legislation which would prevent the buyers or others from being misled by an apparent possession of goods which was belied by legal transactions, which were unknown to the world at large. In 1878, the Bills of Sale Act, 1878, destroyed the validity of assignments and the like without delivery unless registered, and in 1882, the Bills of Sale Act (1878) Amendment Act, 1882, made similar provisions in respect of agreements to secure money on goods remaining in the apparent possession of the borrower. The heredity of the section which their lordships are now considering can, therefore, be summed up as follows. Its words are identical with those of s. 8 of the Factors Act, 1889, where they first appeared in this exact form. In that Act, it was expressly deemed that "actual custody" should constitute possession. In the Sale of Goods Act, 1893, s. 25(1), the same form of words was again enacted. Part of that section (namely s. 25(2)) contains an implicit reference, and part of it (namely s. 25(3)) an explicit reference, to the Factors Act. There was strong authority for saying that in part of the section (namely, s. 25(2)) "actual custody" constitutes possession. It had never been suggested by 1923, when the same form of words was first enacted in New South Wales, that there could be written into another part of s. 25 (namely, s. 25(1)) an implied proviso that actual custody should *not* constitute possession if the possession, though continuous, became attributable to a bailment—thus giving to possession a meaning different from that which it had under the rest of the section and different from that which it had under a previous and co-existing section in identical terms (Factors Act, 1889, s. 8). There is, therefore, the strongest reason for supposing that the words "continues ... in possession" were intended to refer to the continuity of physical possession regardless of any private transactions between the seller and purchaser which might alter the legal title under which the possession was held.

Their lordships do not think that such a view of the law which they believe Parliament to have intended could in practice create any adverse effect. It would mean that, when a person sells a car to a finance house in order to take it back on hire-purchase, the finance house must take physical delivery if it is to avoid the risk of an innocent purchaser acquiring title to it. In any event, however, such arrangements where there is no delivery are not without some jeopardy owing to the Bills of Sale Acts. It seems to their lordships that *Staff Motor Guarantee, Ltd. v. British Wagon Co., Ltd.* (and *Eastern Distributors, Ltd. v. Goldring* in so far as it followed it), was wrongly decided. Even if it were rightly decided, it would not cover the facts of this case. For, even assuming that a separate agreement of bailment, following a sale, without any break in the seller's physical possession, were sufficient to break its continuity for the purposes of the section, here there was no such separate bailment. Motordom's continued physical possession was solely attributable to the arrangement which constituted the sale. It was a term of the sale by Motordom to the respondent that Motordom should be entitled to retain possession of the cars for the purpose of selling them to customers. Motordom only received ninety per cent of the price on the sale to the respondent, and it cannot be argued that the sale ended at that stage. It would be absurd to suppose that either party intended Motordom to sell its stock for ninety per cent of its value without getting a right to any further benefit. The transaction by which Motordom sold the cars to the respondent was inextricably mixed with Motordom's right to keep the cars for display at its premises. In their lordships' opinion, Motordom, having sold the goods whose ownership is disputed, continued in possession of them. In spite of counsel for the respondent's arguments, their lordships cannot question the learned trial judge's conclusions as to the bona fides of the appellant and its lack of notice of the previous sale. No doubt those arguments were put to him at the trial, but, having heard and seen the witnesses, he did not accept the arguments.

Appeal allowed.

NOTES

1) Auto dealers have long looked to sales finance companies and other financial intermediaries to help them carry their inventory of new and used vehicles. In Canada, the typical instrument for providing inventory financing has been the wholesale conditional sale agreement in the case of new vehicles, and the chattel mortgage agreement in the case of used vehicles. See further, J.S. Ziegel, "The Legal Problems of Wholesale Financing of Durable Goods in Canada" (1963), 41 *Can. Bar Rev.* 54 and R.M. Goode and J.S. Ziegel, *Hire-Purchase and Conditional Sale* (1965), chapter 17. Both types of agreement are subject to the registration and other requirements of the provincial PPSAs. The Australian States, like the United Kingdom, do not have equivalent legislation. In most States, the bills of sale legislation is still in force. The bills of sale legislation requires chattel

mortgage agreements to be registered, but it does not extend to conditional sales or other forms of title retention arrangement. The bills of sale legislation has never been popular (in part due to its technical requirements) and in the inventory financing field lawyers have navigated their way round it by the use of various types of sale and leaseback or bailment agreements such as were used in the *Pacific Motor Auctions* case. See generally, R.M. Goode, *Hire-Purchase Law and Practice*, 2nd ed. (1970), chapter 28. Such subterfuges would probably not withstand attack under the Canadian PPSAs. The PPSAs catch every transaction that is in substance a security agreement, regardless of form: see OPPSA, s. 2, discussed in volume III of the previous edition of this casebook, chapter 2.

2) Note the differences in language and scope between s. 2 of the Factors Act (Ont.) and s. 25(1) of the SGA (Ont.)—differences that were crucial to the outcome in the *Pacific Motor Auctions* case. Can the contrasting philosophies be justified and, if so, on what grounds?

3) *Pacific Motor Auctions* is authority for the proposition that the seller's possession of the goods after sale must be continuous. Does this mean that any interruption of the seller's possession, however short, will exclude s. 25(1)? Does the underlying rationale of s. 25(1) require such a strict reading? Consider the following two examples.

a) A agrees to buy a used car from X, a car dealer, and pays for the car. However, X agrees to make some repairs to the car before it is delivered to A. Before A has a chance to collect it, X resells the car to B, a good faith purchaser.

b) The facts are the same as above, except that A takes away the car immediately after purchase and, as agreed, returns it after the weekend so that X can make the repairs. After the car has been returned, X resells it to B.

How will B fare under s. 25(1) in both situations?

Note that, in contrast to the facts of the *Pacific Motor Auctions* case, neither of these problems involves a security interest (A is the car owner, not a financier). Therefore SGA s. 25(1) applies, not the PPSA. The *Pacific Motor Auctions* case is important in Canada, despite the PPSAs, because of its relevance to the kinds of fact situations these problems exemplify.

Worcester Works Finance Ltd. v. Cooden Engineering Co. Ltd.

[1972] 1 QB 210, [1971] 3 All ER 708 (CA)

LORD DENNING MR: This case raises again the question of which of two innocent people should suffer owing to the fraud of a third. In June of 1966 the Cooden Engineering Co. Ltd., or their parent company, owned a Ford Zephyr motor car. A dealer called Griffiths (who turned out to be a fraud) wanted to buy it from the Cooden company. He said he had a customer to whom he wanted to resell it. The Cooden company agreed to sell it to Griffiths for the sum of £525. Griffiths gave them his cheque dated June 21, 1966, for £525. He took delivery of the car and the logbook with it. On July 14, 1966, he was registered with the registration authority as the owner of the car. In point of fact, he did not pay for the car. His cheque was returned dishonoured. But more of that hereafter.

While Griffiths still had the car, he made arrangements with the man called Millerick (whom one suspects was in the fraud) by means of which Griffiths got money from a finance company called Worcester Works Finance Ltd. Griffiths and Millerick filled up documents which on the face of them appeared to evidence the following transaction: on July 14, 1966, Griffiths invoiced this car to Worcester Works Finance Ltd. at a price of £645, less initial payment of £195, leaving £450. Worcester Finance paid the £450 to Griffiths and thus became the owners of the car. By a hire-purchase agreement dated July 18, 1966, Worcester Finance let the car on hire-purchase terms to Millerick at a total hire-purchase price of £757 7s. 6d. payable at £20 15s. 10d. a month for 26 months. Millerick signed a delivery receipt acknowledging that he had taken delivery of the car.

Those documents told a false story. Millerick never took delivery, never paid any deposit, or any instalment of hire charges. The truth was that Griffiths took the car to Millerick's house. He left it outside. He went in and got Millerick to sign the documents. Griffiths then went off in the car with the documents. He sent the documents up to the Worcester Finance company and got £450 from them on the faith of the documents. Worcester Finance did not see the car or have anything to do with it. They simply received the documents, assumed they were genuine, and paid out the £450. Griffiths retained the car in his own possession. Millerick never had it.

Let me return to the original transaction. The Cooden company had sold the car to Griffiths and received a cheque from him for £525. They presented the cheque for payment but it was dishonoured. It was re-presented and still dishonoured. It was dishonoured three times. As they had not been paid, the Cooden company on August 15, 1966, determined to repossess the car. They sent a man along to Griffith's premises. The car was still in Griffiths' custody. So the Cooden company took possession of it. So far as the Cooden company were concerned, they thought that the cheque not having been met, they were entitled to retake possession, and they did so. The man who retook it said: "We all thought it belonged to the Cooden company, because the cheque had been dishonoured." After the Cooden company had got the car back, they used it in their own fleet of self-drive cars.

Now I must return to Griffiths again. He had, as I have said, received £450 from Worcester Finance, and paid out nothing. But he did not want his fraud to be discovered. So he—no doubt in league with Millerick—kept up the hire instalments for some months. He paid some £240, but then stopped altogether. (That still left Griffiths well in hand.) After that, Griffiths kept the finance company quiet for a time by asking for a settlement figure at which Millerick could buy the car. The finance company quoted £310, being the balance of the hire-purchase price. But nothing was ever paid.

I come back now to the Cooden company. They used the car in their own fleet for a time, but afterwards let it out on hire-purchase themselves: and they registered their interest with the Hire-Purchase Information Bureau. In consequence Worcester Finance got to know that the car was in the hands of the Cooden company. Thereupon Worcester claimed that the car was theirs. Now they bring this action for damages for conversion. They have limited their claim of £315 0s. 10d., which was the balance of the hire-purchase price. Worcester Finance rely on the documents which were executed, which on the face of them give them the title to the car. They claim £315 which is the balance outstanding, recoverable in conversion.

The Cooden company in answer rely on the provisions of section 25(1) of the Sale of Goods Act 1893, which says:

. . .

The Cooden company apply that section in this way: They say that Griffiths was a person who, having sold goods to the finance company, continued in possession of them.

The judge has found (and it is no longer disputed) that when the Cooden company delivered the car and logbook to Griffiths and received the cheque for £525, that was then a completed sale to Griffiths. That was in June of 1966. So Griffiths was the owner of the car at that time and was in possession of it. Then when Griffiths on July 14, 1966, invoiced the car to Worcester Finance, he was "a person who had sold goods" to the finance company: and was thus within the opening words of section 25(1). So far there is no difference between the parties.

The question is whether Griffiths comes within the words: was he a person who "continues or is in possession of the goods." The material word here is "continues." The words "or is" have been explained in a New Zealand case—*Mitchell v. Jones* (1905), 24 NZLR 932—which was approved by the Privy Council in *Pacific Motor Auctions Pty. Ltd. v. Motor Credits (Hire Finance) Ltd.*, [1965] AC 867. They refer only to a case where a person who sold the goods had not got the goods when he sold them, but they came into his possession afterwards. Those words "or is" do not apply to this case, because Griffiths, at the time when he sold the car to Worcester Finance, was already in possession of it. The only relevant word is therefore "continues." Was Griffiths a person who, having sold goods, "continues in possession of the goods"?

Mr. Jacob, who appears for Worcester Finance, submits that the words "continues in possession" mean continues in *lawful* possession. He says that, after Griffiths sold the car to the finance company, he ought to have delivered it to the hirer Millerick: and that, by retaining it himself, he retained it unlawfully; and he was, vis-à-vis the finance company, a trespasser. He was in possession of it without their consent at all. In support of this contention Mr. Jacob relied on two cases: *Staffs Motor Guarantee Ltd. v. British Wagon Co. Ltd.*, [1934] 2 KB 305, applied in this court in *Eastern Distributors Ltd. v. Goldring (Murphy, Third Party)*, [1957] 2 QB 600. In those cases it was held that the words "continues in possession" mean continues in possession as seller and not as bailee: and accordingly, if the person who had sold goods continued in possession as a bailee, he did not "continue in possession" within the meaning of the section. But those cases are no longer good law. They were disapproved by the Privy Council in *Pacific Motor Auctions Pty. Ltd. v. Motor Credits (Hire Finance) Ltd.*, [1965] AC 867: and, although decisions of the Privy Council are not binding in this court, nevertheless when the Privy Council disapprove of a previous decision of this court, or cast doubt on it, then we are at liberty to depart from previous decision. I am glad to depart from those earlier cases and to follow the Privy Council. The words "continues in possession" refer to the continuity of physical possession regardless of any private transactions between the seller and purchaser which might alter the legal title under which the possession was held: *per* Lord Pearce, at 888.

It does not matter what private arrangement may be made by the seller with the purchaser—such as whether the seller remains bailee or trespasser, or whether he is lawfully in possession or not. It is sufficient if he remains continuously in possession of the goods that he has sold to the purchaser. If so, he can pass a good title to a bona fide third person, and the original purchaser will be ousted. But there must be a continuity of physical possession. If there is a substantial break in the continuity, as for instance, if the seller actually delivers over the goods to a purchaser who keeps them for a time, and then the seller afterwards gets them back, then the section might not apply.

Applying these principles it is plain that Griffiths was a person who, having sold goods to the finance company, "continued in possession" of them until the time when they were retaken by the Cooden company.

The next question is whether the retaking by the Cooden company was "the delivery or transfer" by Griffiths of the goods to the Cooden company under a "disposition" thereof. Griffiths did not actually deliver or transfer the car to the Cooden company. But he acquiesced in their retaking it. That was, I think, tantamount to a delivery or transfer by him. But was it under a "disposition" thereof?

Mr. Jacob argued that there was no disposition here: there was, he said, only a retaking by the Cooden company. To my mind the word "disposition" is a very wide word. In *Carter v. Carter*, [1896] 1 Ch. 62, at 67, Stirling J said that it extends "to all acts by which a new interest (legal or equitable) in the property is effectually created." That was under an entirely different statute, but I would apply that wide meaning in this section. When the Cooden company retook this car (because the cheque had not been met) there was clearly a transfer back to them of property in the goods. They would not thereafter be able to sue on the cheque. By retaking the goods they impliedly gave up their remedy on the cheque. That retransfer of the property back to the Cooden company was a "disposition" within the section.

The last question is whether at the time when the Cooden company retook the car they received "the same in good faith and without notice of the previous sale," that is, without notice of the sale by Griffiths to the finance company. The word "notice" here means actual notice, that is to say, knowledge of the sale or deliberately turning a blind eye to it. Our commercial law does not like constructive notice. It will have nothing to do with it. I am quite clear that the Cooden company acted in good faith without notice of the sale to the finance company. They had sold a car and been given a dud cheque for it; and were just retaking it.

So all the requisites of section 25(1) are satisfied. The retaking by the Cooden company has the same effect as if it was expressly authorised by Worcester Finance. It is equivalent to a transfer by Griffiths back to the Cooden company with the express authority of the finance company. So the Cooden company acquired a good title to the car.

This result is consonant with the object of section 25. Worcester Finance did not see the car at all. They did not take possession of it. They simply received documents from the dealer Griffiths and handed out money to him. They relied on his honesty. He was dishonest. He got £450 out of them by a trick. In contrast, the Cooden company actually had possession of the car, sold it to Griffiths, and when his cheque was dishonoured, they retook it. Plainly as a matter of commercial good sense the title should remain in the Cooden company and not in Worcester Finance. The Cooden company are protected by section 25. The car is theirs.

I think the judge was right in the conclusion to which he came, and I would dismiss the appeal.

Appeal dismissed.

[Concurring judgments were delivered by Phillimore and Megaw LJJ.]

NOTES

1) SGA s. 25(1), unlike SGA s. 25(2), does not require the seller to be in possession of the goods with the buyer's permission or knowledge. Does this distinction make sense?

2) *Vowles v. Island Finances Ltd.*, [1940] 4 DLR 357 (BCCA) anticipated the decision in *Worcester Works Finance*. The facts were as follows. M, an auto dealer, entered into a conditional sale agreement with H for the sale of a vehicle. M assigned the agreement to I and the agreement was registered under British Columbia's Conditional Sales Act. H did not take delivery of the car and M, in whose possession it remained, sold it to V under a cash sale. I seized the car from V and V sued for its recovery, or alternatively its value. The British Columbia Court of Appeal held, among other things, that the assignment from M to I constituted a sale and that, since I had not taken possession of the vehicle, V was entitled to invoke the seller in possession provision of the British Columbia SGA. The court assumed, apparently without argument, that the seller in possession provision was intended to apply to the assignment of a financing agreement, but this is debatable. Does the history of the provision, as related in the *Pacific Motor Auctions* case, throw any light on the issue? If the same facts arose today, they would be governed by the PPSA. In Ontario, the main relevant provisions are OPPSA ss. 21(2) (assignment of security interests), 25(1) (continuation of security interest in proceeds) and 28(1) (transactions in the ordinary course of business): see volume III of the previous edition of this casebook, especially chapter 9.

3) The Ontario bills of sale legislation was repealed in 1989: Personal Property Security Act, SO 1989, c. 16, s. 84(1). For discussion of the relationship between SGA s. 25(2) and the bills of sale legislation, see the third edition of this casebook, volume III, at 425-26. See also Comment, "Repeal of Bills of Sale Legislation" (1984), 9 *CBLJ* 117. For the OLRC's recommendations, see Sales Report, at 302-5.

BUYER IN POSSESSION

Helby v. Matthews

[1895] AC 471 (HL)

See chapter 2, *supra*.

Shaw v. Commissioner of Police of the Metropolis

[1987] 3 All ER 405 (CA)

LLOYD LJ: Mr. Natalegawa, a student from Indonesia, acquired a red Porsche motor car, for which he paid £16,750. In March 1984 he decided to return home to complete his studies. So on 6 April 1984 he advertised the car for sale in the Evening Standard. The price was £17,250. On 15 April a man calling himself Jonathan London spoke to him on the telephone. He said he was a car dealer who was interested in purchasing the car on behalf of a client. On 16 April Mr. Natalegawa, who I shall refer to as "the claimant," let him have the car. On 1 May Mr. London agreed to sell the car to another car dealer, Mr. Tom Shaw. Mr. Shaw trades in association with Nidd Vale Motors Ltd. I shall refer to them together as "the plaintiffs." The price was £11,500. It was to be paid by a banker's draft for £10,000, and the balance in cash. The plaintiffs obtained a banker's draft dated 1 May from the Midland Bank, made out in favour of Mr. London. The following day a representative of the plaintiffs met Mr. London. They drove together in the car to a bank in Chiswick, where Mr. London had opened an account the previous week. The plaintiffs' representative gave Mr. London the banker's draft. Mr. London took it into the bank, and attempted to cash it. But the bank was unwilling to give him cash, whereupon Mr. London disappeared, and has not been seen since.

In due course the police were called, and took possession of the car. The banker's draft has never been cashed. Within a few days Midland Bank reimbursed the plaintiffs with the amount of the draft, against the plaintiffs' undertaking to indemnify the bank should the draft be presented hereafter. The date of the indemnity is 5 May 1984.

On 30 October 1984 the plaintiffs commenced proceedings against the Metropolitan Police Commissioner claiming that the car belonged to them. In December 1984 the police issued an interpleader summons. On 28 January 1985 Master Grant ordered an issue to be tried. Lengthy affidavits were sworn on either side. On 7 October 1986 Master Grant, in a judgment of which we only have a note, but which, even from the note, appears to have been exceptionally careful and clear, decided the issue in favour of the claimant. He added the comment that he was glad that the law should, in this case, accord with justice.

It is, of course, a frequent occurrence that the courts have to decide which of two innocent parties is to suffer by the fraud of a third. In *Central Newbury Car Auctions Ltd. v. Unity Finance Ltd.*, [1956] 3 All ER 905 at 909, [1957] 1 QB 371 at 379 Denning LJ described it as the "ever-recurring question" and "the familiar contest between the original owner who had been deceived into parting with his property, and the innocent purchaser who has been deceived into buying it." In such cases it is often very difficult to say where justice lies. What makes the present case unique in my experience is that the plaintiffs, so far from suffering as a result of London's fraud will, if they succeed, have obtained a car without having had to pay for it. If they fail, they will have suffered nothing except the loss of their bargain. They are not a penny out of pocket. They still have the £1,500 in cash, and although there is a theoretical possibility that they might have to honour the indemnity which they gave in favour of the Midland Bank, the chances of that happening in practice must now be regarded as extremely remote. So it is not surprising that the master regarded his decision in favour of the claimant in the present case as according with the justice of the case.

Counsel for the plaintiffs, who argued a difficult case with great skill, accepted that the burden was on him to show that the property in the car had passed to the plaintiffs. He sought to discharge that burden in two stages. First, by submitting that London had bought, or agreed to buy, the car from the claimant, and second by relying on s. 25 of the Sale of Goods Act 1979. That section provides:

> (1) Where a person having bought or agreed to buy goods obtains, with the consent of the seller, possession of the goods or the documents of title to the goods, the delivery or transfer by that person, or by a mercantile agent acting for him, of the goods or documents of title, under any sale, pledge, or other disposition thereof, to any person receiving the same in good faith and without notice of any lien or other right of the original seller in respect of the goods, has the same effect as if the person making the delivery or transfer were a mercantile agent in possession of the goods or documents of title with the consent of the owner ...

As to the first step in the argument of counsel for the plaintiff, there was a good deal of evidence from which the master might have inferred that the claimant had sold the car to Mr. London. Thus on 1 May, shortly before Mr. London agreed to sell to the plaintiffs, the claimant gave Mr. London, at London's request, a letter in the following terms:

> This letter serves to certify that I, A.D.H. NATALEGAWA Have sold the Porsche 3.3 *TURBO* Registration number NVS 958V to MR. JONATHAN LONDON of ... and from the date shown below no longer have any legal responsibility connected with that car. [Signed] A.D.H. NATALEGAWA 18 March 1984.

The claimant also signed the notification of sale or transfer slip attached to the car registration certificate showing that he had sold the car to Mr. London on 18 March 1984, in return for which Mr. London gave the claimant a postdated cheque in the sum of £17,250 which subsequently proved to be valueless. Even if the claimant had originally dealt with Mr. London as an agent, or intermediary, the documents to which I have just referred show, according to counsel, that the claimant was "backing it both ways"; in other words, if Mr. London should fail to find a buyer for the car, then he had agreed to buy the car himself. Counsel for the plaintiffs relied on a statement taken by the police on 3 May 1984, in which the claimant said, in unambiguous terms, that he was selling the car to London, and that he had accepted the cheque as payment.

The difficulty with that argument is that it is contrary to the claimant's affidavit, in which he was equally specific that Mr. London was acting as his agent in respect of the sale at all material times, and that he had not in fact sold the car to him as a purchaser.

These inconsistencies could have been explored if the plaintiffs had applied to cross-examine the claimant on his affidavit. But they did not. In those circumstances the master was entitled to accept the evidence contained in the claimant's affidavit, in preference to the statement which he had previously given to the police. The master held that there never was a purported sale between the claimant and London. I see no ground on which we ought to interfere with that finding.

It follows that Mr. London never bought or agreed to buy the car, and that the argument of counsel for the plaintiffs fails at the first stage. Since s. 25 only applies, according to its terms, when a person has bought or agreed to buy goods, the second stage of the argument does not arise. But for completeness I should add the following points.

(i) It was not suggested that Mr. London was a mercantile agent acting in the ordinary course of business so as to enable him to pass a good title under s. 2 of the Factors Act 1889, irrespective of s. 25 of the 1979 Act.

(ii) I would respectfully disagree with the master's view that the car registration certificate and the other documents to which I have referred were documents of title. In *Joblin v. Watkins & Roseveare (Motors) Ltd.*, [1949] 1 All ER 47 it was held that a car registration book is not a document of title; see also *Pearson v. Rose & Young Ltd.*, [1950] 2 All ER 1027 at 1033, [1951] 1 KB 275 at 289 per Denning L.J and *Central Newbury Car Auctions Ltd. v. United Finance Ltd.*, [1956] 3 All ER 905 at 914, [1957] 1 QB 371 at 387 per Hodson LJ.

(iii) Since preparing this judgment I have read the very recent judgment of the Court of Appeal in *National Employers Mutual General Insurance Association Ltd. v. Jones*, [1987] 3 All ER 385, in which it fell to the court to consider s. 25 in some detail. However, there is nothing in that decision which throws any light on the present case.

That brings me to the only point of difficulty in the case. If the plaintiffs cannot rely on s. 25 of the 1979 Act, are they nevertheless entitled to rely on s. 21? That section provides:

> (1) Subject to this Act, where goods are sold by a person who is not their owner, and who does not sell them under the authority or with the consent of the owner, the buyer acquires no better title to the goods than the seller had, unless the owner of the goods is by his conduct precluded from denying the seller's authority to sell ...

Counsel for the plaintiffs submits that the claimant is precluded by his conduct from denying Mr. London's authority to sell, since he represented that Mr. London had been the owner of the car since 18 March 1984, and that the plaintiffs relied on that representation. Counsel did not develop the point at any great length, and did not cite any authority. Nevertheless it deserves attention.

In *Central Newbury Car Auctions Ltd. v. United Finance Ltd.* it was decided that the mere possession by an intermediate seller of the car and the registration book with the consent of the owner does not preclude the owner from asserting his title.

The owner does not thereby represent that the intermediate seller has authority to sell. But here the facts go much further. The signature of the notification of sale or transfer slip, and above all, the document stating in so many words that the claimant had sold the car to Mr. London, is the clearest possible representation, intended to be relied on by the ultimate purchaser, that the claimant had transferred the ownership to Mr. London. So far as any representation goes, therefore, the case comes within the principles stated in *Henderson & Co. v. Williams*, [1895] 1 QB 521 and *Eastern Distributors Ltd. v. Goldring*, [1957] 2 All ER 525, [1957] 2 QB 600; and, if the plaintiffs had bought the car, I should have held that they had acquired a good title against the claimant, and, in practice, against all the world, by virtue of s. 21 of the 1979 Act or, alternatively, by virtue of common law estoppel by representation, if it be different.

But the critical factor in the present case is that the plaintiffs did not buy the car. They agreed to buy it. It was expressly, and in my view rightly, conceded that the property in the car was not intended to pass until Mr. London was paid. So when Mr. London went into the bank to cash the banker's draft, the moment had not yet come when the property was to pass from Mr. London to the plaintiffs. That moment never did come. Does that make a difference? The master has held that it does. In my view he was right.

The meaning of the word "sold" in the phrase "where goods are sold" in s. 21 of the 1979 Act does not appear to have been considered in any decided case or text book, except by Professor Atiyah in *Sale of Goods* (7th edn, 1985) p. 266 and Professor Guest in *Benjamin's Sale of Goods* (2nd edn, 1981) p. 465. Professor Atiyah says: "It may be that the words 'where goods are sold' must be given their strict significance and do not cover cases of an agreement to sell." The authority cited in *Anderson v. Ryan*, [1967] IR 34. In that case a car dealer agreed to sell a car to which he had no title. But he obtained title before he delivered the car. It was argued that the buyer could have no better title than the seller had had at the time of the agreement. Not surprisingly, that argument was rejected. I doubt if that decision helps much either way in the present case.

Professor Guest expresses the view in *Benjamin's Sale of Goods* p. 465, n. 31 that the principle stated in s. 21 applies not only to sale, but also where goods are pledged or otherwise disposed of for value to a third party. But there is no suggestion that the section applies to an agreement to sell. On principle, it seems to me that s. 21 does not apply to an agreement to sell. It can only apply where the intermediate seller has purported to transfer the property in the goods, whether the general property or perhaps the special property. Section 21 is the first of a group of six sections, all of which are concerned with the transfer of title. Thus s. 22 provides that a buyer who buys in a market overt acquires a good title, provided he buys in good faith without notice of any want of title on the part of the seller. Section 23 makes similar provision in the case of a buyer who buys from a seller with a voidable title. It was no doubt for the same reason that the phrase "sale, pledge, or other disposition" in ss. 24 and 25 was held by the Court of Appeal to be confined to cases where there had been a transfer of property, or some interest in property. Transfer of possession is not enough: see *Worcester Works Finance Ltd. v. Cooden Engineering Co. Ltd.*, [1971] 3 All ER 708 at 714, [1972] 1 QB 210 at 220, where Megaw LJ said: "'Disposition' must involve some transfer of an interest in property, in the technical sense of the word 'property,' as contrasted with mere possession."

If that is true of the word "disposition" in ss. 24 and 25 of the 1979 Act, a word which, as a matter of ordinary usage, is capable of a very wide meaning, it must be equally true of the word "sale" in s. 21 of the Act. So I would hold that "sale" in s. 21 does not include an agreement to sell, which, by definition, involves no transfer of property: see s. 2(5) of the 1979 Act. Since it is conceded that the transaction between Mr. London and the plaintiffs never got beyond an agreement to sell, it must follow that s. 21 does not apply.

The second half of s. 21 and ss. 22 to 25 are all statutory exceptions to the rule nemo dat quod non habet, a rule which is expressed in statutory form in the first half of s. 21. In the present case the plaintiffs fail, not because they cannot bring themselves within any of the exceptions to the rule (though they fail for that reason also in the case of s. 25), but for the more fundamental reason that Mr. London never even purported to give what he did not have. If he had purported to transfer the property in the car, then I should have held, as I have already said, that the case fell within *Henderson & Co. v. Williams*, [1895] 1 QB 521 and *Eastern Distributors Ltd. v. Goldring*, [1957] 2 All ER 525, [1957] 2 QB 600. But as he never purported to transfer the property, neither s. 21 nor common law estoppel helps. ...

Appeal dismissed.

[Stocker and Fox LJJ concurred in Lloyd JA's judgment.]

Newtons of Wembley Ltd. v. Williams

[1965] 1 QB 560, [1964] 3 WLR 888 (CA)

[The plaintiffs sold a 1960 model Sunbeam Rapier to one Marks, who registered it on November 23, 1959. Marks sold the car back to the plaintiffs in part exchange for another car on January 22, 1962. On June 15, 1962, the plaintiffs sold the car to one Andrew in return for a cheque, for £735. The written contract of sale provided that the property in the car was not to pass to Andrew until the plaintiffs had received the whole of the purchase price, and if payment as made by cheque until clearance of the cheque. Andrew drove away the car, and was registered as owner of it with the Middlesex County Council on the same day. On Monday, June 18, 1962, the plaintiffs were told by their bank that Andrew's cheque would not be met. The plaintiffs sent a "stop" notice to the Hire Purchase Information Bureau and authorised two men to trace and seize the car. The men were not successful. The plaintiffs also informed the police.

In July, 1962, one Biss came to London from Wincanton in order to purchase a car for himself. He went to Warren Street which was a regular centre for dealings in used cars. Biss met Andrew, who was a complete stranger to him, and agreed to buy the car for £550, which he paid in cash. Biss took the car to Wincanton, and on July 12 sold it to the defendant, who was also a car dealer, in return for a cheque for £505.

Later in July an employee of the defendant offered the car in part exchange to Douglas Seaton (Yeovil) Ltd., who communicated with the Hire Purchase Information Bureau. They informed the plaintiffs of the car's whereabouts. The defendant refused the plaintiff's demand for the return of the car. Andrew was sought by the police on a variety of charges and on September 14, he pleaded guilty inter alia, to obtaining the Sunbeam Rapier from the plaintiffs by means of false pretences.

The plaintiffs brought action against the defendant in detinue for the return of the car or its value and, alternatively, for damages for conversion.]

Sellers LJ stated the facts relating to the sale of the car to Andrew and continued: When the plaintiffs found on Monday, June 18, 1962, that the cheque was not to be met and that there was no probability of it being met as the bank account or accounts of the man Andrew were not in funds and there were many claims against them, they sought at once to recover the car and to rescind the contract. The judge found [1964] 1 WLR 1028, at 1032 that they took all the available steps they could to recover the car and disaffirm the sale, and that the contract between the plaintiffs and Andrew was rescinded on or about June 20—rescinded by the unequivocal acts or conduct of the plaintiffs, applying the decision of this court in *Car & Universal Finance Co. Ltd. v. Caldwell*, [1964] 2 WLR 600: so that, whether the title to the car had ever passed to Andrew or not, it being a case clearly of false pretences as the judge found, the title had re-vested in the plaintiffs by June 20, 1962. It may well be that the intention of the parties, if this was viewed as a bona fide transaction, was that the property in the car, the title to the car, had not passed in any case because it was not to pass by reason of a clause which provided that payment should be made on or before delivery and that until clearance of cheque or receipt of cash for the full purchase price by the plaintiffs the vehicle would remain their property. But it matters not: by June 20 the ownership of the car was with the plaintiffs. [His Lordship stated the facts occurring after June 20, 1962, and continued:] Both parties have claimed the car in these proceedings, and the matter came for consideration before Davies LJ, sitting at first instance as an additional judge of the Queen's Bench Division. He found that the defendant was entitled to retain the car. The plaintiffs appeal from that decision and seek to establish before this court that the defendant has no title to the car. The title he seeks to advance is the title of Biss, when Biss was the buyer, or the purported buyer, of the car from Andrew in the Warren Street market on or about July 6, 1962.

Quite clearly, at common law, Andrew at that date had no title to give, and at common law Biss obtained no title. It was submitted before us that at that stage Andrew was a complete stranger in this matter, that the case is clear, and that possession should be given to the plaintiffs, or damages in lieu thereof. But in fact Andrew was not a complete stranger. Andrew had in fact the possession of the car, which had been given to him or which he had obtained when he acquired the car on the handing over of the cheque on June 15.

In those circumstances, notwithstanding the position at common law—or because of it—the defendant has relied on the Factors Act, 1889 [RSO 1970, c. 156]; and the question which arises in this case is whether the transaction between Andrew and Biss can be brought within the provisions of that Act.

I turn first to section 9. It is one of two sections, sections 8 and 9, dealing with dispositions by sellers and buyers of goods, section 8 dealing with the disposition by a seller remaining in possession, section 9 with disposition by a buyer obtaining possession.[2] [His Lordship read section 9 and continued:] Andrew had bought the goods and obtained them with the consent of the plaintiffs. He had subsequently delivered them on a sale to Biss and, if Biss was a person receiving the same in good faith and without notice of any lien or other right of the original seller, then this section provides that the transaction shall have the same effect as if the person making the delivery, i.e., Andrew, were a mercantile agent in possession of the goods or documents of title with the consent of the owner. So the first part of section 9 is complied with on the facts of this case, and the question arises whether the second part, the receiving of the goods in good faith (and it is not suggested that Biss had notice of any lien or other right of the original seller), had been complied with, and whether, treating Andrew as a mercantile agent, the requirements of section 9 in that respect have been complied with.

That requires a consideration in the first place of the question: What is a mercantile agent? In section 1(1) [Ont. s. 1(1)(c)]:

> The expression "mercantile agent" shall mean a mercantile agent having in the customary course of his business as such agent authority either to sell goods, or to consign goods for the purpose of sale, or to buy goods, or to raise money on the security of goods.

That description is to be applied to Andrew on the facts of this case.

Section 2(1) concerns the powers of a mercantile agent with respect to the disposition of goods thus.

> Where a mercantile agent is, with the consent of the owner, in possession of goods ... any sale ... made by him when acting in the ordinary course of business of a mercantile agent, shall, subject to the provisions of this Act, be as valid as if he were expressly authorised by the owner of the goods to make the same; provided that the person taking under the disposition acts in good faith, and has not at the time of the disposition notice that a person making the disposition has not authority to make the same.

One of the points taken by the plaintiffs was that although at the outset Andrew was a person who had obtained, with the consent of the seller, possession of the goods, at the time when this transaction took place that consent no longer operated: it had been withdrawn by the rescission of the contract. But Andrew was in possession of the goods of the plaintiffs, a possession which he had obtained at the outset with their consent. Section 2(2) provides that "Where a mercantile agent has, with the consent of the owner, been in possession of goods ... any sale ... which would have been valid if the consent had continued, shall be valid notwithstanding the determination of the consent. ..." That is an express provision which altered the law as it had been laid down in an earlier case, *Fuentes v. Montis* (1868), LR 3 CP 268; aff'd. LR 4 CP

---

2   These sections do not appear in the Ontario Factors Act, but almost identical provisions appear in the Ontario SGA, ss. 25(1) and (2). [eds.]

93, some time in 1868. Notwithstanding that which the plaintiffs had done to terminate their contract and withdraw their consent, they had in fact—true, through inability to do otherwise—left the possession of their car with Andrew.

The only other question which arises is how far section 9, on its true construction, takes the ultimate sub-buyer (the defendant in the present case), relying, as he does, on what happened between Andrew and Biss. The judge treated section 9 as placing Andrew in the position of a mercantile agent, but with the obligation on the defendant of establishing not only that Biss took in good faith (I leave out the other requirement of no notice of the plaintiffs' rights; nothing arose on that), but also that in the transaction between Andrew and Biss (Andrew being treated as a mercantile agent in accordance with section 9), Andrew was "acting in the ordinary course of business of a mercantile agent." There is a possible construction, which was urged upon us by the defendant, that Andrew must be deemed to be acting under section 9 as a mercantile agent, and it must be assumed or deemed that he was acting in the ordinary course of business of a mercantile agent; and investigations were made in other parts of the Act of 1889, in particular section 8, to see whether any support could be had for that view.

Section 8 makes a different provision. It states that where a person, having sold goods, continues, or is, in possession of the goods and then sells them, then, providing the person who receives them does so in good faith and without notice of the previous sale, the transaction will have "the same effect as if the person making the delivery or transfer were expressly authorised by the owner of the goods to make the same." The words are different in section 9, and for myself I do not find much help, on constructing section 9, from looking at section 8, except for the fact that since they are different they are intended to have a different effect.

Before one takes too favourable a view for the sub-buyer and too harsh a view against the true owner of the goods as to the cases where section 9 can be invoked, one must remember that it is taking away a right which would have existed at common law, and for myself I should not be prepared to enlarge it more than the words clearly permitted and required. It seems to me that all section 9 can be said clearly to do is to place the buyer in possession in the position of a mercantile agent when he has in fact in his possession the goods of somebody else, and it does no more than clothe him with that fictitious or notional position on any disposition of those goods. Section 2(1) makes it clear that the sub-buyer from a mercantile agent, to whom that section applies, has in order to obtain the full advantage of the subsection, to establish that the mercantile agent was acting in the ordinary course of business. It is said that that is a somewhat vague phrase, and we have been referred to some authorities with regard to that. It may be that in some cases precisely what is in "the ordinary course of business" of a mercantile agent may call for some special investigation, but on the face of it it seems to me that it envisages a transaction by a mercantile agent and is to be derived from such evidence as is either known to the court or established by evidence as to what would be the ordinary course of business.

We were referred to *Oppenheimer v. Attenborough & Son*, [1908] 1 KB 221 (CA). That was a case on a different point as to the range of the business; and the meaning of "in the ordinary course of business" was considered in the judgment, but I need not refer any further to it.

The question arises here on the evidence whether this transaction is to be said to have been in the ordinary course of business of a mercantile agent. Counsel for the plaintiffs sought to establish that a transaction taking place in this somewhat unusual market, the street kerb in Warren Street, was, on the face of it, something which was not an ordinary business transaction in any way, by a mercantile agent or anybody else, but was to some extent suspect. But the judge had evidence about this and he said and I think it is within the knowledge of the court, that there had been an established market in secondhand cars in this area on this very site for a long time. Although he said that he had some doubt at one time about the sale to Biss being in the ordinary course of business, for, as he pointed out, there were no business premises, the sale was in the street, and it was for cash, yet he came to the conclusion, which I think cannot be challenged, that there was in Warren Street and its neighbourhood an established street market for cash dealing in cars. When one looks at what took place in that area and finds the prospective buyer coming up and getting into contact with the prospective seller in regard to a car, with an offer and an acceptance, trial of the car and a looking over it and some questions asked and a delivery—I do not find anything to indicate that it was not in the ordinary course of business of a mercantile agent. It seems to me that the defendant has established that essential fact.

That leaves only the other matter which has to be proved, likewise by the defendant, as to whether Biss acted in good faith. If he did, then the requirements of section 9 are complete, and the result follows that he obtained a good title, as if the goods had been sold to him with the consent of the plaintiffs.

[Sellers LJ reviewed the evidence and concluded:]

I think that that was established, and I would dismiss this appeal.

Appeal dismissed.

[Concurring judgments were delivered by the other members of the court.]

NOTES

1) The buyer in possession provision was instrumental in the shaping of secured financing patterns in the United Kingdom. It led to the emergence of the hire-purchase agreement. The House of Lords confirmed in *Helby v. Matthews, supra* chapter 2, that a properly drawn hire-purchase agreement is not an agreement under which the hirer buys or agrees to buy goods and so the section does not apply and the owner's title is safe. Note how the court in *Helby v. Matthews* distinguished *Lee v. Butler*. Hire-purchase did not achieve the same popularity in Canada. This is because the provinces enacted conditional sales legislation at an early date, and this served to entrench the conditional sales agreement as the preferred method of transacting. See further, note 5, below.

2) For discussion of the *Newtons'* case from Canadian perspectives, see Comment (1965), 43 *Can. Bar Rev.* 639 and *GMAC v. Hubbard* (1978), 87 DLR (3d) 39 (NBCA).

3) In *Brandon v. Leckie; Avco Corp. v. Borgal* (1972), 29 DLR (3d) 633; [1972] 6 WWR 113 (Alta. SC), a mobile home was stolen from each of the plaintiffs. Subsequently, they were purchased by a Calgary auto dealer from one G. Young. The dealer in turn sold the mobile homes to the defendants who acquired them in good faith. The true owners sought to recover the homes in the hands of the defendants or damages in lieu thereof. It was admitted that the dealer was not a buyer in possession of the goods with the consent of the true owners, but it was argued that this did not matter because the concluding words of the Alberta equivalent of s. 25(2) provide that a disposition by a buyer in possession of the goods (which, it was argued, the dealer was, vis-à-vis the person from whom he bought the homes) has the same effect as if the person making the delivery were in possession of the goods "with the consent of the owner." The defendants contended that "owner" should be given its literal meaning. What result? See also *McCallem v. Goldman* (1983), 38 OR (2d) 436 (Co. Ct.) where the same issue arose and *Brandon v. Leckie* was followed.

In the United Kingdom the issue was regarded as sufficiently important to require the attention of the House of Lords. In *National Employers Mutual General Insurance Association Ltd. v. Jones*, [1990] 2 AC 24, the dispute was over title to a Ford Fiesta car which had belonged to a Miss Hopkins. The car was stolen from her, sold by the thief, and then passed through several hands by purchase and sale until it was bought in good faith by Jones for £2,650. Miss Hopkins' insurers indemnified her for the loss of her car and so acquired her rights to the car. They demanded the car back from Jones. He refused and this action ensued. The county court judge found in favour of the appellants. Jones appealed and a divided Court of Appeal affirmed. A unanimous House of Lords also affirmed.

Jones's defence was that he was protected by s. 25(1) of the UK Sale of Goods Act 1979 (formerly s. 25(2) of the 1893 Act) since the subsection conferred on the innocent purchaser the same protection as if the person making the delivery or transfer were a mercantile agent in possession of the goods or documents of title "*with the consent of the owner.*" Speaking for the House of Lords, Lord Goff rejected the argument that there was any evidence that Parliament intended the quoted words to mean anything more than that the goods or document of title must have been entrusted to the buyer with the seller's consent from whom the third party acquired the goods. After a careful examination of the history of the British Factors Act and s. 25 of the Sale of Goods Act, Lord Goff concluded (at p. 432):

> For s. 9 to have any such effect would constitute a change in policy of a fundamental kind, of which there is no evidence whatsoever in the remainder of the 1889 Act. I add for good measure that, when, in 1893, s. 9 was effectively incorporated (with changes which are immaterial for present purposes) as s. 25(2) of the Sale of Goods Act 1893, it was incorporated into an Act of Parliament which expressly maintained the fundamental principle *nemo dat quod non habet* in s. 21(1) of the Act (now s. 21(1) of the 1979 Act). The succeeding sections enact what appear to be minor exceptions to that fundamental principle; yet, if the appellant's contention were to be correct, s. 25(2) would have made not so much an exception to the principle, but would have substantially amounted to a reversal of it.

4) *Gamer's Motor Centre (Newcastle) Pty. Ltd. v. Natwest Wholesale Australia Pty. Ltd.* (1987), 163 CLR 236 concerned a floor plan for the financing of a dealer's secondhand

car inventory similar to the arrangement in the *Pacific Motor Auctions* case. Cars in the dealer's inventory were sold to the respondent finance company and bailed back to the dealer without ever leaving the dealer's possession. The dealer acquired a number of cars from the appellant under a conditional sales agreement. It then purported to sell them to the respondent pursuant to the floor plan arrangement. The appellant and respondent each claimed title to the cars. The issue was whether the buyer in possession provision (s. 28(2) of the New South Wales SGA) applied in the respondent's favour. There was no doubt that the dealer fitted the description of a "person having bought or agreed to buy goods" (compare *Lee v. Butler*, *supra*). However, the dealer had remained in possession of the cars at all relevant times. How could it be said that there was a "delivery or transfer" to the respondent as required by the subsection? A majority of the Australian High Court held that constructive (or symbolic) delivery was sufficient. According to Mason CJ (at 250), constructive delivery occurred in the following way:

> the dealer, having agreed to buy and having taken possession of the vehicles from Gamer, then delivered the receipts to Natwest against which cheques were subsequently drawn in favour of the dealer. ... The delivery receipt had a dual operation. When read with the agreement, it evidenced the terms of the agreement for sale to Natwest, that agreement being made on delivery of the receipt, and acknowledged that the dealer held the vehicle for and on behalf of Natwest. And the receipt also operated as an acknowledgment that the dealer held the vehicle as bailee for Natwest pursuant to the agreement. ... The delivery of the receipt is something apart from the sale so that the constructive delivery which it evidences is something more than a mere change in the right to possession arising from the sale from the dealer to Natwest.

There is strong authority for saying that for the buyer in possession provision to apply, the buyer (X) must take actual delivery of the goods from or with the consent of the true owner (A). Constructive possession is not enough. The High Court in *Gamers* was at pains to emphasize that delivery by X to the purchaser (B) is a different question. Why is it a different question? In terms of the policy underlying the section, why should actual possession be necessary in the one context but not the other?

5) Before the adoption of the PPSAs by the Canadian provinces, starting with the full proclamation of the Ontario PPSA in 1976, instalment sales of durable goods whereby the buyer obtained possession of the goods and the seller retained title until the price had been fully paid were governed by conditional sales legislation. This required registration of the conditional sale agreement where the buyer was allowed to obtain possession of the goods before title passed. There was a conflict between this legislation and SGA s. 25(2). Most of the provincial conditional sales acts or ordinances were adopted before the turn of the 20th century and, in most cases, long before the provinces adopted the British Sale of Goods Act. The unspoken assumption was that, if the seller complied with the registration requirements, the seller retained good title against third parties as well as against the buyer since the *nemo dat* rule was the governing rule in the 19th century and the seller had done what was required of him to give notice of his interest to the world. SGA s. 25(2) was totally inconsistent with this philosophy and had the Canadian legislators been on their toes they would have noticed the conflict and dealt with it. Even so, it is surprising that some Canadian courts were willing to give primacy to the mandate of

s. 25(2) without any serious attempt to examine the history and philosophy of the registration requirements. See Ziegel, "Registration Statutes and the Doctrine of Constructive Notice" (1985), 63 *Can. Bar Rev.* 629.

All this should now be part of commercial law history. When the OPPSA was first adopted in 1967 (although not fully proclaimed until 1976), a new s. 25(3) was also added to the SGA providing that s. 25(2) does not apply to goods the possession of which has been obtained by a buyer under a security agreement whereby the seller retains a security interest under the OPPSA. Inexplicably, however, the subsection was never proclaimed! Fortunately, the conditional seller had another bow to her string since s. 69 of the OPPSA (now s. 73) also provided that where there is a conflict between the OPPSA and any other general or special Act (other than the Consumer Protection Act), the provisions of the OPPSA were to prevail. The old OPPSA also contained conflict of laws provisions dealing with goods brought into Ontario which were subject to an extraprovincial security interest and requiring reperfection of the security interest in Ontario. These provisions also appear, in a revised form, in ss. 5 to 8 of the current OPPSA, and are discussed in volume III of the previous edition of this casebook. The other provincial PPSAs have similar provisions.

VOIDABLE TITLE

Lewis v. Averay

[1972] 1 QB 198 (CA)

LORD DENNING MR: This is another case where one of two innocent persons has to suffer for the fraud of a third. It will no doubt interest students and find its place in the textbooks.

Mr. Lewis is a young man who is a post-graduate student of chemistry. He lives at Clifton near Bristol. He had an Austin Cooper "S" motor car. He decided to sell it. He put an advertisement in the newspaper offering it for £450. On May 8, 1969, in reply to the advertisement a man—I will simply call him the "rogue," for so he was—telephoned and asked if he could come and see the car. He did not give his name. He said he was speaking from Wales, in Glamorganshire. Mr. Lewis said he could come and see it. He came in the evening to Mr. Lewis's flat. Mr. Lewis showed him the car, which was parked outside. The rogue drove it and tested it. He said he liked it. They then went along to the flat of Mr. Lewis's fiancee, Miss Kershaw (they have since married). He told them he was Richard Green and talked much about the film world. He led both of them to believe that he was the well-known film actor, Richard Greene, who played Robin Hood in the "Robin Hood" series. They talked about the car. He asked to see the logbook. He was shown it and seemed satisfied. He said he would like to buy the car. They agreed a price of £450. The rogue wrote out a cheque for £450 on the Beckenham Branch of the Midland Bank. He signed it "R. A. Green." He wanted to take the car at once. But Mr. Lewis was not willing for him to have it until the cheque was cleared. To hold him off, Mr. Lewis said there were one or two small jobs he would like to do on the car before letting him have it, and that would give time for the cheque to be cleared. The rogue said: "Don't worry about those small jobs. I would like to take the car now." Mr. Lewis said: "Have you anything to prove that you are Mr. Richard Green?" The rogue thereupon brought out a special pass of admission to Pinewood Studios, which had an official stamp on it. It bore the name of Richard A. Green and the address, and also a photograph which was plainly the photograph of this man, who was the rogue.

On seeing this pass, Mr. Lewis was satisfied. He thought this man was really Mr. Richard Greene, the film actor. By that time it was 11 o'clock at night. Mr. Lewis took the cheque and let the rogue have the car and the logbook and the Ministry of Transport test certificate. Each wrote and signed a receipt evidencing the transaction. Mr. Lewis wrote:

Received from
Richard A. Green, 59 Marsh Rd., Beckenham, Kent
the sum of £450 in return for Austin Cooper S Reg.
No. AHT 484B chassis No. CA257—549597
                              Keith Lewis.

The rogue wrote:

Received logbook No. 771835 and M.O.T. for Mini-
Cooper S No. AHT 484B
                              R. A. Green.

Next day, May 9, 1969, Mr. Lewis put the cheque into the bank. A few days later the bank told him it was worthless. The rogue had stolen a cheque book and written this £450 on a stolen cheque.

Meanwhile, while the cheque was going through, the rogue sold the car to an innocent purchaser. He sold it to a young man called Mr. Averay. He was at the time under 21. He was a music student in London at the Royal College of Music. His parents live at Bromley. He was keen to buy a car. He put an advertisement in the "Exchange and Mart," seeking a car for £200. In answer he had a telephone call from the rogue. He said he was speaking from South Wales. He said that he was coming to London to sell a car. Mr. Averay arranged to meet him on May 11, 1969. The rogue came with the car. Young Mr. Averay liked it, but wanted to get the approval of his parents. They drove it to Bromley. The parents did approve. Young Mr. Averay agreed to buy it for £200. The rogue gave his name as Mr. Lewis. He handed over the car and logbook to young Mr. Averay. The logbook showed the owner as Mr. Lewis. In return Mr. Averay, in entire good faith, gave the rogue a cheque for £200. The rogue signed this receipt:

Sale of Cooper S to A. J. Averay.

Received £200 for the Cooper S Registration No.
AHT 484B, the said car being my property absolutely,
there being no hire purchase charges outstanding or
other impediment to selling the car.
                              Keith Lewis
                              May 13, 1969.

A fortnight later, on May 29, 1969, Mr. Averay wanted the workshop manual for the car. So his father on his behalf wrote to the name and address of the seller as given in the logbook—that is, Mr. Lewis. Then, of course, the whole story came to light. The rogue had cashed the cheque and disappeared. The police have tried to trace him, but without success.

Now Mr. Lewis, the original owner of the car, sues young Mr. Averay. Mr. Lewis claims that the car is still his. He claims damages for conversion. The judge found in favour of Mr. Lewis and awarded damages of £330 for conversion.

The real question in the case is whether on May 8, 1969, there was a contract of sale under which the property in the car passed from Mr. Lewis to the rogue. If there was such a contract, then, even though it was voidable for fraud, nevertheless Mr. Averay would get a good title to the car. But if there was no contract of sale by Mr. Lewis to the rogue—either because there was, on the face of it, no agreement between the parties, or because any apparent agreement was a nullity and void ab initio for mistake, then no property would pass from Mr. Lewis to the rogue. Mr. Averay would not get a good title because the rogue had no property to pass to him.

There is no doubt that Mr. Lewis was mistaken as to the identity of the person who handed him the cheque. He thought that he was Richard Greene, a film actor of standing and worth: whereas in fact he was a rogue whose identity is quite unknown. It was under the influence of that mistake that Mr. Lewis let the rogue have the car. He would not have dreamed of letting him have it otherwise.

What is the effect of this mistake? There are two cases in our books which cannot, to my mind, be reconciled the one with the other. One of them is *Phillips v. Brooks Ltd.*, [1919] 2 KB 243, where a jeweller had a ring for sale. The other is *Ingram v. Little*, [1961] 1 QB 31, where two ladies had a car for sale. In each case the story is very similar to the present. A plausible rogue comes along. The rogue says he likes the ring, or the car, as the case may be. He asks the price. The seller names it. The rogue says he is prepared to buy it at that price. He pulls out a cheque book. He writes, or prepares to write, a cheque for the price. The seller hesitates. He has never met this man before. He does not want to hand over the ring or the car not knowing whether the cheque will be met. The rogue notices the seller's hesitation. He is quick with his next move. He says to the jeweller in *Phillips v. Brooks*: "I am Sir George Bullough of 11 St. James's Square"; or to the ladies in *Ingram v. Little*: "I am P.G.M. Hutchinson of Stanstead House, Stanstead Road, Caterham"; or to the post-graduate student in the present case: "I am Richard Greene, the film actor of the Robin Hood series." Each seller checks up the information. The jeweller looks up the directory and finds there is a Sir George Bullough at 11 St. James's Square.

The ladies check up too. They look at the telephone directory and find there is a "P.G.M. Hutchinson of Stanstead House, Stanstead Road, Caterham." The post-graduate student checks up too. He examines the official pass of the Pinewood Studios and finds that it is a pass for "Richard A. Green" to the Pinewood Studios with this man's photograph on it. In each case the seller feels that this is sufficient confirmation of the man's identity. So he accepts the cheque signed by the rogue and lets him have the ring, in the one case, and the car and logbook in the other two cases. The rogue goes off and sells the goods to a third person who buys them in entire good faith and pays the price to the rogue. The rogue disappears. The original seller presents the cheque. It is dishonoured. Who is entitled to the goods? The original seller? Or the ultimate buyer? The courts have given different answers. In *Phillips v. Brooks* the ultimate buyer was held to be entitled to the ring. In *Ingram v. Little* the original seller was held to be entitled to the car. In the present case the deputy county court judge has held the original seller entitled.

It seems to me that the material facts in each case are quite indistinguishable the one from the other. In each case there was, to all outward appearance, a contract: but there was a mistake by the seller as to the identity of the buyer. This mistake was fundamental. In each case it led to the handing over of the goods. Without it the seller would not have parted with them.

This case therefore raises the question: What is the effect of a mistake by one party as to the identity of the other? It has sometimes been said that if a party makes a mistake as to the identity of the person with whom he is contracting there is no contract, or, if there is a contract, it is a nullity and void, so that no property can pass under it. This has been supported by a reference to the French jurist Pothier; but I have said before, and I repeat now, his statement is no part of English law. I know that it was quoted by Lord Haldane in *Lake v. Simmons*, [1927] AC 487, 501, and, as such, misled Tucker J in *Sowler v. Potter*, [1940] 1 KB 271, into holding that a lease was void whereas it was really voidable. But Pothier's statement has given rise to such refinements that it is time it was dead and buried altogether.

For instance, in *Ingram v. Little*, [1961] 1 QB 31 the majority of the court suggested that the difference between *Phillips v. Brooks*, [1919] 2 KB 243 and *Ingram v. Little* was that in *Phillips v. Brooks* the contract of sale was concluded (so as to pass the property to the rogue) before the rogue made the fraudulent misrepresentation: see [1961] 1 QB 31, 51, 60: whereas in *Ingram v. Little* the rogue made the fraudulent misrepresentation before the contract was concluded. My own view is that in each case the property in the goods did not pass until the seller let the rogue have the goods.

Again it has been suggested that a mistake as to the identity of a person is one thing: and a mistake as to his attributes is another. A mistake as to identity, it is said, avoids a contract: whereas a mistake as to attributes does not. But this is a distinction without a difference. A man's very name is one of his attributes. It is also a key to his identity. If then, he gives a false name, is it a mistake as to his identity? or a mistake as to his attributes? These fine distinctions do no good to the law.

As I listened to the argument in this case, I felt it wrong that an innocent purchaser (who knew nothing of what passed between the seller and the rogue) should have his title depend on such refinements. After all, he has acted with complete circumspection and in entire good faith: whereas it was the seller who let the rogue have the goods and thus enabled him to commit the fraud. I do not, therefore, accept the theory that a mistake as to identity renders a contract void. I think the true principle is that which underlies the decision of this court in *King's Norton Metal Co. Ltd. v. Edridge Merrett & Co. Ltd.* (1897), 14 TLR 98 and of Horridge J in *Phillips v. Brooks*, [1919] 2 KB 243, which has stood for these last 50 years. It is this: When two parties have come to a contract—or rather what appears, on the face of it, to be a contract—the fact that one party is mistaken as to the identity of the other does not mean that there is no contract, or that the contract is a nullity and void from the beginning. It only means that the contract is voidable, that is, liable to be set aside at the instance of the mistaken person, so long as he does so before third parties have in good faith acquired rights under it.

Applied to the cases such as the present, this principle is in full accord with the presumption stated by Pearce LJ and also Devlin LJ in *Ingram v. Little*, [1961] 1 QB 31, 61, 66. When a dealing is had between a seller like Mr. Lewis and a person who is actually there present before him, then the presumption in law is that there is a contract, even though there is a fraudulent impersonation by the buyer representing himself as a different man than he is. There is a contract made with the very person there, who is present in person. It is liable no doubt to be avoided for fraud, but it is still a good contract under which title will pass unless and until it is avoided. In support of that presumption, Devlin LJ quoted, at p. 66, not only the English case of *Phillips v. Brooks*, but other cases in the United States where "the courts hold that if A appeared in person before B, impersonating C, an innocent purchaser from A gets the property in the goods against B." That seems to me to be right in principle in this country also.

In this case Mr. Lewis made a contract of sale with the very man, the rogue, who came to the flat. I say that he "made a contract" because in this regard we do not look into his intentions, or into his mind to know what he was thinking or into the mind of the rogue. We look to the outward appearances. On the face of the dealing, Mr. Lewis made a contract under which he sold the car to the rogue, delivered the car and the logbook to him, and took a cheque in return. The contract is evidenced by the receipts which were signed. It was, of course, induced by fraud. The rogue made false representations as to his identity, but it was still a contract, though voidable for fraud. It was a contract under which this property passed to the rogue, and in due course passed from the rogue to Mr. Averay, before the contract was avoided.

Though I very much regret that either of these good and reliable gentlemen should suffer, in my judgment it is Mr. Lewis who should do so. I think the appeal should be allowed and judgment entered for the defendant.

Appeal allowed.

[Phillimore and Megaw LJJ agreed that the appeal should be allowed.]

Car & Universal Finance Co. Ltd. v. Caldwell

[1965] 1 QB 525 (QB and CA)

[The defendant, Caldwell, was the owner of a Jaguar car. On 12 January 1960 he sold it for £975 to Norris. Norris gave Caldwell a deposit of £10 and a cheque for £965. He drove the car away. Caldwell banked the cheque the next day, but it was dishonoured. He immediately notified the police and the Automobile Association of the fraud. Later, Norris purported to sell the car to Motobella Ltd., a car dealership. It was agreed that Motobella had notice of Norris's defect in title. Motobella then purported to sell the car to G. & C. Finance Ltd., a hire-purchase company. G. & C.

Finance later sold the car to a dealer who in turn sold it to the plaintiffs. The plaintiffs acted in good faith and without notice of any defect in title.]

LORD DENNING MR (sitting as an additional judge of the Queen's Bench Division): This case raises the familiar question which of two innocent persons is to suffer for the fraud of a third? [His Lordship referred to the facts and continued:] The principal question in this case is whether Caldwell did succeed in avoiding the sale by the steps which he took of going to the bank, the police and the A.A., before the rogue sold the car to Motobella. It is said by Mr. Tapp, for the plaintiffs, that a man from whom goods have been obtained by false pretences cannot avoid the transaction unless he does an act which unequivocally shows his election to avoid it; and, furthermore, communicates his election to the other side, that is, to the other party to the contract. The avoidance does not, it is said, take place until it is communicated. In this case, therefore, the avoidance did not take place on the morning of January 13 when Caldwell went to the police. It would not take place until Caldwell discovered Norris and Foster and communicated his election to them. Mr. Tapp conceded, however, that it was avoided by January 29, 1960, on which date Motobella had sold the car to G. & C. Finance who had acquired a good title.

In support of this supposed requirement of communication Mr. Tapp referred me particularly to the judgment of Lord Blackburn in *Scarf v. Jardine* in which he said that a man did not elect to avoid a contract simply because in his own mind he decided to avoid it or even made a note in his own book about it. An election, he indicated, was not complete until he had communicated it to the other side in such a way as to lead the opposite party to believe that he had made that choice. Then he had completed his election and could go no further. Mr. Tapp also referred me to a passage in *Benjamin on Sale* which appears in the 2nd ed. (1873), and in the 8th ed. (1950), p. 441, which says: "The rescission is the legal consequence of his election to reject it, and takes date from the time at which he announces this election to the opposite party." Those passages seem to support Mr. Tapp's contention that Caldwell's acts on the morning of January 13 did not amount to an election to avoid the contract, because they were not communicated to the opposite party.

I appreciate the force of that argument but I cannot accept it. In principle, it seems to me that a seller can avoid a contract by an unequivocal act of election which demonstrates clearly that he elects to rescind it and to be no longer bound by it. It is sufficient if he asserts his intention to rescind "in the plainest and most open manner competent to him." I take those words from the speech of Lord Hatherley in *Reese River Silver Mining Co. v. Smith*. Lord Hatherley goes on to give communication as one of the ways in which an election can be demonstrated, but not, I think, in such a way as to make it essential, a sine qua non. I would ask this simple question: How is a man in the position of Caldwell ever to be able to rescind the contract when a fraudulent person absconds as Norris did here? If his right to rescind is to be a real right, when the rogue absconds, it must be sufficient if he does all that he can in the circumstances unequivocally to make it known. It is not sufficient for him, of course, to keep it in his own mind or write down a note in his own private sitting room. However, conduct such as we have here, namely, telling the bank, the police and the A.A.,

"Find this car if you possibly can. Get it back. It is mine," seems to me an unequivocal act of rescission.

If you take comparable cases of election, none of them requires communication as an essential pre-requisite. Take forfeiture, which Lord Blackburn took as his guide. If a lessor elects to determine a lease for forfeiture, it is sufficient for him to issue a writ for possession. The forfeiture dates from the issue of the writ, not from the time it is served. Or if the lessor does an act which, if done by a stranger, would be a trespass, it is an entry. The forfeiture dates from the time of the re-entry, even though the lessee is away and does not know anything about it. Next take ratification: where a person has a right to ratify an unauthorised act made professedly on his behalf by an agent, any unequivocal act of affirmation is sufficient. Again, take repudiation: if a contract is repudiated by a party and the other has a right to elect whether to accept it or not, any unequivocal act clearly evincing his election is sufficient. Take, finally, the affirmation of a contract: Mr. Lincoln referred me to *In re Hop and Malt Exchange and Warehouse Co., ex parte Briggs*, where it was held that an affirmation by instructing a broker to re-sell, (which was an unequivocal act), was sufficient affirmation even though not communicated.

I hold, therefore, that where a seller of goods has a right to avoid a contract for fraud, he sufficiently exercises his election if he at once, on discovering the fraud, takes all possible steps to regain the goods even though he cannot find the rogue or communicate with him. That is what Caldwell did here by going to the police and asking them to get back the car. I, therefore, hold that on January 13 the contract of sale to these rogues was avoided and Caldwell then became the owner of the car again. It was only after he avoided it (so that it was once again his property), that these rogues purported to sell it to Motobella and Motobella purported to sell it to G. & C. Finance. Those sales were ineffective to pass the property because it had already been re-vested in Caldwell.

Judgment for plaintiff.

[This part of Lord Denning's judgment was affirmed on appeal: [1965] 1 QB 535.]

REFORM

OLRC Sales Recommendations

(at 316-18)

1. The revised Sale of Goods Act should not adopt a general *possession vaut titre* principle. Rather, the basic *nemo dat* doctrine should be affirmed.

2. The exceptions to the *nemo dat* doctrine contained in sections 22, 24 and 25 of the existing Sale of Goods Act should be retained in the revised Act, subject to the amendments and modifications set out below.

3. The *nemo dat* rule should not apply in the circumstances set out in section 22 of the existing Act. However, the exception to the rule now recognized in the case of

conduct by the owner precluding him from denying the authority of the person in possession to sell the goods should be broadened to include cases where the owner has failed to exercise reasonable care in the entrustment of the goods and the buyer has exercised reasonable care in buying the goods and has acted in good faith.

4. As under section 24 of the existing Act, a seller who has a voidable title to goods should be able to pass good title to a person who buys in good faith and without notice of the seller's defective title. For purposes of this exception to the *nemo dat* rule, the distinction between void and voidable titles should be abolished. The revised Act should, accordingly, contain a provision stating that a purchaser of goods shall be deemed to have a voidable title notwithstanding that the transferor of the goods was deceived as to the identity of the purchaser or the presence of some other mistake affecting the validity of the contract of sale, and also in circumstances similar to those set out in UCC 2-403(1)(b), (c) and (d).

5. The revised Act should provide that, where the seller has or is deemed to have a voidable title, a purported avoidance of the contract by the owner of the goods shall have no effect on a third party, unless the goods are recovered by the owner before they are delivered to the third party by the person in possession of the goods.

6. Subject to the following amendments, the revised Act should contain a provision comparable to section 25 of the existing Sale of Goods Act, which recognizes an exception to the *nemo dat* rule in the case of a transfer of goods, or of a document of title, by buyers and sellers in possession:

(a) The power of a seller in possession to transfer a better title to goods than he himself has should apply whether he is, or continues, in possession of the goods in his capacity as seller, or otherwise.

(b) The power of a buyer or seller in possession to transfer a better title than he himself has shall not apply where a security interest governed by The Personal Property Security Act has been created in the seller or buyer out of possession, or where, prior to the disposition to the third party, a notice in the prescribed form has been filed under The Personal Property Security Act.

(c) The power of a buyer or seller in possession to pass a better title to a third person than he himself has shall be contingent upon his originally being in possession of the goods, or of a document of title thereto, with the consent of the other party to the transaction; and in all other respects, the conditions governing the dispositive powers of buyers and sellers in possession should be the same.

(d) The protection of the provision in the revised Act comparable to section 25 should be confined to a buyer or lessee who receives the goods in good faith and for value from the person in possession.

(e) The scope of the provision in the revised Act comparable to section 25 should be enlarged to cover a prospective buyer, as well as an actual buyer, in possession of the goods. A prospective buyer should be defined to mean a person who receives goods under a sale on approval or contract of sale or return or with an option to purchase, and a person whose offer to buy the goods has been accepted subject to the approval of a third person or the fulfilment of some other condition.

7. The revised Act should not incorporate a general *market overt* rule with respect to sales, including sales of lost or stolen goods, made at retail premises.

8. The revised Act should contain a further exception to the *nemo dat* doctrine, along the lines of UCC 2-403(2), in the case of goods entrusted to a merchant who deals in goods of the kind entrusted. Any entrusting of possession of goods to a merchant who deals in goods of that kind should give him power to transfer all rights of the entruster to a buyer or lessee in the ordinary course of business. "Entrusting" should be defined in the revised Act as in UCC 2-403(3).

9. In light of recommendation No. 8, *supra*, The Factors Act should be reviewed with a view to determining the desirability of its retention.

10. The ability of a buyer or seller in possession, or of a merchant to whom goods have been entrusted, to pass better title than he himself has should apply even though the owner has revoked his consent to possession of the goods by the other party, unless the goods are recovered by the owner before they have been delivered to the third party.

11. Except in the case of entrustment of goods to a merchant who deals in goods of that kind, the court should be able, where it considers it fair, to order that the owner of goods may recover the goods from the person in possession upon repaying to the person in possession the price paid by the person in possession for the goods, together with such reliance losses as the person in possession would otherwise suffer and as the court may order to be paid.

12. The Bills of Sale Act should be repealed.

CHAPTER FIFTEEN

Buyer's Obligations and Seller's Remedies for Buyer's Breach

INTRODUCTION

Compared to the seller's obligations, the buyer's obligations in a typical cash sale are relatively simple and straightforward. The buyer's obligations are to accept delivery of the goods in accordance with the contractual terms, express or implied, and to pay for them. See SGA ss. 26-27.

As in the case of any other creditor, the seller's overriding concern is to obtain payment for the goods or damages for non-payment. The position differs fundamentally depending on whether we are dealing with a cash sale or a credit sale. ("Cash sale" is not a term of art but means a sale where payment is required on or before delivery of the goods: *cf.* SGA s. 27.) The present chapter is only concerned with cash sales. The seller's rights and remedies in secured credit sales are dealt with in volume III of the previous edition of this casebook.

Even in cash sales the position is not as simple as one might suppose. The SGA distinguishes between the seller's "real" rights and its "personal" remedies. Real rights are those which the seller may exercise against the goods and consist of the right to detain the goods, stoppage in transit, and the right to resell for non-payment. See SGA ss. 37-46. The first and third rights are still of great practical importance; stoppage in transit, on the other hand, has lost much of its practical impact because of faster modes of transportation, modern credit techniques, and the ubiquitous use of letters of credit in international sales transactions.

So far as personal remedies are concerned, the seller will always be entitled to sue for damages. As in the converse case of damage claims by the buyer, the recoverable measure of damages will be governed by the rules in *Hadley v. Baxendale*. See SGA s. 48(2). The difference is that the seller will rarely seek to recover consequential damages (why not?), although in principle it should be entitled to do so. If there is an "available market" for the goods, the seller's damages will *prima facie* be governed by SGA s. 48(3). The seller would prefer of course to be able to sue for the price (because that spares him the onus of proving damages and disposing of the goods) but its right to do so depends on the circumscribed rules of s. 47. Finally, the seller may also be entitled to retain any deposit or part payments already made by the buyer and this may satisfy the seller if it has suffered only nominal damages. The table following this note illustrates in simplified form the seller's alternative remedies in the principal types of situation. The reader will note the heavy hand of property concepts in determining the seller's right of specific performance—that is, to sue for the price.

Seller's Remedies for Non-Payment of Price (Cash Sales)

Real Rights   *Personal Remedies*

A. Where Goods Not Yet in Buyer's Possession

1) *Property has passed:*
a) Vendor's lien: s. 39
b) Stoppage in transit: s. 42
 	
c) Right of resale: s. 46
	a) Action for price: s. 47(1)
	b) Acceptance of buyer's repudiation and rescission of contract:
	   i) claim for damages: s. 48(1)
	   ii) forfeiture of deposit or part payment. *Cf.* SGA s. 57

2) *Property has not passed but goods are specific or ascertained:* a) Vendor's right of retention: s. 38(2) b) Stoppage in transit: s. 42 c) Right of resale: s. 46	a) No action for price unless s. 47(2) applies b) Same as in (1)
Sale of future or unascertained goods: No real rights because no goods have been appropriated to the contract.	a) Same as in (2) b) Same as in (1)

B. Where Goods in Buyer's Possession

No statutory right to reclaim goods; seller's rights depend on terms of contract unless buyer has procured goods by fraudulent means.	a) Same as in (1)

Common Payment Terms in Ontario Manufacturing Contracts[1]

	Always or Often	% Mid	Rarely or Never
a) Payment in advance of delivery in one lump sum	0.4	8.0	91.2
b) Payment in instalments in advance of delivery as work on order progresses	2.3	14.1	83.7
c) Payment on delivery	3.9	31.6	64.6
d) Payment within 30 days of delivery	82.3	15.2	2.5
e) Payment within 60 days of delivery	13.4	28.3	58.3
f) Payment more than 60 days after delivery	1.8	15.8	82.5
g) Payment in instalments (types of usual arrangements to be detailed)	3.4	13.9	82.7
h) Other	5.5	4.9	89.7

1   Source: OLRC Sale of Goods Project. (The headings in the original table have been changed slightly. [eds.])

Note on Documentary Draft Sales

Even in Chalmers's day, except in retail sales, face-to-face sales were declining in importance in favour of shipment contracts, and the importance of shipments to a distant point has grown apace since then. In such circumstances, how is the seller to ensure in a cash sale that the goods are not released to the buyer without payment? If the seller uses its own carrier (an uncommon practice in Canada for out-of-town shipments) there is no problem: it will simply instruct the driver to require cash on delivery. Theoretically, the C.O.D. method could also be applied to an independent carrier in inland transportation, but apparently it is not used widely.

Instead, since the last century the more common method has been for the carrier to issue a bill of lading to the order of the seller. The seller endorses the bill of lading and forwards it through its bank to an agent (also usually a bank) located in the city of the buyer's place of business. Attached to the bill of lading will be the seller's draft on the buyer for the price of the goods—a "sight" draft if payment is due on presentment of the draft; a "time" draft if payment is due at a later date. The agent will be authorized to release the bill of lading, and any other incidental documents, on acceptance of the draft by the buyer in the case of a time draft and payment if it is a sight draft. Documentary draft sales are no longer common in Canada in domestic sales, but they still retain their importance in overseas sales, usually in conjunction with letter of credit payment arrangements.

A distinctive feature of such documentary sales requiring payment against documents of title is that, by the express or implied terms of the parties' agreement, the buyer is not entitled to inspect the goods before payment of the price, whether or not the goods are available for inspection at the time. *Cf.* UCC 2-513(3), 2-319(4), 2-320(4); *E. Clemens Horst Co. v. Biddell Bros.*, [1912] AC 18. This is a necessary provision because ordinarily the documents are presented to the buyer or his agent well before the goods reach their destination and because the seller wants its money promptly. It also means however that the buyer runs the risk that the goods may be defective, although the buyer can protect itself by requiring a certificate of inspection of the goods from an independent appraiser at the place of shipment as a condition of its payment. "Stand-by" letters of credit in favour of the buyer are also popular in export agreements with some Middle Eastern countries. See further volume II, chapter 7 of the previous edition of this casebook.

The documentary sale therefore ensures that the seller does not lose control of the goods before it has been paid; it does not, however, itself ensure payment if the buyer has lost interest in the goods or has become insolvent. The seller will then have to try and find an alternative buyer for goods that may have no ready market and that are located perhaps thousands of miles from the point of shipment. It is the office of the letter of credit to insulate the seller from this considerable risk in overseas trade. The salient features of letter of credit law are examined in volume II, chapter 7 of the previous edition of this casebook. In the post-war period the governments of many exporting countries have become heavily involved in providing export credit insurance and guarantee facilities to their exporters where the importer is not able or willing to pay cash and insists on credit terms from the exporter. In Canada, federal assistance is provided through the Export Development Corporation (EDC), a Crown instrumentality established by the Export Development Act, RSC 1985, c. E-20, as am. See further Charles E. O'Connor, "Payment and

Financing Mechanisms in International Trade," in Ziegel and Graham (eds.), *New Dimensions in International Trade Law: A Canadian Perspective* (1982), chapter 3.

ACTIONS FOR THE PRICE

Colley v. Overseas Exporters

[1921] 3 KB 302, [1921] All ER Rep. 596

McCARDIE J: This action is brought upon a writ specially indorsed within Order XIV to recover the sum of 985*l*. 17*s*. 4*d*. alleged to be due from the defendants to the plaintiff as the price of goods. The only question is whether that liquidated sum is due. No question arises as yet as to damages against the defendants. The case raises a point of legal interest and practical utility as to the circumstances under which the purchase price of goods can be sued for. The facts are not in dispute. They can be briefly stated. The plaintiff is a leather merchant at Sheffield. The defendants are merchants at Sheffield. On December 17, 1920, the plaintiff sold to the defendants a quantity of leather belting of stated sizes and qualities and at certain prices "f.o.b. Liverpool." The goods were not specific within the definition clause (s. 62) of the Sale of Goods Act, 1893. They were unascertained at the date of the bargain. On January 26, 1921, the defendants sent shipping instructions to the plaintiff. These directed that the goods should be packed for export and marked as ordered, and then said: "*S/S Kenuta*. Closing despatch 2/2/21 and 5/2/21. Consign to Alexandra Dock Station, Liverpool, c/o Daniel Maccabe, Ld., 17 Brunswick St., Liverpool, advising them of despatch." On February 3 the plaintiff wrote to Maccabe, Ld., who are shipping agents at Liverpool: "We have today despatched by the Great Central Railway Co. (Alexandra Dock Station) to *S/S Kenuta* to the order of Overseas Exporters Ltd. of Sheffield 7 cases of leather belting." The goods left Sheffield and reached their destination in Liverpool to be dealt with by Maccabe, Ld., in order to carry out the plaintiff's obligation to put them on board. A series of misfortunes then occurred. The *Kenuta* was withdrawn from service by her owners, who then proposed to substitute another ship. This second ship was however inadequate for the intended voyage. Then a third vessel was put forward as a substitute, but, an accident having occurred to a fourth vessel of the same owners, the third ship had to be used to replace that damaged vessel. So a further ship was put forward—namely, *The Sorota*, which was then at Glasgow. She however could not reach Liverpool because of a strike. The result was that on April 14, 1921, the day on which the writ was issued, the goods were still unshipped and the plaintiff was still unpaid. Prior to April 13 Daniel Maccabe, Ld., sent a note of their charges, amounting to 1*l*. 4*s*., to the plaintiff, and on April 13 he gave them a cheque for that sum. He of course was responsible for these charges, as the cost of getting the goods aboard fell on him under the contract. Such are the facts. The defendants committed no deliberate breach of contract; they suffered a series of misfortunes. They failed however to name an effective ship. The plaintiff on his part did all he could to carry out his obligations. Under these circumstances the plaintiff seeks to recover the price of the goods in question. The able argument of Mr. Willes for the plaintiff rested on two well-known passages in the judgment of Lord Blackburn in *Mackay v. Dick*, 6 App. Cas. 251, 263, 264. The first passage is this:

> I think I may safely say, as a general rule, that where in a written contract it appears that both parties have agreed that something shall be done, which cannot effectually be done unless both concur in doing it, the construction of the contract is that each agrees to do all that is necessary to be done on his part for the carrying out of that thing, though there may be no express words to that effect.

The second passage is this:

> It would follow in point of law that the defender having had the machine delivered to him, was by his contract to keep it, unless on a fair test according to the contract it failed to do the stipulated quantity of work, in which case he would be entitled to call on the pursuers to remove it. And *by his own default* he can now never be in a position to call upon the pursuers to take back the machine, on the ground that the test had not been satisfied, he must, as far as regards that, keep, and consequently pay for it.

I will consider later on the facts in *Mackay v. Dick*. The contention of Mr. Willes before me was that inasmuch as the defendants' own fault had here prevented the goods from being put on board they were disabled from saying that the price, which would have been payable if and when the goods had actually been put on board, was not now due to the plaintiff. This is a novel and interesting submission. An action for the price of goods is, of course, essentially an action for a liquidated sum. It involves special and technical elements. By special bargain the price of goods may be payable before delivery or before the property has passed from vendor to buyer: see *Pordage v. Cole* (1669), 1 Wms. Saund. 320; *Leake on Contracts*, 6th ed., at 487-88; *Workman, Clark & Co. v. Lloyd Brazileno*, [1908] 1 KB 968; and s. 49 of the Sale of Goods Act, 1893. In ordinary cases and unless otherwise agreed delivery of the goods and payment of the price are concurrent conditions: see s. 28 of the Sale of Goods Act, 1893. Now the full meaning of the word "price" is not actually defined by the Sale of Goods Act, except perhaps in s. 1, which says: "A contract of sale of goods is a contract whereby the seller transfers or agrees to transfer the property in goods to the buyer for a money consideration, called the price." The circumstances however under which a claim to the price may be made (as distinguished from a claim of damages for breach of contract) are indicated in s. 49 of that Act [Ont. s. 47(1)] ... Here sub-s, 2 of s, 49 does not apply, as it apparently did in *Workman, Clark & Co. v. Lloyd Brazileno*, [1908] 1 KB 968, where the price was payable by stated instalments on stated dates. The parties before me here made no special agreement as to the payment of the price. Nor can it be said that sub-s. 1 of s. 49 applies here, for the property in the goods has not in fact and law passed to the buyer. Several rules for the passing of property in sale of goods contracts are indicated in ss. 16, 17, 18, and also in s. 32. The Act does not deal specifically with f.o.b. or c.i.f. contracts. Judicially settled rules exist however with respect to them. I need only to deal with f.o.b. contracts. The presumed intention (see s. 18 of the Act) of the parties has been settled. It seems clear that in the absence of special agreement the property and risk in goods does not in the case of an f.o.b. contract pass from the seller to the buyer till the goods are actually put on board: see *Browne v. Hare* (1859), 4 H. & N. 822; *Inglis v. Stock* (1885), 10 App. Cas. 263; *Wimble v. Rosenberg*, [1913] 3 KB 743, 747; *Benjamin on Sale*, 6th ed., at 785, where several useful cases are collected. Unless therefore the principle involved in the words of Lord Blackburn in the second passage cited from *Mackay v. Dick* applies here the plaintiff will fail. Does the principle go to the extent submitted by Mr. Willes? It is well to consider *Mackay v. Dick*. The headnote says: "If, in the case of a contract of sale and delivery, which makes acceptance of the thing sold and payment of the price conditional on a certain thing being done by the seller, the buyer prevents the possibility of the seller fulfilling the condition, the contract is to be taken as satisfied." If this headnote be given its full apparent effect then the principle it suggests would be most far reaching, and the results extraordinary. The facts in *Mackay v. Dick* must be remembered. Concisely put they were these. By a contract in two letters the seller agreed to sell and deliver at the buyer's works a digging machine. The price of 1125*l*. was payable after the machine had satisfactorily performed certain tests. If it failed to perform them the buyer was to remove the machine. The machine was actually delivered into the buyer's possession. Owing however to the buyer's own default it did not perform the tests. He refused to pay the price, and the seller thereupon brought his action for the 1125*l*. The plaintiff succeeded on the principle stated by Lord Blackburn. It is to be clearly noted that a specific machine was fully delivered by the seller to the buyer. Apparently the property in the machine actually passed to the buyer. It is true that *Mackay v. Dick* fell to be decided by Scotch law. The decision was given by the House of Lords in 1881, twelve years before the Sale of Goods Act, 1893. Scotch law then rested on the civil law and not on English common law, and the transfer of property in goods therefore possessed special features derived from Roman jurisprudence: see *Erskine's Principles of the Law of Scotland*, 19th ed., at 322; *Chalmers' Sale of Goods*, 8th ed., at 9; *Brown on Sale of Goods*, 2nd ed., at 114. It seems clear however that under Scotch law the property in the digging machine had passed to the buyer on delivery: see Erskine (*sup.*), at 322. Hence I think that the sale and delivery of the machine must in *Mackay v. Dick* be deemed to have been complete, and payment of the price was therefore subject only to the "resolutive condition" imposed by the clause as to the test: see *Chalmers' Sale of Goods*, 8th ed., at 6, 7, and the cases there cited as to resolutive conditions. Default by the buyer as to the test was proved, and thus the seller got his judgment for the price. The actual decision in *Mackay v. Dick* does not therefore aid the plaintiff here. The real question is as to the extent to which the principle indicated by Lord Blackburn in the second passage I have quoted operates to make a price payable which, apart from that principle, would not be payable. Although, as I have said, *Mackay v. Dick* turned on Scotch law yet I think that that principle is equally well settled in English law. It has frequently been asserted in well-known text books based on English law: see *Addison on Contracts*, 11th ed., at 624; *Leake on Contracts*, 6th ed., at 479. In *Chitty on Contracts*, 17th ed., at 833, the matter is put very broadly thus: "If on a contract of sale payment is conditional on a certain thing being done by the seller, and the buyer prevents the possibility of the condition being fulfilled, the seller may recover the price." So too in *Benjamin on Sale*, 6th ed., at 641, there is this passage: "As long ago as 1787 Ashhurst J in delivering the opinion of the King's Bench in *Hotham v. East*

India Co. (1787), 1 TR 638, 645 said that it was evident from common sense that if the performance of a condition precedent by the plaintiff had been rendered impossible by the neglect or default of the defendant 'it is equal to performance.'" The principle moreover has been frequently applied in the Courts and is illustrated by *Braithwaite v. Foreign Hardwood Co.*, [1905] 2 KB 543. Nowhere is that principle more luminously dealt with or the English decisions more aptly cited than in *Pollock on Contracts*, 9th ed., at 294-96. It is a corollary and amplification of the rule asserted in the first passage cited by me from Lord Blackburn's judgment. This rule is recognized by the text books as embodied in English law, and has been widely applied by high tribunals as of obvious justice and convenience: see, e.g., *Sprague v. Booth*, [1909] AC 576, 580; *Kleinert v. Abosso Gold Mining Co.* (1913), 58 Sol. J 34. I respectfully followed those authorities in *Harrison v. Walker*, [1919] 2 KB 453. Now in deciding whether the argument of Mr. Willes in this case be sound, and in determining the extent to which the principle stated in the second cited passage from Lord Blackburn may be applied, it is necessary to remember the law which existed before the Act of 1893 was passed. In former days an action for the price of goods would only lie upon one or other of two counts. First, upon the *indebitatus* count for goods sold and delivered, which was pleaded as follows: "Money payable by the defendant to the plaintiff for goods sold and delivered by the plaintiff to the defendant": *Bullen and Leake, Precedent of Pleading*, 3rd ed., at 38. This count would not lie before delivery: *Boulter v. Arnott* (1833), 1 Cr. & M 333. The count was applicable where upon a sale of goods the property had passed and the goods had been delivered to the purchaser and the price was payable at the time of action brought. Secondly, upon the *indebitatus* count for goods bargained and sold, which was pleaded as follows: "Money payable by the defendant to the plaintiff for goods bargained and sold by the plaintiff to the defendant": *Bullen and Leake*, at 39. This count was applicable where upon a sale of goods the property had passed to the purchaser and the contract had been completed in all respects except delivery, and the delivery was not a part of the consideration for the price or a condition precedent to its payment. If the property had not passed the count would not lie: *Atkinson v. Bell* (1828), 8 B & C 277. In my view the law as to the circumstances under which an action will lie for the price of goods has not been changed by the Sale of Goods Act, 1893. That enactment appears to crystallise and confirm the old law; *Chalmers' Sale of Goods*, 8th ed., at 112. By the definition clause of that Act, s. 62, "sale" is to include a bargain and sale as well as a sale and delivery. A sale or, as it is called for distinction, an executed contract of sale is a contract plus a conveyance: *Chalmers (sup.)*, at 8. The existing condition of the law is put in *Benjamin on Sales*, 6th ed., at 946, where it is rightly stated that the old principles "are by implication preserved by s. 49 of the code." And the learned editor adds: "Where the property has not passed, the seller's claim must, as a general rule, be special for damages for non-acceptance." An exception to the general rule is to be found in the cases provided for by s. 49, sub-s. 2, of the code. In my opinion (subject to what I say hereafter as to estoppel) no action will lie for the price of goods until the property has passed, save only in the special cases provided for by s. 49, sub-s. 2. This seems plain both on the code and on common law principle. I have searched in vain for authority to the contrary. A clear distinction exists between cases where the default of the buyer has occurred after the property has passed and cases where the default has been before the property has passed. To the former cases *Mackay v. Dick* may be applied on appropriate facts. To the latter cases *Mackay v. Dick* does not apply so as to enable the buyer to recover the price as distinguished from damages for breach of contract. To hold that *Mackay v. Dick* applies where the property has not passed would lead to extraordinary results. Here the substantial allegation against the defendants is that their default prevented the plaintiff from passing the property and so entitling him to the price. Just the same default however would, in substance, have been committed if the defendants had repudiated the contract before the goods had been sent from Sheffield. So too every buyer who refuses to take delivery of unascertained goods and thereby prevents the transference of property in them from the seller commits a similar default. If the ingenious contention of Mr. Willes were correct it would be difficult to imagine a case of sale of goods, even though unascertained, to which *Mackay v. Dick* would not apply. The pages of *Benjamin on Sales* will afford many appropriate illustrations of this. An interesting decision on the matter is that of Atkin J in *Stein Forbes v. County Tailoring Co.* (1916), 115 LT 215. There the purchasers of goods under a c.i.f. contract (payment to be net cash against documents on arrival of steamer) refused to take up the documents when ready. Atkin J held that s. 49, sub-s. 2, of the Code did not apply, and that as the property in the goods had not passed the sellers could recover damages only and not the price.

Judgment for the defendants.

Stein, Forbes and Co. v. County Tailoring Company

(1916), 115 *Law Times* 215

[The defendants agreed to buy from the plaintiffs several shipments of sheepskins. Payment was to be "net cash against documents on arrival of the steamer." On arrival of the third shipment, the defendants refused to take up the documents. The plaintiffs sued for the price of the shipment alleging either that payment was due "on a day certain irrespective of delivery" within the meaning of s. 49(2) of the British Act (Ont. s. 47(2)) or, alternatively, that title to the sheepskins had passed to the defendants and that payment was therefore due under s. 47(1). The defendants raised several defences. The following extract from Atkin J's judgment deals only with the above two issues:]

ATKIN J: ... The result is that I think the defendants have broken the contract. The material question that remains is as to the plaintiffs' remedy. The plaintiffs have sued only for the price. If they are not entitled to the price they ask for leave to amend and claim damages. I intimated that I should give leave, but the defendants intimated that they were not prepared with evidence on that footing, and should require an adjournment if such was the relief that the plaintiffs were entitled to. I think the defendants' request not unreasonable, and, therefore, there must be an adjournment unless I come to the conclusion that the plaintiffs are entitled to recover the price.

Mr. Wright contended that the plaintiffs were entitled to the price, even though the property in the goods had not passed to the defendants, on the ground that here was a sum certain payable at a fixed time and that, as the defendants had prevented delivery, they could not rely upon non-delivery as a condition precedent.

I do not think that he can establish his claim on that footing. This is not the case of a day being appointed for payment of money and the day happening before the thing which is the consideration for the payment. In such a case, which falls within one of the well-known rules in the notes to *Portage v. Cole* (1 William Saunders, 5th edit., p. 320), the money can be claimed before performance. Such a case is provided for by the Sale of Goods Act 1893 s. 49, sub-s. 2 [see Ont. SGA, s. 47(2)] ...

But this is not a case where the price is payable on a day certain irrespective of delivery. On the contrary, it is payable expressly against delivery. I think, therefore, no action will lie for the price on this ground.

But it was further said by Mr. Wright that the property in fact had passed to the defendants and that upon the plaintiffs being willing to transfer possession they were entitled to the price as in the case of goods bargained and sold. I think that there are many objections to this view. At what time property passes under a contract of sale depends upon the intention of the parties.

[Atkin J quoted ss. 16-17 of the British Act and continued:]

The Act provides certain rules for ascertaining the intention of the parties unless a different intention appears. Many cases have dealt with the problem as to when property passes in contracts of sale on c.i.f. terms. Mr. Wright contends that as soon as the goods are unconditionally appropriated to the contract and the seller holds the documents at the disposal of the buyer the property passes. The value of that proposition depends on the meaning of unconditionally.

I doubt whether goods are appropriated unconditionally if the seller does not mean the buyer to have them unless he pays for them. But it seems to me impossible to lay down a general rule applicable to all c.i.f. contracts. The overruling question is: Does the intention of the parties appear in the course of the making and the fulfilment of the contract? By sect. 19 of the Sale of Goods Act 1893, sub-ss. 1, 2, and 3, it is provided as follows [see Ont. SGA, s. 19, rules 1 to 3] ...

In the present case, the goods were shipped at New York on behalf of the plaintiffs, and the bill of lading was taken to the order of the banking firm who financed the transaction for the plaintiffs. On arrival of the ship the plaintiffs had to take up the bill of lading from the bankers; and, inasmuch as the defendants would not take up the documents, the plaintiffs had to take delivery of the goods from the ship. It seems quite plain that the seller or his banker reserved the *jus disponendi*.

It was said that the property passed to the buyer on shipment, but the seller only reserved his unpaid vendor's lien. That view seems to me inconsistent with the section I have read and with every business probability. In the majority of cases where the seller takes the bill of lading to his order the goods come forward through a banker, and it seems to me very improbable that the seller means to give to the banker or the banker to take a document representing goods the property in which is in some third person, the only security given being a right to retain possession till the fine is paid. I think the intention is to keep the property in the seller till payment.

Then it is said, whatever the original intention may be, at any rate the property passes when there is an appropriation of specific goods, as by the invoice in this case, and a tender or a willingness to tender. It would be a remarkable intention in a commercial man to keep the property on shipment in order to secure payment, but yet in taking the necessary steps to procure payment by appropriation and tender to part with the property before payment is in fact made. I think that in such cases the ordinary inference to be drawn is that the seller does not intend to part with the property, except against payment. It seems to me that this view is confirmed by the statutory provisions in sect. 19, sub-sect. 3, which I have read.

Unless the property has passed I do not think that in this case the plaintiffs can sue for the price; and in my opinion it has not passed. The plaintiff's claim, therefore, is for damages. The case will be adjourned to enable the defendants to deal with the question of damages in case the parties cannot agree.

Case adjourned.

NOTES

1) As will be noted, ss. 47(1) and (2) of the Ontario Act are based on different principles. Section 47(1) proceeds from the premise that once the seller has fulfilled its primary obligation of transferring title to the buyer, the buyer must meet its reciprocal obligation of paying the price. (Note, however, that s. 47(1) makes no reference to the seller's equally fundamental obligation of tendering delivery even though s. 27 provides that, unless otherwise agreed, delivery of the goods and payment of the price are concurrent conditions. Clearly the two sections must be read together.) The theory of s. 47(2) is that, like any other obligation, the buyer may agree to make payment on an agreed date independently of the seller's performance of its obligations.

2) In any event, both subsections give rise to considerable difficulties—subs. (1), because the time of passing of title is often difficult to determine and because forcing the buyer to accept goods it is no longer interested in may be economically inefficient; and subs. (2) because it is not obvious why the buyer's promise to pay at a fixed time should be treated as a specifically enforceable debt and not as an obligation whose breach will give rise to an action for damages. *Cf.* the lack of mutuality with respect to the buyer's right to enforce the seller's obligations specifically under s. 50.

3) As *Stein Forbes* shows, in the past the courts have shown a marked (but not consistent) inclination to apply s. 47(2) very narrowly, so much so that Benjamin argues (*Benjamin's Sale of Goods*, 5th ed. (1997), para. 16-024) that "the better view is a day can be 'certain' under [s. 47(2)] only if it is fixed in advance by the contract in such a way that it can be determined independently of the action of either party or of any third person. If, for example, an instalment of the price becomes due when the seller has reached a specified stage in the construction of the goods, it is submitted that the instalment should not be held to be payable 'on a day certain' within the meaning of this subsection." The authors

admit, however, that dicta in an early Court of Appeal decision, *Workman, Clark & Co. v. Brazileno*, [1908] 1 KB 968, at 977, 981, cast doubt on their submission. This is because the judgments in that case, while not discussing the meaning of a day certain, "assume that the seller could sue for instalments falling due as he reached the specified stage of construction of the ship, for example, when the keel was laid." (Benjamin, *ibid.*)

4) *UCC 2-709*. The Code's approach to the seller's entitlement to sue for the price in cash sales is very different from the SGA approach. True to its general approach, the locus of title to the goods is irrelevant and the issue is whether the buyer has accepted the goods. If the buyer has, it is liable for the price; but if it refuses to accept the goods the seller is remitted to a claim in damages: UCC 2-709(1)(a); 2-708. The theory of the Code is that the seller is usually in a better position to dispose of unwanted goods than is the buyer, and that it is economically wasteful to force goods on an unwilling buyer. There is an exception to the basic rule, in the case of goods identified to the contract, if the seller is unable after reasonable effort to resell them at a reasonable price or the circumstances reasonably indicate that such effort will be unavailing: UCC 2-709(1)(b). It will be seen, therefore, that the seller's right to claim the price is put on the same footing as the buyer's right under UCC 2-716 to claim specific performance of the seller's obligation to perform.

The OLRC Sales Report, while admitting that the Code had not found the complete solution to a difficult problem, nevertheless supported the thrust of UCC 2-709. The Report's reasons were as follows (at 417):

> We support the thrust of UCC 2-709. We appreciate that it can be argued that the Code swings the pendulum too far in the buyer's favour, and that, at least in some circumstances, the seller should be able to sue for the price even though the goods have not been accepted by the buyer. For example, there may be concern about the inadequacy of remitting the seller to a claim for damages and the dilemma that may confront him where the goods are rejected at a distant place. We believe, however, that these apprehensions can be satisfactorily answered. So far as the first point is concerned (the inadequacy of damages), at least in theory the Code's damage provisions, like those in The Sale of Goods Act, attempt to make the seller whole. The real issue is whether it is the seller or the buyer who should have the burden of disposing of the goods. The Code answers this question in terms of a balance of convenience. It may be argued that a wrongly rejecting buyer does not deserve much sympathy; but this proves too much. The argument could lead to the seller's being entitled to sue for the price even where the goods are still in his possession, and this would be even more favourable to him than the present law. So far as the second point is concerned (the rejection of goods at a distant place), UCC 2-603 comes to the seller's assistance by requiring the buyer's co-operation in disposing of the goods where the seller has no agent or place of business at the market of rejection. It is also reasonable to expect that, in such a case, a court will be more inclined to find that the goods are not readily resaleable than would be the case where the goods have never left the seller's premises.

Why would a merchant seller want to force goods for which there is a ready market on an unwilling buyer? Is the Code's approach equally apt for private sales?

SELLER'S RIGHT OF RESALE

R.V. Ward Ltd. v. Bignall

[1967] 1 QB 534, [1967] 2 All ER 449 (CA)

[The following statement of facts is taken from the judgment of Sellers LJ:]

In May, 1965, the plaintiff seller wished to sell two motor vehicles, a Vanguard Estate car and a Ford Zodiac, for which, by advertisement, it was asking £395 and £490 respectively. The defendant buyer, who is a dealer in motor vehicles, saw the advertisement and on May 6, 1965, he went to Mr. Ward's private house. There he examined both the vehicles and then offered Mr. Ward, for the seller, £850 for the two, which was accepted. No log books were produced or even mentioned. The buyer paid £25 in cash and went off to get the balance of £825 in cash from his bank, and it was arranged that he would return with the balance of the price and pay it to Mrs. Ward. Whilst away the buyer had second thoughts. The Vanguard had been advertised as 1962 and the buyer thought that so to describe it was a misrepresentation or a misdescription. He told Mr. Ward that he would not, in the circumstances, proceed with the purchase. The buyer offered to pay £800 instead of £850. That was refused. The buyer then offered to take the Zodiac alone for £500 and that was refused.

On the same day the seller consulted its solicitors. They wrote a letter to the buyer in which they quoted what the buyer had written on the back of one of the seller's cards: "A.M. Bignall Purchased Vanguard Estate Ford Zodiac for sum of £850 [signed] A.M. Bignall £25 deposit paid as seen and approved." In view of the argument before this court it is necessary to quote further from the letter. It continues:

> In view of the foregoing it is our view that ownership of the said motor cars passed to yourself. Mr. Ward further states that you left his home for the purpose of obtaining the balance of the agreed purchase price in cash, but that on your return, you informed Mrs. Ward in the absence of Mr. Ward that you did not intend to purchase the Vanguard but would only purchase the Ford which conversation you later repeated to Mr. Ward over the telephone. As mentioned above, ownership of the two cars has now passed to yourself, and all that remains is for you to collect the same, and to pay to our clients the balance of the agreed purchase price. We have advised [the seller] that a binding agreement has been made by you to purchase the said motor cars, and that failure by you to take possession thereof, and to pay the balance of the agreed purchase price will place you in breach of the said agreement, and will entitle them to recover against you by way of damages, such sum below the price agreed by you, should it be necessary to sell them elsewhere. In these circumstances please accept this letter as notice calling upon you to take delivery of the said cars and to pay the balance due of £825, on or before Tuesday next May 11, failing which our clients will consider you in breach of the said agreement, will dispose of the said motor cars for the best price they can obtain, and in the event of them receiving a price below that agreed by yourself, will look to you for the difference after giving credit for the £25 already paid by you.

The buyer did nothing except to consult a solicitor and to maintain that there had been misrepresentation.

On Oct. 12, 1965, the seller's solicitors wrote to the buyer's solicitor and, after denying that there had been any misrepresentation and pointing out that the buyer had inspected both vehicles before arriving at the contract, the letter continues:

> In an effort to mitigate the damage following [the buyer's] repudiation [the seller] sold the said Vanguard for £350 but [its] efforts to procure a purchaser for the Zodiac have been completely fruitless.

The Vanguard was sold on or about May 24, 1965, without any further communication to the buyer up to that date than the letter of May 6. The seller also endeavoured to sell the Zodiac, but it has remained unsold and in the seller's possession throughout. Apparently without any further communication between the parties, the writ in this action was taken out on Feb. 9, 1966.

That in its terms was a claim for damages, being the balance of the contract price £825 less the £350 received from the sale of the Vanguard plus £22 10s. advertising expenses in respect of the two cars since the date of the contract, a total of £497 10s. When the matter came before Deputy Judge Ellison the buyer pursued two defences. First, …

Secondly, the defence relied on the buyer's offer to buy the Zodiac for £500 and the seller's refusal of it and said that the seller had failed to mitigate its loss. The judgment held that this was not an unfettered offer. It was to be substituted for the contract to buy the two vehicles. This was clearly right, but judgment was thereupon entered for the seller for £497 10s. damages and costs.

DIPLOCK LJ: This is an appeal from a judgment of the deputy county court judge at Woolwich County Court in what appeared to be a simple action for damages for non-acceptance of goods. The appeal is as to quantum of damages only. [Sellers LJ] has already stated the facts [see above]. The main issue in the action was whether it was a term of the contract that the Vanguard should be a 1962 model. The judge held that it was not, and there is no appeal from that decision. The legal consequence of that finding was that the buyer's refusal to go on with the contract was a wrongful repudiation of the contract. The seller could elect to treat that as rescinding the contract, giving him an immediate right to damages for non-acceptance. Alternatively, he could hold the buyer to the contract. That he chose to do, and communicated his intention to the buyer both orally and by a letter written by his solicitors on May 6 which my lord has already read. That letter states the opinion of the sellers' solicitors that the property had passed to the buyer. That opinion was no doubt based on section 18, r. 1, of the Sale of Goods Act, 1893. The governing rule, however, is in section 17, and in modern times very little is needed to give rise to the inference that the property in specific goods is to pass only on delivery or payment. I think that I should have inferred that in this case: but I do not find it necessary to form any final conclusion on the matter, on which the judge made no finding.

Whether or not the property had passed on May 6, 1965, the seller was only liable to deliver upon payment or tender of the balance of the purchase price (see the Sale of Goods Act, s. 28) and was entitled until then to retain possession, either by virtue of his lien as an unpaid seller if the property had passed (Sale of Goods Act, s. 39(1)), or by virtue of his right to withhold delivery if the property had not passed (subs. (2) of the same section). In either case, the unpaid seller has a right to resell the goods if he gives notice of his intention to do so and the buyer does not within a reasonable time pay or tender the price (Sale of Goods Act, s. 48(3)). The note in the current edition of Chalmers that the right of resale only arises where the seller exercises his right of lien or stoppage in transitu, that is, where the property has passed to the buyer, is in my view wrong. This subsection enables a seller in possession of the goods to make time of payment of the purchase price of the essence of the contract whether the property has passed or not. The seller cannot have greater rights of resale if the property has already passed to the buyer than those which he would have if the property had remained in him.

The letter of May 6, 1965, contained notice to resell on or after May 11. Whether that was a reasonable time or not does not matter. The buyer never tendered the price, and on or before May 24 the seller resold the Vanguard for £350. He advertised the Zodiac for sale, but failed to find a buyer at the advertised price, and on October 12, 1965, offered to deliver it to the buyer against payment of £475, being the balance of the original purchase price of £850 for the two cars less the deposit of £25 and the £350 received on resale of the Vanguard car.

The letter of October 12, 1965, in which that offer was made expressed the intention of the seller to institute proceedings against the buyer for the sum of £475 "as the balance of money due and payable ... for goods bargained and sold." When the writ was issued on February 9, 1966, however, the cause of action was not framed as an action for the balance of the purchase price under section 49(1) of the Sale of Goods Act but as an action for damages for non-acceptance under section 50(1), although the particulars of damage were inappropriate to an action for damages for non-acceptance. In the particulars of damage in the statement of claim credit was given, against the balance of the purchase price of £825, for the sum of £350 for which the Vanguard has been sold, but no credit was given for the market price of the Zodiac.

At the trial neither party, nor the judge, seems to have given his mind to the question of where the property in the Zodiac lay by that date. The only argument as to the *quantum* of damages was based on the contention that the seller ought to have mitigated his damage by accepting the buyer's offer to purchase the Zodiac alone for £500 on May 6, 1965. That contention was ill-founded. At the date of that offer the contract of sale of the two cars was still in being. The offer to buy the Zodiac alone was a proposal by the buyer to rescind that contract by mutual consent coupled with an offer to enter into a fresh contract of sale of the Zodiac alone. The seller, as he was entitled to do, refused to rescind the existing contract of sale at that date, and no question of mitigating his damages then arose. The judge appears tacitly to have accepted the view that the seller was under a duty to mitigate his damage as soon as the buyer wrongfully repudiated the contract but to have taken the view that his rejection of the buyer's offer of £500 for the Zodiac was not a breach of that duty for the reason that the seller was entitled to test the market before accepting any offer to buy either or both of the cars. The judge awarded the seller the damages which he claimed and made no allowance for the value of the Zodiac, which the seller still retains.

If the seller, at the date of the issue of the writ, had been in a position to bring an action for the balance of the purchase price and had done so, the measure of damages awarded by the judge would have been correct and the seller would have been entitled to retain possession of the Zodiac by virtue of his unpaid seller's lien until the judgment was satisfied (Sale of Goods Act, s. 43(2)). If, however, he were only in a position to claim damages for non-acceptance, which was what he did, the *prima facie* measure of his damages would be the difference between the contract price and the market price of the two cars (Sale of Goods Act, s. 50(1) and (3)), and any reasonable costs, such as those of advertising, incurred by him in reselling the cars. The onus of proving the market price of both cars lay upon the seller. The evidence of the sale of the Vanguard at £350 on May 24, 1965, was evidence of the market price of the Vanguard. Evidence of the price at which he had advertised the Zodiac but failed to sell it was some evidence that its market price was less than those figures, which ranged from £490 on May 25, 1965, to £450 on July 1, 1965. The lowest figure at which it was offered was, however, rather late in date, and in order to avoid any necessity for a new trial the parties have very sensibly agreed on a figure of £450 as the market price of the Zodiac at about the end of May, 1965. If, therefore, the seller's only right at the date of the issue of the writ on February 9, 1966, was for damages for non-acceptance, the appeal must be allowed and the damages awarded reduced by £450 from £497 10s. to £47 10s.

In this court it has been contended on behalf of the seller that, when an unpaid seller who retains possession of goods the property in which has passed to the buyer exercises his statutory right of resale under section 48(3) of the Sale of Goods Act, he does not thereby elect to treat the contract as rescinded, but remains entitled to recover the purchase price from the buyer although he must give credit for the net proceeds of sale of any of the goods which he has sold. Authority for this proposition is to be found in the judgment of Finnemore J in *Gallagher v. Shilcock*, [1949] 2 KB 765 and the question in this appeal is whether that judgment is right or not.

Finnemore J based his conclusion on his view as to the construction of section 48 of the Sale of Goods Act, and in particular upon the contrast between the express reference in subsection (4) of section 48 to the contract being rescinded when goods are resold under an express right of resale and the absence of any reference to rescission in subsection (3) of section 48. With great respect, however, I think that that disregards basic principles of the law of contract, and that there is another explanation for the contrast between the two subsections.

Rescission of a contract discharges both parties from any further liability to perform their respective primary obligations under the contract, that is to say, to do thereafter those things which by their contract they had stipulated they would do. Where rescission occurs as a result of one party exercising his right to treat a breach by the other party of a stipulation in the contract as a repudiation of the contract, this gives rise to a secondary obligation of the party in breach to compensate the other party for the loss occasioned to him as a consequence of the rescission, and this secondary obligation is enforceable in an action for damages. Until, however, there is rescission by acceptance of the repudiation, the liability of both parties to perform their primary obligations under the contract continues. Thus, under a contract for the sale of goods which has not been rescinded, the seller remains liable to transfer the property in the goods to the buyer and to deliver possession of them to him until he has discharged those obligations by performing them, and the buyer remains correspondingly liable to pay for the goods and to accept possession of them.

The election by a party not in default to exercise his right of rescission by treating the contract as repudiated may be evinced by words or by conduct. Any act which puts it out of his power to perform thereafter his primary obligations under the contract, if it is an act which he is entitled to do without notice to the party in default, must amount to an election to rescind the contract. If it is an act which he is not entitled to do, it will amount to a wrongful repudiation of the contract on his part which the other party can in turn elect to treat as rescinding the contract.

Part IV of the Sale of Goods Act, sections 38 to 48 [Ont. ss. 37-46], deals with the rights of an unpaid seller both before the property in the goods has passed to the buyer and after it has passed. The mere fact that the seller is unpaid does not necessarily mean that the buyer is in breach of the contract, or, if he is, that his breach is one which entitles the seller to exercise his right to treat the contract as repudiated. Section 39(1) and (2) states what the unpaid seller's rights are in relation to the possession of the goods before and after the property has passed to the buyer. Subsection (1)(c) provides that he shall have "a right of resale as limited by this Act." Sections 41 to 47 deal in greater detail with the exercise by the unpaid seller of his rights in relation to the possession of the goods after the property has passed to the buyer. Section 48 [Ont. s. 46] deals with several topics. Subsection (1) reads as follows: "Subject to the provisions of this section, a contract of sale is not rescinded by the mere exercise by an unpaid seller of his right of lien ... or stoppage in transitu."

If the contract provided for delivery upon a specified date, the seller's conduct in failing to deliver on that date would put it out of his power to perform one of his primary obligations under the contract if time were of the essence of the contract. It was, therefore, necessary, or at least prudent, to provide expressly that if his failure to deliver were in the mere exercise of a lien or right of stoppage in transitu it did not discharge his liability to deliver the goods upon tender of the contract price, or the buyer's liability to accept the goods and to pay for them.

Subsection (2) deals with a different topic, videlicet, the title of a new buyer to whom the goods are resold by the seller. If the property in the goods at the time of the resale remained in the seller, the new buyer would obtain a good title at common law and would require no statutory protection. The subsection is, therefore, limited to cases where the property in the goods at the time of resale had already passed to the original buyer, and provides that, where the seller is in possession of the goods in the exercise of his unpaid seller's lien or right of stoppage in transitu, the new buyer shall acquire a good title, and this is so whether or not the seller had a right of resale as against the original buyer.

Subsection (3) reads as follows: ...

This is the provision of the Act which confers "a right of resale as limited by this Act," referred to in section 39(1)(c) [Ont. s. 38(1)(c)]. The right dealt with in this subsection is a right as against the original buyer. As a stipulation as to time of payment is not deemed to be of the essence of a contract of sale unless a different intention appears from the terms of the contract (Sale of Goods Act, s. 10(1)), failure by the buyer to pay on the stipulated date is not conduct by him which entitles the unpaid seller to treat the contract as repudiated. He remains liable to deliver the goods to the buyer upon tender of the contract price (Sale of Goods Act, s. 28). Apart from this subsection, if the unpaid seller resold the goods before or after the property had passed to the original buyer, he would remain liable to the original buyer for damages for non-delivery if the original buyer tendered the purchase price after the resale, and if the property had already passed to the original buyer at the time of the resale he would be liable to an alternative action by the original buyer for damages for conversion. The purpose of the subsection is to make time of payment of the essence of the contract whenever the goods are of a perishable nature, and to enable an unpaid seller, whatever the nature of the goods, to make payment within a reasonable time after notice of the essence of the contract. As already pointed out, an unpaid seller who resells the goods before the property has passed puts it out of his power to perform his primary obligation to the buyer to transfer the property in the goods to the buyer and, whether or not the property has already passed, to deliver up possession of the goods to the buyer. By making the act of resale on which the unpaid seller is entitled to perform, the subsection empowers the seller by his conduct in doing that act to exercise his right to treat the contract as repudiated by the buyer, that is, as rescinded, with the consequence that the buyer is discharged from any further liability to perform his primary obligation to pay the purchase price, and becomes subject to the secondary obligation to pay damages for non-acceptance of the goods. If the contract were not rescinded by the resale the seller would still be entitled to bring an action against the buyer for the price of the goods although, no doubt, he would have to credit the buyer with the proceeds of the resale. If that were the intention of the subsection one would have expected it to provide this in express terms. That it was not the intention is, however, apparent from the words used to define the remedy of the unpaid seller who has exercised his right of resale, videlicet, to "recover from the original buyer damages for any loss occasioned by his breach of contract." It is, of course, well-established that where a contract for the sale of goods is rescinded after the property in the goods has passed to the buyer the rescission divests the buyer of his property in the goods.

Subsection (4) deals with the consequences of a resale by a seller, not necessarily an "unpaid seller" as defined in section 38, made in the exercise of an express right of resale reserved in the contract on the buyer making default. If such an express right were exercisable after the property in the goods had passed to the buyer, its exercise might, on one view, be regarded as an alternative mode of performance of the seller's primary obligation under the contract, and the resale as being made by the seller as agent for the buyer. It was, therefore, necessary to provide expressly that the exercise of an express power of resale should rescind the original contract of sale. That is, in my view, the explanation of the express reference to rescission in subsection (4). The absence of a similar express reference to rescission in subsection (3) is no sufficient ground for ascribing to subsection (3) a meaning which the actual words of the subsection would appear to contradict and which would, in my view, conflict with the general principles of the law of contract.

In the present case the unpaid seller only resold part of the goods which he had contracted to sell to the original buyer. This makes no difference, however. His primary duty under the contract was to deliver both cars to the buyer. If he delivered only one, the buyer would be entitled to reject it (Sale of Goods Act, s. 30(1)). By his conduct in selling the Vanguard on May 24, 1965, the unpaid seller put it out of his power to perform his primary obligation under the contract. He thereby elected to treat the contract as rescinded. The property in the Zodiac thereupon reverted to him, and his only remedy against the buyer after May 24, 1965, was for damages for non-acceptance of the two cars, of which the prima facie measure is the difference between the contract price and their market value on May 24, 1965.

I, too, would allow this appeal, and enter judgment for the plaintiffs for £47 10s. instead of £497 10s.

Appeal allowed.

[Sellers LJ delivered a separate concurring judgment; Russell LJ concurred without giving reasons.]

NOTES

1) Why should the exercise of the seller's right of resale necessarily be regarded as a rescission of the sale? Would it not be just as logical to treat it as an enforcement of the seller's security interest? For the Code's resale provisions, see UCC 2-706.

2) How would *Ward v. Bignall* be decided under UCC 2-709(1)(b)? Should a court, in applying the section, permit partial specific performance of the buyer's obligation to accept and pay for the goods?

3) The OLRC Sales Report (at 401-3) shows that SGA s. 46 is more conspicuous for the questions it fails to answer than for the questions it does answer. Do you agree with this analysis? Consider the following questions:

a) Absent s. 46, would the seller be entitled to cancel the contract and/or to resell the goods at common law?

b) If a seller sells the goods pursuant to the statutory provision for less than the contract price, is it entitled to sue for the difference or must it prove its damages in the ordinary way under SGA s. 48?

c) Is the seller free to sue for damages under SGA s. 48 and to disregard the results of a favourable sale under SGA s. 46?

d) If the seller has sold at a profit, should it be accountable to the buyer for the surplus?

On all of these questions and for the corresponding position under UCC 2-706, see OLRC Sales Report, at 401-3 and 408-15.

Commission Car Sales (Hastings) Ltd. v. Saul

[1957] NZLR 144 (SC)

[The respondent Saul entered into a contract with the appellant company for the purchase of a Plymouth motor-car at a price of £1,200. The purchase price was to be paid by the trading-in of an Oldsmobile motor-car which was valued at £300 and was also treated as a deposit. The balance was to be paid in cash within a few days. The respondent returned the Plymouth car to the company, and refused to carry on with the purchase. A few days later, the company served upon the respondent a notice stated to be given under s. 49 of the (New Zealand) Sale of Goods Act [Ont. s. 46], indicating that if the balance of the purchase price was not paid within seven days the Plymouth car would be resold and that the respondent would remain responsible for any damages suffered by the company. The respondent ignored the notice. Eventually the Plymouth car was sold for £1,000.

The respondent brought action to recover the amount of the deposit. The company counterclaimed for £110 10s. 9d.,[2] being its loss on the resale of the Plymouth (£100); cost of repainting the car (£35); general loss of commission or profit on resale of the car (£110), and costs of serving the notice under s. 49 of the Sale of Goods Act 1908 (£5 10s. 9d.).

The Magistrate allowed the respondent's claim in full, and gave judgment on the counterclaim in favour of the appellant for the amount of its counterclaim, £110 10s. 9d. The appellant appealed against the judgment in favour of the respondent.]

TURNER J: When the respondent returned the Plymouth car to the appellant and intimated that he would not pay for it, he repudiated liability under the contract for its purchase. By accepting the car, the appellant must be taken to have treated the contract as discharged by breach. Doing this, the appellant was clearly entitled, as Mr. Monagan concedes, to treat any deposit as forfeited. This result follows equally when a deposit is (as here) also a payment on account of the purchase price. The Oldsmobile car, which had been traded in by the respondent, must be treated in precisely the same way as a monetary payment by way of deposit which is also a payment on account of purchase moneys: this follows in the present case from the form of the pleadings as finally amended, and from Mr. Monagan's concession at the hearing. The result must therefore be that, immediately after the return of the Plymouth, the appellant was entitled to keep the Oldsmobile (see, for instance, *Howe v. Smith* (1884), 27 Ch. D. 89); and, further, it would seem to follow from *Fitt v. Cassanet* (1842), 4 Man. & G 898; 134 ER 369 that any final surplus on resale of the Plymouth also became the property of the vendor.

Different considerations apply to a case where a vendor, never having lost possession of the goods, resells them under his statutory power upon default being made in payment of the purchase price. In *Gallagher v. Shilcock*, [1949] 2 KB 765; [1949] 1 All ER 921, Finnemore J held that where this happens, the whole of the money received by the vendor—deposit and resale price combined—must be accounted for, and any net surplus over and above the original purchase price must be refunded. But that decision expressly depended upon the fact that where a purchaser defaults in payment upon a contract for the sale of goods, time is not of the essence, and his default does not result in rescission. It was deduced from this proposition that, there

---

2 The Report does not indicate how this sum was arrived at and it does not jibe with the breakdown of the respondent's claim given in the Report. [eds.]

being no rescission, such a vendor does not resell "as the full and untrammelled owner," and that, therefore, he must account not only for the actual proceeds of the resale, but, necessarily, in doing so effectively, also for the deposit.

The present case is quite a different one. Here the vendor sold, to mitigate his damages, a car of which the ownership and possession had passed from him and had later been restored to him: his acts were those which the common law empowers him to do. I am perfectly clear, moreover, that the vendor in the case before me was not able, even if he wished to do so, to exercise the statutory power of sale given by s. 49 of the Sale of Goods Act 1908, for this power is given by the Act only to those vendors who have never lost possession of the goods sold: *cf. Chalmers on Sale of Goods*, 12th ed., 135. Mr. Monagan contends, however, that though as a matter of law the appellant did not at the time have the power to sell under s. 49, he must now be taken so to have sold (incurring thereby the responsibilities attaching to vendors so selling, as laid down in *Gallagher v. Shilcock*) by reason of the notice given on February 4, 1955. It was contended that the appellant, by intimating that he would hold the respondent liable for any final deficiency on resale pursuant to s. 49, became estopped thereby from refusing to give credit when actually a final surplus was realized.

It will perhaps be as well if I now set out the notice that was given on February 4. It was in the following terms:

To:
> Edgar Dalmage Saul,
> Farmer,
> Takapau.

COMMISSION CAR SALES LIMITED, a duly incorporated Company having its registered office in Karamu Road, Hastings, and carrying on business there as car salesmen HEREBY GIVES YOU NOTICE that it intends on or after the expiry of seven (7) clear days from the service of this notice upon you in exercise of its right as an unpaid seller to resell the 1952 "Cranbrook" Plymouth Sedan Motor vehicle Registered No. 358274 which you agreed to buy from it on the 27th day of January, 1955, AND TAKE FURTHER NOTICE that after the resale the said Company intends to take proceedings to recover from you damages for any loss occasioned by your breach of contract.

This Notice is given in terms of Section 49 of the "Sale of Goods Act 1908."

DATED at Hastings this 4th day of February, 1955.

COMMISSION CAR SALES LIMITED by its Solicitor and duly authorised agent.

I am of opinion that Mr. Monagan's submission must fail. It must be remembered, I think, throughout their consideration that the appellant had, before giving notice, already treated the contract as discharged by breach, and had accepted re-delivery of the Plymouth car. He thenceforward had the right to resell, and so to sue in damages for any net deficiency. It is true that if he so sued, he would have had to give credit for the deposit, for it would be unreal to allege a net deficiency unless the deposit was taken into account; but he could either (a) keep the deposit and resell, retaining the whole proceeds; or (b) resell, suing for any net deficiency after giving credit for the deposit: *cf. Howe v. Smith* (1884), 27 Ch. D. 89, 105 *per* Fry LJ. But he could not resell under s. 49; he had, and could have, no rights under that section, nor could the purchaser have any such rights. The section was simply inapplicable.

I think that the notice given by the appellant on February 4 must be treated simply as a nullity. It was given by a party who mistook his legal position and thought, erroneously as it turned out, that he was bound to give notice whereby time was made of the essence, when already the contract had been repudiated and treated as discharged by breach. The notice contains no express misrepresentation of fact upon which any estoppel could be founded; nor do I find that it contains any such implied representation of fact. Expressions of intention will not found an estoppel, nor will misrepresentations of law. Moreover, I do not see in any case that the respondent has shown, or can show, that he has moved to his detriment in reliance upon the notice.

Appeal allowed.

NOTES

1) *Commission Car Sales v. Saul* was decided before *Ward v. Bignall, supra.* Would it have been decided differently if it had come later? The New South Wales Supreme Court decision in *Wherry v. Watson; Classic Auto Search Pty. Ltd. v. Watson* (1990), ASC s. 56-004 suggests not. In that case, the buyer of a rare 1963 model S3 Bentley paid the seller a deposit by cheque, but the cheque was dishonoured. The seller immediately wrote to the buyer returning the dishonoured cheque and notifying him that the sale was off. He then sold the car to someone else. The buyer sued for specific performance of the original agreement, alleging that the seller had not validly exercised his right of resale and that the contract was still on foot. The buyer's argument ran as follows: (1) when the cheque was dishonoured, the seller became an "unpaid seller" within the meaning of the SGA; (2) an unpaid seller of goods has only such rights as s. 42 of the Act (Ont. s. 38) provides for; and (3) s. 42 (Ont. s. 38) read in conjunction with s. 50(3) (Ont. s. 46(3)) gives the seller a right of resale, but only if the seller first gives the buyer notice of his intention to resell and thereafter gives the buyer a reasonable opportunity to pay or tender the purchase price. Powell J rejected this argument. He held as follows: (1) the unpaid seller's rights under the SGA are an extension of, not a limitation on, the seller's common law rights; (2) at common law, an unpaid seller has the right to terminate the contract if the buyer repudiates and, following termination, to resell the goods; (3) in regard to the payment of a deposit, time is of the essence; (4) the dishonouring of the buyer's cheque for the deposit resulted in the buyer committing a "fundamental breach" of the contract; and (5) this entitled the buyer at common law to terminate the agreement without giving the buyer an opportunity to recover his position. *Commission Car Sales (Hastings) Ltd. v. Saul* was not referred to.

2) In *Saul*, upon the buyer's refusal to pay the balance of the price, would the seller have been entitled to repossess the Plymouth vehicle without the buyer's consent? *Cf.* UCC 2-702 and OLRC Sales Report, at 398. Why should the seller's unpaid lien not extend, for a limited period at any rate, even after the buyer has acquired possession of the goods? Can the buyer's voluntary return of the vehicle, and its acceptance by the seller,

be treated as an accord and satisfaction of all outstanding claims between the parties? Should it have been so treated here?

3) *Semble*, equity's power to relieve from forfeiture of payments, as accepted by Denning and Somervell LJJ in *Stockloser v. Johnson* (*infra*, this chapter) was not raised before Turner J. Would it have made a difference if it had been?

MEASUREMENT OF DAMAGES IN LOST VOLUME SALES

Charter v. Sullivan

[1957] 2 QB 117, [1957] 1 All ER 809 (CA)

[The defendant Sullivan appealed from a judgment of Judge Rawlins in which the judge awarded the plaintiff Charter, a motor-car dealer, £97 15s. damages against the defendant for breach of a contract for the sale by the plaintiff to the defendant of a "Hillman Minx" motor-car. The contract was entered into on June 29 or 30, 1955, when the defendant called at the plaintiff's showroom and agreed to buy a new "Hillman Minx" de luxe saloon motor-car which the plaintiff had in stock, together with extras at a total price of £773 17s. At this price the sale, if completed, would have given the plaintiff a profit of £97 15s., of which £90 2s. 6d. was attributable to the car and the balance to the extras. A term of the bargain was that the plaintiff was to take in part exchange at the price of £350 a "Commer" van belonging to the defendant. On or about July 2, 1955, the defendant found that another dealer would be prepared to give him, as he thought, better terms, and on July 5, 1955, he wrote to the plaintiff a letter in which he refused to take the car. Some seven or 10 days later the plaintiff resold the car to another purchaser, Wigley, for the same price as the defendant had agreed to pay, namely, £773 17s., including the extras which had been fitted at the defendant's request.

The "Hillman Minx" car was a product of the motor manufacturing organization known as the Rootes Group, and the plaintiff was an area dealer for that organization, covering the North Hampshire area. In accordance with the usual practice in the trade, the retail price of the cars was fixed by the manufacturers, so that the profit realizable by a dealer on the sale of a new car remained constant.

No point was made on either side of the fact that the defendant was to give another vehicle in part-exchange, nor was any distinction drawn between the car itself and the extra items. The case was argued before the Court of Appeal on the footing that this was a sale for cash; and, although different considerations might apply to the extras as compared with the car itself, £773 17s. was treated as the fixed retail price simply of the car as supplied by the manufacturers and £97 15s. as the profit resulting from a sale of the car at that price.

The sole issue before the court was the measure of damages.]

JENKINS LJ: I turn now to consider what, on the undisputed facts of the case, is in the eye of the law the true measure of the damages, if any, over and above merely nominal damages, which the plaintiff has suffered through the defendant's failure to take and pay for the car he agreed to buy.

Consideration of this question must inevitably begin with a reference to section 50 of the Sale of Goods Act, 1893. [His Lordship read s. 50 (Ont. SGA, s. 48) and continued:] Mr. Collard, for the defendant, argued that in the present case there was an available market for "Hillman Minx" de luxe saloon cars within the meaning of section 50(3) of the Act, and accordingly that the measure of damages ought, in accordance with the *prima facie* rule laid down by the subsection, to be ascertained by the difference between the contract price and the market or current price at the time of the defendant's refusal to perform his contract.

The result of this argument, if accepted, would be that the plaintiff could claim no more than nominal damages, because the market or current price could only be the fixed retail price, which was necessarily likewise the price at which he sold to the defendant and resold to Wigley.

But the plaintiff is a motor-car dealer whose trade for the present purpose can be described as consisting in the purchase of recurrent supplies of cars of the relevant description from the manufacturers, and selling the cars so obtained, or as many of them as he can, at the fixed retail price. He thus receives, on each sale he is able to effect, the predetermined profit allowed by the fixed retail price, and it is obviously in his interest to sell as many cars as he can obtain from the manufacturers. The number of sales he can effect, and consequently the amount of profit he makes, will be governed, according to the state of trade, either by the number of cars he is able to obtain from the manufacturers, or by the number of purchasers he is able to find. In the former case demand exceeds supply, so that the default of one purchaser involves him in no loss, for he sells the same number of cars as he would have sold if that purchaser had not defaulted. In the latter case supply exceeds demand, so that the default of one purchaser may be said to have lost him one sale.

Accordingly, it seems to me that even if there was within the meaning of section 50(3) an available market for cars of the description in question, and even if the fixed retail price was the market or current price within the meaning of the same subsection, the prima facie rule which it prescribes should be rejected in favour of the general rule laid down by subsection (2); for it does not by any means necessarily follow that, because the plaintiff sold at the fixed retail price to Wigley the car which the defendant had agreed to buy at the selfsame fixed retail price, but refused to take, therefore the plaintiff suffered no "loss directly and naturally resulting, in the ordinary course of events" from the defendant's breach of contract.

This makes it strictly unnecessary to decide whether there was in the present case an available market for cars of the description in question within the meaning of section 50(3). But I would find it difficult to hold that there was. Given default by some purchaser of one of his cars of the relevant description, the plaintiff's only alternative mode of disposal would be to sell it at the fixed retail price to some other purchaser. He could endeavour to find another purchaser by displaying the car in his saleroom, circularising or canvassing old customers or the public at large, and advertising by posters or in newspapers. The car would obviously be of interest to retail customers (i.e., the car-using public as distinct from the trade) and any purchaser he might succeed in finding would necessarily have to be a purchaser at the fixed retail price. At that price there might be no takers, in which case the plaintiff would be left with the car on his hands. Section 50(3) seems to me to postulate a market in which there is a market or current price, i.e., a price fixed by supply and demand at which (be it more or less than the contract price) a purchaser can be found. If the only price at which a car can be sold is the fixed retail price and no purchaser can be found at that price, I do not think it can reasonably be said that there is a market or current price or that there is an available market. If the state of the trade were such that the plaintiff could sell at the fixed retail price all the cars he could get, so that the defendant's default did not result in the plaintiff effecting one sale less than he would otherwise have effected, it may well be that the plaintiff could not make out his claim to anything more than nominal damages. I am, however, inclined to think that this would not be on account of the necessary equality of the contract price and the fixed retail price at which alone the car could be sold, taken for the present purpose as the market or current price within the meaning of section 50(3), but because on an application of the general principle laid down by section 50(2) the plaintiff would be found to have suffered no damage.

In *Thompson (W.L.) Ltd. v. Robinson (Gunmakers) Ltd.*, [1955] Ch. 177, Upjohn J had before him a claim for damages in a case resembling the present case to the extent that the damages were claimed in respect of the defendants' refusal to perform a contract with the plaintiffs for the purchase from the plaintiffs of a car (in that instance a "Standard Vanguard" car) which, like the car in the present case, could only be sold by the plaintiffs at a fixed retail price. It is, however, important to note that the case to which I am now referring proceeded on certain admissions, including an admission to the effect that in the relevant district at the date of the contract (which was also the date of the breach) "there was no shortage of 'Vanguard' models to meet all immediate demands in the locality," which I take to mean, in effect, that the supply of such cars exceeded the demand. In these circumstances the plaintiffs by agreement with their suppliers rescinded their contract with them, and returned the car. In the ensuing action the plaintiffs claimed from the defendants damages amounting to the profit the plaintiffs would have made on the sale of the car to the defendants if the defendants had duly completed their purchase of it, and the judge held them entitled to those damages. The defendants raised the same argument as has been raised by the defendant in the present case, namely, that there was an available market for a car of the kind in question, within the meaning of section 50(3), that there was a market or current price in the shape of the fixed retail price, and that as the fixed retail price was the same as the contract price the plaintiffs had suffered no damage. In the course of his judgment Upjohn J at 185 Ch. referred to James LJ's definition of a market in *Dunkirk Colliery Co. v. Lever* (1878), 9 Ch. D. 20, 24, 25. James LJ said this:

> Under those circumstances the only thing that we can do is to send it back to the referee with an intimation that we are of opinion upon the facts (agreeing with the Master of the Rolls in that respect), that the facts do not warrant the application of the principle mentioned in the award, namely, that there was what may be properly called a market. What I understand by a market in such a case as this is, that when the defendant refused

to take the 300 tons the first week or the first month, the plaintiffs might have sent it in waggons somewhere else, where they could sell it, just as they sell corn on the Exchange, or cotton at Liverpool: that is to say, that there was a fair market where they could have found a purchaser either by themselves or through some agent at some particular place. That is my notion of the meaning of a market under those circumstances.

Upjohn J (at 186 Ch.) also referred to the Scottish case of *Marshall & Co. v. Nicoll & Son*, 1919 SC (HL) 129 where it was held in the Court of Session that there was an available market within the meaning of section 51(3) of the Sale of Goods Act, 1893, for annealed steel sheets although they were not kept in stock and were not purchasable in the open market. In the House of Lords the decision was affirmed, but their Lordships would seem to have been equally divided on the question whether there was an available market for the goods. In this state of the authorities, the judge felt himself bound by *Dunkirk Colliery Co. v. Lever*, and held, in effect, that James LJ's definition in that case prevented him from holding that in the case then before him there was an available market within the meaning of section 50(3).

Upjohn J (at 187 Ch.) went on to propound a more extended meaning for the phrase "available market" in these terms:

Had the matter been res integra I think that I should have found that an "available market" merely means that the situation in the particular trade in the particular area was such that the particular goods could freely be sold, and that there was a demand sufficient to absorb readily all the goods that were thrust on it, so that if a purchaser defaulted, the goods in question could readily be disposed of.

He went on to say, in effect, that in the case then before him there was no available market because the supply of "Vanguard" cars at the material time exceeded the demand.

I doubt if James LJ's observations in *Dunkirk Colliery Co. v. Lever* should be literally applied as an exhaustive definition of an available market in all cases. On the other hand, I do not find Upjohn J's definition entirely satisfactory. I will not, however, attempt to improve upon it, but will content myself with the negative proposition that I doubt if there can be an available market for particular goods in any sense relevant to section 50(3) of the Sale of Goods Act, 1893, unless those goods are available for sale in the market at the market or current price in the sense of the price, whatever it may be, fixed by reference to supply and demand as the price at which a purchaser for the goods in question can be found, be it greater or less than or equal to the contract price. The language of section 50(3) seems to me to postulate that in the cases in which it applies there will, or may, be a difference between the contract price and the market or current price, which cannot be so where the goods can only be sold at a fixed retail price.

Accordingly, I am of opinion that whether there was in this case "an available market" within the meaning of section 50(3) or not, it is a case in which section 50(2) should be applied to the exclusion of section 50(3).

It remains, therefore, to ascertain the loss (if any) "naturally resulting, in the ordinary course of events" from the defendant's breach of contract, and the measure of that loss must, in my opinion, be the amount, if any, of the profit the plaintiff has lost by reason of the defendant's failure to take and pay for the car he agreed to buy. This accords with the view taken by Upjohn J in *Thompson (W.L.) Ltd. v. Robinson (Gun-makers) Ltd.*, and also with the principle stated in *In re Vic Mill Ltd.*, [1913] 1 Ch. 465 which Upjohn J applied.

Appeal allowed.

[Hodson and Sellers LJJ delivered concurring judgments.]

NOTES

1) The principle that a lost-volume seller is entitled to recover his lost profit from a repudiating buyer has also been adopted in Canada. See *Victory Motors Ltd. v. Bayda*, [1973] 3 WWR 747 (Sask. Div. Ct.), followed in *Sanford v. Senger*, [1977] 3 WWR 399 (Sask.) and *Canadian Union College v. Camsteel Industries Ltd.* (1979), 9 Alta. LR (2d) 167. How would the principle in *Charter v. Sullivan* operate in the following circumstances:

a) there is a glut of new cars on the market and the dealer, in order to reduce his inventory, sells the car below the agreed price;

b) the market picks up strength and the dealer is able to sell the vehicle for a better price than agreed upon in his contract with the defendant?

2) In *Sanford v. Senger, supra*, defendant agreed to purchase a reconditioned cash register from plaintiff for $2,400. Plaintiff agreed to give defendant $600 credit on a trade-in and the balance was to be financed through a leasing company. Defendant repudiated the contract and plaintiff sold the register to another buyer for $1,600 after spending $201 to convert the machine to the second buyer's use. Plaintiff sued the defendant for damages. Walker DCJ, purporting to follow *Victory Motors v. Bayda*, assessed damages as follows (*ibid.*, at 409):

Agreed sale price	$2,400
Less cost of machine to the plaintiff	450
	$1,950
Less cost of conversion	715
Loss of profit	$1,235
Cost of conversion for sale to third party	201
Less labour on first conversion which was useful in the second conversion	10
	$1,426

Was this a proper case for applying the lost-volume principle and, if it was, did the court arrive at the correct mathematical result?

3) UCC 2-708(2) deals expressly with the assessment of damages in a lost-volume sale, but its wording has attracted much critical comment. See OLRC Sales Report, at 420-21, and the literature cited on 421, n. 130. Nevertheless, the Report recommended the adoption of a modified version of UCC 2-708(2). *Ibid.*, at 421-22.

The soundness of the economic assumptions on which the lost-volume is based has also come under critical scrutiny by lawyer economists. See, *inter alia*, Goetz and Scott, "Measuring Seller's Damages: The Lost Profit Puzzle" (1979), 31 *Stan. L Rev.* 323 and "Comments" (1973), 24 *Case W. Res. L Rev.* 684 *et seq.*

4) Does the lost-volume rule also apply to the sale of used goods? In *Lazenby Garages Ltd. v. Wright*, [1976] 2 All ER 770 the Court of Appeal held that it did not apply to the sale of used cars. On February 14, 1974, the plaintiffs, who were dealers in secondhand motor cars, purchased a secondhand BMW 2002 for £1,325. On February 19 the defendant agreed to buy it from them for £1,670 for delivery on March 1. On February 20 the defendant repudiated the agreement. The plaintiffs resold the car on April 23 for £1,770. They sued the defendant for breach of contract and claimed £345 by way of damages. They arrived at this amount by taking the difference between the price they had paid for the BMW and the price at which they had agreed to sell it to the defendant. The trial judge allowed the plaintiffs one-half of the damages claimed by them and reasoned that, had the defendant performed his contract, there was a 50 per cent chance that the plaintiffs would have sold an extra car.

The Court of Appeal reversed and held that the judge had erred in applying the lost-volume principle to the sale of a used car. The reason Lord Denning MR gave was that (at 772):

> But it is entirely different in the case of a secondhand car. Each secondhand car is different from the next, even though it is the same make. The sales manager of the garage admitted in evidence that some secondhand cars, of the same make, even of the same year, may sell better than others of the same year. Some may sell quickly, others sluggishly. You simply cannot tell why. But they are all different.

Lawton LJ agreed (*ibid.*) and quoted the evidence of the plaintiffs' own sales manager: "No one can say what makes a secondhand car sellable. It is the same with new cars. Cars vary as to date, mileage, sound of engine, wear and tear, upholstery etc."

5) The market price test was developed at common law in the early part of the 19th century in the assessment of damage claims by seller or buyer and, as the OLRC Sales Report observes (at 521), it has much to commend it. In optimum conditions it provides a ready yardstick for the quantification of damages, and at the same time it reaffirms the innocent party's obligation to mitigate its damages by taking those steps that a reasonably prudent person would take in its place. Nevertheless, the Commission felt the market price test had become encrusted with unnecessary technicalities and was too rigid in its statutory form. The Commission was particularly concerned about the unsettled meaning of "available market" and the uncertainties concerning the time and place for determining the market price. The Commission therefore favoured the adoption of a revised market price test to read as follows (Report, at 527):

> 9.10(3) Where at the agreed time for performance and in circumstances amounting to a substantial breach the buyer wrongfully neglects or refuses to accept and pay for the goods and section 9.9 does not apply, the measure of damage is *prima facie* to be ascertained by the difference between the contract price and the price that could have been obtained by a commercially reasonable disposition of the goods within or at a reasonable time and place after the seller learned of the buyer's breach, less any expenses saved in consequence of the buyer's breach.

For further analysis of the market test, see R. Lawson, "An Analysis of the Concept of 'Available Market'" (1969), 43 *ALJ* 106; D.W.M. Waters, "The Concept of Market in the

Sale of Goods" (1958), 36 *Can. Bar Rev.* 360; and Fridman, *Sale of Goods in Canada*, 3rd ed., at 389-400.

6) An important feature of the market price test is that it is a hypothetical test—the question is not what damages the seller (or buyer) actually suffered, but what damages it is deemed to have suffered. This raises two important issues: (a) should the seller be entitled to recover its actual damages; and (b) should the buyer be entitled to show that the seller suffered *less* than the market price damages? UCC 2-706 and 2-712 answer the first question affirmatively (2-706 deals with a resale by the seller; 2-712 with a covering purchase by the buyer); but are markedly silent on the second. American authors are divided on the correct answer. See OLRC Sales Report, at 409-10. The SGA is silent on both points, but the accepted learning is that the seller's actual resale price, where there is an available market, is only of evidentiary value and does not bind the court. Conversely, when sued for the market price measure of damage the buyer is not entitled to prove that the seller suffered lesser damages. See OLRC Report, at 501 (dealing with the converse case of a defaulting seller). The Privy Council's decision in *Wertheim v. Chicoutimi Pulp Co.*, [1911] AC 301 (PC) runs counter to the current of authority and is reproduced *infra* in chapter 17. Article 75 of the UN International Sales Convention provides:

> If the contract is avoided and if, in a reasonable manner and within a reasonable time after avoidance, the buyer has bought goods in replacement or the seller has resold the goods, the party claiming damages may recover the difference between the contract price and the price in the substitute transaction as well as any further damages recoverable under article 74.

Article 76 further provides that if the injured party "has not made a purchase or resale under article 75" and there is a current price for the goods, it may recover the market-price/contract-price difference by way of damages. It will be seen, therefore, that under the Sales Convention the injured party is bound by its election, although there is nothing in Art. 75 requiring it to give the other party notice of its election.

ANTICIPATORY REPUDIATION AND MEASUREMENT OF DAMAGES

Tai Hing Cotton Mill Ltd. v. Kamsing Knitting Factory

[1978] 1 All ER 515, [1979] AC 91 (PC)

LORD KEITH OF KINKEL: This case, which comes before the Board on appeal from the Full Court of the Supreme Court of Hong Kong, raises a question as to the proper method of assessing damages for breach of contract where the breach is an anticipatory one.

The facts are as follows. By written contract dated 23rd March 1971 the appellants, who are yarn manufacturers in Hong Kong, agreed to sell to the respondents, who carry on business there as manufacturers of cloth and knitwear, 1,500 bales of cotton yarn at the price of HK $1,335 per bale, each bale to contain 400 lbs. of yarn. The contract stated that delivery was to be "Apr. 1971-Dec. 1971," but it was common ground that neither party intended this to be a binding term of the contract, their intention in fact being that the respondents should have the right to call, on reasonable notice, for deliveries as and when they required them. Deliveries commenced in

July 1971 and continued in varying amounts thereafter. From late in 1971 or early in 1972 the appellants did not supply all the quantities requested by the respondents, and from February 1973 they delivered only very small amounts. There were no deliveries after May 1973. On 21st July 1973 the respondents sent to the appellants a letter complaining about their delivery record and concluding:

> In order to complete the captioned contract you are earnestly requested to deliver to us daily at least 4 bales *i.e.* 1,600-lbs. starting from the 26th of this month. Your co-operation and prompt attention is absolutely essential.

The appellants replied by letter dated 31st July 1973, stating that they were treating the contract as cancelled on the ground that the respondents had not taken delivery of all the goods within the period stipulated in the contract, i.e. April to December 1971. The appellants now accept that they were not entitled so to do. The respondents did not accept the cancellation, but sought through the Hong Kong Chinese Textile Mills Association to put pressure on the appellants to continue deliveries. These efforts were unsuccessful, and on 28th November 1973 the respondents issued and served on the appellants a writ claiming damages for breach of contract, alleging in their statement of claim that the appellants' letter of 31st July 1973 constituted a wrongful repudiation of the contract. As at 31st July 1973 there were 424.20 bales of yarn remaining undelivered under the contract. The respondents' claim for damages was based on the difference between the contract price of HK $1,335 per bale and the market price of similar yarn at 31st July 1973, which was said to be HK $3,325 per bale. The market price was proved to be HK $3,300 per bale in August 1973, but evidence was given by a witness for the respondents that the market price began to fall in September 1973, and continued to do so until January 1975 when it reached HK $1,800 per bale.

The case was tried before Briggs CJ who on the 19th February 1975 gave judgment in favour of the respondents for damages amounting to HK $451,773. He arrived at this figure on the basis of evidence that the respondents had on 30th May 1973 purchased 40,000 lbs. of yarn from another source in order to make good deficiencies in the appellant's deliveries under the contract, at a price of HK $2,400 per bale. The learned Chief Justice's award represents the difference between that price and the contract price of HK $1,335 per bale, namely HK $1,065, multiplied by the number of bales undelivered under the contract, namely 424.20. He appears to have taken the view that the respondents were under a duty to mitigate their loss by purchasing the whole amount of yarn undelivered at the market price prevailing on 30th May 1973. That view is clearly untenable, since on the evidence there was no breach of contract by the appellants until a considerably later date.

The appellants appealed to the Full Court of Hong Kong on the ground that damages should have been assessed on the basis of the prices at which the respondents had purchased yarn to make good deficiencies in contractual deliveries at dates even earlier than 30th May 1973. At the hearing of the appeal, however, they accepted that they could not maintain that submission unless it could be established that they were in breach of contract at such earlier dates. They sought leave to amend their pleadings with a view to making a case of that nature, but the Full Court refused leave.

The respondents entered a cross-appeal on the ground that the learned Chief Justice erred in assessing the damages as at 30th May 1973, and that he should have done so on the basis of the market price of yarn on 31st July 1973, the date when the appellants repudiated the contract. By order dated 19th September 1975, against which the appellants appeal to Her Majesty in Council, the Full Court (Huggins, McMullin and Cons JJ) unanimously dismissed the appellants' appeal and by a majority (Huggins and McMullin JJ, Cons J dissenting) allowed the respondents' cross-appeal. The order accordingly fixed the damages at the sum of HK $833,553, representing the difference between the contract price of HK $1,335 per bale and the market price of HK $3,300 per bale at 31st July 1973, multiplied by the number of bales undelivered.

The principal question in the appeal is whether the majority of the Full Court were right in holding that damages for the appellants' admitted breach of contract fell to be ascertained as at 31st July 1973, the date of the appellants' repudiation of the contract, notwithstanding that the respondents did not accept the repudiation, and rescind the contract, until they issued and served their writ in the present action on 28th November 1973.

The answer to that question turns on the proper construction of s. 53 of the Hong Kong Sale of Goods Ordinance, which provides [see Ont. SGA, s. 49] ...

These provisions are identical with those of s. 51 of the [United Kingdom] Sale of Goods Act 1893, except that in the latter the words "for delivery" and "neglect or" in the latter part of sub-s. (3) do not appear. Their Lordships do not consider that this difference can properly lead to any distinction of construction between the two enactments.

In the Full Court both Huggins and McMullin JJ took the view that the present contract was one which did not fix any time for delivery, that the appellants on 31st July 1973 intimated their refusal to deliver the balance of the contractual goods, and that the second limb of s. 53(3) consequently required that damages be ascertained by reference to market price at 31st July 1973. Cons J dissented on this matter, and he therefore was in favour of dismissing the cross-appeal and allowing the learned Chief Justice's assessment of damages to stand.

Before this Board it was contended for the appellants that the second limb of sub-s. (3) did not apply to cases of anticipatory breach of contract, that damages fell to be assessed by reference to market price at the time when the goods ought to have been delivered, and that such time was a reasonable period (say, one month) after the last date on which the respondents might have called for delivery of the balance of the contractual goods. That date was 28th November 1973, being the date on which the respondents, by issuing and serving their writ, had accepted the appellant's repudiation and rescinded the contract. Thus the damages fell to be ascertained by reference to the market price of comparable goods at 28th December 1973, and since the respondents had led no evidence about market price on that date they had failed to prove any loss and the damages should be nominal.

In support of their proposition that the second limb of s. 53(3) does not apply in cases of anticipatory breach of contract the appellants relied strongly on *Millet v. Van Heek & Co.*, [1920] 3 KB 535. That case concerned contracts for the sale of quantities of cotton waste by sellers in Rochdale to buyers in Holland. The contracts were entered into in 1916, at a time when government licences were required for the export of cotton waste from the United Kingdom but were freely granted. In 1917, however, the export of cotton waste was completely prohibited. The parties then agreed that deliveries under the contract would be resumed as soon as the export embargo was lifted, but in August 1918 the sellers wrote to the buyers refusing to be bound to make any further deliveries, and in October 1918 the buyers accepted this repudiation. The export embargo was removed in January 1919, and shortly afterwards the sellers started proceedings for a declaration that the contract had been frustrated. The buyers counterclaimed for damages. It was held in the Divisional Court, on appeal from a decision of the Official Referee on the matter of damages, that the parties had entered into a contract for suspension of deliveries until a reasonable time after the removal of the embargo, and that after the expiration of that reasonable time deliveries should be resumed and continued in conformity with the original contracts. Bray J, delivering the judgment of the court, went on to express the opinion that a contract providing for delivery within a reasonable time was not, within the meaning of s. 51(3) of the 1893 Act, a contract for delivery at a fixed time, even if the contract was for delivery within a reasonable time after some future date. He then said [1920] 3 KB 535, at 542, 543:

> The next point was whether this case fell within the rule mentioned in the last two lines of s. 51, sub-s. 3. We hold that this rule cannot apply to this case. It does not apply to a case where the breach is an anticipatory breach. We hold that there is no specific rule in s. 51 within which the present case falls, except the rule in sub-s. 2 and that this case must be decided according to that rule, but with the light thrown upon it by sub-s. 3.

This judgment was affirmed by the Court of Appeal (Bankes, Warrington and Atkin LJJ) on the ground that the second limb of s. 51(3) had no application to the case of an anticipatory breach by repudiation of the contract before the time for performance arrives, the question whether a contract for delivery within a reasonable time is not a contract for delivery at a fixed time being reserved. Atkin LJ said [1921] 2 KB 369, at 376, 377:

> I think that the construction of s. 51, sub-s. 3, of the Sale of Goods Act, 1893, contended for by the appellants would, if it were admitted, introduce a very serious anomaly into the administration of the law relating to the sale of goods, because the position is this: It is admitted that, if a contract is made for the sale of goods deliverable in the future by specified installments at specified dates, and before the time has arrived for performance the contract is repudiated, and the repudiation is accepted, the damages have to be measured in reference to the dates on which the contract ought to have been performed. That is beyond controversy. The law was so laid down by Cockburn CJ in *Frost v. Knight*, in the Exchequer Chamber, and it was the law at the time when the code of 1893 was passed; and there is no reason to suppose that the code intended to alter it. The Lord Chief Justice said (1872), LR 7 Exch. 111, at 113: "The promisee may, if he thinks proper, treat the repudiation of the other party as a wrongful putting an end to the contract, and may at once bring his action as on a breach of it; and in such action he will be entitled to such damages as would have arisen from the non-performance of

the contract at the appointed time, subject, however, to abatement in respect of any circumstances which may have afforded him the means of mitigating his loss." Therefore, if it was such a contract as I have suggested for delivery by fixed instalments at fixed times, then, although the action is brought in respect of the accepted repudiation, the damages would have to be assessed with reference to those fixed times. But it is said that, if no times have been expressed in the contract, and the contract would be construed by law as one for delivery by reasonable instalments over a reasonable time, even though those times might be ascertained as a question of fact by the jury, the plaintiff suing may not merely have an option, but is compelled, to fix his damages in reference to the market price at the time when the repudiation takes place. That, it seems to me, would introduce an anomaly entirely without any kind of principle to justify it. I am satisfied that the code never intended to make that distinction, or to vary what was the rule of law at the time when it was passed, a rule which has been recorded in countless decisions since the doctrine of repudiation of contract has received its development in *Frost v. Knight*—namely, that the damages are to be fixed in reference to the time for performance of the contract subject to questions of mitigation. Therefore, I think that the view taken by the Divisional Court is right on this point.

. . .

Counsel for the respondents, while accepting that the second limb of s. 51(3) of the Sale of Goods Act 1893 and of s. 53(3) of the Hong Kong ordinance did not apply to cases of anticipatory breach where the contract stipulated a fixed time for delivery, argued that it did apply to such cases where no fixed time was stipulated, and that *Millet v. Van Heek & Co.* was wrongly decided. He referred to a number of cases decided between the passing of the 1893 Act and the date of *Millet v. Van Heek & Co.*, which all appear to have this in common, that no specific reference was made to the relevant provisions of the Act and that it was not contended that the damages fell to be ascertained as at the date when the goods ought to have been delivered. ...

In their Lordships' opinion the cases referred to by counsel for the respondents are not authoritative on the point of issue and have in themselves no persuasive effect. The force of his argument resides essentially in the plain terms of the second limb of s. 51(3). Their Lordships are attracted by the consideration that this may have been enacted in order to provide a universal rule of simple application for cases where the contract fixes no time for delivery, as where delivery is to be within a reasonable time or on demand by the purchaser. In such cases there may be great difficulty in determining when the contract ought to have been performed, and there could be much convenience in assessing damages as at the date of repudiation by the seller, assuming the buyer accepts it. Further, if the enactment is not intended to apply to a repudiation in such cases, it is difficult to see what content it can have. It could not apply, in cases where delivery is to be made on demand by the buyer, to a refusal to deliver following on a demand duly made, because the demand, having been made in accordance with the contract, would fix the time for delivery. It might be intended to apply, where delivery is to be made within a reasonable time, to a refusal to deliver intimated at the expiry of the period of reasonable time, but if so nothing significant would have been added to the first limb. It may well be, however, that the enactment was introduced into the subsection without consideration in depth of the juristic position, and that on analysis it proves, exceptionally, to have no content whatever. It would be surprising if the first limb of one and the same subsection were intended to be a specific application of the general principle in the preceding subsection, and the second limb to be a radical departure from it. If Parliament had intended to introduce a new rule of the nature contended for, their Lordships would have expected this to be done by clearer and more specific language than appears in the second limb of sub-s. (3).

Atkin LJ, in the course of that part of his judgment in *Millet v. Van Heek & Co.* which dealt with the question whether the second limb of s. 51(3) applied to cases of anticipatory breach, expressed the view that it was anomalous that a plaintiff should not only have the option, but be compelled, to fix his damages in reference to the time when the repudiation takes place. It appears to their Lordships that a plaintiff in such a case is not necessarily so compelled. He is not required to accept the repudiation, and if he does not do so the repudiation has no effect. He may wait until there has been an actual failure by the defendant to perform the contract, either on account of an unmet demand or on account of a reasonable time having elapsed without delivery. In this event the damages would be assessed, not at the date of the unaccepted repudiation, but at the date of the actual failure to perform. A more important consideration, in their Lordships' view, is that if the plaintiff did accept the repudiation, and if the market were to fall substantially up to the time when in the event the contract ought to have been performed, the plaintiff would be placed in a better position than if there had been due performance. This would represent an important inroad on a fundamental principle of assessment of damages, namely, that they should be no more than compensatory.

In the result, their Lordships have not been satisfied that *Millet v. Van Heek & Co.* was wrongly decided, and considering that the decision has stood for 57 years without being subjected to any published criticism, and has no doubt been acted on in many cases, they are of opinion that it ought to be applied in the present case. Their Lordships therefore affirm the principle that the second limb of s. 51(3) of the 1893 Act and of s. 53(3) of the Hong Kong ordinance, does not apply in any case of anticipatory breach of contract.

. . .

Appeal allowed.

NOTE

The *Tai Hing Cotton Mill* case was about a breach of contract *by the buyer*. The provision in issue was s. 53 of the Hong Kong Sale of Goods Ordinance (s. 49 of the Ontario SGA, damages for non-delivery). Buyers' remedies are dealt with in the next chapter. Section 48 of the Ontario SGA governs the seller's right to damages for non-acceptance by the buyer. Sections 48(3) and 49(3) are mirror-image provisions and, therefore, the *Tai Hing Cotton Mill* case is equally relevant to the construction of s. 48(3). See *Benjamin's Sale of*

Goods, 5th ed. (1997), para. 16-075, which explains acceptance by the seller of the buyer's anticipatory repudiation as follows:

> If the seller accepts the buyer's anticipatory repudiation, he may sue immediately for damages for breach of contract; but in those situations in which there is an available market for the goods, the relevant date for ascertaining the market price remains prima facie (and subject to any requirement of mitigation) the date fixed for delivery, since that is the date when the contract ought to be performed. If the action is heard before the date for delivery arrives, the court should attempt to estimate what the market price is likely to be at that future date. The seller cannot advance the relevant date for ascertaining the market price merely by exercising his option to accept the anticipatory breach: a lower market price at the time of repudiation should not increase the damages. Thus, it is submitted that the provision in section 50(3) that, when no time is fixed for acceptance, damages should be assessed by reference to the market price "at the time of the refusal to accept" should not apply to an anticipatory breach by the buyer.

Paragraph 16-076 goes on to explain the rules that apply where the seller elects not to accept the buyer's anticipatory repudiation.

RELIEF FROM FORFEITURE OF MONIES PAID

Stockloser v. Johnson

[1954] 1 QB 476, [1954] 1 All ER 630 (CA)

[The defendant was the owner of plant and machinery used in connection with the operation of two quarries, known respectively as the Washington and "Playhatch" quarries. The defendant let the Washington plant and machinery to the "Renown" company in exchange for royalty payments and subsequently entered into a similar arrangement with another company, Dow-Mac (Quarries) Ltd., with respect to the Playhatch plant and machinery.

In 1950 the plaintiff agreed to purchase from the defendant the plant and machinery at the two quarries together with the benefit of the hiring agreements. Payment was to be made by instalments. By clause 5 of the agreement it was provided that if the purchaser made default in an instalment for a period exceeding 28 days the vendor was entitled, on giving 14 days' notice to rescind,

> to retake possession of the plant, machinery and appliances specified in the schedule hereto and again to enter into enjoyment of the said agreement and the fruits thereof as though this agreement had never been executed. And in such event all payments made hereunder by the purchaser to the vendor shall be forfeited to the vendor who shall retain the same.

The plaintiff encountered difficulties from the outset and in December, 1951, he defaulted in the payment of instalments on both agreements. On February 25, 1952, the defendant gave notices rescinding both agreements.

The plaintiff at no time expressed his readiness or ability to make further payments if the defendant were willing to waive his right to rescind, but he brought the present action claiming the return of the instalments paid under the agreements. The plaintiff contended that the retention of the instalments by the defendant amounted to the exaction of a penalty, from which he was entitled to be relieved.

Hallett J gave judgment refusing the plaintiff relief in respect of the instalment paid under the "Playhatch" agreement, but granting him relief, subject to certain deductions, in respect of the instalments paid under the Washington agreement.

The defendant appealed, and the plaintiff cross-appealed.]

DENNING LJ: There was acute contest as to the proper legal principles to apply in this case. On the one hand, Mr. Neil Lawson urged us to hold that the buyer was entitled to recover the instalments at law. He said that the forfeiture clause should be ignored because it was of a penal character, and once it was ignored, it meant that the buyer was left with a simple right to repayment of his money on the lines of *Dies v. British and International Mining and Finance Corporation*, [1939] 1 KB 724 subject only to a cross-claim for damages. In asking us to ignore the forfeiture clause, Mr. Lawson relied on the familiar tests which are used to distinguish between penalties and liquidated damages, and said that these tests had been applied in cases for the repayment of money, citing *Barton v. Capewell* (1893), 68 LT 857 and *Commissioner of Public Works v. Hills*, [1906] AC 368. In neither of those cases, however, was the point argued or discussed, and I do not think they warrant Mr. Lawson's proposition. There is, I think, a plain distinction between penalty cases, strictly so called, and cases like the present.

It is this: when one party seeks to exact a penalty from the other, he is seeking to exact payment of an extravagant sum either by an action at law or by appropriating to himself moneys belonging to the other party, as in *Commissioner of Public Works v. Hills*. The claimant invariably relies, like Shylock, on the letter of the contract to support his demand, but the courts decline to give him their aid because they will not assist him in an act of oppression: see the valuable judgments of Somervell and Hodson LJJ in *Cooden Engineering Co. v. Stanford*, [1953] 1 QB 86.

In the present case, however, the seller is not seeking to exact a penalty. He only wants to keep money which already belongs to him. The money was handed to him in part payment of the purchase price and, as soon as it was paid, it belonged to him absolutely. He did not obtain it by extortion or oppression or anything of that sort, and there is an express clause—a forfeiture clause, if you please—permitting him to keep it. It is not the case of a seller seeking to enforce a penalty, but a buyer seeking restitution of money paid. If the buyer is to recover it, he must, I think, have recourse to somewhat different principles from those applicable to penalties, strictly so called.

On the other hand, Mr. Beney urged us to hold that the buyer could only recover the money if he was able and willing to perform the contract, and for this purpose he ought to pay or offer to pay the instalments which were in arrear and be willing to pay the future instalments as they became due; and he relied on *Mussen v. Van Dieman's Land Co.*, [1938] Ch. 253. I think that this contention goes too far in the opposite direction. If the buyer was seeking to re-establish the contract, he would of course have to pay up the arrears and to show himself willing to perform the contract in the future, just as a lessee, who has suffered a forfeiture, has to do when he seeks to re-establish the lease. So, also, if the buyer were seeking specific performance he would have to show himself able and willing to perform his part. But the buyer's object here is not to re-establish the contract. It is to get his money back, and to do this I do not think that it is necessary for him to go so far as to show that he is ready and willing to perform the contract.

I reject, therefore, the arguments of counsel at each extreme. It seems to me that the cases show the law to be this: (1) *When there is no forfeiture clause.* If money is handed over in part payment of the purchase price, and then the buyer makes default as to the balance, then, so long as the seller keeps the contract open and available for performance, the buyer cannot recover the money; but once the seller rescinds the contract or treats it as at the end owing to the buyer's default, then the buyer is entitled to recover his money by action at law, subject to a cross-claim by the seller for damages: see *Palmer v. Temple* (1839), 9 Ad. & El. 508; *Mayson v. Clouet*, [1924] AC 980; *Dies v. British and International Co.*, [1939] 1 KB 724; *Williams on Vendor and Purchaser*, 4th ed., at 1006. (2) *But when there is a forfeiture clause or the money is expressly paid as a deposit, (which is equivalent to a forfeiture clause)*, then the buyer who is in default cannot recover the money at law at all. He may, however, have a remedy in equity, for, despite the express stipulation in the contract, equity can relieve the buyer from forfeiture of the money and order the seller to repay it on such terms as the court thinks fit. That is, I think, shown clearly by the decision of the Privy Council in *Steedman v. Drinkle*, [1916] 1 AC 275, where the Board consisted of a strong three, Viscount Haldane, Lord Parker and Lord Sumner.

The difficulty is to know what are the circumstances which give rise to this equity; but I must say that I agree with all that Somervell LJ has said about it, differing herein from the view of Romer LJ. Two things are necessary: first, the forfeiture clause must be of a penal nature, in this sense, that the sum forfeited must be out of all proportion to the damage, and secondly, it must be unconscionable for the seller to retain the money. Inasmuch as the only case in which this jurisdiction has been exercised is *Steedman v. Drinkle*, I have examined the record and would draw attention to the circumstances of that case. The agreement was in effect a hire-purchase agreement of land. The purchase-money was payable by instalments over six years, completion to be at the end of the six years, and meanwhile the purchasers were to be let into possession of the land as tenants with the instalments ranking as rent. In case of default the vendor was at liberty to cancel the contract and retain the payments which had been made. The purchasers paid the first instalment and went into possession, but they failed to pay the second instalment which was due at the end of the first year. The value of the land had risen greatly during that year and the vendor seized upon the purchaser's default as giving him the opportunity to rescind the contract. Without previous warning, the vendor gave notice cancelling the contract. The purchasers at once tendered the amount due but the vendor refused to accept it. The purchasers issued a writ for specific performance and meanwhile remained in possession of the land taking the crops off it. They failed to get specific performance in the first court, then succeeded in the Court of Appeal, but failed again in the Privy Council on the ground that time was expressly of the essence of the contract. Nevertheless, the Privy Council relieved the purchasers from forfeiture of the sums already paid. The purchasers would no doubt have to give credit for the crops they had taken from the land during the three years or more that they had been in possession, but subject to that credit they would get their money back.

In the later case of *Mussen v. Van Dieman's Land Co.*, [1938] Ch. 253 Farwell J said that the whole basis of the decision in *Steedman v. Drinkle* was that the purchasers were ready and willing to perform the contract; but I think that that is much too narrow an explanation. Readiness and willingness is essential in specific performance, and in relief from forfeiture of leases, but not in relief from forfeiture of sums paid. The basis of the decision in *Steedman v. Drinkle* was, I think, that the vendor had somewhat sharply exercised his right to rescind the contract and retake the land, and it was unconscionable for him also to forfeit the sums already paid. Equity could not specifically enforce the contract, but it could and would relieve against the forfeiture.

In the course of the argument before us Somervell LJ put an illustration which shows the necessity for this equity even though the buyer is not ready and willing to perform the contract. Suppose a buyer has agreed to buy a necklace by instalments, and the contract provides that, on default in payment of any one instalment, the seller is entitled to rescind the contract and forfeit the instalments already paid. The buyer pays 90 per cent of the price but fails to pay the last instalment. He is not able to perform the contract because he simply cannot find the money. The seller thereupon rescinds the contract and retakes the necklace and resells it at a higher price. Surely equity will relieve the buyer against forfeiture of the money on such terms as may be just.

Again, suppose that a vendor of property, in lieu of the usual 10 per cent deposit, stipulates for an initial payment of 50 per cent of the price as a deposit and a part payment; and later, when the purchaser fails to complete, the vendor resells the property at a profit and in addition claims to forfeit the 50 per cent deposit. Surely the court will relieve against the forfeiture. The vendor cannot forestall this equity by describing an extravagant sum as a deposit, any more than he can recover a penalty by calling it liquidated damages.

These illustrations convince me that in a proper case there is an equity of restitution which a party in default does not lose simply because he is not able and willing to perform the contract. Nay, that is the very reason why he needs the equity. The equity operates, not because of the plaintiff's default, but because it is in the particular case unconscionable for the seller to retain the money. In short, he ought not unjustly to enrich himself at the plaintiff's expense. This equity of restitution is to be tested, I think, not at the time of the contract, but by the conditions existing when it is invoked. Suppose, for instance, that in the instance of the necklace, the first instalment was only 5 per cent of the price; and the buyer made default on the second instalment. There would be no equity by which he could ask for the first instalment to be repaid to him any more than he could claim repayment of a deposit. But it is very different after 90 per cent has been paid. Again, delay may be very material. Thus in *Mussen's* case the court was much influenced by the fact that the purchaser had allowed nearly six years to elapse before claiming restitution. He had already had a good deal of land conveyed to him and, during his six years delay, values had so greatly changed that it may be that he had his money's worth. At any rate, it was not unconscionable for the defendant to retain the money.

Applying these principles to the present case, even if one regards the forfeiture clause as of a penal nature—as the judge did and I am prepared to do—nevertheless I do not think that it was unconscionable for the seller to retain the money. The buyer seems to have gambled on the royalties being higher than they were. He thought that they would go a long way to enable him to pay the instalments; but owing to bad weather they turned out to be smaller than he had hoped and he could not find the additional amount necessary to pay the instalments. The judge summarized the position neatly when he said that the purchaser "is in the position of a gambler who has lost his stake and is now saying that it is for the court of equity to get it back for him." He said, "if it is a question of what is unconscionable, or, to use a word with a less legal flavour, unfair, I can see nothing whatever unfair in the defendant retaining the money." With that finding of the judge I entirely agree and think that it disposes of the purchaser's claim to restitution.

Despite this finding, however, the judge did allow the buyer to recover the instalments he had paid on the Washington quarry. The reason was because, after the buyer made default, the seller bought up the interest of the Renown company in the quarry and thereby disabled himself from fulfilling the contract with the buyer if called upon to do so. I do not myself think that in this case that makes any difference. It might have done if there had been no forfeiture clause and the buyer was claiming at law for the return of his instalment; because then the buyer would have to show that the seller had treated the contract as at the end, see *Palmer v. Temple*, 9 Ad. & El. 508, 521. But the buyer here cannot claim at law. There is a forfeiture clause which prevents him doing so. He can only claim in equity; and he does not gain an equity simply because the seller has bought up the quarry. I do not think, therefore, that the judge was right in allowing the buyer to recover the instalments which he had paid on the Washington quarry. The buyer should not be allowed to recover anything. I agree that the appeal of the seller should be allowed, but the cross-appeal should be dismissed.

Appeal allowed;
cross-appeal dismissed.

[In a separate concurring judgment, Somervell LJ expressed the same view of the law as Denning LJ. Romer LJ agreed with the result but disagreed on the main question whether equity will grant relief from forfeiture of instalments paid under a contract of sale. He adopted the position that there was no justification for disturbing contractual stipulations between freely consenting parties where there are no elements of pressure or duress. He thought that the precedents cited by Denning LJ only stood for the proposition that the court will, in a proper case, give a defaulting purchaser further time to make the payments in arrear if he is able and willing to do so.]

NOTES

1) *Stockloser v. Johnson* involved a claim for relief from forfeiture of instalments. Denning LJ does not state clearly whether equity's power applies equally to payments in the form of deposits. In principle it should make no difference and subsequent Canadian

decisions have not distinguished between these two situations. The broad equity is also supported in S.M. Waddams, *The Law of Contracts*, 4th ed. (1999), at paras. 465-469.

2) The subsequent history of the majority doctrine in *Stockloser v. Johnson* is related in the following extract from the OLRC's *Report on Amendment of the Law of Contract* (at 149-50). The extract also includes an overview of some relevant statutory provisions:

> The wide jurisdiction enunciated in *Stockloser v. Johnson* has been greeted coolly by subsequent lower courts in England and there is apparently no reported case where an English court has granted relief to a defaulting buyer from forfeiture of payments made. Canadian courts have been much more positive in their response. The buyer has sought relief from forfeiture in at least thirteen reported cases between 1954 and 1985, and has succeeded in four. The buyer failed in the other nine cases not because the courts denied their jurisdiction to grant relief, but because they did not feel the buyer had made out a meritorious case. *Stockloser v. Johnson* was also referred to by the Supreme Court of Canada in *Dimensional Investments Ltd. v. The Queen* [[1968] SCR 93], but the Court reserved its opinion on the status of the equitable doctrine in Canada.
>
> In Canada, the common law and equitable positions are also affected by various statutory provisions, which are both general and particular in character. The general provision in Ontario is section 111 of the *Courts of Justice Act, 1984* affirming the courts' jurisdiction to grant relief from penalties and forfeitures. The significance of the provision is not clear. In *Snider v. Harper* [(1922), 66 DLR 149, at 151 (CA)], Stuart JA of the Appellate Division of the Supreme Court of Alberta expressed the view that the parallel section in the Alberta Act created a new source of judicial power, whereas in *Emerald Christmas Tree Co. v. Boel & Sons Enterprises Ltd.* [[1979] 13 BCLR 122] the British Columbia Court of Appeal held that the parallel British Columbia provision was only declaratory of the existing law and did not confer a new type of discretion. In any event it seems unlikely that section 111 of the *Courts of Justice Act, 1984* and its predecessors were meant to freeze the courts' discretionary powers to the types of relief available at the time the section was first adopted.
>
> The particular statutory provisions in Canada protecting a buyer's payments differ widely in character. Some, like the provisions in conditional sales legislation, now superseded in Ontario by the *Personal Property Security Act*, seek to protect the buyer's payments by giving him a statutory right to redeem the goods even after they have been repossessed by the seller. The personal property security Acts, on the other hand, contain comprehensive statutory regimes regulating the parties' rights after the debtor's default and in effect making it difficult for a seller to retain the goods *and* any payments made by the buyer without the buyer's consent. Still another example is provided by the Saskatchewan *Agreements of Sale Cancellation Act* which does not permit cancellation of instalment agreements for the sale of land without a court order. These provisions apply only to particular types of transaction. While they may be helpful in indicating what types of relief may be afforded in cases where the normal equitable approach is inadequate or inappropriate, they provide little guidance about the proper scope of the courts' power to grant relief from forfeiture as a matter of general principle. ...

3) In *Stockloser v. Johnson*, Romer LJ would have been prepared to grant relief if the vendor had been guilty of fraud, sharp practice, or other unconscionable conduct. He said that there was "nothing inequitable *per se* in a vendor, whose conduct is not open

to criticism in other respects, insisting on his contractual right to retain instalments of purchase-money already paid": [1954] 1 QB 476, at 501. In other words, Romer LJ insisted on proof of procedural unconscionability, whereas for Denning and Somervell LJJ, substantive unconscionability (in the form of a windfall to the vendor) was enough. In Canada, the law seems to have been settled in favour of the majority view (see note 2, above), but in England and Australia, Romer LJ's view is preferred: see G.H. Treitel, *The Law of Contract*, 10th ed. (1999), at 940; R.P. Meagher, W.M.C. Gummow and J.R.F. Lehane, *Equity Doctrines and Remedies*, 3rd ed. (1992), para. [1827]. Compare the attitude of the English and Australian courts in cases where the purchaser *is* ready and willing to perform: *Shiloh Spinners v. Harding*, [1973] AC 691 (HL); *Legione v. Hateley* (1983), 152 CLR 406 (HCA); and *Stern v. McArthur* (1988), 165 CLR 489. *Stern v. McArthur* reveals a division of opinion in Australia on whether proof of substantive unconscionability is enough: see Meagher, Gummow and Lehane, *op. cit.*, para. [1829].

4) For the Code's treatment of the forfeiture problem, see UCC 2-718(2) and (3), and note its assimilation of the law of penalty and forfeiture clauses. The same approach appears in s. 2-516(c) of the (American) Uniform Land Transactions Act and, in a wider setting, in s. 374 of the Restatement of the Law of Contracts 2nd (1979).

UCC 2-718(2) and (3) read:

> (2) Where the seller justifiably withholds delivery of goods because of the buyer's breach, the buyer is entitled to restitution of any amount by which the sum of his payments exceeds
>
>> (a) the amount to which the seller is entitled by virtue of terms liquidating the seller's damages in accordance with subsection (1), or
>>
>> (b) in the absence of such terms, twenty per cent of the value of the total performance for which the buyer is obligated under the contract or $500, whichever is smaller.
>
> (3) The buyer's right to restitution under subsection (2) is subject to offset to the extent that the seller establishes
>
>> (a) a right to recover damages under the provisions of this Article other than subsection (1), and
>>
>> (b) the amount or value of any benefits received by the buyer directly or indirectly by reason of the contract.

Do you prefer the Code's solution to the vaguer equitable doctrine enunciated in *Stockloser v. Johnson*? The Code's provisions are discussed in Robert J. Nordstrom, "Restitution on Default and Article 2 of the Uniform Commercial Code" (1966), 19 *Van. L Rev.* 1113.

5) The English Law Commission put forward a number of alternative statutory proposals in its Working Paper No. 61 on *Penalty Clauses and Forfeiture of Monies Paid* (1975), but these have not so far resulted in a final report. There appears to be little interest among practitioners in England in changing the status quo. The OLRC Contract Law Amendment Report is much less hesitant. It suggests (at 153) collapsing the legal distinction between stipulated damage clauses and forfeiture of payment clauses and subjecting the validity of both to a general unconscionability test. Do you support this approach? How does it differ from the majority doctrine in *Stockloser v. Johnson*?

CHAPTER SIXTEEN

Buyer's Remedies for Breach of Seller's Obligations: Right of Rejection

As we have seen in earlier chapters, the law imposes heavy obligations on a seller, especially if he is a merchant-seller and therefore subject to the implied conditions in SGA ss. 15-16. The purpose of the present chapter is to examine the contractual remedies available to an aggrieved buyer and the important issues—exegetical and policywise—which they raise. As will be seen, from the seller's point of view the remedial structure matches in severity the heavy substantive obligations imposed on the seller. In practice, therefore, a well-drafted agreement will almost invariably modify, or perhaps exclude altogether, the statutory and common law remedies available to the buyer. (Disclaimer and exception clauses are considered in chapter 18.) This important qualifier should be borne in mind in studying the materials in this chapter.

OLRC Sales Report

at 433

Under existing law, an aggrieved buyer has a variety of remedies, not all of which are spelled out in the Ontario Sale of Goods Act. The nature of these remedies will vary with the nature of the breach and the time it comes to light, the type of goods and the nature of the damages. If the seller, prior to the delivery date, notifies the buyer that he will not meet his delivery obligation, the buyer is confronted with an anticipatory breach which, at his election, he may ignore or accept. If the buyer accepts the repudiation, the agreement, subject to the buyer's right to sue for damages, is deemed at an end. Where there is no anticipatory repudiation but the seller fails to deliver at the proper time, the buyer is usually limited to an action in damages for non-delivery. Exceptionally, however, he may be entitled to an order for specific performance or to other forms of specific relief. If goods are tendered but are non-conforming in character, the buyer usually has an option. If the non-conformity involves breach of a condition and the contract does not involve a sale of specific goods the property in which has passed to the buyer, the buyer may reject and, once again, sue for damages

591

for non-delivery or content himself with a restitutionary claim for the return of any payments he may have made. If he elects to retain the goods he does not waive his claim to damages. This will be equally true if the non-conformity does not come to light until after the buyer is deemed to have accepted the goods; Anglo-Canadian law does not recognize a general right to rescind on account of a latent defect, except where the seller has been guilty of fraud or, possibly, innocent misrepresentation. Where the buyer is entitled to sue for damages for breach of the contract of sale, his damages will be assessed on the same basis of compensation for loss as in claims by the seller in the reverse situation, and subject to the rules of foreseeability enunciated in *Hadley v. Baxendale*. The buyer may also be entitled to sue in tort if the defective goods caused personal injury or damage to other property.

The Interaction of Sections 12(3) and 19, Rule 1

Home Gas Ltd. v. Streeter

[1953] 2 DLR 842, 8 WWR (NS) 689 (Sask. CA)

GORDON JA (for the court): The plaintiff is a company having what appears to be a head office or main office for Saskatchewan in the City of Saskatoon, with a local agent or representative in the City of North Battleford where it has a showroom. On May 18, 1951, the defendant and her husband went to the plaintiff's show-room in North Battleford for the purpose of buying a gas stove. Neither of them had any experience with gas stoves before. They did not like any on display and one Palmer, the plaintiff's agent, told them that he had a fully automatic demonstrator in his trailer, and the defendant's husband went to inspect it in the trailer. Palmer gave the defendant a description of the stove over the telephone and the defendant decided to buy it. Her husband completed the deal. The price installed was to be $398.21. The defendant's husband swears that the cost of installation was to be approximately $100. On May 19, 1951, the defendant gave a cheque to Palmer at her home for $75 as a deposit on the transaction. On September 29, 1951, more than 4 months after the order had been given this stove was installed at the defendant's home and connected up to two tanks of propane gas, the fuel used in the stove. After it was installed Palmer said that he required the balance in cash or a cheque and the cheque sued upon for $323.21 was given.

During the installation the defendant complained that she smelled gas in the room, but Palmer assured her that it was merely some gas that had escaped during the installation. At the conclusion Palmer said: Try it for 4 days and then I will be back to check it thoroughly again and will bring a thermometer to check the oven. No demonstration was made after installation but the next day the defendant tried to use it. The burners in the oven would not light at all. Eventually when they got them to light the oven would not bake properly, it burnt food being baked on the bottom and the top was uncooked. One top burner did not light at all and instead of the burners being lit by the pilot light they had to be lit with a match. The day that the stove was first used was a Sunday, it having been installed on Saturday. On the Monday following the defendant endeavoured to get in touch with Palmer on the telephone a number of times but could not get in touch with him. Trips to the plaintiff's show-room at North Battleford were likewise fruitless. According to the evidence the defendant and her husband have never seen it open since their first visit.

A month after the stove was installed the defendant's husband was in Saskatoon and called at the office of the plaintiff and saw the manager in charge, telling him all about his complaints. The manager then called up Palmer at North Battleford and asked him to go and see the stove and put it in proper operating condition.

During the first 3 weeks after the stove had been installed the defendant had used one of the tanks of gas endeavouring to get it to work and at Christmas time after the installation she again tried until the second tank of gas was exhausted. This was used in a period of about 3 weeks. On cross-examination of the defendant, counsel for the plaintiff brought out the fact that she had written four letters to the plaintiff, one of which was dated February 13, I presume 1952, in which she stated "unless I hear from you immediately we intend to take action against you." None of these letters were produced or filed as exhibits.

On the 26th or 27th of January, 1952, Palmer appeared with a Mr. Jones who was represented to be the plaintiff's manager at Winnipeg. I presume that his visit was that promised by the manager when the defendant's husband visited Saskatoon about a month after the installation, which would be about the end of October. They looked at the stove but did nothing to it. Jones and Palmer were then told all the defects of the stove. Jones told them that one burner would have to be replaced and Jones told Palmer to come back the following day to check the oven. He never came back.

The defendant then wrote the manufacturer of the stove on April 8th and on April 25th the defendant received a letter in reply from the distributors of this particular stove who have their office in Saskatoon. I do not name them because I do not think that they should be implicated in what I consider despicable treatment meted out to this defendant by the plaintiff company. The distributors promised that they would have a sales representative in the district and try and have the stove satisfactorily adjusted, although they stressed that it was not their responsibility. This representative of the distributors did call at the end of April and said that he would do anything that he could to have the plaintiff look after it.

Early in May, 1952, Mr. Olsen, stated to be a representative of the plaintiff from Saskatoon came and looked at the stove but did nothing to it although he was told all of the complaints. At the time of the visit from Mr. Olsen the stove had been disconnected and was in a different room from that in which it had been installed.

The evidence does not disclose the date on which the payment of the cheque was stopped, but attached to the cheque is a bank notation dated October 5, 1951, showing the reason for nonpayment was "payment stopped," so it would have been prior to that date. The above are the undisputed facts and on these facts the plaintiff asks the Court to give it judgment for the amount of the cheque.

It is now necessary to look at the pleadings. The statement of claim is a simple one asking for payment of the cheque. The statement of defence sets forth, first there was no consideration for the cheque, alternatively that the plaintiff "warranted that the goods were reasonably fit for the purpose that they were required," that there was a breach of the warranty and particulars as disclosed in the above are given. There was no reply.

On the argument before us at counsel for the defendant who was not the counsel at the trial or the solicitor on the record took the position that the evidence clearly disclosed that the stove was sold on the condition that it would be a useful stove and that the defendant had rejected the stove and that the plaintiff could not succeed on the cheque. Counsel for the plaintiff, on the other hand, contends that the stove was accepted by the defendant at least by Christmas time 1951 when it was used while burning the second tank of gas and contends that as there is no counterclaim for damages or set-off against the cheque the plaintiff is entitled to judgment for the amount of the cheque and the defendant is entitled to nothing by virtue of the failure of his solicitor to set up a counterclaim.

The learned trial Judge held that the defendant accepted the stove which had been delivered to her and had used it for the two periods of time set forth and that she had no right to reject it or repudiate the contract. The learned trial Judge stated that he was following the decision of the Ontario Court of Appeal in *Sedgwick v. Lloyd*, [1951] OWN 469, and gave the plaintiff judgment for its claim and costs.

I do not think for one moment that the defendant ever intended to accept the stove but it may be that she is bound by the authorities and is limited to her right to damages.

To analyze the evidence a little more carefully, it will be noted that 3 days after the stove was installed the defendant did her best to get in touch with Palmer and at various times until about the end of October when her husband went to Saskatoon and saw the plaintiff's manager at that city and that in his presence Palmer was called and asked to go and see the stove and put it in operating condition. Up to that time it could not be said that the stove had been accepted. Then following various other efforts to get in touch with Palmer, after waiting from this time until the day before Christmas, nothing was done, when another effort was made to get the stove to work unsuccessfully. On the 26th or 27th day of January Jones came from Winnipeg and stated that a burner would have to be replaced and that the oven would be checked. The letters written by the defendant are not produced and we only know that in the letter of February 13th the defendant threatened the plaintiff with action.

If there was ever a case where a purchaser was entitled to reject the goods this is it. On the other hand the law in respect to the rejection of goods is very clear. No particular form of notice of rejection is necessary. The buyer may return the goods or offer to return them and it is sufficient to signify his rejection of them by stating that they are not according to the contract and they are held at the vendor's risk: see *Grimoldby v. Wells* (1875), LR 10 CP 391 at 395. As far as I can find from the evidence the defendant although trying desperately to have the stove put in order, did not reject it.

Further s-s. (3) of s. 13 of the Sale of Goods Act, RSS 1940, c. 284, provides as follows: [see Ont. SGA, s. 12(3)].

The stove in this case falls within the description of "specific goods" and there was no express or implied term in the contract of sale that it could be rejected. I have already stated that the stove was not rejected. This does not, however, fortunately for the defendant, mean that she has no redress.

The learned trial Judge stated that he was following the case of *Sedgwick v. Lloyd*, *supra*, but unfortunately he did not do it. In that case the Court of Appeal of Ontario while allowing the appeal referred the matter back to the trial Judge to determine the amount of damages caused by the breach of warranty.

Appeal allowed in part.

NOTES

1) Was the court's attention drawn to *Varley v. Whipp* (*supra*, chapter 6)? Would it have made a difference if it had been? The rule in section 12(3) is usually ascribed to *Street v. Blay* (1831), 2 B. & Ad. 456, 109 ER 1212. Do you think it is a sensible rule? Section 12(3) was amended by s. 4(1) of the English Misrepresentation Act, 1967, by deleting the rule. See now Sale of Goods Act, 1979, s. 11(4). None of the Canadian provinces appears so far to have copied the English example.

2) Without referring to *Home Gas Ltd. v. Streeter*, in *Wojakowski v. Pembina Dodge Chrysler Ltd.*, [1976] 5 WWR 97 (Man.), Morse J refused to apply literally the Manitoba equivalent of Ont. SGA, s. 12(3), although he also found that no property in the goods had in fact passed to the buyer. The case arose out of a contract for the sale of an automobile. The automobile was delivered by the seller, but proved to be unsatisfactory. It was therefore agreed that the seller should provide another automobile. Certain defects were noticed at the time of possession or shortly afterwards, which the seller agreed to correct. The repairs were not made, or not made to the plaintiff's satisfaction; indeed the problems were aggravated by the drive shaft falling off while the plaintiff was driving the vehicle. Shortly afterwards the plaintiff refused to have anything further to do with the automobile and brought action claiming rescission of the agreement and the return of the purchase money. Morse J allowed the claim and disposed of the SGA s. 12(3) issue as follows (at 102-3):

> I am of the view that the contract between the plaintiff and the defendant was for specific goods. Specific goods are defined by s. 2(1)(n) of the Act to mean: "goods identified and agreed upon at the time a contract of sale is made." There is no question that the second automobile purchased by the plaintiff was identified and agreed upon at the time the plaintiff agreed to buy it. However, I do not believe it can be said that the property in the automobile at any time passed to the plaintiff within the meaning of s. 13(3) of the Act. It is pointed out in Chalmers' Sale of Goods, 15th Ed., at 51, that: "A literal application of [the equivalent section in the English Act] might often mean that a purchaser of specific goods would be unable ever to reject the goods and treat the contract as repudiated." I am of the view that a literal interpretation cannot and should not be given to the words in question and that, as is indicated in the authorities referred to in Chalmers (51, footnotes (k) and (l)), until the goods are accepted by the purchaser, only a conditional property passes and that this is not a passing of property for the purpose of s. 13(3). See, for example, *Taylor v. Combined Buyers Ltd.*, [1924] NZLR. 627; *Leaf v. International Galleries*, [1950] 2 KB 86, [1950] 1 All ER 693; and, to the contrary, 14 MLR 173. The evidence satisfies me that the plaintiff in this case never unconditionally accepted the second automobile (and see s. 37 of the Act). Even at

the outset, plaintiff accepted the automobile on the basis that certain painting work was to be done by the defendant. Thereafter, the plaintiff made additional complaints which the defendant agreed to remedy. Up to the date on which the plaintiff elected to repudiate the contract, i.e., approximately 27th November 1975, the automobile had not been repainted, the leak in the trunk had not been repaired, and the rust in the trunk had not been removed. In my opinion, therefore, the plaintiff never accepted the second automobile and the property in that automobile never passed to her within the meaning of s. 13(3) of the Act. ...

3) The student will note that, both at common law and under the SGA, the buyer's right of rejection is limited to cases where there is breach of a condition; a breach of warranty is not sufficient. On the other hand, the right to reject does not depend on the gravity of the breach. *Cf. IBM v. Shcherban, supra,* chapter 7. Do these rules conform to reasonable commercial practices? What rules would you substitute in their place? *Cf.* the recommendations in the OLRC Sales Report discussed at the end of this chapter.

For the Code's treatment of the buyer's right to reject, see UCC 2-508, 2-601, 2-606, and 2-608. And see further, J. Honnold, "Buyer's Right of Rejection: A Study in the Impact of Codification Upon a Commercial Problem" (1948-49), *U. Pa. L Rev.* 457 and G.L. Priest, "Breach and Remedy for Tender of Nonconforming Goods Under the Uniform Commercial Code: An Economic Approach" (1978), 91 *Harv. L Rev.* 960.

The Interpretation of SGA Sections 33 and 34

Hardy & Company v. Hillerns and Fowler

[1923] 2 KB 490, [1923] All ER Rep. 275 (CA)

BANKES LJ: This case raises a question of law as to the proper construction to be placed on s. 35 of the Sale of Goods Act. Messrs. Hillerns & Fowler bought a large quantity of Rosario or Sante Fé wheat to be shipped from a port in Uruguay to Hull at a certain price including freight and insurance, payment to be by cash in London against shipping documents. The ship sailed and arrived in Hull on March 18. On March 20 the buyers' bankers in London took up the shipping documents. On the 21st the ship commenced to discharge the wheat, and on the same day the buyers sold to sub-purchasers portions of the wheat so discharged, 200 qrs. to a purchaser at Barnsley, 100 qrs. to a purchaser at Nottingham, and 500 qrs. to a purchaser at Southwell. In order to fulfil those sub-contracts they on the same day, March 21, despatched the quantities so sold by rail to Barnsley and Nottingham respectively, and to Southwell by barge. They had taken samples of wheat on the 21st, which samples had raised a suspicion that the cargo was not according to the contract description. But they allowed the discharge to continue, and on the 22nd took further samples, which satisfied them that their suspicions were well founded, and on the 23rd they gave the sellers notice that they rejected the wheat. Upon those facts the sellers contended that under the terms of s. 35 the buyers must be deemed to have accepted the goods and lost their right of rejection. The arbitration tribunal found that the wheat was not in accordance with the contract, but that owing to the difficulty of getting a fairly representative sample until a considerable portion of the cargo had been discharged it was reasonable for the buyers to delay making up their mind to reject until the 23rd.

The question now arises whether the buyers by so reselling and forwarding to the sub-purchasers portions of the wheat had lost the right to reject and were confined to their remedy in damages. The construction which Greer J has placed upon ss. 34 and 35 of the Sale of Goods Act [Ont. ss. 33-34] is one with which I entirely agree. Sect. 34 gives a buyer to whom goods have been delivered, which he has not previously examined, a reasonable opportunity of examining them before he shall be deemed to have accepted them. Then s. 35 [Ont. s. 34] provides as follows: [The Lord Justice read the section.] I understand that to mean that if during the currency of the reasonable time within which the examination is to be made the buyer does certain things, one of which is an "action in relation to (the goods) which is inconsistent with the ownership of the seller," he shall be deemed to have accepted them. Sect. 35 is, in my opinion, independent of s. 34, and it is quite immaterial for the purposes of that section that the reasonable time for examining the goods had not expired when the act was done. The finding therefore of the arbitration tribunal that in the present case that time had not expired may be disregarded.

It remains to be considered whether the act of reselling to the sub-purchasers was an act which was inconsistent with the ownership of the sellers. Mr. Le Quesne has argued that s. 35 has no application to this case, because the contract under which the wheat was sold to the buyers was a c.i.f. contract, and that upon the bank taking up the shipping documents upon March 20 the property passed to the buyers, and that consequently when they resold on the 21st there was no ownership left in the sellers with which that act of resale could be inconsistent. It seems to me that that is attempting to put a meaning on the language of the section which it cannot reasonably bear. I understand the section to refer to an act which is inconsistent with the seller being the owner at the material date; and the material date for the purposes of this case is not the date of the resale, but the date of the notice of rejection, upon receipt of which the ownership revested in the sellers. It is with that revested ownership that in my opinion the act of resale was inconsistent. And it was inconsistent with it for this reason: Where under a contract of sale goods are delivered to the buyer which are not in accordance with the contract, so that the buyer has a right to reject them, the seller upon receipt of notice of rejection is entitled to have the goods placed at his disposal so as to allow of his resuming possession forthwith, and if the buyer has done any act which prevents him from so resuming possession that act is necessarily inconsistent with his right. It is not enough that the buyer should, as in the present case, be in a position to give the seller possession at some later date, he must be able to do so at the time of the rejection. For these reasons I have come to the conclusion that the decision of Greer J was right and that the appeal should be dismissed.

ATKIN LJ: This case raises, not I think for the first time, an important question as to the relation of s. 34, sub-s. 1, of the Sale of Goods Act to s. 35.

[Atkin LJ read the two sections (Ont. ss. 33-34) and continued:]

A possible view of those two sections is that s. 34 limits the provisions of s. 35, and that under the latter section the buyer is not, even in the events there specified, to be deemed to have accepted the goods unless he has had reasonable time and opportunity for examining them. That seems to have been the view taken by the editors of the two last editions of *Benjamin on Sale*. It is there said (6th ed., at 857) that: "Section 35 contemplates a later stage of the transaction than s. 34(1). Under s. 34(1) where the buyer has not previously examined the goods, he is *not* deemed to have accepted them until he has been able to examine them." By s. 35 it is necessary to prove some further fact in order to show that the buyer has accepted them. The words "some further fact" would seem to presume that it was necessary to prove that he had a reasonable opportunity of examination as well as that he did the act mentioned in s. 35. That is no doubt a possible view, but it seems to me to be incorrect. Indeed it was not so argued by Mr. Le Quesne. And I think the reason is obvious. It is that given by the learned judge. One of the acts upon the doing of which the buyer is deemed to have accepted the goods is that "he intimates to the seller that he has accepted them." I think it is plain that such an intimation may be made before he has had a reasonable opportunity of examination, and if such an intimation is made then it appears to me that without more s. 35 operates, and he is to be deemed to have accepted them. In the same way when he does an act in relation to the goods which is inconsistent with the ownership of the seller the section must be treated as coming into operation notwithstanding that the reasonable opportunity of examining them has not expired; and for instance where a man having had goods delivered to him turns them or part of them at once into his mill and uses them in the manufacture. In the present case the tribunal of appeal have found that the buyer had not had a reasonable opportunity of examination until March 23, a date which is subsequent to the act relied on by the sellers as being inconsistent with their ownership; but that finding is, in my opinion, immaterial. Therefore we have here to face the problem whether the act of the buyers in reselling the dispatching the goods was inconsistent with the ownership of the sellers. If it was, they must be deemed to have accepted them. I should like to point out, in reference to that provision, that all the words of the section must have effect given to them. The words are: "When the goods have been delivered to him"—that is to the buyer— "and he does any act" of the kind specified. That means that the buyer must have got delivery before he does the act. Here the arbitrators have found the buyers did not obtain delivery of 1877 qrs. on March 21, and that it was out of the wheat so delivered to them that they on the same day forwarded the various parcels to their sub-purchasers. It was however said on behalf of the buyers that before they did so the property in the cargo had already passed to them, and that therefore the sub-sales by them could not be inconsistent with the ownership of the sellers. What is the precise position with regard to the passing of the property under a c.i.f. contract it is perhaps not necessary here to determine. My own view is that if the goods are not in accordance with the contract the property does not pass to the purchaser upon his taking up the documents if he has not had at that time an opportunity of ascertaining whether the goods are in conformity with the contract. Though it may be that the property passes subject to its being revested when the buyer exercises his right of rejection. But it does not seem to me to matter much for the purposes of this case which of those two views is correct. In either view what happened here was enough to take away the buyers' right of rejection. If the possession was transferred by the buyers to third persons in circumstances which were inconsistent either with the goods being the property of the sellers at the time of such transfer, or inconsistent with their being restored to the sellers upon the notice of rejection being given, it appears to me that the transfer was an act which was inconsistent with the ownership of the sellers; and under those circumstances I think that it is quite immaterial that the sub-purchasers may afterwards, by agreement or otherwise, have returned the goods to the buyers. Such return cannot avail to restore a right of rejection which has been lost. That being so I think that the buyers must be content with their claim in damages.

Appeal dismissed.

[Younger LJ concurred without separate reasons.]

NOTES

1) *Hardy*'s case raises difficult issues of exegesis and policy:

a) What was the ratio of the decision? The re-dispatch of the goods by the buyer? The passing of title? The fact that at the time of rejection the goods were (or were assumed to be) still in the sub-buyer's hands?

b) Is there hardship to the seller in requiring him to take back goods at a place other than the place of delivery? Would the logic of the reasoning in *Hardy* also lead us to the same conclusion where a chain store buyer with many retail outlets distributes the goods within the chain before the defects come to light? *Cf.* UCC 2-513, which provides *inter alia* that, unless otherwise agreed, the buyer has a right before acceptance to inspect the goods at any reasonable time and place and in any reasonable manner. What accounts for the English Court of Appeal's unwillingness in *Hardy* to read a similar provision into the SGA?

c) Assuming the goods are nonconforming and that, absent a restrictive reading of Ont. SGA s. 34, the buyer would have a right to reject the goods, what accounts for the seller's unwillingness to take the goods back? Is it due to the seller's suspicion that the buyer is not acting in good faith or, at any rate, would be in a better position to dispose of the goods than the seller? Is it due to the seller's belief that the buyer may have difficulties proving its damages and that paying damages may be cheaper for the seller than having to take the goods back?

d) *Hardy* was distinguished by the Ontario Court of Appeal in *A.J. Frank & Sons Ltd. v. Northern Peat Co. Ltd.* (1963), 39 DLR (2d) 721, on the grounds that by the terms of the agreement the goods were to be inspected at the ultimate point of destination and that at the time of rejection they were still in the buyer's possession. For a similar decision, see *Hammer and Barrow v. Coca-Cola*, [1962] NZLR 723. *Hardy* was statutorily reversed in England by s. 4(2) of the Misrepresentation Act, 1967, but the drafting is unclear and is criticized in the OLRC Sales Report, at 470-71. For a post-1967 decision giving effect to the amendment (but without referring to it), see *Manifatture Tessile Laniera Wolltex v. J.B. Ashley Ltd.*, [1979] 2 Lloyd's Rep. 28

(CA). No Canadian province has so far adopted a s. 4(2) type amendment and the Sales Report, at 471, recommends the total deletion of the inconsistent act rule.

2) As Bingham J makes clear in *Tradax Export S.A. v. European Grain & Shipping Ltd.*, [1983] 2 Ll. Rep. 100, at 107-8, the inconsistent act rule only applies to conduct by the buyer after he has received the goods and before he has rejected them. What is the position where the buyer continues to make use of the goods *after* rejection or commits other acts inconsistent with the revesting of title in the seller?

The question is of great practical importance because the buyer may have invested all his savings in a high cost item (for example, a new car or a mobile home) and may not be in a position to replace it, even though it is defective, until he recovers the purchase price from the seller. Alternatively, even if shortage of funds is not an impediment, the buyer may need the continued use of the chattel in its business because replacement of the chattel will take several months. (This was true, for example, in *Public Utilities Comm. v. Burroughs Business Machines Ltd.* (1975), 6 OR (2d) 257 (CA), discussed below.)

Some American cases have held that continued use of the goods after rejection nullifies the earlier rejection. See OLRC Sales Report, at 472, n. 173. A less dogmatic position was taken by Bingham J in *Tradax v. European Grain*, *supra*, who reasoned (at 107) that it depends on the particular circumstances:

> A finding that the buyers clearly rejected the goods and claimed arbitration does not in my judgment conclude this question in their favour. It might emerge, as it did in *Chapman v. Morton*, (1843), 11 M & W 534, that the buyers were saying one thing and doing another, so as to invalidate their written statements or throw doubt on the bona fides or the unequivocal nature of their rejection. Or they might act in such a way as to create an estoppel against themselves. Or they might enter into a new agreement with the sellers involving an express or implied withdrawal of their rejection or a retransfer of title to them. It does, however, seem to me quite plain that once the buyers have proved what, on its face, amounted to a clear and unequivocal rejection of the goods and claim for arbitration, it is for the sellers to prove, if they can, that the apparent effect of the buyers' conduct was destroyed by other conduct having a different and inconsistent effect and not for the buyers to establish the negative case that they did nothing subsequently to disentitle themselves from asserting their rejection.

He also expressed his agreement with the following passage in Chalmers, *Sale of Goods*, 18th ed., at 197:

> If the seller refuses to take the goods back when tendered, the buyer may still not deal with the goods as his own, for the property in them has re-vested in the seller. In exceptional cases where the goods are liable to deteriorate, he may be able to sell them as agent of necessity for the seller. Generally, however, he would probably be better advised to commence proceedings against the seller and apply to the court for an order for sale. If the buyer deals with the goods without an order for sale and in circumstances in which he cannot claim to be an agent of necessity, then unless perhaps the seller's refusal is in such terms as to entitle the buyer to do as he wishes with the goods, the buyer may be liable to the seller for conversion. Probably, however, in such a case the seller could not claim that the buyer's conduct in selling the goods was inconsistent with a bona fide intention to reject them.

In *PUC v. Burroughs Business Machines, supra,* the Ontario Court of Appeal held that the plaintiff's continued use of Burrough's computer after they had purported to reject it did not nullify the rejection. Brooke JA gave the following reason for reaching this conclusion (at 268):

> I do not think that the effect of this conduct subsequently to November, 1969, when the Commission advised Burroughs that it must reject the computer should be viewed so as to cast doubt upon that decision, nor should it be regarded as a ground for denying the respondent the remedy to rescission. The decision to continue using the computer until the new one was delivered was dictated by goods business judgment as to the best course to follow. If Burroughs had wished, it was open to it to take possession of the machine at any time after the Commission told the said defendant that it had rejected it. But it made no such effort for a number of reasons. I think it is a fair inference from the evidence that Burroughs, like the Commission, was concerned about the very great cost and perhaps loss to the Commission which would follow immediately as a result of the removal of the computer and tacitly agreed that it was advisable for it to pursue the course it did until a new unit was installed and operational. ...

Would he have been of the same opinion if Burroughs had not acquiesced in PUC's continued use of the machine?

The Uniform Commercial Code provides:

> **2-602.**(2) Subject to the provisions of the two following sections on rejected goods (Sections 2-603 and 2-604).
>
> (a) after rejection any exercise of ownership by the buyer with respect to any commercial unit is wrongful as against the seller;

The OLRC Sales Report (at 472) apparently read "wrongful" as meaning that the buyer's acts would nullify the earlier rejection, which seems doubtful. In any event, the Report felt that UCC 2-602(2) was too rigid and it recommended the following substitutional provision:

> after rejection, use of the goods or other acts of ownership by the buyer are *prima facie* wrongful as against the seller but do not nullify the rejection unless the seller has been materially prejudiced thereby.

Is this formulation entirely satisfactory? Should the buyer's continued use be treated as wrongful at all where he has reasonable grounds for continuing to use the goods? Would it be better to provide in such cases that the buyer shall not be liable in conversion or other damages, but may be required to pay a reasonable sum for the use of the chattel? The Amendments to Article 2 of the UCC approved by the ALI in May 2001 (see, *supra*, chapter 1 of this casebook) contain the following provision in amended s. 2-608:

> (4) If a buyer uses the goods after a rightful rejection or justifiable revocation of acceptance, the following rules apply:
>
> (a) ... .
>
> (b) any use of the goods that is reasonable under the circumstances is not wrongful as against the seller and is not an acceptance, but in any appropriate case the buyer shall be obligated to seller for the value of the use to the seller.

Rafuse Motors Ltd. v. Mardo Construction Ltd.

(1963), 41 DLR (2d) 340, 48 MPR 296 (NSCA)

COFFIN J: This appeal arises from an action on a promissory note made by the defendant to the plaintiff.

The plaintiff (appellant), a body corporate, whose chief place of business is Bridgewater in the County of Lunenburg, is a dealer and distributor for Ford Motor Co. and its subsidiaries, and the defendant (respondent), is a body corporate, whose president and general manager is Mr. George Zinck.

The defendant held a contract for a consolidated school at New Ross in the County of Lunenburg, and in order to complete this contract, Mr. George Zinck decided it would be necessary to use a tractor. Early in January, 1960, he was approached by Mr. Cliff Oxner, salesman for Rafuse Motors Limited, who wanted to sell a tractor. Mr. Zinck told him that the only tractor in which he would be interested was a Major tractor. As a result an order for a Major tractor was executed for the price of $4,673, of which $1,500 cash was to be paid on delivery, balance to be secured by a note.

Mr. Zinck was asked what discussions he had with Mr. Oxner relating to the use of this tractor by Mardo Construction Ltd.

> A. I told him that I had this contract at New Ross, which he was aware of, and I wanted this equipment of a certain type to be used on this job. I explained to him what I was going to do with it and what I wanted it for and why I wanted it.
>
> Q. Do you recall how the name Major or Fordson Major came into the conversation? A. Because I had a Fordson Major tractor before that—a couple of years.
>
> Q. What, if anything, did you say about it? A. I told him I wanted that tractor because I was acquainted with it and had good satisfaction with it prior to this.

A few weeks later Mr. Zinck was advised by Mr. Oxner that he could not get the front end loader for this tractor and that he could supply a Ford tractor complete with all the equipment made by the Ford Motor Co. that was equal to the Fordson Major.

Mr. Zinck said that Mr. Oxner told him: "It would do everything that the Fordson Major would do on this particular job. I told him I wouldn't buy it if he felt it wouldn't do the job because I was disappointed because I wanted the Fordson Major."

This suggested tractor was the 871 Ford tractor.

Mr. Zinck said that he told Mr. Oxner he would take this tractor if it was equal to the Fordson Major, and late in February, 1960, this tractor was delivered to Mr. Zinck's brother's home outside of Chester.

This history of the use of this equipment should be set out in some detail.

1. It was first used around the home outside of Chester to remove snow. Mr. Zinck found it did not do the job that he expected because it seemed too light. Mr. Oxner and Mr. McAfee of the Ford Motor Co. tried the tractor and suggested tractor chains. They were unobtainable nor could Rafuse Motors supply half-tracks, so Mr. Zinck obtained half-tracks from Harbour Motors in Dartmouth, Nova Scotia.

He then found the tractor too light in the rear, and on Mr. Oxner's suggestion he had a set of wheel weights made by Hillis Foundry in Halifax.

The tractor remained in the Chester area until about April 5, 1960.

2. It was taken to New Ross to remove snow from a building that had just been steel framed for the New Ross school. There certain break-downs occurred in the tractor:

. . .

At this point Mr. Zinck said he complained to Mr. Oxner, Mr. L.S. Rafuse and Mr. McAfee who told him the difficulties were in the manufacture and they would "replace them, and they felt sure it would be all right from now on."

. . .

(e) Something broke in the rear end again. I quote Mr. Zinck on this point:

> I called Mr. Oxner at Bridgewater and told him the tractor was broken down, that I was finished with it and wouldn't accept and couldn't accept it. It was a continual breakdown and it was costing us money, plus the fact that you couldn't get the parts without delay.

His evidence is that thereupon Mr. Oxner asked him to call Seffern's Garage to pick up the tractor which they did, and that he has had nothing to do with the tractor since that time. The tractor left his possession around the first of July having performed about 135 hours of work from the time it came on the site not earlier than April 5, 1960. It is apparent from the facts that the time lost in breakdowns was approximately 27 days exclusive of the last collapse of the rear end.

The particulars of the sale of the tractor 871 and equipment are set out in ex. S/5, the total purchase price being $5,055, and on February 22, 1960, the defendant paid the plaintiff $1,500 and gave a promissory note for the balance of $3,555. The defendant (respondent) refused to pay the note, and the plaintiff (appellant) then launched this action on the note for $3,555 principal and $160.20 interest to October 14, 1960, together with interest on the principal at 7% per annum from that date.

The defence alleged failure to deliver the tractor as agreed upon and total failure of consideration. In the alternative the defendant alleged that the consideration for the note was the delivery to the defendant of a Ford 871 tractor with equipment on the express condition that it was the equivalent of a Fordson Major tractor, and adequate for specific work by the plaintiff in carrying out a contract to construct a school building at New Ross, Lunenburg County.

The defendant counterclaimed alleging the contract to supply a Fordson Major diesel tractor and equipment, the failure to deliver, the agreement to substitute the Ford 871 tractor with equipment equivalent to the Fordson Major, the guarantee by the plaintiff that the Ford 871 would do the specific work required, and the acceptance by the defendant of the Ford 871 tractor subject to these conditions and on a trial basis $1,500 being paid as a down payment. The counterclaim further alleged that the defendant gave the tractor a reasonable trial and the plaintiff every opportunity to make good its deficiencies until its final rejection. The reply denied these allegations and the defence to counterclaim denied the surrender of possession and stated that the plaintiff had no knowledge of what happened to the tractor.

. . .

IV. Was there an acceptance of the 871 and equipment by the defendant? I now refer to the Sale of Goods Act, s. 36 [Ont. s. 34]: ...

There is no evidence that the defendant ever intimated to the plaintiff that he had accepted the unit.

The question here is whether the defendant did any act in relation to the unit inconsistent with the ownership of the seller or retained the unit for an unreasonable time without intimating to the plaintiff its rejection.

In the *Alabastine* case, *supra*, Meredith, CJO, said, at 819-20 DLR, at 409 OLR:

> It is, I think, the proper conclusion on the evidence that the "trying out" of the engine was, as understood by both parties, to be for the purpose of discovering whether or not it answered the conditions of the contract, and what was done by the respondent in "trying out" the engine cannot be treated as an acceptance of it, or as evidence that it had been accepted by the respondent.

Brodeur J, in *Schofield v. Emerson Brantingham Implement Co.* 43 DLR 509 at 524-5, 57 SCR 203 at 225, [1918] 3 WWR 434 at 450 dealt with the matter of inducements and encouragements by the vendor:

> The company knew the purpose for which Schofield required the engine and he has certainly relied on their skill and ability to furnish him with an engine suitable for that purpose. The engine not having developed the quantity of horse-power for which it was sold, the respondent company has certainly not fulfilled its contract.
>
>   It is true that there was a settlement made; but that settlement was obtained by continuous representation that the machine would develop the horse-power they contracted for. This engine, it was claimed, would get better with wear, etc. As a question of fact, the company sent after that settlement some experts to try and make it right. They have never succeeded, and it seems to me that the machine, having never been fit for the purpose for which it was purchased, and the settlement having been obtained under certain representations which proved absolutely incorrect, the respondent cannot avail itself of that settlement and the plaintiff should succeed.

I should mention the remarks of Henderson JA, in *Cork v. Greavette Boats Ltd.*, [1940] 4 DLR 202 at 206, [1940] OR 352 at 365, where the plaintiff "deferred the exercise of his right of rejection upon representations made to him that the boat would be made satisfactory. ..."

In considering whether the time is or is not reasonable any inducement by the seller to extend the period of trial of the goods is relevant: 34 *Hals.*, 3rd., at 112.

I agree with the learned trial Judge that Mr. Steele had encouraged Zinck to give the tractor a fair trial. Mr. Zinck said on cross-examination at 85-86:

> Well, it was sometime before the tractor broke down the last time Mr Steele was to see me and told me he had got a call from Rafuse Motors and he was going to come to see me and I told him I was finished with the tractor and he explained to me why it broke down and it was part of the fault of the manufacturer and it was now cured and if I would give it a fair trial he assured me it would do the work.

In fact the whole history of the dealings between the plaintiff and the defendant as shown by the constant efforts to make the equipment work corroborated by the statements in the various letters from the plaintiff to the Ford Company, justify the findings of the learned trial Judge, that any delay in rejection and any acts inconsistent with the plaintiff's ownership were due to the inducements of the plaintiff.

From the time the defendant first operated the unit for snow removal in the Chester area to the final break-down, complaints were being made to the plaintiff. The defendant did everything possible to comply with the suggestion of both plaintiff and Ford Company officials to give the unit a fair trial.

Even before he gave his final notice of rejection, Mr. Zinck told Mr. Oxner that he would pay no more money unless they could prove "it was able to do the work I purchased it for."

I can find nothing in the evidence to persuade me that there was an acceptance under any of the elements contained in s. 36 of the Sale of Goods Act.

Appeal dismissed.

[Currie and MacDonald JJ concurred; Ilsley CJ and MacQuarrie J dissented in part on another question.]

NOTES

1) The Uniform Commercial Code deals with situations such as arose in *Rafuse Motors* under the heading of "revocation of acceptance." UCC 2-608(1) provides:

> (1) The buyer may revoke his acceptance of a lot or commercial unit whose non-conformity substantially impairs its value to him if he has accepted it
>   (a) on the reasonable assumption that its non-conformity would be cured and it has not been seasonally cured; or
>   (b) without discovery of such non-conformity if his acceptance was reasonably induced either by the difficulty of discovery before acceptance or by the seller's assurances.

Is this a preferable approach? Is it correct to speak of the buyer having accepted the goods at all when he is only continuing to use the chattel because of the seller's assurances, or is this only a matter of semantics?

2) What is the position when the buyer rejects the goods but on the wrong grounds? Can he later justify his action on the right grounds. In *Colfax Inc. v. General Foods Ltd.* (1980), 10 BLR 174 at 189-90, which involved a sale of edible oils by instalments, Van Camp J said:

> The question has been raised about the effect of the statement of the grounds for rescission in the letter of April 18th, 1975. At that time, the defendant did not know the exact components of the product which was being delivered and used. The defendant's knowledge was that there was palm oil in the product being delivered, and it was on the grounds of that palm oil that the defendant rescinded. The defendant carefully did not state that it was because of the presence of the palm oil. Mr. Neff was not yet convinced, in spite of the testing that had

been done. He had not had a thorough analysis, and he protected himself by using the wording of "Failing to deliver frying shortening prepared from the ingredients specified," or, "Which does not comply with our requirements."

My attention was directed to the decision in *Braithwaite v. Foreign Hardwood Co.*, [1905] 2 KB 543 (CA). That decision has been considered by several Courts who have differed as to its interpretation.

In *Taylor v. Oakes Roncoroni & Co.* (1922), 127 LT 267, 27 Com. Cas. 261 (CA), to which I have already referred, it is stated that the decision was that a buyer who repudiates for the wrong reasons cannot offer, as a defence, the fact that the seller was unable or unwilling to perform.

Mr. Justice Devlin, in *Universal Cargo Carriers Corpn. v. Citati*, [1957] 2 QB 401 at 443, [1957] 2 All ER 70, [1957] 1 Lloyd's Rep. 174 [affirmed [1957] 1 WLR 979, [1957] 3 All ER 234, [1957] 2 Lloyd's Rep. 191 (CA)], said:

> It is now well settled that a rescission or repudiation, if given for a wrong reason or for no reason at all, can be supported if there are at the time facts in existence which would have provided a good reason.

In *Stockloser v. Campbell Const. Co.*, [1934] OWN 108, the Ontario Court of Appeal was considering a situation where the kind of material which the plaintiffs were supplying, and proposed to continue to supply, did not meet the requirements of the contract. Chief Justice Mulock said [at 110]:

> Although the defendant in its letter repudiating the contract assigned only one reason, it is entitled to justify such repudiation by any other grounds actually in existence at the time of such repudiation. ...

The first three cases cited by Madam Justice Van Camp involved cases of anticipatory repudiation by the buyer before the seller's performance had become due. They are not entirely in point therefore in determining the buyer's position where the goods have been tendered and are rejected by him. Nevertheless, the Anglo-Canadian position is generally understood to be as stated by her. Its reasonableness, however, is another matter. UCC 2-605(1) provides:

> **2-605.**(1) The buyer's failure to state in connection with rejection a particular defect which is ascertainable by reasonable inspection precludes him from relying on the unstated defect to justify rejection or to establish breach
>
> (a) where the seller could have cured it if stated seasonably; or
>
> (b) between merchants when the seller has after rejection made a request in writing for a full and final written statement of all defects on which the buyer proposes to rely.

The OLRC Sales Report (at 478) recommended the adoption in the revised Ontario Act of a provision similar to clause (a) but not of clause (b). Since clause (a) is predicated on a right to cure (a right recognized in UCC 2-508) it obviously would do no good in Ontario unless Ontario law also adopted a right to cure as recommended in the Report. Suppose in *IBM v. Shcherban, supra*, the buyer had initially refused to accept the machine on the grounds of late delivery; should he subsequently have been allowed to justify his rejection because of the missing glass face?

3) Under SGA s. 35 the buyer may rescind by intimating to the seller that the goods are rejected. Under the Business Practices Act, s. 4(5) and (6) the notice must be given in writing and delivered personally or by registered mail. But under the Consumer Protection Act, s. 21(2) (which deals with contracts not signed at the seller's place of business) notice is not sufficient and the buyer must return the goods to the seller, albeit at the seller's expense. Is there any reason for the lack of uniformity? Which method of rescission is best in the consumer context? For the commercial situation? Is there a conflict between the BPA and the CPA?

Hart-Parr Company v. Jones

[1917] 2 WWR 888 (Sask. SC)

LAMONT J: By an order in writing dated August 1, 1913, the defendant requested the plaintiff company, who are the manufacturers of tractors, to ship to him one of their 30 brake, gas tractors and a 4 furrow 14 inch stubble bottom plough, for which he agreed to pay $2,755. Before giving the order the defendant made known to the plaintiffs that he wanted an engine that would operate satisfactorily his threshing separator and that would pull satisfactorily the ploughs which he contemplated purchasing. In pretended compliance with the order the plaintiffs shipped to him an engine of the size and shape of the one ordered, freshly painted so as to look like a new engine. The defendant and the plaintiffs' experts endeavoured in the fall of 1913 to make the engine satisfactorily drive the defendant's separator, but failed to do so. In November an expert named Ginter went to the defendant's to fix up the engine so that it would plough, but when he got the engine operating the ground was frozen so that ploughing was practically impossible. In March the defendant requested the company to send up an expert to start the engine ploughing. In April or the beginning of May the expert arrived and the defendant and the expert examined the engine. The paint in places, owing probably to winter weather, had come off and the parts of the engine thus exposed bore such evidence that the engine had not been a new one when delivered, that certain suspicions along that line which the defendant had entertained were confirmed. He asked the expert about it, but the expert replied that the company's manager at Regina had forbidden him to say whether or not the engine was a rebuilt one. The defendant, becoming satisfied that the company had delivered to him a second-hand engine, drew it to his barn and notified the representatives of the company that it was not the article he had ordered and that it was at his place at the company's risk.

Not receiving the purchase price, the plaintiffs have brought this action for the full amount. The defendant resists payment on the ground (1) that the engine delivered was not the one he ordered and that he refused to accept it, and (2) that there was a total failure of consideration.

On the evidence I find that the engine delivered was not new, but was a second-hand engine with some new parts put in, the whole being newly painted to look like a new engine. I accept the evidence of the defendant that he notified the company that it was an old engine as soon as he was really sure of that fact and that thereafter he made no use of the machine.

On the argument it was not disputed that both parties understood the order to call for a new engine. That such was the meaning of the order I have no hesitation in holding. The delivery of a second-hand engine was not therefore, a compliance with the order.

· · ·

In this case, the engine ordered was not delivered. Did the defendant accept the second-hand engine in fulfillment of his order?

Secs. 33(1) and 34 of The Sale of Goods Act are as follows: ...

What took place in this case is very similar to what occurred in *Alabastine Co. v. Canada Producer & Gas Engine Co.* (1914), 30 OLR 394, 23 OWR 841, 4 OWN 486. There, the plaintiffs ordered from the defendants a three cylinder 19 × 20 natural gas engine and fittings, in accordance with specifications which were made part of the agreement, for $6,000. The specifications required the engine to develop 250 h.p. The title was to remain in the defendants until fully paid for. The engine was delivered in August and set up by the defendant company's engineer about September 8, and commenced to run September 10. From the start there was trouble with the engine and it could not be made to work satisfactorily. At times it would work fairly well for a while and then some part would go wrong. On March 25, 1912, the engine went to pieces. The plaintiffs had paid $5,500 of the purchase price. They sued for a rescission of the contract and a return of the money paid. In giving the judgment of the Court of Appeal, Meredith CJO, at 406, said:

> It is reasonably clear, we think, that there was no such acceptance of the engine as precluded the respondent from rejecting it if it did not fulfil the requirements of the contract. It was being "tried out" from September, when it was set up in the respondent's factory, until the time of the break-down in the following March. The evidence, no doubt, shows that throughout this period the respondent's manager was hoping, and perhaps believing, that the appellant would succeed in making such changes in the engine as would put it in a condition to meet the requirements of the contract, but there is nothing to show that the respondent at any time accepted the engine as answering those requirements, and, besides this, by the terms of the contract, "the title to the machinery or material" furnished was to remain in the appellant until the purchase-price should by fully paid.

This case is authority for the proposition that, where the property has not passed, the receipt of the engine, payment of part of the purchase money and attempted use from September to the following March does not necessarily constitute acceptance. In the case at bar, also, the property has not passed. The defendant received the engine in August; he commenced to thresh in the fall and threshed in all about 30 days, threshing only 20,000 bushels. According to the plaintiffs' own letter they had an expert on the engine 14½ days in the fall. In the spring the defendant rejected the engine.

In November 1913, when the expert Ginter was out attempting to put the engine in shape so that it would plough, he obtained the defendant's signature to the following:

Hart-Parr Co.

Charles City, Iowa.

Gentlemen:

Your Mr. W.C. Ginter called at my request and has spent 4 days rendering the desired assistance on engine No. 2405 and leaves the same in good running order and it is satisfactory to me.

John Jones

This the defendant signed because the expert represented that it was necessary for him to obtain a voucher for the days that he had spent on the defendant's engine. I do not place any reliance upon it as an acceptance of the engine. It was not signed for that purpose, and at the very time it was signed the ground was frozen too hard to make any real trial of the ploughing capacity of the engine. Under the circumstances, this acknowledgement cannot, in my opinion, be considered as an intimation to the seller by the defendant that he accepted the engine. The property in the engine was and still is in the plaintiff company.

Then, did the defendant retain the engine an unreasonable length of time before he intimated that he rejected it?

Ordinarily, the receipt of an article and its retention for eight months would afford strong evidence of acceptance, although not necessarily conclusive. Along with the lapse of time the circumstances must be taken into consideration. In this case two circumstances must not be lost sight of: (1) that from the early part of November until April there was no opportunity of "trying out" the engine, (2) the conduct of the plaintiffs' agents.

In 25 *Halsbury*, at 231, the learned author says:

> 401. In determining what is a reasonable time for the rejection of the goods by the buyer, regard is had to the conduct of the seller, as where he has induced the buyer to prolong the trial of the goods, or has by his silence acquiesced in a further trial.

In *Heilbutt v. Hickson*, LR 7 CP 438; 41 LJ CP 228, the plaintiffs contracted for the purchase of 30,000 pairs of army shoes as per sample, to be inspected and quality approved before shipment. The plaintiffs inspected, received, paid for and shipped to Lille, 4,950 pairs. It was then discovered that the soles of some of the shoes contained paper. The defendants then gave a letter to the plaintiffs agreeing to take back any shoes that might be rejected by the French authorities in consequence of containing paper. The plaintiffs then took delivery of 12,000 additional pairs. The French authorities rejected the whole. The plaintiffs sued for damages, which they claimed to be the whole cost of the shoes with freight, insurance and cartage added and loss of profit. They were held to be entitled. In appeal, the majority of the Court based its judgment on the fact that the letter gave the plaintiffs a right to reject the shoes at Lille, but Brett LJ, while agreeing with the judgment, expressed a decided opinion that the right of the plaintiffs would have been the same under the original bargain and independently of the latter; holding that, where a buyer has a right to reject goods upon inspection at a certain place and the vendors or those for whose acts they are responsible prevent the buyer from making an effective inspection at the place, he is not bound by such inspection. His Lordship, at 456, says:

The defect, though known to the defendants' servants, was a secret defect, not discoverable by any reasonable exercise of care or skill on an inspection in London. By the necessary inefficacy of the inspection in London, an inefficacy caused by this kind of fault, *viz*: a secret defect of manufacture which the defendants' servants committed— the apparent inspection in London could be of no more practical effect than no inspection at all. If it could be of no practical effect, there could not, as has been observed, be any effective, and, therefore, any real practical inspection until an inspection at Lille.

This view seems to be approved of in *Halsbury's Laws of England*, vol. 25, at 229. Applying the principles there laid down to the facts before us, it would justify the conclusion that the plaintiffs' servants by painting the engine made the inspection on the part of the defendant when it was delivered ineffective, and it was not until the spring of 1914 when the paint came off that an effective inspection could be made.

On the whole, I have reached the conclusion that what took place in this case was not such an acceptance of the engine as prevented the defendant from rejecting it when he did. If, however, what took place did amount to an acceptance, it seems clear to me that that acceptance was induced by the act of the plaintiffs' servants in concealing from the defendant the fact that he was not getting a new engine.

Action dismissed; counterclaim allowed.

NOTES

1) George purchased a school bus. Three months after the delivery of the vehicle he received a "recall" notice from the manufacturer advising him that the brackets supporting the exhaust system were not strong enough and needed to be replaced. Can George reject the vehicle and demand the return of his money?

2) *Hart-Parr v. Jones* seems to go a substantial distance toward recognizing a right of rejection because of a latent defect even after a substantial time for inspection has elapsed. Is this consistent with the history and rationale of ss. 33-34? Was Lamont J's judgment influenced by the apparently fraudulent conduct of the plaintiff and by the fact that the plaintiff had wilfully concealed the fact that the engine was second-hand and not new? Should a right of revocation of acceptance be explicitly recognized as it is in UCC 2-608 quoted earlier? Civil law systems which trace their roots to Roman law have long recognized such a right in the so-called "redhibitory" action to rescind the transaction on the grounds of a latent defect. See, for example, Quebec Civil Code, art. 1522 *et seq.* and *cf.* UN International Sales Convention, art. 38-40. Where lies the balance of convenience in such circumstances—the "allocative" and "distributive" costs, to borrow from the economists' lexicon? Or does it depend on the facts of each case? For an economic analysis of the Code's provisions and case law, see G.L. Priest, "Breach and Remedy for Tender of Non-conforming Goods under the Uniform Commercial Code: An Economic Approach" (1978), 91 *Harv. L Rev.* 960. The OLRC supports the Code approach. See Sales Report, at 472-75.

Part Rejection and Part Acceptance in Indivisible Contracts

William Barker (Junior) and Co. Ltd. v. Ed. T. Agius, Ltd.

(1927), 33 Com. Cas. 120, 43 TLR 751 (KB)

[The buyers, William Barker (Junior) and Co., Limited, agreed to buy from the sellers, Ed. T. Agius, Limited, a quantity of German coal. The coal was shipped at Hamburg on a vessel chartered by the buyers, some of it being in the holds and the remainder on deck and covering the hatch covers. When the vessel reached Liverpool it had to wait for a discharging berth. The captain became alarmed because the cargo in the holds was heating. In order to reach it he offered to buy the cargo on deck. The buyers agreed to do so with a view to helping him, and to secure the safety of the ship. The captain had the cargo moved into the bunkers and the covers were taken off the hatches. Only then did the buyers for the first time inspect the cargo in the holds and they found that it was not of the contract description. They then gave notice of rejection of the *whole* cargo, but the sellers contended that as the buyers had dealt with part of the cargo by selling it to the captain the right had been lost. The arbitrator decided in favour of the buyers, subject to the opinion of the court on a special case.]

SALTER J: The next question that is put is whether on the true construction of the documents and on the facts as found by me the applicants had and validly exercised a right to reject the under deck cargo. Those are two questions. Had they a legal right to reject this part of the delivery which is called the under deck cargo? If they had, did they validly exercise it? I will deal with the two questions in that order.

· · ·

Now [the first question], I think, having regard to the authorities, is a question of some difficulty. I will deal with it first as if I were free from authority. It involves a consideration of three sections of the Sale of Goods Act: section 11, subsection 1(c) [Ont. s. 12(3)]; section 30, subsection 3 [Ont. s. 29(3)], and section 35 [Ont. s. 34]. It is convenient, I think, to look first at section 35: "The buyer is deemed to have accepted the goods"—I am reading only the material parts— "when he does any act in relation to them which is inconsistent with the ownership of the seller." I have no doubt that if a buyer takes part of the goods and sells them that he does an act in relation to the goods which have been delivered to him which is inconsistent with the ownership of the seller; he cannot have a right to deal with part of the goods. Now I turn to section 11, 1(c), and I will read the first subsection: "In England or Ireland (a) Where a contract of sale is subject to any condition to be fulfilled by the seller, the buyer may waive the condition, or may elect to treat the breach of such condition as a breach of warranty, and not as a ground for treating the contract as repudiated." Paragraph (c): "Where a contract of sale is not severable, and the buyer has accepted the goods, or part thereof"—I am again reading only the material words— "the breach of any condition to be fulfilled by the seller can only be treated as a breach of warranty, and not as a ground for rejecting the goods and treating the contract as repudiated." I should have thought, if I were free from authority, that that clause governs this case. In my opinion this is not a severable contract. It is a contract for the sale of a cargo of briquettes which, within small limits, may vary in amount but which will be ascertained on delivery on board the ship, for an agreed lump sum which will be ascertained by multiplying the tons by 34s., the price. It is one contract and it is not severable. The buyer has accepted part of the goods. He has sold and delivered 25 tons of it, and, therefore the breach of this condition to be fulfilled by the seller can only be treated as a breach of warranty and not as a ground for rejecting the goods and treating the contract as repudiated. I should like to say that it is clear that rejection in this connexion means rescission. If a seller tenders to a buyer goods which are not in accordance with the contract and the buyer says to the seller, "This is not a performance of the contract; go and get proper goods and perform your contract," in a sense he rejects those goods. But that kind of refusal is not what is meant by rejection in this Act. So far from being a rescission or treating the contract as repudiated, that is an insistence on the contract. "Rejection" here means that the buyer might say to the seller: "This tender in purported performance of the contract is a fundamental breach of the contract and it entitles me, if I please, to treat the contract as repudiated by you, and I do so treat it as rescinded." Now where a buyer has accepted the whole of the goods, there can be no question that after that he cannot claim to reject and rescind, and it seems to me that if this clause were concerned only with rejection of the whole of the goods it would have been unnecessary to say anything about severable contracts. The words "Where a contract of sale is not severable" must have been inserted in view of the words "or part thereof," and if I were left to myself I should say that that means that where the buyer of goods has so dealt with part of the goods that he has rendered it impossible for him to return the whole of the goods the subject of the one contract, so that the parties cannot be restored to their former position, he cannot then claim to return either the whole of the goods—which is obviously impossible here as the buyer has sold part of them—or the part which remains in his hands. Supposing he has had delivery to him in purported performance of a contract for an agreed lump sum 100 tons of goods 5 tons of which are of contract quality and 95 tons are not, if he sells and delivers the 5 tons to a sub-purchaser, keeping the 95 tons in his hands, he cannot after that claim to return to the seller the 95 tons, to recover from the seller 95 percent of the contract price, and to retain the 5 tons at a rate applicable to 100 tons which no one would think of applying to so small a quantity as 5 tons, and then leave the matter so that neither party has any further rights against the other, the contract having been neither repudiated nor rescinded nor performed as a whole. I should have thought that such a position was impossible and that the purchaser who has resold part of the goods delivered in performance of one inseverable contract cannot after that throw back that part which is bad upon the seller, but that he is remitted to his remedy in damages in respect of that part of the delivery which is not in accordance with the contract. That brings me to section 30, sub-section 3, and it is said that section 11, 1(c) and section 35 must be read in conjunction with and in the light of section 30, sub-section 3. Section 30 deals with such matters as delivery of the wrong quantity, delivery of too large a quantity, and, under sub-section 3, delivery of mixed goods. Sub-section 1 provides that where the seller delivers to the buyer a quantity of goods less than he contracted to sell, the buyer may reject them, but if the buyer accepts the goods so delivered he must pay for them at the contract rate. Sub-section 2 says, "Where the seller delivers to the buyer a quantity of goods larger than he contracted to sell, the buyer may accept the goods included in the contract and reject the rest, or he may reject the whole. If the buyer accepts the whole of the goods so delivered he must pay for them at the contract rate." Then sub-section 3 deals with mixed goods: "Where the seller delivers to the buyer the goods he contracted to sell mixed with goods of a different description not included in the contract the buyer may accept the goods which are in accordance with the contract and reject the rest, or he may reject the whole." If I were free to read that section as *res nova* I should have thought it referred only to the goods of surplus delivery and admixture. I should be disposed to give to the word "mixed" a much more definite meaning than was given to it by Rowlatt J in the case of *Moore and Co. v. Landauer and Co.*, [1921] 2 KB 519 reported in the Court below in 1921, 1 KB 73. He said in that case that he thought it meant no more than "accompanied by." I should have thought that it meant much more than "accompanied by." If a man buys a horse and the seller delivers a horse and a donkey it would not require an Act of Parliament, I should think, to say he must keep the horse and return the donkey. I think that a good deal was meant to depend here on the word "mixed." I should have thought that it refers to the case, and only the case, where the seller has delivered the whole of the goods he contracted to deliver, the whole quantity and all of the right description and quality, but he has intermixed with those goods goods which are wholly alien to the contract, goods of a different description not included in his contract. Then the position is that the goods which are in accordance with the contract mixed with those which are not, cannot be separated out without trouble and expense, and then the section would simply say if the buyer chooses to go to that trouble and expense he can accept the goods which are in accordance with the contract and reject those which are not, but that he need not go to that trouble and expense. The seller cannot say to him, "All the goods I contracted to sell of the agreed quantity are there and, therefore, you must take them and sort them out for yourself." He cannot say that. The buyer may, if he pleases, reject the whole. That reading does not touch section 35 or section 11, and that is the way in which I should read it if I were free to read it for myself. But it has not been so read, and the question for me is whether the observations and decisions in three cases to which I now have to refer are such that it is my duty to read section 30, subsection 3, as giving to the buyers in this case a right to accept the 25 tons and to reject, in the sense in which I have defined that word, the balance; that is to say, the right to accept the 25 tons and to pay for them at 34s. a ton and no more, and to return to the sellers the rest of the goods and to recover from them the whole of the contract price except 25 tons at 34s. a ton, with the result that after that neither party has any right against the other. The contract is in a sense repudiated, in a sense performed, neither wholly repudiated nor wholly performed. That is the right which the buyers here are claiming and which it is said section 30, subsection 3, gives them; and the question is whether these three cases show that I ought so to hold.

Now the first of these cases is the case of *Moore and Company v. Landauer and Company*, [1921] 2 KB 519. In that case there was one contract for the sale of canned fruit, "the buyers stipulated that they should be packed in cases containing 30 tins each, payment to be per dozen tins. The sellers tendered the whole quantity ordered, but about one-half was packed in cases each containing 24 tins only." Those were the facts. It was held that the buyers were entitled to reject the whole consignment. The question being considered was whether they were bound to accept the whole, but it is to my mind quite clear that Rowlatt J regarded section 30, subsection 3, as being a section by which on facts such as exist in this case the buyer might accept the part of the goods in accordance with the contract and reject the part which was not, in the sense that he might make a partial rescission of the contract and accept part performance. That case went to the Court of Appeal, where the decision of Rowlatt J was upheld, but the decision is not of much importance in this case. It was held that as part of the goods was not in accordance with the contract the buyers were entitled to reject the whole. But I think it is quite clear that the Court took the view that the meaning of section 30, subsection 3, is that where the seller delivers the whole quantity partly of the contract quality and partly not, the buyer is at liberty to accept the part which is of the contract quality and to reject the rest in the sense of rescinding the contract in respect of the rest. In that case section 11 was not referred to and there was no reason why it should be; and there was certainly no reason why section 35 should be referred to.

The next case is the case of *J. and J. Cunningham, Limited v. Robert A. Munro & Company, Limited*, [1922] 28 Com. Cas. 42. That was a special case stated under section 19 for a Divisional Court. There was a contract for the sale of 200 tons of Dutch bran, f.o.b., Rotterdam, for October shipment. The buyers' ship was to be loaded at Rotterdam, and there was some delay. When loading began it was found that the bran was heated, and the buyers refused to accept any more than 384 bags which had already been put on board. The sellers contended that the buyers had no right to reject and that the bran remained at the risk of the buyers. Various other questions were raised there, but it is to my mind clear that the claim was to reject the portion other than the 384 bags; in fact, the buyers resold the 384 bags, just as in the present case, and they claimed to reject the balance. The first question was whether they were entitled to reject the balance and it was held that they were. In that case I should have expected section 11 and section 35 would have been considered, seeing that the buyers had exercised the rights of owners over part of the goods delivered, but I do not find that that was done. But it is quite clear that that Court considered section 30, subsection 3, as a section which would give the buyers the right which they claimed in this case, a right of partial rejection.

The third case contains a dictum of Greer J. It is the case of *E. Hardy & Company (London), Limited v. Hillerns and Fowler*, [1923] 2 KB 490, reported in the Court below in 28 Com. Cas. 193. That was a case in which the buyers, when the cargo was in process of unloading, without waiting to make a complete inspection of the cargo, resold and delivered parcels of it to sub-buyers. They afterwards claimed to reject the whole; and it was held that they had no such right. That I should have thought was a fairly simple matter, but Greer J, on a further question of a right to reject part having been raised, said: "I shall only answer the question which is raised, not expressly but inferentially, by the case stated—namely, whether the rejection which in fact took place, rejection of the whole quantity, was or was not a valid rejection. If my view is desired on that other point, I should add that in my judgment there has not been an acceptance of part and a rejection of the balance; that can be done where part of the goods is obviously in accordance with the contract and part is not; but where the same objection applies to the whole quantity and notwithstanding the objection to the whole quantity a portion has been accepted, there cannot be a rejection of the remainder. As the point is not raised by the case stated my views on it are *obiter* and need not be regarded as any authority for the proposition." I think that considered observations by Greer J, even though *obiter*, are by no means to be neglected; and what is more, those observations were expressly approved, of course *obiter*, by Bankes LJ when that case was considered in the Court of Appeal.

I have come to the conclusion that in view of these authorities, while it may be possible to say that they are not strictly speaking decisions which I am bound to follow, it would not be right for me to follow what would have been my own reading of these sections; and in view of those authorities and in deference to those authorities I hold that the buyers had in this case a right to accept the 25 tons and to reject the remainder.

[Salter J went on to find, however, in response to the second question, that the buyers had not made an effective rejection since they had purported to reject the whole cargo and not merely the non-conforming part of it. He accordingly held that the buyers were restricted to a claim in damages for breach of warranty.]

NOTES

1) *Benjamin's Sale of Goods*, 4th ed., paras. 12-027 *et seq.*, expresses considerable sympathy with Salter J's reasoning. However, the authors concede that the authorities are against him and that Ont. SGA s. 29(3) applies "not only to cases where the full contract goods are delivered mixed with other, additional goods, but also to cases where the contract amount only is delivered and it contains an admixture of goods of a different description; and that the buyer's right to accept the contract goods and reject the rest applies though he may be said to have accepted part." With respect to the meaning of description in SGA s. 29(3), see *Runnymede Iron & Steel Ltd. v. Rossen Engineering & Construction Co.* (1961), 30 DLR (2d) 410 (SCC) (held that "relaying rails" unfit for relaying without repair were goods of a different description and not simply goods of inferior quality). Is there any justification for restricting s. 29(3) to goods of the wrong description? Why should it not also apply to defects in quality?

2) The Uniform Sales Act did not expressly reject the partial acceptance rule, but it was substantially undermined by the New York Court of Appeals in a leading case, *Portfolio v. Rubin* (1922), 125 NE 843, and the process has been completed in Article 2. UCC 2-601 provides *inter alia* that if the goods or the tender of delivery fail in any respect to conform to the contract, the buyer may reject the whole, accept the whole, or accept any commercial unit or units and reject the rest. "Commercial unit" is defined in UCC 2-105(6) as meaning "such a unit of goods as by commercial usage is a single whole for purposes of sale and division materially affects its character or value on the market or in use." The

OLRC recommended adoption of the Code's approach where the non-conformity amounts to a substantial breach. See Sales Report, at 447. Does UCC 2-601 mean that the buyer has complete freedom of action—that, for example, he can retain part of the conforming goods and reject the rest, or that he can retain only part of the non-conforming goods? How could the section be read to avoid such unreasonable results? Curiously, judging by the paucity of reported Code cases, the issue does not appear so far to have arisen for decision.

3) The UK Sale and Supply of Goods Act 1994 amended s. 11(4) of the SGA [Ont. s. 12(3)] by adding new s. 35A, which provides:

> If the buyer—
> (a) has the right to reject the goods by reason of a breach on the part of the seller that affects some or all of them, but
> (b) accepts some of the goods, including, where there are any goods unaffected by the breach, all such goods,
> he does not by accepting them lose the right to reject the rest.

Is this provision open to the same objections as those noted by the OLRC with respect to UCC 2-601?

Instalment Contracts

Maple Flock Co. Ltd. v. Universal Furniture Products (Wembley) Ltd.

[1934] 1 KB 148, [1933] All ER Rep. 15 (CA)

LORD HEWART CJ (for the court): The appellant company are manufacturers of rag flock, and the respondents are manufacturers of furniture and bedding for which they use such flock. The action was brought by the appellants for breach by the respondents of a contract in writing, dated March 14, 1932, for the sale by the appellants to the respondents of 100 tons of black lindsey flock at 15*l*. 2*s*. 6*d*. per ton, to be delivered in three loads per week as required. It was further stipulated that there should be a written guarantee that all flock supplied under the contract should conform to the Government standard. The load was 1½ tons or 60 bags. The government standard was that required under the Rag Flock Act, 1911, which had been fixed by regulation under the Act at not more than 30 parts of chlorine in 100,000 parts of flock. The Act made it a penal offence punishable by fine for any person (*inter alia*) to sell or have in his possession for sale or use or to use flock not conforming to that standard. A person charged under the Act might, however, if he could prove that he bought it from some one resident in the United Kingdom under a warranty that it complied with the Government standard, and that he had taken reasonable steps to ascertain and did in fact believe in the accuracy of the warranty, bring the seller before the Court by information and transfer the burden of the offence to him.

The appellant company duly gave a written guarantee as required by the contract and deliveries were at once commenced and continued of 1½ tons each. The sixteenth of these deliveries was made on April 29, 1932, and, according to the respondent's evidence, was duly accepted and the stuff put into use; a further delivery was made on April 29, 1932, and another on May 2, 1932. On that latter date the respondents notified the appellants that a sample drawn from the delivery of April 28, 1932, had been analysed and showed a contamination of 250 parts of chlorine, instead of the maximum allowed by law of 30 parts. The respondents thereupon claimed to rescind the contract; the appellants protested, and some negotiations took place, during which two more deliveries were tendered and taken, each of 1½ tons. Eventually the respondents adhered to their claim that they were entitled to rescind, and the writ was issued by the appellants claiming damages on the ground that the refusal of the respondents to take further deliveries was wrongful.

· · ·

The decision of this case depends on the true construction and application of s. 31, sub-s. 2, of the Sale of Goods Act, 1893, which is in the following terms: "Where there is a contract for the sale of goods to be delivered by stated instalments, which are to be separately paid for, and the seller makes defective deliveries in respect of one or more instalments, or the buyer neglects or refuses to take delivery of or pay for one or more instalments, it is a question in each case depending on the terms of the contract and the circumstances of the case, whether the breach of contract is a repudiation of the whole contract or whether it is a severable breach giving rise to a claim for compensation but not to a right to treat the whole contract as repudiated." That sub-section was based on decisions before the Act, and has been the subject of decisions since the Act. A contract for the sale of goods by instalments is a single contract, not a complex of as many contracts as there are instalments under it. The law might have been determined in the sense that any breach of condition in respect of any one or more instalments would entitle the party aggrieved to claim that the contract has been repudiated as a whole; or on the other hand the law as established might have been that any breach, however serious, in respect of one or more instalments should not have consequences extending beyond the particular instalment or instalments or affecting the contract as a whole. The subsection, however, which deals equally with breaches by the buyer or the seller, requires the Court to decide on the merits of the particular case what effect, if any, the breach or breaches should have on the contract as a whole.

The language of the Act is substantially based on the language used by Lord Selborne LC in *Mersey Steel and Iron Co. v. Naylor, Benzon & Co.*, 9 App. Cas. 434 where he said: "I am content to take the rule as stated by Lord Coleridge in *Freeth v. Burr* (1874), LR 9 CP 208, which is in substance, as I understand it, that you must look at the actual circumstances of the case in order to see whether the one party to the contract is relieved from its future performance by the conduct of the other; you must examine what that conduct is, so as to see whether it amounts to a renunciation, to an absolute refusal to perform the contract, such as would amount to a rescission if he had the power to rescind, and whether the other party may accept it as a reason for not performing his part" (at 438). In *Freeth v. Burr* Lord Coleridge CJ stated the true question to be: "Whether the acts and conduct of the party evince an intention no longer to be bound by the contract" (at 213). These were both cases of breach by the buyer and not making punctual payment, and in each case it was clear that the buyer had some justification for the course he took. The case of breach by the seller in making defective deliveries may raise different questions. Lord Selborne in the passage above quoted did not refer to any questions of intention, but said that what is to be examined is the conduct of the party. Lord Coleridge in *Freeth v. Burr*, citing *Hoare v. Rennie* (1859), 5 H & N 19, on the question of the seller's breach, states this one aspect of the rule: "Where by the non-delivery of part of the thing contracted for the whole object of the contract is frustrated, the party making default renounces on his part all the obligations of the contract" (at 214). In other words, the true test will generally be, not the subjective mental state of the defaulting party, but the objective test of the relation in fact of the default to the whole purpose of the contract.

Since the Act, the sub-section has been discussed by a Divisional Court in *Millars' Karri and Jarrah Company (1902) v. Weddel, Truner & Co.*, 14 Com. Cas. 25, where the contract being for 1100 pieces of timber, the first instalment of 750 pieces was rejected by the buyers; an arbitrator awarded "that the said shipment was, and is, so far from complying with the requirements of the said contract as to entitle the buyers to repudiate and to rescind the whole contract and to refuse to accept the said shipment and all further shipments under the said contract." The Court upheld the award. Bigham J thus stated what in his opinion was the true test. "Thus, if the breach is of such a kind, or takes place in such circumstances as reasonably to lead to the inference that similar breaches will be committed in relation to subsequent deliveries, the whole contract may there and then be regarded as repudiated and may be rescinded. If, for instance, a buyer fails to pay for one delivery in such circumstances as to lead to the inference that he will not be able to pay for subsequent deliveries; or if a seller delivers goods differing from the requirements of the contract, and does so in such circumstances as to lead to the inference that he cannot, or will not, deliver any other kind of goods in the future, the other contracting party will be under no obligation to wait to see what may happen; he can at once cancel the contract and rid himself of the difficulty" (at 29). Walton J concurred.

This ruling was more recently applied in *Robert A. Munro & Co. v. Meyer*, [1930] 2 KB 312, where under a contract for the sale of 1500 tons of bone meal, 611 tons were delivered which were seriously adulterated. The sellers were middlemen, who relied on their suppliers, the manufacturers, for correct delivery; when the buyers discovered that the deliveries did not conform to the contract they claimed that they were entitled to treat the whole contract as repudiated by the sellers. It was held that they were right in so claiming, on the ground that "in such a case as this, where there is a persistent breach, deliberate so far as the manufacturers are concerned, continuing for nearly one-half of the total contract quantity, the buyer, if he ascertains in time what the position is, ought to be entitled to say that he will not take the risk of having put upon him further deliveries of this character" (at 331). On the other hand in *Taylor v. Oakes Roncoroni & Co.*, 27 Com. Cas. 261, Greer J, as he then was, and the Court of Appeal, declined to hold that the buyers were entitled to refuse to go on with the contract, but held that the breach was a severable breach, as it was a case "where the instalment delivered failed in a slight but appreciable degree to come up to the standard required by the contract description."

With the help of these authorities we deduce that the main test to be considered in applying the sub-section to the present case are, first, the ratio quantitatively which the breach bears to the contract as a whole, and secondly the degree of probability or improbability that such a breach will be repeated. On the first point, the delivery complained of amounts to no more than 1½ tons out of a contract for 100 tons. On the second point, our conclusion is that the chance of the breach being repeated is practically negligible. We assume that the sample found defective fairly represents the bulk; but bearing in mind the judge's finding that the breach was extraordinary and that the appellant's business was carefully conducted, bearing in mind also that the appellants were warned, and bearing in mind that the delivery complained of was an isolated instance out of 20 satisfactory deliveries actually made both before and after the instalment objected to, we hold that it cannot reasonably be inferred that similar breaches would occur in regard to subsequent deliveries. Indeed, we do not understand that the learned Judge came to any different conclusion. He seems, however, to have decided against the appellants on a third and separate ground, that is, that a delivery not satisfying the Government requirements would or might lead to the respondents being prosecuted under the Act. Though we think he exaggerates the likelihood of the respondents in such a case being held responsible, we do not wish to underrate the gravity to the respondents of their being even prosecuted. But we cannot follow the Judge's reasoning that the bare possibility, however remote, of this happening would justify the respondents in rescinding in this case. There may indeed be such cases, as also cases where the consequences of a single breach of contract may be so serious as to involve a frustration of the contract and justify rescission, or furthermore, the contract might contain an express condition that a breach would justify rescission, in which case effect would be given to such a condition by the Court. But none of these circumstances can be predicated of this case. We think the deciding factor here is the extreme improbability of the breach being repeated, and on that ground, and on the isolated and limited character of the breach complained of, there was, in our judgment, no sufficient justification to entitle the respondents to refuse further deliveries as they did.

Appeal allowed.

NOTES

1) *Assurance of performance.* Suppose a buyer cannot satisfy the court that the seller is likely to breach the balance of the contract (and vice versa), should this be the end of the matter? To change the facts entirely, suppose a seller who has agreed to build to order a large and expensive machine hears widespread rumours that the buyer is in serious financial difficulties and is not paying its creditors on time. Must the seller continue to manufacture until such time as the buyer actually cancels the contract or would you advise the manufacturer to discontinue anyway without awaiting the buyer's request? The Code responds to these types of cases with the following important provision:

2-609.(1) A contract for sale imposes an obligation on each party that the other's expectation of receiving due performance will not be impaired. When reasonable grounds for insecurity arise with respect to the performance of either party the other may in writing demand adequate assurance of due performance and until he receives such assurance may if commercially reasonable suspend any performance for which he has not already received the agreed return.

(2) Between merchants the reasonableness of grounds for insecurity and the adequacy of any assurance offered shall be determined according to commercial standards.

(3) Acceptance of any improper delivery or payment does not prejudice the aggrieved party's right to demand adequate assurance of future performance.

(4) After receipt of a justified demand failure to provide within a reasonable time not exceeding thirty days such assurance of due performance as is adequate under the circumstances of the particular case is a repudiation of the contract.

The SGA contains no similar provision nor does Anglo-Canadian common law recognize a doctrine corresponding to UCC 2-609. The OLRC Sales Report endorsed the soundness of the section and recommended adoption of a similar provision in Ontario. See Report, at 528-31.

2) Apart from the question of the right to cancel the whole contract where there has only been a breach with respect to one or more instalments, instalment contracts raise other questions of which the following is a sampling:

a) *The definition of "instalment contract."* The OLRC Sales Report, at 541-47, argues that the requirements in SGA s. 30(2) that the contract must envisage deliveries of "stated instalments" "to be separately paid for" are too rigid, and expresses a preference for the test in UCC 2-612(1), *viz.* whether the contract is one "which requires or authorizes the delivery of goods in separate lots to be separately accepted." Applying either of these tests, how would you characterize the following transactions: (i) a basketful of groceries tendered for the purchase at the checkout counter of a supermarket; (ii) an order for a three-piece made to measure man's suit; (iii) an agreement to supply a restaurant with its daily requirements of bread, payment to be made at the end of each month?

b) *Effect of breach of the whole contract on previously accepted instalments.* Two questions arise under this head: (1) must the buyer be in a position to return any previously accepted instalments as a condition of his right to cancel the contract because of a subsequent breach? and (2) should the buyer be *entitled* to return any previously accepted instalments if he elects to do so?

The first question is much easier to answer than the second. (Can you see why?) Apropos the second question, the OLRC Sales Report observes (at 549-50):

Under this heading, two separate questions must be considered. The first is whether the buyer must be in a position to return any previously accepted instalments as a condition of his right to cancel the contract because of a subsequent breach. The second question is whether the buyer is *entitled* to return any previously accepted instalments if he elects to do so.

The first question is much easier to answer than the second. The buyer's right to cancel is not dependent on his ability to return previous instalments. This position can be justified by analogy to section 29(3) of the Ontario Sale of Goods Act. This subsection entitles the buyer to reject goods that do not conform to the contract description that have formed part of a single delivery, while retaining those goods that are conforming. More simply, this result can be justified on the basis that it is inherent in the concept of a divisible contract. Both The Sale of Goods Act and the Uniform Commercial Code appear to assume implicity that this is the position, and no contrary case law has appeared since 1893. The point would not appear, therefore, to call for specific treatment in the revised Act.

The second question is much more difficult. At first glance, it might be thought that, if the contract is divisible, it should no more be possible for the buyer to force previously accepted instalments back on the seller than it should be possible for the seller to insist on complete rescission. The meagre case law appears to support this proposition. To the extent that they discuss the problem at all, the textwriters appear to be divided in their views, and neither the Ontario Sale of Goods Act nor Article 2 of the Uniform Commercial Code addresses itself directly to the issue.

The position is complicated because discussions of this question do not always observe the distinction between entire and divisible contracts. If the manufacturer of a machine delivers part of it and then repudiates, it can be persuasively argued that the buyer should be able to revoke his "acceptance" of the part that has already been delivered. This conclusion rests, however, on the assumption that the machine constitutes a single functional unit and that the contract was indivisible. There was, in reality, no true "acceptance" of the part; at best there was only a conditional acceptance, dependant upon satisfactory performance of the balance of the contract. This example throws a little light on what the rule should be where the instalment that has been delivered and accepted constitutes a commercial unit in its own right.

Nevertheless, on balance the Commission concluded that the equities favour the buyer and that he should be allowed to return previously delivered instalments provided certain conditions are met: Report, at 550. Do you support this recommendation?

Recasting the Buyer's Rights of Rejection

From the preceding materials (as well as the materials in chapter 4) it will be obvious that there are many difficulties in the existing Canadian Sale of Goods Acts involving the buyer's rights of rejection, and equally that they suffer from significant uncertainties and ambiguities. Anglo-Canadian law is not alone in finding it difficult to settle on a right set of solutions to what, after all, constitutes one of the most controversial areas of modern sales law; other statutory regimes exhibit the same frailties. Apart from the historical factors, much of the difficulty stems from the fact that a single statutory formula is expected to encompass an infinite range of goods, a wide diversity of parties, and any number of possible breaches of the seller's obligations giving rise to the buyer's grievances.

If we look at the remedial regimes presented by three modern, or relatively modern, sales codes or international conventions, we find the following alternative models:

1) *Current Canadian law.* Generally speaking, the right of rejection only exists for breach of a condition. However, since all of the major implied terms (title, description, merchantability, fitness and conformity to sample) are characterized as conditions and since time of delivery in commercial transactions is equally so treated by the courts, this means in effect that in most cases the buyer is given a very broad right of rejection regardless of the severity of the breach or the actual prejudice to him. From the seller's point of view, the hardship to him is accentuated by the fact that Anglo-Canadian law does not recognize a right of cure after the contractual time for delivery has expired. (See

OLRC Report, at 449-50.) The conception of innominate terms of sale, so vigorously espoused by Lord Denning in *Cehave*'s case, *supra*, chapter 4, has so far borne little fruit in the sales area and is unlikely to do so in face of the predominantly *a priori* characterization of the implied terms of the SGA.

However, the picture is not quite as bleak as may appear at first sight. The combination of the inconsistent act rule and the short period of time allowed in ss. 33-34 for the rejection of goods means that a court can often find that it is too late for the buyer to reject. The temptation must be particularly strong when the breach is only minor. In Canada the ghost of s. 12(3) (recall *Varley v. Whipp, supra*, chapter 6) can also be resurrected although it was never designed for this purpose and can just as easily result in denying the buyer the right to reject altogether. Somewhat more promising is the flexibility inherent in the concepts of merchantability and fitness for purpose. If a buyer seeks to reject goods on trivial grounds, it is often possible for a court to deny the remedy by arguing that s. 15 does not require the goods to be in perfect condition, only that they must be "reasonably fit" for their purpose, and that the test of merchantability is satisfied if there are some persons who would be willing to buy the goods in their existing condition without an abatement in price.

A well-advised seller contemplating this complex scenario will no doubt conclude that he is better off having the contract spell out the consequences of non-conforming goods instead of entrusting himself to the uncertainties of the SGA and the vagaries of litigation.

2) *Section 15A of the UK Sale of Goods Act 1979.* As noted in chapter 4, *supra*, this important amendment, adopted in 1994, denies a buyer the right to reject goods for breach of the implied terms of description, quality, fitness, and conformity with sample where "(b) the breach is so slight that it would be unreasonable for him to reject [the goods]." The amendment does not affect a consumer buyer. Also, the burden is on the seller to prove that the buyer is not entitled to reject because the breach is *de minimis*. Does s. 15A envisage various degrees of slightness of breach or can "so slight" be read as synonymous with non-material? Note too that s. 15A does not affect the buyer's right to reject for breach of an express term of the contract, though a court may be able to overcome the difficulty by treating the term as an innominate term—neither warranty nor condition— but only giving the buyer a right of rejection for material breaches.

3) *Uniform Commercial Code.* American contract law generally adopts a substantial breach test as the basis for cancellation of a contract. The perfect tender rule in UCC 2-601 constitutes a striking exception since it provides that

> Subject to the provisions of this Article on breach in installment contracts (Section 2-612) and unless otherwise agreed under the sections on contractual limitations of remedy (Sections 2-718 and 2-719), if the goods or the tender of delivery fail in any respect to conform to the contract, the buyer may
>
>   (a) reject the whole; or
>
>   (b) accept the whole; or
>
>   (c) accept any commercial unit or units and reject the rest.

For the historical reasons for this dichotomy, see OLRC Sales Report, at 451-52 and Honnold, "Buyer's Right of Rejection" (1949), 97 *U. Pa. L Rev.* 457. There are important exceptions to the perfect tender rule. As a result, it has been claimed by White and

Summers that the rule has been so much eroded "that little is left of it; the law would be little changed if 2-601 gave the right to reject only upon 'substantial' nonconformity." See further, OLRC Report, at 452-55. The important exceptions leading to this opinion include the seller's right to cure a nonconformity under UCC 2-508, the restriction of the buyer's right to revoke his acceptance under UCC 2-608 to cases where the nonconformity is of such a character as substantially to impair the value of the goods to him, and the adoption of the substantial impairment test in UCC 2-612 to sales by instalments.

4) *ULIS and CISG.* Under both the Hague Uniform Law on the International Sale of Goods and its successor, the Vienna Sales Convention (both previously described in chapter 1), the buyer can only avoid the contract where the seller has committed a "fundamental breach" of his obligations. See ULIS, art. 20-32, 33-49, CISG art. 49(1)(a), and OLRC Report, at 456-59. Both conventions also confer on the seller a limited right to cure a nonconformity and *semble* also confer on the buyer a right to demand cure.

A striking feature of CISG (and of civilian systems of sales law generally) is its uncluttered and title-free approach to the exercise of the buyer's right of rejection. The only restrictions are (1) that the buyer must examine the goods, or cause them to be examined, within as short a period as is practicable in the circumstances (art. 38(1)), and (2) that he loses the right to rely on a lack of conformity of the goods if he does not give notice to the seller specifying the nature of the lack of conformity within a reasonable time after he has discovered it or ought to have discovered it (art. 39(1)). He loses the right, in any event, if notice of the nonconformity is not given within two years of delivery of the goods (art. 39(2)).

5) *OLRC recommendations.* As previously indicated (*supra* chapter 4), the Sales Report was of the view that the system of *a priori* characterization of terms in the SGA had little to commend it. It preferred instead a buyer's right of rejection based on a substantial breach test. ("Substantial breach" is defined in s. 1.1(24) of the draft bill as "a breach of contract that the party in breach foresaw or ought reasonably to have foreseen as likely to impair substantially the value of the contract to the other party"). The Report also favoured giving the seller the right to cure a nonconforming tender or delivery (s. 7.7) if the nonconformity can be cured without unreasonable prejudice, risk, or inconvenience to the buyer and the type of cure offered by the seller is reasonable in the circumstances (s. 7.7(2)). Arrestingly, the Report also entitles *the buyer* to demand cure if the demand is made seasonably and before the buyer has accepted the goods, whether or not the nonconformity amounts to a substantial breach of the contract (s. 7.7(4)). Finally, the buyer is given the right to revoke his acceptance of goods on grounds substantially similar to those in UCC 2-608.

It may fairly be concluded, then, that the Sales Report shows a strong partiality toward saving the bargain if it can be done on reasonable terms and that it gives the seller a strong incentive to do so. However, its recommendations are not uncontroversial and they raise, *inter alia*, the following questions:

a) Does a substantial breach test provide a better accommodation of the seller's and buyer's competing interests than the existing SGA provisions? Will it lead to more litigation? Will it preclude a consumer buyer from rejecting a new car, for example, on the grounds of cosmetic defects? Does the buyer have such a right now under the typical motor vehicle warranty?

b) If a substantial breach test is adopted, what justification is there for also giving the seller a right to cure? Are the safeguards built into the exercise of the right sufficient to protect the buyer against abuses? Under UCC 2-508, American courts have adopted conflicting positions with respect to whether the right to cure extends to substantial defects. See Sales Report, at 453-55. Once again the OLRC recommendation was influenced by standard industry clauses. See Report, at 462. For purposes of a right to cure, should a distinction be drawn between major defects manifesting themselves at the time of delivery (in which case no right to cure is given) and defects that only appear after the buyer has had the goods for some time (in which case there is a right to cure). What about defects in title?

c) Since sellers will anyway draft their own remedial provisions as part of the terms of sale, do we need to agonize so much over what constitutes an optimally efficient statutory regime?

For further discussion of the above themes, see J. Honnold, "Buyer's Right of Rejection" (1948-49), 97 *U. Pa. L Rev.* 457; G.H. Treitel, "Some Problems of Breach of Contract" (1967), 30 *Mod. L Rev.* 139, 149 *et seq.*; E.A. Peters, (1963), 73 *Yale LJ* 199, 210 *et seq.*; W.D. Hawkland, (1962), 46 *Minn. L Rev.* 697; J.S. White and R.S. Summers, *Uniform Commercial Code*, 5th ed. (2000), chapter 8; and J.S. Ziegel, "The Remedial Provisions in the Vienna Sales Convention: Some Common Law Perspectives" in Galston and Smit (eds.), *International Sales: The United Nations Convention on Contracts for the International Sale of Goods*, chapter 9 (Matthew Bender, 1984).

CHAPTER SEVENTEEN

Buyer's Remedies: Damages, Specific Performance and Other Remedies

THE MEASURE OF DAMAGES

Whether or not the buyer has a right to reject non-conforming goods, and chooses to exercise it, the buyer is also entitled to claim damages. The SGA only concerns itself with damage claims sounding in contract. However, s. 57(1) preserves the rules of the common law except insofar as they are inconsistent with the express provisions of the Act. Moreover, even the contractual damage provisions are incomplete.

Section 49 deals with damage claims arising out of the seller's failure to deliver and is the counterpart to the seller's right to damages for the buyer's failure to accept and pay for the goods. Section 51 is concerned with damage claims involving a breach of the seller's warranties or conditions where the buyer elects or is obliged to retain the goods. It will be seen therefore that the Act fails to deal explicitly with the right to claim damages following the rejection of non-conforming goods. A tender of non-conforming goods not accepted by the buyer is equivalent to no delivery at all and such a tender should, therefore, attract the provisions of s. 49. Further, only by implication does the Act deal with the effect of a delayed delivery. It may also be noted that delayed delivery, breach of which is not waived, involves at least the breach of a warranty giving rise to a claim under s. 51. (Can you see why?)

The present section examines, non-exhaustively, some aspects of the existing damage rules, all of which proceed from the general contract principle that, subject to the rules of remoteness and the duty to mitigate, the buyer is entitled to be put in the same position as if the seller had not breached its obligations. This principle is so fundamental and so well established that one would not expect it to give rise to so much litigation in practice. It is obvious, however, from the pervasive use of disclaimer and limited liability clauses that many sellers do not find the general default rule at all congenial. Chapter 18 of the casebook therefore addresses the important topic of disclaimer clauses and the extent to which they are enforceable.

The Compensatory Basis of Damages and the Market Price Measure

Wertheim v. Chicoutimi Pulp Co.

[1911] AC 301, [1908-10] All ER Rep. 707 (PC)

LORD ATKINSON: This is an appeal from the judgment of the Court of King's Bench for the Province of Quebec (Appeal Side), dated October 3, 1908, affirming in part and reserving in part a judgment of the Superior Court of that Province, dated November 12, 1907.

By the former judgment the respondent company was condemned in a sum of $2434 and costs.

The [respondent] company carry on the manufacture of wood pulp at the town of Chicoutimi, which is situate on the river Saguenay, a tributary of the St. Lawrence in the Province of Quebec. The [appellant] is the sole partner in a German firm of merchants carrying on a business at Hamburg in Germany. He has an agent at Manchester named Reichenbach, where he trades in the pulp he imports from Canada and elsewhere, and an agent at New York named Goldman.

He claims in this action to recover damages from the respondents under three separate heads for three separate breaches of a contract entered into between them on March 13, 1900, to deliver at Chicoutimi f.o.b. 3000 tons of moist wood pulp between September 1 and November 1 in that year, at a price which was equivalent to 25s. per ton.

. . .

The first breach relied upon consists in the respondents having delayed in delivery of this quantity of pulp till the month of June, 1901; the second in the alleged inferior quality of the pulp actually delivered; and the third in its alleged deficiency in weight. In the view which their Lordships take of the appellant's claim under the second and third heads, it is unnecessary to deal with the amount demanded in respect of each. The first was the main claim. In respect of it the appellant claimed to recover 27s. 6d. per ton on the 3000 tons mentioned in the contract, that being the difference between the market price of such pulp at Manchester, the ultimate destination of the pulp, at the time it should have been delivered, namely, 70s. per ton, and its market price there at the time it was in fact delivered, namely, 42s. 6d. per ton; the difference between the market values of the pulp at these respective times being, according to Sir Robert Finlay's contention on behalf of the appellant, the well-established and indisputable measure of damages for delay in breach of contract in delivery of goods. The appellant in reality never sustained this loss nor anything like it, because he sold the goods under contracts, some anterior in date to the contract sued upon, the other anterior in date to the actual delivery, at the price of 65s. per ton, which is only 5s. per ton less than the top market price for which the pulp could presumably have been sold in Manchester had it arrived there in November, 1900, the contract time. Yet so rigid, it is insisted, is this formula or rule, that the resales must be ignored as collateral and irrelevant matters and damages be awarded for a loss which in reality has never been sustained. That, however, is not the only peculiarity of the appellant's claim. He admits that 13*s.* per ton would cover all the costs and expenses of the transport of the pulp from Chicoutimi to Manchester. It would thus cost him when delivered there 38*s.* per ton in all. If the pulp had been delivered in November and the appellant had sold it then at the highest market price, namely, 70*s.* per ton, he would have made a profit on it of 32*s.* per ton; but if the appellant was to succeed in this action, he would have received from the subvendees the price at which the goods were actually sold, namely, 65*s.* per ton, plus 27*s.* 6*d.* per ton, from the respondents in the shape of damages, making together 92*s.* 6*d.* per ton, or 22*s.* 6*d.* per ton more than if the contract had never been broken at all.

One cannot but feel that the reasoning which leads to results so unjust and anomalous must be fallacious.

On the assumption that by this delay in delivering the pulp the respondents were guilty of a breach of their contract—a point to be dealt with presently—and that the appellant was therefore entitled to recover some damages in respect of it, the main question for decision is on what principle and by what rule those damages are to be measured under the circumstances of this case. That question has given rise, apparently, to much conflict of judicial opinion. By the judgment and decree appealed from, the damages seem to have been fixed at 5*s.* per ton, that being the difference between the full market value of the pulp at Manchester when it should have reached that town and the rate at which it was sold when it in fact reached it. The rate per ton so fixed is, in their Lordships' opinion, the highest rate at which it could properly be fixed, since it covers the loss actually sustained. And it is the general intention of the law that, in giving damages for breach of contract, the party complaining should, so far as it can be done by money, be placed in the same position as he would have been in if the contract had been performed: *Irvine v. Midland Ry. Co. (Ireland)* (1880), 6 LR Ir. at 63, approved of by Palles CB in *Hamilton v. Magill* (1883), 12 LR Ir. at 202. That is a ruling principle. It is a just principle. The rule which prescribes as a measure of damages the difference in market prices at the respective times above mentioned is merely designed to apply this principle and, as stated in one of the American cases cited, it generally secures a complete indemnity to the purchaser. But it is intended to secure only an indemnity. The market value is taken because it is presumed to be the true value of the goods to the purchaser. In the case of non-delivery, where the purchaser does not get the goods he purchased, it is assumed that these would be worth to him, if he had them, what they would fetch in the open market; and that, if he wanted to get others in their stead, he could obtain them in that market at that price. In such a case, the price at which the purchaser might in anticipation of delivery have resold the goods is properly treated, where no question of loss of profit arises, as an entirely irrelevant matter: *Rodocanachi v. Milburn*, 18 QBD 67. The purchaser not having got his goods should receive by way of damages enough to enable him to buy similar goods in the open market. Similarly, when the delivery of goods purchased is delayed, the goods are presumed to have been at the time they should have been delivered worth to the purchaser what he could then sell them for, or buy others like them for, in the open market, and when they are in fact delivered they are similarly presumed to be, for the same reason, worth to the purchaser what he could then sell for in that market, but if in fact the purchaser, when he obtains possession of the

goods, sells thems at a price greatly in advance of the then market value, that presumption is rebutted and the real value of the goods to him is proved by the very fact
of this sale to be more than market value, and the loss he sustains must be measured
by that price, unless he is, against all justice, to be permitted to make a profit by the
breach of contract, be compensated for a loss he never suffered, and be put, as far
money can do it, not in the same position in which he would have been if the contract
had been performed, but in a much better position.

. . .

Appeal dismissed.

Bence Graphics International Ltd. v. Fasson U.K. Ltd.

[1997] 1 All ER 979 (CA)

OTTON LJ: The defendants appeal against a judgment of Morland J whereby he
ordered that there be judgment for the plaintiffs for £564,328.54 together with interest. The defendants seek to set aside the judgment and assert that in substitution there
be judgment for the plaintiffs for the sum of £22,000 (being the admitted value of
returned goods) together with interest or alternatively that there be a new trial or that
an assessment of damages according to the correct measure (being that contended for
by the defendants) be directed in any event.

The sole issue raised on this appeal is whether the correct measure of damages
was (as the judge found) the difference in market value or the actual losses (if any)
suffered by the plaintiffs under or arising from a breach of contract for onward sales.

Background

The defendants were one of a small number of suppliers of cast vinyl film, one of the
uses for which is to manufacture decals which are used to identify bulk containers,
this being the only end use intended in the case of film sold by them to the plaintiffs.
The plaintiffs' manufacturing process involved screen printing words, numbers or
symbols on the film and cutting it to size. The decals were then attached to the containers by reason of the self-adhesive character of the vinyl. Between 1981 and 1985
the defendants supplied to the plaintiffs film to the value of £564,328. This was to
produce in excess of 100,000 decals. Of the decals manufactured from the defendants' film, 93 per cent went for use on Sea Containers Ltd. ("S.C.L.") who were an
important customer of the plaintiffs and who imposed their own specifications for
containers and decals on manufacturers. S.C.L. owned the containers and leased them
to shipping lines and others so that the containers passed out of physical possession
of the owners for the vast majority of their life and were used all over the world.

It was common ground that the standard requirement in the container industry for
such decals was that they should have a "guaranteed minimum five year life." The
defendants know this to be so. Moreover it was a term of the contract between the

parties that the film would be of such a nature as to survive in use in good legible condition for a period of five years at least.

The plaintiffs alleged that the film did not fulfil the warranties with which it was sold, was not reasonably fit for its intended purpose and was not of merchantable quality. The reason for the defective condition was that the polymer constituting the film had insufficient stabiliser against the effects of ultraviolet light and became degraded upon such exposure. The defendants were at pains in their promotional literature to assure customers that their film would be of such a nature as to survive in use in good legible condition for a period of five years at least. The Dutch manufacturing associate of the defendants incorrectly formulated the film sold to the plaintiffs by putting insufficient ultraviolet stabiliser in the film so that, in use, it tended to degrade over a period eventually making some decals illegible. There were extensive complaints from customers of S.C.L. about the poor performance of the film. However, only one claim relating to 349 Tsujii containers was met by the plaintiffs who applied new decals at their expense and the defendants paid an agreed amount to the plaintiffs in compensation. There was also an intimation of a claim from S.C.L. which has so far not been pursued. The plaintiffs retained about £22,000 worth of unused and defective material.

By the statement of claim served in August 1988 the plaintiffs claimed for the difference in value (i.e. the recovery of the whole purchase price). By an amendment served three years later the claim was enlarged to include an alternative claim for indemnity against "all claims" by customers of the plaintiff. The defendants sought to rely on exclusion clauses contained in their standard trading terms. However, on the penultimate and final days of the trial the defendants made several admissions including that their terms did not operate so as to exclude or limit their liability for any breach and that they were in breach of their warranty that their product was durable for five years. Thus in the concluding stages of the trial the only issue left to the judge was the proper measure of damage. The defendants conceded that at least the plaintiffs were entitled to be reimbursed in the sum of £22,000 in respect of the stock returned to them. The judge accurately summarised the position thus:

> In the present case the plaintiffs have not suffered a loss in the shape of a claim for damages from their customers in respect of the decals processed by them from the defective Fasson 940 sold to them by the defendants to whom they have paid the contract price. Although they have suffered no such loss, they have been exposed and remain exposed to claims from their customers and they have been put to the expense of investigating and answering complaints. Also their commercial reputation may have suffered.

The judge found, applying section 53(3) of the Sale of Goods Act 1979, that the plaintiffs were entitled to the difference between the value of the goods at the time of delivery and the value they would have had if they had fulfilled the warranties.

At the heart of this appeal is the defendants' assertion that the judge misdirected himself in defining the issue as to the proper measure of damages which fell for determination.

Section 53 of the Sale of Goods Act 1979 [Ont. SGA, s. 51] has the sidenote "Remedy for Breach of Warranty":

(1) Where there is a breach of warranty by the seller, or where the buyer elects (or is compelled) to treat any breach of a condition on the part of the seller as a breach of warranty, the buyer is not by reason only of such breach of warranty entitled to reject the goods; but he may—(a) set up against the seller the breach of warranty in diminution or extinction of the price, or (b) maintain an action against the seller for damages for the breach of warranty. (2) The measure of damages for breach of warranty is the estimated loss directly and naturally resulting, in the ordinary course of events, from the breach of warranty. (3) In the case of breach of warranty of quality such loss is prima facie the difference between the value of the goods at the time of delivery to the buyer and the value they would have had if they had fulfilled the warranty. (4) The fact that the buyer has set up the breach of warranty in diminution or extinction of the price does not prevent him from maintaining an action for the same breach of warranty if he has suffered further damage.

Section 54 [Ont. SGA, s. 52] provides:

Nothing in this Act affects the right of the buyer or the seller to recover interest or special damages in any case where by law interest or special damages may be recoverable, or to recover money paid where the consideration for the payment of it has failed.

The Sale of Goods Act 1979 lays down the basic principles for remoteness of damage in language derived from the leading case of *Hadley v. Baxendale* (1854), 9 Exch. 341 where the main proposition was:

Where two parties have made a contract which one of them has broken, the damages which the other party ought to receive in respect of such breach of contract should be such as may fairly and reasonably be considered either as arising naturally, i.e. according to the usual course of things, from such breach of contract itself, or such as may reasonably be supposed to have been in the contemplation of both parties, at the time they made the contract, as the probable result of the breach of it;

per Alderson B., at p. 354.

The principles in *Hadley v. Baxendale* have been interpreted and restated by the Court of Appeal (see *Victoria Laundry (Windsor) Ltd. v. Newman Industries Ltd.*, [1949] 2 KB 528) and in the House of Lords in *C. Czarnikow Ltd. v. Koufos*, [1969] 1 AC 350. In the latter case the word "directly" is eliminated and more emphasis is placed on the "reasonable contemplation" of the parties. Such moderately differing formulations of the common law principles for remoteness of damage in contract are still based on *Hadley v. Baxendale*, 9 Exch. 341. Lord Reid in *C. Czarnikow Ltd. v. Koufos*, [1969] 1 AC 350 stated, at p. 385:

The crucial question is whether, on the information available to the defendant when the contract was made, he should, or the reasonable man in his position would, have realised that such loss was sufficiently likely to result from the breach of contract to make it proper to hold that the loss flowed naturally from the breach or that loss of that kind should have been within his contemplation.

Lord Upjohn stated, at p. 424:

the broad rule as follows: What was in the assumed contemplation of both parties acting as reasonable men in the light of the general or special facts (as the case may be) known to both parties in regard to damages as the result of a breach of contract. ...

The so-called second rule in *Hadley v. Baxendale*, 9 Exch. 341 applies when the loss caused by the breach of contract is greater than, or different from, what would have been in "normal" circumstances. The rule is that:

if the special circumstances under which the contract was actually made were communicated by the plaintiffs to the defendants, and thus known to both parties, the damages resulting from the breach of such a contract, which they would reasonably contemplate, would be the amount of injury which would ordinarily follow from a breach of contract under the special circumstances so known and communicated:

pp. 354-355.

Section 53(2) lays down the basic rule in terms of *Hadley v. Baxendale*. The second rule is not expressly incorporated in the Sale of Goods Act 1979 but is considered to be impliedly accepted by the wording of section 54: "Nothing in this Act affects the right of the buyer or the seller to recover ... special damages in any case where by law ... special damages may be recoverable": see *Benjamin Sale of Goods*, 4th ed. (1992), Appendix A, p. 1768, para. A-023.

The judgment

The judge approached the problem thus. He said:

In my judgment—the main issue which I have to determine in this action is whether the prima facie measure of damages is displaced by some other measure. At the time the contracts were made what may the court reasonably suppose to have probably been in the contemplation of the parties as to the remedy to be available to the plaintiffs in the event of breach of the warranty of quality, assuming the parties to have applied their minds to the contingency of there being such a breach? ... Unless the court is satisfied on the balance of probabilities that some other measure of damages was objectively in the contemplation of the parties when the contract was made, the prima facie measure set out in section 53(3) remains un-displaced if as the result of transactions by the buyer with other parties either the buyer may recover a windfall or the seller's liability may be limited to the prima facie measure albeit that the buyer's loss is much greater. ...

A plaintiff will only be restricted in his claim for damages (by reduction from the prima facie measure) as a result of special circumstances when those special circumstances have been brought home to him in such a way as to show that he has accepted or is taken to have accepted the risk that he will not be able to claim damages in respect of defective goods supplied to him unless his customer of his processed goods brings a claim against him. ... Not only at the time that the contract was made must the parties be viewed objectively to have contemplated that the plaintiff is taking the risk of having his normal measure of damages restricted in the event that his customer does not claim against him although he may still suffer loss because his customer may not re-order from him because of the defective quality of the goods supplied to him but also they must be taken to have contemplated that the defendant is taking the risk that the damages awarded against him will not be limited to the prima facie measure but that he will be exposed to a potential open-ended liability that he will have to indemnify the plaintiff in respect of any claim made by a customer against him. ... The defendants have failed to satisfy me on the balance of probabilities that having regard to all the circumstances in which the contract was made the parties must be taken to have contemplated that the section 53(3) measure of damages was displaced.

Mr. Stephen Grime on behalf of the defendants submits that the judge misdirected himself in defining the issue as to the measure of damages which fell for determination. He submits that the principal issue which the judge had to decide was as to whether at the time of the making of the relevant contracts the parties contemplated that the loss which would be suffered by the plaintiffs in the event of a serious breach of warranty of quality resulting in premature deterioration in service of the decals made from the defendants' goods was (i) diminution in the value of goods supplied by the defendants or (ii) liability in damages to purchasers of the decals together with loss of business and goodwill and any incidental loss and expense. The judge wrongly defined the issue as being as to the parties' contemplation of the legal remedy which was available to the plaintiffs in the event of breach of contract rather than as to their contemplation of the nature of the financial loss which the plaintiffs would be likely to suffer upon breach.

Leading counsel advanced the following propositions. (1) In case of sale of goods where a term as to quality is broken, the measure of damages depends upon the contemplation of the parties as to the consequence of a breach of the type committed, such contemplation being based on either their imputed or actual knowledge at the time of contracting. (2) There will be imputed to parties knowledge of facts which they had learnt as to the nature and background of their respective businesses (first limb of *Hadley v. Baxendale* so called). (3) In the Sale of Goods Act 1979, section 53(3) the words "prima facie" are not an expression of special quality or merit being attached to difference in value measure but more a reflection of the trading/mercantile conditions of times. Where the sale contract is not made between merchants dealing in a market the displacement burden is a light one. (4) Actual knowledge of special circumstances may extend the ambit of potential damages: section 54. (5) In some cases the finding as to contemplation of the parties as to the consequences of breach may be to show that breach will give rise to difference in value measure under section 53(3) and special damages under section 54. The claimant will not be limited if he wishes to choose one or both. (6) In other cases the finding as to contemplation of the parties as to the consequences of breach will show that the possible measures are alternatives. (7) Where the measures are alternatives it is for the court to choose the correct measure, not the claimant. (8) Where the court chooses one or other measure, the effect of the choice may reduce the amount of damages which may be claimed or increase it.

Mr. Andrew Moran on behalf of the plaintiffs submits that the judge did not misdirect himself in defining the issue as to the measure of damages which fell for determination. The issue was whether the loss claimed by the plaintiff was too remote a consequence of a breach of contract. In approaching this issue the judge was correct to proceed to the measure prescribed by section 53(2) and (3) of the Act as the starting point and then to consider whether on the facts of this case, the defendants had satisfied him that the prima facie measure was displaced by some other measure. This was to be resolved by asking the question, what loss to the plaintiffs is it reasonable to suppose would have been in the contemplation of the parties as a "serious possibility" or "a not unlikely result" had they had in mind the breach when they made their contract? The time of assessment is the time of making the contract. The judge both correctly defined the issue and expressed a proper approach to its resolution. Section 53(2) lays down a rule defining the measure of damages as a particular "loss" and section 53(3) is the exposition is how "such loss" is ordinarily calculated.

Leading counsel advanced the following propositions. (1) In a case of sale of goods when a term as to quality is broken the court should resolve any issue as to the measure of damage by first recourse to section 53, Sale of Goods Act 1979. In doing so the court is objectively ascertaining what loss would have been in the contemplation of the parties at the time of making the contract had they been made aware that a breach of the type which in fact occurred would occur. (2) The reference to "loss" in paragraph 1 does not involve the precise detail of the damage or the precise manner of its happening: it is enough for the innocent party to show that loss of that kind is not unlikely or a serious possibility. (3) The parties are deemed to contemplate loss which directly and naturally results in the ordinary course of events. In the ordinary course of events when goods of defective quality are delivered such loss is prima facie the difference in value. This principle is of universal application and not confined to mercantile or trading conditions of the time when the predecessor of the Act appeared. (4) Additional actual or imputed knowledge proved by a party seeking to rely on it, may demonstrate that particular loss would have been in the contemplation of the parties either (i) as a serious possibility of additional loss or, (ii) (as in a chain sale proper) as the exclusive kind of loss that might be suffered. In (i) the party suffering loss may confine his claim to the loss which the parties are deemed to contemplate as in (3) above, or he may add a claim for additional loss in contemplation. In (ii) he is confined to a claim for the exclusive loss so contemplated. (5) It is for the judge to resolve as a question of fact whether such additional knowledge as is relied on, demonstrates that some exclusive alternative loss was in contemplation.

Conclusion

I take as my starting point that section 53(3) lays down only a prima facie rule, from which the court may depart in appropriate circumstances. The burden of proof lies upon the person who seeks such a departure. The plaintiffs do not suggest that it is only open to a buyer to rebut the presumption. In my view, there is no reason in logic or principle why a seller cannot, in appropriate circumstances, seek to discharge the burden and displace the presumption: see *Biggin & Co. Ltd. v. Permanite Ltd.*, [1951] 1 KB 422, 435-436.

The situation often arises where the buyer seeks to displace the presumption and recover losses other than the diminution in value. Where a seller knows that the buyer intended to resell the goods and ought reasonably to have contemplated that a breach of his undertaking as to the description or condition of goods would be not unlikely to cause the buyer to lose the profit he hoped to make on the resale, or potential sub-sale, the buyer may recover damages in respect of such loss of profits caused by a breach of the seller's undertaking: see *Chitty on Contracts*, 27th ed. (1994), vol. 2, pp. 1290-1291, para. 41-315.

Situations arise where the court is satisfied and finds as a fact that it was within the contemplation of the parties, at the time of making the contract that:

> (a) the buyer intended to resell, or probably would do so, and that his sub-buyer would probably resell, and so on, so that there would be a series of sub-sales or "string con-tracts" of the same goods; and (b) that each contract in the series would, or probably would, contain the same, or a similar, contractual undertaking as to the description or condition of the goods; and (c) that it was not unlikely that a breach of the seller's undertaking would cause the buyer and each sub-buyer in the series to be in breach of his undertaking to his own buyer; and (d) that it was not unlikely that, in the case of such a breach, the ultimate buyers would recover damages from their sellers, so that liability would in turn be passed up the chain of sellers and buyers. In these circum-stances, the buyer who has paid to his sub-buyer damages and costs for breach of the undertaking in the first contract of sub-sale (which the sub-buyer claimed from the buyer, as the result of similar payments of compensation between successive sub-buyers down the chain) may recover the amount paid by him to the sub-buyer, together with his own reasonable costs in reasonably defending the sub-buyer's claim against him; the dam-ages and costs paid or incurred by the buyer are taken as the measure of damages for the seller's breach of the original contract [see *Hammond & Co. v. Bussey* (1887), 20 QBD 79, *Kasler and Cohen v. Slavouski*, [1928] 1 KB 78]:

per *Chitty on Contracts*, 27th ed., p. 1295, para. 41-321.

In the present case there was no series or "string" of contracts. The same goods were not sold on. Even so the string contract cases illustrate graphically how the court is permitted to and will depart from the presumption in order to do justice between the parties based on a finding of fact of what the parties reasonably contemplated.

If the buyer uses the goods to make some product out of them the value of the goods is not taken. In *Holden (Richard) Ltd. v. Bostock and Co. Ltd.* (1902), 18 TLR 317 where sugar was sold to brewers to be used for brewing beer and because of arsenic in the sugar the beer was rendered poisonous and was destroyed by the brew-ers the value of the beer at its market price in their cellars was allowed, inter alia as damages. Similarly in *Bostock & Co. Ltd. v. Nicholson & Sons Ltd.*, [1904] 1 KB 725 where commercial sulphuric acid warranted free from arsenic was used by the buyer for making brewers' sugar, one of its ordinary uses, he recovered not only the price paid for the acid rendered worthless to him by the breach of warranty but the value of other ingredients spoilt by being mixed with the acid.

In *McGregor on Damages*, 15th ed. (1988), at p. 519, para. 808, it is stated:

> In all these cases, it is once again vital that the use to which the goods have been put by the buyer is one that the seller either contemplated or must be taken to have contem-

plated: otherwise the damage will be too remote. If the buyer adopts the ordinary use of the goods, as where food sold for human consumption is eaten by him, or adopts one of the ordinary and well recognised uses although not the only one, as in *Bostock v. Nicholson*, or adopts even a use which is not the predominant one provided it is a use which is sufficiently common, as in *Hardwick Game Farm v. Suffolk Agricultural Poultry Producers Association*, [1969] 2 AC 31, where contaminated groundnut extractions were supplied for compounding into poultry food and the compound was fed to pheasants and partridges, he will recover under the first rule in *Hadley v. Baxendale*. If however he puts them to some special use, he will recover only if this intention is communicated to the seller, i.e. under the second rule in *Hadley v. Baxendale*. Here, as elsewhere, the dividing line between the first and second rules is not always clear in the cases.

Mr. Moran in argument invoked the principle that where the seller delivers defective goods but the buyer is nevertheless able to perform a sub-contract by delivering the goods to his sub-buyer, the buyer's damages against the seller cannot be reduced by taking this into account. He relied upon the decision of the Court of Appeal in *Slater v. Hoyle & Smith Ltd.*, [1920] 2 KB 11 where the buyer bought cotton cloth from the seller in order to fulfil another contract which the buyer had already made with a sub-buyer. The seller delivered cloth which was not up to the contractual quality, but the buyer was able to perform the sub-contract by delivering the same cloth. The sub-buyer paid the full price under the sub-contract. The buyer sued the seller for damages. The court awarded the buyer damages assessed at the normal measure, namely, the difference between the market price at the time and place of delivery of cloth up to the contractual quality and the market price, at the time and place of delivery of the cloth actually delivered. Scrutton LJ said, at p. 23:

> If the buyer is lucky enough, for reasons with which the seller has nothing to do, to get his goods through on the sub-contract without a claim against him, this on principle cannot affect his claim against the seller any more than the fact that he had to pay very large damages on his sub-contract would affect his original seller.

In my judgment the decision in *Slater*'s case can be narrowly distinguished from the instant case. In *Slater*'s case the sub-sale was of the same goods albeit after bleaching; the seller did not know of the contemplated sub-sale. In the instant case the goods were substantially converted or processed by the buyer and the sellers were aware of the precise use to which the film was to be put at the time the contract was made. I recognise Auld LJ's reservations.

This last case must be considered in the light of the dicta of Devlin J in *Biggin & Co. Ltd. v. Permanite Ltd.*, [1951] 1 KB 422, 435-436:

> Damages which arise under the so-called "second rule" in *Hadley v. Baxendale*, 9 Exch. 341, are sometimes referred to as if they were an increased sum which the plaintiff could obtain if he could show "special circumstances," or as if the rule embodied a measure of damage specially beneficial to the plaintiff which he could invoke if he fulfilled the necessary conditions. It is, no doubt, true that it generally operates in favour of a plaintiff rather than against him, but I think that it is capable of doing either.

and later, at p. 436:

> It has often been held … that the profit actually made on a sub-sale which is outside the contemplation of the parties cannot be used to reduce the damages measured by a notional loss in market value. If, however, a sub-sale is within the contemplation of the parties, I think that the damages must be assessed by reference to it, whether the plaintiff likes it or not. Suppose that the only fault in the compound was its incompatibility with bitumen felt, the chance that it might produce bad results would certainly reduce its market value before use. But if it is the plaintiff's liability to the ultimate user that is contemplated as the measure of damage and if in fact it is used without injurious results so that no such liability arises, the plaintiff could not claim the difference in market value, and say that the sub-sale must be disregarded. I say this so as to make it clear, that although I have come to the conclusion that, if the plaintiffs' basic claim fails, they can to some extent rely on the alternative of difference in market value, it is not because I think the plaintiffs have an option in the matter.

Lord Pearce in *C. Czarnikow Ltd. v. Koufos*, [1969] 1 AC 350 made a similar point when he said, at p. 416:

> … of course the extension of the horizon need not always increase the damages; it might introduce a knowledge of particular circumstances, e.g. a sub-contract, which show that the plaintiff would in fact suffer less damage than a more limited view of the circumstances might lead one to expect.

In my judgment, once the goods had been converted in a manner which was contemplated by the parties, *Slater v. Hoyle & Smith Ltd.*, [1920] 2 KB 11 has no application, the damages must be assessed by reference to the sub-sale "whether the plaintiff likes it or not." Thus the plaintiff does not have the option to choose which outcome is most favourable to him. It is for the court to determine the correct measure of damage, not the aggrieved party. Where the court determines the proper measure the effect of the choice may reduce the amount of damages claimed or increase it.

. . .

AULD LJ: I agree with the conclusion of Otton LJ and his general reasoning, but wish to add some words on the effect of section 53(3) of the Act of 1979 and on mercantile contracts where the parties obviously contemplate that the buyer will sell on the subject matter of the contract in its existing or in an altered form or as part of some other thing.

As to section 53(3), there is, in my view, a danger of giving it a primacy in the code of section 53 that it does not deserve. The starting point in a claim for breach of a warranty of quality is not to determine whether one or other party has "displaced" the prima facie test in that subsection. The starting point is the *Hadley v. Baxendale* principle reproduced in section 53(2) applicable to a breach of any warranty, namely an estimation on the evidence, of "the … loss directly and naturally resulting in the ordinary course of events from the breach of warranty." The evidence may be such that the prima facie test in section 53(3) never comes into play at all.

The *Hadley v. Baxendale* principle is recovery of true loss and no more (or less), namely to put the complaining party, so far as money can do it, in the position he would have been if the contract had been performed. Where there is evidence showing the nature of the loss that the parties must be taken to have contemplated in the event of breach, it is not to be set aside by applying the prima facie test in section 53(3) simply because calculation of such contemplated loss would be difficult. Equally, it should not be set aside in that way so as to produce a result where the claimant will clearly recover more than his true loss.

Where, as here, the contract of sale is between two merchants both of whom contemplate that the subject matter of the sale is to be sold on in whatever form, it offends the *Hadley v. Baxendale* principle to rule out mutual contemplation by them of damage arising from the buyer's onward sale simply because the subject matter is to be altered or incorporated in another product, or because the terms of the sub-sale may not be identical to those in the sale. It is equally offensive to that principle to describe the subject matter, as Mr. Moran did, as "worthless" or of "no value" to the buyer at the time of delivery if it appeared then to be of the contract quality and he was able to incorporate it in his product and sell it on without claim or provable prospective claim. Put shortly, and drawing on the analysis of Scarman LJ in *H. Parsons (Livestock) Ltd. v. Uttley Ingham & Co. Ltd.*, [1978] QB 791, 807, the sort of question the judge should have asked is: "What would the parties have thought about the probable loss to the buyer in the event of a latent defect in film at the time of delivery later causing trouble?"

Those observations run contrary to the judgments of this court in *Slater v. Hoyle & Smith Ltd.*, [1920] 2 KB 11, though they are of a piece with the approach of Devlin J in *Biggin & Co. Ltd. v. Permanite Ltd.*, [1951] 1 KB 422. In my view, the time has come for the former case to be reconsidered at least in the context of claims by a buyer for damages for breach of warranty where he has successfully sold on the subject matter of the contract in its original or modified form without claims from his buyers. With respect to Otton LJ, I do not think that the case is materially distinguishable from the present on the two bases that he suggests.

As to the first, the seller's knowledge of the buyer's intended use of the goods, the report in *Slater v. Hoyle & Smith Ltd.*, [1920] 2 KB 11 states that the seller did not know of the buyer's onward sale contracts. However, that must simply mean that he did not know of the specific contracts; for there can be no doubt that, in contracting to sell 3,000 pieces of unbleached cloth of a certain quality, the seller knew that he was dealing with a commercial buyer who would sell them on either unprocessed or processed to some degree, and must be taken to have contemplated that loss could result from such onward sales if the cloth was not of the required quality. The fact that the seller in this case had more detailed knowledge of the use to which the buyer would put the film is not a material distinction in determining the measure of damages as distinct from their precise calculation.

Second, as to what happened to the goods, the buyer in *Slater*'s case did in fact process them before selling them on; he bleached the unbleached pieces of cloth. That does not seem to me to be materially different for this purpose from incorporating the goods in a manufactured product for onward sale.

The Court of Appeal in *Slater*'s case had to reason around two decisions to the effect that where there has been delivery of goods to the buyer his onward sale may be taken into account in the assessment of damages. The first was a decision of the Privy Council, *Wertheim v. Chicoutimi Pulp Co.*, [1911] AC 301, where their Lordships held that the damages for late delivery should take account of the price actually obtained by the buyer in his onward sale. Lord Atkinson, giving the judgment of the Board, said, at pp. 307-308 [see *supra*, this chapter]. ...

Lord Atkinson's reasoning in that case, in particular the distinction between cases of non-delivery and late delivery and the relevance of the onward sale price in the latter case, was approved and restated by Lord Dunedin in the House of Lords in *Williams Bros. v. Ed. T. Agius Ltd.*, [1914] AC 510, a case of non-delivery. He said, at pp. 522-523:

> It is certain that Lord Atkinson, who delivered the judgment in that case, did not think that he was going against *Rodocanachi*'s case, for he says so in terms. Nor, in my mind, is there any discrepancy between the two judgments. *Wertheim*'s case was a case, not of delivery withheld, but of delivery delayed. The buyer, therefore, got the goods, and the only damage he had suffered was in delay. Now, delay might have prejudiced him; but the amount of prejudice was no longer a matter of speculation, it had been put to the test by the goods being actually sold; and he was rightly, as I think, only held entitled to recover the difference between the market price at the date of due delivery and the price he actually got. But when there is no delivery of the goods the position is quite a different one. The buyer never gets them, and he is entitled to be put in the position in which he would have stood if he had got them at the due date. That position is the position of a man who has goods at the market price of the day—and barring special circumstances, the defaulting seller is neither mulct in damages for the extra profit which the buyer would have got owing to a forward resale at over the market price ... nor can he take benefit of the fact that the buyer has made a forward resale at under the market price.

See also per Lord Atkinson, at p. 529, and the unusual case of *R. Pagnan & Fratelli v. Corbisa Industrial Agrocapuaria Limitada*, [1970] 1 WLR 1306, where a buyer, having initially rejected goods because of their defective quality, later accepted them after negotiating a reduced price which was less than the market price for similar goods at the date of the seller's breach. The Court of Appeal held that the prima facie market price rule in section 53(3) did not apply because the buyer had suffered no loss.

In *Slater*'s case [1920] 2 KB 11 all the members of the court were disinclined to extend the decision in *Wertheim*'s case [1911] AC 301 to a claim for breach of warranty of quality. Bankes LJ [1920] 2 KB 11, 15, confined it in any event to a sub-sale of the identical goods, relying on reasoning of Lord Dunedin in *Williams Bros. v. Ed. T. Agius Ltd.*, [1914] AC 510, 523 about the difficulty of establishing damages based on the terms of a sub-sale in a non-delivery case. Warrington LJ [1920] 2 KB 11, 17-18, appears to have been of the view—though he did not explain why—that section 53(3) of the Sale of Goods Act 1893 (56 & 57 Vict. c. 71) (corresponding to section 53(3) of the Act of 1979) was the right principle governing delivery of inferior goods to those provided for by the contract and that what the buyer did with the goods was irrelevant. Scrutton LJ, at p. 22, expressed the view that the *Rodocanachi* principle, 18 QBD 67 as to non-delivery applied equally to delivery of inferior goods, because if the buyer fulfils his sub-contract by buying in the market, he is left with the inferior goods at their market value against the market value of sound goods. Alternatively, if he applies the inferior goods to a sub-sale the damages he may have to pay to his buyer may be calculable differently from those in the contract with his seller. He acknowledged that, on this approach, the buyer may recover more than his true loss, but he cited examples of the same principle resulting in a recovery of less than the true loss.

With respect to the Court of Appeal in that case, and to the authors of the supporting comments in *McGregor on Damages*, 15th ed., p. 502, para. 774 and *Chitty on Contracts*, 27th ed., vol. 2, p. 1280, para. 41-300, note 91, it seems to me that they wrongly: (1) overlooked the basic rule in section 53(2) as to what would have been in the ordinary and natural contemplation of the parties in a commercial contract such as it was, namely, that the buyer could well be prejudiced in his onward dealing with the goods if they were defective; (2) disregarded the reasoning of the Privy Council in *Wertheim v. Chicoutimi Pulp Co.*, [1911] AC 301 as approved and re-stated by Lords Dunedin and Atkinson in *Williams Bros. v. Ed. T. Agius Ltd.*, [1914] AC 510 that where there has been delivery in a mercantile contract and it can be seen what the buyer has done with the goods, it is possible and proper to measure his actual loss by reference to that outcome; (3) had too much regard to practicality at the expense of principle in relying on possible difficulties of establishing causation and assessment where the goods sold have been subjected to some process or where the terms of the contract and sub-contract may for that or some other reason be different; and (4) were seemingly content to award a buyer more than the evidence clearly showed he had lost.

As Devlin J made plain in his consideration in *Biggin & Co. Ltd. v. Permanite Ltd.*, [1951] 1 KB 422, 436 of the supposed two rules in *Hadley v. Baxendale*, 9 Exch. 341, the critical matter in determining the earlier question as to the applicability or not of the prima facie rule in section 53(3) is the contemplation of the parties:

> ... there is only one area of indemnity to be explored, and that is what is within the prevision of the defendant as a reasonable man in the light of the knowledge, actual or implied, which he has at the time of the contract. It has often been held ... that the profit actually made on a sub-sale which is outside the contemplation of the parties cannot be used to reduce the damages measured by a notional loss in market value. If, however, a sub-sale is within the contemplation of the parties, I think that the damages must be assessed by reference to it, whether the plaintiff likes it or not. ... If it is the plaintiff's liability to the ultimate user that is contemplated as the measure of damage and if in fact it is used without injurious results so that no such liability arises, the plaintiff could not claim the difference in market value, and say that the subsale must be disregarded.

The judge directed himself broadly to the question of the notional contemplation of the parties in the event of a latent defect in the film putting the buyer in breach of his contract to the container manufacturers. However, apart from a brief summary of the relevant circumstances and posing a series of unanswered questions about uncertainties as to the extent of the damages if calculated on that basis, he has not made a reasoned finding as to their notional contemplation. His approach was a paraphrase of a passage in *McGregor on Damages*, 15th ed., pp. 161-162, para. 264 relating to contracting parties' knowledge of "special circumstances." He asked whether there were "special circumstances" known at the time to the buyer which he should be taken as having accepted so as to restrict his claim "by reduction from the prima facie measure" or by which the seller should have contemplated exposing himself to an "open-ended liability" of indemnity.

In my view, that was a wrong approach. This was not a "special circumstances" case or one where the possible damages were so remote or open-ended as not to have been within the parties' contemplation. It was eminently a case in which they would have contemplated that, in the event of a breach by the seller discovered only after the decals had been in use, the buyer might wish to pass on to it claims for damages from dissatisfied customers.

I add a few words about chain contracts. In *Dexters Ltd. v. Hill Crest Oil Co. (Bradford) Ltd.*, [1926] 1 KB 348 (CA), Bankes, Warrington and Scrutton LJJ expressed the view, obiter, that all the contracts in a chain must be the same if recoverable damages are to be passed along the chain. However, as the editors of *McGregor on Damages*, at p. 522, para. 815, observe, that approach is "a little too strict." The matter was considered by Devlin J in *Biggin & Co. Ltd. v. Permanite Ltd.*, [1951] 1 KB 422. He said, at p. 433, that he agreed with the reasoning that lay behind the view, namely that material variations in contracts down the line could lead to contractual claims for damages not contemplated by the original seller. However, he clearly regarded the matter as one of fact for determination in each case, not as a rigid principle of law that all contracts in the chain must be in the same terms. He said, at pp. 433-434:

> I respectfully adopt this principle, but I have still to determine how it should be applied in this case, and also what degree of variation in descriptions breaks the chain. ... To understand the application of the principle it is necessary to understand its basis. Like every principle in this branch of the law, it stems from the broad rule that the damage is to be measured by those consequences of the breach which the parties as reasonable men would, if they had thought about it, have foreseen and accepted as natural and probable. If the variation to a description is such that it is impossible to say whether the injury that ultimately results would have flowed from the breach of the original warranty, the parties must as reasonable men be presumed to have put the liability for the injury outside their contemplation as a measure of compensation. If this is, as I believe, the nature of the principle, it must be applied very differently according to whether the injury for which the defendant is being asked to pay is a market loss or physical damage. In the former case (which I think is what the Lords Justices were considering in *Dexters Ltd. v. Hill Crest Oil Co. (Bradford) Ltd.*, [1926] 1 KB 348) any variation that is more than a matter of words is likely to be fatal, because there is no way of telling its effect on the market value. In the latter case the nature of the physical damage will show whether the variation was material or not.

As Mr. Stephen Grime submitted on behalf of the seller, the point is essentially one of causation, namely whether there is sufficient similarity between the sale contract and the subsequent contract(s) to enable a finding that breach by the seller of the sale contract has in fact caused the breach of the subsequent contract(s). Clearly, as he also submitted, a substantial change to goods sold as a result of the buyer subjecting them to a manufacturing process may break the chain of causation between the breach of the contract sued upon and any claim arising under a subsequent contract. However, that is unlikely on the facts of this case—a five-year film life without deterioration was stipulated by the container owner, the container manufacturer and the decal manufacturer, the buyer, in the contracts into which they respectively entered along the chain.

I therefore conclude, as Otton LJ has done, that this is plainly a case in which the parties must be taken as having contemplated that any latent defect in the vinyl film at the time of delivery or at the time of conversion by the buyer into the decals might when later discovered render the buyer vulnerable to claims for damages which it would wish to pass back to the seller. On the material before the judge, there appear to have been no material differences between the contracts in the chain which would have put damage claimed at any point in the chain outside the imputed contemplation of the buyer and seller, given their knowledge that the vinyl film and the decals into which it was converted were required to serve their purpose for a minimum of five years. I am accordingly of the view that the appeal should be allowed and that there should be an order in the terms stated by Otton LJ.

Appeal allowed.

NOTES ON WERTHEIM AND BENCE GRAPHICS

1) In the 19th century the English courts developed the market price test as determining the measure of damages suffered by a buyer where the seller has failed to deliver the goods and there is an available market where the buyer could have procured replacement goods. In such cases the buyer's measure of damages will be the difference between the contract price and the market price at the time the goods should have been delivered. The market price test appears in the Ontario SGA, s. 50(3) (buyer's failure to accept goods) and s. 51(3) (seller's failure to deliver goods). The SGA contains no explicit market price test where the goods are delivered but are of inferior quality, but the courts have applied the test anyway. See, e.g., *Slater v. Hoyle & Smith*, [1920] 2 KB 11 (CA). As Auld LJ's judgment explains in *Bence Graphics*, the market price test is only a derivation from the general foreseeability test for the measurement of contract damages and no significance attaches to the fact that s. 53(3) of the SGA, dealing with damages for defective goods, makes no specific reference to the market price test.

2) Before the market price test can be applied, there must be an available market. "Available market" is a term of art and is encumbered with a substantial body of case law that is discussed in the leading British and Canadian sales texts. Much more significant, in conceptual terms, is the question of when the courts will be willing to allow greater or lesser damages than those to which the aggrieved buyer or seller would be entitled by applying the market price test. The case law is huge and by no means consistent. *Wertheim* and *Bence Graphics* have been selected for discussion in this chapter: the first because it has been much criticized by commentators and is difficult to reconcile with the orthodox

learning on the market price test, and the second because of Auld LJ's refreshing attempt to restate both the market price test and the exceptions to it in modern and principled terms.

3) The 19th century position, as expounded by the English Court of Appeal in the leading case of *Rodocanachi v. Milburn* (1886), 18 QBD 67, was that evidence about the actual loss suffered by the seller or buyer was inadmissible as "extraneous" to the market price test. In other words, once the court determined that the circumstances required the application of the market price test, it was no longer relevant to enquire what damages the seller or buyer had actually suffered. In this sense, the market price test has been given the status of a liquidated damages type rule. So, for example, in *Williams Bros. Ltd. v. Ed. T. Agius Ltd.*, [1914] AC 510, the House of Lords refused to reduce the market price damages awarded against the defaulting seller despite evidence that the buyer's actual damages were substantially less because the buyer had actually resold goods of the same description at a price lower than what happened to be the market price at the time fixed for delivery. See *Benjamin's Sale of Goods*, 5th ed., para. 17-016. Similarly, in *Slater v. Hoyle & Smith*, [1920] 2 KB 11 (CA), where the buyer complained that the cotton delivered by the seller was not of the contractual quality, the buyer was able to recover market price damages even though a sub-buyer from the buyer had raised no objections to the quality and had paid the full price agreed to in the subcontract. The courts will allow exceptions to the market price rule if it can be shown that the parties had contracted in contemplation of the goods being resold by the buyer or (see *Bence Graphics*) of the goods being processed and then resold by the buyer. However, the cases are not consistent in spelling out the precise test in the case of chain contracts: must the seller actually *know* that the buyer intends to resell those very goods, or is it sufficient to show that the seller knew that a subsale was "probable" (see Benjamin, para. 17-029, discussing *Hall v. Pim*, [1928] All ER 763 (HL), and must the terms of the subsale be identical, or is it sufficient if they are substantially the same?

4) *Wertheim*'s case is troubling because it appears to give the go-by to these traditional tests and to adopt the radical proposition that the buyer will not be allowed to recover more than its actual losses in the case of a subsale—not on the basis that the parties actually contemplated a subsale at the time of the original contract, but because it would be unjust to give the buyer a windfall. Yet in *Williams v. Agius, supra*, Lord Dunedin supported the result in *Wertheim* (while denying the seller in that case the benefit of the buyer's reduced loss), as did Auld LJ more recently in *Bence Graphics*. In *Slater v. Smith, supra*, on the other hand, the Court of Appeal strongly criticized *Wertheim*'s departure from principle. Your editors reconcile these different readings of *Wertheim* on the footing that Lord Dunedin in *Williams v. Agius* and Auld LJ in *Bence Graphics* treated the contract as having been made in contemplation of a subsale and therefore as taking it out of the basic market price test rule.

5) The Uniform Commercial Code contains the following "cover" provision:

2-712.(1) After a breach within the preceding section the buyer may "cover" by making in good faith and without unreasonable delay any reasonable purchase of or contract to purchase goods in substitution for those due from the seller.

(2) The buyer may recover from the seller as damages the difference between the cost of cover and the contract price together with any incidental or consequential damages as hereinafter defined (Section 2-715), but less expenses saved in consequence of the seller's breach.

(3) Failure of the buyer to effect cover within this section does not bar him from any other remedy.

(A corresponding provision entitling the seller to recover damages on the basis of the actual resale price following the buyer's repudiation appears in UCC 2-706. Article 76 of the UN Sales Convention combines both sides of this rule in a single provision.) Do these provisions simply simplify proof of market price damages, or do they also cast light on the other questions discussed in the preceding paragraphs?

Types of Recoverable Damages

Bowlay Logging Ltd. v. Domtar Ltd.

[1978] 4 WWR 105, 87 DLR (3d) 325 (BCSC)

BERGER J: The defendant Domtar Limited is a pole and pile manufacturer. It has a yard in Golden, British Columbia, where poles and piles are prepared for transportation to its wood treatment plants on the prairies. Until 1972 a local contractor logged Domtar's timber quota for it. Not all the timber was suitable for poles and piles, so the poles and piles were sorted from the other logs at the site and hauled to Domtar's yard in Golden. The sawlogs were hauled away to Briscoe Sawmills.

Domtar wished to increase its quota from 48,000 cubic feet to 1,750,000 cubic feet in order to establish a secure supply of timber, so it obtained Timber Sale A03518 from the British Columbia Forest Service to be logged in 1972, additional timber sales to be obtained in subsequent years. Domtar expected to produce 10,000 cunits (1,000,000 cubic feet) from the timber sale. A series of meetings was held between Ron Dyck, of Domtar, and Donald Bremner, Clifford Bowles and Greg Lay. The outcome of the meetings was that the latter three established the plaintiff Bowlay Logging Limited to log Domtar's timber sale. Bremner was the principal financial backer. Lay, and then Bowles, ran the company's operations at the timber sale.

The parties entered into a contract under which Bowlay was to log Timber Sale A03518. Before the end of the year the arrangement was at an end. The timber sale had not been completely logged off. There were allegations of breach of contract. This lawsuit, brought by Bowlay, was the outcome.

[Berger J, after reviewing the evidence, found that Domtar was in breach of failing to supply an adequate number of trucks for the plaintiff's use and then turned to consider the question of damages:]

This brings me to the issue of damages. Bowlay's claim is not for loss of profits, but for compensation for expenditures made in part performance. Bowlay is not in a position to claim damages for loss of profits, because it cannot prove that if it had gone on to complete the contract it would have made any money. Bowlay, since it cannot prove any loss of profits, is seeking to recover its losses for actual outlay. These came to $232,905. The payments received from Domtar for deliveries of logs came to $108,128.57. Bowlay's claim is for the balance, $124,776.43.

While it is true that the parties contemplated that the contract might be renewed on an annual basis, I think Bowlay's claim for damages must be limited to damages in respect of Bowlay's losses on Timber Sale A03518. Any claim based on the loss of expected profits on future timber sales would be too uncertain and remote. In any event, Bowlay has limited its claim to compensation for expenditures made in part performance. It has not advanced any claim for loss of profits.

The cases say that a plaintiff can sue for expenses incurred in part performance of a contract when the contract has been ended by breach. In *Cullinane v. Br. "Rema" Mfg. Co. Ltd.*, [1954] 1 QB 292; [1953] 2 All ER 1237 (CA), Lord Evershed said at 303:

> As a matter of principle also, it seems to me that a person who has obtained a machine, such as the plaintiff obtained, being a machine which was mechanically in exact accordance with the order given but which was unable to perform a particular function which it was warranted to perform, may adopt one of two courses. He may say, when he discovers its incapacity, that it was not what he wanted, that it is quite useless to him, and he may claim to recover the capital cost he has incurred, deducting anything he can obtain by disposing of the material that he got. A claim of that kind puts the plaintiff in the same position as though he had never made the contract at all. In other words, he is back where he started; and, if it were shown that the profit-earning capacity was in fact very small, the plaintiff would probably elect so to base his claim. But, alternatively, where the warranty in question relates to performance, he may, in my judgment, make his claim on the basis of the profit which he has lost because the machine as delivered fell short in its performance of that which it was warranted to do.

See also *McRae v. Commonwealth Disposals Commn.* (1951), 84 CLR 377.

In *Anglia Television v. Reed*, [1972] 1 QB 60, [1971] 3 All ER 690 (CA), Lord Denning MR held that a plaintiff had the right to sue for expenditures made in part performance. He said, at 64:

> If he has not suffered any loss of profits—or if he cannot prove what his profits would have been—he can claim in the alternative the expenditure which has been thrown away, that is, wasted, by reason of the breach. That is shown by *Cullinane v. Br. "Rema" Mfg. Co. Ltd.*, [*supra*, at 303 and 308].

But Domtar has raised an issue not reached by these cases. Mr. Harvey says that even if there was a breach of contract Domtar is not bound to compensate Bowlay for their expenses—at any rate certainly not the full measure of those expenses—because the operation was losing money. If it had continued it would have lost more money. Domtar says that in fact Bowlay's losses on full performance would have exceeded its losses in expenses "thrown away." It is said that in these circumstances Bowlay cannot recover any damages.

May a claim for expenses made in part performance be sustained where the defendant shows that the plaintiff was engaged in a losing operation and, even if there had been no breach and the contract had been fully performed, would inevitably have suffered a loss on the contract? Should the defendant be entitled to have the losses that would have been incurred deducted from the plaintiff's claim for compensation for expenses made in part performance? What if the plaintiff's losses, in the event the contract had been fully performed, would have exceeded the claim for expenses? To what extent should the plaintiff be entitled to recover in such a case?

McGregor on Damages, 13th ed. (1972), at 28, commenting on the *Anglia* case, said:

> This decision however does not cover the case where the plaintiff has made a bad bargain, and it is still an open question whether in such circumstances he should be allowed to opt for the alternative measure. The argument on the one side is that he should not be entitled to more than the normal measure would give him; the argument on the other is that a defendant in breach should not be entitled to object to a claim for the alternative measure even though not dictated by law or by the difficulties of proof.

Mr. Shaw says that the plaintiff should be entitled to recover all of its expenses by way of outlay, and that no deduction should be made even if the plaintiff would have suffered a net loss if the contract had been fully performed. He relies on a judgment of the United States Supreme Court: *US v. Behan* (1884), 110 US 338, Bradley J, speaking for the court, said, at 345-46:

> When a party injured by the stoppage of a contract elects to rescind it, then, it is true, he cannot recover any damages for a breach of the contract, either for outlay or for loss of profits; he recovers the value of his services actually performed as upon a *quantum meruit*. There is then no question of losses or profits. But when he elects to go for damages for the breach of the contract, the first and most obvious damage to be shown is, the amount which he has been induced to expend on the faith of the contract, including a fair allowance for his own time and services. If he chooses to go further and claims for the loss of anticipated profits, he may do so, subject to the rules of law as to the character of profits which may be thus claimed. It does not lie, however, in the mouth of the party, who has voluntarily and wrongfully put an end to the contract, to say that the party injured has not been damaged at least to the amount of what he has been induced fairly and in good faith to lay out and expend, including his own services, after making allowance for the value of materials on hand; at least it does not lie in the mouth of the party in fault to say this, unless he can show that the expenses of the party injured have been extravagant and unnecessary for the purpose of carrying out the contract.

If it is only "extravagant and unnecessary expenses" that the defendant may insist be deducted from the plaintiff's claim, then what about expenses legitimately incurred, but in an unprofitable venture? The implication in the *Behan* case is that the defendant may not have them deducted from the plaintiff's claim for compensation for expenses. Bradley J went on, at 346-47:

> The party who voluntarily and wrongfully puts an end to a contract and prevents the other party from performing it, is estopped from denying that the injured party has not been damaged to the extent of his actual loss and outlay fairly incurred.

The *Behan* case was decided in the last century. It has been rejected in the United States in this century.

Professor L.L. Fuller and William R. Perdue, Jr., in "The Reliance Interest in Contract Damages": 1 (1936-37), 46 *Yale LJ* 52, concluded that the principle enunciated in the *Behan* case compromised the basic notion of restitutio in integrum. They urged, at 79, that the law ought to reflect the following proposition:

> We will not in a suit for reimbursement for losses incurred in reliance on a contract knowingly put the plaintiff in a better position than he would have occupied had the contract been fully performed.

In *L. Albert & Son v. Armstrong Rubber Co.* (1949), 178 F.2d 182, [Learned] Hand CJ, speaking for the Circuit Court of Appeals, Second Circuit, held that on a claim for compensation for expenses in part performance the defendant was entitled to deduct whatever he could prove the plaintiff would have lost if the contract had been fully performed. Hand CJ expressed his concurrence with the formula laid down by Professor Fuller. See also *Re Yeager Co.* (1963), 227 F. Supp. 92.

It has been said by the United States Circuit Court of Appeals in *Dade County v. Palmer and Baker Engineers Inc.* (1965), 339 F.2d 208, that, where the defendant alleges that full performance by the plaintiff would have resulted in a net loss to the plaintiff, the burden of proof is on the defendant. Accepting then that the onus is on the defendant, what has the defendant been able to prove in the case at bar?

Mr. Dunn, a chartered accountant called by Domtar, prepared a list of expenses of the Bowley logging operation. The list is not complete. But Mr. Dunn says that when the revenues of the operation are measured against the expenses, whether on a cash basis or an accrual basis, there is no footing on which the operation could have been regarded as a profitable one. I think he is right about this.

. . .

The law of contract compensates a plaintiff for damages resulting from the defendant's breach; it does not compensate a plaintiff for damages resulting from his making a bad bargain. Where it can be seen that the plaintiff would have incurred a loss on the contract as a whole, the expenses he has incurred are losses flowing from entering into the contract, not losses flowing from the defendant's breach. In these circumstances, the true consequence of the defendant's breach is that the plaintiff is released from his obligation to complete the contract—or in other words, he is saved from incurring further losses.

If the law of contract were to move from compensating for the consequences of breach to compensating for the consequences of entering into contracts, the law would run contrary to the normal expectations of the world of commerce. The burden of risk would be shifted from the plaintiff to the defendant. The defendant would become the insurer of the plaintiff's enterprise. Moreover, the amount of the damages would increase not in relation to the gravity or consequences of the breach but in relation to the inefficiency with which the plaintiff carried out the contract. The greater his expenses owing to inefficiency, the greater the damages.

The fundamental principle upon which damages are measured under the law of contract is restitutio in integrum. The principle contended for here by the plaintiff would entail the award of damages not to compensate the plaintiff but to punish the defendant. So it has been argued that a defendant ought to be able to insist that the plaintiff's damages should not include any losses that would have been incurred if the contract had been fully performed. According to Treitel, *Law of Contract*, 3rd ed. (1970), at 798:

> It is uncertain whether the plaintiff can recover his entire expenses if those exceed the benefit which he would have drived from the contract, had there been no breach.

Ogus, in *Damages* (1973), has said that (at 347), "it is not yet clear whether English law imposes this limitation."

The tendency in American law is to impose such a limitation. And I think Canadian law ought to impose it too.

The onus is on the defendant. But the onus has been met. The only conclusion that I can reach on the evidence is that if the plaintiff had fully performed the contract its losses would have continued at the rate that the figures show they were running at up to the time when the logging operation was closed down.

The case at bar takes the matter farther than any of the cases cited, because here the defendant has shown that the losses the plaintiff would have incurred on full performance exceed the expenditures actually made in part performance. No award for loss of outlay can therefore be made. There is no escaping the logic of this: see *Corbin on Contracts*, 1964, at 205-206:

> If, on the other hand, it is proved that full performance would have resulted in a net loss to the plaintiff, the recoverable damages should not include the amount of this loss. *If the amount of his expenditure at the date of breach is less than the expected net loss, he should be given judgment for nominal damages only.* If the expenditures exceed this loss, he should be given judgment for the excess. (The italics are mine.)

On a conservative view of the evidence as a whole, the notional loss (had there been full performance) may be said to be in the amount of $124,653.60, calculated as follows:

A. *Plaintiff's claim* $232,905.00
    Less: 108,128.57

                                     $124,776.43
    Less: 28th March 1972 payment: see Ex. 39, Sched. I 179.34

                                       $124,597.09

B. *Full Contract Price*: See Ex. 38, Sched. IV $120,443.40
    Less: 2,793.24

                                       $117,650.16

C. *Probable Loss on Full Performance of Contract*
    Expenses on partial completion, i.e., incurred by Bowlay $232,905.00
    Rate of $3.50/ccf (W.C. Bowles' rate) applied to 2,283.23 ccf
        left cut but not skidded (2685.39 ccf × $3.50) 9,398.76

                                       $242,303.76
    Less: Full contract price 117,650.16

    Loss there would have been on full performance $124,653.60

D. *Deduct Loss on Full Performance from*
   Plaintiff's Claim for Part Performance

Plaintiff's claim (A)	$124,597.09
Less: Loss (C)	124,653.60
Amount Recoverable	$ – 56.51

The plaintiff is entitled nevertheless to nominal damages for the breach of contract in the sum of $250.

Judgment for plaintiff for nominal damages.

NOTES

Bowlay Logging was followed by the English Court of Appeal in *C & P Haulage (a firm) v. Middleton*, [1983] 3 All ER 94, discussed by A.S. Burrows in "Comment" (1984), 100 *LQR* 27. See also *CCC Films (London) Ltd. v. Impact Quadrant Films Ltd.*, [1985] 1 QB 16 and *Benjamin's Sale of Goods*, 5th ed. at para. 17-060. In his comment on *Bowlay Logging* in (1979), 3 *CBLJ* 198, Professor Baer raises the following issues:

1) *Have some issues been overlooked?* Professor Baer finds it incredible that experienced loggers could so seriously misjudge their costs over such a short logging period. He also wonders whether the plaintiffs had incurred additional expenditures caused by the breach that are disclosed in the judgment. Would this have made a difference to the outcome?

2) *The relevance of future timber sales.* Professor Baer conjectures that the plaintiffs might have been willing to undertake an unprofitable contract in the short term in the hope of long-term benefits in the form of future profitable contracts. He notes that the contract was renewable annually subject to negotiation. Assuming this meant there was an obligation by Domtar to renew (does it?), he wonders whether Berger J was correct in stating that "[a]ny claim based on the loss of expected profits on future timber sales would be too uncertain and remote." He notes that this would depend on the foreseeability rules in *Hadley v. Baxendale*.

3) *Is the Corbin formula right?* Professor Baer queries whether the Corbin formula adopted by Berger J (and incorporated in s. 333(d) of the *Restatement*; see now Rest. 2nd, Tent. Draft No. 14, §363) is not too harsh and whether the plaintiff should not be entitled to recover at least at the contract rate for the work he has performed. "It is one thing to say that the innocent party should not get more than the contract rate and thereby pass onto the defendant his own improvident bargaining, inefficiency or risk. However, it is quite another thing to say that all losses should be deducted from a claim to expenses so as to give the plaintiff less than the rate for work performed" (at 205). Do you agree? Is a claim to be paid for part performance a claim for reliance losses? Professor Baer also notes that in the present case, applying the Corbin formula, Domtar had actually overpaid the plaintiffs and he asks whether Domtar would have been successful in a counterclaim to recover the difference.

4) *Restitution.* Under this head Professor Baer considers the question whether the plaintiffs could have improved their position by framing their claim in restitution and seeking

to recover the value of the benefits conferred on Domtar, thus by-passing the difficulties inherent in their damages claim. It is well settled in Anglo-Canadian law that a buyer can recover the purchase price where there has been a total failure of consideration regardless of any expectancy losses. *Cf. Rowland v. Divall, supra,* chapter 5. In other cases (such as the present), where the benefit conferred is of a non-pecuniary kind, the position is unsettled. American opinion favours the view that where the aggrieved party has fully performed his part of the contract and no performance by the other party remains due other than payment of a definite sum of money, the aggrieved party cannot recover more as restitution than she would have recovered in full performance: *Restatement* §§350-351; Rest. 2nd, Tent. Draft No. 14, §387(2). If the aggrieved party has only partly performed, the American position is less clear. The first Rest., §347, Comment *c*, made the contract price a relevant criterion but not a conclusive one; Rest. 2nd, §387, Comment *d*, at 230, firmly limits the aggrieved party's maximum restitutionary recovery to the contract price. Professor Baer regards the distinction between partly and fully performed contractual obligations as illogical. His concluding observation, however, is that "[i]f the plaintiff could at least get the contract rate by claiming restitution, it should get as much by claiming damages based on reliance" (at 209). For further discussion of these difficult issues, see J.P. Dawson, "Restitution or Damages?" (1959), 20 *Ohio St. LJ* 175; G.E. Palmer, "The Contract Price as a Limit on Restitution for Defendant's Breach" (1959), 20 *Ohio St. LJ* 264; and English Law Commission, *Pecuniary Restitution on Breach of Contract* (Working Paper No. 65, 1975), at 39-44, 65-66.

Election Between Recovery of Reliance and Expectation Losses

Cullinane v. British "Rema" Mfg. Co. Ltd.

[1954] 1 QB 292, [1953] 2 All ER 1257 (CA)

[The plaintiff agreed to buy from the defendants a pulverizing and drying plant to be built according to specification. The defendants also warranted that the plant would be capable of pulverizing the plaintiff's clay at the rate of 6 tons per hour. The purchase price was £6,578. The plant was delivered about April 1, 1950, but it was never capable of pulverizing clay at the rate of 6 tons per hour. It could only handle 2 tons per hour and was therefore commercially useless to the plaintiff. The plaintiff kept the machine and brought an action for damages for breach of warranty. They computed their damages under five separate heads as follows:

PARTICULARS OF DAMAGE

A. Cost of buildings erected and work done by the plaintiff to house, support, accommodate, and generally be ancillary to the plant supplied by the defendants.

	£	s.	d.	£	s.	d.
Total cost	4,559	1	5			
Subtract estimated break-up value of buildings	2,000	0	0	£ 2,559	1	5

B. Cost of plant supplied
    by the defendants   6,578   0   0

    Subtract estimated residual
      value of the plant   3,289   0   0   £ 3,289   0   0

C. Cost of associated and
    ancillary plant and charges—

    (Items) Total   3,343   0   0
    Subtract estimated residual
      value of the plant   1,671   0   0   £ 1,672   0   0

D. Interest on capital at 4 per cent from
    April 1, 1950 to December 15, 1951
    (and continuing until settlement of
    claim for damages)—

                              A.   4,559   0   0
                              B.   6,578   0   0
                              C.   3,343   0   0

                                  14,480   0   0
    Subtract interest at 4 per cent for the
    same period on the balance of the
    purchase price   1,078   0   0

                                       £13,402   0   0
    On which interest is   £   915   16   0

E. Loss of profit.

    (A) Per annum
        Receipts from warranted output of
        six tons per hour on a 47-hour week:
        14,664 tons per annum at
          £1 17s. 6d. per ton   £27,495   0   0
    Subtract
        Depreciation at 10 per cent and
          maintenance at 5 per cent on plant
          and buildings (on £14,480)   2,172   0   0
        Running costs   6,433   2 10
        Office expenses   1,030   0   0
    Interest on capital   579   4   0   £10,214   6 10

        Estimated net profit per annum   £17,280 13   2
    (B) From April 1, 1950, to December 15,
        1951, and continuing   £29,521   2   6
    Total of A, B, C, D and E   £37,956 19 11
    Subtract balance of the purchase price of
      the plant outstanding and due from the
      plaintiff to the defendants   £ 1,078   0   0

                                                           £36,878 19 11

In reply to a request for further and better particulars, the plaintiff stated inter alia that under E.(B) the words "and continuing" covered the period from December 15, 1951, to the date of trial of the action. The defendants in their defence denied the warranty and any breach thereof and also alleged that the plaintiff had failed to mitigate his damages by failing to take steps to procure another plant.

The action was heard before an Official Referee and he found that the plaintiff was entitled to the following damages: Under A., £2,559 1s. 5d; under B., £2,389 0s. 0d.; under C., £1,522 0s. 0d.; under D. (calculated to Apr. 1, 1953) £1,608 4s. 9d.; and under E., £8,913 1s. 0d.—Total, £17,891 7s. 2d. Less sum counterclaimed by defendants, £1,078 0s. 0d.—£16,813 7s. 2d.

The defendants appealed.]

EVERSHED MR: This appeal relates only to the proper measure of the damages which flow from what has been found to be a breach of warranty in regard to certain plant manufactured by the defendants and supplied to the plaintiff. The nature of the plant and of the warranty alleged and found to have been broken is sufficiently stated in the statement of claim as amended thus: [see *supra*, statement of facts.] The plant was delivered about April 1, 1950.

It is, in my judgment, extremely important to have clearly in mind the nature of the contract and particularly of the warranty. The plant, I understand, was built according to a detailed specification, and there is no doubt that the plant as supplied conformed strictly with the specification. Unfortunately, however, as the official referee found, the plant did not satisfy the warranty, because it was incapable of producing dry clay powder at the requisite speed. The gist of the warranty lies in the last few words, which I read, "at the rate of six tons per hour." The machine was capable of handling the plaintiff's clay and of cutting, drying and grinding it so as to produce a dry clay powder, but not at the rate of six tons per hour. The productive capacity turned out to be at a considerably less rate, and I understand that the difference in rate, commercially speaking, was the difference between a profitable and an unprofitable commercial venture.

The plaintiff, in his statement of claim, further particularized the damage which he alleged he had suffered. [His Lordship referred to the particulars of damage set out above and continued:] It is, I think, obvious that damages of approximately £37,000 was a very large sum to claim for plant for which the purchase price was about £6,000 and which was to be used in an enterprise which seems (from my reading of the official referee's judgment) to have been of a somewhat speculative character. The total amount awarded was considerably less, namely, £16,813 odd. That reduction is attributable entirely, or almost entirely, to a reduction of the sum awarded for loss of profit. [His Lordship referred to the particulars of the award, and continued:] The argument in this court of the defendants has been that the award really involves giving damages twice over to the plaintiff. The machine was made precisely according to the specification. It was delivered and is now in the plaintiff's possession and it is working, though it does not perform its productive function in the way that was warranted. The principle upon which damages for breach of contract are awarded has been stated many times and was carefully considered by Asquith LJ in delivering the judgment of this court in *Victoria Laundry (Windsor) Ld. v. Newman Industries*, [1949] 2 KB 528, at 539. The court has read passages from that judgment which are expository of the original principle laid down in *Hadley v. Baxendale* (1854), 9 Exch. 341, and it will, I think, suffice to quote the passage from *Hadley v. Baxendale* (at 354) which forms the text, so to speak, of Asquith LJ's later exposition:

> Where two parties have made a contract which one of them has broken, the damages which the other party ought to receive in respect of such breach of contract should be such as may fairly and reasonably be considered either arising naturally, that is according to the usual course of things, from such breach of contract itself, or such as may reasonably be supposed to have been in the contemplation of both parties, at the time they made the contract, as the probable result of the breach of it.

In the present case it is plain that to the knowledge of the defendants this machine was required to perform a particular function, and the warranty given shows what the function was that the machine was designed to perform. There is, therefore, no doubt at all that the plaintiff is entitled to rely on the second part of the passage I have read, and to claim as damages the business loss which must reasonably be supposed to have been, in the contemplation of both parties at the time when they made the contract, the probable result of the breach. In other words, this plaintiff is not confined to the loss which might be called the natural result of having a machine which turned out to be worth less than the purchase price he has paid for it.

Reference was made to the Sale of Goods Act, 1893; but that Act, which put into statutory form long established principles, does not for present purposes, to my mind, add anything to what I have already stated based on my citation from *Hadley v. Baxendale*. But it is perhaps right to note that section 53 of the Sale of Goods Act, 1893, is directed particularly to the remedy for breach of warranty. Subsection (2) provides: "The measure of damages for breach of warranty is the estimated loss directly and naturally resulting, in the ordinary course of events, from the breach of warranty." Subsection (3) provides: "In the case of breach of warranty of quality such loss is prima facie the difference between the value of the goods at the time of delivery to the buyer and the value they would have had if they answered to the warranty." Those two subsections do not, I think, assist, or qualify the general statement applicable here, that the plaintiff, who got a machine which in the event failed to live up to the performance warranted, should be put in the same position (so far as that can be done by money) as he would have been in if the machine had been as warranted.

I have read the material part of the statement of claim, and it is plain from the case as pleaded that the plaintiff was alleging entitlement to the total capital loss he had suffered by having laid out, approximately, £14,000 and then finding himself with material which was only worth £7,000, also to the loss of the profit which this machine, if it had been as warranted, would have brought him during its mechanical life. It is fair to say that in making his computation of damages for loss of profit, he did deduct from each annual sum a figure of 10 per cent of the total original capital outlay in respect of depreciation.

It appears from the finding of the official referee that the useful life of the machine was ten years—that is to say, it would have continued to perform its mechanical functions for a period of ten years: so that if there had been clay to grind and markets in which the ground clay could have been sold it would have brought emoluments to the plaintiff for that period. I base that statement on the passage of the judgment where the official referee said:

> If the plant had been as warranted Mr. Davies gave its probable life as ten years. I find that it was within the contemplation of the defendants that this plant would be used, not as a museum piece but as a means for making a profit by the sale of its products. If the plant had been as warranted the plaintiff's intention was to use it for its life, or for so long as it could provide profit. At the end of that time it would be useless.

It seems to me, as a matter of principle, that the full claim of damages in the form in which it is pleaded was not sustainable, in so far as the plaintiff sought to recover both the whole of his original capital loss and also the whole of the profit which he would have made. I think that that is really a self-evident proposition, because a claim for loss of profits could only be founded upon the footing that the capital expenditure had been incurred. As I have said, however, there was a deduction made in respect of depreciation at 10 per cent; and if the estimated life of the plant is taken as ten years it follows that, during the period of ten years, while profits must be assumed to have been earned, the whole of the capital cost would have been written off. In other words, if the estimation of damages under head (E) had been carried on for the whole period of ten years, the sum total under heads (A), (B) and (C), having been elaborately worked out, would have all been deducted again in the course of calculating (E).

As a matter of principle also, it seems to me that a person who has obtained a machine, such as the plaintiff obtained, being a machine which was mechanically in exact accordance with the order given but which was unable to perform a particular function which it was warranted to perform, may adopt one of two courses. He may say, when he discovers its incapacity, that it was not what he wanted, that it is quite useless to him, and he may claim to recover the capital cost he has incurred, deducting anything he can obtain by disposing of the material that he got. A claim of that kind puts the plaintiff in the same position as though he had never made the contract at all. In other words, he is back where he started; and, if it were shown that the profit-earning capacity was in fact very small, the plaintiff would probably elect so to base his claim. But, alternatively, where the warranty in question relates to performance, he may, in my judgment, make his claim on the basis of the profit which he has lost because the machine as delivered fell short in its performance of which it was warranted to do. If he chooses to base his claim on that footing, it seems to me that depreciation has nothing whatever to do with it.

During the course of the argument many analogies were taken, and I find some assistance from the simple agricultural analogy of the cow. If, for example, A sells to B a heifer for £100, and warrants that for the next five lactations she will produce milk at the rate of four gallons a day, but it is discovered that the cow's performance is not at the rate of four gallons a day but is only one gallon a day, and if a one-gallon-a-day cow is worth not £100 but £10, then the buyer might elect to follow one of two courses. He could claim to recover the difference between the £100 which he had paid for a four-gallon-a-day heifer and £10, the true value of the one-gallon-a-day heifer, and he could recover the difference, £90. That would put him in the position in which he would have been if he had bought, and intended to buy, the cow which in fact he got. Alternatively, he might say: "I keep this cow and I shall sue you for the loss I have suffered because her performance was not as warranted: I am getting not four gallons but one gallon a day, and, therefore, I am losing what I would have got on the sales (less necessary expenditure) of, approximately, an extra thousand gallons a year." If the latter course is chosen it seems to me, as I have indicated, that the depreciated or depreciating, value of the cow has nothing whatever to do with the claim. So much, I think, is conceded; and it has, therefore, seemed to the court that it would be impossible to combine in this case a claim for the capital loss with a claim for the total loss of profit; and it would be impossible to recover, in the hypothetical case, both the £90 (being the capital loss on the cow) and the full amount of the loss due to the shortage of milk.

But in the course of these proceedings there occurred an event which has given rise, as I think, to the whole difficulty. Head (E) of the statement of claim, subparagraph (B), reads: "From April 1, 1950, to December 15, 1951, and continuing," and the defendants asked the plaintiff to give particulars of the words "and continuing." They were asking the plaintiff to state for what period of time he was alleging and intending to prove loss of profit. The actual words of the request, which are of importance, are: "Of the words 'and continuing,' stating precisely what period is referred to and the amount of loss of profit (if any) claimed in respect of such period." The plaintiff's answer was: "'and continuing' is the period from December 15, 1951, to the date of trial of this action." That seems to me to be a clear and unequivocal statement by the plaintiff that, so far as his claim was based on loss of profit, he was only claiming loss of profit up to the date of the trial and that he did not propose to claim or to seek to prove loss of profit beyond that date.

The effect of that statement in the particulars left the statement of claim as a claim for the full amount of the capital loss (arrived at by setting out under each head the total sum actually spent and deducting from that the estimated break-up, or residual, value of the buildings and plant at the date, I suppose, of the statement of claim plus a claim for loss of profit in addition; but subject to this qualification, that in the computation for loss of profit there remained in the statement of claim the item of depreciation at 10 per cent per annum on the original capital cost.

· · ·

But whatever may be the answer to these problems, I come back to the point which I left a little time ago. I think that the plaintiff could choose to claim on the basis that he had wasted capital, and that he ought to be put in the position he would have been if he had never bought this machine; or, alternatively, he was entitled to say: "I have got the machine: what I am claiming is the loss I have suffered because its performance falls short of that which was warranted; therefore I have not made profitable sales which I would have made, and I claim, accordingly, the loss of such profits." The second alternative being the larger, he was entitled to choose that; but, in my judgment, he should be limited to it. By stating that his claim for lost profit was limited to three years, he was not, in my judgment, then entitled to claim (as he, admittedly, could not claim if he had not placed the limitation of the profit) both for loss of capital *and* for loss of profit. It is said that he might do that if in the computation of profits he made due allowance for depreciation. But in my judgment depreciation has nothing to do with the profit which was lost as a consequence of the breach of warranty. And the effect of so reducing the profit would appear to be that the plaintiff first recovers for loss of capital and then has to bring into account against the profit part of what he has recovered for loss of capital.

Upon the question whether the plaintiff could have claimed for loss of profit up to the date of the hearing and have claimed an additional sum because he was at that date left with a machine which was less valuable than the machine as warranted, I say only that the plaintiff has not so claimed. If he had done so, the second part of the claim would appear to be no more than a method of computing profit for the possible profit-earning period after the date of the hearing.

MORRIS LJ (dissenting): It seems to me that the basis on which damages were pleaded on behalf of the plaintiff was permissible and logical.

Perhaps I can illustrate by figures why I express this view. Supposing that a machine cost £10,000 and had a life of ten years, and supposing it were found that there would be net profits of £2,000 a year. At the end of ten years, with fulfilment of the warranty, the purchaser would have received £20,000, and allowing for the £10,000 which he had spent in buying the machine he would make £10,000 profit. Supposing that the machine was delivered to him, and supposing he paid £10,000 for it, and supposing it is found to be entirely valueless, the purchaser might say: "I am claiming simply my profits, that is £20,000." But it seems to me that he could, alternatively, say: "out of £2,000 received by me each year I would have allocated £1,000 each year over the ten years to pay for the plant, and so my net profit would have been £1,000 a year. Instead of claiming £20,000 I put it in this way: I claim back the £10,000 I have paid for the plant, which is valueless, and I claim the profits which I would have made, that is £1,000 a year over ten years, £10,000." In either way of statement, the amount of the claim is exactly the same. It seems to me that in the statement of claim the matter was put in the latter way. It was pleaded on behalf of the plaintiff that, by reason of the breach of warranty, he was out of pocket. He had spend sums for the plant and for accessory plant and for buildings. He said: "I want those sums back, less, of course, the present scrap value of what I have got, and in addition I want the profits which I would have made, namely, my net profits: out of the profits that I would have received each year" (and the life of this plant was ten years) "I make an allocation of one-tenth and, making that allowance, I arrive at my net profits." It seems to me that it is permissible and logical to formulate the claim in that way.

Appeal allowed, judgment varied
by substituting £10,521 for £16,813.

H. Street
Principles of the Law of Damages

(1962), at 245

It is submitted therefore that in circumstances like the *Cullinane* case the plaintiff can always recover his expenditure (other than the purchase price of the warranted goods) contemplated by the parties. He can also always claim the difference between the price and the market value of the goods. If, however, it were reasonable for him to use the machine for a certain period in order to see whether it could measure up to the warranty then he could claim the difference between the profit he would have made had the machine been as warranted and that which he in fact made during this period. He could not recover in any event for loss of profit beyond the period when he ought reasonably to have ceased using the machine and either replaced it or discontinued his operation. In such a case, his loss of profit (struck after an allowance for depreciation) should be recoverable in addition to his reliance expenditures on other plant and his capital loss on the machine. In his dissenting judgment, Morris LJ took a position not unlike that taken here. He appeared to treat the three years as a reasonable period during which the plaintiff tried to operate the machine with a view of profit, and justified an award of three years' loss of profits on that account.

R.G. McLean Ltd. v. Canadian Vickers Ltd.

(1970), 15 DLR (3d) 15, [1971] 1 OR 207 (CA)

ARNUP JA (for the court): [This] action arises from the sale by the defendant to the plaintiff of a two-colour press. The plaintiff had previously purchased from the Mann company a two-colour press and, after considerable discussion between the parties, it was decided that the plaintiff should purchase a second press as identical as possible to the first one, with the idea of running them in tandem. By using both presses it would be possible to print two-colour material using one press and an additional two colours using the other, and thereby turn out a finished product in four colours. The parties entered into a written contract dated September 30, 1964, covering the sale by the defendant to the plaintiff of the second press at a price of $75,850, plus applicable taxes, with an adjustment in the price dependent upon the rate of exchange. The agreement was expressed to be "subject to the conditions of sale of goods attached hereto ... ."

. . .

The learned trial Judge correctly found on the evidence [[1969] 2 OR 249 at 251; 5 DLR (3d) 100 at 102] that "the new press was expected to turn out the highest quality offset lithographic printing. Anything less was not within the contemplation of the buyer or seller." Following the installation of the new press in the plaintiff's premises in Toronto, a long series of difficulties ensued. Some of these were capable of being repaired and were minor in nature, and were in fact repaired by the defendant or by the plaintiff itself. Problems continued, however, throughout the fall of 1965 and the early winter of 1966. Representatives of the defendant were sent out from England to try to locate the source of the trouble. Many things were tried but in the end it became obvious to the defendant that, whatever the trouble was, it could not be pinpointed and they were unable to fix it.

It was at this point (which was shortly before March 30, 1966) that the defendant finally offered to take back the press and to refund the payments made by the plaintiff. The plaintiff refused this suggestion, pointing out that it had already incurred more than $36,000 in expenses and direct losses. The offer, however, was not conditional upon the plaintiff agreeing to forego any claim for damages. This becomes significant in considering the question of damages, which I shall deal with later.

[Arnup JA reviewed the trial judge's finding that the defendants, by supplying a machine totally incapable of doing the job for which it was intended, had committed a fundamental breach of contract and considered the effect of this finding on the disclaimer clauses in the agreement. (For their terms, see the judgment of Coffin JA in *Canso Chemicals Ltd. v. Canadian Westinghouse Co. Ltd.*, *infra*, chapter 18.) Arnup JA held the disclaimer clauses inapplicable and continued:]

The next question therefore is: what damages should be awarded to the plaintiff on the basis of these findings? In effect, the award by the learned trial Judge in favour of the plaintiff falls into three categories:

(i) He dismissed entirely the claim of the defendant for the purchase price of the machine. This claim was for $59,782.75.

(ii) He awarded $50,549.47 in respect of a list of items which he appears to have thought were in the nature of special damages. These are as follows [[1969] 2 OR 249 at 261, 5 DLR (3d) 100 at 112]:

losses on Ontario 66 book	$18,338.25
losses due to lost press hours	6,968.00
" " " " "	5,769.79
losses incurred while Canadian mechanic of G. Mann Co. testing for print	643.50
loss incurred while mechanic from England G. Mann Co. working on press	8,190.00
13,750 sheets used in testing press	1,616.00
1,500 sheets used in testing press	129.59
plate making time, plate metal test plates	244.00
blankets spoiled	600.00
supervision and plant engineer's time spent with mechanics of George Mann Co.	2,286.27
installation cost on No. 7 press	4,542.46
loss incurred while press being tested during visit of L. Wright, George Mann Co.	1,221.42
	$50,549.47

(iii) He allowed $50,554.50 for "loss of business profits."

Dealing with item (iii) first, the learned trial Judge stated [at 264 OR, 115 DLR] that he had been furnished, during the trial, and after the accountants for both sides had examined the plaintiff's records, "with a statement (ex. 87) showing the various items of damage and the amounts, the amounts being agreed to, as I understand it, as accurate." He further said that that statement showed the loss of business as $50,554.50.

In this the learned Judge was clearly under a misapprehension. While the figure of $50,554.50 for loss of business profits continued to be shown in a column on ex. 87, it was made quite clear at the trial by counsel for the plaintiff that that amount was *not* being agreed to and that the issue with respect to it was at large. The learned trial Judge's allowance, under this heading, being based entirely upon a mistaken impression of the agreement between counsel, therefore cannot stand, and, while I have endeavoured on the basis of the record and the evidence as it exists to ascertain what a suitable allowance would be for loss of business profits, or indeed whether any such allowance should be made at all, I have found it impossible to do so on this record. This is partly due to the fact that in my view, as will appear, the basis upon which the over-all claim for damages was put forward is erroneous.

Turning next to the dismissal of the claim for the price, this could only have been done on the basis that a claim for breach of warranty had been established in an amount which exceeded the claim for the price. The plaintiff was quite entitled to set up the breach of warranty in diminution or extinction of the purchase price, and to claim any amount of damages over and above the amount of the price which he could establish, but in this case the learned trial Judge has not taken into account, in otherwise assessing the plaintiff's damages, the fact that he had in effect already allowed the plaintiff $59,782.75 by way of damages for breach of warranty when he dismissed the claim against the plaintiff for the price.

Since the damages are to be assessed on the basis that the contract was still in force, the plaintiff is entitled to be compensated (subject to questions of mitigation) to the extent that it will be in approximately the same position as it would have been in if the contract had been performed according to its terms: *Wertheim v. Chicoutimi Pulp Co.*, [1911] AC 301 at 307, and see the cases referred to in *Sunshine Exploration Ltd. et al. v. Dolly Varden Mines Ltd. (N.P.L.)*, [1970] SCR 2, 8 DLR (3d) 441, 70 WWR 418. If the contract had been performed, and profits earned by use of the machine, the plaintiff would have had to pay the purchase price. In any calculation of damages, on a basis as if the contract had been performed, the purchase price must stand as a debit against the plaintiff; any damages awarded in its favour can be used to extinguish the purchase price, but only the excess can then be allowed to the plaintiff by way of further damages.

This conclusion is supported by the judgment of the English Court of Appeal in *Cullinane v. British "Rema" Manufacturing Co. Ltd.*, [1954] 1 QB 292. Mr. Starr attacked the reasoning of the majority of the Court in that case and invited us to adopt instead the reasons for judgment of Morris LJ (as he then was), in his dissenting judgment at 313. A close reading of the case does not indicate that the divergence of opinion between the majority and Morris LJ, on the point involved here was as great as was indicated by Mr. Starr, but, in any event, I do not think that case assists Mr. Starr so far as the actual purchase price of the machine is concerned. There is a useful discussion of the case in Street, *Principles of the Law of Damages* (1962), at 243-45. While the learned author criticizes the actual decision of the majority on the facts of that case, he does indicate at 244 that to give a purchaser both a refund of the purchase price and expenditures made would be double compensation.

Coming then to item (ii), it seems quite clear to me that there is overlapping as to at least three items in this list into the heading of damages "loss of business profits." These items are:

losses on Ontario 66 book	$18,338.25
losses due to lost press hours	6,968.00
losses due to lost press hours	5,769.79

These items in themselves total $31,076.04.

It was further argued before us that other items in this list, while treated by the plaintiff as being direct loss through expense incurred, or as outlays made for which no return was received, nevertheless included supervision and overhead (including supervision and overhead on the "Ontario 66 book job" itself), and hence further overlapping has taken place. There is much force in this argument but, since, for the reasons I have already stated, it is not possible for me to arrive at the assessment which I think would have been proper in this case, I do not pursue the mathematics of this matter further.

Before arriving at my final conclusion with respect to damages, I must deal with the arguments advanced to us that the plaintiff had failed to mitigate its damages. It was suggested that once the plaintiff had realized the difficulties being encountered with the new press, it should have run certain work on the old press instead of continuing to run it on the new one. I regard this as a counsel of perfection, particularly since some of these damages as claimed were sustained before it had become clear that nothing but trouble could ensue from further attempts to use the new press.

The more serious points of mitigation, however, arise from the argument of the defendant that by February, 1966, the plaintiff had concluded that there were serious problems with the press, yet went ahead knowing of these problems and of sufficient facts that any prudent person in the position of the plaintiff should have known that the press could never properly perform its function. The first proposition made by counsel for the defendant is founded on the offer of the defendant, already referred to, to remove the press and refund the purchase price. No evidence was referred to in the argument which would indicate that there was any condition, express or implied, that the plaintiff must accept such offer in full settlement and forego any claim for damages. The plaintiff's answer to this contention was that it had already spent so much money and had sustained such losses that it could not afford to buy another press to replace the one purchased from the defendant. In my opinion, this argument cannot prevail. The plaintiff could not refuse the unconditional offer made, retain the obviously defective press and "run up the damages" to the prejudice of the defendant. The frailties (if any) of the plaintiff's credit, or its inability to purchase a new press from available assets, cannot be set up to destroy the effect of the defendant's offer. If the plaintiff had a good cause of action for damages by March, 1966 (and I have already found that it had), any delay in actually collecting such damages would not in law be the fault of the defendant nor a valid excuse for the plaintiff's failure to mitigate its damages by accepting the offer.

The second point arises independently of the offer, but on facts existing at approximately the same time. As I have indicated, the plaintiff should have known by February or March, 1966, that the difficulties concerning the press were so serious that it was entitled to treat the breach of contract as a fundamental one, enabling it to treat the contract as at the end, and demand back its money (only a portion of the purchase price had then been paid), and sue for damages. In my opinion, once the innocent party is in a position to make this election, in a case where the other party has purported to complete its performance, he cannot make an election which has the effect of increasing the burden upon the wrong-doer. The effect in law is almost precisely the same as the effect of the offer, *i.e.*, the plaintiff could not elect to keep the press, knowing it could never properly perform its function and that its continued operation would only result in future losses, and thereby "run up the damages" against the defendant. This seems to me to be the clear and logical conclusion which follows from the conclusion that the right of election arose.

The situation would undoubtedly be different in a case of an instalment contract, or one requiring the performance of a series of future acts. In such case, when fundamental breach occurs, the innocent party may decide he wants the rest of the contract performed and he is entitled to require that that be done. In this case no further acts of performance on the part of the defendant were called for by the contract; it was what had already been done that either was, or was not, a performance of its contractual obligations.

I am therefore of the opinion that the plaintiff did fail to mitigate its damages and that in the assessment of damages a date which I will arbitrarily take as being March 30, 1966, should be treated as being the "cutoff date"; no damages should be payable by the defendant in respect of events occurring after that date.

Finally, it was argued before us that there was no evidence to show what work was lost to the plaintiff by reason of the press being shut down, or what work was available for tender by it. Instead, the accountant who gave evidence on behalf of the plaintiff appears to have based his figures on pre-contract estimates rather than actual contracts performed. He made estimates based on the number of available hours of press run and the estimated profit which might have been made by running at full capacity during those available hours, and from this he arrived at a mathematical conclusion. Furthermore, in taking into consideration the assessment of "loss of business profits," the profit picture for this company in the four years preceding 1966 was not such as to make certain by any means that the purchase of a second press identical to the one it already had was going to change its profit position (which had varied from small losses to small profits) into one of very substantial profit.

I therefore conclude that there must be a new assessment of damages in this case. Having regard to the extent to which the issues have already been canvassed with respect to damages, I see no reason to send this matter back to a trial Judge for a reassessment of damages, and I therefore would refer it to the Master at Toronto to assess the damages arising from the breach of contract. In so doing the Master will observe these principles:

1. The plaintiff is to be treated as being liable to pay the balance of the purchase price, if it elects to assert a claim for damages for breach of warranty in excess of the price.

2. No damages should be allowed in respect of any matter occurring subsequent to March 30, 1966.

3. The Master, when he comes to deal with "loss of business profits" generally, is to ensure that there is no duplication with items claimed for losses within the plant which include an allowance for supervision and overhead.

4. In assessing any claim that may be asserted for "loss of business profits" the Master will satisfy himself that work sufficient to earn the profits claimed was in fact available in the periods in question, and could have been obtained and performed by the plaintiff.

5. In assessing such loss of profits, the Master should take into account the work which was actually done, so that any estimate of the work which could have been done but for the defects in the machine will not include (as the estimates of the accountant at this trial clearly did include) the expenses and time of work actually done.

Appeal allowed in part.

Sunnyside Greenhouses Ltd. v. Golden West Seeds Ltd.

(1972), 27 DLR (3d) 434, [1972] 4 WWR 420 (Alta. CA);
aff'd. 33 DLR (3d) 384n (SCC)

CLEMENT JA (for the court): This section arises out of a contract for the sale of goods by Golden West Seeds Ltd. to Sunnyside Greenhouses Ltd. Cullen J, at trial found that there was implied in the contract a condition that the goods were reasonably fit for the purposes of Sunnyside and a condition that they were of merchantable quality, within s. 17(2) and (4) of the Sale of Goods Act, now RSA 1970, c. 327; and also an express warranty relating to the fitness for purpose. He further found that the condition and warranty were breached and awarded damages in the sum of $5,690. It was not open to Sunnyside in the circumstances to claim rescission of the contract by reason of the breaches of condition, and it sued for damage pursuant to s. 53 of the Act. Sunnyside has appealed the amount of the award, and Golden West has appealed against the finding that there was implied in the contract a condition that the goods were of merchantable quality.

Sunnyside carries on a business of producing and growing plants in greenhouses for sale to the public and to stores. The roof coverings of greenhouses, with which we are here concerned, require to be of a material that allows sunlight to pass through and reach the growing plants, in addition to protecting them from the weather and enabling the enclosed areas to be maintained at suitable temperatures. Golden West carries on the business of supplier of the requirements for the operation of commercial greenhouses, including roof coverings. It had been supplier to Sunnyside for many years and knew its operation and requirements, including those for roof coverings.

In 1965 Sunnyside moved its operation to a new site, on which it constructed 18 greenhouses 20 × 70 ft. in area with the long axis of each running east and west, together with a connecting house 20 × 250 ft. In the spring of that year Golden West had, in addition to an existing agency, taken on an agency for the sale of a relatively new greenhouse roof covering of plastic panels known as Takiron PVC. They were made of polyvinyl chloride. The salesman of Golden West brought this product to the attention of Sunnyside as suitable for the roof covering of its new greenhouses, and after discussions the latter ordered the panels at a cost of $10,472.82, together with amounts for fittings and hardware with which we are not concerned. Delivery was made at the end of October except for a small quantity delivered in February, 1966.

The length of time during which the plastic panels would maintain their transparency to sunlight was of major importance to Sunnyside and was a substantial part of the discussions leading to the order. Representations in this regard were made that the panels would have a useful life of from seven to ten years. In addition to finding the implied conditions above referred to, the trial Judge found that the representations amounted to an express warranty that the fitness of the panels in respect of transparency would endure for not less than seven years. On the facts it was reasonable for him to infer the warranty: *Traders Finance Corp. Ltd. v. Haley* (1966), 57 DLR (2d) 15 at 19 [aff'd. *sub nom. Ford Motor Co. of Canada Ltd. v. Haley* (1967), 62 DLR (2d) 329, [1967] SCR 437, 60 WWR 497]. I agree with his conclusions both as to the implied conditions and the express warranty. In this view it is not necessary to deal with the appeal in respect of the implied condition of merchantable quality, although if it were I would affirm the finding of Cullen J.

Installation of the panels on eight of the greenhouses was completed by December, 1965, when work shut down temporarily because of winter conditions. The remainder were completed by the end of April, 1966. The labour cost of installation of all of the panels amounted to $4,300.

Sunnyside grew two crops in the course of each year, one for the spring and one for the winter trade. The trial Judge found that the panels

> ... functioned very well in 1966. In 1967 the panels on the southern exposure started to turn milky and hence became somewhat opaque, but the crops were average. In 1968 the panels on the south side became brownish. The crop was showing signs of "dropping off," although the year 1968 was a "reasonable" year. In 1969 the southern panels had reached such a stage of discolouration and opaqueness that it was necessary to move and manoeuvre the bedding plants from one position to another in order that they might utilize what sunlight was available. The Christmas crop of 1969 did not mature.

I should observe here that the increasing discolouration and opacity of the panels was caused by the action of the ultra-violet rays of sunlight (which is most powerful during the summer months) on their chemical composition. This may be categorized as a latent defect. Sunlight during the late fall and winter is weaker and of shorter daily duration, and the increased opacity of the south panels more effectively screened the required sunlight from the plants during this period. These could not then be manoeuvred as in the spring, since the manoeuvring had included moving them to outside cold frames which are unsuitable for winter conditions. At the end of October, 1969,

Sunnyside had replaced the south panels of two greenhouses with fibreglass, and in July, 1970, it replaced all of the remaining south panels. The labour cost for this work amounted to $1,760.

The north panels did not deteriorate so rapidly. They received direct sunlight only during the early hours of the morning and the late hours of the afternoon in the summer months. They had gradually developed a discolouration which by the time of the trial in the spring of 1971 was described as markedly apparent; from which the inference is inevitable that their opacity had increased in like measure. Direct evidence was lacking to show what contribution, if any, this deterioration made to the failure of the winter crop of 1969 to mature, and there is evidence that the winter crop of 1970, after replacing the south panels with fibreglass, was normal in comparison with earlier years. Sunnyside gave evidence that it intended to replace these panels also in the summer of 1971 at a labour cost also of $1,760, although in fact it was stated on appeal that this had been postponed to 1972. The outcome of the winter crop of 1971 is, of course, not in evidence. I will return to this subject in discussing damages.

In assessing damages, Cullen J, took into account s. 53 of the Sale of Goods Act: [Ont. s. 51] ... He also referred amongst other authorities to *Ford Motor Co. of Canada Ltd. v. Haley* (1967), 62 DLR (2d) 329, [1967] SCR 437, 60 WWR 497, and *Massey-Harris Co. Ltd. v. Skelding*, [1934] 3 DLR 193, [1934] SCR 431, discussed by this Division in *Evanchuk Transport Ltd. v. Canadian Trailmobile Ltd.* (1971), 21 DLR (3d) 246, [1971] 5 WWR 317. The principle there expressed is that upon a breach of an implied condition for fitness of purpose [*sic*], where the buyer is compelled by the circumstances of the case to seek his remedy in damages rather than rescission, the damage is *prima facie* the amount of the full purchase price, subject to diminution by such residual value, if any, to the buyer that the seller may be able to establish. In so far as the panels alone are concerned, the evidence at trial was directed to assessment of damage on this principle.

In respect of the south panels, Cullen J, held in effect that there had been no breach of the implied condition of fitness, nor of the related express warranty of duration of fitness, during the first three years of the prospective minimum of seven years of useful life, or, to put it another way, their residual value to Sunnyside was three years of useful life. He thus found that the recovery of the purchase price should be diminished by three-sevenths, which by calculation results in damages on this head of $2,992.23. Sunnyside does not seriously contend that this is an inadequate measure of its damage in respect of the south panels.

However, in respect of the north panels, Cullen J, said:

> The panels on the northern exposure are still in use and are still performing whatever function northern-exposure panels are required to perform in this area.

With respect, to me the evidence falls short of showing that the north panels were of full value to Sunnyside throughout the whole of the seven years. As above noted, the discolouration of these panels had become markedly apparent by the spring of 1971. There is, I think, an almost irresistible inference that north light has some value in the growth of indoor plants. All greenhouses are so equipped, and it is common experience that some plants will grow satisfactorily with only north light. North panels should let in the light, for such growing powers as it has. They were no longer performing that function during the last two years of the seven-year expectancy, and Golden West has not established residual value to Sunnyside in respect of these two years. I would allow the appeal on this head and award damages, calculated in similar fashion, of $1,496.12.

As pointed out by Cullen J, we are not concerned here with the principles applicable on rescission of a contract: the claim is for damages which are to be assessed in accordance with s. 53 of the Act. The recovery of the *prima facie* measure of damages prescribed by *Ford Motor Co. of Canada Ltd. v. Haley* does not exhaust the possibilities of recovery under the section, the several additional heads of damage have been put forward which require consideration.

The first head is the sum of $4,300 for installation of the panels. Cullen J, allowed the portion of it attributable to the south panels, but in view of my opinion in respect of the north panels I am of opinion that the whole sum is assessable and should be allowed at $4,300 to Sunnyside. This was an expense that was unavoidable in order to make the intended use of the panels, and as the panels have to be replaced (including those of which the replacement was postponed), the expense was wasted by reason of the breaches. There is authority for such assessment. For example, in *McRae v. Commonwealth Disposals Commission* (1951), 84 CLR 377, the High Court of Australia, in circumstances treated as a case of breach by non-delivery of a stranded tanker, said at 415:

> ... we are of opinion that the plaintiffs were entitled to recover damages in this case for breach of contract, and that their damages are to be measured by reference to expenditure incurred and wasted in reliance on the Commission's promise that a tanker existed at the place specified.

Recovery was allowed of the purchase price of the tanker and also damages on several heads, including the expenses incurred and wasted in preparation for salvaging the tanker.

The next head of damage is the cost of removing the panels, for which Cullen J, made an allowance in respect of the south panels, and if it is allowable counsel have agreed that the proper amount is $1,760. He made no allowance for the ultimate removal of the north panels since he had found there had been no breaches from which damage had resulted to Sunnyside in respect of them. The item is put forward as an expense caused by the breach, a subject which is discussed in *Mayne and McGregor on Damages*, 12th ed. (1961), para. 29, and dealt with in *Smeed v. Foord* (1859), 1 El. & El. 602, 120 ER 1035. It was contended on behalf of Golden West that this expenditure was not the direct and natural consequence of the breach, since it was in contemplation by both parties that the panels would in any event have to be replaced after a period of time; and that if the matter were to be taken into account at all it should only be on the footing that the replacement was at an earlier date than contemplated and the proper compensation in that state of affairs is interest on the expenditures actually made in advance of the time at which they would otherwise be made. I am of opinion that this is the correct view. The expense was not caused by the breach: only the earlier outlay of the money. Interest will be allowed on the expenditure in respect of the south panels, amounting to $2,600, for four years at 5%. This amounts to $460. In respect of the north panels, the evidence warrants an allowance of interest for one year in the amount of $115. The aggregate on this head is $575, which is allowed.

The last head is the damage claimed in respect of the failure of the 1969 winter crop to mature. The trial Judge disallowed this claim, saying:

> There is a suggestion that the sales of the fall crop were down by $2,400 to $2,800 in 1969 as compared with 1966, 1967, 1968 and 1970. Whether this is attributable to the failure of maturity of the Christmas crop or to some other reason has not been made clear in the evidence.

The gross sales of the fall crop for those years, and the year 1969, are as follows:

1966	$6,684.35
1967	$7,141.35
1968	$6,654.00
1969	$4,274.00
1970	$7,181.00

The average gross sales for the years other than 1969 is $6,915, and the 1969 gross sales were below this average by some $2,640. The trial Judge found that the 1969 fall crop failed to mature by reason of the breach of condition of fitness for purpose, and I think he erred in rejecting the foregoing figures, and related evidence, as proof of damage. The related evidence was that the operating expenses in growing the 1969 fall crop which failed to mature, were exactly the same as if the crop had matured satisfactorily. The loss in gross sales resulted from Sunnyside being unable to supply its customers because of the crop failure. It is not put forward as special damage for loss of particular customers but rather as general damage arising from loss of crop with which to supply customers. Damages of this nature were allowed, for example, in *Gull v. Saunders & Stuart* (1913), 17 CLR 82.

The remaining issue for consideration is whether these damages, which are akin to loss of profit, can be given in addition to recovery of the capital loss through the breaches and the expenses wasted thereby. In so far as such damages fairly come within s. 53, I am of opinion that they can also be recovered. They were allowed in *Grosvenor Hotel Co. v. Hamilton*, [1894] 2 QB 836, a case in which a tenant brought action against his landlord for the commission of a nuisance in respect of the demised premises of such extent that they became useless to the tenant and he moved out. The tenant claimed for the value of the term of the lease which he had thereby lost (*i.e.*, capital loss), and also for the consequential loss of expenses of moving and loss of profits occasioned by the move. Damages on these heads were awarded at trial, and were sustained on appeal although with some reduction in respect of the moving expenses. Lindley LJ, said at 840:

> There being then a good cause of action, the question of damages arises. It is contended for the plaintiffs [the landlord who was suing for rent and against whom the tenant counterclaimed] that the damages consist solely in the loss of the term. If the term were of value the defendant could recover its value by way of damages; but to say that the damages are confined to the value of the term is erroneous in point of law. The damages

are whatever loss results to the injured party as a natural consequence of the wrongful act of the defendant.

Similarly, in *Hydraulic Engineering Co. Ltd. v. McHaffie, Goslett, & Co.* (1878), 4 QBD 670, damages were assessed both for the expenses wasted by the purchaser and the profit he lost by reason of the seller's breach. In *Gull v. Saunders & Stuart*, damages were awarded in respect of capital loss, as well as for consequential loss of crops. I think that the correct principle is that loss of profit (or similar loss) which is the direct and natural consequence of the breach, may be claimed for the period during which the breach is the effective cause of the loss, in addition to other heads of damage which fairly come within s. 53.

In determining the period during which the breach is the effective cause of the loss, regard must be had to the duty of mitigation stated in the leading case of *British Westinghouse Electric & Mfg. Co., Ltd. v. Underground Electric Railways Co. of London Ltd.*, [1912] AC 673. There Viscount Haldane LC, said at 689:

> The fundamental basis is thus compensation for pecuniary loss naturally flowing from the breach; but this first principle is qualified by a second, which imposes on the plaintiff the duty of taking all reasonable steps to mitigate the loss consequent on the breach, and debars him from claiming any part of the damage which is due to his neglect to take steps.

When such loss is a direct and natural consequence of the breach, as it unquestionably is in the present case, then I am of opinion it may be assessed for such period of time as it is incurred before reasonable steps in mitigation of loss can become effective. It was not suggested that Sunnyside was dilatory in replacing the south panels and on considering the evidence I am clearly of opinion that they acted with reasonable dispatch in all of the circumstances. The loss of crop occurred during this period. Had they delayed unreasonably in replacing the panels, then I would have thought that a succeeding crop loss would not have been the direct and natural consequence of the breach, but rather the consequence of the default of Sunnyside in acting reasonably in mitigation. [Clement JA concluded his judgment by discussing *Cullinane*'s case, *supra*. He pointed out that the majority judgment in that case overlooked the plaintiff's duty to mitigate his damages, and that it was this duty to mitigate that affected the amount of damages recoverable by the plaintiff in the present case.]

Appeal allowed; cross-appeal dismissed.

Notes on Measurement of Damages for Loss of Revenue-Producing Property

Cullinane, *McLean*, and *Sunnyside* raise the following basic questions: (1) is the buyer bound to elect between recovery of his capital loss (that is, diminished value of the equipment) and loss of prospective revenue from the property (that is, his expectancy); (2) how are the lost profits to be calculated; and (3) is impecuniosity a defence to the buyer's failure to mitigate his damages?

The Duty To Elect and Measurement of Lost Profits

The first question is considered by Professor M.G. Baer in an admirable comment in (1973), 51 *Can. Bar Rev.* 490. He argues that the courts in *Cullinane* and *McLean* were mistaken in putting the buyer to his election and that there is no incompatibility in allowing the recovery of reliance and expectancy losses (that is, lost profits), provided lost profits are defined as those profits that remain after deduction of depreciation and all other relevant expenditures. In other words, he agrees with Morris LJ's approach in *Cullinane*. This approach also won the support of the High Court of Australia in *T.C. Industrial Plant Pty. Ltd. v. Robert's Queensland Pty. Ltd.* (1963-64), 37 ALJR 289, but it is open to several objections, some of which are discussed by Nahum Biger and Andrea Rosen, "A Framework for the Assessment of Damages" (1981), 5 *CBLJ* 302.

The authors point out that "two major concepts govern the accurate measurement of an injured party's expected and actual financial positions: cash flow analysis and the time value of money. Related to these concepts are two important subsidiary issues: depreciation and the residual value of capital assets." The importance and the proper method of measuring each of these factors is explained by them in the following extracts (at 308-26):

(1) *Cash flow valuation*

As Professor Baer has pointed out, much of the confusion surrounding the damage assessment issue stems from a loose use of the term "profits." What Professor Baer has not adequately appreciated, however, is that the problem extends beyond the definitional issue. In fact, the use of any accounting profit figures to measure business performance may lead to improper valuations of such performance. Accurate assessment of the damage to an injured party should be based not on the plaintiffs "book profits" (or "losses"), but rather on an analysis of his differential cash position. More colloquially put, the relevant questions are: What is the plaintiff's position at the bank now, and what would it have been had the contract been performed?

Accounting practices fail to provide direct answers to such questions. For instance, in accordance with Generally Accepted Accounting Principles (GAAP), many non-cash expenses, notably depreciation and amortization, are charged against revenues to arrive at a net income figure. The arbitrary nature of these allocations has led many accountants to question the usefulness of the income statement in analyzing a firm's performance. The result has been increased reliance on the "Statement of Changes in Financial Position," a relatively new financial report which does not require non-working capital expense allocations.

Just as the accounting profession has turned to cash flow analysis for a more objective evaluation of economic performance, so should the legal profession in assessing consequential economic damages. Indeed, where a contract breach results in loss of business earnings, a truly accurate measure of the damage to an innocent party can be determined only if the analytical focus is on the plaintiff's cash rather than "book profit" position.

· · ·

(2) *The time value of money*

In listing the issues involved in investment analysis, one crucial factor was ignored. This factor, the investor's "cost of capital," is related to a broader concept, that of the time value of money. Simply stated, $1 now is worth more than $1 to be received a year from now, and each is worth more than $1 due in two years. After all, $1 received now can be invested and earn interest for one or two years. For the moment, denote the best rate at which it can be invested as "k."

If we invest A_0 now and can get k, the value of A_0 one year hence is $A_1 = A_0 (1 + k)$. If the investment is for two years and the first year's proceeds are invested for another year at k, the future value two years hence is: $A_2 = A_0(1 + k)(1 + k) = A_0(1 + k)^2$. In general, the future value of A_0, n years hence, is: $A_n = A_0(1 + k)^n$.

If k is assumed to be .10 (10%), then one dollar invested for one year will be worth $1(1.10) = 1.10$ in one year. Invested for two years the dollar will be worth $1(1.10)^2 = 1.21$, because the $1.10 is reinvested to earn 10% for one more year.

In the example of cash flow analysis presented above, the manufacturer received $7,000 less per anum for four years and $9,000 less for one year than he would have if the machine had performed as warranted. The $7,000 lost in the first year could have been invested for five years at "k," the $7,000 lost the second year could have been invested at "k" for four years, and so on. Investment opportunity at the rate of "k" was lost. Hence, "k" is termed the *opportunity cost* by economists. ...

. . .

(3) *Duty to mitigate*

The foregoing example is completely correct only in so far as the plaintiff's duty to mitigate is not at issue. If the plaintiff's failure to mitigate were deemed unreasonable by the court, then it would be necessary to consider the potential for mitigation in the assessment of damages. Specifically, it would be necessary to adjust the measurement of the plaintiff's so-called actual position to reflect what it would have been had proper mitigation taken place. This presumed actual position, rather than that attained in the absence of mitigation would then be compared to the expected position to derive the measure of damages.

Consider again the manufacturer example above. Suppose the court has concluded that the plaintiff should have taken mitigating actions, and could reasonably have done so by undertaking major repairs to the machine in year 2 at a cost of $8,000. Suppose also that as a result of such repairs, the court estimates that the plaintiff would have been able to earn $27,000 revenues in each of years 3, 4 and 5, instead of the $20,000 earned without the repairs. The annual variable expenses would then have been $8,100 per year, and with $1,000 fixed cost total operating expenses would have been $9,100 per year. Furthermore, assume that with the value added by the repairs the residual value of the machine at the time of trial would have been $5,400 and with the building total residual value would have been $13,400. Under such circumstances the differential cash flow, computed with recognition of the plaintiff's duty to mitigate, would be as follows:

	Start	Year 1	Year 2	Year 3	Year 4	Year 5
Expected	($100,000)	$20,000	$20,000	$20,000	$20,000	$34,000
Presumed actual given mitigation	(100,000)	13,000	13,000 (8,000)	17,900	17,900	31,300
Difference	—	$ 7,000	$15,000	$ 2,100	$ 2,100	$ 2,700

Assuming as before an interest rate of 12%, the loss for which damage should be awarded is:

$$\$7,000(1.12)^4 + \$15,000(1.12)^3 + \$2,100(1.12)^2 + \$2,700 = \$39,774.80$$

Thus, as would be expected, the damage award computed with explicit consideration of the plaintiff's duty to mitigate and his failure to do so would be about $7,000 lower than otherwise.

(4) *Depreciation*

Since *Rema*, Canadian courts and commentators have been confused about the issue of depreciation. As the widget example above demonstrates, depreciation must be ignored when cash flow figures are constructed; the annual cash flow figures will represent net annual income from the project before depreciation. There are two reasons for this approach. The first is technical: depreciation allowance does not involve any cash flows and therefore depreciation is not to be subtracted from income. The second reason is more profound: each investment project is assumed to have some limited "useful life," at the end of which the value of the investment will be either zero or some greatly diminished salvage value. In assessing a plaintiff's financial position, consideration of the salvage value instead of the original investment already assures consideration of the loss of value of this investment. A further subtraction of depreciation charges against annual operating income figures would be tantamount to double-counting. Thus, the majority in *Rema* was basically correct in ignoring depreciation expenses, the fact that the capital assets had depreciated was already taken into account in the plaintiff's assessment of their break-up value. The break-up or salvage value was substantially less than the original capital investment in the assets; depreciation of the assets during three years of use is accounted for in the difference.

Whether or not there is a contract breach, assets usually deteriorate in value over time. Thus, at any point throughout their economic life, capital assets will have a market value lower than their original price. Although this residual asset value incorporates depreciation, it does not by itself, or in conjunction with the original value, define the injured party's loss in the event of a contract breach. Again, what is important is the difference between the plaintiff's actual and expected positions; that is, the difference between the actual residual value of the assets and what the residual value would have been if the contract had been performed. In *Rema*, for example, after three years of use, the actual break-up value of the capital assets was £6,960, or £7,520 less than the original investment. However, had the machines performed at the rate warranted, their residual value would have been considerably greater. Presumably a three-year-old, six ton-per-hour machine would have been worth considerably more than a three-year-old, two ton-per-hour machine. In other words, an accurate measurement of the plaintiff's loss would have had to account for the fact that the breach left the plaintiff with used defective assets instead of just used assets.

· · ·

(5) *Residual asset value*

The term "residual value" refers to the net market value of investment assets at any given point during the economic life of the assets. Clearly, in measuring an injured party's expected and actual economic positions, a cash value assessment of all assets must be made. In the case of capital assets, the relevant value is their net realizable value; that is, market value net of the removal and selling costs which may have to be incurred in order to dispose of the asset.

It seems elementary to insist that the value of an asset to an injured party is its market value (more precisely, its net realizable value) and not its book value. After all, book value is determined solely by the choice of depreciation method and reflects an arbitrary allocation of depreciation expenses against the asset's original cost. Yet this point has not been understood by either courts or commentators. For example, implicit in the dissent of Morris LJ in the *Rema* case is the notion that an asset's residual value can be assessed on the basis of straight line depreciation. That is, where, as in *Rema*, an asset has an economic life of ten years and its value is assessed after three, this value is determined to be seven-tenths of the purchase price.

There are three major flaws in this valuation approach. In the first place, an asset will probably not deteriorate in an even pattern; however, this is the assumption inherent in straight line depreciation. In addition, straight line depreciation is based on the original cost of the asset. So even if an asset's value did diminish in equal amounts every year, it is incorrect to calculate residual value with reference to the asset contracted for instead of the asset actually received. After all, if the assets received were not defective in some way, there would be no claim for damages. The very fact that the asset was defective when purchased means that its true value when new was considerably less than the price paid for it. Hence, it is improper to determine residual asset values through use of a depreciation method based on this price. As noted above, the asset is not simply used; it is used *and* defective.

The third flaw in the use of straight line depreciation to measure residual asset value is its failure to account for the time value of money. This is the major error in the reasoning of Lord Justice Morris in his dissent in *Rema*. At any positive interest rate, deduction of depreciation expenses from annual revenues does not accurately account for an asset's deterioration in economic value, *even when its residual value is zero*. Thus, it is not correct to say as did the High Court of Australia that "x + y − x + x = x + y."

These conceptual problems are eliminated when an asset's residual value is defined in terms of its market value. Where a market for the asset in question exists, ascertainment of this value will be straightforward. Complications arise, however, when a market value cannot be easily determined. In such a case, the asset's worth must be defined in terms of its future productive ability. The asset will generate earnings in the form of net cash inflows. These cash flows must be evaluated as of a particular point in time using the firm's cost of capital. The capitalized value of the earnings, or their "present value," represents the asset's true worth. In essence, this is how the market establishes asset prices. The absence of a market means this value must be calculated with reference only to the asset's value to a particular firm instead of to the market as a whole.

Applying the above principles to the facts in *Sunnyside*, Biger and Rosen conclude that "Sunnyside's true economic loss was only $8,117.17, about two-thirds of the $12,003.35 awarded as damages by the Appellate Division. While the difference in this case was only $3,886.18 and may seem trivial to some, the results will certainly not be trivial where the financial stakes are much greater."

Professor Baer, in a short reply ("A Framework or Straightjacket: A Reply to Biger and Rosen" (1981-82), 6 *CBLJ* 367), admitted that "Lawyers should be familiar with the modern, and usually more precise, terminology used by accountants and economists in place of the more ambiguous terms lawyers share with the public." Nevertheless, "at the risk of sounding narrow-minded or anti-intellectual," he insisted that "such terminology does not necessarily provide for more accurate insight or lead to more appropriate legal solutions." Do you agree? Are damage awards a matter of "insight"?

The Duty To Mitigate Damages, Impecuniosity, and Contributory Negligence

The Duty To Mitigate

The aggrieved party's duty to mitigate his damages is as much a part of sales law as it is of general contract law, and it underlies the market price damages rule in SGA ss. 48 and 49. As will have been seen, the mitigation rule was applied in both *McLean* and *Sunnyside* and explains why the buyer with defective goods on his hands cannot simply sit back and do nothing: he must act as a reasonable person would have acted to mitigate his damages.

Difficulties may arise because the buyer often cannot afford to buy substitutional goods or take other mitigating steps, or may not be able to do so until he recovers the purchase price or damages from the seller. Or again the buyer may suffer aggravated damages because he was relying on the expected stream of income from the seller's equipment to help pay for some of his other debts. This happened for example in *Freedhoff v. Pomalift Industries Ltd.*, [1971] 2 OR 773 (CA). Nevertheless, in *McLean* the court held that impecuniosity is no defence to the buyer's failure to mitigate, and in *Freedhoff* it denied damages ascribable to the buyer's impecuniosity on the grounds that they were too remote. However, this position may be too rigid and does not appear to be consistent with the views expressed in *Muhammad Issa el Sheik Ahmad v. Ali*, [1947] AC 414, and *Trans Trust SPRL v. Danubian Trading Co. Ltd.*, [1952] 2 QB 297 (CA). In the latter case, Denning LJ observed (at 306):

> It was also said that the damages were the result of the impecuniosity of the sellers and that it was a rule of law that such damages are too remote. I do not think there is any such rule. In the case of a breach of contract, it depends on whether the damages were reasonably foreseeable or not. In the present case they clearly were.

(Somervell and Romer LJJ expressed similar views.) On the other hand, the Ontario position is consistent with the decision in "*The Liesbosch*," [1933] AC 449 (HL), a leading case on the assessment of damages in tort. See further, OLRC Sales Report, at 502-3, and note that American law appears to support Denning's dictum. See, for example, *REB Inc. v. Ralston Purina* (1975), 525 F.2d 749 (10 CCA), cited in Shanker (1978-79), 3 *CBLJ* at 367.

The status of the *Liesbosch* "rule" was also commented upon by the Court of Appeal in *Perry v. Sidney Phillips & Son*, [1982] 3 All ER 705. The plaintiff successfully sued the defendants in contract and tort for a negligently prepared survey report on which he had relied in the purchase of a house. As part of his loss he claimed damages for the distress and discomfort of living in a house which was in a defective condition. His excuse for not doing the repairs was that he could not afford to do so and that the defendant's denial of liability also deterred him from carrying out the repairs.

The Court of Appeal upheld the trial judge's allowance of damages under this head. Lord Denning said (at 709) that L. Wright's statement in the *Liesbosch* "must be restricted to the facts of the *Liesbosch* case. It is not of general application." Oliver LJ was more

guarded. He admitted that if impecuniosity was the plaintiff's only reason for not carrying out the repairs *Liesbosch* might well have provided an answer for the defendants.
However, the plaintiff's conduct in not carrying out the repairs was quite reasonable for
other reasons. Kerr LJ observed that L Wright's judgment in the *Liesbosch* "is consistently being attenuated in more recent decisions of this court," and continued (at 712-13):

> If it is reasonably foreseeable that the plaintiff may be unable to mitigate or remedy the
> consequence of the other party's breach as soon as he would have done if he had been
> provided with the necessary means to do so from the other party, then it seems to me that
> the principle of the *Liesbosch* case no longer applies in its full rigour. In the *Liesbosch* case,
> as I see it, it was not reasonably foreseeable that the plaintiff would be put into the
> difficulties in which he was put by the other party's breach of duty.

The *Liesbosch* case was also distinguished, and *Perry v. Sydney Phillips & Son* favourably cited, by the Saskatchewan Court of Appeal in its recent decision in *Kozak v. Gruza*
(1990), 63 DLR (4th) 129, which involved a claim for damages in conversion. The court
made it clear that the plaintiff's impecuniosity would not preclude a claim for damages
if the impecuniosity was foreseeable by the usual tests of foreseeability. It remains to
be seen to what extent this trend toward isolating the *Liesbosch* rule results in its total
elimination.

Contributory Negligence

Although the issue did not arise in *Cullinane*, *McLean*, or *Sunnyside*, the buyer may itself
been negligent in its handling, maintenance or use of the goods. It happened for example
in *Lambert v. Lewis*, [1980] 2 WLR 299 (CA), discussed *supra*, chapter 4. There the trial
judge found, in the action by the plaintiffs against the owner of the trailer and the manufacturer of the towing hitch, that the owner had been contributorily negligent in not discovering the defect before the time of the accident and held him responsible for 25 per
cent of the damages. Not surprisingly, in the claim by the owner over against the retailer
for breach of the implied conditions of quality (SGA s. 15), the retailer relied on these
findings and sought an abatement of the damages for which he might be held responsible,
if not indeed a full discharge. The trial judge responded favourably but the Court of Appeal
unanimously reversed this part of his judgment. The Court of Appeal's reasoning is summarized in the following extract from the headnote ([1980] 2 WLR 299 at 300):

> although the negligence of the owner triggered off the accident, the basic cause of that
> accident was the faulty design of the towing hitch and, since the owner's conduct was
> neither so unreasonable as to be beyond the contemplation of the retailers nor such as to
> break the chain of causation between the warranty and the accident, the damage sustained
> was a natural consequence of the retailer's breach of warranty and accordingly they were
> liable to indemnify the owner to the extent that he had been found 25 per cent liable to the
> plaintiffs in damages.

The court followed its earlier decision in the leading case of *Mowbray v. Merryweather*,
[1895] 2 QB 640, and subsequent decisions to the same effect. In *Mowbray v. Merryweather*,

… a chain supplied by the defendants was defective and caused an accident to the plaintiff's servant, who recovered damages from the plaintiff. It was held that the plaintiff's liability to pay damages to the servant was a natural consequence of the defendant's breach of contract and was such as might reasonably have been supposed to have been in the contemplation of the parties when the contract was entered into and that accordingly the damages were not too remote.

The House of Lords unanimously reversed the Court of Appeal's decision in *Lambert v. Lewis*. See [1981] 1 All ER 1185, [1982] AC 271. Speaking for the House of Lords, Lord Diplock held that the Court of Appeal had misapplied *Mowbray v. Merryweather* and that the *ratio decidendi* in that case was subject to the following implied limitation enunciated by Winn LJ in *Hadley v. Droitwich Construction Co. Ltd.*, [1967] 3 All ER 911, at 914:

… in a case where A has been held liable to X, a stranger, for negligent failure to take a certain precaution, he may recover over from someone with whom he has a contract only if, by that contract, the other contracting party has warranted that he *need not*—there is no necessity to—take the very precautions for the failure to take which he has been liable in law to [X]. (Winn LJ's emphasis.)

Lord Diplock continued (at 276-77):

The implied warranty of fitness for a particular purpose relates to the goods at the time of delivery under the contract of sale in the state in which they were delivered. I do not doubt that it is a continuing warranty that the goods will continue to be fit for that purpose for a reasonable time after delivery, so long as they remain in the same apparent state as that in which they were delivered, apart from normal wear and tear. What is a reasonable time will depend on the nature of the goods, but I would accept that in the case of the coupling the warranty was still continuing up to the date, some three to six months before the accident, when it first became known to the farmer that the handle of the locking mechanism was missing. Up to that time the farmer would have had a right to rely on the dealers' warranty as excusing him from making his own examination of the coupling to see if it were safe; but, if the accident had happened before then, the farmer would not have been held to have been guilty of any negligence to the plaintiff. After it had become apparent to the farmer that the locking mechanism of the coupling was broken, and consequently that it was no longer in the same state as when it was delivered, the only implied warranty which could justify his failure to take the precaution either to get it mended or at least to find out whether it was safe to continue to use it in that condition would be a warranty that the coupling could continue to be safely used to tow a trailer on a public highway notwithstanding that is was in an obviously damaged state. My Lords, any implication of a warranty in these terms needs only to be stated to be rejected. So the farmer's claim against the dealers fails in limine. In the state in which the farmer knew the coupling to be at the time of the accident, there was no longer any warranty by the dealers of its continued safety in use on which the farmer was entitled to rely.

The Court of Appeal reasoned that, since there was no break in the chain of causation between negligence of the manufacturers, which consisted in the defective design of the coupling, and the plaintiff's damage, there could be no such break between the dealers' breach of warranty, which likewise consisted in the defective design of the coupling, and the farmer's loss occasioned by his share of the liability for the plaintiff's damage. With respect, this reasoning was erroneous. The farmer's liability arose not from the defective design of the coupling but from his own negligence in failing, when he knew that the coupling was damaged, to have it repaired or to ascertain if it was still safe to use. The issue of causation, therefore, on which the farmer's claim against the dealers depended was whether *his* negligence resulted directly and naturally, in the ordinary course of events, from the dealer's breach of warranty. Manifestly it did not.

The reasoning in *Mowbray* has been criticized by Glanville Williams, *Joint Torts and Contributory Negligence* (1951), at 219 *et seq.*, as being illogical (can you see why?) and he argues strongly that contributory negligence should be a defence to an unintentional breach of contract regardless of the exact verbal mechanism by which the defence may be introduced: "the fact remains that, whatever the language, the subject of enquiry is whether the negligence of the plaintiff has concurred with that of the defendant to produce the misfortune for which damages are claimed" (at 214). Other authors simply cite *Mowbray v. Merryweather* without questioning the soundness of the court's reasoning. See, for example, *McGregor on Damages*, 14th ed., paras. 638-639, 644; and *Benjamin's Sale of Goods*, 2nd ed., para. 1415.

In *Lambert v. Lewis* no issue was raised as to the court's power to apportion damages between the owner and retailer—it was treated as an all or nothing proposition. Given the facts, this was understandable since there was no evidence that the retailer had been negligent although it is not clear that this is a conclusive answer. Nevertheless the question remains highly relevant. So far as the answer depends on the construction of language substantially the same as that of the Ontario Negligence Act, RSO 1980, c. 315 as am., the answer may well be no. It has been repeatedly held in Ontario that s. 2, which deals with claims for contribution between wrongdoers "where damages have been caused or contributed to by the fault or neglect of two or more persons," is limited to claims between tortfeasors. See, for example, *Dominion Chain Co. Ltd. v. Eastern Construction Co. Ltd.* (1976), 68 DLR (3d) 385 (Ont. CA); aff'd. [1978] 2 SCR 1346. Presumably the same interpretation will be applied to s. 4, which deals with the defence of contributory negligence in actions based on "the fault or negligence" of the defendant. (Glanville Williams, *op. cit.*, chapter 11, argues for the applicability of the differently worded English Act; and see also *West Coast Finance Ltd. v. Gunderson, Stokes, Walton & Co. Ltd.* (1974), 44 DLR (3d) 232 (BCSC), rev'd. on other grounds 56 DLR (3d) 460 (CA), and S.M. Waddams, *The Law of Contracts*, 2nd ed. (1984), at 580-83.)

The Foreseeability Test

Koufos v. Czarnikow Ltd. ("The Heron II")

[1967] 3 WLR 1491, [1969] 1 AC 350 (HL)

LORD REID: My Lords, by charterparty of October 15, 1960, the respondents chartered the appellant's vessel, *Heron II*, to proceed to Constanza, there to load a cargo of 3,000 tons of sugar; and to carry it to Basrah, or, in the charterer's option, to Jeddah.

The vessel left Constanza on November 1, 1960. The option was not exercised and the vessel arrived at Basrah on December 2, 1960. The umpire has found that "a reasonably accurate prediction of the length of the voyage was twenty days." But the vessel had in breach of contract made deviations which caused a delay of nine days.

It was the intention of the respondents to sell the sugar "promptly after arrival at Basrah and after inspection by merchants." The appellant did not know this, but he was aware of the fact that there was a market for sugar at Basrah. The sugar was in fact sold at Basrah in lots between December 12 and 22, 1960, but shortly before that time the market price had fallen, partly by reason of the arrival of another cargo of sugar. It was found by the umpire that if there had not been this delay of nine days the sugar would have fetched £32 10s. 0d. per ton. The actual price realised was only £31 2s. 9d. per ton. The respondent claimed that they were entitled to recover the difference as damages for breach of contract. The appellant admits that he is liable to pay interest for nine days on the value of the sugar and certain minor expenses but denies that fall in market value can be taken into account in assessing damages in this case.

. . .

So the question for decision is whether a plaintiff can recover as damages for breach of contract a loss of a kind which the defendant, when he made the contract, ought to have realised was not unlikely to result from a breach of contract causing delay in delivery. I use the words "not unlikely" as denoting a degree of probability considerably less than an even chance but nevertheless not very unusual and easily foreseeable.

For over a century everyone has agreed that remoteness of damage in contract must be determined by applying the rule (or rules) laid down by a court including Lord Wensleydale (then Parke B), Martin B and Alderson B in *Hadley v. Baxendale*. But many different interpretations of that rule have been adopted by judges at different times. So I think that one ought first to see just what was decided in that case, because it would seem wrong to attribute to that rule a meaning which, if it had been adopted in that case, would have resulted in a contrary decision of that case.

In *Hadley v. Baxendale* the owners of a flour mill at Gloucester which was driven by a steam engine delivered to common carriers, Pickford & Co., a broken crankshaft to be sent to engineers in Greenwich. A delay of five days in delivery there was held to be in breach of contract and the question at issue was the proper measure of damages. In fact the shaft was sent as a pattern for a new shaft and until it arrived the mill could not operate. So the owners claimed £300 as loss of profit for the five days by which resumption of work was delayed by this breach of contract. But the carriers did not know that delay would cause loss of this kind.

Alderson B, delivering the judgment of the court, said (at 355-56):

We find that the only circumstances here communicated by the plaintiffs to the defendants at the time the contract was made, were, that the article to be carried was the broken shaft of a mill, and that the plaintiffs were the millers of that mill. But how do these circumstances show reasonably that the profits of the mill must be stopped by an unreasonable delay in the delivery of the broken shaft by the carrier to the third person? Suppose the plaintiffs had another shaft in their possession put up or putting up at the time, and that they only wished to send back the broken shaft to the engineer who made it; it is clear that this would be quite consistent with the above circumstances, and yet the unreasonable delay in the delivery would have no effect upon the intermediate prof-its of the mill. Or, again, suppose that at the time of the delivery to the carrier, the machinery of the mill had been in other respects defective, then, also, the same results would follow.

Then, having said that in fact the loss of profit was caused by the delay, he continued (at 356):

> But it is obvious that, in the great multitude of cases of millers sending off broken shafts to third persons by a carrier under ordinary circumstances, such consequences would not, in all probability, have occurred.

Alderson B clearly did not and could not mean that it was not reasonably foresee-able that delay might stop the resumption of work in the mill. He merely said that in the great multitude—which I take to mean the great majority—of cases this would not happen. He was not distinguishing between results which were foreseeable or unforeseeable, but between results which were likely because they would happen in the great majority of cases, and results which were unlikely because they would only happen in a small minority of cases. He continued (at 354):

> It follows, therefore, that the loss of profits here cannot reasonably be considered such a consequence of the breach of contract as could have been fairly and reasonably con-templated by both the parties when they made this contract.

He clearly meant that a result which will happen in the great majority of cases should fairly and reasonably be regarded as having been in the contemplation of the parties, but that a result which, though foreseeable as a substantial possibility, would only happen in a small minority of cases should not be regarded as having been in their contemplation. He was referring to such a result when he continued (at 356):

> For such loss would neither have flowed naturally from the breach of this contract in the great multitude of such cases occurring under ordinary circumstances, nor were the special circumstances, which perhaps, would have made it a reasonable and natural consequence of such breach of contract, communicated to or known by the defendants.

I have dealt with the latter part of the judgment before coming to the well known rule because the court were there applying the rule and the language which was used in the latter part appears to me to throw considerable light on the meaning which they must have attached to the rather vague expressions used in the rule itself. The rule (at 354) is that the damages "should be such as may fairly and reasonably be considered either arising naturally, i.e., according to the usual course of things, from such breach of contract itself, or such as may reasonably be supposed to have been in the contem-plation of both parties, at the time they made the contract, as the probable result of the breach of it."

I do not think that it was intended that there were to be two rules or that two different standards or tests were to be applied. The last two passages which I quoted from the end of the judgment applied to the facts before the court which did not include any special circumstances communicated to the defendants; and the line of reasoning there is that because in the great majority of cases loss of profit would not in all probability have occurred, it followed that this could not reasonably be considered as having been fairly and reasonably contemplated by both the parties, for it would not have flowed naturally from the breach in the great majority of cases.

I am satisfied that the court did not intend that every type of damage which was reasonably foreseeable by the parties when the contract was made should either be considered as arising naturally, i.e., in the usual course of things, or be supposed to have been in the contemplation of the parties. Indeed the decision makes it clear that a type of damage which was plainly foreseeable as a real possibility but which would only occur in a small minority of cases cannot be regarded as arising in the usual course of things or be supposed to have been in the contemplation of the parties: the parties are not supposed to contemplate as grounds for the recovery of damage any type of loss or damage which on the knowledge available to the defendant would appear to him as only likely to occur in a small minority of cases.

In cases like *Hadley v. Baxendale* or the present case it is not enough that in fact the plaintiff's loss was directly caused by the defendant's breach of contract. It clearly was so caused in both. The crucial question is whether, on the information available to the defendant when the contract was made, he should, or the reasonable man in his position would, have realised that such loss was sufficiently likely to result from the breach of contract to make it proper to hold that the loss flowed naturally from the breach or that loss of that kind should have been within his contemplation.

The modern rule of tort is quite different and it imposes a much wider liability. The defendant will be liable for any type of damage which is reasonably foreseeable as liable to happen even in the most unusual case, unless the risk is so small that a reasonable man would in the whole circumstances feel justified in neglecting it. And there is good reason for the difference. In contract, if one party wishes to protect himself against a risk which to the other party would appear unusual, he can direct the other party's attention to it before the contract is made, and I need not stop to consider in what circumstances the other party will then be held to have accepted responsibility in that event. But in tort there is no opportunity for the injured party to protect himself in that way, and the tortfeasor cannot reasonably complain if he has to pay for some very unusual but nevertheless foreseeable damage which results from his wrongdoing. I have no doubt that today a tortfeasor would be held liable for a type of damage as unlikely as was the stoppage of Hadley's Mill for lack of a crankshaft: to anyone with the knowledge the carrier had that may have seemed unlikely but a chance of it happening would have been seen to be far from negligible. But it does not at all follow that *Hadley v. Baxendale* would today be differently decided.

. . .

For a considerable time there was a tendency to set narrow limits to awards of damages. Such phrases were used as that the damage was not "the immediate and necessary effect of the breach of contract" (*per* Cockburn CJ in *Hobbs v. London and South Western Railway Co.* (1875), LR 10 QB 111 at 118). *The Parana* was decided during that period. But later a more liberal tendency can be seen. I do not think it useful to review the authorities in detail but I do attach importance to what was said in this House in *R. & H. Hall Ltd. v. W.H. Pim (Junior) & Co. Ltd.* (1928), 33 Com. Cas. 324.

In that case Pim sold a cargo of wheat to Hall but failed to deliver it. Hall had resold the wheat but as a result of Pim's breach of contract lost the profit which they would have made on their sub-sale. Three of their Lordships dealt with the case on the basis that the relevant question was whether it ought to have been in the contemplation of the parties that a resale was probable. The finding (at 329) of the arbitrators was:

> The arbitrators are unable to find that it was in the contemplation of the parties or ought to have been in the contemplation of Messrs. Pim at that time that the cargo would be resold or was likely to be resold before delivery; in fact, the chances of its being resold as a cargo and of its being taken delivery of by Messrs. Hall were about equal.

On that finding the Court of Appeal (1927), 32 Com. Cas. 144, at 151 had decided in favour of Pim, saying that, as the arbitrators had stated as a fact that the chances of the cargo being resold or not being resold were equal, it was therefore "idle to speak of a likelihood or of a probability of a resale."

Viscount Dunedin pointed out that it was for the court to decide what was to be supposed to have been in the contemplation of the parties, and then said (at 329-30):

> I do not think that "probability" ... means that the chances are all in favour of the event happening. To make a thing probable, it is enough, in my view, that there is an even chance of its happening. That is the criterion I apply: and in view of the facts, as I have said above, I think there was here in the contemplation of parties the probability of a resale.

He did not have to consider how much less than a 50 per cent chance would amount to a probability in this sense.

Lord Shaw of Dunfermline went rather further. He said (at 333):

> To whatever extent in a contract of goods for future delivery the extent of damages is in contemplation of parties is always extremely doubtful. The main business fact is that they are thinking of the contract being performed and not of its being not performed. But with regard to the latter if their contract shows that there were instances or stages which made ensuing losses or damage a not unlikely result of the breach of a contract, then all such results must be reckoned to be within not only the scope of the contract, but the contemplation of parties as to its breach.

Lord Phillimore was less definite and perhaps went even further. He said (at 337) that the sellers of the wheat knew that the buyers "might well sell it over again and make a profit on the resale"; and that being so they "must be taken to have consented to this state of things and thereby to have made themselves liable to pay" the profit on a resale.

It may be that there was nothing very new in this but I think that *Hall*'s case must be taken to have established that damages are not to be regarded as too remote merely because, on the knowledge available to the defendant when the contract was made, the chance of the occurrence of the event which caused the damage would have appeared to him to be rather less than an even chance. I would agree with Lord Shaw that it is generally sufficient that that event would have appeared to the defendant as not unlikely to occur. It is hardly ever possible in this matter to assess probabilities with any degree of mathematical accuracy. But I do not find in that case or in cases which preceded it any warranty for regarding as within the contemplation of the parties any event which would not have appeared to the defendant, had he thought about it, to have a very substantial degree of probability.

But then it has been said that the liability of defendants has been further extended by *Victoria Laundry (Windsor) Ltd. v. Newman Industries Ltd.*, [1949] 2 KB 528. I do not think so. The plaintiffs bought a large boiler from the defendants and the defendants were aware of the general nature of the plaintiffs' business and of the plaintiffs' intention to put the boiler into use as soon as possible. Delivery of the boiler was delayed in breach of contract and the plaintiffs claimed as damages loss of profit caused by the delay. A large part of the profits claimed would have resulted from some specially lucrative contracts which the plaintiffs could have completed if they had had the boiler: that was rightly disallowed because the defendants had no knowledge of these contracts. But Asquith LJ then said (at 543):

> It does not, however, follow that the plaintiffs are precluded for recovering some general (and perhaps conjectural) sums for loss of business in respect of dyeing contracts to be reasonably expected, any more than in respect of laundering contracts to be reasonably expected.

It appears to me that this was well justified on the earlier authorities. It was certainly not unlikely on the information which the defendants had when making the contract that delay in delivering the boiler would result in loss of business: indeed it would seem that that was more than an even chance. And there was nothing new in holding that damages should be estimated on a conjectural basis. This House had approved of that as early as 1813 in *Hall v. Ross* (1813), Dow. 201.

But what is said to create a "landmark" is the statement of principles by Asquith LJ (at 539-40). This does to some extent go beyond the older authorities and in so far as it does so, I do not agree with it. In paragraph (2) it is said (at 539) that the plaintiff is entitled to recover "such part of the loss actually resulting as was at the time of the contract reasonably foreseeable as liable to result from the breach." To bring in reasonable foreseeability appears to me to be confusing measure of damages in contract with measure of damages in tort. A great many extremely unlikely results are reasonably foreseeable: it is true that Lord Asquith may have meant foreseeable as a likely result, and if that is all he meant I would not object further than to say that I think that the phrase is liable to be misunderstood. For the same reason I would take exception to the phrase "liable to result" in paragraph (5). Liable is a very vague word but I think that one would usually say that when a person foresees a very improbable result he foresees that it is liable to happen.

I agree with the first half of paragraph (6). For the best part of a century it has not been required that the defendant could have foreseen that a breach of contract must necessarily result in the loss which has occurred. But I cannot agree with the second half of that paragraph. It has never been held to be sufficient in contract that the loss was foreseeable as "a serious possibility" or "a real danger" or as being "on the cards."

It is on the cards that one can win £100,000 or more for a stake of a few pence—several people have done that. And anyone who backs a hundred to one chance regards a win as a serious possibility—many people have won on such a chance. And the *Wagon Mound (No. 2)*, [1967] AC 617 could not have been decided as it was unless the extremely unlikely fire should have been foreseen by the ship's officer as a real danger. It appears to me that in the ordinary use of language there is wide gulf between saying that some event is not unlikely or quite likely to happen and saying merely that it is a serious possibility, a real danger, or on the cards. Suppose one takes a well-shuffled pack of cards, it is quite likely or not unlikely that the top card will prove to be a diamond: the odds are only 3 to 1 against. But most people would not say that it is quite likely to be the nine of diamonds for the odds are then 51 to 1 against. On the other hand I think that most people would say that there is a serious possibility or a real danger of its being turned up first and of course it is on the cards. If the tests of "real danger" or "serious possibility" are in future to be authoritative then the *Victoria Laundry* case would indeed be a landmark because it would mean that *Hadley v. Baxendale* would be differently decided today. I certainly could not understand any court deciding that, on the information available to the carrier in that case, the stoppage of the mill was neither a serious possibility nor a real danger. If those tests are to prevail in the future then let us cease to pay lip service to the rule in *Hadley v. Baxendale*. But in my judgment to adopt these tests would extend liability for breach of contract beyond what is reasonable or desirable. From the limited knowledge which I have of commercial affairs I would not expect such an extension to be welcomed by the business community and from the legal point of view I can find little or nothing to recommend it.

Appeal dismissed.

[Concurring judgments were delivered by the other law lords, though the test of forseeability preferred by them was expressed in slightly different terms, *viz.*, whether there was a "serious possibility" or a "real danger" of the type or damages occurring claimed to have been suffered by the plaintiff, or whether such damages were "liable to result" or "not unlikely to result."]

NOTES

1) As will be noted, *The Heron II* is essentially a gloss on *Hadley v. Baxendale*, the foundation of the modern rule governing the measurement of damages in contract cases. The House of Lords did not question the soundness of the rule itself. For a fascinating description of the legal and business matrix in which *Hadley v. Baxendale* was decided, see R. Danzig, "*Hadley v. Baxendale*: A Study in the Industrialization of the Law" (1975), 4 *J Legal Studies* 249. In view of the limited reach of *The Heron II*, will the decision make the damages assessment rules more acceptable to sellers?

2) Article 74 of the UN International Sales Convention provides as follows:

Damages for breach of contract by one party consist of a sum equal to the loss, including loss of profit, suffered by the other party as a consequence of the breach. Such damages may not exceed the loss which the party in breach foresaw or ought to have foreseen at the time of the conclusion of the contract, in the light of the facts and matters of which he then knew or ought to have known, as a possible consequence of the breach of contract.

Is its test of foreseeability the same as the tests favoured in *The Heron II*?

3) For a thorough discussion of the problems associated with the foreseeability test, see K. Swinton, "Foreseeability: Where Should the Award of Contract Damages Cease?" Study 3 in Reiter and Swan (eds.), *Studies in Contract Law* (1980), 61.

H. Parsons (Livestock) Ltd. v. Uttley Ingham & Co. Ltd.

[1977] 3 WLR 990, [1978] QB 791 (CA)

LORD DENNING MR: The plaintiffs, H. Parsons (Livestock) Ltd., have a fine herd of nearly 700 pigs at their farm in Derbyshire. They call it the Wayside Herd. They manage it most efficiently. They feed the pigs on special pignuts. They use about 10 tons a month of these pignuts. In order to store and handle the pignuts, the plaintiffs bought in 1968 a big hopper called a bulk feed storage hopper. They bought it from the makers, the defendants, Uttley Ingham & Co. Ltd., who are sheet-metal workers. The plaintiffs paid £270 for it. It was a huge round metal bin 28 feet high and 8 feet 6 inches in diameter. It was cylindrical at the top and tapering down into a cone. It had a lid on the top with a ventilator in it. The pignuts go into the top and come out at the bottom.

The first hopper was so successful that in 1971 the plaintiffs ordered a second one to be just the same as the first. It cost £275. The defendants accepted the order in a letter of April 23, 1971, in these terms:

> We are very pleased to book your order for one bulk hopper exactly as supplied in 1968. ... Hopper fitted with ventilated top and complete with filler and breather pipes. ... Ex works price £275. Carriage charges £15. We deliver in an upright position on your prepared concrete base and bolt down ... tipping the hopper off the back of the vehicle.

On August 2, 1971, the defendants delivered the hopper to the site. It was exactly the same as the first, but when the delivery man erected it in position he forgot to adjust the ventilator. He left it closed. It was fastened with a piece of tape which had been put on so as to stop it rattling on the journey. No one noticed the mistake, because the ventilator was at the top of the hopper 28 feet above the ground. The delivery man went off. The plaintiffs used the hopper. They put pignuts into it just as they did with the first hopper. On August 12, 1971, they filled it with 9½ tons of pignuts; on September 10, 8½ tons; on October 1, 8 tons.

At first all was well. But on September 28 a small number of the nuts appeared to be mouldy. The plaintiffs did not think this would harm the pigs. So they went on feeding them. Early in October more nuts turned mouldy. But still the plaintiffs were not unduly concerned. As a rule, mouldy nuts do not harm pigs. On Saturday, October 9, there was a bigger proportion of mouldy nuts; and some of the pigs were showing signs of illness. About six of the 21 sows suckling litters were very loose, and about seven or eight were not eating all their ration of nuts. Over the weekend the plaintiffs became really concerned. They did not know the cause. They telephoned the suppliers of the nuts. They telephoned the veterinary surgeon. The suppliers of nuts came. The veterinary surgeon came. They stopped feeding the pigs with nuts from the hopper. They got some bagged foods and fed them from the bags. They telephoned the defendants. On Friday, October 15, a representative of the defendants came. He climbed up to the top of the hopper. He found the ventilator closed. He opened it. When he came down, he said to the plaintiffs: "That appears to be your trouble."

It was indeed the trouble. After much evidence by experts, the judge found that the closed ventilator was the cause. But the effects remained so as to affect the herd greatly. A large number of the pigs suffered an attack of E. coli, which is very bad for pigs. It was triggered off by the eating of the mouldy nuts. The infection spread rapidly; 254 pigs died of a value of £10,000. They also lost sales and turnover resulting in big financial loss. The total claim is £20,000 or £30,000. The question is whether that damage is recoverable from the makers of the hopper, or whether it is too remote.

The judge's findings

The judge had before him the speeches in the House of Lords in *C. Czarnikow Ltd. v. Koufos*, [1969] 1 AC 350 about remoteness of damage. That case draws a distinction between contract and tort. Remoteness in contract depends on what the parties "reasonably contemplated at the time of the contract," whereas in tort it depends on what could "reasonably be foreseen at the time of the wrongful act or omission." But the judge did not think either of those tests was applicable. He based his decision on the implied term that the goods should be reasonably fit for the purpose under the implied condition of section 14(1) of the Sale of Goods Act 1893, as it then was. He held that this was an "absolute warranty" and that, in case of a breach, the seller was liable for all the damage of which the breach was a cause. The judge said, significantly:

> The plaintiffs do not have to prove that the toxicity or its results were foreseeable to either party ... there is no need to have recourse to the question of the presumed contemplation.

But, in case he was wrong on this point and that, being a breach of contract, he ought to consider what was "reasonably contemplated at the time of the contract," the judge went on to consider the facts in regard to it. He inquired whether the "damage that occurred through the outbreak of E. coli was within the reasonable contemplation of the parties." After considering the evidence, he said:

> Although I sympathise with the plaintiffs, who have no doubt suffered heavy loss as a result in fact on my findings of a breach of contract, I would not consider that I would be justified in finding that in the spring of 1971 at the time of the contract either a farmer in the position of the plaintiffs or a hopper manufacturer in the position of the defendants would reasonably have contemplated that there was either a very substantial degree of possibility or a real danger or serious possibility that the feeding of mouldy

pignuts in the condition described by Mr. Parsons would cause illness in the pigs that ate them, even on an intensive farm such as that of the plaintiffs.

Applying the speeches in *C. Czarnikow Ltd. v. Koufos*, [1969] 1 AC 350, that finding would mean that the illness and death of the pigs was too remote to be an admissible head of damage.

The terms of contract

The judge derived his "absolute warranty" from section 14(1) of the Sale of Goods Act 1893 about reasonable fitness for the purpose. I agree that the warranty in section 14(1) is absolute in this sense: if the goods are unfit owing to a latent defect, which could not be discovered by any amount of care, nevertheless the seller is liable. But I do not think this absoluteness means that the seller is liable for all consequences of a breach, however remote the consequences may be. He is only liable, as section 53(2) of the Act of 1893 says, for "the estimated loss directly and naturally resulting, in the ordinary course of events, from the breach of warranty." That section is an attempted codification of the rule in *Hadley v. Baxendale* (1854), 9 Exch. 341 and should be so interpreted.

But I am not sure that section 14(1) was really appropriate here. The contract was divisible into two parts: the sale of the hopper and the erection of it. Under the second part, the maker was under a duty to use reasonable care in erecting the hopper. But even so, here again the maker would not be liable for all consequences. He would only just be liable for such damage "as may fairly and reasonably be considered either arising naturally, i.e., according to the usual course of things, from such breach:" see *Hadley v. Baxendale*, 9 Exch. 341, at 354. That is virtually the same as section 53(2).

On either view, therefore, the maker is not liable for all the consequences, but only for such damage as is not too remote in law. So I turn to examine the judge's findings of fact in regard to it.

The judge's findings of fact

As I read the judge's findings of fact, he was of opinion that the makers of the hopper could reasonably contemplate the following consequences as the result of the breach: (i) that the ventilator would remain closed whilst the hopper was in use; (ii) that the pignuts stored in it would become mouldy for want of proper ventilation; (iii) that the pignuts would be fed to the pigs in a mouldy condition.

But the judge, in the important extract I have already read from his judgment, was also of opinion that the makers would not reasonably contemplate that there was a serious possibility that the mouldy nuts would cause the pigs to become ill. There may have been a slight possibility, but not a serious possibility. It was so slight that the plaintiff pig farmers (who fed the nuts to the pigs knowing that they were mouldy) did not themselves feel any concern about feeding the mouldy nuts to the pigs.

By making that last finding the judge has presented us with a nice problem of remoteness of damage. Mr. Drake submitted that it means that the plaintiffs should fail. The action is for breach of contract. It has, he says, been held by the House of Lords that a contract-breaker is only liable for the consequences which he may reasonably contemplate as a *serious* possibility and not for those which he can only foresee as a *slight* possibility.

There is no problem here about causation. The closed ventilator was clearly the cause, or one of the causes, of the deaths of the pigs. There was an unbroken sequence all the way. There was no intervening human action such as gave rise to the discussion on causation in *Weld-Blundell v. Stephens*, [1920] AC 956 or *Dorset Yacht Co. Ltd. v. Home Office*, [1970] AC 1004, at 1030. The only problem here is with remoteness of damage.

The law as to remoteness

Remoteness of damage is beyond doubt a question of law. In *C. Czarnikow Ltd. v. Koufos*, [1969] AC 350 the House of Lords said that, in remoteness of damage, there is a difference between contract and tort. In the case of a *breach of contract*, the court has to consider whether the consequences were of such a kind that a reasonable man, at the time of making the contract, would *contemplate* them as being of a very substantial degree of probability. (In the House of Lords various expressions were used to describe this degree of probability, such as, not merely "on the cards" because that may be too low: but as being "not unlikely to occur" (see 383 and 388); or "likely to result or at least not unlikely to result" (see 406); or "liable to result" (see 410); or that there was a "real danger" or "serious possibility" of them occurring (see 415).)

In the case of a *tort*, the court has to consider whether the consequences were of such a kind that a reasonable man, at the time of the tort committed, would *foresee* them as being of a much lower degree of probability. (In the House of Lords various expressions were used to describe this, such as, it is sufficient if the consequences are "liable to happen in the most unusual case" (see 385) or in a "very improbable" case (see 389); or that "they may happen as a result of the breach, however unlikely it may be, unless it can be brushed aside as far-fetched" (see 422).)

I find it difficult to apply those principles universally to all cases of contract or to all cases of tort: and to draw a distinction between what a man "contemplates" and what he "foresees." I soon begin to get out of my depth. I cannot swim in this sea of semantic exercises—to say nothing of the different degrees of probability—especially when the cause of action can be laid either in contract or in tort. I am swept under by the conflicting currents. I go back with relief to the distinction drawn in legal theory by Professors Hart and Honore in their book *Causation in the Law* (1959), at 281-287. They distinguish between those cases in contract in which a man has suffered no damage to person or property, but only *economic loss*, such as, loss of profit or loss of opportunities for gain in some future transaction: and those in which he claims damages for an *injury actually done* to his person or *damage actually done* to his property (including his livestock) or for ensuing expense (*damnum emergens*) to which he has actually been put. In the law of *tort*, there is emerging a distinction between economic loss and physical damage: see *Spartan Steel & Alloys Ltd. v. Martin & Co. (Contractors) Ltd.*, [1973] QB 27, at 36-37. It underlies the words of Lord

Wilberforce in *Anns v. Merton London Borough Council*, [1977] 2 WLR 1024, at 1039 recently, where he classified the recoverable damage as "material, physical damage." It has been much considered by the Supreme Court of Canada in *Rivtow Marine Ltd. v. Washington Iron Works and Walkem Machinery & Equipment Ltd.*, [1973] 6 WWR 692 and by the High Court of Australia in *Caltex Oil (Australia) Pty. Ltd. v. Dredge Willemstad* (1976), 51 ALGR 270.

It seems to me that in the law of *contract*, too, a similar distinction is emerging. It is between loss of profit consequent on a breach of contract and physical damage consequent on it.

Loss of profit cases

I would suggest as a solution that in the former class of case—loss of profit cases—the defaulting party is only liable for the consequences if they are such as, at the time of the contract, he ought reasonably to have *contemplated* as a *serious* possibility or real danger. You must assume that, at the time of the contract, he had the very kind of breach in mind—such a breach as afterwards happened, as for instance, delay in transit—and then you must ask: ought he reasonably to have *contemplated* that there was a *serious* possibility that such a breach would involve the plaintiff in loss of profit? If yes, the contractor is liable for the loss unless he has taken care to exempt himself from it by a condition in the contract—as, of course, he is able to do if it was the sort of thing which he could reasonably contemplate. The law of this class of case is now covered by the three leading cases of *Hadley v. Baxendale*, 9 Exch. 341; *Victoria Laundry (Windsor) Ltd. v. Newman Industries Ltd.*, [1949] 2 KB 528; and *C. Czarnikow Ltd. v. Koufos*, [1969] 1 AC 350. These were all "loss of profit" cases: and the test of "reasonable contemplation" and "serious possibility" should, I suggest, be kept to that type of loss or, at any rate, to economic loss.

Physical damage cases

In the second class of case—the physical injury or expense case—the defaulting party is liable for any loss or expense which he ought reasonably to have *foreseen* at the time of the breach as a possible consequence, even if it was only a *slight* possibility. You must assume that he was aware of his breach, and then you must ask: ought he reasonably to have foreseen, at the time of the breach, that something of this kind might happen in consequence of it? This is the test which has been applied in cases of tort ever since *The Wagon Mound* cases [1961] AC 388 and [1967] 1 AC 388 and [1967] 1 AC 617. But there is a long line of cases which support a like test in cases of contract.

One class of case which is particularly apposite here concerns latent defects in goods; in modern words "product liability." In many of these cases the manufacturer is liable in contract to the immediate party for a breach of his duty to use reasonable care and is liable in tort to the ultimate consumer for the same want of reasonable care. The ultimate consumer can either sue the retailer in contract and pass the liability up the chain to the manufacturer, or he can sue the manufacturer in tort and thus by-pass the chain. The liability of the manufacturer ought to be the same in either case. In nearly all these cases the defects were outside the range of anything that was in fact contemplated, or could reasonably have been contemplated, by the manufacturer or by anyone down the chain to the retailers. Yet the manufacturer and others in the chain have been held liable for the damage done to the ultimate user, as for instance the death of the young pheasants in *Hardwick Game Farm v. Suffolk Agricultural Poultry Producers Association*, [1969] 2 AC 31 and of the mink in *Christopher Hill Ltd. v. Ashington Piggeries Ltd.*, [1972] AC 441. Likewise, the manufacturers and retailers were held liable for the dermatitis caused to the wearer in the woollen underwear case of *Grant v. Australian Knitting Mills Ltd.*, [1936] AC 85, even though they had not the faintest suspicion of any trouble. So were the manufacturers down the chain to the subcontractors for the disintegrating roofing tiles in *Young & Marten Ltd. v. McManus Childs Ltd.*, [1969] 1 AC 454.

Another familiar class of case is where the occupier of premises is under the common duty of care, either in pursuance of a contract with a visitor or under the Occupiers Liability Act 1957. If he fails in that duty and a visitor is injured, the test of remoteness must be the same no matter whether the injured person enters by virtue of a contract or as a visitor by permission without a contract. No matter whether in contract or tort, the damages must be the same. Likewise, when a contractor is doing work on premises for a tenant and either the tenant or a visitor is injured—the test of remoteness is the same no matter whether the person injured is a tenant under the contract or a visitor without a contract; see *AC Billings & Sons Ltd. v. Riden*, [1958] AC 240.

Yet another class of case is where a hospital authority renders medical services in contract to a paying patient and gratuitously to another patient without any contract. The paying patient can sue in contract for negligence. The poor patient can sue in tort: see *Cassidy v. Ministry of Health*, [1951] 2 KB 343, at 359-60. The test of remoteness should be the same whether the hospital authorities are sued in contract or in tort: see *Esso Petroleum Co. Ltd. v. Mardon*, [1976] QB 801, at 802.

Instances could be multiplied of injuries to persons or damages to property where the defendant is liable for his negligence to one man in contract and to another in tort. Each suffers like damage. The test of remoteness is, and should be, the same in both.

Coming to the present case, we were told that in some cases the makers of these hoppers supply them direct to the pig farmer under contract with him, but in other cases they supply them through an intermediate dealer—who buys from the manufacturer and resells to the pig farmer on the self-same terms—in which the manufacturer delivers direct to the pig farmer. In the one case the pig farmer can sue the manufacturer in contract. In the other in tort. The test of remoteness should be the same. It should be the test in tort.

Conclusion

The present case falls within the class of case where the breach of contract causes physical damage. The test of remoteness in such cases is similar to that in tort. The contractor is liable for all such loss or expense as could reasonably have been foreseen, at the time of the breach, as a possible consequence of it. Applied to this case, it means that the makers of the hopper are liable for the death of the pigs. They ought reasonably to have foreseen that, if the mouldy pignuts were fed to the pigs, there was a possibility that they might become ill. Not a serious possibility. Nor a real danger. But still a slight possibility. On that basis the makers were liable for the illness suffered by the pigs. They suffered from diarrhoea at the beginning. This triggered off the deadly E. coli. That was a far worse illness than could then be foreseen. But that does not lessen this liability. The type or kind of damage was foreseeable even though the extent of it was not: see *Hughes v. Lord Advocate*, [1963] AC 837. The makers are liable for the loss of the pigs that died and of the expenses of the vet and such like, but not for loss of profit on future sales or future opportunities of gain: see *Simon v. Pawson & Leafs Ltd.* (1932), 38 Com. Cas. 151.

So I reach the same result as the judge, but by a different route. I would dismiss the appeal.

Appeal dismissed.

NOTE

Separate concurring judgments were rendered by Orr and Scarman LJJ but based on different reasoning. They did not agree with Lord Denning MR that the test of remoteness in contract to be applied with respect to physical damages differs from that with respect to claims for loss of profit. They reached the same conclusion as Lord Denning because (*per* Scarman LJ) they approved of the following statement in *McGregor on Damages*, 13th ed., at 131-32: "… in contract as in tort, it should suffice that, if physical injury or damage is within the contemplation of the parties, recovery is not to be limited because the degree of physical injury or damage could not have been anticipated." What then is the practical difference between the two approaches?

Cf. UCC 2-715(2), which provides that "Consequential damages resulting from the seller's breach include … (b) injury to person or property proximately resulting from any breach of warranty."

What justification is there for applying a different test of foreseeability for some types of damages? The seller's superior ability to insure against the loss? The need to maximize the deterrent against negligent conduct? Are you persuaded by Lord Denning's reasoning that claims arising out of physical injury should be governed by the same test of remoteness whether the claim sounds in contract or tort? If this reasoning is sound why are tort claims for defective goods still subject to proof of negligence?

Damage Claims in Private Sales

OLRC Sales Report

at 489-91

The existing law in respect of the assessment of damages does not distinguish between different types of seller. *Prima facie*, it may seem anomalous that the law should place damage claims against a private seller on the same footing as damage claims against a merchant seller. It may be thought that a persuasive case could be made for restricting the liability of a private seller to restitutionary damages, or, at any rate, to protecting him against claims for consequential damages in the absence of wilful breach of the contract, fraud or negligence. We have recommended in an earlier chapter an expanded definition of express warranty. We noted that a representor (including a private seller) could be liable for expectation and reliance losses, and for consequential, as well as direct damages, should there be a breach of an express warranty as so expanded. We considered the implications of this change of definition in the case of representations made by a private seller and the possibility of drawing a distinction between commercial and private sales. For reasons stated, we decided not to recommend an adoption of this distinction. We pointed out, however, that it may be that a different rule of damages should be adopted generally in non-commercial sales, and that we would explore this possibility at a later stage of this Report. We have reached that stage of the Report and we now turn to consider this more general issue.

The possibility that a private seller may be held liable for expectation and other non-restitutionary claims is not confined to breaches of an express warranty. The possibility also exists where he is sued for breach of any other contractual obligation, such as late delivery or breach of the implied conditions of title and description. The suggestion that a distinction should be drawn between the measure of the damages recoverable from a merchant seller and non-merchant seller is not novel since, with respect to latent defects in the goods sold, such a distinction already appears to exist in substance, if not in form, in various civil law systems.

There are, however, persuasive reasons against the adoption of such a distinction in the revised Act. First, to the best of our knowledge, no other common law jurisdiction has so far introduced the distinction in its sales legislation and, in the context of express warranties, it was not supported in the New South Wales Working Paper. Secondly, there is little evidence that the problem is a significant one. Most of the heavy damage claims appear to involve breaches of the conditions of merchantability and fitness, and these implied terms do not apply to private sales. Again, in so sensitive an area as damages, a flexible approach is preferable to a rigid distinction between different types of sale. Finally, it may be thought that if different damage rules are to be applied to private transactions the distinction should be drawn across a wider contractual area and not confined to sales law.

We are ourselves divided about the merits of introducing the distinction in the revised Act, but we agree that this problem warrants further examination. Accordingly, we recommend that it be remitted for this purpose to the Law of Contract Amendment Project.

NOTE

The OLRC Law of Contract Amendment Report (1987) does not in fact discuss the question.

SPECIFIC PERFORMANCE, ACTIONS IN DETINUE
AND REPLEVIN REMEDIES

Specific Performance

In re Wait

[1927] 1 Ch. 606, [1926] All ER Rep. 433 (CA)
See, *supra*, chapter 13

Sky Petroleum Ltd. v. VIP Petroleum Ltd.

[1974] 1 All ER 954, [1974] 1 WLR 576 (Ch.)

GOULDING J: This is a motion for an injunction brought by the plaintiff company, Sky Petroleum Ltd., as buyer, under a contract dated 11th March 1970 made between the defendant company. VIP Petroleum Ltd., as seller, of the one part and the plaintiff company of the other part. That contract was to operate for a period of ten days, subject to certain qualifications, and thereafter on an annual basis unless terminated by either party giving to the other not less than three months written notice to that effect. It was a contract at fixed prices, subject to certain provisions which I need not now mention. Further, the contract obliged the plaintiff company—and this is an important point—to take its entire requirement of motor gasoline and diesel fuel under the contract, with certain stipulated minimum yearly quantities.

After the making of the agreement, it is common knowledge that the terms of trade in the market for petroleum and its different products changed very considerably, and I have little doubt that the contract is now disadvantageous to the defendant company. After a long correspondence, the defendant company, by telegrams dated 15th and 16th November 1973, has purported to terminate the contract under a clause therein providing for termination by the defendant company if the plaintiff company fails to conform with any of the terms of the bargain. What is alleged is that the plaintiff company has exceeded the credit provisions of the contract and has persistently been, and now is, indebted to the defendant company in larger amounts than were provided for. So far as that dispute relates, as for the purposes of this motion it must, to the date of the purported termination of the contract, it is impossible for me to decide it on the affidavit evidence. It involves not only a question of construction of the contract, but also certain disputes on subsequent arrangements between the parties and on figures in the accounts. I cannot decide it on motion and the less I say about it the better.

What I have to decide is whether any injunction should be granted to protect the plaintiff company in the meantime. There is trade evidence that the plaintiff company has no great prospect of finding any alternative source of supply for the filling stations which constitute its business. The defendant company has indicated its willingness to continue to supply the plaintiff company, but only at prices which, according to the plaintiff company's evidence, would not be serious prices from a commercial point of view. There is, in my judgment, so far as I can make out on the evidence before me, a serious danger that unless the court interferes at this stage the plaintiff company will be forced out of business. In those circumstances, unless there is some specific reason which debars me from doing so, I should be disposed to grant an injunction to restore the former position under the contract until the rights and wrongs of the parties can be fully tried out.

. . .

Now I come to the most serious hurdle in the way of the plaintiff company which is the well-known doctrine that the court refuses specific performance of a contract to sell and purchase chattels not specific or ascertained. That is a well-established and salutary rule and I am entirely unconvinced by counsel for the plaintiff company when he tells me that an injunction in the form sought by him would not be specific enforcement at all. The matter is one of substance and not of form and it is, in my judgment, quite plain that I am for the time being specifically enforcing the contract if I grant an injunction. However the ratio behind the rule is, as I believe, that under the ordinary contract for the sale of non-specific goods, damages are a sufficient remedy. That, to my mind, is lacking in the circumstances of the present case. The evidence suggests, and indeed it is common knowledge, that the petroleum market is in an unusual state in which a would-be buyer cannot go out into the market and contract with another seller, possibly at some sacrifice as to price. Here, the defendant company appears for practical purposes to be the plaintiff company's sole means of keeping its business going, and I am prepared so far to depart from the general rule as to try to preserve the position under the contract until a later date. I therefore propose to grant an injunction.

Order accordingly.

NOTES

1) As has been previously observed (*supra*, chapter 13), the real issue in cases such as *In re Wait* is whether the buyer who has paid for goods should have a preferred claim against them in the event of the seller's insolvency or whether he should rank equally with the seller's general creditors.

2) The reason for the restriction of SGA s. 50 to a sale of specific or ascertained goods is unclear. Professor Treitel has argued that the restriction did not exist in the pre-1893 law: see G.H. Treitel, "Specific Performance in the Sale of Goods," [1966] *J Bus. Law* 211. The restriction was not copied in the Uniform Sales Act and does not appear in UCC 2-716, the Code provision on specific performance. The OLRC in its Sales Report (at 443) has recommended liberalizing the language of SGA s. 50 so as to allow a decree of specific performance in respect of any type of goods, whether or not the contract involves a sale of specific goods. Assuming this recommendation is adopted, will it help a buyer in a future *In re Wait* or *Carlos Federspiel* (both *supra*, chapter 13) type of situation? Will he be able to persuade the court that damages are not an adequate remedy

because the seller is insolvent? Is this what equity means by "inadequacy"? Will the buyer be in a stronger position if he can show that title to the goods has passed to him prior to the seller's insolvency? For the Code's approach see UCC 2-502 and OLRC Sales Report, at 441-43, and *cf. Cohen v. Roche, infra*, this chapter.

3) The decision in *Sky Petroleum* appears to be quite incompatible with the reasoning in *In re Wait*. Can you see why? It is striking that Goulding J's judgment makes no reference to the case and equally surprising that *Benjamin's Sale of Goods*, 5th ed., makes no reference to *Sky Petroleum*! In *In re London Wine (Shippers) Co. Ltd.* (1986), PCC 121, Oliver J was inclined to think that the contract in the *Sky Petroleum* case was strictly not a contract of sale of goods, but "a long-term supply contract under which successive sales would arise if orders were placed and accepted," but he went on to hold that even if *Sky Petroleum* was evidence of a jurisdiction to grant specific performance outside s. 52, it was still not possible to grant a decree where the goods were not ascertained, and the buyer had no proprietary interest in the goods: Atiyah, *The Sale of Goods*, 8th ed., p. 554, n. 11. Do you find Oliver J's distinction persuasive?

A willingness to overlook the restriction in SGA s. 50 also appears in various Canadian cases but again without discussion of the statutory difficulties. See R.J. Sharpe, "Specific Relief for Contract Breach," Study 5 in B.J. Reiter and J. Swan, eds., *Studies in Contract Law* (1980), 123, esp. at 131-32. *Cf.* the decision in *Humboldt Flour Mills Co. Ltd. v. Boscher* (1975), 50 DLR (3d) 477 (Sask. QB), in which Bence CJQB refused to continue an interim injunction to restrain the defendant from selling mustard seed grown and produced in 1973 to anyone other than the plaintiff. The defendant had previously agreed with the plaintiff to plant 500 lbs. of mustard seed and to deliver on the demand of the plaintiff all the mustard produced. The court rested its decision on the absence of a contract for the sale of specific or ascertained goods; the judgment does not disclose whether damages afforded an adequate remedy.

4) Civil law jurisdictions, in contrast to the common law, frequently regard specific performance as a primary remedy and leave it to the plaintiff to decide whether to make do with the substitutional damages remedy. This Romanist approach is also adopted in the International Sales Convention, though in deference to common law sensitivities this rule does not apply where a court would not order specific performance under its own law in respect of a domestic contract. See art. 28 of the Convention. The contrast between the civilian and common law approach is not as marked as may appear at first sight because of weaknesses in the enforcement mechanism of civil law jurisdictions, as well as for other reasons. See further J.P. Dawson, "Specific Performance in France and Germany" (1959), 57 *Mich. L Rev.* 495 and *cf.* Treitel, "Remedies for Breach of Contracts" in *International Encyclopedia of Comparative Law* (1976), vol. VII, c. 16. The "orthodox" economic view is that the common law discretionary remedy is preferable because it promotes the more efficient use of resources. See R. Posner, *Economic Analysis of Law*, 5th ed. (1998), at 130-32 and *cf.* A.T. Kronman, "Specific Performance" (1978), 45 *U. Chi. L Rev.* 351.

Actions in Detinue

Cohen v. Roche

[1927] 1 KB 169, 95 LJKB 945

[The plaintiff, a dealer in antique furniture, was the successful bidder for a set of Hepplewhite chairs owned by the defendant, an auctioneer, and sold by him at a public auction. The defendant refused to release the chairs, alleging the existence of a "knock out" agreement between the plaintiff and another dealer. Consequently the plaintiff brought this action claiming specific delivery of the chairs or damages in lieu thereof. The following extract from McCardie J's judgment deals with the plaintiff's claim to have the chairs delivered to him.]

McCARDIE J: I now take the final point in the case. The plaintiff sued in detinue only. The writ and statement of claim contain no alternative demand for damages for breach of contract. They ask (a) for delivery up of the chairs or payment of their value, and (b) damages for detention. I have however allowed an amendment whereby the statement of claim asks damages for breach of contract. The plaintiff vigorously contends he is entitled as of right, once a binding contract is established, to an order for the actual delivery of the chairs, and that he is not limited to damages for breach of bargain. This point raises a question of principle and practice. Here I may again state one or two of the facts. The Hepplewhite chairs in lot 145 possessed no special features at all. They were ordinary Hepplewhite furniture. The plaintiff bought them in the ordinary way of his trade for the purpose of ordinary resale at a profit. He had no special customer in view. The lot was to become a part of his usual trade stock.

The form of order in detinue cases for the delivery of goods is, in substance, this: "It is this day adjudged that the plaintiff do have a return of the chattels in the statement of claim mentioned and described (here set out description) or recover against the defendant their value (here set out value) ... and damages for their detention": see the observations of Rowlatt J in *Bailey v. Gill*, [1919] 1 KB 41, 42. By Order XLVIII., r. 1, however, the Court has power to direct that execution shall issue for the delivery of the goods, without giving to the defendant the option to retain the property upon payment of the assessed value. Now in the case before me, the plaintiff desires to secure a warrant for the compulsory and specific delivery of the chairs to him: see *Benjamin on Sale*, 6th ed., at 1121 (n.). I do not doubt that upon the purchase of specific items in lot 145 the plaintiff gained the property in such items: see *Tarling v. Baxter* (1827), 6 B. & C. 360 and s. 18 of the Sale of Goods Act, 1893. *Prima facie*, therefore, he would be entitled to possession on payment or tender of the price. Here the plaintiff was willing to pay the price, and it seems clear that the defendant waived a formal legal tender. The defendant did not object to the cheque as a cheque, inasmuch as the plaintiff's credit was perfectly good: see *Polglass v. Oliver* (1831), 2 Cr. & J 15, and *Jones v. Arthur* (1890), 8 Dowl. PC 442, and *Roscoe's Nisi Prius*, 19th ed., at 594. Tender divests lien (see *Martindale v. Smith* (1841), 1 QB 389), and I will assume that waiver of tender will produce the same result as actual tender in divesting a defendant of his right to assert a vendor's lien: see the cases at 886-89 of

Benjamin on Sale, 6th ed. It therefore follows that the plaintiff here was entitled to launch his action of detinue: see *Benjamin on Sale*, 6th ed., at 1120 and 1081.

But at this point there arise other considerations. In *Chinery v. Viall* (1860), 5 HN 288 it was laid down that as between buyer and seller the buyer cannot recover larger damages by suing in tort instead of contract: see too *Benjamin on Sale*, 6th ed., at 1080 (z.). Bearing *Chinery v. Viall* in mind, it is necessary next to mention s. 52 of the Sale of Goods Act, 1893, which provides that in any action for breach of contract to deliver specific or ascertained goods the Court may, if it thinks fit, on the application of the plaintiff, direct by its judgment that the contract shall be performed specifically without giving the defendant the option of retaining the goods on payment of damages. It has been held that s. 52 applies to all cases where the goods are ascertained, whether the property therein has passed to the buyer or not: see *Per* Parker J in *Jones v. Earl of Tankerville*, [1909] 2 Ch. 440, at 445. It seems clear that the discretionary provisions of s. 52 cannot be consistent with an absolute right of a plaintiff to an order for compulsory delivery under a detinue judgment in such a case as the present. How, then, does the law stand as to detinue? In my view the power of the Court in an action of detinue rests upon a footing which fully accords with s. 52 of the Sale of Goods Act, 1893. In *Whitely, Ld. v. Hilt*, [1918] 2 KB 808, at 819 (an action of detinue) Swinfen Eady MR said: "The power vested in the Court to order the delivery up of a particular chattel is discretionary, and ought not to be exercised when the chattel is an ordinary article of commerce and of no special value or interest, and not alleged to be of any special value to the plaintiff, and where damages would fully compensate. In equity, where a plaintiff alleged and proved the money value of the chattel, it was not the practice of the Court to order its specific delivery: see *Dowling v. Betjamann*" (1862), 2 J & H 544 in its several parts. In the present case the goods in question were ordinary articles of commerce and of no special value of interest, and no grounds exist for any special order for delivery. The judgment should be limited to damages for breach of contract. The plaintiff in his evidence said that the chairs were worth from 70*l.* to 80*l.* With this I agree. I assess the damages at the sum of 15*l.*

Judgment for plaintiff.

NOTE

Actions in detinue were abolished in England by the Torts (Interference with Goods) Act 1977, s. 2(1), and replaced by an omnibus remedy in s. 3 for "wrongful interference" with goods. Section 3(2) enables the following relief to be given against the person in possession or control of the goods:

> (a) an order for delivery of the goods, and for payment of any consequential damages, or
>
> (b) an order for delivery of the goods, but giving the defendant the alternative of paying damages by reference to the value of the goods, together in either alternative with payment of any consequential damages, or
>
> (c) damages.

Section 1 defines "wrongful interference" or "wrongful interference with goods" as meaning

    (a) conversion of goods (also called trover),

    (b) trespass to goods,

    (c) negligence so far as it results in damage to goods or to an interest in goods,

    (d) subject to section 2, any other tort so far as it results in damage to goods or to an interest in goods.

The Replevin Remedy

OLRC Sales Report

at 439-40

At common law, an action in replevin only lay where the person suing for replevin alleged a wrongful seizure of his goods. The restitutionary remedy could not be invoked where the seller merely refused to deliver goods that had been in his lawful possession all the time. In this respect, the Replevin Act [RSO 1970, c. 412] appears to have made an important change in the law. Section 2 of the Act permits the owner or other person capable of maintaining an action for damages to bring a replevin action for the recovery of goods "wrongfully ... detained," as well as for those wrongfully distrained or otherwise wrongfully taken. Assuming that title has passed to the buyer, it would appear that he is entitled to compel delivery by a recalcitrant seller by following the prescribed procedure, and it has been so held on a number of occasions.

The reason for the extension in Ontario of the common law remedy of replevin is obscure, and it is not clear whether the draftsman appreciated a potential conflict with the rules of specific performance and the action in detinue. Presumably, the extension reflects the judgment of the legislature that, where the person suing for replevin claims superior proprietary or possessory rights, the person resisting the order for replevin should not be given the option of paying damages. However this may be, it appears anomalous that a buyer to whom title has passed should be able to obtain relief in a replevin action, and yet not be able to obtain an order for specific performance under the Sale of Goods Act. The Replevin Act does not, however, fall within our terms or reference and we refrain from offering any recommendations for its amendment beyond drawing attention to this conflict.

NOTE

The Replevin Act, RSO 1980, c. 449, was repealed by the Courts of Justice Act, 1984, SO 1984, c. 11, and replaced by s. 117 of the latter Act, now RSO 1990, c. C-43, s. 104. Section 104 authorizes the court, on motion, to make an interim order for the recovery of possession of personal property where an action has been begun for the possession of such property. Section 104 applies to cases where it is alleged that the defendant is unlawfully detaining the property, as well as to cases where it is alleged the property was unlawfully taken from the plaintiff. The procedural mechanics for obtaining an interim order appear in Rule 44 of the Rules of Civil Procedure. Note carefully that under s. 104 the granting of such an order is discretionary with the court.

CHAPTER EIGHTEEN

Disclaimers and Limitations of Liability, Choice of Law and Jurisdictional Clauses, and Class Actions

INTRODUCTION

As will have been gathered from the preceding chapters, the buyer's position under the Sale of Goods Act is generally very favourable and if its provisions were mandatory the story would have a simple ending. In fact the real position is much more complex.

The complications are caused by the following factors. In the first place, the SGA provisions are only presumptive and can be freely varied or excluded by agreement between the parties (s. 53). Needless to say, sellers freely avail themselves of this right. Second, at the retail level the sale is frequently accompanied by some form of financing arrangement either directly between the buyer and the seller or between the buyer and a third party, with the seller only playing an indirect role. In either event, if the buyer's promissory note or the agreement evidencing the sale is held by a third party, the question arises whether the buyer is entitled to raise defences or claim a set-off because the goods are defective or the seller has committed some other breach of the sale agreement. In the consumer context there is yet another formidable barrier the buyer may have to surmount. If she cannot resolve her difficulties with the seller amicably, can she afford to litigate or are there other channels she can pursue to find a solution to his problem? The present chapter is primarily concerned with the effectiveness of disclaimer clauses; the problems created by the intervention of a third-party financer are dealt with in chapter 3 of volume II of the previous edition of this casebook. Unfortunately, space does not permit further treatment of the consumer's remedial and procedural problems beyond the discussion found *supra*, in chapters 3 and 16.

THE ROLE OF DISCLAIMER CLAUSES

It is a rare agreement in written form that does not contain a disclaimer or limitation of liability clause of some description. For a classification of the clauses, see OLRC Warranties Report, at 47, and OLRC Sales Report, at 462. In the retail field such clauses are usually coupled with a manufacturer's express warranty, which is frequently less favourable to the buyer than the statutory warranties and conditions usually displaced by the express warranty. See *supra*, chapters 9 and 10.

The judicial and legislative response to disclaimer clauses constitutes one of the most remarkable chapters in modern contract law. The story is told by Lord Denning, with his usual verve and style, in *Geo. Mitchell (Chesterhall) Ltd. v. Finney Lock Seeds Ltd.*, [1982] 3 WLR 1036 (CA). Before World War II, the courts mainly limited themselves to constructional techniques in trying to blunt the sharp edges of such clauses and legislation, which, though not unimportant, were restricted to a few discrete areas. The absence, until recently, of comprehensive legislation (and in Canada there is still no comprehensive legislation) and growing judicial concern no doubt account for the much more complex judicial reaction in the post-war period.

It was inevitable that some courts would seek a more explicit policing tool than was covertly provided by constructional techniques. Not surprisingly, in England Lord Denning led the crusade. It was he who first announced the proposition in *Karsales (Harrow) Ltd. v. Wallis*, [1956] 2 All ER 866 (CA), that no exception clause, however sweeping, could excuse a seller from fulfilling his fundamental obligations, thus ushering in the era of the doctrine of "fundamental breach" and "breach of a fundamental term."

The principal question before the House of Lords in the *Suisse Atlantique* case ([1967] 1 AC 361) was whether the doctrine was compatible with the concept of freedom of contract. The law lords said no and indicated that it was for Parliament, not the courts, to declare whether exception clauses should be banned on grounds of public policy. But the House of Lords had reckoned without Lord Denning's ingenuity and the ambiguities in several of the law lords' own judgments. Dicta by Lord Reid and Lord Upjohn in *Suisse Atlantique* were seized upon by Lord Denning and his fellow judges in *Harbutt's "Plasticine" Ltd. v. Wayne Tank & Pump Co. Ltd.*, [1970] 1 QB 447 (CA), to justify their conclusion that a disclaimer clause ceases to have effect once the agreement is terminated because of breach of the contract by the party seeking to rely on the clause. The gap was enlarged still further as a result of the decision in *Wathes (Western) Ltd. v. Austins (Menswear) Ltd.*, [1976] 1 Lloyd's Rep. 14 (CA), holding that the disclaimer clause was of no effect even though the innocent party had affirmed the contract after the breach. Thus, to all intents and purposes, *Suisse Atlantique* had been successfully undermined, a fact that Lord Denning skilfully demonstrated in the Court of Appeal's judgment in *Photo Production Ltd. v. Securicor Transport Ltd.*, [1978] 3 All ER 146. It was a challenge which the House of Lords could not and did not ignore in its judgment in *Photo Production Ltd.*, [1980] AC 837.

Prior to its reversal by the House of Lords, the doctrine of *Harbutt's "Plasticine"* only exerted a modest influence on appellate decisions in Canada. However, this made little difference because, with almost unfailing regularity, the courts managed to find, as a matter of construction, that the parties could not have intended the disclaimer clause to apply to the circumstances before them. No wonder then that some judges declared, prior to *Photo Production*, that "'the fundamental term' doctrine is 'alive and prospering' in Canada": *Heffron v. Imperial Parking Co.* (1974), 3 OR (2d) 722, at 731. See also *Murray v. Sperry Rand Corp.* (1979), 96 DLR (3d) 113, at 122 (Ont. HCJ). In England, much of the old learning on disclaimer clauses has become largely academic because of the provisions in the Unfair Contract Terms Act 1977 (now supplemented by the European Union Directive on Unfair Terms of April 5, 1993) applying a test of reasonableness in some cases (see ss. 2-4, 6(3), and (8)) and outlawing disclaimer clauses altogether in others (see ss. 6(1) and (2), and 7(2)). Outside the consumer sales area, there is no comparable legislation in Canada and the common law case law is still very relevant. *Photo Production* is still regularly cited but, prior to the 1989 decision of the Supreme Court of Canada in *Hunter Engineering Co. Inc. v. Syncrude Canada Ltd.*, reproduced below, Canadian courts were divided in their reactions. Some paid lip service to *Photo Production*, but continued to disregard disclaimer or limitation of liability clauses where the defendant had committed a fundamental breach of its obligations. See, for example, *Cathcart Inspection Services Ltd. v. Purolator Courier Ltd.* (1981), 128 DLR (3d) 227, aff'd. (1982) 139 DLR (3d) 371 (Ont. CA), *Thomas Equipment Ltd. v. Sperry Rand Can. Ltd.* (1982), 135 DLR (3d) 197 (NBCA), and the BC Court of Appeal's judgment in *Hunter Engineering*. The Supreme Court itself reintroduced the fundamental breach doctrine through the back door in its judgment in *Beaufort Realties (1964) Inc. v. Belcourt Construction (Ottawa) Ltd.*, [1980] 2 SCR 718. In other cases, such as *Gafco Enterprises Ltd. v. Schofield*, [1984] 4 WWR 135 (Alta. CA), reproduced below, and *Canadian Dominion Leasing Corp. v. Geo. A. Welch & Co.* (1981), 125 DLR (3d) 723 (Ont.), the disclaimer clause has been upheld even though the defendant may have committed a fundamental breach.

The Supreme Court's decision in *Hunter Engineering* arguably ushers in a new era for several reasons. First, both Dickson CJ and Wilson J in their elaborate judgments firmly embrace *Photo Production* and its requirement that exculpatory clauses be given a natural and unforced construction. Second, both judges rejected the doctrine of fundamental breach as a relevant element in the construction of such clauses although, somewhat anomalously, Wilson J was willing to retain a role for the doctrine in determining whether a disclaimer clause should be enforced in the light of the gravity of the breach committed by the defendant. Third, the two judges accepted unconscionability as a valid defence to an exculpatory clause that would otherwise be enforceable. This is the most explicit acknowledgment so far by the Supreme Court of the appropriateness of the unconscionability defence in this branch of commercial law. The judgments in *Hunter Engineering* are frequently cited in subsequent cases involving disclaimer clauses, but it is too early to assess their impact on Canadian law.

In the interests of space, the cases reproduced in the first part of this chapter are limited to the Supreme Court's judgment in *Hunter Engineering* and the Alberta Court of Appeal's judgment in *Gafco Enterprises Ltd. v. Schofield*.

JUDICIAL REACTIONS

Hunter Engineering Co., Inc. v. Syncrude Canada Ltd.

(1989), 57 DLR (4th) 321 (SCC)

[Syncrude purchased gearboxes for its tar sands extraction plant in Alberta under separate contracts governed by Ontario law, one with Hunter and another with Allis-Chalmers. Syncrude provided specifications detailing the intended use and purpose of the gearboxes, but not how they were to be constructed. The contracts with Hunter and Allis-Chalmers each contained an express warranty with a time limit. The contract with Allis-Chalmers also expressly excluded any other warranty "statutory or otherwise." After the expiry of the time-limit of the express warranties, the gear boxes failed because of a design defect in the welding of the gear boxes.

Syncrude repaired the gear boxes at its own expense and then brought action against the defendants for breach of implied conditions under the Ontario Sale of Goods Act. At trial Syncrude was successful against Hunter but failed against Allis-Chalmers. The British Columbia Court of Appeal held both defendants liable.

On further appeal and cross-appeal to the Supreme Court of Canada, all the judges were agreed that the welding design details were Hunter's responsibility, and that the failure of the gear boxes constituted a breach of s. 15(1) of the Ontario Act. Further, the presence of an express warranty did not exclude the statutorily implied condition. Wilson J held (McIntyre and L'Heureux-Dubé JJ concurring) that the breach did not amount to a fundamental breach of the sellers' obligations. All members of the court also agreed that a disclaimer or limitation of liability clause was not per se invalid because it involved a breach of the seller's fundamental obligations unless (per Dickson CJ, La Forest J concurring) it was unconscionable or unless (per Wilson J, L'Heureux-Dubé concurring) it ought not to be enforced in the circumstances of the breach. (As will be seen, Wilson J also accepted the defence of unconscionability although she gives it a different scope from Dickson CJ.)

The following extracts from the judgments of Dickson CJ and Wilson J deal with their treatment of the doctrine of fundamental breach.]

DICKSON CJ:

IV Fundamental Breach

It will now be convenient to consider the liability to Syncrude of Allis-Chalmers and in turn of Hunter US on the third party claim of Allis-Chalmers. The facts can be briefly stated. The purchase agreement contained in para. 8 a warranty modified, as stated earlier, to exclude statutory warranties or conditions. Paragraph 14 of the agreement read:

C. Paragraph 14—Limitation of Liability

Notwithstanding any other provision in this contract or any applicable statutory provisions neither the Seller nor the Buyer shall be liable to the other for special or consequential damages or damages for loss of use arising directly or indirectly from any breach of this contract, fundamental or otherwise or from any tortious acts or omissions of their respective employees or agents and in no event shall the liability of the Seller exceed the unit price of the defective product or of the product subject to late delivery.

The price of the 14 conveyor systems and accessories purchased from Allis-Chalmers was $4,166,464. The agreed cost of the repairs was $400,000; including prejudgment interest, $535,000. In the face of the contractual provisions, Allis-Chalmers can only be found liable under the doctrine of fundamental breach.

The Court of Appeal differed with the trial judge on the question of fundamental breach. At trial Gibbs J, at pp. 74-6, quoted with approval from the judgment of Stratton JA, as he then was, in *Sperry Rand Canada Ltd. v. Thomas Equipment Ltd.* (1982), 135 DLR (3d) 197 at pp. 205-6, 40 NBR (2d) 271 (NBCA), and the judgment of Harradence JA in *Gafco Enterprises Ltd. v. Schofield*, [1983] 4 WWR 135 at pp. 139-41, 25 Alta. LR (2d) 238, 23 BLR 9 (Alta. CA).

Applying the principle of these cases to the purchase order and the nature of the defect in the bull gears, Gibbs J concluded that the case for fundamental breach had not been made out. He said at pp. 77-8:

> As to the nature of the defect, in my opinion it was not so fundamental that it went to the root of the contract. The contract between the parties was still a contract for gearboxes. Gearboxes were supplied. They were capable of performing their function and did perform it for in excess of a year which, given the agreed time limitations, was the "cost free to Syncrude" period contemplated by the parties. It was conceded that the gearboxes were not fit for the service. However, the unfitness, or defect, was repairable and was repaired at a cost significantly less than the original purchase price. No doubt the bull gear is an important component of the gearbox but no more important than the engine in an automobile and in the *Gafco Ent.* case the failure of the engine was not a sufficiently fundamental breach to lead the Court to set aside the contract of sale. On my appreciation of the evidence Syncrude got what it bargained for … It has not convinced me that there was fundamental breach.

On appeal, Anderson JA reviewed a number of authorities including the judgment of Seaton JA in *Beldessi v. Island Equipment Ltd.* (1973), 41 DLR (3d) 147 (BCCA), and held that Allis-Chalmers was in fundamental breach because Syncrude was deprived of substantially the whole benefit of the contract.

In reaching that conclusion he said at p. 393:

> It follows that the cost of repair was not significantly less than the original purchase price but, on the contrary, the cost of repair constituted 86 per cent of the purchase price. Moreover, the expected life of a gearbox is 20 years. The expected life of a bull gear is at least ten years. The bull gear failed within less than two years after Syncrude's operations commenced.

He rejected as without merit the argument of counsel for Allis-Chalmers that Syncrude's contract with Allis-Chalmers was not just a "contract for gearboxes" but was rather a contract for the purchase of a package of 14 conveyor systems for a price of over $4,000,000, and viewed in relation to the total purchase price actually paid by Syncrude, the cost of repair of one component, whether it is considered to be the bull gear or the gearbox, was indeed "significantly less than the original purchase price."

Hunter US, ultimately liable on account of the third-party claim against it, submits that the British Columbia Court of Appeal was wrong on this branch of the case because the effect of its decision is to re-establish the doctrine of fundamental breach as a rule of law invalidating a clause limiting liability.

Counsel submits that in England, since *Suisse Atlantique Société d'Armement Maritime S.A. v. N.V. Rotterdamsche Kolen Centrale*, [1967] 1 AC 361, the doctrine of fundamental breach has been rejected as a rule of law invalidating exemption clauses. At p. 405, Lord Reid said: "In my view no such rule of law ought to be adopted." In commenting upon that decision, Professor P.S. Atiyah in his text, the *Sale of Goods*, 6th ed. (London: Pitman, 1980), at p. 157, says, "This was not in all respects an easy decision to understand ... ." With that statement I am in full agreement. Professor Atiyah continues:

> ... but the principal point to emerge from the *Suisse Atlantique* case was the firm and unanimous holding that the "doctrine" of fundamental breach is not a rule of law but merely a rule of construction. Parties are free to make whatever provision they desire in their contracts, but it is a rule of construction that an exemption clause does not protect a party from liability for fundamental breach. It follows that if the contract by express provision does protect a party from such a result and the court thinks that the provision was intended to operate in the circumstances which have occurred, the provision must be given full effect.

It was contended by Hunter US that, at bar, the Court of Appeal approached the matter by asking whether the warranty in the contract excluded liability for fundamental breach. Upon finding it did not, the Court of Appeal then found as a fact, contrary to the finding of fact made by the trial judge, that the breach was fundamental, and awarded the buyer the full amount of its claim.

It was submitted that by doing this, the Court of Appeal erroneously adopted the approach (as it did in *Beldessi v. Island Equipment Ltd.*, *supra*, upon which it relied so heavily in this case) that to be effective a limitation of liability clause must expressly exclude liability for fundamental breach. It was submitted this approach involves returning to the notion of treating fundamental breach as something which, as a rule of law, will displace the terms of the contract; to paraphrase Lord Bridge's decision in *George Mitchell (Chesterhall) Ltd. v. Finney Lock Seeds Ltd.*, [1983] 2 All ER 737 (HL) at p. 741: it reintroduces by the back door a doctrine which the *Suisse Atlantique* case, and cases following, had evicted by the front.

Allis-Chalmers adopted in its entirety the argument of Hunter US with respect to the fundamental breach issue. The argument in the factum of Allis-Chalmers was directed to the further question whether the Court of Appeal erred in failing to construe properly the warranty clause in ascertaining whether it applied to the instant breach.

Allis-Chalmers argued that the words of cl. 8 are clear and fairly susceptible of only one meaning, and the Court of Appeal erred in failing to give effect to them; instead of giving effect to the language of the contract, the Court of Appeal imported its own implied warranty and erroneously embarked on a consideration of whether cl. 8 was effective to eliminate the "essential undertaking of Allis-Chalmers to provide gearboxes capable of meeting the requirements of the extraction process." In proceeding in this fashion, the Court of Appeal in effect resurrected a term analogous to the implied statutory warranty of fitness for the purpose required, which the parties had expressly excluded. By importing this additional term into the contract the court rewrote the bargain which the parties had made for themselves.

Syncrude argues in response that the seller's fundamental obligation does not derive from, and is not dependent upon, the existence of express or implied warranties or conditions. It is inherent in the contract of sale.

. . .

The House of Lords' cases decided that liability for breach of a fundamental term may be excluded by a suitably worded exclusion clause. However, counsel contended that there is a rule of construction that exemption clauses must be very clearly worded if they are to be sufficient to exclude liability for fundamental breach. It was said that this approach to the construction of a contract was confirmed in this court in *Beaufort Realties (1964) Inc. v. Chomedey Aluminum Co. Ltd.* (1980), 116 DLR (3d) 193, [1980] 2 SCR 718, 13 BLR 119.

On the application of the principles to the present case, Syncrude asked the question whether Allis-Chalmers and Syncrude intended that Allis-Chalmers could supply gearboxes which were so fundamentally defective as to require complete replacement, or in this case, complete reconstruction, after 15 months' service, at Syncrude's sole cost. Syncrude would give a negative response to this question.

I have had the advantage of reading the reasons for judgment prepared by my colleague, Justice Wilson, in this appeal and I agree with her disposition of the liability of Allis-Chalmers. In my view, the warranty clauses in the Allis-Chalmers contract effectively excluded liability for defective gearboxes after the warranty period expired. With respect, I disagree, however, with Wilson J's approach to the doctrine of fundamental breach. I am inclined to adopt the course charted by the House of Lords in *Photo Production Ltd. v. Securicor Transport Ltd.*, [1980] AC 827, and to treat fundamental breach as a matter of contract construction. I do not favour, as suggested by Wilson J, requiring the court to assess the reasonableness of enforcing the contract terms after the court has already determined the meaning of the contract based on ordinary principles of contract interpretation. In my view, the courts should not disturb the bargain the parties have struck, and I am inclined to replace the doctrine of fundamental breach with a rule that holds the parties to the terms of their agreement, provided the agreement is not unconscionable.

The doctrine of fundamental breach in the context of clauses excluding a party from contractual liability has been confusing at the best of times. Simply put, the doctrine has served to relieve parties from the effects of contractual terms, excluding liability for deficient performance where the effects of these terms have seemed particularly harsh. Lord Wilberforce acknowledged this in *Photo Production*, at p. 843:

> 1. The doctrine of "fundamental breach" in spite of its imperfections and doubtful parentage has served a useful purpose. There was a large number of problems, productive of injustice, in which it was worse than unsatisfactory to leave exception clauses to operate.

In cases where extreme unfairness would result from the operation of an exclusion clause, a fundamental breach of contract was said to have occurred. The consequence of fundamental breach was that the party in breach was not entitled to rely on the contractual exclusion of liability but was required to pay damages for contract breach. In the doctrine's most common formulation, by Lord Denning in *Karsales (Harrow) Ltd. v. Wallis*, [1956] 1 WLR 936 (CA), fundamental breach was said to be a rule of law that operated regardless of the intentions of the contracting parties. Thus, even if the parties excluded liability by clear and express language, they could still be liable for fundamental breach of contract. This rule of law was rapidly embraced by both English and Canadian courts.

A decade later in the *Suisse Atlantique* case, the House of Lords rejected the rule of law concept in favour of an approach based on the true construction of the contract. The Law Lords expressed the view that a court considering the concept of fundamental breach must determine whether the contract, properly interpreted, excluded liability for the fundamental breach. If the parties clearly intended an exclusion clause to apply in the event of fundamental breach, the party in breach would be exempted from liability. In *B.G. Linton Construction Ltd. v. CNR Co.* (1974), 49 DLR (3d) 548, [1975] 2 SCR 678, [1975] 3 WWR 97, this court approved of the *Suisse Atlantique* formulation. The renunciation of the rule of law approach by the House of Lords and by this court, however, had little effect on the practice of lower courts in England or in Canada. Lord Denning quickly resuscitated the rule of law doctrine in *Harbutt's "Plasticine" Ltd. v. Wayne Tank & Pump Co. Ltd.*, [1970] 1 QB 447 (CA).

Finally, in 1980, the House of Lords definitively rejected the rule of law approach to fundamental breach in *Photo Production, supra*. In that case, the plaintiff, Photo Production, had contracted with Securicor, a company in the business of supplying security services, to provide four nightly patrols of its factory. At issue was whether Securicor was liable for a fire deliberately set by one of its employees in the course of his duties at the Photo Production factory. The contract between the two parties contained the following limitation clause (at p. 840):

> Under no circumstances shall the company [Securicor] be responsible for any injurious act or default by any employee of the company unless such act or default could have been foreseen and avoided by the exercise of due diligence on the part of the company as his employer; nor, in any event, shall the company be held responsible for (a) any loss suffered by the customer through burglary, theft, fire or any other cause, except insofar as such loss is solely attributable to the negligence of the company's employees acting within the course of their employment. ...

The limitation clause clearly excluded liability for fire with the exception of fires started by negligent acts. Securicor argued it could not be liable under the contract for the fire that occurred. Photo Production contended that Securicor was liable for the damage done to the factory under the doctrine of fundamental breach.

Lord Wilberforce rejected Photo Production's argument. He began by reviewing the fractured history of the doctrine of fundamental breach and then forecefully repudiated the rule of law concept. Lord Wilberforce reiterated the thoughts articulated in *Suisse Atlantique*, stating at pp. 842-3, he had no doubt as to

> ... the main proposition that the question whether, and to what extent, an exclusion clause is to be applied to a fundamental breach, or a breach of a fundamental term, or indeed to any breach of contract, is a matter of construction of the contract.

The policy behind this approach is stated by Lord Wilberforce at p. 843 as follows:

> At the stage of negotiation as to the consequences of a breach, there is everything to be said for allowing the parties to estimate their respective claims according to the contractual provisions they have themselves made, rather than for facing them with a legal complex so uncertain as the doctrine of fundamental breach must be. ...
>
> At the judicial stage there is still more to be said for leaving cases to be decided straightforwardly on what the parties have bargained for rather than on analysis, which becomes progressively more refined, of decisions in other cases leading to inevitable appeals.

Lord Wilberforce proceeded to examine the contract between Securicor and Photo Production to determine exactly what the parties had provided, at p. 846:

> As a preliminary, the nature of the contract has to be understood. Securicor undertook to provide a service of periodical visits for a very modest charge ... It would have no knowledge of the value of the plaintiffs' factory: that, and the efficacy of their fire precautions, would be known to the respondents. In these circumstances nobody could consider it unreasonable, that as between these *two equal parties* the risk assumed by Securicor should be a modest one, and that the respondents should carry the substantial risk of damage or destruction.
>
> The duty of Securicor was, as stated, to provide a service. There must be implied an obligation to use due care in selecting their patrolmen, to take care of the keys and, I would think, to operate the service with due and proper regard to the safety and security of the premises. The breach of duty committed by Securicor lay in a failure to discharge this latter obligation. Alternatively it could be put upon a vicarious responsibility for the wrongful act ... This being the breach, does condition 1 apply? It is drafted in strong terms, "under no circumstances" ... "any injurious act or default by any employee." *These words have to be approached with the aid of the cardinal rules of construction that they must be read contra proferentem and that in order to escape from the consequences of one's own wrongdoing, or that of one's servant, clear words are necessary, I think that these words are clear.* The respondents in facts [*sic*] relied upon them for an argument that since they exempted from negligence they must be taken as not exempting from the consequence of deliberate acts. But this is a perversion of the rule that if a clause can cover something other than negligence, it will not be applied to negligence. *Whether, in addition to negligence it covers other, e.g., deliberate, acts, remains a matter of construction requiring, of course, clear words. I am of the opinion that it does, and being free to construe and apply the clause, I must hold that liability is excluded.* (Emphasis added.)

Lord Diplock alluded to the importance of negotiated risk allocation at p. 851:

> My Lords, the reports are full of cases in which what would appear to be very strained constructions have been placed on exclusion clauses, mainly in what to-day would be called consumer contracts and contracts of adhesion. ... In commercial contracts negotiated between business-men capable of looking after their own interests and of deciding how risks inherent in the performance of various kinds of contract can be most economically borne (generally by insurance), it is, in my view, wrong to place a strained

construction upon words in an exclusion clause which are clear and fairly susceptible of one meaning only even after due allowance has been made for the presumption in favour of the implied primary and secondary obligations.

In *Beaufort Realties (1964) Inc., supra*, Ritchie J, delivering the judgment of this court, stated, at p. 196 DLR, p. 723 SCR:

> Stated bluntly, the difference of opinion as to the true intent and meaning of their Lordships' judgment in the *Suisse Atlantique* case centered around the question of whether a rule of law exists to the effect that a fundamental breach going to the root of a contract eliminates once and for all the effect of all clauses exempting or excluding the party in breach from rights which it would otherwise have been entitled to exercise, or whether the true construction of the contract is the governing consideration in determining whether or not an exclusionary clause remains unaffected and enforceable notwithstanding the fundamental breach. The former view was espoused by Lord Denning MR and is illustrated by his judgment which he delivered on behalf of the Court of Appeal in the *Photo Production* case, *supra* ...

and at p. 197 DLR, p. 725 SCR:

> It has been concurrently found by the learned trial judge and the Court of Appeal that art. 6 of this contract constituted an exclusionary or exception clause and Madam Justice Wilson adopted the same considerations as those which governed the House of Lords in the *Photo* case in holding that the question of whether such a clause was applicable where there was a fundamental breach was to be determined according to the true construction of the contract. I concur in this approach to the case.

As Wilson J notes in her reasons, Canadian courts have tended to pay lip service to contract construction but to apply the doctrine of fundamental breach as if it were a rule of law. While the motivation underlying the continuing use of fundamental breach as a rule of law may be laudatory, as a tool for relieving parties from the effects of unfair bargains, the doctrine of fundamental breach has spawned a host of difficulties; the most obvious is how to determine whether a particular breach is fundamental. From this very first step the doctrine of fundamental breach invites the parties to engage in games of characterization, each party emphasizing different aspects of the contract to show either that the breach that occurred went to the very root of the contract or that it did not. The difficulty of characterizing a breach as fundamental for the purposes of exclusion clauses is vividly illustrated by the differing views of the trial judge and the Court of Appeal in the present case.

The many shortcomings of the doctrine as a means of circumventing the effects of unfair contracts are succinctly explained by Professor Waddams (*The Law of Contracts*, 2nd ed. (Toronto: CLB Inc., 1984), at pp. 352-53):

> The doctrine of fundamental breach has, however, many serious deficiencies as a technique of controlling unfair agreements. The doctrine requires the court to identify the offending provision as an "exemption clause," then to consider the agreement apart from the exemption clause, to ask itself whether there would have been a breach of that part of the agreement and then to consider whether that breach was "fundamental."

These enquiries are artificial and irrelevant to the real questions at issue. An exemption clause is not always unfair and there are many unfair provisions that are not exemption clauses. It is quite unsatisfactory to look at the agreement apart from the exemption clause, because the exemption clause is itself part of the agreement, and if fair and reasonable a perfectly legitimate part. Nor is there any reason to associate unfairness with breach or with fundamental breach. …

More serious is the danger that suppression of the true criterion leads, as elsewhere, to the striking down of agreements that are perfectly fair and reasonable.

Professor Waddams makes two crucially important points. One is that not all exclusion clauses are unreasonable. This fact is ignored by the rule of law approach to fundamental breach. In the commercial context, clauses limiting or excluding liability are negotiated as part of the general contract. As they do with all other contractual terms, the parties bargain for the consequences of deficient performance. In the usual situation, exclusion clauses will be reflected in the contract price. Professor Waddams' second point is that exclusion clauses are not the only contractual provisions which may lead to unfairness. There appears to be no sound reason for applying special rules in the case of clauses excluding liability than for other clauses producing harsh results.

In light of the unnecessary complexities the doctrine of fundamental breach has created, the resulting uncertainty in the law, and the unrefined nature of the doctrine as a tool for averting unfairness, I am much inclined to lay the doctrine of fundamental breach to rest, and where necessary and appropriate, to deal explicitly with unconscionability. In my view, there is much to be gained by addressing directly the protection of the weak from over-reaching by the strong, rather than relying on the artificial legal doctrine of "fundamental breach." There is little value in cloaking the inquiry behind a construction that takes on its own idiosyncratic traits, sometimes at odds with concerns of fairness. This is precisely what has happened with the doctrine of fundamental breach. It is preferable to interpret the terms of the contract, in an attempt to determine exactly what the parties agreed. If on its true construction the contract excludes liability for the kind of breach that occurred, the party in breach will generally be saved from liability. Only where the contract is unconscionable, as might arise from situations of unequal bargaining power between the parties, should the courts interfere with agreements the parties have freely concluded. The courts do not blindly enforce harsh or unconscionable bargains and, as Professor Waddams has argued, the doctrine of "fundamental breach" may best be understood as but one manifestation of a general underlying principle which explains judicial intervention in a variety of contractual settings. Explicitly addressing concerns of unconscionability and inequality of bargaining power allows the courts to focus expressly on the real grounds for refusing to give force to a contractual term said to have been agreed to by the parties.

I wish to add that, in my view, directly considering the issues of contract construction and unconscionability will often lead to the same result as would have been reached using the doctrine of fundamental breach, but with the advantage of clearly addressing the real issues at stake. …

Turning to the case at bar, I am of the view that Allis-Chalmers is not liable for the defective gearboxes. The warranty provision of the contract between Allis-Chalmers and Syncrude clearly limited the liability of Allis-Chalmers' to defects appearing within one year from the date of placing the equipment into service. The trial judge found that the defects in the gearboxes did not become apparent until after the warranty of Allis-Chalmers had expired. It is clear, therefore, that the warranty clause excluded liability for the defects that materialized, and subject to the existence of any unconscionability between the two parties there can be no liability on the part of Allis-Chalmers. I have no doubt that unconscionability is not an issue in this case. Both Allis-Chalmers and Syncrude are large and commercially sophisticated companies. Both parties knew or should have known what they were doing and what they had bargained for when they entered into the contract. There is no suggestion that Syncrude was pressured in any way to agree to terms to which it did not wish to assent. I am therefore of the view that the parties should be held to the terms of their bargain and that the warranty clause freed Allis-Chalmers from any liability for the defective gearboxes.

WILSON J:

. . .

(iii) *Fundamental breach*

Fundamental breach has been the subject of many judicial definitions. It has been described as "a breach going to the root of the contract" (*Suisse Atlantique Société d'Armement Maritime S.A. v. N.V. Rotterdamsche Kolen Centrale*, [1967] 1 AC 361 (HL), *per* Lord Reid at p. 399) and as one which results "in performance totally different from what the parties had in contemplation" (*R.G. McLean Ltd. v. Canadian Vickers Ltd.* (1970), 15 DLR (3d) 15 at p. 20, [1971] 1 OR 207 (CA), *per* Arnup JA). In *Canso Chemicals Ltd. v. Canadian Westinghouse Co. Ltd.* (1974), 54 DLR (3d) 517, 10 NSR (2d) 306 (CA), MacKeigan CJNS gave nine different definitions from leading Canadian and United Kingdom cases. The definitional uncertainty that has pervaded this area of the law is further illustrated by Fridman, *Law of Contract in Canada*, 2nd ed. (1986), at p. 531, and the cases cited therein.

The formulation that I prefer is that given by Lord Diplock in *Photo Production Ltd. v. Securicor Transport Ltd.*, [1980] AC 827 (HL). A fundamental breach occurs "Where the event resulting from the failure by one party to perform a primary obligation has the effect of depriving the other party of *substantially the whole benefit* which it was the intention of the parties that he should obtain from the contract" (p. 849). (Emphasis added.) This is a restrictive definition and rightly so, I believe. As Lord Diplock points out, the usual remedy for breach of a "primary" contractual obligation (the thing bargained for) is a concomitant "secondary" obligation to pay damages. The other primary obligations of both parties yet unperformed remain in place. Fundamental breach represents an exception to this rule for it gives to the innocent party an additional remedy, an election to "put an end to all primary obligations of both parties remaining unperformed" (p. 849). It seems to me that this exceptional remedy should be available only in circumstances where the foundation of the contract has been undermined, where the very thing bargained for has not been provided.

I do not think the present case involves a fundamental breach. The trial judge had this to say on the question at pp. 77-8:

> As to the nature of the defect, in my opinion it was not so fundamental that it went to the root of the contract. The contract between the parties was still a contract for gearboxes. Gearboxes were supplied. They were capable of performing their function and did perform it for in excess of a year which, given the agreed time limitations, was the "cost free to Syncrude" period contemplated by the parties. It was conceded that the gearboxes were not fit for the service. However, the unfitness, or defect, was repairable and was repaired at a cost significantly less than the original purchase price. No doubt the bull gear is an important component of the gearbox but no more important than the engine in an automobile and in the *Gafco Ent.* case the failure of the engine was not a sufficiently fundamental breach to lead the Court to set aside the contract of sale. On my appreciation of the evidence Syncrude got what it bargained for from Stephens-Adamson. It has not convinced me that there was fundamental breach.

The Court of Appeal, in overturning this finding, seems to have been influenced by two factors: that the repair cost was 85% of the original contract price and that the gear which should have lasted ten years failed after less than two. I will deal with each of these factors in turn.

There is an obvious conflict between the judgments below over the relationship between the size of the contract and the cost of repairs. The Court of Appeal treated the contract for the gearboxes as a discrete transaction in coming to its conclusion. The trial judge, however, was influenced by the fact that the overall contract with Allis-Chalmers was for 14 conveyor systems, only four of which contained extraction gearboxes. The total cost of these systems was in excess of $4M. It seems to me that the trial judge was right to take this into account. If he was, then Allis-Chalmers breached only one aspect of its contract with Syncrude, one "primary obligation." Although the gears were obviously an important component of the conveyor system, their inferior performance did not have the effect of depriving Syncrude of "substantially the whole benefit of the contract" to use Lord Diplock's phrase. The cost of repair was only a small part of the total cost.

Syncrude bargained for and received bull gears. Clearly, they were not very good gears. They were not reasonably fit for the purposes they were intended to serve. But they did work for a period of time and were repairable. There are numerous cases in which serious but repairable defects in machinery of various kinds have been found not to amount to fundamental breach. In *Gafco Enterprises Ltd. v. Schofield*, [1983] 4 WWR 135, 25 Alta. LR (2d) 238, 43 AR 262 (CA), a case relied on by Gibbs J in this case, the purchaser bought a second-hand car for $12,000 which immediately required some $4,000 worth of engine repairs. Harradence JA held that the defects "do not amount to a breach going to the root of the contract. They are repairable, albeit at some expense" (p. 267 AR). Similarly, in *Peters v. Parkway Mercury Sales Ltd.* (1975), 58 DLR (3d) 128, 10 NBR (2d) 703 (CA), a transmission failure shortly after the expiration of a 30-day warranty on a used car was found not to be a fundamental breach. Hughes CJNB said at p. 711 NBR:

> In my view the car which the defendant sold the plaintiff was not essentially different in character from what the parties should have had in contemplation. Although the car was in poorer condition than either party probably knew, I do not think the defects

amounted to "such a congeries of defects as to destroy the workable character of the machine" and consequently the plaintiff's claim for a declaration that there has been a fundamental breach entitling him to rescission if [*sic*] the contract fails.

In *Keefe v. Fort* (1978), 89 DLR (3d) 275, 27 NSR (2d) 353 (SCAD), another case involving a faulty but repairable car, Pace JA said at p. 279 that "the doctrine of fundamental breach was never intended to be applied to situations where the parties have received substantially what they had bargained for."

In the present case the Court of Appeal relied on its own prior judgment in *Beldessi v. Island Equipment Ltd.* (1973), 41 DLR (3d) 147 (BCCA), which it said was "very similar" to this one (p. 390). *Beldessi*, however, involved a log skidding machine which, despite numerous repairs, never worked properly. It was therefore similar to *R.G. McLean Ltd. v. Canadian Vickers Ltd.*, *supra*, in which a printing press could not be made to function adequately. It seems to me that the present case is more akin to those cited above where the purchaser got a poor, but none the less repairable, version of what it contracted for. I do not think that in these circumstances it can be said that the breach undermined the entire contractual setting or that it went to the very root of the contract. It was not, in other words, fundamental. I would therefore allow the appeal by Allis-Chalmers on this issue.

However, if I am wrong in this and the breach by Allis-Chalmers is properly characterized as fundamental, the liability of Allis-Chalmers would, in my view, be excluded by the terms of the contractual warranty.

Prior to 1980, in both the United Kingdom and in Canada, there were two competing views of the consequences of fundamental breach. One held that there was a rule of law that a fundamental breach brought a contract to an end, thereby preventing the contract breaker from relying on any clause exempting liability. This view was most closely identified with Lord Denning in the English Court of Appeal: see *Karsales (Harrow) Ltd. v. Wallis*, [1956] 1 WLR 936 (CA); *Harbutt's "Plasticine" Ltd. v. Wayne Tank & Pump Co. Ltd.*, [1970] 1 QB 447 (CA). The other view was that exemption clauses should be construed by the same rules of contract interpretation whether a fundamental breach had occurred or not. Whether or not liability was excluded was to be decided simply on the construction of the contract: see *Suisse Atlantique*, *supra*; *Traders Finance Corp. v. Halverson* (1968), 2 DLR (3d) 666 (BCCA); *R.G. McLean Ltd. v. Canadian Vickers Ltd.*, *supra*.

In England the issue was unequivocally resolved by the House of Lords in favour of the construction approach in the *Photo Production* case. ...

. . .

The construction approach to exclusionary clauses in the face of a fundamental breach affirmed in *Photo Production* was adopted by this court as the law in Canada in *Beaufort Realties (1964) Inc. v. Chomedey Aluminum Co. Ltd.* (1980), 116 DLR (3d) 193, [1980] 2 SCR 718, 13 BLR 119. The court did not, however, reject the concept of fundamental breach. The respondent entered into a construction contract with Beaufort in which it agreed to waive all liens for work and materials provided in the event of a failure to make payments. Such a failure took place and Justice Ritchie had no difficulty in concluding that the failure constituted a fundamental breach. He adopted Lord Wilberforce's construction approach to the exclusion clause and stated at p. 197 DLR, p. 725 SCR, "that the question of whether such a clause was applicable where there was a fundamental breach was to be determined according to the true construction of the contract."

As Professor Waddams noted (see (1981), 15 UBC Law Rev. 189) shortly after this court's decision in *Beaufort Realties*:

> ... the Supreme Court of Canada followed the House of Lords in holding that there is
> no rule of law preventing the operation of exclusionary clauses in cases of fundamental
> breach of contract. The effect of such clauses is now said to depend in each case on the
> true construction of the contract.

Thus, the law in Canada on this point appears to be settled. Some uncertainty, however, does remain primarily with regard to the application of the construction approach. Some decisions of our courts clearly follow the construction approach in both theory and practice. In *Hayward v. Mellick* (1984), 5 DLR (4th) 740, 45 OR (2d) 110, 2 OAC 161 (CA), for example, Weatherston JA noted that as "the courts of this province adopted the doctrine from the English courts, I think we should now follow their lead in rejecting it as a rule of law" (p. 749 DLR, p. 168 OAC). Even when the exclusion clause in issue was "strictly construed" Weatherston JA recognized that "it would be too strained a construction of the disclaimer clause to say that it applies only to representations that are not negligent. I think that effect must be given to it ... ." He went on to hold that the exclusion clause in that case was sufficient to cover any breach of contract.

Commentators seem to be in agreement, however, that the courts, while paying lip service to the construction approach, have continued to apply a modified "rule of law" doctrine in some cases. Professor Fridman in *Law of Contract in Canada*, 2d ed. (1986), has suggested at p. 558 that:

> Under the guise of "construction," some courts appear to be utilizing something very
> much akin to the "rule of law" doctrine. What Canadian courts may be doing is to apply
> a concept of "fair and reasonable" construction in relation to the survival of the exclu-
> sion clause after a fundamental breach, and the application of such a clause where the
> breach in question involves not just a negligent performance of the contract, but the
> complete failure of the party obliged to fulfil the contract in any way whatsoever.

Professor Ogilvie, in a review of Canadian cases decided shortly after *Photo Production*, including *Beaufort Realties* itself, argues that the rule of law approach "has been replaced by a substantive test of reasonableness which bestows on the courts at least as much judicial discretion to intervene in contractual relationships as fundamental breach ever did": see Ogilvie, "The Reception of *Photo Production Ltd. v. Securicor Transport Ltd.* in Canada: *Nec Tamen Consumebatur*" (1982), 27 McGill LJ 424 at p. 441.

Little is to be gained from a review of the recent cases which have inspired these comments. Suffice it to say that the law in this area seems to be in need of clarification. The uncertainty might be resolved in either of two ways. The first way would be to adopt *Photo Production* in its entirety. This would include discarding the concept of fundamental breach. The courts would give effect to exclusion clauses on their true construction regardless of the nature of the breach. Even the party who had committed a breach such that the foundation of the contract was undermined and the very thing bargained for not provided could rely on provisions in the contract limiting or excluding his or her liability. The only relevant question for the court would be: on a true and natural construction of the provisions of the contract did the parties, *at the time the contract was made*, succeed in excluding liability? This approach would have the merit of importing greater simplicity into the law and consequently greater certainty into commercial dealings, although the results of enforcing such exclusion clauses could be harsh if the parties had not adequately anticipated or considered the possibility of the contract's disintegration through fundamental breach.

The other way would be to import some "reasonableness" requirement into the law so that courts could refuse to enforce exclusion clauses in strict accordance with their terms if to do so would be unfair and unreasonable. One far-reaching "reasonableness" requirement which I would reject (and which I believe was rejected in *Beaufort Realties* both by this court and the Ontario Court of Appeal) would be to require that the exclusion clause be *per se* a fair and reasonable contractual term in the contractual setting or bargain made by the parties. I would reject this approach because the courts, in my view, are quite unsuited to assess the fairness or reasonableness of contractual provisions as the parties negotiated them. Too many elements are involved in such an assessment, some of them quite subjective. It was partly for this reason that this court in *Beaufort Realties* and the House of Lords in *Photo Production* clearly stated that exclusion clauses, like all contractual provisions, should be given their natural and true construction. Great uncertainty and needless complications in the drafting of contracts will obviously result if courts give exclusion clauses strained and artificial interpretations in order, indirectly and obliquely, to avoid the impact of what seems to them *ex post facto* to have been an unfair and unreasonable clause.

I would accordingly reject the concept that an exclusion clause in order to be enforceable must be *per se* a fair and reasonable provision at the time it was negotiated. The exclusion clause cannot be considered in isolation from the other provisions of the contract and the circumstances in which it was entered into. The purchaser may have been prepared to assume some risk if he could get the article at a modest price or if he was very anxious to get it. Conversely, if he was having to pay a high price for the article and had to be talked into the purchase, he may have been concerned to impose the broadest possible liability on his vendor. A contractual provision that seems unfair to a third party may have been the product of hard bargaining between the parties and, in my view, deserves to be enforced by the courts in accordance with its terms.

It is, however, in my view an entirely different matter for the courts to determine *after a particular breach has occurred* whether an exclusion clause should be enforced or not. This, I believe, was the issue addressed by this court in *Beaufort Realties*. In *Beaufort* this court accepted the proposition enunciated in *Photo Production* that no rule of law invalidated or extinguished exclusion clauses in the event of fundamental breach but rather that they should be given their natural and true construction so that the parties' agreement would be given effect. Nevertheless the court, in approving the approach taken by the Ontario Court of Appeal in *Beaufort*, recognized at the same time the need for courts to determine whether *in the context of the particular breach which had occurred* it was fair and reasonable to enforce the clause in favour of the party who had committed that breach even if the exclusion clause was clear and unambiguous. The relevant question for the court in *Beaufort* was: is it fair and reasonable in the context of this fundamental breach that the exclusion clause continue to operate for the benefit of the party responsible for the fundamental breach? In other words, should a party be able to commit a fundamental breach secure in the knowledge that no liability can attend it? Or should there be room for the courts to say: this party is now trying to have his cake and eat it too. He is seeking to escape almost entirely the burdens of the transaction but enlist the support of the courts to enforce its benefits.

It seems to me that the House of Lords was able to come to a decision in *Photo Production* untrammelled by the need to reconcile the competing values sought to be advanced in a system of contract law such as ours. We do not have in this country legislation comparable to the United Kingdom's *Unfair Contract Terms Act 1977*. I believe that in the absence of such legislation Canadian courts must continue to develop through the common law a balance between the obvious desirability of allowing the parties to make their own bargains and have them enforced through the courts and the obvious undesirability of having the courts used to enforce bargains in favour of parties who are totally repudiating such bargains themselves. I fully agree with the commentators that the balance which the courts reach will be made much clearer if we do not clothe our reasoning "in the guise of interpretation." Exclusion clauses do not automatically lose their validity in the event of a fundamental breach by virtue of some hard and fast rule of law. They should be given their natural and true construction so that the meaning and effect of the exclusion clause the parties agreed to at the time the contract was entered into is fully understood and appreciated. But, in my view, the court must still decide, having ascertained the parties' intention at the time the contract was made, whether or not to give effect to it in the context of subsequent events such as a fundamental breach committed by the party seeking its enforcement through the courts. Whether the courts address this narrowly in terms of fairness as between the parties (and I believe this has been a source of confusion, the parties being, in the absence of inequality of bargaining power, the best judges of what is fair as between themselves) or on the broader policy basis of the need for the courts (apart from the interests of the parties) to balance conflicting values inherent in our contract law (the approach which I prefer), I believe the result will be the same since the question essentially is: in the circumstances that have happened should the court lend its aid to A to hold B to this clause?

In affirming the legitimate role of our courts at common law to decide whether or not to enforce an exclusion clause in the event of a fundamental breach, I am not unmindful of the fact that means are available to render exclusion clauses unenforceable even in the absence of a finding of fundamental breach. While we do not have legislation comparable to the United Kingdom's *Unfair Contract Terms Act 1977*, we do have some legislative protection in this area. Six provinces prevent sellers from excluding their obligations under Sale of Goods Acts where consumer sales are concerned: see *Consumer Protection Act*, RSO 1980, c. 87, s. 34(1); *Consumer Protection Act*, RSNS 1967, c. 53, s. 20C, as amended by SNS 1975, c. 19; the *Consumer Protection Act*, RSM 1970, c. C200, s. 58(1); *Sale of Goods Act*, RSBC 1979, c. 370, s. 20; *Consumer Product Warranty and Liability Act*, SNB 1978, c. C-18.1, ss. 24-26 (except in so far as an exclusion is fair and reasonable); the *Consumer Products Warranties Act*, RSS 1978, c. C-30, ss. 8 and 11. In addition, some provinces have legislation dealing with unfair business practices which affects the application of some exclusion clauses: see *Business Practices Act*, RSO 1980, c. 55, s. 2(b)(vi); *Trade Practice Act*, RSBC 1979, c. 406, s. 4(e); *Unfair Trade Practices Act*, RSA 1980, c. U-3, s. 4(b), (d); the *Trade Practices Inquiry Act*, RSM 1987, c. T110, s. 2; the *Trade Practices Act*, SN 1978, c. 10, s. 6(d); *Business Practices Act*, SPEI 1977, c. 31, s. 3(b)(vi). Such legislation, in effect, imposes limits on freedom of contract for policy reasons.

There are, moreover, other avenues in our law through which the courts (as opposed to the legislatures) can control the impact of exclusion clauses in appropriate circumstances. Fundamental breach has its origins in that aspect of the doctrine of unconscionability which deals with inequality of bargaining power: see Waddams, "Unconscionability of Contracts" (1976), 39 *Mod. L Rev.* 369. As Professor Ziegel notes in "Comment" (1979), 57 *Can. Bar Rev.* 105 at p. 113:

> The initial impulse that prompted the development of the doctrine of fundamental breach was very sound insofar as it was designed to prevent overreaching of a weaker party by a stronger party. The impulse became distorted when subsequent courts confused cause and effect and treated the doctrine, albeit covertly, as expressing a conclusive rule of public policy regardless of the circumstances of the particular case. *What is needed therefore is a return to a regime of natural construction coupled with an explicit test of unfairness tailored to meet the facts of particular cases.* (Emphasis added.)

The availability of a plea of unconscionability in circumstances where the contractual term is *per se* unreasonable *and* the unreasonableness stems from inequality of bargaining power was confirmed in Canada over a century ago in *Waters v. Donnelly* (1884), 9 OR 391 (Ch.). It has been used on many subsequent occasions: see *Morrison v. Coast Finance Ltd.* (1965), 55 DLR (2d) 710, 54 WWR 257 (BCCA); *Harry v. Kreutziger* (1978), 95 DLR (3d) 231, 9 BCL 166 (CA); *Taylor v. Armstrong* (1979), 99 DLR (3d) 547, 24 OR (2d) 614 (HC).

While this is perhaps not the place for a detailed examination of the doctrine of unconscionability as it relates to exclusion clauses, I believe that the equitable principles on which the doctrine is based are broad enough to cover many of the factual situations which have perhaps deservedly attracted the application of the "fair and reasonable" approach in cases of fundamental breach. In particular, the circumstances surrounding the making of a consumer standard-form contract could permit the purchaser to argue that it would be unconscionable to enforce an exclusion clause. *Davidson v. Three Spruces Realty Ltd.* (1977), 79 DLR (3d) 481, [1977] 4 WWR 460 (BCSC), is a case in point. The plaintiff and others deposited valuables with the defendants. When they were stolen as a result of the latter's negligence a broad exclusion clause was pleaded. Anderson J found the defendant liable for fundamental breach and for misrepresentation but he also expressed the view that the exclusion clause should not be applied because of unconscionability.

. . .

As I have noted, this is not the place for an exposition of the doctrine of unconscionability as it relates to inequality of bargaining power and I do not necessarily endorse the approaches taken in the cases to which I have just referred. I use them merely to illustrate the broader point that in situations involving contractual terms which result from inequality of bargaining power the judicial armory has weapons apart from strained and artificial constructions of exclusion clauses. Where, however, there is no such inequality of bargaining power (as in the present case) the courts should, as a general rule, give effect to the bargain freely negotiated by the parties. The question is whether this is an absolute rule or whether *as a policy matter* the courts should have the power to refuse to enforce a clear and unambiguous exclusion clause freely negotiated by parties of equal bargaining power and, if so, in what circumstances? In the present state of the law in Canada the doctrine of fundamental breach provides one answer.

To dispense with the doctrine of fundamental breach and rely solely on the principle of unconscionability, as has been suggested by some commentators, would, in my view, require an extension of the principle of unconscionability beyond its traditional bounds of inequality of bargaining power. The court, in effect, would be in the position of saying that terms freely negotiated by parties of equal bargaining power were unconscionable. Yet it was the inequality of bargaining power which traditionally was the source of the unconscionability. What was unconscionable was to permit the strong to take advantage of the weak in the making of the contract. Remove the inequality and we must ask, wherein lies the unconscionability? It seems to me that it must have its roots in subsequent events, given that the parties themselves are the best judges of what is fair at the time they make their bargain. The policy of the common law is, I believe, that having regard to the conduct (pursuant to the contract) of the party seeking the indulgence of the court to enforce the clause, the court refuses. This conduct is described for convenience as "fundamental breach." It marks off the boundaries of tolerable conduct. But the boundaries are admittedly uncertain. Will replacing it with a general concept of unconscionability reduce the uncertainty?

When and in what circumstances will an exclusion clause in a contract freely negotiated by parties of equal bargaining power be unconscionable? If both fundamental breach and unconscionability are properly viewed as legal tools designed to relieve parties in light of subsequent events from the harsh consequences of an automatic enforcement of an exclusion clause in accordance with its terms, is there anything to choose between them as far as certainty in the law is concerned? Arguably, unconscionability is even less certain than fundamental breach. Indeed, it may be described as "the length of the Chancellor's foot." Lord Wilberforce may be right that parties of equal bargaining power should be left to live with their bargains regardless of subsequent events. I believe, however, that there is some virtue in a residual power residing in the court to withhold its assistance on policy grounds in appropriate circumstances. ...

The inadequacies of the constructional approach, without the support of an unconscionability doctrine, are neatly illustrated by the following case:

Gafco Enterprises Ltd. v. Schofield

[1983] 4 WWR 135 (Alta. CA)

HARRADENCE JA: The sole issue in this appeal is whether defects which appeared in a used car amount to a fundamental breach entitling the respondent to rescind the contract for sale of the car and sue for damages.

The facts of the case are essentially not in dispute. The appellant is a dealership specializing in the sale of high quality used cars, operating under the name of Select Auto. In August 1980 the appellant acquired a turbo-charged 1980 Volkswagen Scirocco with an odometer reading of 12,723 kilometres. Between that time and October 1980 the vehicle was driven a further 98 kilometres for demonstration purposes. In the first week of October 1980 the respondent visited the appellant's showroom and, while there, inquired about the Scirocco which was on display. He was told by the appellant's general manager that it was a "good car." During negotiations the general manager reduced the asking price and advised the respondent that this was solid value for his dollar.

On 24th October the respondent returned to the dealership and signed a form of agreement to purchase the car for the sum of $12,750. He paid a downpayment of $10 and agreed to pay a further $12,000 upon delivery, with the balance being due at a later date. At no time did the respondent take the car for a test drive, have it checked by an independent mechanic, or even have the engine started in his presence.

The purchase agreement is a two-page document. On the face of the document and in large, clear print were these words: "The purchaser understands and agrees that one of the following applies," followed by four alternative clauses. One of these clauses, clearly marked as applicable, says "no warranty of any kind."

Further, on the back of the agreement are 12 numbered paragraphs setting out the terms of the agreement. The appellant relies upon para. 6 which states:

> 6. Purchaser expressly waives the provisions of the Sale of Goods Act RSA 1970 [c. 327; now RSA 1980, c. S-2] and amendments thereto with respect to warranties, conditions and representations, whether express or implied or otherwise and warrants that no representations have been made by dealer, its servants or employees with respect to vehicle purchased to induce him to enter into this contract. Purchaser acknowledges he has inspected vehicle and it is satisfactory in every respect and hereby accepts same on an *"as is" basis* without warranty or guarantee except as provided in paragraph 8 hereof. (The italics are mine.)

Paragraph 8 provides:

> 8. This Purchase Agreement comprises the entire agreement made between the parties hereto and no other terms other than those contained herein, or statements of any nature not contained herein, regarding this agreement will be recognized.

Paragraph 10 provides:

> 10. It is expressly agreed that used goods are not warranted by dealer as to year, model, mileage or otherwise howsoever unless by authorized written warranty.

At the bottom of the front page of the agreement just above the signature it states:

> 1. I/We have read and understand the terms of the back hereof and agree to them as part of this Agreement as if they were printed above my/our signature.
>
> 2. The front and back of this order comprise the entire agreement effecting this purchase and no other agreement or understanding of any nature concerning the same has been made.

The general manager of the appellant gave evidence at trial that while they would normally give a warranty on a car of this age, it was their policy not to give a warranty on a turbo-charged car.

The respondent testified that he did not read the contract before signing it nor during the two weeks that the document was in his possession before completion. The respondent was given a photocopy of the agreement. On 7th November 1980 he returned to the dealership, paid the sum of $12,000 by way of a bank draft and agreed to pay the balance of $740 within a month. He was then given possession of the car.

Earlier that day employees of the appellant had moved the car out of the show-room and at that time discovered water leaking from the water pump. The respondent was advised that he could bring the car into the service department the next morning to have the water pump replaced at the appellant's expense. He was further advised that he should not drive the car too hard and that he might hear a "popping" noise as a result of the leak.

After driving the vehicle off the appellant's premises, the respondent heard a popping noise. Before he had gone three miles he began to hear a clangy or tinny noise emanating from the engine. Although he was aware that this noise was different from the one about which he had been warned, he did not stop the car as there were no other outward signs of a problem. He drove directly home, did not drive the car that evening, and returned the car to the service department the next morning. In total he drove the car approximately eight miles.

On the afternoon of 8th November 1980, the respondent was informed that there was serious engine damage which could cost up to $4,000 to repair. At this point the respondent decided to rescind the contract.

The cause of the damage to the engine was the deterioration of the "babbit," which is a soft white metal used to coat the bearings in the engine. The evidence at trial indicated that this type of deterioration results from friction heat when the oil barrier between the metal surfaces breaks down. An expert witness called by the respondents testified at the trial that a minor engine problem caused by deterioration of the babbit can become a major problem, displaying symptoms such as the clangy tinny noise in as little as thirty seconds. The same witness estimated that it would cost at least $2,600 to repair the Scirocco engine. There was no evidence to suggest that the damage was related to the leaking water pump. Indeed, the respondent did not prove precisely what caused the damage.

There is no suggestion of any fraud, bad faith or intentional misrepresentation on the part of the appellants and their employees.

Following unsuccessful attempts to resolve the dispute, the respondent brought an action for rescission of the contract and for damages. The appellant counterclaimed for $740, which was the amount owing on the contract.

The learned trial judge held that the defects in the car amounted to a fundamental breach of the contract which disentitled the seller from relying on the exemption clause and justified the buyer in treating the contract as at an end. He granted rescission of the contract, return of the amount paid and special damages of $2,930.15, being the amount of interest that the respondent was required to pay on a $12,000 bank loan which he had obtained in order to purchase the car.

On the argument of this appeal counsel for the respondent conceded that the exemption clause is part of the contract between the parties. It was not suggested that the clause should not be binding for want of notice or unreasonableness. Although the plaintiff pleaded the provisions of the Unfair Trade Practices Act, 1975 (2nd Sess.) (Alta.), c. 33 [now RSA 1980, c. U-3], in his statement of claim, it appears that this claim was not pursued. It was not raised on the appeal.

Thus the sole issue for determination in this appeal is whether the defects in the Scirocco amount to a fundamental breach which entitles the buyer to bring the contract to an end and to bring an action for damages.

. . .

[Harradence JA quoted from some of the judgments in *Suisse Atlantique* and *Photo Production*, and continued:]

I am, with respect, of the view that the learned trial judge erred in his approach to this case. While there may have been some doubt in the past, it is now clear that there is no substantive rule of law that nullifies an exclusionary clause where there has been a fundamental breach. The question of whether there has been a fundamental breach or whether an exclusionary clause is applicable to such a breach is to be determined according to a true construction of the entire contract, including any exclusionary or exemption clauses contained therein. Within the limits that exemption clauses should not be construed so as to deprive one party's stipulations of all contractual force, they must be given effect where their meaning is plain.

I now turn to a consideration of the facts of this case. Paraphrasing the words of Lord Wilberforce in *Suisse Atlantique, supra*, were it not for para. 6, the defect in the engine was sufficiently serious to justify the refusal of further performance by the respondent. Paragraph 6, however, is clearly and unambiguously worded in its waiver of the protection of the Sale of Goods Act. When taken together with the words "no warranty of any kind," which appear in block letters on the fact of the contract, and the disclaimer from warranties in para. 10, it is clear that the parties contemplated that the risk of defects in the automobile was to be borne by the buyer. This is not to imply that, in the words of Lord Wilberforce, the clause has so wide an ambit as in effect to deprive the seller's stipulations of all contractual force.

The defects in the Scirocco do not amount to a breach going to the root of the contract. They are repairable, albeit at some expense. Taking into consideration the wording of the contract, the value of the car, and the nature of the defects, I come to the same conclusion as Hughes CJNB in *Peters v. Parkway Mercury Sales Ltd.* (1975), 58 DLR (3d) 128, 10 NBR (2d) 703 at 711 (CA), who stated:

> In my view the car which the defendant sold the plaintiff was not essentially different in character from what the parties should have had in contemplation. Although the car was in poorer condition than either party probably knew, I do not think the defects amounted to "such a congeries of defects as to destroy the workable character of the machine" and consequently the plaintiff's claim for a declaration that there has been a fundamental breach entitling him to rescission of the contract fails.

That case involved the purchase of a used car which developed a transmission failure shortly after the expiration of a 30-day warranty.

In the result, I would allow the appeal and dismiss the respondent's action.

Appeal allowed.

QUESTIONS

1) If Harradence JA had applied a test of reasonableness to the disclaimer provisions in the above case, would he have reached a different decision? Was Mr. Schofield the author of his own misfortune? Should he have insisted on a minimum warranty? Should he at least have test-driven the car before he agreed to buy it, or was he entitled to rely on the general reputation of the dealership and the verbal representations made to him before the purchase?

2) The following cases illustrate both the continuing influence of old constructional techniques and the impact of *Hunter Engineering*. In *Kordas v. Stokes Seeds Ltd.* (1993), 96 DLR (4th) 129 (OCA), the plaintiff farmer, who had bought cabbage seed from the defendant, claimed that the defendant had not delivered the contractually agreed seeds. The judgment leaves it unclear whether there was a breach of the implied condition of description or only a breach of the implied condition of fitness or merchantability. In any event, Finlayson JA did not address these issues, but only whether the trial judge had been correct in finding that the defendant had breached a fundamental term of the contract. He held that the trial judge had been mistaken and cited *Hunter Engineering*, but it is not clear whether he appreciated that Dickson CJ had rejected the fundamental breach doctrine in its entirety as a basis for disallowing a disclaimer clause. On the issue of unconscionability, Finlayson JA found that the disclaimer clause was clear and unambiguous and that the parties were dealing at arm's length, and therefore rejected the defence. The judgment is very short on this point and, surprisingly, does not refer to the judgments of the Court of Appeal and the House of Lords in the *Finney Lock Seeds Ltd.* case cited and partially reproduced later in this chapter.

In *Gregorio v. Intrans-Corp.* (1994), 115 DLR (4th) 200 (OCA), the plaintiff bought a truck from the first defendant, a dealer, who ordered it from the second defendant, a Canadian-based subsidiary of the US manufacturer. The plaintiff signed a purchase order on May 12, 1984, and on August 2, 1984, received and signed for a written warranty which gave a limited 1-year warranty but excluded all implied warranties and any claims for consequential damages. The plaintiff paid the price on August 2, 1984, and the truck was delivered the following day. The truck's steering proved to be defective and, after numerous attempts by the defendants to correct the defects, the plaintiff sued for rescission of the contract and/or damages. He succeeded at trial.

On appeal by the defendants, the Ontario Court of Appeal found (1) that the contract was formed on May 12, 1984, and that there was no consideration to support the variation in its terms as allegedly embodied in the warranty document of August 2, 1984. The Court also held (2) that since the document only excluded "implied warranties," it did not cover the implied conditions of fitness and merchantability under the SGA; (3) that there was no ground for identifying the second defendant with the US manufacturer and that the latter was not liable in contract or tort to the plaintiff; and (4) that the second defendant was in breach of its s. 15 SGA statutory obligations to the dealer and therefore obliged to indemnify the dealer in respect of the dealer's liability to the plaintiff.

In view of its findings under (2) and (3), the Court did not deem it necessary to consider whether the exclusionary provisions in the warranty were also unenforceable on the grounds of unconscionability.

3) In *Geo. Mitchell (Chesterhall) Ltd. v. Finney Lock Seeds Ltd.*, [1982] 3 WLR 1036, at 1045, Lord Denning claimed the following results for the combined effect of the English Law Commission's two reports on Exemption Clauses and the enacting legislation in the Supply of Goods (Implied Terms) Act 1973 and the Unfair Contract Terms Act 1977:

> To my mind it heralds a revolution in our approach to exemption clauses; not only where they exclude liability altogether and also where they limit liability; not only in the specific categories in the Unfair Contract Terms Act 1977, but in other contracts too. Just as in other fields of law we have done away with the multitude of cases on "common employment," "last opportunity," "invitees" and "licensees" and so forth, so also in this field we should do away with the multitude of cases on exemption clauses. We should no longer have to go through all kinds of gymnastic contortions to get round them. We should no longer have to harass our students with the study of them. We should set about meeting a new challenge. It is presented by the test of reasonableness.

If this is a correct assessment of the British situation, why have the Canadian courts been so reluctant to apply an explicit fairness test? Do the provinces not have an equally impressive body of law reform reports and legislation (summarized below) indicating concern about unfair provisions? Does the fault lie with counsel in not citing these sources or is the reason due to judicial reluctance to be influenced by extra-judicial precedents and by legislation not directly addressed to the issue before the court?

3) *Problem.* S, a franchised dealer for M's equipment, sells a machine to B. When delivering the machine to B, S hands him the manufacturer's handbook containing M's express performance warranty. The warranty is of the usual "replace or repair" kind and excludes all other liabilities and obligations by M. S's written contract with B contains no express disclaimer clause and makes no reference to M's warranty. The machine proves to be defective. In an action by B, can S rely on the limited nature of M's warranty? Would

it make a difference if B had made use of M's warranty or if M's warranty purported to cover the dealer's liability as well as its own? See *Langille v. Scotia Gold Cooperative Limited* (1979), 33 NSR (2d) 157, esp. 166 *et seq.*, and *cf. Davis v. Chrysler Canada Ltd.* (1977), 26 NSR (2d) 410 and *International Terminal Operators Ltd. v. Miida Electronics Inc.*, [1986] 1 SCR 752. In England, contracts for the benefit of third parties are now statutorily enforceable as a result of the Contracts (Rights of Third Parties) Act, (UK) 1999, c. 31. However, the Act permits contracting parties to opt out of the Act. Many provincial law reform reports in Canada have recommended legislative recognition of third party contracts, but none of the recommendations has so far been implemented. However, in *Fraser River Pile & Dredge Ltd. v. Can-Dive Services Ltd.*, [1999] 2 SCR 108, after long-time adherence to the common law rule, the Supreme Court announced its readiness to make principled exceptions to the rule. See further John D. McCamus, "Loosening the Privity Fetters: Should Common Law Canada Recognize Contracts for the Benefit of Third Parties?" (2001), 35 *CBLJ* 173.

LEGISLATIVE REACTIONS

Summary of Provisions

The following is an outline of some of the more important statutory attempts to cope with disclaimer clauses:

A. General Regulation Of Unconscionability

1) *Sales legislation*
   a) UCC 2-302 gives courts the power to refuse to enforce a contract or clause that is unconscionable.
   b) The OLRC Sales Report recommended the adoption of a modified version of UCC 2-302, including a non-exhaustive list of factors which a court may consider in determining whether a clause is unconscionable. See pp. 160-62, Draft Bill s. 5.2. (The Law of Contract Amendment Report, c. 6 contains a parallel recommendation with respect to all types of contract.)
2) *Consumer legislation*
   a) Sections 2(2) and 3 of the BPA prohibit "unfair practices" which include "unconscionable consumer representations." Would an unconscionable exemption clause fall within this provision?

B. Specific Regulation Of Disclaimer Clauses

1) *Contract legislation*
   a) Section 2(1) of the Unfair Contract Terms Act 1977 (UK), c. 50, prohibits exclusionary clauses purporting to restrict or exclude liability for death or personal injury resulting from negligence. Section 2(2) provides for similar control over the exclusion of other types of loss or damage caused by negligence.

Section 3 of the Act prevents a party from disclaiming contractual liability based on standard form clauses or where the other party is a consumer, unless the disclaimer clauses satisfy the requirement of reasonableness (as amplified in s. 11).

Other relevant provisions in the Act are ss. 7 and 8.

2) *Sales legislation*

a) UCC 2-316 provides specific guidelines concerning the circumstances and manner in which express or implied warranties may be modified or excluded. UCC 2-719 governs the limitation or modification of contractual remedies. Consequential damages may be limited or excluded unless the limitation or exclusion is unconscionable. In cases of injury to the person by consumer goods, limitation of consequential damages is deemed to be *prima facie* unconscionable.

b) The Unfair Contract Terms Act 1977, s. 6, provides that liability for breach of the implied terms of title under the SGA (UK) and Supply of Goods (Implied Terms) Act 1973 cannot be excluded by contractual clauses; implied terms as to description or sample, quality or fitness *are* excludable as against a non-consumer, subject to an overriding requirement of reasonableness.

c) The OLRC Sales Report (at 227-35, 241) recommended against adoption of provisions similar to UCC 2-316, but supported adoption of a modified version of UCC 2-719(3). This deems an exclusion or limitation of damages for breach to be *prima facie* unconscionable in the case of injury to person. Clauses purporting to exclude liability for negligent acts, it recommended, should be controlled by the general unconscionability provision (*supra*). The Report also contains recommendations relating to disclaimer clauses and privity of contract.

3) *Consumer legislation*

a) Section 34(2) of the CPA provides that any term in a "consumer sale" which purports to vary or negative any of the implied conditions or warranties in the SGA is void. Examine the section carefully. Does it also apply to limitation of liability clauses or clauses otherwise limiting the buyer's remedies?

b) Section 8(1) of Bill 110, dealing with the sale of "consumer products," provided that "any warranty under this Act or the availability or scope of any remedy otherwise available for the breach thereof" could not be negatived, excluded, restricted, or diminished by terms of acknowledgments—any such term would be void if it purported to do so.

c) The Saskatchewan Consumer Protection Act, SS 1996 c. C-30.1, s. 44, provides that (with the exception of used consumer products) the provisions of the Act and regulations cannot be waived, limited, or modified in effect and that any agreement which attempts to do so is void. Section 45(3) provides that no express warranty shall "disclaim, exclude or limit a statutory warranty prescribed by section 48."

d) Section 2(3) of the New Brunswick Consumer Product Warranty and Liability Act, SNB 1978, c. C-18.1, as am., provides that the Act applies "notwithstanding any agreement, notice, disclaimer, waiver, acknowledgment or other thing to the contrary." Sections 24-26 govern the exclusion of warranties and remedies. In the case of a contract for the sale or supply of a consumer product, an agreement excluding or restricting remedies provided by the Act for breach of express warranties is subject to an overriding requirement of reasonableness and fairness. Remedies provided for breach of any part of an express warranty which forms part of the description of a consumer product cannot be excluded or restricted (s. 25(4)). Section 26 deals with the situation of a buyer acting in the course of a business and permits the exclusion or restriction of any warranty or remedy provided by the Act but such agreement is ineffective with respect to any "consumer loss" for which the seller would be liable if no such agreement had been made.

e) Section 10 of the Quebec Consumer Protection Act, SQ 1978, c. 9, as am., provides that: "Any stipulation whereby a merchant is liberated from the consequences of his own act or the act of his representatives is prohibited." Section 44 prohibits exclusion clauses in a "conventional warranty" unless "clearly indicated in separate and successive clauses."

Which of the above approaches do you prefer? What are the relevant weaknesses of the various attempts to control the use of disclaimer clauses? There is a dearth of authority interpreting and applying the above provisions of the Canadian consumer legislation. Why should this be so? For an early decision applying the disclaimer clause provisions in the Saskatchewan Conditional Sales Act (see now RSS 1978, c. C-25, as am.), see *Relland Motors Ltd. v. Foy* (1959), 20 DLR (2d) 558 (Sask. CA).

C. Disclaimer Clauses in Particular Types of Sale Agreement

The agricultural machinery and farm implement acts of the prairie provinces (later joined by PEI) have long regulated the use of disclaimer clauses in sale agreements for this type of product. For the details, see OLRC Warranties Report, at 96-100.

Judicial Application

R.W. Green Ltd. v. Cade Bros. Farms

[1978] 1 Ll. L. Rep. 602 (QB)

[The sellers, who were seed potato merchants, had over a period of years done a considerable volume of business with the buyers, who carried on a substantial farming business. The sales were subject to the sellers' standard conditions of sale which were based on a standard form of conditions produced by the National Association of Seed Potato Merchants in collaboration with the National Farmers Union.

In January 1974 the buyers ordered twenty tons of uncertified King Edward potatoes at a price of £28 per ton. The potatoes were delivered to the buyers' farm on February 5, 1974. On February 18 the buyers complained to the sellers about the condition of the potatoes, but the sellers persuaded the buyers that although the potatoes looked dull and there was a bit of gangrene, the percentage was within accepted limits of tolerance.

The sellers were mistaken and, after the potatoes were planted, it became obvious that they were inherently unhealthy. On October 9, 1974, an official report was obtained and this revealed that the potatoes were infected with a virus which could only be detected by examination of the growing crop in the previous season.

As a result of this infection the crop was very poor and the buyers suffered a heavy loss of profit.

The sellers brought action claiming £2,273 in respect of the seed potatoes they had sold the buyers. The buyers admitted the debt but raised a counterclaim for the loss of profits they had suffered. By way of defence to the counterclaim the sellers relied on clause 5 of the conditions of sale, which read as follows:

> If the Purchaser considers he has grounds for rejection of the Seed notwithstanding that the goods have passed in transit from the point of loading, he shall, if requested by the Seller clear the goods and take all necessary measures to mitigate damage or loss without prejudice to the claim of either party. Time being the essence of this Contract, however, notification of rejection, claim or complaint must be made to the Seller, giving a statement of the grounds for such rejection, claim or complaint within three days (within ten days in the case of rejection, claim or complaint specifically in respect of Skinspot, Gangrene or Dry Rot) after the arrival of the Seed at its destination. The place of rejection is the place of delivery in all cases. Notwithstanding the foregoing it shall not be competent to the Purchaser to reject, claim or complain for any reason unless the Seed Potatoes shall have been properly stored during the period after their arrival at their destination. The Seller shall replace any Seed properly rejected by the Purchaser unless otherwise agreed. It is specifically provided and agreed that compensation and damages payable under any claim or claims arising out of this contract under whatsoever pretext shall not under any circumstances amount in aggregate to more than the contract price of the potatoes forming the subject of the claim or claims.]

GRIFFITHS J: The crop that was grown was of poor quality and fetched only £14.50 per ton, and was unfit for pre-packing. The market price of a healthy crop was £29.50 per ton, to which must be added a pre-packing profit of £7.41 per ton. Some small allowance must be made for the fact that even in a healthy crop not all the potatoes are fit for pre-packing. These basic facts are taken from the evidence of the defendants' accountant and the Cade brothers, and I accept it. After the arithmetic has been done, it shows a total loss of profit on the crop of £5822.00.

Can the farmers recover these damages from the seed potato merchants? The first ground upon which they rely in their pleadings depends upon establishing that Mr. Richardson sold the seed potatoes as corresponding to the original sample he produced in September, 1973, and further, that he gave Mr. Stanley Cade an oral warranty that the seed potatoes were as good as the others and would produce just as good results. On my findings of fact that way of putting the case fails. I find that there was no such oral warranty and that it was not a sale by sample related to the original 100 tons.

Alternatively the defendants rely upon the implied terms that the seed potatoes were of merchantable quality and were reasonably fit for their purpose—s. 14, Sale of Goods Act, 1893. As the consignment was infected with potato virus Y at the time of sale, they were not reasonably fit for growing a crop of potatoes; nor were they of merchantable quality. The plaintiffs do not seek to argue that there were no breaches of these two implied terms, but say that they are relieved of the liability to pay damages by virtue of cl. 5 of their conditions of sale.

On the pleadings the defendants disputed that this sale was made subject to the plaintiffs' standard conditions of sale, but in the light of Mr. Stanley Cade's frank admission that he understood that all his business with the plaintiffs was done upon their standard trading conditions, this line of defence has no longer been pursued. However, although the defendants concede that the sale was subject to the plaintiffs' standard conditions, they say that cl. 5 does not protect the plaintiffs from the consequences of their breaches. Firstly, they say that it would not be fair or reasonable to allow the plaintiffs to rely upon cl. 5 in the circumstances of this case, and they rely upon s. 55, sub-ss. (4) and (5) of the Sale of Goods Act, 1893, as amended by s. 4 of the Supply of Goods (Implied Terms) Act, 1973. Secondly they say that in any event, upon its true construction, cl. 5 is of no application to the latent defect such as the presence of virus Y disease in these potatoes. Thirdly, and finally, they say that the plaintiffs were in fundamental breach of the contract or alternatively in breach of a fundamental term of the contract, and thus not entitled to rely upon cl. 5 of the contract of sale.

This contract, like any commercial contract, must be considered and construed against the background of the trade in which it operates. The plaintiffs' conditions are based upon a standard form of conditions produced by the National Association of Seed Potato Merchants. They are used by a large majority of seed potato merchants and, apart from amendments to accommodate a change to metrication, they have been in use in their present form for over 20 years. They have evolved over a much longer period as the result both of trade practice and discussions between the Association and the National Farmers' Union. They are therefore not conditions imposed by the strong upon the weak; but are rather a set of trading terms upon which both sides are apparently content to do business.

It is also important to have in mind the distinction between certified and uncertified seed. The Ministry of Agriculture provides a service whereby its inspectors will inspect a potato crop during the growing season, and if it appears healthy will issue a certificate to that effect. There are various grades of certificate indicating the percentage of virus infected plants in the growing crop, ranging from an H certificate based on a tolerance of 2 per cent., to an FS certificate, based on a tolerance of 0.001 per cent. If a farmer buys certified seed, he pays a little more for it to cover the costs of the inspection and certification. The certificate cannot be an absolute guarantee that the seed will not be infected, but according to Mr. Cook it is on the whole a fairly reliable system, and I have no doubt provided a very real safeguard against buying an infected batch of seed. The farmer who buys uncertified seed does not have this safeguard which is provided by the independent examination of the Ministry, and must as a general rule by taking a greater risk of buying infected seed, but of course he gets it at a cheaper price.

With these considerations in mind, I now look at cl. 5; it is headed "REJECTION AND CLAIMS" and it reads: [see statement of facts].

On my findings no complaint was made about the potatoes until 13 days after delivery. The plaintiffs therefore say that the claim is out of time and barred by the condition that it must be made within three, or in certain cases 10, days of delivery. The plaintiffs' directors, in their evidence, explained that such a term was necessary in the trade because potatoes are a very perishable commodity and may deteriorate badly after delivery, particularly if they are not properly stored. So it was thought reasonable to give the farmer three days to inspect and make his complaint, and in the case of certain specific types of damage which might take longer to become apparent, 10 days. This appears to me to be a very reasonable requirement in the case of damage that is discoverable by reasonable inspection. But the presence of virus Y in the potatoes was not discoverable by inspection, and the complaint that was made did not relate to this defect, which neither the farmer nor the potato merchant suspected.

Section 55 sub-s. (4) of the Sale of Goods Act as amended by s. 4 of the Supply of Goods (Implied Terms) Act, 1973, provides as follows:

> In the case of a contract for sale of goods, any term of that or any other contract exempting from all or any of the provisions of section 13, 14 or 15 of this Act shall be void in the case of a consumer sale and shall, in any other case, not be enforceable to the extent that it is shown that it would not be fair or reasonable to allow reliance on the term.

Sub-section 5 provides:

> In determining for the purposes of subsection 4 above whether or not reliance on any such term would be fair or reasonable regard shall be had to all the circumstances of the case and in particular to the following matters; [—and then, by provision (d):—] Where the term exempts from all or any of the provisions of section 13, 14 or 15 of this Act if some condition is not complied with, whether it was reasonable at the time of the contract to expect that compliance with that condition would be practicable.

At the time this contract was made no one would expect it to have been practicable for the farmer to complain of virus Y in the potatoes within three days of delivery, for the simple reason that he would not know of its presence. It would therefore, in my judgment, not be fair or reasonable that this claim should be defeated because no complaint was made within three or 10 days of delivery. I therefore declare that that part of cl. 5 is unenforceable in this action and provides no defence to the plaintiffs.

Is the claim to be limited to the contract price of the potatoes? Mr. Harvey submits that upon its true construction, cl. 5 applies only to patent defects; he argues that as that part of the condition that deals with notification of complaints could only have been intended to apply to patent—that is, to reasonably discoverable—defects, it follows that the limitation of the damages in the latter part of the condition must also be similarly restricted to patent defects. I cannot accept this construction. In the first place I doubt if, as a matter of construction, the parts of the condition dealing with complaints is restricted to patent defects; it appears, as drafted, to cover all complaints, but the Court has avoided the harsh consequences of this construction by declaring it unenforceable pursuant to its statutory power. However, even assuming that it should be construed as limited to complaints in respect of patent defects, I can see no reason to read a similar restriction into the very wide wording of the final sentence of the condition, which I now repeat:

> … It is specifically provided and agreed that compensation and damages payable under any claim or claims arising out of this contract under whatsoever pretext shall not under

any circumstances amount in aggregate to more than the contract price of the potatoes forming the subject of the claim or claims.

This is clear language, easily intelligible, and I do not believe that any farmer who read it would say to himself "Ah; now that only applies to patent defects."

Furthermore, it is made clear by the terms of cl. 3(a) that the condition is intended to cover defects not patent at the time of delivery, for that condition provides:

Seed potatoes sometimes develop diseases after delivery. It being impossible to ascertain the presence of such diseases by the exercise of reasonable skill and judgment the Seller cannot accept any responsibility should any disease develop after delivery other than as provided under clause 5.

In my judgment, as a matter of construction cl. 5 limits the defendants' claim to the contract price of the potatoes.

Should I exercise my discretion under s. 55, as amended, of the Sale of Goods Act and declare it to be unenforceable, because it would not be fair or reasonable to let the plaintiffs rely upon it?

I have considered the matters to which I am particularly directed to have regard by s. 55(5), in so far as they are relevant in this case. The parties were of equal bargaining strength; the buyer received no inducement to accept the term. True, it appears that he could not easily have bought potatoes without this term in the contract, but he had had the protection of the National Farmers' Union to look after his interests as the contract evolved and he knew that he was trading on these conditions.

No moral blame attaches to either party; neither of them knew, nor could be expected to know, that the potatoes were infected. There was of course a risk; it was a risk that the farmer could largely have avoided by buying certified seed, but he chose not to do so. To my mind the contract in clear language places the risk in so far as damage may exceed the contract price, on the farmer. The contract has been in use for many years with the approval of the negotiating bodies acting on behalf of both seed potato merchants and farmers, and I can see no grounds upon which it would be right for the Court to say in the circumstances of this case that such a term is not fair or reasonable.

[Griffiths J proceeded to deal with, and to dismiss, counsel's argument that because the defendants had committed a fundamental breach of their contractual obligations they should not be entitled to rely on cl. 5 to limit their liability in respect of them. He concluded:]

Furthermore, it appears to me that now Parliament has given the Judge a discretion to declare such a clause unenforceable if he thinks that it is not fair and reasonable, there will in the future be little need to resort to the doctrine of the fundamental breach in this type of action, and that the Court should not strain to give an artificially restricted meaning to an exclusion clause when it has the other remedy close at hand to do justice between the parties.

Judgment for plaintiff.

NOTE

Section 55(4) of the amended British Sale of Goods Act 1893 has now been replaced by ss. 6(2) and 11 of the Unfair Contract Terms Act 1977. None of the Canadian common law provinces has so far adopted an unconscionability provision similar to s. 55(4). Is this fatal? Could the doctrine be adopted judicially, as it has been in other parts of contract law, or by analogy with the statutory powers in s. 2 of the BPA? Can statutes serve as a source of judicial law? On these questions see further Ziegel, Comment on *Green v. Cade Bros. Farms* (1979), 57 *Can. Bar Rev.* 105.

George Mitchell (Chesterhall) Ltd. v. Finney Lock Seeds Ltd.

[1983] 2 AC 803

LORD BRIDGE OF HARWICH: My Lords, the appellants are seed merchants. The respondents are farmers in East Lothian. In December 1973 the respondents ordered from the appellants 30lb. of dutch winter white cabbage seeds. The seeds supplied were invoiced as "Finney's Late Dutch Special." The price was £201 60. "Finney's Late Dutch Special" was the variety required by the respondents. It is a Dutch winter white cabbage which grows particularly well in the area of East Lothian where the respondents farm, and can be harvested and sold at a favourable price in the spring. The respondents planted some 63 acres of their land with seedlings grown from the seeds supplied by the appellants to produce their cabbage crop for the spring of 1975. In the event, the crop proved to be worthless and had to be ploughed in. This was for two reasons. First, the seeds supplied were not "Finney's Late Dutch Special" or any other variety of Dutch winter white cabbage, but a variety of autumn cabbage. Secondly, even as autumn cabbage the seeds were of very inferior quality.

The issues in the appeal arise from three sentences in the conditions of sale endorsed on the appellants' invoice and admittedly embodied in the terms on which the appellants contracted. For ease of reference it will be covenient to number the sentences. Omitting immaterial words they read as follows:

> 1. In the event of any seeds or plants sold or agreed to be sold by us not complying with the express terms of the contract of sale ... or any seeds or plants proving defective in varietal purity we will, at our option, replace the defective seeds or plants, free of charge to the buyer or will refund all payments made to us by the buyer in respect of the defective seeds or plants and this shall be the limit of our obligation.

> 2. We hereby exclude all liability for any loss or damage arising from the use of any seeds or plants supplied by us and for any consequential loss or damage arising out of such use or any failure in the performance of or any defect in any seeds or plants supplied by us or for any other loss or damage whatsoever save for, at our option, liability for any such replacement or refund as aforesaid.

> 3. In accordance with the established custom of the seed trade any express or implied condition, statement or warranty, statutory or otherwise, not stated in these conditions is hereby excluded.

I will refer to the whole as "the relevant condition" and to the parts as "clauses 1, 2 and 3" of the relevant condition.

The first issue is whether the relevant condition, on its true construction in the context of the contract as a whole, is effective to limit the appellants' liability to a refund of £201 60, the price of the seeds ("the common law issue"). The second issue is whether, if the common law issue is decided in the appellants' favour, they should nevertheless be precluded from reliance on this limitation of liability pursuant to the provisions of the modified section 55 of the Sale of Goods Act 1979 which is set out in paragraph 11 of Schedule 1 to the Act and which applies to contracts made between May 18, 1973, and February 1, 1978 ("the statutory issue").

The learned trial judge, Parker J, [1981] 1 Lloyd's Rep. 476, at 480, on the basis of evidence that the seeds supplied were incapable of producing a commercially sale-able crop, decided the common law issue against the appellants on the ground that "what was supplied ... was in no commercial sense vegetable seed at all" but was "the delivery of something wholly different in kind from that which was ordered and which the defendants had agreed to supply." He accordingly found it unnecessary to decide the statutory issue, but helpfully made some important findings of fact, which are very relevant if that issue falls to be decided. He gave judgment in favour of the respondents for £61,513 78 damages and £30,756 00 interest. Nothing now turns on these figures, but it is perhaps significant to point out that the damages awarded do not represent merely "loss of anticipated profit," as was erroneously suggested in the appellants' printed case. The figure includes, as Mr. Waller very properly accepted, all the costs incurred by the respondents in the cultivation of the worthless crop as well as the profit they would have expected to make from a successful crop if the proper seeds had been supplied.

In the Court of Appeal, the common law issue was decided in favour of the appellants by Lord Denning MR, [1983] QB 284, at 296 who said: "On the natural interpretation, I think the condition is sufficient to limit the seed merchants to a refund of the price paid or replacement of the seeds." Oliver LJ, [1983] QB 284, at 305, 306, decided the common law issue against appellants primarily on the ground akin to that of Parker J, albeit somewhat differently expressed. Fastening on the words "agreed to be sold" in clause 1 of the relevant condition, he held that the clause could not be construed to mean "in the event of the seeds sold or agreed to be sold by us not being the seeds agreed to be sold by us." Clause 2 of the relevant condition he held to be "merely a supplement" to clause 1. He thus arrived at the conclusion that the appellants had only succeeded in limiting their liability arising from the supply of seeds which were correctly described as "Finney's Late Dutch Special" but were defective in quality. As the seeds supplied were not "Finney's Late Dutch Special," the relevant condition gave them no protection. Kerr LJ, [1983] QB 284, at 313, in whose reasoning Oliver LJ also concurred, decided the common law issue against the appellants on the ground that the relevant condition was ineffective to limit the appellants' liability for a breach of contract which could not have occurred without negligence on the appellants' part, and that the supply of the wrong variety of seeds was such a breach.

The Court of Appeal, however, were unanimous in deciding the statutory issue against the appellants.

[Lord Bridge proceeded to examine the reasoning of the members of the Court of Appeal on the proper construction of the disclaimer clauses, and expressed his agreement with Lord Denning's conclusion. He continued:]

The relevant subsections of the modified section 55 provide as follows:

(1) Where a right, duty or liability would arise under a contract of sale of goods by implication of law, it may be negatived or varied by express agreement ... but the preceding provision has effect subject to the following provisions of this section. ... (4) In the case of a contract of sale of goods, any term of that or any other contract exempting from all or any of the provisions of section 13, 14 or 15 above is void in the case of a consumer sale and is, in any other case, not enforceable to the extent that it is shown that it would not be fair or reasonable to allow reliance on the term. (5) In determining for the purposes of subsection (4) above whether or not reliance on any such term would be fair or reasonable regard shall be had to all the circumstances of the case and in particular to the following matters—(a) the strength of the bargaining positions of the seller and buyer relative to each other, taking into account, among other things, the availability of suitable alternative products and sources of supply; (b) whether the buyer received an inducement to agree to the term or in accepting it had an opportunity of buying the goods or suitable alternatives without it from any source of supply; (c) whether the buyer knew or ought reasonably to have known of the existence and extent of the term (having regard, among other things, to any custom of the trade and any previous course of dealing between the parties); (d) whether the term exempts from all or any of the provisions of section 13, 14, or 15 above if some condition is not complied with, whether it was reasonable at the time of the contract to expect that compliance with that condition would be practicable; (e) whether the goods were manufactured, processed, or adapted to the special order of the buyer. ... (9) Any reference in this section to a term exempting from all or any of the provisions of any section of this Act is a reference to a term which purports to exclude or restrict, or has the effect of excluding or restricting, the operation of all or any of the provisions of that section, or the exercise of a right conferred by any provision of that section, or any liability of the seller for breach of a condition or warranty implied by any provision of that section.

The contract between the appellants and the respondents was not a "consumer sale," as defined for the purpose of these provisions. The effect of clause 3 of the relevant condition is to exclude, inter alia, the terms implied by sections 13 and 14 of the Act that the seeds sold by description should correspond to the description and be of merchantable quality and to substitute therefor the express but limited obligations undertaken by the appellants under clauses 1 and 2. The statutory issue, therefore, turns on the words in subsection (4) "to the extent that it is shown that it would not be fair or reasonable to allow reliance on" this restriction of the appellants' liabilities, having regard to the matters referred to in subsection (5).

This is the first time your Lordships' House has had to consider a modern statutory provision giving the court power to override contractual terms excluding or restricting liability, which depends on the court's view of what is "fair and reasonable." The particular provision of the modified section 55 of the Act of 1979 which applies in the instant case is of limited and diminishing importance. But the several provisions of the Unfair Contract Terms Act 1977 which depend on "the requirement of reasonableness," defined in section 11 by reference to what is "fair and reasonable," albeit in a different context, are likely to come before the courts with increasing frequency. It may, therefore, be appropriate to consider how an original decision as to what is "fair and reasonable" made in the application of any of these provisions should be approached by an appellate court. It would not be accurate to describe such a decision as an exercise of discretion. But a decision under any of the provisions referred to will have this in common with the exercise of a discretion, that, in having regard to the various matters to which the modified section 55(5) of the Act of 1979, or section 11 of the Act of 1977 direct attention, the court must entertain a whole range of considerations, put them in the scales on one side or the other, and decide at the end of the day on which side the balance comes down. There will sometimes be room for a legitimate difference of judicial opinion as to what the answer should be, where it will be impossible to say that one view is demonstrably wrong and the other demonstrably right. It must follow, in my view, that, when asked to review such a decision on appeal, the appellate court should treat the original decision with the utmost respect and refrain from interference with it unless satisfied that it proceeded upon some erroneous principle or was plainly and obviously wrong.

Turning back to the modified section 55 of the Act of 1979, it is common ground that the onus was on the respondents to show that it would not be fair or reasonable to allow the appellants to rely on the relevant condition as limiting their liability. It was argued for the appellants that the court must have regard to the circumstances as at the date of the contract, not after the breach. The basis of the argument was that this was the effect of section 11 of the Act of 1977 and that it would be wrong to construe the modified section 55 of the Act as having a different effect. Assuming the premise is correct, the conclusion does not follow. The provisions of the Act of 1977 cannot be considered in construing the prior enactment now embodied in the modified section 55 of the Act of 1979. But, in any event, the language of subsections (4) and (5) of that section is clear and unambiguous. The question whether it is fair or reasonable to allow reliance on a term excluding or limiting liability for a breach of contract can only arise after the breach. The nature of the breach and the circumstances in which it occurred cannot possibly be excluded from "all the circumstances of the case" to which regard must be had.

The only other question of construction debated in the course of the argument was the meaning to be attached to the words "to the extent that" in subsection (4) and, in particular, whether they permit the court to hold that it would be fair and reasonable to allow partial reliance on a limitation clause and, for example, to decide in the instant case that the respondents should recover, say, half their consequential damage. I incline to the view that, in their context, the words are equivalent to "in so far as" or "in circumstances in which" and do not permit the kind of judgment of Solomon illustrated by the example. But for the purpose of deciding this appeal I find it unnecessary to express a concluded view on this question.

My Lords, at long last I turn to the application of the statutory language to the circumstances of the case. Of the particular matters to which attention is directed by

paragraphs (a) to (e) of section 55(5), only those in (a) to (c) are relevant. As to paragraph (c), the respondents admittedly knew of the relevant condition (they had dealt
with the appellants for many years) and, if they had read it, particularly clause 2, they
would, I think, as laymen rather than lawyers, have had no difficulty in understanding what it said. This and the magnitude of the damages claimed in proportion to the
price of the seeds sold are factors which weigh in the scales in the appellants' favour.

The question of relative bargaining strength under paragraph (a) and of the opportunity to buy seeds without a limitation of the seedsman's liability under paragraph
(b) were inter-related. The evidence was that a similar limitation of liability was universally embodied in the terms of trade between seedsmen and farmers and had been
so for very many years. The limitation had never been negotiated between representative bodies but, on the other hand, had not been the subject of any protest by the
National Farmers' Union. These factors, if considered in isolation, might have been
equivocal. The decisive factor, however, appears from the evidence of four witnesses
called for the appellants, two independent seedsmen, the chairman of the appellant
company, and a director of a sister company (both being wholly-owned subsidiaries
of the same parent). They said that it had always been their practice, unsuccessfully
attempted in the instant case, to negotiate settlements of farmers' claims for damages
in excess of the price of the seeds, if they thought that the claims were "genuine" and
"justified." This evidence indicated a clear recognition by seedsmen in general, and
the appellants in particular, that reliance on the limitation of liability by the relevant
condition would not be fair or reasonable.

Two further factors, if more were needed, weight the scales in favour of the
respondents. The supply of autumn, instead of winter, cabbage seeds was due to the
negligence of the appellants' sister company. Irrespective of its quality, the autumn
variety supplied could not, according to the appellants' own evidence, be grown commercially in East Lothian. Finally, as the trial judge found, seedsmen could insure
against the risk of crop failure caused by supplying the wrong variety of seeds without materially increasing the price of seeds.

My Lords, even if I felt doubts about the statutory issue, I should not, for the
reasons explained earlier, think it right to interfere with the unanimous original decision of that issue by the Court of Appeal. As it is, I feel no such doubts. If I were making
the original decision, I should conclude without hesitation that it would not be fair or
reasonable to allow the appellants to rely on the contractual limitation of their liability.

Appeal dismissed.

[Concurring judgments were delivered by the other law lords.]

NOTES

1) In the course of his judgment, Lord Bridge refers to the "important" distinction
drawn by Lord Fraser in *Securicor II (Ailsa Craig Fishing Co. v. Malvern Fishing Co.)*,
[1983] 1 WLR 964 (HL), between exclusion and limitation clauses, and implicitly supports Lord Fraser's view that the first type of clause should be construed more strictly
than the second? Is the distinction viable? Taking the *Geo. Mitchell* facts as an example,

was the plaintiff significantly better off because the agreement entitled him to a refund of the purchase price (£201.60) rather than excluding all liability?

2) How strong an inference can be drawn from the evidence in the present case that on other occasions, when the sellers received complaints about defective goods, they had attempted to settle them out of court if they thought the claims were justified? If the sellers did not intend to rely on the limitation clauses why did they put them in to begin with?

3) How should a court determine the issue of reasonableness if *neither* party can readily obtain insurance (or self-insure) against the type of loss that has occurred? What should the court do if *both* parties can insure for the loss and indeed have done so?

4) How important is the issue of the seller's negligence? In *Securicor I* the House of Lords appears to have discounted it in construing the exclusion clause. The issue of reasonableness was not before the House. However, several of the law lords made it clear that they still thought the clause was a reasonable one. If a seller can exclude its liability or reduce it to a nominal amount despite its negligence, what incentive does it have to exercise care? Should the seller perhaps be held liable for a percentage of the buyer's loss? (The question is of particular importance in the carrier and courier cases where the bailees have long been accustomed to limiting their liability to a nominal amount.)

CHOICE OF LAW AND JURISDICTIONAL CLAUSES, AND CLASS ACTIONS

In the evolving North American—indeed international—trade environment where it is as easy and almost as common for consumers to buy high unit goods and services outside Canada as it is to buy them domestically, consumers may face additional hurdles in enforcing warranty claims beyond the ubiquitous disclaimer clauses discussed in the preceding pages. One is the jurisdictional issue: will the consumer be able to sue the foreign supplier in the provincial courts? The contract itself may foreclose the question by providing that suit can only be brought at the supplier's place of business in the foreign state. The contract may also require all disputes between supplier and buyer to be resolved by arbitration and may also affect the buyer's right to bring a class action. The following case is a recent example of judicial treatment of these issues.

Rudder v. Microsoft Corp.

(1999), 40 CPC (4th) 394, 2 CPR (4th) 474 (Ont. SC)

WINKLER J: This is a motion by the defendant Microsoft for a permanent stay of this intended class proceeding. The motion is based on two alternative grounds, first that the parties have agreed to the exclusive jurisdiction, and venue, of the courts, in King County in the State of Washington in respect of any litigation between them, and secondly, that in any event, Ontario is not the appropriate forum for the conduct of this proceeding and that the service ex juris of the Statement of Claim ought to be set aside.

The Microsoft Network ("MSN"), is an online service, providing, inter alia, information and services including Internet access to its members. The service is provided to members, around the world, from a "gateway" located in the State of Washington through computer connections most often made over standard telephone lines.

The proposed representative plaintiffs in this action were subscriber members of MSN. Both are law school graduates, one of whom is admitted to the Bar in Ontario while the other worked as a legal researcher. They were associated with the law firm which originally represented the intended class. The plaintiffs claim under the Class Proceedings Act, 1992, SO, C.6 on behalf of a Canada-wide class defined as:

> All persons resident in Canada who subscribed for the provision of Internet access or information or services from or through MSN, The Microsoft Network, since September 1, 1995.

This class is estimated to contain some 89,000 MSN members across Canada.

The plaintiffs claim damages for breach of contract, breach of fiduciary duty, misappropriation and punitive damages in the total amount of $75,000,000.00 together with an accounting and injunctive relief. The plaintiffs allege that Microsoft has charged members of MSN and taken payment from their credit cards in breach of contract and that Microsoft has failed to provide reasonable or accurate information concerning accounts. The Statement of Claim was served on Microsoft at its offices in Redmond, Washington on January 5, 1998.

The contract which the plaintiffs allege to have been breached is identified by MSN as a "Member Agreement." Potential members of MSN are required to electronically execute this agreement prior to receiving the services provided by the company. Each Member Agreement contains the following provision:

> 15.1 This Agreement is governed by the laws of the State of Washington, U.S.A., and you consent to the exclusive jurisdiction and venue of courts in King County, Washington, in all disputes arising out of or relating to your use of MSN or your MSN membership.

The defendant relies on this clause in support of its assertion that the intended class proceeding should be permanently stayed.

Although the plaintiffs rely on the contract as the basis for their causes of action, they submit that the court ought not to give credence to the "forum selection clause" contained within. It is stated in support of this contention that the representative plaintiffs read only portions of the Member Agreement and thus had no notice of the forum selection clause. Alternatively, the plaintiffs contend, in any event, that the Washington courts are not appropriate for the conduct of this lawsuit.

I cannot accede to these submissions. In my view, the forum selection clause is dispositive and there is nothing in the factual record which persuades me that I should exercise my discretion so as to permit the plaintiffs to avoid the effect of the contractual provision. Accordingly, an order will go granting the relief sought by the defendant. My reasons follow.

Analysis and Disposition

Forum selection clauses are generally treated with a measure of deference by Canadian courts. Madam Justice Huddart, writing for the court in *Sarabia v. "Oceanic*

Mindoro" (1996), 4 CPC (4th) 11 (BCCA), leave to appeal denied [1997] SCCA No. 69, adopts the view that forum selection clauses should be treated the same as arbitration agreements. She states at 20:

> Since forum selection clauses are fundamentally similar to arbitration agreements, ... there is no reason for forum selection clauses not to be treated in a manner consistent with the deference shown to arbitration agreements. Such deference to forum selection clauses achieves greater international commercial certainty, shows respect for the agreements that the parties have signed, and is consistent with the principle of international comity.

Huddart JA further states at 21 that "a court is not bound to give effect to an exclusive jurisdiction clause" but that the choice of the parties should be respected unless "there is strong cause to override the agreement." The burden for a showing of a "strong cause" rests with the plaintiff and the threshold to be surpassed is beyond the mere "balance of convenience." The approach taken by Huddart JA is consistent with that adopted by courts in Ontario. (See *Holo-Deck Adventures Ltd. v. Orbotron Inc.* (1996), 8 CPC (4th) 376 (Gen. Div.); *Mithras Management Ltd. v. New Visions Entertainment Corp.* (1992), 90 DLR (4th) 726 (Ont. Gen. Div.).)

The plaintiffs contend, first, that regardless of the deference to be shown to forum selection clauses, no effect should be given to the particular clause at issue in this case because it does not represent the true agreement of the parties. It is the plaintiffs submission that the form in which the Member Agreement is provided to potential members of MSN is such that it obscures the forum selection clause. Therefore, the plaintiffs argue, the clause should be treated as if it were the fine print in a contract which must be brought specifically to the attention of the party accepting the terms. Since there was no specific notice given, in the plaintiffs' view, the forum selection clause should be severed from the Agreement which they otherwise seek to enforce.

The argument advanced by the plaintiffs relies heavily on the alleged deficiencies in the technological aspects of electronic formats for presenting the terms of agreements. In other words, the plaintiffs contend that because only a portion of the Agreement was presented on the screen at one time, the terms of the Agreement which were not on the screen are essentially "fine print."

I disagree. The Member Agreement is provided to potential members of MSN in a computer readable form through either individual computer disks or via the Internet at the MSN website. In this case, the plaintiff Rudder, whose affidavit was filed on the motion, received a computer disk as part of a promotion by MSN. The disk contained the operating software for MSN and included a multi-media sign up procedure for persons who wished to obtain the MSN service. As part of the sign-up routine, potential members of MSN were required to acknowledge their acceptance of the terms of the Member Agreement by clicking on an "I Agree" button presented on the computer screen at the same time as the terms of the Member Agreement were displayed.

. . .

I have viewed the Member Agreement as it was presented to Rudder during the sign-up procedure. All of the terms of the Agreement are displayed in the same format. Although there are certain terms of the Agreement displayed entirely in upper-case letters, there are no physical differences which make a particular term of the agreement more difficult to read than any other term. In other words, there is no fine print as that term would be defined in a written document. The terms are set out in plain language, absent words that are commonly referred to as "legalese." Admittedly, the entire Agreement cannot be displayed at once on the computer screen, but this is not materially different from a multi-page written document which requires a party to turn the pages. Furthermore, the structure of the sign-up procedure is such that the potential member is presented with the terms of membership twice during the process and must signify acceptance each time. Each time the potential member is provided with the option of disagreeing which terminates the process. The second time the terms are displayed occurs during the online portion of the process and at that time, the potential member is advised via a clear notice on the computer screen of the following:

> ... The membership agreement includes terms that govern how information about you and your membership may be used. To become a MSN Premier member, you must select "I Agree" to acknowledge your consent to the terms of the membership agreement. If you click "I Agree" without reading the membership agreement, you are still agreeing to be bound by all of the terms of the membership agreement, without limitation. ...

· · ·

It is plain and obvious that there is no factual foundation for the plaintiffs' assertion that any term of the Membership Agreement was analogous to "fine print" in a written contract. What is equally clear is that the plaintiffs seek to avoid the consequences of specific terms of their agreement while at the same time seeking to have others enforced. Neither the form of this contract nor its manner of presentation to potential members are so aberrant as to lead to such an anomalous result. To give effect to the plaintiffs' argument would, rather than advancing the goal of "commercial certainty," to adopt the words of Huddart JA in *Sarabia*, move this type of electronic transaction into the realm of commercial absurdity. It would lead to chaos in the marketplace, render ineffectual electronic commerce and undermine the integrity of any agreement entered into through this medium.

On the present facts, the Membership Agreement must be afforded the sanctity that must be given to any agreement in writing. The position of selectivity advanced by the plaintiffs runs contrary to this stated approach, both in principle and on the evidence, and must be rejected. Moreover, given that both of the representative plaintiffs are graduates of law schools and have a professed familiarity with Internet services, their position is particularly indefensible.

Having found that the terms of the Member Agreement, including the forum selection clause, bind the plaintiffs, I turn to a consideration of whether it is appropriate to exercise my discretion to override the forum clause agreed to by the parties. In my view, the submissions made by the defendant are compelling. On the facts of this case, it would not be appropriate for this court to permit the plaintiff to continue this action in Ontario contrary to the forum selection clause.

Simply put, I find that the plaintiffs have not met the burden of showing a "strong cause" as to why the forum selection clause should not be determinative. In *Sarabia*, Huddart JA referred to the English case, *"Eleftheria" (The) (Cargo Owners) v. "Eleftheria" (The)*, [1969] 2 All ER 641, as the decision most often followed in Canada in setting out the factors that a court will consider in determining whether it should exercise its discretion and refuse to enforce a forum selection clause in an agreement.

The factors to consider may be paraphrased as follows:

(1) in which jurisdiction is the evidence on issues of fact situated, and the effect of that on the convenience and expense of trial in either jurisdiction;

(2) whether the law of the foreign country applies and its differences from the domestic law in any respect;

(3) the strength of the jurisdictional connections of the parties;

(4) whether the defendants desire to enforce the forum selection clause is genuine or merely an attempt to obtain a procedural advantage;

(5) whether the plaintiffs will suffer prejudice by bringing their claim in a foreign court because they will be

    (a) deprived of security for the claim; or

    (b) be unable to enforce any judgment obtained; or

    (c) be faced with a time-bar not applicable in the domestic court; or

    (d) unlikely to receive a fair trial.

When these factors are applied within the factual matrix of this case, it is apparent that the plaintiffs cannot meet the threshold of a "strong cause." Most of the activities associated with the provision of services pursuant to the Member Agreements that are the subject of the allegations in the Statement of Claim are carried out in King County, Washington. This includes the business management of accounts of MSN members, member authentication, policy-making regarding member accounts, billing and customer service. All of the computers in which MSN content and information are contained are located in King County. The sheer size of the intended class means that there is a potential that voluminous amounts of billing statements and related information, which is most likely to be located in Washington, will be required as evidence. Furthermore, the MSN witnesses are located at the company's center of operations in King County.

Since I have found that the forum selection clause applies in this case, by operation of that clause the choice of law agreed to by the parties is the law of the State of Washington. Regardless of whether this action [were to be] tried in Ontario or elsewhere, the law to be applied would remain the same.

Microsoft has demonstrated substantial connection to the State of Washington, and in particular to King County. The plaintiffs, on the other hand, propose to represent a Canada-wide class whose connections to Ontario are not readily apparent on the evidence before the court. Class proceedings may be conducted under both the federal and state court systems in the State of Washington and while the test for certification may be somewhat more advantageous to the plaintiffs in Ontario, it is not sufficiently so as to permit me to ignore the other factors which clearly favour the defendant in this case. Moreover, in the interests of international comity, and in the absence of any evidence to the contrary, there is nothing to suggest that the plaintiffs would not receive a fair trial in the State of Washington. Indeed, considering that the defendant is resident there, it would be more advantageous to the plaintiffs, in respect of enforcement, if a judgment were obtained from a court in that jurisdiction.

Motion allowed.

Class Action Remedies

As we have tried to emphasize throughout this book, conferring protective rights on consumers is not sufficient. Just as important—perhaps more—is providing effective remedies for the enforcement of those rights. In theory, the consumer has a wide panoply of remedies at her disposal, but the reality is very different. Writing a letter or making a phone call may be ineffectual; litigating (even in the Small Claims Courts) is time consuming and expensive. Even if she wins, the consumer may only gain a Pyrrhic victory if, as often turns out to be the case, the defendant company is judgment proof.

In theory, federal and provincial consumer protection agencies have broad mandates, but differ widely in their willingness and capacity to intervene effectively on behalf of consumers. As indicated in chapter 1 of this casebook, over the past 20 years both provincial and federal governments have generally retreated from the high-profile activist position adopted by them in the 1960s and 1970s.

Class action legislation is important in this context because it puts a powerful new tool at the consumer's disposal—a tool that does not depend on governmental largesse for its effectiveness. Class actions (or, to give them their historical title, representative actions) were first introduced in Equity and were then absorbed in England and Canada in the general rules of practice and procedure. However, the courts interpreted the practice rules very narrowly and plaintiffs were additionally deterred by the cost factors. The Supreme Court of Canada's decision in *Naken v. General Motors Canada Ltd.*, [1983] 1 SCR 72, confirmed the Court's unwillingness to revitalize the rules; the Court also made it clear that it thought it was a job for the legislatures.

In the United States, Rule 23 of the Federal Rules of Civil Procedure led the way in facilitating class actions for consumer and other purposes, and in spelling out the detailed rules necessary for handling the sequential stages in what are often complex procedural and substantive issues. The seminal report of the Ontario Law Reform Commission, *Report on Class Actions* (Toronto: Queen's Printer, 1982), recommended a Rule 23 type model for enactment in Ontario. However, the OLRC's recommendation was not enacted until 1992. See now the Class Proceedings Act, SO 1992, c. 6. Meanwhile, Quebec had beaten Ontario to the draw by adopting its own Class Actions Law in 1978. British Columbia's Class Proceedings Act followed in 1995. These are the only three provinces so far with class action legislation. However, other provinces have recently indicated their interest in climbing on the bandwagon as well.[1]

---

1 A political science student may well wonder why the other provinces and the local bars have been so slow. Can you suggest a reason?

The effectiveness of a class action as a remedial tool depends heavily on a sympathetic judiciary. This is because under all the Acts a class action cannot proceed unless a court has first certified that the action is appropriate for class action treatment and that there are major issues of law of fact that are common to the members of the class and that can most efficiently be resolved in a class action format.

Canadian courts have in fact, and on the whole, responded very positively. As a result, class actions have become a popular and well-established remedial mechanism in the Canadian legal firmament. The reported cases cover a full spectrum of legal issues and involve public law issues as well as private law suits. For a sampling of the rich diversity, see Branch and McMaster, *Class Actions in Canada* (Canada Law, looseleaf), Appendix 1, "Summary of Class Certification Decisions." The Appendix lists 161 cases. As one would expect, contract, misleading advertising, product liability, and mass tort cases account for a high percentage of the total number, but competition law, securities law, and employment law are represented as well. In short, the potential is as great as plaintiff counsels' imagination and enterprise. The plaintiffs' bar is attracted to class litigation because the payoff for a successful action can be very high (in the Canadian Red Cross tainted blood litigation, court approved counsel fees ran to many millions of dollars) and because a large number of very small claims can be aggregated into one very large one.

Vehicle Purchase Agreement

(NAME OF DEALER)			DATE
PURCHASER	HOME PHONE NO	BUSINESS PHONE NO	OCCUPATION
ADDRESS	APT NO	CITY	PROVINCE	POSTAL CODE
DRIVER'S LIC NO.	INSURANCE CO	POLICY NO	EXPIRY DATE	INS. AGENT

I, THE PURCHASER, AGREE TO PURCHASE THE FOLLOWING VEHICLE FROM YOU, THE DEALER, ON THE TERMS SET OUT ON THE FRONT AND BACK OF THIS PAGE.

VEHICLE DESCRIPTION

☐ NEW ☐ USED	☐ POLICE VEHICLE ☐ TAXICAB	☐ DAILY RENTAL ☐ OTHER	YEAR	MAKE	MODEL	COLOUR
V.I.N			STOCK NO			SAFETY STANDARDS CERTIFICATE NO
IF MANUFACTURER WARRANTY APPLICABLE TIME IS MEASURED FROM	19	DISTANCE TRAVELLED	KM ☐ MI ☐	PURCHASER'S INITIAL

BASIC VEHICLE AND OPTIONS

BASIC VEHICLE (MSRP)

OPTIONAL EXTRAS

TOTAL BASIC VEHICLE AND OPTIONAL EXTRAS PRICE ▶

TOTAL ▶

PRE-DELIVERY EXPENSE

TOTAL SALE PRICE ▶

PURCHASE PRICE AND PAYMENT

TOTAL SALE PRICE	▶
FREIGHT	
FEDERAL AIR CONDITIONER TAX	
TAX FOR FUEL CONSUMPTION	
ADMINISTRATION FEE	

PRODUCT NAME AND DESCRIPTION	WARRANTY PERIOD		DATE OF COMMENCEMENT
	NO. OF MONTHS	NO. OF KMS	

TOTAL VEHICLE PRICE	▶
TRADE-IN ALLOWANCE	
TOTAL VEHICLE PRICE LESS TRADE-IN ALLOWANCE	
PROVINCIAL SALES TAX ON TOTAL VEHICLE PRICE LESS TRADE-IN ALLOWANCE	
G.S.T. ON TOTAL VEHICLE PRICE ($)	
LICENSE FEE ☐ TRANSFER ☐ NEW PLATES	
FUEL (INCLUDES G.S.T.)	

TRADE-IN DESCRIPTION AND LIEN DISCLOSURE

☐ DAILY RENTAL ☐ POLICE VEHICLE ☐ TAXICAB	V.I.N	
YEAR	MAKE	MODEL
COLOUR	G.S.T REGISTRANT NO.	G.S.T ON TRADE IN $
DISTANCE TRAVELLED ☐ KM ☐ MI	LIEN HOLDER	AMT OF OUTSTANDING LIENS $
REMARKS		

PAYOUT ON LIENS AGAINST TRADE-IN

G.S.T. REGISTRANT NO. ( )	
FUEL TAX CONSERVATION REBATE	
TOTAL PURCHASE PRICE	▶
DEPOSIT ☐ CASH ☐ CARD ☐ CHEQUE	
AMOUNT FINANCED (SUBJECT TO LENDER'S APPROVAL)	
AMOUNT DUE ON DELIVERY	▶

FINANCING TERMS

PRINCIPAL AMOUNT	
LIFE INSURANCE (IF REQUESTED)	
ACCIDENT AND HEALTH INSURANCE (IF REQUESTED)	
LOSS OF INCOME INSURANCE (IF REQUESTED)	
P.S.T. ON TOTAL INSURANCE	
REGISTRATION FEE	
TOTAL TO BE FINANCED (SUBJECT TO LENDER'S APPROVAL)	
COST OF BORROWING	%
AMOUNT OF PAYMENTS $	NO. OF PAYMENTS	PAYMENT START DATE

ACCEPTANCE OF TERMS

I HAVE READ THE TERMS ON THE FRONT AND BACK OF THIS PAGE AND AGREE THAT YOU HAVE NOT MADE ANY PROMISES TO ME, NOR ARE THERE ANY OTHER TERMS RELATING TO THIS AGREEMENT, EXCEPT AS WRITTEN ON THE FRONT AND BACK OF THIS PAGE AND THAT THIS AGREEMENT WILL ONLY BE EFFECTIVE WHEN SIGNED BY YOUR AUTHORIZED REPRESENTATIVE

X _____ X _____
  PURCHASER'S SIGNATURE   CO-SIGNER (IF ANY)

NAME AND POSITION OF AUTHORIZED REPRESENTATIVE

SIGNATURE OF AUTHORIZED REPRESENTATIVE   REG NO
X

SALESPERSON'S NAME

SALESPERSON'S SIGNATURE   REG NO
X

739

ADDITIONAL TERMS

1.   **Distance Travelled.**   You represent to me that to the best of your knowledge the distance travelled by the Vehicle is as shown on the other side of this page and, in the case of a Trade-In, I represent to you that to the best of my knowledge the distance travelled by the Trade-In is as shown on the other side of this page.

2.   **Original Pollution Equipment.**   You will ensure, in the case of a used Vehicle, and I will ensure in the case of a Trade-In, that all original pollution control equipment on the vehicle certified under the Motor Vehicle Safety Act of Canada is intact and operational at the time of delivery.

3.   **Safety Standards Certificate and Transfer Documents.**   I acknowledge that the motor vehicle permit for the Vehicle cannot be transferred to me unless I obtain a Safety Standards Certificate. If I do not request a Safety Standards Certificate you will deliver the Vehicle to me with an Unfit Motor Vehicle Permit and I will be responsible, at my sole cost, for removing the Vehicle from your premises. I authorize you on my behalf to make all applications and obtain all permits required to transfer the Vehicle in accordance with this Agreement.

4.   **Trade-Ins.**   I will transfer the Trade-In to you at the time that you deliver the Vehicle to me, or at such earlier time as we may agree to, free and clear of all liens (other than the liens which I have disclosed to you on the other side of this page). At the time of transfer, the Trade-In will be equipped and in the same condition, except for reasonable wear and tear, as it is on the date of this Agreement. If the Trade-In is not in the same condition, I may pay you for all necessary repairs or agree to reduce the Trade-In Allowance by the cost of the repairs. If we are unable to make arrangements which are satisfactory to both of us for the payment of any necessary repairs, this Agreement will be cancelled and you will be entitled to deduct your damages from my Deposit. If I transfer the Trade-In to you prior to the Vehicle being delivered to me, the Trade-In will form part of my Deposit.

5.   **Manufacturer's Suggested Retail Price.**   If the Vehicle is new the Basic Vehicle Price and the prices of the Optional Extras are the manufacturer's suggested retail prices. If the Vehicle is being ordered by you from the manufacturer and there is any increase in the manufacturer's suggested retail prices after the date of this Agreement, the increases will be added to the Total Basic Vehicle and Optional Extras Price. If I refuse to pay the increase in the Amount Due on Delivery, you will have the right to waive the increase or cancel this Agreement and return my Deposit.

6.   **Payment of Additional and Increased Taxes.**   If any federal or provincial taxes relating to the Vehicle or my purchase of the Vehicle under this Agreement are increased after the date of this Agreement and prior to the taking delivery of the Vehicle, I will pay you the amount of the increased taxes at the time of delivery.

7.   **Financing Information.**   If financing is to be provided to me, you represent to me that you have complied with Section 24 of the Consumer Protection Act of Ontario.

8.   **Ownership Transfers Only Upon Payment in Full.**   I agree that I will not become the owner of the Vehicle or have any other interest whatsoever in the Vehicle until I have paid the Amount Due on Delivery in full (including the amount of any increases resulting from increased taxes or changes in the manufacturer's suggested retail prices). I will pay you by certified cheque unless we otherwise agree.

9.   **Delays in Delivery of the Vehicle.**   If the Vehicle is to be ordered from the manufacturer and you are unable to deliver the Vehicle to me within 90 days of the date of this Agreement, you will notify me in writing of the reason for the delay and thereafter either one of us may cancel this Agreement by giving written notice of the cancellation to the other person. Unless we agree in writing to a new delivery date, this Agreement will be cancelled automatically at the end of the 5 day period following my receipt of your notice of the delay. If you are unable to deliver the Vehicle to me by the new delivery date, this Agreement will be cancelled automatically. If this Agreement is cancelled for any of the above reasons, you will return my Deposit and neither one of us will have any further obligations under this Agreement.

10.   **Failure to Accept Delivery or to Pay.**   If I fail to accept delivery of the Vehicle within 7 days of you notifying me by registered mail that the Vehicle is available for delivery, or if I fail to pay you the full Amount Due on Delivery, you will be entitled, in addition to any other rights or remedies you may have, to cancel this Agreement and to deduct the amount of your damages from my Deposit.

11.   **Explanation of Damages.**   If you keep any part of my Deposit you will provide me with a written calculation and brief explanation of your damages.

12.   **Dealing with Trade-Ins as Deposits.**   If my Deposit includes a Trade-In, you may sell it and upon the completion of the sale my Deposit will be increased by the amount of the Trade-In Allowance, less any amounts paid by you to reduce any outstanding liens. If I am entitled to the return of my Deposit and you have not sold the Trade-In, you will transfer the Trade-In back to me and I will pay you for the Safety Standards Certificate and all other costs associated with transferring the Trade-In back into my name, all repairs and improvements which you may have made to the Trade-In and for all payments which you may have made to reduce any outstanding liens.